PROFESSIONAL
VISUAL STUDIO® 2010

D0128109

INTRODUCTION xxxix

CHAPTER 1   A Quick Tour 3
CHAPTER 2   The Solution Explorer, Toolbox, and Properties. 15
CHAPTER 3   Options and Customizations 33
CHAPTER 4   The Visual Studio Workspace 53
CHAPTER 5   Find and Replace and Help 73
CHAPTER 6   Solutions, Projects, and Items 89
CHAPTER 7   IntelliSense and Bookmarks 119
CHAPTER 8   Code Snippets and Refactoring 137
CHAPTER 9   Server Explorer. 159
CHAPTER 10   Modeling with the Class Designer 175
CHAPTER 11   Unit Testing 191
CHAPTER 12   Documentation with XML Comments 219
CHAPTER 13   Code Consistency Tools. 245
CHAPTER 14   Code Generation with T4 263
CHAPTER 15   Project and Item Templates 291
CHAPTER 16   Language-Specific Features 311
CHAPTER 17   Windows Forms Applications 335
CHAPTER 18   Windows Presentation Foundation (WPF). 351
CHAPTER 19   Office Business Applications. 379
CHAPTER 20   ASP.NET Web Forms. 399
CHAPTER 21   ASP.NET MVC. 437
CHAPTER 22   Silverlight. 471
CHAPTER 23   Dynamic Data 485
CHAPTER 24   SharePoint. 513
CHAPTER 25   Windows Azure. 533
CHAPTER 26   Visual Database Tools. 549
CHAPTER 27   DataSets and DataBinding. 559

CHAPTER 28   Language Integrated Queries (LINQ)............................587

CHAPTER 29   The ADO.NET Entity Framework................................ 621

CHAPTER 30   Reporting...645

CHAPTER 31   Windows Communication Foundation (WCF)..................... 681

CHAPTER 32   Windows Workflow Foundation (WF)........................... 701

CHAPTER 33   Client Application Services 725

CHAPTER 34   Synchronization Services.....................................745

CHAPTER 35   WCF RIA Services 757

CHAPTER 36   Configuration Files..773

CHAPTER 37   Connection Strings 795

CHAPTER 38   Resource Files 805

CHAPTER 39   Using the Debugging Windows.............................. 827

CHAPTER 40   Debugging with Breakpoints.................................845

CHAPTER 41   DataTips, Debug Proxies, and Visualizers.....................857

CHAPTER 42   Debugging Web Applications 871

CHAPTER 43   Advanced Debugging Techniques............................887

CHAPTER 44   Upgrading with Visual Studio 2010 905

CHAPTER 45   Build Customization...911

CHAPTER 46   Assembly Versioning and Signing 929

CHAPTER 47   Obfuscation, Application Monitoring, and Management 937

CHAPTER 48   Packaging and Deployment................................. 961

CHAPTER 49   Web Application Deployment 983

CHAPTER 50   The Automation Model 1001

CHAPTER 51   Add-Ins..1009

CHAPTER 52   Macros 1025

CHAPTER 53   Managed Extensibility Framework (MEF) 1033

CHAPTER 54   Visual Studio Ultimate for Architects 1061

CHAPTER 55   Visual Studio Ultimate for Developers........................ 1075

CHAPTER 56   Visual Studio Ultimate for Testers...........................1095

CHAPTER 57   Team Foundation Server 1111

INDEX...1139

PROFESSIONAL

Visual Studio® 2010

Nick Randolph
David Gardner
Michael Minutillo
Chris Anderson

WILEY
Wiley Publishing, Inc.

Professional Visual Studio® 2010

Published by
Wiley Publishing, Inc.
10475 Crosspoint Boulevard
Indianapolis, IN 46256
www.wiley.com

Copyright © 2010 by Wiley Publishing, Inc., Indianapolis, Indiana

Published simultaneously in Canada

ISBN: 978-0-470-54865-3

Manufactured in the United States of America

10 9 8 7 6 5 4 3 2 1

For general information on our other products and services please contact our Customer Care Department within the United States at (877) 762-2974, outside the United States at (317) 572-3993 or fax (317) 572-4002.

Wiley also publishes its books in a variety of electronic formats. Some content that appears in print may not be available in electronic books.

Library of Congress Control Number: 2010922566

To my beautiful Cynthia

—NICK RANDOLPH

To my wife Julie

—DAVID GARDNER

For Barbara, amore sempre

—MICHAEL MINUTILLO

For my parents, Michael and Narelle

—CHRIS ANDERSON

ABOUT THE AUTHORS

NICK RANDOLPH currently runs Built To Roam which focuses on building rich mobile applications. Previously, Nick was co-founder and Development Manager for nsquared solutions where he led a team of developers to build inspirational software using next wave technology. Prior to nsquared, Nick was the lead developer at Intilecta Corporation where he was integrally involved in designing and building their application framework.

After graduating with a combined Engineering (Information Technology)/Commerce degree, Nick went on to be nominated as a Microsoft MVP in recognition of his work with the Perth .NET user group and his focus on mobile devices. He is still an active contributor in the device application development space via his blog at `http://community.softteq.com/blogs/nick/` and via the Professional Visual Studio web site, `www.professionalvisualstudio.com/`.

Nick has been invited to present at a variety of events including Tech Ed Australia, MEDC and Code camp. He has also authored articles for MSDN Magazine (ANZ edition), two books entitled *Professional Visual Studio 2005* and *Professional Visual Studio 2008*, and helped judge the 2004, 2005, 2007 and 2008 world finals for the Imagine Cup.

DAVID GARDNER is a seasoned .NET developer and the Chief Software Architect at Intilecta Corporation. David has an ongoing passion to produce well-designed, high-quality software products that engage and delight users. Since the mid 90s, He has worked as a solutions architect, consultant, and developer and has lent his expertise to organizations in Australia, New Zealand, and Malaysia.

David is a regular speaker at the Perth .NET user group and has presented at events including Microsoft TechEd and the Microsoft Executive Summit. He holds a Bachelor of Science (Computer Science) and is a Microsoft Certified Systems Engineer. David was co-author of *Professional Visual Studio 2008*, and blogs about Visual Studio and .NET at `www.professionalvisualstudio.com`.

MICHAEL MINUTILLO is a .NET software engineer with a Bachelor of Science degree in Computer Science. A self-described "Indiscriminate Information Sponge," he started writing .NET software in early 2000 to fund his university studies and has been an active member of the .NET community ever since.

Michael is a regular attendee at the Perth .NET Community of Practice where he has given presentations on the new features of C#, ASP.NET MVC and Test-Driven Philosophy. In 2009 Michael started the Perth ALT.NET User Group which meets monthly to discuss software engineering tools and practices in the .NET development space.

Michael maintains a technical blog at `http://wolfbyte-net.blogspot.com` and can be contacted at `http://twitter.com/wolfbyte`.

CHRIS ANDERSON has been a professional developer for over 10 years, specializing in building desktop, Web, and mobile business applications using Microsoft technologies for industries as wide ranging as accounting, property valuation, mining, the fresh produce industry, pet cremations, logistics, field services, sales, and construction. He holds a Bachelor of Engineering in Computer Systems with a Diploma in Engineering Practise. Chris is a co-owner of Peer Placements (a specialist recruitment firm for software developers) in addition to working as a consultant and author. Currently specializing in Silverlight (particularly in relation to building business applications in Silverlight), Chris has spoken on this topic at Code Camp Australia 2009, TechEd Australia 2009, Silverlight Code Camp Australia 2010, and numerous Sydney Silverlight Designer and Developer Network (SDDN) meetings for which he is a co-organizer. Chris maintains a blog at `http://chrisa.wordpress.com` and can be found on Twitter at `http://twitter.com/christhecoder`.

ABOUT THE TECHNICAL EDITOR

JOE BENNETT has been consulting as a developer and software solutions architect for more than 20 years and has been working with .NET exclusively since the beta for version 1.0. He is passionate about building well-architected, robust software for organizations of all sizes, and loves sharing his knowledge and experience with other developers.

Joe is the Chief Software Architect at Carolina Software Consultants, LLC and a past President of the Triangle .NET User Group located in the Triangle area of North Carolina. He frequently speaks at meetings and events and holds a Bachelor of Science degree in Computer Science from the University of Houston.

CREDITS

ACQUISITIONS EDITOR
Paul Reese

PROJECT EDITOR
Kelly Talbot

TECHNICAL EDITOR
Joe Bennett

PRODUCTION EDITOR
Eric Charbonneau

COPY EDITOR
Kim Cofer

EDITORIAL DIRECTOR
Robyn B. Siesky

EDITORIAL MANAGER
Mary Beth Wakefield

ASSOCIATE DIRECTOR OF MARKETING
David Mayhew

PRODUCTION MANAGER
Tim Tate

VICE PRESIDENT AND EXECUTIVE GROUP PUBLISHER
Richard Swadley

VICE PRESIDENT AND EXECUTIVE PUBLISHER
Barry Pruett

ASSOCIATE PUBLISHER
Jim Minatel

PROJECT COORDINATOR, COVER
Lynsey Stanford

PROOFREADERS
Scott Klemp and Beth Prouty, Word One

INDEXER
Johnna Vanhoose Dinse

COVER DESIGNER
Michael E. Trent

COVER IMAGE
© Eric Delmar/istockphoto

ACKNOWLEDGMENTS

THE PROCESS OF WRITING this book for Visual Studio 2010 has been frustrating at times; however, the journey of investigating new or forgotten features has reignited my passion for being a developer and working with one of the premiere development tools on the market. As with the previous two editions, this was a time-demanding exercise and I must again thank my partner, Cynthia, who consistently encouraged me to "get it done," so that we can once again have a life.

I would especially like to thank everyone at Wrox who has helped me re-learn the art of technical writing—in particular, Kelly Talbot, whose attention to detail has resulted in consistency throughout the book despite there being four authors contributing to the process, and Paul Reese (whose ability to get us back on track was a life-saver), who made the whole process possible.

I have to pass on a big thank you to my co-authors, Dave, Mike and Chris, who agreed to work with me on this edition. I doubt that I really gave an accurate representation of exactly how much work would be involved, and I really appreciated having co-authors of such high caliber to bounce ideas off of and share the workload.

Lastly, I would like to thank all of my fellow Australian MVP developers and the Microsoft staff, who were always able to answer any questions along the way.

—NICK RANDOLPH

WRITING A BOOK IS WITHOUT A DOUBT among the most rewarding and challenging activities I've ever undertaken. I thought it would be easier the second time around, but alas I was quickly proven wrong. However, in the process I have amassed a wealth of knowledge that I never would have found the time to learn otherwise.

The production behind this book is significant, and I am especially thankful to the team at Wrox who worked tirelessly behind the scenes to bring it to fruition. Without Paul Reese and Kelly Talbot working as hard as they did to cajole the next chapter out of us, we never would have gotten this finished. It was a pleasure to be in such experienced hands, and I thank them for their patience and professionalism.

A huge thank you goes to my co-authors Nick Randolph, Michael Minutillo, and Chris Anderson, whose excellent contributions have improved this book significantly over the previous edition. I enjoyed collaborating on such a big project and the ongoing conversations about the latest cool feature that we'd just discovered.

My appreciation and thanks go to Gabriel Torok, Bill Leach, and Mike Moores from PreEmptive Solutions; Jonathan Carter from Microsoft; and SharePoint extraordinaire Jeremy Thake, whose feedback and suggestions greatly improved various chapters. Also thanks to my fellow coffee drinkers and .NET developers who (unintentionally) remind me how much I still have to learn about .NET development.

Special thanks to my parents, John and Wendy, who have always been there for me and who have always provided me with the encouragement and support I needed to achieve my goals. Special thanks also to my daughters Jasmin and Emily, who gave up countless cuddles and tickles so that Daddy could find the time to write this book. I promise I'll do my best to catch up on the tickles that I owe you and pay them back with interest.

Most of all I would like to thank my extraordinarily supportive wife and best friend, Julie. She knew exactly what she was getting herself into when I agreed to write this book, and yet she still offered her full encouragement and support. Julie did way more than her fair share for our family when I needed to drop everything except work and writing, and I am truly grateful for her love and friendship.

—David Gardner

FIRST AND FOREMOST I'd like to thank my co-authors Nick and Dave for inviting me to join them on this adventure. That act of trust and faith has sustained me during several very early morning writing sessions. When I first appeared on the Perth .NET scene Nick and Dave welcomed me with loads of friendly advice and conversation. It's an atmosphere that the community here retains to this day. A special thanks goes to Chris for racing me to the finish line. When one day we finally meet in person, I think I owe you a drink.

Like most first-time authors I had no real clue what I was getting myself into when I agreed to write this book. Thanks to the team at Wrox for patiently educating me. Special thanks goes to Kelly Talbot who continually worked to keep me on schedule and who coordinated the team that made my sections readable. Editing a technical book of this size has got to be an interesting challenge and ensuring consistency across four authors must make it particularly difficult.

Writing a book is a great way to teach you just how much you still have to learn. While researching material I was constantly surprised by the little corners of Visual Studio that I hadn't previously been aware of, but there was always someone hanging out on twitter with a useful link or comment. There are too many of you to thank individually, so in true twitter style I'll just say thanks and know that you are all listening.

Finally, I would particularly like to thank Barbara, the wonderful woman I am so lucky to be married to. When Nick and Dave first approached me about being involved in this book, I don't think either of us realized the impact it would have on our lives. Barbara gave me the courage and the support to step up to the challenge and was ready to be banished from the house for whole weekends at a time, taking the kids on wonderful (and tiring) adventures so that I could get a chapter completed. To her and to my three beautiful children, Chiara, Caleb and Will, I promise I can come with you on the next adventure. And I won't write any more books for a while. I promise.

—Michael Minutillo

WHEN I WAS INVITED TO JOIN Nick, Dave, and Michael in writing this book, I had no idea what I was getting myself into. Writing is a gruelling and time-consuming process — far more than I could have ever imagined. Each chapter is almost like writing a thesis in itself, but on a strict time budget, only to move onto the next once it's done. Knowing that thousands of people would be reading my chapters and relying on the information that they contain only added to the stress, but I am quite proud of what we've managed to produce, and hope that it gives you the skills and knowledge to become a Visual Studio power user. It's been a big learning curve, and I came to realize how much I think and produce solely in code rather than in English. There's a definite skill in effectively expressing concepts in the written form, and I have a newfound appreciation and respect for those who do it so well.

I'd like to thank Nick and Dave for inviting me to be a part of the team. I was very much honored to be asked and to actually be involved in this project. My thanks go to all three of my co-authors: Nick, Dave, and Michael. Despite being located at opposite sides of Australia I think we've worked remarkably well as a team, and I appreciate all your effort, feedback, and encouragement. My thanks also go to our editor Kelly Talbot, who kept us in check and valiantly (if not always successfully) attempted to keep us on schedule. While I have received help from a number of people at Microsoft, I must particularly thank Dustin Campbell and John Vulner who provided me with some valuable help and answers.

On a personal note, I would like to thank my parents Michael and Narelle, whose hard work, generosity, and love have been my inspiration.

—CHRIS ANDERSON

CONTENTS

INTRODUCTION   *xxxix*

PART I: INTEGRATED DEVELOPMENT ENVIRONMENT

CHAPTER 1: A QUICK TOUR   3

Getting Started   3
Installing Visual Studio 2010   3
Running Visual Studio 2010   5
The Visual Studio IDE   7
Developing, Building, Debugging, and Deploying Your
First Application   9
Summary   13

CHAPTER 2: THE SOLUTION EXPLORER, TOOLBOX, AND PROPERTIES   15

The Solution Explorer   15
Common Tasks   17
The Toolbox   22
Arranging Components   24
Adding Components   25
Properties   26
Extending the Properties Window   28
Summary   32

CHAPTER 3: OPTIONS AND CUSTOMIZATIONS   33

The Start Page   33
Customizing the Start Page   34
Code Behind with User Controls   36
Window Layout   39
Viewing Windows and Toolbars   39
Navigating Open Items   40
Docking   41
The Editor Space   43
Fonts and Colors   43
Visual Guides   44

Full-Screen Mode	45
Tracking Changes	46
Other Options	**46**
Keyboard Shortcuts	46
Projects and Solutions	48
Build and Run	49
VB Options	50
Importing and Exporting Settings	**51**
Summary	**52**

CHAPTER 4: THE VISUAL STUDIO WORKSPACE   **53**

The Code Editor	**53**
The Code Editor Window Layout	53
Regions	54
Outlining	55
Code Formatting	55
Navigating Forward/Backward	57
Additional Code Editor Features	57
Split View	58
Tear Away (Floating) Code Windows	58
Creating Tab Groups	59
Advanced Functionality	59
The Command Window	**61**
The Immediate Window	**62**
The Class View	**63**
The Error List	**64**
The Object Browser	**64**
The Code Definition Window	**66**
The Call Hierarchy Window	**66**
The Document Outline Tool Window	**68**
HTML Outlining	68
Control Outlining	69
Reorganizing Tool Windows	**70**
Summary	**71**

CHAPTER 5: FIND AND REPLACE AND HELP   **73**

Quick Find/Replace	**73**
Quick Find	74
Quick Replace	75
Find Options	75

Wildcards 75
Regular Expressions 76
Find and Replace Options 77
Find/Replace in Files **78**
Find in Files 78
Find Dialog Options 79
Results Window 79
Replace in Files 80
Find Symbol **81**
Navigate To **82**
Incremental Search **82**
Accessing Help **83**
Navigating and Searching the Help System 84
Configuring the Help System 85
Summary **86**

PART II: GETTING STARTED

CHAPTER 6: SOLUTIONS, PROJECTS, AND ITEMS

89

Solution Structure **89**
Solution File Format **91**
Solution Properties **92**
Common Properties 92
Configuration Properties 93
Project Types **94**
Project Files Format **96**
Project Properties **96**
Application 97
Compile (Visual Basic Only) 100
Build (C# and F# Only) 102
Build Events (C# and F# Only) 103
Debug 103
References (Visual Basic Only) 105
Resources 106
Services 107
Settings 108
Reference Paths (C# and F# Only) 108
Signing 109
My Extensions (Visual Basic Only) 110
Security 111

Publish   111
Code Analysis (VSTS Premium and Ultimate Editions Only)   112
Web Application Project Properties   **113**
Web   113
Silverlight Applications   114
Package/Publish Web   115
Package/Publish SQL   116
Web Site Projects   **116**
Summary   **117**

CHAPTER 7: INTELLISENSE AND BOOKMARKS   **119**

IntelliSense Explained   **119**
General IntelliSense   120
Completing Words and Phrases   121
Parameter Information   127
Quick Info   128
JavaScript IntelliSense   **128**
The JavaScript IntelliSense Context   129
Referencing another JavaScript File   129
IntelliSense Options   **130**
General Options   131
Statement Completion   132
C#-Specific Options   132
Extended IntelliSense   **132**
Code Snippets   133
XML Comments   133
Adding Your Own IntelliSense   133
Bookmarks and the Bookmark Window   **133**
Summary   **135**

CHAPTER 8: CODE SNIPPETS AND REFACTORING   **137**

Code Snippets Revealed   **138**
Storing Code Blocks in the Toolbox   138
Code Snippets   138
Using Snippets in C#   139
Using Snippets in VB   140
Surround With Snippet   141
Code Snippets Manager   142
Creating Snippets   143
Reviewing Existing Snippets   144

Accessing Refactoring Support   **147**
Refactoring Actions   **148**
  Extract Method   148
  Encapsulate Field   150
  Extract Interface   151
  Reorder Parameters   153
  Remove Parameters   154
  Rename   154
  Promote Variable to Parameter   155
  Generate Method Stub   156
  Organize Usings   156
Summary   **157**

CHAPTER 9: SERVER EXPLORER   **159**

Server Connections   **159**
  Event Logs   160
  Management Classes   162
  Management Events   164
  Message Queues   167
  Performance Counters   169
  Services   172
Data Connections   **173**
SharePoint Connections   **174**
Summary   **174**

CHAPTER 10: MODELING WITH THE CLASS DESIGNER   **175**

Creating a Class Diagram   **176**
The Design Surface   **177**
The Toolbox   **178**
  Entities   178
  Connectors   179
The Class Details   **180**
The Properties Window   **181**
Layout   **181**
Exporting Diagrams   **182**
Code Generation and Refactoring   **182**
  Drag-and-Drop Code Generation   182
  IntelliSense Code Generation   184
  Refactoring with the Class Designer   185

Modeling Power Toys for Visual Studio   **186**
   Visualization Enhancements   186
   Functionality Enhancements   187
Summary   **188**

PART III: DIGGING DEEPER

CHAPTER 11: UNIT TESTING   191

Your First Test Case   **192**
   Identifying Tests using Attributes   200
   Additional Test Attributes   200
Asserting the Facts   **202**
   The Assert Class   203
   The StringAssert Class   203
   The CollectionAssert Class   204
   The ExpectedException Attribute   204
Initializing and Cleaning Up   **206**
   TestInitialize and TestCleanup   206
   ClassInitialize and ClassCleanup   206
   AssemblyInitialize and AssemblyCleanup   207
Testing Context   **207**
   Data   207
   Writing Test Output   210
Advanced Unit Testing   **211**
   Custom Properties   211
   Testing Private Members   213
Testing Code Contracts   **214**
Managing Large Numbers of Tests   **216**
Summary   **217**

CHAPTER 12: DOCUMENTATION WITH XML COMMENTS   219

Inline Commenting   **220**
XML Comments   **220**
   Adding XML Comments   221
   XML Comment Tags   222
Using XML Comments   **235**
   IntelliSense Information   237
Generating Documentation with GhostDoc   **237**

Compiling Documentation with Sandcastle   238
Task List Comments   241
Summary   243

CHAPTER 13: CODE CONSISTENCY TOOLS   245

Source Control   245
  Selecting a Source Control Repository   246
  Accessing Source Control   248
  Offline Support for Source Control   253
Coding Standards   254
  Code Analysis with FxCop   254
  Style Using StyleCop   258
  Code Contracts   258
Summary   260

CHAPTER 14: CODE GENERATION WITH T4   263

Creating a T4 Template   264
T4 Building Blocks   268
  Expression Blocks   268
  Statement Blocks   268
  Class Feature Blocks   270
How T4 Works   272
T4 Directives   275
  Template Directive   275
  Output Directive   275
  Assembly Directive   276
  Import Directive   276
  Include Directive   277
Troubleshooting   278
  Design-Time Errors   278
  Compiling Transformation Errors   279
  Executing Transformation Errors   279
  Generated Code Errors   280
Generating Code Assets   280
Preprocessed Text Templates   284
  Using Preprocessed Text Templates   286
  Differences Between a Standard T4 Template   288
Tips and Tricks   289
Summary   290

CHAPTER 15: PROJECT AND ITEM TEMPLATES 291

Creating Templates 291
Item Template 291
Project Template 295
Template Structure 296
Template Parameters 298
Template Locations 299
Extending Templates 299
Template Project Setup 299
IWizard 301
Generating the Extended Project Template 306
Starter Kits 308
Online Templates 308
Summary 309

CHAPTER 16: LANGUAGE-SPECIFIC FEATURES 311

Hitting a Nail with the Right Hammer 311
Imperative 312
Declarative 312
Dynamic 312
Functional 313
What's It All Mean? 314
A Tale of Two Languages 314
Compiling without PIAs 315
Generic Variance 316
Visual Basic 321
Lambdas and Anonymous Methods 321
Implicit Line Continuation 322
Automatic Properties with Initial Values 322
Collection Initializers and Array Literals 323
Nullable Optional Parameters 324
Visual Basic PowerPacks 325
C# 325
Late Binding with Dynamic Lookup 325
Named and Optional Parameters 326
F# 327
Your First F# Program 327
Exploring F# Language Features 330
Summary 331

PART IV: RICH CLIENT APPLICATIONS

CHAPTER 17: WINDOWS FORMS APPLICATIONS — 335

Getting Started	335
The Windows Form	336
Appearance Properties	338
Layout Properties	338
Window Style Properties	338
Form Design Preferences	338
Adding and Positioning Controls	341
Vertically Aligning Text Controls	342
Automatic Positioning of Multiple Controls	342
Tab Order and Layering Controls	344
Locking Control Design	344
Setting Control Properties	345
Service-Based Components	346
Smart Tag Tasks	346
Container Controls	347
Panel and SplitContainer	347
FlowLayoutPanel	348
TableLayoutPanel	348
Docking and Anchoring Controls	349
Summary	350

CHAPTER 18: WINDOWS PRESENTATION FOUNDATION (WPF) — 351

What Is WPF?	352
Getting Started with WPF	353
XAML Fundamentals	355
The WPF Controls	357
The WPF Layout Controls	358
The WPF Designer and XAML Editor	360
Working with the XAML Editor	361
Working with the WPF Designer	362
The Properties Tool Window	364
Data Binding Features	367
Styling Your Application	371
Windows Forms Interoperability	372
Hosting a WPF Control in Windows Forms	372
Hosting a Windows Forms Control in WPF	374
Debugging with the WPF Visualizer	376
Summary	377

CHAPTER 19: OFFICE BUSINESS APPLICATIONS   **379**

Choosing an Office Project Type   **380**
Document-Level Customizations   381
Application-Level Add-Ins   381
Creating a Document-Level Customization   **382**
Your First VSTO Project   382
Protecting the Document Design   385
Adding an Actions Pane   386
Creating an Application Add-In   **388**
Some Outlook Concepts   388
Creating an Outlook Form Region   389
Debugging Office Applications   **392**
Unregistering an Add-In   392
Disabled Add-Ins   394
Deploying Office Applications   **394**
Summary   **396**

PART V: WEB APPLICATIONS

CHAPTER 20: ASP.NET WEB FORMS   **399**

Web Application vs. Web Site Projects   **400**
Creating Web Projects   **401**
Creating a Web Site Project   401
Creating a Web Application Project   404
Other Web Projects   406
Starter Kits, Community Projects, and Open-Source Applications   406
Designing Web Forms   **407**
The HTML Designer   407
Positioning Controls and HTML Elements   409
Formatting Controls and HTML Elements   411
CSS Tools   412
Validation Tools   416
Web Controls   **417**
Navigation Components   418
User Authentication   418
Data Components   420
Web Parts   423
Master Pages   **424**

Rich Client-Side Development	**425**
Developing with JavaScript	426
Working with ASP.NET AJAX	427
Using AJAX Control Extenders	429
ASP.NET Web Site Administration	**431**
Security	432
Application Settings	433
ASP.NET Configuration in IIS	434
Summary	**434**

CHAPTER 21: ASP.NET MVC — **437**

Model View Controller	**438**
Getting Started with ASP.NET MVC	**439**
Choosing a Model	**440**
Controllers and Action Methods	**441**
Rendering a UI with Views	**443**
Advanced MVC	**451**
Routing	451
Action Method Parameters	456
Areas	459
Validation	461
Partial Views	463
Custom View Templates	463
Dynamic Data Templates	464
jQuery	468
Summary	**470**

CHAPTER 22: SILVERLIGHT — **471**

What is Silverlight?	**472**
Getting Started with Silverlight	**473**
Navigation Framework	**478**
Theming	**479**
Enabling Running Out of Browser	**481**
Summary	**484**

CHAPTER 23: DYNAMIC DATA — **485**

Creating a Dynamic Data Web Application	**486**
Adding a Data Model	487
Exploring a Dynamic Data Application	489

Customizing the Data Model   **491**

Scaffolding Individual Tables   491

Customizing Individual Data Fields   492

Adding Custom Validation Rules   494

Customizing the Display Format   496

Customizing the Presentation   **498**

Page Templates   499

Field Templates   502

Entity Templates   506

Filter Templates   509

Enabling Dynamic Data for Existing Projects   **511**

Summary   **512**

CHAPTER 24: SHAREPOINT   **513**

Preparing the Development Environment   **514**

Installing the Prerequisites   515

Installing SharePoint 2010   517

Exploring SharePoint 2010   **518**

Creating a SharePoint Project   **520**

Building Custom SharePoint Components   **524**

Developing Web Parts   524

Creating Content Types and Lists   525

Adding Event Receivers   527

Creating SharePoint Workflows   528

Working with Features   **529**

Packaging and Deployment   **530**

Summary   **532**

CHAPTER 25: WINDOWS AZURE   **533**

The Windows Azure Platform   **534**

The Development Fabric   535

Table, Blob, and Queue Storage   536

Application Deployment   540

Tuning Your Application   543

SQL Azure   **544**

AppFabric   **545**

Service Bus   545

Access Control Service   545

Summary   **546**

PART VI: DATA

CHAPTER 26: VISUAL DATABASE TOOLS — 549

Database Windows in Visual Studio 2010 — 549
  Server Explorer — 550
  The Data Sources Window — 556
Editing Data — 556
Previewing Data — 557
Summary — 558

CHAPTER 27: DATASETS AND DATABINDING — 559

DataSets Overview — 559
  Adding a Data Source — 561
  The DataSet Designer — 563
Binding Data — 565
  BindingSource — 567
  BindingNavigator — 569
  Data Source Selections — 570
  Saving Changes — 573
  Inserting New Items — 575
  Validation — 576
  Customized DataSets — 578
  BindingSource Chains and the DataGridView — 579
Working with Data Sources — 581
  The Web Service Data Source — 583
  Browsing Data — 584
Summary — 586

CHAPTER 28: LANGUAGE INTEGRATED QUERIES (LINQ) — 587

LINQ Providers — 588
Old-School Queries — 588
Query Pieces — 590
  From — 591
  Select — 592
  Where — 592
  Group By — 593
  Custom Projections — 594
  Order By — 594
Debugging and Execution — 596
LINQ to XML — 597

VB XML Literals 598
Paste XML as XElement 599
Creating XML with LINQ 600
Querying XML **602**
Schema Support **603**
LINQ to SQL **605**
Creating the Object Model 606
Querying with LINQ to SQL 608
Binding LINQ to SQL Objects 614
LINQPad **618**
Summary **618**

CHAPTER 29: THE ADO.NET ENTITY FRAMEWORK **621**

What Is the Entity Framework? **622**
Comparison with LINQ to SQL 622
Entity Framework Concepts 623
Getting Started **624**
Creating an Entity Model **624**
The Entity Data Model Wizard 624
The Entity Framework Designer 626
Creating/Modifying Entities 630
Creating/Modifying Entity Associations 634
Entity Inheritance 635
Validating an Entity Model 635
Updating an Entity Model with Database Changes 635
Querying the Entity Model **636**
LINQ to Entities Overview 636
Getting an Object Context 636
CRUD Operations 637
Navigating Entity Associations 641
Advanced Functionality **642**
Updating a Database from an Entity Model 642
Adding Business Logic to Entities 643
Plain Old CLR Objects (POCO) 643
Summary **643**

CHAPTER 30: REPORTING **645**

Getting Started with Reporting **645**
Designing Reports **647**
Defining Data Sources 648

Reporting Controls 650

Expressions, Placeholders, and Aggregates 661

Custom Code 663

Report Layout 668

Subreports 670

The Report Wizard 672

Rendering Reports **673**

The Report Viewer Controls 673

Generating the Report 674

Rendering Reports to Different Formats 675

Deploying Reports **677**

Summary **677**

PART VII: APPLICATION SERVICES

CHAPTER 31: WINDOWS COMMUNICATION FOUNDATION (WCF) **681**

What Is WCF? **681**

Getting Started **682**

Defining Contracts **683**

Creating the Service Contract 684

Creating the Data Contract 685

Configuring WCF Service Endpoints **688**

Hosting WCF Services **691**

Consuming a WCF Service **696**

Summary **699**

CHAPTER 32: WINDOWS WORKFLOW FOUNDATION (WF) **701**

What Is Windows Workflow Foundation? **701**

Why Use Windows Workflow? **702**

Workflow Concepts **703**

Activities 703

Control Flow Activities 704

Expressions 705

Workflow Run Time/Scheduler 705

Bookmarks 705

Persistence 706

Tracking 706

Getting Started **707**

The Workflow Foundation Designer   **709**
Creating a Workflow   **712**
    Designing a Workflow   713
    Writing Code Activities   715
    Executing a Workflow   716
    Debugging Workflows   718
    Testing Workflows   719
Hosting the Workflow Designer   **719**
Summary   **723**

CHAPTER 33: CLIENT APPLICATION SERVICES   **725**

Client Services   **725**
Role Authorization   **729**
User Authentication   **731**
Settings   **733**
Login Form   **738**
Offline Support   **740**
Summary   **743**

CHAPTER 34: SYNCHRONIZATION SERVICES   **745**

Occasionally Connected Applications   **746**
Server Direct   **746**
Getting Started with Synchronization Services   **749**
Synchronization Services over N-Tiers   **751**
Background Synchronization   **752**
Client Changes   **755**
Summary   **756**

CHAPTER 35: WCF RIA SERVICES   **757**

Getting Started   **757**
Domain Services   **760**
Domain Operations   **762**
    Query Operations   762
    Insert/Update/Delete Operations   763
    Other Operation Types   763
Consuming a Domain Service in Silverlight   **764**
Summary   **769**

PART VIII: CONFIGURATION AND RESOURCES

CHAPTER 36: CONFIGURATION FILES 773

.Config Files	**773**
Machine.Config	773
Web.Config	774
App.Config	774
Security.Config	775
ApplicationHost.Config	775
Configuration Schema	**775**
Section: configurationSections	775
Section: startup	777
Section: runtime	777
Section: system.runtime.remoting	778
Section: system.net	778
Section: cryptographySettings	779
Section: system.diagnostics	779
Section: system.web	779
Section: compiler	780
Configuration Attributes	780
Application Settings	**782**
Using appSettings	782
Project Settings	783
Dynamic Properties	784
Custom Configuration Sections	785
User Settings	**790**
Referenced Projects with Settings	**792**
Summary	**793**

CHAPTER 37: CONNECTION STRINGS 795

Connection String Wizard	**795**
SQL Server Format	**800**
In-Code Construction	**801**
Encrypting Connection Strings	**803**
Summary	**804**

CHAPTER 38: RESOURCE FILES 805

What are Resources?	**805**
Text File Resources	806
Resx Resource Files	807

Binary Resources 807
Adding Resources 808
Embedding Files as Resources 808
Naming Resources 809
Accessing Resources 809
Designer Files 810
Resourcing Your Application **811**
Control Images 813
Satellite Resources **813**
Cultures 813
Creating Culture Resources 814
Loading Culture Resource Files 814
Satellite Culture Resources 815
Accessing Specifics **816**
Bitmap and Icon Loading 816
Cross-Assembly Referencing 816
ComponentResourceManager 816
Coding Resource Files **817**
ResourceReader and ResourceWriter 818
ResxResourceReader and ResxResourceWriter 818
Custom Resources **819**
Summary **823**

PART IX: DEBUGGING

CHAPTER 39: USING THE DEBUGGING WINDOWS **827**

The Code Window **827**
Breakpoints 828
DataTips 828
The Breakpoints Window **828**
The Output Window **829**
The Immediate Window **830**
The Watch Windows **831**
QuickWatch 831
Watch Windows 1–4 832
Autos and Locals 833
The Code Execution Windows **833**
Call Stack 833
Threads 834
Modules 834
Processes 835

The Memory Windows	**835**
Memory Windows 1–4	836
Disassembly	836
Registers	836
IntelliTrace (Ultimate Edition Only)	**837**
The Parallel Debugging Windows	**838**
Parallel Stacks	839
Parallel Tasks	840
Exceptions	**841**
Customizing the Exception Assistant	842
Unwinding an Exception	843
Summary	**843**

CHAPTER 40: DEBUGGING WITH BREAKPOINTS	**845**
Breakpoints	**845**
Setting a Breakpoint	846
Adding Break Conditions	848
Working with Breakpoints	850
Tracepoints	**852**
Creating a Tracepoint	852
Tracepoint Actions	852
Execution Control	**853**
Stepping Through Code	853
Moving the Execution Point	855
Edit and Continue	**855**
Rude Edits	855
Stop Applying Changes	856
Summary	**856**

CHAPTER 41: DATATIPS, DEBUG PROXIES, AND VISUALIZERS	**857**
DataTips	**858**
Debugger Attributes	**859**
DebuggerBrowsable	859
DebuggerDisplay	860
DebuggerHidden	861
DebuggerStepThrough	862
DebuggerNonUserCode	862
DebuggerStepperBoundary	862
Type Proxies	**863**
Raw View	865
Visualizers	**865**

Advanced Techniques	**867**
Saving Changes to Your Object	867
Summary	**869**

CHAPTER 42: DEBUGGING WEB APPLICATIONS — 871

Debugging Server-Side ASP.NET Code	**872**
Web Application Exceptions	874
Edit and Continue	876
Error Handling	876
Debugging Client-Side JavaScript	**877**
Setting Breakpoints in JavaScript Code	878
Debugging Dynamically Generated JavaScript	878
Debugging ASP.NET AJAX JavaScript	879
Debugging Silverlight	**879**
Tracing	**880**
Page-Level Tracing	881
Application-Level Tracing	882
Trace Output	882
The Trace Viewer	883
Custom Trace Output	884
Health Monitoring	**884**
Summary	**886**

CHAPTER 43: ADVANCED DEBUGGING TECHNIQUES — 887

Start Actions	**887**
Debugging with Code	**890**
The Debugger Class	890
The Debug and Trace Classes	890
Debugging Running Applications	**892**
Attaching to a Windows Process	892
Attaching to a Web Application	893
Remote Debugging	894
.NET Framework Source	**896**
Multi-Threaded and Parallelized Application Debugging	**897**
Debugging SQL Server Stored Procedures	**899**
Mixed-Mode Debugging	**899**
Post-Mortem Debugging	**900**
Generating Dump Files	900
Debugging Dump Files	901
Summary	**902**

PART X: BUILD AND DEPLOYMENT

CHAPTER 44: UPGRADING WITH VISUAL STUDIO 2010 — 905

Upgrading from Visual Studio 2008 — 905
Upgrading to .NET Framework 4.0 — 909
Summary — 910

CHAPTER 45: BUILD CUSTOMIZATION — 911

General Build Options — 911
Manual Dependencies — 914
The Visual Basic Compile Page — 915
   Advanced Compiler Settings — 916
   Build Events — 917
C# Build Pages — 919
MSBuild — 920
   How Visual Studio Uses MSBuild — 921
   The MSBuild Schema — 923
   Assembly Versioning via MSBuild Tasks — 925
Summary — 927

CHAPTER 46: ASSEMBLY VERSIONING AND SIGNING — 929

Assembly Naming — 929
Version Consistency — 932
Strongly Named Assemblies — 933
The Global Assembly Cache — 933
Signing an Assembly — 934
Summary — 936

CHAPTER 47: OBFUSCATION, APPLICATION MONITORING, AND MANAGEMENT — 937

The MSIL Disassembler — 938
Decompilers — 939
Obfuscating Your Code — 941
   Dotfuscator Software Services — 941
   Obfuscation Attributes — 945
   Words of Caution — 948
Application Monitoring and Management — 949
   Tamper Defense — 950

Runtime Intelligence Instrumentation and Analytics 952
Application Expiry 956
Application Usage Tracking 957
Summary **959**

CHAPTER 48: PACKAGING AND DEPLOYMENT — 961

Windows Installers **961**
Building an Installer 962
Customizing the Installer 966
Adding Custom Actions 970
The Service Installer 973
ClickOnce **976**
One Click to Deploy 976
One Click to Update 980
Summary **982**

CHAPTER 49: WEB APPLICATION DEPLOYMENT — 983

Web Site Deployment **984**
Publish Web Site 984
Copy Web Site 985
Web Application Deployment **986**
Publishing a Web Application 986
Packaging a Web Application 987
web.config Transformations 989
Web Project Installers **991**
The Web Platform Installer **992**
Extending the Web Platform Installer 993
Summary **997**

PART XI: CUSTOMIZING AND EXTENDING VISUAL STUDIO

CHAPTER 50: THE AUTOMATION MODEL — 1001

Visual Studio Extensibility Options **1001**
The Visual Studio Automation Model **1002**
An Overview of the Automation Model 1002
Solutions and Projects 1004
Windows and Documents 1005
Commands 1006

Debugger   1007
Events   1007
Summary   **1008**

CHAPTER 51: ADD-INS   1009

Developing an Add-In   **1009**
The Add-in Wizard   1010
Project Structure   1012
Testing Your Add-in   1013
The .AddIn File   1014
The Connect Class   1015
Creating a Tool Window   1015
Accessing the Visual Studio Automation Model   1018
Handling Visual Studio Events   1020
Deploying Add-ins   **1022**
Summary   **1023**

CHAPTER 52: MACROS   1025

Understanding Macros   **1025**
The Macro Explorer Tool Window   **1026**
The Macros IDE   **1026**
Creating a Macro   **1027**
How to Record a Macro   1028
How to Develop a Macro   1028
Running a Macro   **1030**
Deploying Macros   **1030**
Summary   **1031**

CHAPTER 53: MANAGED EXTENSIBILITY FRAMEWORK (MEF)   1033

Getting Started with MEF   **1034**
Imports and Exports   1036
Contracts   1037
Catalogs   1040
Advanced MEF   1041
The Visual Studio 2010 Editor   **1041**
The Text Model Subsystem   1042
The Text View Subsystem   1042
The Classification Subsystem   1043
The Operations Subsystem   1043

Extending the Editor	**1044**
Editor Extension Points	1045
Editor Services	1050
The Check Comment Highlighter Extension	1050
Summary	**1057**

PART XII: VISUAL STUDIO ULTIMATE (AVAILABLE ONLINE)

CHAPTER 54: VISUAL STUDIO ULTIMATE FOR ARCHITECTS   **1061**

Modeling Projects	**1061**
UML Diagrams	1062
UML Model Explorer	1066
Using Layer Diagrams to Verify Application Architecture	1066
Linking to Team Foundation Server	1068
Exploring Code	**1068**
The Architecture Explorer	1068
Dependency Graphs	1070
Generate Sequence Diagram	1072
Summary	**1073**

CHAPTER 55: VISUAL STUDIO ULTIMATE FOR DEVELOPERS   **1075**

Code Metrics	**1075**
Lines of Code	1076
Depth of Inheritance	1077
Class Coupling	1077
Cyclomatic Complexity	1078
Maintainability Index	1078
Excluded Code	1078
Managed Code Analysis Tool	**1078**
C/C++ Code Analysis Tool	**1079**
Profiling Tools	**1080**
Configuring Profiler Sessions	1080
Reports	1082
Stand-Alone Profiler	**1083**
IntelliTrace	**1084**
Database Tools	**1086**
SQL-CLR Database Project	1086
Offline Database Schema	1086
Data Generation	1089
Database Refactoring	1090

Schema Compare 1091
Data Compare 1092
Static Analysis 1093
Transact-SQL Editor 1093
Best Practices 1093
Summary **1094**

CHAPTER 56: VISUAL STUDIO ULTIMATE FOR TESTERS 1095

Automated Tests **1095**
Web Performance Tests 1096
Load Tests 1099
Database Unit Test 1100
Coded UI Test 1101
Generic Tests 1102
Ordered Test 1102
Relating Code and Tests **1103**
Code Coverage 1103
Test Impact Analysis 1105
Visual Studio Test Management **1105**
Test and Lab Manager **1106**
Testing Center 1106
Lab Center 1108
Summary **1110**

CHAPTER 57: TEAM FOUNDATION SERVER 1111

Team Project **1112**
Process Templates **1112**
Work Item Tracking **1113**
Work Item Queries 1114
Work Item Types 1115
Adding Work Items 1116
Work Item State 1116
Excel and Project Integration **1117**
Excel 1117
Project 1118
Version Control **1119**
Working from Solution Explorer 1120
Check Out 1121
Check In 1121
Resolve Conflicts 1122

Working Offline   1124
Label   1124
History   1125
Annotate   1125
Shelve   1125
Branch   1126
Merge   1128

Team Foundation Build   **1128**

Reporting and Business Intelligence   **1130**

Team Portal   **1132**
Documents   1132
Process Guidance   1132
SharePoint Lists   1132
Dashboards   1132

Team System Web Access   **1133**

Administering TFS   **1134**

TFS Automation and Process Customization   **1135**
Work Item Types   1135
Customizing the Process Template   1136

Summary   **1137**

INDEX   *1139*

INTRODUCTION

Visual Studio 2010 is an enormous product no matter which way you look at it. Incorporating the latest advances in Microsoft's premiere programming languages, Visual Basic and C#, along with a host of improvements and new features in the user interface, can be intimidating to both newcomers and experienced .NET developers.

Professional Visual Studio 2010 looks at every major aspect of this developer tool, showing you how to harness each feature and offering advice about how best to utilize the various components effectively. It shows you the building blocks that make up Visual Studio 2010, breaking the user interface down into manageable chunks for you to understand.

It then expands on each of these components with additional details about exactly how it works both in isolation and in conjunction with other parts of Visual Studio 2010 to make your development efforts even more efficient.

WHO THIS BOOK IS FOR

Professional Visual Studio 2010 is for all developers new to Visual Studio as well as those programmers who have some experience but want to learn about features they may have previously overlooked.

If you are familiar with the way previous versions of Visual Studio worked, you may want to skim over Part I, which deals with the basic constructs that make up the user interface, and move on to the remainder of the book where the new features found in Visual Studio 2010 are discussed in detail. While you may be familiar with most of Part I, it is worth reading this section in case there are features of Visual Studio 2010 that you haven't seen or used before.

If you're just starting out, you'll greatly benefit from the first part, where basic concepts are explained and you're introduced to the user interface and how to customize it to suit your own style.

WHAT THIS BOOK COVERS

Microsoft Visual Studio 2010 is arguably the most advanced integrated development environment (IDE) available for programmers today. It is based on a long history of programming languages and interfaces and has been influenced by many different iterations of the theme of development environments.

The next few pages introduce you to Microsoft Visual Studio 2010, how it came about, and what it can do for you as a developer. If you're already familiar with what Visual Studio is and how it came to be, you may want to skip ahead to the next chapter and dive into the various aspects of the integrated development environment itself.

A Brief History of Visual Studio

Microsoft has worked long and hard on its development tools. Actually, its first software product was a version of BASIC in 1975. Back then, programming languages were mainly interpretive languages in which the computer would process the code to be performed line by line. In the past three decades, programming has seen many advances, one of the biggest by far being development environments aimed at helping developers be efficient at producing applications in their chosen language and platform.

In the 32-bit computing era, Microsoft started releasing comprehensive development tools, commonly called IDEs (integrated development environments), which contained not just a compiler but also a host of other features to supplement it, including a context-sensitive editor and rudimentary IntelliSense features that helped programmers determine what they could and couldn't do in a given situation. Along with these features came intuitive visual user interface designers with drag-and-drop functionality and associated tool windows that gave developers access to a variety of properties for the various components on a given window or user control.

Initially, these IDEs were different for each language, with Visual Basic being the most advanced in terms of the graphical designer and ease of use, and Visual C++ having the most power and flexibility. Under the banner of Visual Studio 6, the latest versions of these languages were released in one large development suite along with other "Visual" tools such as FoxPro and InterDev. However, it was obvious that each language still had a distinct environment in which to work, and as a result, development solutions had to be in a specific language.

One Comprehensive Environment

When Microsoft first released Visual Studio .NET in 2002, it inherited many features and attributes of the various, disparate development tools the company had previously offered. Visual Basic 6, Visual InterDev, Visual C++, and other tools such as FoxPro all contributed to a development effort that the Microsoft development team mostly created on its own. The team had some input from external groups, but Visual Studio .NET 2002 and .NET 1.0 were primarily founded on Microsoft's own principles and goals.

Visual Studio .NET 2003 was the next version released, and it provided mostly small enhancements and big fixes. Two years later, Visual Studio 2005 and the .NET Framework 2.0 were released. Subsequently Visual Studio 2008, coupled with the .NET Frameworks 3.0 and 3.5, was then released. These were both major releases with new foundation framework classes that went far beyond anything Microsoft had released previously. However, the most significant part of these releases was realized in the IDE where the various components continued to evolve in a cohesive way to provide you with an efficient tool set where everything was easily accessible.

The latest release, Visual Studio 2010 and .NET Framework 4.0, builds on this strong foundation. With the code shell being re-written to use Windows Presentation Foundation, many of the now out-dated designers have been given a new lease of life. In addition there are new designers to assist with building Silverlight applications and built-in support for building Office applications.

Visual Studio 2010 comes in several versions: Express, Professional, Premium and Ultimate. The majority of this book deals with the Professional Edition of Visual Studio 2010, but some parts utilize features found only in the Premium and Ultimate editions. If you haven't used these editions before, read through Chapters 54 to 57 (available online) for an overview of the features they offer over and above the Professional Edition.

HOW THIS BOOK IS STRUCTURED

This book's first section is dedicated to familiarizing you with the core aspects of Visual Studio 2010. Everything you need is contained in the first five chapters, from the IDE structure and layout to the various options and settings you can change to make the user interface synchronize with your own way of doing things.

From there, the remainder of the book is broken into 11 parts:

➤ **Getting Started:** In this part, you learn how to take control of your projects and organize them in ways that work with your own style.

➤ **Digging Deeper:** Though the many graphical components of Visual Studio that make a programmer's job easier are discussed in many places throughout this book, you often need help when you're in the process of actually writing code. This part deals with features that support the coding of applications such as IntelliSense, code refactoring, and creating and running unit tests In the latest version of the .NET Framework, enhancements were added to support dynamic languages and move towards feature parity between the two primary .NET languages, C# and VB. This part covers changes to these languages, as well as looking at a range of features that will help you write better and more consistent code.

➤ **Rich Client** and **Web Applications:** For support building everything from Office add-ins to cloud applications, Visual Studio enables you to develop applications for a wide range of platforms. These two parts cover the application platforms that are supported within Visual Studio 2010, including ASP.NET and Office, WPF, Silverlight 2 and ASP.NET MVC.

➤ **Data:** A large proportion of applications use some form of data storage. Visual Studio 2010 and the .NET Framework include strong support for working with databases and other data sources. This part examines how to use DataSets, the Visual Database Tools, LINQ, Synchronization Services and ADO.NET Entity Framework to build applications that work with data. It also shows you how you can then present this data using Reporting.

➤ **Application Services:** Through the course of building an application you are likely to require access to services that may or may not reside within your organization. This part covers core technologies such as WCF, WF, Synchronization Services and WCF RIA Services that you can use to connect to these services.

➤ **Configuration and Internationalization:** The built-in support for configuration files allows you to adjust the way an application functions on the fly without having to rebuild it. Furthermore, resource files can be used to both access static data and easily localize an application into foreign languages and cultures. This part of the book shows how to use .NET configuration and resource files.

➤ **Debugging:** Application debugging is one of the more challenging tasks developers have to tackle, but correct use of the Visual Studio 2010 debugging features will help you analyze the state of the application and determine the cause of any bugs. This part examines the rich debugging support provided by the IDE.

➤ **Build and Deployment:** In addition to discussing how to build your solutions effectively and getting applications into the hands of your end users, this part also deals with the process of upgrading your projects from previous versions.

➤ **Customizing and Extending Visual Studio:** If the functionality found in the previous part isn't enough to help you in your coding efforts, Microsoft has made Visual Studio 2010 even more extensible. This part covers the automation model, how to write add-ins and macros, and then how to use a new extensibility framework, MEF, to extend Visual Studio 2010.

➤ **Visual Studio Ultimate (available online):** The final part of the book examines the additional features only available in the Premium and Ultimate versions of Visual Studio 2010. In addition, you'll also learn how the Team Foundation Server provides an essential tool for managing software projects.

Though this breakdown of the Visual Studio feature set provides the most logical and easily understood set of topics, you may need to look for specific functions that will aid you in a particular activity. To address this need, references to appropriate chapters are provided whenever a feature is covered in more detail elsewhere in the book.

WHAT YOU NEED TO USE THIS BOOK

To use this book effectively, you'll need only one additional item — Microsoft Visual Studio 2010 Professional Edition. With this software installed and the information found in this book, you'll be able to get a handle on how to use Visual Studio 2010 effectively in a very short period of time.

This book assumes that you are familiar with the traditional programming model, and it uses both the C# and Visual Basic (VB) languages to illustrate features within Visual Studio 2010. In addition, it is assumed that you can understand the code listings without an explanation of basic programming concepts in either language. If you're new to programming and want to learn Visual Basic, please take a look at *Beginning Visual Basic 2010* by Thearon Willis and Bryan Newsome. Similarly, if you are after a great book on C#, track down *Beginning Visual C# 2010*, written collaboratively by a host of authors.

Some chapters discuss additional products and tools that work in conjunction with Visual Studio. The following are all available to download either on a trial basis or for free:

➤ **Code Snippet Editor:** This is a third-party tool developed for creating code snippets in VB. The Snippet Editor tool is discussed in Chapter 8.

➤ **Sandcastle:** Using Sandcastle, you can generate comprehensive documentation for every member and class within your solutions from the XML comments in your code. XML comments and Sandcastle are discussed in Chapter 12.

➤ **SQL Server 2008:** The installation of Visual Studio 2010 includes an install of SQL Server 2008 Express, enabling you to build applications that use database files. However, for more comprehensive enterprise solutions, you can use SQL Server 2008 instead. Database connectivity is covered in Chapter 26.

➤ **Visual Studio 2010 Premium or Ultimate edition:** These more advanced versions of Visual Studio introduce tools for other parts of the development process such as testing and design. They are discussed in Chapters 54-57 that are available online.

➤ **Team Foundation Server:** The server product that provides application lifecycle management throughout Visual Studio 2010. This is covered in Chapter 57.

CONVENTIONS

To help you get the most from the text and keep track of what's happening, we've used a number of conventions throughout the book.

> *Boxes with a warning icon like this one hold important, not-to-be forgotten information that is directly relevant to the surrounding text.*

> *The pencil icon indicates notes, tips, hints, tricks, or asides to the current discussion.*
>
> *As for styles in the text:*
>
> ➤ *We highlight new terms and important words when we introduce them.*
>
> ➤ *We show keyboard strokes like this: Ctrl+A.*
>
> ➤ *We show file names, URLs, and code within the text like so:* persistence.properties.
>
> ➤ *We present code in two different ways:*
>
> ```
> We use a monofont type with no highlighting for most code
> examples.
> We use bold to emphasize code that's particularly important in the
> present context or to show changes from a previous code snippet.
> ```

SOURCE CODE

As you work through the examples in this book, you may choose either to type in all the code manually, or to use the source code files that accompany the book. All the source code used in this book is available for download at `http://www.wrox.com`. When at the site, simply locate the book's title (use the Search box or one of the title lists) and click the Download Code link on the book's detail page to obtain all the source code for the book. Code that is included on the Web site is highlighted by the following icon:

Available for download on Wrox.com

Listings include the filename in the title. If it is just a code snippet, you'll find the filename in a code note such as this:

code snippet filename

 Because many books have similar titles, you may find it easiest to search by ISBN; this book's ISBN is 978-0-470-54865-3.

Once you download the code, just decompress it with your favorite compression tool. Alternately, you can go to the main Wrox code download page at `http://www.wrox.com/dynamic/books/download.aspx` to see the code available for this book and all other Wrox books.

ERRATA

We make every effort to ensure that there are no errors in the text or in the code. However, no one is perfect, and mistakes do occur. If you find an error in one of our books, like a spelling mistake or faulty piece of code, we would be very grateful for your feedback. By sending in errata you may save another reader hours of frustration and at the same time you will be helping us provide even higher quality information.

To find the errata page for this book, go to `http://www.wrox.com` and locate the title using the Search box or one of the title lists. Then, on the book details page, click the Book Errata link. On this page you can view all errata that has been submitted for this book and posted by Wrox editors. A complete book list including links to each book's errata is also available at `www.wrox.com/misc-pages/booklist.shtml`.

If you don't spot "your" error on the Book Errata page, go to `www.wrox.com/contact/techsupport.shtml` and complete the form there to send us the error you have found. We'll check the information and, if appropriate, post a message to the book's errata page and fix the problem in subsequent editions of the book.

P2P.WROX.COM

For author and peer discussion, join the P2P forums at p2p.wrox.com. The forums are a Web-based system for you to post messages relating to Wrox books and related technologies and interact with other readers and technology users. The forums offer a subscription feature to e-mail you topics of interest of your choosing when new posts are made to the forums. Wrox authors, editors, other industry experts, and your fellow readers are present on these forums.

At http://p2p.wrox.com you will find a number of different forums that will help you not only as you read this book, but also as you develop your own applications. To join the forums, just follow these steps:

1. Go to p2p.wrox.com and click the Register link.

2. Read the terms of use and click Agree.

3. Complete the required information to join as well as any optional information you wish to provide and click Submit.

4. You will receive an e-mail with information describing how to verify your account and complete the joining process.

> *You can read messages in the forums without joining P2P but in order to post your own messages, you must join.*

Once you join, you can post new messages and respond to messages other users post. You can read messages at any time on the Web. If you would like to have new messages from a particular forum e-mailed to you, click the Subscribe to this Forum icon by the forum name in the forum listing.

For more information about how to use the Wrox P2P, be sure to read the P2P FAQs for answers to questions about how the forum software works as well as many common questions specific to P2P and Wrox books. To read the FAQs, click the FAQ link on any P2P page.

PART I
Integrated Development Environment

▶ **CHAPTER 1:** A Quick Tour

▶ **CHAPTER 2:** The Solution Explorer, Toolbox, and Properties

▶ **CHAPTER 3:** Options and Customizations

▶ **CHAPTER 4:** The Visual Studio Workspace

▶ **CHAPTER 5:** Find and Replace and Help

1

A Quick Tour

WHAT'S IN THIS CHAPTER?

➤ Installing and getting started with Visual Studio 2010

➤ Creating and running your first application

➤ Debugging and deploying an application

Ever since we have been developing software, there has been a need for tools to help us write, compile, debug, and deploy our applications. Microsoft Visual Studio 2010 is the next iteration in the continual evolution of a best-of-breed integrated development environment (IDE).

This chapter introduces the Visual Studio 2010 user experience and shows you how to work with the various menus, toolbars, and windows. It serves as a quick tour of the IDE, and as such it doesn't go into detail about what settings can be changed or how to go about customizing the layout, because these topics are explored in the following chapters.

GETTING STARTED

With each iteration of the Visual Studio product, the installation process has been incrementally improved, meaning that you can now get up and running with Visual Studio 2010 with minimal fuss. This section walks you through the installation process and getting started with the IDE.

Installing Visual Studio 2010

When you launch Visual Studio 2010 setup, you see the dialog in Figure 1-1 showing you the three product installation stages. As you would imagine, the first stage is to install the product itself. The other two stages are optional. You can either install the product documentation locally, or use the online (and typically more up-to-date) version. It is recommended that you do search for service releases because it ensures you are working with the most recent version of the product and associated tools.

FIGURE 1-1

As you progress through the setup process you are prompted to provide feedback to Microsoft (left image, Figure 1-2) and agree to the licensing terms for the product (right image, Figure 1-2).

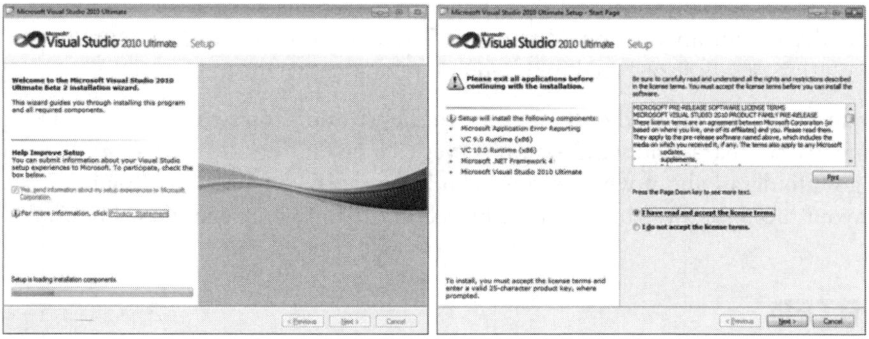

FIGURE 1-2

The Visual Studio 2010 setup process has been optimized for two general categories of developers: those writing managed, or .NET, applications, and those writing native, or C++, applications (left image, Figure 1-3). The Customize button allows you to select components from the full component tree as shown in the right image of Figure 1-3.

FIGURE 1-3

Once you have selected the components you want to install, you see the updated progress dialog in the left image of Figure 1-4. Depending on which components you already have installed on your computer, you may be prompted to restart your computer midway through the installation process. When all the components have been installed, you see the setup summary dialog in the right image of Figure 1-4. You should review this to ensure that no errors were encountered during installation.

FIGURE 1-4

Running Visual Studio 2010

When you launch Visual Studio the Microsoft Visual Studio 2010 splash screen appears. Like a lot of splash screens, it provides information about the version of the product and to whom it has been licensed, as shown in Figure 1-5.

FIGURE 1-5

> *An interesting fact about the splash screen is that while a large portion of Visual Studio now uses WPF to display its content, the new splash screen in Visual Studio 2010 is still done in native code so that it displays as soon as possible after you start Visual Studio. A significant amount of time went into hand crafting the wave at the bottom of the splash screen, so make sure you marvel at it whenever you're sitting there patiently waiting for Visual Studio to load.*

The first time you run Visual Studio 2010, you see the splash screen only for a short period before you are prompted to select the default environment settings. It may seem unusual to ask those who haven't used a product before how they imagine themselves using it. Because Microsoft has consolidated a number of languages and technologies into a single IDE, that IDE must account for the subtle (and sometimes not so subtle) differences in the way developers work.

If you take a moment to review the various options in this list, as shown in Figure 1-6, you'll find that the environment settings that are affected include the position and visibility of various windows, menus, and toolbars, and even keyboard shortcuts. For example, if you select the General Development Settings option as your default preference, this screen describes the changes that will be applied. Chapter 3 covers how you can change your default environment settings at a later stage.

FIGURE 1-6

> *A tip for Visual Basic .NET developers coming from previous versions of Visual Studio is that they should not use the Visual Basic Development Settings option. This option has been configured for VB6 developers and will only infuriate Visual Basic .NET developers, because they will be used to different shortcut key mappings. We recommend that you use the general development settings, because these will use the standard keyboard mappings without being geared toward another development language.*

THE VISUAL STUDIO IDE

Depending on which set of environment settings you select, when you click the Start Visual Studio button you will most likely see a dialog indicating that Visual Studio is configuring the development environment. When this process is complete, Visual Studio 2010 opens, ready for you to start work, as shown in Figure 1-7.

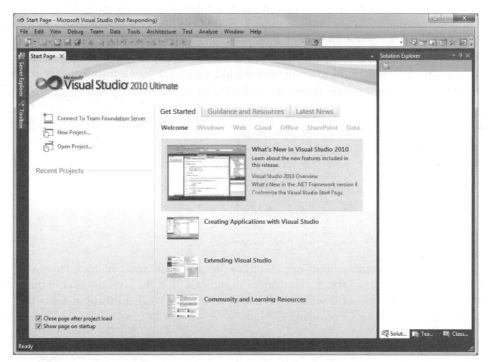

FIGURE 1-7

Regardless of the environment settings you selected, you see the Start Page in the center of the screen. However, the contents of the Start Page and the surrounding toolbars and tool windows can vary.

> *If you click the grey rounded rectangle with the text "Download the latest information for developers to the Start Page," this pulls down news items from an RSS feed specified in the environment settings you specified. Each item is displayed in summary within the rectangle, allowing you to click through to the full article. You can customize this feed by changing the Start Page News Channel property on the Environment ➪ Startup node of the Options dialog, accessible via the Options item on the Tools menu.*

Before you launch into building your first application, it's important to take a step back and look at the components that make up the Visual Studio 2010 IDE. Menus and toolbars are positioned along the top of the environment, and a selection of subwindows, or panes, appears on the left, right, and bottom of the main window area. In the center is the main editor space: whenever you open a code file, an XML document, a form, or some other file, it appears in this space for editing. With each file you open, a new tab is created so that you can toggle among opened files.

On either side of the editor space is a set of tool windows: these areas provide additional contextual information and functionality. In the case of the general developer settings, the default layout includes the Solution Explorer and Class View on the right, and the Server Explorer and Toolbox on the left. The tool windows on the left are in their collapsed, or *unpinned*, state. If you click a tool window's title, it expands; it collapses again when it no longer has focus or you move the cursor to another area of the screen. When a tool window is expanded, you see a series of three icons at the top right of the window, similar to those shown in the left image of Figure 1-8.

FIGURE 1-8

If you want the tool window to remain in its expanded, or *pinned*, state, you can click the middle icon, which looks like a pin. The pin rotates 90 degrees to indicate that the window is now pinned. Clicking the third icon, the X, closes the window. If later you want to reopen this or another tool window, you can select it from the View menu.

> *Some tool windows are not accessible via the View menu; for example, those having to do with debugging, such as threads and watch windows. In most cases these windows are available via an alternative menu item; in the case of the debugging windows, it is the Debug menu.*

The right image in Figure 1-8 shows the context menu that appears when the first icon, the down arrow, is clicked. Each item in this list represents a different way of arranging the tool window. As you would imagine, the Float option allows the tool window to be placed anywhere on the screen, independent of the main IDE window. This is useful if you have multiple screens, because you can move the various tool windows onto the additional screen, allowing the editor space to use the maximum screen real estate. Selecting the Dock as Tabbed Document option makes the tool window into an additional tab in the editor space. In Chapter 4, you learn how to effectively manage the workspace by docking and pinning tool windows.

Developing, Building, Debugging, and Deploying Your First Application

Now that you have seen an overview of the Visual Studio 2010 IDE, this section walks through creating a simple application that demonstrates working with some of these components. This is, of course, the mandatory "Hello World" sample that every developer needs to know, and it can be done in either Visual Basic .NET or C#, depending on what you feel more comfortable with.

1. Start by selecting File ⇨ New ⇨ Project. This opens the New Project dialog, as shown in Figure 1-9. If you have worked with earlier versions of Visual Studio you will notice that this dialog has had a significant facelift. There is still the tree on the left side of the dialog for grouping templates based on language and technology, but now there is also a search box in the top-right corner. The right pane of this dialog displays additional information about the project template you have selected. Lastly, you can select the version of the .NET Framework that the application will target using the drop-down at the top of the dialog.

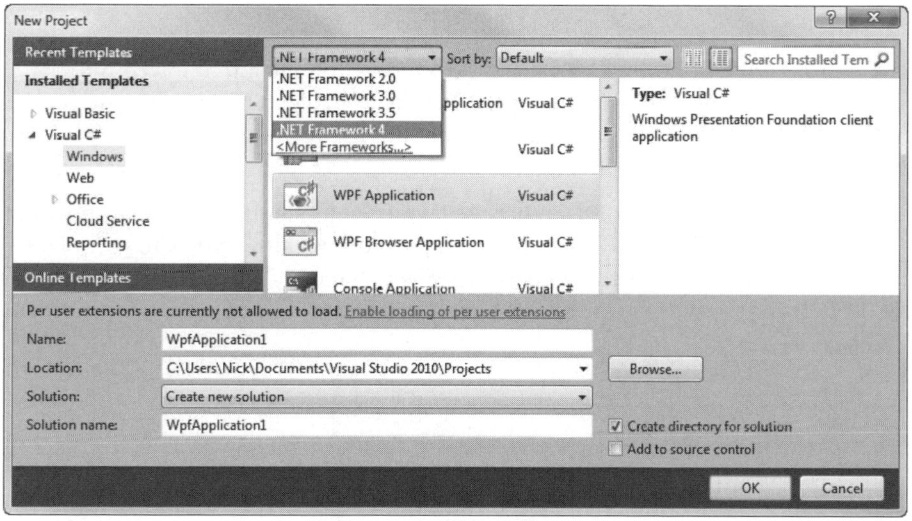

FIGURE 1-9

Select the WPF Application from the Templates area (this item exists under the root Visual Basic and Visual C# nodes, or under the sub-node Windows) and set the Name to **GettingStarted,** before selecting OK. This should create a new WPF application project, which includes a single startup window and is contained within a GettingStarted solution, as shown in the Solution Explorer window of Figure 1-10. This startup window has automatically opened in the visual designer, giving you a graphical representation of what the window will look like when you run the application. You will notice that the Properties tool window has appeared at the bottom of the right tool windows area.

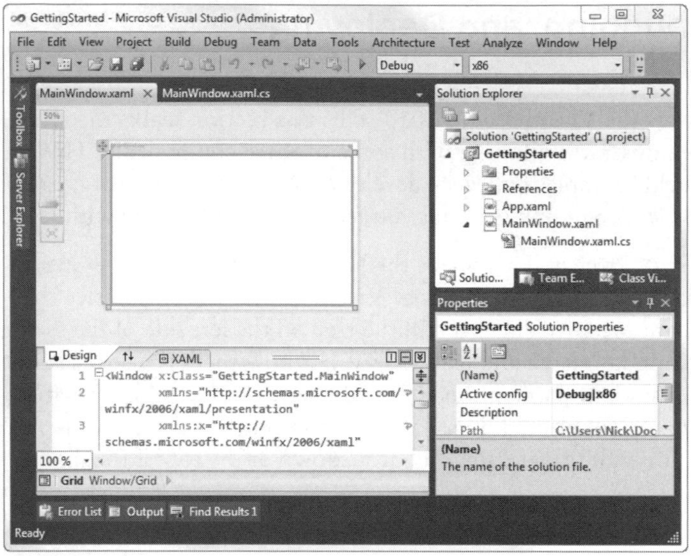

FIGURE 1-10

2. Click the Toolbox tool window, which causes the window to expand, followed by the pin icon, which pins the tool window open. To add controls to the window, select the appropriate items from the Toolbox and drag them onto the form. Alternatively, you can double-click the item and Visual Studio automatically adds them to the window.

3. Add a button and textbox to the form so that the layout looks similar to the one shown in Figure 1-11. Select the textbox and select the Properties tool window (you can press F4 to automatically open the Properties tool window). Change the name of the control to **txtToSay**. Repeat for the Button control, naming it **btnSayHello** and setting the *Content* property to **Say Hello!**

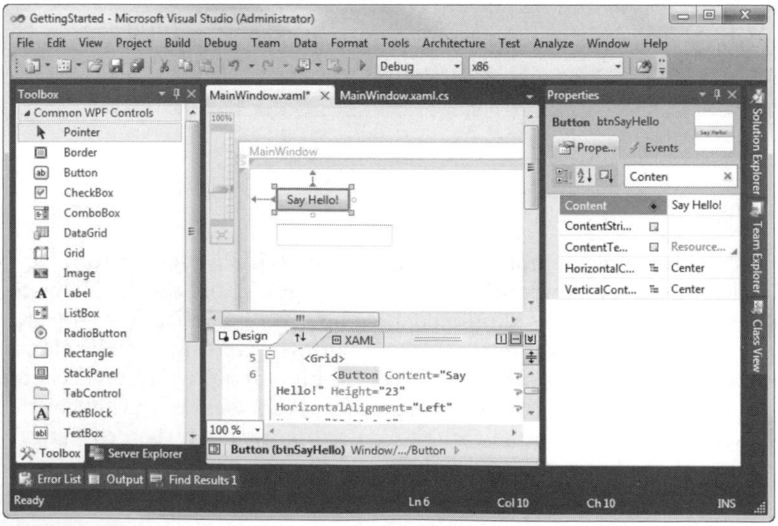

FIGURE 1-11

You can quickly locate a property by typing its name into the search field located beneath the Name field. In Figure 1-11 "Conten" has been entered in order to reduce the list of Properties so that it's easier to locate the Content property.

You will also notice that after you add controls to the window, the tab is updated with an asterisk (*) after the text to indicate that there are unsaved changes to that particular item. If you attempt to close this item while changes are pending, you are asked if you want to save the changes. When you build the application, any unsaved files are automatically saved as part of the build process.

> *One thing to be aware of is that some files, such as the solution file, are modified when you make changes within Visual Studio 2010 without your being given any indication that they have changed. If you try to exit the application or close the solution, you are still prompted to save these changes.*

4. Deselect all controls and then double-click the button. This not only opens the code editor with the code-behind file for this form, it also creates and wires up an event handler for the click event on the button. Figure 1-12 shows the code window after a single line has been added to echo the message to the user.

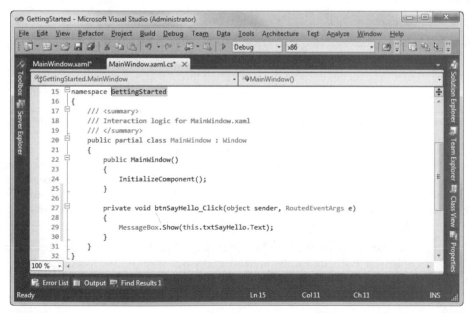

FIGURE 1-12

5. Before you build and execute your application, place the cursor somewhere on the line containing `Messagebox.Show` and press F9. This sets a breakpoint — when you run the application by pressing F5 and then click the "Say Hello!" button, the execution halts at this line. Figure 1-13 illustrates this breakpoint being reached. The data tip, which appears when the mouse hovers over the line, shows the contents of the `txtToSay.Text` property.

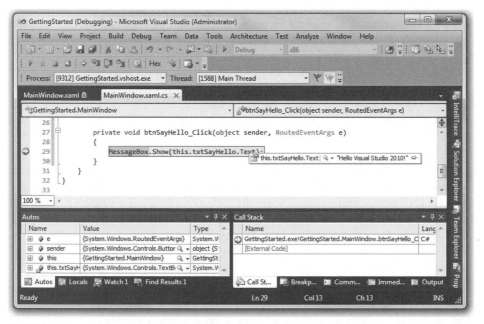

FIGURE 1-13

The layout of Visual Studio in Figure 1-13 is significantly different from the previous screenshots, because a number of new tool windows are visible in the lower half of the screen, and new command bars are visible at the top. When you stop the application you will notice that Visual Studio returns to the previous layout. Visual Studio 2010 maintains two separate layouts: design time and run time. Menus, toolbars, and various windows have default layouts for when you are editing a project, whereas a different setup is defined for when a project is being executed and debugged. You can modify each of these layouts to suit your own style and Visual Studio 2010 will remember them.

6. The last step is to deploy your application. Whether you're building a rich client application using Windows Forms or WPF, or a web application, Visual Studio 2010 has the ability to publish your application. Double-click the Properties node in Solution Explorer and select the Publish node to display the options for publishing your application, as shown in Figure 1-14.

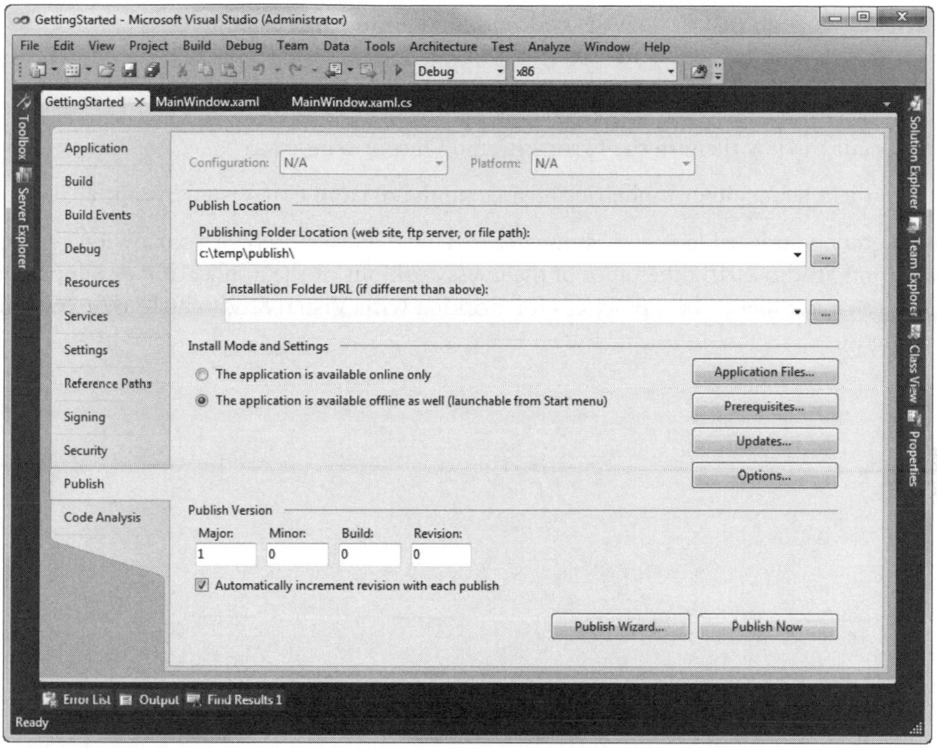

FIGURE 1-14

In Figure 1-14, the publishing folder has been set to a local path, but you can specify a network folder, an IIS folder, or an FTP site instead. Once you have specified where you want to publish to, clicking Publish Now publishes your application to that location.

SUMMARY

You've now seen how the various components of Visual Studio 2010 work together to build an application. The following list outlines the typical process of creating a solution:

1. Use the File menu to create a solution.

2. Use the Solution Explorer to locate the window that needs editing and double-click the item to show it in the main workspace area.

3. Drag the necessary components onto the window from the Toolbox.

4. Select the window and each component in turn, and edit the properties in the Properties window.

5. Double-click the window or a control to access the code behind the component's graphical interface.

6. Use the main workspace area to write code and design the graphical interface, switching between the two via the tabs at the top of the area.

7. Use the toolbars to start the program.

8. If errors occur, review them in the Error List and Output windows.

9. Save the project using either toolbar or menu commands, and exit Visual Studio 2010.

In subsequent chapters, you learn how to customize the IDE to more closely fit your own working style, and how Visual Studio 2010 takes a lot of the guesswork out of the application development process. You also see a number of best practices for working with Visual Studio 2010 that you can reuse as a developer.

2

The Solution Explorer, Toolbox, and Properties

➤ Arranging files with the Solution Explorer

➤ Adding projects, items and references to your solution

➤ Working with the Properties tool window

➤ Include your own properties in the Properties tool window

In Chapter 1 you briefly saw and interacted with a number of the components that make up the Visual Studio 2010 IDE. Now you get an opportunity to work with three of the most commonly used tool windows — the Solution Explorer, the Toolbox, and Properties.

Throughout this and other chapters you see references to keyboard shortcuts, such as Ctrl+S. In these cases, we assume the use of the general development settings, as shown in Chapter 1. Other profiles may have different key combinations.

THE SOLUTION EXPLORER

Whenever you create or open an application, or for that matter just a single file, Visual Studio 2010 uses the concept of a solution to tie everything together. Typically, a solution is made up of one or more projects, each of which in turn can have multiple items associated with it. In the past these items were typically just files, but increasingly projects are made up of items that may consist of multiple files, or in some cases no files at all. Chapter 6 goes into more detail about projects, the structure of solutions, and how items are related.

The Solution Explorer tool window (Ctrl+Alt+L) provides a convenient visual representation of the solution, projects, and items, as shown in Figure 2-1. In this figure you can see three projects presented in a tree: a C# WPF application, a C# WCF service library, and a VB class library.

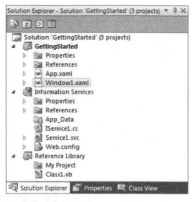

Each project has an icon associated with it that typically indicates the type of project and the language it is written in. There are some exceptions to this rule, such as setup projects that don't have a language.

One node is particularly noticeable, because the font is boldfaced. This indicates that this project is the startup project — in other words, the project that is launched when you select Debug ➪ Start Debugging or press F5. To change the

FIGURE 2-1

startup project, right-click the project you want to nominate and select Set as StartUp Project. It is also possible to nominate multiple projects as startup projects via the Solution Properties dialog, which you can reach by selecting Properties from the right-click menu of the Solution node.

> *With certain environment settings (see "Let's Get Started" in Chapter 1), the Solution node is not visible when only a single project exists. The problem with this is that it becomes difficult to access the Solution Properties window. To get the Solution node to appear you can either add another project to the solution or check the Always Show Solution item from the Projects and Solutions node in the Options dialog, accessible via Tools ➪ Options.*

The toolbar across the top of the Solution Explorer enables you to customize the way the contents of the window appear to you, as well as giving you shortcuts to the different views for individual items. For example, the first button, Show All Files, expands the solution listing to display the additional files and folders, shown in Figure 2-2. You can see that the My Project node is actually made up of multiple files, which hold settings, resources, and information about the assembly.

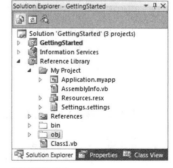

In this expanded view you can see all the files and folders contained under the project structure. Unfortunately, if the file system changes, the Solution Explorer does not automatically update to reflect these changes. The second button, Refresh, can be used to make sure you are seeing the correct list of files and folders.

FIGURE 2-2

The Solution Explorer toolbar is contextually aware, with different buttons displayed depending on what type of node is selected. This is shown in Figure 2-2, where a folder not contained in the project (as indicated by the faded icon color) is selected and the remaining buttons from Figure 2-1 are not visible. In short, these buttons when visible can be used to view code (in this case, the `Window1.xaml.cs` file) or open the designer, which displays both the design and xaml views of the `Window1.xaml` file. Figure 2-2 also shows the Class Diagram button.

> *If you don't already have a class diagram in your project, clicking the View Class Diagram button will insert one and automatically add all the classes. For a project with a lot of classes, this can be quite time consuming and will result in a large and unwieldy class diagram. It is generally a better idea to manually add one or more class diagrams, which gives you total control.*

Common Tasks

In addition to providing a convenient way to manage projects and items, the Solution Explorer has a dynamic context menu that gives you quick access to some of the most common tasks, such as building the solution or individual projects, accessing the build configuration manager, and opening files. Figure 2-3 shows how the context menu varies depending on which item is selected in the Solution Explorer.

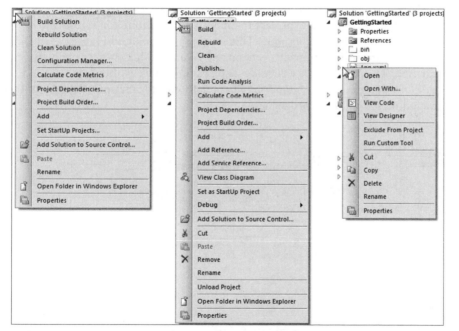

FIGURE 2-3

The first items in the left-hand and center menus relate to building either the entire solution or the selected project. In most cases, selecting Build is the most efficient option, because it only builds projects that have changed. However, in some cases you may need to force a Rebuild, which builds all dependent projects regardless of their states. If you just want to remove all the additional files that are created during the build process, you can invoke Clean. This option can be useful if you want to package your solution in order to e-mail it to someone — you wouldn't want to include all the temporary or output files that are created by the build.

For most items in the Solution Explorer, the first section of the context menu is similar to the right-hand menu in Figure 2-3: the default Open and Open With items allow you to determine how the item will be opened. This is of particular use when you are working with XML resource files. Visual Studio 2010 opens this file type using the built-in resource editor, but this prevents you from making certain changes and doesn't support all data types you might want to include (Chapter 38 goes into how you can use your own data types in resource files), Using the Open With menu item, you can use the XML Editor instead.

> *The context menu for the Solution, Project, and Folder nodes contains the Open Folder in Windows Explorer item. This enables you to open Windows Explorer quickly to the location of the selected item, saving you the hassle of having to navigate to where your solution is located and then find the appropriate subfolder.*

Adding Projects and Items

The most common activities carried out in the Solution Explorer are the addition, removal, and renaming of projects and items. To add a new project to an existing solution, you select Add ⇨ New Project from the context menu off the Solution node. This invokes the dialog in Figure 2-4, which has undergone a few minor changes since previous versions of Visual Studio. Project templates can now be sorted and searched. The pane on the right side displays information about the selected project, such as the type of project and its description (Chapter 15 covers creating your own Project and Item templates, including setting these properties).

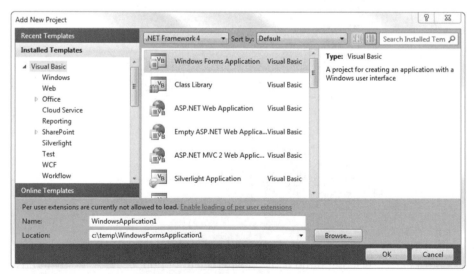

FIGURE 2-4

In the Installed Templates hierarchy on the left of the Add New Project dialog, the templates are primarily arranged by language and then by technology. The templates include Office project types, enabling you to build both application- and document-level add-ins for most of the Office products. Though the Office add-ins still make use of Visual Studio Tools for Office (VSTO), this is built into Visual Studio 2010 instead of being an additional installer. You'll see in Chapter 19 how you can use these project types to build add-ins for the core Office applications. There are also tabs for Recent Templates and Online Templates. The Online Templates can be sorted and searched in the same way as your Installed Templates, although the sort criteria has been extended to include creation date, ratings, and downloaded frequency.

The other thing you will notice in this dialog is the ability to select different framework versions. If you have existing projects that you don't want to have to migrate forward to the new version of the .NET Framework, you can still immediately take advantage of the new features, such as improved IntelliSense. The alternative would have been to have both Visual Studio 2010 and a previous version installed in order to build projects for earlier framework versions. The framework selection is also included in the search criteria, limiting the list of available project templates to those that are compatible with the selected .NET Framework version.

> *When you open your existing solutions or projects in Visual Studio 2010, they will still go through the upgrade wizard (see Chapter 44 for more information) but will essentially make only minor changes to the solution and project files. Unfortunately, these minor changes, which involve the inclusion of additional properties, will break your existing build process if you are using a previous version of MSBuild. For this reason, you will still need to migrate your entire development team across to using Visual Studio 2010.*

One of the worst and most poorly understood features in Visual Studio is the concept of a Web Site project. This is distinct from a Web Application project, which can be added via the aforementioned Add New Project dialog. To add a Web Site project you need to select Add ➪ Web Site from the context menu off the Solution node. This displays a dialog similar to the one shown in Figure 2-5, where you can select the type of web project to be created. In most cases, this simply determines the type of default item that is to be created in the project.

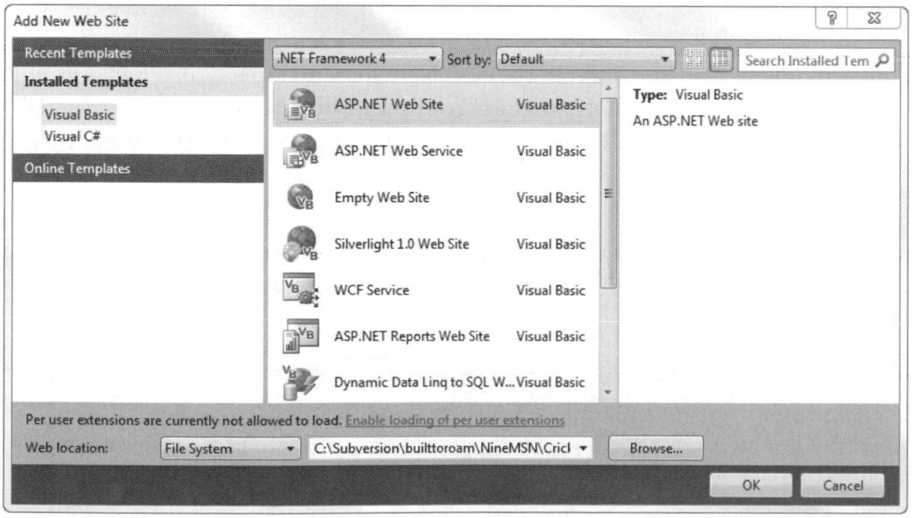

FIGURE 2-5

> *It is important to note that the types of web projects listed in Figure 2-5 are the same as the types listed under the Web node in the Add New Project dialog. However, understand that they will not generate the same results, because significant differences exist between Web Site projects (created via the Add New Web Site dialog) and Web Application projects (created via the Add New Project dialog). The differences between these project types are covered in detail in Chapter 20.*

Once you have a project or two, you will need to start adding items. You do this via the Add context menu item off the project node in the Solution Explorer. The first submenu, New Item, launches the Add New Item dialog, as seen in Figure 2-6.

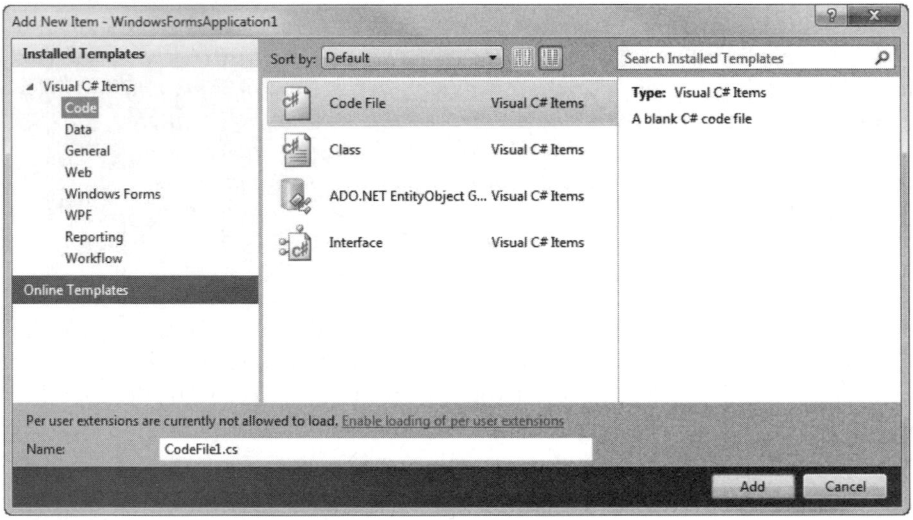

FIGURE 2-6

Like the New Project and New Web Site dialogs, the Add New Item dialog has also had a facelift. In addition to listing only those item templates that are relevant to the project you have selected, this dialog enables you to search the installed templates, as well as go online to look for templates generated by third parties.

Returning to the Add context menu, you will notice a number of predefined shortcuts such as User Control and Class. These do little more than bypass the stage of locating the appropriate template within the Add New Item dialog. The Add New Item dialog is still displayed, because you need to assign a name to the item being created.

> *It is important to make the distinction that you are adding items rather than files to the project. Though a lot of the templates contain only a single file, some, like the Window or User Control, will add multiple files to your project.*

Adding References

Each new software development technology that is released promises better reuse, but few are able to actually deliver on this promise. One way that Visual Studio 2010 supports reusable components is via the references for a project. If you expand out any project you will observe a number of .NET Framework libraries, such as System and System.Core, that need to be referenced by a project in order to be built. Essentially, a reference enables the compiler to resolve type, property, field, and method names back to the assembly where they are defined. If you want to reuse a class from a third-party library, or even your own .NET assembly, you need to add a reference to it via the Add Reference context menu item on the project node of the Solution Explorer.

When you launch the Add Reference dialog, shown in Figure 2-7, Visual Studio 2010 interrogates the local computer, the Global Assembly Cache, and your solution in order to present a list of known libraries that can be referenced. This includes both .NET and COM references that are separated into different lists, as well as projects and recently used references. In previous versions of Visual Studio this dialog was notoriously slow to load. If the component you need to reference isn't present in the appropriate list, you can choose the Browse tab, which enables you to locate the file containing the component directly in the file system. By initially loading the list of projects within your solution and presenting that as the default tab, then lazy loading the content for the remaining tabs, this dialog now displays almost instantly.

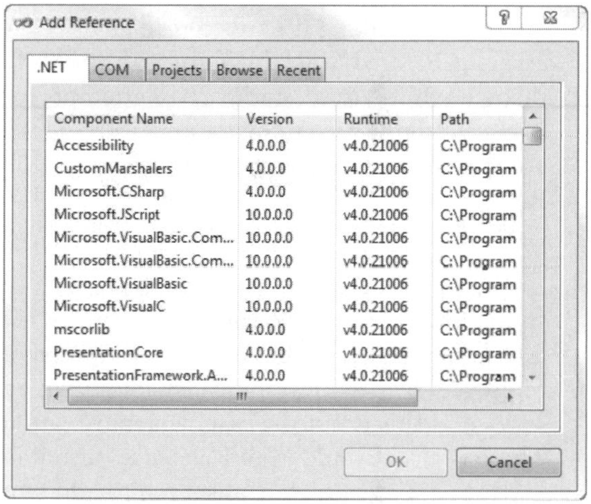

FIGURE 2-7

As in other project-based development environments going back as far as the first versions of VB, you can add references to projects contained in your solution, rather than adding the compiled binary components. The advantage to this model is that it's easier to debug into the referenced component and helps ensure you are running the latest version of all components, but for large solutions this may become unwieldy.

> *When you have a solution with a large number of projects (large can be relevant to your computer but typically anything over 20), you may want to consider having multiple solutions that reference subsets of the projects. This will continue to give you a nice debugging experience throughout the entire application while improving Visual Studio performance during both loading and building of the solution. Alternatively, you may want to create different build configurations (see Chapter 45) to build a subset of the projects.*

Adding Service References

The other type of reference that the Solution Explorer caters to is service references. In previous versions of Visual Studio this was referred to as web references, but with the advent of the Windows Communication Foundation (WCF) there is now a more generic Add Service Reference menu item. This invokes the Add Service Reference dialog, which you can see in Figure 2-8. In this example the drop-down feature of the Discover button has been used to look for Services in Solution.

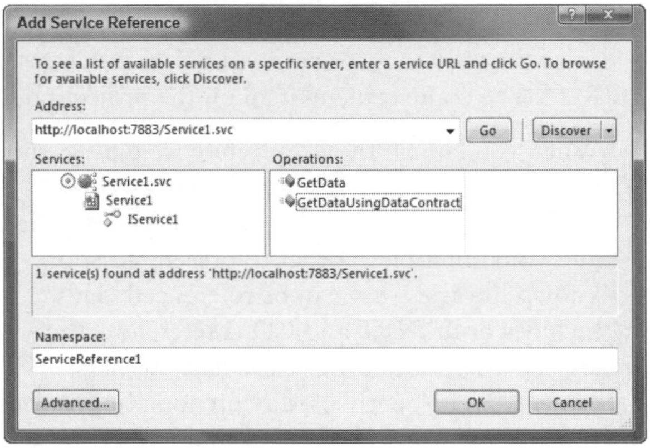

Unfortunately, this dialog is another case of Microsoft not understanding the usage pattern properly. Though the dialog itself is resizable, the status response message area is not, making it hard to read any errors generated. Luckily, if any errors are thrown while Visual Studio 2010 attempts to access the service information, it provides a hyperlink that opens the Add Service Reference Error dialog. This generally gives you enough information to resolve the problem.

FIGURE 2-8

In the lower left-hand corner of Figure 2-8 is an Advanced button. The Service Reference Settings dialog that this launches enables you to customize which types are defined as part of the service reference. By default, all local system types are assumed to match those being published by the service. If this is not the case, you may want to adjust the values in the Data Type area of this dialog. There is also an Add Web Reference button in the lower left-hand corner of the Service Reference Settings dialog, which enables you to add more traditional .NET Web service references. This might be important if you have some limitations or are trying to support intersystem operability. Adding services to your application is covered in more detail in Chapter 31 on WCF.

THE TOOLBOX

One of the major advantages over many other IDEs that Microsoft has offered developers is true drag-and-drop placement of elements during the design of both web and rich client applications. These elements are all available in what is known as the Toolbox (Ctrl+Alt+X), a tool window accessible via the View menu, as shown in Figure 2-9.

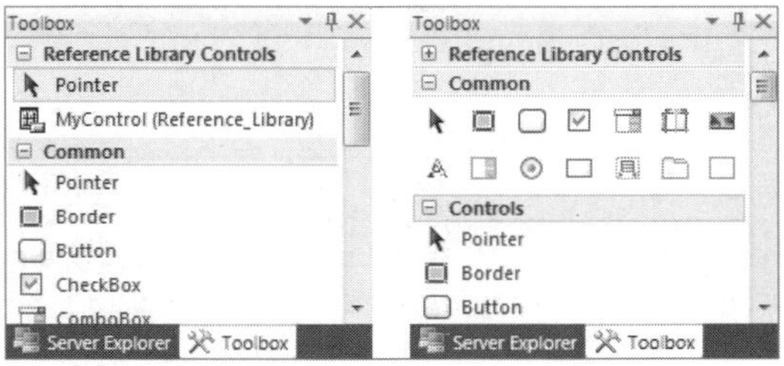

FIGURE 2-9

The Toolbox window contains all of the available components for the currently active document being shown in the main workspace. These can be visual components, such as buttons and textboxes; invisible, service-oriented objects, such as timers and system event logs; or even designer elements, such as class and interface objects used in the Class Designer view.

> *An interesting feature of the Toolbox is that you can copy snippets of code into the Toolbox by simply selecting a region and dragging it onto the Toolbox. You can rename and reorder your code snippets, making it really useful for presentations or storing chunks of code you use frequently.*

Visual Studio 2010 presents the available components in groups rather than as one big mess of components. This default grouping enables you to more easily locate the controls you need — for example, data-related components are in their own Data group.

By default, groups are presented in List view (see the left side of Figure 2-9). Each component is represented by its own icon and the name of the component. This differs from the old way of displaying the available objects, in which the Toolbox was simply a stacked list of icons that left you guessing as to what some of the more obscure components were, as shown with the Common Controls group on the right side of Figure 2-9. You can change the view of each control group individually — right-click anywhere within the group area and deselect the List View option in the context menu.

Regardless of how the components are presented, the way they are used in a program is usually the same: click and drag the desired component onto the design surface of the active document, or double-click the component's entry for Visual Studio to automatically add an instance. Visual components, such as buttons and textboxes, appear in the design area where they can be repositioned, resized, and otherwise adjusted via the property grid. Non-visual components, such as the Timer control, appear as icons, with associated labels, in a non-visual area below the design area, as shown in Figure 2-10.

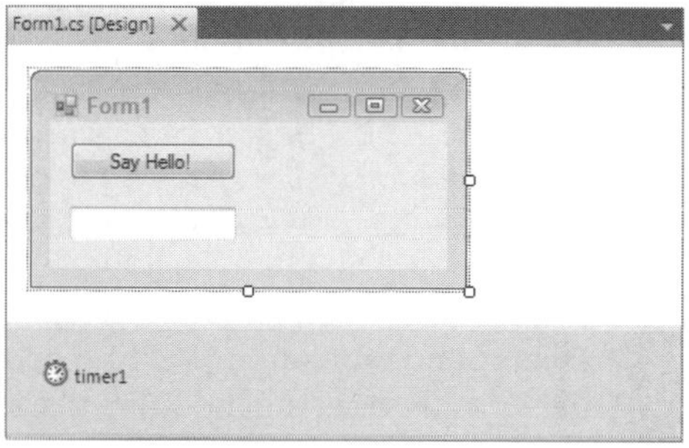

FIGURE 2-10

At the top left-hand side of Figure 2-9 is a group called Reference Library Controls with a single component, MyControl. "Reference_Library" is actually the name of a class library that is defined in the same solution, and it contains the MyControl control. When you start to build your own components or controls, instead of your having to manually create a new tab and go through the process of adding each item, Visual Studio 2010 automatically interrogates all the projects in your solution. If any components or controls are identified (essentially any class that implements *System .ComponentModel.IComponent* or *System.Windows.FrameworkElement* for WPF), a new tab is created for that project and the appropriate items are added with a default icon and class name (in this case MyControl), as you can see on the left in Figure 2-9. For components, this is the same icon that appears in the non-visual part of the design area when you use the component.

> *Visual Studio 2010 interrogates all projects in your solution, both at startup and after build activities. This can take a significant amount of time if you have a large number of projects. If this is the case, you should consider disabling this feature by setting the AutoToolboxPopulate property to false under the Windows Forms Designer node of the Options dialog (Tools ⇨ Options).*

To customize how your items appear in the Toolbox, you need to add a 16×16 pixel bitmap to the same project as your component or control. Next, select the newly inserted bitmap in the Solution Explorer and navigate to the Properties window. Make sure the Build property is set to Embedded Resource. All you now need to do is attribute your control with the `ToolboxBitmap` attribute:

VB

```
<ToolboxBitmap(GetType(MyControl), "MyControlIcon.bmp")>
Public Class MyControl
```

C#

```
[ToolboxBitmap(typeof(MyControl), "MyControlIcon.bmp")]
public class MyControl
```

This attribute uses the type reference for MyControl to locate the appropriate assembly from which to extract the `MyControlIcon.bmp` embedded resource. Other overloads of this attribute can use a file path as the only argument. In this case you don't even need to add the bitmap to your project.

> *Unfortunately, you can't customize the way the automatically generated items appear in the Toolbox. However, if you manually add an item to the Toolbox and select your components, you will see your custom icon. Alternatively, if you have a component and you drag it onto a form, you will see your icon appear in the non-visual space on the designer.*

It is also worth noting that customizing the Toolbox and designer experience for Windows Presentation Foundation (WPF) controls uses the notion of a Metadata store instead of attributes. This typically results in additional assemblies that can be used to tailor the design experience in both Visual Studio 2010 and Expression Blend.

Arranging Components

Having Toolbox items in alphabetical order is a good default because it enables you to locate items that are unfamiliar. However, if you're only using a handful of components and are frustrated by having to continuously scroll up and down, you can create your own groups of controls and move existing object types around.

Repositioning an individual component is easy. Locate it in the Toolbox and click and drag it to the new location. When you're happy with where it is, release the mouse button and the component will move to the new spot in the list. You can move it to a different group in the same way — just keep dragging the component up or down the Toolbox until you've located the right group. These actions work in both List and Icon views.

If you want to copy the component from one group to another, rather than move it, hold down the Ctrl key as you drag, and the process will duplicate the control so that it appears in both groups.

Sometimes it's nice to have your own group to host the controls and components you use the most. To create a new group in the Toolbox, right-click anywhere in the Toolbox area and select the Add Tab command. A new blank tab will be added to the bottom of the Toolbox with a prompt for you to name it. Once you have named the tab, you can then add components to it by following the steps described in this section.

When you first start Visual Studio 2010, the items within each group are arranged alphabetically. However, after moving items around, you may find that they're in a bewildering state and decide that you simply need to start again. All you have to do is right-click anywhere within the group and choose the Sort Items Alphabetically command.

By default, controls are added to the Toolbox according to their class names. This means you end up with some names that are hard to understand, particularly if you add COM controls to your Toolbox. Visual Studio 2010 enables you to modify a component's name to something more understandable.

To change the name of a component, right-click the component's entry in the Toolbox and select the Rename Item command. An edit field will appear inline in place of the original caption, enabling you to name it however you like, even with special characters.

If you've become even more confused, with components in unusual groups, and you have lost sight of where everything is, you can choose Reset Toolbox from the same right-click context menu. This restores all of the groups in the Toolbox to their original states, with components sorted alphabetically and in the groups in which they started.

> *Remember: Selecting Reset Toolbox deletes any of your own custom-made groups of commands, so be very sure you want to perform this function!*

Adding Components

Sometimes you'll find that a particular component you need is not present in the lists displayed in the Toolbox. Most of the main .NET components are already present, but some are not. For example, the WebClient class component is not displayed in the Toolbox by default. Managed applications can also use COM components in their design. Once added to the Toolbox, COM objects can be used in much the same way as regular .NET components, and if coded correctly you can program against them in precisely the same way, using the Properties window and referring to their methods, properties, and events in code.

To add a component to your Toolbox layout, right-click anywhere within the group of components you want to add it to and select Choose Items. After a moment (this process can take a few seconds on a slower machine, because the machine needs to interrogate the .NET cache to determine all the possible components you can choose from), you are presented with a list of .NET Framework components, as Figure 2-11 shows.

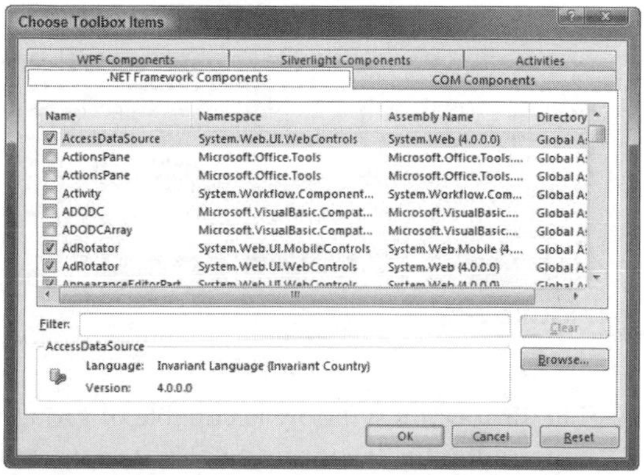

FIGURE 2-11

Scroll through the list to locate the item you want to add to the Toolbox and check the corresponding checkbox. You can add multiple items at the same time by selecting each of them before clicking the OK button to apply your changes. At this time you can also remove items from the Toolbox by deselecting them from the list. Note that this removes the items from any groups to which they belong, not just from the group you are currently editing.

If you're finding it hard to locate the item you need, you can use the Filter box, which filters the list based on name, namespace, and assembly name. On rare occasions the item may not be listed at all. This can happen with nonstandard components, such as ones that you build yourself or that are not registered in the Global Assembly Cache (GAC). You can still add them by using the Browse button to locate the physical file on the computer. Once you've selected and deselected the items you need, click the OK button to save them to the Toolbox layout.

COM components, WPF components, Silverlight Components, and (Workflow) Activities can be added in the same manner. Simply switch over to the relevant tab in the dialog window to view the list of available, properly registered COM components to add. Again, you can use the Browse button to locate controls that may not appear in the list.

PROPERTIES

One of the most frequently used tool windows built into Visual Studio 2010 is the Properties window (F4), as shown in Figure 2-12. The Properties window is made up of a property grid and is contextually aware, displaying only relevant properties of the currently selected item, whether that item is a node in the Solution Explorer or an element in the form design area. Each line represents a property with its name and corresponding value in two columns. The right side of Figure 2-12 shows the updated property grid for WPF applications, which includes a preview icon and search capabilities.

FIGURE 2-12

The Properties window is capable of grouping properties, or sorting them alphabetically — you can toggle this layout using the first two buttons at the top of the Properties window. It has built-in editors for a range of system types, such as colors, fonts, anchors, and docking, which are invoked when you click into the value column of the property to be changed. When a property is selected, as shown in the center of Figure 2-12, the property name is highlighted and a description is presented in the lower region of the property grid.

In the Properties window, read-only properties are indicated in gray and you will not be able to modify their values. The value SayHello for the Text property on the left side of Figure 2-12 is boldfaced, which indicates that this is not the default value for this property. Similarly on the right side of Figure 2-12 the Text property has a filled-in black square between the property name and value, indicating the value has been specified. If you inspect the following code that is generated by the designer, you will notice that a line exists for each property that is boldfaced in the property grid — adding a line of code for every single property on a control would significantly increase the time to render the form.

Available for download on Wrox.com

VB

```vb
Me.btnSayHello.Location = New System.Drawing.Point(12, 12)
Me.btnSayHello.Name = "btnSayHello"
Me.btnSayHello.Size = New System.Drawing.Size(100, 23)
Me.btnSayHello.TabIndex = 0
Me.btnSayHello.Text = "Say Hello!"
Me.btnSayHello.UseVisualStyleBackColor = True
```

Code snippet Form1.Designer.vb

Available for download on Wrox.com

C#

```csharp
this.btnSayHello.Location = new System.Drawing.Point(12, 12);
this.btnSayHello.Name = "btnSayHello";
this.btnSayHello.Size = new System.Drawing.Size(100, 23);
this.btnSayHello.TabIndex = 0;
this.btnSayHello.Text = "Say Hello!";
this.btnSayHello.UseVisualStyleBackColor = true;
```

Code snippet Form1.Designer.cs

> *For Web and WPF applications, the properties set in the Properties window are persisted as markup in the aspx or xaml file, respectively. As with the Windows forms designer, only those values in the Properties window that have been set are persisted into markup.*

In addition to displaying properties for a selected item, the Properties window also provides a design experience for wiring up event handlers. The Properties window on the left of Figure 2-13 illustrates the event view that is accessible via the fourth button, the lightning bolt, across the top of the Properties window. In this case, you can see that there is an event handler for the click event. To wire up another event you can either select from a list of existing methods via a drop-down list in the value column, or you can double-click the value column. This creates a new event-handler method and wires it up to the event. If you use the first method you will notice that only methods that match the event signature are listed.

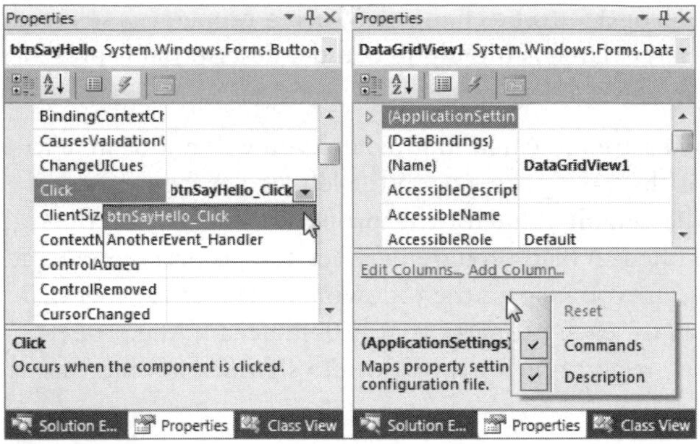

FIGURE 2-13

Certain components, such as the `DataGridView`, expose a number of commands, or shortcuts, that can be executed via the Properties window. On the right side of Figure 2-13 you can see two commands for the `DataGridView`: Edit Columns and Add Column. When you click either of these command links, you are presented with a dialog for performing that action.

If the Properties window has only a small amount of screen real estate, it can be difficult to scroll through the list of properties. If you right-click in the property grid you can uncheck the Command and Description checkboxes to hide these sections of the Properties window.

Extending the Properties Window

You have just seen how Visual Studio 2010 highlights properties that have changed by boldfacing the value. The question that you need to ask is, How does Visual Studio 2010 know what the default value is? The answer is that when the Properties window interrogates an object to determine what properties to display in the property grid, it looks for a number of design attributes. These attributes can be used to control which properties are displayed, the editor that is used to edit the value, and what the default value is. To show how you can use these attributes on your own components, start with adding a simple automatic property to your component:

Available for download on Wrox.com

VB

```
Public Property Description As String
```

Code snippet MyControl.vb

Available for download on Wrox.com

C#

```
public string Description { get; set; }
```

Code snippet MyControl.cs

The Browsable Attribute

By default, all public properties are displayed in the property grid. However, you can explicitly control this behavior by adding the `Browsable` attribute. If you set it to `false` the property will not appear in the property grid.

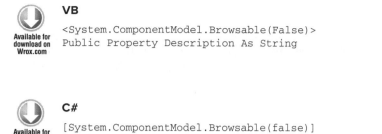

VB

```
<System.ComponentModel.Browsable(False)>
Public Property Description As String
```

Code snippet MyControl.vb

C#

```
[System.ComponentModel.Browsable(false)]
public string Description { get; set; }
```

Code snippet MyControl.cs

DisplayName Attribute

The DisplayName attribute is somewhat self-explanatory; it enables you to modify the display name of the property. In our case, we can change the name of the property as it appears in the property grid from Description to VS2010 Description.

VB

```
<System.ComponentModel.DisplayName("VS2010 Description")>
Public Property Description As String
```

Code snippet MyControl.vb

C#

```
[System.ComponentModel.DisplayName("VS2010 Description")]
public string Description { get; set; }
```

Code snippet MyControl.cs

Description

In addition to defining the friendly or display name for the property, it is also worth providing a description, which appears in the bottom area of the Properties window when the property is selected. This ensures that users of your component understand what the property does.

VB

```
<System.ComponentModel.Description("My first custom property")>
Public Property Description As String
```

Code snippet MyControl.vb

C#

```
[System.ComponentModel.Description("My first custom property")]
public string Description { get; set; }
```

Code snippet MyControl.cs

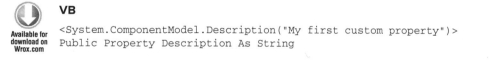

Category

By default, any property you expose is placed in the Misc group when the Properties window is in grouped view. Using the `Category` attribute, you can place your property in any of the existing groups, such as Appearance or Data, or a new group if you specify a group name that doesn't exist.

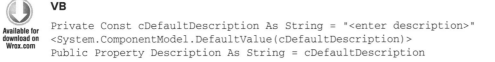

VB

```
<System.ComponentModel.Category("Appearance")>
Public Property Description As String
```

Code snippet MyControl.vb

C#

```
[System.ComponentModel.Category("Appearance")]
public string Description { get; set; }
```

Code snippet MyControl.cs

DefaultValue

Earlier you saw how Visual Studio 2010 highlights properties that have changed from their initial or default values. The `DefaultValue` attribute is what Visual Studio 2010 looks for to determine the default value for the property.

VB

```
Private Const cDefaultDescription As String = "<enter description>"
<System.ComponentModel.DefaultValue(cDefaultDescription)>
Public Property Description As String = cDefaultDescription
```

Code snippet MyControl.vb

C#

```
private const string cDefaultDescription = "<enter description>";
private string mDescription = cDefaultDescription;
[System.ComponentModel.DefaultValue(cDefaultDescription)]
public string Description
{
    get
    {
        return mDescription;
    }
    set
    {
        mDescription = value;
    }
}
```

Code snippet MyControl.cs

In this case, if the value of the `Description` property is set to "`<enter description>`", Visual Studio 2010 removes the line of code that sets this property. If you modify a property and want to return to the default value, you can right-click the property in the Properties window and select Reset from the context menu.

> *It is important to note that the* `DefaultValue` *attribute does not set the initial value of your property. It is recommended that if you specify the* `DefaultValue` *attribute you also set the initial value of your property to the same value, as done in the preceding code.*

AmbientValue

One of the features we all take for granted but that few truly understand is the concept of ambient properties. Typical examples are background and foreground colors and fonts: unless you explicitly set these via the Properties window they are inherited — not from their base classes, but from their parent control. A broader definition of an ambient property is a property that gets its value from another source.

Like the `DefaultValue` attribute, the `AmbientValue` attribute is used to indicate to Visual Studio 2010 when it should not add code to the designer file. Unfortunately, with ambient properties you can't hard-code a value for the designer to compare the current value to, because it is contingent on the property's source value. Because of this, when you define the `AmbientValue` attribute this tells the designer to look for a function called `ShouldSerializePropertyName`. In our case, it would be `ShouldSerializeDescription`, and this method is called to determine whether the current value of the property should be persisted to the designer code file.

VB

```vb
Private mDescription As String = cDefaultDescription
<System.ComponentModel.AmbientValue(cDefaultDescription)>
Public Property Description As String
    Get
        If Me.mDescription = cDefaultDescription AndAlso
                            Me.Parent IsNot Nothing Then
            Return Parent.Text
        End If
        Return mDescription
    End Get
    Set(ByVal value As String)
        mDescription = value
    End Set
End Property

Private Function ShouldSerializeDescription() As Boolean
    If Me.Parent IsNot Nothing Then
        Return Not Me.Description = Me.Parent.Text
```

```
        Else
            Return Not Me.Description = cDefaultDescription
        End If
End function
```

Code snippet MyControl.vb

C#

```
private string mDescription = cDefaultDescription;
[System.ComponentModel.AmbientValue(cDefaultDescription)]
public string Description{
    get{
        if (this.mDescription == cDefaultDescription &&
            this.Parent != null){
            return Parent.Text;
        }
        return mDescription;
    }
    set{
        mDescription = value;
    }
}

private bool ShouldSerializeDescription(){
    if (this.Parent != null){
        return this.Description != this.Parent.Text;
    }
    else{
        return this.Description != cDefaultDescription;
    }
}
```

Code snippet MyControl.cs

When you create a control with this property, the initial value would be set to the value of the DefaultDescription constant, but in the designer you would see a value corresponding to the Parent.Text value. There would also be no line explicitly setting this property in the designer code file, as reflected in the Properties window by the value being non-boldfaced. If you change the value of this property to anything other than the DefaultDescription constant, you will see that it becomes bold and a line is added to the designer code file. If you reset this property, the underlying value is set back to the value defined by AmbientValue, but all you will see is that it has returned to displaying the Parent.Text value.

SUMMARY

In this chapter you have seen three of the most common tool windows in action. Knowing how to manipulate these windows can save you considerable time during development. However, the true power of Visual Studio 2010 is exposed when you start to incorporate the designer experience into your own components. This can be useful even if your components aren't going to be used outside your organization. Making effective use of the designer can improve not only the efficiency with which your controls are used, but also the performance of the application you are building.

3

Options and Customizations

WHAT'S IN THIS CHAPTER?

➤ Customizing the Visual Studio 2010 start page

➤ Tweaking options

➤ Controlling window layout

Now that you're familiar with the general layout of Visual Studio 2010, it's time to learn how you can customize the IDE to suit your working style. In this chapter you learn how to manipulate tool windows, optimize the code window for maximum viewing space, and change fonts and colors to reduce developer fatigue.

As Visual Studio has grown, so too has the number of settings that you can adjust to optimize your development experience. Unfortunately, unless you've periodically spent time sifting through the Options dialog (Tools ➪ Options), it's likely that you've overlooked one or two settings that might be important. Through the course of this chapter, you see a number of recommendations of settings you might want to investigate further.

A number of Visual Studio add-ins will add their own nodes to the Options dialog because this provides a one-stop shop for configuring settings within Visual Studio. Note also that some developer setting profiles, as selected in Chapter 1, show only a cut-down list of options. In this case, checking the Advanced checkbox shows the complete list of available options.

THE START PAGE

By default, when you open a new instance of Visual Studio 2010 you see what is known as the Start Page. You can adjust this behavior from the Environment ➪ Startup node of the Options dialog. Other alternatives are to display the Home Page (which you can set via the Environment ➪ Web Browser node), the last loaded solution, open or new project dialogs, or no action at all.

The reason that most developers stick with the Start Page is that it provides a useful starting point from which to jump to any number of actions. In the left image of Figure 3-1, you can see that there are links down the left side for connecting to Team Foundation Server and for creating or opening projects. There is also a list of recent projects allowing you to quickly open projects that you have recently been working on. Hovering the mouse over the left side of a project displays a horizontal pin. Clicking the pin changes the orientation to vertical to indicate that the project has been pinned to the Recent Projects list. Alternatively, you can right-click a project and either open the containing folder (useful if you want to locate the project on disk rather than actually opening it) or remove the project from the list. In the lower-left corner there are two checkboxes that control whether the Start Page is closed after opening a project and whether it's displayed at startup. If for whatever reason the Start Page is closed and you want to open it again, you can do so by selecting the View ⇨ Start Page menu item.

On the right side of the Start Page are a series of tabs. The Get Started tab (the left image of Figure 3-1) contains various subsections on a variety of topics including Windows, Web, Office and the Cloud. Click on any of these to find information on how to get started working with these technologies and what's new in Visual Studio 2010.

On the Guidance and Resources tab (the center image of Figure 3-1) are links to topics pertaining to best practices, how-to's, and other reference material on designing, building, testing and deploying software using Visual Studio 2010.

FIGURE 3-1

Finally, the Latest News tab (the right image of Figure 3-1) keeps you abreast of the latest happenings around Visual Studio 2010 and the .NET Framework. You can either use the default RSS feed or specify your own feed that you want to be displayed within the Start Page.

Customizing the Start Page

In Visual Studio 2010, the Start Page is in fact a WPF control that is hosted within the IDE shell. As such, it is possible to tailor the Start Page to feature information or actions that are relevant to you. Rather than modifying the default Start Page, Visual Studio supports user-specific or Custom Start Pages. By default, this features is disabled so before you can start customizing your Start Page you have to enable the Allow Custom Start Page checkbox on the Environment ⇨ Startup tab of the Options dialog.

Because the Start Page is just a WPF control, you could simply create a new WPF control project and build your page from scratch. However, in most cases it is much simpler to start with the default Start Page and tailor it to suit your needs. To do this you need to copy the default Start Page from where it is installed into your Documents folder.

1. Copy the contents of the directory `C:\Program Files\Microsoft Visual Studio 10.0\Common7\IDE\StartPages\<culture>` into the directory `C:\Users\<user name>\Documents\Visual Studio 10\StartPages` (you may need to create this folder because it may not exist by default).

2. Double-click the project file `StartPage.csproj` to open the project in Visual Studio 2010, as shown in Figure 3-2.

As you can see from Figure 3-2, you are able to modify the Start Page using either the WPF designer or directly in the XAML page. The XAML page is broken down into a number of sections. The best place to get started is where the `TabItem` tags are defined for the existing tabs. To create an additional tab, copy one of the existing tags and modify it to include your own content. For example, add the following tag after the Latest News tab to add information pertaining to your company.

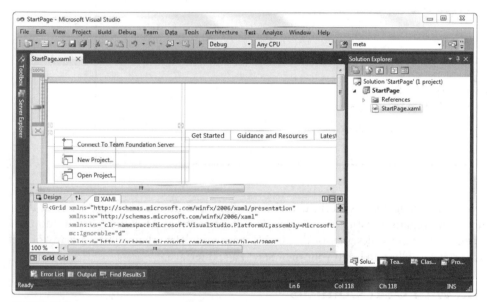

FIGURE 3-2

XAML

```xml
<!-- Company Tab -->
<TabItem Header="Company" Height="Auto" x:Uid="Company_Tab"
        DataContext="{Binding Links.Content, Converter=
                    {StaticResource StringToXmlDataProviderConverter}}">
    <Grid>
        <Grid.RowDefinitions>
            <RowDefinition Height="Auto"></RowDefinition>
            <RowDefinition Height="*"></RowDefinition>
        </Grid.RowDefinitions>
        <TextBlock Foreground="#E8E8E8" Margin="15" TextWrapping="Wrap"
            x:Uid="Information_Paragraph" >
            The Company has put a lot of effort into writing this custom
```

```
                    Start Page so that you can quickly access information relevant to
                    your job, the projects you are working on etc.
            </TextBlock>
        </Grid>
    </TabItem>
```

As soon as you save this change, if you click back to the Start Page tab in Visual Studio 2010 you will notice that your changes have already been applied, giving you a new Company tab, as shown in Figure 3-3.

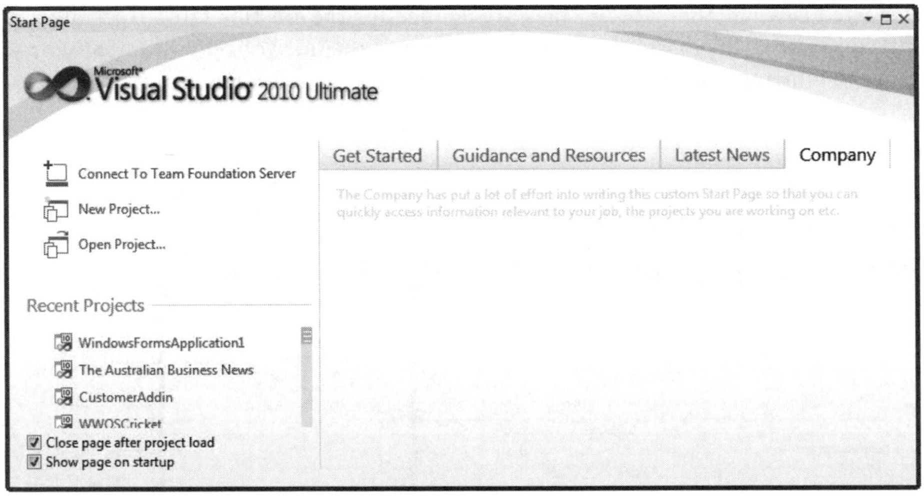

FIGURE 3-3

Of course, if you want to do away with the default Start Page layout, you can remove any of the existing elements and replace it with your own layout, information, and functionality. To do this, select the elements either in the designer or the XAML page and delete them. Then use any of the WPF controls in your Toolbox to build your own Start Page interface.

Code Behind with User Controls

To extend the functionality of the Start Page further you may want to execute code on particular events. The Start Page itself doesn't support having a code-behind file in which to code event handlers. However, you can encapsulate your functionality into a user control that can then be used on your Start Page.

With your Start Page project open, created in the previous section, add a new project in which to place the control you are going to create. To do this, select File ➪ Add ➪ New Project and select the WPF User Control Library from the Windows node under either the VB or C# node. Give the project a name, such as CompanyStartPageControls, and click OK. Now, follow these steps to create a button that launches your company web site:

1. Rename UserControl1.xaml to **CompanyPortalControl.xaml** in Solution Explorer.

2. Double-click the CompanyPortalControl.xaml file in Solution Explorer to open it in the designer.

3. Replace the XAML with the following markup that creates a button with a Click event handler.

XAML

```xaml
<UserControl x:Class="CompanyStartPageControls.CompanyPortalControl"
             xmlns="http://schemas.microsoft.com/winfx/2006/xaml/presentation"
             xmlns:x="http://schemas.microsoft.com/winfx/2006/xaml">
    <Grid>
        <Button Click="LaunchWebsite">Company Website</Button>
    </Grid>
</UserControl>
```

4. Right-click the `CompanyPortalControl.xaml` file in Solution Explorer and select View Code.

5. Replace the code with the following, which implements the `Click` event handler for the button to launch the company web site.

VB

```vb
Class CompanyPortalControl
    Private Sub LaunchWebsite(ByVal sender As Object, ByVal e As RoutedEventArgs)
        System.Diagnostics.Process.Start("http://www.builttoroam.com")
    End Sub
End Class
```

C#

```csharp
namespace CompanyStartPageControls{
    public partial class CompanyPortalControl : UserControl{
        public CompanyPortalControl(){
            InitializeComponent();
        }
        private void LaunchWebsite(object sender, RoutedEventArgs e){
            System.Diagnostics.Process.Start(
                            @"http://www.builttoroam.com");
        }
    }
}
```

You have now created a control with basic functionality encapsulated within it. Follow these steps to now use this control within your Start Page:

1. Right-click the StartPage project within Solution Explorer and select Add Reference. From the Projects tab, select the CompanyStartPageControls project and click OK.

2. Force a rebuild of your solution by selecting the Build ⇨ Rebuild Solution menu item.

3. Double-click the `StartPage.xaml` file in Solution Explorer to open the designer.

4. In the Toolbox you will now see a tab for CompanyStartPageControls, in which you will find your CompanyPortalControl. Drag this item onto the StartPage beneath the information about the Company. The Company TabItem XAML should now look like the following.

XAML

```xaml
<!-- Company Tab -->
<TabItem Header="Company" Height="Auto" x:Uid="Company_Tab"
         DataContext="{Binding Links.Content, Converter=
                      {StaticResource StringToXmlDataProviderConverter}}">
    <Grid>
        <Grid.RowDefinitions>
            <RowDefinition Height="Auto"></RowDefinition>
            <RowDefinition Height="*"></RowDefinition>
        </Grid.RowDefinitions>
        <TextBlock Foreground="#E8E8E8" Margin="15" TextWrapping="Wrap"
            x:Uid="Information_Paragraph" >
            The Company has put a lot of effort into writing this custom
            Start Page so that you can quickly access information relevant to your
            job, the projects you are working on etc.
        </TextBlock>
        <my:CompanyPortalControl Grid.Row="1" HorizontalAlignment="Left"
                              Margin="6,12,0,0" VerticalAlignment="Top" />
    </Grid>
</TabItem>
```

If you now save all files (Ctrl+Shift+S) and select the Start Page tab in Visual Studio 2010, you will see an error as the assembly containing your CompanyPortalControl cannot be found. To fix this issue, you need to copy the `CompanyStartPageControls.dll` into the `c:\Program Files\ Microsoft Visual Studio 10.0\Common7\IDE\StartPageAssemblies` directory. This directory doesn't exist by default, so you will need to create it prior to copying the assembly in there.

Once you have copied `CompanyStartPageControls.dll`, you need to restart Visual Studio. Your start page should display as shown in Figure 3-4.

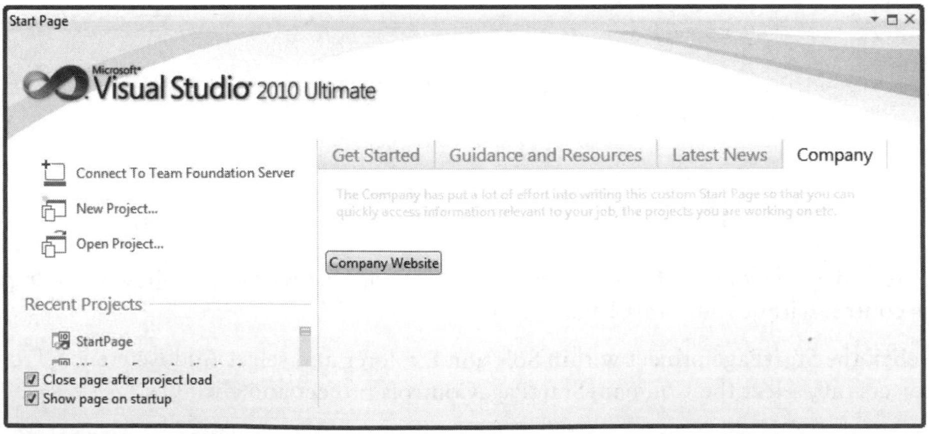

FIGURE 3-4

If you click the Company Website button, it will launch your company portal in your external web browser, directly from the Start Page.

WINDOW LAYOUT

If you are unfamiliar with Visual Studio, the behavior of the numerous tool windows may strike you as erratic, because they seem to appear in random locations and then come and go when you move between writing code (design time) and running code (run time). In actual fact, Visual Studio 2010 remembers the locations of tool windows in each of these modes. This way you can optimize the way you write and debug code.

As you open different items from the Solution Explorer, you'll see that the number of toolbars across the top of the screen varies depending on the type of file being opened. Each toolbar has a built-in association to specific file extensions so that Visual Studio knows to display the toolbar when a file with one of those extensions is opened. If you close a toolbar when a file is open that has a matching file extension, Visual Studio will remember this when future files with the same extension are opened.

> You can reset the association between toolbars and the file extensions via the Customize dialog (Tools ⇨ Customize). Select the appropriate toolbar and click the Reset button.

Viewing Windows and Toolbars

Once a tool window or toolbar has been closed it can be difficult to locate it again. Luckily, most of the most frequently used tool windows are accessible via the View menu. Other tool windows, mainly related to debugging, are located under the Debug menu.

All the toolbars available in Visual Studio 2010 are listed under the View ⇨ Toolbars menu item. Each toolbar that is currently visible is marked with a tick against the appropriate menu item. You can also access the list of toolbars by right-clicking in any empty space in the toolbar area at the top of the Visual Studio window.

Once a toolbar is visible, you can customize which buttons are displayed, either via View ⇨ Toolbars ⇨ Customize or under the Tools menu. Alternatively, as shown in Figure 3-5, if you select the down arrow at the end of a toolbar you will see a list of all the buttons available on that toolbar, from which you can check the buttons you want to appear on the toolbar.

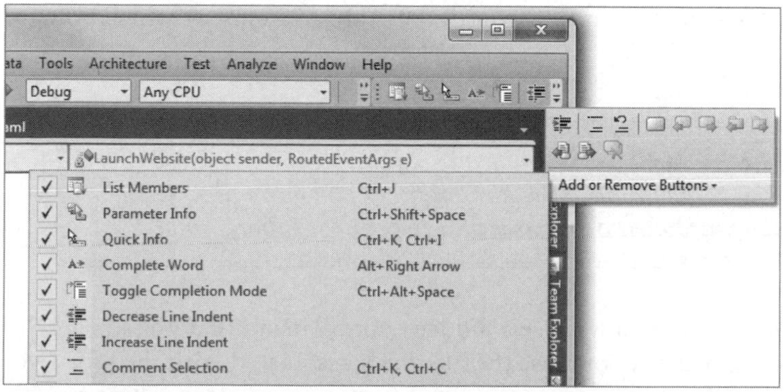

FIGURE 3-5

Navigating Open Items

After opening multiple items you'll notice that you run out of room across the top of the editor space and that you can no longer see the tabs for all the items you have open. Of course, you can go back to the Solution Explorer window and select a specific item. If the item is already open it will be displayed without reverting to its saved state. However, it is still inconvenient to have to find the item in the Solution Explorer.

Luckily, Visual Studio 2010 has a number of shortcuts to the list of open items. As with most document-based applications, Visual Studio has a Windows menu. When you open an item its title is added to the bottom section of this menu. To display an open item just select the item from the Windows menu, or click the generic Windows item, which displays a modal dialog from which you can select the item you want.

Another alternative is to use the drop-down menu at the end of the tab area of the editor space. Figure 3-6 shows the drop-down list of open items from which you can select the item you want to access.

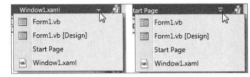

FIGURE 3-6

Figure 3-6 (right) is the same as Figure 3-6 (left) except for the drop-down icon. This menu also displays a down arrow, but this one has a line across the top. This line indicates that there are more tabs than can fit across the top of the editor space.

Another way to navigate through the open items is to press Ctrl+Tab, which displays a temporary window, as shown in Figure 3-7. It is a temporary window because when you release the Ctrl key it disappears. However, while the window is open you can use the arrow keys or press Tab to move among the open windows.

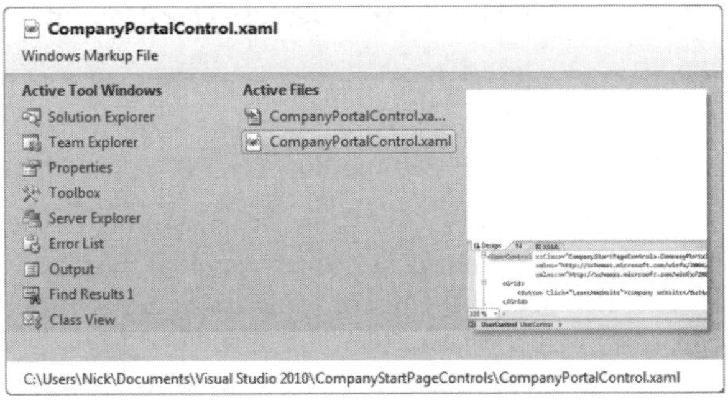

FIGURE 3-7

The Ctrl+Tab window is divided into three sections, which include the active tool windows, active files (this should actually be active items because it contains some items that don't correspond to a single file), and a preview of the currently selected item. As the number of either active files or active tool windows increases, the windows expand vertically until there are 15 items, at which point an additional column is formed.

> *If you get to the point where you are seeing multiple columns of active files, you might consider closing some or all of the unused files. The more files Visual Studio 2010 has open, the more memory it uses and the slower it performs.*

If you right-click the tab of an open item, you will see a hidden context menu that gives you a quick way to do common tasks such as save or close the file that's associated with the tab. Two particularly useful actions are Close All But This and the Open Containing Folder. These are self-descriptive as the former closes all tabs other than the one you clicked to get the context menu, while the latter opens the folder that contains the file in Windows Explorer. Now that all windows are dockable, there are also actions to Float or Dock as Tabbed Document, which are enabled depending on what state the tab is in.

Docking

Each tool window has a default position, which it will resume when it is opened from the View menu. For example, View ⇨ Toolbox opens the Toolbox docked to the left edge of Visual Studio. Once a tool window is opened and is docked against an edge, it has two states, pinned and unpinned. As you saw in Chapter 1, you can toggle between these states by clicking the vertical pin to unpin the tool window or the horizontal pin to pin the tool window.

You will notice that as you unpin a tool window it slides back against the edge of the IDE, leaving visible a tag displaying the title of the tool window. This animation can be annoying and time-consuming when you have tool windows unpinned. On the Environment node of the Options dialog, you can control whether Visual Studio should automatically adjust the visual experience based on client performance. Alternatively, you can elect to uncheck the Enable rich client visual experience option.

Most developers accept the default location of tool windows, but occasionally you may want to adjust where the tool windows appear. Visual Studio 2010 has a sophisticated system for controlling the layout of tool windows. In Chapter 1 you saw how you could use the drop-down, next to the Pin and Close buttons at the top of the tool window, to make the tool window floating, dockable, or even part of the main editor space (using the Tabbed Document option).

When a tool window is dockable, you have a lot of control over where it is positioned. In Figure 3-8 you can see the top of the Properties window, which has been dragged away from its default position at the right of the IDE. To begin dragging, you need to make sure the tool window is pinned and then click either the title area at the top of the tool window or the tab at the bottom of the tool window and drag the mouse in the direction you want the window to move. If you click in the title area you'll see that all tool windows in that section of the IDE will also be moved. Clicking the tab results in only the corresponding tool window moving.

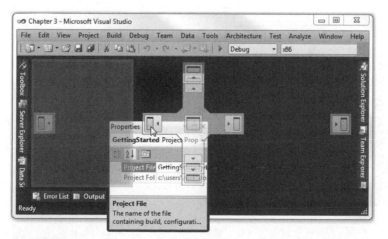

FIGURE 3-8

As you drag the tool window around Visual Studio 2010, you'll see that translucent icons appear at different locations around the IDE. These icons are a useful guide to help you position the tool window exactly where you want. In Figure 3-9 the Data Sources tool window has been pinned against the left side. Now when the Properties window is positioned over the left icon of the center image, the blue shading again appears on the inside of the existing tool window. This indicates that the Properties tool window will be pinned to the right of the Data Sources tool window and visible if this layout is chosen. If the far left icon was selected, the Properties tool window would again be pinned to the left of the IDE, but this time to the left of the Data Sources window.

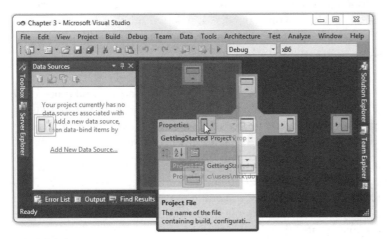

FIGURE 3-9

Alternatively, if the Properties tool window is dragged over the Data Sources tool window as in Figure 3-10, the center image will move over the existing tool window. This indicates that the Properties tool window will be positioned within the existing tool window area. As you drag the window over the different quadrants, you will see that the blue shading again indicates where the tool window will be positioned when the mouse is released. In Figure 3-10 it indicates that the Properties tool window will appear below the Data Sources tool window.

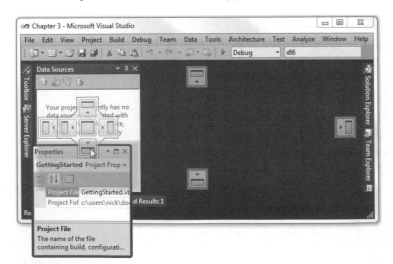

FIGURE 3-10

> *It should be noted that if you have a large screen or multiple screens, it is worth spending time laying out the tool windows you use frequently. With multiple screens, using floating tool windows means that you can position them away from the main editor space, maximizing your screen real estate. If you have a small screen you may find that you continually have to adjust which tool windows are visible, so becoming familiar with the docking and layout options is essential.*

THE EDITOR SPACE

Like most IDEs, Visual Studio 2010 has been built up around the central code-editing window. Over time, it has evolved and is now much more than a simple text editor. Though most developers will spend considerable time writing code in the editor space, an increasing number of designers are available for performing tasks such as building forms, adjusting project settings, and editing resources. Regardless of whether you are writing code or doing form design, you are going to spend a lot of your time within Visual Studio 2010 in the editor space. Because of this, it is important for you to know how to tweak the layout so you can work more efficiently.

Fonts and Colors

Some of the first things that presenters change in Visual Studio are the fonts and colors used in the editor space, in order to make the code more readable. However, it shouldn't just be presenters who adjust these settings. Selecting fonts and colors that are easy for you to read and that aren't harsh on the eyes will make you more productive and enable you to code for longer without feeling fatigued. Figure 3-11 shows the Fonts and Colors node of the Options dialog, where you can make adjustments to the font, size, color, and styling of different display items. One thing to note about this node in the Options dialog is that it is very slow to load, so try to avoid accidentally clicking it.

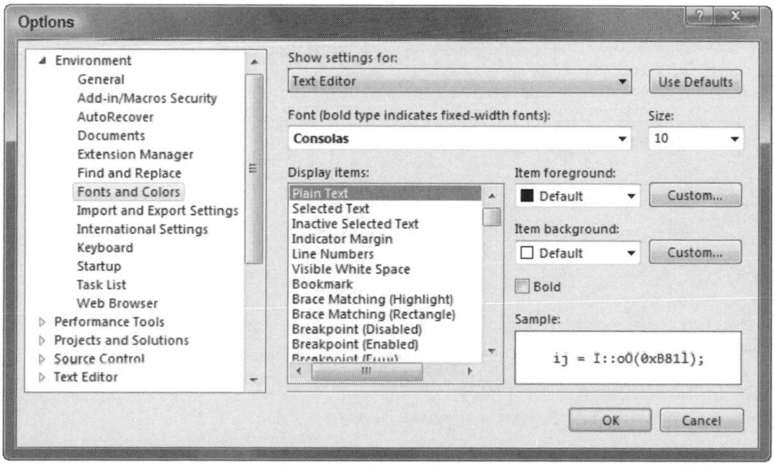

FIGURE 3-11

To adjust the appearance of a particular text item within Visual Studio 2010, you first need to select the area of the IDE that it applies to. In Figure 3-11 the Text Editor has been selected, and has been used to determine which items should appear in the Display Items list. Once you have found the relevant item in this list, you can make adjustments to the font and colors.

> *Some items in this list, such as Plain Text, are reused by a number of areas within Visual Studio 2010, which can result in some unpredictable changes when you tweak fonts and colors.*

When choosing a font, remember that proportional fonts are usually not as effective for writing code as non-proportional fonts (also known as fixed-width fonts). As indicated in Figure 3-11, fixed-width fonts are distinguished in the list from the variable-width types so they are easy to locate.

Visual Guides

When you are editing a file, Visual Studio 2010 automatically color-codes the code based on the type of file. For example, VB code highlights keywords in blue, variable names and class references are in black, and string literals are in red. In Figure 3-12 you can see that there is a line running up the left side of the code. This is used to indicate where the code blocks are. You can click the minus sign to condense the btnSayHello_Click method or the entire Form1 code block.

Various points about visual guides are illustrated in Figures 3-12 to 3-14. Those readers familiar with VB.NET will realize that Figure 3-12 is missing the end of the line where the method is set to handle the Click event of the btnSayHello button. This is because the rest of the line is being obscured by the edge of the code window. To see what is at the end of the line, the developer has to either scroll the window to the right or use the keyboard to navigate the cursor to the end of the line. In Figure 3-13, word wrap has been enabled via the Options dialog (see the Text ⇨ Editor ⇨ All Languages ⇨ General node).

```
Public Class Form1
    Private Sub btnSayHello_Click(ByVal sender As System.Object, ByVal e As System.EventArgs)
        MessageBox.Show(Me.txtToSay.Text)
    End Sub
End Class
```

FIGURE 3-12

```
Public Class Form1
    Private Sub btnSayHello_Click(ByVal sender As System.Object, ByVal e As System.EventArgs)
Handles btnSayHello.Click
        MessageBox.Show(Me.txtToSay.Text)
    End Sub
End Class
```

FIGURE 3-13

```
1  Public Class Form1
2      Private Sub btnSayHello_Click(ByVal sender As System.Object, ByVal e As System.EventArgs)
   Handles btnSayHello.Click
3          MessageBox.Show(Me.txtToSay.Text)
4      End Sub
5  End Class
```

FIGURE 3-14

Unfortunately, enabling word wrapping can make it hard to work out which lines have been wrapped. Luckily, Visual Studio 2010 has an option (immediately below the checkbox to enable word wrapping in the Options dialog) that can display visual glyphs at the end of each line that will indicate a line has been wrapped to the next line, as you can see in Figure 3-14. In this figure you can also see two other visual guides. On the left, outside the code block markers, are line numbers. These can be enabled via the Line Numbers checkbox below both the Word Wrap and Visual Glyphs checkboxes. The other guide is the dots that represent space in the code. Unlike the other visual guides, this one can be enabled via the Edit ➪ Advanced ➪ View White Space menu item when the code editor space has focus.

Full-Screen Mode

If you have a number of tool windows and multiple toolbars visible, you will have noticed that you quickly run out of space for actually writing code. For this reason, Visual Studio 2010 has a full-screen mode that you can access via the View ➪ Full Screen menu item. Alternatively, you can press Shift+Alt+Enter to toggle in and out of full-screen mode. Figure 3-15 shows the top of Visual Studio 2010 in full-screen mode. As you can see, no toolbars or tool windows are visible and the window is completely maximized, even to the exclusion of the normal Minimize, Restore, and Close buttons.

```
File  Edit  View  Project  Build  Debug  Team  Data  Tools  Architecture  Test  Analyze  Window  Help   Full Screen
Form1.vb  ×
Form1                                                          ▾  (Declarations)
   1  Public·Class·Form1
   2      Private·Sub·btnSayHello_Click(ByVal·sender·As·System.Object,·ByVal·e·As·System.EventArgs)·Handles·btnSayHello.Click
   3          ····MessageBox.Show(Me.txtToSay.Text)
   4      ····End·Sub
   5  End·Class
100 %  ▾
Ready                                              Ln 1         Col 1       Ch 1                     INS
```

FIGURE 3-15

If you are using multiple screens, full-screen mode can be particularly useful. Undock the tool windows and place them on the second monitor. When the editor window is in full-screen mode you still have access to the tool windows, without having to toggle back and forth. If you undock a code window this will not be set to full screen.

Tracking Changes

To enhance the experience of editing, Visual Studio 2010 uses line-level tracking to indicate which lines of code you have modified during an editing session. When you open a file to begin editing there will be no line coloring. However, when you begin to edit you will notice that a yellow mark appears next to the lines that have been modified. In Figure 3-16 you can see that the `MessageBox` line has been modified since this file was last saved.

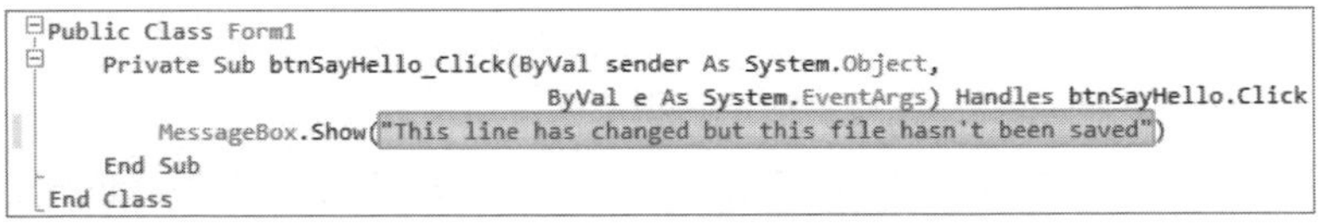

```
Public Class Form1
    Private Sub btnSayHello_Click(ByVal sender As System.Object,
                           ByVal e As System.EventArgs) Handles btnSayHello.Click
        MessageBox.Show("This line has changed but this file hasn't been saved")
    End Sub
End Class
```

FIGURE 3-16

When the file is saved, the modified lines will change to having a green mark next to them. In Figure 3-17 the first `MessageBox` line has changed since the file was opened, but those changes have been saved to disk. However, the second `MessageBox` line has not yet been saved.

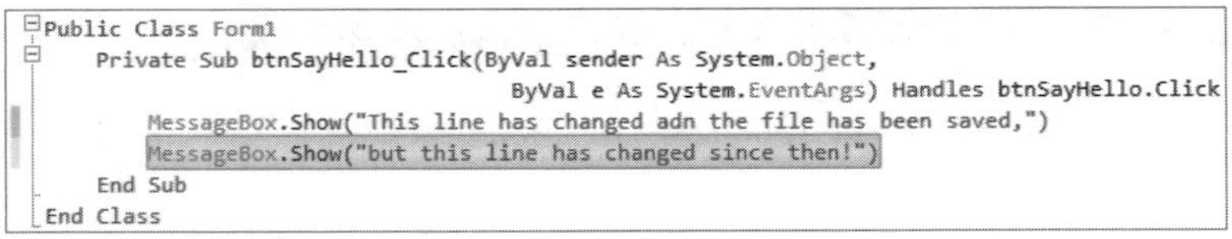

```
Public Class Form1
    Private Sub btnSayHello_Click(ByVal sender As System.Object,
                           ByVal e As System.EventArgs) Handles btnSayHello.Click
        MessageBox.Show("This line has changed adn the file has been saved,")
        MessageBox.Show("but this line has changed since then!")
    End Sub
End Class
```

FIGURE 3-17

> *If you don't find tracking changes to be useful, you can disable this feature by unchecking the Text Editor ⇨ General ⇨ Track Change item in the Options dialog.*

OTHER OPTIONS

Many options that we haven't yet touched on can be used to tweak the way Visual Studio operates. Through the remainder of this chapter you will see some of the more useful options that can help you be more productive.

Keyboard Shortcuts

Visual Studio 2010 ships with many ways to perform the same action. Menus, toolbars, and various tool windows provide direct access to many commands, but despite the huge number available, many more are not accessible through the graphical interface. Instead, these commands are accessed (along with most of those in the menus and toolbars) via keyboard shortcuts.

These shortcuts range from the familiar Ctrl+Shift+S to save all changes, to the obscure Ctrl+Alt+E to display the Exceptions dialog window. As you might have guessed, you can set your own keyboard shortcuts and even change the existing ones. Even better, you can filter the shortcuts to operate only in certain contexts, meaning you can use the same shortcut differently depending on what you're doing.

Figure 3-18 shows the Keyboard node in the Environment section of the Options dialog with the default keyboard mapping scheme selected. If you want to change to use a different keyboard mapping scheme, simply select it from the drop-down and hit the Reset button.

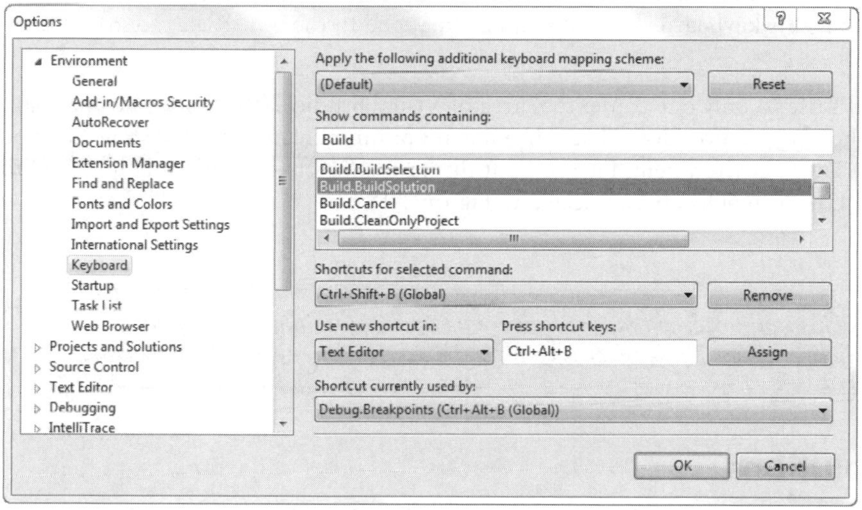

FIGURE 3-18

> The keyboard mapping schemes are stored as VSK files at `C:\Program Files\ Microsoft Visual Studio 10.0\Common7\IDE`. This is the keyboard mapping file format used in versions of Visual Studio prior to Visual Studio 2005. To import keyboard mappings from Visual Studio 2005, use the import settings feature (see the end of this chapter); for earlier versions, copy the appropriate VSK file into the aforementioned folder, and you will be able to select it from the mapping scheme drop-down the next time you open the Options dialog.

The listbox in the middle of Figure 3-18 lists every command that is available in Visual Studio 2010. Unfortunately, this list is quite extensive and the Options dialog is not resizable, which makes navigating this list difficult. To make it easier to search for commands, you can filter the command list using the Show Commands Containing textbox. In Figure 3-18 the word *Build* has been used to filter the list down to all the commands starting with or containing that word. From this list the `Build.BuildSolution` command has been selected. Because there is already a keyboard shortcut assigned to this command, the Shortcuts for Selected Command drop-down and the Remove button have been enabled. It is possible to have multiple shortcuts for the same command, so the drop-down enables you to remove individual assigned shortcuts.

> *Having multiple shortcuts is useful if you want to keep a default shortcut — so that other developers feel at home using your setup — but also add your own personal one.*

The remainder of this dialog enables you to assign a new shortcut to the command you have selected. Simply move to the Press Shortcut Keys textbox and, as the label suggests, press the appropriate keys. In Figure 3-18 the keyboard chord Ctrl+Alt+B has been entered, but this shortcut is already being used by another command, as shown at the bottom of the dialog window. If you click the Assign button, this keyboard shortcut will be remapped to the `Build.BuildSolution` command.

To restrict a shortcut's use to only one contextual area of Visual Studio 2010, select the context from the Use New Shortcut In drop-down list. The Global option indicates that the shortcut should be applied across the entire environment, but we want this new shortcut to work only in the editor window, so the Text Editor item has been selected in Figure 3-18.

> *Chapter 52 deals with macros that you can create and maintain to make your coding experience easier. These macros can also be assigned to keyboard shortcuts.*

Projects and Solutions

Several options relate to projects and solutions. The first of these is perhaps the most helpful — the default locations of your projects. By default, Visual Studio 2010 uses the standard Documents and Settings path common to many applications (see Figure 3-19), but this might not be where you'll want to keep your development work.

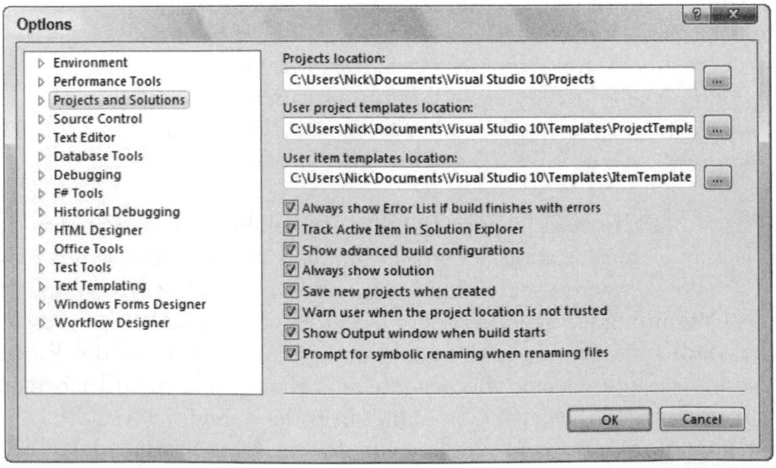

FIGURE 3-19

You can also change the location of template files at this point. If your organization uses a common network location for corporate project templates, you can change the default location in Visual Studio 2010 to point to this remote address rather than map the network drive.

You can adjust a number of other options to change how projects and solutions are managed in Visual Studio 2010. One of particular interest is Track Active Item in Solution Explorer. With this option enabled, the layout of the Solution Explorer changes as you switch among items to ensure the current item is in focus. This includes expanding (but not collapsing again) projects and folders, which can be frustrating on a large solution because you are continually having to collapse projects so that you can navigate.

Another option that relates to solutions, but doesn't appear in Figure 3-19, is to list miscellaneous files in the Solution Explorer. Say you are working on a solution and you have to inspect an XML document that isn't contained in the solution. Visual Studio 2010 will happily open the file, but you will have to reopen it every time you open the solution. Alternatively, if you enable Environment Documents Show Miscellaneous Files in Solution Explorer via the Options dialog, the file will be temporarily added to the solution. The miscellaneous files folder to which this file is added is shown in Figure 3-20.

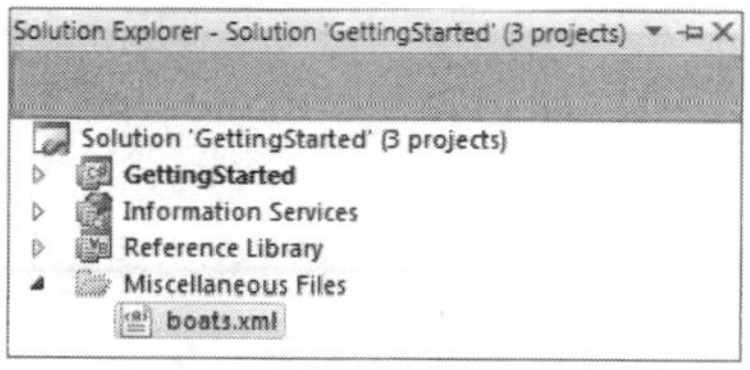

FIGURE 3-20

> *Visual Studio 2010 will automatically manage the list of miscellaneous files, keeping only the most recent ones, based on the number of files defined in the Options dialog. You can get Visual Studio to track up to 256 files in this list, and files will be evicted based on when they were last accessed.*

Build and Run

The Projects and Solutions ➪ Build and Run node, shown in Figure 3-21, can be used to tailor the build behavior of Visual Studio 2010. The first option to notice is Before Building. With the default option of Save All Changes, Visual Studio will apply any changes made to the solution prior to compilation. In the event of a crash during the build process or while you're debugging the compiled code, you can be assured that your code is safe. You may want to change this option to Prompt to Save All Changes if you don't want changes to be saved prematurely, though this is not recommended. This setting will inform you of unsaved modifications made in your solution, enabling you to double-check those changes prior to compilation.

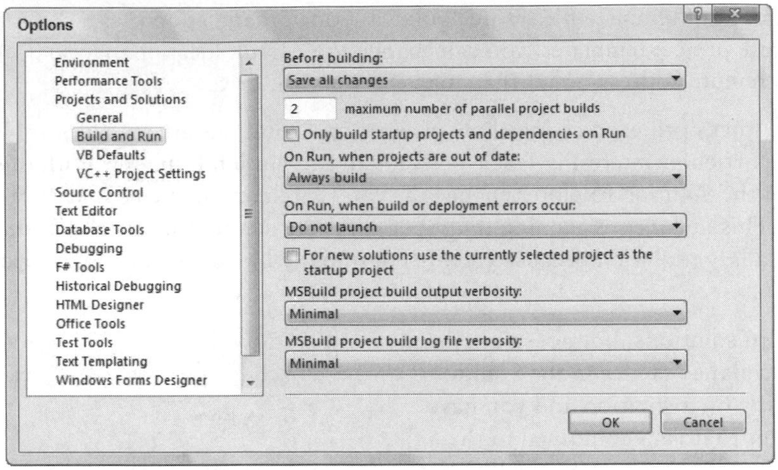

FIGURE 3-21

To reduce the amount of time it takes to build your solution, you may want to increase the maximum number of parallel builds that are performed. Visual Studio 2010 can build in parallel only those projects that are not dependent, but if you have a large number of independent projects this might yield a noticeable benefit. Be aware that on a single-core or single-processor machine this may actually increase the time taken to build your solution.

Figure 3-21 shows that projects will Always Build when they are out of date, and that if there are build errors the solution will not launch. Both these options can increase your productivity, but be warned that they eliminate dialogs letting you know what's going on.

> *The last option worth noting in Figure 3-21 is MSBuild project build output verbosity. In most cases the Visual Studio 2010 build output is sufficient for debugging build errors. However, in some cases, particularly when building ASP.NET projects, you will need to increase verbosity to diagnose the build error. New to this version of the Visual Studio 2010 is the ability to control the log file verbosity independently of the output.*

VB Options

VB programmers have four compiler options that can be configured at a project or a file level. You can also set the defaults on the Projects and Solutions ⇨ VB Defaults node of the Options dialog. Previous versions of VB had an Option Explicit, which forced variables to be defined prior to their use in code. When it was introduced, many experts recommended that it be turned on permanently because it did away with many runtime problems in VB applications that were caused by improper use of variables.

Option Strict takes enforcing good programming practices one step further by forcing developers to explicitly convert variables to their correct types, rather than let the compiler try to guess the proper conversion method. Again, this results in fewer runtime issues and better performance.

We advise strongly that you use Option Strict to ensure that your code is not implicitly converting variables inadvertently. If you are not using Option Strict, with all the new language features, you may not be making the most effective use of the language.

IMPORTING AND EXPORTING SETTINGS

Once you have the IDE in exactly the configuration you want, you may want to back up the settings for future use. You can do this by exporting the IDE settings to a file that can then be used to restore the settings or even transfer them to a series of Visual Studio 2010 installations, so that they all share the same IDE setup.

The Environment ⇨ Import and Export Settings node in the Options dialog enables you to specify a team settings file. This can be located on a network share, and Visual Studio 2010 will automatically apply new settings if the file changes.

To export the current configuration, select Tools ⇨ Import and Export Settings to start the Import and Export Settings Wizard, shown in Figure 3-22. The first step in the wizard is to select the Export option and which settings are to be backed up during the export procedure.

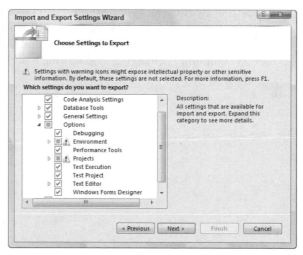

As shown in Figure 3-22, a variety of grouped options can be exported. The screenshot shows the Options section expanded, revealing that the Debugging and Projects settings will be backed up along with the Text Editor and Windows Forms Designer configurations. As the small exclamation icons indicate, some settings are not included in the export by default, because they contain information that may infringe on

FIGURE 3-22

your privacy. You will need to select these sections manually if you want them to be included in the backup. Once you have selected the settings you want to export, you can progress through the rest of the wizard, which might take a few minutes depending on the number of settings being exported.

Importing a settings file is just as easy. The same wizard is used, but you select the Import option on the first screen. Rather than simply overwriting the current configuration, the wizard enables you to back up the current setup first.

You can then select from a list of preset configuration files — the same set of files from which you can choose when you first start Visual Studio 2010 — or browse to a settings file that you created previously. Once the settings file has been chosen, you can then choose to import only certain sections of the configuration, or import the whole lot.

The wizard excludes some sections by default, such as External Tools or Command Aliases, so that you don't inadvertently overwrite customized settings. Make sure you select these sections if you want to do a full restore.

If you just want to restore the configuration of Visual Studio 2010 to one of the default presets, you can choose the Reset All Settings option in the opening screen of the wizard, rather than go through the import process.

SUMMARY

This chapter covered only a core selection of the useful options available to you as you start to shape the Visual Studio interface to suit your own programming style; many other options are available. These numerous options enable you to adjust the way you edit your code, add controls to your forms, and even select the methods to use when debugging code.

The settings within the Visual Studio 2010 Options page also enable you to control how and where applications are created, and even to customize the keyboard shortcuts you use. Throughout the remainder of this book, you'll see the Options dialog revisited according to specific functionality such as compiling, debugging, and writing macros.

4

The Visual Studio Workspace

WHAT'S IN THIS CHAPTER?

➤ Using the code editor

➤ Exploring the core Visual Studio tool windows

➤ Reorganizing your workspace

So far you have seen how to get started with Visual Studio 2010 and how to customize the IDE to suit the way that you work. In this chapter, you learn to take advantage of some of the built-in commands, shortcuts, and supporting tool windows that will help you to write code and design forms.

THE CODE EDITOR

As a developer you're likely to spend a considerable portion of your time writing code, which means that knowing how to tweak the layout of your code and being able to navigate it effectively are particularly important. Visual Studio 2010 introduces an all new WPF-based code editor that provides numerous new features from what was available in previous versions of Visual Studio.

The Code Editor Window Layout

When you open a code file for editing you are working in the code editor window, as shown in Figure 4-1. The core of the code editor window is the code pane in which the code is displayed.

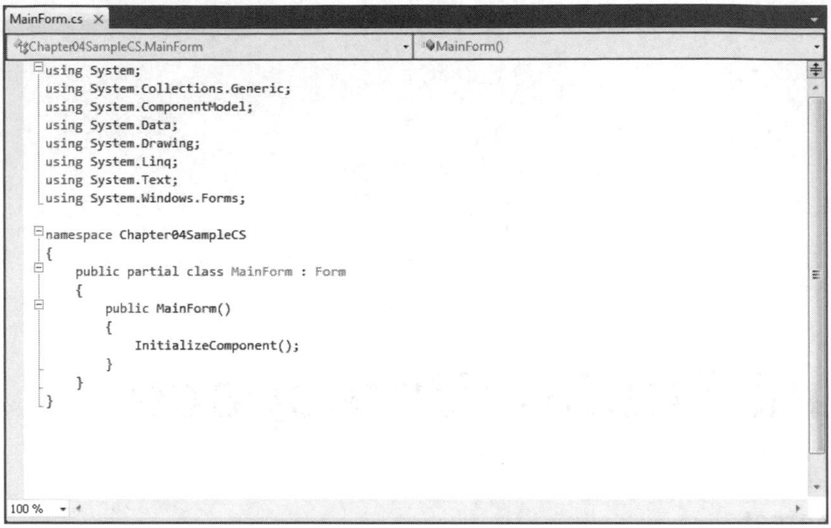

```
MainForm.cs  ×
Chapter04SampleCS.MainForm                    MainForm()
using System;
using System.Collections.Generic;
using System.ComponentModel;
using System.Data;
using System.Drawing;
using System.Linq;
using System.Text;
using System.Windows.Forms;

namespace Chapter04SampleCS
{
    public partial class MainForm : Form
    {
        public MainForm()
        {
            InitializeComponent();
        }
    }
}
100 %
```

FIGURE 4-1

Above the code pane are two drop-down lists that can help you navigate the code file. The first drop-down lists the classes in the code file, and the second one lists the members of the selected class in the first drop-down. These are listed in alphabetical order, making it easier to find a method or member definition within the file.

As you modify the code in the code editor window, lines of code that you've modified since the file has been opened are marked in the left-hand margin (which can be seen in Figure 4-2) — yellow for unsaved changes and green for those that have been saved.

Regions

Effective class design usually results in classes that serve a single purpose and are not overly complex or lengthy. However, there will be times when you have to implement so many interfaces that your code file will become unwieldy. In this case, you have a number of options, such as partitioning the code into multiple files or using regions to condense the code, thereby making it easier to navigate.

The introduction of partial classes (where the definition of a class can be split over two or more files) means that at design time you can place code into different physical files representing a single logical class. The advantage of using separate files is that you can effectively group all methods that are related, for example, methods that implement an interface. The problem with this strategy is that navigating the code then requires continual switching between code files.

An alternative is to use named code regions to condense sections of code that are not currently in use. In Figure 4-2 you can see that two regions are defined, Constructor and IComparable. Clicking the minus sign next to #Region condenses the region into a single line and clicking the plus sign expands it again.

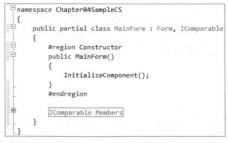

```
namespace Chapter04SampleCS
{
    public partial class MainForm : Form, IComparable
    {
        #region Constructor
        public MainForm()
        {
            InitializeComponent();
        }
        #endregion

        IComparable Members
    }
}
```

FIGURE 4-2

You don't need to expand a region to see the code within it. Simply hover the mouse cursor over the region and a tooltip displays the code within it.

Outlining

In addition to regions that you have defined, Visual Studio 2010 has the ability to auto-outline your code, making it easy to collapse methods, comments, and class definitions. Auto-outlining is enabled by default, but if it's not enabled you can enable it using the Edit ➪ Outlining ➪ Start Automatic Outlining menu item.

Figure 4-3 shows four condensable regions. One is a defined region called Constructor, however there are also three other automatic regions, outlining the class, the XML comments, and the constructor method (which has been collapsed). Automatic outlines can be condensed and expanded in the same way as regions you define manually.

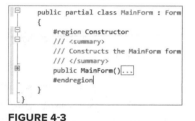

```
public partial class MainForm : Form
{
    #region Constructor
    /// <summary>
    /// Constructs the MainForm form
    /// </summary>
    public MainForm()...
    #endregion
}
```

FIGURE 4-3

The Edit ➪ Outlining menu provides a number of commands to help in toggling outlining, such as collapsing the entire file to just method/property definitions (Edit ➪ Outlining ➪ Collapse to Definitions) and expanding it to display all collapsed code again (Edit ➪ Outlining ➪ Stop Outlining). The other way to expand and condense regions is via the keyboard shortcut Ctrl+M, Ctrl+M. This shortcut toggles between the two layouts.

One trick for C# developers is that Ctrl+] enables you to easily navigate from the beginning of a region, outline, or code block to the end and back again.

Code Formatting

By default, Visual Studio 2010 assists you in writing readable code by automatically indenting and aligning. However, it is also configurable so that you can control how your code is arranged. Common to all languages is the ability to control what happens when you create a new line. In Figure 4-4 you can see that there is a Tabs node under the Text Editor ➪ All Languages node of the Options dialog. Setting values here defines the default value for all languages, which you can then overwrite for an individual language using the Basic ➪ Tabs node (for VB.NET), C# ➪ Tabs, or other language nodes.

By default, the indenting behavior for both C# and VB.NET is smart indenting, which will, among other things, automatically add indentation as you open and close enclosures. Smart indenting is not available for all languages, in which case block indenting is used.

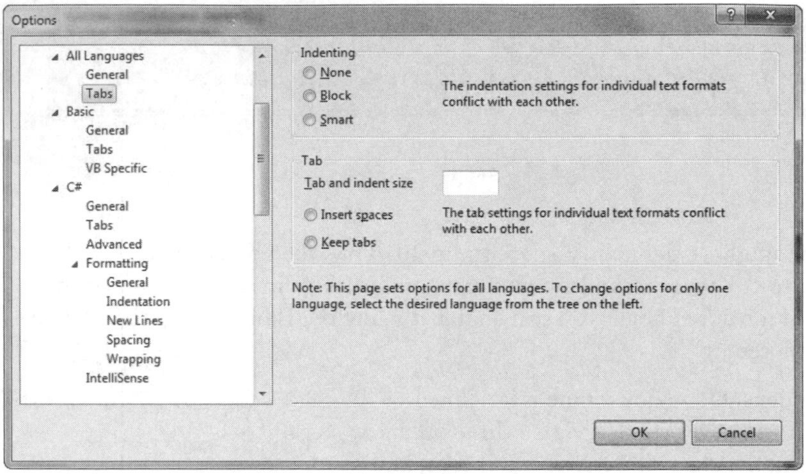

FIGURE 4-4

> *If you are working on a small screen, you might want to reduce the tab and indent sizes to optimize screen usage. Keeping the tab and indent sizes the same ensures that you can easily indent your code with a single tab keypress.*
>
> *What is interesting about this dialog is the degree of control C# users have over the layout of their code. Under the VB Specific node is a single checkbox entitled "Pretty listing (reformatting) of code," which if enabled keeps your code looking uniform without your having to worry about aligning methods, closures, class definitions, or namespaces. C# users, on the other hand, can control nearly every aspect of how the code editor reformats code, as you can see from the additional nodes for C# in Figure 4-4.*

Visual Studio's Smart Indenting does a pretty good job of automatically indenting code as it is written or pasted into the code editor, but occasionally you can come across code that has not been properly formatted, making it difficult to read. To have Visual Studio reformat the entire document and set the brace locations and line indentations, select Edit ⇨ Advanced ⇨ Format Document or press Ctrl+K, Ctrl+D. To reformat just the selected code block, select Edit ⇨ Advanced ⇨ Format Selection or press Ctrl+K, Ctrl+F.

When writing code, to indent an entire block of code one level without changing each line individually, simply select the block and press Tab. Each line will have a tab inserted at its start. To unindent a block one level, select it and press Shift+Tab.

> *You may have noticed the Tabify/Untabify Selected Lines commands under the Edit ⇨ Advanced menu and wondered how these differ from the Format Selection command. These commands simply convert leading spaces in lines to tabs and vice versa, rather than recalculating the indenting as the Format Selection command does.*

Navigating Forward/Backward

As you move within and between items, Visual Studio 2010 tracks where you have been, in much the same way that a web browser tracks the sites you have visited. Using the Navigate Forward and Navigate Backward items from the View menu, you can easily go back and forth between the various locations in the project that you have made changes to. The keyboard shortcut to navigate backward is Ctrl+−. To navigate forward again it is Ctrl+Shift+−.

Additional Code Editor Features

The Visual Studio code editor is very rich with far more features than we can cover in depth here. However, here are a few additional features that you may find useful.

Reference Highlighting

A new feature in Visual Studio 2010 is reference highlighting. All uses of the symbol (such as a method or property) under the cursor within its scope are highlighted (as shown in Figure 4-5). This makes it easy to spot where else this symbol is used within your code. You can easily navigate between the uses by Ctrl+Shift+Up/Down.

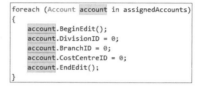

```
foreach (Account account in assignedAccounts)
{
    account.BeginEdit();
    account.DivisionID = 0;
    account.BranchID = 0;
    account.CostCentreID = 0;
    account.EndEdit();
}
```

FIGURE 4-5

Code Zooming

You can use Ctrl+Mouse Wheel to zoom in and out of your code (effectively making the text larger or smaller). This feature can be especially useful when presenting to a group to enable the people at the back of the audience to see the code being demonstrated. The bottom left-hand corner of the code editor also has a drop-down enabling you to select from some predefined zoom levels.

Word Wrap

You can turn on word wrap in the code editor from the options. Go to Tools ➪ Options, expand the Text Editor node, select the All Languages subnode, and select the Word Wrap option. You can also choose to display a return arrow glyph where text has been wrapped by selecting the Show Visual Glyphs for Word Wrap option below the Word Wrap option.

You can turn this on for the current project by selecting Edit ➪ Advanced ➪ Word Wrap.

```
10  namespace Chapter04SampleCS
11  {
12      public partial class MainForm : Form
13      {
14          #region Constructor
15          /// <summary>
16          /// Constructs the MainForm form
17          /// </summary>
18          public MainForm()
19          {
20              InitializeComponent();
21          }
22          #endregion
23      }
24  }
25
```

Line Numbers

To keep track of where you are in a code file you may find it useful to turn on line numbers in the code editor (as shown in Figure 4-6). To turn line numbers on, go to Tools ➪ Options, expand the Text Editor node, select the All Languages subnode, and select the Line Numbers option.

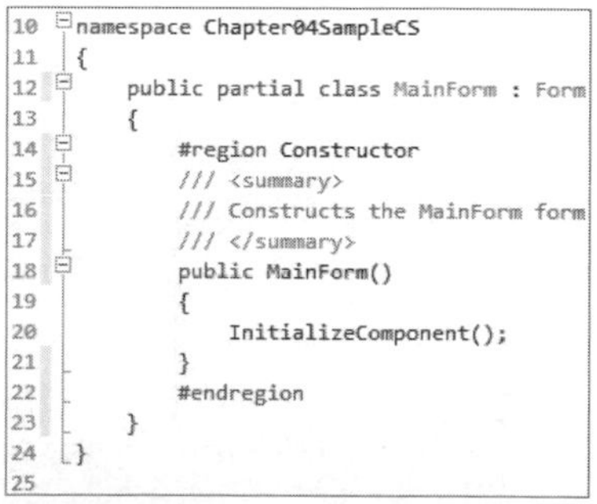

FIGURE 4-6

Split View

Sometimes you want to view two different parts of the same code file at the same time. Split view enables you to do this by splitting the active code editor window into two horizontal panes separated by a splitter bar. These can then be scrolled separately to display different parts of the same file simultaneously (as shown in Figure 4-7).

To split a code editor window, select Split from the Window menu. Alternatively, drag the handle directly above the vertical scroll bar down to position the splitter bar.

Drag the splitter bar up and down to adjust the size of each pane. To remove the splitter simply double-click the splitter bar, or select Remove Split from the Window menu.

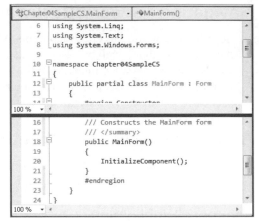

FIGURE 4-7

Tear Away (Floating) Code Windows

A welcome new feature in Visual Studio 2010 for those with multiple monitors is the ability to "tear off" or float code editor windows (and tool windows) and move them outside the main Visual Studio IDE window (as shown in Figure 4-8), including onto another monitor. This allows you to now make use of the extra screen real-estate that having multiple monitors provides by enabling multiple code editor windows to be visible at the same time over separate monitors. To tear off a window, make sure it has the focus and then select Float from the Window menu. Alternatively, right-click the title bar of the window and select Float from the drop-down menu, or simply click and drag the tab for that window (effectively tearing it away from its docked position) and position it where you want it to be located.

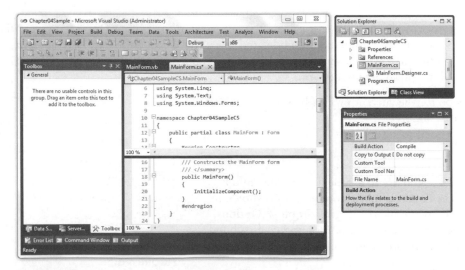

FIGURE 4-8

You may find halving the code editor window in split view (discussed in the previous section) in order to view different parts of a file at the same time too much of a limited view, so you might want to use the floating code windows feature instead to open another code editor window for the same file, and place it, say, on a different screen (if you have a multiple monitor setup). The trick to doing this (because double-clicking the file again in the Solution Explorer simply activates the existing code editor window instance for that file) is to select New Window from the Window menu. This will open the file currently being viewed in another window which you can then tear away and position as you please.

Creating Tab Groups

If you don't have the privilege of having more than one monitor, it is still possible to view more than one code editor window at the same time. You do this by creating tab groups, and tiling these groups to display at the same time. As their name would indicate, a tab group is a group of code editor window tabs, with each tab group appearing in a separate tile. Multiple tab groups can be created, limited only by the amount of screen real-estate they will occupy. You can choose to tile the tab groups vertically or horizontally, although you cannot use a mix of the two.

To start this process you need to have more than one tab open in the code editor window. Ensure a code editor tab has the focus, then select Window ⇨ New Horizontal Tab Group or Window ⇨ New Vertical Tab Group from the menu displayed. This starts a new tab group and creates a tile for it (as shown in Figure 4-9).

Alternatively, you can simply drag a tab below or beside an existing one and dock it to achieve the same effect.

You can drag tabs between tab groups or move them between tab groups using Window ⇨ Move to Next Tab Group and Window ⇨ Move to Previous Tab Group. These options are also available from the drop-down menu when right-clicking a tab.

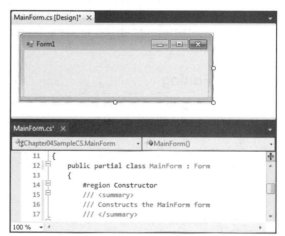

FIGURE 4-9

To restore the user interface to having a single tab group again, move the tabs from the new tab group(s) back into the original one again and the tiling will be removed.

Advanced Functionality

To be a truly productive developer it can help to know various advanced features available in the code editor that are hidden away but can save you a lot of time. Here are some of the most useful commands that aren't immediately obvious within the code editor.

Commenting/Uncommenting a Code Block

Often you need to comment or uncomment a block of code, and you don't want to have to add/remove the comment characters to/from the start of each line, especially when there are many lines in the block. Of course, in C# you could wrap the block of code between a /* and */ to comment it out, but this type of comment isn't available in Visual Basic, and it can be problematic in C# when commenting out a block that already contains a comment using this style.

Visual Studio provides a means to comment/uncomment a block of code easily, by selecting the block, then selecting Edit ➪ Advanced ➪ Comment Selection to comment it out, or selecting Edit ➪ Advanced ➪ Uncomment Selection to uncomment it.

The easiest way to access these commands (you are likely to use these often) is via their shortcuts. Press Ctrl+K, Ctrl+C to comment a block of code, and Ctrl+K, Ctrl+U to uncomment it. The Text Editor toolbar is another simple means to access these commands.

Block Selection

Also known as box selection, column selection, rectangle selection, or vertical text selection, block selection is the ability to select text in a block (as shown in Figure 4-10) instead of the normal behavior of selecting lines of text (stream selection). To select a block of text, hold down the Alt key while selecting text with the mouse, or use Shift+Alt+Arrow with the keyboard. This feature can come in handy when, for example, you have code lined up and want to remove a vertical portion of that code (such as a prefix on variable declarations).

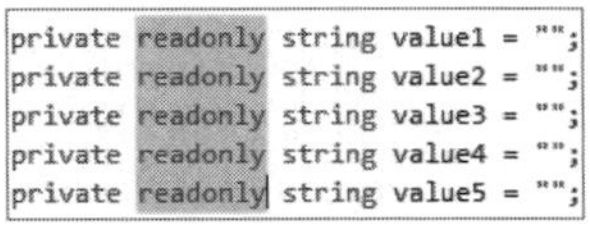

```
private readonly string value1 = "";
private readonly string value2 = "";
private readonly string value3 = "";
private readonly string value4 = "";
private readonly string value5 = "";
```

FIGURE 4-10

Multiline Editing

Multiline editing is a new feature available in Visual Studio 2010 that extends the abilities of block selection. In previous versions, after selecting a vertical block of text you could only delete, cut, or copy the block. With Visual Studio 2010 you can now type after selecting a vertical block of text, which will replace the selected text with what's being typed on each line. This can be handy for changing a group of variables from private to protected, for example.

> *You can also insert text across multiple lines by creating a block with zero width and simply starting to type.*

The Clipboard Ring

Visual Studio keeps track of the last 20 snippets of text that have been copied or cut to the clipboard. To paste text that was previously copied to the clipboard but overwritten, instead of the normal Ctrl+V when pasting, use Ctrl+Shift+V. Pressing V while holding down Ctrl+Shift cycles through the entries.

Full-Screen View

You can maximize the view for editing the code by selecting View ➪ Full Screen, or using the Shift+Alt+Enter shortcut. This effectively maximizes the code editor window, hiding the other tool windows and the toolbars. To return to the normal view, press Shift+Alt+Enter again or click the Full-Screen toggle button that has been added to the end of the menubar.

Go To Definition

To quickly navigate to the definition of the class, method, or member under the cursor, right-click ⇨ Go To Definition, or simply press F12.

Find All References

You can find where a method or property is called by right-clicking its definition and selecting Find All References from the drop-down menu, or placing the cursor in the method definition and pressing Shift+F12. This activates the Find Symbol Results tool window and displays the locations throughout your solution where that method or property is referenced. You can then double-click a reference in the results window to navigate to that result in the code editor window.

> *This feature has somewhat been made obsolete by the new Call Hierarchy window, discussed later in this chapter. However, it can still be a quick way to view where a method is used without navigating through the Call Hierarchy window.*

THE COMMAND WINDOW

As you become more familiar with Visual Studio 2010, you will spend less time looking for functionality and more time using keyboard shortcuts to navigate and perform actions within the IDE. One of the tool windows that's often overlooked is the Command window, accessible via View ⇨ Other Windows ⇨ Command Window (Ctrl+Alt+A). From this window you can execute any existing Visual Studio command or macro, as well as any additional macros you may have recorded or written. Figure 4-11 illustrates the use of IntelliSense to show the list of commands that can be executed from the Command window. This list will include all macros defined within the current solution.

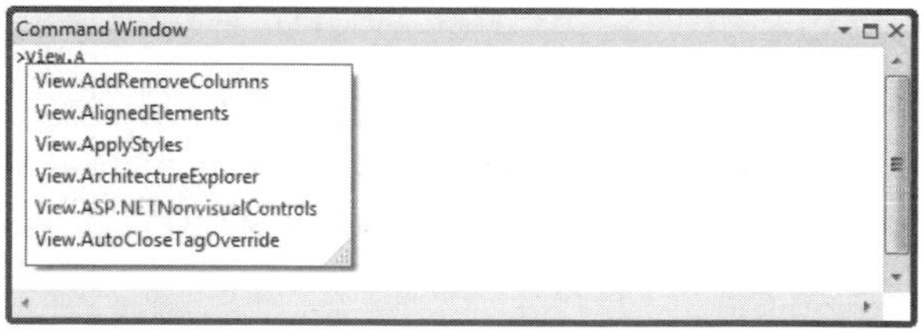

FIGURE 4-11

A full list of the Visual Studio commands is available via the Environment ⇨ Keyboard node of the Options dialog (Tools ⇨ Options). The commands all have a similar syntax based on the area of the IDE that they are derived from. For example, you can open the debugging output window (Debug ⇨ Windows ⇨ Output) by typing `Debug.Output` into the Command window.

The commands fall into three rough groups. Many commands are shortcuts to either tool windows (which are made visible if they aren't already open) or dialogs. For example, `File.NewFile` opens the new file dialog. Other commands query information about the current solution or the debugger. Using `Debug.ListThreads` lists the current threads, in contrast to `Debug.Threads`, which opens the Threads tool window. The third type includes those commands that perform an action without displaying a dialog. This would include most macros and a number of commands that accept arguments (a full list of these, including the arguments they accept, is available within the MSDN documentation). There is some overlap between these groups: for example, the `Edit.Find` command can be executed with or without arguments. If this command is executed without arguments, the Find and Replace dialog is displayed. Alternatively, the following command will find all instances of the string `MyVariable` in the current document (`/d`) and place a marker in the code window border against the relevant lines (`/m`):

```
>Edit.Find MyVariable /m /d
```

Although there is IntelliSense within the Command window, you may find typing a frequently used command somewhat painful. Visual Studio 2010 has the ability to assign an alias to a particular command. For example, the `alias` command can be used to assign an alias, `e?`, to the find command used previously:

```
>alias e? Edit.Find MyVariable /m /d
```

With this alias defined you can easily perform this command from anywhere within the IDE: press Ctrl+Alt+A to give the Command Window focus, then type **e?** to perform the find-and-mark command.

You will have imported a number of default aliases belonging to the environment settings when you began working with Visual Studio 2010. You can list these using the `alias` command with no arguments. Alternatively, if you want to find out what command a specific alias references, you can execute the command with the name of the alias. For example, querying the previously defined alias, `e?`, would look like the following:

```
>alias e?
alias e? Edit.Find SumVals /m /doc
```

Two additional switches can be used with the `alias` command. The `/delete` switch, along with an alias name, removes a previously defined alias. If you want to remove all aliases you may have defined and revert any changes to a predefined alias, you can use the `/reset` switch.

THE IMMEDIATE WINDOW

Quite often when you are writing code or debugging your application, you will want to evaluate a simple expression either to test a bit of functionality or to remind yourself of how something works. This is where the Immediate window comes in handy. This window enables you to run expressions as you type them. Figure 4-12 shows a number of statements — from basic assignment and print operations to more advanced object creation and manipulation.

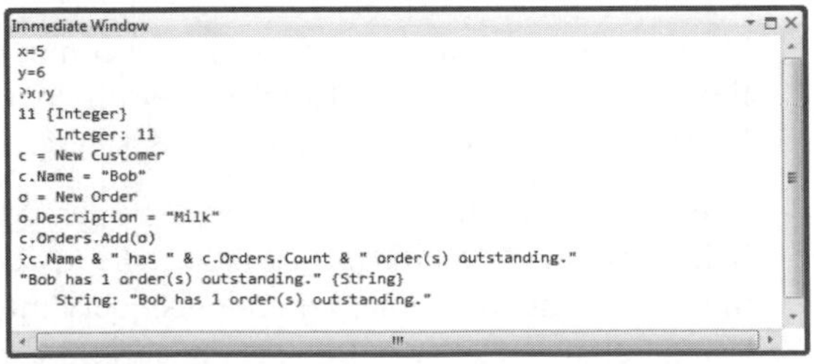

FIGURE 4-12

> *In Visual Basic you can't do explicit variable declaration in the Immediate window (for example, Dim x as Integer), but instead you do this implicitly via the assignment operator. The example shown in Figure 4-12 shows a new customer being created, assigned to a variable c, and then used in a series of operations. When using C#, new variables in the Immediate window must be declared explicitly before they can be assigned a value.*

The Immediate window supports a limited form of IntelliSense, and you can use the arrow keys to track back through the history of previous commands executed. Variable values can be displayed by means of the Debug.Print statement. Alternatively, you can use its ? alias. Neither of these are necessary in C#; simply type the variable's name into the window and press Enter to print its value.

When you execute a command in the Immediate window while in design mode, Visual Studio will build the solution before executing the command. If your solution doesn't compile, the expression cannot be evaluated until the compilation errors are resolved. If the command execute code has an active breakpoint, the command will break there. This can be useful if you are working on a particular method that you want to test without running the entire application.

You can access the Immediate window via the Debug ⇨ Windows ⇨ Immediate menu or the Ctrl+Alt+I keyboard chord, but if you are working between the Command and Immediate windows you may want to use the predefined aliases cmd and immed, respectively.

> *Note that in order to execute commands in the Immediate window you need to add > as a prefix (for example, >cmd to go to the Command window); otherwise Visual Studio tries to evaluate the command.*
>
> *Also, you should be aware that the language used in the Immediate window is that of the active project. The examples shown in Figure 4-12 will work only if a Visual Basic project is currently active.*

THE CLASS VIEW

Although the Solution Explorer is probably the most useful tool window for navigating your solution, it can sometimes be difficult to locate particular classes and methods. The Class View tool window provides you with an alternative view of your solution that lists namespaces, classes, and methods so that you can easily navigate to them. Figure 4-13 shows a simple Windows application that contains a single form (MainForm), which is selected in the class hierarchy. Note that there are two Chapter04Sample nodes. The first is the name of the project (not the assembly as you might expect), and the second is the namespace that MainForm belongs to. If you were to expand the References node, you would see a list of assemblies that this project references. Drilling further into each of these would yield a list of namespaces, followed by the classes contained in the assembly.

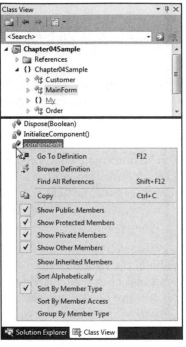

In the lower portion of Figure 4-13 you can see the list of members that are available for the class `Form1`. Using the right-click shortcut menu, you can either filter this list based on accessibility, sort and group the list, or use it to navigate to the selected member. For example, clicking Go To Definition on `InitializeComponent()` would take you to the `Form1. Designer.vb` file.

The Class View is useful for navigating to generated members, which are usually in a file hidden in the default Solution Explorer view (such as the designer file in the previous example). It can also be a useful way to navigate to classes that have been added to an existing file — this would result in multiple classes in the same file, which is not a recommended practice. Because the file does not have a name that matches the class name, it becomes hard to navigate to that class using the Solution Explorer; hence the Class View is a good alternative.

FIGURE 4-13

THE ERROR LIST

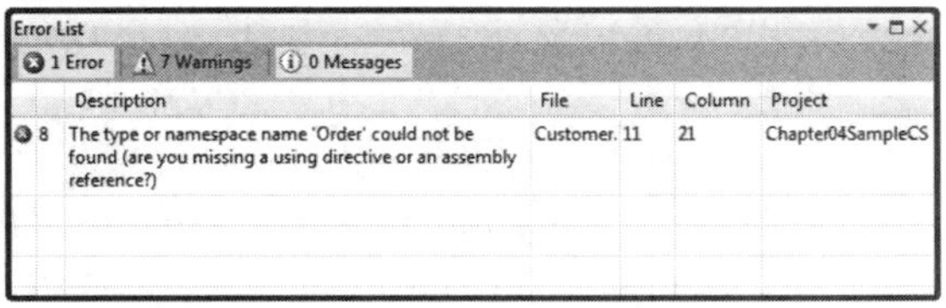

The Error List window displays compile errors, warnings, and messages for your solution, as shown in Figure 4-14. You can open the Error List window by selecting View ⇨ Error List, or by using the keyboard shortcut Ctrl+\, Ctrl+E. Errors will appear in the list as you edit code

FIGURE 4-14

and when you compile the project. Double-clicking an error in the list opens the file and takes you to the line of code that is in error.

You can filter the entries in the list by toggling the buttons above the list to select the types of errors (Errors, Warnings, and/or Messages) you want to display.

THE OBJECT BROWSER

Another way of viewing the classes that make up your application is via the Object Browser. Unlike most other tool windows, which appear docked to a side of Visual Studio 2010 by default, the Object Browser appears in the editor space. To view the Object Browser window, select

View ⇨ Object Browser, or by using the keyboard shortcut Ctrl+Alt+J (or F2, depending on your keyboard settings). As you can see in Figure 4-15, at the top of the Object Browser window is a drop-down box that defines the object browsing scope. This includes a set of predefined values, such as All Components, .NET Framework 4.0, and My Solution, as well as a Custom Component Set. Here, My Solution is selected and a search string of `sample` has been entered. The contents of the main window are then all the namespaces, classes, and members that match this search string.

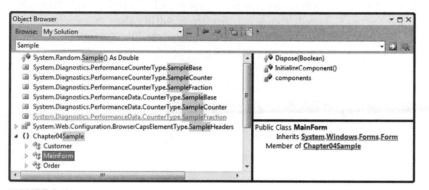

FIGURE 4-15

In the top right-hand portion of Figure 4-15 you can see the list of members for the selected class (`MainForm`), and in the lower window the full class definition, which includes its base class and namespace information. One of the options in the Browse drop-down of Figure 4-15 is a Custom Component Set. To define what assemblies are included in this set you can either click the ellipsis next to the drop-down or select Edit Custom Component Set from the drop-down itself. This presents you with an edit dialog similar to the one shown in Figure 4-16.

Selecting items in the top section and clicking Add inserts that assembly into the component set. Similarly, selecting an item in the lower section and clicking Remove deletes that assembly from the component set. Once you have finished customizing the component set, it will be saved between Visual Studio sessions.

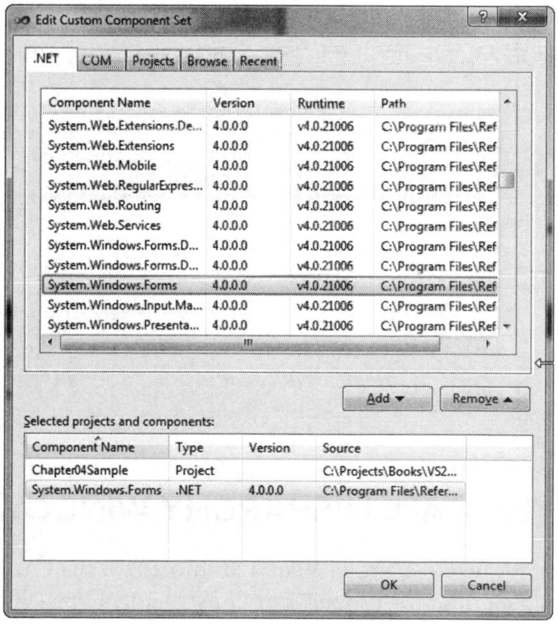

FIGURE 4-16

THE CODE DEFINITION WINDOW

When navigating around your code you might come across a method call that you'd like to view the code for without leaving your current position in the code editor. This is where the Code Definition window can come in handy, to show the source of the method when the cursor has been placed within a reference to it (as shown in Figure 4-17). Access it via View ➪ Other Windows ➪ Code Definition window (Ctrl+\, Ctrl+D). It's just like another code editor window with many of the same commands available (such as inserting a breakpoint, view call hierarchy, and so on), but is read-only. To edit the code for that method, right-click anywhere within the Code Definition window and select Edit Definition. The source code file for this method will be opened in a code editor window and the method definition will be navigated to.

```
MainWindow.xaml.cs  ×
FinancialReporting.MainWindow                    ▼   Save(object sender, ExecutedRoutedEventArgs e)    ▼
           private void Save(object sender, ExecutedRoutedEventArgs e)
           {
               if (IsActiveScreenValid())
                   SaveAllData();
           }
100 %  ◄  ◄                        III                                             ►

Code Definition Wi...ainWindow.xaml.cs)  ×  Call Hierarchy     Task List     Error List
           private bool SaveAllData()
           {
               bool success = true;

               this.Cursor = Cursors.Wait;

               // Save the dictionaries
               try
               {
                   DictionaryCache.Divisions.Save();
100 %  ◄                            III                                             ►
```

FIGURE 4-17

> You can also use the Code Definition window with the Class View and the Object Browser windows to view the code for the selected member of a class.

THE CALL HIERARCHY WINDOW

A new feature in Visual Studio 2010, the Call Hierarchy window displays all the calls to and from a method (or property or constructor, but each henceforth referred to as methods), enabling you to see where a method is being used and additionally what calls it makes to other methods. This enables you to easily follow the execution path and the flow of the code.

To view the call hierarchy for a method, select a method definition in the code editor window and select View Call Hierarchy from the right-click context menu. This adds the method to the tree in the Call Hierarchy window with two subnodes — Calls To (MethodName) and Calls From (MethodName), as shown in Figure 4-18.

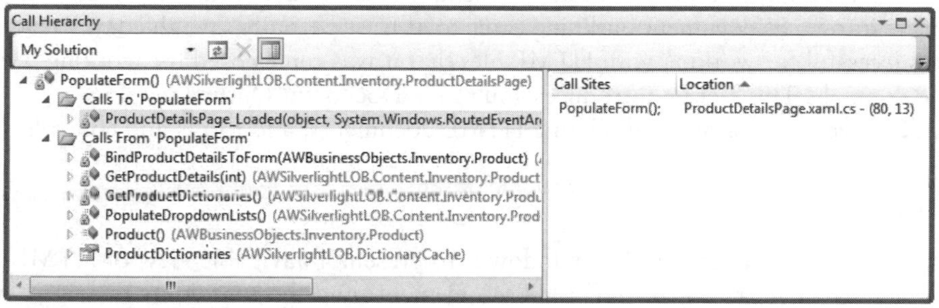

FIGURE 4-18

Expanding the Calls To (MethodName) lists all the methods that call the specified method. Expanding the Calls From (MethodName) lists all the other methods that are called by the specified method.

The Call Hierarchy window allows you to drill down through the results to build a hierarchy of the program execution flow — seeing which methods call the specified method, which methods call them, and so on.

Double-clicking a method navigates to that method definition in the code editor window.

> *You can view the call hierarchy for methods in the Class View window or the Object Browser window also, by right-clicking the method and selecting View Call Hierarchy from the drop-down menu.*

Despite the fact that the Call Hierarchy window can be left floating or be docked, it doesn't work in the same way as the Code Definition window. Moving around the code editor window to different methods will not display the call hierarchy automatically for the method under the cursor — instead you will need to explicitly request to view the call hierarchy for that method, at which point it will be added to the Call Hierarchy window. The Call Hierarchy window can display the call hierarchy for more than just one method and each time you view the call hierarchy for a method it is added to the window rather than replacing the call hierarchy currently being viewed. When you no longer need to view the call hierarchy for a method, select it in the window and press Delete (or the red cross in the toolbar) to remove it.

> *This window can come in very handy when working on an unfamiliar project or refactoring a project.*

THE DOCUMENT OUTLINE TOOL WINDOW

Editing HTML files, using either the visual designer or code view, is never as easy as it could be, particularly when you have a large number of nested elements. When Visual Studio .NET first arrived on the scene, a feature known as document outlining came to at least partially save the day. In fact, this feature was so successful for working with HTML files that it was repurposed for working with non-web forms and controls. This section introduces you to the Document Outline window and demonstrates how effective it can be at manipulating HTML documents, and forms and controls.

HTML Outlining

The primary purpose of the Document Outline window is to present a navigable view of HTML pages so that you could easily locate the different HTML elements and the containers they were in. Because it is difficult to get HTML layouts correct, especially with the many .NET components that could be included on an ASP.NET page, the Document Outline view provides a handy way to find the correct position for a specific component.

Figure 4-19 shows a typical HTML page. Without the Document Outline window, selecting an element in the designer can be rather tricky if it's small or not visible in the designer. The Document Outline pane (View ⇨ Other Windows ⇨ Document Outline), on the left of Figure 4-19, enables you to easily select elements in the hierarchy to determine where in the page they are located, and to enable you to set their properties.

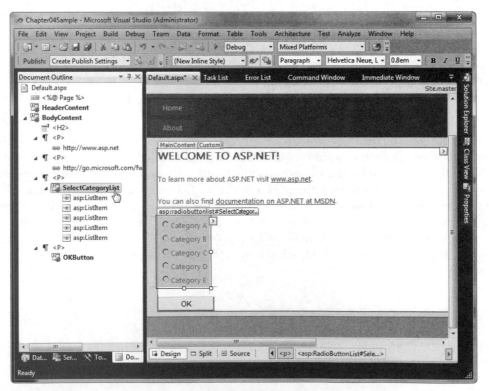

FIGURE 4-19

Visual Studio analyzes the content of the currently active file and populates it with a tree view containing every element in the page hierarchy. The Name or ID value of each element will be displayed in the tree (if they are assigned one), while unnamed elements are simply listed with their HTML tags.

As you select each entry in the Document Outline window, the Design view is updated to select the component and its children. In Figure 4-19, the `SelectCategoryList` RadioButtonList control's tag is selected in the Document Outline window, highlighting the control in the Design view, and enabling you to see where it is located on the page. Correspondingly, selecting a control or element in the Design view will select the corresponding tag in the page hierarchy in the Document Outline window (although you will need to set the focus back to the Document Outline window for it to update accordingly).

Control Outlining

The Document Outline window has been available in Visual Studio since the first .NET version for HTML files but has been of little use for other file views. When Visual Studio 2003 was released, an add-in called the Control view was developed that allowed a similar kind of access to Windows Forms.

The tool was so popular that Microsoft incorporated its functionality into the Document Outline tool window, so now you can browse Windows Forms in the same way.

Figure 4-20 shows a typical complex form, with many panels to provide structure and controls to provide the visual elements. Each component is represented in the Document Outline by its name and component type. As each item is selected in the Document Outline window, the corresponding visual element is selected and displayed in the Design view.

This means that when the item is in a menu (as is the case in Figure 4-20) Visual Studio automatically opens the menu and selects the menu item ready for editing. As you can imagine, this is an incredibly useful way of navigating your form layouts, and it can often provide a shortcut for locating wayward items.

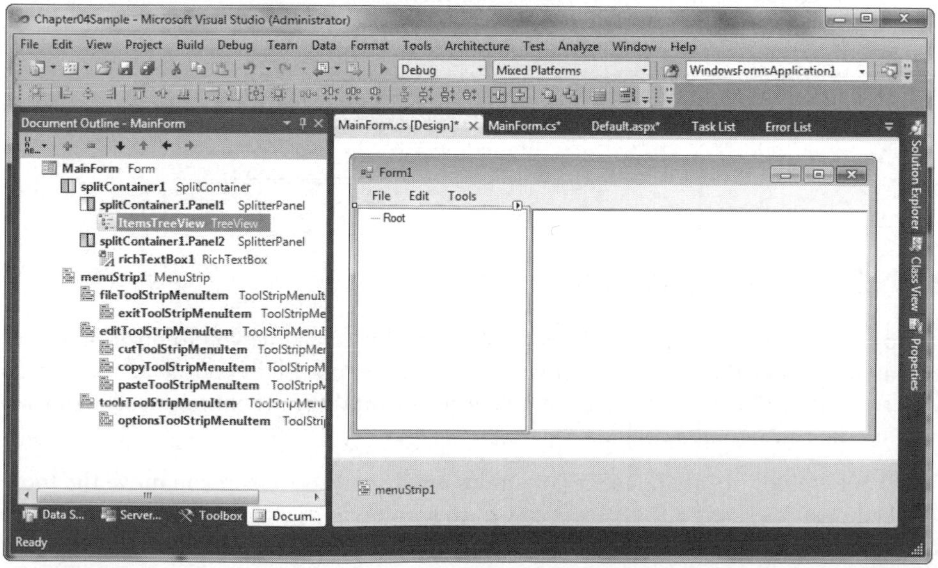

FIGURE 4-20

The Document Outline window has more functionality when used in Control Outline mode than just a simple navigation tool. Right-clicking an entry gives you a small context menu of actions that can be performed against the selected item. The most obvious is to access the Properties window.

One tedious chore is renaming components after you've added them to the form. You can select each one in turn and set its Name property in the Properties window, but using the Document Outline window you can simply choose the Rename option in the context menu and Visual Studio will automatically rename the component in the design code, thus updating the Name property for you without your needing to scroll through the Properties list.

Complex form design can sometimes produce unexpected results. This often happens when a component is placed in an incorrect or inappropriate container control. In such a case you'll need to move the component to the correct container. Of course, you have to locate the issue before you even know that there is a problem.

The Document Outline window can help with both of these activities. First, using the hierarchical view, you can easily locate each component and check its parent container elements. The example shown in Figure 4-20 indicates that the TreeView control is in Panel1, which in turn is in SplitContainer, which is itself contained in a ContentPanel object. In this way you can easily determine when a control is incorrectly placed on the form's design layout.

When you need to move a component it can be quite tricky to get the layout right. In the Document Outline window it's easy. Simply drag and drop the control to the correct position in the hierarchy. For example, dragging the TreeView control to Panel2 results in its sharing the Panel2 area with the ListView control.

You also have the option to cut, copy, and paste individual elements or whole sets of containers and their contents by using the right-click context menu. The copy-and-paste function is particularly useful, because you can duplicate whole chunks of your form design in other locations on the form without having to use trial and error to select the correct elements in the Design view, or resort to duplicating them in the code-behind in the `Designer.vb` file.

> *When you cut an item, remember to paste it immediately into the destination location.*

REORGANIZING TOOL WINDOWS

The Visual Studio IDE has been designed to be very customizable to enable you to position tool windows such that you can be the most productive and can make full use of your available screen real estate. You can dock tool windows, have them floating, or minimize them to the edge of the IDE displaying only their tab using auto hide.

When dragging a tool window around, a series of guides are displayed to help you move the tool window to a docked position. Drag the tool window onto a guide to dock the window. Dragging over a part of a guide highlights the part of the IDE that the tool window would be docked to if you were to drop it there (as shown in Figure 4-21).

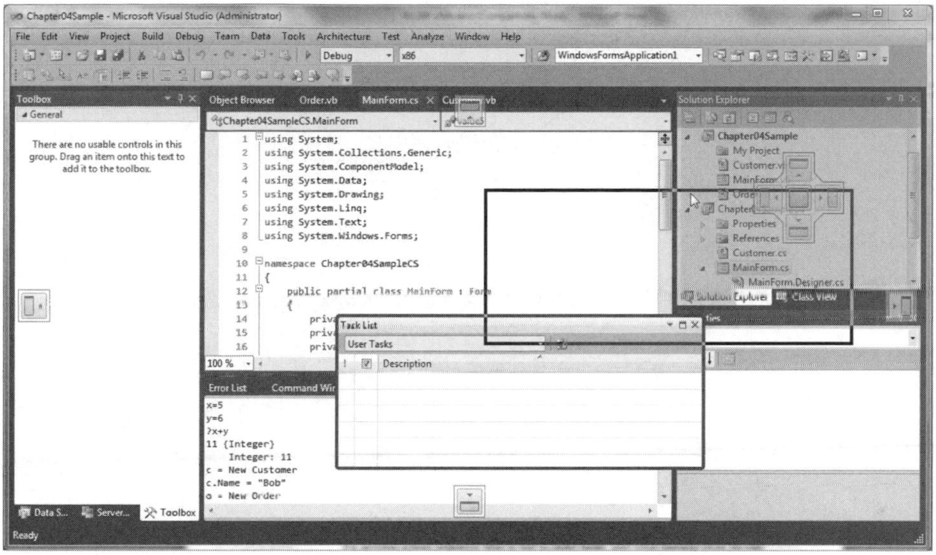

FIGURE 4-21

To float a docked tool window simply click and drag it to a new position (making sure not to drop it on top of one of the guides that appears). Pressing the Ctrl key while moving the window will prevent the guides from appearing and the window from snapping to them. When a tool window is docked and part of a tab group (that is, windows that occupy the same space and can be switched between by clicking their tabs), clicking and dragging the tab for the tool window moves just that window, whereas clicking and dragging the title bar for the tool window moves the entire tab group.

To access a tool window that is set to auto hide, put your mouse over its tab to make it slide out. To put a tool window into auto hide mode, click the pushpin button in the title bar for the window, and click it again while in the auto hide mode to return it to its docked position.

> *After dragging a tool window out of its docked position and moving it elsewhere (such as onto another monitor), simply double-click its title bar while holding the Ctrl key to return it to its previously docked position.*

SUMMARY

In this chapter you have seen a number of tool windows that can help you not only write code but also prototype and try it out. Making effective use of these windows will dramatically reduce the number of times you have to run your application in order to test the code you are writing. This, in turn, will improve your overall productivity and eliminate idle time spent waiting for your application to run.

5
Find and Replace and Help

WHAT'S IN THIS CHAPTER?

➤   Using Visual Studio's various Find and Replace tools

➤   Navigating Visual Studio's local help system

To be a productive developer, you need to be able to navigate your way around a code base and find what you need quickly. Visual Studio 2010 provides not just one but a number of search functions, each suited to particular searching tasks. The first part of this chapter discusses each of these search functions and when and where to use them.

Visual Studio 2010 is an immensely complex development environment that encompasses multiple languages based on an extensive framework of libraries and components. You will find it almost impossible to know everything about the IDE, let alone each of the languages or even the full extent of the .NET Framework. As both the .NET Framework and Visual Studio evolve, it becomes increasingly difficult to stay abreast of all the changes; moreover, it is likely that you need to know only a subset of this knowledge. Of course, you'll periodically need to obtain more information on a specific topic. To help you in these situations, Visual Studio 2010 comes with comprehensive documentation in the form of the MSDN Library, Visual Studio 2010 Edition. The second part of this chapter walks you through the methods of researching documentation associated with developing projects in Visual Studio 2010.

QUICK FIND/REPLACE

The simplest means of searching in Visual Studio 2010 is via the Quick Find dialog.

The find-and-replace functionality in Visual Studio 2010 is split into two broad tiers with a shared dialog and similar features: *Quick Find*, and the associated *Quick Replace*, are for searches that you need to perform quickly on the document or project currently open in the IDE. These two tools have limited options to filter and extend the search, but as you'll see in a moment, even those options provide a powerful search engine that goes beyond what you'll find in most applications.

 This search tool is best suited for when you need to do a simple text-based search/replace (as opposed to searching for a symbol).

Quick Find

Quick Find is the term that Visual Studio 2010 uses to refer to the most basic search functionality. By default, it enables you to search for a simple word or phrase within the current document, but even Quick Find has additional options that can extend the search beyond the active module, or even incorporate wildcards and regular expressions in the search criteria.

To start a Find action, press the standard keyboard shortcut Ctrl+F or select Edit Find and Replace Quick Find. Visual Studio will display the basic Find and Replace dialog, with the default Quick Find action selected (see Figure 5-1).

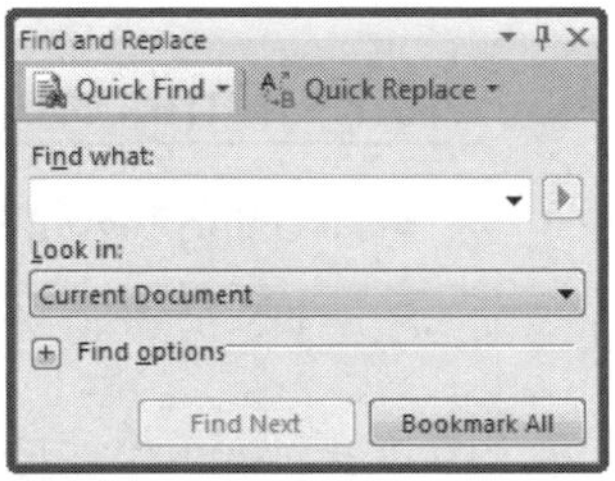

FIGURE 5-1

Type the search criteria into the Find what textbox, or select from previous searches by clicking the drop-down arrow and scrolling through the list of criteria that have been used. By default, the scope of the search is restricted to the current document or window you're editing, unless you have a number of lines selected, in which case the default scope is the selection. The Look in drop-down list gives you additional options based on the context of the search itself, including Selection, Current Block, Current Document, Current Project, Entire Solution, and All Open Documents.

Find-and-replace actions will always wrap around the selected scope looking for the search terms, stopping only when the find process has reached the starting point again. As Visual Studio finds each result, it highlights the match and scrolls the code window so you can view it. If the match is already visible in the code window, Visual Studio does not scroll the code. Instead, it just highlights the new match. However, if it does need to scroll the window, it attempts to position the listing so the match is in the middle of the code editor window.

 Once you have performed the first Quick Find search, you no longer need the dialog to be visible. You can simply press F3 to repeat the same search.

In the Standard toolbar there is a Quick Find box, as shown in Figure 5-2. This box actually has multiple purposes. The keyboard shortcut Ctrl+/ will place focus on the box. You can then enter a search phrase and press Enter to find the next match in the currently open file. If you prefix what

FIGURE 5-2

you type with >, Visual Studio 2010 attempts to execute the command as if it had been entered into the Command window (see Chapter 4 for more information).

Quick Replace

Performing a Quick Replace is similar to performing a Quick Find. You can switch between Quick Find and Quick Replace by clicking their respective buttons at the top of the dialog window. If you want to go directly to Quick Replace, you can do so with the keyboard shortcut Ctrl+H or the menu command Edit Find and Replace Quick Replace. The Quick Replace options (see Figure 5-3) are the same as those for Quick Find, but with an additional field where you can specify what text should be used in the replacement.

The Replace With field works in the same way as Find What — you can either type a new replacement string or, with the drop-down list provided, choose any you've previously entered.

FIGURE 5-3

A simple way to delete recurring values is to use the replace functionality with nothing specified in the Replace With text area. This enables you to find all occurrences of the search text and decide if it should be deleted.

Find Options

Sometimes you will want to filter the search results in different ways, and that's where the find options come into play. First, to display the options section (available in all find-and-replace actions), click the expand icon next to Find Options. The dialog will expand to show a set of checkbox options and drop-down lists from which you can choose, as shown in Figure 5-4.

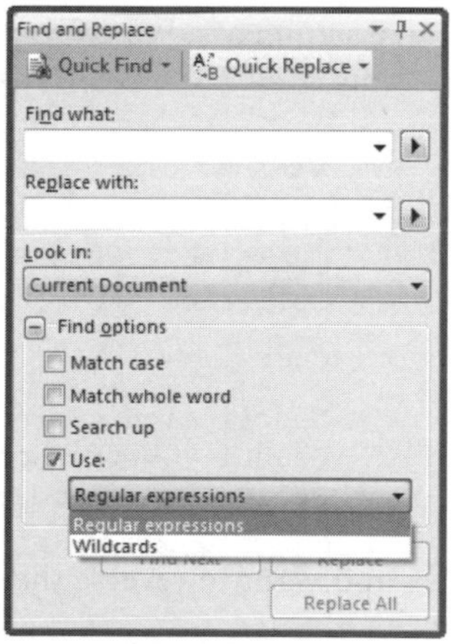

These options enable you to refine the search to be case-sensitive (Match Case) or an exact match (Match Whole Word). You can also change the direction of the search (Search Up), and specify that you are performing a more advanced search that is using wildcards or regular expressions.

FIGURE 5-4

Wildcards

Wildcards are simple text symbols that represent one or more characters, and are familiar to many users of Windows applications. Figure 5-5 illustrates the Expression Builder when the wildcard option is specified under the Use drop-down. Although additional characters can be used in a wildcard search, the most common characters are ? for a single character and * for multiple characters that are unknown or variable in the search.

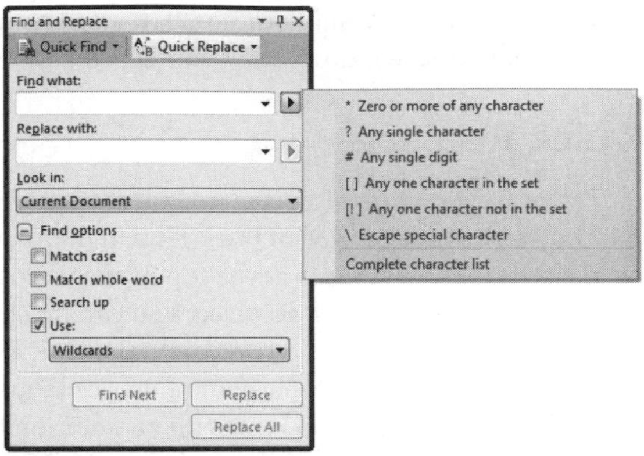

Regular Expressions

Regular expressions take searching to a whole new level, with the capability to do complex text matching based on the full RegEx engine built into Visual Studio 2010. Although this book doesn't go into great detail on the advanced matching capabilities of regular expressions, it's worth mentioning the additional help provided by the Find and Replace dialog if you choose to use them in your search terms.

Figure 5-6 again shows the Expression Builder, this time for building a regular expression as specified in the Use drop-down. From here you can easily build your regular expressions with a menu showing the most commonly used regular expression phrases and symbols, along with English descriptions of each.

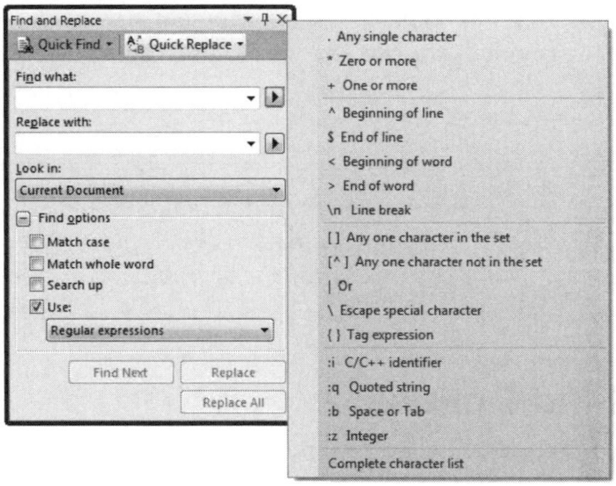

An example of where using regular expressions might come in handy is when reversing assignments. For example, if you have this code:

VB

```
Description = product.Description
Quantity = product.Quantity
SellPrice = product.SellPrice
```

C#

```
Description = product.Description;
Quantity = product.Quantity;
SellPrice = product.SellPrice;
```

and want to reverse the assignments like so:

VB

```
product.Description = Description
product.Quantity = Quantity
product.SellPrice = SellPrice
```

FIGURE 5-5

FIGURE 5-6

C#

```
product.Description = Description;
product.Quantity = Quantity;
product.SellPrice = SellPrice;
```

this would be a perfect use for performing a Quick Replace with regular expressions rather than modifying each line of code manually. Ensure you select regular expressions in the find options, and enter the following as the "text" to find:

VB

```
{<.*} = {.*}
```

C#

```
{<.*} = {.*};
```

and the following as the replace with "text":

VB

```
\2 = \1
```

C#

```
\2 = \1;
```

As a brief explanation, you are searching for two groups (defined by the curly brackets) separated by an equals sign. The first group is searching for the first character of a word (<) and then any characters (.*). The second group is searching for any characters until an end-of-line character is found in the VB example or a semicolon is found in the C# example. Then when you do the replace, you are simply inserting the characters from the second group found in its place, an equals sign (surrounded by a space on each side), then the characters from the first group found (followed by a semicolon in the C# example). If you aren't familiar with regular expressions it may take some time to get your head around it, but it is a very quick and easy way to perform an otherwise rather mundane manual process.

> *Note that the regular expressions used in the Quick Find tool don't have exactly the same syntax as the standard regular expressions you might find in the .NET Framework, with a few differences present between the two.*

Find and Replace Options

You can further configure the find-and-replace functionality with its own set of options in the Tools ⮑ Options dialog. Found in the Environment group, the Find and Replace options enable you to enable/disable displaying informational and warning messages, as well as to indicate whether the Find what field should be automatically filled with the current selection in the editor window. There is also an option to hide the Find dialog after performing a Quick Find or Quick Replace, which can be handy if you typically look only for the first match.

FIND/REPLACE IN FILES

The *Find in Files* and *Replace in Files* commands enable you to broaden the search beyond the current solution to whole folders and folder structures, and even to perform mass replacements on any matches for the given criteria and filters. Additional options are available to you when using these commands, and search results can be placed in one of two tool windows so you can easily navigate them.

> *This search tool is best suited when you need to do a simple text-based search/ replace across files that are not necessarily a part of your current solution.*

Find in Files

The really powerful part of the search engine built into Visual Studio is found in the Find in Files command. Rather than restrict yourself to files in the current solution, Find in Files gives you the ability to search entire folders (along with all their subfolders), looking for files that contain the search criteria.

The Find in Files dialog, shown in Figure 5-7, can be invoked via the menu command Edit ➪ Find and Replace ➪ Find in Files. Alternatively, if you have the Quick Find dialog open, you can switch over to Find in Files mode by clicking the small drop-down arrow next to Quick Find and choosing Find in Files. You can also use the keyboard shortcut Ctrl+Shift+F to launch this dialog.

Most of the Quick Find options are still available to you, including wildcard and regular expressions searching, but instead of choosing a scope from the project or solution, you use the Look In field to specify where the search is to be performed. Either type the location you want to search or click the ellipsis to display the Choose Search Folders dialog, shown in Figure 5-8.

FIGURE 5-7

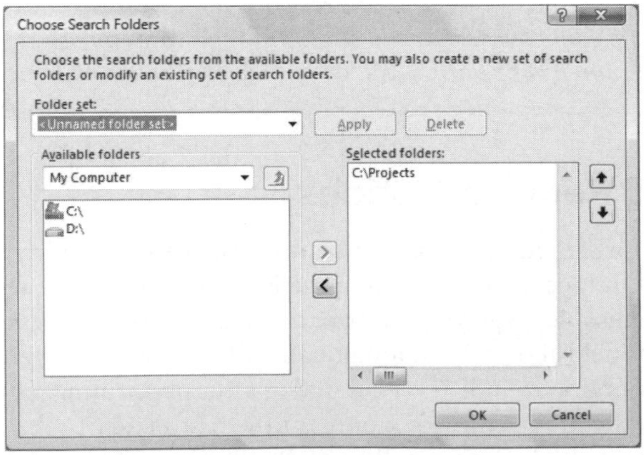

FIGURE 5-8

You can navigate through the entire filesystem, including networked drives, and add the folders you want to the search scope. This enables you to add disparate folder hierarchies to the one single search. Start by using the Available Folders list on the left to select the folder(s) that you would like to search. Add them to the Selected Folders list by clicking the right arrow. Within this list you can adjust the search order using the up and down arrows. Once you have added folders to the search, you can simply click OK to return a semicolon-delimited list of folders. If you want to save this set of folders for future use you can enter a name into the Folder Set drop-down and click Apply.

> *The process of saving search folders is less than intuitive, but if you think of the Apply button as more of a Save button then you can make sense of this dialog.*

Find Dialog Options

The options for the Find in Files dialog are similar to those for the Quick Find dialog. Because the search is being performed on files that are not necessarily open within the IDE or are even code files, the Search Up option is therefore not present. There is an additional filter that can be used to select only specific file types to search in.

The Look at these file types drop-down list contains several extension sets, each associated with a particular language, making it easy to search for code in Visual Basic, C#, J#, and other languages. You can type in your own extensions too, so if you're working in a non-Microsoft language, or just want to use the Find in Files feature for non-development purposes, you can still limit the search results to those that correspond to the file types you want.

In addition to the Find options are configuration settings for how the results will be displayed. For searching, you can choose one of two results windows, which enables you to perform a subsequent search without losing your initial action. The results can be quite lengthy if you show the full output of the search, but if you're interested only in finding out which files contain the information you're looking for, check the Display Filenames Only option and the results window will be populated with only one line per file.

Results Window

When you perform a Find in Files action, results are displayed in one of two Find Results windows. These appear as open tool windows docked to the bottom of the IDE workspace. For each line that contains the search criteria, the results window displays a full line of information, containing the filename and path, the line number that contained the match, and the actual line of text itself, so you can instantly see the context (see Figure 5-9).

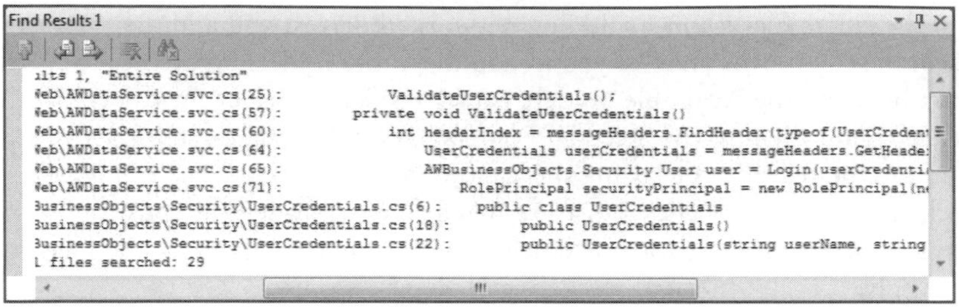
Find Results 1
ults 1, "Entire Solution"
Web\AWDataService.svc.cs(25): ValidateUserCredentials();
Web\AWDataService.svc.cs(57): private void ValidateUserCredentials()
Web\AWDataService.svc.cs(60): int headerIndex = messageHeaders.FindHeader(typeof(UserCreden
Web\AWDataService.svc.cs(64): UserCredentials userCredentials = messageHeaders.GetHeade
Web\AWDataService.svc.cs(65): AWBusinessObjects.Security.User user = Login(userCredenti
Web\AWDataService.svc.cs(71): RolePrincipal securityPrincipal = new RolePrincipal(n
BusinessObjects\Security\UserCredentials.cs(6): public class UserCredentials
BusinessObjects\Security\UserCredentials.cs(18): public UserCredentials()
BusinessObjects\Security\UserCredentials.cs(22): public UserCredentials(string userName, string
l files searched: 29

FIGURE 5-9

Along the edge of each results window is a small toolbar, as shown in Figure 5-10 (left), for navigation within the results themselves. These commands are also accessible through a context menu, as shown in Figure 5-10 (right).

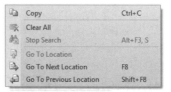

Copy Ctrl+C
Clear All
Stop Search Alt+F3, S
Go To Location
Go To Next Location F8
Go To Previous Location Shift+F8

FIGURE 5-10

Simply double-click a specific match to navigate to that line of code.

Replace in Files

Although it's useful to search a large number of files and find a number of matches to your search criteria, even better is the Replace in Files action. Accessed via the keyboard shortcut Ctrl+Shift+H or the drop-down arrow next to Quick Replace, Replace in Files performs in much the same way as Find in Files, with all the same options.

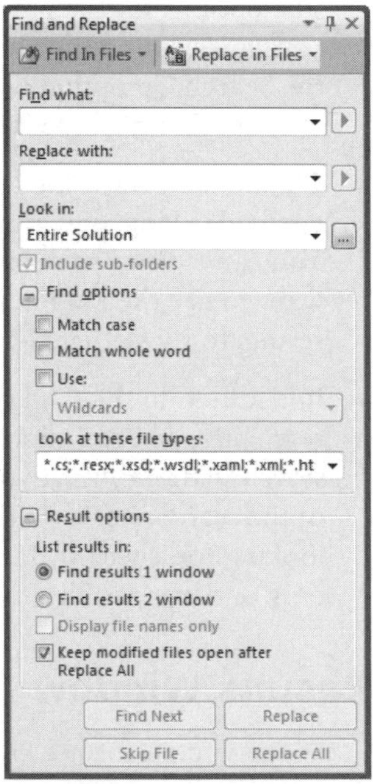
Find and Replace
Find In Files
Replace in Files
Find what:
Replace with:
Look in:
Entire Solution
Include sub-folders
Find options
Match case
Match whole word
Use:
Wildcards
Look at these file types:
.cs;.resx;*.xsd;*.wsdl;*.xaml;*.xml;*.ht
Result options
List results in:
Find results 1 window
Find results 2 window
Display file names only
Keep modified files open after Replace All
Find Next
Replace
Skip File
Replace All

FIGURE 5-11

The main difference is that you can enable an additional Results option when you're replacing files. When you're performing a mass replacement action like this, it can be handy to have a final confirmation before committing changes. To have this sanity check available to you, select the Keep Modified Files Open After Replace All checkbox (shown at the bottom of Figure 5-11).

Note that this feature works only when you're using Replace All; if you just click Replace, Visual Studio will open the file containing the next match and leave the file open in the IDE anyway.

Important: If you leave this option unchecked and perform a mass replacement on a large number of files, they will be changed permanently without your having any recourse to an undo action. Be very sure that you know what you're doing.

Whether or not you have this option checked, after performing a Replace All action, Visual Studio reports back to you how many changes were made. If you don't want to see this dialog box, you have an option to hide the dialog with future searches.

FIND SYMBOL

The Find Symbol search tool enables you to search for a class, method, property, or other types of symbols. Whereas the standard Quick Find function is essentially a plaintext search across your selected scope (current document, current project, and so on), Find Symbol is limited to searching only for symbols.

You can invoke the Find Symbol dialog by the keyboard shortcut Alt+F12 or the menu command Edit ⇨ Find and Replace ⇨ Find Symbol. Alternatively, you can switch the normal Find and Replace dialog over to Find Symbol by clicking the drop-down arrow next to Quick Find or Find in Files.

The Find Symbol dialog (see Figure 5-12) has slightly different options from the dialogs for the other Find actions. Rather than having its scope based on a current document or solution like Quick Find, or on the filesystem like Find in Files, Find Symbol can search through your whole solution, a full component list, or even the entire .NET Framework. In addition, you can include any references added to the solution as part of the scope. To create your own set of components in which to search, click the ellipsis next to the Look in field and browse through and select the .NET and COM components registered in the system, or browse to files or projects.

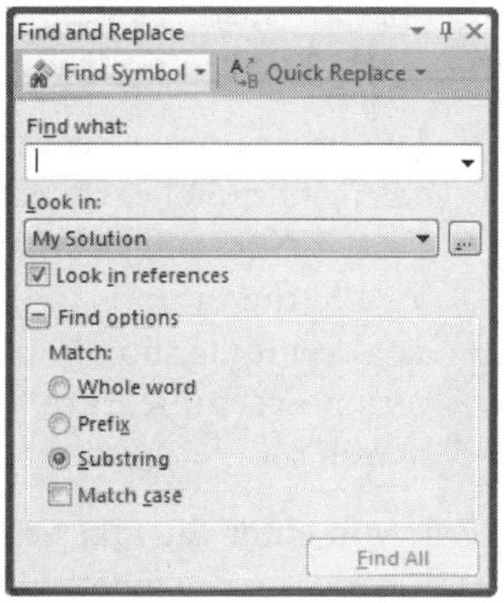

FIGURE 5-12

> The Find options are also simplified. You can search only for whole words, substrings (the default option), or prefixes.

After you click Find All, the search results are compiled and presented in a special tool window entitled Find Symbol Results. By default, this window shares space with the Find Results windows at the bottom of the IDE, and displays each result with any references to the particular object or component. This is extremely handy when you're trying to determine where and how a particular object is used or referenced from within your project.

> This search tool is best suited for when you need to search for all instances of a symbol and retrieve a list of all matches within the selected scope so you can easily navigate to a number of the results. By limiting the search scope to only symbols, you aren't searching extraneous text such as comments, code within methods, and so on. The search is also not limited to just your code but can also search the .NET Framework and referenced assemblies.

NAVIGATE TO

Navigate To is a powerful new search tool in Visual Studio 2010, providing an alternative to the standard find functions when searching for symbols. Like Find Symbol, you are limited to only searching for symbols; a number of differences between this and how Find Symbol operates can make this more useful.

As opposed to Find Symbol, Navigate To displays live results as you type the search text. The more of the search text you type, the more the results are narrowed down. Double-clicking one of the results closes the dialog and navigates to that result.

One of the most unique features of the Navigate To dialog, however, is in how it searches. Say you are looking for a class named ProductSummary. In this search tool, spaces are essentially AND operators, so typing *prod sum* as the search text (that is, searching for *prod* and *sum* in the same symbol name) returns the ProductSummary class as a result, as would typing in *sum prod*.

The other unique search capability that it has is its camel case searching. To find the ProductSummary class you can simply search for *PS* (the capitals in its name) to return it as a result (as shown in Figure 5-13) — a very powerful feature found only in this search tool.

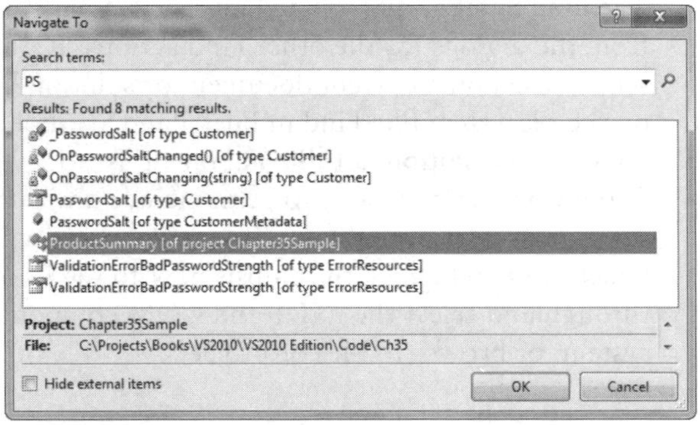

If you enter the text to search for in lowercase, the matching will be non-case-specific. However, if you enter an uppercase character as a part of the search text, the search will become case-specific.

FIGURE 5-13

The shortcut to open the Navigate To dialog is Ctrl+, (comma).

> *This search tool is best suited for when you need to search for and navigate to a single instance of a symbol, with the benefits of "live" results as you type and its partial/camel case search capabilities.*

INCREMENTAL SEARCH

If you're looking for something in the current code window and don't want to bring up a dialog, the Incremental Search function might be what you need. Invoked by either the Edit ⇨ Advanced ⇨ Incremental Search menu command or the keyboard shortcut Ctrl+I, Incremental Search locates the next match based on a plaintext search of what you type. To search up the document instead of down use Ctrl+Shift+I.

Immediately after invoking Incremental Search, simply begin typing the text you need to find. The mouse pointer will change to a set of binoculars and a down arrow. As you type each character, the editor will move to the next match for the text you entered. For example, typing *f* would find the first word containing an *f* — such as *offer*. Typing an *o* would then move the cursor to the first word containing *fo* — such as *form*; and so on.

If you enter the text to search for in lowercase, the matching will be non-case-specific. However, if you enter an uppercase character as a part of the search text, the search will become case-specific.

> *This search tool is really mostly for use in the same situations as you might use the Quick Find tool, but it searches only the current file and doesn't have the additional options that Quick Find does. It does keep the Quick Find dialog from getting in the way if you don't require these advanced search features. However, you are better off using the Quick Find dialog if you want to find a result, make a change, then find the next result, as when finding the next result you would have to start typing the incremental search text all over again.*

ACCESSING HELP

You are exposed to a wide range of technologies as a developer. Not only do they evolve at a rapid pace, but you are constantly being bombarded with additional new technologies which you must get up to speed on quickly. It's impossible to know everything about these technologies, and being a developer involves constantly learning. Often, knowing how to find information on using these technologies is as important a skill as being able to actually implement them. Luckily, there are a multitude of information sources on these technologies from which you can draw on. The inclusion of IntelliSense into IDEs over a decade ago was one of the most useful tools for helping developers write code, but it's rarely a substitute for a full blown help system that provides all the ins and outs of a technology. Visual Studio's help system provides this support for developers.

The easiest way to get help for Visual Studio 2010 is to use the same method you would use for almost every Windows application ever created — press the F1 key, the universal shortcut key for help. Visual Studio 2010 has a brand new help system which uses Microsoft Help 3. Rather than using a special "shell" to host the help and enable you to navigate around and search it, the help system now runs in a browser window. To support some of the more complex features of the help system such as the search functionality (when using the offline help), there is now a help listener application that runs in your system tray and serves these requests. You'll also note that the address in the browser's address bar points to a local web server on your machine. The online and offline help modes look and behave very similarly to one another, but this chapter specifically focuses on the offline help.

> *You may find that you receive a Service Unavailable message when using the help system. The likely cause of this error is that the help listener is no longer running in your system tray. Simply open the help system from within Visual Studio and the help listener will be automatically started again.*

The help system in Visual Studio is contextual. This means that if the cursor is currently positioned on or inside a class definition in a project and you press F1, the help window will open immediately with a mini-tutorial about what the class statement is and how to use it, as shown in Figure 5-14.

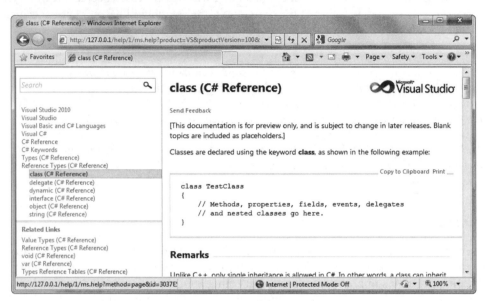

FIGURE 5-14

This is incredibly useful because more often than not if you simply press F1, the help system will navigate directly to the help topic that deals with the problem you're currently researching.

However, in some situations you will want to go directly to the table of contents within the help system. Visual Studio 2010 enables you to do this through the Visual Studio Documentation menu item in its main Help menu (see Figure 5-15).

In addition to the several help links you also have shortcuts to MSDN forums and for reporting a bug.

FIGURE 5-15

Navigating and Searching the Help System

Navigating through the help system should be very familiar, as it is essentially the same as navigating the Web. On the left-hand side of the browser window you will find links to pages in the same part of the help system as the page being currently viewed, and you will also find links that might be related to the current page.

In the top left of the browser window, you will find a search text box. Enter your search query here (in much the same way you would in a search engine like Google or Bing). This search is a full text search of the pages in the help system, and your query does not necessarily need to appear in the title of the pages. This will take you to the results, which are again provided in a manner similar to the results from a search engine. A one-line extract from the page of each result is displayed to help you determine if it is the article you are after, and you can click through to view the corresponding page.

Configuring the Help System

When you first start using the help system, it's a good idea to configure it to your needs. To do so, select the Help ➪ Manage Help Settings menu. This opens the Help Library Manager dialog, as shown in Figure 5-16.

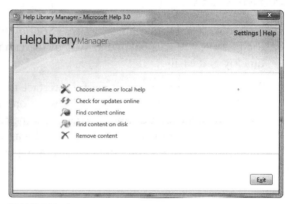

The first option, Choose online or local help, opens another screen in the dialog that enables you to select whether you will be using the online or offline help. If you select the online option, pressing F1 or opening the help from the Help menu will automatically navigate to the appropriate page in the documentation on MSDN online (for the current context in Visual Studio). Selecting the offline option

FIGURE 5-16

will navigate to the appropriate page in the documentation installed locally (assuming that the documentation has actually been installed on your machine).

The advantage of the online help over the offline help is that it will always be up to date and won't consume space on your hard drive (assuming you don't install the help content). The disadvantage is that you must always have an active Internet connection, and at times (depending on your bandwidth) it may be slower than the offline version to access. Essentially it is a trade-off, and you must choose the most appropriate option for your work environment.

The Check for updates online option will check if there are any updates to each of the product documentation sets that are currently installed. A screen will show the documentation sets that are installed and do a check for updates for each. When the checks are complete, it will show an estimated download size at the bottom of the dialog. Be aware that these documentation sets can be rather large, and only continue with the update if you have the bandwidth to download files of that size.

The Find content online option enables you to download and add additional product documentation sets to your offline library. The dialog will obtain a list of the available documentation sets and their size from the Internet. You can then click the Add hyperlink button next to each documentation set that your want to download. Again, be aware that these files can be rather large.

The Find content on disk option enables you to install documentation sets from local media, such as a CD/DVD, SD card, or hard drive. You will need to navigate to a manifest file (which has a .msha extension) that accompanies the documentation, and the Help Library Manager will take it from there and handle the installation of the related documentation.

The final option is Remove content, which enables you to remove product documentation sets from your local disk and free some disk space. The screen will show the documentation sets that are currently installed, and you can uninstall a documentation set by pressing the Remove hyperlink button next to its name.

SUMMARY

As you've seen in this chapter, Visual Studio 2010 comes with a number of search-and-replace tools, each best suited to a particular type of search task to enable you to navigate and modify your code quickly and easily.

The new help system is a powerful interface to the documentation that comes with Visual Studio 2010. The ability to switch easily between online and local documentation ensures that you can balance the speed of offline searches with the relevance of information found on the Web. And the abstract paragraphs that are shown in all search results, regardless of their locations, help reduce the number of times you might click a false positive.

PART II
Getting Started

▶ **CHAPTER 6:** Solutions, Projects, and Items

▶ **CHAPTER 7:** IntelliSense and Bookmarks

▶ **CHAPTER 8:** Code Snippets and Refactoring

▶ **CHAPTER 9:** Server Explorer

▶ **CHAPTER 10:** Modeling with the Class Designer

6

Solutions, Projects, and Items

➤ Creating and configuring solutions and projects

➤ Controlling how an application is compiled, debugged, and deployed

➤ Configuring the many project-related properties

➤ Including resources and settings with an application

➤ Enforcing good coding practices with the Code Analysis Tools

➤ Modifying the configuration, packaging, and deployment options for web applications

Other than the simplest applications, such as Hello World, most applications require more than one source file. This raises a number of issues, such as how the files will be named, where they will be located, and whether they can be reused. Within Visual Studio 2010, the concept of a *solution*, containing a series of *projects*, made up of a series of *items*, is used to enable developers to track, manage, and work with their source files. The IDE has a number of built-in features that aim to simplify this process, while still allowing developers to get the most out of their applications. This chapter examines the structure of solutions and projects, looking at available project types and how they can be configured.

SOLUTION STRUCTURE

Whenever you're working within Visual Studio, you will have a solution open. When you're editing an ad hoc file, this will be a temporary solution that you can elect to discard when you have completed your work. However, the solution enables you to manage the files that you're currently working with, so in most cases saving the solution means that you can return to what you were doing at a later date without having to locate and reopen the files on which you were working.

> *Solutions should be thought of as a container of related projects. The projects within a solution do not need to be of the same language or project type. For example, a single solution could contain an ASP.NET web application written in Visual Basic, an F# library, and a C# WPF application. The solution allows you to open all these projects together in the IDE and manage the build and deployment configuration for them as a whole.*

The most common way to structure applications written within Visual Studio is to have a single solution containing a number of projects. Each project can then be made up of a series of both code files and folders. The main window in which you work with solutions and projects is the Solution Explorer, shown in Figure 6-1.

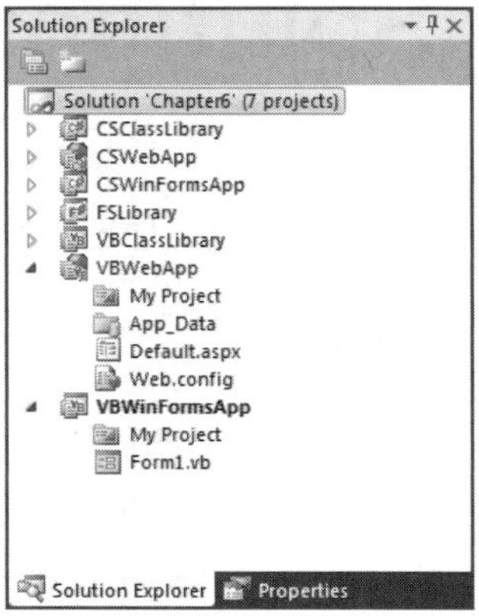

Within a project, folders are used to organize the source code and have no application meaning associated with them (with the exception of web applications, which can have specially named folders that have specific meaning in this context). Some developers use folder names that correspond to the namespace to which the classes belong. For example, if class `Person` is found within a folder called DataClasses in a project called FirstProject, the fully qualified name of the class could be `FirstProject.DataClasses.Person`.

FIGURE 6-1

Solution folders are a useful way to organize the projects in a large solution. Solution folders are visible only in the Solution Explorer — a physical folder is not created on the filesystem. Actions such as Build or Unload can be performed easily on all projects in a solution folder. Solution folders can also be collapsed or hidden so that you can work more easily in the Solution Explorer. Projects that are hidden are still built when you build the solution. Because solution folders do not map to a physical folder, they can be added, renamed, or deleted at any time without causing invalid file references or source control issues.

> *Miscellaneous Files is a special solution folder that can be used to keep track of other files that have been opened in Visual Studio but are not part of any projects in the solution. The Miscellaneous Files solution folder is not visible by default. You can find the settings to enable it under Tools ⇨ Options ⇨ Environment ⇨ Documents.*

There is a common misconception that projects necessarily correspond to .NET assemblies. Although this is generally true, it is possible for multiple projects to represent a single .NET assembly. However, this case is not supported by Visual Studio 2010, so this book assumes that a project will correspond to an assembly.

In Visual Studio 2010, although the format for the solution file has not changed, you cannot open a solution file that was created with Visual Studio 2010 with Visual Studio 2008. However, project files can be opened with both Visual Studio 2008 and Visual Studio 2010.

In addition to tracking which files are contained within an application, solution and project files can record other information, such as how a particular file should be compiled, project settings, resources, and much more. Visual Studio 2010 includes non-modal dialog for editing project properties, whereas solution properties still open in a separate window. As you might expect, the project properties are those properties pertaining only to the project in question, such as assembly information and references, whereas solution properties determine the overall build configurations for the application.

SOLUTION FILE FORMAT

Visual Studio 2010 actually creates two files for a solution, with extensions `.suo` and `.sln` (solution file). The first of these is a rather uninteresting binary file, and hence difficult to edit. It contains user-specific information — for example, which files were open when the solution was last closed and the location of breakpoints. This file is marked as hidden, so it won't appear in the solution folder using Windows Explorer unless you have enabled the option to show hidden files.

> *Occasionally the* `.suo` *file becomes corrupted and causes unexpected behavior when building and editing applications. If Visual Studio becomes unstable for a particular solution, you should exit and delete the* `.suo` *file. It will be re-created by Visual Studio the next time the solution is opened.*

The `.sln` solution file contains information about the solution, such as the list of projects, build configurations, and other settings that are not project-specific. Unlike many files used by Visual Studio 2010, the solution file is not an XML document. Instead it stores information in blocks, as shown in the following example solution file:

```
Microsoft Visual Studio Solution File, Format Version 11.00
# Visual Studio 10
Project("{F184B08F-C81C-45F6-A57F-5ABD9991F28F}") = "FirstProject",
    "FirstProject\FirstProject.vbproj", "{D4FAF2DD-A26C-444A-9FEE-2788B5F5FDD2}"
EndProject
Global
    GlobalSection(SolutionConfigurationPlatforms) = preSolution
        Debug|Any CPU = Debug|Any CPU
    EndGlobalSection
    GlobalSection(ProjectConfigurationPlatforms) = postSolution
        {D4FAF2DD-A26C-444A-9FEE-2788B5F5FDD2}.Debug|Any CPU.ActiveCfg = Debug|Any CPU
        {D4FAF2DD-A26C-444A-9FEE-2788B5F5FDD2}.Debug|Any CPU.Build.0 = Debug|Any CPU
    EndGlobalSection
    GlobalSection(SolutionProperties) = preSolution
        HideSolutionNode = FALSE
    EndGlobalSection
EndGlobal
```

In this example, the solution consists of a single project, FirstProject, and a `Global` section outlining settings that apply to the solution. For instance, the solution itself will be visible in the Solution Explorer because the `HideSolutionNode` setting is `FALSE`. If you were to change this value to `TRUE`, the solution name would not be displayed in Visual Studio.

> *As long as a solution consists of projects that do not target the .NET Framework version 4.0, you can open the solution with Visual Studio 2008 by performing a quick edit to the* `.sln` *file. Simply replace the first two lines of the file with the following, and the solution will open with no errors:*
>
> ```
> Microsoft Visual Studio Solution File, Format Version 10.00
> # Visual Studio 2008
> ```

SOLUTION PROPERTIES

You can reach the solution Properties dialog by right-clicking the Solution node in the Solution Explorer and selecting Properties. This dialog contains two nodes to partition Common and Configuration properties, as shown in Figure 6-2.

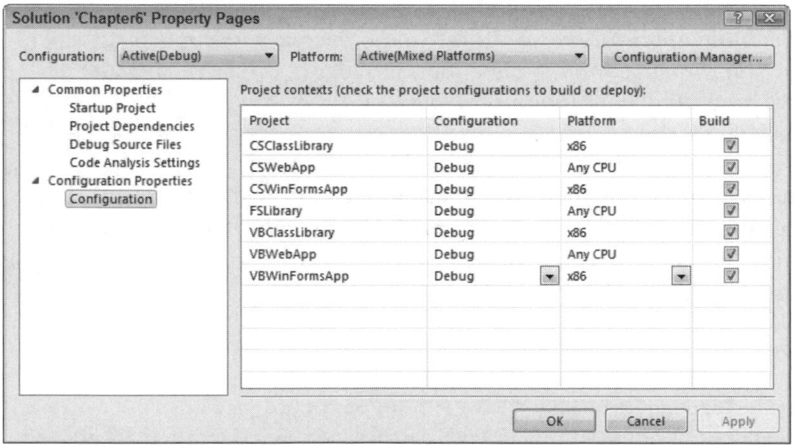

FIGURE 6-2

The following sections describe the Common and Configuration properties nodes in more detail.

Common Properties

You have three options when defining the Startup Project for an application, and they're somewhat self-explanatory. Selecting Current Selection starts the project that has current focus in the Solution Explorer. Single Startup ensures that the same project starts up each time. This is the default selection, because most applications have only a single startup project. The last option, Multiple

Startup Projects, allows for multiple projects to be started in a particular order. This can be useful if you have a client/server application specified in a single solution and you want them both to be running. When running multiple projects, it is also relevant to control the order in which they start up. Use the up and down arrows next to the project list to control the order in which projects are started.

The Project Dependencies section is used to indicate other projects on which a specific project is dependent. For the most part, Visual Studio will manage this for you as you add and remove project references for a given project. However, sometimes you may want to create dependencies between projects to ensure that they are built in the correct order. Visual Studio uses its list of dependencies to determine the order in which projects should be built. This window prevents you from inadvertently adding circular references and from removing necessary project dependencies.

In the Debug Source Files section, you can provide a list of directories through which Visual Studio can search for source files when debugging. This is the default list that is searched before the Find Source dialog is displayed. You can also list source files that Visual Studio should not try to locate. If you click Cancel when prompted to locate a source file, the file will be added to this list.

The Code Analysis Settings section is available only in the Visual Studio Team Suite editions. This allows you to select the static code analysis rule set that will be run for each project. Code Analysis is discussed in more detail later in the chapter.

Configuration Properties

Both projects and solutions have build configurations associated with them that determine which items are built and how. It can be somewhat confusing because there is actually no correlation between a project configuration, which determines how things are built, and a solution configuration, which determines which projects are built, other than they might have the same name. A new solution will define both Debug and Release (solution) configurations, which correspond to building all projects within the solution in Debug or Release (project) configurations.

For example, a new solution configuration called Test can be created, which consists of two projects: MyClassLibrary and MyClassLibraryTest. When you build your application in Test configuration, you want MyClassLibrary to be built in Release mode so you're testing as close to what you would release as possible. However, to be able to step through your test code, you want to build the test project in Debug mode.

When you build in Release mode, you don't want the Test solution to be built or deployed with your application. In this case, you can specify in the Test solution configuration that you want the MyClassLibrary project to be built in Release mode, and that the MyClassLibraryTest project should not be built.

> *You can switch between configurations easily via the Configuration drop-down on the standard toolbar. However, it is not as easy to switch between platforms, because the Platform drop-down is not on any of the toolbars. To make this available, select View ⇨ Toolbars ⇨ Customize. From the Build category on the Commands, the Solution Platforms item can be dragged onto a toolbar.*

You will notice that when the Configuration Properties node is selected from the Solution Properties dialog as shown in Figure 6-2, the Configuration and Platform drop-down boxes are enabled. The Configuration drop-down contains each of the available solution configurations (Debug and Release by default), Active, and All. Similarly, the Platform drop-down contains each of the available platforms. Whenever these drop-downs appear and are enabled, you can specify the settings on that page on a per-configuration and/or per-platform basis. You can also use the Configuration Manager button to add additional solution configurations and/or platforms.

When adding additional solution configurations, there is an option (checked by default) to create corresponding project configurations for existing projects (projects will be set to build with this configuration by default for this new solution configuration), and an option to base the new configuration on an existing configuration. If the Create Project Configurations option is checked and the new configuration is based on an existing configuration, the new project configurations will copy the project configurations specified for the existing configuration.

The options available for creating new platform configurations are limited by the types of CPU available: Itanium, x86, and x64. Again, the new platform configuration can be based on existing configurations, and the option to create project platform configurations is also available.

The other thing you can specify in the solution configuration file is the type of CPU for which you are building. This is particularly relevant if you want to deploy to 64-bit architecture machines.

You can reach all these solution settings directly from the right-click context menu from the Solution node in the Solution Explorer window. Whereas the Set Startup Projects menu item opens the solution configuration window, the Configuration Manager, Project Dependencies, and Project Build Order items open the Configuration Manager and Project Dependencies window. The Project Dependencies and Project Build Order menu items will be visible only if you have more than one project in your solution.

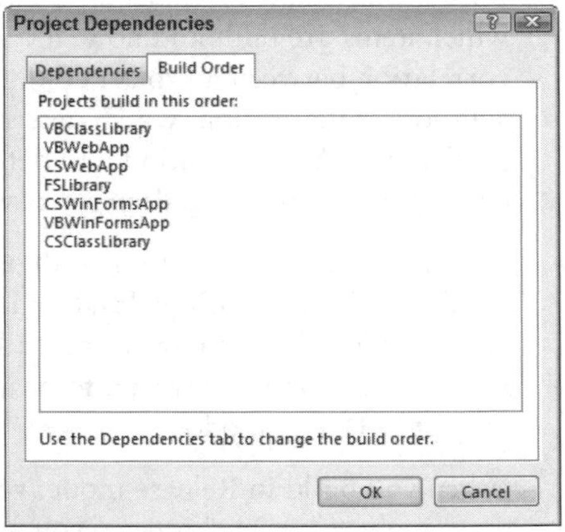

When the Project Build Order item is selected, this opens the Project Dependencies window and lists the build order, as shown in Figure 6-3. This tab reveals the order in which projects will be built, according to the dependencies. This can be useful if you are maintaining references to project binary assemblies rather than project references, and it can be used to double-check that projects are being built in the correct order.

FIGURE 6-3

PROJECT TYPES

Within Visual Studio, the projects for Visual Basic and C# are broadly classified into different categories. With the exception of Web Site projects, which are discussed separately later in this chapter, each project contains a project file (.vbproj or .csproj) that conforms to the MSBuild schema. Selecting a project template creates a new project, of a specific project type, and populates it with initial classes and settings. Following are some of the more common categories of projects as they are grouped under Visual Studio:

➤ **Windows:** The Windows project category is the broadest category and includes most of the common project types that run on end-user operating systems. This includes the Windows Forms executable projects, Console application projects, and Windows Presentation Foundation (WPF) applications. These project types create an executable (.exe) assembly that is executed directly by an end user. The Windows category also includes several types of library assemblies that can easily be referenced by other projects. These include both class libraries and control libraries for Windows Forms and WPF applications. A class library reuses the familiar DLL extension. The Windows Service project type can also be found in this category.

➤ **Web:** The Web category includes the project types that run under ASP.NET. This includes ASP.NET web applications, XML web services, and control libraries for use in web applications and rich AJAX-enabled web applications.

➤ **Office:** As its name suggests, the Office category creates managed code add-ins for Microsoft Office products, such as Outlook, Word, or Excel. These project types use Visual Studio Tools for Office (VSTO), and are capable of creating add-ins for most products in both the Office 2003 and Office 2007 product suite.

➤ **SharePoint:** Another self-describing category, this contains projects that target Windows SharePoint Services, such as SharePoint Workflows or Team Sites.

➤ **Database:** The Database category contains a project type for creating code that can be used with SQL Server. This includes stored procedures, user-defined types and functions, triggers, and custom aggregate functions.

➤ **Reporting:** This category includes a project type that is ideal for quickly generating complex reports against a data source.

➤ **Silverlight:** This contains project types for creating Silverlight Applications or Class Library projects.

➤ **Test:** The Test category includes a project type for projects that contain tests using the MSTest unit testing framework.

➤ **WCF:** This contains a number of project types for creating applications that provide Windows Communication Foundation (WCF) services.

➤ **Workflow:** This contains a number of project types for sequential and state machine workflow libraries and applications.

The New Project dialog box in Visual Studio 2010, shown in Figure 6-4, allows you to browse and create any of these project types. The target .NET Framework version is listed in a drop-down selector in the top right-hand corner of this dialog box. If a project type is not supported by the selected .NET Framework version, such as a WPF application under .NET Framework 2.0, that project type will not be displayed.

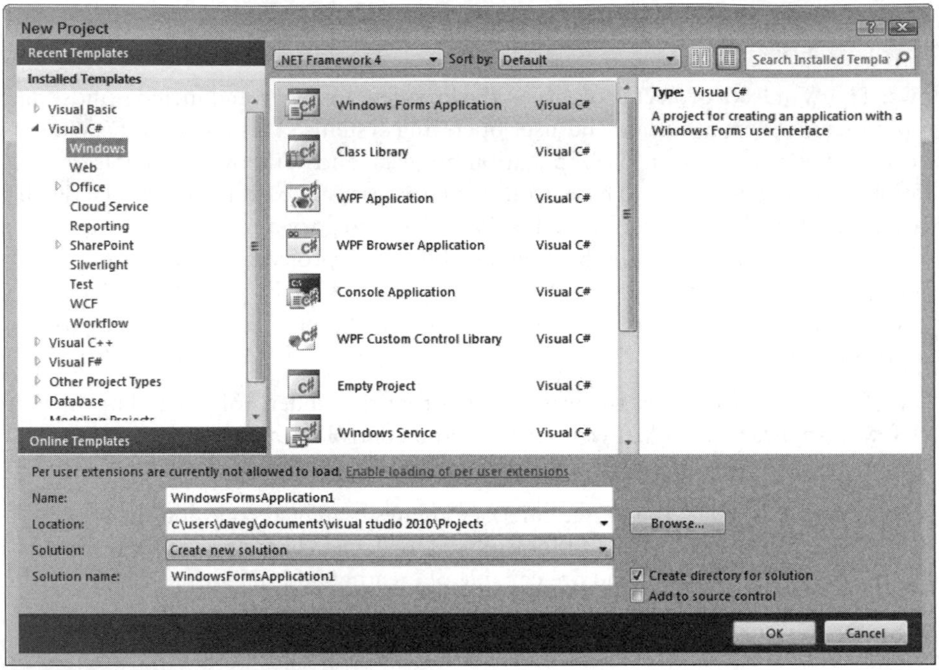

FIGURE 6-4

PROJECT FILES FORMAT

The project files (`.csproj`, `.vbproj`, or `.fsproj`) are text files in an XML document format that conforms to the MSBuild schema. The XML schema files for the latest version of MSBuild are installed with the .NET Framework, by default in `C:\WINDOWS\Microsoft.NET\Framework\ v4.0.20506\MSBuild\Microsoft.Build.Core.xsd`.

> *To view the project file in XML format, right-click the project and select Unload. Then right-click the project again and select Edit <project name>. This will display the project file in the XML editor, complete with IntelliSense.*

The project file stores the build and configuration settings that have been specified for the project and details about all the files that are included in the project. In some cases, a user-specific project file is also created (`.csproj.user or .vbproj.user`), which stores user preferences such as startup and debugging options. The `.user` file is also an XML file that conforms to the MSBuild schema.

PROJECT PROPERTIES

You can reach the project properties by either right-clicking the Project node in Solution Explorer and then selecting Properties, or by double-clicking My Project (Properties in C#) just under the Project node. In contrast to solution properties, the project properties do not display in a modal dialog. Instead they appear as an additional tab alongside your code files. This was done in part to make it easier to navigate between code files and project properties, but it also makes it possible to open project properties of multiple projects at the same time. Figure 6-5 illustrates the project settings for a Visual Basic Windows Forms project. This section walks you through the vertical tabs on the project editor for both Visual Basic and C# projects.

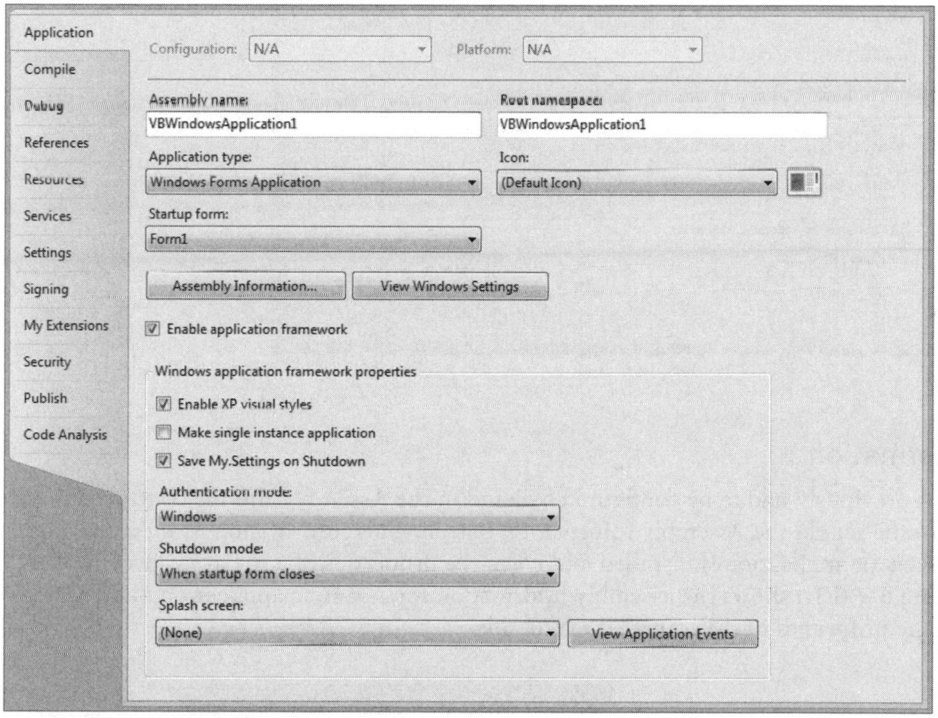

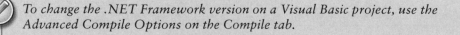

FIGURE 6-5

The project properties editor contains a series of vertical tabs that group the properties. As changes are made to properties in the tabs, a star is added to the corresponding vertical tab. This functionality is limited, however, because it does not indicate which fields within the tab have been modified.

Application

The Application tab, visible in Figure 6-5 for a Visual Basic Windows Forms project, enables the developer to set the information about the assembly that will be created when the project is compiled. These include attributes such as the output type (that is, Windows or Console Application, Class Library, Windows Service, or a Web Control Library), application icon, and startup object. The Application tab for C# applications, shown in Figure 6-6, has a different format, and provides options such as the ability to select the target .NET Framework version.

> *To change the .NET Framework version on a Visual Basic project, use the Advanced Compile Options on the Compile tab.*

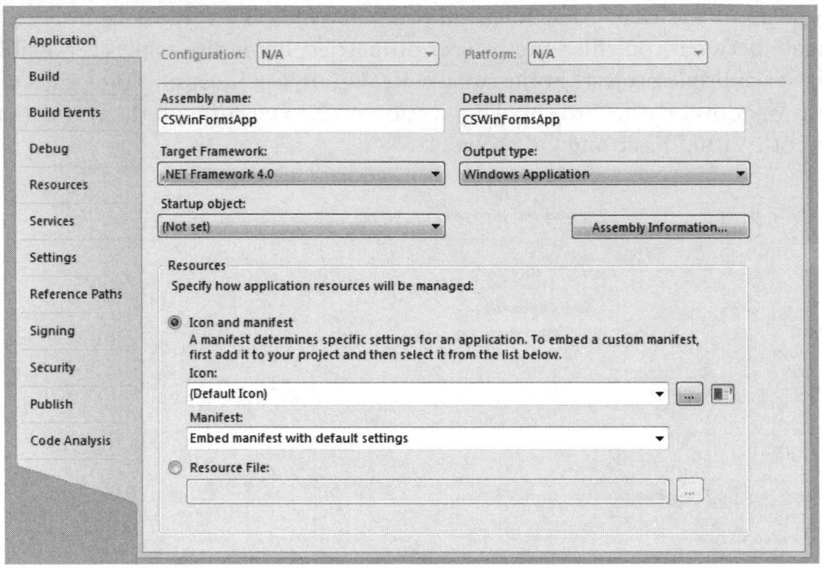

FIGURE 6-6

Assembly Information

Attributes that previously had to be configured by hand in the AssemblyInfo file contained in the project can also be set via the Assembly Information button. This information is important, because it shows up when an application is installed and when the properties of a file are viewed in Windows Explorer. Figure 6-7 (left) shows the assembly information for a sample application and Figure 6-7 (right) shows the properties of the compiled executable.

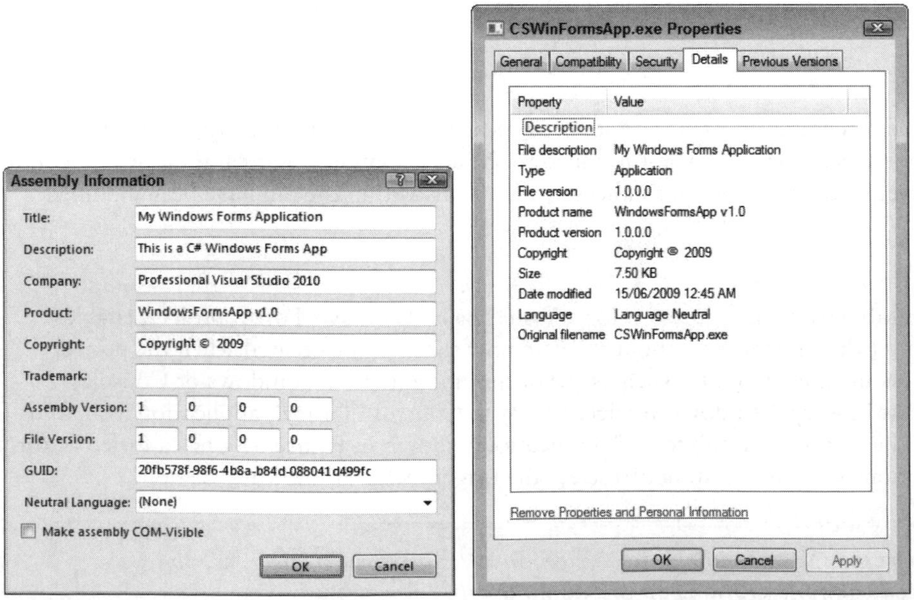

FIGURE 6-7

Each of the properties set in the Assembly Information dialog is represented by an attribute that is applied to the assembly. This means that the assembly can be queried in code to retrieve this information. In Visual Basic, the `My.Application.Info` namespace provides an easy way to retrieve this information.

User Account Control Settings

Visual Studio 2010 provides support for developing applications that work with User Account Control (UAC) under Windows Vista and Windows 7. This involves generating an assembly manifest file, which is an XML file that notifies the operating system if an application requires administrative privileges on startup. In Visual Basic applications, the View Windows Settings button on the Application tab can be used to generate and add an assembly manifest file for UAC to your application. The following code shows the default manifest file that is generated by Visual Studio.

```xml
<?xml version="1.0" encoding="utf-8"?>
<asmv1:assembly manifestVersion="1.0" xmlns="urn:schemas-microsoft-com:asm.v1"
        xmlns:asmv1="urn:schemas-microsoft-com:asm.v1"
        xmlns:asmv2="urn:schemas-microsoft-com:asm.v2"
        xmlns:xsi="http://www.w3.org/2001/XMLSchema-instance">
  <assemblyIdentity version="1.0.0.0" name="MyApplication.app"/>
  <trustInfo xmlns="urn:schemas-microsoft-com:asm.v2">
    <security>
      <requestedPrivileges xmlns="urn:schemas-microsoft-com:asm.v3">
        <!-- UAC Manifest Options
            If you want to change the Windows User Account Control level replace the
            requestedExecutionLevel node with one of the following.

        <requestedExecutionLevel  level="asInvoker" />
        <requestedExecutionLevel  level="requireAdministrator" />
        <requestedExecutionLevel  level="highestAvailable" />

            If you want to utilize File and Registry Virtualization for backward
            compatibility then delete the requestedExecutionLevel node.
        -->
        <requestedExecutionLevel level="asInvoker" />
      </requestedPrivileges>
      <applicationRequestMinimum>
        <defaultAssemblyRequest permissionSetReference="Custom" />
        <PermissionSet ID="Custom" SameSite="site" />
      </applicationRequestMinimum>
    </security>
  </trustInfo>
</asmv1:assembly>
```

If the UAC-requested execution level is changed from the default `asInvoker` to `require Administrator`, Windows will present a UAC prompt when the application is launched. If you have UAC enabled, Visual Studio 2010 will also prompt to restart in administrator mode if an application requiring admin rights is started in Debug mode. Figure 6-8 shows the prompt that is shown on Windows allowing you to restart Visual Studio in administrator mode.

If you agree to the restart, Visual Studio will not only restart with administrative privileges, it will also reopen your solution including all files you had opened. It will even remember the last cursor position.

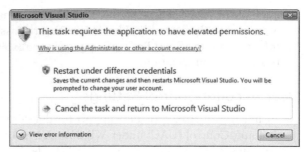

FIGURE 6-8

Application Framework (Visual Basic Only)

Additional application settings are available for Visual Basic Windows Forms projects because they can use the Application Framework that is exclusive to Visual Basic. This extends the standard event model to provide a series of application events and settings that control the behavior of the application. You can enable the Application Framework by checking the Enable Application Framework checkbox. The following three checkboxes control the behavior of the Application Framework:

➤ **Enable XP Visual Styles:** XP visual styles are a feature that significantly improves the look and feel of applications running on Windows XP or later, because it provides a much smoother interface through the use of rounded buttons and controls that dynamically change color as the mouse passes over them. Visual Basic applications enable XP styles by default and can be disabled from the Project Settings dialog, or controlled from within code through the EnableVisualStyles method on the Application class.

➤ **Make Single Instance Application:** Most applications support multiple instances running concurrently. However, an application opened more than two or three times may be run only once, with successive executions simply invoking the original application. Such an application could be a document editor, whereby successive executions simply open a different document. This functionality can be easily added by marking the application as a single instance.

➤ **Save My.Settings on Shutdown:** Selecting the Save My.Settings on Shutdown option ensures that any changes made to user-scoped settings will be preserved, saving the settings provided prior to the application shutting down.

This section also allows you to select an authentication mode for the application. By default this is set to Windows, which uses the currently logged-on user. Selecting Application-defined allows you to use a custom authentication module.

You can also identify a form to be used as a splash screen when the application is first launched, and specify the shutdown behavior of the application.

Compile (Visual Basic Only)

The Compile section of the project settings, as shown in Figure 6-9, enables the developer to control how and where the project is built. For example, the output path can be modified so that it points to an alternative location. This might be important if the output is to be used elsewhere in the build process.

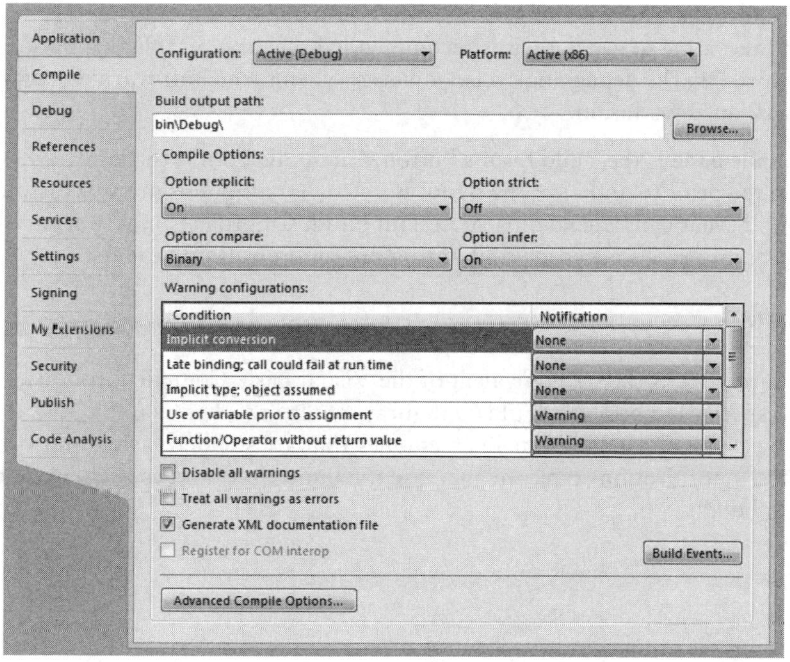

FIGURE 6-9

The Configuration drop-down selector at the top of the tab page allows different build settings for the Debug and Release build configuration.

If your dialog is missing the Configuration drop-down selector, you need to check the Show Advanced Build Configurations property in the Projects and Solutions node of the Options window, accessible from the Tools menu. Unfortunately, this property is not checked for some of the setting profiles — for example, the Visual Basic Developer profile.

Some Visual Basic–specific properties can be configured in the Compile pane. Option Explicit determines whether variables that are used in code have to be explicitly defined. Option Strict forces the type of variables to be defined, rather than it being late-bound. Option Compare determines whether strings are compared using binary or text comparison operators. Option Infer specifies whether to allow local type inference in variable declarations or whether the type must be explicitly stated.

> *All four of these compile options can be controlled at either the Project or File-level. File-level compiler options will override the Project-level options.*

The Compile pane also defines a number of different compiler options that can be adjusted to improve the reliability of your code. For example, unused variables may only warrant a warning, whereas a path that doesn't return a value is more serious and should generate a build error. It is possible either to disable all these warnings or treat all of them as errors.

Visual Basic developers also have the capability to generate XML documentation. Of course, because the documentation takes time to generate, it is recommended that you disable this option for debug builds. This will speed up the debugging cycle; however, when turned off warnings will not be given for missing XML documentation.

The last element of the Compile pane is the Build Events button. Click this button to view commands that can be executed prior to and after the build. Because not all builds are successful, the execution of the post-build event can depend on a successful build. C# projects have a separate Build Events tab in the project properties pages for configuring pre- and post-build events.

Build (C# and F# Only)

The Build tab, shown in Figure 6-10, is the C# equivalent of the Visual Basic Compile tab. This tab enables the developer to specify the project's build configuration settings. For example, the Optimize code setting can be enabled, which results in assemblies that are smaller, faster, and more efficient. However, these optimizations typically increase the build time, and as such are not recommended for the Debug build.

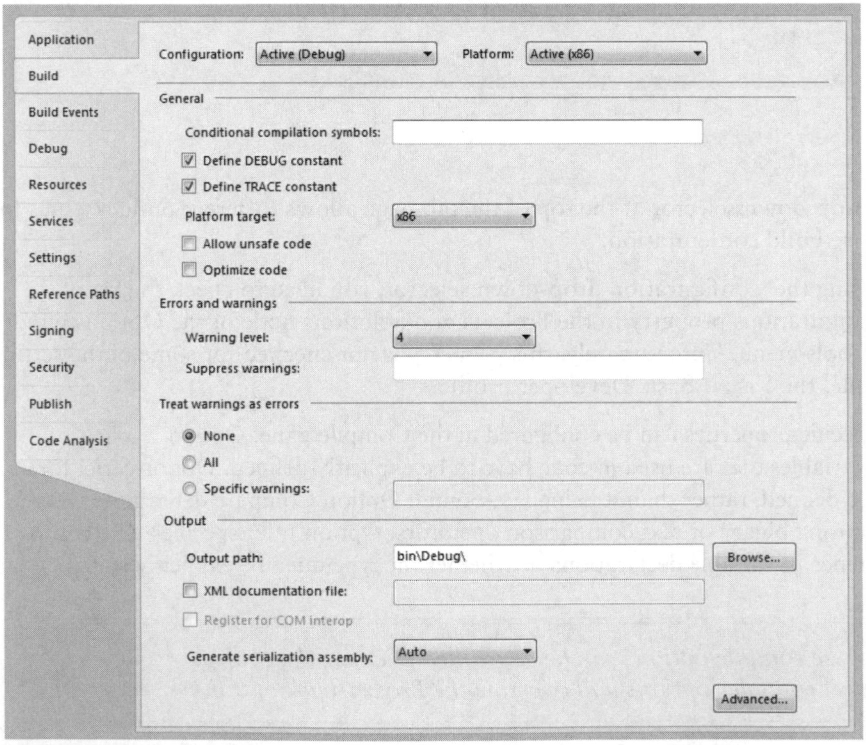

FIGURE 6-10

On the Build tab, the DEBUG and TRACE compilation constants can be enabled. Alternatively, you can easily define your own constants by specifying them in the Conditional compilation symbols textbox. The value of these constants can be queried from code at compile-time. For example, the DEBUG constant can be queried as follows:

C#

```
#if(DEBUG)
    MessageBox.Show("The debug constant is defined");
#endif
```

VB

```
#If DEBUG Then
    MessageBox.Show("The debug constant is defined")
#End If
```

The compilation constants are defined on the Advanced Compiler Settings dialog, which can be displayed by clicking the Advanced Compile Options... button on the Compile tab.

The Configuration drop-down selector at the top of the tab page allows different build settings for the Debug and Release build configuration. You can find more information on the Build options in Chapter 45.

Build Events (C# and F# Only)

The Build Events tab allows you to perform additional actions before or after the build process. In Figure 6-11, you can see a post-build event that executes the FXCop Static Code Analysis tool after every successful build.

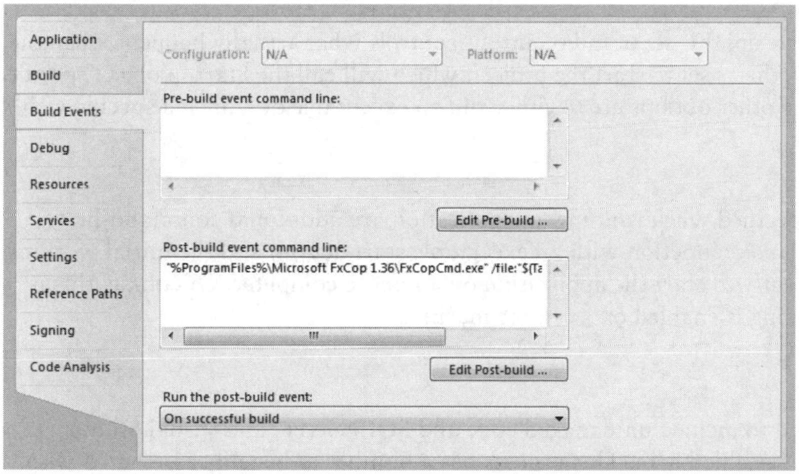

FIGURE 6-11

You can use environment variables such as *ProgramFiles* in your command lines by enclosing them with the percent character. A number of macros are also available, such as *ProjectPath*. These macros are listed on the Edit Pre-build and Edit Post-build dialog box.

Debug

The Debug tab, shown in Figure 6-12, determines how the application will be executed when run from within Visual Studio 2010. This tab is not visible for web applications — instead the Web tab is used to configure similar options.

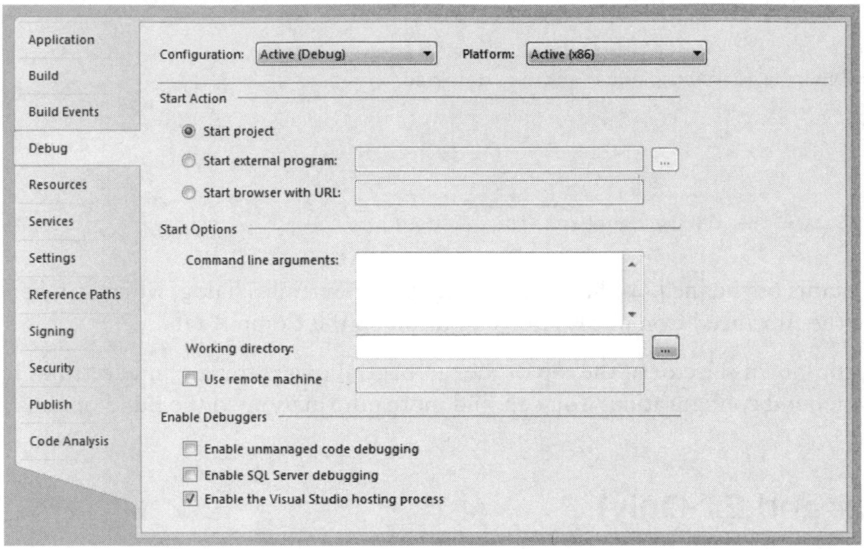

FIGURE 6-12

Start Action

When a project is set to start up, this set of radio buttons controls what actually happens when the application is run. Initially, this is set to start the project, which will call the Startup object specified on the Application tab. The other options are to either run an executable or launch a specific web site.

Start Options

The options that can be specified when running an application are additional command-line arguments (generally used in conjunction with an executable start action) and the initial working directory. You can also specify to start the application on a remote computer. Of course, this is possible only when debugging is enabled on a remote machine.

Enable Debuggers

Debugging can be extended to include unmanaged code and SQL Server. The Visual Studio hosting process can also be enabled here. This process has a number of benefits associated with the performance and functionality of the debugger. The benefits fall into three categories. First, the hosting process acts as a background host for the application you are debugging. In order to debug a managed application, various administrative tasks must be performed, such as creating an AppDomain and associating the debugger, which take time. With the hosting process enabled, these tasks are handled in the background, resulting in a much quicker load time during debugging.

Second, in Visual Studio 2010, it is quite easy to create, debug, and deploy applications that run under partial trust. The hosting process is an important tool in this process because it gives you the ability to run and debug an application in partial trust. Without this process, the application would run in full trust mode, preventing you from debugging the application in partial trust mode.

The last benefit that the hosting process provides is design-time evaluation of expressions. This is in effect an optical illusion, because the hosting process is actually running in the background. However, using the Immediate window as you're writing your code means that you can easily evaluate expressions, call methods, and even hit breakpoints without running up the entire application.

References (Visual Basic Only)

The References tab enables the developer to reference classes in other .NET assemblies, projects, and native DLLs. Once the project or DLL has been added to the references list, a class can be accessed either by its full name, including namespace, or the namespace can be imported into a code file so the class can be referenced by just the class name. Figure 6-13 shows the References tab for a project that has a reference to a number of framework assemblies.

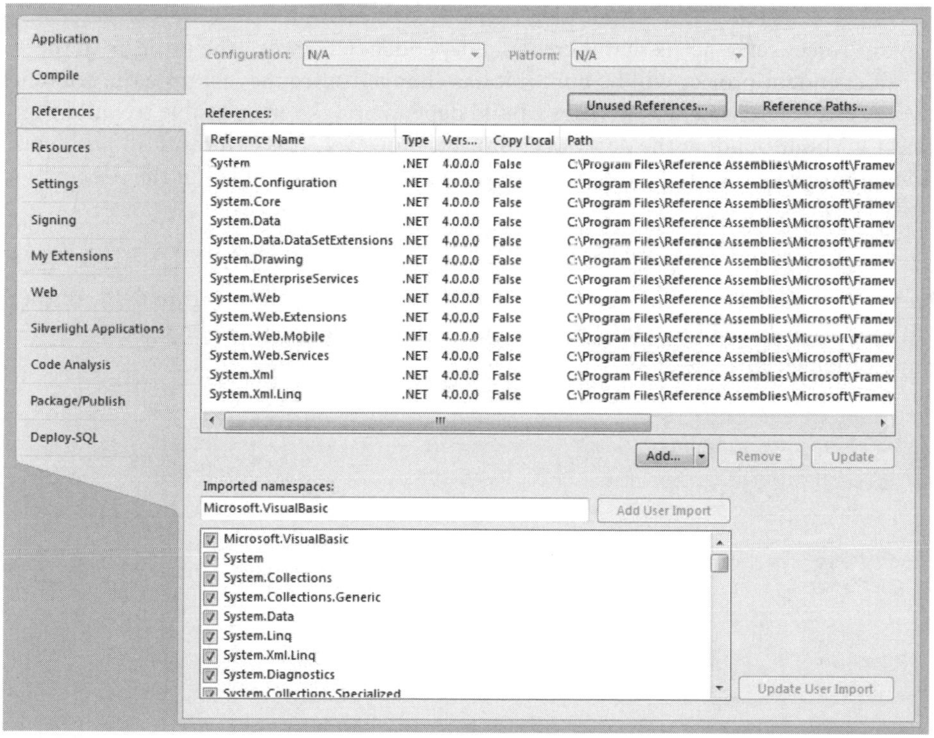

FIGURE 6-13

One of the features of this tab for Visual Basic developers is the Unused References button, which performs a search to determine which references can be removed. It is also possible to add a reference path, which will include all assemblies in that location.

Once an assembly has been added to the reference list, any public class contained within that assembly can be referenced within the project. Where a class is embedded in a namespace (which might be a nested hierarchy), referencing a class requires the full class name. Both Visual Basic and

C# provide a mechanism for importing namespaces so that classes can be referenced directly. The References section allows namespaces to be globally imported for all classes in the project, without them being explicitly imported within the class file.

References to external assemblies can either be File references or Project references. File references are direct references to an individual assembly. File references are created by using the Browse tab of the Add Reference dialog box. Project references are references to a project within the solution. All assemblies that are outputted by that project are dynamically added as references. Project references are created by using the Project tab of the Add Reference dialog box.

> *You should generally not add a File reference to a project that exists in the same solution. If a project requires a reference to another project in that solution, a Project reference should be used.*

The advantage of a Project reference is that it creates a dependency between the projects in the build system. The dependent project will be built if it has changed since the last time the referencing project was built. A File reference doesn't create a build dependency, so it's possible to build the referencing project without building the dependent project. However, this can result in problems with the referencing project expecting a different version from what is included in the output.

Resources

Project resources can be added and removed via the Resources tab, shown in Figure 6-14. In the example shown, four icons have been added to this application. Resources can be images, text, icons, files, or any other serializable class.

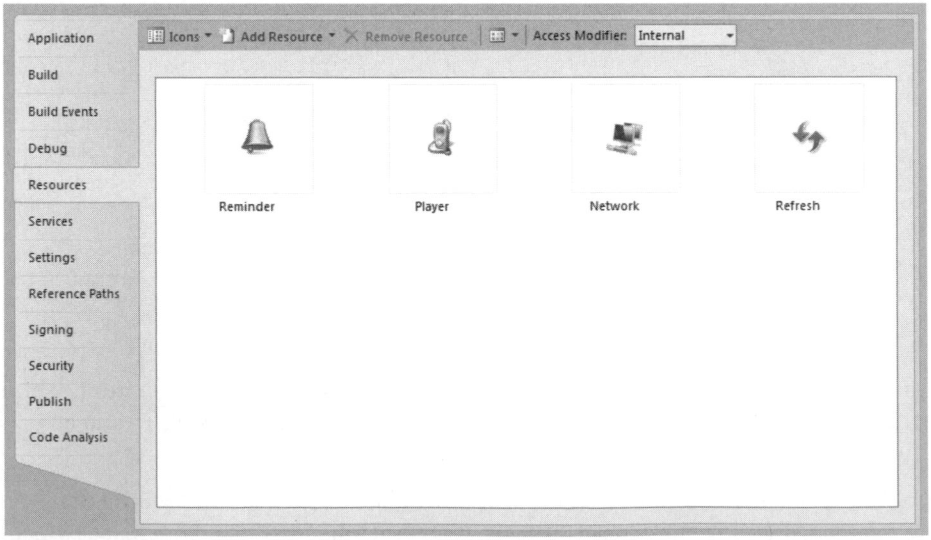

FIGURE 6-14

This interface makes working with resource files at design time very easy. Chapter 38 examines in more detail how resource files can be used to store application constants and internationalize your application.

Services

Client application services allow Windows-based applications to use the authentication, roles, and profile services that were introduced with Microsoft ASP.NET 2.0. The client services enable multiple web- and Windows-based applications to centralize user profiles and user-administration functionality.

Figure 6-15 shows the Services tab, which is used to configure client application services for Windows applications. When enabling the services, the URL of the ASP.NET service host must be specified for each service. This will be stored in the `app.config` file. The following client services are supported:

➤ **Authentication:** This enables the user's identity to be verified using either the native Windows authentication, or a custom forms-based authentication that is provided by the application.

➤ **Roles:** This obtains the roles an authenticated user has been assigned. This enables you to allow certain users access to different parts of the application. For example, additional administrative functions may be made available to admin users.

➤ **Web Settings:** This stores per-user application settings on the server, which allows them to be shared across multiple computers and applications.

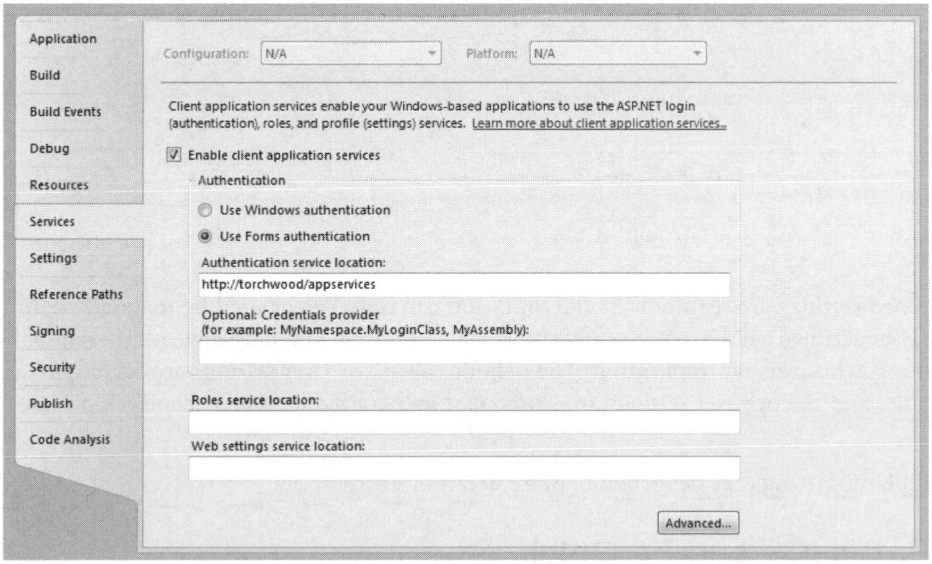

FIGURE 6-15

Client application services utilize a provider model for web services extensibility. The service providers include offline support that uses a local cache to ensure that it can still operate even when a network connection is not available.

Client application services are discussed further in Chapter 33.

Settings

Project settings can be of any type and simply reflect a name/value pair whose value can be retrieved at run time. Settings can be scoped to either the Application or the User, as shown in Figure 6-16. Settings are stored internally in the Settings.settings file and the app.config file. When the application is compiled this file is renamed according to the executable being generated — for example, *SampleApplication.exe.config*.

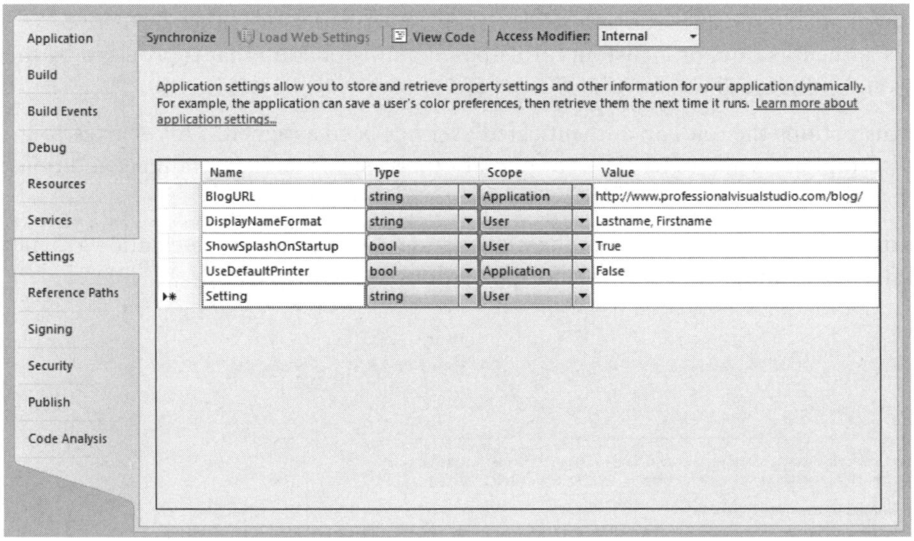

FIGURE 6-16

Application-scoped settings are read-only at run time, and can only be changed by manually editing the config file. User settings can be dynamically changed at run time, and may have a different value saved for each user who runs the application. The default values for User settings are stored in the app.config file, and the per-user settings are stored in a user.config file under the user's private data path.

Application and User settings are described in more detail in Chapter 36.

Reference Paths (C# and F# Only)

The Reference Paths tab, shown in Figure 6-17, is used to specify additional directories that are searched for referenced assemblies.

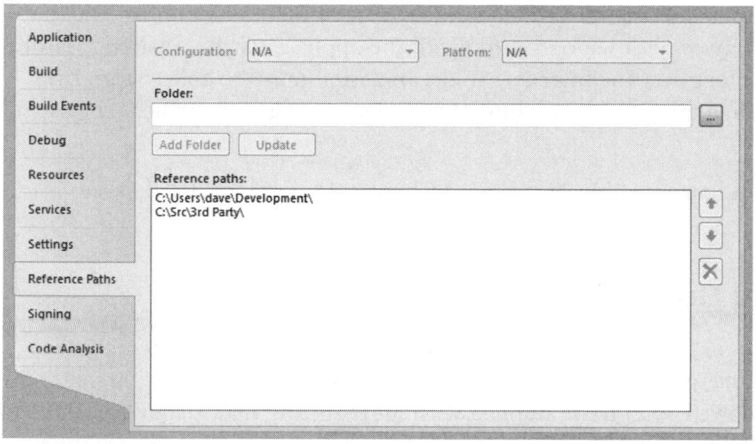

FIGURE 6-17

When an assembly reference has been added, Visual Studio resolves the reference by looking in the following directories in order:

1. The project directory.

2. Directories specified in this Reference Paths list.

3. Directories displaying files in the Add Reference dialog box.

4. The obj directory for the project. This is generally only relevant to COM interop assemblies.

Signing

Figure 6-18 shows the Signing tab, which provides developers with the capability to determine how assemblies are signed in preparation for deployment. An assembly can be signed by selecting a key file. A new key file can be created by selecting <New...> from the file selector drop-down.

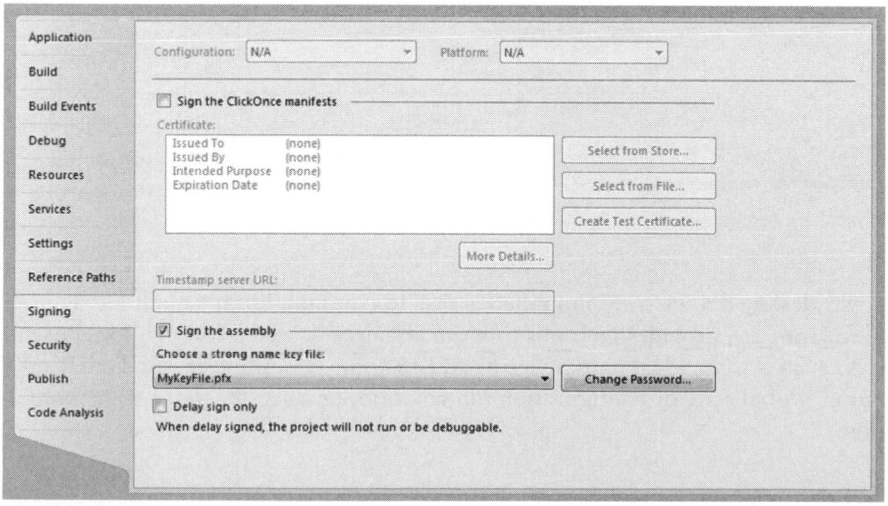

FIGURE 6-18

The ClickOnce deployment model for applications enables an application to be published to a web site where a user can click once to download and install the application. Because this model is supposed to support deployment over the Internet, an organization must be able to sign the deployment package. The Signing tab provides an interface for specifying the certificate to use to sign the ClickOnce manifests.

Chapter 46 provides more detail on assembly signing and Chapter 48 discusses ClickOnce deployments.

My Extensions (Visual Basic Only)

The My Extensions tab, shown in Figure 6-19, allows you to add reference to an assembly that extends the Visual Basic My namespace, using the extension methods feature. Extension methods were initially introduced to enable LINQ to be shipped without requiring major changes to the base class library. They allow developers to add new methods to an existing class, without having to use inheritance to create a subclass or recompile the original type.

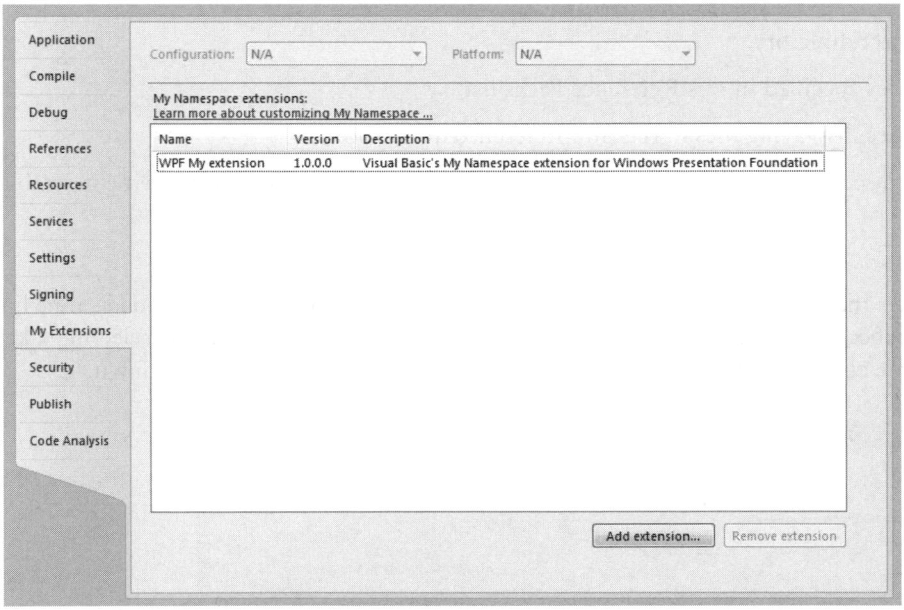

FIGURE 6-19

The My namespace was designed to provide simplified access to common library methods. For example, My.Application.Log provides methods to write an entry or exception to a log file using a single line of code. As such it is the ideal namespace to add custom classes and methods that provide useful utility functions, global state or configuration information, or a service that can be used by multiple applications.

Security

Applications deployed using the ClickOnce deployment model may be required to run under limited or partial trust. For example, if a low-privilege user selects a ClickOnce application from a web site across the Internet, the application will need to run with partial trust as defined by the Internet zone. This typically means that the application can't access the local filesystem, has limited networking ability, and can't access other local devices such as printers, databases, and computer ports.

The Security tab, illustrated in Figure 6-20, allows you to define the trust level that is required by your application to operate correctly.

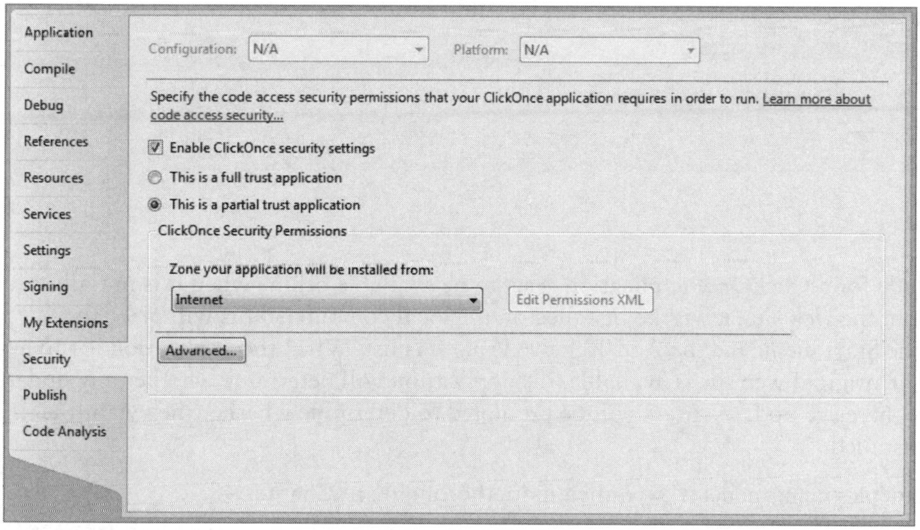

FIGURE 6-20

Modifying the permission set that is required for a ClickOnce application may limit who can download, install, and operate the application. For the widest audience, specify that an application should run in partial trust mode with security set to the defaults for the Internet zone. Alternatively, specifying that an application requires full trust ensures that the application has full access to all local resources, but will necessarily limit the audience to local administrators.

Publish

The ClickOnce deployment model can be divided into two phases: initially publishing the application and subsequent updates, and the download and installation of both the original application and subsequent revisions. You can deploy an existing application using the ClickOnce model using the Publish tab, shown in Figure 6-21.

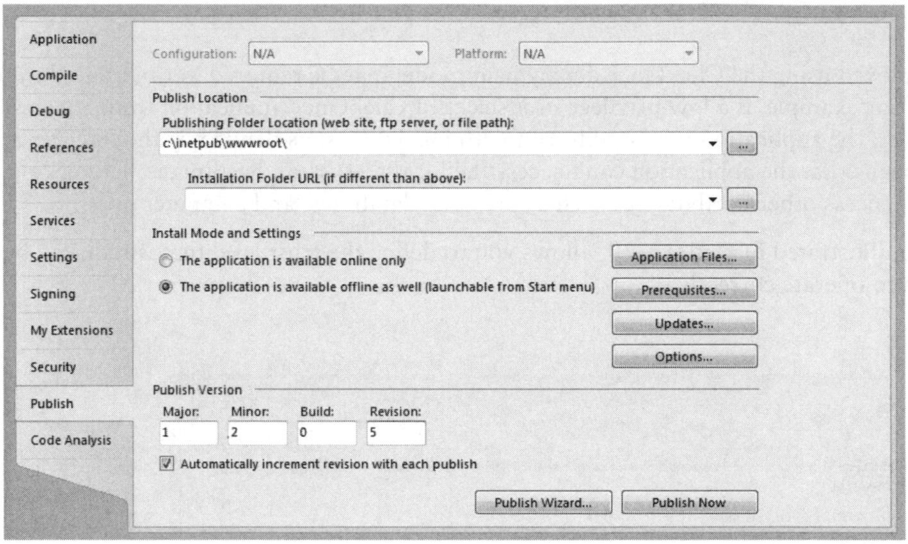

FIGURE 6-21

If the install mode for a ClickOnce application is set to be available offline when it is initially downloaded from the web site, it will be installed on the local computer. This will place the application in the Start menu and the Add/Remove Programs list. When the application is run and a connection to the original web site is available, the application will determine whether any updates are available. If there are updates, users will be prompted to determine whether they want the updates to be installed.

The ClickOnce deployment model is explained more thoroughly in Chapter 48.

Code Analysis (VSTS Premium and Ultimate Editions Only)

Most developers who have ever worked in a team have had to work with an agreed-upon set of coding standards. Organizations typically use an existing standard or create their own. Unfortunately, standards are useful only if they can be enforced, and the only way that this can be effectively done is using a tool. In the past this had to be done using an external utility, such as FXCop. The VSTS Premium and Ultimate Editions of Visual Studio 2010 have the capability to carry out static code analysis from within the IDE.

The Code Analysis tab, shown in Figure 6-22, can be used to enable code analysis as part of the build process. Because this can be quite a time-consuming process, it may be included only in release or test build configurations. Regardless of whether code analysis has been enabled for a project, it can be manually invoked from the Build menu.

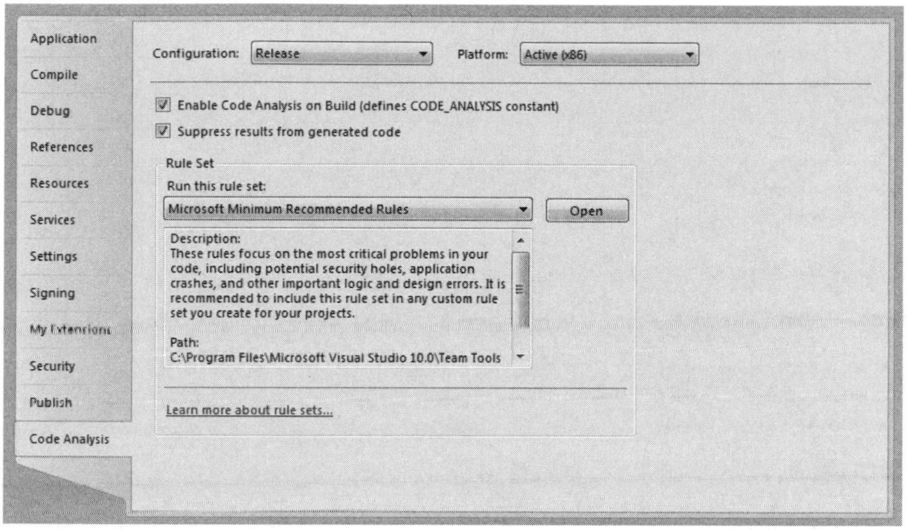

FIGURE 6-22

Not all rules defined in the Code Analysis pane are suitable for all organizations or applications. This pane gives the developer control over which rules are applied, and whether they generate a warning or a build error. Deselecting the rule in the Rules column disables the rule. Double-clicking a cell in the Status column toggles what happens when a rule fails to be met between a warning and a build error.

FXCop is covered in Chapter 13 and the native Visual Studio Code Analysis tools are discussed further in Chapter 55.

WEB APPLICATION PROJECT PROPERTIES

Due to the unique requirements of web applications, four additional project property tabs are available to ASP.NET Web Application projects. These tabs control how web applications are run from Visual Studio as well as the packaging and deployment options.

Web

The Web tab, shown in Figure 6-23, controls how Web Application projects are launched when executed from within Visual Studio. Visual Studio ships with a built-in web server suitable for development purposes. The Web tab enables you to configure the port and virtual path that this runs under. You may also choose to enable NTLM authentication.

> *The Edit and Continue option allows editing of code-behind and standalone class files during a debug session. Editing of the HTML in an* `.aspx` *or* `.ascx` *page is allowed regardless of this setting; however, editing inline code in an* `.aspx` *page or an* `.ascx` *file is never allowed.*

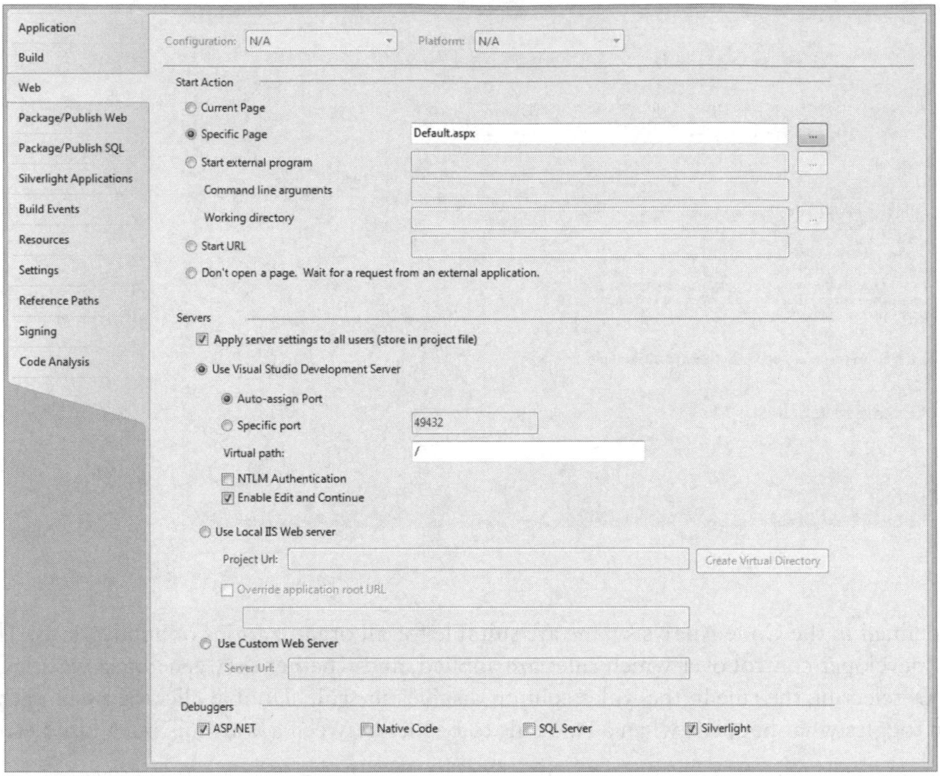

FIGURE 6-23

The debugging options for web applications are explored in Chapter 42.

Silverlight Applications

The Silverlight Applications tab provides an easy way to provide a link to a Silverlight project and host it within an ASP.NET Web Application.

When you add a Silverlight application to a Web Application project, you can select an existing Silverlight project if one exists in the current solution, or create a new Silverlight project as shown in Figure 6-24. The dialog box allows you to select the location and language for the new project, as well as options for how the Silverlight application will be included in the current web application.

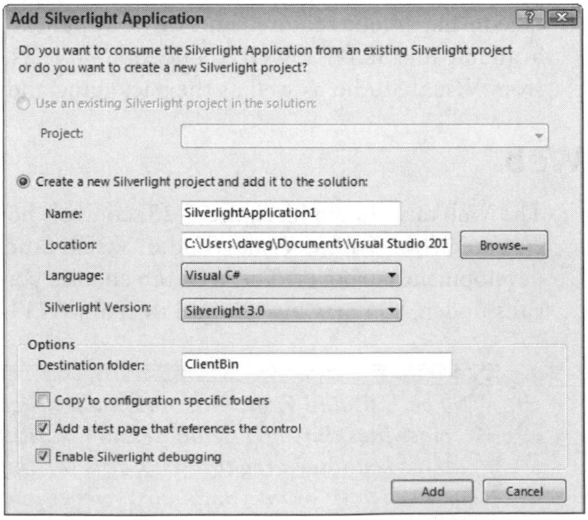

FIGURE 6-24

If you accept the defaults when you add a new Silverlight application, Visual Studio will create a reference to the new project and generate three files in the web application: a static HTML page, an ASP.NET web form, and a JavaScript file that contains logic for loading Silverlight applications and installing the run time if required.

Chapter 22 explores the development of Silverlight applications and the options for hosting them within an existing web application.

Package/Publish Web

Application deployment has always been a difficult challenge, especially when it comes to complex web applications. A typical web application comprises not only a large number of source files and assemblies, but also images, style sheets, and JavaScript files. To complicate matters further, it may be dependent on a specific configuration of the IIS web server.

Visual Studio 2010 simplifies this process by allowing you to package a Web Application project with all of the necessary files and settings contained in a single compressed (.zip) file. Figure 6-25 shows the packaging and deployment options that are available to an ASP.NET Web Application.

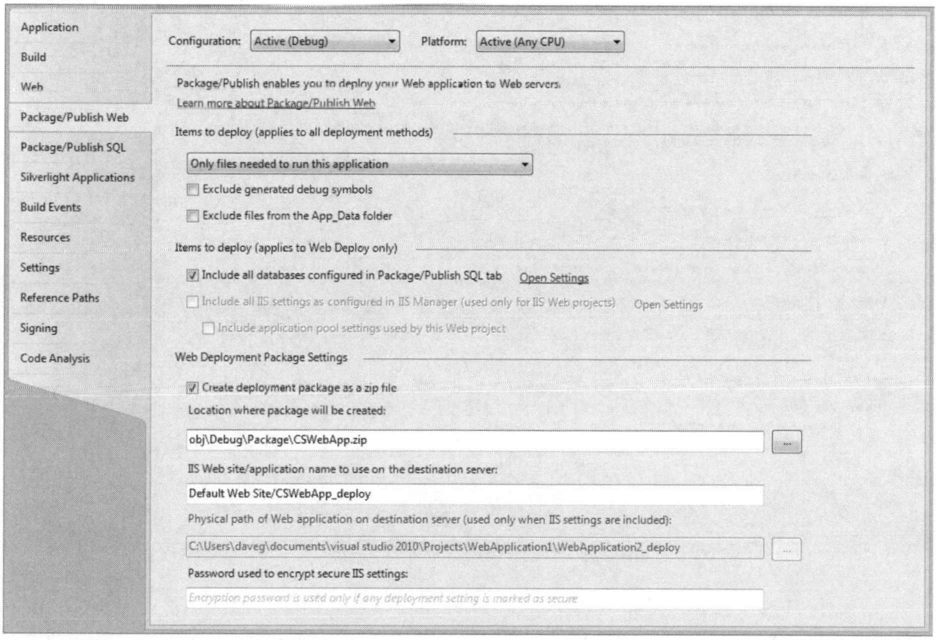

FIGURE 6-25

Further discussion on web application deployment is included in Chapter 49.

Package/Publish SQL

All but the simplest of web applications are backed by a database of some description. For ASP.NET Web applications this is typically a SQL Server database.

The Visual Studio 2010 web packaging and deployment functionality includes support for packaging one or more SQL Server databases. As illustrated in Figure 6-26, when you create a package you can specify a connection string for your source database and allow Visual Studio to create SQL scripts for the database schema only or schema and data. You can also provide custom SQL scripts to be executed either before or after the auto-generated script.

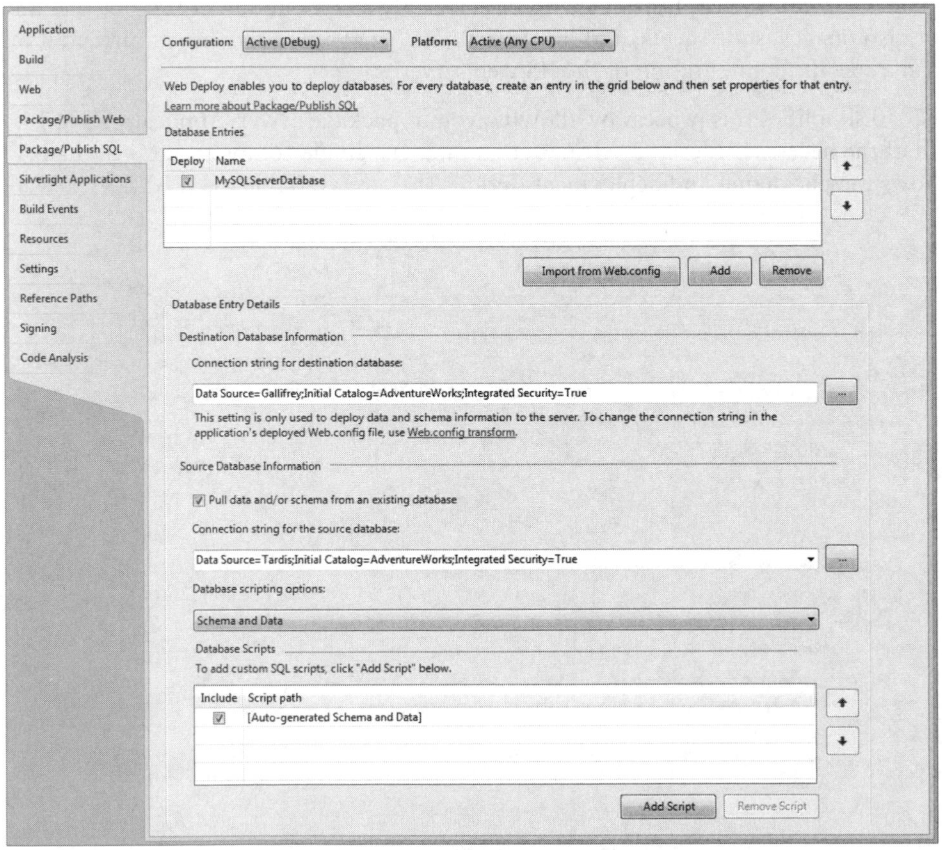

FIGURE 6-26

Chapter 49 explores the web application deployment options in more detail.

WEB SITE PROJECTS

The Web Site project functions quite differently from other project types. Web Site projects do not include a .csproj or .vbproj file, which means they have a number of limitations in terms of build options, project resources, and managing references. Instead, Web Site projects use the folder structure to define the contents of the project. All files within the folder structure are implicitly part of the project.

Web Site projects provide the advantage of dynamic compilation, which allows pages to be edited without rebuilding the entire site. The file can be saved and simply reloaded in the browser. As such they enable extremely short code and debug cycles. Microsoft first introduced Web Site projects with Visual Studio 2005; however, it was quickly inundated with customer feedback to reintroduce the Application Project model, which had been provided as an additional download. By the release of Service Pack 1, Web Application projects were back within Visual Studio as a native project type.

> *Since Visual Studio 2005, an ongoing debate has been raging about which is better — Web Site projects or Web Application projects. Unfortunately, there is no simple answer to this debate. Each has its own pros and cons, and the decision comes down to your requirements and your preferred development workflow.*

You can find further discussion on Web Site and Web Application projects in Chapter 20.

SUMMARY

In this chapter you have seen how a solution and projects can be configured using the user interfaces provided within Visual Studio 2010. In particular, this chapter showed you how to do the following:

- ➤ Create and configure solutions and projects.
- ➤ Control how an application is compiled, debugged, and deployed.
- ➤ Configure the many project-related properties.
- ➤ Include resources and settings with an application.
- ➤ Enforce good coding practices with the Code Analysis Tools.
- ➤ Modify the configuration, packaging, and deployment options for web applications.

In subsequent chapters many of the topics, such as building and deploying projects and the use of resource files, are examined in more detail.

7

IntelliSense and Bookmarks

WHAT'S IN THIS CHAPTER?

➤ Improving efficiency with contextual help

➤ Detecting and fixing simple errors

➤ Reducing keystrokes

➤ Generating code

➤ Navigating source code with bookmarks

One thing that Microsoft has long been good at is providing automated help as you write your code. Older versions of Visual Basic had a limited subset of this automated intelligence known as IntelliSense, but with the introduction of Visual Studio .NET, Microsoft firmly established the technology throughout the whole IDE. With recent releases of Visual Studio, IntelliSense has become so pervasive that it has been referred to as IntelliSense Everywhere.

This chapter illustrates the many ways in which IntelliSense helps you write your code. Among the topics covered are detecting and repairing syntax errors, harnessing contextual information, and variable name completion. You also learn how to set and use bookmarks in your code for easier navigation.

INTELLISENSE EXPLAINED

IntelliSense is the general term for automated help and actions in a Microsoft application. The most commonly encountered aspects of IntelliSense are those wavy lines you see under words that are not spelled correctly in Microsoft Word, or the small visual indicators in a Microsoft Excel spreadsheet that inform you that the contents of the particular cell do not conform to what was expected.

Even these basic indicators enable you to quickly perform related actions. Right-clicking a word with red wavy underlining in Word displays a list of suggested alternatives. Other applications have similar features.

The good news is that Visual Studio has had similar functionality for a long time. In fact, the simplest IntelliSense features go back to tools such as Visual Basic 6. With each release of Visual Studio, Microsoft has refined the IntelliSense features, making them more context-sensitive and putting them in more places so that you should always have the information you need right at your fingertips.

In Visual Studio 2010, the IntelliSense name is applied to a number of different features from visual feedback for bad code and smart tags for designing forms to shortcuts that insert whole slabs of code. These features work together to provide you with deeper insight, efficiency, and control of your code. Some of the features new to Visual Studio 2010, such as suggestion mode and Generate From Usage, are designed to support the alternative style of application development known as test-driven development (TDD).

General IntelliSense

The simplest feature of IntelliSense gives you immediate feedback about bad code in your code listings. Figure 7-1 shows one such example, in which an unknown data type is used to instantiate an object. Because the data type is unknown where this code appears, Visual Studio draws a red (C#) or blue (VB) wavy line underneath to indicate a problem.

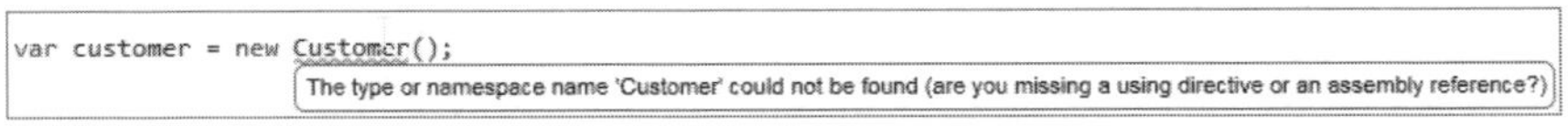

```
var customer = new Customer();
                   The type or namespace name 'Customer' could not be found (are you missing a using directive or an assembly reference?)
```

FIGURE 7-1

> The formatting of this color feedback can be adjusted in the Fonts and Colors group of Options.

Hovering the mouse over the offending piece of code displays a tooltip to explain the problem. In this example the cursor was placed over the data type, with the resulting tooltip "The type or namespace name 'Customer' could not be found."

Visual Studio is able to look for this kind of error by continually precompiling the code you write in the background, and looking for anything that will produce a compilation error. If you were to add the `Customer` class to your project, Visual Studio would automatically process this and remove the IntelliSense marker.

Figure 7-2 displays the smart tag associated with the error. This applies only to errors for which Visual Studio 2010 can offer you corrective actions. Just below the problem code, a small blue (C#)

or red (VB) rectangle is displayed. Placing the mouse cursor over this marker displays the smart tag action menu associated with the type of error — in this case the action menu provides options for generating your Customer class from what Visual Studio is able to determine from the way you have used it.

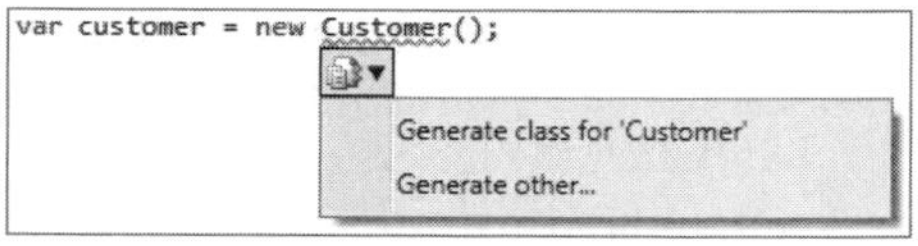

FIGURE 7-2

The standard shortcut key used by all Microsoft applications to activate an IntelliSense smart tag is Shift+Alt+F10, but Visual Studio 2010 provides the more wrist-friendly Ctrl+. shortcut for the same action.

The smart tag technology found in Visual Studio is not solely reserved for the code window. In fact, Visual Studio 2010 also includes smart tags on visual components when you are editing a form or user control in Design view (see Figure 7-3).

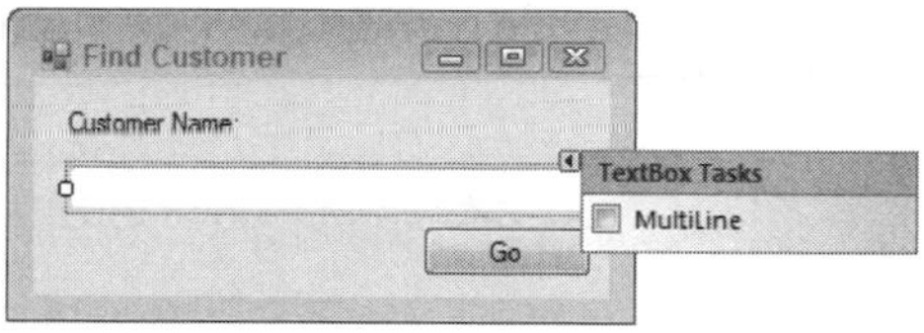

FIGURE 7-3

When you select a control that has a smart tag, a small triangle appears at the top-right corner of the control itself. Click this button to open the smart tag Tasks list — Figure 7-3 shows the Tasks list for a standard TextBox control.

The keyboard shortcuts for opening smart tags also work for visual controls.

Completing Words and Phrases

The power of IntelliSense in Visual Studio 2010 becomes apparent as soon as you start writing code. As you type, various drop-down lists are displayed to help you choose valid members, functions, and parameter types, thus reducing the number of potential compilation errors before you even finish writing your code. Once you become familiar with the IntelliSense behavior, you'll notice that it can greatly reduce the amount of code you actually have to write. This can be a significant savings to developers using more verbose languages such as Visual Basic.

In Context

In Visual Studio 2010, IntelliSense appears almost as soon as you begin to type within the code window. Figure 7-4 illustrates the IntelliSense displayed during the creation of a For loop in Visual Basic. On the left side of the image, IntelliSense appeared as soon as the *f* was entered, and the list of available words progressively shrank as each subsequent key was pressed. As you can see, the list is made up of all the alternatives, whether they be statements, classes, methods, or properties, that match the letters entered (in this case those containing the word `For`).

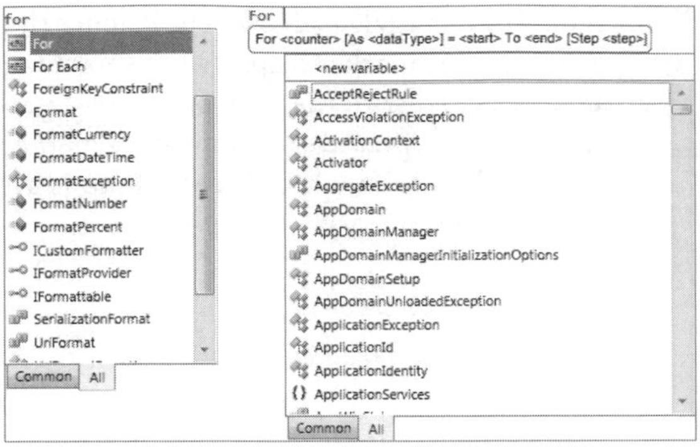

Notice the difference in the right-hand image of Figure 7-4, where a space has been entered after the word `for`. Now the IntelliSense list has expanded to include all the alternatives that could be entered at this position in the code. In addition, there is a tooltip that indicates the syntax of the `For` statement. Lastly, there is a `<new variable>` item just above the IntelliSense list. This is to indicate that it's possible for you to specify a new variable at this location.

FIGURE 7-4

> *The `<new variable>` item appears only for Visual Basic users.*

Although it can be useful that the IntelliSense list is reduced based on the letters you enter, this feature is a double-edged sword. Quite often you will be looking for a variable or member but won't quite remember what it is called. In this scenario, you might enter the first couple of letters of a guess and then use the scrollbar to locate the right alternative. Clearly, this won't work if the letters you have entered have already eliminated the alternative. To bring up the full list of alternatives, simply hit the Backspace key with the IntelliSense list visible.

In previous versions of Visual Studio, IntelliSense has only been able to help you find members that began with the same characters that you typed into the editor. In Visual Studio 2010 this is no longer true. Now it is possible to find words that appear in the middle of member names as well. It does this by looking for word boundaries within the member names. Figure 7-5 shows an example in C# where typing `Console.in` will find `In`, `InputEncoding`, `OpenStandardInput`, `SetIn`, and `TreatControlCAsInput` but does not find `LargestWindowHeight` despite the fact that it contains the substring "in."

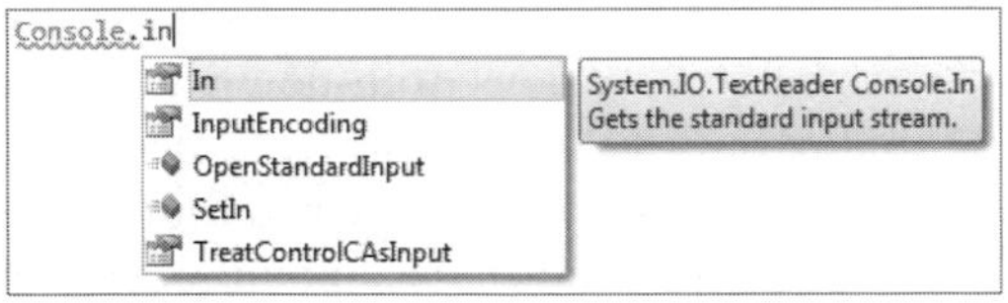

FIGURE 7-5

> *If you know exactly what you are looking for, you can save even more keystrokes by typing the first character of each word in uppercase. As an example, if you type `System.Console.OSI`, then `OpenStandardInput` will be selected by IntelliSense.*

If you find that the IntelliSense information is obscuring other lines of code, or you simply want to hide the list, you can press Esc. Alternatively, if you simply want to view what is hidden behind the IntelliSense list without closing it completely, you can hold down the Ctrl key. This makes the IntelliSense list translucent, enabling you to read the code behind it, as shown in Figure 7-6.

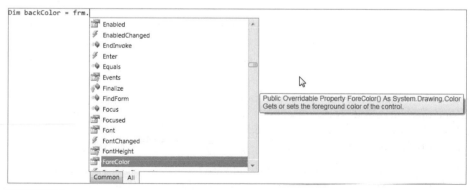

FIGURE 7-6

The IntelliSense list is not just for informational purposes. You can select an item from this list and have Visual Studio actually insert the full text into the editor window for you. You have a number of ways to select an item from the list. You can double-click the desired item with the mouse; you can use the arrow keys to change which item is highlighted and then press the Enter or Tab keys to insert the text; and finally, when an item is highlighted in the list it will automatically be selected if you enter a *commit character*. Commit characters are those that are not normally allowed within member names. Examples include parentheses, braces, mathematical symbols, and semicolons.

List Members

Because IntelliSense has been around for so long, most developers will be familiar with the member list that appears when you type the name of an object and immediately follow it by a period. This indicates that you are going to refer to a member of the object, and Visual Studio automatically displays a list of members available to you for that object (see Figure 7-7). If this is the first time you've accessed the member list for a particular object, Visual Studio simply shows the member list in alphabetical order with the top of the list visible. However, if you've used it before, it highlights the last member you accessed to speed up the process for repetitive coding tasks.

Figure 7-7 also shows another helpful aspect of the member list for Visual Basic programmers. The Common and All tabs (at the bottom of the member list) enable you to view either just the commonly used members or a comprehensive list.

FIGURE 7-7

> *Only Visual Basic gives you the option to filter the member list down to commonly accessed properties, methods, and events.*

Suggestion Mode

By default, when Visual Studio 2010 shows the IntelliSense member list, one member is selected and as you type, the selection is moved to the item in the list that best matches the characters entered. If you press Enter, Space, or type one of the commit characters (such as an open parenthesis), the currently selected member is inserted into the editor window. This default behavior is known as *"completion mode."*

In most cases completion mode provides the desired behavior and can save you a great deal of typing, but it can be problematic for some activities. One such activity is test-driven development where references are frequently made to members that have not yet been defined. This causes IntelliSense to select members that you didn't intend it to and insert text that you do not want.

To avoid this issue Microsoft has introduced a new IntelliSense mode into Visual Studio 2010 called *suggestion mode.* When IntelliSense is in suggestion mode one member in the list will have focus but will not be selected by default. As you type, IntelliSense moves the focus indicator to the item that most closely matches the characters you typed, but it will not automatically select it. Instead, the characters that you type are added to the top of the IntelliSense list and if you type one of the commit characters or press Space or Enter, the exact string that you typed is inserted into the editor window.

> *You can still make a selection from the IntelliSense list by using the arrow keys. Also, you can select the item that has focus in the member list by pressing the Tab key.*

Figure 7-8 shows an example of the problem that suggestion mode is designed to address. On the left-hand side we are writing a test for a new method called `Load` on the `CustomerData` class. The `CustomerData` class does not have a method called `Load` yet but it does have a method called `LoadAll`.

On the right-hand side of Figure 7-8 we have typed `Load` followed by the open parenthesis character. IntelliSense has incorrectly assumed that we wanted the `LoadAll` method and has inserted it into the editor.

FIGURE 7-8

To avoid this behavior we can turn on suggestion mode by pressing Ctrl+Alt+Space. Now when we type `Load` it appears at the top of the IntelliSense list. When we type the open parenthesis character we get `Load` as originally intended (see Figure 7-9).

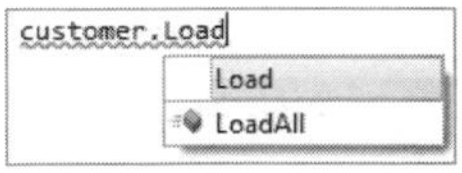

FIGURE 7-9

> *IntelliSense remains in suggestion mode until you press Ctrl+Alt+Space again to revert back to completion mode.*

Stub Completion

In addition to word and phrase completion, the IntelliSense engine has another feature known as *stub completion*. This feature can be seen in Visual Basic when you create a function by writing the declaration of the function and pressing Enter. Visual Studio automatically reformats the line, adding the appropriate ByVal keyword for parameters that don't explicitly define their contexts, and also adding an End Function line to enclose the function code. Another example can be seen when editing an XML document. When you type the open tag of a new element, Visual Studio automatically puts the closing tag in for you.

Visual Studio 2010 takes stub completion an extra step by enabling you to do the same for interface and method overloading. When you add certain code constructs such as an interface in a C# class definition, Visual Studio gives you the opportunity to automatically generate the code necessary to implement the interface. To show you how this works, the following steps outline a task in which the IntelliSense engine generates an interface implementation in a simple class:

1. Start Visual Studio 2010 and create a C# Windows Forms Application project. When the IDE has finished generating the initial code, open Form1.cs in the code editor.

2. At the top of the file, add a using statement to provide a shortcut to the System.Collections namespace:

   ```
   using System.Collections;
   ```

3. Add the following line of code to start a new class definition:

   ```
   public class MyCollection: IEnumerable
   ```

   As you type the IEnumerable interface, Visual Studio first adds a red wavy line at the end to indicate that the class definition is missing its curly braces, and then adds a smart tag indicator at the beginning of the interface name (see Figure 7-10).

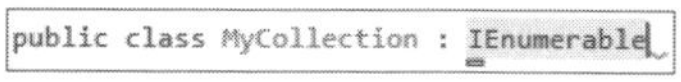

   ```
   public class MyCollection : IEnumerable
   ```

   FIGURE 7-10

4. Hover your mouse pointer over the smart tag indicator. When the drop-down icon appears, click it to open the menu of possible actions, as shown in Figure 7-11.

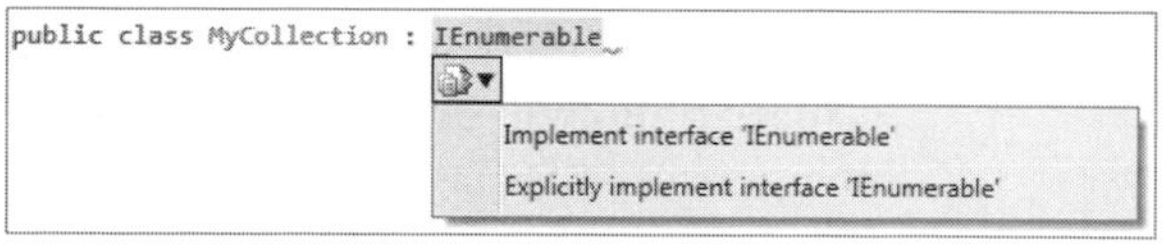

   ```
   public class MyCollection : IEnumerable
   ```
   Implement interface 'IEnumerable'
   Explicitly implement interface 'IEnumerable'

   FIGURE 7-11

5. Click either of the options to "implement interface 'IEnumerable'" and Visual Studio 2010 automatically generates the rest of the code necessary to implement the minimum interface

definition. Because it detects that the class definition itself isn't complete, it also adds the braces to correct that issue at the same time. Figure 7-12 shows what the final interface will look like.

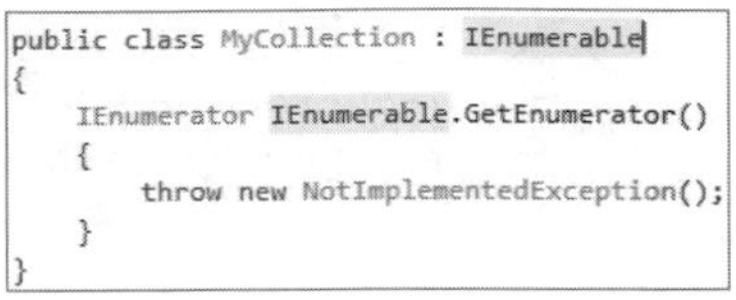

```
public class MyCollection : IEnumerable
{
    IEnumerator IEnumerable.GetEnumerator()
    {
        throw new NotImplementedException();
    }
}
```

FIGURE 7-12

Event handlers can also be automatically generated by Visual Studio 2010. The IDE does this much as it performs interface implementation. When you write the first portion of the statement (for instance, `myBase.OnClick +=`), Visual Studio gives you a suggested completion that you can select simply by pressing Tab.

Generate From Usage

Rather than generating code from a definition that already exists, sometimes it is more convenient to generate the definition of a code element from the way you have used it. This is especially true if you practice test-driven development where you write tests for classes that have not been defined yet. It would be convenient to be able to generate the classes from the tests themselves and this is the purpose of the Generate From Usage feature in C# and Visual Basic.

To understand how you might use this in practice, the following steps outline the creation of a very simple `Customer` class by writing some client code that uses it and then generating the class from that usage:

1. Start Visual Studio 2010 and create a C# Command Line project. When the IDE is ready open the `Program.cs` file.

2. Update the `Main` method with the following code:

   C#
   ```
   Customer c = new Customer
   {
     FirstName = "Joe",
     LastName = "Smith"
   };

   Console.WriteLine(c.FullName);
   c.Save();
   ```

3. You should see a red wiggly line underneath both instances of the class name `Customer`. Right-click one of them and select Generate ⇨ Class. This should create a new class in your project called `Customer`. If you open `Customer.cs` you will see an empty class declaration. Visual Studio will discover that `FirstName`, `LastName`, `FullName`, and `Save` are not members on this class.

4. For each property that does not exist, right-click it and select Generate ⇨ Property. Now go and look at `Customer.cs` again and note that Visual Studio has been able to provide an implementation for you.

5. You can do the same for the `Save` method by right-clicking and selecting Generate ⇨ Method Stub.

> *Though generated properties and classes can be used straight away, method stubs are generated to throw a* NotImplementedException.

If the undefined code that you are trying to generate is a type, you will have the option to Generate Class or Generate Other. If you select Generate Other, the Generate New Type dialog is shown (see Figure 7-13). This dialog gives you more options to configure your new type including whether you want a class, enumeration, interface, or structure; whether the new type should be public, private, or internal; and where the new type should go.

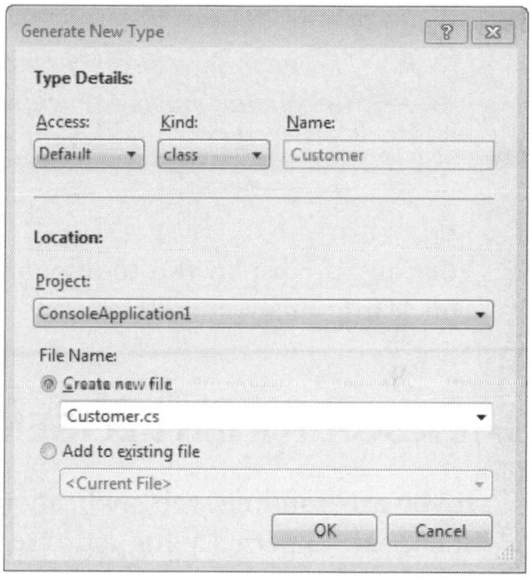

FIGURE 7-13

Parameter Information

In old versions of Microsoft development tools, such as Visual Basic 6, as you created the call to a function, IntelliSense would display the parameter information as you typed. Thankfully, this incredibly useful feature is still present in Visual Studio 2010.

The problem with the old way parameter information was displayed was that it would only be shown if you were actually modifying the function call. Therefore, you could see this helpful tooltip as you created the function call or when you changed it but not if you were just viewing the code. The result was that programmers sometimes inadvertently introduced bugs into their code because they intentionally modified function calls so they could view the parameter information associated with the calls.

Visual Studio 2010 eliminates that risk by providing an easily accessible command to display the information without modifying the code. The keyboard shortcut Ctrl+Shift+Space displays the information about the function call, as displayed in Figure 7-14. You can also access this information through the Edit ➪ IntelliSense ➪ Parameter Info menu command.

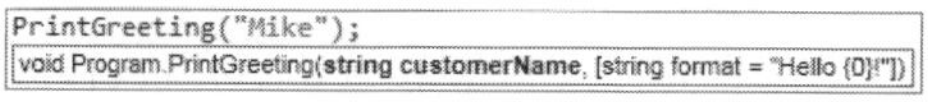

```
PrintGreeting("Mike");
```
`void Program.PrintGreeting(`**`string customerName`**`, [string format = "Hello {0}!"])`

FIGURE 7-14

> *In Figure 7-14 the* PrintGreeting *method takes two parameters. The second parameter is optional and displays in square brackets with an assignment showing its default value if you don't provide one. VB programmers will be familiar with this syntax but it is new to C# 4.0.*

Quick Info

In a similar vein, sometimes you want to see the information about an object or interface without modifying the code. The Ctrl+K, Ctrl+I keyboard shortcut displays a brief tooltip explaining what the object is and how it was declared (see Figure 7-15).

> *The keyboard shortcuts for each VS2010 install depend on the settings selected (i.e. Visual Basic Developer, Visual C# Developer, and so on). All of the shortcut keys in this chapter are based on using the General Developer Profile setting.*

You can also display this tooltip through the Edit ⇨ IntelliSense ⇨ Quick Info menu command.

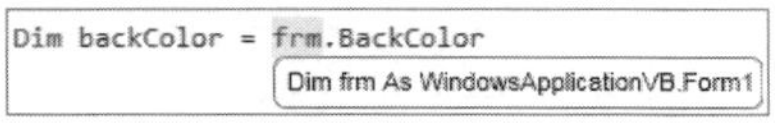

```
Dim backColor = frm.BackColor
                 Dim frm As WindowsApplication\VB.Form1
```

FIGURE 7-15

JAVASCRIPT INTELLISENSE

If you are building web applications, you will find yourself working in JavaScript to provide a richer client-side experience for your users. Unlike C# and Visual Basic, which are compiled languages, JavaScript is an interpreted language, which means that traditionally the syntax of a JavaScript program has not been verified until it is loaded into the browser. Although this can give you a lot of flexibility at run time, it requires discipline, skill, and a heavy emphasis on testing to avoid a large number of common mistakes.

In addition to this, while developing JavaScript components for use in a browser, you must keep track of a number of disparate elements. This can include the JavaScript language features themselves, HTML DOM elements, and handwritten and third-party libraries. Luckily Visual Studio 2010 is able to provide a full IntelliSense experience for JavaScript, which will help you to keep track of all of these elements and warn you of syntax errors.

As you type JavaScript into the code editor window, Visual Studio lists keywords, functions, parameters, variables, objects, and properties just as if you were using C# or Visual Basic. This works for built-in JavaScript functions and objects as well as those you define in your own custom scripts and those found in third-party libraries. Visual Studio is also able to detect and highlight syntax errors in your JavaScript code.

> *Since Internet Explorer 3.0 Microsoft, has maintained its own dialect of JavaScript called JScript. Technically, the JavaScript tools in Visual Studio 2010 are designed to work with Jscript, so you will sometimes see menu options and window titles containing this name. In practice, the differences between the two languages are so minor that the tools work equally well with either one.*

The JavaScript IntelliSense Context

To prevent you from accidentally referring to JavaScript elements that are not available, Visual Studio 2010 builds up an "IntelliSense context" based on the location of the JavaScript block that you are editing. The context is made up of the following items:

➤ The current script block. This includes inline script blocks for `.aspx`, `.ascx`, `.master`, `.html`, and `.htm` files.

➤ Any script file imported into the current page via a `<script />` element or a ScriptManager control. In this case the imported script file must have the `.js` extension.

➤ Any script files that are referenced with a references directive (see the section "Referencing another JavaScript File" later in this chapter).

➤ Any references made to XML Web Services.

➤ The items in the Microsoft AJAX Library (if you are working in an AJAX-enabled ASP.NET web application).

> *Visual Studio keeps track of files in the context and updates JavaScript IntelliSense whenever one of them changes. Sometimes this update may be pending and the JavaScript IntelliSense data will be out of date. You can force Visual Studio to update the JavaScript IntelliSense data by selecting Edit ⇨ IntelliSense ⇨ Update JScript IntelliSense.*

Occasionally something will go wrong and Visual Studio will be unable to build a JavaScript IntelliSense context. Often, though, Visual Studio will be able to determine what caused the error and provide you with feedback that you can use to correct the issue. In Figure 7-16, Visual Studio has detected that we have made a reference to a JavaScript file that does not exist. When you add the file to the project, Visual Studio will detect its presence and remove the error indicator and error message. Although this error detection normally happens as a background process you can force Visual Studio to check a page by selecting Edit ⇨ Advanced ⇨ Validate Document.

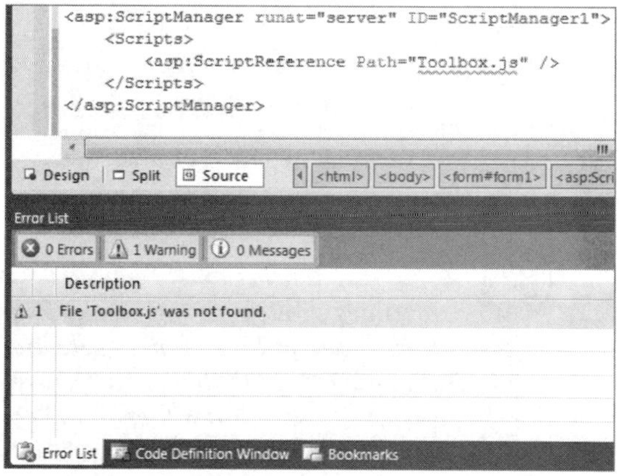

FIGURE 7-16

Referencing another JavaScript File

Sometimes one JavaScript file builds upon the base functionality of another. When this happens they are usually referenced together by any page using them but have no direct reference explicitly defined. Because there is no explicit reference, Visual Studio 2010 is unable to add the file with the base functionality to the JavaScript IntelliSense context and you won't get full IntelliSense support.

To allow Visual Studio to discover the base file and add it to the context you can provide a reference to it by using a references directive. A references directive is a special kind of comment that provides information about the location of another file. You can use references directives to make a reference to any of the following:

➤ **Other JavaScript files:** This includes .js files and JavaScript embedded in assemblies. It does not include absolute paths so the file you reference must be a part of the current project.

➤ **Web Service (.asmx) files:** These also must be a part of the current project and Web Service files in Web Application projects are not supported.

➤ **Pages containing JavaScript:** One page may be referred to in this way. If any page is referenced, no other references can be made.

Following are some examples of references directives. These must appear before any other code in your JavaScript file.

JavaScript

```
// JavaScript file in current folder
/// <reference path="Toolbox.js" />

// JavaScript file in parent folder
/// <reference path="../Toolbox.js" />

// JavaScript file in a path relative to the root folder of the site
/// <reference path="~/Scripts/Toolbox.js" />

// JavaScript file embedded in Assembly
/// <reference name="Ajax.js" path="System.Web.Extensions, …" />

// Web Service file
/// <reference path="MyService.asmx" />

// Standard Page
/// <reference path="Default.aspx" />
```

> *A few restrictions exist on how far references directives will work. First, references directives that refer to a path outside of the current project are ignored. Second, references directives are not recursively evaluated so only those in the file currently being edited are used to help build the context. References directives inside other files in the context are not used.*

INTELLISENSE OPTIONS

Visual Studio 2010 sets up a number of default options for your experience with IntelliSense, but you can change many of these in the Options dialog if they don't suit your own way of doing things. Some of these items are specific to individual languages.

General Options

The first options to look at are in the Environment section under the Keyboard group. Every command available in Visual Studio has a very specific entry in the keyboard mapping list (see the Options dialog shown in Figure 7-17, accessible via Tools ➪ Options).

You can override the predefined keyboard shortcuts or add additional ones. The commands for the IntelliSense features are shown in Table 7-1.

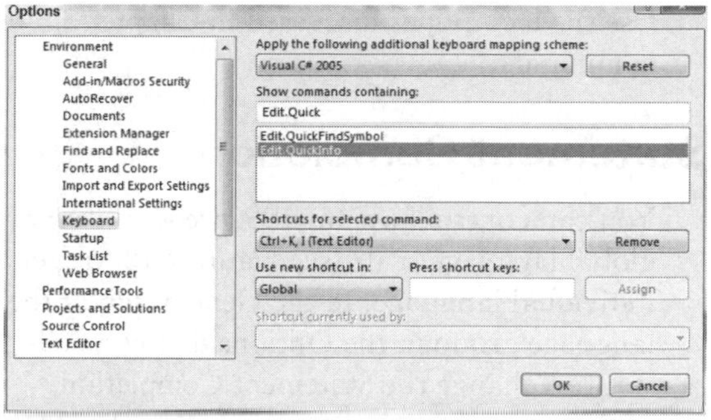

FIGURE 7-17

TABLE 7-1: IntelliSense commands

COMMAND NAME	DEFAULT SHORTCUT	COMMAND DESCRIPTION
Edit.QuickInfo	Ctrl+K, Ctrl+I	Displays the Quick Info information about the selected item
Edit.CompleteWord	Ctrl+Space	Attempts to complete a word if there is a single match, or displays a list to choose from if multiple items match
Edit.ToggleConsumeFirstCompletionMode	Ctrl+Alt+Space	Toggles IntelliSense between suggestion and completion modes
Edit.ParameterInfo	Ctrl+Shift+Space	Displays the information about the parameter list in a function call
Edit.InsertSnippet	Ctrl+K, Ctrl+X	Invokes the Code Snippet dialog, from which you can select a code snippet to insert code automatically (see the next chapter)
Edit.GenerateMethodStub	Ctrl+K,Ctrl+M	Generates the full method stub from a template
Edit.ImplementAbstractClassStubs	None	Generates the abstract class definitions from a stub
Edit.ImplementInterfaceStubsExplicitly	None	Generates the explicit implementation of an interface for a class definition
Edit.ImplementInterfaceStubsImplicitly	None	Generates the implicit implementation of an interface for a class definition

Use the techniques discussed in Chapter 3 to add additional keyboard shortcuts to any of these commands.

Statement Completion

You can control how IntelliSense works on a global language scale (see Figure 7-18) or per individual language. In the General tab of the language group in the Options dialog, you want to change the Statement Completion options to control how member lists should be displayed, if at all.

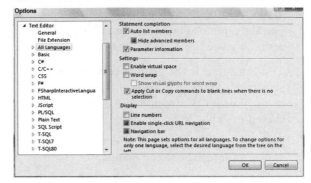

C#-Specific Options

Besides the general IDE and language options for IntelliSense, some languages, such as C#, provide an additional IntelliSense tab in their

FIGURE 7-18

own sets of options. Displayed in Figure 7-19, the IntelliSense for C# can be further customized to fine-tune how the IntelliSense features should be invoked and used.

First, you can turn off completion lists so they do not appear automatically, as discussed earlier in this chapter. Some developers prefer this because the member lists don't get in the way of their code listings. If the completion list is not to be automatically displayed, but instead only shown when you manually invoke it, you can choose what is to be included in the lists in addition to the normal entries, including keywords and code snippet shortcuts.

To select an entry in a member list, you can use any of the characters shown in the Selection In Completion List section, or optionally after the spacebar is pressed. Finally, as mentioned previously, Visual Studio automatically highlights the member in a list that was last used. You can turn this feature off for C# or just clear the history.

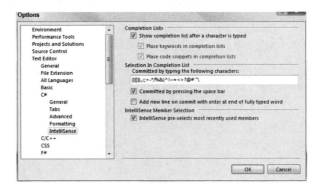

FIGURE 7-19

EXTENDED INTELLISENSE

In addition to the basic aspects of IntelliSense, Visual Studio 2010 also implements extended IDE functionality that falls into the IntelliSense feature set. These features are discussed in detail in other chapters in this book, as referenced in the following discussion, but this section provides a quick summary of what's included in IntelliSense.

Code Snippets

Code snippets are sections of code that can be automatically generated and pasted into your own code, including associated references and `using` statements, with variable phrases marked for easy replacement. To invoke the Code Snippets dialog, press Ctrl+K, Ctrl+X. Navigate the hierarchy of snippet folders (shown in Figure 7-20) until you find the one you need. If you know the shortcut for the snippet, you can simply type it and press Tab, and Visual Studio invokes the snippet without displaying the dialog. In Chapter 8, you see just how powerful code snippets are.

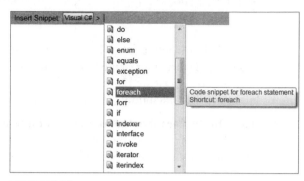

FIGURE 7-20

XML Comments

XML comments are described in Chapter 12 as a way of providing automated documentation for your projects and solutions. However, another advantage of using XML commenting in your program code is that Visual Studio can use it in its IntelliSense engine to display tooltips and parameter information beyond the simple variable-type information you see in normal user-defined classes.

Adding Your Own IntelliSense

You can also add your own IntelliSense schemas, normally useful for XML and HTML editing, by creating a correctly formatted XML file and installing it into the `Common7\Packages\schemas\xml` subfolder inside your Visual Studio installation directory (the default location is `C:\Program Files\Microsoft Visual Studio 10.0`). An example of this would be extending IntelliSense support for the XML editor to include your own schema definitions. The creation of such a schema file is beyond the scope of this book, but you can find schema files on the Internet by searching for "IntelliSense schema in Visual Studio."

BOOKMARKS AND THE BOOKMARK WINDOW

Bookmarks in Visual Studio 2010 enable you to mark places in your code modules so you can easily return to them later. They are represented by indicators in the left margin of the code, as shown in Figure 7-21.

To toggle between bookmarked and not bookmarked on a line, use the shortcut Ctrl+K, Ctrl+K. Alternatively, you can use the Edit ➪ Bookmarks ➪ Toggle Bookmark menu command to do the same thing.

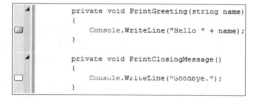

FIGURE 7-21

> *Remember that* toggle *means just that. If you use this command on a line already bookmarked, it removes the bookmark.*

Figure 7-21 shows a section of the code editor window with two bookmarks set. The top bookmark is in its normal state, represented by a shaded blue rectangle. The lower bookmark has been disabled and is represented by a solid white rectangle. Disabling a bookmark enables you to keep it for later use while excluding it from the normal bookmark-navigation functions.

To enable or disable a bookmark use the Edit ➪ Bookmarks ➪ Enable Bookmark toggle menu command. Use the same command to re-enable the bookmark. This seems counterintuitive because you actually want to disable an active bookmark, but for some reason the menu item isn't updated based on the cursor context.

> *You may want to set up a shortcut for disabling and enabling bookmarks if you plan on using them a lot in your code management. To do so, access the Keyboard Options page in the Environment group in Options and look for* `Edit.EnableBookmark`.

Along with the ability to add and remove bookmarks, Visual Studio provides a Bookmarks tool window, shown in Figure 7-22. You can display this tool window by pressing Ctrl+K, Ctrl+W or via the View Bookmark Window menu item. By default, this window is docked to the bottom of the IDE and shares space with other tool windows, such as the Task List and Find Results windows.

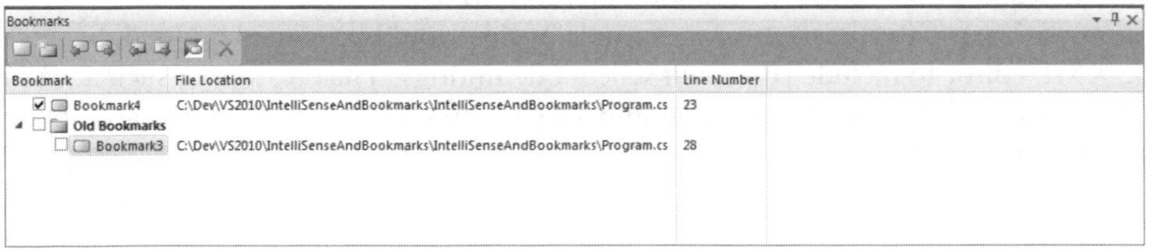

FIGURE 7-22

Figure 7-22 illustrates some useful features of bookmarks in Visual Studio 2010. The first feature is the ability it gives you to create folders that can logically group the bookmarks. In the example list, notice that a folder named Old Bookmarks contains a bookmark named Bookmark3.

To create a folder of bookmarks, click the New Folder icon in the toolbar along the top of the Bookmarks window (it's the second button from the left). This creates an empty folder (using a default name of Folder1, followed by Folder2, and so on) with the name of the folder in focus so that you can make it more relevant. You can move bookmarks into the folder by selecting their entries in the list and dragging them into the desired folder. Note that you cannot create a hierarchy of folders, but it's unlikely that you'll want to. Bookmarks can be renamed in the same way as folders, and for permanent bookmarks renaming can be more useful than accepting the default names of Bookmark1, Bookmark2, and so forth. Folders are not only a convenient way of grouping bookmarks; they also provide an easy way for you to enable or disable a number of bookmarks in one go, simply by using the checkbox beside the folder name.

To navigate directly to a bookmark, double-click its entry in the Bookmarks tool window. Alternatively, if you want to cycle through all of the enabled bookmarks defined in the project, use the Previous Bookmark (Ctrl+K, Ctrl+P) and Next Bookmark (Ctrl+K, Ctrl+N) commands. You can restrict this navigation to only the bookmarks in a particular folder by first selecting a bookmark in the folder and then using the Previous Bookmark in Folder (Ctrl+Shift+K, Ctrl+Shift+P) and Next Bookmark in Folder (Ctrl+Shift+K, Ctrl+Shift+N) commands.

The last two icons in the Bookmarks window are Toggle All Bookmarks, which can be used to disable (or re-enable) all of the bookmarks defined in a project, and Delete, which can be used to delete a folder or bookmark from the list.

> *Deleting a folder also removes all the bookmarks contained in the folder. Visual Studio provides a confirmation dialog to safeguard against accidental loss of bookmarks. Deleting a bookmark is the same as toggling it off.*

Bookmarks can also be controlled via the Bookmarks submenu, which is found in the Edit main menu. In Visual Studio 2010, bookmarks are also retained between sessions, making permanent bookmarks a much more viable option for managing your code organization.

Task lists are customized versions of bookmarks that are displayed in their own tool windows. The only connection that still exists between the two is that there is an Add Task List Shortcut command still in the Bookmarks menu. Be aware that this does not add the shortcut to the Bookmarks window but instead to the Shortcuts list in the Task List window.

SUMMARY

IntelliSense functionality extends beyond the main code window. Various other windows, such as the Command and Immediate tool windows, can harness the power of IntelliSense through statement and parameter completion. Any keywords, or even variables and objects, known in the current context during a debugging session can be accessed through the IntelliSense member lists.

IntelliSense in all its forms enhances the Visual Studio experience beyond most other tools available to you. Constantly monitoring your keystrokes to give you visual feedback or automatic code completion and generation, IntelliSense enables you to be extremely effective at writing code quickly and correctly the first time. In the next chapter you dive into the details behind code snippets, a powerful addition to IntelliSense.

In this chapter you've also seen how you can set and navigate between bookmarks in your code. Becoming familiar with using the associated keystrokes will help you improve your coding efficiency.

8

Code Snippets and Refactoring

WHAT'S IN THIS CHAPTER?

➤ Using code snippets

➤ Creating your own code snippets

➤ Refactoring code

One of the advantages of using an Integrated Development Environment (IDE) over a plain text editor is that it's designed to help you be more productive and efficient by enabling you to write code faster. Two of Visual Studio 2010's most powerful features that help increase your productivity are its support for code snippets and the refactoring tools that it provides.

Code snippets are small chunks of code that can be inserted into an application's code base and then customized to meet the application's specific requirements. They do not generate full-blown applications or whole files, unlike project and item templates. Instead, code snippets are used to insert frequently used code structures or obscure program code blocks that are not easy to remember. In the first part of this chapter you see how using code snippets can improve your coding efficiency enormously.

This chapter also focuses on Visual Studio 2010's refactoring tools — refactoring being the process of reworking code to improve it without changing its functionality. This might entail simplifying a method, extracting a commonly used code pattern, or even optimizing a section of code to make it more efficient.

Although refactoring tools are implemented for C# in Visual Studio, unfortunately they haven't been implemented for VB. In order to fill this hole in functionality in previous versions of Visual Studio, Microsoft licensed the VB version of Refactor! from Developer Express. For Visual Studio 2010, CodeRush Xpress (also from Developer Express) takes over from Refactor! to implement refactoring for VB. Even though Microsoft has licensed CodeRush Xpress, it still needs to be downloaded and installed separately from Visual Studio (as an add-in). You can download it from the VB developer center at `http://msdn.microsoft.com/vbasic/`; follow the links to Downloads, then Tools and Utilities.

CodeRush Xpress provides a range of additional refactoring support that complements the integrated support available for C# developers. However, this chapter's discussion is restricted to the built-in refactoring support provided within Visual Studio 2010 (for C# developers) and the corresponding action in CodeRush Xpress (for VB developers).

CODE SNIPPETS REVEALED

Code snippets have been around in a variety of forms for a long time but generally required third-party add-ins for languages such as VB 6 and the early versions of Visual Studio. Visual Studio 2010 includes extensive code snippet support that allows a block of code along with predefined replacement variables to be inserted into a file, making it easy to customize the inserted code to suit the task at hand.

Storing Code Blocks in the Toolbox

Before looking at code snippets, this section looks at the simplest means Visual Studio provides to insert predefined blocks of text into a file. Much like it can hold controls to be inserted on a form, the Toolbox can also hold blocks of text (such as code) that can be inserted into a file. To add a block of code (or other text) to the Toolbox, simply select the text in the editor and drag it over

onto the Toolbox. This creates an entry for it in the Toolbox with the first line of the code as its name. You can rename, arrange, and group these entries like any other element in the Toolbox. To insert the code block you simply drag it from the Toolbox to the desired location in a file as shown in Figure 8-1, or simply double-click the Toolbox entry to insert it at the current cursor position in the active file.

FIGURE 8-1

> *Many presenters use this simple feature to quickly insert large code blocks when writing code live in presentations.*

This is the simplest form of "code snippet" behavior in Visual Studio 2010, but with its simplicity comes limited functionality, such as the lack of ability to modify and share them. Nevertheless, this method of keeping small sections of code can prove useful in some scenarios to maintain a series of code blocks for short-term use.

Code Snippets

Now we come to a much more useful way to insert blocks of code into a file: *code snippets*. Code snippets are defined in individual XML files, each containing a block of code that programmers may want to insert into their code, and may also include replaceable parameters making it easy to then customize the inserted snippet for the current task. They are integrated with Visual Studio's IntelliSense, making them very easy to find and insert into a code file.

> *VB code snippets also have the ability to add assembly references and insert* `Imports` *statements.*

Visual Studio 2010 ships with many predefined code snippets for the two main languages, VB and C#, along with snippets for JavaScript, HTML, and XML. These snippets are arranged hierarchically in a logical fashion so that you can easily locate the appropriate snippet. Rather than locate the snippet in the Toolbox, you can use menu commands or keyboard shortcuts to bring up the main list of groups.

In addition to the predefined code snippets, you can create your own code snippets and store them in this code snippet library. Because each snippet is stored in a special XML file, you can even share them with other developers.

Following are three scopes under which a snippet can be inserted:

➤ **Class Declaration:** The snippet actually generates an entire class.

➤ **Member Declaration:** This snippet scope includes code that defines members, such as methods, properties, and event handler routines. This means it should be inserted outside an existing member.

➤ **Member Body:** This scope is for snippets that are inserted into an already defined member, such as a method.

Using Snippets in C#

Insert Snippet is a special kind of IntelliSense that appears inline in the code editor. Initially, it displays the words "Insert Snippet" along with a drop-down list of code snippet groups from which to choose. Once you select the group that contains the snippet you require (using up and down arrows, followed by the Tab key), it shows you a list of snippets, and you can simply double-click the one you need (alternatively, pressing Tab or Enter with the required snippet selected has the same effect).

To insert a code snippet in C#, simply locate the position where you want to insert the generated code, and then the easiest way to bring up the Insert Snippet list is to use the keyboard shortcut combination of Ctrl+K, Ctrl+X. You have two additional methods to start the Insert Snippet process. The first is to right-click at the intended insertion point in the code window and select Insert Snippet from the context menu that is displayed. The other option is to use the Edit ➪ IntelliSense ➪ Insert Snippet menu command.

At this point, Visual Studio brings up the Insert Snippet list, as Figure 8-2 demonstrates. As you scroll through the list and hover the mouse pointer over each entry, a tooltip is displayed to indicate what the snippet does and a shortcut that can be used to insert it.

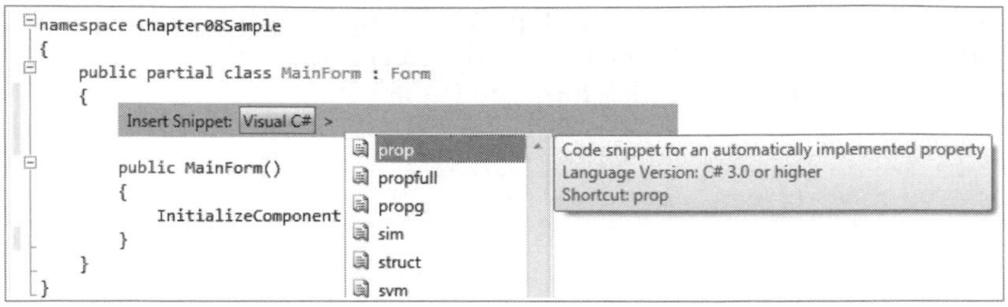

FIGURE 8-2

To use the shortcut for a code snippet, simply type it into the code editor (note that it appears in the IntelliSense list) and press the Tab key twice to insert the snippet at that position.

Figure 8-3 displays the result of selecting the Automatically Implemented Property snippet. To help you modify the code to your own requirements, the sections you would normally need to change (the replacement variables) are highlighted, with the first one conveniently selected.

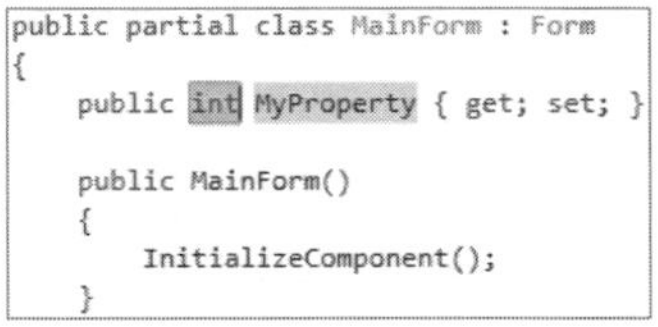

FIGURE 8-3

When you are changing the variable sections of the generated code snippet, Visual Studio 2010 helps you even further. Pressing the Tab key moves to the next highlighted value, ready for you to override the value with your own. Shift+Tab navigates backward, so you have an easy way of accessing the sections of code that need changing without needing to manually select the next piece to modify. Some code snippets use the same variable for multiple pieces of the code snippet logic. This means changing the value in one place results in it changing in all other instances.

To hide the highlighting of these snippet variables once you are done you can simply continue coding, or press either Enter or Esc.

Using Snippets in VB

Code snippets in VB have additional features over what is available in C#, namely the ability to automatically add references to assemblies in the project, and insert Imports statements into a file that the code needs in order to compile.

To use a code snippet you should first locate where you want the generated code to be placed in the program listing and position the cursor at that point. You don't have to worry about the associated references and Imports statements; they will be placed in the correct location. Then, as with C# snippets, you can use one of the following methods to display the Insert Snippet list:

➤ Use the keyboard chord Ctrl+K, Ctrl+X

➤ Right-click and choose Insert Snippet from the context menu

➤ Run the Edit ⇨ IntelliSense ⇨ Insert Snippet menu command

VB also has an additional way to show the Insert Snippet List: simply type ? and press Tab.

Let's navigate through the hierarchy and insert a snippet named Draw a Pie Chart. Figure 8-4 demonstrates how you might navigate through the hierarchy to find the snippet and insert it into your project.

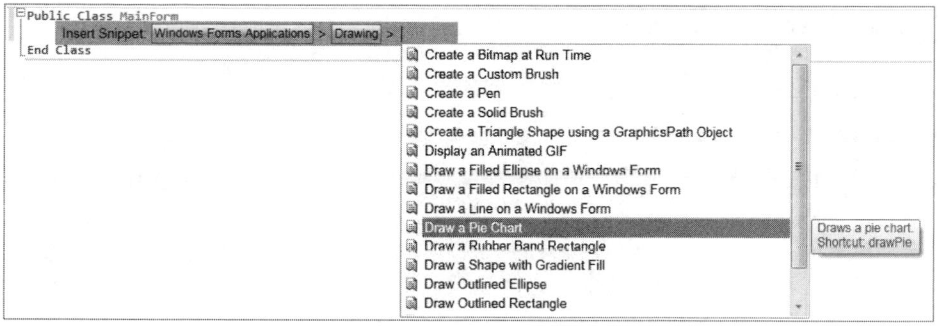

FIGURE 8-4

You might have noticed in Figure 8-4 that the tooltip text includes the words "Shortcut: drawPie." This text indicates that the selected code snippet has a text shortcut that you can use to automatically invoke the code snippet behavior without navigating the code snippet hierarchy. As with C# all you need to do is type the shortcut into the code editor and press the Tab key *once* for it to be inserted. In VB the shortcut isn't case-sensitive, so this example can be generated by typing the term "drawpie" and pressing Tab. Note that shortcuts don't appear in IntelliSense in VB as they do in C#.

After inserting the code snippet, if it contains replacement variables you can enter their values then navigate between these by pressing Tab as described for C#. To hide the highlighting of these snippet variables once you are done, you can simply continue coding, or right-click and select Hide Snippet Highlighting. If you want to highlight all the replacement variables of the code snippets inserted since the file was opened, right-click and select Show Snippet Highlighting.

Surround With Snippet

The last refactoring action, available in C# (and VB with CodeRush Xpress), is the capability to surround an existing block of code with a code snippet. For example, to wrap an existing block with a conditional try-catch block, right-click and select Surround With, or select the block of code and press Ctrl+K, Ctrl+S. This displays the Surround With dialog that contains a list of surrounding snippets that are available to wrap the selected line of code, as shown in Figure 8-5.

FIGURE 8-5

Selecting the `try` snippet results in the following code:

VB

```
Public Sub MethodXYZ(ByVal name As String)
    Try
        MessageBox.Show(name)
```

```vb
        Catch ex As Exception
            Throw
        End Try
End Sub
```

C#

```csharp
public void MethodXYZ(string name)
{
    try
    {
        MessageBox.Show(name);
    }
    catch (Exception)
    {
        throw;
    }
}
```

Code Snippets Manager

The Code Snippets Manager is the central library for the code snippets known to Visual Studio 2010. You can access it via the Tools ➪ Code Snippet Manager menu command or the keyboard shortcut chord Ctrl+K, Ctrl+B.

When it is initially displayed, the Code Snippets Manager shows the HTML snippets available, but you can change it to display the snippets for the language you are using via the Language drop-down list. Figure 8-6 shows how it looks when you're editing a C# project. The hierarchical folder structure follows the same set of folders on the PC by default, but as you add snippet files from different locations and insert them into the different groups, the new snippets slip into the appropriate folders.

If you have an entire folder of snippets to add to the library, such as when you have a corporate setup and need to import the company-developed snippets, you use the Add button. This brings up a dialog that you use to browse to the required folder. Folders added in this fashion appear at the root level of the tree — on the same level as the main groups of default snippets. However, you can add a folder that contains subfolders, which will be added as child nodes in the tree.

Removing a folder is just as easy — in fact, it's dangerously easy. Select the root node that you want to remove and click the Remove button. Instantly, the node and all child nodes

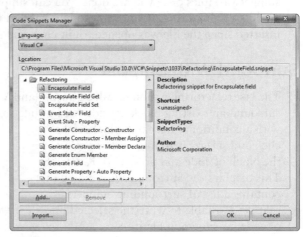

FIGURE 8-6

and snippets are removed from the Snippets Manager without a confirmation window. If you do this by accident you are best off clicking the Cancel button and opening the dialog again. If you've made changes you don't want to lose, you can add them back by following the steps explained in the previous walkthrough, but it can be frustrating trying to locate a default snippet folder that you inadvertently deleted from the list.

The location for the code snippets that are installed with Visual Studio 2010 is deep within the installation folder. By default, the code snippet library when running on 32-bit Windows is installed in `%programfiles%\Microsoft Visual Studio 10.0\VB\Snippets\1033` for VB snippets and `%programfiles%\Microsoft Visual Studio 10.0\VC#\Snippets\1033` for C# (for 64-bit Windows, replace `%programfiles%` with `%programfiles(x86)%`). Individual snippet files can be imported into the library using the Import button. The advantage of this method over the Add button is that you get the opportunity to specify the location of each snippet in the library structure.

Creating Snippets

Visual Studio 2010 does not ship with a code snippet creator or editor. However, Bill McCarthy's Snippet Editor allows you to create, modify, and manage your snippets (including support for VB, C#, HTML, JavaScript, and XML snippets). Starting as an internal Microsoft project, the Snippet Editor is now an open source project hosted on CodePlex where Bill fixed the outstanding issues and proceeded to add functionality. With the help of other MVPs it is now also available in a number of different languages. You can download the snippet editor from `http://snippeteditor.codeplex.com`.

Creating code snippets by manually editing the `.snippet` XML files can be a tedious and error-prone process, so the Snippet Editor makes it a much more pleasant experience. When you start the Snippet Editor you will notice a drop-down list in the top left-hand corner — make sure you select Visual Studio 2010. Below this is a tree containing all the snippets known to Visual Studio 2010. By expanding a node you'll see a set of folders similar to those in the code snippet library (see Figure 8-7).

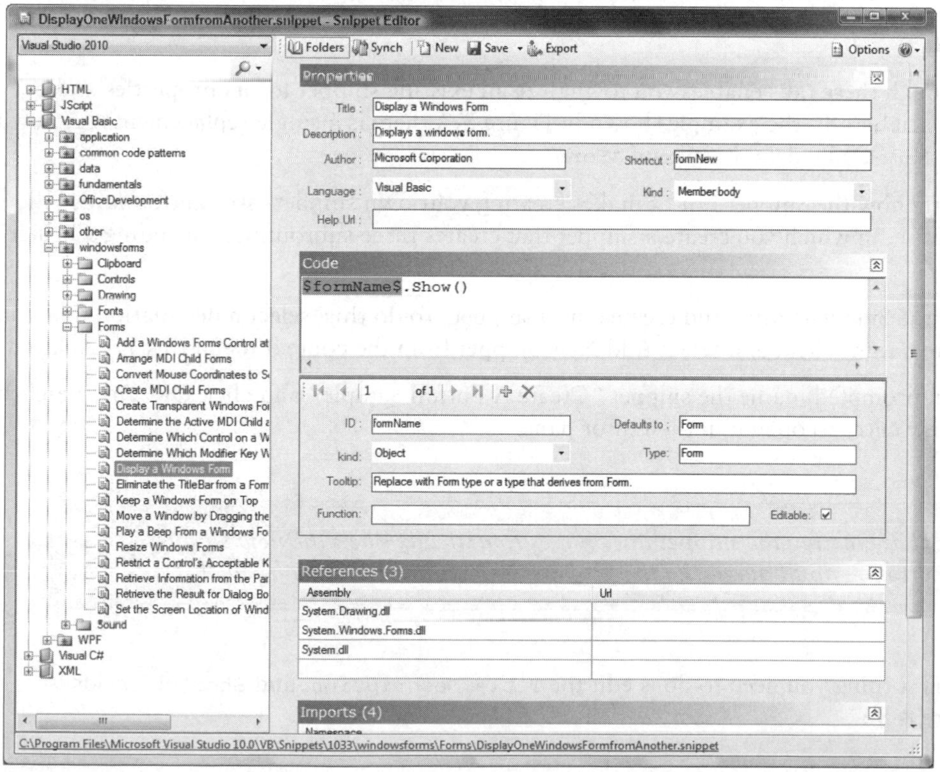

FIGURE 8-7

Reviewing Existing Snippets

An excellent feature of the Snippet Editor is the view it offers of the structure of any snippet file in the system. This means you can browse the default snippets installed with Visual Studio, which can provide insight into how to better build your own snippets.

Browse to the snippet you're interested in and double-click its entry to display it in the Editor window. Figure 8-7 shows a simple snippet to Display a Windows Form. Four main panes contain all the associated information about the snippet. From top to bottom, these panes are described in Table 8-1.

TABLE 8-1: Information Panes for Snippets

PANE	FUNCTION
Properties	The main properties for the snippet, including title, shortcut, and description.
Code	Defines the code for the snippet, including all Literal and Object replacement regions.
References	If your snippet will require assembly references, this tab enables you to define them.
Imports	Similar to the References tab, this tab enables you to define any `Imports` statements that are required in order for your snippet to function correctly.

Browsing through these tabs enables you to analyze an existing snippet for its properties and replacement variables. In the example shown in Figure 8-7, there is a single replacement region with an ID of `formName` and a default value of `"Form"`.

To demonstrate how the Snippet Editor makes creating your own snippets straightforward, follow this next exercise, in which you create a snippet that creates three subroutines, including a helper subroutine:

1. Start the Snippet Editor and create a new snippet. To do this, select a destination folder in the tree, right-click, and select Add New Snippet from the context menu that is displayed.

2. When prompted, name the snippet "Create A Button Sample" and click OK. Double-click the new entry to open it in the Editor pane.

> Note that creating the snippet does not automatically open the new snippet in the Editor — don't overwrite the properties of another snippet by mistake!

3. The first thing you need to do is edit the `Title`, `Description`, and `Shortcut` fields (see Figure 8-8):

➤ `Title`: Create A Button Sample

➤ `Description`: This snippet adds code to create a button control and hook an event handler to it

➤ `Shortcut`: CreateAButton

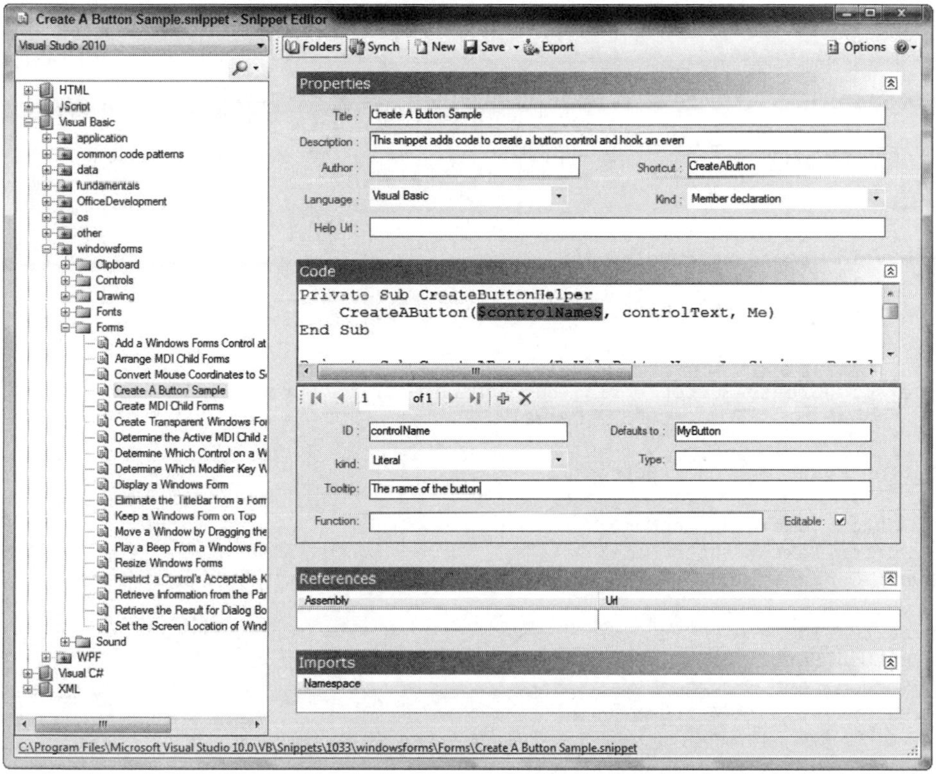

FIGURE 8-8

4. Because this snippet contains member definitions, set the Type to "Member Declaration."

5. In the Editor window, insert the code necessary to create the three subroutines:

VB

```
Private Sub CreateButtonHelper
    CreateAButton(controlName, controlText, Me)
End Sub

Private Sub CreateAButton(ByVal ButtonName As String, _
                          ByVal ButtonText As String, _
                          ByVal Owner As Form)
    Dim MyButton As New Button

    MyButton.Name = ButtonName
```

```
    MyButton.Text = ButtonName
    Owner.Controls.Add(MyButton)

    MyButton.Top = 0
    MyButton.Left = 0
    MyButton.Text = ButtonText
    MyButton.Visible = True

    AddHandler MyButton.Click, AddressOf ButtonClickHandler
End Sub

Private Sub ButtonClickHandler(ByVal sender As System.Object, _
                        ByVal e As System.EventArgs)
    MessageBox.Show("The " & sender.Name & " button was clicked")
End Sub
```

C#

```
private void CreateButtonHelper()
{
    CreateAButton(controlName, controlText, this);
}

private void CreateAButton(string ButtonName, string ButtonText,
                        Form Owner)
{
    Button MyButton = new Button();

    MyButton.Name = ButtonName;
    MyButton.Text = ButtonName;
    Owner.Controls.Add(MyButton);

    MyButton.Top = 0;
    MyButton.Left = 0;
    MyButton.Text = ButtonText;
    MyButton.Visible = true;

    MyButton.Click += MyButton_Click;
}

private void  MyButton_Click(object sender, EventArgs e)
{
    MessageBox.Show("The " + sender.Name + " button was clicked");
}
```

6.   You will notice that your code differs from that shown in Figure 8-8 in that the word `controlName` does not appear highlighted. In Figure 8-8, this argument has been made a replacement region. You can do this by selecting the entire word, right-clicking, and selecting Add Replacement (or alternatively, clicking the Add button in the area below the code window).

7.   Change the replacement properties like so:

   ➤   `ID:` `controlName`

   ➤   `Defaults to:` `"MyButton"`

   ➤   `Tooltip:` The name of the button

8. Repeat this for `controlText`:

> ➤ ID: `controlText`

> ➤ Defaults to: `"Click Me!"`

> ➤ Tooltip: The text property of the button

Your snippet is now done and ready to be used. You can use Visual Studio 2010 to insert the snippet into a code window.

ACCESSING REFACTORING SUPPORT

There are a number of ways to invoke the refactoring tools in Visual Studio 2010, including from the right-click context menu, smart tags, and the Refactor menu in the main menu (for C# developers only).

Figure 8-9 shows the Refactor context menu available for C# developers. The full list of refactoring actions available to C# developers within Visual Studio 2010 includes Rename, Extract Method, Encapsulate Field, Extract Interface, Promote Local Variable to Parameter, Remove Parameters, and Reorder Parameters. You can also use Generate Method Stub and Organize Usings, which can be loosely classified as refactoring.

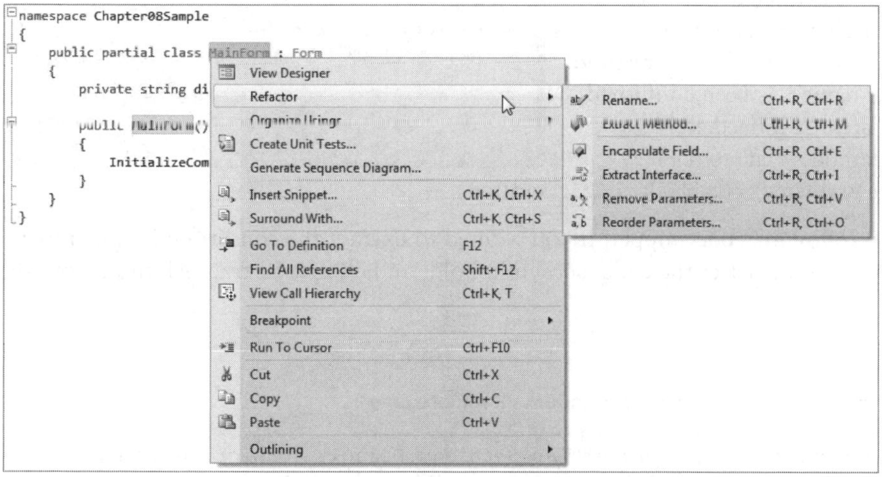

```
namespace Chapter08Sample
{
    public partial class MainForm : Form
    {
        private string di
        
        public MainForm()
        {
            InitializeCom
        }
    }
}
```

🖵 View Designer		
Refactor ▶	ab✓ Rename...	Ctrl+R, Ctrl+R
Organize Usings ▶	🖉 Extract Method...	Ctrl+R, Ctrl+M
🗐 Create Unit Tests...	🖉 Encapsulate Field...	Ctrl+R, Ctrl+E
Generate Sequence Diagram...	🖳 Extract Interface...	Ctrl+R, Ctrl+I
🖹 Insert Snippet... Ctrl+K, Ctrl+X	▲⋋ Remove Parameters...	Ctrl+R, Ctrl+V
🖹 Surround With... Ctrl+K, Ctrl+S	⬚ᵇ Reorder Parameters...	Ctrl+R, Ctrl+O
🖵 Go To Definition F12		
Find All References Shift+F12		
🖫 View Call Hierarchy Ctrl+K, T		
Breakpoint ▶		
⋅☰ Run To Cursor Ctrl+F10		
✂ Cut Ctrl+X		
🗐 Copy Ctrl+C		
🗐 Paste Ctrl+V		
Outlining ▶		

FIGURE 8-9

The built-in refactoring support provided by Visual Studio 2010 for VB developers is limited to the symbolic Rename and Generate Method Stub. Additional refactoring support for VB developers is provided by CodeRush Xpress, which can be accessed via the right-click context menu (which dynamically changes so that only valid refactoring actions are displayed), or via the smart tags (as shown in Figure 8-10) that it displays when a refactoring is available for the current selection (which can be clicked, or activated by pressing Ctrl+`).

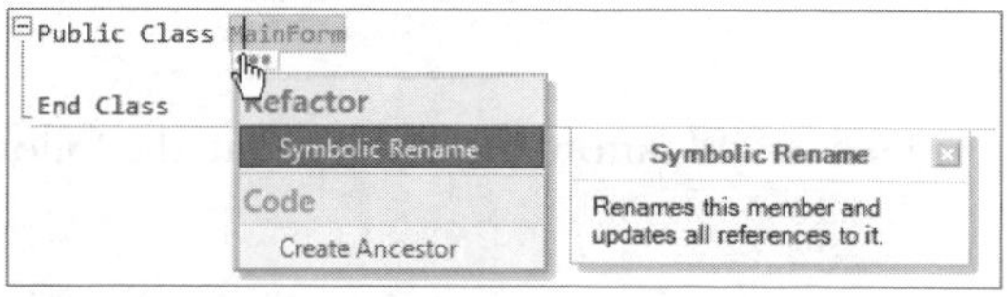

```
Public Class MainForm

End Class
```

Refactor	
Symbolic Rename	**Symbolic Rename** ☒
Code	Renames this member and updates all references to it.
Create Ancestor	

FIGURE 8-10

CodeRush Xpress adds support for all of the refactoring tools that C# has, and it adds many more (to both languages). Examples of additional refactorings include Create Overload, Flatten Conditional, Inline Temp, Introduce Constant, Introduce Local, Move Declaration Near Reference, Move Initialization to Declaration, Remove Assignments to Parameters, Rename, Reorder Parameters, Replace Temp with Query, Reverse Conditional, Safe Rename, Simplify Expression, Split Initialization from Declaration, and Split Temporary Variable.

REFACTORING ACTIONS

The following sections describe each of the refactoring options and provide examples of how to use built-in support for both C# and CodeRush Xpress for VB.

Extract Method

One of the best ways to start refactoring a long method is to break it up into several smaller methods. The Extract Method refactoring action is invoked by selecting the region of code you want moved out of the original method and selecting Extract Method from the context menu. In C#, this will prompt

you to enter a new method name, as shown in Figure 8-11. If there are variables within the block of code to be extracted that were used earlier in the original method, they automatically appear as variables in the method signature. Once the name has been confirmed, the new method is created immediately after the original method. A call to the new method replaces the extracted code block.

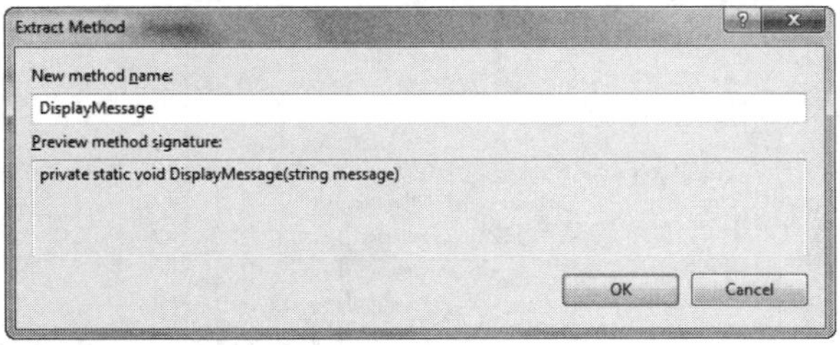

FIGURE 8-11

For example, in the following code snippet, if you wanted to extract the conditional logic into a separate method, you would select the code, shown in bold, and choose Extract Method from the right-click context menu:

C#
```
private void button1_Click(object sender, EventArgs e)
{
    string connectionString = Properties.Settings.Default.ConnectionString;
    if (connectionString == null)
    {
        connectionString = "DefaultConnectionString";
    }
    MessageBox.Show(connectionString);
    /* ... Much longer method ... */
}
```

This would automatically generate the following code in its place:

C#
```
Private void button1_Click(object sender, EventArgs e)
{
```

```
        string connectionString = Properties.Settings.Default.ConnectionString;
        connectionString = ValidateConnectionString(output);
        MessageBox.Show(connectionString);
        /* ... Much longer method ... */
    }

    private static string ValidateConnectionString(string connectionString)
    {
        if (connectionString == null)
        {
            connectionString = "DefaultConnectionString";
        }
        return connectionString;
    }
```

CodeRush Xpress handles this refactoring action slightly differently for VB developers. After you select the code you want to replace, CodeRush Xpress prompts you to select a place in your code where you want to insert the new method. This can help developers organize their methods in groups, either alphabetically or according to functionality.

Figure 8-12 illustrates the aid that appears which enables you to position where the method should be inserted using the cursor keys.

```
Private Sub Button1_Click(ByVal sender As System.Object,
                ByVal e As System.EventArgs) Handles Button1.Click
    Dim connectionString As String = My.MySettings.Default.ConnectionString

    If connectionString Is Nothing Then
        connectionString = "DefaultConnectionString"
    End If

    MessageBox.Show(connectionString)
    'Much longer method
End Sub
End Class
```

Extract Method – Targeting

Key	Behavior
Up	Move the target picker **up**.
Down	Move the target picker **down**.
Num Enter or Enter	✓ **Declare new method** at target location.
Esc	✗ **Cancel** this refactoring.

FIGURE 8-12

After selecting the insert location, CodeRush Xpress inserts the new method, giving it an arbitrary name. In doing so it highlights the method name, enabling you to rename the method either at the insert location or where the method is called (see Figure 8-13).

Using the Extract Method refactoring on the following code:

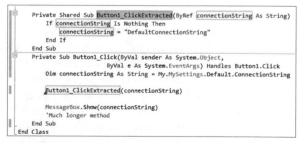

```
Private Shared Sub Button1_ClickExtracted(ByRef connectionString As String)
    If connectionString Is Nothing Then
        connectionString = "DefaultConnectionString"
    End If
End Sub
Private Sub Button1_Click(ByVal sender As System.Object,
                ByVal e As System.EventArgs) Handles Button1.Click
    Dim connectionString As String = My.MySettings.Default.ConnectionString

    Button1_ClickExtracted(connectionString)

    MessageBox.Show(connectionString)
    'Much longer method
End Sub
End Class
```

FIGURE 8-13

VB

```
Private Sub Button1_Click(ByVal sender As System.Object,
                ByVal e As System.EventArgs) Handles Button1.Click
```

```
    Dim connectionString As String = My.MySettings.Default.ConnectionString
    If connectionString Is Nothing Then
        connectionString = "DefaultConnectionString"
    End If
    MessageBox.Show(connectionString)
    'Much longer method
End Sub
```

And renaming the method to give it an appropriate name will result in the following code:

VB

```
Private Sub Button1_Click(ByVal sender As System.Object,
                          ByVal e As System.EventArgs) Handles Button1.Click
    Dim connectionString As String = My.MySettings.Default.ConnectionString
    ValidateConnectionString(connectionString)
    MessageBox.Show(connectionString)
    'Much longer method
End Sub

Private Shared Sub ValidateConnectionString(ByRef connectionString As String)
    If connectionString Is Nothing Then
        connectionString = "DefaultConnectionString"
    End If
End Sub
```

Encapsulate Field

Another common task when refactoring is to encapsulate an existing class variable with a property. This is what the Encapsulate Field refactoring action does. To invoke this action, select the variable you want to encapsulate and then choose the appropriate refactoring action from the context menu. This gives you the opportunity to name the property and elect where to search for references to the variable, as shown in Figure 8-14.

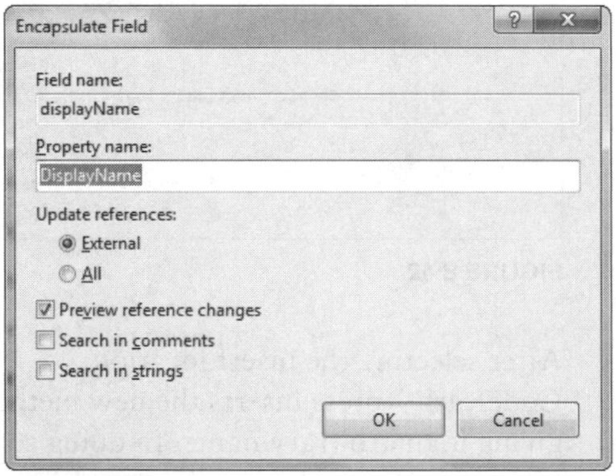

The next step after specifying the new property name is to determine which references to the class variable should be replaced with a reference to the new property. Figure 8-15 shows the preview window that

FIGURE 8-14

is returned after the reference search has been completed. In the top pane is a tree indicating which files and methods have references to the variable. The checkbox beside each row indicates whether a replacement will be made. Selecting a row in the top pane brings that line of code into focus in the lower pane. Once each of the references has been validated, the encapsulation can proceed. The class variable is updated to be private, and the appropriate references are also updated.

The Encapsulate Field refactoring action using CodeRush Xpress works in a similar way, except that it automatically assigns the name of the property based on the name of the class variable. The interface for updating references is also different, as shown in Figure 8-16. Instead of a modal dialog,

CodeRush Xpress presents a visual aid that can be used to navigate through the references (or you can navigate between references using the Tab key). Where a replacement is required, click the check mark or press Enter. Unlike the C# dialog box, in which the checkboxes can be checked and unchecked as many times as needed, once you accept a replacement there is no way to undo this action.

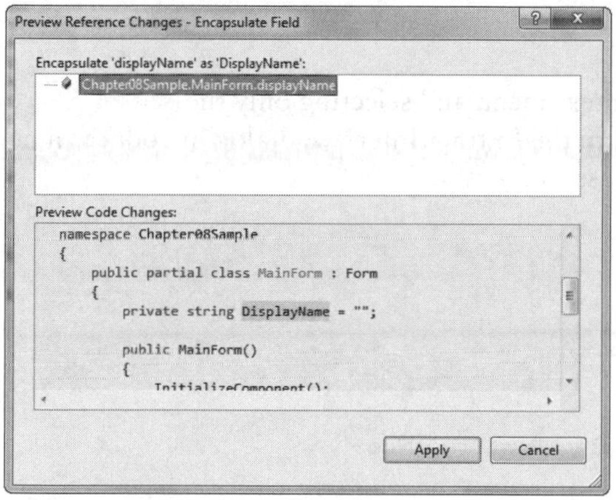

FIGURE 8-15

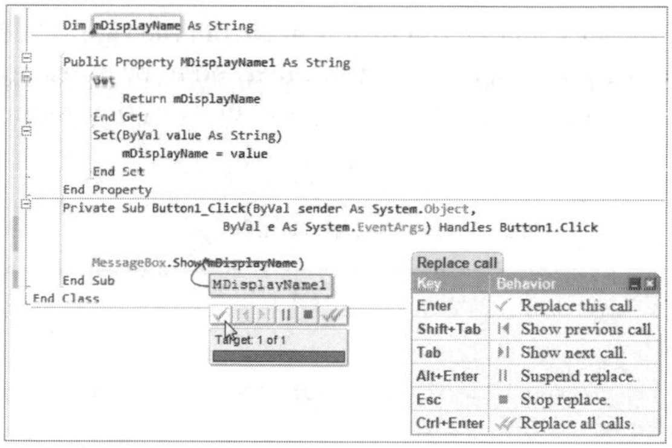

FIGURE 8-16

Extract Interface

As a project goes from prototype or early-stage development to a full implementation or growth phase, it's often necessary to extract the core methods for a class into an interface to enable other implementations or to define a boundary between disjointed systems. In the past you could do this by copying the entire method to a new file and removing the method contents so you were just left with the interface stub. The Extract Interface refactoring action enables you to extract an interface based on any number of methods within a class. When this refactoring action is invoked on a class, the dialog in Figure 8-17 is displayed, which enables you to select which methods are included in the interface. Once selected, those methods are added to the new interface. The new interface is also added to the original class.

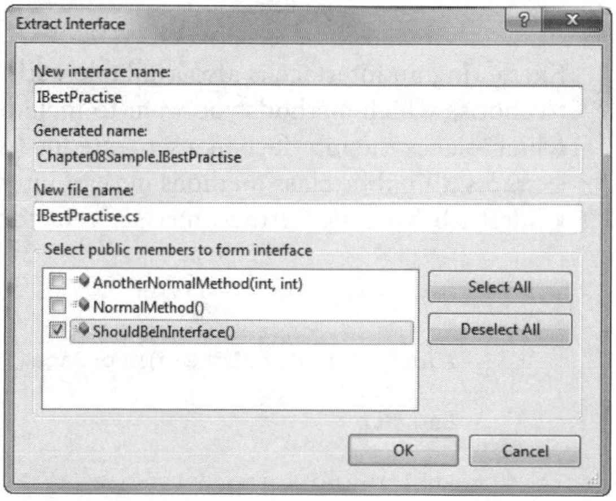

In the following example, the first method needs to be extracted into an interface:

FIGURE 8-17

C#

```csharp
public class ConcreteClass
{
    public void ShouldBeInInterface()
```

```
        { /* ... */ }

        public void AnotherNormalMethod(int ParameterA, int ParameterB)
        { /* ... */ }

        public void NormalMethod()
        { /* ... */ }
    }
```

Selecting Extract Interface from the right-click context menu and selecting only the
`ShouldBeInInterface` method to be extracted from the Extract Interface dialog introduces a new
interface (in a new file) and updates the original class as follows:

C#

```
interface IBestPractice
{
    void ShouldBeInInterface();
}

public class ConcreteClass: Chapter08Sample.IBestPractice
{
    public void ShouldBeInInterface()
    { /* ... */ }

    public void NormalMethod(int ParameterA, int ParameterB)
    { /* ... */ }

    public void AnotherNormalMethod()
    { /* ... */ }
}
```

Extracting an interface is also available within CodeRush Xpress, however it doesn't allow you
to choose which methods you want to include in the interface. Unlike the C# interface extraction,
which places the interface in a separate file (which is recommended), CodeRush Xpress simply
extracts all public class methods into an interface in the same code file. For example, using
CodeRush Xpress's Extract Interface refactoring action on the following class:

VB

```
Public Class ConcreteClass
    Public Sub ShouldBeInInterface()
        '...
    End Sub

    Public Sub NormalMethod(ByVal ParameterA As Integer,
                            ByVal ParameterB As Integer)
        '...
    End Sub

    Public Sub AnotherNormalMethod()
        '...
    End Sub
End Class
```

Will result in the following code:

VB

```vb
Public Interface IConcreteClass
    Sub ShouldBeInInterface()
    Sub NormalMethod(ByVal ParameterA As Integer, ByVal ParameterB As Integer)
    Sub AnotherNormalMethod()
End Interface

Public Class ConcreteClass
    Implements IConcreteClass
    Public Sub ShouldBeInInterface() Implements IConcreteClass.ShouldBeInInterface
        '...
    End Sub

    Public Sub NormalMethod(ByVal ParameterA As Integer,
                            ByVal ParameterB As Integer) _
                            Implements IConcreteClass.NormalMethod
        '...
    End Sub

    Public Sub AnotherNormalMethod() Implements IConcreteClass.AnotherNormalMethod
        '...
    End Sub
End Class
```

Reorder Parameters

Sometimes it's necessary to reorder parameters. This is often for cosmetic reasons, but it can also aid readability and is sometimes warranted when implementing interfaces. The Reorder Parameters dialog, shown in Figure 8-18, enables you to move parameters up and down in the list according to the order in which you want them to appear.

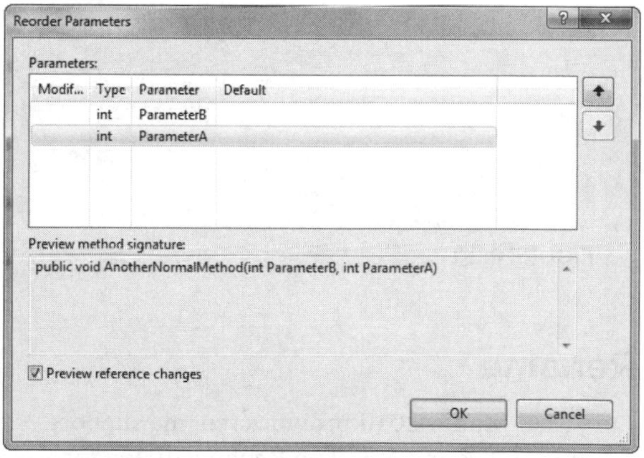

Once you establish the correct order, you're given the opportunity to preview the changes. By default, the parameters in every reference to this method are reordered according to the new order. The Preview dialog, similar to the one shown in Figure 8-15, enables you to control which references are updated.

The CodeRush Xpress experience for reordering parameters is somewhat more intuitive than the native action for C#. Again, the creators have opted for visual aids instead of a modal dialog, as shown in Figure 8-19. You can move the selected parameter left or

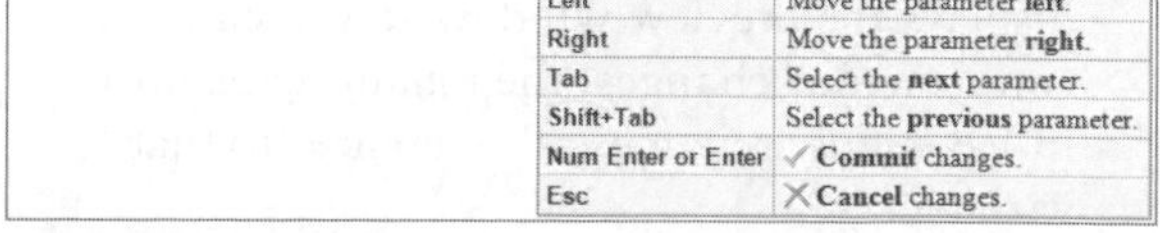

FIGURE 8-18

FIGURE 8-19

right in the parameter list and navigate between parameters with the Tab key. Once the parameters are in the desired order, the search and replace interface, illustrated in Figure 8-16, enables the developer to verify all updates.

Remove Parameters

When removing a parameter from a method, using the refactoring function to do this considerably reduces the amount of searching that has to be done for compile errors that can occur when a parameter is removed. The other time this action is particularly useful is when there are multiple overloads for a method, and removing a parameter may not generate compile errors; in such a case, runtime errors may occur due to semantic, rather than syntactical, mistakes.

Figure 8-20 illustrates the Remove Parameters dialog that is used to remove parameters from the parameters list. If a parameter is accidentally removed, it can be easily restored until the correct parameter list is arranged. As the warning on this dialog indicates, removing parameters can often result in unexpected functional errors, so it is important to review the changes made. Again, you can use the preview window to validate the proposed changes.

CodeRush Xpress only supports removing unused parameters, as shown in Figure 8-21.

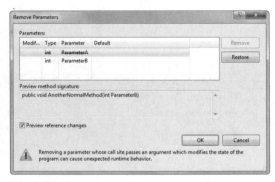

FIGURE 8-20

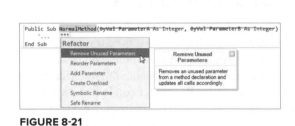

FIGURE 8-21

Rename

Visual Studio 2010 provides rename support in both C# and VB. The Rename dialog for C# is shown in Figure 8-22; it is similar in VB although it doesn't have the options to search in comments or strings.

Unlike the C# rename support, which displays the preview window so you can confirm your changes, the rename capability in VB simply renames all references to that variable.

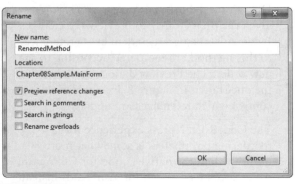

FIGURE 8-22

Promote Variable to Parameter

One of the most common refactoring techniques is to adapt an existing method to accept an additional parameter. Promoting a method variable to a parameter makes the method more generic. It also promotes code reuse. Intuitively, this operation would introduce compile errors wherever the method was referenced. However, the catch is that the variable you are promoting to a parameter must have an initial constant value. This value is added as a parameter value to all the method references to prevent any changes to functionality. Starting with the following snippet, if the method variable output is promoted, you end up with the second snippet:

VB

```
Private Sub MethodA()
    MethodB()
End Sub

Private Sub MethodB()
    Dim output As String = "Test String"
    MessageBox.Show(output)
End Sub
```

C#

```
public void MethodA()
{
    MethodB();
}
public void MethodB()
{
    string output = "Test String";
    MessageBox.Show( output);
}
```

After the variable is promoted, you can see that the initial value is now being passed through as a parameter wherever this method is referenced:

VB

```
Private Sub MethodA()
    MethodB("Test String")
End Sub

Private Sub MethodB(ByVal output As String)
    MessageBox.Show(output)
End Sub
```

C#

```
public void MethodA()
{
    MethodB("Test String");
}
public void MethodB(string output)
{
    MessageBox.Show( output);
}
```

Generate Method Stub

As you write code, you may realize that you need to call a method that you haven't written yet. For example, the following snippet illustrates a new method that you need to generate at some later stage:

VB

```vb
Private Sub MethodA()
    Dim InputA As String
    Dim InputB As Double
    Dim OutputC As Integer = NewMethodIJustThoughtOf(InputA, InputB)
End Sub
```

C#

```csharp
public void MethodA()
{
    string InputA;
    double InputB;
    int OutputC = NewMethodIJustThoughtOf(InputA, InputB);
}
```

Of course, the preceding code generates a build error because this method has not been defined. Using the Generate Method Stub refactoring action (available as a smart tag in the code itself), you can generate a method stub. As you can see from the following sample, the method stub is complete with input parameters and output type:

VB

```vb
Private Function NewMethodIJustThoughtOf(ByVal InputA As String,
                                         ByVal InputB As Double) As Integer
    Throw New NotImplementedException
End Function
```

C#

```csharp
private int NewMethodIJustThoughtOf(string InputA, double InputB)
{
    throw new Exception("The method or operation is not implemented.");
}
```

Organize Usings

It's good practice to maintain a sorted list of Using statements in each file (in C#), and only reference those namespaces that are actually required within that file. The Organize Usings menu (available from the context menu when right-clicking in the code editor as shown in Figure 8-23) can help you in both these cases.

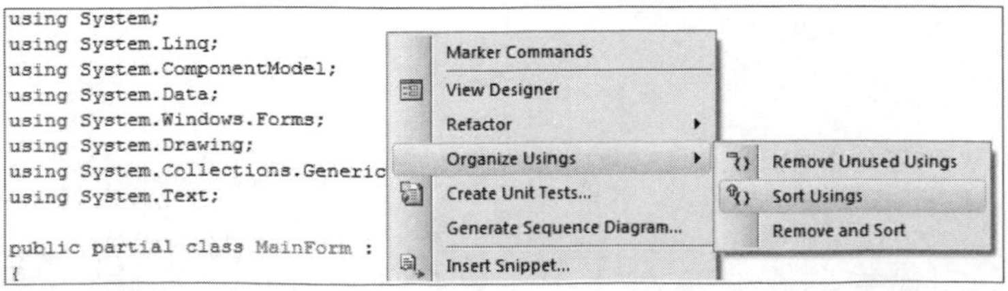

FIGURE 8-23

After a major refactoring of your code you may find that you have a number of using directives at the top of your code file that are no longer being used. Rather than going through a process of trial and error to determine what is and isn't being used, you can use an operation in Visual Studio to do this for you by right-clicking in the code editor and choosing Organize Usings ➪ Remove Unused Usings (C# only). Using directives, using aliases, and external assembly aliases not being used in the code file are removed.

> *VB developers don't have a way to sort and remove unused* Imports *statements. However, on the References tab on the Project Properties dialog, it's possible to mark namespaces to be imported into every code file. This can save significantly on the number of* Imports *statements. On this page you also have the ability to remove unused assembly references.*

It's good practice to organize the using directives in alphabetical order to make it easy to manage what namespaces are being referenced. To save you doing this manually you can right-click in the code editor and choose Organize Usings ➪ Sort Usings to have Visual Studio do this for you. The using directives from the System namespace appear first, then the using directives from other namespaces appear in alphabetical order. If you have aliases defined for namespaces, these are moved to the bottom of the list, and if you are using external assembly aliases (using the extern keyword in C#), these are moved to the top of the list.

To sort using directives and remove those that are not being used in one action, right-click in the code editor and choose Organize Usings ➪ Remove and Sort.

> *The default Visual Studio template code files have the using statements at the top of the file outside the namespace block. However, if you are following the StyleCop guidelines these specify that using statements should be contained within the namespace block. The Organize Usings functions handle either situation based upon the current location of the using statements in the file and retaining that location.*

SUMMARY

Code snippets are a valuable inclusion in the Visual Studio 2010 feature set. You learned in this chapter how to use them, and how to create your own, including variable substitution (and Imports and reference associations for VB snippets). With this information you'll be able to create your own library of code snippets from functionality that you use frequently, saving you time in coding similar constructs later.

This chapter also provided examples of each of the refactoring actions available within Visual Studio 2010. Although VB developers do not get complete refactoring support out of the box, CodeRush Xpress provides a wide range of refactoring actions that enable them to easily refactor their projects.

9

Server Explorer

➤ Querying hardware resources and services on local and remote computers

➤ Using the Server Explorer to easily add code that works with computer resources to your applications

The Server Explorer is one of the few tool windows in Visual Studio that is not specific to a solution or project. It allows you to explore and query hardware resources and services on local or remote computers. You can perform various tasks and activities with these resources, including adding them to your applications.

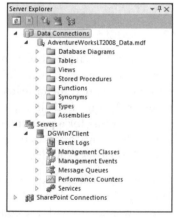

FIGURE 9-1

The Server Explorer, shown in Figure 9-1, has three types of resources to which it can connect. The first, under the Servers node, enables you to access hardware resources and services on a local or remote computer. This functionality is explored in detail in this chapter. The second type of resources is under the Data Connections node and allows you to work with all aspects of data connections, including the ability to create databases, add and modify tables, build relationships, and even execute queries. Chapter 26 covers the Data Connections functionality in detail. Finally, you can add a connection to a SharePoint server and browse SharePoint-specific resources such as Content Types, Lists, Libraries, and Workflows. SharePoint connections are covered in more detail in Chapter 24.

SERVER CONNECTIONS

The Servers node would be better named Computers, because it can be used to attach to and interrogate any computer to which you have access, regardless of whether it is a server or a desktop workstation. Each computer is listed as a separate node under the Servers node. Below each computer node is a list of the hardware, services, and other components that belong to that computer. Each of these contains a number of activities or tasks that can be performed. Several software vendors have components that plug into and extend the functionality provided by the Server Explorer.

To access Server Explorer, select Server Explorer on the View menu. By default, the local computer appears in the Servers list. To add another computer, right-click the Servers node and select Add Server from the context menu.

Entering a computer name or IP address initiates an attempt to connect to the machine using your credentials. If you do not have sufficient privileges, you can elect to connect using a different username by clicking the appropriate link. The link appears to be disabled, but clicking it does bring up a dialog, shown in Figure 9-2, in which you can provide an alternative username and password.

FIGURE 9-2

> *You will need Administrator privileges on any server that you want to access through the Server Explorer.*

Event Logs

The Event Logs node gives you access to the machine event logs. You can launch the Event Viewer from the right-click context menu. Alternatively, as shown in Figure 9-3, you can drill into the list of event logs to view the events for a particular application. Clicking any of the events displays information about the event in the Properties window.

Although the Server Explorer is useful for interrogating a machine while writing your code, the true power comes with the component creation you get when you drag a resource node onto a Windows Form. For example, if you drag the Application node onto a Windows Form, you get an instance of the `System.Diagnostics.EventLog` class added to the nonvisual area of the designer. You can then write an entry to this event log using the following code:

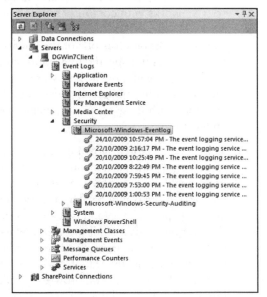

FIGURE 9-3

Available for download on Wrox.com

C#

```csharp
this.eventLog1.Source = "My Server Explorer App";
this.eventLog1.WriteEntry("Something happened",
                System.Diagnostics.EventLogEntryType.Information);
```

Code snippet Form1.cs

VB

```vb
Me.EventLog1.Source = "My Server Explorer App"
Me.EventLog1.WriteEntry("Something happened",
                    System.Diagnostics.EventLogEntryType.Information)
```

Code snippet Form1.vb

> *Because the preceding code creates a new Source in the Application Event Log,*
> *it requires administrative rights to execute. If you are running Windows Vista or*
> *Windows 7 with User Account Control enabled, you should create an*
> *application manifest. This is discussed in Chapter 6.*

After you run this code, you can view the results directly in the Server Explorer. Click the Refresh
button on the Server Explorer toolbar to ensure that the new Event Source is displayed under the
Application Event Log node.

For Visual Basic programmers, an alternative to adding an `EventLog` class to your code is to use
the built-in logging provided by the `My` namespace. For example, you can modify the previous code
snippet to write a log entry using the `My.Application.Log.WriteEntry` method:

VB

```vb
My.Application.Log.WriteEntry("Button Clicked", TraceEventType.Information)
```

You can also write exception information using the `My.Application.Log.WriteException`
method, which accepts an exception and two optional parameters that provide additional
information.

Using the `My` namespace to write logging information has a number of additional benefits.
In the following configuration file, an `EventLogTraceListener` is specified to route log
information to the event log. However, you can specify other trace listeners — for example,
the `FileLogTraceListener`, which writes information to a log file by adding it to the
`SharedListeners` and `Listeners` collections:

```xml
<?xml version="1.0" encoding="utf-8" ?>
<configuration>
    <system.diagnostics>
        <sources>
            <source name="DefaultSource" switchName="DefaultSwitch">
                <listeners>
                    <add name="EventLog"/>
                </listeners>
            </source>
        </sources>
        <switches>
            <add name="DefaultSwitch" value="Information"/>
        </switches>
```

```
        <sharedListeners>
            <add name="EventLog"
                type="System.Diagnostics.EventLogTraceListener"
                initializeData="ApplicationEventLog"/>
        </sharedListeners>
    </system.diagnostics>
</configuration>
```

This configuration also specifies a switch called `DefaultSwitch`. This switch is associated with the trace information source via the `switchName` attribute and defines the minimum event type that will be sent to the listed listeners. For example, if the value of this switch were `Critical`, events with the type Information would not be written to the event log. The possible values of this switch are shown in Table 9-1.

TABLE 9-1: Values for DefaultSwitch

DEFAULTSWITCH	EVENT TYPES WRITTEN TO LOG
Off	No Events
Critical	Critical Events
Error	Critical and Error Events
Warning	Critical, Error, and Warning Events
Information	Critical, Error, Warning, and Information events
Verbose	Critical, Error, Warning, Information, and Verbose events
ActivityTracing	Start, Stop, Suspend, Resume, and Transfer events
All	All Events

Note that there are overloads for both `WriteEntry` and `WriteException` that do not require an event type to be specified. In this case the event types will default to Information and Error, respectively.

Management Classes

Figure 9-4 shows the full list of management classes available via the Server Explorer. Each node exposes a set of functionalities specific to that device or application. For example, right-clicking the Printers node enables you to add a new printer connection, whereas right-clicking the named node under My Computer enables you to add the computer to a domain or workgroup. The one thing common to all these nodes is that they provide a strongly typed wrapper around the Windows Management Instrumentation (WMI) infrastructure. In most cases, it is simply a matter of dragging the node

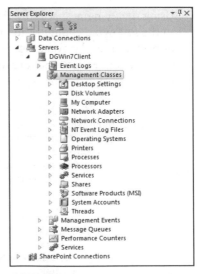

FIGURE 9-4

representing the information in which you're interested across to the form. From your code you can then access and manipulate that information.

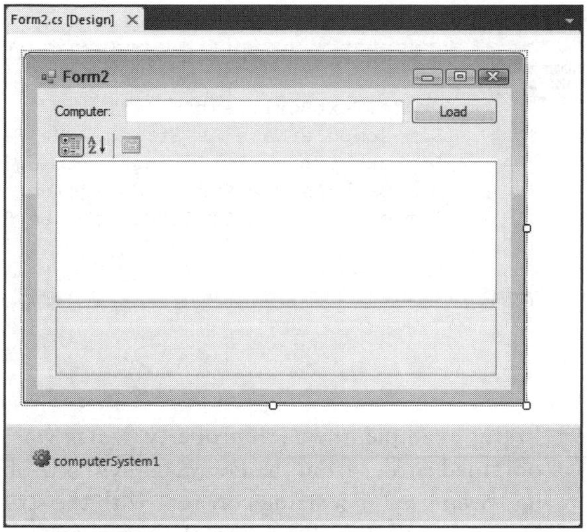

To give you an idea of how these wrappers can be used, this section walks through how you can use the management classes to retrieve information about a computer. Under the My Computer node, you will see a node with the name of the local computer. Selecting this node and dragging it onto the form gives you a `ComputerSystem` component in the nonvisual area of the form. Also add a Label control, a TextBox control, a Button, and a PropertyGrid control from the All Windows Forms tab on the Toolbox and arrange them on the Form as shown in Figure 9-5.

FIGURE 9-5

If you look in the Solution Explorer, you will see that it has also added a custom component called `root.CIMV2.Win32_ComputerSystem` (or similar depending on the computer configuration). This custom component is generated by the Management Strongly Typed Class Generator (`Mgmtclassgen.exe`) and includes the `ComputerSystem` and other classes, which will enable you to expose WMI information.

If you click the `computerSystem1` object on the form, you can see the information about that computer in the Properties window. In this application, however, you're not that interested in that particular computer; that computer was selected as a template to create the `ComputerSystem` class. The `ComputerSystem1` object can be deleted, but before deleting it, take note of the `Path` property of the object. The `Path` is used, combined with the computer name entered in the form in Figure 9-5, to load the information about that computer. You can see this in the following code that is added to the button click event handler for the Load button:

C#

```csharp
const string compPath = "\\\\{0}\\root\\CIMV2:Win32_ComputerSystem.Name=\"{0}\"";

if (!string.IsNullOrEmpty(this.textBox1.Text))
{
    string computerName = this.textBox1.Text;
    string pathString = string.Format(compPath, computerName);
    var path = new System.Management.ManagementPath(pathString);
    ROOT.CIMV2.ComputerSystem cs = new ROOT.CIMV2.ComputerSystem(path);

    this.propertyGrid1.SelectedObject = cs;
}
```

Code snippet Form2.cs

VB

```vb
Const compPath As String = "\\{0}\root\CIMV2:Win32_ComputerSystem.Name=""{0}"""

If Not Me.TextBox1.Text = "" Then
    Dim computerName As String = Me.TextBox1.Text
    Dim pathString As String = String.Format(compPath, computerName)
    Dim path As New System.Management.ManagementPath(pathString)
    Dim cs As New ROOT.CIMV2.ComputerSystem(path)

    Me.PropertyGrid1.SelectedObject = cs
End If
```

Code snippet Form2.vb

In this example, the Path property, which was obtained earlier from the computerSystem1 object, has been used in a string constant with the string replacement token {0} where the computer name should go. When the button is clicked, the computer name entered into the textbox is combined with this path using String.Format to generate the full WMI path. The path is then used to instantiate a new ComputerAccount object, which is in turn passed to the PropertyGrid control. The result of this at run time is shown in Figure 9-6.

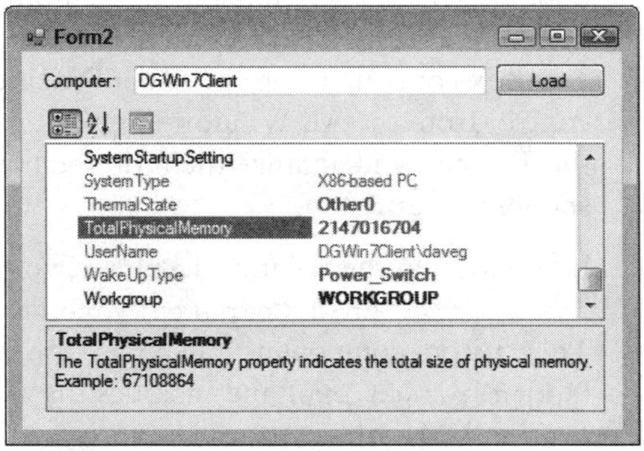

FIGURE 9-6

Though most properties are read-only, for those fields that are editable, changes made in this PropertyGrid are immediately committed to the computer. This behavior can be altered by changing the AutoCommit property on the ComputerSystem class.

Management Events

In the previous section you learned how you can drag a management class from the Server Explorer onto the form and then work with the generated classes. The other way to work with the WMI interface is through the Management Events node. A management event enables you to monitor any WMI data type and have an event raised if an object of that type is created, modified, or deleted. By default, this node is empty, but you can create your own by right-clicking the Management Events node and selecting Add Event Query, which invokes the dialog shown in Figure 9-7.

Use this dialog to locate the WMI data type in which you are interested. Because there are literally thousands of these, it is useful to use the Find box. In Figure 9-7, the search term "process" was entered, and the class CIM Processes was found

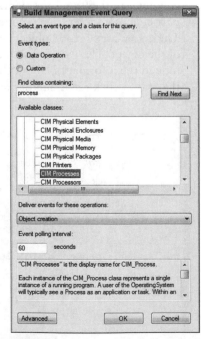

FIGURE 9-7

under the root\CIMV2 node. Each instance of this class represents a single process running on the system. You are only interested in being notified when a new process is created, so ensure that Object Creation is selected from the drop-down menu.

After clicking OK, a CIM Processes Event Query node is added to the Management Events node. If you open a new instance of an application on your system, such as Notepad, you will see events being progressively added to this node. In the Build Management Event Query dialog shown in Figure 9-7, the default polling interval was set to 60 seconds, so you may need to wait up to 60 seconds for the event to show up in the tree once you have made the change.

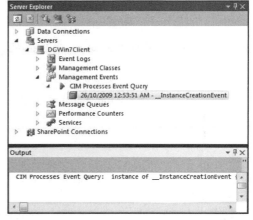

When the event does finally show up, it appears along with the date and time in the Server Explorer, and it also appears in the Output window, as shown in the lower pane of Figure 9-8. If you select the event, you will notice that the Properties window is populated with a large number of properties that don't really make any sense. However, once you know which of the properties to query, it is quite easy to trap, filter, and respond to system events.

FIGURE 9-8

To continue the example, drag a CheckBox control and a ListBox control from the Toolbox onto a new Windows Form.

Next drag the CIM Processes Event Query node from the Server Explorer onto a new form. This generates an instance of the `System.Management.ManagementEventWatcher` class, with properties configured so it will listen for the creation of a new process. The actual query can be accessed via the `QueryString` property of the nested `ManagementQuery` object. As with most watcher classes, the `ManagementEventWatch` class triggers an event when the watch conditions are met — in this case, the `EventArrived` event. To handle this event, add the following code:

Available for download on Wrox.com

C#

```csharp
private void managementEventWatcher1_EventArrived(System.Object sender,
                               System.Management.EventArrivedEventArgs e)
{
    foreach (System.Management.PropertyData p in e.NewEvent.Properties)
    {
        if (p.Name == "TargetInstance")
        {
            var mbo = (System.Management.ManagementBaseObject)p.Value;
            string[] sCreatedProcess = {(string)mbo.Properties["Name"].Value,
                               (string)mbo.Properties["ExecutablePath"].
                               Value };
            this.BeginInvoke(new LogNewProcessDelegate(LogNewProcess),
                    sCreatedProcess);
        }
    }
}
```

```csharp
delegate void LogNewProcessDelegate(string ProcessName, string ExePath);
private void LogNewProcess(string ProcessName, string ExePath)
{
    this.listBox1.Items.Add(string.Format("{0}-{1}", ProcessName, ExePath));
}

private void checkBox1_CheckedChanged(System.Object sender, System.EventArgs e)
{
    if (this.checkBox1.Checked)
    {
        this.managementEventWatcher1.Start();
    }
    else
    {
        this.managementEventWatcher1.Stop();
    }
}
```

Code snippet Form3.cs

VB

```vbnet
Private Sub ManagementEventWatcher1_EventArrived(ByVal sender As System.Object, _
                        ByVal e As System.Management.EventArrivedEventArgs)
    For Each p As System.Management.PropertyData In e.NewEvent.Properties
        If p.Name = "TargetInstance" Then
            Dim mbo As System.Management.ManagementBaseObject = _
                    CType(p.Value, System.Management.ManagementBaseObject)
            Dim sCreatedProcess As String() = {mbo.Properties("Name").Value, _
                                    mbo.Properties("ExecutablePath").Value}
            Me.BeginInvoke(New LogNewProcessDelegate(AddressOf LogNewProcess), _
                    sCreatedProcess)
        End If
    Next
End Sub

Delegate Sub LogNewProcessDelegate(ByVal ProcessName As String, _
                        ByVal ExePath As String)
Private Sub LogNewProcess(ByVal ProcessName As String, ByVal ExePath As String)
    Me.ListBox1.Items.Add(String.Format("{0}-{1}", ProcessName, ExePath))
End Sub

Private Sub CheckBox1_CheckedChanged(ByVal sender As System.Object, _
                                    ByVal e As System.EventArgs) _
                                    Handles CheckBox1.CheckedChanged
    If Me.CheckBox1.Checked Then
        Me.ManagementEventWatcher1.Start()
    Else
        Me.ManagementEventWatcher1.Stop()
    End If
End Sub
```

Code snippet Form3.vb

In the event handler, you need to iterate through the `Properties` collection on the `NewEvent` object. Where an object has changed, two instances are returned: `PreviousInstance`, which holds the state at the beginning of the polling interval, and `TargetInstance`, which holds the state at the end of the polling interval. It is possible for the object to change state multiple times within the same polling period. If this is the case, an event will be triggered only when the state at the end of the period differs from the state at the beginning of the period. For example, no event is raised if a process is started and then stopped within a single polling interval.

The event handler constructs a new `ManagementBaseObject` from a value passed into the event arguments to obtain the display name and executable path of the new process. Since UI controls can only be updated from the UI thread, you cannot directly update the ListBox. Instead you must call `BeginInvoke` to execute the `LogNewProcess` function on the UI thread. Figure 9-9 shows the form in action.

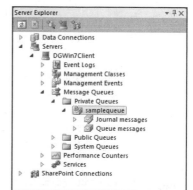

FIGURE 9-9

Message Queues

The Message Queues node, expanded in Figure 9-10, gives you access to the message queues available on your computer. You can use three types of queues: private, which will not appear when a foreign computer queries your computer; public, which will appear; and system, which is used for unsent messages and other exception reporting.

> *To use the Message Queues node, you need to ensure that MSMQ is installed on your computer. You can do this via Programs and Features in the Control Panel. Select the* Turn Windows Features On or Off *task menu item and then select the checkbox to enable the Microsoft Message Queue (MSMQ) Server feature.*

In Figure 9-10, a message queue called samplequeue has been added to the Private Queues node by selecting Create Queue from the right-click context menu. Once you have created a queue, you can create a properly configured instance of the `MessageQueue` class by dragging the queue onto a new Windows Form. To demonstrate the functionality of the `MessageQueue` object, add two TextBoxes and a button to the form, laid out as shown in Figure 9-11. The Send button is wired up to use the `MessageQueue` object to send the message entered in the first textbox. In the `Load` event for the form, a background thread is created that continually polls the queue to retrieve messages, which will populate the second textbox:

FIGURE 9-10

Available for download on Wrox.com

```csharp
C#
public Form4()
{
    InitializeComponent();
    var monitorThread = new System.Threading.Thread(MonitorMessageQueue);
```

```csharp
    monitorThread.IsBackground = true;
    monitorThread.Start();
    this.Button1.Click +=new EventHandler(btn_Click);
}

private void btn_Click(object sender, EventArgs e)
{
    this.messageQueue1.Send(this.TextBox1.Text);
}

private void MonitorMessageQueue()
{
    var m = default(System.Messaging.Message);
    while (true)
    {
        try
        {
            m = this.messageQueue1.Receive(new TimeSpan(0, 0, 0, 0, 50));
            this.ReceiveMessage((string)m.Body);
        }
        catch (System.Messaging.MessageQueueException ex)
        {
            if (!(ex.MessageQueueErrorCode ==
                    System.Messaging.MessageQueueErrorCode.IOTimeout))
            {
                throw ex;
            }
        }
        System.Threading.Thread.Sleep(10000);
    }
}

private delegate void MessageDel(string msg);
private void ReceiveMessage(string msg)
{
    if (this.InvokeRequired)
    {
        this.BeginInvoke(new MessageDel(ReceiveMessage), msg);
        return;
    }
    this.TextBox2.Text = msg;
}
```

Code snippet Form4.cs

VB

```vbnet
Private Sub Form_Load(ByVal sender As Object, ByVal e As System.EventArgs) _
                    Handles Me.Load
    Dim monitorThread As New Threading.Thread(AddressOf MonitorMessageQueue)
    monitorThread.IsBackground = True
    monitorThread.Start()
End Sub
```

```
    Private Sub btn_Click(ByVal sender As System.Object, ByVal e As System.EventArgs) _
                        Handles Button1.Click
        Me.MessageQueue1.Send(Me.TextBox1.Text)
    End Sub

    Private Sub MonitorMessageQueue()
        Dim m As Messaging.Message
        While True
            Try
                m = Me.MessageQueue1.Receive(New TimeSpan(0, 0, 0, 0, 50))
                Me.ReceiveMessage(m.Body)
            Catch ex As Messaging.MessageQueueException
                If Not ex.MessageQueueErrorCode = _
                        Messaging.MessageQueueErrorCode.IOTimeout Then
                    Throw ex
                End If
            End Try
            Threading.Thread.Sleep(10000)
        End While
    End Sub

    Private Delegate Sub MessageDel(ByVal msg As String)
    Private Sub ReceiveMessage(ByVal msg As String)
        If Me.InvokeRequired Then
            Me.BeginInvoke(New MessageDel(AddressOf ReceiveMessage), msg)
            Return
        End If
        Me.TextBox2.Text = msg
    End Sub
```

Code snippet Form4.vb

Note in this code snippet that the background thread is never explicitly closed. Because the thread has the `IsBackground` property set to `True`, it is automatically terminated when the application exits. As with the previous example, because the message processing is done in a background thread, you need to switch threads when you update the user interface using the `BeginInvoke` method. Putting this all together, you get a form like the one shown in Figure 9-11.

As messages are sent to the message queue, they appear under the appropriate queue in Server Explorer. Clicking the message displays its contents in the Properties window.

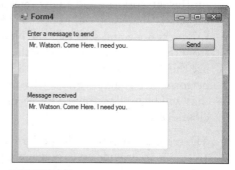

FIGURE 9-11

Performance Counters

One of the most common things developers forget to consider when building an application is how it will be maintained and managed. For example, consider an application that was installed a year ago and has been operating without any issues. All of a sudden, requests start taking an unacceptable amount of time. It is clear that the application is not behaving correctly, but there is no way to determine the cause of the misbehavior. One strategy for identifying where the performance issues are is to use performance counters. Windows has many built-in performance counters that can be used to monitor operating system activity, and a lot of third-party software also installs performance counters so administrators can identify any rogue behavior.

The Performance Counters node in the Server Explorer tree, expanded in Figure 9-12, has two primary functions. First, it enables you to view and retrieve information about the currently installed counters. You can also create new

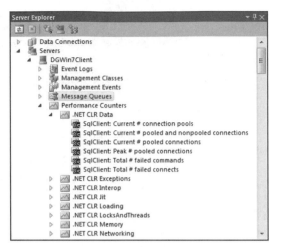

FIGURE 9-12

performance counters, as well as edit or delete existing counters. As you can see in Figure 9-12, under the Performance Counters node is a list of categories and under those is a list of counters.

 You must be running Visual Studio with Administrator rights to view the Performance Counters under the Server Explorer.

To edit either the category or the counters, select Edit Category from the right-click context menu for the category. To add a new category and associated counters, right-click the Performance Counters node and select Create New Category from the context menu. Both of these operations use the dialog shown in Figure 9-13. Here, a new performance counter category has been created that will be used to track a form's open and close events.

The second function of the Performance Counters section is to provide an easy way for you to access performance counters via your code. By dragging a performance counter category onto a form, you gain access to read and write to that performance counter. To continue with this chapter's example, drag the new My Application performance counters, Form Open and Form Close, onto a new

FIGURE 9-13

Windows Form. Also add a couple of textboxes and a button so you can display the performance counter values. Finally, rename the performance counters so they have friendly names. This should give you a form similar to the one shown in Figure 9-14.

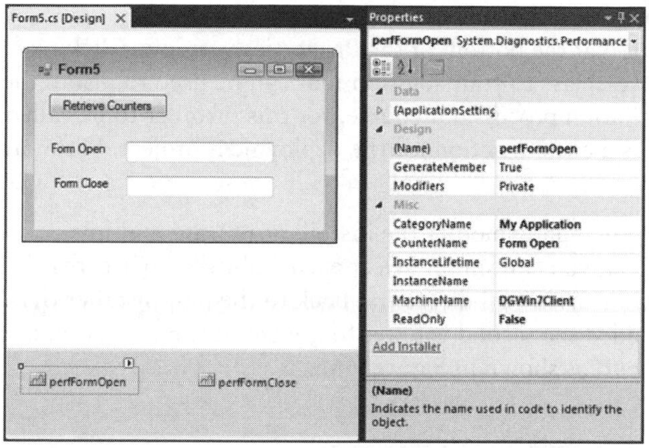

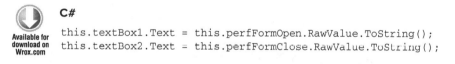

FIGURE 9-14

In the properties for the selected performance counter, you can see that the appropriate counter — in this case, Form Close — has been selected from the My Application category. You will also notice a `MachineName` property, which is the computer from which you are retrieving the counter information, and a `ReadOnly` property, which needs to be set to `False` if you want to update the counter. (By default, the `ReadOnly` property is set to `True`.) To complete this form, add the following code to the Retrieve Counters button click event handler:

Available for download on Wrox.com

C#

```
this.textBox1.Text = this.perfFormOpen.RawValue.ToString();
this.textBox2.Text = this.perfFormClose.RawValue.ToString();
```

Code snippet Form5.cs

Available for download on Wrox.com

VB

```
Me.textBox1.Text = Me.perfFormOpen.RawValue
Me.textBox2.Text = Me.perfFormClose.RawValue
```

Code snippet Form5.vb

You also need to add code to the application to update the performance counters. For example, you might have the following code in the Form `Load` event handlers:

C#

```
this.perfFormOpen.Increment();
```

VB

```
Me.perfFormOpen.Increment()
```

When you dragged the performance counter onto the form, you may have noticed a *smart tag* (small arrow that appears near the top-right corner when a control is selected) on the performance counter component that had a single item, Add Installer. When the component is selected, as in Figure 19-14, you will notice the same action at the bottom of the Properties window. Clicking this action in either place adds an `Installer` class to your solution that can be used to install the performance counter as part of your installation process. Of course, for this installer to be called, the assembly it belongs to must be added as a custom action for the deployment project. For more information on custom actions, see Chapter 48.

Prior to Visual Studio 2008, you needed to manually modify the installer to create multiple performance counters. In the current version, you can simply select each additional performance counter and click Add Installer. Visual Studio 2010 will direct you back to the first installer that was created and will have automatically added the second counter to the `Counters` collection of the `PerformanceCounterInstaller` component, as shown in Figure 9-15.

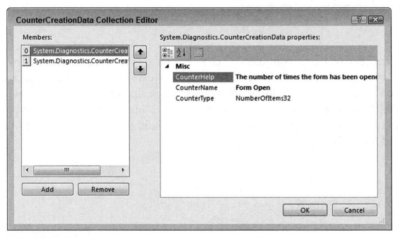

FIGURE 9-15

You can also add counters in other categories by adding additional `PerformanceCounterInstaller` components to the design surface. You are now ready to deploy your application with the knowledge that you will be able to use a tool such as PerfMon to monitor how your application is behaving.

Services

The Services node, expanded in Figure 9-16, shows the registered services for the computer. Each node indicates the state of that service in the bottom-right corner of the icon. Possible states are Stopped, Running, or Paused. Selecting a service displays additional information about the service, such as other service dependencies, in the Properties window.

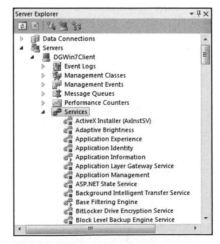

FIGURE 9-16

As with other nodes in the Server Explorer, each service can be dragged onto the design surface of a form. This generates a `ServiceController` component in the nonvisual area of the form. By default, the `ServiceName` property is set to the service that you dragged across from the Server Explorer, but this can be changed to access information and control any service. Similarly, the `MachineName` property can be changed to connect to any computer to which you have access. The following code shows how you can stop a Service using `ServiceController` component:

C#

```csharp
this.serviceController1.Refresh();
if (this.serviceController1.CanStop)
{
    if (this.serviceController1.Status ==
            System.ServiceProcess.ServiceControllerStatus.Running)
    {
        this.serviceController1.Stop();
        this.serviceController1.Refresh();
    }
}
```

Code snippet Form6.cs

VB

```vb
Me.ServiceController1.Refresh()
If Me.ServiceController1.CanStop Then
    If Me.ServiceController1.Status = _
            ServiceProcess.ServiceControllerStatus.Running Then
        Me.ServiceController1.Stop()
        Me.ServiceController1.Refresh()
    End If
End If
```

Code snippet Form6.vb

In addition to the three main states — Running, Paused, or Stopped — other transition states are ContinuePending, PausePending, StartPending, and StopPending. If you are about to start a service that may be dependent on another service that is in one of these transition states, you can call the `WaitForStatus` method to ensure that the service will start properly.

DATA CONNECTIONS

The Data Connections node allows you to connect to a database and perform a large range of administrative functions. You can connect to a wide variety of data sources including any edition of SQL Server, Microsoft Access, Oracle, or a generic ODBC data source. Figure 9-17 shows the Server Explorer connected to a SQL Server database file.

The Server Explorer provides access to the Visual Database, which will allow you to perform a large range of administrative functions on the connected database. You can create databases, add and modify tables, views, and stored procedures, manage indexes, execute queries, and much more. Chapter 26 covers all aspects of the Data Connections functionality.

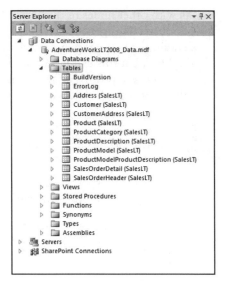

FIGURE 9-17

SHAREPOINT CONNECTIONS

New to Visual Studio 2010 is the ability to connect to a Microsoft Office SharePoint Server with the Server Explorer. This feature allows you to navigate and view many of the SharePoint resources and components.

The Server Explorer only provides read-only access to SharePoint resources — you cannot, for example, create or edit a list definition. Even so, it can be useful to have ready access to this information in Visual Studio when developing a SharePoint application. As with many of the components under the Servers Node you can also drag and drop certain SharePoint resources directly onto the design surface of your SharePoint project.

Using the Server Explorer to browse SharePoint resources is covered in detail in Chapter 24.

SUMMARY

In this chapter you learned how the Server Explorer can be used to manage and work with computer resources and services. Chapter 22 continues the discussion on the Server Explorer, covering the Data Connections node in more detail. Chapter 24 wraps it all up with an in-depth look at managing SharePoint resources using the Server Explorer.

10

Modeling with the Class Designer

WHAT'S IN THIS CHAPTER?

➤ Using the Class Designer to create a graphical visualization of your class architecture

➤ Easily generating and refactoring your classes with the Class Designer

➤ Using the Modeling Power Toys for Visual Studio 2010 add-in to better work with large class hierarchies

Traditionally, software modeling has been performed separately from coding, often during a design phase that is completed before coding begins. More often than not, the modeling diagrams that are constructed during design are not kept up to date as the development progresses, and they quickly lose their value as design changes are inevitably made.

The Class Designer in Visual Studio 2010 brings modeling into the IDE, as an activity that can be performed at any time during a development project. Class diagrams are constructed dynamically from the source code, which means that they are always up to date. Any change made to the source code is immediately reflected in the class diagram, and any change to the diagram is also made to the code.

This chapter looks at the Class Designer in detail and explains how you can use it to design, visualize, and refactor your class architecture.

CREATING A CLASS DIAGRAM

The design process for an application typically involves at least a sketch of the classes that are going to be created and how they interact. Visual Studio 2010 provides a design surface, called the Class Designer, onto which classes can be drawn to form a class diagram. Fields, properties, and methods can then be added to the classes, and relationships can be established between classes. Although this design is called a class diagram, it supports classes, structures, enumerations, interfaces, abstract classes, and delegates.

There is more than one way to add a Class Diagram to your project. One way to add a Class Diagram is through the Add New Item dialog, as shown in Figure 10-1. This will create a new blank Class Diagram within the project.

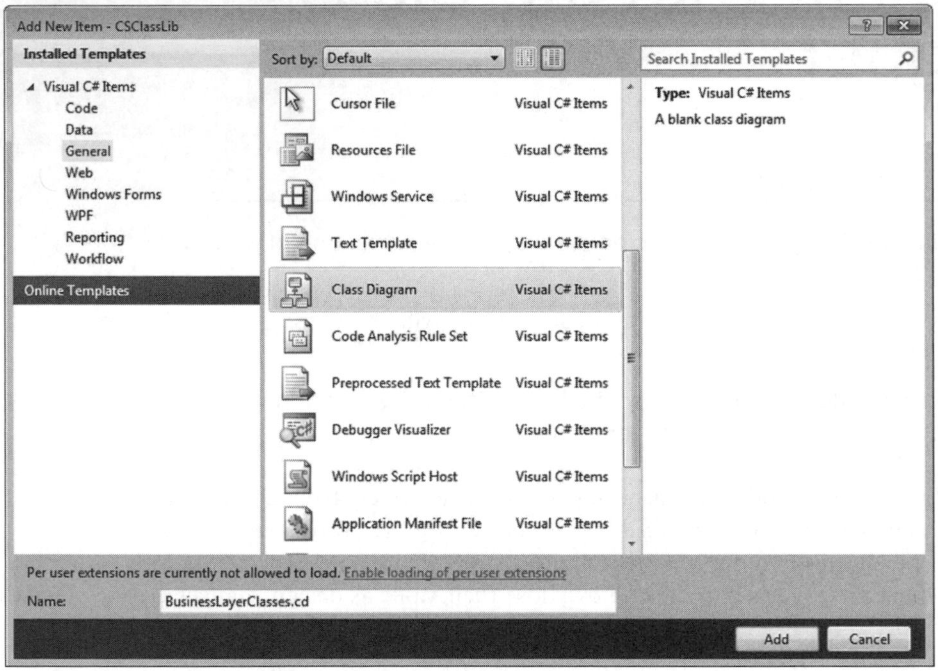

FIGURE 10-1

You can also add a new Class Diagram to your project by selecting the View Class Diagram button from the toolbar in the Solution Explorer window or by right-clicking a project or class and selecting the View Class Diagram menu item. If the project is selected when you create a Class Diagram in this way, Visual Studio will automatically add all the types defined within the project to the initial class diagram. Although this may be desirable in some instances, for a project that contains a large number of classes the process of creating and laying out the diagram can be quite time consuming.

Unlike some tools that require all types within a project to be on the same diagram, the class diagram can include as many or as few of your types as you want. This makes it possible to add multiple class diagrams to a single solution.

The scope of the Class Designer is limited to a single project. You cannot add types to a class diagram that are defined in a different project, even if it is part of the same solution.

The Class Designer can be divided into four components: the design surface, the Toolbox, the Class Details window, and the property grid. Changes made to the class diagram are saved in a `.cd` file, which works in parallel with the class code files to generate the visual layout shown in the Class Designer.

THE DESIGN SURFACE

The design surface of the Class Designer enables the developer to interact with types using a drag-and-drop-style interface. You can add existing types to the design surface by dragging them from either the class view or the Solution Explorer. If a file in the Solution Explorer contains more than one type, they are all added to the design surface.

Figure 10-2 shows a simple class diagram that contains two classes, `Customer` and `Order`, and an enumeration, `OrderStatus`. Each class contains fields, properties, methods, and events. There is an association between the classes, because a `Customer` class contains a property called `Orders` that is a list of `Order` objects, and the `Order` class implements the IDataErrorInfo interface. All this information is visible from this class diagram.

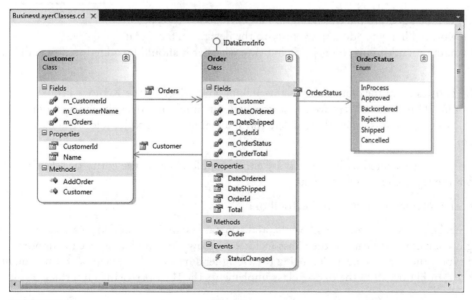

FIGURE 10-2

Each class appears as an entity on the class diagram, which can be dragged around the design surface and resized as required. A class is made up of fields, properties, methods, and events. In Figure 10-2, these components are grouped into compartments. You can select alternative layouts for the class diagram, such as listing the components in alphabetical order or grouping the components by accessibility.

The Class Designer is often used to view multiple classes to get an understanding of how they are associated. In this case, it is convenient to hide the components of a class to simplify the diagram. To hide all the components at once, use the toggle in the top-right corner of the class on the design surface. If only certain components need to be hidden, they can be individually hidden, or the entire compartment can be hidden, by right-clicking the appropriate element and selecting the Hide menu item.

THE TOOLBOX

To facilitate items being added to the class diagram there is a Class Designer tab in the Toolbox. To create an item, drag the item from the Toolbox onto the design surface or simply double-click it. Figure 10-3 shows the Toolbox with the Class Designer tab visible. The items in the Toolbox can be classified as either entities or connectors. Note the Comment item, which can be added to the Class Designer but does not appear in any of the code; it is there simply to aid documentation of the class diagram.

FIGURE 10-3

Entities

The entities that can be added to the class diagram all correspond to types in the .NET Framework. When you add a new entity to the design surface, you need to give it a name. In addition, you need to indicate whether it should be added to a new file or an existing file.

You can remove entities from the diagram by right-clicking and selecting the Remove From Diagram menu item. This does not remove the source code; it simply removes the entity from the diagram. In cases where it is desirable to delete the associated source code, select the Delete Code menu item.

You can view the code associated with an entity by either double-clicking the entity or selecting View Code from the right-click context menu.

The following list explains the entities in the Toolbox:

> **Class:** Fields, properties, methods, events, and constants can all be added to a class via the right-click context menu or the Class Details window. Although a class can support nested types, they cannot be added using the Designer surface. Classes can also implement interfaces. In Figure 10-2, the `Order` class implements the IDataErrorInfo interface.

➤ **Enum:** An enumeration can only contain a list of members that can have a value assigned to them. Each member also has a summary and remarks property, but these appear only as an XML comment against the member.

➤ **Interface:** Interfaces define properties, methods, and events that a class must implement. Interfaces can also contain nested types, but recall that adding a nested type is not supported by the Designer.

➤ **Abstract Class:** Abstract classes behave the same as classes except that they appear on the design surface with an italic name and are marked as Abstract (C#) or MustInherit (VB).

➤ **Structure:** A structure is the only entity, other than a comment, that appears on the Designer in a rectangle. Similar to a class, a structure supports fields, properties, methods, events, and constants. It, too, can contain nested types. However, unlike a class, a structure cannot have a destructor.

➤ **Delegate:** Although a delegate appears as an entity on the class diagram, it can't contain nested types. The only components it can contain are parameters that define the delegate signature.

Connectors

Two types of relationships can be established between entities. These are illustrated on the class diagram using connectors, and are explained in the following list:

➤ **Inheritance:** The Inheritance connector is used to show the relationship between classes that inherit from each other.

➤ **Association:** Where a class makes reference to another class, there is an association between the two classes. This is shown using the Association connector.

If a relationship is based around a collection — for example, a list of Order objects — this can be represented using a *collection association*. A collection association called Orders is shown in Figure 10-2 connecting the Customer and Order classes.

A *class association* can be represented as either a field or property of a class, or as an association link between the classes. You can use the right-click context menu on either the field or property or the association to toggle between the two representations.

> *To show a property as a collection association you need to right-click the property in the class and select Show as Collection Association. This hides the property from the class and displays it as a connector to the associated class on the diagram.*

THE CLASS DETAILS

You can add a component to an entity by right-clicking and selecting the appropriate component to add. Unfortunately, this is a time-consuming process and doesn't afford you the ability to add method parameters or return values. The Class Designer in Visual Studio 2010 includes a Class Details window, which provides a user interface that enables components to be quickly entered. This window is illustrated in Figure 10-4 for the Customer class previously shown in Figure 10-2.

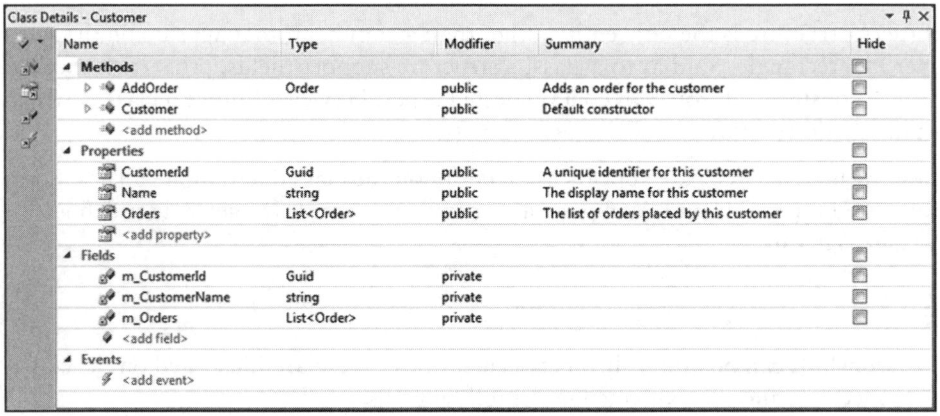

Name	Type	Modifier	Summary	Hide
▲ **Methods**				☐
▷ AddOrder	Order	public	Adds an order for the customer	☐
▷ Customer		public	Default constructor	☐
<add method>				
▲ Properties				☐
CustomerId	Guid	public	A unique identifier for this customer	☐
Name	string	public	The display name for this customer	☐
Orders	List<Order>	public	The list of orders placed by this customer	☐
<add property>				
▲ Fields				☐
m_CustomerId	Guid	private		☐
m_CustomerName	string	private		☐
m_Orders	List<Order>	private		☐
<add field>				
▲ Events				
<add event>				

FIGURE 10-4

On the left side of the window are buttons that can aid in navigating classes that contain a large number of components. The top button can be used to add methods, properties, fields, or events to the class. The remaining buttons can be used to bring any of the component groups into focus. For example, the second button is used to navigate to the list of methods for the class. You can navigate between components in the list using the up and down arrow keys.

Because Figure 10-4 shows the details for a class, the main region of the window is divided into four alphabetical lists: Methods, Properties, Fields, and Events. Other entity types may have other components, such as Members and Parameters. Each row is divided into five columns that show the name, the return type, the modifier or accessibility of the component, a summary, and whether the item is hidden on the design surface. In each case, the Summary field appears as an XML comment against the appropriate component. Events differ from the other components in that the Type column must be a delegate. You can navigate between columns using the left and right arrow keys, Tab (next column), and Shift+Tab (previous column).

To enter parameters on a method, use the right arrow key to expand the method node so that a parameter list appears. Selecting the Add Parameter node adds a new parameter to the method. Once added, the new parameter can be navigated to by using the arrow keys.

THE PROPERTIES WINDOW

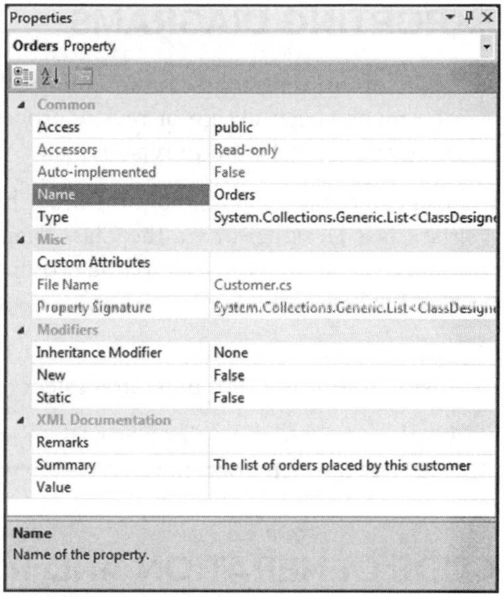

Although the Class Details window is useful it does not provide all the information required for entity components. For example, properties can be marked as read-only, which is not displayed in the Class Details window. The Properties window in Figure 10-5 shows the full list of attributes for the Orders property of the Customer class.

Figure 10-5 shows that the Orders property is read-only and that it is not static. It also shows that this property is defined in the Customer.cs file. With partial classes, a class may be separated over multiple files. When a partial class is selected, the File Name property shows all files defining that class as a comma-delimited list. Although some of these properties are read-only in this window, they can, of course, be adjusted within the appropriate code file.

FIGURE 10-5

LAYOUT

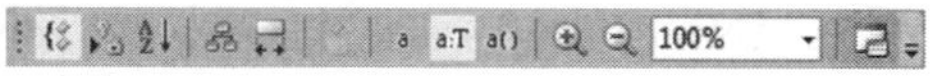

Because the class diagram is all about visualizing classes, you have several toolbar controls at your disposal to create the layout of the entities on the

FIGURE 10-6

Designer. Figure 10-6 shows the toolbar that appears as part of the Designer surface.

The first three buttons control the layout of entity components. From left to right, the buttons are Group by Kind, Group by Access, and Sort Alphabetically.

The next two buttons are used to automate the process of arranging the entities on the design surface. On the left is the Layout Diagram button, which automatically repositions the entities on the design surface. It also minimizes the entities, hiding all components. The right button, Adjust Shapes Width, adjusts the size of the entities so that all components are fully visible. If a single component is selected, the "Adjust Shapes Width" button adjusts the width of only that component. If no components are selected, the width of all components are adjusted.

Entity components, such as fields, properties, and methods, can be hidden using the Hide Member button.

The display style of entity components can be adjusted using the next three buttons. The left button, Display Name, sets the display style to show only the name of the component. This can be extended to show both the name and the component type using the Display Name and Type button. The right button, Display Full Signature, sets the display style to be the full component signature. This is often the most useful, although it takes more space to display.

The remaining controls on the toolbar enable you to zoom in and out on the Class Designer, and to display the Class Details window.

EXPORTING DIAGRAMS

Quite often, the process of designing which classes will be part of the system architecture is a part of a much larger design or review process. Therefore, it is a common requirement to export the class diagram for inclusion in reports.

You can export a class diagram either by right-clicking the context menu from any space on the Class Designer or via the Class Diagram menu. Either way, selecting the Export Diagram as Image menu item opens a dialog prompting you to select an image format and filename for saving the diagram.

You can also copy and paste an image directly into Microsoft Word or a drawing program such as Visio. To do this, you must first select one or more classes on the diagram.

Lastly, you can also print Class Diagrams directly from Visual Studio through the normal File ⇨ Print menu option.

CODE GENERATION AND REFACTORING

One of the core goals of Visual Studio 2010 and the .NET Framework is to reduce the amount of code that developers have to write. This goal is achieved in two ways: either reduce the total amount of code that has to be written or reduce the amount that actually has to be written manually. The first approach is supported through a very rich set of base classes included in the .NET Framework. The second approach, reduce the amount of code that is written manually, is supported by the code generation and refactoring tools included with the Class Designer.

Drag-and-Drop Code Generation

Almost every action performed on the class diagram results in a change in the underlying source code, and essentially provides some level of code generation. We've already covered a number of these changes, such as adding a property or method to a class in the Class Details window. However, some more advanced code generation actions can be performed by manipulating the class diagram.

As explained earlier in the chapter, you can use the Inheritance connector to establish an inheritance relationship between a parent class and an inheriting class. When you do this, the code file of the derived class is updated to reflect this change. However, when the parent class is abstract, as in the case of the Product class in Figure 10-7, the Class Designer can perform some additional analysis and code generation. If the parent class is an abstract class and contains any abstract members, those members are automatically implemented in the inheriting classes. This is shown in Figure 10-7 (right) where the abstract properties Description, Price, and SKU have been added to the Book class. The method GetInventory() was not implemented because it was not marked as abstract.

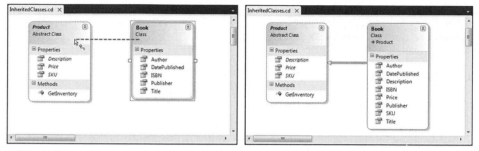

FIGURE 10-7

The Inheritance connector can be used in one more way that results in automatic code generation. In Figure 10-8 (left) an interface, ICrudActions, has been added to the diagram. When the Inheritance connector is dragged from a class to the interface, all the members of the interface are implemented on the class, as shown in Figure 10-8 (right).

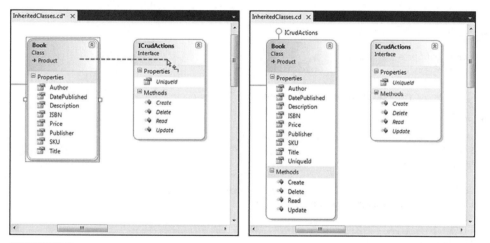

FIGURE 10-8

The following code shows the code that is automatically generated when the ICrudActions interface is added to the Book class.

C#

```csharp
#region ICrudActions Members
    public Guid UniqueId
    {
        get
        {
            throw new NotImplementedException();
        }
        set
        {
            throw new NotImplementedException();
        }
    }
```

```csharp
    public void Create()
    {
        throw new NotImplementedException();
    }

    public void Update()
    {
        throw new NotImplementedException();
    }

    public void Read()
    {
        throw new NotImplementedException();
    }

    public void Delete()
    {
        throw new NotImplementedException();
    }
#endregion
```

Visual Basic

```vbnet
#Region ICrudActions Members
    Public Property UniqueId As Guid
        Get
            throw new NotImplementedException()
        End Get
        Set
            throw new NotImplementedException()
        End Set
    End Property

    Public Sub Create()
        throw new NotImplementedException()
    End Sub

    Public Sub Update()
        throw new NotImplementedException()
    End Sub

    Public Sub Read()
        throw new NotImplementedException()
    End Sub

    Public Sub Delete()
        throw new NotImplementedException()
    End Sub
#End Region
```

IntelliSense Code Generation

The rest of the code generation functions in the Class Designer are available under the somewhat unintuitively named IntelliSense submenu. Because these code generation functions apply only to classes, this menu is visible only when a class or abstract class has been selected on the diagram. The two code generation functions included on this menu are Implement Abstract Class and Override Members.

The Implement Abstract Class function ensures that all abstract members from the base class are implemented in the inheriting class. To access this function, right-click the inheriting class, choose IntelliSense, and then choose Implement Abstract Class.

Somewhat related is the Override Members function, which is used to select public properties or methods from a base class that you would like to override. To access this function, right-click the inheriting class, choose IntelliSense, and then choose Override Members. The dialog box shown in Figure 10-9 is displayed, populated with the base classes and any properties or methods that have not already been overridden.

FIGURE 10-9

Refactoring with the Class Designer

In Chapter 8 you saw how Visual Studio 2010 provides support for refactoring code from the code editor window. The Class Designer also exposes a number of these refactoring functions when working with entities on a class diagram.

The refactoring functions in the Class Designer are available by right-clicking an entity, or any of its members, and choosing an action from the Refactor submenu. The following refactoring functions are available:

➤ **Rename Types and Type Members:** Allows you to rename a type or a member of a type on the class diagram or in the Properties window. Renaming a type or type member changes it in all code locations where the old name appeared. You can even ensure that the change is propagated to any comments or static strings.

➤ **Encapsulate Field:** Enables you to quickly create a new property from an existing field, and then seamlessly update your code with references to the new property.

➤ **Reorder or Remove Parameters (C# only):** Enables you to change the order of method parameters in types, or to remove a parameter from a method.

➤ **Extract Interface (C# only):** You can extract the members of a type into a new interface. This function allows you to select only a subset of the members that you want to extract into the new interface.

> *You can also use the standard Windows Cut, Copy, and Paste actions to copy and move members between types.*

MODELING POWER TOYS FOR VISUAL STUDIO

Although the Class Designer is a very useful tool for designing and visualizing a class hierarchy, it can be cumbersome and unwieldy when trying to work with very large diagrams. To ease this burden you can either break up the diagram into multiple class diagrams, or install the Modeling Power Toys for Visual Studio 2010.

Modeling Power Toys is a free add-in to Visual Studio that extends the functionality of the Class Designer in several ways. It includes enhancements that enable you to work more effectively with large diagrams including panning and zooming, improved scrolling, and diagram search. It also provides functions that address some of the limitations of the Class Designer such as the ability to create nested types and new derived classes and display XML comments.

The add-in, including source code, is available from `http://modeling.codeplex.com/`. The download includes an MSI file for easy installation.

Visualization Enhancements

The Modeling Power Toys for Visual Studio 2010 provides some very useful enhancements for visualizing and working with large class diagrams. The diagram search feature is one of the more useful; it allows you to search the entities on a diagram for a specific search term. The search dialog, shown in Figure 10-10, is invoked via the standard Find menu item or Ctrl+F shortcut.

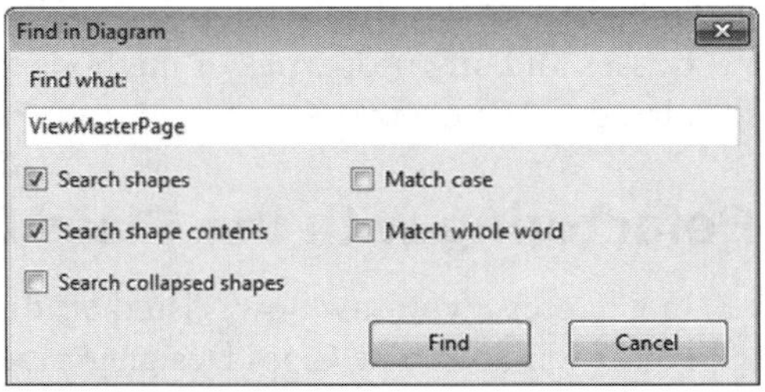

FIGURE 10-10

Another useful tool for large diagrams is the panning tool, which provides an easy way to see an overview of the entire diagram and navigate to different areas without changing the zoom level. You can invoke this tool by clicking a new icon that appears in the bottom right of the window, which displays the panning window, as shown in Figure 10-11.

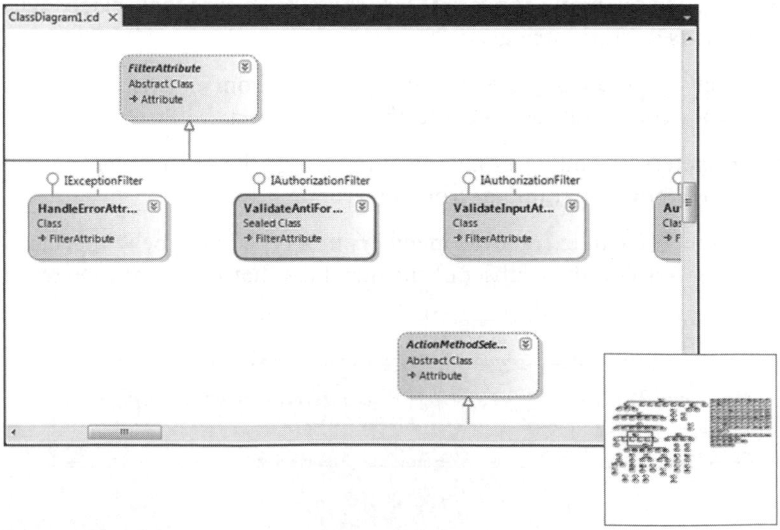

FIGURE 10-11

The Modeling Power Toys also allows quite fine control over what is displayed on the diagram via the filtering options. These are available via the Class Diagram menu, and include:

➤ **Hide Inheritance Lines:** Hides all inheritance lines in the selection.

➤ **Show All Inheritance Lines:** Shows all hidden inheritance lines on the diagram.

➤ **Show All Public Associations:** Shows all possible public associations on the diagram.

➤ **Show All Associations:** Shows all possible associations on the diagram.

➤ **Show Associations As Members:** Shows all association lines as members.

➤ **Hide Private:** Hides all private members.

➤ **Hide Private and Internal:** Hides all private and/or internal members.

➤ **Show Only Public:** Hides all members except for public; all hidden public members are shown.

➤ **Show Only Public and Protected:** Hides all members except for public and protected; hidden public and/or protected members are shown.

➤ **Show All Members:** Shows all hidden members.

Functionality Enhancements

Modeling Power Toys includes a number of enhancements that address some of the functional limitations of the Class Designer. Though the Class Designer can display nested types, you cannot create them using the design surface.

This constraint is addressed by the Modeling Power Toys by enabling you to add nested types including classes, enumerations, structures, or delegates. You can also easily add several new member types, such as read-only properties and indexers.

There are also some improvements around working with interfaces. Often it is difficult to understand what members of a class have been used to implement an interface. The Modeling Power Toys simplifies this by adding a Select Members menu item to the interface lollipop label on a type. For example, in Figure 10-12, the Select Members command is being invoked on the IStatus interface.

In addition to those mentioned here, many other minor enhancements and functionality improvements are provided by the Modeling Power Toys that add up to make it a very useful extension.

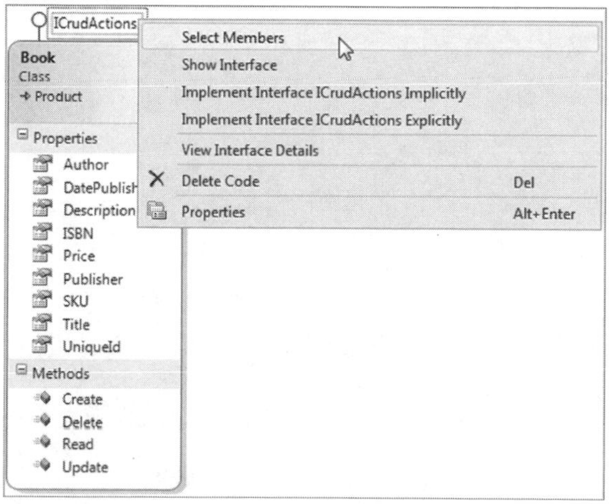

FIGURE 10-12

SUMMARY

This chapter focused on the Class Designer, one of the best tools built into Visual Studio 2010 for generating and understanding code. The design surface and supporting toolbars and windows provide a rich user interface with which complex class hierarchies and associations can be modeled and designed.

PART III
Digging Deeper

▶ **CHAPTER 11:** Unit Testing

▶ **CHAPTER 12:** Documentation with XML Comments

▶ **CHAPTER 13:** Code Consistency Tools

▶ **CHAPTER 14:** Code Generation with T4

▶ **CHAPTER 15:** Project and Item Templates

▶ **CHAPTER 16:** Language-Specific Features

11

Unit Testing

WHAT'S IN THIS CHAPTER?

➤ Generating a test harness from existing code

➤ Making assertions about the behavior of your code

➤ Executing custom code during test life-cycle events

➤ Creating data-driven tests

➤ Testing private members and code contracts

➤ Managing lists of tests

Application testing is one of the most important parts of writing software. Research into the costs of software maintenance have revealed that a software defect can cost up to 25 times more to fix if it makes it to a production environment than if it had been caught during development. At the same time, a lot of testing involves repetitive, dull, and error-prone work that must be undertaken every time you make a change to your code base. The easiest way to counter this is to produce repeatable automated tests that can be executed by a computer on demand. This chapter looks at a specific type of automated testing that focuses on individual components, or units, of a system. Having a suite of automated unit tests gives you the power to verify that your individual components all work as specified even after making radical changes to them.

Visual Studio 2010 has a built-in framework for authoring, executing, and reporting on test cases. Originally included only in the Team System Edition of Visual Studio, many of the testing tools are now available in the Professional Edition. This means a much wider audience can now more easily obtain the benefits of automated, robust testing. This chapter focuses on creating, configuring, running, and managing a suite of unit tests as well as adding support to drive the tests from a set of data.

YOUR FIRST TEST CASE

Writing test cases is not a task that is easily automated, because the test cases have to mirror the functionality of the software being developed. However, at several steps in the process code stubs can be generated by a tool. To illustrate this, start with a fairly straightforward snippet of code to learn to write test cases that fully exercise the code. Setting the scene is a Subscription class with a public property called CurrentStatus, which returns the status of the current subscription as an enumeration value:

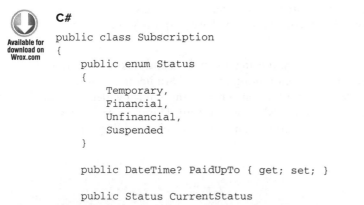

VB

```vb
Public Class Subscription
    Public Enum Status
        Temporary
        Financial
        Unfinancial
        Suspended
    End Enum

    Public Property PaidUpTo As Nullable(Of Date)

    Public ReadOnly Property CurrentStatus As Status
        Get
            If Not Me.PaidUpTo.HasValue Then Return Status.Temporary
            If Me.PaidUpTo > Now Then
                Return Status.Financial
            Else
                If Me.PaidUpTo >= Now.AddMonths(-3) Then
                    Return Status.Unfinancial
                Else
                    Return Status.Suspended
                End If
            End If
        End Get
    End Property
End Class
```

Code snippet Subscriptions\Subscription.vb

C#

```csharp
public class Subscription
{
    public enum Status
    {
        Temporary,
        Financial,
        Unfinancial,
        Suspended
    }

    public DateTime? PaidUpTo { get; set; }

    public Status CurrentStatus
```

```
            {
                get
                {
                    if (this.PaidUpTo.HasValue == false)
                        return Status.Temporary;
                    if (this.PaidUpTo > DateTime.Today)
                        return Status.Financial;
                    else
                    {
                        if (this.PaidUpTo >= DateTime.Today.AddMonths(-3))
                            return Status.Unfinancial;
                        else
                            return Status.Suspended;
                    }
                }
            }
        }
    }
```

Code snippet Subscriptions\Subscription.cs

As you can see from the code snippet, four code paths need to be tested for the `Current Status` property. To test this property you create a separate `SubscriptionTest` test class in a new test project, into which you add a test method that contains the code necessary to instantiate a `Subscription` object, set the `PaidUpTo` property, and check that the `CurrentStatus` property contains the correct result. Then you keep adding test methods until all of the code paths through the `CurrentStatus` property have been executed and tested.

Fortunately, Visual Studio automates the process of creating a new test project, creating the appropriate `SubscriptionTest` class and writing the code to create the `Subscription` object. All you have to do is complete the test method. It also provides a runtime engine that is used to run the test case, monitor its progress, and report on any outcome from the test. Therefore, all you have to do is write the code to test the property in question. In fact, Visual Studio generates a code stub that executes the property being tested. However, it does not generate code to ensure that the `Subscription` object is in the correct initial state; this you must do yourself.

You can create empty test cases from the Test menu by selecting the New Test item. This prompts you to select the type of test to create, after which a blank test is created in which you need to manually write the appropriate test cases. However, you can also create a new unit test that contains much of the stub code by selecting the Create Unit Tests menu item from the right-click context menu of the main code window. For example, right-clicking within the `CurrentStatus` property and selecting this menu item brings up the Create Unit Tests dialog displayed in Figure 11-1. This dialog shows all the members of all the classes within the current solution and enables you to select the items for which you want to generate a test stub.

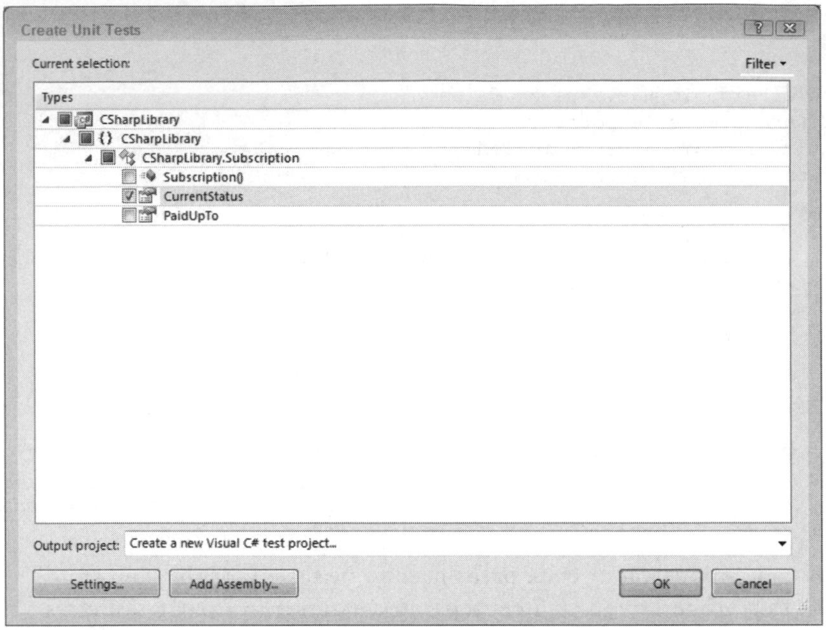

FIGURE 11-1

If you have a unit test project already in your solution you can generate your new test class into it by selecting it from the Output Project drop-down list; otherwise, keep the default selection and Visual Studio will create a new test project for you. Unlike alternative unit test frameworks such as NUnit, which allow test classes to reside in the same project as the source code, the testing framework within Visual Studio requires that all test cases reside in a separate test project. When test cases are created from the dialog shown in Figure 11-1, they are named according to the name of the member and the name of the class to which they belong.

> You can alter this naming convention in the Test Generation Settings dialog, which you can access by clicking the Settings button. You will find other settings that allow you to control how the test code is generated as well.

With the CurrentStatus property checked as in Figure 11-1, clicking the OK button generates the following code (some comments and commented-out code have been removed from this code):

VB

Available for download on Wrox.com

```vb
<TestClass()>
Public Class SubscriptionTest

        Private testContextInstance As TestContext

        Public Property TestContext() As TestContext
```

```vb
        Get
            Return testContextInstance
        End Get
        Set(ByVal value As TestContext)
            testContextInstance = value
        End Set
    End Property

    <TestMethod()>
    Public Sub CurrentStatusTest()
        Dim target As Subscription = New Subscription()
' TODO: Initialize to an appropriate value
        Dim actual As Subscription.Status
        actual = target.CurrentStatus
        Assert.Inconclusive("Verify the correctness of this test method.")
    End Sub
End Class
```

Code snippet SubscriptionTests\SubscriptionTest.vb

Available for
download on
Wrox.com

C#

```csharp
[TestClass()]
public class SubscriptionTest
{

    private TestContext testContextInstance;

    public TestContext TestContext
    {
        get
        {
            return testContextInstance;
        }
        set
        {
            testContextInstance = value;
        }
    }


    [TestMethod()]
    public void CurrentStatusTest()
    {
        Subscription target = new Subscription();
// TODO: Initialize to an appropriate value
        Subscription.Status actual;
        actual = target.CurrentStatus;
        Assert.Inconclusive("Verify the correctness of this test method.");
    }
}
```

Code snippet SubscriptionTests\SubscriptionTest.cs

The test case generated for the CurrentStatus property appears in the final method of this code snippet. (The top half of this class is discussed later in this chapter.) As you can see, the test case was created with a name that reflects the property it is testing (in this case CurrentStatusTest) in a class that reflects the class in which the property appears (in this case SubscriptionTest). One of the difficulties with test cases is that they can quickly become unmanageable. This simple naming convention ensures that test cases can easily be found and identified.

If you look at the test case in more detail, you can see that the generated code stub contains the code required to initialize everything for the test. A Subscription object is created, and a test variable called actual is assigned the CurrentStatus property of that object. All that is missing is the code to actually test that this value is correct. Before going any further, run this test case to see what happens by opening the Test View window, shown in Figure 11-2, from the Test Windows menu.

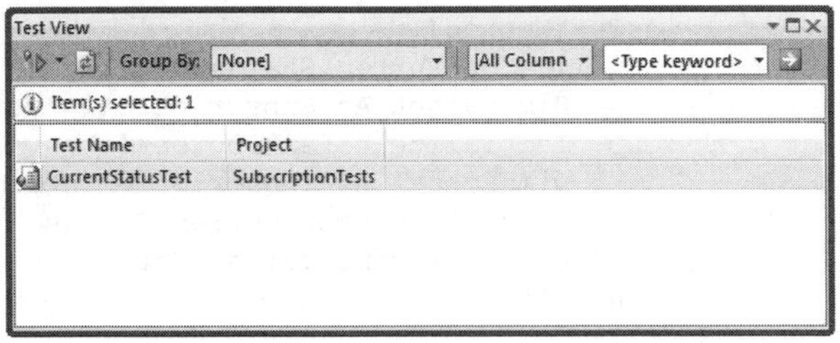

FIGURE 11-2

Selecting the CurrentStatusTest item and clicking the Run Selection button, the first on the left, invokes the test. This also opens the Test Results window, which initially shows the test as being either Pending or In Progress.

> *The Test View is just one way to select and run a test case. If you right-click the test case itself in the code window there is a Run Tests option. There is also a Tests toolbar with an option to run all the tests in the current context. This will run an individual test case, a whole test class, a test assembly, or all tests in the solution depending on the current selection. Finally, you can create lists of tests using the Test List Editor, which you see later in this chapter.*
>
> *In addition to each of these methods you can also set breakpoints in your code and run test cases in the debugger by selecting one of the Debug Tests options from the main toolbar or the Test View window.*

Once the test has completed, the Test Results window will look like the one shown in Figure 11-3.

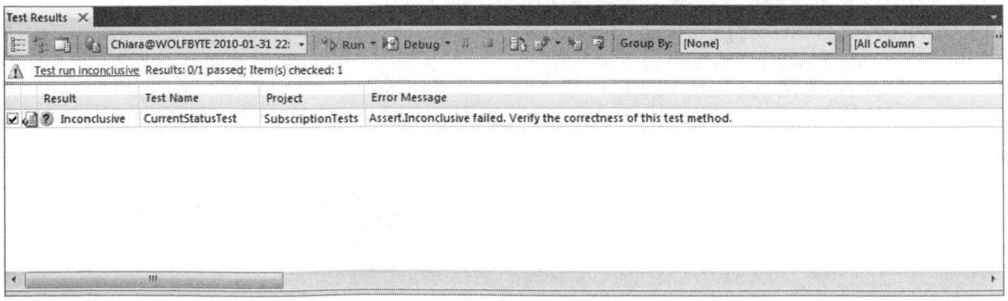

FIGURE 11-3

You can see from Figure 11-3 that the test case has returned an inconclusive result. Essentially, this indicates either that a test is not complete or that the results should not be relied upon, because changes may have been made that would make this test invalid.

You can get more information on the result of any particular test result by double-clicking it. Figure 11-4 shows the result of double-clicking the inconclusive result for the example. The results show basic information about the test, the result, and other useful environmental information such as the computer name, test execution duration, and start and end times.

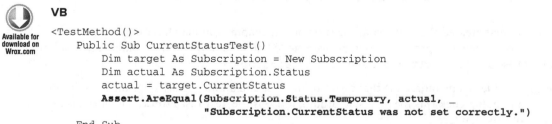

Common Results

Test Run:	dev@DEV-PC 2009-07-13 00:27:31
Test Name:	CurrentStatusTest
Result:	Inconclusive
Duration:	00:00:00.1752708
Computer Name:	DEV-PC
Start Time:	7/13/2009 12:27:31 AM
End Time:	7/13/2009 12:27:34 AM

Error Message   Copy
Assert.Inconclusive failed. Verify the correctness of this test method.

Error Stack Trace   Copy
CSharpTests.SubscriptionTest.CurrentStatusTest() C:\Users\dev\Documents\Visual Studio 10\Projects\UnitTesting\CSharpTests\SubscriptionTest.cs : line 76

FIGURE 11-4

> As well as information about a particular result, you can also get information about a complete test run by clicking the Run Details button in the Test Results window. By default, the Test Results window shows the details of the most recent test run, but Visual Studio stores all of the results from a number of recent test runs and you can use the Test Run drop-down list to browse the results of previous runs.

When test cases are generated by Visual Studio, they are all initially marked as inconclusive by means of the `Assert.Inconclusive` statement. In addition, depending on the test stub that was created, there may be additional TODO statements that will prompt you to complete the test case.

Returning to the code snippet generated for the `CurrentStatusTest` method, you can see both an `Assert.Inconclusive` statement and a TODO item. To complete this test case, remove the TODO comment and replace the `Assert.Inconclusive` statement with `Assert.AreEqual`, as shown in the following code:

Available for download on Wrox.com

VB

```vb
<TestMethod()>
    Public Sub CurrentStatusTest()
        Dim target As Subscription = New Subscription
        Dim actual As Subscription.Status
        actual = target.CurrentStatus
        Assert.AreEqual(Subscription.Status.Temporary, actual, _
                    "Subscription.CurrentStatus was not set correctly.")
    End Sub
```

Code snippet SubscriptionTests\SubscriptionTest.vb

C#

```
[TestMethod()]
public void CurrentStatusTest()
{
    Subscription target = new Subscription();
    Subscription.Status actual;
    actual = target.CurrentStatus;
    Assert.AreEqual(Subscription.Status.Temporary, actual,
                    "Subscription.CurrentStatus was not set correctly.");
}
```

Code snippet SubscriptionTests\SubscriptionTest.cs

Each test shown in the Test Results window has a checkbox next to it allowing it to be selected. When test results are selected, clicking the Run Tests button in the Test Results window causes only those selected tests to be run. By default, after a test run any tests that did not pass are selected. After you fix the code that caused these tests to fail, click the Run Tests button to re-run these test cases and produce a successful result, as shown in Figure 11-5.

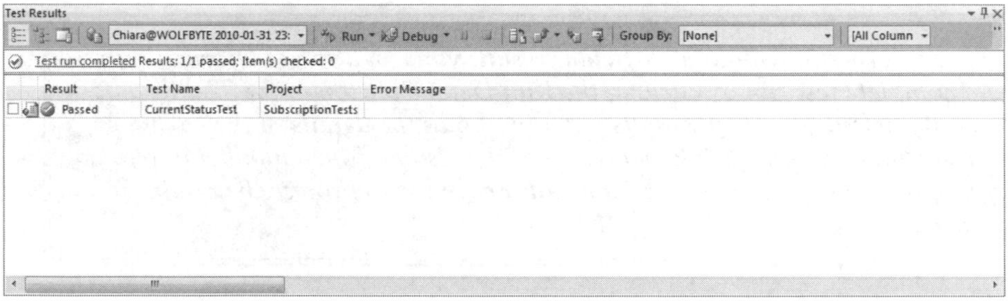

FIGURE 11-5

> *Any test case that makes no assertions is considered to pass, which is why Visual Studio automatically puts an* `Assert.Inconclusive` *warning into generated test cases. By removing this assertion you are indicating that the test case is complete. In this example, we have only exercised one code path and you should add further test cases that fully exercise the other three.*

When you first created the unit test at the start of this chapter you may have noticed that, in addition to the new test project, two items were added under a new solution folder called Solution Items. These are `Chapter11.vsmdi` and `Local.testsettings`.

The `.vsmdi` file is a metadata file that contains information about the tests within the solution. When you double-click this file in Visual Studio, it opens the Test List Editor, which is discussed at the end of this chapter.

The `.testsettings` file is a Test Run Configuration file. This is an XML file that stores settings that control how a set of tests, called a *test run*, is executed. You can create and save multiple run configurations that represent different scenarios, and then make a specific run configuration active using the Test ➪ Select Active Test Run Configuration menu item. This defines which of the test run configurations should be used when tests are run.

> *If you are using the Ultimate edition of Visual Studio then you might also have a* `TraceAndTestImpact.testsettings` *file when you create a new test project. This Test Run Configuration is used by Visual Studio to implement the Test Impact Analysis feature which is covered in Chapter 56.*

When you double-click to open the `Local.testsettings` file, it launches a special-purpose editor. Within this editor you can configure a test run to copy required support files to a deployment directory, or link to custom startup and cleanup scripts. The editor also includes a Test Timeouts section, shown in Figure 11-6, which enables you to define a timeout after which a test will be aborted or marked as failed. This is useful if a global performance limit has been specified for your application (for example, if all screens must return within five seconds).

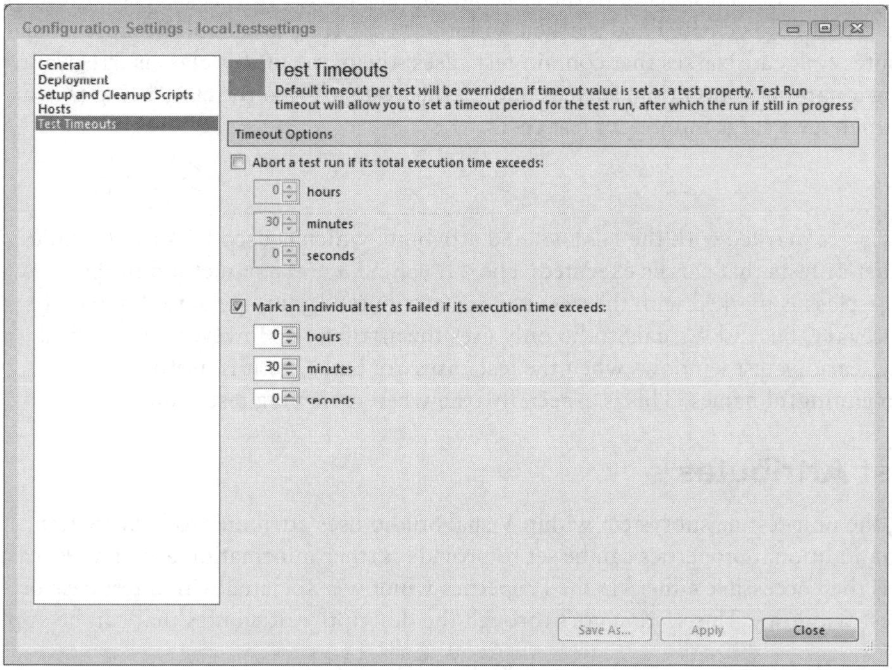

FIGURE 11-6

Most of these settings can be overridden on a per-method basis by means of test attributes, which are discussed in the next section.

Identifying Tests using Attributes

Before going any further with this scenario, take a step back and consider how testing is carried out within Visual Studio 2010. As mentioned earlier, all test cases have to exist within test classes that themselves reside in a test project. But what really distinguishes a method, class, or project as containing test cases? Starting with the test project, if you look at the underlying XML project file, you will see that there is virtually no difference between a test project file and a normal class library project file. In fact, the only difference appears to be the project type: When this project is built it simply outputs a standard .NET class library assembly. The key difference is that Visual Studio recognizes this as a test project and automatically analyzes it for any test cases in order to populate the various test windows.

Classes and methods used in the testing process are marked with an appropriate attribute. The attributes are used by the testing engine to enumerate all the test cases within a particular assembly.

TestClass

All test cases must reside within a test class that is appropriately marked with the `TestClass` attribute. Although it may appear that there is no reason for this attribute other than to align test cases with the class and member that they are testing, you will later see some benefits associated with grouping test cases using a test class. In the case of testing the `Subscription` class, a test class called `SubscriptionTest` was created and marked with the `TestClass` attribute. Because Visual Studio uses attributes to locate classes that contain test cases, the name of this class is irrelevant. However, adopting a naming convention, such as adding the Test suffix to the class being tested, makes it easier to manage a large number of test cases.

TestMethod

Individual test cases are marked with the `TestMethod` attribute, which is used by Visual Studio to enumerate the list of tests that can be executed. The `CurrentStatusTest` method in the `SubscriptionTest` class is marked with the `TestMethod` attribute. Again, the actual name of this method is irrelevant, because Visual Studio only uses the attributes. However, the method name is used in the various test windows when the test cases are listed, so it is useful for test methods to have meaningful names. This is especially true when reviewing test results.

Additional Test Attributes

As you have seen, the unit-testing subsystem within Visual Studio uses attributes to identify test cases. A number of additional properties can be set to provide further information about a test case. This information is then accessible either via the Properties window associated with a test case or within the other test windows. This section goes through the descriptive attributes that can be applied to a test method.

Description

Because test cases are listed by test method name, a number of tests may have similar names, or names that are not descriptive enough to indicate what functionality they test. The `Description` attribute, which takes a `String` as its sole argument, can be applied to a test method to provide additional information about a test case.

Owner

The `Owner` attribute, which also takes a `String` argument, is useful for indicating who owns, wrote, or is currently working on a particular test case.

Priority

The `Priority` attribute, which takes an `Integer` argument, can be applied to a test case to indicate the relative importance of a test case. Though the testing framework does not use this attribute, it is useful for prioritizing test cases when you are determining the order in which failing, or incomplete, test cases are resolved.

Test Categories

The `TestCategory` attribute accepts a single `String` identifying one user-defined category for the test. Like the `Priority` attribute the `TestCategory` attribute is essentially ignored by Visual Studio but is useful for sorting and grouping related items together. A test case may belong to many categories but must have a separate attribute for each one.

Work Items

The `WorkItem` attribute can be used to link a test case to one or more work items in a work-item-tracking system such as Team Foundation Server. If you apply one or more `WorkItem` attributes to a test case, you can review the test case when making changes to existing functionality. You can read more about Team Foundation Server in Chapter 57.

Ignore

It is possible to temporarily prevent a test method from running by applying the `Ignore` attribute to it. Test methods with the `Ignore` attribute will not be run and will not show up in the results list of a test run.

> *You can apply the `Ignore` attribute to a test class as well to switch off all of the test methods within it.*

Timeout

A test case can fail for any number of reasons. A performance test, for example, might require a particular functionality to complete within a specified time frame. Instead of the tester having to write complex multi-threading tests that stop the test case once a particular timeout has been reached, you can apply the `Timeout` attribute to a test case with a timeout value in milliseconds, as shown in the following code. This ensures that the test case fails if that timeout is reached.

VB

```
<TestMethod()>
<Owner("Mike Minutillo")>
<Description("Tests the functionality of the Current Status Property")>
<Priority(3)>
<Timeout(10000)>
<TestCategory("Financial")>
Public Sub CurrentStatusTest()
    Dim target As Subscription = New Subscription
    Dim actual As Subscription.Status
    actual = target.CurrentStatus
    Assert.AreEqual(Subscription.Status.Temporary, actual, _
                    "Subscription.CurrentStatus was not set correctly.")
End Sub
```

Code snippet SubscriptionTests\SubscriptionTest.vb

C#

```
[TestMethod()]
[Owner("Mike Minutillo")]
[Description("Tests the functionality of the Current Status Method")]
[Priority(3)]
[Timeout(10000)]
[TestCategory("Financial")]
public void CurrentStatusTest()
{
    Subscription target = new Subscription();
    Subscription.Status actual;
    actual = target.CurrentStatus;
    Assert.AreEqual(Subscription.Status.Temporary, actual,
                    "Subscription.CurrentStatus was not set correctly.");
}
```

Code snippet SubscriptionTests\SubscriptionTest.cs

This snippet augments the original `CurrentStatusTest` method with some of these attributes to illustrate their usage. In addition to providing additional information about what the test case does and who wrote it, this code assigns the test case a priority of 3 and a category of `"Financial"`. Lastly, the code indicates that this test case should fail if it takes more than 10 seconds (10,000 milliseconds) to execute.

ASSERTING THE FACTS

So far, this chapter has examined the structure of the test environment and how test cases are nested within test classes in a test project. What remains is to look at the body of the test case and review how test cases either pass or fail. (When a test case is generated, you saw that an `Assert .Inconclusive` statement is added to the end of the test to indicate that it is incomplete.)

The idea behind unit testing is that you start with the system, component, or object in a known state, and then run a method, modify a property, or trigger an event. The testing phase comes at the end, when you need to validate that the system, component, or object is in the correct state. Alternatively, you may need to validate that the correct output was returned from a method or property. You do this by attempting to assert a particular condition. If this condition is not true, the testing system reports this result and ends the test case. A condition is asserted, not surprisingly, via the Assert class. There is also a StringAssert class and a CollectionAssert class, which provide additional assertions for dealing with String objects and collections of objects, respectively.

The Assert Class

The Assert class in the UnitTesting namespace, not to be confused with the Debug.Assert or Trace.Assert method in the System.Diagnostics namespace, is the primary class used to make assertions about a test case. The basic assertion has the following format:

VB

```
Assert.IsTrue(variableToTest, "Output message if this fails")
```

C#

```
Assert.IsTrue(variableToTest, "Output message if this fails");
```

As you can imagine, the first argument is the condition to be tested. If this is true, the test case continues operation. However, if it fails, the output message is emitted and the test case exits with a failed result.

This statement has multiple overloads whereby the output message can be omitted or String formatting parameters supplied. Because quite often you won't be testing a single positive condition, several additional methods simplify making assertions within a test case:

- ➤ IsFalse: Tests for a negative, or false, condition
- ➤ AreEqual: Tests whether two arguments have the same value
- ➤ AreSame: Tests whether two arguments refer to the same object
- ➤ IsInstanceOfType: Tests whether an argument is an instance of a particular type
- ➤ IsNull: Tests whether an argument is nothing

This list is not exhaustive — several more methods exist, including negative equivalents of those listed. Also, many of these methods have overloads that allow them to be invoked in several different ways.

The StringAssert Class

The StringAssert class does not provide any additional functionality that cannot be achieved with one or more assertions via the Assert class. However, it not only simplifies the test case code by making it clear that String assertions are being made; it also reduces the mundane tasks associated with testing for particular conditions. The additional assertions are as follows:

➤ `Contains`: Tests whether a `String` contains another `String`

➤ `DoesNotMatch`: Tests whether a `String` does not match a regular expression

➤ `EndsWith`: Tests whether a `String` ends with a particular `String`

➤ `Matches`: Tests whether a `String` matches a regular expression

➤ `StartsWith`: Tests whether a `String` starts with a particular `String`

The CollectionAssert Class

Similar to the `StringAssert` class, `CollectionAssert` is a helper class that is used to make assertions about a collection of items. Some of the assertions are as follows:

➤ `AllItemsAreNotNull`: Tests that none of the items in a collection is a null reference

➤ `AllItemsAreUnique`: Tests that no duplicate items exist in a collection

➤ `Contains`: Tests whether a collection contains a particular object

➤ `IsSubsetOf`: Tests whether a collection is a subset of another collection

The ExpectedException Attribute

Sometimes test cases have to execute paths of code that can cause exceptions to be raised. Though exception coding should be avoided, conditions exist where this might be appropriate. Instead of writing a test case that includes a `Try-Catch` block with an appropriate assertion to test that an exception was raised, you can mark the test case with an `ExpectedException` attribute. For example, change the `CurrentStatus` property to throw an exception if the `PaidUp` date is prior to the date the subscription opened, which in this case is a constant:

VB

```vb
Public Const SubscriptionOpenedOn As Date = #1/1/2000#
Public ReadOnly Property CurrentStatus As Status
    Get
        If Not Me.PaidUpTo.HasValue Then Return Status.Temporary
        If Me.PaidUpTo > Now Then
            Return Status.Financial
        Else
            If Me.PaidUpTo >= Now.AddMonths(-3) Then
                Return Status.Unfinancial
            ElseIf Me.PaidUpTo > SubscriptionOpenedOn Then
                Return Status.Suspended
            Else
                Throw New ArgumentOutOfRangeException( _
        "Paid up date is not valid as it is before the subscription opened.")
            End If
        End If
    End Get
End Property
```

Code snippet Subscriptions\Subscription.cs

C#

```csharp
public static readonly DateTime SubscriptionOpenedOn = new DateTime(2000, 1, 1);
public Status CurrentStatus
{
    get
    {
        if (this.PaidUpTo.HasValue == false)
            return Status.Temporary;
        if (this.PaidUpTo > DateTime.Today)
            return Status.Financial;
        else
        {
            if (this.PaidUpTo >= DateTime.Today.AddMonths(-3))
                return Status.Unfinancial;
            else if (this.PaidUpTo >= SubscriptionOpenedOn)
                return Status.Suspended;
            else
                throw new ArgumentOutOfRangeException(
                  "Paid up date is not valid as it is before the subscription opened");
        }
    }
}
```

Code snippet Subscriptions\Subscription.vb

Using the same procedure as before, you can create a separate test case for testing this code path, as shown in the following example:

VB

```vb
<TestMethod()>
<ExpectedException(GetType(ArgumentOutOfRangeException),
    "Argument exception not raised for invalid PaidUp date.")>
Public Sub CurrentStatusExceptionTest()
    Dim target As Subscription = New Subscription

    target.PaidUpTo = Subscription.SubscriptionOpenedOn.AddMonths(-1)

    Dim expected = Subscription.Status.Temporary

    Assert.AreEqual(expected, target.CurrentStatus, _
                    "This assertion should never actually be evaluated")
End Sub
```

Code snippet SubscriptionTests\SubscriptionTest.vb

C#

```csharp
[TestMethod()]
[ExpectedException(typeof(ArgumentOutOfRangeException),
    "Argument Exception not raised for invalid PaidUp date.")]
public void CurrentStatusExceptionTest()
{
```

```
            Subscription target = new Subscription();
            target.PaidUpTo = Subscription.SubscriptionOpenedOn.AddMonths(-1);

            var expected = Subscription.Status.Temporary;

            Assert.AreEqual(expected, target.CurrentStatus,
                "This assertion should never actually be evaluated");
        }
```

Code snippet SubscriptionTests\SubscriptionTest.cs

The `ExpectedException` attribute not only catches any exception raised by the test case; it also ensures that the type of exception matches the type expected. If no exception is raised by the test case, this attribute will cause the test to fail.

INITIALIZING AND CLEANING UP

Despite Visual Studio generating the stub code for test cases you are to write, typically you have to write a lot of setup code whenever you run a test case. Where an application uses a database, that database should be returned to its initial state after each test to ensure that the test cases are completely repeatable. This is also true for applications that modify other resources such as the file system. Visual Studio provides support for writing methods that can be used to initialize and clean up around test cases. (Again, attributes are used to mark the appropriate methods that should be used to initialize and clean up the test cases.)

The attributes for initializing and cleaning up around test cases are broken down into three levels: those that apply to individual tests, those that apply to an entire test class, and those that apply to an entire test project.

TestInitialize and TestCleanup

As their names suggest, the `TestInitialize` and `TestCleanup` attributes indicate methods that should be run before and after each test case within a particular test class. These methods are useful for allocating and subsequently freeing any resources that are needed by all test cases in the test class.

ClassInitialize and ClassCleanup

Sometimes, instead of setting up and cleaning up after each test, it can be easier to ensure that the environment is in the correct state at the beginning and end of running an entire test class. Previously, we explained that test classes are a useful mechanism for grouping test cases; this is where you put that knowledge to use. Test cases can be grouped into test classes that contain one method marked with the `ClassInitialize` attribute and another marked with the `ClassCleanup` attribute. These methods must both be marked as `static`, and the one marked with `ClassInitialize` must take exactly one parameter that is of type `UnitTesting.TestContext`, which is explained later in this chapter.

> *When you use the Create Unit Test menu to generate a unit test, it generates stubs for the* TestInitialize, TestCleanup, ClassInitialize, *and* ClassCleanup *methods in a source code region that is commented out.*

AssemblyInitialize and AssemblyCleanup

The final level of initialization and cleanup attributes is at the assembly, or project, level. Methods that are intended to initialize the environment before running an entire test project, and cleaning up after, can be marked with the AssemblyInitialize and AssemblyCleanup attributes, respectively. Because these methods apply to any test case within the test project, only a single method can be marked with each of these attributes. Like the class-level equivalents, these methods must both be static and the one marked with AssemblyInitialize must take a parameter of type UnitTesting.TestContext.

For both the assembly-level and class-level attributes, it is important to remember that even if only one test case is run, the methods marked with these attributes will also be run.

> *It is a good idea to put the methods marked with* AssemblyInitialize *and* AssemblyCleanup *together into their own test class to make them easy to find. If there is more than one method marked with either of these attributes, then running any tests in the project results in a runtime error.*

TESTING CONTEXT

When you are writing test cases, the testing engine can assist you in a number of ways, including by managing sets of data so you can run a test case with a range of data, and by enabling you to output additional information for the test case to aid in debugging. This functionality is available through the TestContext object that is generated within a test class and passed into the AssemblyInitialize and ClassInitialize methods.

Data

The CurrentStatusTest method generated in the first section of this chapter tested only a single path through the CurrentStatus property. To fully test this method, you could have written additional statements and assertions to set up and test the Subscription object. However, this process is fairly repetitive and would need to be updated if you ever changed the structure of the CurrentStatus property. An alternative is to provide a DataSource for the CurrentStatusTest method whereby each row of data tests a different path through the property. To add appropriate data to this method, use the following process:

1. Create a local SQL CE database and database table to store the various test data. In this case, create a database called LoadTest with a table called `Subscription_CurrentStatus`. The table has an Identity `bigint` column called Id, a nullable `datetime` column called PaidUp, and an `nvarchar(20)` column called Status.

2. Add appropriate data values to the table to cover all paths through the code. Test values for the `CurrentStatus` property are shown in Figure 11-7.

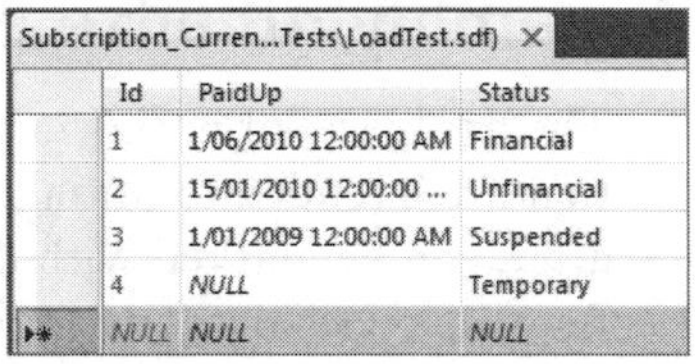

	Id	PaidUp	Status
	1	1/06/2010 12:00:00 AM	Financial
	2	15/01/2010 12:00:00 ...	Unfinancial
	3	1/01/2009 12:00:00 AM	Suspended
	4	NULL	Temporary
▶*	NULL	NULL	NULL

Subscription_Curren...Tests\LoadTest.sdf) ✕

FIGURE 11-7

3. Select the appropriate test case in the Test View window and open the Properties window. Select the Data Connection String property and click the ellipsis button to open the Connection Properties dialog.

4. Use the Connection Properties dialog to connect to the database created in Step 1. You should see a connection string similar to the following:

```
data source=|DataDirectory|\LoadTest.sdf
```

5. If the connection string is valid, a drop-down box appears when you select the `DataTable` property, enabling you to select the database table you created in Step 1.

6. To open the test case in the main window, return to the Test View window and select Open Test from the right-click context menu for the test case. Notice that a `DataSource` attribute has been added to the test case. This attribute is used by the testing engine to load the appropriate data from the specified table. This data is then exposed to the test case through the `TestContext` object.

> *If you are using a SQL Server CE database, you'll also get a* DeploymentItem *attribute added by default. This ensures that the database will be copied if the test assembly is deployed to another location.*

7. Modify the test case to access data from the `TestContext` object and use the data to drive the test case, which gives you the following `CurrentStatusTest` method:

VB

```
<DataSource("System.Data.SqlServerCe.3.5", _
        "data source=|DataDirectory|\LoadTest.sdf", _
        "Subscription_CurrentStatus", DataAccessMethod.Sequential)> _
<DeploymentItem("SubscriptionTests\LoadTest.sdf")> _
<TestMethod()>_
Public Sub CurrentStatusDataTest()
    Dim target As Subscription = New Subscription
```

```
        If Not IsDBNull(Me.TestContext.DataRow.Item("PaidUp")) Then
            target.PaidUpTo = CType(Me.TestContext.DataRow.Item("PaidUp"), Date)
        End If
        Dim val As Subscription.Status = _
                CType([Enum].Parse(GetType(Subscription.Status), _
                CStr(Me.TestContext.DataRow.Item("Status"))), Subscription.Status)

        Assert.AreEqual(val, target.CurrentStatus, _
            "Subscripiton.CurrentStatus was not set correctly.")
    End Sub
```

Code snippet SubscriptionTests\SubscriptionTest.vb

Available for download on Wrox.com

C#

```
[DataSource("System.Data.SqlServerCe.3.5",
  "data source=|DataDirectory|\\LoadTests.sdf",
  "Subscription_CurrentStatus",
  DataAccessMethod.Sequential)]
[DeploymentItem("SubscriptionTests\\LoadTests.sdf")]
[TestMethod()]
public void CurrentStatusDataTest()
{
  var target = new Subscription();
  var date = this.TestContext.DataRow["PaidUp"] as DateTime?;
  if (date != null)
  {
    target.PaidUpTo = date;
  }

  var val = Enum.Parse(typeof(Subscription.Status),
    this.TestContext.DataRow["Status"] as string);

  Assert.AreEqual(val, target.CurrentStatus,
    "Subscription.CurrentStatus was not set correctly.");

}
```

Code snippet SubscriptionTests\SubscriptionTest.cs

When this test case is executed, the `CurrentStatusTest` method is executed four times (once for each row of data in the database table). Each time it is executed, a `DataRow` object is retrieved and exposed to the test method via the `TestContext.DataRow` property. If the logic within the `CurrentStatus` property changes, you can add a new row to the `Subscription_CurrentStatus` table to test any code paths that may have been created.

Before moving on, take one last look at the `DataSource` attribute that was applied to the `CurrentStatusTest`. This attribute takes four arguments, the first three of which are used to determine which `DataTable` needs to be extracted. The remaining argument is a `DataAccessMethod` enumeration, which determines the order in which rows are returned from the `DataTable`. By default, this is `Sequential`, but it can be changed to `Random` so the order is different every time the test is run. This is particularly important when the data is representative of end user data but does not have to be processed in any particular order.

> *Data-driven tests are not just limited to database tables; they can be driven by Excel spreadsheets or even from Comma-Separated Values (CSV) files.*

Writing Test Output

Writing unit tests is all about automating the process of testing an application. Because of this, these test cases can be executed as part of a build process, perhaps even on a remote computer. This means that the normal output windows, such as the console, are not a suitable place for outputting test-related information. Clearly, you also don't want test-related information interspersed throughout the debugging or trace information being generated by the application. For this reason, there is a separate channel for writing test-related information so it can be viewed alongside the test results.

The `TestContext` object exposes a `WriteLine` method that takes a `String` and a series of `String`. `Format` arguments that can be used to output information to the results for a particular test. For example, adding the following line to the `CurrentStatusDataTest` method generates additional information with the test results:

Available for download on Wrox.com

VB

```
TestContext.WriteLine("No exceptions thrown for test id {0}", _
    CInt(Me.TestContext.DataRow.Item(0)))
```

Code snippet SubscriptionTests\SubscriptionTest.vb

C#

```
TestContext.WriteLine("No exceptions thrown for test id {0}",
                this.TestContext.DataRow[0]);
```

Code snippet SubscriptionTests\SubscriptionTest.cs

> *Although you should use the* `TestContext.WriteLine` *method to capture details about your test executions, the Visual Studio test tools will collect anything written to the standard error and standard output streams and add that data to the Test Results window.*

After the test run is completed, the Test Results window is displayed, listing all the test cases that were executed in the test run along with their results. The Test Results Details window, shown in

Figure 11-8, displays any additional information that was outputted by the test case. You can view this window by double-clicking the test case in the Test Results window.

In Figure 11-8, you can see in the Additional Information section the output from the `WriteLine` method you added to the test method. Although you added only one line to the test method, the `WriteLine` method was executed for each row in the database table. The Data Driven Test Results section of Figure 11-8 provides more information about each of the test passes, with a row for each row in the table. Your results may differ from those shown in Figure 11-8, depending on the code you have in your `Subscription` class.

CurrentStatusDataTest [Results]	×	SubscriptionTest.cs

Common Results

Test Run:	dev@DEV-PC 2009-07-13 01:31:57
Test Name:	CurrentStatusDataTest
Result:	Passed
Duration:	00:00:00.8688445
Computer Name:	DEV-PC
Start Time:	7/13/2009 1:31:58 AM
End Time:	7/13/2009 1:32:00 AM

Additional Information

No exceptions thrown for test id 1
No exceptions thrown for test id 2
No exceptions thrown for test id 3
No exceptions thrown for test id 4

Data Driven Test Results: 4 of 4 passed

Result	Duration	Data Row	Error Message
Passed	00:00:00.0769824	0	
Passed	00:00:00.0045662	1	
Passed	00:00:00.0059468	2	
Passed	00:00:00.0080552	3	

FIGURE 11-8

ADVANCED UNIT TESTING

Up until now, you have seen how to write and execute unit tests. This section goes on to examine how you can add custom properties to a test case, and how you can use the same framework to test private methods and properties.

Custom Properties

The testing framework provides a number of test attributes that you can apply to a method to record additional information about a test case. This information can be edited via the Properties window and updates the appropriate attributes on the test method. At times you might want to drive your test methods by specifying your own properties, which can also be set using the Properties window. To do this, add `TestProperty` attributes to the test method. For example, the following code adds two attributes to the test method to enable you to specify an arbitrary date and an expected status. This might be convenient for ad hoc testing using the Test View and Properties window:

Available for download on Wrox.com

VB

```vb
<TestMethod()>
<TestProperty("SpecialDate", "1/1/2008")>
<TestProperty("SpecialStatus", "Suspended")>
Public Sub SpecialCurrentStatusTest()
    Dim target As New Subscription

    target.PaidUpTo = CType(Me.TestContext.Properties.Item("SpecialDate"), _
        Date)

    Dim val As Subscription.Status = _
        [Enum].Parse(GetType(Subscription.Status), _
        CStr(Me.TestContext.Properties.Item("SpecialStatus")))

    Assert.AreEqual(val, target.CurrentStatus, _
```

```
        "Correct status not set for Paidup date {0}", target.PaidUpTo)
End Sub
```

Code snippet SubscriptionTests\SubscriptionTest.vb

Available for
download on
Wrox.com

C#

```
[TestMethod]
[TestProperty("SpecialDate", "1/1/2008")]
[TestProperty("SpecialStatus", "Suspended")]
public void SpecialCurrentStatusTest()
{
    var target = new Subscription();

    target.PaidUpTo = this.TestContext.Properties["SpecialDate"] as DateTime?;

    var val = Enum.Parse(typeof(Subscription.Status),
        this.TestContext.Properties["SpecialStatus"] as string);

    Assert.AreEqual(val, target.CurrentStatus,
        "Correct status not set for Paidup date {0}", target.PaidUpTo);

}
```

Code snippet SubscriptionTests\SubscriptionTest.cs

By using the Test View to navigate to this test case and accessing the Properties window, you can see that this code generates two additional properties, SpecialDate and SpecialStatus, as shown in Figure 11-9.

You can use the Properties window to adjust the SpecialDate and SpecialStatus values. Unfortunately, the limitation here is that there is no way to specify the data type for the values. As a result, the property grid displays and enables edits as if they were String data types.

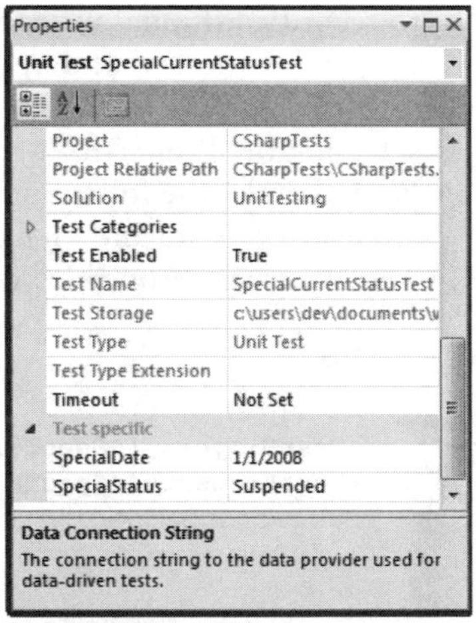

FIGURE 11-9

In the previous version of Visual Studio the TestContext.Properties dictionary was not automatically filled in and you had to do this by hand in your TestInitialize method. In Visual Studio 2010 this is all handled for you.

Testing Private Members

One of the selling points of unit testing is that it is particularly effective for testing the internals of your class to ensure that they function correctly. The assumption here is that if each of your components works in isolation, there is a better chance that they will work together correctly; and in fact, you can use unit testing to test classes working together. However, you might be wondering how well the unit-testing framework handles testing private methods.

One of the features of the .NET Framework is the capability to reflect over any type that has been loaded into memory and to execute any member regardless of its accessibility. This functionality does come at a performance cost, because the reflection calls obviously include an additional level of redirection, which can prove costly if done frequently. Nonetheless, for testing, reflection enables you to call into the inner workings of a class and not worry about the potential performance penalties for making those calls.

The other, more significant issue with using reflection to access non-public members of a class is that the code to do so is somewhat messy. Fortunately, Visual Studio 2010 does a very good job of generating a wrapper class that makes testing even private methods easy. To show this, return to the `CurrentStatus` property, change its access from `public` to `private`, and rename it `PrivateCurrentStatus`. Then regenerate the unit test for this property as you did earlier.

The following code snippet is the new unit-test method that is generated:

VB

```vb
<TestMethod(), _
 DeploymentItem("Subscriptions.dll")> _
Public Sub PrivateCurrentStatusTest()
    Dim target As Subscription_Accessor = New Subscription_Accessor()
    ' TODO:  Initialize to an appropriate value
    Dim actual As Subscription.Status
    actual = target.PrivateCurrentStatus
    Assert.Inconclusive("Verify the correctness of this test method.")
End Sub
```

Code snippet SubscriptionTests\SubscriptionTest.vb

C#

```csharp
[TestMethod()]
[DeploymentItem("Subscriptions.dll")]
public void PrivateCurrentStatusTest()
{
    Subscription_Accessor target = new Subscription_Accessor();
    Subscription.Status actual;
    actual = target.PrivateCurrentStatus;
    Assert.Inconclusive("Verify the correctness of this test method.");
}
```

Code snippet SubscriptionTests\SubscriptionTest.cs

As you can see, the preceding example uses an instance of a new `Subscription_Accessor` class to access the `PrivateCurrentStatus` property. This is a class that was auto-generated and compiled into a new assembly by Visual Studio. A new file was also added to the test project with the `.accessor` extension, which is what causes Visual Studio to create the new accessor classes.

You can add a private accessor class to a test project without generating a unit test. To do this, open the class that you want a private accessor for and select Create Private Accessor from the context menu of the editor.

> *You don't need to create a private accessor for every class in a project individually. Each .accessor file actually relates of a single project and creates an accessor class for all of the classes in that project.*

TESTING CODE CONTRACTS

If you are using the new Code Contracts feature described in Chapter 13, then you might want to write tests that verify the behavior of your contracts. The simplest way to do this is to open the Code Contracts project properties page and uncheck the Assert on Contract Failure checkbox. When you do this the Code Contracts API will raise exceptions instead of causing Assertion failures. You can check for these exceptions with an `ExpectedException` attribute if you know the type of exception to expect. By default, the Code Contracts tools generate the exceptions that will be thrown and their type cannot be known at runtime. Many of the contract methods have an overload which accepts an exception type as a generic parameter.

Here is a simple class which performs a mathematical operation on positive integers and a unit test to check the case where a negative number is passed in.

Available for download on Wrox.com

VB

```vb
Class Calculator
    Public Function Factorial(ByVal n As Integer) As Integer
        Contract.Requires(Of ArgumentOutOfRangeException)(n >= 0, "n")

        If n = 0 Then Return 1
        Return n * Factorial(n - 1)

    End Function
End Class


<TestMethod(), ExpectedException(GetType(ArgumentOutOfRangeException))>
Public Sub NegativeTest()

  Dim generator As New Calculator()
  Dim actual = generator.Factorial(-1)

  Assert.Fail("Contract not working")
End Sub
```

Code snippet CodeContracts1\CalculatorTests.vb

C#

```csharp
class Calculator
{
  public int Factorial(int n)
  {
    Contract.Requires<ArgumentOutOfRangeException>(n >= 0, "n");

    if (n == 0) return 1;
    return n * Factorial(n - 1);
  }
}

[TestMethod, ExpectedException(typeof(ArgumentOutOfRangeException))]
public void NegativeTest()
{
  var generator = new Calculator();
  var actual = generator.Factorial(-1);

  Assert.Fail("Contract not working");
}
```

Code snippet CodeContracts1\CalculatorTests.cs

Although this method of testing Code Contracts works, it is not really recommended as it may cover up errors in the code. A better option is to hook into the Code Contracts system and override its default behavior from within the test project itself. You do this by registering for the `ContractFailed` event on the static `Contract` class inside of an `AssemblyInitialize` method. Inside of the event handler you tell the Code Contracts API that you have handled the contract failure and that you would like to throw an appropriate exception.

VB

```vbnet
<AssemblyInitialize()>
Public Shared Sub AssemblyInitialize(ByVal testContext As TestContext)

    AddHandler Contract.ContractFailed, Sub(sender As Object,
                        e As ContractFailedEventArgs)
                        e.SetHandled()
                        e.SetUnwind()
                    End Sub
End Sub

<TestMethod(), ExpectedException(GetType(Exception), AllowDerivedTypes:=True)>
Public Sub NegativeTest()

  Dim generator As New Calculator()
```

```
    Dim actual = generator.Factorial(-1)

    Assert.Fail("Contract not working")
End Sub
```

Code snippet CodeContracts2\CalculatorTests.vb

C#

```
[AssemblyInitialize]
public static void AssemblyInitialize(TestContext testContext)
{
  Contract.ContractFailed += (s, e) =>
  {
    e.SetHandled();
    e.SetUnwind();
  };
}

[TestMethod, ExpectedException(typeof(Exception), AllowDerivedTypes = true)]
public void NegativeTest()
{
  var generator = new Calculator();
  var actual = generator.Factorial(-1);
  Assert.Fail("Contract not working");
}
```

Code snippet CodeContracts2\CalculatorTests.cs

> When Code Contracts are configured to cause Asserts, the intended exception
> is lost, so the code sample checks for any subclass of `Exception`. *The
> actual exception that gets thrown is a* `System.Diagnostics.Contracts`
> `.ContractException`, *which is private to the .NET Framework, so you can't
> detect it directly.*

MANAGING LARGE NUMBERS OF TESTS

Visual Studio provides both the Test View window and the Test List Editor to display a list of all of the tests in a solution. The Test View window, which was shown earlier in the chapter in Figure 11-2, simply displays the unit tests in a flat list. However, if you have hundreds, or even thousands, of unit tests in your solution, trying to manage them with a flat list will quickly become unwieldy.

The Test List Editor enables you to group and organize related tests into test lists. Because test lists can contain both tests and other test lists, you can further organize your tests by creating a logical, hierarchical structure. All the tests in a test list can then be executed together from within Visual Studio, or via a command-line test utility.

You can open the Test List Editor from the Test Windows menu, or you can double-click the Visual Studio Test Metadata (.vsmdi) file for the solution. Figure 11-10 shows the Test List Editor for a solution with a number of tests organized into a hierarchical structure of related tests.

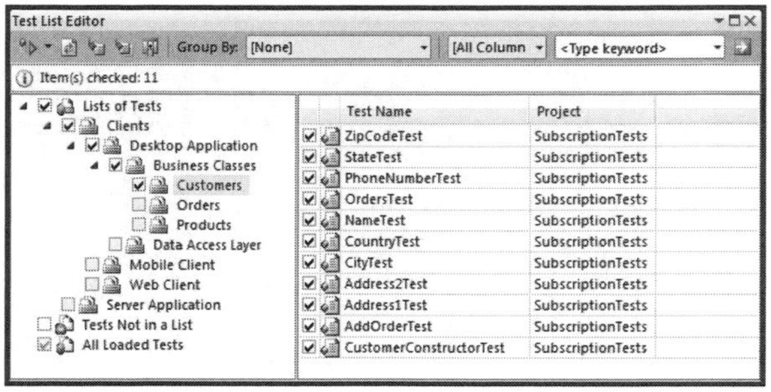

On the left in the Test List Editor window is a hierarchical tree of test lists available for the current solution. At the bottom of the tree are two project lists, one showing all the test

FIGURE 11-10

cases (All Loaded Tests) and one showing those test cases that haven't been put in a list (Tests Not in a List). Under the Lists of Tests node are all the test lists created for the project.

To create a new test list, click Test ⇨ Create New Test List. Test cases can be dragged from any existing list into the new list. Initially, this can be a little confusing because a test will be moved to the new list and removed from its original list. To add a test case to multiple lists, either hold the Ctrl key while dragging the test case or copy and paste the test case from the original list to the new list.

After creating a test list, you can run the whole list by checking the box next to the list in the Test Manager. The Run button executes all lists that are checked. Alternatively, you can run the list with the debugger attached using the Debug Checked Tests menu item.

SUMMARY

This chapter described how you can use unit testing to ensure the correct functionality of your code. The unit-testing framework within Visual Studio is quite comprehensive, enabling you to both document and manage test cases.

You can fully exercise the testing framework using an appropriate data source to minimize the repetitive code you have to write. You can also extend the framework to test all the inner workings of your application.

Visual Studio Premium and Ultimate contain even more functionality for testing, including the ability to track and report on code coverage, and support for load and web application testing. Chapter 56 provides more detail on these advanced testing capabilities.

Documentation with XML Comments

WHAT'S IN THIS CHAPTER?

➤ Adding inline documentation to your code using XML comments

➤ Using the GhostDoc Visual Studio Add-In to automatically generate XML comments

➤ Producing stand-alone documentation from XML comments with Sandcastle

➤ Using Task List comments to keep track of pending coding tasks and other things to do

Documentation is a critical, and often overlooked, feature of the development process. Without documentation, other programmers, code reviewers, and project managers have a more difficult time analyzing the purpose and implementation of code. You can even have problems with your own code once it becomes complex, and having good internal documentation can aid in the development process.

XML comments are a way of providing that internal documentation for your code without having to go through the process of manually creating and maintaining a separate document. Instead, as you write your code, you include metadata at the top of every definition to explain the intent of your code. Once the information has been included in your code, it can be consumed by Visual Studio to provide Object Browser and IntelliSense information.

GhostDoc is a free third-party add-in for Visual Studio that can automatically insert an XML comment block for a class or member.

Sandcastle is a set of tools that act as a documentation compiler. These tools can be used to easily create standalone documentation in Microsoft compiled HTML help or Microsoft Help 2 format from the XML comments you have added to your code.

INLINE COMMENTING

All programming languages supported by Visual Studio provide a method for adding inline documentation. By default, all inline comments are highlighted in green.

C# supports both single line comments and comment blocks. Single line comments are denoted by `//` at the beginning of the comment. Block comments typically span multiple lines and are opened by `/*` and closed off by `*/`, as shown in the following code:

C#

```csharp
// Calculate the factorial of an integer
public int Factorial(int number)
{
    /* This function calculates a factorial using an
     * iterative approach.
     */
    int intermediateResult = 1;
    for (int factor = 2; factor <= number; factor++)
    {
        intermediateResult = intermediateResult * factor;
    }
    return intermediateResult;    //The calculated factorial
}
```

VB just uses a single quote character to denote anything following it to be a comment, as shown in the following code:

VB

```vb
' Calculate the factorial of an integer
Public Function Factorial(ByVal number As Integer) As Integer
    ' This function calculates a factorial using an
    ' iterative approach.
    '
    Dim intermediateResult As Integer = 1
    For factor As Integer = 2 To number
        intermediateResult = intermediateResult * factor
    Next
    Return intermediateResult 'The calculated factorial
End Function
```

XML COMMENTS

XML comments are specialized comments that you include in your code. When the project goes through the build process, Visual Studio can optionally include a step to generate an XML file based on these comments to provide information about user-defined types such as classes and individual members of a class (user defined or not), including events, functions, and properties.

XML comments can contain any combination of XML and HTML tags. Visual Studio performs special processing on a particular set of predefined tags, as you see throughout the bulk of this chapter. Any other tags are included in the generated documentation file as is.

Adding XML Comments

XML comments are added immediately before the property, method, or class definition they are associated with. Visual Studio automatically adds an XML comment block when you type the shortcut code /// in C# before a member or class declaration. In some cases the XML comments will already be present in code generated by the supplied project templates, as shown in Figure 12-1.

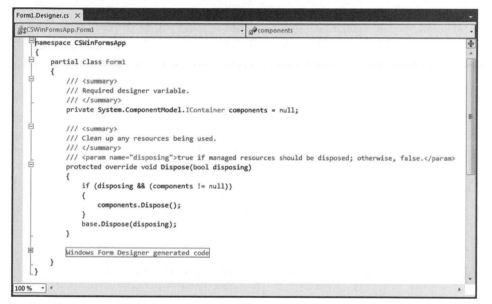

FIGURE 12-1

> The automatic insertion of the summary section can be enabled or disabled in the Visual Studio options. Select Tools ➪ Options, and then choose Text Editor ➪ C# ➪ Advanced from the navigation tree. Uncheck the "Generate XML documentation comments for ///" option to disable this feature.

Adding an XML comment block to VB is achieved by using the '' shortcut code. In this way it replicates the way C# documentation is generated.

In both languages, once the comments have been added, Visual Studio automatically adds a collapsible region to the left margin so you can hide the documentation when you're busy writing code. Hovering over the collapsed area displays a tooltip message containing the first few lines of the comment block.

XML Comment Tags

Though you can use any kind of XML comment structure you like, including your own custom XML tags, Visual Studio's XML comment processor recognizes a number of predefined tags and automatically formats them appropriately. The Sandcastle document compiler, which is discussed later in this chapter, has support for a number of additional tags, and you can supplement these further with your own XML schema document.

> *If you need to use angle brackets in the text of a documentation comment, use the entity references* <; *and* >;.

Because documentation is so important, the next section of this chapter details each of these predefined tags, their syntax, and how you would use them in your own documentation.

The <c> Tag

The <c> tag indicates that the enclosed text should be formatted as code, rather than normal text. It's used for code that is included in a normal text block. The structure of <c> is simple, with any text appearing between the opening and closing tags being marked for formatting in the code style.

```
<c>code-formatted text</c>
```

The following example shows how <c> might be used in the description of a property:

C#

```
/// <summary>
/// The <c>UserId</c> property is used in conjunction with other properties
/// to setup a user properly. Remember to set the <c>Password</c> field too.
/// </summary>
public string UserId { get; set; }
```

VB

```
''' <summary>
''' The <c>UserId</c> property is used in conjunction with other properties
''' to setup a user properly. Remember to set the <c>Password</c> field too.
''' </summary>
Public Property UserId() As String
```

The <code> Tag

If the amount of text in the documentation you need to format as code is more than just a phrase within a normal text block, you can use the <code> tag instead of <c>. This tag marks everything within it as code, but it's a block-level tag, rather than a character-level tag. The syntax of this tag is a simple opening and closing tag with the text to be formatted inside, as shown here:

```
<code>
Code-formatted text
Code-formatted text
</code>
```

The `<code>` tag can be embedded inside any other XML comment tag. The following code shows an example of how it could be used in the summary section of a property definition:

C#

```
/// <summary>
/// The <c>UserId</c> property is used in conjunction with other properties
/// to setup a user properly. Remember to set the <c>Password</c> field too.
/// For example:
/// <code>
/// myUser.UserId = "daveg"
/// myUser.Password = "xg4*Wv"
/// </code>
/// </summary>
public string UserId { get; set; }
```

VB

```
''' <summary>
''' The <c>UserId</c> property is used in conjunction with other properties
''' to setup a user properly. Remember to set the <c>Password</c> field too.
''' For example:
''' <code>
''' myUser.UserId = "daveg"
''' myUser.Password = "xg4*Wv"
''' </code>
''' </summary>
Public Property UserId() As String
```

The <example> Tag

A common requirement for internal documentation is to provide an example of how a particular procedure or member can be used. The `<example>` tags indicate that the enclosed block should be treated as a discrete section of the documentation, dealing with a sample for the associated member. Effectively, this doesn't do anything more than help organize the documentation, but used in conjunction with an appropriately designed XML style sheet or processing instructions, the example can be formatted properly.

The other XML comment tags, such as `<c>` and `<code>`, can be included in the text inside the `<example>` tags to give you a comprehensively documented sample. The syntax of this block-level tag is simple:

```
<example>
Any sample text goes here.
</example>
```

Using the example from the previous discussion, the following code moves the <code> formatted text out of the <summary> section into an <example> section:

C#

```
/// <summary>
/// The <c>UserId</c> property is used in conjunction with other properties
/// to setup a user properly. Remember to set the <c>Password</c> field too.
/// </summary>
/// <example>
/// <code>
/// myUser.UserId = "daveg"
/// myUser.Password = "xg4*Wv"
/// </code>
/// </example>
public string UserId { get; set; }
```

VB

```
''' <summary>
''' The <c>UserId</c> property is used in conjunction with other properties
''' to setup a user properly. Remember to set the <c>Password</c> field too.
''' </summary>
''' <example>
''' <code>
''' myUser.UserId = "daveg"
''' myUser.Password = "xg4*Wv"
''' </code>
''' </example>
Public Property UserId() As String
```

The <exception> Tag

The <exception> tag is used to define any exceptions that could be thrown from within the member associated with the current block of XML documentation. Each exception that can be thrown should be defined with its own <exception> block, with an attribute of cref identifying the fully qualified type name of an exception that could be thrown. Note that the Visual Studio 2010 XML comment processor checks the syntax of the exception block to enforce the inclusion of this attribute. It also ensures that you don't have multiple <exception> blocks with the same attribute value. The full syntax is as follows:

```
<exception cref="exceptionName">
Exception description.
</exception>
```

Extending the examples from the previous tag discussions, the following code adds two exception definitions to the XML comments associated with the UserId property: System. TimeoutException, and System.UnauthorizedAccessException.

C#

```
/// <summary>
/// The <c>UserId</c> property is used in conjunction with other properties
/// to setup a user properly. Remember to set the <c>Password</c> field too.
```

```
/// </summary>
/// <exception cref="System.TimeoutException">
/// Thrown when the code cannot determine if the user is valid within a reasonable
/// amount of time.
/// </exception>
/// <exception cref="System.UnauthorizedAccessException">
/// Thrown when the user identifier is not valid within the current context.
/// </exception>
/// <example>
/// <code>
/// myUser.UserId = "daveg"
/// myUser.Password = "xg4*Wv"
/// </code>
/// </example>
public string UserId { get; set; }
```

VB

```
''' <summary>
''' The <c>UserId</c> property is used in conjunction with other properties
''' to setup a user properly. Remember to set the <c>Password</c> field too.
''' </summary>
''' <exception cref="System.TimeoutException">
''' Thrown when the code cannot determine if the user is valid within a reasonable
''' amount of time.
''' </exception>
''' <exception cref="System.UnauthorizedAccessException">
''' Thrown when the user identifier is not valid within the current context.
''' </exception>
''' <example>
''' <code>
''' myUser.UserId = "daveg"
''' myUser.Password = "xg4*Wv"
''' </code>
''' </example>
Public Property UserId() As String
```

The <include> Tag

You'll often have documentation that needs to be shared across multiple projects. In other situations, one person may be responsible for the documentation while others are doing the coding. Either way, the <include> tag will prove useful. The <include> tag enables you to refer to comments in a separate XML file so they are brought inline with the rest of your documentation. Using this method, you can move the actual documentation out of the code, which can be handy when the comments are extensive.

The syntax of <include> requires that you specify which part of the external file is to be used in the current context. The path attribute is used to identify the path to the XML node, and uses standard XPath terminology:

```
<include file="filename" path="XPathQuery" />
```

The external XML file containing the additional documentation must have a path that can be navigated with the attribute you specify, with the end node containing an attribute of name to uniquely identify the specific section of the XML document to be included.

You can include files in either VB or C# using the same tag. The following code takes the samples used in the <exception> tag discussion and moves the documentation to an external file:

C#

```
/// <include file="externalFile.xml" path="MyDoc/Properties[@name='UserId']/*" />
public string UserId { get; set; }
```

VB

```
''' <include file="externalFile.xml" path="MyDoc/Properties[@name='UserId']/*" />
Public Property UserId() As String
```

The external file's contents would be populated with the following XML document structure to synchronize it with what the <include> tag processing expects to find:

```
<MyDoc>
  <Properties name="UserId">
    <summary>
      The <c>sender</c> object is used to identify who invoked the procedure.
    </summary>
    <summary>
      The <c>UserId</c> property is used in conjunction with other properties
      to setup a user properly. Remember to set the <c>Password</c> field too.
    </summary>
    <exception cref="System.TimeoutException">
      Thrown when the code cannot determine if the user is valid within a
      reasonable amount of time.
    </exception>
    <exception cref="System.UnauthorizedAccessException">
      Thrown when the user identifier is not valid within the current context.
    </exception>
    <example>
      <code>
        myUser.UserId = "daveg"
        myUser.Password = "xg4*Wv"
      </code>
    </example>
  </Procedures>
</MyDoc>
```

The <list> Tag

Some documentation requires lists of various descriptions, and with the <list> tag you can generate numbered and unnumbered lists along with two-column tables. All three take two parameters for each entry in the list — a term and a description — represented by individual XML tags, but they instruct the processor to generate the documentation in different ways.

To create a list in the documentation, use the following syntax, where `type` can be one of the following values — `bullet`, `numbered`, or `table`:

```
<list type="type">
    <listheader>
        <term>termName</term>
        <description>description</description>
    </listheader>
    <item>
        <term>myTerm</term>
        <description>myDescription</description>
    </item>
</list>
```

The `<listheader>` block is optional, and is usually used for table-formatted lists or definition lists. For definition lists, the `<term>` tag must be included, but for bullet lists, numbered lists, or tables the `<term>` tag can be omitted.

The XML for each type of list can be formatted differently using an XML style sheet. An example of how to use the `<list>` tag appears in the following code. Note how the sample has omitted the `listheader` tag, because it was unnecessary for the bullet list:

C#

```
/// <summary>
/// This function changes a users password. The password change could fail for
/// several reasons:
/// <list type="bullet">
/// <item>
/// <term>Too Short</term>
/// <description>The new password was not long enough.</description>
/// </item>
/// <item>
/// <term>Not Complex</term>
/// <description>The new password did not meet the complexity requirements. It
/// must contain at least one of the following characters: lowercase, uppercase,
/// and number.
/// </description>
/// </item>
/// </list>
/// </summary>
public bool ChangePwd(string oldPwd, string newPwd)
{
    //...code...
    return true;
}
```

VB

```
''' <summary>
''' This function changes a users password. The password change could fail for
''' several reasons:
''' <list type="bullet">
''' <item>
```

```
''' <term>Too Short</term>
''' <description>The new password was not long enough.</description>
''' </item>
''' <item>
''' <term>Not Complex</term>
''' <description>The new password did not meet the complexity requirements. It
''' must contain at least one of the following characters: lowercase, uppercase,
''' and number.
''' </description>
''' </item>
''' </list>
''' </summary>
Public Function ChangePwd(ByVal oldPwd As String, ByVal newPwd As String) _
                        As Boolean
    '...code...
    Return True
End Function
```

The <para> Tag

Without using the various internal block-level XML comments such as `<list>` and `<code>`, the text you add to the main `<summary>`, `<remarks>`, and `<returns>` sections all just runs together. To break it up into readable chunks, you can use the `<para>` tag, which simply indicates that the text enclosed should be treated as a discrete paragraph. The syntax is simple:

```
<para>This text will appear in a separate paragraph.</para>
```

The <param> Tag

To explain the purpose of any parameters in a function declaration, you can use the `<param>` tag. This tag will be processed by the Visual Studio XML comment processor with each instance requiring a name attribute that has a value equal to the name of one of the properties. Enclosed between the opening and closing `<param>` tag is the description of the parameter:

```
<param name="parameterName">Definition of parameter.</param>
```

The XML processor will not allow you to create multiple `<param>` tags for the one parameter, or tags for parameters that don't exist, producing warnings that are added to the Error List in Visual Studio if you try. The following example shows how the `<param>` tag is used to describe two parameters of a function:

C#

```
/// <param name="oldPwd">Old password-must match the current password</param>
/// <param name="newPwd">New password-must meet the complexity requirements</param>
public bool ChangePwd(string oldPwd, string newPwd)
{
    //...code...
    return true;
}
```

VB

```
''' <param name="oldPwd">Old password-must match the current password</param>
''' <param name="newPwd">New password-must meet the complexity requirements</param>
Public Function ChangePwd(ByVal oldPwd As String, ByVal newPwd As String) _
                        As Boolean
    '...code...
    Return True
End Function
```

> *The* <param> *tag is especially useful for documenting preconditions for a method's parameters, such as if a null value is not allowed.*

The <paramref> Tag

If you are referring to the parameters of the method definition elsewhere in the documentation other than the <param> tag, you can use the <paramref> tag to format the value, or even link to the parameter information depending on how you code the XML transformation. The compiler does not require that the name of the parameter exist, but you must specify the text to be used in the name attribute, as the following syntax shows:

```
<paramref name="parameterName" />
```

Normally, <paramref> tags are used when you are referring to parameters in the larger sections of documentation such as the <summary> or <remarks> tags, as the following example demonstrates:

C#

```
/// <summary>
/// This function changes a users password. This will throw an exception if
/// <paramref name="oldPwd" /> or <paramref name="newPwd" /> are nothing.
/// </summary>
/// <param name="oldPwd">Old password-must match the current password</param>
/// <param name="newPwd">New password-must meet the complexity requirements</param>
public bool ChangePwd(string oldPwd, string newPwd)
{
    //...code...
    return true;
}
```

VB

```
''' <summary>
''' This function changes a users password. This will throw an exception if
''' <paramref name="oldPwd" /> or <paramref name="newPwd" /> are nothing.
''' </summary>
''' <param name="oldPwd">Old password-must match the current password</param>
''' <param name="newPwd">New password-must meet the complexity requirements</param>
Public Function ChangePwd(ByVal oldPwd As String, ByVal newPwd As String) _
                        As Boolean
```

```
        '...code...
        Return True
End Function
```

The <permission> Tag

To describe the code access security permission set required by a particular method, use the <permission> tag. This tag requires a `cref` attribute to refer to a specific permission type:

```
<permission cref="permissionName">
    description goes here
</permission>
```

If the function requires more than one permission, use multiple <permission> blocks, as shown in the following example:

C#

```
/// <permission cref="System.Security.Permissions.RegistryPermission">
/// Needs full access to the Windows Registry.
/// </permission>
/// <permission cref="System.Security.Permissions.FileIOPermission">
/// Needs full access to the .config file containing application information.
/// </permission>
public string UserId { get; set; }
```

VB

```
''' <permission cref="System.Security.Permissions.RegistryPermission">
''' Needs full access to the Windows Registry.
''' </permission>
''' <permission cref="System.Security.Permissions.FileIOPermission">
''' Needs full access to the .config file containing application information.
''' </permission>
Public Property UserId() As String
```

The <remarks> Tag

The <remarks> tag is used to add an additional comment block to the documentation associated with a particular method. Discussion on previous tags has shown the <remarks> tag in action, but the syntax is as follows:

```
<remarks>
    Any further remarks go here
</remarks>
```

Normally, you would create a summary section, briefly outline the method or type, and then include the detailed information inside the <remarks> tag, with the expected outcomes of accessing the member.

The <returns> Tag

When a method returns a value to the calling code, you can use the <returns> tag to describe what it could be. The syntax of <returns> is like most of the other block-level tags, consisting of an opening and closing tag with any information detailing the return value enclosed within:

```
<returns>
    Description of the return value.
</returns>
```

A simple implementation of <returns> might appear like the following code:

C#

```
/// <summary>
/// This function changes a user's password.
/// </summary>
/// <returns>
/// This function returns:
/// <c>True</c> which indicates that the password was changed successfully,
/// or <c>False</c> which indicates that the password change failed.
/// </returns>
public bool ChangePwd(string oldPwd, string newPwd)
{
    //...code...
    return true;
}
```

VB

```
''' <summary>
''' This function changes a user's password.
''' </summary>
''' <returns>
''' This function returns:
''' <c>True</c> which indicates that the password was changed successfully,
''' or <c>False</c> which indicates that the password change failed.
''' </returns>
Public Function ChangePwd(ByVal oldPwd As String, ByVal newPwd As String) _
                            As Boolean
    '...code...
    Return True
End Function
```

In addition to return value of a function, the <returns> tag is especially useful for documenting any post-conditions that should be expected.

The <see> Tag

You can add references to other items in the project using the <see> tag. Like some of the other tags already discussed, the <see> tag requires a cref attribute with a value equal to an existing member, whether it is a property, method, or class definition. The <see> tag is used inline with other areas of the documentation such as <summary> or <remarks>. The syntax is as follows:

```
<see cref="memberName" />
```

When Visual Studio processes the <see> tag it produces a fully qualified address that can then be used as the basis for a link in the documentation when transformed via style sheets. For example, referring to an application with a class containing a function named ChangePwd would result in the following cref value:

```
<see cref="applicationName.className.ChangePwd"/>
```

The following example uses the <see> tag to provide a link to another function called CheckUser:

C#
```
/// <remarks>
/// Use <see cref="CheckUser" /> to verify that the user exists before calling
/// ChangePwd.
/// </remarks>
public bool ChangePwd(string oldPwd, string newPwd)
{
    //...code...
    return true;
}
```

VB
```
''' <remarks>
''' Use <see cref="CheckUser" /> to verify that the user exists before calling
''' ChangePwd.
''' </remarks>
Public Function ChangePwd(ByVal oldPwd As String, ByVal newPwd As String) _
                         As Boolean
    '...code...
    Return True
End Function
```

> *In VB only, if the member specified in the* cref *value does not exist, Visual Studio will use IntelliSense to display a warning and add it to the Error List.*

The <seealso> Tag

The <seealso> tag is used to generate a separate section containing information about related topics within the documentation. Rather than being inline like <see>, the <seealso> tags are defined outside the other XML comment blocks, with each instance of <seealso> requiring a cref attribute containing the name of the property, method, or class to which to link. The full syntax appears like so:

```
<seealso cref="memberName" />
```

Modifying the previous example, the following code shows how the <seealso> tag can be implemented in code:

C#

```
/// <remarks>
/// Use <see cref="CheckUser" /> to verify that the user exists before calling
/// ChangePwd.
/// </remarks>
/// <seealso cref="ResetPwd" />
public bool ChangePwd(string oldPwd, string newPwd)
{
    //...code...
    return true;
}
```

VB

```
''' <remarks>
''' Use <see cref="CheckUser" /> to verify that the user exists before calling
''' ChangePwd.
''' </remarks>
''' <seealso cref="ResetPwd" />
Public Function ChangePwd(ByVal oldPwd As String, ByVal newPwd As String) _
                         As Boolean
    '...code...
    Return True
End Function
```

The <summary> Tag

The <summary> tag is used to provide the brief description that appears at the top of a specific topic in the documentation. As such it is typically placed before all public and protected methods and classes. In addition, the <summary> area is used for Visual Studio's IntelliSense engine when using your own custom-built code. The syntax to implement <summary> is as follows:

```
<summary>
    A description of the function or property goes here.
</summary>
```

The <typeparam> Tag

The <typeparam> tag provides information about the type parameters when dealing with a generic type or member definition. The <typeparam> tag expects an attribute of name containing the type parameter being referred to:

```
<typeparam name="typeName">
    Description goes here.
</typeparam>
```

You can use <typeparam> in either C# or VB, as the following code shows:

C#

```
/// <typeparam name="T">
/// Base item type (must implement IComparable)
/// </typeparam>
public class myList<T> where T : IComparable
{
    //...code...
}
```

VB

```
''' <typeparam name="T">
''' Base item type (must implement IComparable)
''' </typeparam>
Public Class myList(Of T As IComparable)
    '...code...
End Class
```

The <typeparamref> Tag

If you are referring to a generic type parameter elsewhere in the documentation other than the <typeparam> tag, you can use the <typeparamref> tag to format the value, or even link to the parameter information depending on how you code the XML transformation.

```
<typeparamref name="parameterName" />
```

Normally, <typeparamref> tags are used when you are referring to parameters in the larger sections of documentation such as the <summary> or <remarks> tags, as the following code demonstrates:

C#

```
/// <summary>
/// Creates a new list of arbitrary type <typeparamref name="T"/>
/// </summary>
/// <typeparam name="T">
/// Base item type (must implement IComparable)
/// </typeparam>
public class myList<T> where T : IComparable
{
    //...code...
}
```

VB

```
''' <summary>
''' Creates a new list of arbitrary type <typeparamref name="T"/>
''' </summary>
''' <typeparam name="T">
''' Base item type (must implement IComparable)
''' </typeparam>
```

```
Public Class myList(Of T As IComparable)
    '...code...
End Class
```

The <value> Tag

Normally used to define a property's purpose, the <value> tag gives you another section in the XML where you can provide information about the associated member. The <value> tag is not used by IntelliSense.

```
<value>The text to display</value>
```

When used in conjunction with a property, you would normally use the <summary> tag to describe what the property is for, whereas the <value> tag is used to describe what the property represents:

C#

```
/// <summary>
/// The <c>UserId</c> property is used in conjunction with other properties
/// to setup a user properly. Remember to set the <c>Password</c> field too.
/// </summary>
/// <value>
/// A string containing the UserId for the current user
/// </value>
public string UserId { get; set; }
```

VB

```
''' <summary>
''' The <c>UserId</c> property is used in conjunction with other properties
''' to setup a user properly. Remember to set the <c>Password</c> field too.
''' </summary>
''' <value>
''' A string containing the UserId for the current user
''' </value>
Public Property UserId() As String
```

USING XML COMMENTS

Once you have the XML comments inline with your code, you'll most likely want to generate an XML file containing the documentation. In VB this setting is on by default, with an output path and filename specified with default values. However, C# has the option turned off as its default behavior, so if you want documentation you'll need to turn it on manually.

To ensure that your documentation is being generated where you require, open the property pages for the project through the Solution Explorer's right-click context menu. Locate the project for which you want documentation, right-click its entry in the Solution Explorer, and select Properties.

The XML documentation options are located in the Build section (see Figure 12-2). Below the general build options is an Output section that contains a checkbox that enables XML documentation file generation. When this checkbox is checked, the text field next to it becomes available for you to specify the filename for the XML file that will be generated.

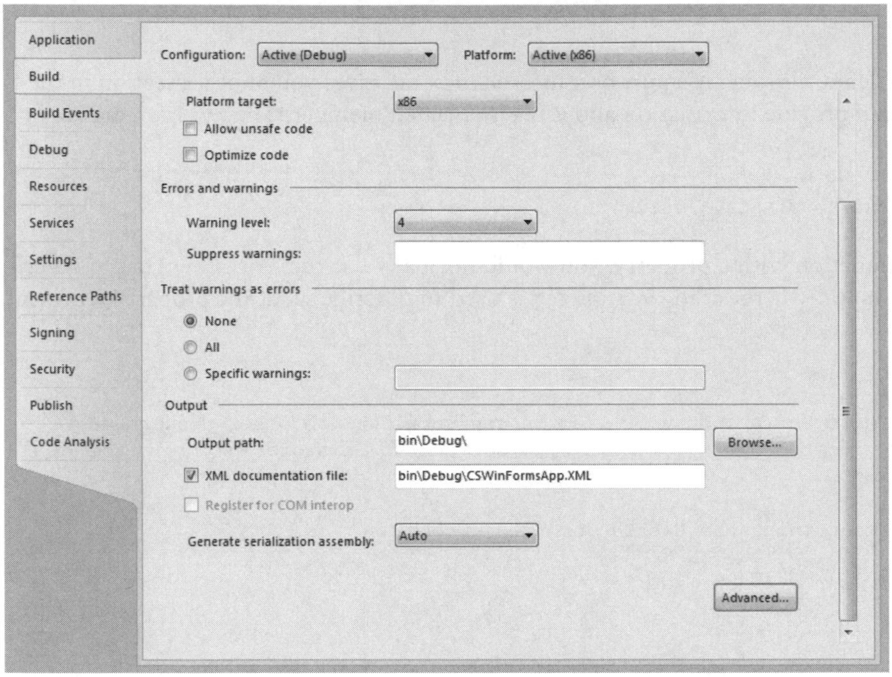

FIGURE 12-2

For VB applications, the option to generate an XML documentation file is on the Compile tab of the project properties.

Once you've saved these options, the next time you perform a build, Visual Studio adds the /doc compiler option to the process so that the XML documentation is generated as specified.

> *Generating an XML documentation file will slow down the compile time. If this is impacting your development or debugging cycle, you can disable it for the Debug build while leaving it enabled for the Release build.*

The XML file that is generated will contain a full XML document that you can apply XSL transformations against, or process through another application using the XML document object model. All references to exceptions, parameters, methods, and other "see also" links will be included as fully addressed information, including namespace, application, and class data. Later in this chapter you see how you can make use of this XML file to produce professional-looking documentation using Sandcastle.

IntelliSense Information

The other useful advantage of using XML comments is how Visual Studio consumes them in its own IntelliSense engine. As soon as you define the documentation tags that Visual Studio understands, it will generate the information into its IntelliSense, which means you can refer to the information elsewhere in your code.

You can access IntelliSense in two ways. If the member referred to is within the same project or is in another project within the same solution, you can access the information without having to build or generate the XML file. However, you can still take advantage of IntelliSense even when the project is external to your current application solution.

The trick is to ensure that when the XML file is generated by the build process, it must have the same name as the .NET assembly being built. For example, if the compiled output is `MyApplication.exe`, the associated XML file should be named `MyApplication.xml`. In addition, this generated XML file should be in the same folder as the compiled assembly so that Visual Studio can locate it.

GENERATING DOCUMENTATION WITH GHOSTDOC

Although most developers will agree that documentation is important, it still takes a lot of time and commitment to write. The golden rule of "if it's easy the developer will have more inclination to do it" means that any additional enhancements to the documentation side of development will encourage more developers to embrace it.

> *You can always take a more authoritarian approach to documentation and use a source code analysis tool such as StyleCop to enforce a minimum level of documentation. StyleCop ships with almost 50 built-in rules specifically for verifying the content and formatting of XML documentation. StyleCop is discussed in more detail in chapter 13.*

GhostDoc is an add-in for Visual Studio that attempts to do just that, providing the capability to set up a keyboard shortcut that automatically inserts the XML comment block for a class or member. However, the true power of GhostDoc is not in the capability to create the basic stub, but to automate a good part of the documentation itself.

Through a series of lists that customize how different parts of member and variable names should be interpreted, GhostDoc generates simple phrases that get you started in creating your own documentation. For example, consider the list shown in Figure 12-3, where words are defined as trigger points for "Of the" phrases. Whenever a variable or member name has the string "color" as part of its name, GhostDoc attempts to create a phrase that can be used in the XML documentation.

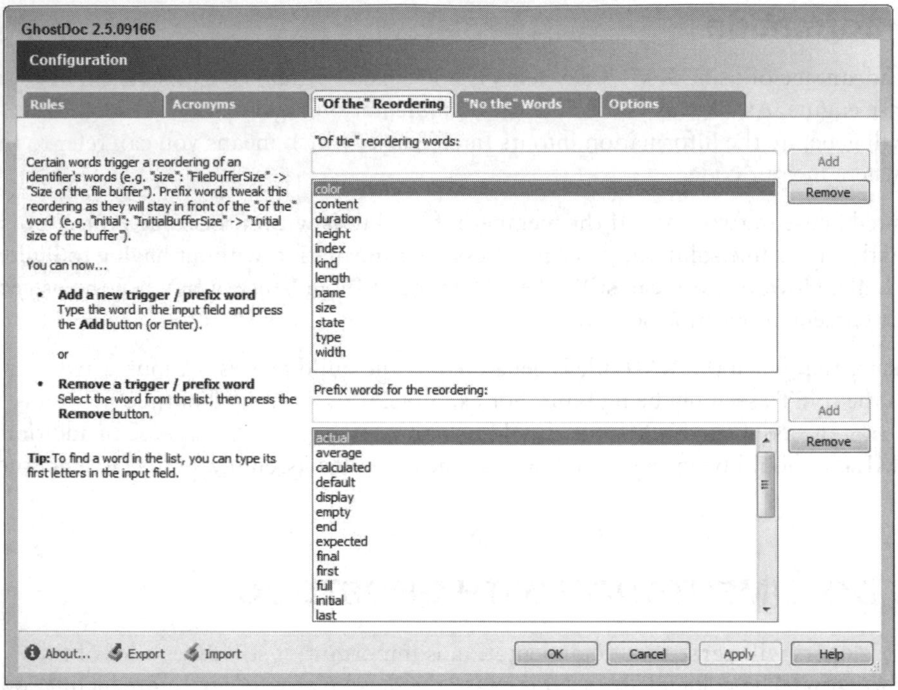

FIGURE 12-3

For instance, a property called `NewBackgroundColor` will generate a complete phrase of `New color of the background`. The functionality of GhostDoc also recognizes common parameter names and their purpose. Figure 12-4 shows this in action with a default `Click` event handler for a button control. The `sender` and `e` parameters were recognized as particular types in the context of an event handler, and the documentation that was generated by GhostDoc reflects this accordingly.

```
        /// <summary>
        /// Handles the Click event of the btnClose control.
        /// </summary>
        /// <param name="sender">The source of the event.</param>
        /// <param name="e">The <see cref="System.EventArgs"/> instance containing the event data.</param>
        private void btnClose_Click(object sender, EventArgs e)
        {
            this.Close();
        }
```

FIGURE 12-4

GhostDoc is an excellent resource for those who find documentation difficult. You can find it at its official web site, `http://submain.com/ghostdoc`.

COMPILING DOCUMENTATION WITH SANDCASTLE

Sandcastle is a set of tools published by Microsoft that act as documentation compilers. These tools can be used to easily create very professional-looking external documentation in Microsoft compiled HTML help (`.chm`) or Microsoft Help 2 (`.hsx`) format.

The primary location for information on Sandcastle is the Sandcastle blog at `http://blogs.msdn.com/sandcastle/`. There is also a project on CodePlex, Microsoft's open source project hosting site, at `http://sandcastle.codeplex.com/`. You can find documentation, a discussion forum, and a link to download the latest Sandcastle installer package on this site.

By default, Sandcastle installs to `c:\Program Files\Sandcastle`. When it is run, Sandcastle creates a large number of working files and the final output file under this directory. Unfortunately all files and folders under Program Files require administrator permissions to write to, which can be problematic particularly if you are running on Windows Vista with UAC enabled. Therefore it is recommended that you install it to a location where your user account has write permissions.

Out of the box, Sandcastle is used from the command line only. A number of third-parties have put together GUI interfaces for Sandcastle, which are linked to on the Wiki.

To begin, open a Visual Studio 2010 Command Prompt from Start Menu ⇨ All Programs ⇨ Microsoft Visual Studio 2010 ⇨ Visual Studio Tools, and change directory to `<Sandcastle Install Directory>\Examples\sandcastle\`.

> *The Visual Studio 2010 Command Prompt is equivalent to a normal command prompt except that it also sets various environment variables, such as directory search paths, which are often required by the Visual Studio 2010 command-line tools.*

In this directory you will find an example class file, `test.cs`, and an MSBuild project file, `build.proj`. The example class file contains methods and properties that are commented with the standard XML comment tags that were explained earlier in this chapter, as well as some additional Sandcastle-specific XML comment tags. You can compile the class file and generate the XML documentation file by entering the following command:

```
csc /t:library test.cs /doc:example.xml
```

Once that has completed, you are now ready to generate the documentation help file. The simplest way to do this is to execute the example MSBuild project file that ships with Sandcastle. This project file has been hard-coded to generate the documentation using `test.dll` and `example.xml`. Run the MSBuild project by entering the following command:

```
msbuild build.proj
```

The MSBuild project will call several Sandcastle tools to build the documentation file including MRefBuilder, BuildAssembler, and XslTransform.

> *Rather than manually running Sandcastle every time you build a release version, it would be better to ensure that it is always run by executing it as a post-build event. Chapter 6 describes how to create a build event.*

You may be surprised at how long the documentation takes to generate. This is partly because the MRefBuilder tool uses reflection to inspect the assembly and all dependant assemblies to obtain information about all of the types, properties, and methods in the assembly and all dependant assemblies. In addition, anytime it comes across a base .NET Framework type, it will attempt to resolve it to the MSDN online documentation in order to generate the correct hyperlinks in the documentation help file.

> *The first time you run the MSBuild project, it generates reflection data for all of the .NET Framework classes, so you can expect it to take even longer to complete.*

By default, the `build.proj` MSBuild project generates the documentation with the vs2005 look-and-feel, as shown in Figure 12-4, in the directory `<Sandcastle Install Directory>\Examples\sandcastle\chm\`. You can choose a different output style by adding one of the following options to the command line:

```
/property:PresentationStyle=vs2005
/property:PresentationStyle=hana
/property:PresentationStyle=prototype
```

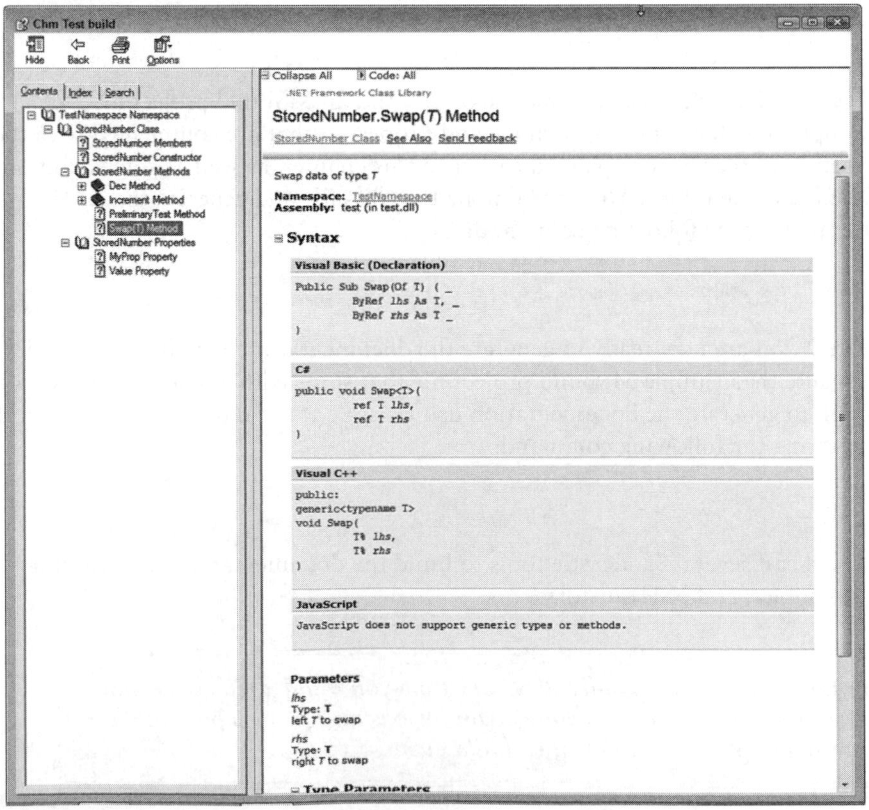

FIGURE 12-5

The following code shows the source code section from the example class file, `test.cs`, which relates to the page of the help documentation shown in Figure 12-5.

```
/// <summary>
/// Swap data of type <typeparamref name="T"/>
/// </summary>
/// <param name="lhs">left <typeparamref name="T"/> to swap</param>
/// <param name="rhs">right <typeparamref name="T"/> to swap</param>
/// <typeparam name="T">The element type to swap</typeparam>
public void Swap<T>(ref T lhs, ref T rhs)
{
    T temp;
    temp = lhs;
    lhs = rhs;
    rhs = temp;
}
```

The default target for the `build.proj` MSBuild project is "Chm," which builds a CHM compiled HTML Help file for the `test.dll` assembly. You can also specify one of the following targets on the command line:

```
/target:Clean  - removes all generated files
/target:HxS    - builds HxS file for Visual Studio in addition to CHM
```

> *The Microsoft Help 2 (.HxS) is the format that the Visual Studio help system uses. You must install the Microsoft Help 2.x SDK in order to generate .HxS files. This is available and included as part of the Visual Studio 2010 SDK.*

TASK LIST COMMENTS

The Task List window is a feature of Visual Studio 2010 that allows you to keep track of any coding tasks or outstanding activities you have to do. Tasks can be manually entered as User Tasks, or automatically detected from the inline comments. You can open the Task List window by selecting View ⇨ Task List, or using the keyboard shortcut CTRL+\, CTRL+T. Figure 12-6 shows the Task List window with some User Tasks defined.

> *User Tasks are saved in the solution user options (.suo) file, which contains user-specific settings and preferences. It is not recommended that you check this file into source control and, as such, User Tasks cannot be shared by multiple developers working on the same solution.*

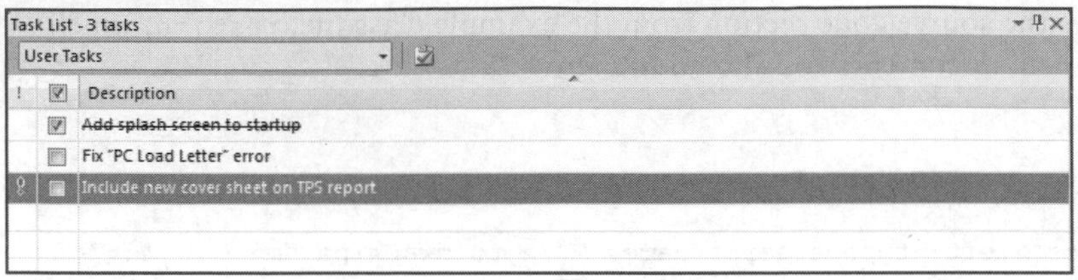

FIGURE 12-6

> The Task List has a filter in the top-left corner that toggles the code between Comment Tasks and manually entered User Tasks.

When you add a comment into your code that begins with a *comment token*, the comment will be added to the Task List as a Comment Task. The default comment tokens that are included with Visual Studio 2010 are TODO, HACK, UNDONE, and UnresolvedMergeConflict.

The following code shows a TODO comment. Figure 12-7 shows how this comment appears as a task in the Task List window. You can double-click the Task List entry to go directly to the comment line in your code.

C#

```csharp
using System;
using System.Windows.Forms;

namespace CSWindowsFormsApp
{
    public partial class Form1 : Form
    {
        public Form1()
        {
            InitializeComponent();
            //TODO: The database should be initialized here
        }
    }
}
```

FIGURE 12-7

You can edit the list of comment tokens from an options page under Tools ⇨ Options ⇨ Environment ⇨ Task List, as shown in Figure 12-8. Each token can be assigned a priority — Low, Normal, High. The default token is TODO and it cannot be renamed or deleted. You can, however, adjust its priority.

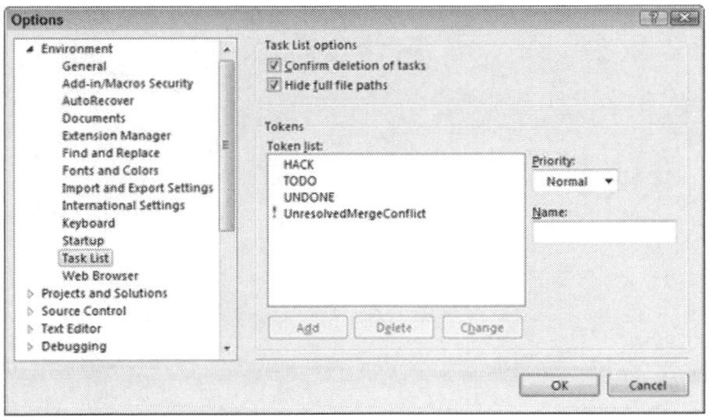

In addition to User Tasks and Comments, you can also add shortcuts to code within the Task List. To create a Task List Shortcut, place the cursor on the location for the shortcut within the code editor and select Edit ⇨ Bookmarks ⇨ Add Task List Shortcut. This will place an arrow icon in the gutter of the code editor, as shown in Figure 12-9.

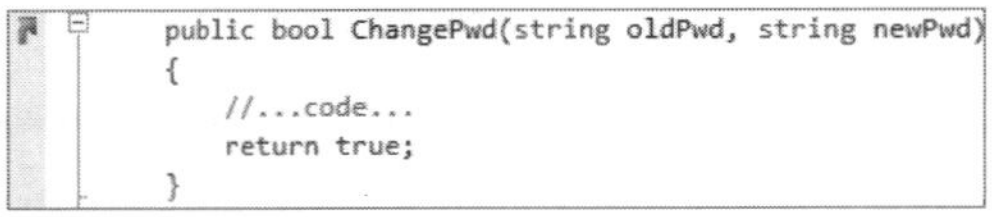

FIGURE 12-8

```
public bool ChangePwd(string oldPwd, string newPwd)
{
    //...code...
    return true;
}
```

FIGURE 12-9

If you now go to the Task List window you will see a new category called Shortcuts listed in the drop-down list, as shown in Figure 12-10. By default the description for the shortcut will contain the line of code; however, you can edit this and enter whatever text you like. Double-clicking an entry takes you to the shortcut location in the code editor.

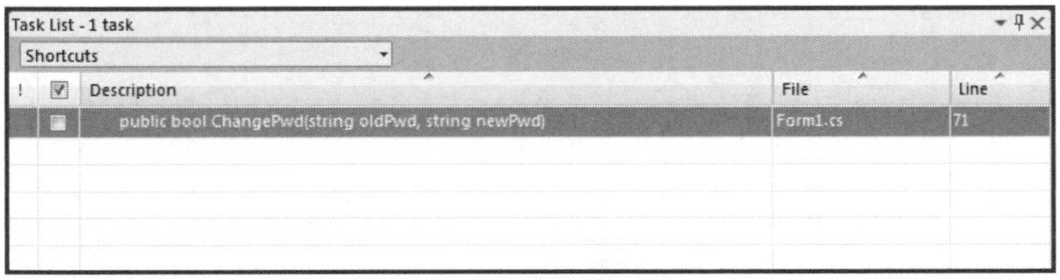

!	☑	Description	File	Line
	▣	public bool ChangePwd(string oldPwd, string newPwd)	Form1.cs	71

Task List - 1 task
Shortcuts

FIGURE 12-10

As with User Tasks, Shortcuts are stored in the .suo file, and aren't typically checked into source control or shared among users. Therefore, they are a great way to annotate your code with private notes and reminders.

SUMMARY

XML comments are not only extremely powerful, but also very easy to implement in a development project. Using them enables you to enhance the existing IntelliSense features by including your own custom-built tooltips and Quick Info data. You can automate the process of creating XML comments with the GhostDoc Visual Studio add-in. Using Sandcastle, you can generate professional-looking standalone documentation for every member and class within your solutions. Finally, Task List comments are useful for keeping track of pending coding tasks and other outstanding activities.

Code Consistency Tools

WHAT'S IN THIS CHAPTER?

➤ Working with source control

➤ Creating, adding, and updating code in a source repository

➤ Defining and enforcing code standards

➤ Adding contracts to your code

If you are building a small application by yourself, it's very easy to understand how all the pieces fit together and to make changes to accommodate new or changed requirements. Unfortunately, even on such a small project the code base can easily go from being very well structured and organized to being a mess of variables, methods, and classes. This problem is amplified if the application is large, complex, and has multiple developers working on it concurrently.

In this chapter, you will learn about how you and your team can use features of Visual Studio 2010 to write and maintain consistent code. The first part of this chapter is dedicated to the use of source control to assist you in tracking changes to your code base over time. Use of source control facilitates sharing of code and changes among a team but more importantly gives you a history of changes made to an application over time.

In the remainder of the chapter you will learn about FxCop and StyleCop, which can be used to set up and enforce coding standards. Adhering to a set of standards and guidelines ensures the code you write will be easier to understand, leading to fewer issues and shorter development times. You'll also see how you can use Code Contracts to write higher quality code.

SOURCE CONTROL

Many different methodologies for building software applications exist, and though the theories about team structure, work allocation, design, and testing often differ, one point that they agree on is that there should be a repository for all source code for an application.

Source control is the process of storing source code (referred to as checking code in) and accessing it again (referred to as checking code out) for editing. When we refer to source code, we mean any resources, configuration files, code files, or even documentation that is required to build and deploy an application.

Source code repositories also vary in structure and interface. Basic repositories provide a limited interface through which files can be checked in and out. The storage mechanism can be as simple as a file share, and no history may be available. Yet this repository still has the advantage that all developers working on a project can access the same file, with no risk of changes being overwritten or lost. More sophisticated repositories not only provide a rich interface for checking in and out, they also assist with file merging and conflict resolution. They can also be used from within Visual Studio to manage the source code. Other functionality that a source control repository can provide includes versioning of files, branching, and remote access.

Most organizations start using a source control repository to provide a mechanism for sharing source code between participants in a project. Instead of developers having to manually copy code to and from a shared folder on a network, the repository can be queried to get the latest version of the source code. When a developer finishes his or her work, any changes can simply be checked into the repository. This ensures that everyone in the team can access the latest code. Also, having the source code checked into a single repository makes it easy to perform regular backups.

Version tracking, including a full history of what changes were made and by whom, is one of the biggest benefits of using a source control repository. Although most developers would like to think that they write perfect code, the reality is that quite often a change might break something else. Being able to review the history of changes made to a project makes it possible to identify which change caused the breakage. Tracking changes to a project can also be used for reporting and reviewing purposes, because each change is date stamped and its author indicated.

Selecting a Source Control Repository

Visual Studio 2010 does not ship with a source control repository, but it does include rich support for checking files in and out, as well as merging and reviewing changes. To make use of a repository from within Visual Studio 2010, it is necessary to specify which repository to use. Visual Studio 2010 supports deep integration with Team Foundation Server (TFS), Microsoft's premier source control and project tracking system. In addition, Visual Studio supports any source control client that uses the Source Code Control (SCC) API. Products that use the SCC API include Microsoft Visual SourceSafe, and the free, open-source source-control repositories Subversion and CVS.

> *You would be forgiven for thinking that Microsoft Visual SourceSafe is no longer available, considering that all the press mentions is TFS. However, Microsoft Visual SourceSafe 2005 is still available and compatible with Visual Studio 2010. There will, however, be a new licensing option for TFS, which is specifically designed for small development teams as a replacement for SourceSafe.*

To make Visual Studio 2010 easy to navigate and work with, any functionality that is not available is typically hidden from the menus. By default, Visual Studio 2010 does not display the source control menu item. To get this item to appear, you must configure the source control provider information under the Options item on the Tools menu. The Options window, with the Source Control tab selected, is shown in Figure 13-1.

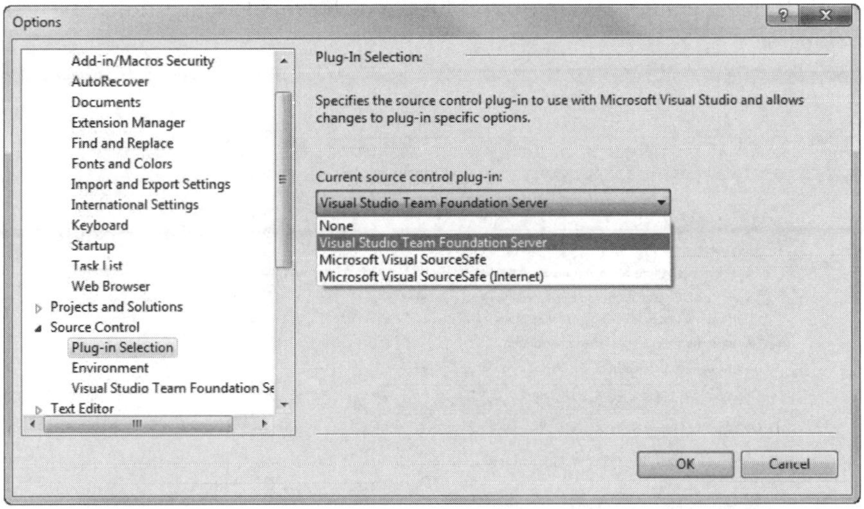

FIGURE 13-1

Initially, very few settings for source control appear. However, once a provider has been selected, additional nodes are added to the tree to control how source control behaves. These options are specific to the source control provider that has been selected.

The remainder of this chapter focuses on the use of Visual SourceSafe with Visual Studio 2010. Chapter 57 covers the use of Team Foundation, which offers much richer integration and functionality as a source control repository.

> *The Internet-based version of Visual SourceSafe uses a client-server model that runs over HTTP or HTTPS, instead of accessing the source code repository through a file share. Additional setup is required on the server side to expose this functionality.*

Once a source control repository has been selected from the plug-in menu, it is necessary to configure the repository for that machine. For Visual SourceSafe, this includes specifying the path to the repository, the user with which to connect, and the settings to use when checking files in and out of the repository.

Environment Settings

Most source control repositories define a series of settings that must be configured for Visual Studio 2010 to connect to and access information from the repository. These settings are usually unique to the repository, although some apply across most repositories.

In Figure 13-2 the Environment tab is shown, illustrating the options that control when files are checked in and out of the repository. These options are available for most repositories. The drop-down menu at the top of the pane defines a couple of profiles, which provide suggestions for different types of developers.

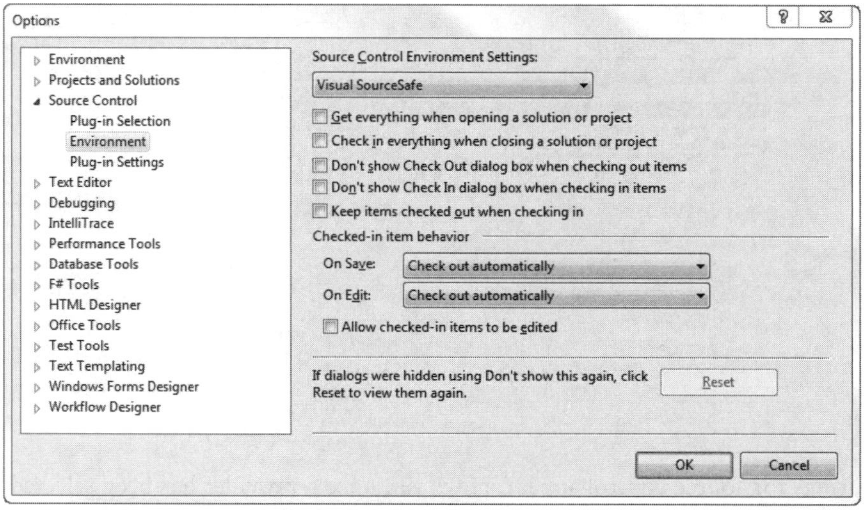

FIGURE 13-2

Plug-In Settings

Many source control repositories need some additional settings for Visual Studio 2010 to connect to the repository. These are specified in the Plug-in Settings pane, which is customized for each repository. Some repositories, such as SourceSafe, do not require specific information regarding the location of the repository until a solution is added to source control. At that point, SourceSafe requests the location of an existing repository or enables the developer to create a new repository.

Accessing Source Control

This section walks through the process of adding a solution to a new Visual SourceSafe 2010 repository, although the same principles apply regardless of the repository chosen. This process can be applied to any new or existing solution that is not already under source control. We also assume here that Visual SourceSafe is not only installed, but that it has been selected as the source control repository within Visual Studio 2010.

Creating the Repository

The first step in placing a solution under source control is to create a repository in which to store the data. It is possible to place any number of solutions in the same repository, although this means that it is much harder to separate information pertaining to different projects. Furthermore, if a repository is corrupted, it may affect all solutions contained within that repository.

To begin the process of adding a solution to source control, navigate to the File menu and select Source Control ⇨ Add Solution to Source Control, as shown in Figure 13-3. Alternatively, if you are creating a new solution, there is a checkbox entitled "Add to Source Control" on the New Project dialog that you can check to immediately add your new solution to a source control repository.

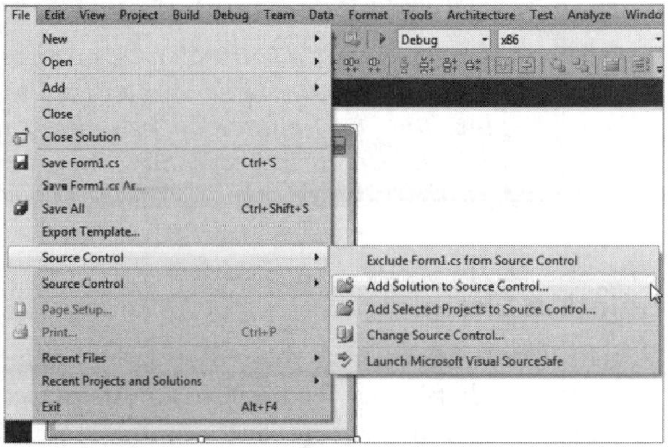

FIGURE 13-3

If this is the first time you have accessed SourceSafe, this opens a dialog box that lists the available databases, which at this stage will be empty. Clicking the Add button initiates the Add SourceSafe Database Wizard, which steps you through either referencing an existing database, perhaps on a server or elsewhere on your hard disk, or creating a new database.

To create a new SourceSafe database you need to specify a location for the database and a name. You must also specify the type of locking that is used when checking files in and out. Selecting the Lock-Modify-Unlock model allows only a single developer to check out a file at any point in time. This prevents two people from making changes to the same file at the same time, which makes the check-in process very simple. However, this model can often lead to frustration if multiple developers need to adjust the same resource. Project files are a common example of a resource that multiple developers may need to be able to access at the same time. In order to add or remove files from a project, this file must be checked out. Unless developers are diligent about checking the project file back in after they add a new file, this can significantly slow down a team.

An alternative model, Copy-Modify-Merge, allows multiple developers to check out the same file. Of course, when they are ready to check the file back in, there must be a process of reconciliation to ensure that their changes do not overwrite any changes made by another developer. Merging changes can be a difficult process and can easily result in loss of changes or a final code set that neither compiles nor runs. This model offers the luxury of allowing concurrent access to files, but suffers from the operational overhead during check in.

Adding the Solution

Once a SourceSafe repository has been created, the Add to SourceSafe dialog appears, which prompts you for a location for your application and a name to give it in the repository. SourceSafe works very similarly to a network file share — it creates folders under the root ($/) into which it places the files under source control.

> *Although it is no longer required with SourceSafe, many development teams align the SourceSafe folder structure to the directory structure on your computer. This is still considered a recommended practice because it encourages the use of good directory and folder structures.*
>
> *The Source Code Control (SCC) API assumes that the* .sln *solution file is located in the same folder or a direct parent folder as the project files. If you place the* .sln *solution file in a different folder hierarchy than the project files, then you should expect some "interesting" source control maintenance issues.*

Solution Explorer

The first difference that you will see after adding your solution to source control is that Visual Studio 2010 adjusts the icons within the Solution Explorer to indicate their source control status. Figure 13-4 illustrates three file states. When the solution is initially added to the source control repository, the files all appear with a little padlock icon next to the file type icon. This indicates that the file has been checked in and is not currently checked out by anyone. For example, the Solution file and Properties have this icon.

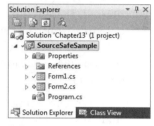

FIGURE 13-4

Once a solution is under source control, all changes are recorded, including the addition and removal of files. Figure 13-4 illustrates the addition of Form2.cs to the solution. The plus sign next to Form2.cs indicates that this is a new file. The tick next to the SourceSafeSample project and Form1.cs signifies that the files are currently checked out. In the scenario where two people have the same file checked out, this will be indicated with a double tick next to the appropriate item.

Checking In and Out

Files can be checked in and out using the right-click shortcut menu associated with an item in the Solution Explorer. When a solution is under source control, this menu expands to include the items shown on the left in Figure 13-5.

FIGURE 13-5

Before a file can be edited, it must be checked out. This can be done using the Check Out for Edit menu item. Once a file is checked out, the shortcut menu expands to include additional options, including Check In, View Pending Checkins, Undo Checkout, and more, as shown on the right in Figure 13-5.

Pending Changes

In a large application, it can often be difficult to see at a glance which files have been checked out for editing, or recently added or removed from a project. The Pending Checkins window (accessible from the right-click context menu off the Solution Explorer or via the View menu), shown in Figure 13-6, is very useful for seeing which files are waiting to be checked into the repository. It also provides a space into which a comment can be added. This comment is attached to the files when they are checked into the repository so that the reason for the change(s) can be reviewed at a later date.

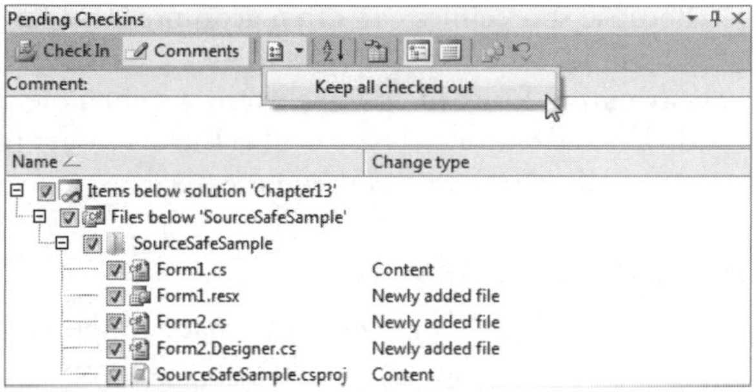

To check a file back in, you should ensure that there is a check against the file in the list, add an appropriate comment in the space provided, and then select the Check In button. Depending on the options you have specified, you may also receive a confirmation dialog prior to the item's being checked in. If the Keep All Checked Out option shown in

FIGURE 13-6

Figure 13-6 is checked, the files being checked in will remain in the checked out state, even after the check in has completed successfully. This can be useful if you are in the middle of a set of changes and want to commit your current changes so that other developers can access them.

One option that many developers prefer is to set Visual Studio to automatically check out a file when it is edited. This saves the often unnecessary step of having to check the file out before editing. However, it can result in files being checked out prematurely; for example, if a developer accidentally makes a change in the wrong file. Alternatively, a developer may decide that changes made previously are no longer required and wish to revert to what is contained in the repository. The last button on the Toolbar contained within the Pending Checkins window is an Undo Checkout button. This retrieves the current version from the repository, in the process overwriting the local changes that were made by the developer. This option is also available via the right-click shortcut menu.

Before checking a file into the repository, it is a good idea for someone to review any changes that have been made. In fact, some organizations have a policy requiring that all changes be reviewed before being checked in. Selecting the Compare Versions menu item brings up an interface that highlights any differences between two versions of a file. Figure 13-7 shows that a Form Load event handler has been added to `Form1.vb`. Although not evident in Figure 13-7, the type of change is also color coded; additions (such as the Say_HelloButton_Click method) are highlighted in green text, and red and blue lines indicate deleted and changed lines.

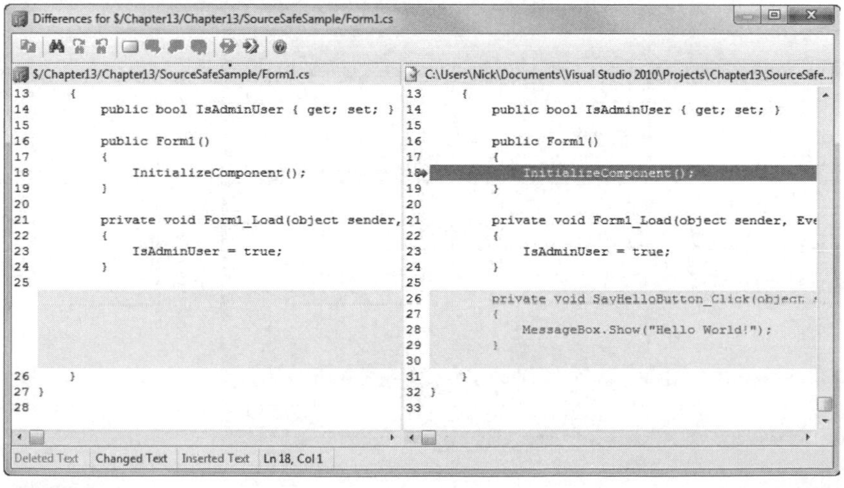

![Differences for $/Chapter13/Chapter13/SourceSafeSample/Form1.cs showing a two-pane comparison of code versions]

FIGURE 13-7

Because source files can often get quite large, this window provides some basic navigation shortcuts. The Find option can be used to locate particular strings. Bookmarks can be placed to ease navigation forward and backward within a file. The most useful shortcuts are the Next and Previous difference buttons. These enable the developer to navigate through the differences without having to manually scroll up and down the file.

Merging Changes

Occasionally, changes might be made to the same file by multiple developers. In some cases, these changes can be automatically resolved if they are unrelated, such as the addition of a method to an existing class. However, when changes are made to the same portion of the file, there needs to be a process by which the changes can be mediated to determine the correct code.

Figure 13-8 illustrates the Merge dialog that is presented to developers when they attempt to check in a file that has been modified by another developer. The top half of the dialog shows the two versions of the file that are in conflict. Each pane indicates where that file differs from the original file that the developer checked out. The left pane shows what is now in the source repository, while the right pane shows the changes the developer has made. In this case, both versions had a message box inserted, and it is up to the developer to determine which of the messages is correct.

Unlike the Compare Versions dialog, the Merge dialog has been designed to facilitate developer interaction. From the top panes, changes made in either version can be accepted or rejected by simply clicking the change. The highlighting changes to indicate that a change has been accepted, and that piece of code is inserted into the appropriate place in the code presented in the lower pane. The lower pane also allows the developer to enter code, although it does not support IntelliSense or error detection.

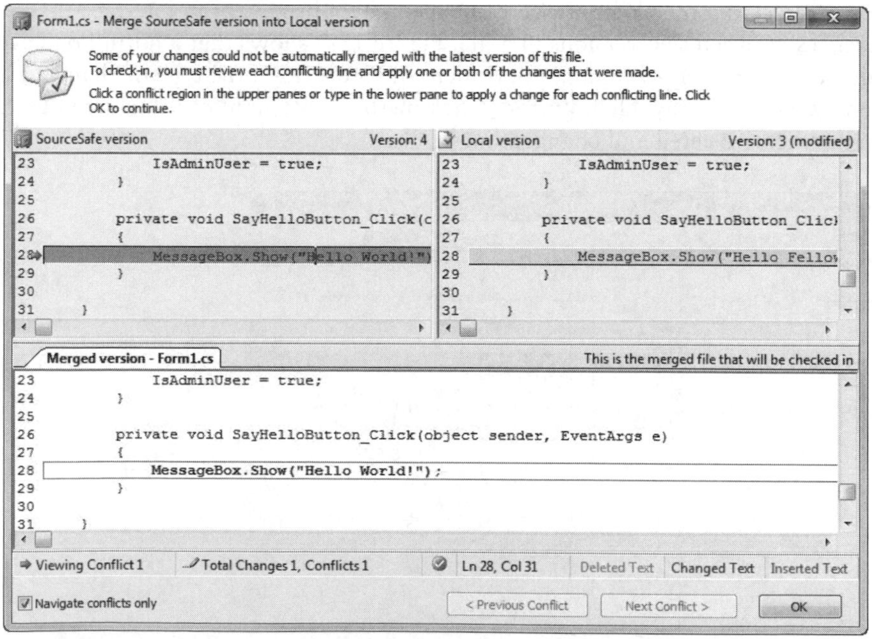

FIGURE 13-8

Once the conflicts have been resolved, clicking the OK button saves the changes to your local file. The merged version can then be checked into the repository.

History

Any time a file is checked in and out of the SourceSafe repository, a history is recorded of each version of the file. Use the View History option on the right-click shortcut menu from the Solution Explorer to review this history. Figure 13-9 shows a brief history of a file that had four revisions checked in. This dialog enables developers to view previous versions, look at details (such as the comments), get the particular version (overwriting the current file), and check out the file. Additional functionality is provided to compare different versions of the file, pin a particular version, roll the file back to a previous version (which will erase newer versions), and report on the version history. When you select View History, you can also constrain the list by a date range and/or by user.

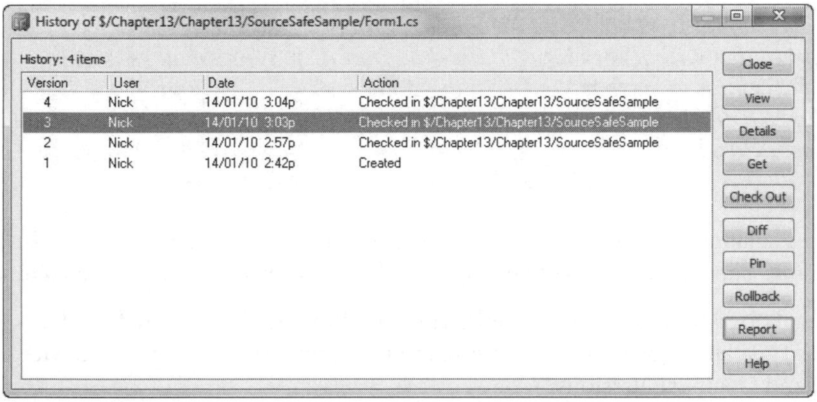

FIGURE 13-9

Pinning

The History window (refer to Figure 13-9) can be used to pin a version of the file. Pinning a version of a file makes that version the current version. When a developer gets the current source code from the repository, the pinned version is returned. Pinning a version of a file also prevents anyone from checking out that file. This can be useful if changes that have been checked are incomplete or are causing errors in the application. A previous version of the file can be pinned to ensure that other developers can continue to work while the problem is resolved.

Offline Support for Source Control

Visual Studio 2010 provides built-in offline support for Visual SourceSafe when the source code repository is not available. A transient outage could occur for many reasons — the server may be down, a network outage may have occurred, or you could be using your laptop at home.

If you open a solution in Visual Studio that has been checked into Visual SourceSafe, and the source code repository is not available, you are first prompted to continue or select a different repository. You may also be asked if you want to try to connect using HTTP. Assuming you select No for both of these prompts, you are presented with four options on how to proceed, as shown in Figure 13-10.

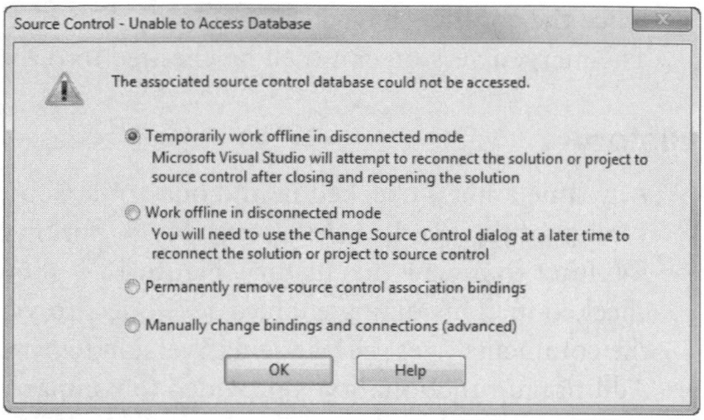

FIGURE 13-10

If the issue is transient, you should select the first option: Temporarily Work Offline in Disconnected Mode. This allows you to check out files and continue editing source code.

> *The first time you attempt to check out a file while working in disconnected mode, you are presented with a very large dialog box that displays a small essay. The basic gist of this message is that Visual Studio will actually be simulating a checkout on your behalf, and you may need to manually merge changes when you go to check code back in.*

The next time you open the solution and the source code repository is available, Visual Studio automatically checks out any "simulated" checkouts that occurred while working in disconnected mode.

Many of the source control operations are not available while working in disconnected mode. These are operations that typically depend on direct access to the server, such as Check In, Merge Changes, View History, and Compare Versions.

CODING STANDARDS

As software development projects and teams grow, there is a tendency for code to rapidly become a mixed-bag of styles, standards, and approaches. This can lead to a maintenance nightmare, often resulting in new features being parked due to an abundance of bugs and issues that need to be addressed. Luckily, some great tools are both built into Visual Studio 2010 and available as Addins that can enforce things like naming conventions, ordering of methods, and ensure appropriate comments are written. In this section you learn about some tools that can be used to improve the consistency of the code you and your team write.

Code Analysis with FxCop

Over several iterations of the .NET Framework and Visual Studio, Microsoft has put together a set of coding standards that development teams can choose to adhere to. These are well documented under the topic of Code Analysis for Managed Code Warnings on MSDN (http://msdn.microsoft.com) and can be enforced using a tool called FxCop, which you can download from the Microsoft download site.

> *Visual Studio 2010 Premium edition and above include the Managed Code Analysis tool, which is essentially a version of FxCop that is integrated into the IDE. This is discussed in Chapter 55.*

Once you have downloaded and installed FxCop you need to run it as a standalone tool from the Start menu. If you want to run FxCop as part of your build process you can run it from the command line using the FxCopCmd.exe found in the install folder. When FxCop launches, it automatically creates and opens a new project. Start by saving the project into the folder alongside the solution file for your application. Then from the Project menu, select Add Targets and select the assemblies (dlls and exes) that make up your application. Click the Analyze button to run the code analysis over your application; the result should look similar to Figure 13-11.

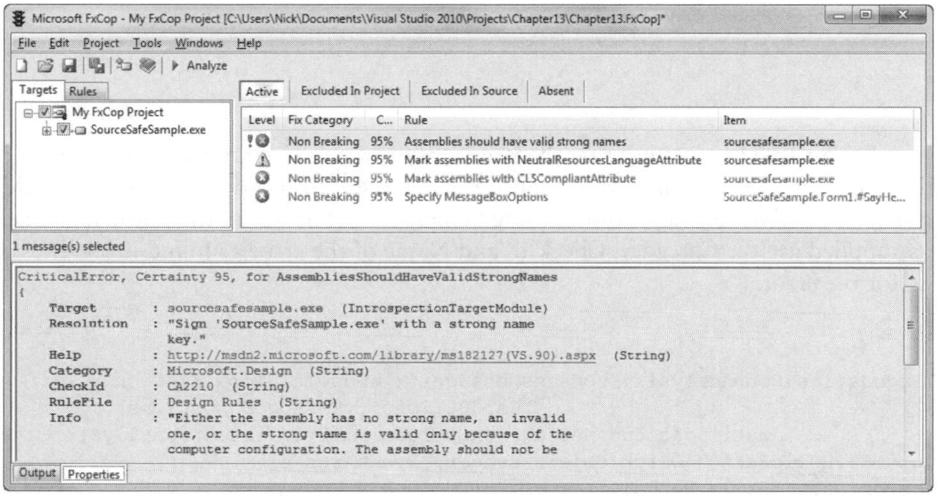

FIGURE 13-11

As you can see from Figure 13-11, there are three errors (including one marked as critical) and one warning. Although you can ignore the warnings, they quite often indicate an area of concern, either to do with the architecture or security of your code, so it is wise to try to minimize or eliminate where possible the number of warnings and errors. In this example, the first error is easy to resolve; you can just code sign the application and the error will go away. However, it may not be possible to mark your assembly with the CLSCompliant attribute, which is what the second error is requiring. So that this error doesn't appear each time in the active errors list, you can right-click the error and select Exclude. You'll be prompted to add a comment so that you can justify the exclusion of that error. Once you click OK, the excluded error will appear in the Excluded In Project tab, as shown in the background of Figure 13-12. Double-clicking this error opens the details for the error, in which you can find your comment in the Notes section.

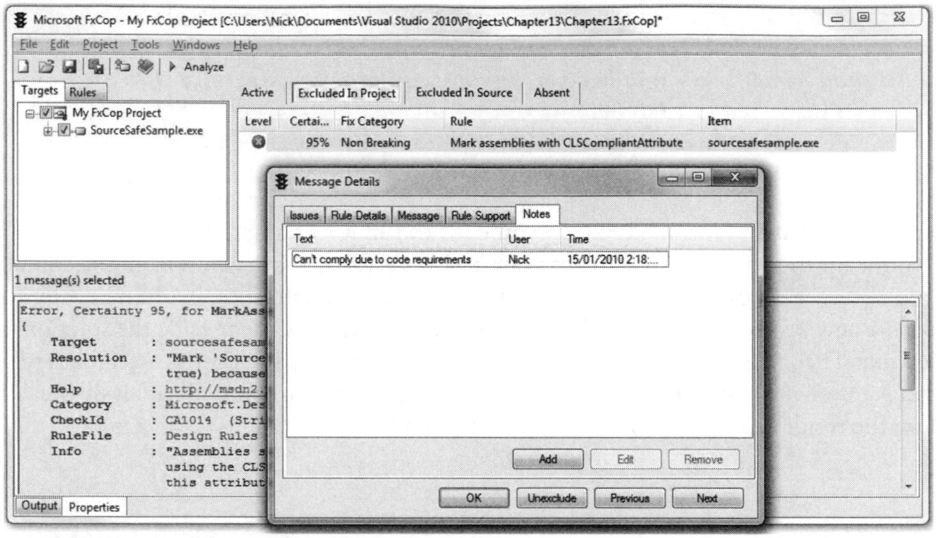

FIGURE 13-12

The third error in Figure 13-11 points out that the `MessageBoxOptions` parameter hasn't been specified. In this case, this is by design so you want to exclude the error in source. To do this, add the `SuppressMessage` attribute to the method calling `MessageBox.Show` as in the following code. The parameters supplied are the Category, CheckId, and Name of the error as found in the Message Details window for the error.

C#

```
[System.Diagnostics.CodeAnalysis.SuppressMessage("Microsoft.Globalization",
                            "CA1300:SpecifyMessageBoxOptions",
                Justification="MessageBoxOptions omitted intentionally")]
private void SayHelloButton_Click(object sender, EventArgs e){
    MessageBox.Show("Hello World!");
}
```

VB

```
<System.Diagnostics.CodeAnalysis.SuppressMessage("Microsoft.Globalization",
                                "CA1300:SpecifyMessageBoxOptions",
                Justification:="MessageBoxOptions omitted intentionally")>
Private Sub SayHelloButton_Click(ByVal sender As System.Object, _
                ByVal e As System.EventArgs) Handles SayHelloButton.Click
    MessageBox.Show("Hello World!")
End Sub
```

To get FxCop to notice the `SuppressMessage` attribute, you also need to set the `CODE_ANALYSIS` compilation flag. You do this by adding the `CODE_ANALYSIS` keyword to the Custom Constants textbox in the Advanced Compile Options dialog (from the Compile tab of the project properties page) for VB, or by adding the same keyword to the Conditional compilation symbols textbox (on the Build tab of the project properties page) for C#. After saving, rebuilding your application and rerunning the Analysis (note that you don't need to restart or even reload the project within FxCop) you will see that the error has been moved to the Excluded in Source tab. Again, double-clicking the error and going to the Notes tab reveals the contents of the `Justification` parameter specified as part of the `SuppressMessage` attribute (you may need to import the `System .Diagnostic.CodeAnalysis` namespace to use this attribute).

You have two other ways to control how FxCop is applied to your code. The first is to use the Targets window to enable/disable the running of rules on sections of code. The left image of Figure 13-13 shows the Targets window with the SourceSafeSample expanded to view the `IsAdminUser` property. In this example the checkboxes have been unchecked to indicate that rules should not be run on this property.

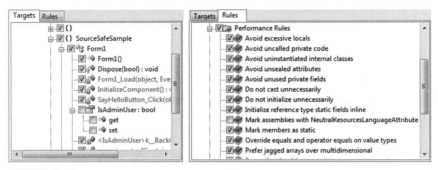

FIGURE 13-13

In the right image of Figure 13-13 you can see the Rules list that has been expanded to show the Mark assemblies with `NeutralResourcesLanguageAttribute` rule. This was the rule that was generating a warning in Figure 13-11 and has been unchecked to prevent this rule being used in the analysis.

> *Excluding an entire rule is generally not a good practice because it can hide errors at a later date. For example, if an assembly is added to the project, this rule will never be run on that assembly, even though it may be important for the rule to be applied to that assembly.*

FxCop comes with a large selection of rules that may or may not align with the way you and your team write code. If you want to enforce your own standards you can extend the default set of rules by writing your own, using the FxCop SDK that comes with FxCop as a reference.

Style Using StyleCop

Although FxCop is great for picking up issues relating to the way that you write your code, it doesn't do much for maintaining a common coding style. For this, you need to download and install StyleCop, which is available by searching for StyleCop on the MSDN code gallery (http://code.msdn.microsoft.com). Unlike FxCop, which runs as a standalone tool, StyleCop integrates into the Visual Studio 2010 IDE,

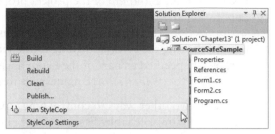

FIGURE 13-14

allowing you to invoke the analysis from Solution Explorer, as shown in Figure 13-14.

After running StyleCop, you will see that any issues are by default reported as warnings, as in Figure 13-5. If you want to enforce StyleCop you need to tell Visual Studio 2010 to treat warnings as errors.

		Description	File	L	C	P.
A	1	SA1600: The class must have a documentation header.	Program.cs	8	1	
⚠	2	SA1633: The file has no header, the header Xml is invalid, or the header is not located at the top of the file.	AssemblyInfo.cs	1	1	
⚠	3	SA1633: The file has no header, the header Xml is invalid, or the header is not located at the top of the file.	Program.cs	1	1	
⚠	4	SA1400: The class must have an access modifier.	Program.cs	8	1	
⚠	5	SA1400: The method must have an access modifier.	Program.cs	14	1	

FIGURE 13-15

As with FxCop you can elect to ignore rules via the StyleCop settings, or suppress rules in specific instances by adding the `SuppressMessage` attribute. You will most likely have to right-click the warning and select Show Error Help to access the Category, CheckId, and Name of the warning you are going to suppress. The format for the `SuppressMessage` arguments are (`"[Category]"`, `"[CheckId]:[Name]"`), so for example, (`"Maintainability Rules"`, `"SA1400: AccessModifierMustBeDeclared"`).

Code Contracts

The last tool that we're going to cover is Microsoft Code Contracts, which at the time of writing is currently available as a download from the Code Contracts project at Microsoft DevLabs (http://msdn.microsoft.com/devlabs). After downloading and installing this tool, you will need to restart Visual Studio 2010 to get the IDE extensions to appear. Once you have reopened your project you will also need to add a reference to `Microsoft.Contracts`, which should be on the .NET tab of the Add References dialog (right-click the project in Solution Explorer and select Add References).

Now you can add contracts in the form of pre- and post-conditions to your code. In the following example you can see a pre-condition set for the `Divide` method that requires (using

`Contract.Requires`) that the denominator is not zero. Similarly, there is a post-condition that ensures (using `Contract.Ensure`) the `Add` method increments the field `currentValue` by the correct amount.

C#

```
private double currentValue;
private double Divide(double denominator){
    Contract.Requires(denominator != 0);
    return currentValue / denominator;
}
private void Add(double valueToAdd){
    Contract.Ensures(currentValue == Contract.OldValue(currentValue) + valueToAdd);
    // Do nothing so that contract fails
}

private void InvokeDivision(){
    currentValue = 7.0;
    double c = Divide(0); // fails validation because b == 0
}
private void InvokeAddition(){
    currentValue = 13.0;
    Add(6);
}
```

VB

```
Private currentValue As Double
Private Function Divide(ByVal denominator As Double) As Double
    Contract.Requires(denominator <> 0)
    Return currentValue / denominator
End Function
Private Sub Add(ByVal valueToAdd As Double)
    Contract.Ensures(currentValue = Contract.OldValue(currentValue) + valueToAdd)
    ' Do nothing so that contract fails
End Sub

Private Sub InvokeDivision()
    currentValue = 7.0
    Dim c = Divide(0.0) 'fails validation because b == 0
End Sub

Private Sub InvokeAddition()
    currentValue = 13.0
    Add(6)
End Sub
```

With these contracts in place, you need to enable contract verification via the Code Contracts tab of the project properties page, as shown in Figure 13-16. Now when you build and run your application, you will see an Assert dialog thrown when either `InvokeDivision` or `InvokeAddition` are called, reflecting the contract that has been violated.

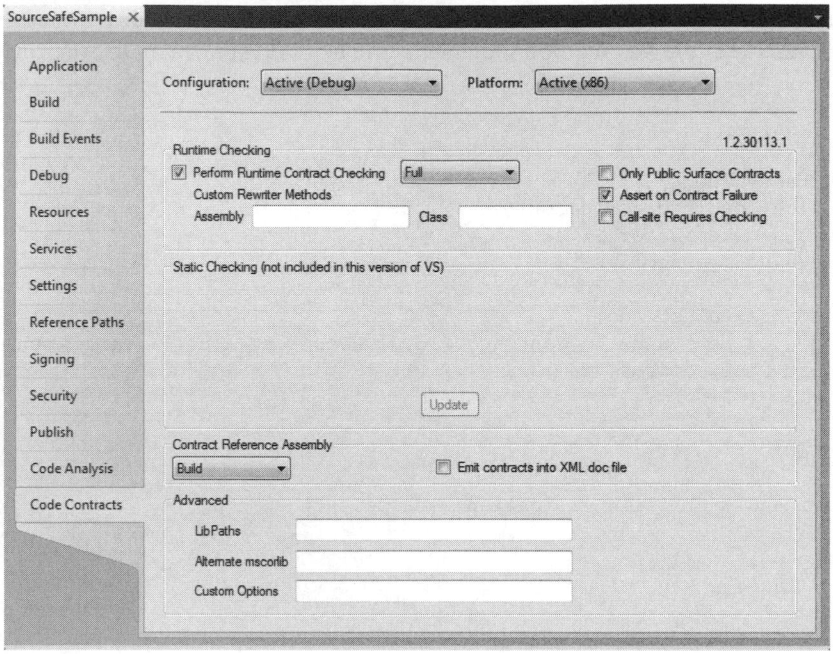

FIGURE 13-16

Here you can see that run time checking has been enabled and that it has been set to raise an Assert on Contract Failure. If you disable this option a `ContractException` is raised instead, which you can handle via code.

> *In Figure 13-16, there is space in the middle for Static Checking options. These are available if you install Code Contracts for Visual Studio 2010 Premium and above. This enables further static checking to attempt to ensure contracts are not violated at design time, rather than waiting for them to fail at run time.*

SUMMARY

This chapter demonstrated Visual Studio 2010's rich interface for using a source control repository to manage files associated with an application. Checking files in and out can be done using the Solution Explorer window, and more advanced functionality is available via the Pending Changes window.

Although SourceSafe is sufficient for individuals and small teams of developers, it has not been designed to scale for a large number of developers. It also doesn't provide any capability to track tasks or reviewer comments against a set of changes. Chapter 57 discusses the advantages and additional functionality that is provided by Team Foundation Server, an enterprise-class source control repository system.

This chapter also introduced you to FxCop, StyleCop, and Code Contracts, which can all be used to improve the quality, reliability, and consistency of your code. Their close integration into or with Visual Studio 2010 makes them invaluable tools for development teams of any size.

14

Code Generation with T4

WHAT'S IN THIS CHAPTER?

➤ Using T4 templates to generate text and code

➤ Troubleshooting T4 templates

➤ Creating Preprocessed T4 template to include templating in your projects

Frequently, when writing software applications you will come across large areas of boilerplate code in which the same pattern is repeated over and over. Working on these areas of code can be time-consuming and tedious, which leads to inattention and easily avoidable errors. Writing this code is a task best suited to automation.

Code generation is a common software engineering practice where some mechanism, rather than a human engineer, is used to write program components automatically. The tool used to generate the code is known as a code generator. A number of commercial and free code generators are available in the market from the very general in nature to those that are targeted toward a very specific task.

Visual Studio 2010 includes a code generator that can generate files from simple template definitions. This code generator is known as the Text Template Transformation Toolkit, or more commonly, T4.

T4 was originally introduced as part of the Domain Specific Languages Toolkit, which was an add-in for Visual Studio 2005. T4 was included out of the box in Visual Studio 2008 but it was poorly documented and there were very few hints in the IDE that it existed. Visual Studio 2010 makes T4 a first-class citizen so that Text Template is now one of the options in the File ➪ New dialog.

This chapter explores the creation, configuration, and execution of T4 templates. You also see how to troubleshoot templates when they go wrong. Finally, you create a Preprocessed Text Template that allows you to create reusable T4 templates that you can easily call from your own code.

CREATING A T4 TEMPLATE

In previous versions of Visual Studio, creating a new T4 template was a hidden feature that involved creating a text file with the .tt extension. In Visual Studio 2010 you can create a T4 template simply by selecting Text Template from the General page of the Add New Item dialog shown in Figure 14-1.

FIGURE 14-1

When a new T4 template is created or saved, Visual Studio displays the warning dialog shown in Figure 14-2. T4 templates execute normal .NET code and can theoretically be used to run *any* sort of .NET code. T4 templates are executed every time they are saved so you will likely see this warning a lot. There is an option to suppress these warnings but it is global to all templates

FIGURE 14-2

in all solutions. If you do turn it off and decide you'd rather have the warnings, you can reactivate them by changing Show Security Message to True in Tools ➪ ptions ➪ Text Templating.

Once the template has been created it appears in the Solution Explorer window as a file with the `.tt` extension. The template file can be expanded to reveal the file it generates. Each template generates a single file, which will have the same name as the template file itself and a different extension. Figure 14-3 shows a template file and the file it generates in Solution Explorer.

FIGURE 14-3

> *If you are using VB you need to enable Show All Files for the project to see the generated file.*

The generated file is initially empty because no output has been defined in the template file. The template file is not empty, however. When it is first generated it contains the following two lines:

```
<#@ template debug="false" hostspecific="false" language="C#" #>
<#@ output extension=".txt" #>
```

Each of these two lines is a T4 *directive*, which controls some aspect of the way in which the template is executed. T4 directives are discussed later in the chapter but there are a few things of interest here. The `template` directive contains an attribute specifying which `language` the template will use. Each template file can include code statements that are executed to generate the final file and this attribute tells Visual Studio which language those statements will be in.

> *The template language has no impact on the file being generated. You can generate a C# file from a template that uses the VB language and vice versa. This defaults to the language of the current project but can be changed. Both C# and VB templates are supported in projects of either language.*

The second thing of note is the `extension` attribute on the `output` directive. The name of the generated file is always the same as that of the template file except that the `.tt` extension is replaced by the contents of this attribute. If Visual Studio recognizes the extension of the generated file, it treats it the same as if you had created it from the Add New Item dialog. In particular, if the extension denotes a code file, such as `.cs` or `.vb`, Visual Studio adds the generated file to the build process of your project.

> *When the output extension of a template is changed, the previously generated file is deleted the next time the template is run. As long as you are not editing the generated file this shouldn't be an issue.*

At the bottom of the template file add a single line containing the words `Hello World` and save the template.

Available for download on Wrox.com

C#

```
<#@ template debug="false" hostspecific="false" language="C#" #>
<#@ output extension=".txt" #>
Hello World
```

Code snippet HelloWorld.tt

Available for download on Wrox.com

VB

```
<#@ template debug="false" hostspecific="false" language="VB" #>
<#@ output extension=".txt" #>
Hello World
```

Code snippet HelloWorld.tt

As was mentioned previously, templates are run every time they are saved, so the generated file will be updated with the new contents of the template. Open up the generated file and you will see the text `Hello World` in there.

Although each individual template file can always be regenerated by opening it and saving it again, Visual Studio also has a button at the top of the Solution Explorer tool window to Transform All Templates (see Figure 14-4). Clicking this button transforms all of the templates in the solution.

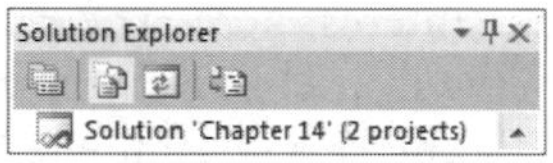

FIGURE 14-4

As was mentioned previously, if the `output` directive specifies an extension that matches the language of the current project, the resulting generated file is included in the project. You will get full IntelliSense from types and members declared within generated files. The next code snippet shows a T4 template along with the code that it generates. The generated class can be accessed by other parts of the program and a small console application demonstrating this follows.

Available for download on Wrox.com

C#

```
<#@ template debug="false" hostspecific="false" language="C#" #>
<#@ output extension=".cs" #>

namespace AdventureWorks {
  class GreetingManager {
    public static void SayHi() {
      System.Console.WriteLine("Aloha Cousin!");
    }
  }
}
```

Code snippet GreetingManager.tt

```
namespace AdventureWorks {
  class GreetingManager {
    public static void SayHi() {
```

```
      System.Console.WriteLine("Aloha Cousin!");
    }
  }
}
```

Code snippet GreetingManager.cs

```
namespace AdventureWorks {
  class Program {
    static void Main(string[] args) {
      GreetingManager.SayHi();
    }
  }
}
```

Code snippet Program.cs

VB

```
<#@ template debug="false" hostspecific="false" language="VB" #>
<#@ output extension=".vb" #>
Public Class GreetingManager
  Public Shared Sub SayHi
    System.Console.WriteLine( "Aloha Cousin!" )
  End Sub
End Class
```

Code snippet GreetingManager.tt

```
Public Class GreetingManager
    Public Shared Sub SayHi()
        System.Console.WriteLine("Aloha Cousin!")
    End Sub
End Class
```

Code snippet GreetingManager.vb

```
Module Module1
  Sub Main()
    GreetingManager.SayHi()
  End Sub
End Module
```

Code snippet Module1.vb

> *Although the rest of your application will get IntelliSense covering your generated code, the T4 template files themselves have no IntelliSense or syntax highlighting in Visual Studio 2010. A few third-party editors and plug-ins are available that provide a richer design-time experience for T4.*

This example works, but it doesn't really demonstrate the power and flexibility that T4 can offer. This is because the template is completely static. To create useful templates, more dynamic capabilities are required.

T4 BUILDING BLOCKS

Each T4 template consists of a number of *blocks* which affect the generated file. The line `Hello World` from the first example is a Text block. Text blocks are copied verbatim from the template file into the generated file. They can contain any kind of text and can contain other blocks.

In addition to Text blocks, three other types of blocks exist: Expression blocks, Statement blocks, and Class Feature blocks. Each of the other types of block is surrounded by a specific kind of markup to identify it. Text blocks are the only type of block that have no special markup.

Expression Blocks

An Expression block is used to pass some computed value to the generated file. Expression blocks normally appear inside of Text blocks and are denoted by <#= and #> tags. Here is an example of a template that outputs the date and time that the file was generated.

Available for
download on
Wrox.com

C#

```
<#@ template debug="false" hostspecific="false" language="C#" #>
<#@ output extension=".txt" #>
This file was generated: <#=System.DateTime.Now #>
```

Code snippet Existential.tt

VB

```
<#@ template debug="false" hostspecific="false" language="VB" #>
<#@ output extension=".txt" #>
This file was generated: <#=System.DateTime.Now #>
```

Code snippet Existential.tt

The expression inside the block may be any valid expression in the template language that is specified in the `template` directive. Every time it is run the template evaluates the expression and then calls `ToString()` on the result. This value is then inserted into the generated file.

Statement Blocks

A Statement block is used to execute arbitrary statements when the template is run. Code inside a Statement block might log the execution of the template, create temporary variables, or delete a file from your computer, so you need to be careful. In fact, the code inside a Statement block can consist of any valid statement in the template language. Statement blocks are commonly used to implement flow control within a template, manage temporary variables, and interact with other systems. A Statement block is denoted by <# and #> tags which are similar to Statement block delimiters but without the equals sign. The following example produces a file with all 99 verses of a popular drinking song.

C#

```
<#@ template debug="false" hostspecific="false" language="C#" #>
<#@ output extension=".txt" #>
<# for( int i = 99; i > = 1; i-- )
   { #>
<#=i #> Bottles of Non-alcoholic Carbonated Beverage on the wall
<#=i #> Bottles of Non-alcoholic Carbonated Beverage
Take one down
And pass it around
<# if( i-1 == 0 ) { #>
There's no Bottles of Non-alcoholic Carbonated Beverage on the wall
<# } else { #>
There's <#=i-1 #> Bottles of Non-alcoholic Carbonated Beverage on the wall
<# } #>

  <# } #>
```

Code snippet DrinkingSong.tt

VB

```
<#@ template debug="false" hostspecific="false" language="VB" #>
<#@ output extension=".txt" #>
<# For i As Integer = 99 To 1 Step -1 #>
  <#= i #> Bottles of Non-alcoholic Carbonated Beverage on the wall
  <#= i #> Bottles of Non-alcoholic Carbonated Beverage
  Take one down
  And pass it around
<# If i - 1 = 0 Then #>
  There's no Bottles of Non-Alcoholic Carbonated Beverage on the wall.
<# Else #>
  There's <#= i-1 #> Bottles of Non-alcoholic Carbonated Beverage on the wall.
<# End If #>

<# Next #>
```

Code snippet DrinkingSong.tt

> *In the preceding example the Statement block contains another Text block,
> which in turn contains a number of Expression blocks. Using these three block
> types alone enables you to create some very powerful templates.*

Although the Statement block in the example contains other blocks, it doesn't need to. From within
a Statement block you can write directly to the generated file using the `Write()` and `WriteLine()`
methods. Here is the example again using this method.

C#

```
<#@ template debug="false" hostspecific="false" language="C#" #>
<#@ output extension=".txt" #>
<#
```

```
for( int i = 99; i > 1; i-- )
{
  WriteLine( "{0} Bottles of Non-alcoholic Carbonated Beverage on the wall", i);
  WriteLine( "{0} Bottles of Non-alcoholic Carbonated Beverage", i );
  WriteLine( "Take one down" );
  WriteLine( "And pass it around" );
  if( i - 1 == 0 ) {
    WriteLine(
      "There's no Bottles of Non-alcoholic Carbonated Beverage on the wall." );
  } else {
    WriteLine(
      "There's {0} Bottles of Non-alcoholic Carbonated Beverage on the wall.",i-1);
  }
  WriteLine( "" );
} #>
```

Code snippet ImperativeDrinkingSong.tt

VB

```
<#@ template debug="false" hostspecific="false" language="VB" #>
<#@ output extension=".txt" #>
<# For i As Integer = 99 To 1 Step -1
  Me.WriteLine("{0} Bottles of Non-alcoholic Carbonated Beverage on the wall", i)
  Me.WriteLine("{0} Bottles of Non-alcoholic Carbonated Beverage", i)
  Me.WriteLine("Take one down")
  Me.WriteLine("And pass it around")
  If i - 1 = 0 Then
    WriteLine("There's no Bottles of Non-Alcoholic Carbonated Beverage on the" &_
      " wall.")
  Else
    WriteLine("There's {0} Bottles of Non-Alcoholic Carbonated Beverage on the" &_
      " wall.",i-1)
  End If
  Me.WriteLine( "" )

Next #>
```

Code snippet ImperativeDrinkingSong.tt

The final generated results for these two templates are the same. Depending on the template, you might find one technique or the other easier to understand. It is recommended that you use one technique exclusively in each template to avoid confusion.

Class Feature Blocks

The final type of T4 block is the Class Feature block. These blocks contain arbitrary code that can be called from Statement and Expression blocks to help in the production of the generated file. This often includes custom formatting code or repetitive tasks. Class Feature blocks are denoted using <#+ and #> tags which are similar to those that denote Expression blocks except that the equals sign in the opening tag becomes a plus character. The following template writes the numbers from −5 to 5 using a typical financial format where every number has two decimal places, is preceded by a dollar symbol, and negatives are written as positive amounts but are placed in brackets.

C#

```
<#@ template debug="false" hostspecific="false" language="C#" #>
<#@ output extension=".txt" #>

Financial Sample Data
<# for( int i = -5; i <= 5; i++ )
   {
     WriteFinancialNumber(i);
        WriteLine( "" );
   } #>
End of Sample Data

 <#+
   void WriteFinancialNumber(decimal amount)
   {
     if( amount < 0 )
       Write("(${0:#0.00})", System.Math.Abs(amount) );
     else
        Write("${0:#0.00}", amount);
   }
   #>
```

Code snippet FinancialData.tt

VB

```
<#@ template debug="true" hostspecific="false" language="VB" #>
<#@ output extension=".txt" #>

Financial Sample Data
<# For i as Integer = -5 To 5
   WriteFinancialNumber(i)
   WriteLine( "" )
 Next   #>
End of Sample Data

<#+
Sub WriteFinancialNumber(amount as Decimal)
  If amount < 0 Then
    Write("(${0:#0.00})", System.Math.Abs(amount) )
  Else
    Write("${0:#0.00}", amount)
  End If
End Sub
#>
```

Code snippet FinancialData.tt

Class Feature blocks can contain Text blocks and Expression blocks but they cannot contain Statement blocks. In addition to this, no Statement blocks are allowed to appear once the first Class Feature block is encountered.

Now that you know the four different types of T4 blocks that can appear within a template file, it's time to see how Visual Studio 2010 is able to use them to generate the output file.

HOW T4 WORKS

The process of generating a file from a T4 template comprises two basic steps. In the first step, the `.tt` file is used to generate a standard .NET class. This class inherits from the `abstract` (`MustInherit`) `Microsoft.VisualStudio.TextTemplating.TextTransformation` class and overrides a method called `TransformText()`.

In the second step, an instance of this class is created and configured, and the `TransformText` method is called. This method returns a string that is used as the contents of the generated file.

Normally, you won't see the generated class file but you can configure the T4 engine to make a copy available by turning debugging on for the template. This simply involves setting the `debug` attribute of the `template` directive to `true` and saving the template file.

After a T4 template is executed in Debug mode a number of files are created in the temporary folder of the system. One of these files will have a random name and a `.cs` or a `.vb` extension (depending on the template language). This file contains the actual generator class.

> *You can find the temporary folder of the system by opening a Visual Studio command prompt and entering the command echo %TEMP%.*

This code contains a lot of pre-processor directives that support template debugging but make the code quite difficult to read. Here are the contents of the code file generated from the `FinancialSample.tt` template presented in the previous section reformatted and with these directives removed.

C#

```csharp
namespace Microsoft.VisualStudio.TextTemplatingBE7601CBE8A6858147D586FD8FC4C6F9
{
  using System;
  public class GeneratedTextTransformation :
        Microsoft.VisualStudio.TextTemplating.TextTransformation
  {
    public override string TransformText()
    {
      try
      {
        this.Write("\r\nFinancial Sample Data\r\n");

        for( int i = -5; i <= 5; i++ )
        {
          WriteFinancialNumber(i);
          WriteLine( "" );
        }

        this.Write("End of Sample Data\r\n\r\n ");
```

```
      }
      catch (System.Exception e)
      {
        System.CodeDom.Compiler.CompilerError error = new~CA
                    System.CodeDom.Compiler.CompilerError();
        error.ErrorText = e.ToString();
        error.FileName = "C:\\dev\\Chapter 14\\Chapter 14\\Finance.tt";
        this.Errors.Add(error);
      }
      return this.GenerationEnvironment.ToString();
    }

    void WriteFinancialNumber(decimal amount)
    {
      if( amount < 0 )
        Write("({0:#0.00})", System.Math.Abs(amount) );
      else
        Write("{0:#0.00}", amount);
    }
  }
}
```

VB

```
Imports System
Namespace Microsoft.VisualStudio.TextTemplating2739DD4202E83EF5273E1D1376F8FC4E
  Public Class GeneratedTextTransformation
    Inherits Microsoft.VisualStudio.TextTemplating.TextTransformation

    Public Overrides Function TransformText() As String
      Try
        Me.Write(""&Global.Microsoft.VisualBasic.ChrW(13) _
          & Global.Microsoft.VisualBasic.ChrW(10) _
          & "Financial Sample Data" _
          & Global.Microsoft.VisualBasic.ChrW(13) _
          & Global.Microsoft.VisualBasic.ChrW(10)) _

        For i as Integer = -5 To 5
          WriteFinancialNumber(i)
          WriteLine( "" )
        Next

        Me.Write("End of Sample Data" _
          & Global.Microsoft.VisualBasic.ChrW(13) _
          & Global.Microsoft.VisualBasic.ChrW(10) _
          & Global.Microsoft.VisualBasic.ChrW(13) _
          & Global.Microsoft.VisualBasic.ChrW(10)&" ")
      Catch e As System.Exception
        Dim [error] As System.CodeDom.Compiler.CompilerError = _
          New System.CodeDom.Compiler.CompilerError()
        [error].ErrorText = e.ToString
        [error].FileName = "C:\\dev\\Chapter 14\\Chapter 14\\Finance.tt"
        Me.Errors.Add([error])
      End Try
      Return Me.GenerationEnvironment.ToString
```

continues

(continued)

```
    End Function

    Sub WriteFinancialNumber(amount as Decimal)
      If amount < 0 Then
        Write("(${0:#0.00})", System.Math.Abs(amount) )
      Else
        Write("${0:#0.00}", amount)
      End If
    End Sub

  End Class
End Namespace
```

Note a few things of interest in this code. First, the template is executed by running the `TransformText()` method. The contents of this method run within the context of a try-catch block where all errors are captured and stored. Visual Studio 2010 knows how to retrieve these errors and displays them in the normal errors tool window.

The next interesting thing is the use of `Write()`. You can see that each Text block has been translated into a single string, which is passed to the `Write()` method. Under the covers this is added to the `GenerationEnvironment` property, which is then converted into a string and returned to the T4 engine.

The Statement blocks and the Class Feature blocks are copied verbatim into the generated class. The difference is in where they end up. Statement blocks appear inside the `TransformText()` method but Class Feature blocks appear after it and exist at the same scope. This should give you some idea as to the kinds of things you could declare within a Class Feature block.

Finally, Expression blocks are evaluated and the result is passed into `Microsoft.VisualStudio` `.TextTemplating.ToStringHelper.ToStringWithCulture()`. This method returns a string, which is then passed back into `Write()` as if it were a Text block. Note that the `ToStringHelper` takes a specific culture into account when producing a string from an expression. This culture can be specified as an attribute of the `template` directive.

When the `TransformText()` method finishes execution it passes a string back to the host environment, which in this case is Visual Studio 2010. It is up to the host to decide what to do with it. Visual Studio uses the `output` directive for this task. Directives are the subject of the next section.

> *Before moving on, the previous paragraph implied that T4 does not need to run inside Visual Studio. There is a command-line tool called* `TextTransform.exe`, *which you can find in the* `%CommonProgramFiles%\microsoft shared\` `TextTemplating\10.0\` *folder (*`C:\Program Files(x86)\Common Files\` `microsoft shared\TextTemplating\10.0\` *on 64-bit machines). Although you can use this to generate files during a build process, T4 itself relies on the presence of certain libraries that are installed with Visual Studio to run. This means that if you have a separate build machine you will need to install Visual Studio on it. Within Visual Studio, files with the* `.tt` *extension are processed with a custom tool referred to as* `TextTemplatingFileGenerator`.

T4 DIRECTIVES

A T4 template can communicate with its execution environment by using directives. Each directive needs to be on its own line and is denoted with `<#@` and `#>` tags. This section discusses the five standard directives.

Template Directive

The `template` directive controls a number of diverse options about the template itself. It contains the following attributes:

> `language`: Defines the .NET language used throughout the template inside of Expression, Statement, and Class Feature blocks. Valid values are `C#` and `VB`.

> `inherits`: Determines the base class of the generated class used to produce the output file. This can be overridden to provide additional functionality from within template files. Any new base class must derive from `Microsoft.VisualStudio.TextTemplating` `.TextTransformation`, which is the default value for the attribute.

> *If you want to inherit from a different base class, you will need to use an* `assembly` *directive (see the "Assembly Directive" section later in this chapter) to make it available to the T4 template.*

> `culture`: Selects a localization culture for the template to be executed within. Values should be expressed using the standard xx-XX notation (en-US, ja-JP, and so on). The default value is a blank string that specifies the Invariant Culture.

> `debug`: Turns on Debug mode. This causes the code file containing the generator class to be dumped into the temporary folder of the system. Can be set to `true` or `false`. Defaults to `false`.

> `hostspecific`: Indicates that the template file is designed to work within a specific host. If set to `true`, a `Host` property is exposed from within the template. When running in Visual Studio 2010 this property is of type `Microsoft.VisualStudio.TextTemplating.VSHost` `.TextTemplatingService`. Defaults to `false`. It is beyond the scope of this book but you can write your own host for T4 and use it to execute template files.

Output Directive

The `output` directive is used to control the file that is generated by the template. It contains two properties.

> `extension`: The extension that will be added to the generator name to create the filename of the output file. The contents of this property basically replace `.tt` in the template file-name. By default, this is `.cs` but it may contain any sequence of characters that the underlying file system will allow.

➤ encoding: Controls the encoding of the generated file. This can be the result of any of the encodings returned by `System.Text.Encoding.GetEncodings()`; that is, UTF-8, ASCII, and Unicode. The default, value is Default, which makes the encoding equal to the current ANSI code page of the system the template is being run on.

Assembly Directive

The `assembly` directive is used to give code within the template file access to classes and types defined in other assemblies. It is similar to adding a reference to a normal .NET project. It has a single attribute called `name`, which should contain one of the following items:

➤ The filename of the assembly: The assembly will be loaded from the same directory as the T4 template.

➤ The absolute path of the assembly: The assembly will be loaded from the exact path provided.

➤ The relative path of the assembly: The assembly will be loaded from the relative location with respect to the directory in which the T4 template is located.

➤ The strong name of the assembly: The assembly will be loaded from the Global Assembly Cache (CAG).

Import Directive

The `import` directive is used to provide easy access to items without specifying their full namespace qualified type name. It works in the same way as the `Import` statement in VB or the `using` statement from C#. It has a single attribute called `namespace`. By default, the `System` namespace is already imported for you. The following example shows a small Statement block both with and without an `import` directive.

C#

```
<#
  var myList = new System.Collections.Generic.List<string>();
  var myDictionary = new System.Collections.Generic.Dictionary<string,
  System.Collections.Generic.List <string>>();
#>
```

Code snippet WithoutImport.tt

VB

```
<#
Dim myList As New System.Collections.Generic.List(Of String)
Dim myDictionary As New System.Collections.Generic.Dictionary(Of System.String,
System.Collections.Generic.List(Of String))
#>
```

Code snippet WithImport.tt

C#

```
<#@ import namespace="System.Collections.Generic" #>
<#
  var myList = new List<string>();
  var myDictionary = new Dictionary<string, List<string>>();
#>
```

Code snippet WithImport.tt

VB

```
<#@ import namespace="System.Collections.Generic" #>

<#
Dim myList As New List(Of String)
Dim myDictionary As New Dictionary(Of String, List(Of String))
#>
```

Code snippet WithImport.tt

> The code that benefits from the `import` and `assembly` directives is the code that is executed when the T4 template is run, not the code that is contained within the final output file. If you want to access resources in other namespaces in the generated output file, you must include `using` or `Import` statements of your own into the generated file and add references to your project as normal.

Include Directive

The `include` directive allows you to copy the contents of another file directly into your template file. It has a single attribute called `file`, which should contain a relative or absolute path to the file to be included. If the other file contains T4 directives or blocks, they are executed as well. The following example inserts the BSD License into a comment at the top of a generated file.

```
' Copyright (c) <#=DateTime.Now.Year#>, <#=CopyrightHolder#>
' All rights reserved.

' Redistribution and use in source and binary forms, with or without
...
```

Code snippet License.txt

C#

```
<#@ template debug="false" hostspecific="false" language="C#" #>
<#@ output extension=".generated.cs" #>

<# var CopyrightHolder = "AdventureWorks Inc."; #>
/*
```

continues

(continued)

```
<#@ include file="License.txt" #>
*/
namespace AdventureWorks {
  // ...
}
```

Code snippet IncludeSample.tt

VB

```
<#@ template debug="false" hostspecific="false" language="VB" #>
<#@ output extension=".vb" #>

<# Dim CopyrightHolder = "AdventureWorks Inc." #>

<#@ include file="License.txt" #>

Namespace AdventureWorks
    ' ...
End Namespace
```

Code snippet IncludeSample.tt

TROUBLESHOOTING

As template files get bigger and more complicated, the potential for errors grows significantly. This is not helped by the fact that errors might occur at several main stages, and each needs to be treated slightly differently. Remember that even though T4 runs these processes one at a time, any might occur when a template file is executed, which occurs every time the file is saved.

When making any changes to T4 template files it is highly recommended that you take small steps to regenerate often and immediately reverse out any change that breaks things.

Design-Time Errors

The first place where errors might occur is when Visual Studio attempts to read a T4 template and use it to create the temporary .NET class. In Figure 14-5 there is a missing hash symbol in the opening tag for the Expression block. The resulting template is invalid. The Error List window at the bottom of Figure 14-5 shows Visual Studio identifying this sort of issue quite

FIGURE 14-5

easily. It is even able to correctly determine the line number where the error occurs.

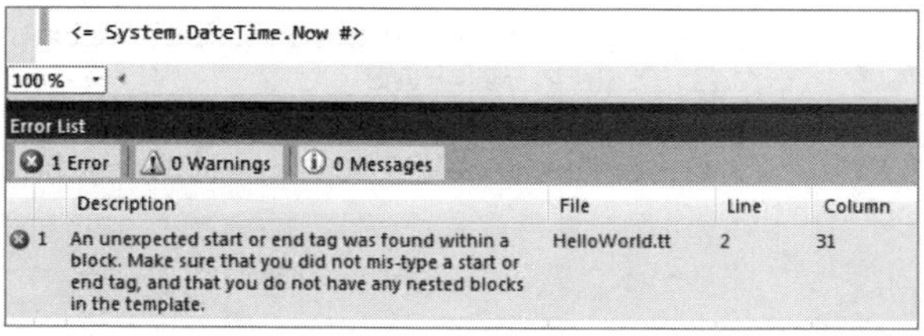

The other type of error that is commonly encountered at design time relates to directive issues. In many cases when a problem arises with an attribute of a directive a warning is raised and the default value is used. When there are no sensible defaults, such as with the import, include, and assembly directives, an error is raised instead.

> *One interesting exception to the way that Visual Studio handles invalid directives is the* extension *attribute of the* output *directive. If the value supplied is invalid in any way, a warning is raised but the generated file is not produced at all. If you have other code that depends on the contents of the generated file, the background compilation process will quickly find a cascade of errors, which can be overwhelming. Check to see if the file is being generated at all before attempting to fix the template by temporarily removing all the contents of the template file except for the* template *and* output *directives.*

Compiling Transformation Errors

The next step in the T4 pipeline where an error might occur is when the temporary .NET code file containing the code generator class is compiled into an assembly. Errors that occur here typically result from malformed code inside Expression, Statement, or Class Feature blocks. Again, Visual Studio does a good a job of finding and exposing these errors but the file and line number references point to the generated file. Each error that is found by the engine at this point is prefixed with the string Compiling Transformation which make them easy to identify.

The first step to fixing these errors is to turn Debug mode on in the template directive. This forces the engine to dump copies of the files that it is using to try and compile the code into the temporary folder. When these files are dumped out, double-clicking the error line in the Error List window opens the temporary file and you can see what is happening. Because this file will be a .cs or .vb file Visual Studio is able to provide syntax highlighting and IntelliSense to help isolate the problem area. Once the general issue has been discovered it is then much easier to find and update the relevant area of the template.

> *One of the other files generated by turning debugging on is a* .cmdline *file, which contains arguments that are passed to* csc.exe *or* vbc.exe *when T4 compiles the template. You can use this file to re-create the compilation process. There is also a file with the* .out *extension, which contains the command line call to the compiler and its results.*

Executing Transformation Errors

The final step in the T4 pipeline that might generate errors is when the code generator is actually instantiated and executed to produce the contents of the generated file. This stage is essentially running arbitrary .NET code and is the most likely to encounter trouble with environmental conditions or faulty logic. Like Compiling Transformation errors, errors found during this stage have a prefix of Executing Transformation, which makes them easy to spot.

The best way of handling Executing Transformation errors is to code defensively. From within the T4 template, if you can detect an error condition such as a file missing or being unable to connect to a database, you can use the Error() method to notify the engine of the specific problem. These errors will appear as Executing Transformation errors just like all of the others, only they'll have a more contextual, and hence, more useful message associated with them:

```
if( !File.Exists(fileName) ) {
  this.Error("Cannot find file");
}
```

In addition to `Error()` there is an equivalent `Warning()` method to raise warnings.

If the T4 template encounters an error that is catastrophic, such as not being able to connect to the database that it gets its data from, it is able to throw an exception to halt the execution process. The details about the exception are gathered and included in the Error List tool window.

Generated Code Errors

Although not technically a part of the T4 process, the generated file can just as easily contain compile-time or run time errors. In the case of compile-time errors, Visual Studio is simply able to detect these as normal. For run time errors it is probably a good idea to unit test complex types anyway, even those that have been generated.

Now that you know what to do when things go wrong, it is time to look at a larger example.

GENERATING CODE ASSETS

When you develop enterprise applications, you will frequently come across reference data that rarely changes and is represented in code as an enumeration type. The task of keeping the data in the database and the values of the enumerated type in sync is time-consuming and repetitive, which makes it a perfect candidate to automate with a T4 template. The template presented in this section connects to the AdventureWorks example database and creates an enumeration based on the contents of the `Sales.ContactType` table.

C#

```
<<#@ template debug="false" hostspecific="false" language="C#" #>
<#@ output extension=".generated.cs" #>

<#@ assembly name="System.Data" #>
<#@ import namespace="System.Data.SqlClient" #>
<#@ import namespace="System.Text.RegularExpressions" #>

<#
var connectionString = "Data Source=.\\SQLEXPRESS; Initial Catalog=AdventureWorks;"
    + "Integrated Security=true;";
var sqlString = "SELECT ContactTypeID, [Name] FROM [Person].[ContactType]";
#>

// This code is generated. Please do not edit it directly
// If you need to make changes please edit ContactType.tt instead
namespace AdventureWorks {
```

```
    public enum ContactType {

<#
using(var conn = new SqlConnection(connectionString))
using(var cmd = new SqlCommand(sqlString, conn))
{
  conn.Open();

  var contactTypes = cmd.ExecuteReader();

  while( contactTypes.Read() )
  {
  #>
    <#= ValidIdentifier( contactTypes[1].ToString() ) #> = <#=contactTypes[0]#>,
  <#}

  conn.Close();
}
#>
  }
}

<#+
  public string ValidIdentifier(string input)
  {
    return  Regex.Replace(input, @"[^a-zA-Z0-9]", String.Empty );
  }
#>
```

Code snippet ContactTypes.tt

VB

```
<#@ template debug="false" hostspecific="false" language="VB" #>
<#@ output extension=".generated.vb" #>

<#@ assembly name="System.Data" #>
<#@ import namespace="System.Data.SqlClient" #>
<#@ import namespace="System.Text.RegularExpressions" #>

<#
Dim ConnectionString as String = "Data Source=.\SQLEXPRESS; " _
& "Initial Catalog=AdventureWorks; Integrated Security=true;"
Dim SqlString as String = "SELECT ContactTypeID,[Name] FROM [Person].[ContactType]"
#>

' This code is generated. Please do not edit it directly
' If you need to make changes please edit ContactType.tt instead
Namespace AdventureWorks
  Enum ContactType

<#
Using Conn As New SqlConnection(ConnectionString), _
```

continues

(continued)

```
      Cmd As New SqlCommand(SqlString, Conn)

   Conn.Open()

   Dim ContactTypes As SqlDataReader = Cmd.ExecuteReader()

   While ContactTypes.Read()
#>
    <#= ValidIdentifier( contactTypes(1).ToString() ) #> = <#=contactTypes(0)#>
<#
  End While
  Conn.Close()
End Using
#>
  End Enum
End Namespace

<#+
  Public Function ValidIdentifier(Input as String) As String
    Return Regex.Replace(Input, "[^a-zA-Z0-9]", String.Empty )
  End Function
#>
```

Code snippet ContactTypes.tt

The first section is made up of T4 directives. The first two specify the language for the template and the extension of the output file. The third attaches an assembly to the generator (to provide access to the System.Data.SqlClient namespace), and the final two import namespaces into the template that the template code requires.

The next section is a T4 Statement block. It contains some variables that the template will be using. Putting them at the top of the template file makes them easier to find later on in case they need to change.

After the variable declarations there is a T4 Text block containing some explanatory comments along with a namespace and an enumeration declaration. These are copied verbatim into the generated output file. It's usually a good idea to provide a comment inside the generated file explaining where they come from and how to edit them. This prevents nasty accidents when changes are erased after a file is regenerated.

The bulk of the rest of the template is taken up by a Statement block. This block creates and opens a connection to the AdventureWorks database using the variables defined in the first Statement block. It then queries the database to retrieve the desired data with a data reader.

For each record retrieved from the database a Text block is produced. This Text block consists of two Expression blocks separated by an equals sign. The second expression merely adds the ID of the Contact Type to the generated output file. The first one calls a helper method called ValidIdentifier, which is defined in a Class Feature block that creates a valid identifier for each contact type by removing all invalid characters from the Contact Type Name.

The generated output file is shown in the following listing. The end result looks fairly simple in comparison to the script that is used to generate it, but this is a little deceiving. The T4 template can remain the same as rows of data are added to and removed from the ContactType table. In fact, the items in the database can be completely re-ordered and your code will still compile. With a little modification this script can even be used to generate enumerated types from a number of different tables at once.

C#

```csharp
// This code is generated. Please do not edit it directly
// If you need to make changes please edit ContactType.tt instead
namespace AdventureWorks {
    public enum ContactType {
        AccountingManager = 1,
        AssistantSalesAgent = 2,
        AssistantSalesRepresentative = 3,
        CoordinatorForeignMarkets = 4,
        ExportAdministrator = 5,
        InternationalMarketingManager = 6,
        MarketingAssistant = 7,
        MarketingManager = 8,
        MarketingRepresentative = 9,
        OrderAdministrator = 10,
        Owner = 11,
        OwnerMarketingAssistant = 12,
        ProductManager = 13,
        PurchasingAgent = 14,
        PurchasingManager = 15,
        RegionalAccountRepresentative = 16,
        SalesAgent = 17,
        SalesAssociate = 18,
        SalesManager = 19,
        SalesRepresentative = 20,
    }
}
```

Code snippet ContactTypes.generated.cs

VB

```vb
' This code is generated. Please do not edit it directly
' If you need to make changes please edit ContactType.tt instead
Namespace AdventureWorks
    Enum ContactType

        AccountingManager = 1
        AssistantSalesAgent = 2
        AssistantSalesRepresentative = 3
        CoordinatorForeignMarkets = 4
        ExportAdministrator = 5
        InternationalMarketingManager = 6
        MarketingAssistant = 7
        MarketingManager = 8
        MarketingRepresentative = 9
        OrderAdministrator = 10
        Owner = 11
        OwnerMarketingAssistant = 12
```

continues

(continued)
```
        ProductManager = 13
        PurchasingAgent = 14
        PurchasingManager = 15
        RegionalAccountRepresentative = 16
        SalesAgent = 17
        SalesAssociate = 18
        SalesManager = 19
        SalesRepresentative = 20
    End Enum
End Namespace
```

Code snippet ContactTypes.generated.vb

PREPROCESSED TEXT TEMPLATES

Text Template Transformation is a powerful technique and it shouldn't be restricted to a design-time activity. Visual Studio 2010 makes it easy to take advantage of the T4 engine to create your own text template generators to use in your own projects. These generators are called Preprocessed Text Templates.

To create a new Preprocessed Text Template, open the Add New Item dialog, select the General page, and select Preprocessed Text Template from the list of items. The newly created file has the same .tt extension as normal T4 template files and contains a single T4 directive:

C#

```
<#@ template language="C#" #>
```

VB

```
<#@ template language="VB" #>
```

Note that there is no output directive. The generated file will have the same filename as the template file but the .tt will be replaced with .vb or .cs depending on your project language. When this file is saved, it generates an output file like the following.

C#

```
// ------------------------------------------------------------------------------
// <auto-generated>
//     This code was generated by a tool.
//     Runtime Version: 10.0.0.0
//
//     Changes to this file may cause incorrect behavior and will be lost if
//     the code is regenerated.
// </auto-generated>
// ------------------------------------------------------------------------------
namespace Chapter_14
{
```

```csharp
using System;

public partial class NewTemplate
{
  // region Fields
  // region Properties
  // region Transform-time helpers

  public virtual string TransformText()
  {
    return this.GenerationEnvironment.ToString();
  }
}
}
```

Code snippet NewTemplate.cs

VB

```vbnet
Imports System
'-------------------------------------------------------------------------
'<auto-generated>
'     This code was generated by a tool.
'     Runtime Version: 10.0.0.0
'
'     Changes to this file may cause incorrect behavior and will be lost if
'     the code is regenerated.
'</auto-generated>
'-------------------------------------------------------------------------
Namespace My.Templates
  Partial Public Class NewTemplate
    ' Region "Fields"
    ' Region "Properties"
    ' Region "Transform-time helpers"
    Public Overridable Function TransformText() As String
      Return Me.GenerationEnvironment.ToString
    End Function
  End Class
End Namespace
```

Code snippet NewTemplate.vb

This is very much like the interim code file that is produced by T4 for a normal template. This generated class is now just a class inside the project, which means you can instantiate it, fill in its properties, and call `TransformText()` on it.

> *Just as with a normal Text Template, Visual Studio uses a Custom Tool to generate the output file of a Preprocessed Text Template. Instead of using the* `TextTemplatingFileGenerator` *custom tool, Preprocessed Text Templates are transformed using the* `TextTemplatingFilePreprocessor` *custom tool, which adds the code generator class to your project instead of the results of executing the code generator.*

Using Preprocessed Text Templates

To demonstrate how to use a Preprocessed Text Template within your own code, this section presents a simple scenario. The project needs to be able to send a standard welcome letter to new club members when they join the AdventureWorks Cycle club. The following Preprocessed Text Template contains the basic letter that is to be produced.

C#

```
<#@ template language="C#" #>
Dear <#=Member.Salutation#> <#=Member.Surname#>,

    Welcome to our Bike Club!

Regards,
The AdventureWorks Team
<#= Member.DateJoined.ToShortDateString() #>
<#+ public ClubMember Member { get; set; } #>
```

Code snippet WelcomeLetter.tt

VB

```
<#@ template language="VB" #>
Dear <#=Member.Salutation#> <#=Member.Surname#>,

    Welcome to our Bike Club!

Regards,
The AdventureWorks Team
<#= Member.DateJoined.ToShortDateString() #>
<#+ Public Member as ClubMember #>
```

Code snippet WelcomeLetter.tt

This file generates a class called `WelcomeLetter` and relies on the following simple data class, which is passed into the template via its `Member` property.

C#

```
public class ClubMember
{
    public string Salutation { get; set; }
    public string Surname { get; set; }
    public DateTime DateJoined { get; set; }
}
```

Code snippet ClubMember.tt

VB

```
Public Class ClubMember
    Public Surname As String
```

```
        Public Salutation As String
        Public DateJoined As Date
    End Class
```

Code snippet ClubMember.tt

Finally, to create the letter you instantiate a `WelcomeLetter` object, set the `Member` property to a `ClubMember` object, and call `TransformText()`.

C#

```csharp
// ...
var member = new ClubMember
{
  Surname = "Fry",
  Salutation = "Mr",
  DateJoined = DateTime.Today
};

var letterGenerator = new WelcomeLetter();

letterGenerator.Member = member;

var letter = letterGenerator.TransformText();
// ...
```

Code snippet Program.cs

VB

```vb
' ...
Dim NewMember As New ClubMember
With NewMember
  .Surname = "Fry"
  .Salutation = "Mr"
  .DateJoined = Date.Today
End With

Dim LetterGenerator As New WelcomeLetter

LetterGenerator.Member = NewMember

Dim Letter = LetterGenerator.TransformText()
' ...
```

Code snippet Module1.vb

This can look a little awkward but `WelcomeLetter` is a partial class so you can change the API to be whatever you want. Often you will find yourself making the constructor of the generator private and create a few static methods to handle the creation and use of generator instances.

C#

```csharp
public partial class WelcomeLetter
{
    private WelcomeLetter() { }
```

continues

(continued)

```csharp
  public static string Create(ClubMember member)
  {
    return new WelcomeLetter { Member = member }.TransformText();
  }
}
```

VB

```vb
Namespace My.Templates
  Partial Public Class WelcomeLetter
    Private Sub New()
    End Sub

    Public Shared Function Create(ByVal Member As ClubMember) As String
      Dim LetterGenerator As New WelcomeLetter()
      LetterGenerator.Member = Member
      Return LetterGenerator.TransformText()
    End Function

  End Class
End Namespace
```

Code snippet WelcomeLetter.Extensions.vb

> The generator contains a `StringBuilder`, *which it uses internally to build up the input when* `TransformText` *is executed. This* `StringBuilder` *is not cleared out when you run the* `TransformText` *method, which means that each time you run it the results are appended to the results of the previous execution. This is why the* `Create` *method presented creates a new* `WelcomeLetter` *object each time instead of keeping one in a* `static` *(*`Shared`*) variable and re-using it.*

Differences Between a Standard T4 Template

Aside from which aspect of the generation process is included in your project, a few other key differences exist between a Preprocessed Text Template and a standard T4 template. First, Preprocessed Text Templates are completely standalone classes. They do not inherit from a base class by default and therefore do not rely on Visual Studio to execute. The `TransformText()` method of the generator class does not run within a `try`/`catch` block so you will need to watch for and handle errors yourself when executing the generator.

Not all T4 directives will make sense in a Preprocessed Text Template, and for those that do some attributes will no longer make much sense. Here is a quick summary.

The `template` directive is still used but not all of the attributes make sense. The `culture` and `language` attributes are fully supported. The `language` attribute must match that of the containing language or the generator class cannot be compiled. The `debug` attribute is ignored because you can control the debug status of the generator class by setting the project configuration as you would with any other class.

The `inherits` attribute is supported and has a significant impact on the generated class. If you do not specify a base class, the generated file will be completely standalone and will contain implementations of all of the helper functions such as `Write` and `Error`. If you do specify a base class, it is up to the base class to specify these implementations and the generated class will rely on those implementations to perform the generation work.

The `hostspecific` attribute is supported and generates a `Host` property on the generator class. This property is of the `Microsoft.VisualStudio.TextTemplating.ITextTemplatingEngineHost` type, which resides in the `Microsoft.VisualStudio.TextTemplating` assembly. It is up to you to add a reference to this assembly to your project and to provide a member of the appropriate type before calling the `TransformText` method.

The `import` directive works as normal. The referenced namespaces are included in the generator code file with `using` statements in C# and `Import` statements in VB. The `include` directive is also fully supported.

The `output` and `assembly` directives are ignored. To add an assembly to the template you simply add a reference to the project as normal. The output filename is selected based on the template filename and the selected language.

Finally, you can set the namespace of the generator class in the Properties window of the template file shown in Figure 14-6. The namespace is normally based on the project defaults and the location of the template file within the folder structure of the project.

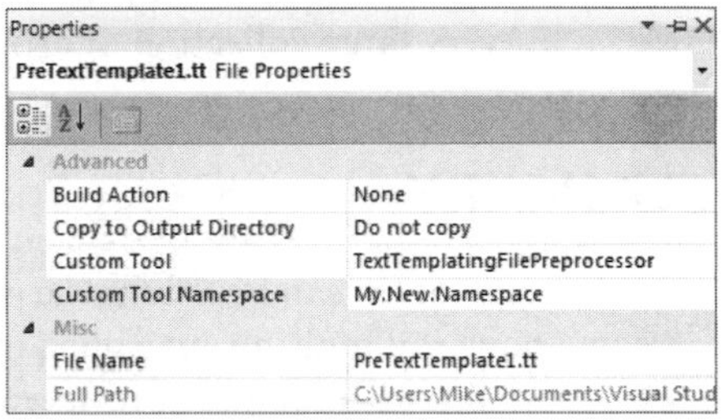

FIGURE 14-6

TIPS AND TRICKS

Following are a few things that might help you to take full advantage of T4:

➤ Write the code you intend to generate first for one specific case as a normal C# or VB code file. Once you are satisfied that everything is working as intended, copy the entire code file into a `.tt` file. Now start slowly making the code less specific and more generic by introducing Statement blocks and Expression blocks, factoring out Class Feature blocks as you go.

➤ Save frequently as you make changes. As soon as a change breaks the generated code or the generator, simply reverse it and try again.

➤ Never make changes directly to a generated file. The next time the template is saved those changes will be lost.

➤ Make generated classes partial. This makes the generated classes extensible, allowing you to keep some parts of the class intact and regenerate the other parts. In fact this is one of the reasons that the partial class functionality exists.

➤ Use an extension that includes the word *generated* such as `.generated.cs` and `.generated.vb`. This is a convention used by Visual Studio itself and will discourage other users from making changes to template files.

➤ Similarly, include a comment toward the top of the generated file stating that the file is generated along with instructions for how to change the contents and regenerate the file.

➤ Make T4 template execution a part of your build process. This ensures that the content of the generated files doesn't get stale with respect to the metadata used to generate it.

➤ If you don't have a lot of things dependent upon the generated code produced by a normal T4 Text Template, switch the custom tool over to make the template a Preprocessed Template while you develop it. This brings the code generator into your project and allows you to write unit tests against it.

➤ Don't use T4 to generate .tt files. If you are trying to use a code generator to generate template files, the level of complexity when things go wrong increases substantially. At this point it might be wise to consider a different strategy for your project.

➤ Finally, an absolutely invaluable resource for anyone getting started with T4 is http://www.olegsych.com. Oleg is a Visual C# MVP who maintains a blog with a very large collection of articles about T4.

SUMMARY

Code generation can be a fantastic productivity gain for your projects and Visual Studio 2010 includes some powerful tools for managing the process out of the box. In this chapter you have seen how to create and use T4 templates to speed up common and generic coding tasks. Learning when and how to apply T4 to your projects increases your productivity and makes your solutions far more flexible.

15

Project and Item Templates

WHAT'S IN THIS CHAPTER?

➤ Creating your own item templates

➤ Creating your own project templates

➤ Adding a wizard to your project templates

Most development teams build a set of standards that specify how they build applications. This means that every time you start a new project or add an item to an existing project, you have to go through a process to ensure that it conforms to the standard. Visual Studio 2010 enables you to create templates that can be reused without having to modify the standard item templates that ship with Visual Studio 2010. This chapter describes how you can create simple templates and then extend them with a wizard that can change how the project is generated using the `IWizard` interface.

CREATING TEMPLATES

Two types of templates exist: those that create new project items and those that create entire projects. Both types of templates essentially have the same structure, as you see later, except that they are placed in different template folders. The project templates appear in the New Project dialog, whereas the item templates appear in the Add New Item dialog.

Item Template

Although it is possible to build a project item template manually, it is much quicker to create one from an existing project item and make changes as required. This section begins by looking at an item template — in this case an About form that contains some basic information, such as the application's version number and who wrote it.

To begin, create a new Windows Forms application (using your language of choice) called StarterProject. Instead of creating an About form from scratch, you can customize the About Box template that ships with Visual Studio. Right-click the StarterProject project, select Add ⇨ New Item, and add a new About Box. Customize the default About form by deleting the logo and first column of the TableLayoutPanel control (by selecting the table layout panel, going to the Properties window, selecting the Columns property, clicking its ellipsis button (…), and deleting column 1). The customized About form is shown in Figure 15-1.

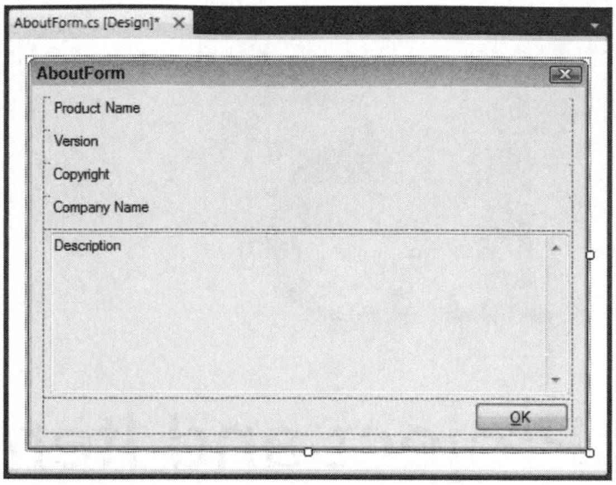

FIGURE 15-1

To make a template out of the About form, select the Export Template item from the File menu. This starts the Export Template Wizard, shown in Figure 15-2. If you have unsaved changes in your solution, you will be prompted to save before continuing. The first step is to determine what type of template you want to create. In this case, select the Item Template radio button and make sure that the project in which the About form resides is selected in the drop-down list.

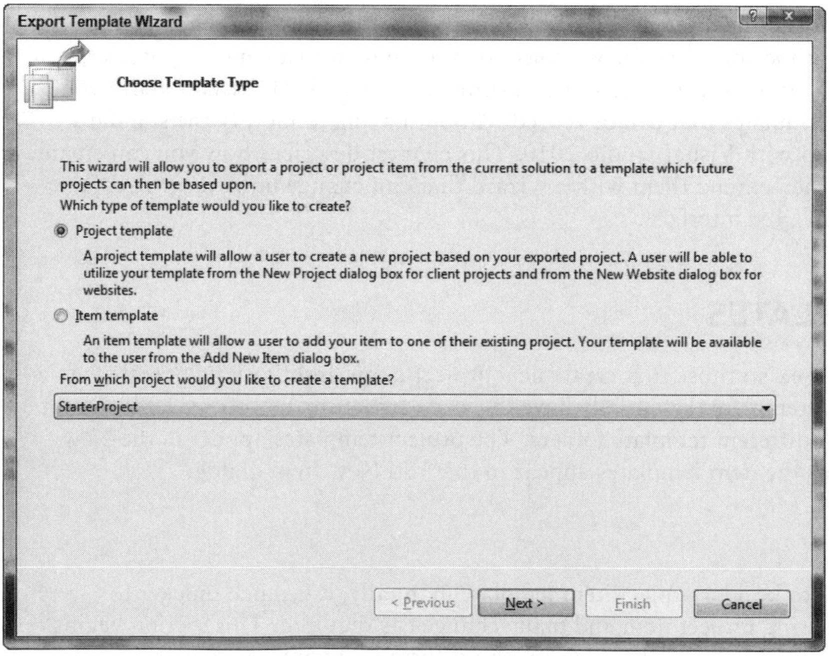

FIGURE 15-2

Click Next. You will be prompted to select the item on which you want to base the template. In this case, select the About form. The use of checkboxes is slightly misleading, because with item templates you can select only a single item on which to base the template (selecting a second item will deselect the item already selected). After you make your selection and click Next, the dialog shown in Figure 15-3 enables you to include any assembly references that you may require. This list is based on the list of references in the project in which that item resides. Because this is a form, include a reference to the `System.Windows.Forms` library, which will be added to a project when adding a new item of this type (if it has not already been added). Otherwise it is possible that the project won't compile if it did not have a reference to this assembly (Class Library projects don't generally reference this assembly by default).

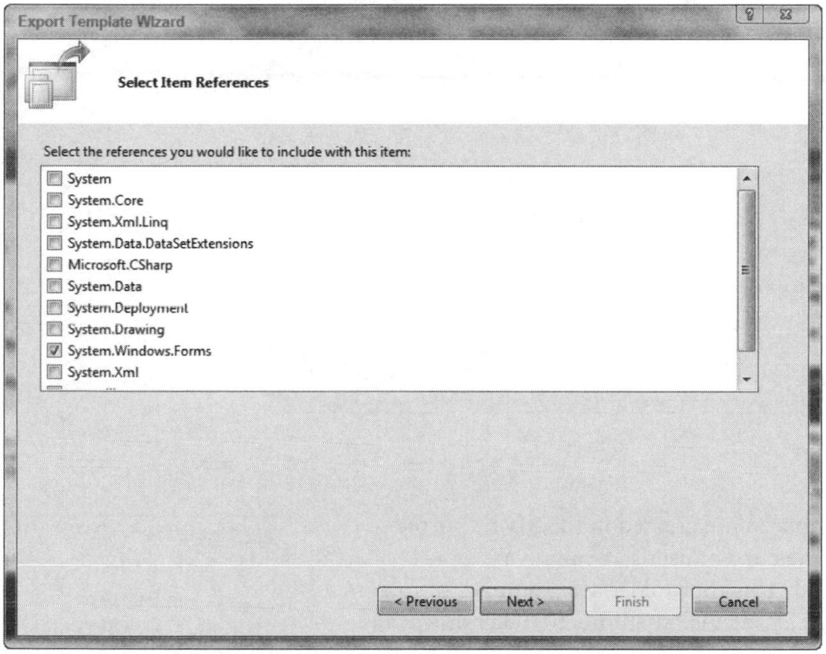

FIGURE 15-3

After selecting an assembly, a warning may be displayed underneath the list stating that the selected assembly isn't preinstalled with Visual Studio and may prevent a user from using your template if the assembly isn't available on their machine. Be aware of this issue, and only select assemblies that your item really needs.

The final step in the Export Template Wizard is to specify some properties of the template to be generated, such as the name, description, and icon that will appear in the Add New Item dialog.

Figure 15-4 shows the final dialog in the wizard. As you can see, there are two checkboxes, one for displaying the output folder upon completion and one for automatically importing the new template into Visual Studio 2010.

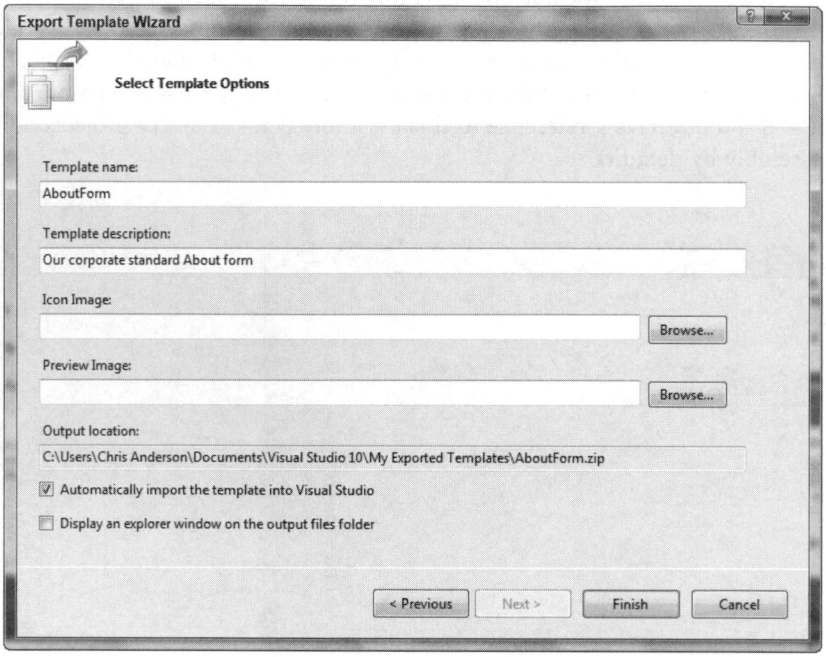

FIGURE 15-4

By default, exported templates are created in the My Exported Templates folder under the current user's `Documents\Visual Studio 2010` folder. Inside this root folder are a number of folders that contain user settings about Visual Studio 2010 (as shown in Figure 15-5).

You will also notice the Templates folder in Figure 15-5. Visual Studio 2010 looks in this folder for additional templates to display when you are creating new items. Two subfolders beneath the Templates folder hold item templates and project templates, respectively. These in turn are divided further by language. If you check the Automatically Import the Template into Visual Studio option on the final page of the Export Template Wizard, the new template will not only be placed in the output folder but will also be copied to the relevant location (depending on language and template type) within the Templates folder. Visual Studio 2010 will automatically display this item template the next time you display the Add New Item dialog, as shown in Figure 15-6.

FIGURE 15-5

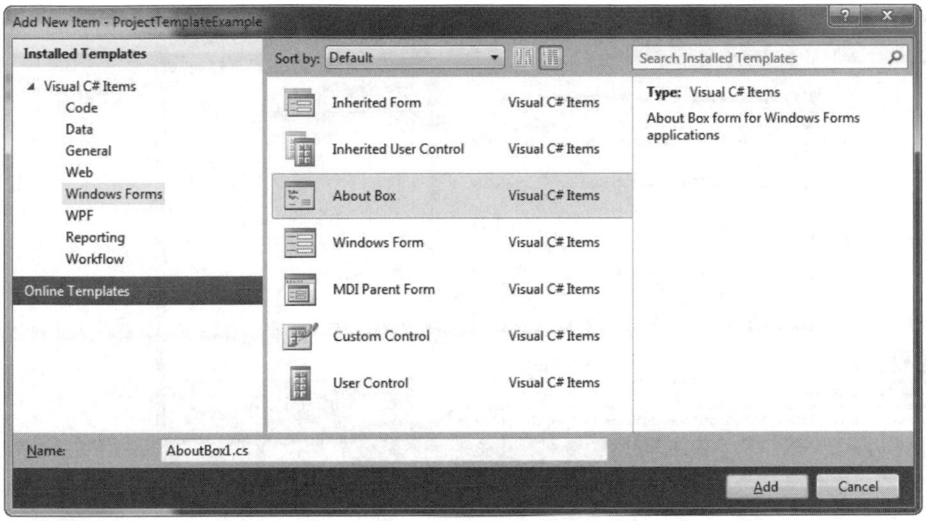

FIGURE 15-6

> If you want an item or project template to appear under an existing category (or one of your own) in the Add New Item / New Project dialog (such as the Windows Forms category), simply create a folder with that name and put the template into it (under the relevant location as described for that template). The next time you open the Add New Item / New Project dialog, the template will appear in the category with the corresponding folder name (or as a new category if a category matching the folder name doesn't exist).

Project Template

You build a project template the same way you build an item template, but with one difference. Whereas the item template is based on an existing item, the project template needs to be based on an entire project. For example, you might have a simple project called ProjectTemplateExample (as shown in Figure 15-7) that has a main form, an About form, and a splash screen.

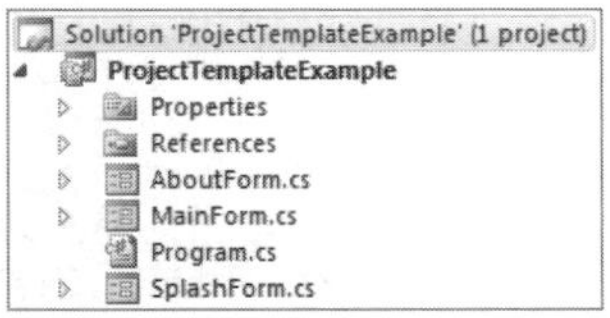

FIGURE 15-7

To generate a template from this project, you follow the same steps you took to generate an item template, except that you need to select Project Template when asked what type of template to generate, and there is no step to select the items to be included (all items within the project will be included in the template). After you've completed the Export Template Wizard, the new project template will appear in the New Project dialog, shown in Figure 15-8.

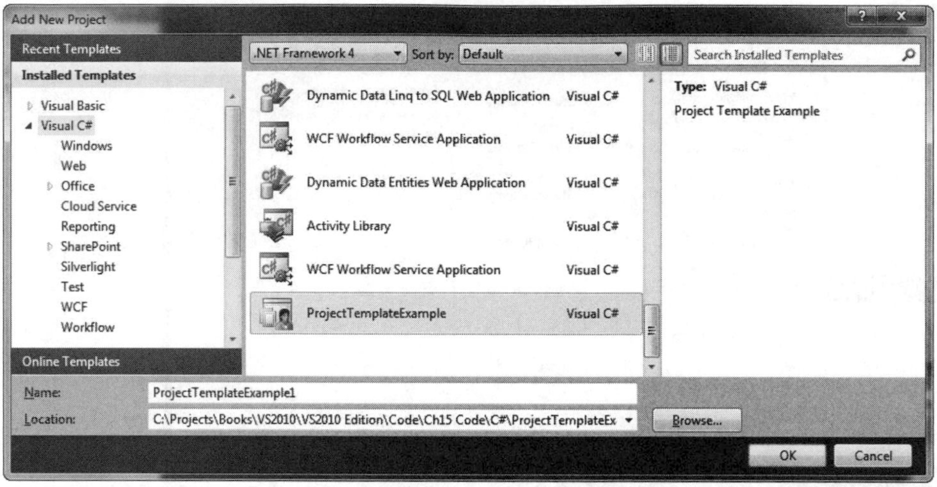

FIGURE 15-8

Template Structure

Before examining how to build more complex templates, you need to understand what is produced by the Export Template Wizard. If you look in the My Exported Templates folder, you will see that all the templates are exported as a single compressed zip file. The zip file can contain any number of files or folders, depending on whether they are templates for single files or full projects. However, the one common element of all template zip files is that they contain a `.vstemplate` file. This file is an XML document that holds the template configuration. The following listing is the `.vstemplate` file that was exported as a part of your project template earlier:

```xml
<VSTemplate Version="2.0.0"
  xmlns="http://schemas.microsoft.com/developer/vstemplate/2005" Type="Project">
  <TemplateData>
    <Name>Project Template Example</Name>
    <Description>Project Template Example</Description>
    <ProjectType>CSharp</ProjectType>
    <ProjectSubType>
    </ProjectSubType>
    <SortOrder>1000</SortOrder>
    <CreateNewFolder>true</CreateNewFolder>
    <DefaultName>Project Template Example</DefaultName>
    <ProvideDefaultName>true</ProvideDefaultName>
    <LocationField>Enabled</LocationField>
    <EnableLocationBrowseButton>true</EnableLocationBrowseButton>
    <Icon>__TemplateIcon.ico</Icon>
  </TemplateData>
  <TemplateContent>
    <Project TargetFileName="ProjectTemplateExample.csproj"
      File="ProjectTemplateExample.csproj" ReplaceParameters="true">
      <ProjectItem ReplaceParameters="true" TargetFileName="AboutForm.cs">
        AboutForm.cs</ProjectItem>
      <ProjectItem ReplaceParameters="true" TargetFileName="AboutForm.Designer.cs">
        AboutForm.Designer.cs</ProjectItem>
```

```
      <ProjectItem ReplaceParameters="true" TargetFileName="AboutForm.resx">
        AboutForm.resx</ProjectItem>
      <ProjectItem ReplaceParameters="true" TargetFileName="MainForm.cs">
        MainForm.cs</ProjectItem>
      <ProjectItem ReplaceParameters="true" TargetFileName="MainForm.Designer.cs">
        MainForm.Designer.cs</ProjectItem>
      <ProjectItem ReplaceParameters="true" ="Program.cs">Program.cs</ProjectItem>
      <Folder Name="Properties" TargetFolderName="Properties">
        <ProjectItem ReplaceParameters="true"
          TargetFileName="AssemblyInfo.cs">AssemblyInfo.cs</ProjectItem>
        <ProjectItem ReplaceParameters="true"
          TargetFileName="Resources.resx">Resources.resx</ProjectItem>
        <ProjectItem ReplaceParameters="true"
          TargetFileName="Resources.Designer.cs">Resources.Designer.cs
          </ProjectItem>
        <ProjectItem ReplaceParameters="true"
          TargetFileName="Settings.settings">Settings.settings</ProjectItem>
        <ProjectItem ReplaceParameters="true"
          TargetFileName="Settings.Designer.cs">Settings.Designer.cs</ProjectItem>
      </Folder>
      <ProjectItem ReplaceParameters="true" TargetFileName="SplashForm.cs">
        SplashForm.cs</ProjectItem>
      <ProjectItem ReplaceParameters="true"
        TargetFileName="SplashForm.Designer.cs">
        SplashForm.Designer.cs</ProjectItem>
      <ProjectItem ReplaceParameters="true" TargetFileName="SplashForm.resx">
        SplashForm.resx</ProjectItem>
    </Project>
  </TemplateContent>
```

At the top of the file, the `VSTemplate` node contains a `Type` attribute that specifies whether this is an item template (`Item`), a project template (`Project`), or a multiple project template (`ProjectGroup`). The remainder of the file is divided into `TemplateData` and `TemplateContent`. The `TemplateData` block includes information about the template itself, such as its name and description and the icon that will be used to represent it in the New Project dialog, whereas the `TemplateContent` block defines the file structure of the template.

In the preceding example, the content starts with a `Project` node, which indicates the project file to use. The files contained in this template are listed by means of the `ProjectItem` nodes. Each node contains a `TargetFileName` attribute that can be used to specify the name of the file as it will appear in the project created from this template. In the case of an item template, the `Project` node is missing and `ProjectItems` are contained within the `TemplateContent` node.

> *It's possible to create templates for a solution that contains multiple projects. These templates contain a separate .vstemplate file for each project in the solution. They also have a global .vstemplate file, which describes the overall template and contains references to each projects' individual .vstemplate files. Creating this file is a manual process, however, as Visual Studio does not currently have a function to export a solution template.*

For more information on the structure of the .vstemplate file, see the full schema at
`%programfiles%\Microsoft Visual Studio 10.0\Xml\Schemas\1033\vstemplate.xsd`.

Template Parameters

Both item and project templates support parameter substitution, which enables replacement
of key parameters when a project or item is created from the template. In some cases these are
automatically inserted. For example, when the About form was exported as an item template, the
class name was removed and replaced with a template parameter, as shown here:

```
Public Class $safeitemname$
```

Table 15-1 lists 14 reserved template parameters that can be used in any project.

TABLE 15-1: Template Parameters

PARAMETER	DESCRIPTION
clrversion	Current version of the common language runtime.
GUID[1-10]	A GUID used to replace the project GUID in a project file. You can specify up to ten unique GUIDs (for example, GUID1, GUID2, and so on).
itemname	The name provided by the user in the Add New Item dialog.
machinename	The current computer name (for example, computer01).
projectname	The name provided by the user in the New Project dialog.
registeredorganization	The registry key value that stores the registered organization name.
rootnamespace	The root namespace of the current project. This parameter is used to replace the namespace in an item being added to a project.
safeitemname	The name provided by the user in the Add New Item dialog, with all unsafe characters and spaces removed.
safeprojectname	The name provided by the user in the New Project dialog, with all unsafe characters and spaces removed.
time	The current time on the local computer.
userdomain	The current user domain.
username	The current username.
webnamespace	The name of the current web site. This is used in any web form template to guarantee unique class names.
year	The current year in the format YYYY.

In addition to the reserved parameters, you can also create your own custom template parameters. You define these by adding a `<CustomParameters>` section to the .vstemplate file, as shown here:

```
<TemplateContent>
    ...
    <CustomParameters>
        <CustomParameter Name="$timezoneName $" Value="(GMT+8:00) Perth"/>
        <CustomParameter Name="$timezoneOffset $" Value="+8"/>
    </CustomParameters>
</TemplateContent>
```

You can refer to this custom parameter in code as follows:

```
string tzName = "$timezoneName$";
string tzOffset = "$timezoneOffset$";
```

When a new item or project containing a custom parameter is created from a template, Visual Studio automatically performs the template substitution on both custom and reserved parameters.

Template Locations

By default, custom item and project templates are stored in the user's personal Documents\Visual Studio 2010\Templates folder, but you can redirect this to another location (such as a shared directory on a network so you are using the same custom templates as your colleagues) via the Options dialog. Go to Tools ➪ Options and select the Projects and Solutions node. You can then select a different location for the custom templates here.

EXTENDING TEMPLATES

Building templates based on existing items and projects limits what you can do. It assumes that every project or scenario will require exactly the same items. Instead of creating multiple templates for each different scenario (for example, one that has a main form with a black background and another that has a main form with a white background), with a bit of user interaction you can accommodate multiple scenarios from a single template. Therefore, this section takes the project template created earlier and tweaks it so users can specify the background color for the main form. In addition, you'll build an installer for both the template and the wizard that you will create for the user interaction.

To add user interaction to a template, you need to implement the IWizard interface in a class library that is then signed and placed in the Global Assembly Cache (GAC) on the machine on which the template will be executed. For this reason, to deploy a template that uses a wizard you also need rights to deploy the wizard assembly to the GAC.

Template Project Setup

Before plunging in and implementing the IWizard interface, follow these steps to set up your solution so you have all the bits and pieces in the same location, which will make it easy to make changes, perform a build, and then run the installer:

1. Create a new project with the Project Template Example project template that you created earlier in the chapter and name it ExtendedProjectTemplateExample. Make sure that this solution builds and runs successfully before proceeding. Any issues with this solution will be harder to detect later, because the error messages that appear when a template is used are somewhat cryptic.

2. Into this solution add a Class Library project, called WizardClassLibrary, in which you will place the `IWizard` implementation.

3. Add to the WizardClassLibrary a new empty class file called `MyWizard`, and a blank Windows Form called ColorPickerForm. These will be customized later.

4. To access the `IWizard` interface, add to the Class Library project `EnvDTE.dll` and `Microsoft.VisualStudio.TemplateWizardInterface.dll` as references, both located at `%programfiles%\Microsoft Visual Studio 10.0\Common7\IDE\PublicAssemblies\`.

5. Finally, you will also need to add a Setup project to the solution. To do this, select File ➪ Add ➪ New Project, expand the Other Project Types category, and then highlight Setup and Deployment. Select the Setup Wizard template and follow the prompts to include both the Primary Output and Content Files from WizardClassLibrary.

This should result in a solution that looks similar to what is shown in Figure 15-9.

As shown in Figure 15-9, when you include the primary output and content files from the Class Library project to the installer it also adds a number of dependencies. Because the template will only be used on a machine with Visual Studio 2010, you don't need any of these dependencies. Exclude them by clicking the Exclude menu item on the right-click context menu. Then perform the following steps to complete the configuration of the Installer project:

FIGURE 15-9

1. When you add primary outputs and content files from projects in the solution to the installer, they are added to the Application folder. However, you want the primary output of the class library to be placed in the GAC, and its content files to go into the user's Visual Studio Templates folder. To move these files, right-click the Installer project and select View ➪ File System from the context menu to open the File System view.

2. By default, the File System view contains the Application folder (which can't be deleted), the User's Desktop folder, and the User's Programs Menu folder. Remove the two user folders by selecting Delete from the right-click context menu.

3. Add both the Global Assembly Cache (GAC) folder and the User's Personal Data folder (Documents) to the file system by right-clicking the File System on Target Machine node and selecting these folders from the list.

4. Into the User's Personal Data folder, add a Visual Studio 2010 folder (right-click and choose Add ➪ Folder), followed by a Templates folder, followed by a ProjectTemplates folder, and

finally followed by Visual C# (if it is a C# project) or Visual Basic (if it's a VB project). The result should look like what is shown in Figure 15-10.

5. To complete the installer, move the primary output from the Application folder into the Global Assembly Cache folder, and then move the

FIGURE 15-10

content files from the Application folder to the ProjectTemplates folder. (Simply drag the files between folders in the File System view.)

IWizard

Now that you've completed the installer, you can start work on the wizard class library. As shown in Figure 15-9, you have a form (ColorPickerForm) and a class (MyWizard). The former is a simple form that can be used to specify the color of the background of the main form. To this form you will need to add a Color Dialog control, called ColorDialog1, a Panel called ColorPanel, a Button called PickColorButton (with the text "Pick Color"), and a Button called AcceptColorButton (with the text "Accept Color").

Rather than use the default icon that Visual Studio uses on the form, you can select a more appropriate icon from the Visual Studio 2010 Image Library. The Visual Studio 2010 Image Library is a collection of standard icons, images, and animations that are used in Windows, Office, and other Microsoft software. You can use any of these images royalty-free to ensure that your applications are visually consistent with Microsoft software.

The Image Library is installed with Visual Studio as a compressed file called `VS2010ImageLibrary.zip`. By default, you can find this under `%programfiles%\Microsoft Visual Studio 10.0\Common7\VS2010ImageLibrary\1033\`. Extract the contents of this zip file to a more convenient location, such as a directory under your profile.

To replace the icon on the form, first go to the Properties window and then select the Form in the drop-down list at the top. On the `Icon` property, click the ellipsis button (...) to load the file selection dialog. Select the icon file you want to use and click OK (for this example we've chosen `VS2010ImageLibrary\Objects\ico_format\WinVista\Settings.ico`).

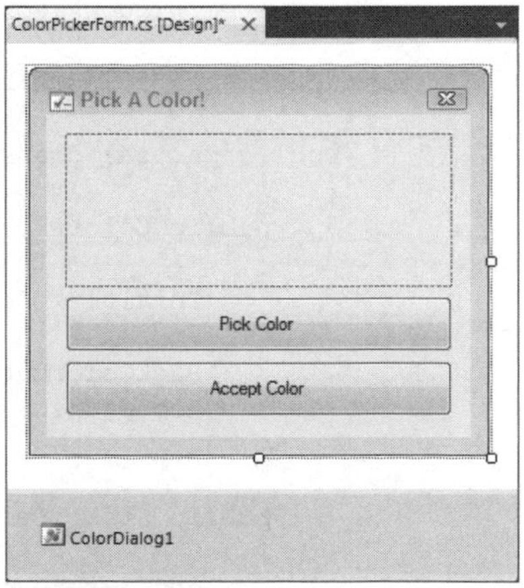

Once completed, the ColorPickerForm should look similar to the one shown in Figure 15-11.

FIGURE 15-11

The following code listing can be added to this form. The main logic of this form is in the event handler for the Pick Color button, which opens the ColorDialog that is used to select a color.

VB

```vb
Public Class ColorPickerForm
    Public ReadOnly Property SelectedColor() As Drawing.Color
        Get
            Return ColorPanel.BackColor
        End Get
    End Property

    Private Sub PickColorButton_Click(ByVal sender As System.Object, _
                        ByVal e As System.EventArgs) Handles
                        PickColorButton.Click
        ColorDialog1.Color = ColorPanel.BackColor
        If ColorDialog1.ShowDialog() = Windows.Forms.DialogResult.OK Then
            ColorPanel.BackColor = ColorDialog1.Color
        End If
    End Sub

    Private Sub AcceptColorButton_Click(ByVal sender As System.Object, _
                        ByVal e As System.EventArgs) Handles
                        AcceptColorButton.Click
        Me.DialogResult = Windows.Forms.DialogResult.OK
        Me.Close()
    End Sub
End Class
```

C#

```csharp
using System;
using System.Drawing;
using System.Windows.Forms;

namespace WizardClassLibrary
{
    public partial class ColorPickerForm : Form
    {
        public ColorPickerForm()
        {
            InitializeComponent();

            PickColorButton.Click += PickColorButton_Click;
            AcceptColorButton.Click += AcceptColorButton_Click;
        }

        public Color SelectedColor
        {
            get { return ColorPanel.BackColor; }
        }

        private void PickColorButton_Click(object sender, EventArgs e)
        {
            ColorDialog1.Color = ColorPanel.BackColor;

            if (ColorDialog1.ShowDialog() == DialogResult.OK)
            {
```

```
            ColorPanel.BackColor = ColorDialog1.Color;
        }
    }

    private void AcceptColorButton_Click(object sender, EventArgs e)
    {
        this.DialogResult = DialogResult.OK;
        this.Close();
    }
}
}
```

The `MyWizard` class implements the `IWizard` interface, which provides a number of opportunities for user interaction throughout the template process. Add some code to the `RunStarted` method, which will be called just after the project-creation process is started. This provides the perfect opportunity to select and apply a new background color for the main form:

VB

```
Imports Microsoft.VisualStudio.TemplateWizard
Imports System.Collections.Generic
Imports System.Windows.Forms

Public Class MyWizard
    Implements IWizard

    Public Sub BeforeOpeningFile(ByVal projectItem As EnvDTE.ProjectItem) _
                                        Implements IWizard.BeforeOpeningFile
    End Sub

    Public Sub ProjectFinishedGenerating(ByVal project As EnvDTE.Project) _
                                    Implements IWizard.ProjectFinishedGenerating
    End Sub

    Public Sub ProjectItemFinishedGenerating _
                            (ByVal projectItem As EnvDTE.ProjectItem) _
                            Implements IWizard.ProjectItemFinishedGenerating
    End Sub

    Public Sub RunFinished() Implements IWizard.RunFinished

    End Sub

    Public Sub RunStarted(ByVal automationObject As Object, _
                    ByVal replacementsDictionary As  _
    Dictionary(Of String, String), _
                    ByVal runKind As WizardRunKind, _
                    ByVal customParams() As Object) _
    Implements IWizard.RunStarted
        Dim selector As New ColorPickerForm
        If selector.ShowDialog = DialogResult.OK Then
            Dim c As Drawing.Color = selector.SelectedColor
            Dim colorString As String = "System.Drawing.Color.FromArgb(" & _
    c.R.ToString & "," & _
```

continues

(continued)

```
        c.G.ToString & "," & _
        c.B.ToString & ")"
                replacementsDictionary.Add _
                                    ("Me.BackColor = System.Drawing.Color.Silver", _
                                     "Me.BackColor = " & colorString)
            End If
        End Sub

        Public Function ShouldAddProjectItem(ByVal filePath As String) As Boolean _
                                    Implements IWizard.ShouldAddProjectItem
            Return True
        End Function
    End Class
```

C#

```csharp
using System;
using System.Drawing;
using System.Windows.Forms;
using System.Collections.Generic;
using Microsoft.VisualStudio.TemplateWizard;

namespace WizardClassLibrary
{
    public class MyWizard : IWizard
    {
        public void BeforeOpeningFile(EnvDTE.ProjectItem projectItem)
        {
        }

        public void ProjectFinishedGenerating(EnvDTE.Project project)
        {
        }

        public void ProjectItemFinishedGenerating(EnvDTE.ProjectItem projectItem)
        {
        }

        public void RunFinished()
        {
        }

        public void RunStarted(object automationObject, Dictionary<string, string>
            replacementsDictionary, WizardRunKind runKind, object[] customParams)
        {
            ColorPickerForm selector = new ColorPickerForm();

            if (selector.ShowDialog() == DialogResult.OK)
            {
                Color c = selector.SelectedColor;
                string colorString = "Color.FromArgb(" +
                    c.R.ToString() + "," +
                    c.G.ToString() + "," +
                    c.B.ToString() + ")";
```

```
            replacementsDictionary.Add
                            ("this.BackColor = System.Drawing.Color.Silver",
                            "this.BackColor = " + colorString);
            }
        }

        public bool ShouldAddProjectItem(string filePath)
        {
            return true;
        }
    }
}
```

In the RunStarted method, you prompt the user to select a new color and then use that response to add a new entry into the replacements dictionary. In this case, you are replacing "Me.BackColor = System.Drawing.Color.Silver" (VB) or "this.BackColor = System.Drawing.Color.Silver" (C#) with a concatenated string made up of the RGB values of the color specified by the user. The replacements dictionary is used when the files are created for the new project, because they will be searched for the replacement keys. Upon any instances of these keys being found, they will be replaced by the appropriate replacement values. In this case, you're looking for the line specifying that the BackColor is Silver, and replacing it with the new color supplied by the user.

The class library containing the implementation of the IWizard interface must contain a strongly named assembly capable of being placed into the GAC. To ensure this, use the Signing tab of the Project Properties dialog to generate a new signing key, as shown in Figure 15-12.

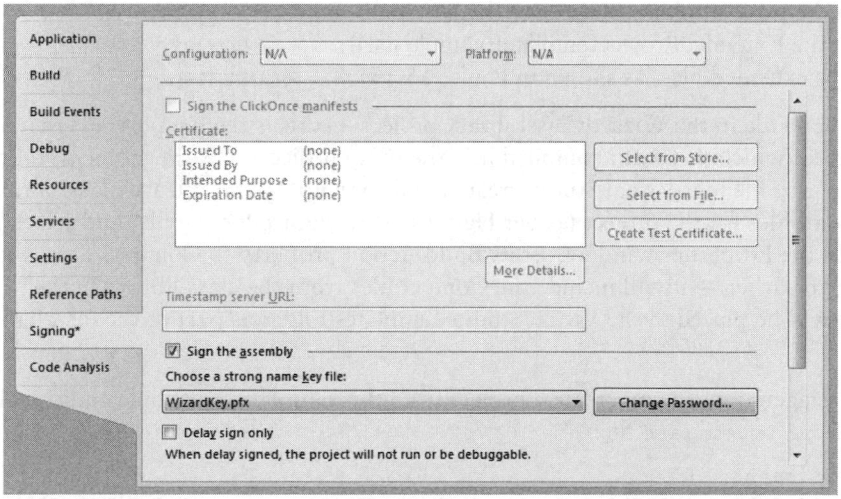

FIGURE 15-12

After you check the Sign the Assembly checkbox, there will be no default value for the key file. To create a new key, select <New . . .> from the drop-down list. Alternatively, you can use an existing key file using the <Browse . . .> item in the drop-down list.

Generating the Extended Project Template

You're basing the template for this example on the ExtendedProjectTemplateExample project, and you need only make minor changes in order for the wizard you just built to work correctly. In the previous section you added an entry in the replacements dictionary, which searches for instances where the `BackColor` is set to `Silver`. If you want the `MainForm` to have the `BackColor` specified while using the wizard, you need to ensure that the replacement value is found. To do this, simply set the `BackColor` property of the `MainForm` to `Silver`. This will add the line `"Me.BackColor = System.Drawing.Color.Silver"` to the `MainForm.Designer.vb` file (VB) or `"this.BackColor = System.Drawing.Color.Silver"` to the `MainForm.Designer.cs` file so that it is found during the replacement phase.

Now you need to associate the wizard with the project template so that it is called when creating a new project from this template. Unfortunately this is a manual process, but you can automate it once you've made these manual changes upon subsequent rebuilds of the project. Start by exporting the ExtendedProjectTemplateExample as a new project template as per the previous instructions. Find the `.zip` file for this template in Windows Explorer and unzip it. Take the `.vstemplate` file and the icon file and put it into the folder containing the ExtendedProjectTemplateExample project. The other files from the unzipped template can be disregarded — you'll note that these are just the same files from the project folder that you will be using in your template's output instead, so you now have all the files you need in the project folder. Make sure that you do *not* include these files in the ExtendedProjectTemplateExample itself; they should appear as excluded files, as shown in Figure 15-13.

FIGURE 15-13

You will notice the `.zip` file in the WizardClassLibrary project — this is the template file that Visual Studio exported (which you want compiled into the setup project). For the moment, take the project template `.zip` file that Visual Studio created and copy it into the WizardClassLibrary project folder. Show all files for the project (as per Figure 15-13), right-click the file, and select Include In Project. In the Properties window, set its Build Action property to Content. This is for the installer you set up earlier — it will include the Content files from the class library in the setup file, and these will be placed in the Visual Studio Templates folder as part of the installation process.

To have the wizard triggered when you create a project from this template, add some additional lines to the `MyTemplate.vstemplate` file:

```
<VSTemplate Version="2.0.0"
 xmlns="http://schemas.microsoft.com/developer/vstemplate/2005" Type="Project">
  <TemplateData>
  ...
  </TemplateData>
```

```
<TemplateContent>
...
</TemplateContent>
<WizardExtension>
  <Assembly>WizardClassLibrary, Version=1.0.0.0, Culture=neutral,
      PublicKeyToken=022e960e5582ca43, Custom=null</Assembly>
  <FullClassName>WizardClassLibrary.MyWizard</FullClassName>
</WizardExtension>
</VSTemplate>
```

The `<WizardExtension>` node added in the sample indicates the class name of the wizard and the strong-named assembly in which it resides. You have already signed the wizard assembly, so all you need to do is determine the `PublicKeyToken` by opening the assembly using Lutz

Roeder's Reflector for .NET (available at `http://www.red-gate.com/products/ reflector/`). If you haven't already built the WizardLibrary you will have to build the project so you have an assembly to open with Reflector. Once you have opened the assembly in Reflector (go to File ⇨ Open and select the assembly) you can see the `PublicKeyToken` of the assembly by selecting it in the tree, as shown in Figure 15-14. The `PublicKeyToken` value in the `.vstemplate` file needs to be replaced with this value you found using Reflector.

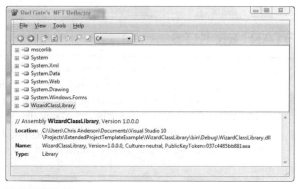

FIGURE 15-14

The last change you need to make to the ExtendedProjectTemplateExample is to add a post-build event command that will zip this project into a project template (this example uses 7-zip, available at `www.7-zip.org`, but any command-line zip utility will work). We will make a call to the 7-zip executable, which will zip the contents of the ExtendedProjectTemplateExample folder (recursively, but excluding the bin and obj folders) into `ExtendedProjectTemplateExample.zip`, and place it into the WizardClassLibrary folder. Note that you may need to change the path as per the location of your zip utility. Put the following command (on one line) as a post-build event:

```
"C:\Program Files\7-Zip\7z.exe" a -tzip ..\..\..\WizardClassLibrary\
ExtendedProjectTemplateExample.zip ..\..\*.* -r -x!bin -x!obj
```

You have now completed the individual projects required to create the project template (ExtendedProjectTemplateExample), added a wizard to modify the project as it is created (WizardClassLibrary), and built an installer to deploy your template to other machines. One last step is to correct the solution dependency list to ensure that the ExtendedProjectTemplateExample is rebuilt (and hence the template zip file re-created) prior to the installer being built. Because there is no direct dependency between the Installer project and the ExtendedProjectTemplateExample, you need to open the solution properties and indicate that there is a dependency, as illustrated in Figure 15-15.

Your solution is now complete and can be used to install the ExtendedProjectTemplateExample and associated `IWizard` implementation. Once the solution is installed, you can create a new project from the ExtendedProjectTemplateExample you have just created.

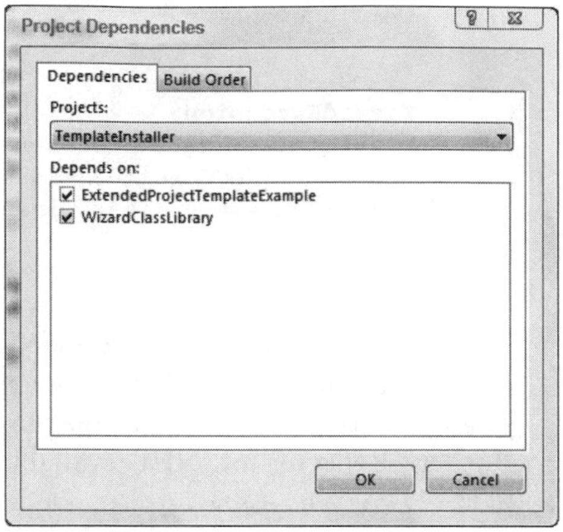

FIGURE 15-15

STARTER KITS

A Starter Kit is essentially the same as a template but differs somewhat in terms of intent. Whereas project templates create the basic shell of an application, Starter Kits create an entire sample application with documentation on how to customize it. Starter Kits will appear in the New Project window in the same way project templates do. Starter Kits can give you a big head start on a project (if you can find one focused toward your project type), and you can create your own to share with others in the same way that you created the project template previously.

ONLINE TEMPLATES

Visual Studio 2010 integrates nicely with the online Visual Studio Gallery (`http://www .visualstudiogallery.com`) enabling you to search for templates created by other developers that they uploaded to the gallery for other developers to download and use. You can browse the gallery and install selected templates from within Visual Studio in two ways: via the Open Project window and from the Extension Manager.

When you open the New Project window in Visual Studio you are looking at the templates installed on your machine; however, you can browse and search the templates available online by selecting Online Templates from the sidebar. Visual Studio will then allow you to browse the templates online. When you select a template it will be downloaded and installed on your machine, and a new project will be created using it.

Visual Studio 2010 introduces a new feature called the Extension Manager (as shown in Figure 15-16), which you can get to from Tools ➪ Extension Manager. The Extension Manager integrates the online Visual Studio Gallery (`http://www.visualstudiogallery.com`) right into Visual Studio itself. It also allows you to browse the Visual Studio Gallery and download and install templates, as well as controls and tools.

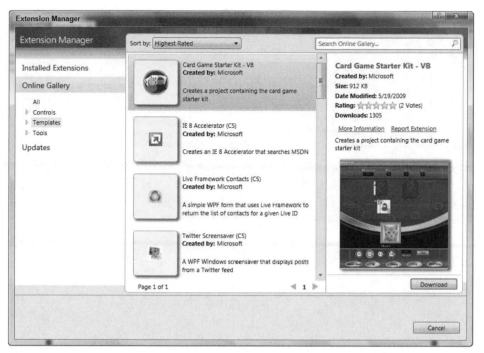

FIGURE 15-16

SUMMARY

This chapter provided an overview of how to create both item and project templates with Visual Studio 2010. Existing projects or items can be exported into templates that you can deploy to your colleagues. Alternatively, you can build a template manually and add a user interface using the `IWizard` interface. From what you learned in this chapter, you should be able to build a template solution that can create a project template, build and integrate a wizard interface, and finally build an installer for your template.

16

Language-Specific Features

WHAT'S IN THIS CHAPTER?

➤ Choosing the right language for the job

➤ Working with the new C# and VB language features

➤ Understanding and getting started with Visual F#

The .NET language ecosystem is alive and well. With literally hundreds of languages targeting the .NET Framework (you can find a fairly complete list at `www.dotnetpowered.com/languages.aspx`), .NET developers have a huge language arsenal at their disposal. Because the .NET Framework was designed with language interoperability in mind, these languages are also able to talk to each other, allowing for a creative cross-pollination of languages across a cross-section of programming problems. You're literally able to choose the right language tool for the job.

This chapter explores some of the latest language paradigms within the ecosystem, each with particular features and flavors that make solving those tough programming problems just a little bit easier. After a tour of some of the programming language paradigms, you learn about some of the new language features introduced in Visual Studio 2010, including one of the newest additions to Microsoft's supported language list: a functional programming language called F#.

HITTING A NAIL WITH THE RIGHT HAMMER

We need to be flexible and diverse programmers. The programming landscape requires elegance, efficiency, and longevity. Gone are the days of picking one language and platform and executing like crazy to meet the requirements of our problem domain. Different nails sometimes require different hammers.

Given that hundreds of languages are available on the .NET platform, what makes them different from each other? Truth be told, most are small evolutions of each other, and are not particularly useful in an enterprise environment. However, it is easy to class these languages into a range of programming paradigms.

Programming languages can be classified in various ways, but I like to take a broad-strokes approach, putting languages into four broad categories: imperative, declarative, dynamic, and functional. This section takes a quick look at these categories and what languages fit within them.

Imperative

Your classic all-rounder — imperative languages describe how, rather than what. Imperative languages were designed from the get-go to raise the level of abstraction of machine code. It's said that when Grace Hopper invented the first-ever compiler, the A-0 system, her machine code programming colleagues complained that she would put them out of a job.

It includes languages where language statements primarily manipulate program state. Object-oriented languages are classic state manipulators through their focus on creating and changing objects. The C and C++ languages fit nicely in the imperative bucket, as do our favorites VB and C#.

They're great at describing real-world scenarios through the world of the type system and objects. They are strict — meaning the compiler does a lot of safety checking for you. Safety checking (or type soundness) means you can't easily change a Cow type to a Sheep type — so, for example, if you declare that you need a Cow type in the signature of your method, the compiler will make sure that you don't hand that method a Sheep instead. They usually have fantastic reuse mechanisms too — code written with polymorphism in mind can easily be abstracted away so that other code paths, from within the same module through to entirely different projects, can leverage the code that was written. They also benefit from being the most popular. They're clearly a good choice if you need a team of people working on a problem.

Declarative

Declarative languages describe what, rather than how (in contrast to imperative, which describes the how through program statements that manipulate state). Your classic well-known declarative language is HTML. It describes the layout of a page: what font, text, and decoration are required, and where images should be shown. Parts of another classic, SQL, are declarative — it describes what it wants from a relational database. A recent example of a declarative language is XAML (eXtensible Application Markup Language), which leads a long list of XML-based declarative languages.

Declarative languages are great for describing and transforming data, and as such, we've invoked them from our imperative languages to retrieve and manipulate data for years.

Dynamic

The dynamic category includes all languages that exhibit "dynamic" features such as late-bound binding and invocation, REPL (Read Eval Print Loops), duck typing (non-strict typing, that is, if an object looks like a duck and walks like a duck it must be a duck), and more.

Dynamic languages typically delay as much compilation behavior as they possibly can to run time. Whereas your typical C# method invocation "Console.WriteLine()" would be statically checked and linked to at compile time, a dynamic language would delay all this to run time. Instead, it looks up the "WriteLine()" method on the "Console" type while the program is actually running, and if it finds it, invokes it at run time. If it does not find the method or the type, the language may expose features for the programmer to hook up a "failure method," so that the programmer can catch these failures and programmatically "try something else."

Other features include extending objects, classes, and interfaces at run time (meaning modifying the type system on the fly); dynamic scoping (for example, a variable defined in the global scope can be accessed by private or nested methods); and more.

Compilation methods like this have interesting side effects. If your types don't need to be fully defined up front (because the type system is so flexible), you can write code that will consume strict interfaces (like COM, or other .NET assemblies, for example) and make that code highly resilient to failure and versioning of that interface. In the C# world, if an interface you're consuming from an external assembly changes, you typically need a recompile (and a fix-up of your internal code) to get it up and running again. From a dynamic language, you could hook the "method missing" mechanism of the language, and when a particular interface has changed simply do some "reflective" lookup on that interface and decide if you can invoke anything else. This means you can write fantastic glue code that glues together interfaces that may not be versioned dependently.

Dynamic languages are great at rapid prototyping. Not having to define your types up front (something you would do straightaway in C#) allows you concentrate on code to solve problems, rather than on the type constraints of the implementation. The REPL (Read Eval Print Loop) allows you to write prototypes line-by-line and immediately see the changes reflected in the program instead of wasting time doing a compile-run-debug cycle.

If you're interested in taking a look at dynamic languages on the .NET platform, you're in luck. Microsoft has released IronPython (`www.codeplex.com/IronPython`), which is a Python implementation for the .NET Framework. The Python language is a classic example of a dynamic language, and is wildly popular in the scientific computing, systems administration, and general programming space. If Python doesn't tickle your fancy, you can also download and try out IronRuby (`www.ironruby.net/`), which is an implementation of the Ruby language for the .NET Framework. Ruby is a dynamic language that's popular in the web space, and though it's still relatively young, it has a huge popular following.

Functional

The functional category focuses on languages that treat computation like mathematical functions. They try really hard to avoid state manipulation, instead concentrating on the results of functions as the building blocks for solving problems. If you've done any calculus before, the theory behind functional programming might look familiar.

Because functional programming typically doesn't manipulate state, the surface area of side effects generated in a program is much smaller. This means it is fantastic for implementing parallel and concurrent algorithms. The holy grail of highly concurrent systems is the avoidance of overlapping "unintended" state manipulation. Dead-locks, race conditions, and broken invariants are classic manifestations of not synchronizing your state manipulation code. Concurrent programming and synchronization through threads, shared memory, and locks is incredibly hard, so why not avoid it altogether? Because functional programming encourages the programmer to write stateless algorithms, the compiler can then reason about automatic parallelism of the code. This means you can exploit the power of multi-core processors without the heavy lifting of managing threads, locks, and shared memory.

Functional programs are terse. There's usually less code required to arrive at a solution than with its imperative cousin. Less code typically means fewer bugs and less surface area to test.

What's It All Mean?

These categories are broad by design: languages may include features that are common to one or more of these categories. The categories should be used as a way to relate the language features that exist in them to the particular problems that they are good at solving.

Languages like C# and VB.NET are now leveraging features from their dynamic and functional counterparts. LINQ (Language Integrated Query) is a great example of a borrowed paradigm. Consider the following C# 3.0 LINQ query:

```
var query =    from c in customers
               where c.CompanyName == "Microsoft"
               select new { c.ID, c.CompanyName };
```

This has a few borrowed features. The `var` keyword says "infer the type of the query specified," which looks a lot like something out of a dynamic language. The actual query itself, `from c in ...`, looks and acts like the declarative language SQL, and the `select new { c.ID ...` creates a new anonymous type, again something that looks fairly dynamic. The code-generated results of these statements are particularly interesting: they're actually not compiled into classic IL (intermediate language); they're instead compiled into what's called an expression tree and then interpreted at run time — something that's taken right out of the dynamic language playbook.

The truth is, these categories don't particularly matter too much for deciding which tool to use to solve the right problem. Cross-pollination of feature sets from each category into languages is in fashion at the moment, which is good for a programmer, whose favorite language typically picks up the best features from each category. Currently the trend is for imperative/dynamic languages to be used by application developers, while functional languages have excelled in solving domain-specific problems.

If you're a .NET programmer, you have even more to smile about. Language interoperation through the CLS (Common Language Specification) works seamlessly, meaning you can use your favorite imperative language for the majority of the problems you're trying to solve, then call into a functional language for your data manipulation, or maybe some hard-core math you need to solve a problem.

A TALE OF TWO LANGUAGES

Since the creation of the .NET Framework there has been an ongoing debate as to which language developers should use to write their applications. In a lot of cases, teams choose between C# and VB based upon prior knowledge of either C/C++, Java, or VB6. However, this decision was made harder by a previous divergence of the languages. In the past, the language teams within Microsoft made additions to their languages independently, resulting in a number of features appearing in one language and not the other. For example, VB has integrated language support for working with XML literals, whereas C# has anonymous methods and iterators. Although these features benefited the users of those languages, it made it difficult for organizations to choose which language to use. In fact, in some cases organizations ended up using a mix of languages attempting to use the best language for the job at hand. Unfortunately, this either means that the development team needs to be able to read and write both languages, or the team gets fragmented with some working on the C# and some on the VB code.

With Visual Studio 2010 and the .NET Framework 4.0, a decision was made within Microsoft to co-evolve the two primary .NET languages, C# and VB. This co-evolution would seek to minimize the differences in capabilities between the two languages (often referred to as feature parity). However, this isn't an attempt to merge the two languages; in fact, it's quite the opposite. Microsoft has clearly indicated that each language may implement a feature in a different way to ensure it is in line with the way developers already write and interact with the language.

In the coming sections, you learn about the language features that have been added in Visual Studio 2010. You start by looking at the features common to both languages before going through changes to the individual languages, most of which are discussed in the context of feature parity and how the introduced feature matches a feature already in the other language.

Compiling without PIAs

Visual Studio 2010 has first-class support for building both document- and application-level add-ins for the main Office applications such as Word and Excel. As part of automating these products, you will want to be able to call into the exposed COM interfaces. You do this by referencing the Primary Interop Assemblies (PIAs) in order to work with the Microsoft Office Object Model. In the past, this then introduced a deployment dependency requiring you to ensure that the PIAs not only existed but were also the version you required. This added unnecessary size and complexity to the deployment of your add-in.

Both VB and C# include support for deploying applications, whether they be add-ins or standalone applications that use Office automation, without relying on the users having the PIAs installed on their machine. In Figure 16-1 you can see that there is a new property that specifies whether the compiler should Embed Interop Types.

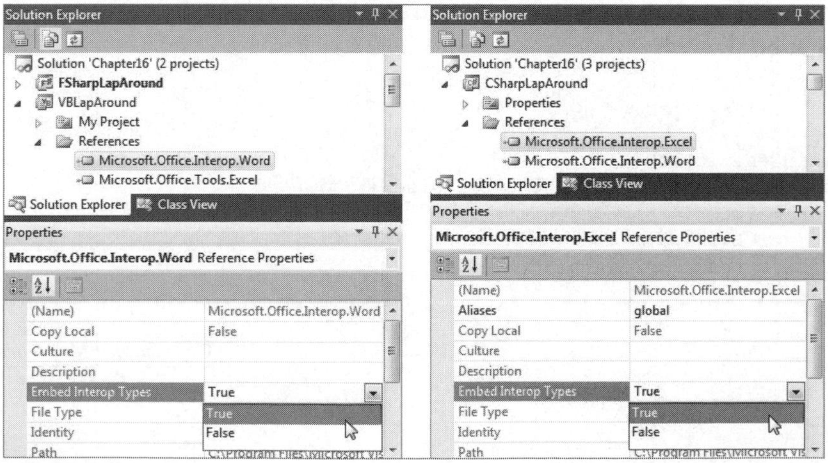

FIGURE 16-1

When the application is compiled, any interop types that are referenced are cloned from the PIAs into the compiled application. In Figure 16-2 you can see that the `Microsoft.Office.Interop.Word.Application` interface as been created within the `CShaperLapAround` executable.

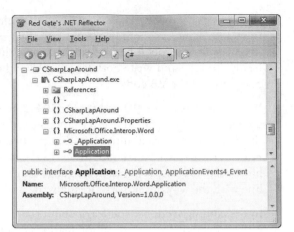

When this application executes, the .NET Framework 4.0 uses a new feature called type *equivalence* to allow COM objects passed between managed assemblies to be cast to a corresponding type in the receiving assembly. This effectively means that two assemblies can both declare managed types that wrap a COM object and for them to be deemed type equivalent as if they both used the same type definition.

FIGURE 16-2

 Because PIA-less compilation relies on type equivalence, which is a feature of .NET Framework 4.0, the Embed Interop Types option is available only for projects that are compiling against the .NET Framework 4.0. With the ability for Visual Studio 2010 to target multiple versions of the framework, it is quite easy to accidentally create projects that are targeting an earlier version of the framework, in which case this option would not be available.

Generic Variance

One of the seemingly confusing aspects of Generics is the role, or lack thereof, of inheritance. Take, for example, the inheritance chain Tortoise, which inherits from Animal, which in turn inherits from Object. You would assume that if you have a List of Tortoise (that is, `List<Tortoise>` in C# or `List(of Tortoise)` in VB) that you could cast it back to a List of Animal. The following code illustrates why this cannot be allowed:

C#

```csharp
private void InvalidGenericCast(){
    List<Tortoise> tortoiseList = new List<Tortoise>();
    List<Animal> animalList = tortoiseList;
    animalList.Add(new Lion());
    var notATortoise = tortoiseList[0];
}
```

Code snippet MainForm.cs

VB

```vb
Public Sub InvalidGenericCast()
    Dim tortoiseList As New List(Of Tortoise)
    Dim animalList As List(Of Animal) = tortoiseList
    animalList.Add(New Lion)
    Dim notATortoise As Tortoise = tortoiseList(0)
End Sub
```

Code snippet MainForm.vb

This code attempts to cast the List of Tortoise to a List of Animal. If this was allowed, a Lion could then be added to the list, because it too inherits from Animal. This would then make the last statement inconsistent because the List of Tortoise would no longer just contain Tortoises.

Though this illustrates a case against being able to cast between generic types, in some circumstances casting between types is allowable. For example, the following code snippet illustrates the List of Tortoise being cast to an IEnumerable of Animal. Because the IEnumerable interface doesn't permit modification of the collection, this is deemed to be a safe or allowable conversion.

C#

```csharp
private void ValidGenericCast(){
    List<Tortoise> tortoiseList = new List<Tortoise>();
    tortoiseList.Add(new Tortoise());
    IEnumerable<Animal> animalList = tortoiseList;
    var firstAnimal = animalList.First();
}
```

Code snippet MainForm.cs

VB

```vb
Public Sub ValidGenericCast()
    Dim tortoiseList As New List(Of Tortoise)
    tortoiseList.Add(New Tortoise)
    Dim animalList As IEnumerable(Of Animal) = tortoiseList
    Dim firstAnimal As Animal = animalList.First()
End Sub
```

Code snippet MainForm.vb

The ability to convert between generic types in this way is referred to as *generic variance*. In some circumstances you want to be able to narrow the type variable, such as in the preceding example, and you want to be able to widen the type variable. These are known as *covariance* and *contravariance*.

Covariance

In the previous example you saw how IEnumerable of Tortoise can be cast to an IEnumerable of Animal. This is what is known as covariance and is allowable because the IEnumerable of T interface has been updated to include the out keyword:

C#

```csharp
public interface IEnumerable<out T> : IEnumerable{
    IEnumerator<T> GetEnumerator();
}
```

VB

```vb
Interface IEnumerable(Of Out T) : Inherits IEnumerable
    Function GetEnumerator() As IEnumerator(Of T)
End Interface
```

Using the out keyword, you too can declare interfaces and delegates that have a variant type parameter. For example, in the following code the IAnimalCreator interface allows for the type parameter to be widened, allowing a conversion from IAnimalCreator of Lion (which MainForm implements) to IAnimalCreator of Animal, which the DoAnimalAction method expects:

C#

```csharp
public interface IAnimalCreator<out T> where T:Animal{
    T CreateAnimal();
}

public partial class MainForm : Form, IAnimalCreator<Lion>{
    public MainForm(){
        InitializeComponent();
        var animal = DoAnimalAction(this);
        MessageBox.Show(animal.GetType().Name);
    }

    private Animal DoAnimalAction(IAnimalCreator<Animal> action) {
        return action.CreateAnimal();
    }

    Lion IAnimalCreator<Lion>.CreateAnimal(){
        return new Lion();
    }
}
```

Code snippet MainForm.cs

VB

```vb
Public Interface IAnimalCreator(Of Out T As Animal)
    Function CreateAnimal() As Animal
End Interface
```

```vb
Public Class MainForm
    Implements IAnimalCreator(Of Lion)

    Public Sub New()

        InitializeComponent()

        Dim animal = DoAnimalAction(Me)
        MessageBox.Show(animal.GetType().Name)

    End Sub

    Public Function DoAnimalAction(ByVal action As IAnimalCreator(Of Animal)) _
                                                                As Animal
        Return action.CreateAnimal()
    End Function

    Public Function CreateAnimal() As Animal _
                            Implements IAnimalCreator(Of Lion).CreateAnimal
        Return New Lion
    End Function
End Class
```

Code snippet MainForm.vb

You can see in this code that the conversion is safe because the `CreateAnimal` method doesn't accept any typed parameter (that is, a type parameter going `in`). Instead, the type parameter defines the type of the return, or `out`, value, making the interface covariant on T.

Contravariance

Cases exist where you also want to be able to widen the type parameter. This is known as contravariance and is used by the IComparer interface. As you can imagine, an IComparer of Animal is also an IComparer of Lion, because if you can compare any animal you should be able to compare Lions. This conversion is allowable because the IComparer interface has been updated to use the `in` keyword.

C#

```csharp
public interface IComparer<in T>{
    public int Compare(T left, T right);
}
```

VB

```vb
Interface IComparer(Of In T)
    Function Compare(left As T, right As T) As Integer
End Interface
```

Again, you can use the `in` keyword to build your own contravariant interfaces or delegates. Using the Animal example again, you can define a method `DoAnotherAnimalAction` that will accept an IAnimalAction of Tortoise. However, the MainForm actually implements IAnimalAction of Animal.

C#

```csharp
public interface IAnimalAction<in T> where T : Animal{
    void Action(T animal);
}

public partial class MainForm : Form, IAnimalAction<Animal>{
    public MainForm(){
        InitializeComponent();
        DoAnotherAnimalAction(this);
    }

    private void DoAnotherAnimalAction(IAnimalAction<Tortoise> action){
        action.Action(new Tortoise());
    }

    void IAnimalAction<Animal>.Action(Animal animal){
        MessageBox.Show("This could be any animal.... " + animal.GetType().Name);
    }
}
```

Code snippet MainForm.cs

VB

```vb
Public Interface IAnimalAction(Of In T As Animal)
    Sub Action(ByVal animal As T)
End Interface

Public Class MainForm
    Implements IAnimalCreator(Of Lion), IAnimalAction(Of Animal)

    Public Sub New()
        InitializeComponent()
        DoAnotherAnimalAction(Me)
    End Sub

    Public Sub DoAnotherAnimalAction(ByVal action As IAnimalAction(Of Tortoise))
        action.Action(New Tortoise)
    End Sub

    Public Function CreateAnimal() As Animal _
                Implements IAnimalCreator(Of Lion).CreateAnimal
        Return New Lion
    End Function

    Public Sub Action(ByVal animal As Animal) _
                    Implements IAnimalAction(Of Animal).Action
        MessageBox.Show("This could be any animal.... " & animal.GetType().Name)
    End Sub
End Class
```

Code snippet MainForm.vb

Looking at this example, you may be wondering why it is safe to perform the conversion between an IAnimalAction of Animal to an IAnimalAction of Tortoise. This operation is safe because the compiler enforces that the contravariant type parameter, T, can only be used as an input parameter. Because a Tortoise can always be converted to an Animal, it is always safe to use a Tortoise as an input parameter for a method that expects an Animal.

VISUAL BASIC

This release of Visual Basic (VB) includes a number of additions that bring it closer to feature parity with C#. It also includes a couple of language-specific features that make it easier for developers to initialize collections and arrays.

Lambdas and Anonymous Methods

One of the key omissions from previous versions of VB was full support for lambdas and anonymous methods. An anonymous method is a method that is defined without a name and a lambda is a special case whereby the expression can be either used to generate a delegate (as with most anonymous methods) or an expression tree (discussed further in Chapter 29 on LINQ). In VB you now have the ability to declare single and multiline anonymous methods.

The following code snippet illustrates a number of features of working with anonymous methods in VB. In the first line an anonymous function is declared that accepts a name parameter and returns a Boolean. Type inference is used to determine that the name parameter should be a string and in fact in this case the `As Boolean` can be omitted because the return type can also be inferred. If the inferred input type is wrong or you wish to make your code more readable you can also specify the type of the input parameter.

Available for download on Wrox.com

VB

```vb
Dim exp = Function(name) As Boolean
                Console.WriteLine("Hello " & name)
                Return name.length > 10
          End Function
Dim exp2 = Sub(name)
                If exp(name) Then
                    Console.WriteLine(name & " is longer than 10 characters")
                End If
           End Sub
exp("Fred")
Dim names = {"Fred", "Joe", "Sandra"}
Array.ForEach(names, exp2)
Array.ForEach(names, Sub(name As String) Console.WriteLine(name))
```

Code snippet MainForm.vb

The second line illustrates that you can create an anonymous method with no return type, also know as a Sub in VB. Both lines return a delegate that can be invoked by supplying a parameter, illustrated in the next two lines. The final line illustrates how you can define an anonymous method in line as part of a method call. Note here that the abbreviated form has been used, as the

Sub is a single line. If your method has multiple lines, you need to use the full notation that includes an `End Sub` or `End Function`, depending on whether it has a return value.

Implicit Line Continuation

Where possible, the VB compiler will infer line continuation. For example, you can now write the following with no line continuation characters:

VB

```
Public Function LongMethodDeclaration(ByVal parameterOne As Integer,
                                      ByVal parameterTwo As Integer,
                                      ByVal parameterThree As Integer,
                                      ByVal parameterFour As Integer,
                                      ByVal parameterFive As Integer,
                                      ByVal parameterSix As Integer) As Integer
        Return parameterOne + parameterTwo + parameterThree +
                   parameterFour + parameterFive + parameterSix
    End Function
```

Code snippet MainForm.vb

In some cases, a line continuation character is still required. For example, if you wanted the parameter list to start on a new line:

VB

```
Public Function LongMethodDeclaration _
                             (ByVal parameterOne As Integer,
                              ByVal parameterTwo As Integer,
```

Implicit line continuation makes writing LINQ expressions with VB much easier, as you can break up the expression over multiple lines without having to add the line break character each time.

Automatic Properties with Initial Values

When defining a class, it is good practice to use encapsulation to hide or encapsulate the functionality of your class. The idea is that if you need to change the implementation, you can do so without affecting other code that uses that class. As such, it is recommended that where you want to expose a field, it should be done via a property. The property can simply be a getter/setter, or it can contain additional functionality, for example, that raises an event when the property value changes. This practice has resulted in large amounts of repetitive code where a property is declared along with a backing field. Although this has been made easier with Visual Studio snippets, it still results in code that is overly verbose.

In Visual Studio 2010, VB now not only has automatic properties — properties that automatically implement the backing field — it also enables you to declare an initial value for the property in the same way as you would for a field. The initial value is set by calling the property setter after the object instance is initialized but prior to any constructor being invoked. The following code illustrates this with the `MaximumWordCount` property:

VB

```vb
Public Property MaximumWordCount As Integer = 10
Public Sub New()
    MessageBox.Show("The maximum word count is " & MaximumWordCount)
    MessageBox.Show("The maximum word count is " & _MaximumWordCount)
```

Code snippet MainForm.vb

Nowhere in this code snippet is the `_MaximumWordCount` field declared. VB exposes the backing field used by the automatic property by simply prepending the property name with an underscore. Although it is not recommended, you can access the field directly from within your class because it is declared with a scope of `Private`.

Collection Initializers and Array Literals

VB now has a compact notation for specifying arrays, illustrated in the following code snippet:

VB

```vb
' Single dimension arrays
Dim a = {56, 34, 29, 12, 35, 872, 34, 12, 66} 'Integer()
Dim b = {1, 5, 3.54, 3.5} 'Double()
Dim c = {"Betty", "Frank"} 'String()
Dim d = {1, "123", New Animal} 'Object()

'Multi-dimension arrays
Dim e = {{1, 2, 3},
        {4, 5, 6}} 'non-jagged array (ie Integer(,) )
Dim f = {({1, 2, 3}),
        ({4}),
        ({5, 6, 7})} 'jagged array (ie Integer()())
```

Code snippet MainForm.vb

Note that the type of the array is inferred from the type of each of the constituent values. As such, the array b is an array of Double because this allows both the first two values, which are Integers, and the remaining values to be inserted. The `Object` array will raise an error if Option Strict is on.

Lists and Dictionaries can also be initialized using a similar compact notation:

VB

```vb
Private listOfNames As New List(Of String) From {"Nick", "Dave", "Mike", "Chris"}
Private cityLookup As New Dictionary(Of String, String) _
                            From {{"Nick", "Sydney"},
                                  {"Dave", "Perth"},
                                  {"Mike", "Perth"},
                                  {"Chris", "Sydney"}}
```

Code snippet MainForm.vb

The initialization of the List and Dictionary is done by invoking the Add method on the newly created instance. You can use a similar compact syntax to add your own object types to a List by creating an extension method, named Add, that will convert a set of input values into an instance of your class.

VB

```vb
Private listOfWeirdObjects As New List(Of MyListClass) From {{"Boo", 45, 67, 4.5},
                                                             {"Foo", 29, 34, 7.4}}
Public Module Extensions
    <Extension()>
    Sub Add(ByVal list As List(Of MyListClass),
            ByVal Name As String,
            ByVal Height As Integer,
            ByVal Weight As Integer,
            ByVal Width As Double)

        list.Add(New MyListClass With {
                                    .Name = Name,
                                    .Height = Height,
                                    .Weight = Weight,
                                    .Width = Width
                                })
    End Sub

End Module
```

Code snippet MainForm.vb

Nullable Optional Parameters

In the past it was not possible for nullable parameters to be optional. Now they can be, allowing you to define methods such as the following:

VB

```vb
Public Sub New()
    MethodWithOptionalParameters(5, parameterThree:=6)
End Sub
Public Function MethodWithOptionalParameters _
                    (Optional ByVal parameterOne As Integer? = Nothing,
                     Optional ByVal parameterTwo As Integer? = 0,
                     Optional ByVal parameterThree As Integer? = Nothing) _
                                                    As Integer
```

Code snippet MainForm.vb

As you can see from the code, for the optional parameters you need to define a default value. Also, when calling the method you may need to use parameter naming (as in `parameterThree:=`) if you wish to skip an optional parameter.

Visual Basic PowerPacks

One of the challenges often put forward by VB6 developers is that doing tasks in .NET requires many more steps or is more complex than it was in VB6. To encourage VB6 developers across to the .NET Framework, VB introduced the `My` namespace, which provides a set of shortcut methods to get frequently performed tasks done.

The VB team has also released the Visual Basic PowerPacks for previous versions of Visual Studio that add a number of useful controls and other classes to aid VB developers.

Visual Studio 2010 ships with the Visual Basic PowerPacks. As you can see in Figure 16-3, an additional tab in the Toolbox contains a number of drawing controls such as Line, Oval, and Rectangle. These can be used to generate simple graphics, such as the one on the right-hand side of Figure 16-3.

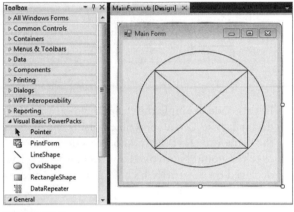

FIGURE 16-3

Although the Visual Basic PowerPacks are available by default to VB developers, there is no reason why C# developers can't access the same controls. To use these controls in a C# project, simply add a reference to the PowerPacks assembly and then add the controls to your Toolbox. From there you can use them on any Windows Forms application.

C#

In this iteration of the C# language there are only a couple of new features that mainly focus around the ability to interop with both native and dynamic languages.

Late Binding with Dynamic Lookup

Interoperability with other languages/technologies can often be quite painful, particularly with dynamic languages where it is not always known up front what methods a class may contain. In the past it was possible to execute these calls, but it often required a fairly in-depth understanding of reflection, and even then required many calls to invoke a single method. The new `dynamic` keyword can be used to allow methods to be late bound:

C#

```
public class DynamicClass{}
public class MoreDynamic : DynamicClass{
```

```
        public void SimpleMethod(){
            MessageBox.Show("Dynamic Invoked");
        }
    }

    public MainForm(){
        InitializeComponent();

        dynamic lateBound = CreateDynamic();
        lateBound.SimpleMethod();
    }

    public object CreateDynamic(){
        return new MoreDynamic();
    }
```

Code snippet MainForm.cs

In this code example the CreateDynamic method returns a MoreDynamic object as just an object. By declaring the lateBound object using the dynamic keyword it is possible to invoke the SimpleMethod the same way as if the method was declared on the object. Without this keyword, the static type checker would be invoked and a compile error would be thrown because the SimpleMethod is not declared on object (which is returned from CreateDynamic and thus would be the inferred type of the lateBound variable).

> One of the challenges with using the dynamic keyword is that the onus is now firmly on you to make sure you get the method naming, type, and number of parameters correct to ensure your code doesn't fail at run time. The dynamic keyword effectively blocks the static type checking at compile time, deferring it to the point where the code is executed.

Named and Optional Parameters

Two features that have been noticeably absent from C# are the ability to define optional parameters and to specify parameters using their names. Both these features contribute to making code more usable and more readable because they do away with unnecessary bloat (that is, specifying null for parameters you don't need/want to specify or having additional method overloads to effectively define optional parameters) and allow parameter values to be named.

C#

```
public MainForm(){
    InitializeComponent();
    var output = MethodWithOptionalParameters(parameterTwo: 15);
}
```

```
     public int MethodWithOptionalParameters(int? parameterOne = null,
                                             int parameterTwo = 5){
   return (parameterOne ?? 0) + parameterTwo;
}
```

Code snippet MainForm.cs

In this code both parameters are optional: the first being a nullable int with a default value of null, the second being a normal int with a default value of 5. Parameters become optional when a default value is specified as part of the method signature. When calling a method with optional parameters, those parameters can simply be omitted. Regardless of whether parameters are optional, you can name each of the parameter values so that someone reading your code can easily understand what the parameter values correspond to. This is particularly important if you are supplying a constant value, as is the case in the preceding code snippet, where the meaning of the constant value is not immediately obvious.

The use of named and optional parameters is particularly useful when working with COM interfaces. These quite often have a number of optional parameters that in the past would have had to be specified. This is no longer the case because those parameters can simply be omitted. Using named parameter values makes it clear which parameters you are supplying.

> *Calling methods using named parameters can make your code more brittle to changes. For example, say you access a third-party control that has a method with a single parameter called* height*. If the control vendor does a version update and changes the parameter name to* controlHeight*, even if the method signature didn't change, your code will no longer be able to locate the* height *parameter, so it will fail.*

F#

F# (pronounced F Sharp) is a relatively new language incubated out of Microsoft Research in Cambridge, England, by the guy that brought generics to the .NET Framework, Don Syme. Microsoft's Developer Division recently welcomed F# to the Visual Studio range of supported languages and it ships in the box with Visual Studio 2010. F# is a multi-paradigm functional language. This means it's primarily a functional language, but supports other flavors of programming, such as imperative and object-oriented programming styles.

Your First F# Program

Fire up Visual Studio 2010 and create a new F# project. As Figure 16-4 shows, the F# Application template is located in the Visual F# node in the New Project dialog. Give it a name and click OK.

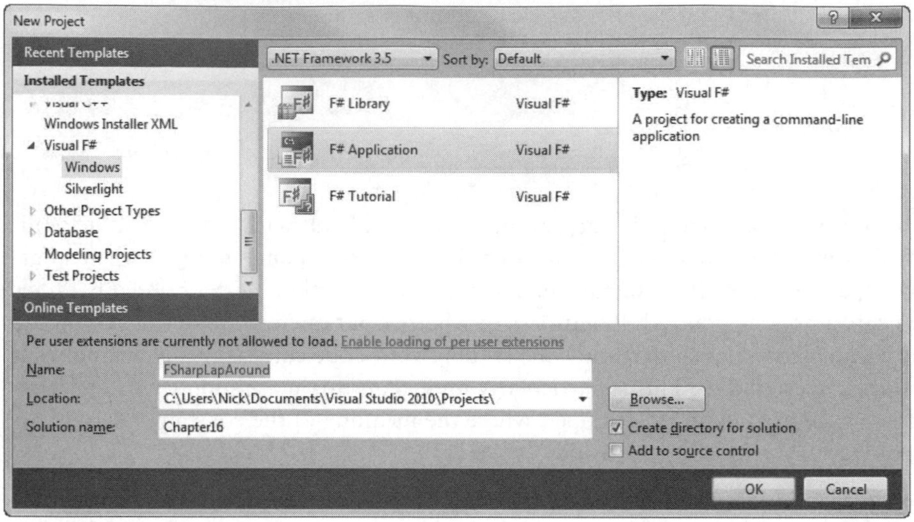

FIGURE 16-4

The F# Application template simply creates an F# project with a single source file, `Program.fs`, which is empty except for a reference to the F# Developer Center, `http://fsharp.net`. If you want to learn more about F# a great place to start is the F# Tutorial template. This creates a normal F# project except for the main source file, `Tutorial.fs`, which contains approximately 280 lines of documentation on how to get started with F#. Walking down this file and checking out what language features are available is an interesting exercise in itself. For now, return to the `Program.fs` and quickly get the canonical "Hello World" example up and running to see the various options available for compilation and interactivity. Add the following code:

```
#light

printfn "Hello, F# World!"
```

The first statement, `#light`, is a compile flag to indicate that the code is written using the optional lightweight syntax. With this syntax, whitespace indentation becomes significant, reducing the need for certain tokens such as `in` and `;;`. The second statement simply prints out `"Hello, F# World!"` to the console.

> *If you have worked with previous versions of F# you may find that your code now throws compiler errors. F# was born out of a research project and it has only now been converted into a commercial offering. As such, there has been a refactoring of the language and some operations have been moved out of FSharp.Core into supporting assemblies. For example, the* `print_endline` *command has been moved into the* `FSharp.PowerPack.dll` *assembly. The F# Powerpack is available for download via the F# Developer Center at* `http://fsharp.net`.

You can run an F# program in two ways. The first is to simply run the application as you would normally (press F5 to start debugging). This compiles and runs your program as shown in Figure 16-5.

FIGURE 16-5

The other way to run an F# program is to use the F# Interactive window from within Visual Studio. This allows you to highlight and execute code from within Visual Studio, and immediately see the result in your running program. It also allows you to modify your running program on the fly!

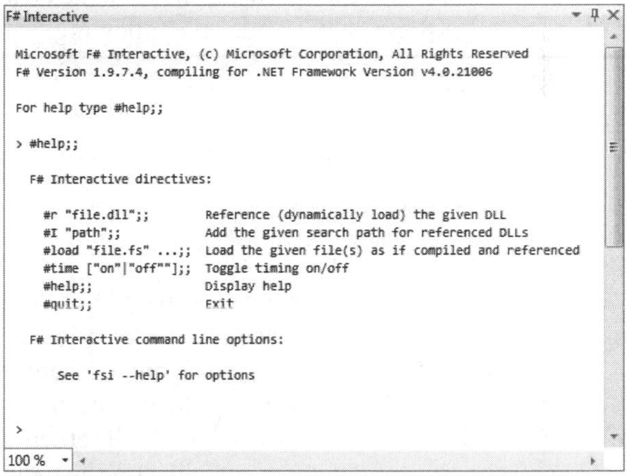

The F# Interactive window is available from the View ➪ Other Windows ➪ F# Interactive menu item, or by pressing the Ctrl+Alt+F key combination, as shown in Figure 16-6.

In the Interactive window, you can start interacting with the F# compiler through the REPL (Read Eval Print Loop) prompt. This means that for every line of F# you type, it will compile and execute that line immediately. REPLs are great if you want to test ideas quickly and modify programs on the fly. They allow for quick algorithm experimentation and rapid prototyping.

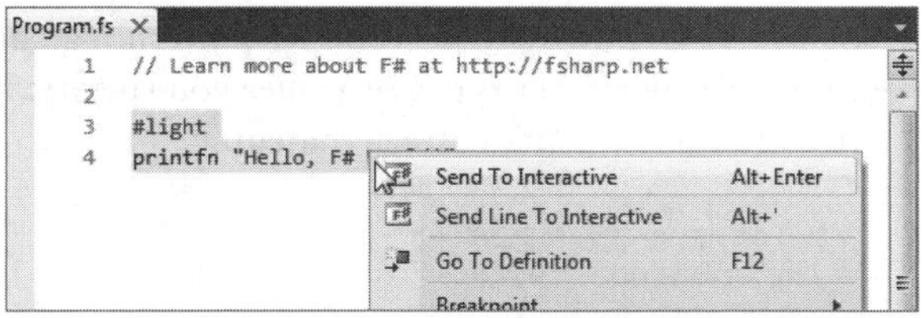

FIGURE 16-6

However, from the REPL prompt in the F# Interactive window, you essentially miss out on the value that Visual Studio delivers through IntelliSense, code snippets, and so on. The best experience is that of both worlds: using the Visual Studio text editor to create your programs, and piping that output through to the Interactive Prompt. You can do this by hitting Alt+Enter on any highlighted piece of F# source code. Alternatively, you can use the right-click context menu to send a selection to the Interactive window, as shown in Figure 16-7.

FIGURE 16-7

Pressing Alt+Enter, or selecting Send To Interactive, pipes the highlighted source code straight to the Interactive Prompt and executes it immediately, as shown in Figure 16-8.

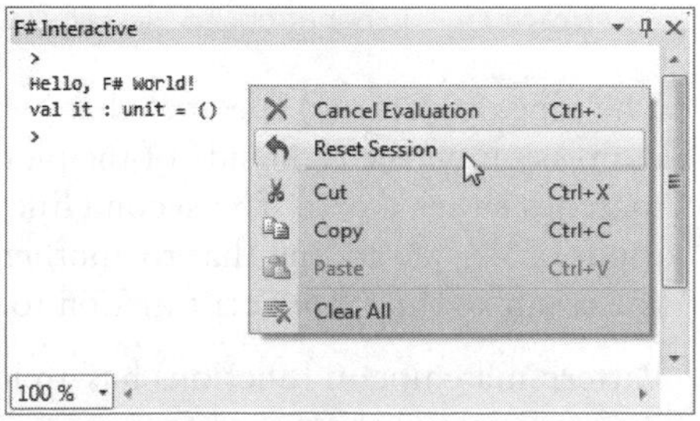

FIGURE 16-8

Figure 16-8 also shows the right-click context menu for the F# Interactive window where you can either Cancel Evaluation (for long running operations) or Reset Session (where any prior state will be discarded).

Exploring F# Language Features

A primer on the F# language is beyond the scope of this book, but it's worth exploring some of the cooler language features that it supports. If anything, it should whet your appetite for F#, and act as a catalyst to learn more about this great language.

A very common data type in the F# world is the list. It's a simple collection type with expressive operators. You can define empty lists, multi-dimensional lists, and your classic flat list. The F# list is immutable, meaning you can't modify it once it's created; you can only take a copy. F# exposes a feature called List Comprehensions to make creating, manipulating, and comprehending lists easier and more expressive. Consider the following:

```
#light

let countInFives = [ for x in 1 .. 20 do if x % 5 = 0  then yield x ]

printf "%A" countInFives
System.Console.ReadLine()
```

The expression in braces does a classic "for" loop over a list that contains elements 1 through 20 (the ". ." expression is shorthand for creating a new list with elements 1 through 20 in it). The "do" is a comprehension that the "for" loop executes for each element in the list. In this case, the action to execute is to "yield" x where the if condition "when x module 5 equals 0" is true. The braces are shorthand for "create a new list with all returned elements in it." And there you have it — a very expressive way of defining a new list on the fly in one line.

F#'s Pattern Matching feature is a flexible and powerful way to create control flow. In the C# world, we have the switch (or simply a bunch of nested "if else's"), but we're usually constrained to the type of what we're switching over. F#'s pattern matching is similar, but more flexible, allowing the test to be over whatever types or values you specify. For example, take a look at defining a Fibonacci function in F# using pattern matching:

```
let rec fibonacci x =
    match x with
    | 0 | 1 -> x
    | _ -> fibonacci (x - 1) + fibonacci (x - 2)

printfn "fibonacci 15 = %i" (fibonacci 15)
```

The pipe operator (|) specifies that you want to match the input to the function against an expression on the right side of the pipe. The first says return the input of the function x when x matches either 0 or 1. The second line says return the recursive result of a call to Fibonacci with an input of x - 1, adding that to another recursive call where the input is x - 2. The last line writes the result of the Fibonacci function to the console.

Pattern matching in functions has an interesting side effect — it makes dispatch and control flow over different receiving parameter types much easier and cleaner. In the C#/VB.NET world, you would traditionally write a series of overloads based on parameter types, but in F# this is unnecessary, because the pattern matching syntax allows you to achieve the same thing within a single function.

Lazy evaluation is another neat language feature common to functional languages that F# also exposes. It simply means that the compiler can schedule the evaluation of a function or an expression only when it's needed, rather than precomputing it up front. This means that you only have to run code you absolutely have to — fewer cycles spent executing and less working set means more speed.

Typically, when you have an expression assigned to a variable, that expression gets immediately executed in order to store the result in the variable. Leveraging the theory that functional programming has no side effects, there is no need to immediately express this result (because in-order execution is not necessary), and as a result, you should only execute when the variable result is actually required. Take a look at a simple case:

```
let lazyDiv = lazy ( 10 / 2 )
printfn "%A" lazyDiv
```

First, the `lazy` keyword is used to express a function or expression that will only be executed when forced. The second line prints whatever is in `lazyDiv` to the console. If you execute this example, what you actually get as the console output is "(unevaluated)." This is because under the hood the input to `printfn` is similar to a delegate. You actually need to force, or invoke, the expression before you'll get a return result, as in the following example:

```
let lazyDiv2 = lazy ( 10 / 2 )
let result = lazyDiv2.Force()
print_any result
```

The `lazyDiv2.Force()` function forces the execution of the `lazyDiv2` expression.

This concept is very powerful when optimizing for application performance. Reducing the amount of working set, or memory, that an application needs is extremely important in improving both startup performance and run time performance. Lazy evaluation is also a required concept when dealing with massive amounts of data. If you need to iterate through terabytes of data stored on disk, you can easily write a Lazy evaluation wrapper over that data, so that you only slurp up the data when you actually need it. The Applied Games Group in Microsoft Research has a great write-up of using F#'s Lazy evaluation feature with exactly that scenario: `http://blogs.technet .com/apg/archive/2006/11/04/dealing-with-terabytes-with-f.aspx`.

SUMMARY

In this chapter you learned about the different styles of programming languages and about their relative strengths and weaknesses. Visual Studio 2010 brings together the two primary .NET languages, C# and VB, with the goal of reaching feature parity. The co-evolution of these languages will help reduce the cost of development teams and projects, allowing developers to more easily switch between languages. You also learned about the newest addition to the supported Microsoft languages, Visual F#. As the scale of problems that we seek to solve increases, so does the complexity introduced by the need to write highly parallel applications. Visual F# can be used to tackle these problems through the execution of parallel operations without adding to the complexity of an application.

PART IV
Rich Client Applications

▶ **CHAPTER 17:** Windows Form Applications

▶ **CHAPTER 18:** Windows Presentation Foundation (WPF)

▶ **CHAPTER 19:** Office Business Applications

17

Windows Forms Applications

WHAT'S IN THIS CHAPTER?

➤ Creating a new Windows Forms application

➤ Designing the layout of forms and controls using the Visual Studio designers and control properties

➤ Using container controls and control properties to ensure that your controls automatically resize when the application resizes

Since its earliest days, Visual Studio has excelled at providing a rich visual environment for rapidly developing Windows applications. From simple drag-and-drop procedures to place graphical controls onto the form, to setting properties that control advanced layout and behavior of controls, the designer built into Visual Studio 2010 provides you with immense power without having to manually create the UI from code.

This chapter walks you through the rich designer support and comprehensive set of controls that are available for you to maximize your efficiency when creating Windows Forms applications.

GETTING STARTED

The first thing you need to get started is to create a new Windows Forms project. Select the File ➪ New ➪ Project menu to create the project in a new solution. If you have an existing solution to which you want to add a new Windows Forms project, select File ➪ Add ➪ New Project.

Windows Forms applications can be created with either VB or C#. In both cases, the Windows Forms Application project template is the default selection when you open the New Project dialog box and select the Windows category, as shown in Figure 17-1.

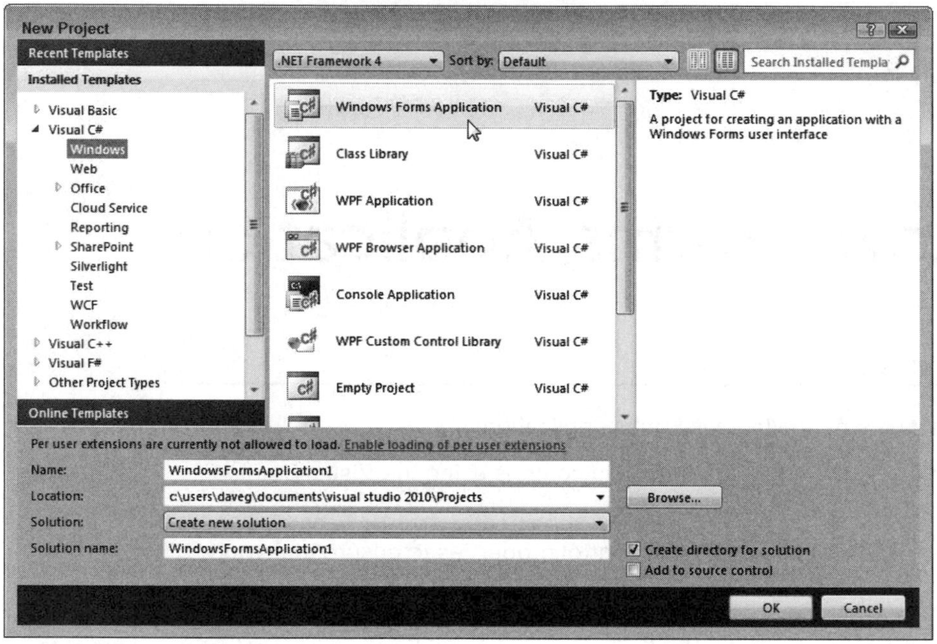

FIGURE 17-1

The New Project dialog allows you to select the .NET Framework version you are targeting. Unlike WPF applications, Windows Forms projects have been available since version 1.0 of the .NET Framework, and will stay in the list of available projects regardless of which version of the .NET Framework you select. After entering an appropriate name for the project, click OK to create the new Windows Forms Application project.

THE WINDOWS FORM

When you create a Windows application project, Visual Studio 2010 automatically creates a single blank form ready for your user interface design (see Figure 17-2). You can modify the visual design of a Windows Form in two common ways: by using the mouse to change the size or position of the form or a control or by changing the value of the control's properties in the Properties window.

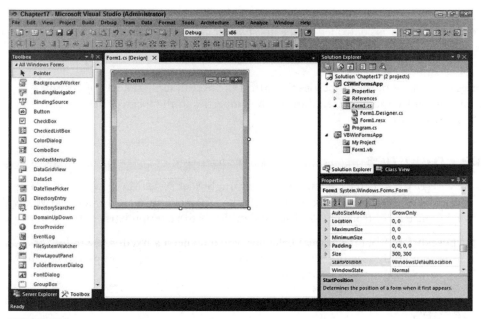

FIGURE 17-2

Almost every visual control, including the Windows Form itself, can be resized using the mouse. Resize grippers appear when the form or control has focus in the Design view. For a Windows Form, these are visible only on the bottom, the right side, and the bottom-right corner. Use the mouse to grab the gripper and drag it to the size you want. As you are resizing, the dimensions of the form are displayed on the bottom right of the status bar.

There is a corresponding property for the dimensions and position of Windows Forms and controls. As you may recall from Chapter 2, the Properties window, shown on the right-hand side of Figure 17-2, shows the current value of many of the attributes of the form. This includes the Size property, a compound property made up of the Height and Width. Click the expand icon to display the individual properties for any compound properties. You can set the dimensions of the form in pixels by entering either an individual value in both the Height and Width properties, or a compound Size value in the format width, height.

The Properties window, shown in Figure 17-3, displays some of the available properties for customizing the form's appearance and behavior.

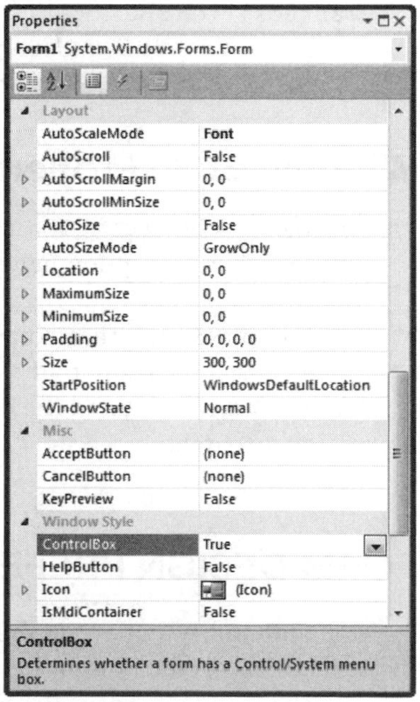

FIGURE 17-3

Properties are displayed in one of two views: either grouped together in categories or in alphabetical order. The view is controlled by the first two icons in the toolbar of the Properties window. The following two icons toggle the attribute list between displaying Properties and Events.

Three categories cover most of the properties that affect the overall look and feel of a form: Appearance, Layout, and Window Style. Many of the properties in these categories are also available on Windows controls.

Appearance Properties

The Appearance category covers the colors, fonts, and form border style. Many Windows Forms applications leave most of these properties as their defaults. The `Text` property is one that you will typically change, because it controls what is displayed in the form's caption bar.

If the form's purpose differs from the normal behavior, you may need a fixed-size window or a special border, as is commonly seen in tool windows. The `FormBorderStyle` property controls how this aspect of your form's appearance is handled.

Layout Properties

In addition to the `Size` properties discussed earlier, the Layout category contains the `MaximumSize` and `MinimumSize` properties, which control how small or large a window can be resized to. The `StartPosition` and `Location` properties can be used to control where the form is displayed in the screen. The `WindowState` property can be used to initially display the form minimized, maximized, or normally according to its default size.

Window Style Properties

The Window Style category includes properties that determine what is shown in the Windows Form's caption bar, including the maximize and minimize boxes, help button, and form icon. The `ShowInTaskbar` property determines whether the form is listed in the Windows taskbar. Other notable properties in this category include the `TopMost` property, which is used to ensure that the form always appears on top of other windows, even when it does not have focus, and the `Opacity` property, which can be used to make a form semi-transparent.

FORM DESIGN PREFERENCES

You can modify some Visual Studio IDE settings that will simplify your user interface design phase. In the Options dialog (shown in Figure 17-4) of Visual Studio 2010, two pages of preferences deal with the Windows Forms Designer.

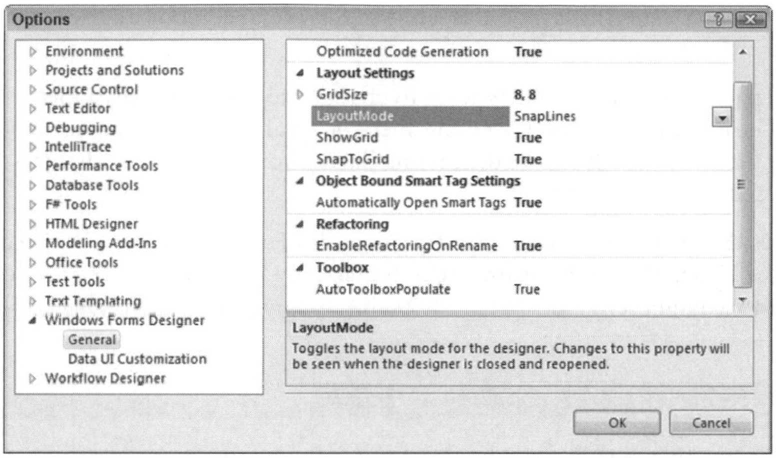

FIGURE 17-4

The main settings that affect your design are the layout settings. By default, Visual Studio 2010 uses a layout mode called SnapLines. Rather than position visible components on the form via an invisible grid, SnapLines helps you position them based on the context of surrounding controls and the form's own borders. You see how to use this new mode in a moment, but if you prefer the older style of form design that originated in Visual Basic 6 and was used in the first two versions of Visual Studio .NET, you can change the LayoutMode property to SnapToGrid.

> *The SnapToGrid layout mode is still used even if the LayoutMode is set to SnapLines. SnapLines only becomes active when you are positioning a control relative to another control. At other times, SnapToGrid will be active and allow you to position the control on the grid vertex.*

The GridSize property is used when positioning and sizing controls on the form. As you move controls around the form, they snap to specific points based on the values you enter here. Most of the time, you'll find a grid of 8 × 8 (the default) too large for fine-tuning, so changing this to something such as 4 × 4 might be more appropriate.

> *Both SnapToGrid and SnapLines are aids for designing user interfaces using the mouse. Once the control has been roughly positioned, you can use the keyboard to fine tune control positions by "nudging" the control with the arrow keys.*

ShowGrid displays a network of dots on your form's design surface when you're in SnapToGrid mode so you can more easily see where the controls will be positioned when you move them. You will need to close the designer and reopen it to see any changes to this setting. Finally, setting the

SnapToGrid property to False deactivates the layout aids while in SnapToGrid mode and results in pure free-form form design.

While you're looking at this page of options, you may want to change the Automatically Open Smart Tags value to False. The default setting of True pops open the smart tag task list associated with any control you add to the form, which can be distracting during your initial form design phase. Smart tags are discussed later in this chapter.

The other page of preferences that you can customize for the Windows Forms Designer is the Data UI Customization section (see Figure 17-5). This is used to automatically bind various controls to data types when connecting to a database.

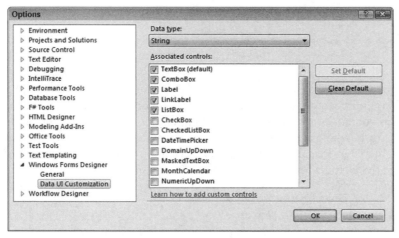

FIGURE 17-5

As you can see in the screenshot, the `String` data type is associated with five commonly used controls, with the TextBox control set as the default. Whenever a database field that is defined as a String data type is added to your form, Visual Studio automatically generates a TextBox control to contain the value.

The other controls marked as associated with the data type (ComboBox, Label, LinkLabel, and ListBox) can be optionally used when editing the data source and style.

> *It's worth reviewing the default controls associated with each data type at this time and making sure you're happy with the types chosen. For instance, all* `DateTime` *data type variables will automatically be represented with a DateTime Picker control, but you may want it to be bound to a MonthCalendar.*

Working with data bound controls is discussed further in Chapter 27.

ADDING AND POSITIONING CONTROLS

You can add two types of controls to a Windows Form: graphical components that actually reside on the form itself, and components that do not have a specific visual interface displaying on the form.

You can add graphical controls to your form in one of two ways. The first method is to locate the control you want to add in the Toolbox and double-click its entry. Visual Studio 2010 will place it in a default location on the form — the first control will be placed adjacent to the top and left borders of the form, with subsequent controls placed down and to the right.

> *If the Toolbox is closed, it won't be automatically displayed next time the Windows Forms designer is opened. You can display it again by selecting View ⇨ Toolbox from the menu.*

The second method is to click and drag the entry on the list onto the form. As you drag over available space on the form, the mouse cursor changes to show you where the control will be positioned. This enables you to directly position the control where you want it, rather than first adding it to the form and then moving it to the desired location. Either way, once the control is on the form, you can move it as many times as you like, so it doesn't really matter how you get the control onto the form's design surface.

> *There is actually a third method to add controls to a form — copy and paste a control or set of controls from another form. If you paste multiple controls at once, the relative positioning and layout of the controls to each other will be preserved. Any property settings will also be preserved, although the control names may be changed because they must be unique.*

When you design your form layouts in SnapLines mode (see the previous section), a variety of guidelines are displayed as you move controls around in the form layout. These guidelines are recommended "best practice" positioning and sizing markers, so you can easily position controls in context to each other and the edge of the form.

Figure 17-6 shows a Button control being moved toward the top-left corner of the form. As it gets near the recommended position, the control snaps to the exact recommended distance from the top and left borders, and small blue guidelines are displayed.

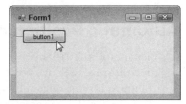

FIGURE 17-6

These guidelines work for both positioning and sizing a control, enabling you to snap to any of the four borders of the form — but they're just the tip of the SnapLines iceberg. When additional components are present on the form, many more guidelines will begin to appear as you move a control around.

In Figure 17-7, you can see a second Button control being moved. The guideline on the left is the same as previously discussed, indicating the ideal distance from the left border of the form. However, now three additional guidelines are displayed. Two blue vertical lines appear on either side of the control, confirming that the control is aligned with both the left and right sides of the other Button control already on the form (this is expected because the buttons are the same width). The other vertical line indicates the ideal gap between two buttons.

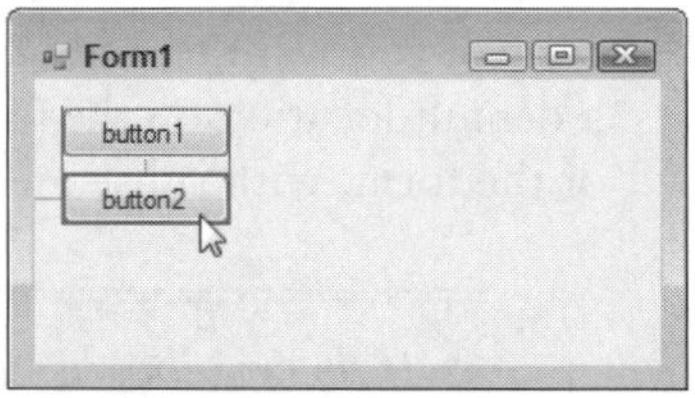

FIGURE 17-7

Vertically Aligning Text Controls

One problem with alignment of controls is that the vertical alignment of the text displayed within a TextBox is different compared to a Label. The problem is that the text within each control is at a different vertical distance from the top border of the control. If you simply align these different controls according to their borders, the text contained within these controls would not be aligned.

As shown in Figure 17-8, an additional guideline is available when lining up controls that have text aspects to them. In this example, the Telephone label is being lined up with the textbox containing the actual Telephone value. A line, colored magenta by default, appears and snaps the control in place. You can still align the label to the top or bottom borders of the textbox by shifting it slightly and snapping it to their guidelines, but this new guideline takes the often painful guesswork out of lining up text.

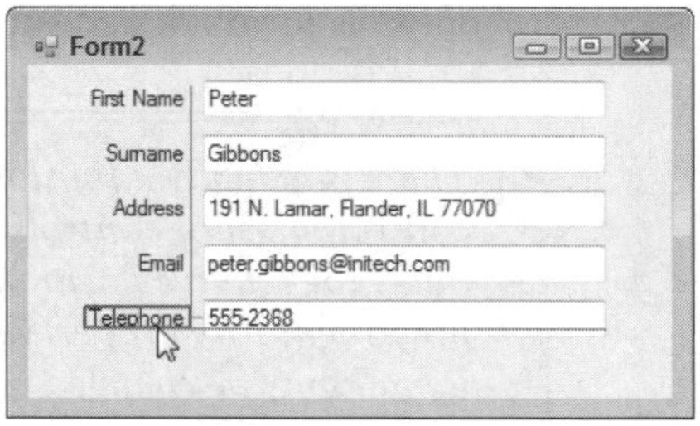

FIGURE 17-8

Note that the other guidelines show how the label is horizontally aligned with the Label controls above it, and it is positioned the recommended distance from the textbox.

Automatic Positioning of Multiple Controls

Visual Studio 2010 gives you additional tools to automatically format the appearance of your controls once they are positioned approximately where you want them. The Format menu, shown in Figure 17-9, is normally only accessible when you're in the Design view of a form. From here you can have the IDE automatically align, resize, and position groups of controls, as well as set the order of the controls in the event that they overlap each other. These commands are also available via the design toolbar and keyboard shortcuts.

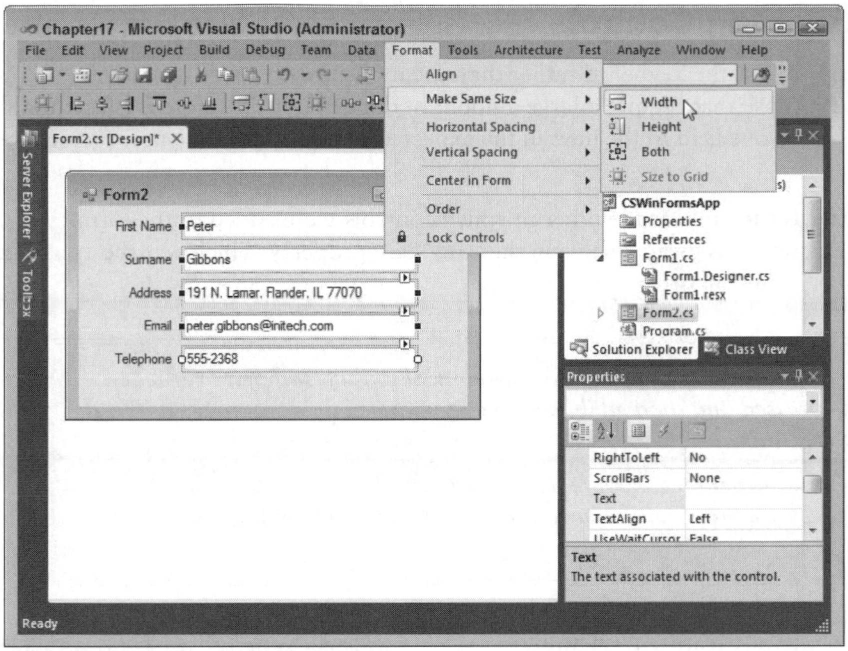

FIGURE 17-9

The form displayed in Figure 17-9 contains several TextBox controls, all with differing widths. This looks messy and should be cleaned up by setting them all to the same width as the widest control. The Format menu provides you with the capability to automatically resize the controls to the same width, using the Make Same Size ⇨ Width command.

> *The commands in the Make Same Size menu use the first control selected as the template for the dimensions. You can first select the control to use as the template, and then add to the selection by holding down the Ctrl key and clicking each of the other controls. Alternatively, once all controls are the same size, you can simply ensure they are still selected and resize the group at the same time with the mouse.*

You can perform automatic alignment of multiple controls in the same way. First, select the item whose border should be used as a base, and then select all of the other elements that should be aligned with it. Next, select Format ⇨ Align and choose which alignment should be performed. In this example, the Label controls have all been positioned with their right edges aligned. This could have been done using the guidelines, but often it's easier to use this mass alignment option.

Two other handy functions are the horizontal and vertical spacing commands. These automatically adjust the spacing between a set of controls according to the particular option you have selected.

Tab Order and Layering Controls

Many users find it faster to use the keyboard rather than the mouse when working with an application, particularly those that require a large amount of data entry. Therefore it is essential that the cursor moves from one field to the next in the expected manner when the user presses the Tab key.

By default, the tab order is the same as the order in which controls were added to the form. Beginning at zero, each control is given a value in the `TabIndex` property. The lower the `TabIndex`, the earlier the control is in the tab order.

> *If you set the `TabStop` property to False, the control will be skipped over when the Tab key is pressed and there will be no way for a user to set its focus without using the mouse.*
>
> *Some controls can never be given the focus, such as a Label. These controls still have a `TabIndex` property; however, they are skipped when the Tab key is pressed.*

Visual Studio provides a handy feature to view and adjust the tab order of every control on a form. If you select View ⇨ Tab Order from the menu, the `TabIndex` values are displayed in the designer for each control, as shown in Figure 17-10. In this example the `TabIndex` values assigned to the controls are not in order, which would cause the focus to jump all over the form as the Tab key is pressed.

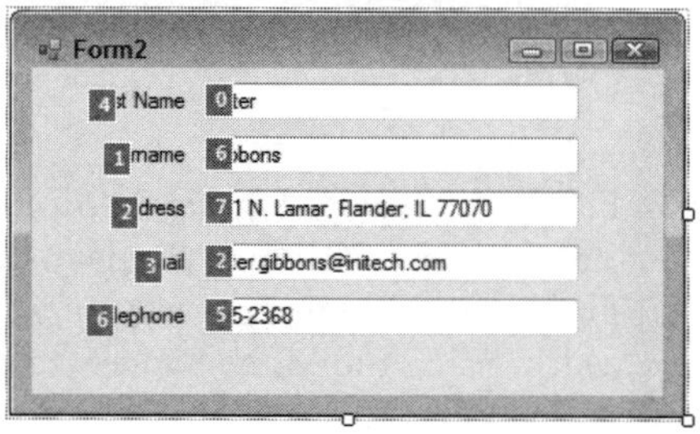

FIGURE 17-10

You can click each control in order to establish a new tab order. Once you have finished, press the Esc key to hide the tab order from the designer.

If more than one control on a form has the same `TabIndex`, the *z-order* is used to determine which control is next in the tab order. The z-order is the layering of controls on a form along the form's z-axis (depth) and is generally only relevant if controls must be layered on top of each other. The z-order of a control can be modified using the *Bring to Front* and *Send to Back* commands under the Format ⇨ Order menu.

Locking Control Design

Once you're happy with your form design you will want to start applying changes to the various controls and their properties. However, in the process of selecting controls on the form, you may inadvertently move a control from its desired position, particularly if you're not using either of the snap layout methods or if you have many controls that are being aligned with each other.

Fortunately, Visual Studio 2010 provides a solution in the form of the Lock Controls command, available in the Format menu. When controls are locked, you can select them to change their properties, but you cannot use the mouse to move or resize them, or the form itself. The location of the controls can still be changed via the Properties grid.

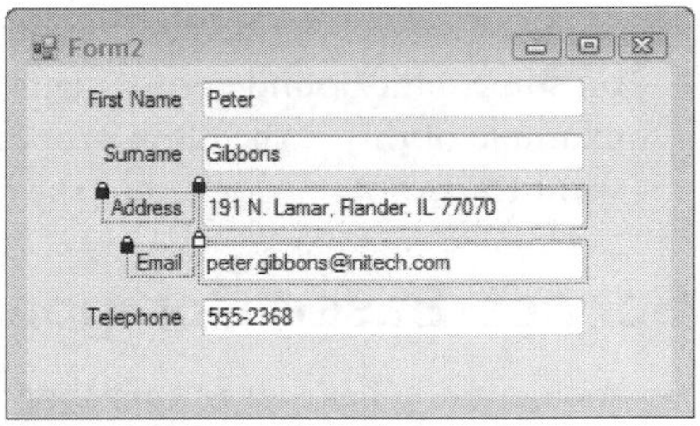

Figure 17-11 shows how small padlock icons are displayed on controls that are selected while the Lock Controls feature is active.

FIGURE 17-11

> You can also lock controls on an individual basis by setting the Locked property of the control to True in the Properties window.

Setting Control Properties

You set the properties on controls using the Properties window, just as you would for a form's settings. In addition to simple text value properties, Visual Studio 2010 has a number of property editor types, which aid you in setting the values efficiently by restricting them to a particular subset appropriate to the type of property.

Many advanced properties have a set of subordinate properties that can be individually accessed by expanding the entry in the Properties window. Figure 17-12 (left) displays the Properties window for a Label, with the Font property expanded to show the individual properties available.

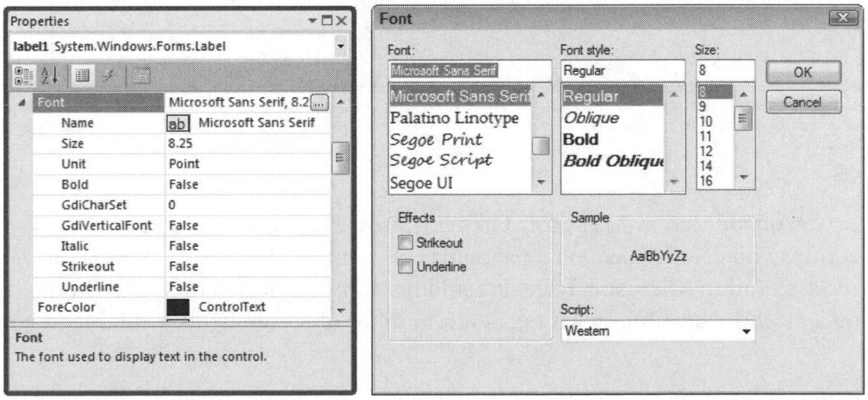

FIGURE 17-12

Many properties also provide extended editors, as is the case for Font properties. In Figure 17-12 (right), the extended editor button in the Font property has been selected, causing the Font dialog to appear.

Some of these extended editors invoke full-blown wizards, such as the Data Connection property on some data-bound components, whereas others have custom-built inline property editors. An example of this is the `Dock` property, for which you can choose a visual representation of how you want the property docked to the containing component or form.

Service-Based Components

As mentioned earlier in this chapter, two kinds of components can be added to a Windows Form — those with visual aspects to them and those without. Service-based components such as timers and dialogs, or extender controls such as tooltip and error provider components, can all be used to enhance your application.

Rather than place these components on the form, when you double-click one in the Toolbox, or drag and drop it onto the design surface, Visual Studio 2010 creates a tray area below the Design view of the form and puts the new instance of the component type there, as shown in Figure 17-13.

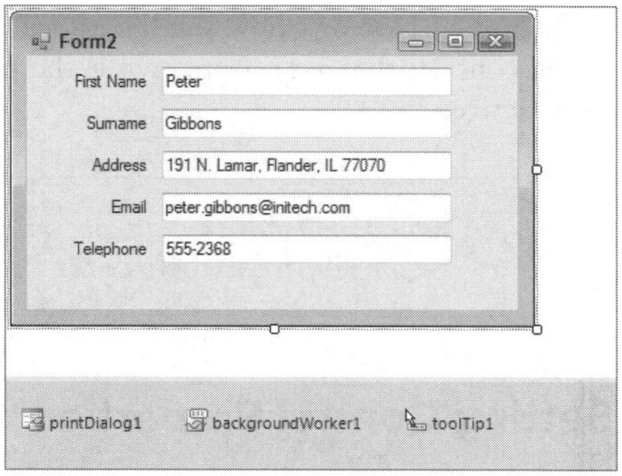

FIGURE 17-13

To edit the properties of one of these controls, locate its entry in the tray area and open the Properties window.

> *In the same way that you can create your own custom visual controls by inheriting from* `System.Windows.Forms.Control`, *you can create non-visual service components by inheriting from* `System.ComponentModel.Component`. *In fact* `System.ComponentModel.Component` *is the base class for* `System.Windows.Forms.Control`.

Smart Tag Tasks

Smart tag technology was introduced in Microsoft Office. It provides inline shortcuts to a small selection of actions you can perform on a particular element. In Microsoft Word, this might be a word or phrase, and in Microsoft Excel it could be a spreadsheet cell. Visual Studio 2010 supports the concept of design-time smart tags for a number of the controls available to you as a developer.

Whenever a selected control has a smart tag available, a small right-pointing arrow is displayed on the top-right corner of the control itself. Clicking this smart tag indicator opens up a Tasks menu associated with that particular control.

Figure 17-14 shows the tasks for a newly added DataGridView control. The various actions that can be taken usually mirror properties available to you in the Properties window (such as the

Multiline option for a TextBox control), but sometimes they provide quick access to more advanced settings for the component.

The Edit Columns and Add Column commands shown in Figure 17-14 are not listed in the DataGridView's Properties list, and the Data Source and Enable settings directly correlate to individual properties (for example, Enable Adding is equivalent to the AllowUserToAddRows property).

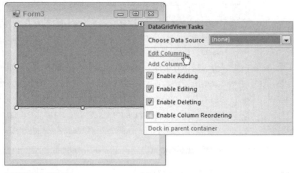

FIGURE 17-14

CONTAINER CONTROLS

Several controls, known as *container controls*, are designed specifically to help you with your form's layout and appearance. Rather than have their own appearance, they hold other controls within their bounds. Once a container houses a set of controls, you no longer need to move the child controls individually, but instead just move the container. Using a combination of Dock and Anchor values, you can have whole sections of your form's layout automatically redesign themselves at run time in response to the resizing of the form and the container controls that hold them.

Panel and SplitContainer

The Panel control is used to group components that are associated with each other. When placed on a form, it can be sized and positioned anywhere within the form's design surface. Because it's a container control, clicking within its boundaries selects anything inside it. In order to move it, Visual Studio 2010 places a move icon at the top-left corner of the control. Clicking and dragging this icon enables you to reposition the Panel.

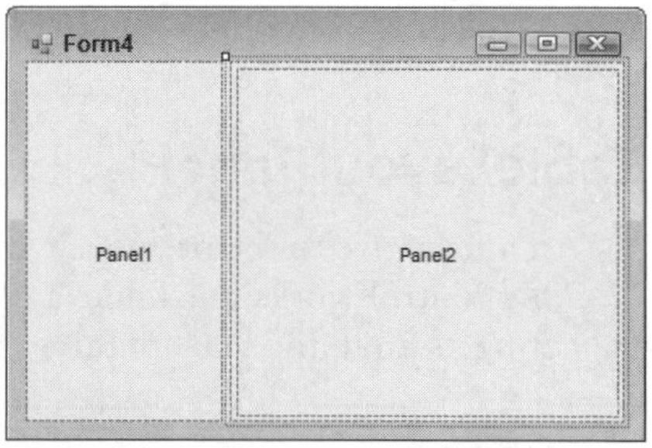

The SplitContainer control (shown in Figure 17-15) automatically creates two Panel controls when added to a form (or another container control). It divides the space into two sections, each of which you can control individually. At run time, users can resize the two spaces by dragging the splitter bar that divides them. SplitContainers can be either vertical (as in Figure 17-15) or horizontal, and they can be contained with other SplitContainer controls to form a complex layout that can then be easily customized by the end user without your needing to write any code.

FIGURE 17-15

> *Sometimes it's hard to select the actual container control when it contains other components, such as in the case of the SplitContainer housing the two Panel controls. To gain direct access to the SplitContainer control itself, you can either locate it in the drop-down list in the Properties window, or right-click one of the Panel controls and choose the Select command that corresponds to the SplitContainer. This context menu contains a Select command for every container control in the hierarchy of containers, right up to the form itself.*

FlowLayoutPanel

The FlowLayoutPanel control enables you to create form designs with a behavior similar to web browsers. Rather than explicitly position each control within this particular container control, Visual Studio simply sets each component you add to the next available space. By default, the controls will flow left to right, and then top to bottom, but you can use the `FlowDirection` property to reverse this order in any configuration depending on the requirements of your application.

Figure 17-16 displays the same form with six button controls housed within a FlowLayoutPanel container. The FlowLayoutPanel's `Dock` property was set to fill the entire form's design surface, so as the form is resized, the container is also automatically sized. As the form gets wider and there is available space, the controls begin to be realigned to flow left to right before descending down the form.

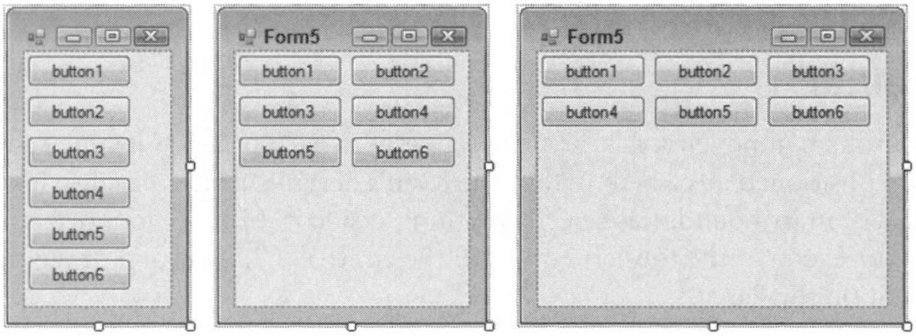

FIGURE 17-16

TableLayoutPanel

An alternative to the previously discussed container controls is the TableLayoutPanel container. This control works much like a table in Microsoft Word or in a typical web browser, with each cell acting as an individual container for a single control.

> *You cannot add multiple controls within a single cell directly. You can, however, place another container control, such as a Panel, within the cell, and then place the required components within that child container.*

Placing a control directly into a cell automatically positions the control to the top-left corner of the table cell. You can use the `Dock` property to override this behavior and position it as required. This property is discussed further later in this chapter.

The TableLayoutPanel container enables you to easily create a structured, formal layout in your form with advanced features, such as the capability to automatically grow by adding more rows as additional child controls are added.

Figure 17-17 shows a form with a TableLayoutPanel added to the design surface. The smart tag tasks were then opened and the Edit Rows and Columns command executed. As a result, the Column and Row Styles dialog is displayed so you can adjust the individual formatting options for each column and row. The dialog displays several tips for designing table layouts in your forms, including spanning multiple rows and columns and how to align controls within a cell. You can change the way the cells are sized here as well as add or remove additional columns and rows.

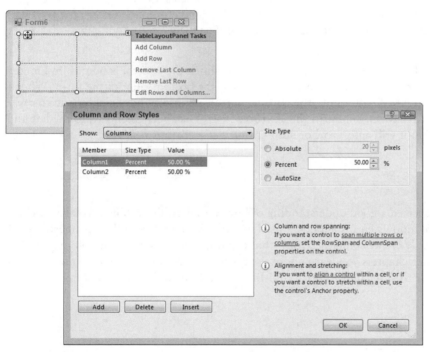

FIGURE 17-17

DOCKING AND ANCHORING CONTROLS

It's not enough to design layouts that are nicely aligned according to the design-time dimensions. At run time, a user will likely resize the form, and ideally the controls on your form will resize automatically to fill the modified space. The control properties that have the most impact on this are `Dock` and `Anchor`. Figure 17-18 shows how the controls on a Windows Form will properly resize once you have set the correct `Dock` and `Anchor` property values.

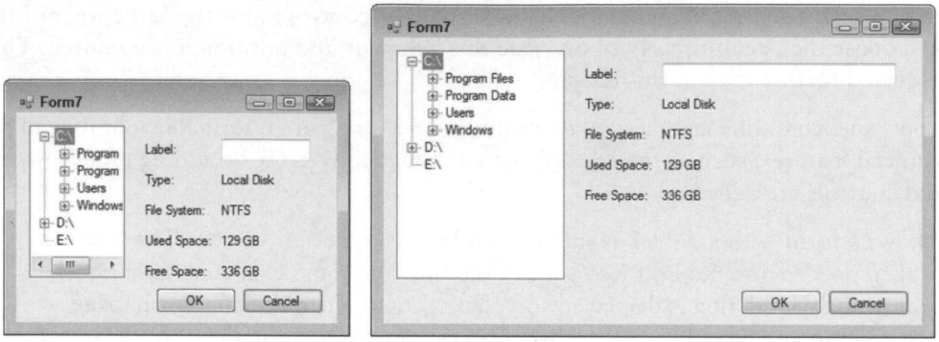

FIGURE 17-18

The Dock property controls which borders of the control are bound to the container. For example, in Figure 17-18 (left), the TreeView control Dock property has been set to Fill to fill the left panel of a SplitContainer, effectively docking it to all four borders. Therefore, no matter how large or small the left-hand side of the SplitContainer is made, the TreeView control will always resize itself to fill the available space.

The Anchor property defines the edges of the container to which the control is bound. In Figure 17-18 (left), the two button controls have been anchored to the bottom-right of the form. When the form is resized, as shown in 17-18 (right), the button controls maintain the same distance between to the bottom-right of the form. Similarly, the TextBox control has been anchored to the left and right, which means that it will auto-grow or auto-shrink as the form is resized.

SUMMARY

In this chapter you received a good understanding of how Visual Studio can help you to quickly design the layout of Windows Forms applications. The various controls and their properties enable you to quickly and easily create complex layouts that can respond to user interaction in a large variety of ways. In later chapters you learn about the specifics of designing the user interfaces for other application platforms, including Office Add-Ins, WPF, Web, and Silverlight applications.

18

Windows Presentation Foundation (WPF)

WHAT'S IN THIS CHAPTER?

➤ Learning the basics of XAML

➤ Creating a WPF application

➤ Styling your WPF application

➤ Hosting WPF content in a Windows Forms project

➤ Hosting Windows Forms Content in a WPF project

➤ Using the WPF Visualizer

When starting a new Windows client application in Visual Studio you have two major technologies to choose from — a standard Windows Forms–based application, or a Windows Presentation Foundation (WPF)–based application. Both are essentially a different API for managing the presentation layer for your application. WPF is extremely powerful and flexible, and was designed to overcome many of the shortcomings and limitations of Windows Forms. In many ways you could consider WPF a successor to Windows Forms. However, WPF's power and flexibility comes with a price in the form of a rather steep learning curve because it does things quite differently than Windows Forms.

This chapter guides you through the process of creating a basic WPF application in Visual Studio 2010. It's beyond the scope of this book to cover the WPF framework in any great detail — it would take an entire book on its own to do so. Instead, what you will see is an overview of Visual Studio 2010's capabilities to help you rapidly build user interfaces using XAML.

WHAT IS WPF?

Windows Presentation Foundation is a presentation framework for Windows. But what makes WPF unique, and why should you consider using it over Windows Forms? Whereas Windows Forms uses the raster-based GDI/GDI+ as its rendering engine, WPF instead contains its own vector-based rendering engine, so it essentially isn't creating windows and controls in the standard Windows manner and look. WPF has taken a radical departure from the way things are done in Windows Forms. In Windows Forms you generally define the user interface using the visual designer, and in doing so it automatically creates the code (in the language your project is targeting) in a .designer file to define that user interface — so essentially your user interface is defined and driven in C# or VB code. However, user interfaces in WPF are actually defined in an XML-based markup language called Extensible Application Markup Language (generally referred to as XAML, pronounced "zammel") specifically designed for this purpose by Microsoft. XAML is the underlying technology to WPF that gives it its power and flexibility, enabling the design of much richer user experiences and more unique user interfaces than was possible in Windows Forms. Regardless of which language your project targets, the XAML defining the user interface will be the same. Consequently, along with the new capabilities of the user interface controls there have been a number of new supporting concepts on the code side of things, such as the introduction of dependency properties (properties that can accept an expression that must be resolved as their value — which is required in many binding scenarios to support XAML's advanced binding capabilities). However, you will find that the code-behind in a WPF application is much the same as a standard Windows Forms application — the XAML side of things is where you need to do most of your learning.

When developing WPF applications, you need to think differently than the way you think when developing Windows Forms applications. A core part of your new thought processes should be to take full advantage of XAML's advanced binding capabilities, with the code-behind no longer acting as the controller for the user interface but serving it instead. Instead of the code "pushing" data into the user interface and telling it what to do, the user interface should ask the code what it should do, and request (that is, "pull") data from it. It's a subtle difference, but it greatly changes the way in which the presentation layer of your application will be defined. Think of it as having a user interface that is now in charge. The code can (and should) act as a decision manager, but no longer provides the muscle.

This "new thinking" has also led to new design patterns for how the code and the user interface elements interact, such as the popular Model-View-ViewModel (MVVM) pattern, which enables much better unit testing of the code serving the user interface and maintains a clean separation between the designer and developer elements of the project. This results in changing the way you write the code-behind, and ultimately changes the way you design your application. This clear separation supports the designer/developer workflow, enabling a designer to work in Expression Blend on the same part of the project as the developer (working in Visual Studio) without clashing.

By taking advantage of the flexibility of XAML, WPF enables you to design unique user interfaces and user experiences. At the heart of this is WPF's styling and templating functionality that separates the look of controls from their behavior. This enables you to alter the appearance of controls easily by simply defining an alternate "style" on that particular use without having to modify the control itself.

Ultimately you could say that WPF uses a much better way of defining user interfaces than Windows Forms does, through its use of XAML to define user interfaces, along with a number of additional supporting concepts thrown in. The bad news is that the flexibility and power of XAML comes with a corresponding steep learning curve that will take some time to climb, even for the experienced developer. If you are a productive developer in Windows Forms, WPF will no doubt create considerable frustration for you while you get your head around its concepts, and it really requires a change in your developer mindset to truly get a grasp on it and how things hold together. Many simple tasks will initially seem a whole lot harder than they should be, and would have been were you to implement the same functionality or feature in Windows Forms. However, if you can make it through this period you will start to see the benefits and appreciate the new possibilities that WPF and XAML provide. Because Silverlight shares a lot conceptually with WPF (both being XAML based, with Silverlight essentially being a subset of WPF), by learning and understanding WPF you are also learning and understanding how to develop Silverlight applications.

> *If you've looked at earlier versions of WPF (those that shipped in the .NET Framework 3.0 and 3.5 versions) you may have noticed that text rendered in WPF often took on a rather blurry appearance instead of being crisp and sharp, generating numerous complaints from the developer community. Fortunately in the .NET Framework 4.0 the text rendering has been vastly improved, and if this has held you back from developing WPF applications previously it is probably time to take another look. Microsoft has demonstrated its faith in WPF by rewriting Visual Studio's code editor in WPF for the 2010 version to take advantage of its power and flexibility.*

GETTING STARTED WITH WPF

When you open the New Project dialog you see a number of built-in project templates for WPF that ship with Visual Studio 2010: WPF Application, WPF Browser Application, WPF Custom Control Library, and WPF User Control Library, as shown in Figure 18-1.

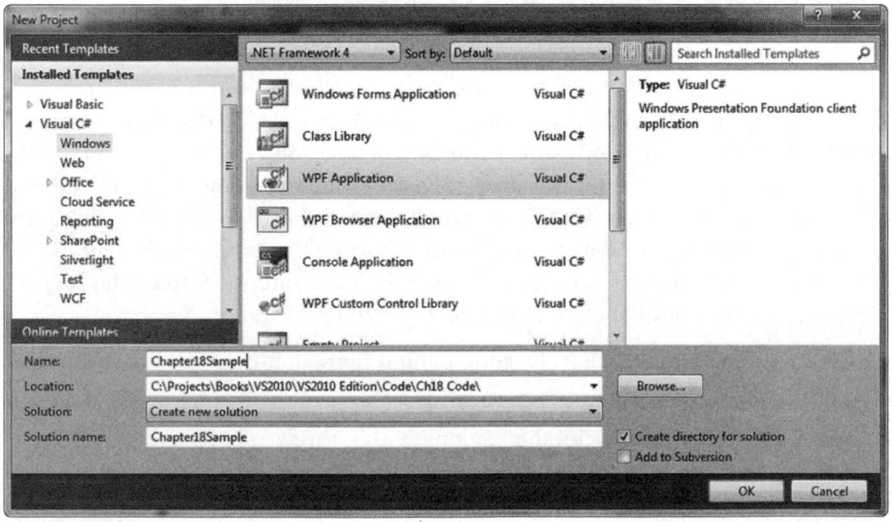

FIGURE 18-1

You will notice that these projects are for the most part a direct parallel to the Windows Forms equivalent. The exception is the WPF Browser Application, which generates an XBAP file that uses the browser as the container for your rich client application (in much the same way as Silverlight does, except an XBAP application targets the full .NET Framework, which must be installed on the client machine).

For this example you create a project using the WPF Application template, but most of the features of Visual Studio 2010 discussed herein apply equally to the other project types. The project structure generated should look similar to Figure 18-2.

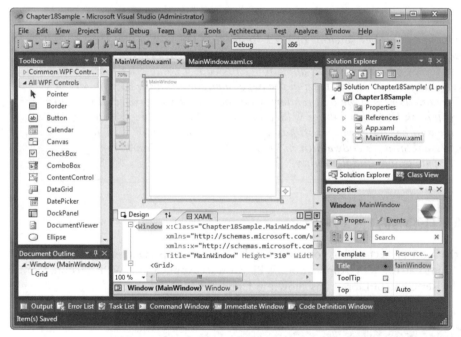

FIGURE 18-2

Here you can see that the project structure consists of App.xaml and MainWindow.xaml, each with a corresponding code-behind file (.cs or .vb), which you can view if you expand out the relevant project items. At this stage the App.xaml contains an Application XAML element, which has a StartupUri attribute used to define which XAML file will be your initial XAML file to load (by default MainWindow.xaml). For those familiar with Windows Forms, this is the equivalent of the startup form. So if you were to change the name of MainWindow.xaml and its corresponding class to something more meaningful, you would need to make the following changes:

➤ Change the filename of the .xaml file. The code-behind file will automatically be renamed accordingly.

➤ Change the class name in the code-behind file, along with its constructor, and change the value of the x:Class attribute of the Window element in the .xaml file to reference the new name of the class (fully qualified with its namespace). Note that the last two steps are automatically performed if you change the class name in the code-behind file first and use the smart tag that appears after doing so to rename the object in all the locations that reference it.

➤ Finally, change the `StartupUri` attribute of the `Application` element in `App.xaml` to point toward the new name of the `.xaml` file (because it is your startup object).

As you can see, a few more changes need to be made when renaming a file in a WPF project than you would have to do in a standard Windows Forms project, however it's reasonably straightforward when you know what you are doing (and using the smart tag reduces the number of steps required).

Working around the Visual Studio layout of Figure 18-2, you can see that the familiar Toolbox tool window attached to the left side of the screen has been populated with WPF controls that are similar to what you would be used to when building a Windows Forms application. Below this window, still on the left side, is the Document Outline tool window. As with both Windows Forms and Web Applications this gives you a hierarchical view of the elements on the current window. Selecting any of these nodes in this window highlights the appropriate control in the main editor window, making it easier to navigate more complex documents. An interesting feature of the Document Outline when working with WPF is that as you hover over an item you get a mini-preview of the control. This helps you identify that you are selecting the correct control.

> *If the Document Outline tool window is not visible it may be collapsed against one of the edges of Visual Studio. Alternatively, you may need to force it to be displayed by selecting it from the View ➪ Other Windows menu.*

On the right side of Figure 18-2 is the Properties tool window. You may note that it has a very similar layout and behavior to the Windows Forms designer Properties tool window. However, this window in the WPF designer has additional features for editing WPF windows and controls. Finally, in the middle of the screen is the main editor/preview space, which is currently split to show both the visual layout of the window (above) and the XAML code that defines it (below).

XAML Fundamentals

If you have some familiarity working with XML (or to some extent HTML), you should find the syntax of XAML relatively straightforward because it is XML based. XAML can have only a single root level node, and elements are nested within each other to define the layout and content of the user interface. Every XAML element maps to a .NET class, and the attribute names map to properties/events on that class. Note that element and attribute names are case sensitive.

Take a look at the default XAML file created for the MainWindow class:

```
<Window x:Class="Chapter18Sample.MainWindow"
    xmlns="http://schemas.microsoft.com/winfx/2006/xaml/presentation"
    xmlns:x="http://schemas.microsoft.com/winfx/2006/xaml"
    Title="MainWindow" Height="300" Width="300">
    <Grid>

    </Grid>
</Window>
```

Here you have Window as your root node, and a Grid element within it. To make sense of it, think of it in terms of "your window contains a grid." The root node maps to its corresponding code-behind class via the x:Class attribute, and also contains some namespace prefix declarations (discussed shortly) and some attributes used to set the value of properties (Title, Height, and Width) of the Window class. The value of all attributes (regardless of type) should be enclosed within quotes.

You'll note two namespace prefixes defined on the root node, both declared using xmlns (the XML attribute used for declaring namespaces). You could consider XAML namespace prefix declarations to be somewhat like the using/Imports statements at the top of a class in C#/VB, but not quite. These declarations assign a unique prefix to the namespaces used within the XAML file, with the prefix used to qualify that namespace when referring to a class within it (that is, specify the location of the class). Prefixes reduce the verbosity of XAML by letting you use that prefix rather than including the whole namespace when referring to a class within it in your XAML file. The prefix is defined immediately following the colon after xmlns. The first definition actually doesn't specify a prefix because it is defining your default namespace (the WPF namespace). However, the second namespace defines x as its prefix (the XAML namespace). Both definitions map to URIs rather than specific namespaces — these are consolidated namespaces (that is, they cover multiple namespaces), and hence reference the unique URI that is used to define that consolidation. However, you don't need to worry about this concept — leave these definitions as they are and simply add your own definitions following them. When adding your own namespace definitions they will almost always begin with clr-namespace and reference a CLR namespace and the assembly that contains it. For example:

```
xmlns:wpf="clr-namespace:Microsoft.Windows.Controls;assemblty=WPFToolkit"
```

Prefixes can be anything of your choosing, but it is best to make them short yet meaningful. Namespaces are generally defined on the root node in the XAML file. This is not necessary because a namespace prefix can be defined at any level in a XAML file, but it is generally a standard practice to keep them together on the root node for maintainability purposes.

If you want to refer to a control in the code-behind or by binding it to another control in the XAML file (such as ElementName binding) you will need to give your control a name. Many controls implement the Name property for this purpose, but you may also find that controls are assigned a name using the x:Name attribute. This is defined in the XAML namespace (hence the x: prefix) and can be applied to any control. If the Name property is implemented (which it will be in most cases because it is defined on the base classes that most controls inherit from), it simply maps to this property anyway and they serve the same purpose. For example:

```
<Button x:Name="OKButton" Content="OK" />
```

is the same as:

```
<Button Name="OKButton" Content="OK" />
```

Either way is technically valid (although in Silverlight most controls don't support the Name attribute and you must use the x:Name attribute instead). Once one of these properties is set, a field is generated (in the automatically generated code that you won't see) that you can use to refer to that control.

The WPF Controls

WPF contains a rich set of controls to use in your user interfaces, roughly comparable to the standard controls for Windows Forms. If you looked at previous versions of WPF you may have noticed a number of controls (such as the Calendar, DatePicker, DataGrid, and so on), which are included in the standard controls for Windows Forms but were not included in the standard controls for WPF. Instead you had to turn to the free WPF Toolkit hosted on CodePlex to obtain these controls. This toolkit was developed by Microsoft over time to help fill this hole in the original WPF release by providing some of the missing controls. With WPF 4.0, however, you will find many of the controls within the WPF Toolkit are now included within WPF's standard controls, providing a reasonably complete set of controls "out of the box." Of course you can still use third-party controls where the standard set doesn't suffice, but now you have a reasonable base to work from.

Although the controls set for WPF is somewhat comparable to that of Windows Forms, you will note that their properties are quite different to their counterparts. For example, there is no longer a Text property on many controls, although you will find a Content property instead. The Content property is used to assign content to the control (hence its name). You can for the most part treat this as you would the Text property for a Windows Forms control and simply assign some text to this property to be rendered. However, the Content property can in fact accept any WPF element, allowing almost limitless ability to customize the layout of a control without necessarily having to create your own custom control — a very powerful feature for designing complex user interfaces. You may also note that many controls don't have properties to accomplish what was pretty straightforward in Windows Forms, and you may find this somewhat confusing. For example, there is no Image property on the WPF Button control to assign an image to a button as there is in Windows Forms. This may initially make you think WPF is very limited in its capabilities, but you would be mistaken because this is where the Content property comes into its own. Because the Content property can have any WPF control assigned to it to define the content of its control you can assign a StackPanel (discussed in the next section) containing both an Image control and a TextBlock control to achieve the same effect. Though this may initially appear to be more work than it would be to achieve the same outcome in Windows Forms, it does enable you to easily lay out the content of the button in whatever form you choose (rather than how the control chooses to implement the layout), and demonstrates the incredible flexibility of WPF and XAML. The XAML for the button in Figure 18-3 is as follows:

```
<Button HorizontalAlignment="Left" VerticalAlignment="Top" Width="100" Height="30">
    <Button.Content>
        <StackPanel Orientation="Horizontal">
            <Image Source="/Chapter18Sample;component/Images/save.png" Width="16"
                Height="16" />
            <TextBlock Margin="5,0,0,0" Text="Save" VerticalAlignment="Center" />
        </StackPanel>
    </Button.Content>
</Button>
```

Other notable property name changes from Windows Forms include the IsEnabled property (which was simply Enabled in Windows Forms) and the Visibility property (which was Visible in Windows Forms). Like IsEnabled, you will notice that most Boolean properties are now prefixed with Is (for example, IsTabStop, IsHitTestVisible,

FIGURE 18-3

and so on), conforming to a standard naming scheme. The `Visibility` property, however, is no longer a Boolean value — instead it is an enumeration that can have the value Visible, Hidden, or Collapsed.

> *Keep an eye on the WPF Toolkit at* `http://wpf.codeplex.com` *because new controls for WPF will continue to be developed and hosted there that you may find useful.*

The WPF Layout Controls

Windows Forms development used absolute placement for controls on its surface (that is, each control had its x and y coordinates explicitly set), although over time the TableLayoutPanel and FlowLayoutPanel controls were added, in which you could place controls to provide a more advanced means of laying out the controls on your form. However, the concepts around positioning controls in WPF are slightly different than how controls are positioned in Windows Forms. Along with controls that provide a specific function (for example, buttons, textboxes, and so on), WPF also has a number of controls that are used specifically for defining the layout of your user interface.

Layout controls are invisible controls that handle the positioning of controls upon their surface. In WPF there isn't a default surface for positioning controls as such — the surface you are working with is determined by the layout controls further up the hierarchy, with a layout control generally used as the element directly below the root node of each XAML file to define the default layout method for that XAML file. The most important layout controls in WPF are the Grid, the Canvas, and the StackPanel, so this section takes a look at each of those. For example, in the default XAML file created for the MainWindow class provided earlier, the `Grid` element was the element directly below the `Window` root node, and thus would act as the default layout surface for that window. Of course you could change this to any layout control in order to suit your requirements, and use additional layout controls within it if necessary to create additional surfaces that change the way their containing controls are positioned.

The next section looks at how to layout your forms using the designer surface, but look at the XAML to use these controls first.

In WPF, if you want to place controls in your form using absolute coordinates (similar to the default in Windows Forms) you would use the Canvas control as a "surface" to place the controls on. Defining a Canvas control in XAML is very straightforward:

```
<Canvas>

</Canvas>
```

To place a control (for example, a TextBox control) within this surface using given X and Y coordinates (relative to the location of the top-left corner of the canvas) we need to introduce the concept of *attached properties* within XAML. The TextBox control doesn't actually have properties to define its location, because its positioning within the layout control it is contained within is totally dependent on the type of control. So correspondingly, the properties that the TextBox control requires in order to specify its position within the layout control must come from the layout control itself (because it will be handling the positioning of the controls within it). This is where attached properties come in. In a nutshell, attached properties are properties that are assigned a value on a control, but the property is actually defined on and belongs to another control higher up in the hierarchy. When using the property, the name of the property is qualified by the name of the control that the property is actually defined on, followed by a period, and then the name of the property on that control you are using (for example, `Canvas.Left`). By setting that value on another control that is hosted within it (such as your textbox), the Canvas control is actually storing that value, and will manage that textbox's position using that value. For example, this is the XAML required to place the textbox at coordinates 15, 10 using the Left and Top properties defined on the Canvas control:

```
<Canvas>
    <TextBox Text="Hello" Canvas.Left="15" Canvas.Top="10" />
</Canvas>
```

While absolute placement is the default for controls in Windows Forms, best practice in WPF is to actually use the Grid control for laying out controls. The Canvas control should be used only sparsely and where necessary, because the Grid control is actually far more powerful for defining form layouts and is a better choice in most scenarios. One of the big benefits of the Grid control is that its contents can automatically resize when its own size is changed. So you can easily design a form that automatically sizes to fill all of the area available to it — that is, the size and location of the controls within it are determined dynamically. The Grid control allows you to divide its area into regions (cells) into which you can place controls. These cells are created by defining a set of rows and columns on the grid, and are defined as values on the `RowDefinitions` and `ColumnDefinitions` properties on the grid. The intersections between rows and columns become the cells that you can place controls within.

To support defining rows and columns, you need to know how to define complex values in XAML. Up until now you have been assigning simple values to controls, which map to either .NET primitive data types, the name of an enumeration value, or have a type converter to convert the string value to its corresponding object. These simple properties had their values applied as attributes within the control definition element. However, complex values cannot be assigned this way because they map to objects (which require the value of multiple properties on the object to be assigned), and must be defined using *property element syntax* instead. Because the `RowDefinitions` and `ColumnDefinitions` properties of the Grid control are collections, they take complex values that need to be defined with property element syntax. For example, here is a grid that has two rows and three columns defined using property element syntax:

```
<Grid>
    <Grid.RowDefinitions>
        <RowDefinition />
        <RowDefinition />
    </Grid.RowDefinitions>
    <Grid.ColumnDefinitions>
        <ColumnDefinition Width="100" />
        <ColumnDefinition Width="150" />
        <ColumnDefinition />
    </Grid.ColumnDefinitions>
</Grid>
```

Note how in order to set the `RowDefinitions` property using property element syntax you need to create a child element of the Grid to define it. Qualifying it by adding Grid before the property name indicates that the property belongs to a control higher in the hierarchy (as with attached properties), and making the property an element in XAML indicates you are assigning a complex value to the specified property on the Grid control.

The `RowDefinitions` property accepts a collection of `RowDefinitions` so you are instantiating a number of `RowDefinition` objects that are then populating that collection. Correspondingly, the `ColumnDefinitions` property is being assigned a collection of `ColumnDefinition` objects. To demonstrate that `ColumnDefinition` (like `RowDefinition`) is actually an object, the `Width` property of the `ColumnDefinition` object has been set on the first two column definitions.

To place a control within a given cell you again make use of attached properties, this time telling the container grid which column and row it should be placed in:

```
<CheckBox Grid.Column="0" Grid.Row="1" Content="A check box" IsChecked="True" />
```

The StackPanel is another important container control for laying out controls. It stacks the controls contained within it either horizontally or vertically (depending on the value of its `Orientation` property). For example, if you had two buttons defined within the same grid cell (without a StackPanel) the grid would position the second button directly over the first. However, if you put the buttons within a StackPanel control it would control the position of the two buttons within the cell and lay them out next to one another.

```
<StackPanel Orientation="Horizontal">
    <Button Content="OK" Height="23" Width="75" />
    <Button Content="Cancel" Height="23" Width="75" Margin="10,0,0,0" />
</StackPanel>
```

THE WPF DESIGNER AND XAML EDITOR

The WPF designer and XAML editor have had a number of improvements since Visual Studio 2008, including stability improvements (the Visual Studio 2008 WPF designer was notoriously unstable), and most notably the designer now supports drag and drop binding.

The WPF designer is similar in layout to Windows Form's designer, but supports a number of unique features. To take a closer look at some of these, Figure 18-4 isolates this window so you can see in more detail the various components.

First you will notice that the window is split into a visual designer at the top and a code window at the bottom. If you prefer the other way around you can simply click the up/down arrows between

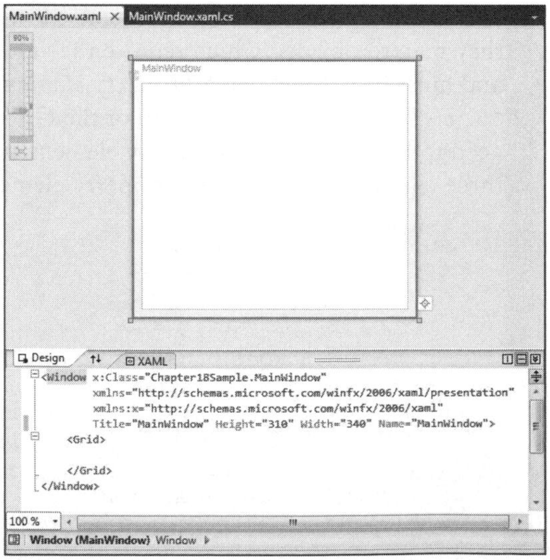

FIGURE 18-4

the Design and XAML tabs. In Figure 18-4 the second icon on the right side is highlighted to indicate that the screen is being split horizontally. Selecting the icon to its left instead splits the screen vertically.

> You will probably find that working in split mode is the best option when working with the WPF designer because you are likely to find yourself directly modifying the XAML regularly but want the ease of use of the designer for general tasks.

If you prefer not to work in split screen mode, you can double-click either the Design or XAML tab. This makes the relevant tab fill the entire editor window as shown in Figure 18-5, and you can click the tabs to switch between each view. To return to split screen mode you just need to click the Expand Pane icon, which is the right-most icon on the splitter bar.

In the designer you'll note the zoom control in the visual designer portion of the editor space. The zoom control allows you to easily zoom in or out on the window or control being edited, which can be extremely handy when making small fiddly adjustments or to get an overview of the whole XAML layout. In this case the screen is zoomed out to 90 percent. There is a mark where 100 percent is on the zoom scale and the button at the bottom of the zoom control allows you to easily

FIGURE 18-5

size the XAML layout so that it expands (or contracts) to fit the designer surface.

The last thing worth noting is the cookie-crumb tracker that is at the bottom of the visual designer window, to the right of the Design and XAML tabs. In this case it only has a single `Window` element, but you will see that as you add more elements to the window this feature becomes quite useful in determining and navigating the control hierarchy for the selected control.

Working with the XAML Editor

Working with the XAML editor is somewhat similar to working with the HTML editor in Visual Studio. Numerous IntelliSense improvements have been made in this editor since Visual Studio 2008, making writing XAML directly very quick and easy.

One neat feature with the XAML editor is the ability to easily navigate to an event handler once it has been assigned to a control. Simply right-click the event handler assignment in XAML and select the Navigate to Event Handler item from the popup menu, as shown in Figure 18-6.

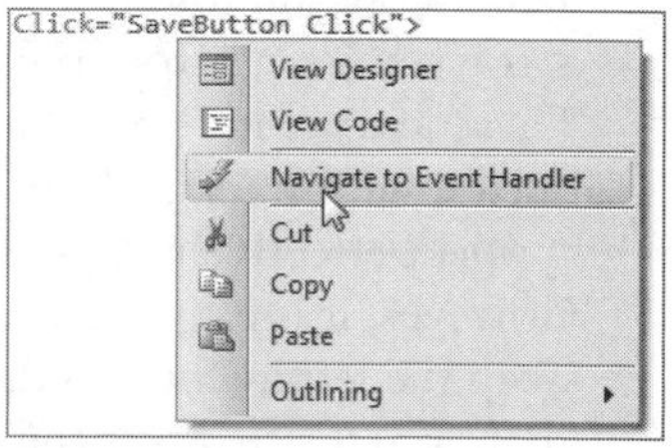

FIGURE 18-6

Working with the WPF Designer

Although it is important to familiarize yourself with writing XAML in the XAML editor, VS2010 also has a very good designer for WPF, comparable to the Windows Forms designer, and in some respects even better. This section takes a look at some of the features of the WPF designer.

Figure 18-7 shows some of the snap lines, guides, and glyphs that are added when you select, move, and resize a control.

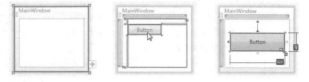

FIGURE 18-7

Note the glyph that appears on the left of the window toward its bottom-left corner in the first image in Figure 18-7. Clicking it allows you to easily switch between the window having a fixed width/height, and having it automatically size to fit its contents. When you click the glyph, the glyph will change (indicating what sizing mode it is in), and the `SizeToContent` property on the window is set accordingly. Clicking the glyph again changes the window back to having a fixed width/height. This option appears only on the root node.

> If you are wondering why the size of the window doesn't change in the designer when you click the glyph for it to size to content, the Height and Width properties of the window are replaced with "designer" height/width properties that retain these values for use by the WPF designer so that the SizeToContent property doesn't interfere while designing the form. These properties are then switched back to the standard Height and Width properties if you return to fixed-size mode.

The second image in Figure 18-7 demonstrates the snap lines that appear when you move a control around the form (or resize it). These snap lines are similar to those in the Windows Forms designer, and help you align controls to a standard margin within their container control, or easily align a control to other controls. Hold down ALT while you move a control if you don't want these snap lines to appear and your control to snap to them.

The third image in Figure 18-7 demonstrates the rulers that appear when you are resizing a control. This feature allows you to easily see the new dimensions of a control as you resize it in order to help you adjust it to a particular size.

You'll note that the third image in Figure 18-7 also contains some anchor points (that is, the two arrows pointing from the left and top of the button to the corresponding edges of its container grid). These arrows indicate that the button has a margin applied to it, dictating the placement of the button within its grid cell. Currently these arrows indicate that the button has a top and left margin applied, effectively "anchoring" its top and left sides to the top and left of the grid containing it. However, it is easy to swap the top anchor so that the button is anchored by its bottom edge, and swap the left anchor so that the button is anchored by its right edge instead. Simply click the top anchor arrow to have the button anchored by its bottom edge, and click the left anchor arrow to have the button anchored by its right edge. The anchor arrows swap position, and you can simply

The WPF Designer and XAML Editor | 363

click them again to return them back to their original anchor points. You can also anchor both sides (that is, left/right or top/bottom) of a control such that it stretches as the grid cell it is hosted within is resized. For example, if the left side of the textbox is anchored to the grid cell you can also anchor its right side by clicking the small circle to the right of the textbox. To remove the anchor from just one side, click the anchor arrow on that side to remove it.

As previously mentioned, the most important control for laying out your form is the Grid control. Take a look at the some of the special support that the WPF designer has for working with this control. By default your `MainWindow.xaml` file was created with a single grid element without any rows or columns defined. Before you commence adding elements you might want to define some rows and columns, which can be used to control the layout of the controls within the form. To do this, start by selecting the grid by clicking in the blank area in the middle of the window, selecting the relevant node from the Document Outline tool window, or placing the cursor within the corresponding grid element in the XAML file itself (when in split view).

When the grid element is selected, a border appears around the top and left edges of the grid, highlighting both the actual area occupied by the grid and the relative sizing of each of the rows and columns, as shown in Figure 18-8. This figure currently shows a grid with two rows and two columns.

FIGURE 18-8

You can add additional rows or columns by simply clicking at a location within the border. Once added, the row or column markers can be selected and dragged to get the correct sizing. You will notice when you are initially placing the markers that there is no information about the size of the new row/column displayed, which is unfortunate; however, these will appear once the marker has been created.

When you move the cursor over the size display for a row or column, three options appear across the top of the grid, as shown in Figure 18-9.

These options allow you to easily specify that the size of the row/column should be fixed (#), a weighted proportion (*), or determined by its contents (Auto).

FIGURE 18-9

> *Weighted proportion is a similar concept to specifying a percentage of the space available (compared to other columns). After fixed and auto-sized columns/rows have been allocated space, columns/rows with weighted proportions will divide up the remaining available space. This division will be equal, unless you prefix the asterisk with a numeric multiplier. For example, say you have a grid with a width of 1000 (pixels) and two columns. If both have * as their specified width, they each will have a width of 500 pixels. However, if one has a width of *, and the other has a width of 3* then the 1000 pixels will divided into 250 pixel "chunks," with one chunk allocated to the first column (thus having a width of 250 pixels), and three chunks will be allocated to the second column (thus having a width of 750 pixels).*

To delete a row or column, click the row or column and drag it outside of the grid area. It will be removed and the controls in the surrounding cells will be updated accordingly.

> *When you create a control by dragging and dropping it on a grid cell, remember to "dock" it to the left and top edges of the grid cell (by dragging it until it snaps into that position). Otherwise a margin will be defined on the control to position it within the grid cell, which is probably not the behavior you will want.*

The Properties Tool Window

When you've placed a control on your form you don't have to return to the XAML editor to set its property values and assign event handlers. Like Windows Forms, WPF has a Properties window, although you will note that there are quite a few differences in WPF's implementation as shown in Figure 18-10.

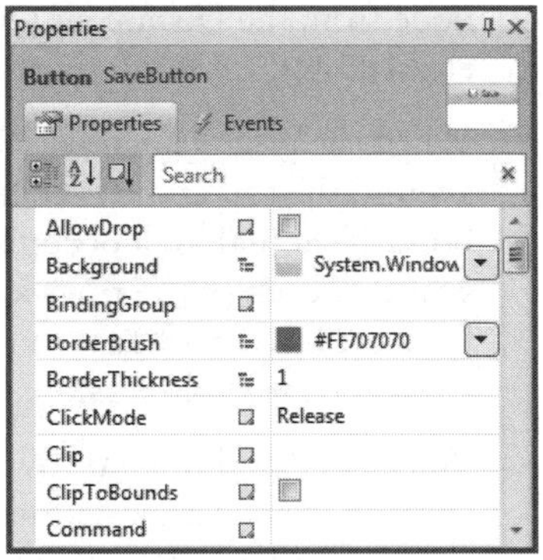

The Properties window has had a huge makeover in terms of functionality from Visual Studio 2008. The Visual Studio 2008 version was very limited in its capabilities, requiring developers to modify the XAML directly in many cases. However, it has been vastly improved in Visual Studio 2010, reducing the need for this.

FIGURE 18-10

The Properties tool window for Windows Forms development allows you to select a control to set the properties for via a drop-down control selector above the properties/events list. However, you will note that this drop-down is missing in WPF's Properties window. Instead you must select the control on the designer, via the Document Outline tool window, or by placing the cursor within the definition of a control in XAML view. A thumbnail preview of the selected control (and any controls it contains) will be displayed in the top left-hand corner of the window, and the qualified type of the control will be displayed next to it.

> *The Properties window can be used while working in both the XAML editor and the designer. However, if you want to use it from the XAML editor the designer must have been loaded (you may need to switch to designer view and back if you have opened the file straight into the XAML editor), and if you have invalid XAML you may find you will need to fix the errors first.*

The Name property for the control is not within the property list, but has a dedicated textbox above the property list. Note that if the control doesn't already have a name it will assign the value to its Name property (rather than x:Name). However, if the x:Name attribute is defined on the control element and you update its name from the Properties window it will continue to use and update that attribute.

Controls can have many properties or events, and navigating through the properties/events lists in Windows Forms to find the one you are after can be a chore. To make finding a specific property easier for developers the WPF Properties window has a search function that dynamically filters the properties list based on what you type into the textbox. Your search string doesn't need to be the start of the property/event name, but retains the property/event in the list if any part of its name contains the search string. Unfortunately this search function doesn't support camel case searching.

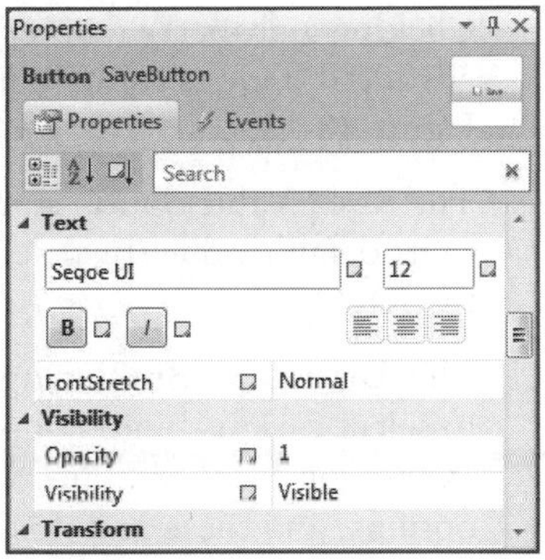

The property list in the WPF designer (like for Windows Forms) can be displayed in either a Categorized or Alphabetical order. You'll note that none of the properties that are objects (such as Margin) can be expanded to show/edit their properties (which they do for Windows Forms). However, if the list is displayed in the Categorized order you will observe a new and unique feature of WPF's property window: category editors. For example, if you select a Button control and browse down to the Text category you will find that it has a special editor for the properties in the Text category to make setting these values a better experience, as shown in Figure 18-11.

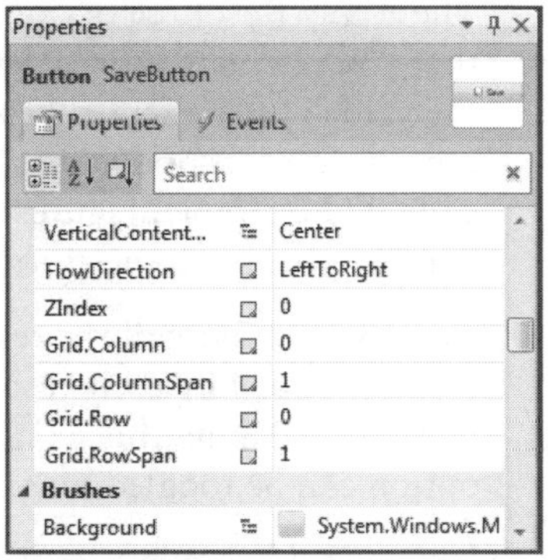

Various attached properties available to a control also appear in the property list, as shown in Figure 18-12.

You may have noticed that each property name has a small icon to its right. This is a new feature in Visual Studio 2010 called *property markers*, which indicate what the source for that property's value is. Placing your mouse cursor over an icon will show a tooltip describing what it means. The icon will change based on where the value is to be sourced from. Figure 18-13 demonstrates these various icons, which are described below:

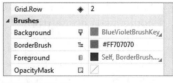

FIGURE 18-11

FIGURE 18-12

FIGURE 18-13

➤ A light gray icon indicates that the property has no value assigned to it and will use its default value.

➤ A black diamond icon indicates that the property has a local value assigned to it (that is, has been given a specific value).

➤ A yellow cylinder icon indicates that the property has a data binding expression assigned to it (discussed later in this chapter).

➤ A paintbrush (with green paint) icon indicates that the property has a resource assigned to it.

➤ A purple tree hierarchy icon indicates that the property is inheriting its value from another control further up the hierarchy.

Clicking a property marker icon displays a popup menu providing some advanced options for assigning the value of that property, as shown in Figure 18-14.

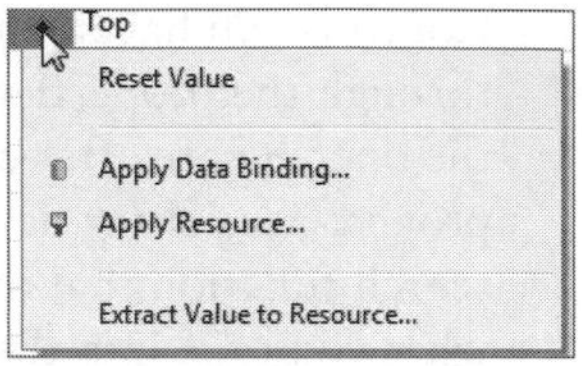

The Reset Value option simply returns the value of the property back to its default value (by deleting the attribute that assigns the value in the XAML).

FIGURE 18-14

The Apply Data Binding option provides a popup editor to select various binding options to create a data binding expression for that value. WPF supports numerous binding options, and these and this window are described further in the next section.

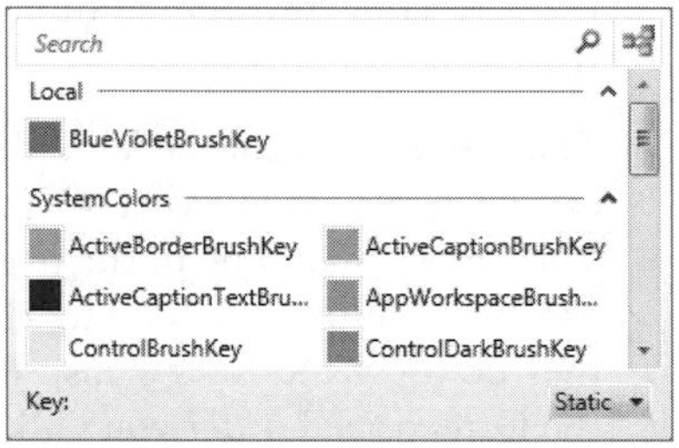

The Apply Resource option enables you to select a resource that you've created (or is defined by WPF) and assign it as the value of the selected property. Resources are essentially reusable objects and values, similar in concept to constants in code. For example, Figure 18-15 shows the popup window that appears when you select this option.

FIGURE 18-15

The resources are all the resources available to this property (that is, within scope and of the same type), grouped by their resource dictionary. Note the icon in the top right-hand corner of the popup window. Clicking this icon also groups the resources by which XAML file they originate from. This option can be toggled on and off.

Figure 18-15 shows a resource of the same type as this property (BlueVioletBrushKey) that is defined within the current XAML file (under the Local grouping). Because this is a property of type SolidColorBrush, the window is displaying all the color brush resources predefined in WPF that you could also choose from.

Returning to the other options in the menu shown in Figure 18-14, the Extract Value to Resource option takes the value of that property and turns it into a resource. The resource is created as a resource of the root node in the XAML file such that it can be reused throughout the file by the unique key you give it. The value of the property is automatically updated to use this resource. For example, using this option on the `Background` property of a control that has a value of #FF8888B7 defines the following resource in `Window.Resources` with the name `BlueVioletBrushKey`:

```
<SolidColorBrush x:Key="BlueVioletBrushKey">#FF8888B7</SolidColorBrush>
```

The control will reference this resource as such:

```
Background="{StaticResource BlueVioletBrushKey}"
```

You can then apply this resource to other controls using the same means in XAML, or you can apply it by selecting the control and the property to apply it to, and using the Apply Resource option on the property marker menu described previously.

In the designer you will find that (as with Windows Forms) double-clicking a control automatically creates an event handler for that control's default event in the code-behind. You can also create event handlers for any of the control's events using the Properties window as you would in Windows Forms. Clicking the lightning icon in the Properties window takes you to the Events view, as shown in Figure 18-16. This shows a list of events that the control can raise, and you can double-click the event to automatically create the appropriate event handler in the code-behind.

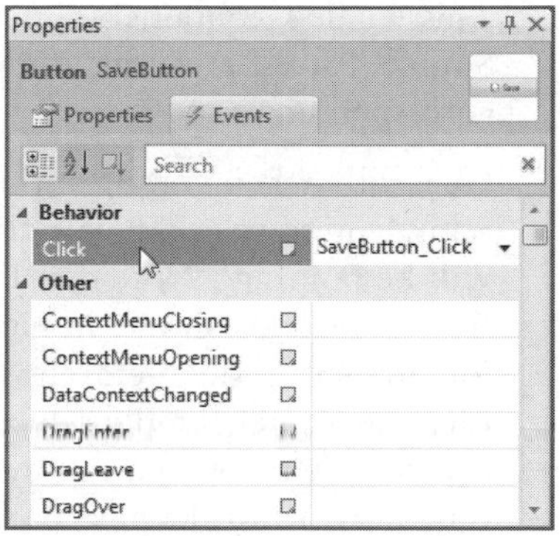

FIGURE 18-16

> *For VB.NET developers, double-clicking the Button control or creating the event via the Properties window wires up the event using the Handles syntax. Therefore, the event handler is not assigned to the event as an attribute. If you use this method to handle the event you won't see the event handler defined in the XAML for the control, and thus you won't be able to use the Navigate to Event Handler menu (from Figure 18-6) when in the XAML editor to navigate to it.*

Data Binding Features

Data binding is a very important concept in WPF, and is one of its core strengths. Data binding syntax can be a bit confusing initially, but Visual Studio 2010 makes creating data bound forms very easy in the designer. Visual Studio 2010 helps with data binding in two ways: with the Apply Data Binding option on a property in the Properties tool window, and the drag and drop data binding support from the Data Sources window. This section looks at these two options in turn.

In WPF you can bind to objects (which also includes datasets, ADO.NET Entity Framework entities, and so on), resources, and even properties on other controls. So there are very rich binding capabilities in WPF and you can bind a property to almost anything you want to. Hand-coding these complex binding expressions in XAML can be quite daunting, but the Apply Data Binding editor enables you to build these expressions via a point-and-click interface.

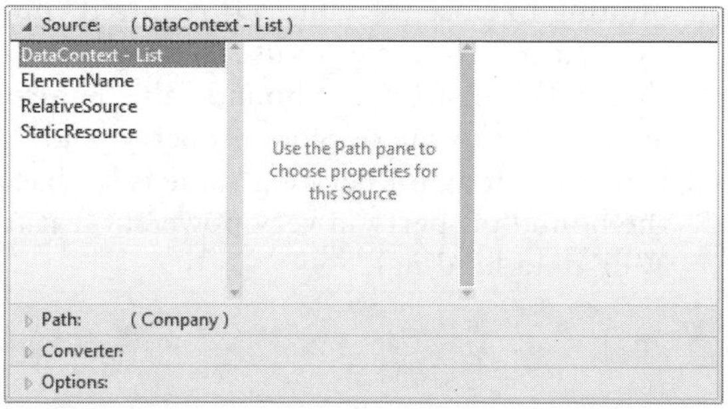

To bind a property on a control first select the control in the designer and find the property you want to bind in the Properties window. Click the property marker icon and select the Apply Data Binding option. Figure 18-17 shows the window that appears.

FIGURE 18-17

This window contains a number of steps (similar to a wizard) that help you create a binding - Source, Path, Converter, and Options in an accordion style layout. Click on a header to open the corresponding step.

Generally when you open the window, you will be presented with the Source step that will allow you to select the binding source (in other words, the source of the data to which you will be binding). Note that this step may be automatically skipped and show the Path selection step instead (as shown in Figure 18-18) if there is already a data context set on the control (or further up the hierarchy). If you want to use one of the other types of bindings (such as ElementName), simply select the header of the Source step to change the preselected binding source. Then you can follow through selecting the options for your binding (select an option then move onto the next pane).

In the example shown in Figure 18-17, you have a Grid control further up the hierarchy to which has been assigned a CollectionViewSource resource (which points to a ViewModel object as the data source) to its DataContext property. The DataContext property's value is inherited by the controls further down the hierarchy, so when applying a data binding to a text box within that grid you can specify that the binding source is the text box's DataContext property (which is shown as having a List assigned to it). Once you have selected your binding source, you can move on to the Path step.

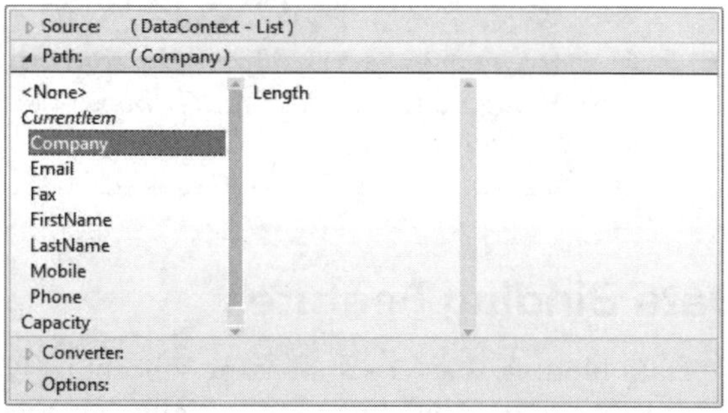

The Path step enables you to select the path on the binding source from which the value to be bound is located. For example, in Figure 18-18 the Company property (which is on the ViewModel that the binding source is bound to) has been selected.

FIGURE 18-18

If that property itself is an object, you can drill down and select the property on that to bind to (and so on). As can be seen in Figure 18-18, the company property (a string) has a Length property that we could bind to if we wished.

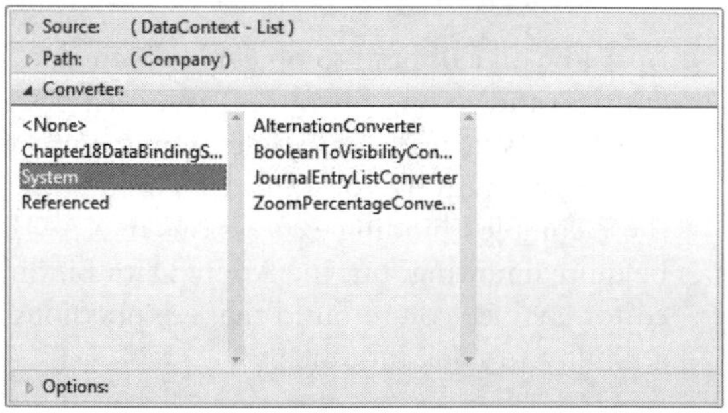

Double-click your final selection in your binding to close the editor. If required you can select a converter to use (see Figure 18-19) that will transform the bound value before assigning it to the selected property, and transform it again before a value is set back on the bound property (a very powerful feature in WPF data binding).

FIGURE 18-19

Various other binding options can also be set from the Options section as shown in Figure 18-20.

As you can see, this binding expression builder makes creating the binding expression much easier, without requiring you to learn the data binding syntax. This is a good way to learn the data binding syntax, because you can then see the expression produced in the XAML.

FIGURE 18-20

Now look at the drag and drop data binding features of Visual Studio 2010. The first step is to create something to bind to. This can be an object, a dataset, or an ADO.NET Entity Framework entity, among many other binding targets. For the purposes of this example you will create an object to bind to. Create a new class in your project called ContactViewModel, and create a number of properties on it such as FirstName, LastName, Company, Phone, Fax, Mobile, and Email (all strings).

> *The name of your object is called ContactViewModel because it is acting as your ViewModel object, which pertains to the Model-View-ViewModel (MVVM) design pattern mentioned earlier. This design pattern will not be fully fleshed out in this example, however, in order to reduce its complexity and save potential confusion.*

Now compile your project (this is important or otherwise the class won't appear in the next step). Return to the designer of your form and select Add New Data Source from the Data menu. Select Object as your data source type, click Next, and select the ContactViewModel class from the tree (you will need to expand the nodes to find it within the namespace hierarchy). Click the Finish button and the Data Sources tool window appears with the ContactViewModel object listed and its properties below, as shown in Figure 18-21.

FIGURE 18-21

Now you are set to drag and drop either the whole object or individual properties onto the form, which will create one or more controls to display its data. By default a DataGrid control will be created to display the data, but if you select the ContactViewModel item, it will show a button that when clicked displays a drop-down menu (as shown in Figure 18-22) allowing you to select between DataGrid, List, and Details.

FIGURE 18-22

➤ The DataGrid option creates a DataGrid control, which has a column for each property of the object.

➤ The List option creates a List control with a data template containing fields for each of the properties.

➤ The Details option creates a Grid control with two columns: one for labels and one for fields. A row will be created for each property on the object, with a Label control displaying the field name (with spaces intelligently inserted before capital letters) in the first column, and a field (whose type depends on the data type of the property) in the second column.

A resource is created in the Resources property of the Window, which points to the ContactViewModel object that can then be used as the data context or items source of the control(s) binding to the object. This can be deleted at a later stage if you want to set the data source from the code-behind. The control(s) will also have the required data binding expressions assigned. The type of control(s) that will be created on the form to display the data will depend on your selection on the ContactViewModel item.

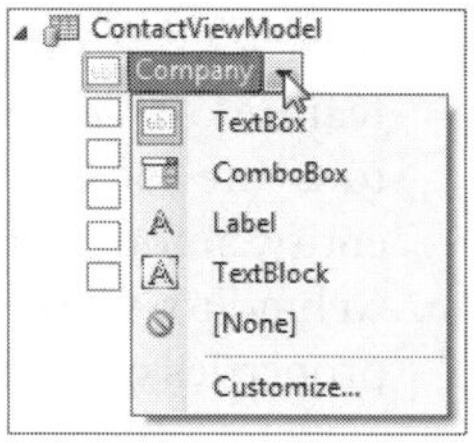

The type of control created for each property will have a default based upon the data type of the property, but like the ContactViewModel item you can select the property to show a button that when clicked displays a drop-down menu allowing you to select a different control type (as shown in Figure 18-23). If the type of control isn't in the list (such as if you want to use a third-party control), you can use the Customize option to add it to the list for the corresponding data type. If you don't want a field created for that property, select None from the menu.

FIGURE 18-23

For this example you will create a details form, so select Details on the ContactViewModel item in the Data Sources window. You can change the control generated for each property if you want, but for now leave each as a textbox and have each property generated in the details form. Now select the ContactViewModel item from the Data Sources window and drop it onto your form. A grid will be created along with a field for each property as shown in Figure 18-24.

Unfortunately there is no way in the Data Sources window to define the order of the fields in the form, so you will need to reorder the controls in the grid manually (either via the designer or by modifying the XAML directly).

FIGURE 18-24

When you look at the XAML generated you will see that this drag and drop data binding feature will save you a lot of work and make the process of generating forms a lot faster and easier.

> *If you write user/custom controls that expose properties that may be assigned a data binding expression you will need to make these dependency properties. Dependency properties are a special WPF/Silverlight concept whose value can accept an expression that needs to be resolved (such as data binding expression). Dependency properties need to be defined differently than standard properties. The discussion of these is beyond the scope of this chapter, but essentially only properties that have been defined as dependency properties can be assigned a data binding expression.*

STYLING YOUR APPLICATION

Up until now, your application has looked very plain — in fact it could be considered much plainer than if you had designed it in Windows Forms. The great thing about WPF, however, is that the visual appearance of the controls is easy to modify, allowing you to completely change the way they look. You can store commonly used changes to specific controls as *styles* (a collection of property values for a control which is stored as a resource that can be defined once and applied to multiple controls), or you can completely redefine the XAML for a control by creating a new *control template* for it. These resources can be defined in the Resources property of any control in your layout along with a key, which can then be used by any controls further down the hierarchy that refer to it by that key. For example, if you wanted to define a resource available for use by any control within your MainWindow XAML file you could define it in Window.Resources. Or if you wanted to be able to use it throughout the entire application you could define it in the Application.Resources property on the Application element in App.xaml.

Taking it one step further, you could define multiple control templates/styles in a resource dictionary and use this as a *theme*. This theme could be applied across your application to automatically style the controls in your user interface and provide a unique and consistent look for your application. This is what this section looks at. Rather than creating your own themes you will actually be using the themes available from the WPF Themes project on CodePlex: http://www.codeplex.com/wpfthemes.

These themes were initially designed (most by Microsoft) for use in Silverlight applications, but have been converted (where it was necessary) so they can be used in WPF applications. Use one of these themes to create a completely different look for your application.

Start by creating a new application and adding some different controls on the form, as shown in Figure 18-25.

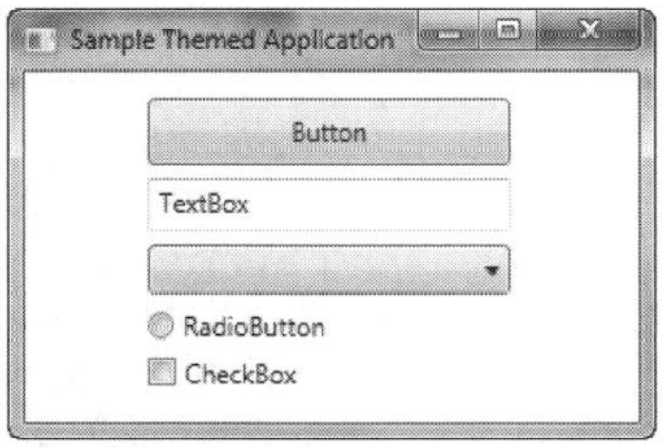

As you can see this looks fairly bland, so try applying a theme and seeing how you can easily change its look completely. When you download the WPF Themes project you will see that it contains a solution with two projects: one providing the themes, and a demonstration project that uses them. You will use the themes slightly differently, however. Run the sample application and find a theme that you like. For the purposes of demonstration choose the Shiny Blue theme. In the WPF.Themes project under the ShinyBlue folder you will find a Theme.xaml file. Copy this into the root of your own project (making sure to include it in your project in Visual Studio).

FIGURE 18-25

Open up App.xaml and add the following XAML code to Application.Resources:

```
<ResourceDictionary>
    <ResourceDictionary.MergedDictionaries>
        <ResourceDictionary Source="Theme.xaml"/>
    </ResourceDictionary.MergedDictionaries>
</ResourceDictionary>
```

This XAML code simply merges the resources from the theme file into your application resources, which will apply the resources application-wide and override the default styling of the controls in your project with the corresponding ones defined in the theme file.

One last change to make is to set the background style for your window(s) to use the style from the theme file (because this isn't automatically assigned). In your `Window` element add the following attribute:

FIGURE 18-26

```
Background="{StaticResource WindowBackgroundBrush}"
```

Now run your project and you will find the controls in your form look completely different, as shown in Figure 18-26.

To change the theme to a different one you can simply replace the `Theme.xaml` file with another one from the WPF.Themes project and recompile your project.

> *If you plan to extensively modify the styles and control templates for your application you may find it much easier to do so in Expression Blend — a tool specifically designed for graphics designers who are working with XAML. Expression Blend is much better suited to designing graphics and animations in XAML, and provides a much better designer for doing so than Visual Studio (which is focused more toward developers). Expression Blend can open up Visual Studio solutions and can also view/edit code and compile projects, although it is really best suited to design-related tasks. This integration of Visual Studio and Expression Blend helps to support the designer/developer workflow. Both these tools can have the same solution/project open at the same time (even on the same machine), enabling you to quickly switch between them when necessary. If a file is open in one when you save a change to a file in the other a notification dialog appears asking if you want to reload the file. To easily open a solution in Expression Blend from Visual Studio, right-click a XAML file and select the Open in Expression Blend option.*

WINDOWS FORMS INTEROPERABILITY

Up until now you have seen how you can build a WPF application, however the likelihood is that you already have a significant code base in Windows Forms and are unlikely to immediately migrate it all to WPF. You may have a significant investment in that code base and not want to rewrite it all for technology's sake. To ease this migration path, Microsoft has enabled WPF and Windows Forms to work together within the same application. Bi-directional interoperability is supported by both WPF and Windows Forms applications, with WPF controls able to be hosted in a Windows Forms application, and Windows Forms controls able to be hosted in a WPF application. This section looks at how to implement each of these scenarios.

Hosting a WPF Control in Windows Forms

To begin with, create a new project in your solution to create the WPF control in. This control (for the purpose of demonstration) will be a simple username and password entry control. From the

Add New Project dialog (see Figure 18-27), select the WPF User Control Library project template. This will already include the XAML and code-behind files necessary for a WPF user control. If you examine the XAML of the control you will see that it is essentially the same as the original XAML for the window you started with at the beginning of the chapter except that the root XAML element is UserControl instead of Window.

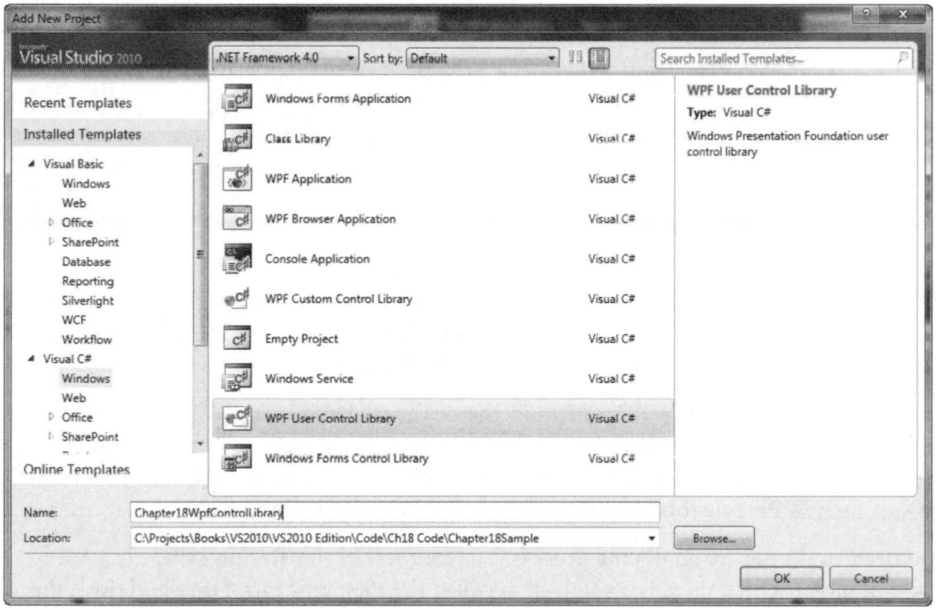

FIGURE 18-27

Rename the control to UserLoginControl, and add a grid, two text blocks, and two textboxes to it as demonstrated in Figure 18-28.

FIGURE 18-28

In the code-behind add some simple properties to expose the contents of the textboxes publicly (getters and setters):

VB

```vb
Public Property UserName As String
    Get
        Return txtUserName.Text
    End Get
    Set(ByVal value As String)
        txtUserName.Text = value
    End Set
End Property

Public Property Password As String
    Get
        Return txtPassword.Text
    End Get
```

```
      Set(ByVal value As String)
          txtPassword.Text = value
      End Set
End Property
```

C#

```
public string Username
{
    get { return txtUserName.Text; }
    set { txtUserName.Text = value; }
}

public string Password
{
    get { return txtPassword.Text; }
    set { txtPassword.Text = value; }
}
```

Now that you have your WPF control, build the project and create a new Windows Forms project to host it in. Create the project and add a reference to your WPF project that contains the control (using the Add Reference menu item when right-clicking the References in the project).

Open up the form that will host the WPF control in the designer. Because the WPF control library you built is in the same solution, your UserLoginControl control will appear in the Toolbox and can simply be dragged and dropped onto the form to be used. This automatically adds an ElementHost control (which can host WPF controls) and references the control as its content.

However, if you need to do this manually the process is as follows. In the Toolbox there is a WPF Interoperability tab, under which there is a single item called the ElementHost. Drag and drop this onto the form, as shown in Figure 18-29, and you will see that there is a smart tag that prompts you to select the WPF control that you want to host. Note that if the control doesn't appear in the drop-down you may need to build your solution.

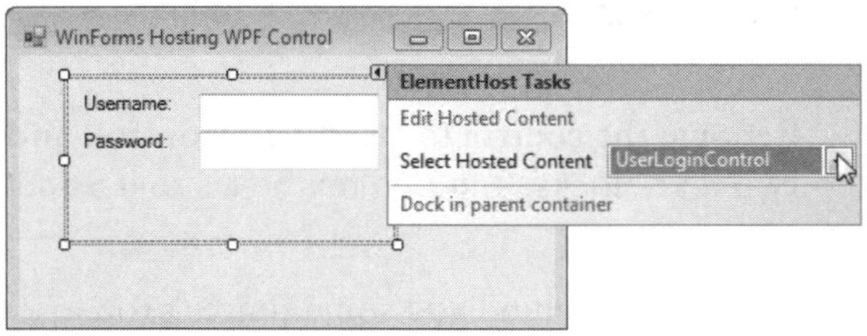

The control will be loaded into the ElementHost control and automatically given a name to refer to it in code (which can be changed via the `HostedContentName` property).

FIGURE 18-29

Hosting a Windows Forms Control in WPF

Now take a look at the opposite scenario — hosting a Windows Forms control in a WPF application. Create a new project using the Class Library project template called Chapter 18 WinFormsControlLibrary. Delete the Class1 class, and add a new User Control item to the project and call it UserLoginControl.

Open this item in the designer and add two text blocks and two textboxes to it as demonstrated in Figure 18-30.

FIGURE 18-30

In the code-behind add some simple properties to expose the contents of the textboxes publicly (getters and setters):

VB

```vb
Public Property UserName As String
    Get
        Return txtUserName.Text
    End Get
    Set(ByVal value As String)
        txtUserName.Text = value
    End Set
End Property

Public Property Password As String
    Get
        Return txtPassword.Text
    End Get
    Set(ByVal value As String)
        txtPassword.Text = value
    End Set
End Property
```

C#

```csharp
public string Username
{
    get { return txtUserName.Text; }
    set { txtUserName.Text = value; }
}

public string Password
{
    get { return txtPassword.Text; }
    set { txtPassword.Text = value; }
}
```

Now that you have your Windows Forms control, build the project and create a new WPF project to host it in. Create the project and add a reference to your Windows Forms project that contains the control (using the Add Reference menu item when right-clicking the References in the project).

Open up the form that will host the Windows Forms control in the designer. Select the WindowsFormsHost control from the Toolbox and drag and drop it onto your form. Unfortunately at this point the designer can't help you and you need to change to the XAML editor. You need to add a namespace prefix definition on the root element:

```
xmlsn:wfapp="clr-namespace:Chapter18WinFormsControlLibrary;
assembly=Chapter18WinFormsControlLibrary"
```

And you can then modify the WindowsFormsHost element to host your control, which when run will render the control as shown in Figure 18-31.

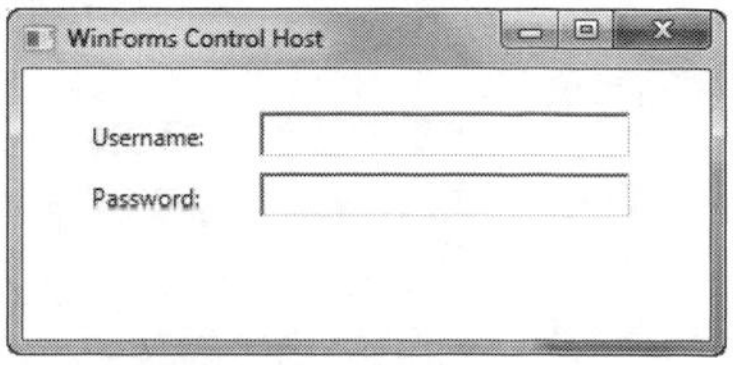

```xml
<WindowsFormsHost x:Name="windowsFormsHost">
    <wfapp:UserLoginControl x:Name="userLoginDetails" />
</WindowsFormsHost>
```

FIGURE 18-31

DEBUGGING WITH THE WPF VISUALIZER

Identifying problems in your XAML/visual tree at runtime can be difficult, but fortunately a new feature called the WPF Visualizer has been added to VS2010 to help you debug your WPF application's visual tree. For example, an element may not be visible when it should be, may not appear where it should, or may not be styled correctly. The WPF Visualizer can help you track down these sorts of problems by enabling you to view the visual tree, view the values of the properties for a selected element, and view where properties are getting their styling from.

In order to open the WPF Visualizer, you must first be in break mode. Using the Autos, Local, or Watch tool window, find a variable that contains a reference to an element in the XAML document to debug. You can then click the little magnifying glass icon next to a WPF user interface element listed in the tool window to open the visualizer (as shown in Figure 18-32). Alternatively you can place your mouse cursor over a variable that references a WPF user interface element (to display the DataTip popup) and click the magnifying glass icon there.

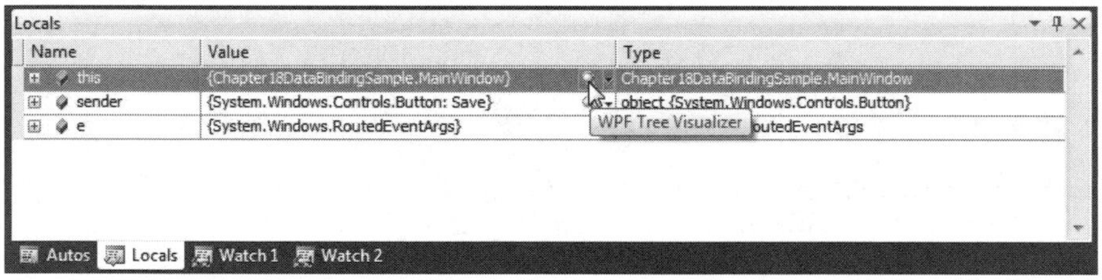

FIGURE 18-32

The WPF Visualizer is shown in Figure 18-33. On the left side of the window you can see the visual tree for the current XAML document and the rendering of the selected element in this tree below it. On the right side is a list of all the properties of the selected element in the tree, their current values, and other information associated with each property.

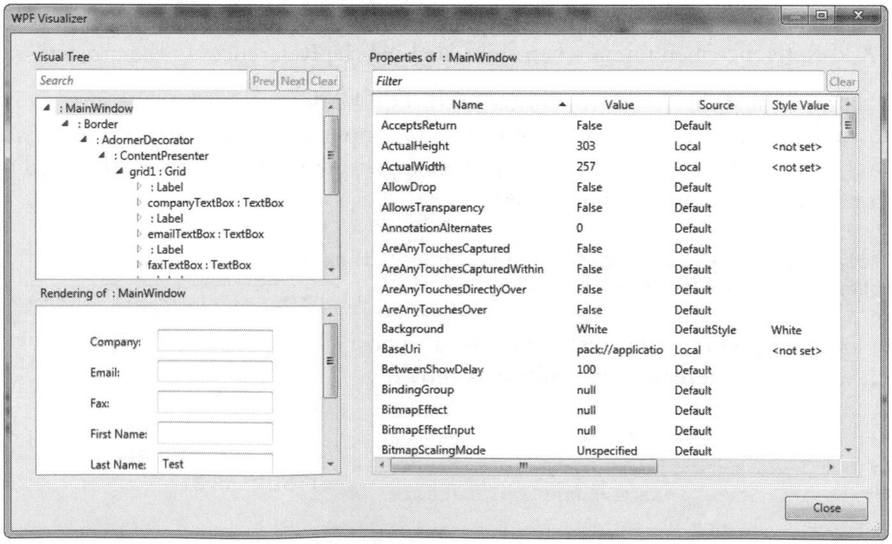

FIGURE 18-33

Because a visual tree can contain thousands of items, finding the one you are after by traversing the tree can be difficult. If you know the name or type of the element you are looking for, you can enter this into the search text box above the tree and navigate through the matching entries using the Next and Prev buttons. You can also filter the property list by entering a part of the property name, value, style, or type that you are searching for.

Unfortunately there's no means to edit a property value or modify the property tree, but inspecting the elements in the visual tree and their property values (and the source of the values) should help you track down problems in your XAML much more easily than in previous versions of Visual Studio.

SUMMARY

In this chapter you have seen how you can work with Visual Studio 2010 to build applications with WPF. You've learned some of the most important concepts of XAML, how to use the unique features of the WPF designer, looked at styling an application, and used the interoperability capabilities between WPF and Windows Forms.

19
Office Business Applications

WHAT'S IN THIS CHAPTER?

➤ Exploring the different ways to extend Microsoft Office

➤ Creating a Microsoft Word document customization

➤ Creating a Microsoft Outlook add-in

➤ Launching and debugging an Office application

➤ Packaging and deploying an Office application

Microsoft Office applications have always been extensible via add-ins and various automation techniques. Even Visual Basic for Applications (VBA), which was widely known for various limitations in accessing system files, had the capability to write applications that used an instance of an Office application to achieve certain tasks, such as Word's spell-checking feature.

When Visual Studio .NET was released in 2002, Microsoft soon followed with the first release of Visual Studio Tools for Office (known by the abbreviation VSTO, pronounced *visto*). This initial version of VSTO didn't really produce anything new except for an easier way of creating application projects that would use Microsoft Word or Microsoft Excel. However, subsequent versions of VSTO quickly evolved and became more powerful, allowing you to build more functional applications that ran on the Office platform.

The latest version of VSTO was shipped as part of Visual Studio 2010. It provides several enhancements over the previous version, including support for Office 2010, expanded support for the Ribbon user interface, and improved packaging and deployment functionality.

This chapter begins with a look at the types of applications you can build with VSTO. It then guides you through the process of creating a document-level customization to a Word document, including a custom Actions Pane. Following this, the chapter provides a walkthrough, showing how to create an Outlook add-in complete with an Outlook Form region. Finally, the chapter provides some important information regarding the debugging and deployment of Office applications.

CHOOSING AN OFFICE PROJECT TYPE

As you would expect, the types of applications you can create using VSTO under Visual Studio has been updated since the previous version. You now have the ability to create applications that target the new Microsoft Office 2010 applications, as well as Microsoft Office 2007 applications.

As with the previous version, add-in applications can be created for almost every product in the Office suite including Excel, InfoPath, Outlook, PowerPoint, Project, Visio, and Word. In the case of Excel and Word, these solutions can either be attached to a single document or be loaded every time that application is launched.

You can create a new Office application by selecting File ➪ New ➪ Project. Select your preferred language (Visual Basic or Visual C#), and then select the Office project category, as shown in Figure 19-1.

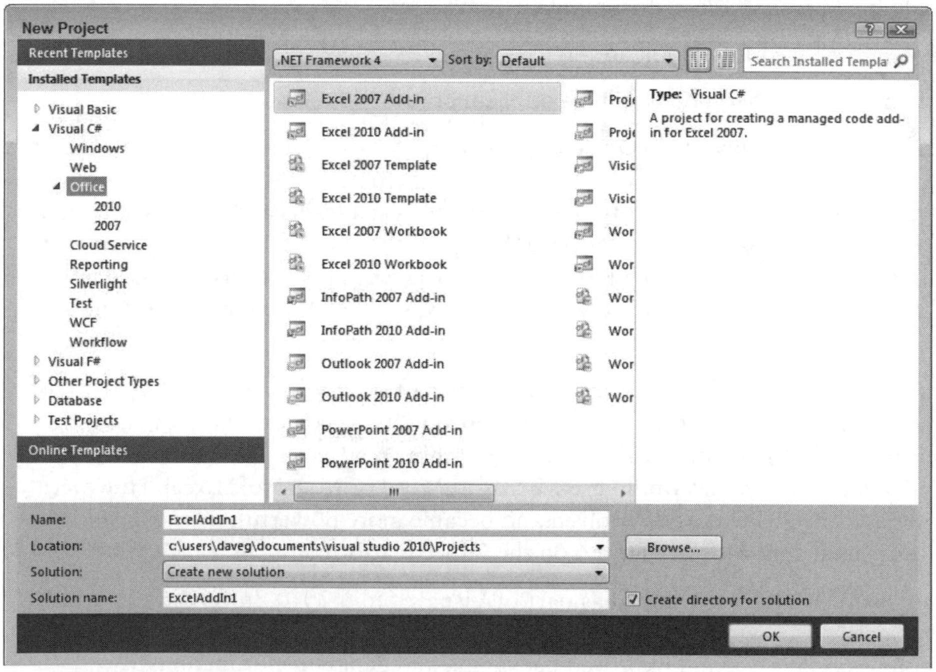

FIGURE 19-1

Two types of project templates are available for Office applications: document-level customizations and application-level add-ins.

Document-Level Customizations

A document-level customization is a solution that is based on a single document. To load the customization, an end user must open a specific document. Events in the document, such as loading the document or clicking buttons and menu items, can invoke event handler methods in the attached assembly. Document-level customizations can also be included with an Office template, which ensures that the customization is included when you create a new document from that template.

Visual Studio 2010 allows you to create document-level customizations for the following types of documents:

➤   Microsoft Excel Workbook

➤   Microsoft Excel Template

➤   Microsoft Word Document

➤   Microsoft Word Template

Using a document-level customization, you can modify the user interface of Word or Excel to provide a unique solution for your end users. For example, you can add new controls to the Office Ribbon or display a customized *Actions Pane* window.

Microsoft Word and Microsoft Excel also include a technology called *smart tags*, which enable developers to track the user's input and recognize when text in a specific format has been entered. Your solution can use this technology by providing feedback or even actions that the user could take in response to certain recognized terms, such as a phone number or address.

Visual Studio also includes a set of custom controls that are specific to Microsoft Word. Called *content controls*, they are optimized for both data entry and print. You see content controls in action later in this chapter.

Application-Level Add-Ins

Unlike a document-level customization, an application-level add-in is always loaded regardless of the document that is currently open. In fact, application-level add-ins will run even if the application is running with no documents open.

Earlier versions of VSTO had significant limitations when it came to application-level add-ins. For example, you could only create add-ins for Microsoft Outlook, and even then you could not customize much of the user interface.

Fortunately, in Visual Studio 2010 such restrictions do not exist, and you can create application-level add-ins for almost every product in the Microsoft Office suite, including Excel, InfoPath, Outlook, PowerPoint, Project, Visio, and Word. This applies equally to version 2007 and version 2010 of Office. You can create the same UI enhancements as you can with a document-level customization, such as adding new controls to the Office Ribbon.

You can also create a custom *Task Pane* as part of your add-in. Task Panes are very similar to the Action Panes that are available in document-level customization projects. However, custom Task Panes are associated with the application, not a specific document, and as such can be created only within an application-level add-in.

An Actions Pane, on the other hand, is a specific type of Task Pane that is customizable and is attached to a specific Word document or Excel workbook. You cannot create an Actions Pane in an application-level add-in.

Also included in Visual Studio 2010 is the ability to create custom Outlook form regions in Outlook add-in projects. Form regions are the screens that are displayed when an Outlook item is opened, such as a Contact or Appointment. You can either extend the existing form regions or create a completely custom Outlook form. Later in this chapter you walk through the creation of an Outlook 2010 add-in that includes a custom Outlook form region.

CREATING A DOCUMENT-LEVEL CUSTOMIZATION

This section walks through the creation of a Word document customization. This demonstrates how to create a document-level customization complete with Word Content Controls and a custom Actions Pane.

> *The example in this section uses Word 2010, which you must have installed locally in order to debug the project. If you only have Word 2007 installed, you can still follow the instructions and create a document-level customization using the Word 2007 project template. Any differences between Word 2010 and Word 2007 have been noted in the instructions.*

Your First VSTO Project

When you create a document-level customization with Visual Studio 2010, you can either create the document from scratch or jump-start the design by using an existing document or template. A great source of templates, particularly for business-related forms, is the free templates available from Microsoft Office Online at `http://office.microsoft.com/templates/`.

> *All of the templates available for download from the Office Online web site are provided in the older Word 97-2003 format (.`dot`). Unfortunately, some features, such as the Word Content Controls, are only available for documents that are saved with the newer Open XML format (.`dotx`). Therefore, you will need to ensure that the template is in the latest format if you wish to use all the available features.*

This example uses the Employee warning notice that is available under the Forms, Employment category. When you download a template from the Office Online web site using Internet Explorer, you are prompted to save it to the default templates location. Once saved, Microsoft Word then opens with a new document based on the template. Save this new document to a convenient folder on your computer as a Word Template in the Open XML format (.`dotx`), as shown in Figure 19-2.

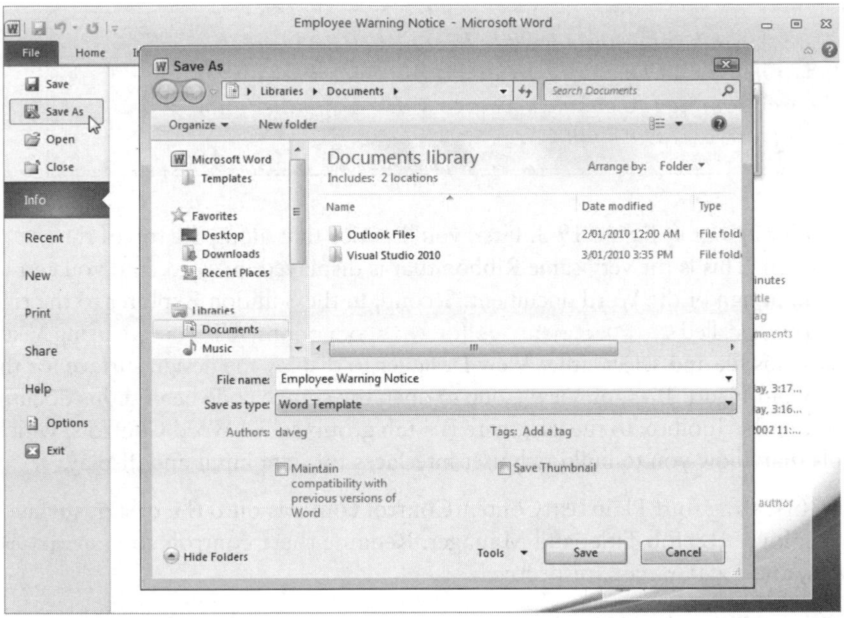

FIGURE 19-2

Next, launch Visual Studio 2010 and select File ➪ New ➪ Project. Filter the project types by selecting your preferred language (C# or Visual Basic) followed by Office, and then choose a new Word 2010 Template. You are presented with a screen that prompts you to create a new document or copy an existing one. Select the option to copy an existing document and then navigate to and select the document template you saved earlier. When you click OK, the project is created and the document opens in the Designer as shown in Figure 19-3.

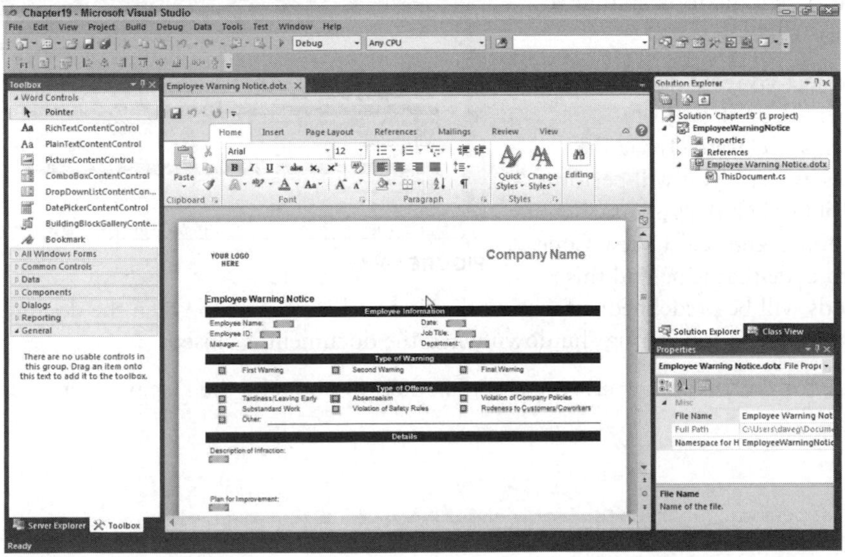

FIGURE 19-3

> *VSTO requires access to Visual Basic for Applications (VBA) even though the projects do not use VBA. Therefore, the first time you create an Office application you are prompted to enable access to VBA. You must grant this access even if you work exclusively in C#.*

A few things are worth pointing out in Figure 19-3. First, you'll notice that along the top of the Designer is the Office Ribbon. This is the very same Ribbon that is displayed in Word, and you can use it to modify the layout and design of the Word document. Second, in the Solution Explorer to the right, the file that is currently open is called `ThisDocument.cs` (or `ThisDocument.vb` if you are using Visual Basic). You can right-click this file and select either View Designer to display the design surface for the document, currently shown in Figure 19-3, or View Code to open the source code behind this document in the code editor. Finally, in the Toolbox to the left, there is a tab group called Word Controls, which contains a set of controls that allow you to build rich user interfaces for data input and display.

To customize this form, first drag four PlainTextContentControl controls onto the design surface for the Employee Name, Employee ID, Job Title, and Manager. Rename these controls to `txtEmpName`, `txtEmpID`, `txtJobTitle`, and `txtManager`, respectively.

Next, drag a DatePickerContentControl for the Date field, and rename it to be `dtDate`. Then drag a DropDownListContentControl next to the Department field, and rename it `ddDept`.

Following this, drag a RichTextContentControl into the Details section of the document, and place it under the Description of Infraction label.

Finally, to clean up the document a little, remove the sections titled Type of Warning and Type of Offense, and all of the text that is below the RichTextContentControl you added. Once you have done this, your form should look similar to what is shown in Figure 19-4.

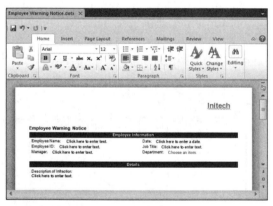

Before you run this project you will need to populate the Department drop-down list. Although you can do this declaratively via the Properties field, for this exercise you will perform it programmatically. Right-click the `ThisDocument` file in the Solution Explorer and select View Code to display the managed code that is behind this

FIGURE 19-4

document. Two methods will be predefined: a function that is run during startup when the document is opened, and a function that is run during shutdown when the document is closed.

Add the following code for the `ThisDocument_Startup` method to populate the Department drop-down list:

C#

```csharp
private void ThisDocument_Startup(object sender, System.EventArgs e)
{
    ddDept.PlaceholderText = "Select your department";
    ddDept.DropDownListEntries.Add("Finance", "Finance", 0);
```

```
        ddDept.DropDownListEntries.Add("HR", "HR", 1);
        ddDept.DropDownListEntries.Add("IT", "IT", 2);
        ddDept.DropDownListEntries.Add("Marketing", "Marketing", 3);
        ddDept.DropDownListEntries.Add("Operations", "Operations", 4);
}
```

Code Snippet ThisDocument.cs

VB

```
Private Sub ThisDocument_Startup() Handles Me.Startup
    ddDept.PlaceholderText = "Select your department"
    ddDept.DropDownListEntries.Add("Finance", "Finance", 0)
    ddDept.DropDownListEntries.Add("HR", "HR", 1)
    ddDept.DropDownListEntries.Add("IT", "IT", 2)
    ddDept.DropDownListEntries.Add("Marketing", "Marketing", 3)
    ddDept.DropDownListEntries.Add("Operations", "Operations", 4)
End Sub
```

Code Snippet ThisDocument.vb

You can now run the project in Debug mode by pressing F5. This compiles the project and opens the document in Microsoft Word. You can test out entering data in the various fields to obtain a feel for how they behave.

Protecting the Document Design

While you have the document open you may notice that in addition to entering text in the control fields that you added, you can also edit the surrounding text and even delete some of the controls. This is obviously not ideal in this scenario. Fortunately, Office and VSTO provide a way to prevent the document from undesirable editing. For this, you will need to show the Developer tab.

For Word 2010, click the File tab and then click the Options button. In the Word Options dialog window, select Customize Ribbon and then check the box next to Developer under the Main Tabs list.

For Word 2007, click the Office button and then click the Word Options button on the bottom of the screen. In the Word Options dialog window, check the box next to the Show Developer Tab in the Ribbon option.

When you stop debugging and return to Visual Studio, you will see a new tab on the toolbar above the Ribbon, as shown in Figure 19-5. This provides some useful functions for Office development-related tasks.

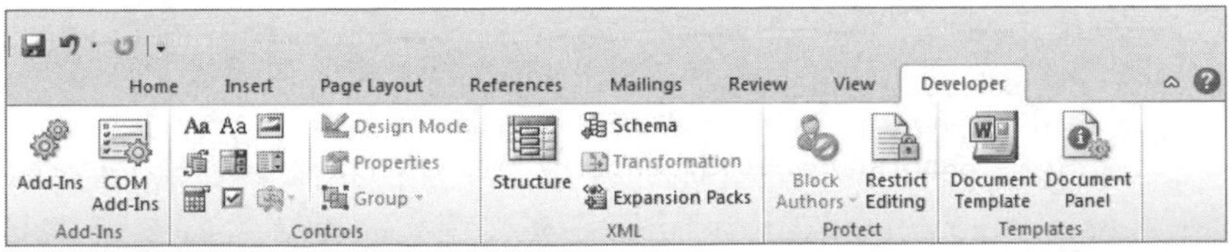

FIGURE 19-5

To prevent the document from being edited, you must perform a couple of steps. First, ensure that the Designer is open and then press Ctrl+A to select everything in the document (text and controls). On the Developer tab click Group ⇨ Group. This allows you to treat everything on the document as a single entity, and easily apply properties to all elements in one step.

With this new group selected, open the Properties window and set the `LockContentControl` property to `True`. Now when you run the project you will find that the standard text on the document cannot be edited or deleted, and you can only input data into the content controls that you have added.

Adding an Actions Pane

The final customization you will add to this document is an Actions Pane window. An Actions Pane is typically docked to one side of a window in Word, and can be used to display related information or provide access to additional information. For example, on an employee leave request form you could add an Actions Pane that retrieved and displayed the current employees' available leave balance.

> An Actions Pane, or custom Task Pane in the case of application-level add-ins, is nothing more than a standard user control. In the case of an Actions Pane, Visual Studio has included an item template; under the covers, however, this does little more than add a standard user control to the project with the Office namespace imported. For application-level add-ins there is no custom Task Panes item template, so you can simply add a standard user control to the project.

To add an Actions Pane to this document customization, right-click the project in the Solution Explorer and select Add ⇨ New Item. Select Actions Pane Control, provide it with a meaningful name, and click Add. The Actions Pane will open in a new designer window. You are simply going to add a button that retrieves the username of the current user and adds it to the document. Drag a button control onto the form and rename it `btnGetName`. Then double-click the control to register an event handler and add the following code for the button click event:

Available for
download on
Wrox.com

C#
```csharp
private void btnGetName_Click(object sender, EventArgs e)
{
    var myIdent = System.Security.Principal.WindowsIdentity.GetCurrent();
    Globals.ThisDocument.txtEmpName.Text = myIdent.Name;
}
```

Code Snippet GetUserName.cs

Available for
download on
Wrox.com

VB
```vb
Private Sub btnGetName_Click(ByVal sender As System.Object, _
                            ByVal e As System.EventArgs) _
                            Handles btnGetName.Click
```

```
        Dim myIdent = System.Security.Principal.WindowsIdentity.GetCurrent()
        Globals.ThisDocument.txtEmpName.Text = myIdent.Name
    End Sub
```

Code Snippet GetUserName.vb

The Actions Pane components are not added automatically to the document because you may want to show different Actions Panes, depending on the context users find themselves in when editing the document. However, if you have a single Actions Pane component and simply want to add it immediately when the document is opened, add the component to the `ActionsPane.Controls` collection of the document at startup, as demonstrated in the following code:

C#

Available for
download on
Wrox.com

```csharp
private void ThisDocument_Startup(object sender, System.EventArgs e)
{
    this.ActionsPane.Controls.Add(new NameOfActionsPaneControl());
}
```

Code Snippet ThisDocument.cs

VB

Available for
download on
Wrox.com

```vb
Private Sub ThisDocument_Startup() Handles Me.Startup
    Me.ActionsPane.Controls.Add(new NameOfActionsPaneControl())
End Sub
```

Code Snippet ThisDocument.vb

For application-level add-ins, add the user control to the `CustomTaskPanes` collection.

The next time you run the project, it will display the document in Word with the Actions Pane window shown during startup, as shown in Figure 19-6.

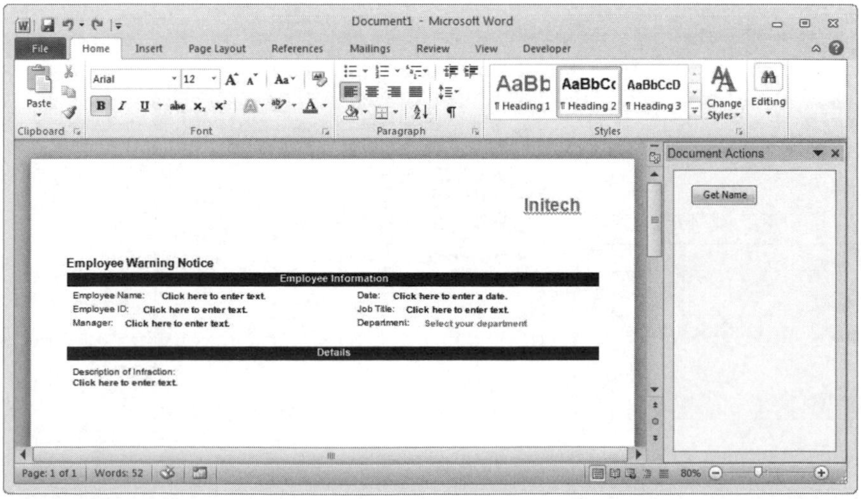

FIGURE 19-6

CREATING AN APPLICATION ADD-IN

This section walks through the creation of an add-in to Microsoft Outlook 2010. This will demonstrate how to create an application-level add-in that includes a custom Outlook form region for a Contact item.

> ⊗ *Never develop Outlook add-ins using your production e-mail account! There's too much risk that you will accidentally do something that you will regret later, such as deleting all of the e-mail in your Inbox. With Outlook, you can create a separate mail profile; one for your normal mailbox and one for your test mailbox.*

Some Outlook Concepts

Before creating an Outlook add-in, it is worth understanding some basic concepts that are specific to Outlook development. Though there is a reasonable degree of overlap, Outlook has always had a slightly different programming model from the rest of the products in the Office suite.

The Outlook object model is a heavily collection-based API. The `Application` class is the highest-level class and represents the Outlook application. This can be directly accessed from code as a property of the add-in; `this.Application` in C# or `Me.Application` in Visual Basic. With the `Application` class you can access classes that represent the *Explorer* and *Inspector* windows.

An Explorer window in Outlook is the main window that is displayed when Outlook is first opened and displays the contents of a folder, such as the Inbox or Calendar. Figure 19-7 (left) shows the Calendar in the Explorer window. The `Explorer` class represents this window, and includes properties, methods, and events that can be used to access the window and respond to actions.

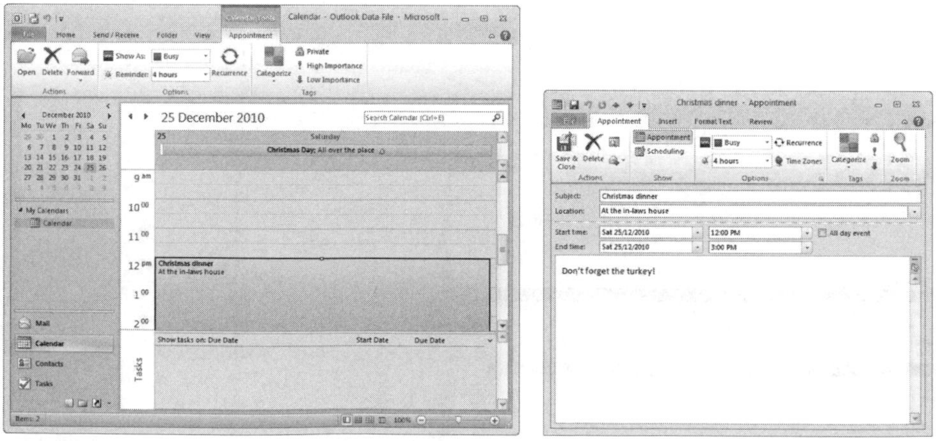

FIGURE 19-7

An Inspector window displays an individual item such as an e-mail message, contact, or appointment. Figure 19-7 (right) shows an Inspector window displaying an appointment item. The `Inspector` class includes properties and methods to access the window, and events that can be handled when certain actions occur within the window. Outlook form regions are hosted within Inspector windows.

The `Application` class also contains a `Session` object, which represents everything to do with the current Outlook session. This object provides you with access to the available address lists, mail stores, folders, items, and other Outlook objects. A mail folder, such as the Inbox or Calendar, is represented by a `MAPIFolder` class and contains a collection of items. Within Outlook, every item has a message class property that determines how it is presented within the application. For example, an e-mail message has a message class of `IPM.Note` and an appointment has a message class of `IPM.Appointment`.

Creating an Outlook Form Region

Now that you understand the basics of the Outlook object model, you can create your first Outlook add-in. In Visual Studio 2010, select File ➪ New ➪ Project. Filter the project types by selecting Visual C# followed by Office, and then choose a new Outlook 2010 Add-in project.

> *If you only have Outlook 2007 installed, select the Outlook 2010 Add-In project instead.*

Unlike a document-level customization, an application-level add-in is inherently code-based. In the case of a Word or Excel add-in, there may not even be a document open when the application is first launched. An Outlook add-in follows a similar philosophy; when you first create an Outlook add-in project, it will consist of a single nonvisual class called `ThisAddIn.cs` (or `ThisAddIn.vb`). You can add code here that performs some actions during startup or shutdown.

To customize the actual user interface of Outlook you can add an Outlook form region. This is a user control that is hosted in an Outlook Inspector window when an item of a certain message class is displayed.

To add a new Outlook form region, right-click the project in the Solution Explorer and select Add ➪ New Item. From the list of available items select Outlook Form Region, provide it with a meaningful name, and click Add. Visual Studio then opens the New Outlook Form Region Wizard that will obtain some basic properties needed to create the new item.

The first step of the wizard asks you to either design a new form or import an Outlook Form Storage (`.ofs`) file, which is a form designed in Outlook. Select Design a New Form Region and click Next.

The second step in the wizard allows you to select what type of form region to create. The wizard provides a handy visual representation of each type of form region, as shown in Figure 19-8. Select the Separate option and click Next.

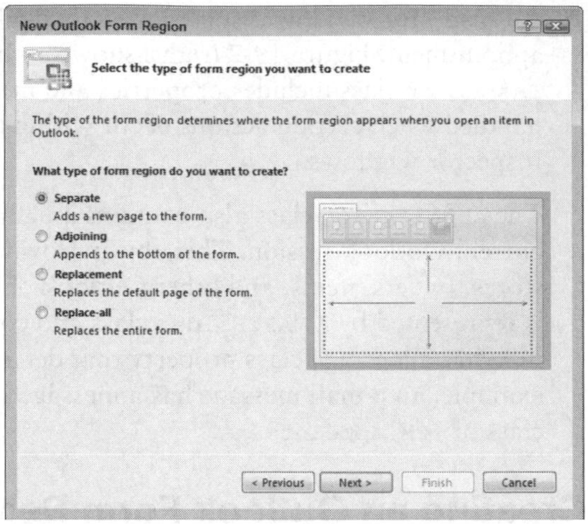

The next step in the wizard allows you to enter a friendly name for the form region, and, depending on the type of form region you've chosen, a title and description. This step also allows you to choose the display mode for the form region. *Compose mode* is displayed when an item is first being created, such as when you create a new e-mail message. *Read mode* is displayed when you subsequently open an e-mail message that has already been sent or received. Ensure that both of these checkboxes are ticked, enter Custom Details as the name, and click Next.

FIGURE 19-8

The final step in the wizard allows you to choose what message classes will display the form region. You can select from any of the standard message classes, such as mail message or appointment, or specify a custom message class. Select the Contact message class as shown in Figure 19-9 and click Finish to close the wizard.

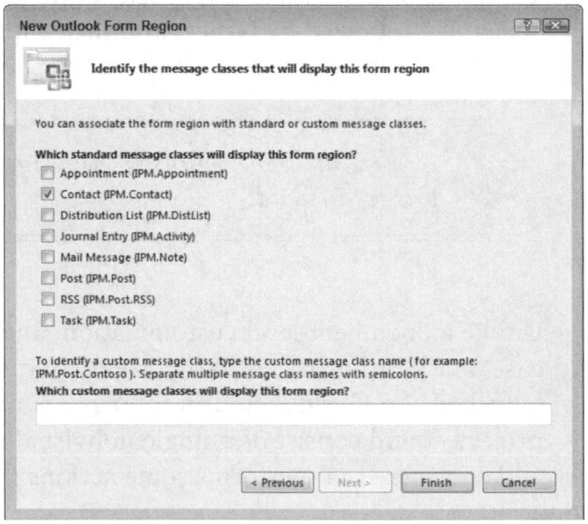

Once the wizard exits, the new form region will be created and opened in the Designer. As mentioned earlier, an Outlook form region, like an Actions Pane and a Task Pane, is simply a user control. However, unlike an Actions Pane, it contains an embedded manifest that defines how the form region appears in Outlook. To access the manifest, ensure that the form is selected in the Designer and open the Properties window. This will show

FIGURE 19-9

a property called `Manifest`, under which you can set various properties to how it appears. This property can also be accessed through code at run time.

In this scenario you will use the Outlook form region to display some additional useful information about a Contact. The layout of an Outlook form region is created in the same way as any other user control. Drag four Label controls and four textbox controls onto the design surface and align them as shown in Figure 19-10. Rename the textbox controls `txtPartner`, `txtChildren`, `txtHobbies`, and `txtProfession`, and change the text on the labels to match these fields.

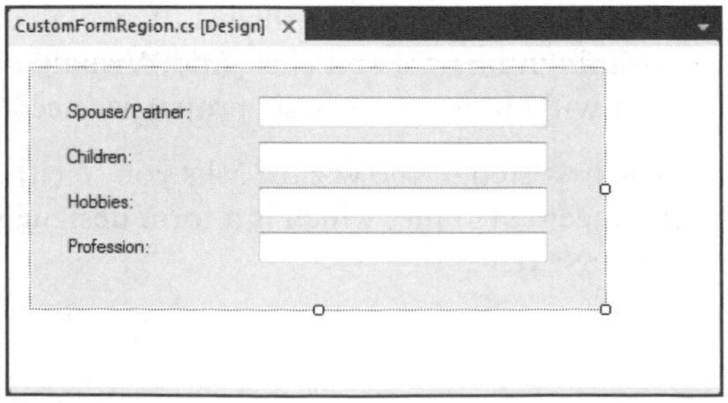

FIGURE 19-10

The `ContactItem` class contains a surprisingly large number of properties that are not obviously displayed in a standard Contact form in Outlook. In fact, with well over 100 contact-specific fields, there is a high chance that any custom property you want to display for a contact is already defined. In this case, the fields displayed on this form (spouse/partner, children, hobbies, and profession) are available as existing properties. You can also store a custom property on the item by adding an item to the `UserProperties` collection.

The code behind the form region will already have stubs for the `FormRegionShowing` and `FormRegionClosed` event handlers. Add the following code to those properties to access the current Contact item and retrieve and save these custom properties:

Available for download on Wrox.com

C#

```csharp
private void CustomFormRegion_FormRegionShowing(object sender, System.EventArgs e)
{
    var myContact = (Outlook.ContactItem)this.OutlookItem;
    this.txtPartner.Text = myContact.Spouse;
    this.txtChildren.Text = myContact.Children;
    this.txtHobbies.Text = myContact.Hobby;
    this.txtProfession.Text = myContact.Profession;
}
private void CustomFormRegion_FormRegionClosed(object sender, System.EventArgs e)
{
    var myContact = (Outlook.ContactItem)this.OutlookItem;
    myContact.Spouse = this.txtPartner.Text;
    myContact.Children = this.txtChildren.Text;
    myContact.Hobby = this.txtHobbies.Text;
    myContact.Profession = this.txtProfession.Text;
}
```

Code Snippet CustomFormRegion.cs

Available for download on Wrox.com

VB

```vb
Private Sub CustomFormRegion_FormRegionShowing(ByVal sender As Object, _
                                    ByVal e As System.EventArgs) _
                                    Handles MyBase.FormRegionShowing
    Dim myContact = CType(Me.OutlookItem, Outlook.ContactItem)
    myContact.Spouse = Me.txtPartner.Text
    myContact.Children = Me.txtChildren.Text
    myContact.Hobby = Me.txtHobbies.Text
    myContact.Profession = Me.txtProfession.Text
End Sub
Private Sub CustomFormRegion_FormRegionClosed(ByVal sender As Object, _
                                    ByVal e As System.EventArgs) _
                                    Handles MyBase.FormRegionClosed
    Dim myContact = CType(Me.OutlookItem, Outlook.ContactItem)
    myContact.Spouse = Me.txtPartner.Text
    myContact.Children = Me.txtChildren.Text
    myContact.Hobby = Me.txtHobbies.Text
    myContact.Profession = Me.txtProfession.Text
End Sub
```

Code Snippet CustomFormRegion.vb

Press F5 to build and run the add-in in Debug mode. If the solution compiled correctly, Outlook will open with your add-in registered. Open the Contacts folder and create a new Contact item. To view your custom Outlook form region, click the Custom Details button in the Show tab group of the Office Ribbon. Figure 19-11 shows how the Outlook form region should appear in the Contact Inspector window.

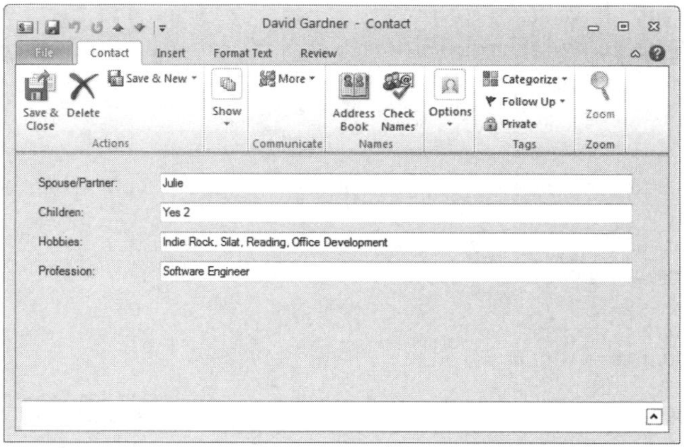

FIGURE 19-11

DEBUGGING OFFICE APPLICATIONS

You can debug Office applications by using much the same process as you would with any other Windows application. All the standard Visual Studio debugger features, such as the ability to insert breakpoints and watch variables, are available when debugging Office applications.

The VSTO run time, which is responsible for loading add-ins into their host applications, can display any errors that occur during startup in a message box or write them to a log file. By default, these options are disabled, and they can be enabled through environment variables.

To display any errors in a message box, create an environment variable called VSTO_SUPPRESSDISPLAYALERTS and assign it a value of 0. Setting this environment variable to 1, or deleting it altogether, will prevent the errors from being displayed.

To write the errors to a log file, create an environment variable called VSTO_LOGALERTS and assign it a value of 1. The VSTO run time will create a log file called <manifestname>.manifest.log in the same folder as the application manifest. Setting the environment variable to 0, or deleting it altogether, will stop errors from being logged.

Unregistering an Add-In

When an application-level add-in is compiled in Visual Studio 2010, it automatically registers the add-in to the host application. Visual Studio will not automatically unregister the add-in from your application unless you run Build ➪ Clean Solution. Therefore, you may find your add-in will continue to be loaded every time you launch the application. Rather than reopen the solution in Visual Studio, you can unregister the add-in directly from Office.

To unregister the application you will need to open the Add-Ins window. Under Outlook 2010, select File ⇨ Options ⇨ Add-ins to bring up the window shown in Figure 19-12. For Outlook 2007, select Tools ⇨ Trust Center from the menu and click Add-ins. For all the other Microsoft Office applications, open the File or Office menu and click the Options button on the bottom of the menu screen.

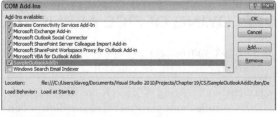

FIGURE 19-12

If it is registered and loaded, your application will be listed under the Active Application Add-ins list. Select COM Add-ins from the drop-down list at the bottom of the window and click the Go button. This brings up the COM Add-Ins window shown in Figure 19-13 that will allow you to remove your add-in from the application.

FIGURE 19-13

You can also disable your add-in by clearing the checkbox next to the add-in name in this window.

Disabled Add-Ins

When developing Office applications, you will inevitably do something that will generate an unhandled exception and cause your add-in to crash. If your add-in happens to crash when it is being loaded, the Office application will disable it. This is called *soft disabling*.

A soft-disabled add-in will not be loaded and will appear in the Trust Center (see Figure 19-12) under the Inactive Application Add-ins list. Visual Studio 2010 will automatically re-enable a soft-disabled add-in when it is recompiled. You can also use the COM Add-Ins window that was displayed earlier in Figure 19-13 to re-enable the add-in by ticking the checkbox next to the add-in name.

An add-in will be flagged to be *hard disabled* when it causes the host application to crash, or when you stop the debugger, while the constructor or the Startup event handler is executing. The next time the Office application is launched, you will be presented with a dialog box similar to the one shown in Figure 19-14. If you select Yes the add-in will be hard disabled.

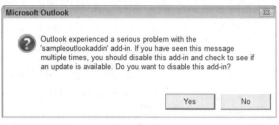

FIGURE 19-14

When an add-in is hard disabled it cannot be re-enabled from Visual Studio. If you attempt to debug a hard-disabled add-in, you will be presented with a warning message that the add-in has been added to the Disabled Items list and will not be loaded.

To remove the application from the Disabled Items list, start the Office application and open the Add-Ins window that was shown earlier in Figure 19-12 (File ⇨ Options ⇨ Add-ins from Outlook 2010, or Tools ⇨ Trust Center from Outlook 2007). Select Disabled Items from the drop-down list at the bottom of the window and click the Go button. This displays the Disabled Items window shown in Figure 19-15. Select your add-in and click Enable to remove it from this list. You must restart the application for this to take effect.

FIGURE 19-15

DEPLOYING OFFICE APPLICATIONS

The two main ways to deploy Office applications are either using a traditional MSI setup project or using the support for ClickOnce deployment that is built into Visual Studio 2010.

In earlier versions of VSTO, configuring code access security was a manual process. Although VSTO hides much of the implementation details from you, in the background it still needs to invoke COM+ code to communicate with Office. Because the Common Language Runtime (CLR) cannot enforce code access security for non-managed code, the CLR requires any applications that invoke COM+ components to have full trust to execute.

Fortunately, the ClickOnce support for Office applications that is built into Visual Studio 2010 automatically deploys with full trust. As with other ClickOnce applications, each time it is invoked it automatically checks for updates.

When an Office application is deployed it must be packaged with the required prerequisites. For Office applications, the following prerequisites are required:

➤ Windows Installer 3.1

➤ .NET Framework 4, .NET Framework 4 Client Profile, or .NET Framework 3.5

➤ Visual Studio 2010 Tools for Office run time

If you are using version 3.5 of the .NET Framework you will also need to package the Microsoft Office primary interop assemblies (PIAs). A PIA is an assembly that contains type definitions of types implemented with COM. The PIAs for Office 2007 and Office 2010 are shipped with Visual Studio Tools for Office, and are automatically included as references when the project is created. In Figure 19-16 (left), you can see a reference to `Microsoft.Office.Interop.Outlook`, which is the PIA for Outlook 2010.

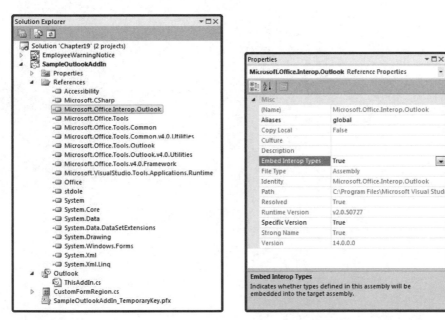

FIGURE 19-16

You do not need to deploy the PIAs with your application if you are using .NET Framework 4 because of a new feature called Type Equivalence. When *Type Equivalence* is enabled, Visual Studio will embed the referenced PIA as a new namespace within the target assembly. CLR then ensures that these types are considered equivalent when the application is executed.

Type Equivalence is enabled for individual references by setting the Embed Interop Types property to True, as shown in Figure 19-16 (right). Rather than include the entire interop assembly, Visual Studio will only embed those portions of the interop assemblies that an application actually uses. This results in smaller and simpler deployment packages.

More information on ClickOnce and MSI setup projects is available in Chapter 48.

SUMMARY

This chapter introduced you to the major features in Visual Studio Tools for Office. It is now very easy to build feature-rich applications using Microsoft Office applications because the development tools are fully integrated into Visual Studio 2010. You can create .NET solutions that customize the appearance of the Office user interface with your own components at both the application level and the document level. This enables you to have unprecedented control over how end users interact with all of the products in the Microsoft Office suite.

PART V
Web Applications

▶ **CHAPTER 20:** ASP.NET Web Forms

▶ **CHAPTER 21:** ASP.NET MVC

▶ **CHAPTER 22:** Silverlight

▶ **CHAPTER 23:** Dynamic Data

▶ **CHAPTER 24:** SharePoint

▶ **CHAPTER 25:** Windows Azure

ASP.NET Web Forms

WHAT'S IN THIS CHAPTER?

➤ The differences between Web Site and Web Application projects

➤ Using the HTML and CSS design tools to control the layout of your web pages

➤ Easily generating highly functional web applications with the server-side web controls

➤ Adding rich client-side interactions to your web pages with JavaScript and ASP.NET AJAX

When Microsoft released the first version of ASP.NET, one of the most talked-about features was the capability to create a full-blown web application in the same way as you would create a Windows application. The abstractions provided by ASP.NET coupled with the rich tooling support in Visual Studio allowed programmers to quickly develop feature-rich applications that ran over the Web in a wholly integrated way.

ASP.NET version 2.0, which was released in 2005, was a major upgrade that included new features such as a provider model for everything from menu navigation to user authentication, more than 50 new server controls, a web portal framework, and built-in web site administration, to name but a few. These enhancements made it even easier to build complex web applications in less time.

Most of the new features in the latest version of ASP.NET and Visual Studio have focused on improving the client-side development experience. These include enhancements to the HTML Designer and CSS editing tools, better IntelliSense support for JavaScript, HTML and JavaScript snippets, and new project templates.

In this chapter you learn how to create ASP.NET Web Applications in Visual Studio 2010, as well as look at many of the features and components that Microsoft has included to make your web development life a little (and in some cases a lot) easier.

WEB APPLICATION VS. WEB SITE PROJECTS

With the release of Visual Studio 2005, a radically new type of project was introduced — the Web Site project. Much of the rationale behind the move to a new project type was based on the premise that web sites, and web developers for that matter, are fundamentally different from other types of applications (and developers), and would therefore benefit from a different model. Although Microsoft did a good job extolling the virtues of this new project type, many developers found it difficult to work with, and clearly expressed their displeasure to Microsoft.

Fortunately, Microsoft listened to this feedback, and a short while later released a free add-on download to Visual Studio that provided support for a new Web Application project type. It was also included with Service Pack 1 of Visual Studio 2005.

The major differences between the two project types are fairly significant. The most fundamental change is that a Web Site project does not contain a Visual Studio project file (.csproj or .vbproj), whereas a Web Application project does. As a result, there is no central file that contains a list of all the files in a Web Site project. Instead, the Visual Studio solution file contains a reference to the root folder of the Web Site project, and the content and layout are directly inferred from its files and subfolders. If you copy a new file into a subfolder of a Web Site project using Windows Explorer, then that file, by definition, belongs to the project. In a Web Application project you must explicitly add all files to the project from within Visual Studio.

The other major difference is in the way the projects are compiled. Web Application projects are compiled in much the same way as any other project under Visual Studio. The code is compiled into a single assembly that is stored in the \bin directory of the web application. As with all other Visual Studio projects, you can control the build through the property pages, name the output assembly, and add pre- and post-build action rules.

On the contrary, in a Web Site project all the classes that aren't code-behind-a-page or user control are compiled into one common assembly. Pages and user controls are then compiled dynamically as needed into a set of separate assemblies.

The big advantage of more granular assemblies is that the entire web site does not need to be rebuilt every time a page is changed. Instead, only those assemblies that have changes (or have a down-level dependency) are recompiled, which can save a significant amount of time, depending on your preferred method of development.

Microsoft has pledged that it will continue to support both the Web Site and Web Application project types in all future versions of Visual Studio.

So which project type should you use? The official position from Microsoft is "it depends," which is certainly a pragmatic, although not particularly useful, position to take. All scenarios are different, and you should always carefully weigh each alternative in the context of your requirements and environment. However, the anecdotal evidence that has emerged from the .NET developer community over the past few years, and the experience of the authors, is that in most cases the Web Application project type is the best choice.

> *Unless you are developing a very large web project with hundreds of pages, it is actually not too difficult to migrate from a Web Site project to a Web Application project and vice versa. So don't get too hung up on this decision. Pick one project type and migrate it later if you run into difficulties.*

CREATING WEB PROJECTS

In addition to the standard ASP.NET Web Application and Web Site projects, Visual Studio 2010 provides support and templates for several specialized web application scenarios. These include web services, WCF services, server control libraries, and reporting applications. However, before we discuss these you should understand how to create the standard project types.

Creating a Web Site Project

As mentioned previously, creating a Web Site project in Visual Studio 2010 is slightly different from creating a regular Windows-type project. With normal Windows applications and services, you pick the type of project, name the solution, and click OK. Each language has its own set of project templates and you have no real options when you create the project. Web Site project development is different because you can create the development project in different locations, from the local file system to a variety of FTP and HTTP locations that are defined in your system setup, including the local Internet Information Services (IIS) server or remote FTP folders.

Because of this major difference in creating these projects, Microsoft has separated out the Web Site project templates into their own command and dialog. Selecting New Web Site from the File ⇨ New submenu displays the New Web Site dialog, where you can choose the type of project template you want to use (see Figure 20-1).

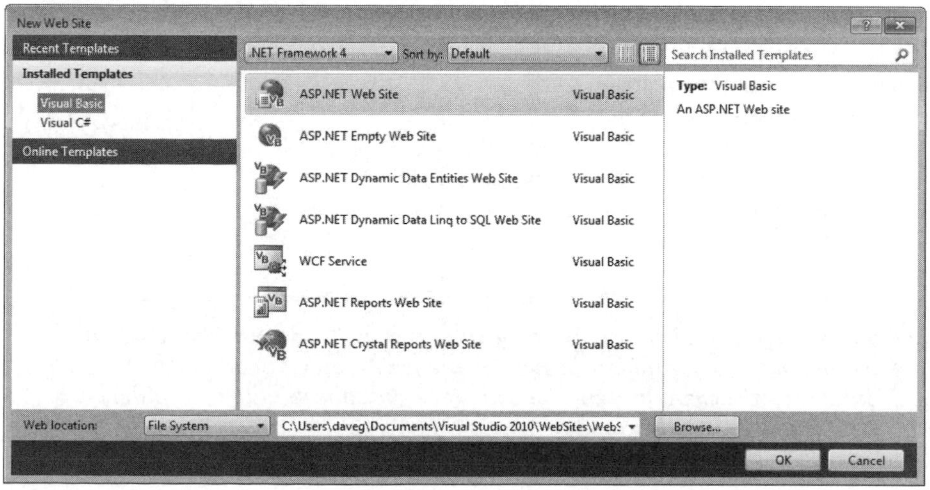

FIGURE 20-1

Most likely, you'll select the ASP.NET Web Site project template. This creates a web site populated with a starter web application that will ensure you your initial application is structured in a logical manner. The template will create a project that demonstrates how to use a master page, menus, the account management controls, CSS, and the jQuery JavaScript library.

In addition to the ASP.NET Web Site project template, there is an Empty Web Site project template that creates nothing more than an empty folder and a reference in a solution file. The remaining templates, which are for the most part variations on the Web Site template, are discussed later in this chapter. Regardless of which type of web project you're creating, the lower section of the dialog enables you to choose where to create the project.

By default, Visual Studio expects you to develop the web site or service locally, using the normal file system. The default location is under the `My Documents/Visual Studio 2010/WebSites` folder for the current user, but you can change this by overtyping the value, selecting an alternative location from the drop-down list, or clicking the Browse button.

The Location drop-down list also contains HTTP and FTP as options. Selecting HTTP or FTP changes the value in the filename textbox to a blank `http://` or `ftp://` prefix ready for you to type in the destination URL. You can either type in a valid location or click the Browse button to change the intended location of the project.

The Choose Location dialog (shown in Figure 20-2) is shown when you click the Browse button and enables you to specify where the project should be stored. Note that this isn't necessarily where the project will be deployed, because you can specify a different destination for that when you're ready to ship, so don't expect that you are specifying the ultimate destination here.

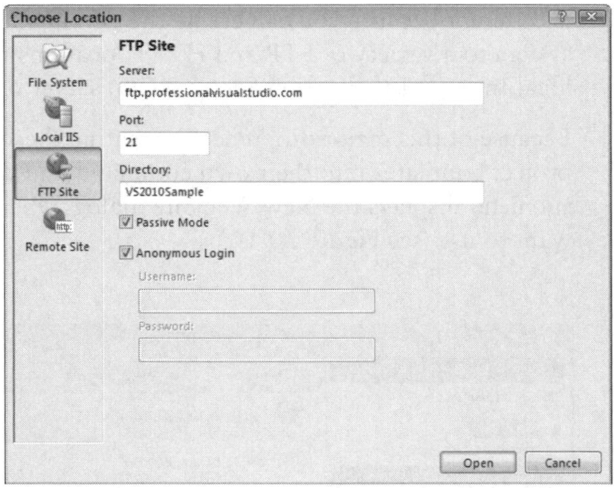

FIGURE 20-2

The File System option enables you to browse through the folder structure known to the system, including the My Network Places folders, and gives you the option to create subfolders where you need them. This is the easiest way of specifying where you want the web project files, and the way that makes the files easiest to locate later.

> Although you can specify where to create the project files, by default the solution file is created in a new folder under the `My Documents/Visual Studio 2010/Projects` folder for the current user. You can move the solution file to a folder of your choice without affecting the projects.

If you are using a local IIS server to debug your Web Site project, you can select the File System option and browse to your wwwroot folder to create the web site. However, a much better option is to use the local IIS location type and drill down to your preferred location under the Default Web Site folders. This interface enables you to browse virtual directory entries that point to web sites that are not physically located within the wwwroot folder structure, but are actually aliases to elsewhere in the file system or network. You can create your application in a new Web Application folder or create a new virtual directory entry in which you browse to the physical file location and specify an alias to appear in the web site list.

The FTP site location type is shown in Figure 20-2, which gives you the option to log in to a remote FTP site anonymously or with a specified user. When you click Open, Visual Studio saves the FTP settings for when you create the project, so be aware that it won't test whether the settings are correct until it attempts to create the project files and save them to the specified destination.

> *You can save your project files to any FTP server to which you have access, even if that FTP site doesn't have .NET installed. However, you will not be able to run the files without .NET, so you will only be able to use such a site as a file store.*

The last location type is a remote site, which enables you to connect to a remote server that has FrontPage extensions installed on it. If you have such a site, you can simply specify where you want the new project to be saved, and Visual Studio 2010 will confirm that it can create the folder through the FrontPage extensions.

Once you've chosen the intended location for your project, clicking OK tells Visual Studio 2010 to create the project files and store them in the desired location. After the web application has finished initializing, Visual Studio opens the `Default.aspx` page and populates the Toolbox with the components available to you for web development.

The Web Site project has only a small subset of the project configuration options available under the property pages of other project types, as shown in Figure 20-3. To access these options, right-click the project and select Property Pages.

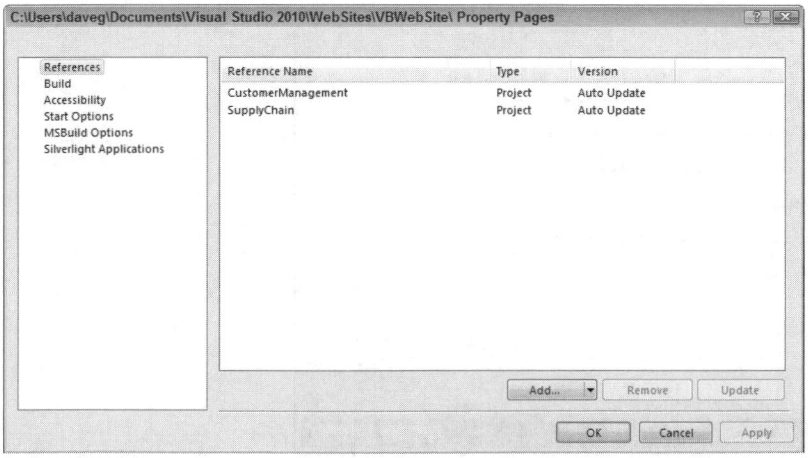

	Reference Name	Type	Version	
References	CustomerManagement	Project	Auto Update	
Build	SupplyChain	Project	Auto Update	
Accessibility				
Start Options				
MSBuild Options				
Silverlight Applications				

C:\Users\daveg\Documents\Visual Studio 2010\WebSites\VBWebSite\ Property Pages

Add... ▾   Remove   Update

OK   Cancel   Apply

FIGURE 20-3

The References property page, shown in Figure 20-3, enables you to define references to external assemblies or web services. If you add a binary reference to an assembly that is not in the Global Assembly Cache (GAC), the assembly is copied to the \bin folder of your web project along with a .refresh file, which is a small text file that contains the path to the original location of the assembly. Every time the web site is built, Visual Studio compares the current version of the assembly in the \bin folder with the version in the original location and, if necessary, updates it. If you have a large number of external references, this can slow the compile time considerably. Therefore, it is recommended that you delete the associated .refresh file for any assembly references that are unlikely to change frequently.

The Build, Accessibility, and Start Options property pages provide some control over how the web site is built and launched during debugging. The accessibility validation options are discussed later in this chapter and the rest of the settings on those property pages are reasonably self-explanatory.

The MSBuild Options property page provides a couple of interesting advanced options for web applications. If you uncheck the Allow This Precompiled Site to be Updatable option, all the content of the .aspx and .ascx pages is compiled into the assembly along with the code-behind. This can be useful if you want to protect the user interface of a web site from being modified. Finally, the Use Fixed Naming and Single Page Assemblies option specifies that each page be compiled into a separate assembly rather than the default, which is an assembly per folder.

The Silverlight Applications property page allows you to add or reference a Silverlight project that can be embedded into the web site. This is discussed in more detail in Chapter 22.

Creating a Web Application Project

Creating a Web Application project with Visual Studio 2010 is much the same as creating any other project type. Select File ➪ New ➪ Project and you are presented with the New Project dialog box, shown in Figure 20-4. By filtering the project types by language and then by the Web category, you are given a selection of templates that is partially similar to those available for Web Site projects.

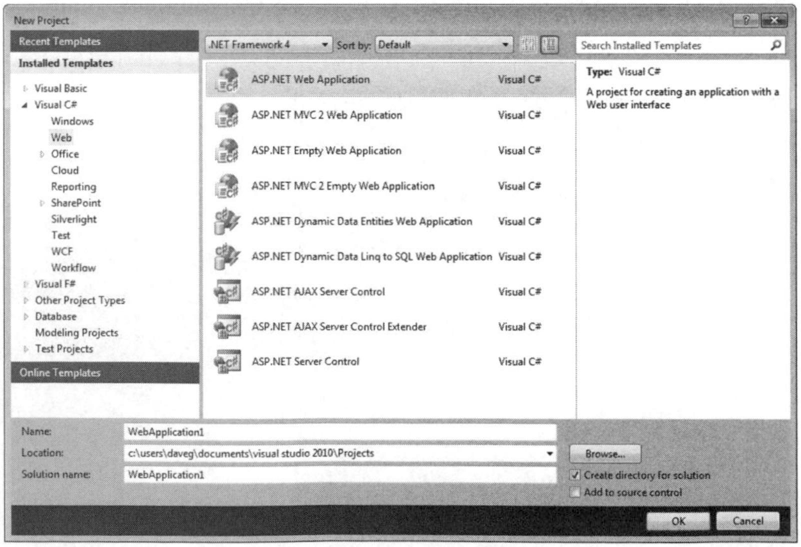

FIGURE 20-4

The notable difference in available project templates is that the reporting template is not available as a Web Application project. However, the Web Application project type includes templates for creating several different types of server controls.

Once you click OK your new Web Application project will be created with a few more items than the Web Site projects. It includes an `AssemblyInfo` file, a References folder, and a My Project item under the Visual Basic or Properties node under C#.

You can view the project properties pages for a Web Application project by double-clicking the Properties or My Project item. The property pages include an additional Web page, as shown in Figure 20-5.

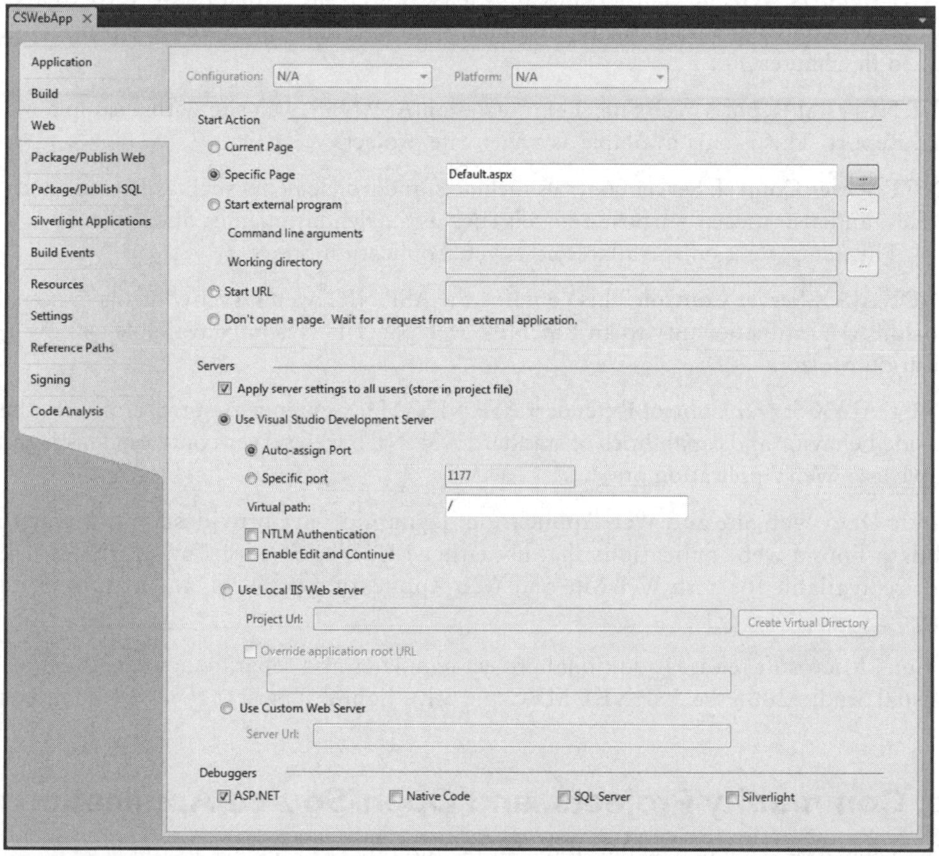

FIGURE 20-5

The options on the Web page are all related to debugging an ASP.NET web application and are covered in Chapter 42, "Debugging Web Applications," and Chapter 43, "Advanced Debugging Techniques."

Other Web Projects

In addition to the standard ASP.NET Web Site and Web Application project templates are templates that provide solutions for more specific scenarios:

➤ **ASP.NET MVC 2 Web Application:** This creates a web application using the Model-View-Controller (MVC) architecture. This is only available as a Web Application project and is discussed in Chapter 21.

➤ **ASP.NET Web Service:** This creates a default Web service called `Sevice.asmx`, which contains a sample Web method. This is only available as a Web Application project when the target is .NET Framework 3.5 or earlier.

➤ **ASP.NET Reports Web Site:** This creates an ASP.NET web site with a report (`.rdlc`) and a ReportViewer control bound to the report. This is only available as a Web Site project and is explained in Chapter 30.

➤ **ASP.NET Crystal Reports Web Site:** This creates an ASP.NET web site with a sample Crystal Report. This is only available as a Web Site project.

➤ **ASP.NET Server Control:** Server controls include standard elements such as buttons and textboxes, and also special-purpose controls such as a calendar, menus, and tree view control. This template is only available as a Web Application project.

➤ **ASP.NET AJAX Server Control:** This contains the ASP.NET web server controls that enable you to add AJAX functionality to an ASP.NET web page. This is only available as a Web Application project.

➤ **ASP.NET AJAX Server Control Extender:** ASP.NET AJAX extender controls improve the client-side behavior and capabilities of standard ASP.NET web server controls. This is only available as a Web Application project.

➤ **Dynamic Data Web Site and Web Application:** Dynamic Data provides a quick way to build data-bound web applications that use either LINQ to SQL or Entity Framework. These are available for both Web Site and Web Application projects, and are covered in Chapter 23.

From time to time, Microsoft releases additional project templates as a separate download. For example, in Visual Studio 2008 the ASP.NET MVC and Silverlight 2.0 project types were released in this manner.

Starter Kits, Community Projects, and Open-Source Applications

One of the best ways to learn any new development technology is to review a sample application. The Microsoft ASP.NET web site contains a list of starter kits and community projects at `http://www.asp.net/community/projects`. These web applications are excellent reference implementations for demonstrating best practices and good use of ASP.NET components and design.

Unfortunately, many of the starter kits have not been maintained and are still running on older versions of the .NET Framework. However, they are still very useful because they demonstrate a wide range of advanced ASP.NET technologies and techniques including multiple CSS themes, master-detail pages, and user management.

The Microsoft ASP.NET site also contains a list of popular open-source projects that have been built on ASP.NET. One of the more comprehensive projects is the DinnerNow.net sample application, available at http://www.dinnernow.net/. Although it is categorized as an open-source application, it is really a reference implementation of many of the latest technologies from Microsoft.

The DinnerNow.net application is a fictitious marketplace where customers can order food from local restaurants for delivery to their homes or offices. In addition to the latest ASP.NET components, it demonstrates the use of IIS7, ASP.NET AJAX Extensions, LINQ, Windows Communication Foundation, Windows Workflow Foundation, Windows Presentation Foundation, Windows Powershell, and the .NET Compact Framework.

Another great place to find a large number of excellent open-source examples is CodePlex, Microsoft's open-source project-hosting web site. Located at http://www.codeplex.com/, CodePlex is a veritable wellspring of the good, the bad, and the ugly in Microsoft open-source applications.

DESIGNING WEB FORMS

One of the strongest features in Visual Studio 2010 for web developers is the visual design of web applications. The HTML Designer allows you to change the positioning, padding, and margins in Design view, using visual layout tools. It also provides a split view that enables you to simultaneously work on the design and markup of a web form. Finally, Visual Studio 2010 supports rich CSS editing tools for designing the layout and styling of web content.

The HTML Designer

The HTML Designer in Visual Studio is one of the main reasons it's so easy to develop ASP.NET applications. Because it understands how to render HTML elements as well as server-side ASP.NET controls, you can simply drag and drop components from the Toolbox onto the HTML Designer surface to quickly build up a web user interface. You can also quickly toggle between viewing the HTML markup and the visual design of a web page or user control.

The modifications made to the View menu of the IDE are a great example of what Visual Studio does to contextually provide you with useful features depending on what you're doing. When you're editing a web page in Design view, additional menu commands become available for adjusting how the design surface appears (see Figure 20-6).

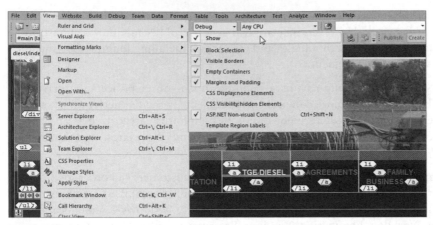

FIGURE 20-6

The three submenus at the top of the View menu — Ruler and Grid, Visual Aids, and Formatting Marks — provide you with a whole bunch of useful tools to assist with the overall layout of controls and HTML elements on a web page.

For example, when the Show option is toggled on the Visual Aids submenu, it draws gray borders around all container controls and HTML tags such as `<table>` and `<div>` so you can easily see where each component resides on the form. It also provides color-coded shading to indicate the margins and padding around HTML elements and server controls. Likewise, on the Formatting Marks submenu you can toggle options to display HTML tag names, line breaks, spaces, and much more. The impact of these options in the HTML Designer can be seen in action in Figure 20-6.

The HTML Designer also supports a split view, shown in Figure 20-7, which shows your HTML markup and visual design at the same time. You activate this view by opening a page in design mode and clicking the Split button on the bottom left of the HTML Designer window.

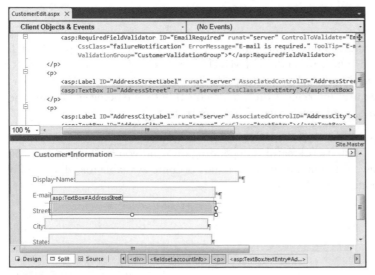

FIGURE 20-7

When you select a control or HTML element on the design surface, the HTML Designer highlights it in the HTML markup. Likewise, if you move the cursor to a new location in the markup, it highlights the corresponding element or control on the design surface.

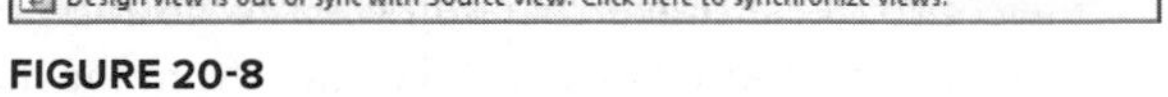

If you make a change to anything on the design surface, that change is immediately reflected in the HTML markup. However, changes to the markup are not always shown in the HTML Designer right away. Instead, you are presented with an information bar at the top of the Design view stating that it is out of sync with the Source view (see Figure 20-8). You can either click the information bar or press Ctrl+Shift+Y to synchronize the views. Saving your changes to the file also synchronizes it.

> 🖉 Design view is out of sync with Source view. Click here to synchronize views.

FIGURE 20-8

> ✐ *If you have a widescreen monitor you can orient the split view vertically to take advantage of your screen resolution. Select Tools ➪ Options and then click the HTML Designer node in the TreeView. You can use a number of settings here to configure how the HTML Designer behaves, including an option called Split Views Vertically.*

Another feature worth pointing out in the HTML Designer is the tag navigator breadcrumb that appears at the bottom of the design window. This feature, which is also in the Silverlight and WPF Designers, displays the hierarchy of the current element or control and all its ancestors. The breadcrumb displays the type of the control or element and the ID or CSS class if it has been defined. If the tag path is too long to fit in the width of the HTML Designer window, the list is truncated and a couple of arrow buttons are displayed so you can scroll through the tag path.

The tag navigator breadcrumb displays the path only from the current element to its top-level parent. It does not list any elements outside that path. If you want to see the hierarchy of all the elements in the current document you should use the Document Outline window, shown in Figure 20-9. Select View ➪ Other Windows ➪ Document Outline to display the window. When you select an element or control in the Document Outline, it is highlighted in the Design and Source views of the HTML Designer. However, selecting an element in the HTML Designer does not highlight it in the Document Outline window.

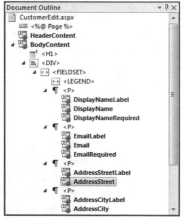

FIGURE 20-9

Positioning Controls and HTML Elements

One of the trickier parts of building web pages is the positioning of HTML elements. Several attributes can be set that control how an element is positioned, including whether it is using a relative or absolute position, the float setting, the z-index, and the padding and margin widths.

Fortunately, you don't need to learn the exact syntax and names of all of these attributes and manually type them into the markup. As with most things in Visual Studio, the IDE is there to assist with the specifics. Begin by selecting the control or element that you want to position in Design view. Then choose Format ⇨ Position from the menu to bring up the Position window shown in Figure 20-10.

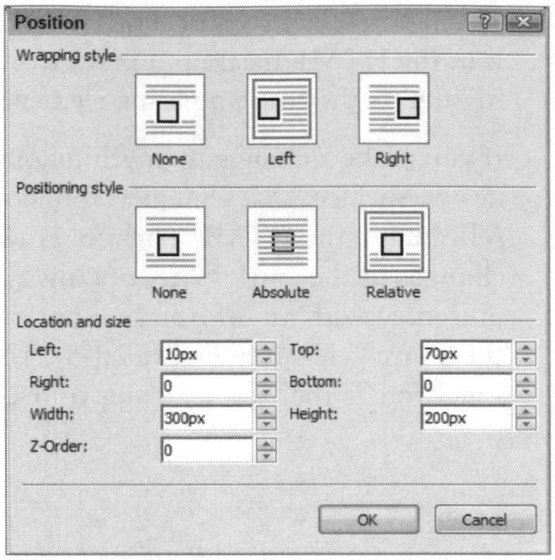

After you click OK, the wrapping and positioning style you have chosen and any values you have entered for location and size are saved to a style attribute on the HTML element.

If an element has relative or absolute positioning, you will be able to reposition it in the Design view. Beware, though, of how you drag elements around the HTML Designer, because you may be doing something you didn't intend! Whenever you select an element or control

FIGURE 20-10

in Design view, a white tag appears at the top-left corner of the element. This displays the type of element, as well as the ID and class name if they are defined.

If you want to reposition an element with relative or absolute positioning, drag it to the new position using the white control tag. If you drag the element using the control itself, it does not modify the HTML positioning, but instead moves it to a new line of code in the source.

Figure 20-11 shows a button that has relative positioning and has been repositioned. The actual location of the element in the normal flow of the document is shown with an empty blue rectangle.

However, this control has been repositioned 45px down and 225px to the right of its original position. The actual control is shown in its new position, and blue horizontal and vertical guidelines are displayed, which indicate that the control is relatively positioned. The guidelines and original position of the element are shown only while it is selected.

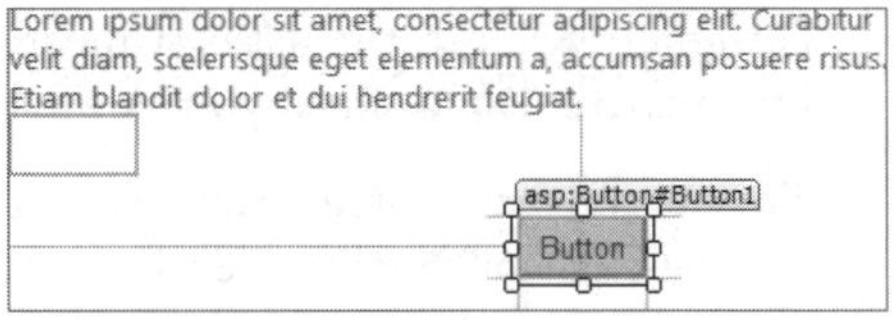

FIGURE 20-11

> If a control uses absolute positioning, the positioning container is highlighted, and two additional guidelines are displayed that extend from the bottom and right of the control to the edge of the container.

The final layout technique discussed here is setting the padding and margins of an HTML element. Many web developers are initially confused about the difference between these display attributes — which is not helped by the fact that different browsers render elements with these attributes differently. Though not all HTML elements display a border, you can *generally* think of padding as the space inside the border, and of margins as the space outside.

If you look very closely within the HTML Designer, you may notice some gray lines extending a short way horizontally and vertically from all four corners of a control. These are only visible when the element is selected in the Design view. These are called *margin handles* and they allow you to set the width of the margins. Hover the mouse over the handle until it changes to a resize cursor, and then drag it to increase or decrease the margin width (see Figure 20-12).

FIGURE 20-12

Finally, within the HTML Designer you can set the padding around an element. If you select an element and then hold down the Shift key, the margin handles become padding handles. Keeping the Shift key pressed, you can drag the handles to increase or decrease the padding width. When you release the Shift key they revert to margin handles again. Figure 20-12 shows how an HTML image element looks in the HTML Designer when the margin and padding widths have been set on all four sides.

At first, this means of setting the margins and padding can feel counterintuitive, because it does not behave very consistently. To increase the top and left margins you must drag the handlers into the element, and to increase the top and left padding you must drag the handlers away. However, just to confuse things, dragging the bottom and right handlers away from the element increases both margin and padding widths.

Once you have your HTML layout and positioning the way you want them, you can follow good practices by using the new CSS tools to move the layout off the page and into an external style sheet. These tools are discussed in the section after next.

Formatting Controls and HTML Elements

In addition to the Position dialog window discussed in the previous section, Visual Studio 2010 provides a toolbar and a range of additional dialog windows that enable you to edit the formatting of controls and HTML elements on a web page.

The Formatting toolbar, shown in Figure 20-13, provides easy access to most of the formatting options. The leftmost drop-down list lets you control how the formatting options are applied and includes options for inline styling or new CSS rules. The next drop-down list includes all the common HTML elements that can be applied to text, including the `<h1>` through `<h6>` headers, `<ul>`, `<ol>`, and `<blockquote>`.

| < Inline Style > | ▾ | ab✓ | 📋 | (None) | ▾ | Helvetica Neue, Lt | ▾ | 0.8em | ▾ | **B** | *I* | U̲ | A | ✐ | ≡▾ | ⋮≡ | ≡ | 📑 | 📑 | ⌄ |

FIGURE 20-13

Most of the other formatting dialog windows are listed as entries on the Format menu. These include windows for setting the foreground and background colors, font, alignment, bullets, and numbering. These dialog windows are similar to those available in any word processor or WYSIWYG interface and their uses are immediately obvious.

The Insert Table dialog window, shown in Figure 20-14, provides a way for you to easily define the layout and design of a new HTML table. Open it by positioning the cursor on the design surface where you want the new table to be placed and selecting Table ⇨ Insert Table.

One final and quite useful feature on the Insert Table and Font dialog windows is under the color selector. In addition to the list of Standard Colors, there is also the Document Colors list, shown in Figure 20-15. This lists all the colors that have been applied in some way or another to the current page, for example as foreground, background, or border colors. This saves you from having to remember custom RGB values for the color scheme that you have chosen to apply to a page.

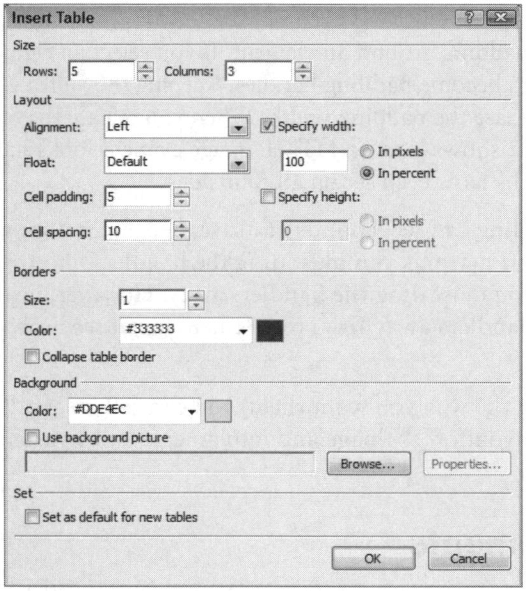

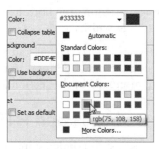

FIGURE 20-14

FIGURE 20-15

CSS Tools

Once upon a time, the HTML within a typical web page consisted of a mishmash of both content and presentation markup. Web pages made liberal use of HTML tags that defined *how* the content should be rendered, such as `<font>`, `<center>`, and `<big>`. Nowadays, designs of this nature are frowned upon — best practice dictates that HTML documents should specify only the content of the web page, wrapped in semantic tags such as `<h1>`, `<ul>`, and `<div>`. Elements requiring special presentation rules should be assigned a `class` attribute, and all style information should be stored in external CSS.

Visual Studio 2010 has several features that provide a rich CSS editing experience in an integrated fashion. As you saw in the previous section, you can do much of the work of designing the layout and styling the content in Design view. This is supplemented by the Manage Styles window, the Apply Styles window, and the CSS Properties window, which are all accessible from the View menu when the HTML Designer is open.

The Manage Styles window lists all the CSS styles that are internal, inline, or in an external CSS file linked through to the current page. The objective of this tool window is to provide you with an overall view of the CSS rules for a particular page, and to enable you to edit and manage those CSS classes.

All the styles are listed in a TreeView with the style sheet forming the top-level nodes, as shown in Figure 20-16. The styles are listed in the order in which they appear in the style sheet file, and you can drag and drop to rearrange the styles, or even move styles from one style sheet to another.

When you hover over a style the tooltip shows the CSS properties in that style, as shown in Figure 20-16. The Options menu drop-down enables you to filter the list of styles to show only those that are applicable to elements on the current page or, if you have an element selected in the HTML Designer, only those that are relevant to the selected element.

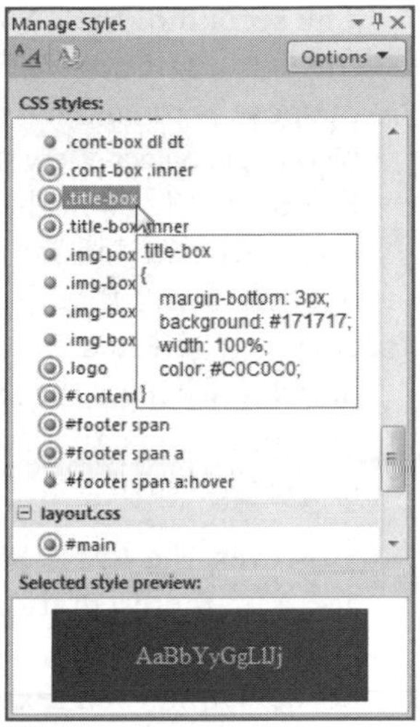

FIGURE 20-16

> The selected style preview, which is at the bottom of the Manage Styles window, is generally not what will actually be displayed in the web browser. This is because the preview does not take into account any CSS inheritance rules that might cause the properties of the style to be overridden.

The Manage Styles window uses a set of icons to provide further visual information about the type of each style. The icons next to the style names have different colors: a red dot indicates an ID-based style, a green dot a class-based style, a blue dot an element-based style, and a yellow dot an inline style.

A circle around a dot indicates that the style is used on the current page. For example, in Figure 20-16 you can quickly see that the title-box CSS class is used on the active web page, whereas the img-box class is not. Finally, the @ symbol is used to indicate an imported external CSS.

When you right-click a style in the Manage Styles window you are given the option to create a new style from scratch, create a new style based on the selected style, or modify the selected style. Any of these three options launch the Modify Style dialog box, shown in Figure 20-17. This dialog provides an intuitive way to define or modify a CSS style. Style properties are grouped into familiar categories, such as Font, Border, and Position, and a useful preview is displayed toward the bottom of the window.

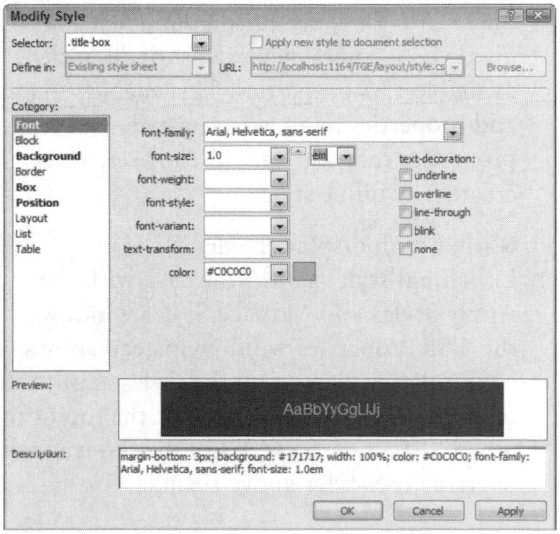

FIGURE 20-17

The second of the CSS windows is the Apply Styles window. Though this has a fair degree of overlap with the Manage Styles window, its purpose is to enable you to easily apply styles to elements on the web page. Select View ⇨ Apply Styles to open the window, shown in Figure 20-18. As in the Manage Styles window, all the available styles are listed in the window and you can filter the list to show only the styles that are applicable to the current page or the currently selected element. The window uses the same icons to indicate whether the style is ID-based, class-based, element-based, or inline. You can also hover over a style to display all the properties in the CSS rule.

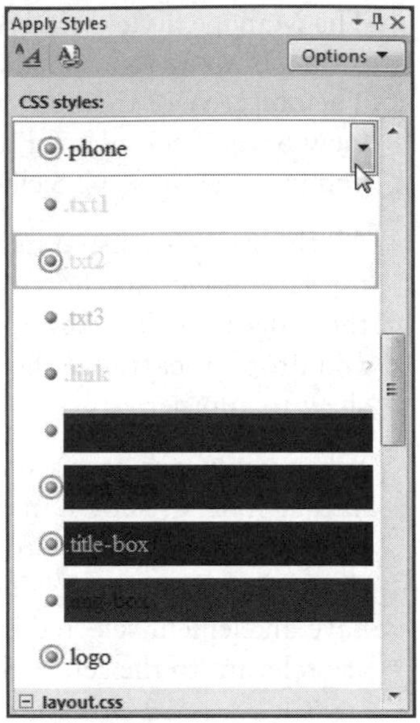

However, the Apply Styles window displays a much more visually accurate representation of the style than the Manage Styles window. It includes the font color and weight, background colors or images, borders, and even text alignment.

When you select an HTML element in the Designer, the styles applied to that element are surrounded by a blue border in the Apply Styles window. This can be seen in Figure 20-18, where the .phone style is active for the selected element. When you hover the mouse over

FIGURE 20-18

any of the styles a drop-down button appears over it, providing access to a context menu. This menu has options for applying that style to the selected element or, if the style has already been applied, for removing it. Simply clicking the style also applies it to the current HTML element.

The third of the new CSS windows in Visual Studio 2010 is the CSS Properties window, shown in Figure 20-19. This displays a property grid with all the styles used by the HTML element that is currently selected in the HTML Designer. In addition, the window gives you a comprehensive list of all of the available CSS properties. This enables you to add properties to an existing style, modify properties that you have already set, and create new inline styles.

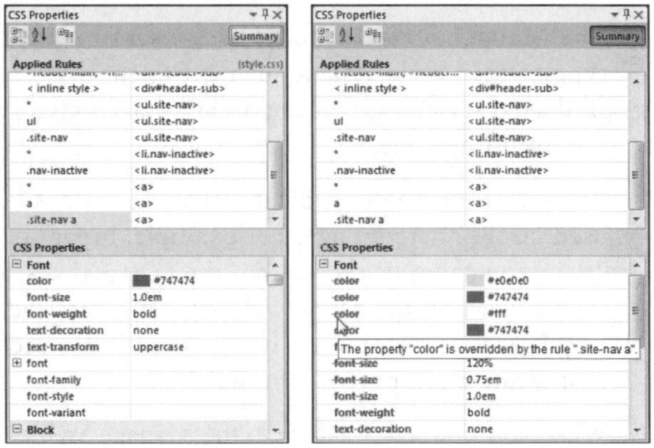

Rather than display the details of an individual style, as was the case with the Apply Styles and Manage Styles windows, the CSS Properties window instead shows

FIGURE 20-19

a cumulative view of all the styles applicable to the current element, taking into account the order of precedence for the styles. At the top of the CSS Properties window is the Applied Rules section, which lists the CSS styles in the order in which they are applied. Styles that are lower on this list override the styles above them.

Selecting a style in the Applied Rules section shows all the CSS properties for that style in the lower property grid. In Figure 20-19 (left) the `.site-nav a` CSS rule has been selected, which has a definition for the `color`, `font-size`, `font-weight`, `text-decoration`, and `text-transform` CSS properties. You can edit these properties or define new ones directly in this property grid.

The CSS Properties window also has a Summary button, which displays all the CSS properties applicable to the current element. This is shown in Figure 20-19 (right). CSS properties that have been overridden are shown with a red strikethrough, and hovering the mouse over the property displays a tooltip with the reason for the override.

Visual Studio 2010 also includes a Target Rule selector on the Formatting toolbar, shown in Figure 20-20, which enables you to control where style changes you made using the formatting toolbars and dialog windows are saved. These include the Formatting toolbar and the dialog windows under the Format menu, such as Font, Paragraph, Bullets and Numbering, Borders and Shading, and Position.

.site-nav a (style.css)
ordered List
Arial, Helvetica, sa
1em
.site-nav a (style.css)
a (style.css)
* (style.css)
(New Auto Class)
(New Inline Style)
Automatic
Apply New Style...

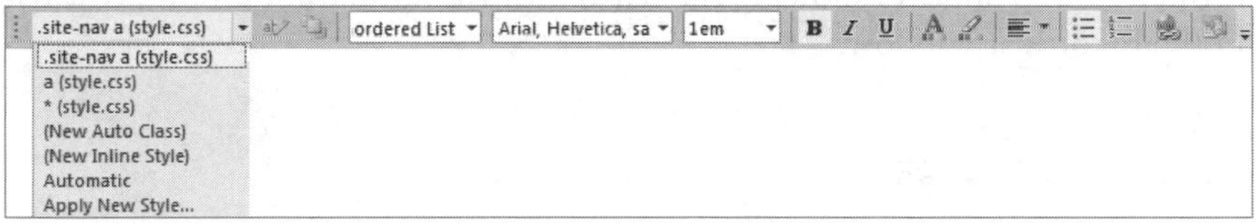

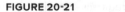

FIGURE 20-20

The Target Rule selector has two modes: Automatic and Manual. In Automatic mode Visual Studio automatically chooses where the new style is applied. In Manual mode you have full control over where the resulting CSS properties are created. Visual Studio 2010 defaults to Manual mode, and any changes to this mode are remembered for the current user.

The Target Rule selector is populated with a list of styles that have already been applied to the currently selected element. Inline styles are displayed with an entry that reads `<inline style>`. Styles defined inline in the current page have `(Current Page)` appended, and styles defined in an external style sheet have the filename appended.

Finally, in Visual Studio 2010 there is now IntelliSense support for CSS in both the CSS editor and HTML editor. The CSS editor, which is opened by default when you double-click a CSS file, provides IntelliSense prompts for all the CSS attributes and valid values, as shown in Figure 20-21. After the CSS styles are defined, the HTML editor subsequently detects and displays a list of valid CSS class names available on the web page when you add the `class` attribute to a HTML element.

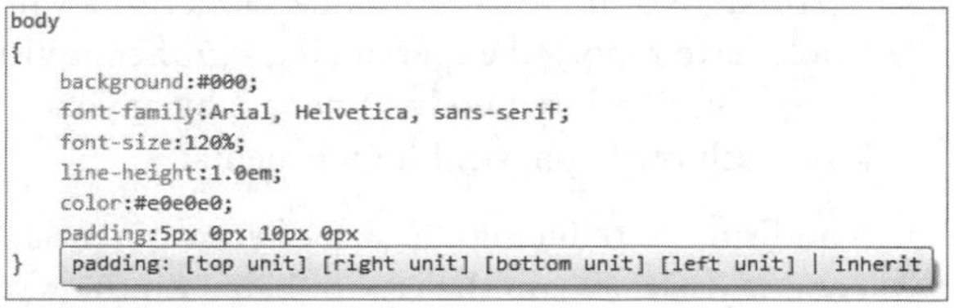

body
{
background:#000;
font-family:Arial, Helvetica, sans-serif;
font-size:120%;
line-height:1.0em;
color:#e0e0e0;
padding:5px 0px 10px 0px
}
padding: [top unit] [right unit] [bottom unit] [left unit] | inherit

FIGURE 20-21

Validation Tools

Web browsers are remarkably good at hiding badly formed HTML code from end users. Invalid syntax that would cause a fatal error if it were in an XML document, such as out-of-order or missing closing tags, will often render fine in your favorite web browser. However, if you view that same malformed HTML code in a different browser, it may look totally different. This is one good reason to ensure that your HTML code is standards-compliant.

The first step to validating your standards compliance is to set the target schema for validation. You can do this from the HTML Source Editing toolbar shown in Figure 20-22.

FIGURE 20-22

Your HTML markup will be validated against the selected schema. Validation works like a background spell-checker, examining the markup as it is entered and adding wavy green lines under the elements or attributes that are not valid based on the current schema. As shown in Figure 20-23, when you hover over an element marked as invalid a tooltip appears showing the reason for the validation failure. A warning entry is also created in the Error List window.

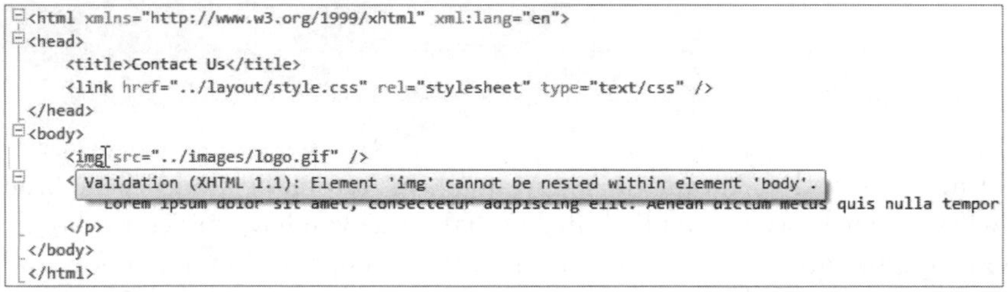

```
<html xmlns="http://www.w3.org/1999/xhtml" xml:lang="en">
<head>
    <title>Contact Us</title>
    <link href="../layout/style.css" rel="stylesheet" type="text/css" />
</head>
<body>
    <img src="../images/logo.gif" />
    < Validation (XHTML 1.1): Element 'img' cannot be nested within element 'body'.
      Lorem ipsum dolor sit amet, consectetur adipiscing elit. Aenean dictum metus quis nulla tempor
    </p>
</body>
</html>
```

FIGURE 20-23

Schema validation will go a long way toward helping your web pages render the same across different browsers. However, it does not ensure that your site is accessible to everyone. There may be a fairly large group of people with some sort of physical impairment who find it extremely difficult to access your site due to the way the HTML markup has been coded.

The World Health Organization has estimated that about 314 million people worldwide are visually impaired (World Health Organization, 2009). In the United States alone, more than 21 million people have reported experiencing significant vision loss (National Center for Health Statistics, 2006). That's a large body of people by anyone's estimate, especially given that it doesn't include those with other physical impairments.

In addition to reducing the size of your potential user base, if you do not take accessibilities into account you may run the risk of being on the wrong side of a lawsuit. A number of countries have introduced legislation that requires web sites and other forms of communication to be accessible to people with disabilities.

Fortunately, Visual Studio 2010 includes an accessibility-validation tool that checks HTML markups for compliance with accessibility guidelines. The Web Content Accessibility Checker, launched from Tools ⇨ Check Accessibility, enables you to check an individual page for compliance against several accessibility guidelines, including Web Content Accessibility Guidelines (WCAG) version 1.0 and the Americans with Disabilities Act Section 508 Guidelines, commonly referred to as Section 508.

Select the guidelines to check for compliance and click Validate to begin. Once the web page has been checked, any issues are displayed as errors or warnings in the Error List window, as shown in Figure 20-24.

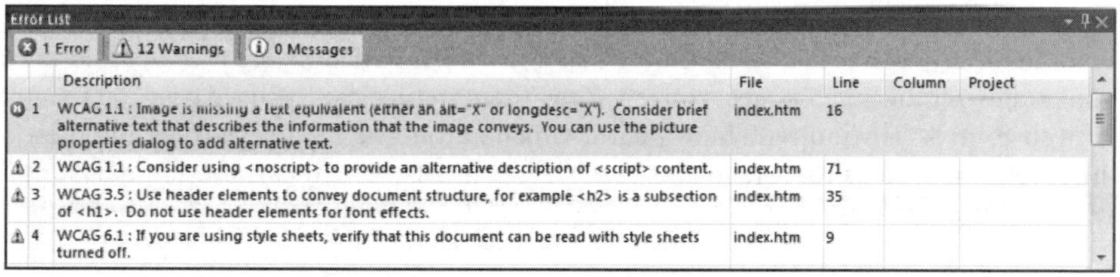

FIGURE 20-24

> *Previous versions of the* ASP.NET *web controls rendered markup that generally did not conform to HTML or accessibility standards. Fortunately, for the most part, this has been fixed in* ASP.NET *version 4.0.*

WEB CONTROLS

When ASP.NET version 1.0 was first released, a whole new way of building web applications was enabled for Microsoft developers. Instead of using HTML elements mingled with a server-side scripting language, as was the case with languages such as classic ASP, JSP, and Perl, ASP.NET introduced the concept of feature-rich controls for web pages that acted in ways similar to their Windows counterparts.

Web controls such as button and textbox components have familiar properties such as `Text`, `Left`, and `Width`, along with just as recognizable methods and events such as `Click` and `TextChanged`. In addition to these, ASP.NET 1.0 provided a limited set of web-specific components, some dealing with data-based information, such as the DataGrid control, and others providing common web tasks, such as an ErrorProvider to give feedback to users about problems with information they entered into a web form.

Subsequent versions of ASP.NET introduced well over 50 web server controls including navigation components, user authentication, web parts, and improved data controls. Third-party vendors have also released numerous server controls and components that provide even more advanced functionality.

Unfortunately, we don't have room in this book to explore all the server controls available to web applications in much detail. In fact, many of the components, such as TextBox, Button, and Checkbox, are simply the web equivalents of the basic user interface controls that you may well be very familiar with already. However, it will be useful to provide an overview of some of the more specialized and functional server controls that reside in the ASP.NET web developers' toolkit.

Navigation Components

ASP.NET includes a simple way to add site-wide navigation to your web applications with the sitemap provider and associated controls. In order to implement sitemap functionality into your projects, you must manually create the site data, by default in a file called Web.sitemap, and keep it up to date as you add or remove web pages from the site. Sitemap files can be used as a data source for a number of web controls, including SiteMapPath, which automatically keeps track of where you are in the site hierarchy, as well as the Menu and TreeView controls, which can present a custom subset of the sitemap information.

Once you have your site hierarchy defined in a Web .sitemap file, the easiest way to use it is to drag and drop a SiteMapPath control onto your web page design surface (see Figure 20-25). This control automatically binds to the default sitemap provider, as specified in the Web.config file, to generate the nodes for display.

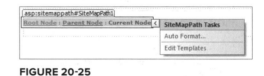

FIGURE 20-25

Though the SiteMapPath control displays only the breadcrumb trail leading directly to the currently viewed page, at times you will want to display a list of pages in your site. The ASP.NET Menu control can be used to do this, and has modes for both horizontal and vertical viewing of the information. Likewise, the TreeView control can be bound to a sitemap and used to render a hierarchical menu of pages in a web site. Figure 20-26 shows a web page with a SiteMapPath, Menu, and TreeView that have each been formatted with one of the built-in styles.

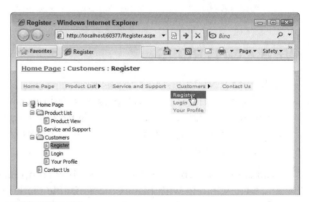

FIGURE 20-26

User Authentication

Perhaps the most significant additions to the web components in ASP.NET version 2.0 were the new user authentication and login components. Using these components, you can quickly and easily create the user-based parts of your web application without having to worry about how to format them or what controls are necessary.

Every web application has a default data source added to its ASP.NET configuration when it is first created. The data source is a SQL Server Express database with a default name pointing to a local file system location. This data source is used as the default location for your user authentication processing, storing information about users and their current settings.

The benefit of having this automated data store generated for each web site is that Visual Studio can have an array of user-bound web components that can automatically save user information without your needing to write any code.

Before you can sign in as a user on a particular site, you first need to create a user account. Initially, you can do that in the administration and configuration of ASP.NET, which is discussed later in this chapter, but you may also want to allow visitors to the site to create their own user accounts. The CreateUserWizard component does just that. It consists of two wizard pages with information about creating an account, and indicates when account creation is successful.

FIGURE 20-27

Once users have created their accounts they need to be able to log in to the site, and the Login control fills this need. Adding the Login component to your page creates a small form containing User Name and Password fields, along with the option to remember the login credentials, and a Log In button (see Figure 20-27).

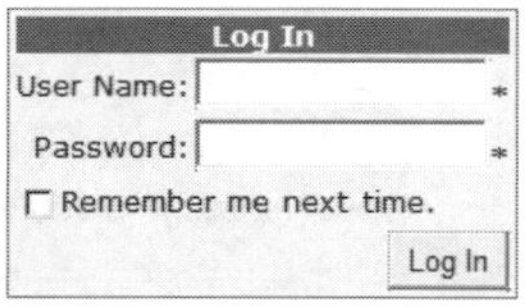

The trick to getting this to work straightaway is to edit your Web.config file and change the authentication to Forms. The default authentication type is Windows, and without the change the web site authenticates you as a Windows user because that's how you are currently logged in. Obviously, some web applications require Windows authentication, but for a simple web site that you plan to deploy on the Internet, this is the only change you need to make in order for the Login control to work properly.

You can also use several controls that will detect whether the user has logged on, and display different information to an authenticated user as opposed to an anonymous user. The LoginStatus control is a simple bi-state component that displays one set of content when the site detects that a user is currently logged in, and a different set of content when there is no logged-in user. The LoginName component is also simple; it just returns the name of the logged-in user.

There are also controls that allow end users to manage their own passwords. The ChangePassword component works in conjunction with the other automatic user-based components to enable users to change their passwords. However, sometimes users forget their passwords, which is where the PasswordRecovery control comes into play. This component, shown in Figure 20-28, has three views: UserName, Question, and Success.

The idea is that users first enter their username so the application can determine and display the security question, and then wait for an answer. If the answer is correct, the component moves to the Success page and sends an e-mail to the registered e-mail address.

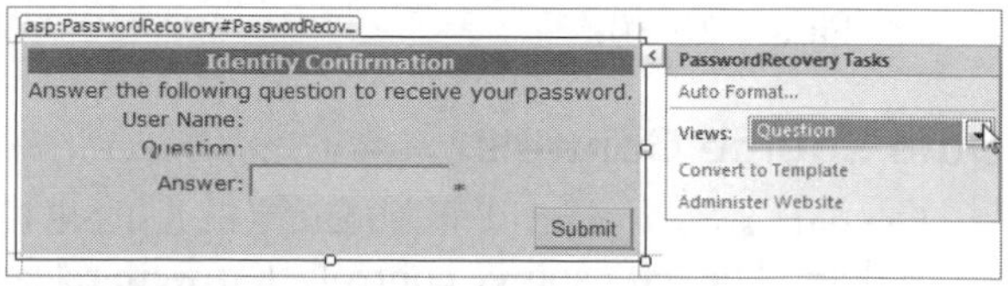

FIGURE 20-28

The last component in the Login group on the Toolbox is the LoginView object. LoginView enables you to create whole sections on your web page that are visible only under certain conditions related to who is (or isn't) logged in. By default, you have two views: the AnonymousTemplate, which is used when no user is logged in, and the LoggedInTemplate, used when any user is logged in. Both templates have an editable area that is initially completely empty.

However, because you can define specialized roles and assign users to these roles, you can also create templates for each role you have defined in your site (see Figure 20-29). The Edit RoleGroups command on the smart-tag Tasks list associated with LoginView displays the typical collection editor and enables you to build role groups that can contain one or multiple roles. When the site detects that the user logs in with a certain role, the display area of the LoginView component is populated with that particular template's content.

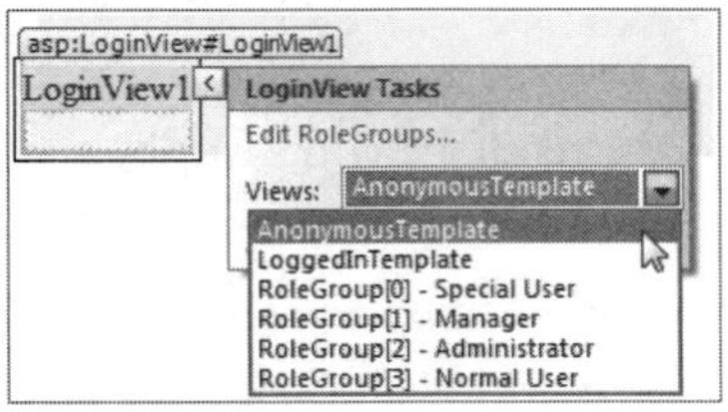

FIGURE 20-29

> See the "ASP.NET Web Site Administration" section later in this chapter for information on how to create and manage roles.

What's amazing about all of these controls is that with only a couple of manual property changes and a few extra entries in the `Web.config` file, you can build a complete user-authentication system into your web application. In fact, as you'll see in the "ASP.NET Web Site Administration" section later in this chapter, you can edit all these settings without needing to edit the `Web.config` file directly. Now that's efficient coding!

Data Components

Data components were introduced to Microsoft web developers with the first version of Visual Studio .NET and have evolved to be even more powerful with each subsequent release of Visual Studio. Each data control has a smart-tag Tasks list associated with it that enables you to edit the individual templates for each part of the displayable area. For example, the DataList has seven templates in all, which can be individually customized (see Figure 20-30).

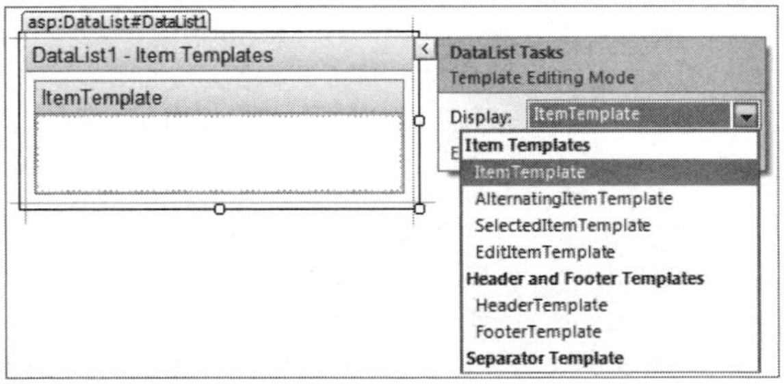

FIGURE 20-30

Data Source Controls

The data source control architecture in ASP.NET provides a really simple way for UI controls to bind to data. The data source controls that were released with ASP.NET 2.0 include SqlDataSource and AccessDataSource for binding to SQL Server or Access databases, ObjectDataSource for binding to a generic class, XmlDataSource for binding to XML files, and SiteMapDataSource for the site navigation tree for the web application.

ASP.NET 3.5 shipped with a LinqDataSource control that enables you to directly bind UI controls to data sources using Language Integrated Query (LINQ). The EntityDataSource control, released with ASP.NET 3.5 SP1, supports data binding using the ADO.NET Entity Framework. These controls provide you with a designer-driven approach that automatically generates most of the code necessary for interacting with the data.

All data source controls operate in a similar way. For the purposes of this discussion, the remainder of this section uses the LinqDataSource as an example.

Before you can use LinqDataSource, you must already have a DataContext class created. The data context wraps a database connection in order to provide object lifecycle services. Chapter 28 explains how to create a new DataContext class in your application.

You can then create a LinqDataSource control instance by dragging it from the Toolbox onto the design surface. To configure the control, launch the Configure Data Source Wizard under the smart tag for the control. Select the data context class, and then choose the data selection details you want to use. Figure 20-31 shows the screen within the Configure Data Source Wizard that enables you to choose the tables and columns to generate a LINQ to SQL query. It is then a simple matter to bind this data source to a UI server control, such as the ListView control, in order to provide read-only access to your data.

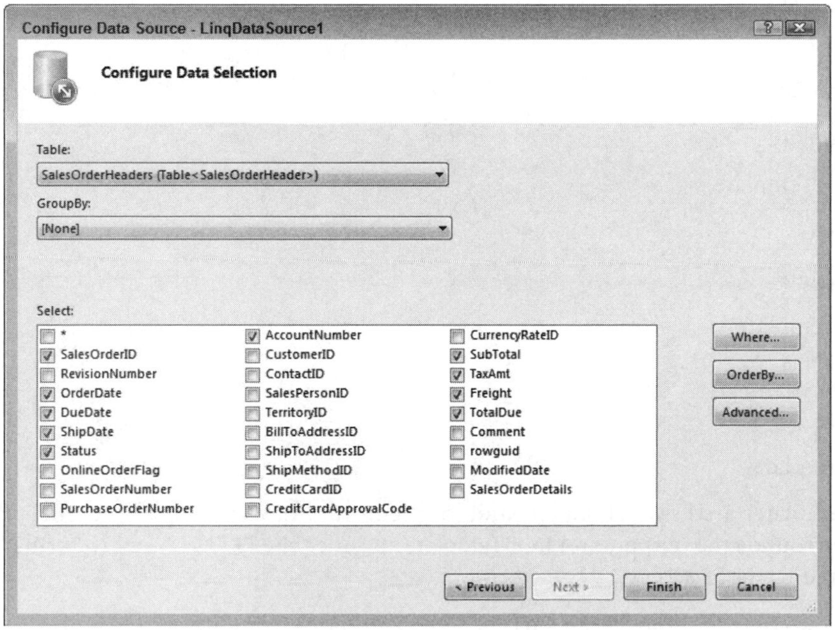

FIGURE 20-31

You can easily take advantage of more advanced data access functionality supported by LINQ, such as allowing inserts, updates, and deletes, by setting the `EnableInsert`, `EnableUpdate`, and `EnableDelete` properties on LinqDataSource to `true`. You can do this either programmatically in code or through the property grid.

You can find more information on LINQ in Chapter 28.

Data View Controls

Once you have specified a data source it is a simple matter to use one of the data view controls to display this data. ASP.NET ships with eight built-in web controls that render data in different ways including Chart, DataList, DetailsView, FormView, GridView, ListView, and Repeater. The Chart control is used to render data graphically using visualizations such as a bar chart or line chart and is discussed in Chapter 30.

A common complaint about the ASP.NET server controls is that developers have very little control over the HTML markup they generate. This is especially true of many of the data view controls such as GridView, which always uses an HTML table to format the data it outputs, even though in some situations an ordered list would be more suitable.

The ListView control provides a good solution to the shortcomings of other data controls in this area. Instead of surrounding the rendered markup with superfluous `<table>` or `<span>` elements, it enables you to specify the exact HTML output that is rendered. The HTML markup is defined in the 11 templates that ListView supports:

➤ AlternatingItemTemplate

➤ EditItemTemplate

➤ EmptyDataTemplate

➤ EmptyItemTemplate

➤ GroupSeparatorTemplate

➤ GroupTemplate

➤ InsertItemTemplate

➤ ItemSeparatorTemplate

➤ ItemTemplate

➤ LayoutTemplate

➤ SelectedItemTemplate

The two most useful templates are LayoutTemplate and ItemTemplate. LayoutTemplate specifies the HTML markup that surrounds the output, and ItemTemplate specifies the HTML used to format each record that is bound to the ListView.

When you add a ListView control to the design surface, you can bind it to a data source and then open the Configure ListView dialog box shown in Figure 20-32, via smart-tag actions. This provides a code-generation tool that automatically produces HTML code based on a small number of predefined layouts and styles.

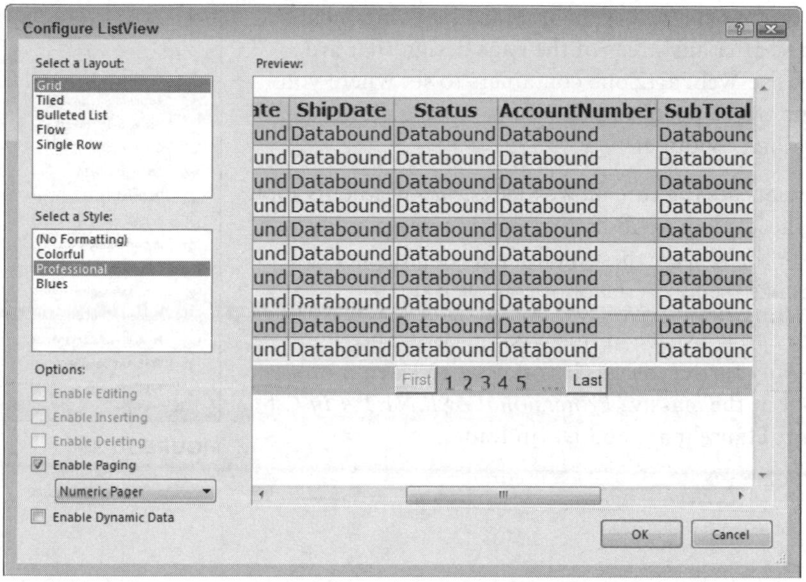

FIGURE 20-32

> *Because you have total control over the HTML markup, the Configure ListView dialog box does not even attempt to parse any existing markup. Instead, if you reopen the window it simply shows the default layout settings.*

Data Helper Controls

The DataPager control is used to split the data that is displayed by a UI control into multiple pages, which is necessary when you're working with very large data sets. It natively supports paging via either a NumericPagerField object, which lets users select a page number, or a NextPreviousPagerField object, which lets users navigate to the next or previous page. As with the ListView control, you can also write your own custom HTML markup for paging by using the TemplatePagerField object.

Finally, the QueryExtender control, new to ASP.NET version 4.0, provides a way to filter data from an EntityDataSource or LinqDataSource in a declarative manner. It is particularly useful for searching scenarios.

Web Parts

Another excellent feature in ASP.NET is the ability to create Web Parts controls and pages. These allow certain pages on your site to be divided into chunks that either you or your users can move around, and show and hide, to create a unique viewing experience. Web Parts for ASP.NET are loosely based on custom web controls but owe their inclusion in ASP.NET to the huge popularity of Web Parts in SharePoint Portals.

With a Web Parts page, you first create a WebPartManager component that sits on the page to look after any areas of the page design that are defined as parts. You then use WebPartZone containers to set where you want customizable content on the page, and then finally place the actual content into the WebPartZone container.

Though these two components are the core of Web Parts, you need only look at the WebParts group in the Toolbox to discover a whole array of additional components (see Figure 20-33). You use these additional components to enable your users to customize their experience of your web site.

Unfortunately, there is not enough space in this book to cover the ASP.NET web controls in any further detail. If you want to learn more, we recommend you check out the massive *Professional ASP.NET 4 in C# and VB* by Bill Evjen, Scott Hanselman, and Devin Rader.

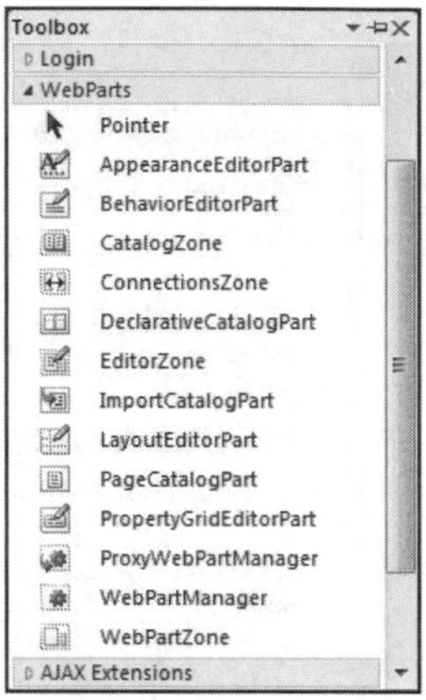

FIGURE 20-33

MASTER PAGES

A very useful feature of web development in Visual Studio is the ability to create *master pages* that define sections that can be customized. This enables you to define a single page design that contains the common elements that should be shared across your entire site, specify areas that can house individualized content, and inherit it for each of the pages on the site.

To add a master page to your Web Application project, use the Add New Item command from the web site menu or from the context menu in the Solution Explorer. This displays the Add New Item dialog, shown in Figure 20-34, which contains a large number of item templates that can be added to a web application. You'll notice that besides Web Forms (.aspx) pages and Web User Controls, you can also add plain HTML files, style sheets, and other web-related file types. To add a master page, select the Master Page template, choose a name for the file, and click Add.

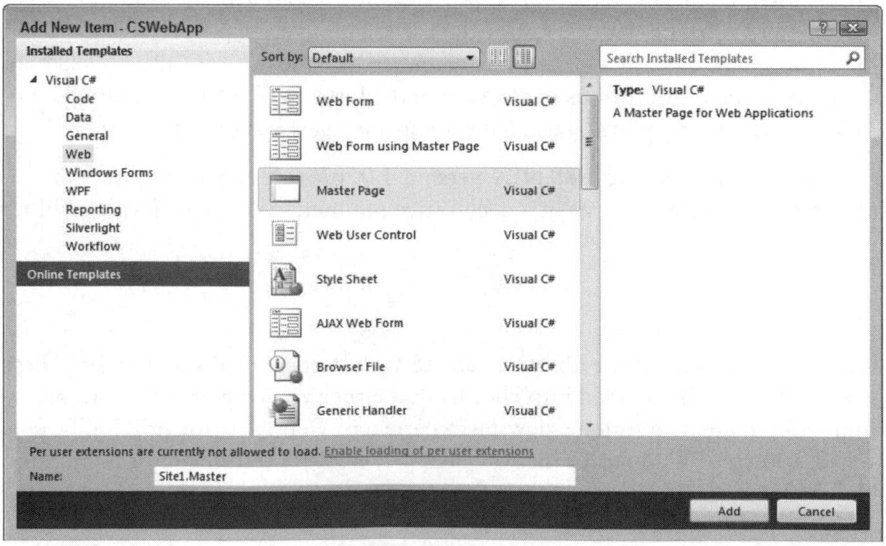

FIGURE 20-34

When a master page is added to your web site, it starts out as a minimal web page template with two empty ContentPlaceHolder components — one in the body of the web page and one in the head. This is where the detail information can be placed for each individual page. You can create the master page as you would any other web form page, complete with ASP.NET and HTML elements, CSSs, and theming.

If your design requires additional areas for detail information, you can either drag a new ContentPlaceHolder control from the Toolbox onto the page, or switch to Source view and add the following tags where you need the additional area:

```
<asp:ContentPlaceHolder Id="aUniqueId" runat="server">
</asp:ContentPlaceHolder>
```

Once the design of your master page has been finalized, you can use it for the detail pages for new web forms in your project.

Unfortunately, the process to add a form that uses a master page is slightly different depending on whether you are using a Web Application or Web Site project. For a Web Application project, rather than adding a new Web Form you should add a new Web Form using Master Page. This displays the Select a Master Page dialog box shown in Figure 20-35. In a Web Site project, the Add New Item window contains a checkbox titled Select Master Page. If you check this, the Select a Master Page dialog is displayed.

FIGURE 20-35

Select the master page to be applied to the detail page and click OK. The new web form page that is added to the project will include one or more Content controls, which map to the ContentPlaceHolder controls on the master page.

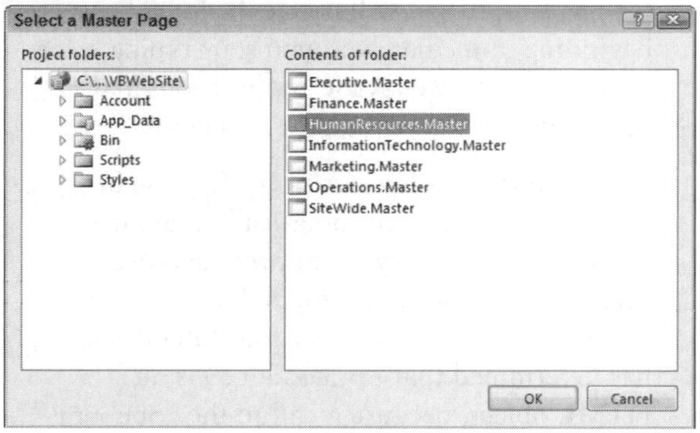

It doesn't take long to see the benefits of master pages and understand why they have become a very popular feature. However, it is even more useful to create nested master pages.

Working with nested master pages is not much different from working with normal master pages. To add one, select Nested Master Page from the Add New Item window. You are prompted to select the parent master page via the Select a Master Page window that was shown in Figure 20-35. When you subsequently add a new content web page, any nested master pages are also shown in the Select a Master Page window.

RICH CLIENT-SIDE DEVELOPMENT

In the past couple of years the software industry has seen a fundamental shift toward emphasizing the importance of the end user experience in application development. Nowhere has that been more apparent than in the development of web applications. Fueled by technologies such as AJAX and an increased appreciation of JavaScript, we are now expected to provide web applications that approach the richness of their desktop equivalents.

Microsoft has certainly recognized this and includes a range of tools and functionality in Visual Studio 2010 that support the creation of rich client-side interactions. There is integrated debugging and IntelliSense support for JavaScript. ASP.NET AJAX is shipped with Visual Studio 2010, and there is support in the IDE for AJAX Control Extenders. These tools make it much easier for you to design, build, and debug client-side code that provides a much richer user experience.

Developing with JavaScript

Writing JavaScript client code has long had a reputation for being difficult, even though the language itself is quite simple. Because JavaScript is a dynamic, loosely typed programming language — very different from the strong typing enforced by Visual Basic and C# — JavaScript's reputation is even worse in some .NET developer circles.

Thus, one of the most useful features of Visual Studio for web developers is IntelliSense support for JavaScript. You will notice the IntelliSense beginning immediately as you start typing, with prompts for native JavaScript functions and keywords such as `var`, `alert`, and `eval`.

Furthermore, the JavaScript IntelliSense in Visual Studio 2010 automatically evaluates and infers variable types to provide more accurate IntelliSense prompts. For example, in Figure 20-36 you can see that IntelliSense has determined that `optSelected` is an HTML object, because a call to the `document` `.getElementByID` function will return that type.

FIGURE 20-36

In addition to displaying IntelliSense within web forms, Visual Studio also supports IntelliSense in external JavaScript files. It also provides IntelliSense help for referenced script files and libraries, such as the Microsoft AJAX library.

Microsoft has extended the XML commenting system in Visual Studio to recognize comments on JavaScript functions. IntelliSense detects these XML code comments and displays the summary, parameters, and return type information for the function.

A couple of limitations could prevent the JavaScript IntelliSense from displaying information in certain circumstances, including:

➤ A syntax or other error in an external referenced script file.

➤ Invoking a browser-specific function or object. Most web browsers provide a set of objects that is proprietary to that browser. You can still use these objects, and in fact many popular JavaScript frameworks do; however, you won't get IntelliSense support for them.

➤ Referencing files that are outside the current project.

Visual Studio constantly monitors changes to files in the project and updates the IntelliSense as they happen. If for some reason you find that Visual Studio isn't displaying the latest information, you can force it to update the IntelliSense by selecting Edit ⇨ IntelliSense ⇨ Update JScript IntelliSense.

One new feature in the latest version of ASP.NET is the `ClientIDMode` property that has been added to web server controls. In previous versions, the value that was generated for the `id` attribute on generated HTML controls made it difficult to reference these controls in JavaScript. The `ClientIDMode` property fixes this by defining two new modes (`Static` and `Predictable`) for generating these ids in a simpler and more predictable way.

The updated JavaScript IntelliSense support, combined with the improved client-side debugging and better control over client IDs, significantly reduces the difficulty of developing JavaScript code with Visual Studio 2010.

Working with ASP.NET AJAX

The ASP.NET AJAX framework provides web developers with a familiar server-control programming approach for building rich client-side AJAX interactions.

ASP.NET AJAX includes both server-side and client-side components. A set of server controls, including the popular UpdatePanel and UpdateProgess controls, can be added to web forms to enable asynchronous partial-page updates without your needing to make changes to any existing code on the page. The client-side Microsoft AJAX Library is a JavaScript framework that can be used in any web application, such as PHP on Apache, and not just ASP.NET or IIS.

The following walkthrough demonstrates how to enhance an existing web page by adding the ASP.NET AJAX UpdatePanel control to perform a partial-page update. In this scenario we have a very simple web form with a DropDownList server control, which has an AutoPostBack to the server enabled. The web form handles the `DropDownList.SelectedIndexChanged` event and saves the value that was selected in the DropDownList to a TextBox server control on the page. The code listing for this page is as follows:

AjaxSampleForm.aspx

```
<%@ Page Language="vb" AutoEventWireup="false"
    CodeBehind="AjaxSampleForm.aspx.vb"
    Inherits="ASPNetWebApp.AjaxSampleForm" %>
<!DOCTYPE html PUBLIC "-//W3C//DTD XHTML 1.0 Transitional//EN"
    "http://www.w3.org/TR/xhtml1/DTD/xhtml1-transitional.dtd">
<html xmlns="http://www.w3.org/1999/xhtml" >
<head runat="server">
    <title>ASP.NET AJAX Sample</title>
</head>
<body>
    <form id="form1" runat="server">
        <div>
        Select an option:
        <asp:DropDownList ID="DropDownList1" runat="server" AutoPostBack="True">
            <asp:ListItem Text="Option 1" Value="Option 1" />
            <asp:ListItem Text="Option 2" Value="Option 2" />
            <asp:ListItem Text="Option 3" Value="Option 3" />
```

```
        </asp:DropDownList>
        <br />
        Option selected:
        <asp:TextBox ID="TextBox1" runat="server"></asp:TextBox>
    </div>
    </form>
</body>
</html>
```

AjaxSampleForm.aspx.vb

```
Public Partial Class AjaxSampleForm
    Inherits System.Web.UI.Page
    Protected Sub DropDownList1_SelectedIndexChanged(ByVal sender As Object, _
                                            ByVal e As EventArgs) _
                                   Handles DropDownList1.SelectedIndexChanged
        System.Threading.Thread.Sleep(2000)
        Me.TextBox1.Text = Me.DropDownList1.SelectedValue
    End Sub
End Class
```

Notice that in the DropDownList1_SelectedIndexChanged method we have added a statement to sleep for two seconds. This will exaggerate the server processing time, thereby making it easier to see the effect of the changes we will make. When you run this page and change an option in the drop-down list, the whole page will be refreshed in the browser.

The first AJAX control that you need to add to your web page is a ScriptManager. This is a nonvisual control that's central to ASP.NET AJAX and is responsible for tasks such as sending script libraries and files to the client and generating any required client proxy classes. You can have only one ScriptManager control per ASP.NET web page, which can pose a problem when you're using master pages and user controls. In that case, you should add the ScriptManager to the topmost parent page, and a ScriptManagerProxy control to all child pages.

After you add the ScriptManager control, you can add any other ASP.NET AJAX controls. In this case, add an UpdatePanel control to the web page, as shown in the following listing. Notice that TextBox1 is now contained within the new UpdatePanel control.

```
<%@ Page Language="vb" AutoEventWireup="false"
    CodeBehind="AjaxSampleForm.aspx.vb"
    Inherits="ASPNetWebApp.AjaxSampleForm" %>
<!DOCTYPE html PUBLIC "-//W3C//DTD XHTML 1.0 Transitional//EN"
    "http://www.w3.org/TR/xhtml1/DTD/xhtml1-transitional.dtd">
<html xmlns="http://www.w3.org/1999/xhtml" >
<head runat="server">
    <title>ASP.NET AJAX Sample</title>
</head>
<body>
    <form id="form1" runat="server">
    <asp:ScriptManager ID="ScriptManager1" runat="server"></asp:ScriptManager>
    <div>
        Select an option:
        <asp:DropDownList ID="DropDownList1" runat="server" AutoPostBack="True">
            <asp:ListItem Text="Option 1" Value="Option 1" />
            <asp:ListItem Text="Option 2" Value="Option 2" />
```

```
                <asp:ListItem Text="Option 3" Value="Option 3" />
            </asp:DropDownList>
            <br />
            Option selected:
            <asp:UpdatePanel ID="UpdatePanel1" runat="server">
                <ContentTemplate>
                    <asp:TextBox ID="TextBox1" runat="server"></asp:TextBox>
                </ContentTemplate>
                <Triggers>
                    <asp:AsyncPostBackTrigger ControlID="DropDownList1"
                                              EventName="SelectedIndexChanged" />
                </Triggers>
            </asp:UpdatePanel>
        </div>
        </form>
    </body>
</html>
```

The web page now uses AJAX to provide a partial-page update. When you now run this page and change an option in the drop-down list, the whole page is no longer refreshed. Instead, just the text within the textbox is updated. In fact, if you run this page you will notice that AJAX is too good at just updating part of the page. There is no feedback and if you didn't know any better you would think that nothing is happening. This is where the UpdateProgress control becomes useful. You can place an UpdateProgress control on the page, and when an AJAX request is invoked the HTML within the ProgressTemplate section of the control is rendered. The following listing shows an example of an UpdateProgress control for our web form:

```
<asp:UpdateProgress ID="UpdateProgress1" runat="server">
    <ProgressTemplate>
        Loading.
    </ProgressTemplate>
</asp:UpdateProgress>
```

The final server control in ASP.NET AJAX that hasn't been mentioned is the Timer control, which enables you to perform asynchronous or synchronous client-side postbacks at a defined interval. This can be useful for scenarios such as checking with the server to see if a value has changed.

Once you have added some basic AJAX functionality to your web application, you can further improve the client user experience by adding one or more elements from the AJAX Control Toolkit, which is discussed in the following section.

Using AJAX Control Extenders

AJAX Control Extenders provide a way to add AJAX functionality to a standard ASP.NET server control. The best-known set of control extenders is the AJAX Control Toolkit, a free open-source library of client behaviors that includes almost 40 control extenders. These either provide enhancements to existing ASP.NET web controls or provide completely new rich-client UI elements. Figure 20-37 shows a Calendar Extender that has been attached to a TextBox control.

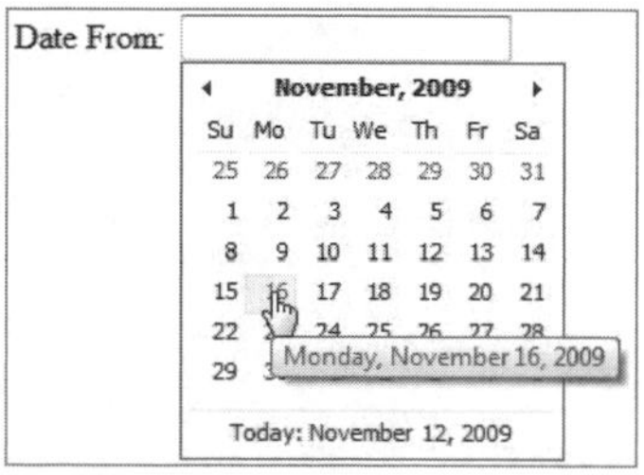

FIGURE 20-37

The ASP.NET AJAX Control Toolkit is available for download via a link from `http://ajaxcontroltoolkit.codeplex.com`. The binary version of the download includes an assembly called `AjaxControlToolkit.dll`. Copy this to a directory where you won't accidentally delete it.

To add the controls to the Visual Studio Control Toolbox, you should first create a new tab to house them. Right-click anywhere in the Toolbox window, choose Add Tab, and then rename the new tab something meaningful, such as AJAX Control Toolkit. Next, right-click in the new tab and select Choose Items. Click the Browse button and locate the `AjaxControlToolkit.dll` to add the AJAX controls to the list of available .NET Framework Components. Click OK and the tab will be populated with all the controls in the AJAX Control Toolkit.

Visual Studio 2010 provides designer support for any AJAX Control Extenders, including the AJAX Control Toolkit. Once you have added the controls to the Toolbox, Visual Studio adds an entry to the smart-tag Tasks list of any web controls with extenders, as shown in Figure 20-38.

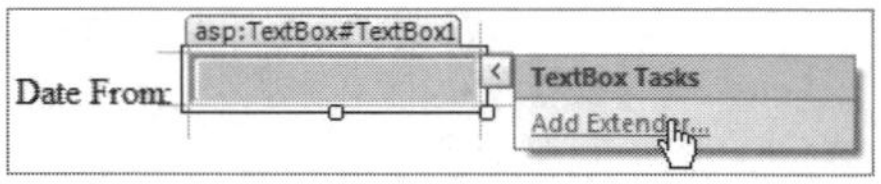

FIGURE 20-38

When you select the Add Extender task it launches the Extender Wizard, shown in Figure 20-39. Choose an extender from the list and click OK to add it to your web form. In most cases, the Extender Wizard will also automatically add a reference to the AJAX Control Toolkit library. However, if it does not you can manually add a binary reference to the `AjaxControlToolkit.dll` assembly.

> *Because the Extender Controls are built on top of ASP.NET AJAX, you will need to ensure that a ScriptManager control is on your web form.*

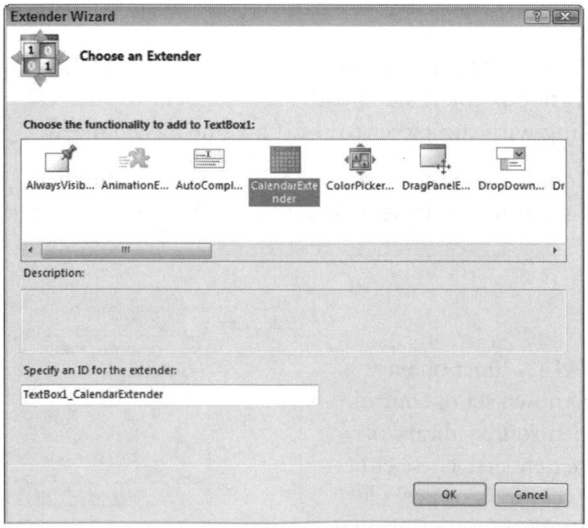

FIGURE 20-39

As shown in Figure 20-40, Visual Studio 2010 includes all the properties for the control extender in the property grid, under the control to which the extender is attached.

Because the AJAX Control Toolkit is open source, you can customize or further enhance any of the control extenders it includes. Visual Studio 2010 also ships with C# and Visual Basic project templates to create your own AJAX Control Extenders and ASP.NET AJAX Controls. This makes it easy to build rich web applications with UI functionality that can be easily reused across your web pages and projects.

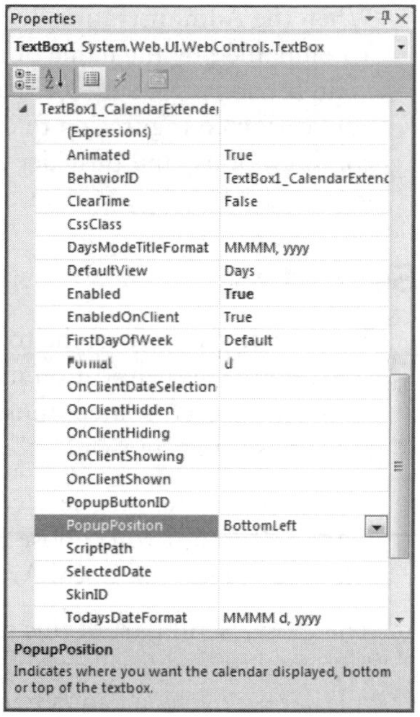

FIGURE 20-40

ASP.NET WEB SITE ADMINISTRATION

Although running your web application with default behavior will work in most situations, sometimes you'll need to manage the application settings beyond simply setting the properties of components and page items. The Web Site Administration Tool provides you with a web-based configuration application that enables you to define various security-related settings, such as users and roles, as well as application-wide settings that can come in handy, such as a default error page, and global SMTP e-mail settings that are used by various components, such as the PasswordRecovery control.

To start the Administration Tool, use the Project ➪ ASP.NET Configuration menu command for Web Application projects, or Website ➪ ASP.NET Configuration for Web Site projects. When the tool is launched, Visual Studio 2010 instantiates a temporary web server on a unique port and opens a web browser to the Administration Tool home page for the application you're currently administering.

You can determine whether the web server is active by looking in the notification area of your taskbar and finding the development server icon connected to the port that Visual Studio 2010 allocated when it was started up. You can stop an active web server by right-clicking its icon in the notification area and selecting Show Details. When the server information is displayed (see Figure 20-41), click the Stop button to stop the specific instance of the development web server.

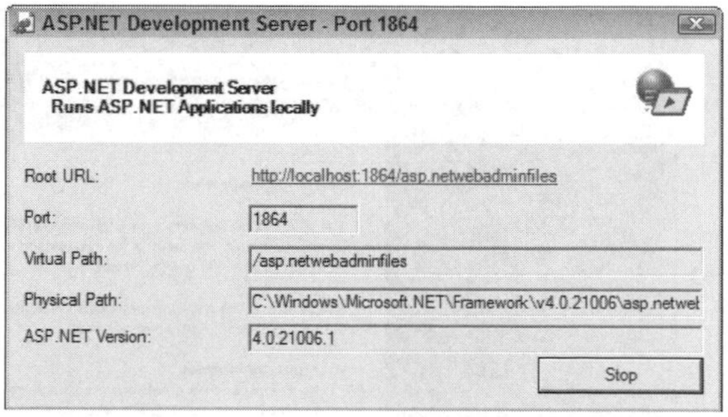

FIGURE 20-41

 Note that stopping an active web server won't affect any other development servers that are currently running.

When the Administration Tool is displayed in your web browser, it shows the application name, accompanied by the name of the current Windows-based authenticated user. The tool has three main sections: security for the creation and maintenance of users, roles, and authentication; application configuration to control application-specific key-value pairs, SMTP settings, and debug configurations; and provider configuration to control the way the user administration data is stored for the site.

Security

The security section of the tool provides you with a summary of the users and roles defined in the site, and the authentication mode. You can change individual settings from this summary page by clicking their associated links, or use the Security Setup Wizard to step through each section of the security settings in turn.

The authentication mode is controlled by the access method page (shown in the wizard in Figure 20-42). If you choose From the Internet, the tool sets the authentication mode to Forms, whereas the From a Local Area Network option results in an authentication mode of Windows.

The most useful part of this tool is the ability it gives you to add and edit roles. In the wizard you'll first need to enable role management by checking the Enable Roles for this Web Site option. Once roles are active you can define them either through the wizard or from the summary page. Each role is defined by a single string value, and it's up to you to control how that role will be used in your web application (with the exception of access rules, which are discussed in a moment).

The next step in the wizard is to create user accounts. The information on this page is a replication of the CreateUserAccount component, and enables you to create an initial user who can serve as administrator for your web site.

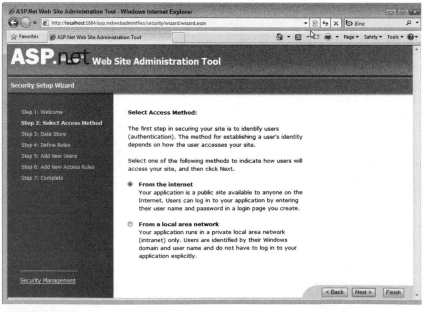

FIGURE 20-42

The access rules page (shown in Figure 20-43) enables you to restrict access to certain parts of your site to a specific role or user, or to grant access only when any user is logged in. As Figure 20-43 shows, by default there is a single rule (which is actually implicitly defined and inherited from the server) that defines full access to the entire site for all users.

Web site processing will look at the rules in the order in which they are defined, stopping at the first rule that applies to the particular context. For example, if you define first a rule that allows access to the Admin folder for anyone belonging to the Administrator's role, and then define a subsequent rule that denies access to the same folder for all users, it will effectively block access to the Admin folder for all users who do not belong to the Administrator's role.

Once you have users, roles, and rules defined in your site, you can then start applying the access by clicking the Manage Users link from the summary security page. This presents you with a list of all users defined in the system. Click the Edit User or Edit Roles link to specify the roles to which each user belongs.

This information can be used to customize the content in your web pages with the LoginView component discussed earlier in this chapter.

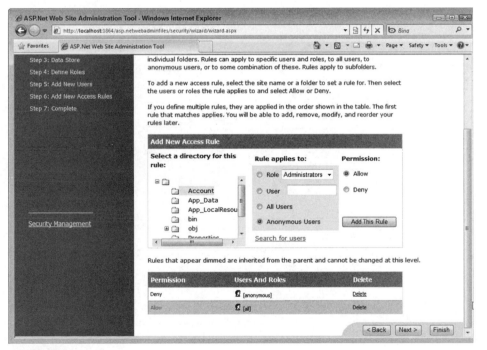

FIGURE 20-43

Application Settings

The application section of the Web Site Administration Tool enables you to define and edit application-specific settings in the form of key-value pairs, as well as to configure SMTP e-mail settings, including the default SMTP mail server and sender's e-mail address.

You can also specify what level of debugging you want to perform on the application, and customize the tracing information being kept as you run the application.

ASP.NET Configuration in IIS

If you have already deployed an ASP.NET application to a production server, you can edit the configuration settings directly within Internet Information Services (IIS), located in the Administrative Tools section of the Control Panel. When ASP.NET is installed on a machine, you'll find that each web site (including virtual directories) will have a set of configuration tools in IIS under the property pages, as shown in Figure 20-44.

The tools included in IIS enable you to manage all the settings you saw earlier, including the creation and management of users, roles, application settings, and SMTP settings. You are also given access to more powerful administration tools that enable you to configure advanced settings such as the .NET compilation behavior, .NET trust level, and session state configuration. These tools enable you to maintain a web application running on any IIS server without needing to resort to editing the `Web.config` configuration file.

FIGURE 20-44

SUMMARY

In this chapter you learned how to create ASP.NET applications using the Web Site and Web Application projects. The improvements to the HTML Designer and the new CSS tools in Visual Studio 2010 provide you with great power over the layout and visual design of web pages. The vast number of web controls included in ASP.NET enables you to quickly put together highly functional web pages. Through the judicious use of JavaScript, ASP.NET AJAX, and control extenders in the AJAX Control Toolkit, you can provide a very rich user experience in your web applications.

Of course, there's much more to web development than we covered here. Chapters 21 and 22 continue the discussion on building rich web applications by exploring the latest web technologies from Microsoft: ASP.NET MVC and Silverlight. Chapter 42 provides detailed information about the tools and techniques available for effective debugging of web applications. Finally, Chapter 49 walks you through the deployment options for web applications. If you are looking for more information after this, you should check out *Professional ASP.NET 4 in C# and VB* by Bill Evjen, Scott Hanselman, and Devin Rader. Weighing in at over 1,600 pages, this is the best and most comprehensive resource available to web developers who are building applications on the latest version of ASP.NET.

ASP.NET MVC

WHAT'S IN THIS CHAPTER?

➤ Understanding the Model-View-Controller design pattern

➤ Developing ASP.NET MVC applications

➤ Designing URL routes

➤ Validating user input

➤ Customizing the ASP.NET MVC View templates

➤ Integrating with jQuery

When Microsoft introduced the first version of the .NET Framework in 2002 it added a new abstraction for the development of web applications called ASP.NET Web Forms. Where traditional Active Server Pages (ASP) had up until this point operated like simple templates containing a mix of HTML markup and server-side code, Web Forms was designed to bring the web application development experience closer to the desktop application programming model. This model involves dragging components from a toolbox onto a design surface and then configuring those components by setting property values and writing code to handle specific events.

Although Web Forms has been and continues to be very successful, it is not without criticism. Without strong discipline it is easy for business logic and data-access concerns to creep into the user interface, making it hard to test without sitting in front of a browser. It heavily abstracts away the stateless request/response nature of the Web, which can make it frustrating to debug. It relies heavily on controls rendering their own HTML markup, which can make it difficult to control the final output of each page.

In 2004, the release of a simple open source framework for building web applications called Ruby on Rails heralded a renewed interest in an architectural pattern called Model-View-Controller (MVC). The MVC pattern divides the parts of a user interface into three classifications with very well-defined roles. This makes applications easier to test, evolve, and maintain.

Microsoft first announced the ASP.NET MVC framework at an ALT.NET conference in late 2007. This framework allows you to build applications based on the MVC architecture while taking advantage of the .NET framework's extensive set of libraries and language options. ASP.NET MVC has been developed in a very open manner with many of its features shaped by community feedback. In fact, in April 2009 the entire source code for the framework was release as open source under the Ms-PL license.

> *Microsoft has been very careful to state that ASP.NET MVC is not a replacement for Web Forms. It is simply an alternative way of building web applications that some people will find preferable. Microsoft has made it very clear that it will continue to support both ASP.NET Web Forms and ASP.NET MVC into the future.*

MODEL VIEW CONTROLLER

If you have never heard of it before you might be surprised to learn that this "new" Model-View-Controller architectural pattern was first described in 1979 by Trygve Reenskaug, a researcher working on an implementation of SmallTalk.

In the MVC architecture, applications are separated into the following components:

➤ **Model:** The model consists of classes that implement domain-specific logic for the application. Although the MVC architecture does not concern itself with the specifics of the data access layer, it is understood that the model should encapsulate any data access code. Generally, the model will call separate data access classes responsible for retrieving and storing information in a database.

➤ **View:** The views are classes that take the model and render it into a format where the user can interact with it.

➤ **Controller:** The controller is responsible for bringing everything together. A controller processes and responds to events, such as a user clicking a button. The controller maps these events onto the model and invokes the appropriate view.

These descriptions aren't really helpful until you understand how they interact together. The request life cycle of an ASP.NET MVC application normally consists of the following:

1. The user performs an action that triggers an event, such as entering a URL or clicking a button. This generates a request to the controller.

2. The controller receives the request and invokes the relevant action on the model. Often this will cause a change in the model's state, although not always.

3. The controller retrieves any necessary data from the model and invokes the appropriate view, passing it the data from the model.

4. The view renders the data and sends it back to the user.

The most important thing to note here is that both the view and controller depend on the model. However, the model has no dependencies, which is one of the key benefits of the architecture. This separation is what provides better testability and makes it easier to manage complexity.

> *Different MVC framework implementations have minor variations in the preceding life cycle. For example, in some cases the view will query the model for the current state, instead of receiving it from the controller.*

Now that you understand the Model-View-Controller architectural pattern, you can begin to apply this newfound knowledge to building your first ASP.NET MVC application.

GETTING STARTED WITH ASP.NET MVC

This section details the creation of a new ASP .NET MVC application and describes some of the standard components. To create a new MVC application, go to File ⇨ New Project and select ASP.NET MVC 2.0 Application from the Web section. Once you give a name to the project and select OK, Visual Studio asks if it should create a unit test project for the application as shown in Figure 21-1. Although this is not required it is highly recommended because improved testability is one of the key advantages of using the MVC framework. You can always add a test project later on if you want.

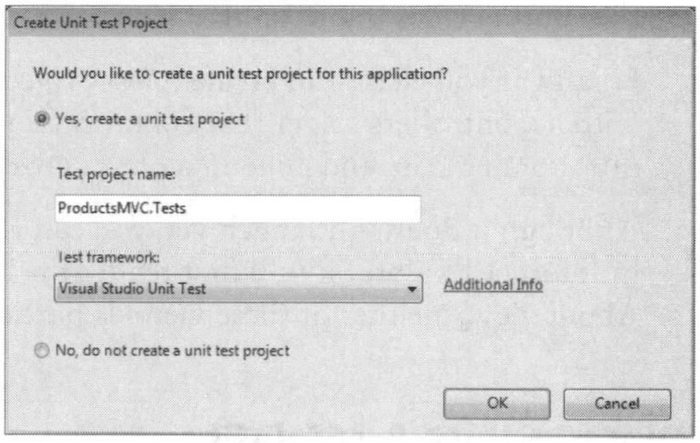

FIGURE 21-1

> *Visual Studio 2010 is able to create test projects for MVC applications using a number of unit testing frameworks. The default choice (shown in Figure 21-1) is to use the built-in unit testing tools in Visual Studio. If you prefer to use a different unit testing technology, see the vendor for instructions on how to add to this list.*

When an ASP.NET MVC application is first created, it generates a number of files and folders. In actual fact, the MVC application that is generated from the project template is a complete application that can be run immediately.

The folder structure that is automatically generated by Visual Studio is shown in Figure 21-2 and includes the following folders:

➤ **Content:** A location to store static content files such as CSS files and images.

➤ **Controllers:** Contains the Controller files. Two sample controllers called `HomeController` and `AccountController` are created by the project template.

➤ **Models:** Contains model files. This is also a good place to store any data access classes that are encapsulated by the model. The MVC project template does not create an example model.

➤ **Scripts:** Contains JavaScript files. By default, this folder contains script files for JQuery and Microsoft AJAX along with some helper scripts to integrate with MVC.

➤ **Views:** Contains the view files. The MVC project template creates a number of folders and files in the Views folder. The Home subfolder contains two example view files that are invoked by the `HomeController`. The Shared subfolder contains a master page that is used by these views.

Visual Studio also creates a `Default.aspx` file, which is simply a placeholder that is needed to ensure IIS loads the MVC application correctly. There is also a `Global.asax` file, which is used to configure the routing rules (more on that later).

Finally, if you elected to create a test project this will be created with a Controllers folder that contains two unit test stubs for the `HomeController` and `AccountController`, respectively.

FIGURE 21-2

Although it doesn't do much yet, you can run the MVC application by pressing F5. When it opens in Internet Explorer it will first render the Index view with a link that allows you to navigate to the About view. Neither of these views is particularly interesting, because they just render static content.

CHOOSING A MODEL

In the previous section it was noted that the MVC project template does not create a sample model for you. In fact, the application is capable of running without a model altogether. While in practice your applications are likely to have a full model, MVC provides no guidance as to which technology you should use. This gives you a great deal of flexibility.

The model part of your application is an abstraction of the business capabilities that the application provides. If you are building an application to process orders or organize a leave schedule, your model should express these concepts. This is not always easy. It is frequently tempting to allow some of these details to creep in the View-controller part of your application.

The examples in this chapter use a simple LINQ to SQL model based on a subset of the AdventureWorksDB sample database as shown in Figure 21-3. You can download this sample database from `http://msftdbprodsamples.codeplex.com/`.

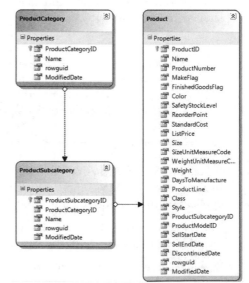

FIGURE 21-3

The next section explains how you can build your own controller, followed by some interesting views that render a dynamic user interface.

CONTROLLERS AND ACTION METHODS

A controller is a class that responds to some user action. Usually, this response involves updating the model in some way and then organizing for a view to present content back to the user. Each controller is capable of listening for and responding to a number of user actions. Each of these is represented in the code by a normal method referred to as an action method.

Begin by right-clicking the Controllers folder in the Solution Explorer and selecting Add ⇨ Controller to display the Add Controller dialog shown in Figure 21-4. This simple dialog allows you to select a name for your new controller. By convention, the MVC framework requires that all controller classes have names that end in "Controller," so this part is already filled in for you. There is also a checkbox allowing you to add some simple functionality. We'll ignore this for now and come back to it later. Give the new controller a name of ProductsController and click Add.

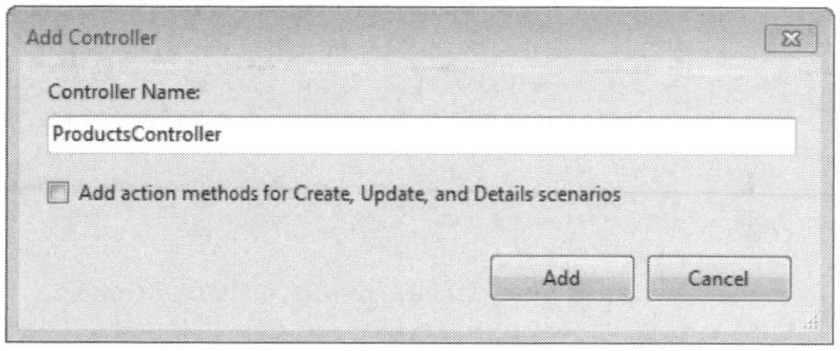

FIGURE 21-4

> You can quickly add a controller to your project by using the Ctrl+M, Ctrl+C shortcut as well.

New controller classes inherit from the System.Web.Mvc.Controller base class, which performs all of the hefty lifting in terms of determining the relevant method to call for an action and mapping of URL and POST parameter values. This means that you can concentrate on the implementation details of your actions, which typically involves invoking a method on a model class and then selecting a view to render.

A newly created controller class will be populated with a default action method called Index. You can add a new action simply by adding a public method to the class. If a method is public, it will be visible as an action on the controller. You can stop a public method from being exposed as an action by adding the System.Web.Mvc.NonAction attribute to the method. The following listing contains the controller class with the default action that simply renders the Index view, and a public method that is not visible as an action:

C#

```
public class ProductsController : Controller
{
  //
  // GET: /Products/

  public ActionResult Index()
```

```
  {
    return View();
  }

  [NonAction]
  public void NotAnAction()
  {
    // This method is not exposed as an action.
  }
}
```

VB

```
Public Class ProductsController
    Inherits System.Web.Mvc.Controller

    '
    ' GET: /Products/

    Function Index() As ActionResult
        Return View()
    End Function

    <NonAction()>
    Sub NotAnAction()
        ' This method is not exposed as an action.
    End Sub

End Class
```

> *The comment that appears above the* Index *method is a convention that indicates how the action is triggered. Each action method is placed at a URL that is a combination of the controller name and the action method name formatted like /controller/action. The comment has no control over this convention but is used to indicate where you can expect to find this action method. In this case it is saying that the index action is triggered by executing an HTTP GET request against the URL /Products/. This is just the name of the controller because an action named* Index *is assumed if one is not explicitly stated by the URL. This convention is revisited in the section on routing.*

The result of the Index method is an object that derives from the System.Web.Mvc.ActionResult abstract class. This object is responsible for determining what happens after the action method returns. A number of standard classes inherit from ActionResult that allow you to perform a number of standard tasks, including redirection to another URL, generating some simple content in a number of different formats, or in this case, rendering a view.

> *The* View *method on the* Controller *base class is a simple method that creates and configures a* System.Web.Mvc.ViewResult *object. This object is responsible for selecting a view and passing it any information that it needs to render its contents.*

It is important to note that `Index` is just a normal .NET method and `ProductsController` is just a normal .NET class. There is nothing special about either of them. This means that you can easily instantiate a `ProductsController` in a test harness, call its `Index` method, and then make assertions about the `ActionResult` object it returns.

Before moving on, update the `Index` method to retrieve a list of Products and pass them onto the view, as shown in the following code listing:

C#

Available for download on Wrox.com

```csharp
public ActionResult Index()
{
    List<Product> products;

    using (var db = new ProductsDataContext())
    {
        products = db.Products.ToList();
    }

    return View(products);
}
```

Code snippet Controllers\ProductsController.cs

VB

Available for download on Wrox.com

```vb
Function Index() As ActionResult
    Dim products As New List(Of Product)

    Using db As New ProductsDataContext
        products = db.Products.ToList()
    End Using

    Return View(products)
End Function
```

Code snippet Controllers\ProductsController.vb

Now that you have created a model and a controller all that is needed is to create the view to display the UI.

RENDERING A UI WITH VIEWS

In the previous section you created an action method that gathers the complete list of products and then passes that list to a view. Each view belongs to a single controller and is stored in a subfolder in the Views folder, which is named after the controller that owns it. Additionally, there is a Shared folder, which contains a number of shared views that are accessible from a number of controllers. When the view engine is looking for a view it checks the controller-specific area first and then checks in the shared area.

> *You can specify the full path to a view as the view name if you need to refer to a view that is not in the normal view engine search areas.*

Each view looks very similar to a standard ASP.NET Web Forms `Page` or `Control` having either an `.aspx` or `.ascx` extension. They contain a mix of HTML markup and code blocks. They can even have master pages and render some standard controls. However, a number of important differences exist that need to be highlighted.

First, a view doesn't have a code-behind page. As such, there is nowhere to add event handlers for any controls that the view renders, including those that normally happen behind the scenes. Instead, it is expected that a controller will respond to user events and that the view will expose ways for the user to trigger action methods. Second, instead of inheriting from `System.Web.Page`, a view inherits from `System.Web.Mvc.ViewPage`. This base class exposes a number of useful properties and methods that can be used to help render the HTML output. One of these properties contains a dictionary of objects that were passed into the view from the controller. Finally, in the markup you will notice that there is no form control with a `runat="server"` attribute. No server form means that there is no View State emitted with the page. The majority of the ASP.NET server controls must be placed inside a server form. Some controls such a Literal or Repeater control will work fine outside a form; however, if you try to use a Button or DropDownList control, your page will throw an exception at run time.

You can create a View in a number of ways, but the easiest is to right-click the title of the action method and select Add View, which brings up the Add View dialog shown in Figure 21-5.

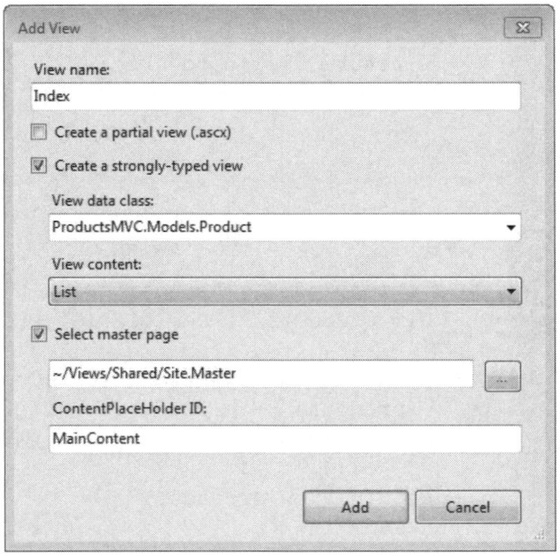

FIGURE 21-5

> *You can use the shortcut Ctrl+M, Ctrl+V when the cursor is inside an action method to open the Add View dialog as well.*

This dialog contains a number of options. By default, the name is set to match the name of the action method. If you change this, you need to change the call to `View` to include the view name as a parameter. Check the box to create a strongly typed view and then choose `Models.Product` from the View Data Class drop-down. If you don't see the Product class straight away you might need to build the application before adding the view.

> *If you do not opt to create a strongly typed view, it will contain a dictionary of objects that will need to be converted back into their real types before you can use them. It is recommended to always use strongly typed views. If you require your views to be weakly typed and you are using C#, you should create a strongly typed view of the new dynamic type and pass it* ExpandoObject *instances.*

Finally, change the View Content drop-down to List. This tells Visual Studio to generate a list page for Product objects. When you click Add, the view should be generated and opened in the main editor window. It will look like this:

C#

```
<%@ Page Title="" Language="C#" MasterPageFile="~/Views/Shared/Site.Master"
Inherits="System.Web.Mvc.ViewPage<IEnumerable<CSProductsMVC.Models.Product>>" %>

<asp:Content ID="Content1" ContentPlaceHolderID="TitleContent" runat="server">
    Index
</asp:Content>

<asp:Content ID="Content2" ContentPlaceHolderID="MainContent" runat="server">

    <h2>Index</h2>

    <table>
        <tr>
            <th></th>
            <th>ProductID</th>
            <th>Name</th>
            <th>ProductNumber</th>
            <th>MakeFlag</th>
            <th>FinishedGoodsFlag</th>
            <th>Color</th>
            <th>SafetyStockLevel</th>
            <th>ReorderPoint</th>
            <th>StandardCost</th>
            <th>ListPrice</th>
            <th>Size</th>
            <th>SizeUnitMeasureCode</th>
            <th>WeightUnitMeasureCode</th>
            <th>Weight</th>
            <th>DaysToManufacture</th>
            <th>ProductLine</th>
            <th>Class</th>
            <th>Style</th>
            <th>ProductSubcategoryID</th>
            <th>ProductModelID</th>
            <th>SellStartDate</th>
            <th>SellEndDate</th>
            <th>DiscontinuedDate</th>
```

```
            <th>rowguid</th>
            <th>ModifiedDate</th>
        </tr>

    <% foreach (var item in Model) { %>

        <tr>
            <td>
                <%= Html.ActionLink("Edit", "Edit", new { id=item.ProductID }) %> |
                <%= Html.ActionLink("Details", "Details", new
                { id=item.ProductID })%>
            </td>
            <td><%= Html.Encode(item.ProductID) %></td>
            <td><%= Html.Encode(item.Name) %></td>
            <td><%= Html.Encode(item.ProductNumber) %></td>
            <td><%= Html.Encode(item.MakeFlag) %></td>
            <td><%= Html.Encode(item.FinishedGoodsFlag) %></td>
            <td><%= Html.Encode(item.Color) %></td>
            <td><%= Html.Encode(item.SafetyStockLevel) %></td>
            <td><%= Html.Encode(item.ReorderPoint) %></td>
            <td><%= Html.Encode(String.Format("{0:F}", item.StandardCost)) %></td>
            <td><%= Html.Encode(String.Format("{0:F}", item.ListPrice)) %></td>
            <td><%= Html.Encode(item.Size) %></td>
            <td><%= Html.Encode(item.SizeUnitMeasureCode) %></td>
            <td><%= Html.Encode(item.WeightUnitMeasureCode) %></td>
            <td><%= Html.Encode(String.Format("{0:F}", item.Weight)) %></td>
            <td><%= Html.Encode(item.DaysToManufacture) %></td>
            <td><%= Html.Encode(item.ProductLine) %></td>
            <td><%= Html.Encode(item.Class) %></td>
            <td><%= Html.Encode(item.Style) %></td>
            <td><%= Html.Encode(item.ProductSubcategoryID) %></td>
            <td><%= Html.Encode(item.ProductModelID) %></td>
            <td><%= Html.Encode(String.Format("{0:g}", item.SellStartDate)) %></td>
            <td><%= Html.Encode(String.Format("{0:g}", item.SellEndDate)) %></td>
            <td><%= Html.Encode(String.Format("{0:g}",
            item.DiscontinuedDate)) %></td>
            <td><%= Html.Encode(item.rowguid) %></td>
            <td><%= Html.Encode(String.Format("{0:g}", item.ModifiedDate)) %></td>
        </tr>

    <% } %>

    </table>

    <p>
        <%= Html.ActionLink("Create New", "Create") %>
    </p>

</asp:Content>
```

Code snippet Views\Products\Index.aspx

VB

```vb
<%@ Page Title="" Language="VB" MasterPageFile="~/Views/Shared/Site.Master"
Inherits="System.Web.Mvc.ViewPage(Of IEnumerable (Of ProductsMVC.Product))" %>

<asp:Content ID="Content1" ContentPlaceHolderID="TitleContent" runat="server">
    Index
</asp:Content>

<asp:Content ID="Content2" ContentPlaceHolderID="MainContent" runat="server">

    <h2>Index</h2>

    <p>
        <%=Html.ActionLink("Create New", "Create")%>
    </p>

    <table>
        <tr>
            <th></th>
            <th>ProductID</th>
            <th>Name</th>
            <th>ProductNumber</th>
            <th>MakeFlag</th>
            <th>FinishedGoodsFlag</th>
            <th>Color</th>
            <th>SafetyStockLevel</th>
            <th>ReorderPoint</th>
            <th>StandardCost</th>
            <th>ListPrice</th>
            <th>Size</th>
            <th>SizeUnitMeasureCode</th>
            <th>WeightUnitMeasureCode</th>
            <th>Weight</th>
            <th>DaysToManufacture</th>
            <th>ProductLine</th>
            <th>Class</th>
            <th>Style</th>
            <th>ProductSubcategoryID</th>
            <th>ProductModelID</th>
            <th>SellStartDate</th>
            <th>SellEndDate</th>
            <th>DiscontinuedDate</th>
            <th>rowguid</th>
            <th>ModifiedDate</th>
        </tr>

    <% For Each item In Model%>

        <tr>
            <td>
                <%=Html.ActionLink("Edit", "Edit", New With
                {.id = item.ProductID})%> |
```

```
            <%=Html.ActionLink("Details", "Details", New With
            {.id = item.ProductID})%>
        </td>
        <td><%= Html.Encode(item.ProductID) %></td>
        <td><%= Html.Encode(item.Name) %></td>
        <td><%= Html.Encode(item.ProductNumber) %></td>
        <td><%= Html.Encode(item.MakeFlag) %></td>
        <td><%= Html.Encode(item.FinishedGoodsFlag) %></td>
        <td><%= Html.Encode(item.Color) %></td>
        <td><%= Html.Encode(item.SafetyStockLevel) %></td>
        <td><%= Html.Encode(item.ReorderPoint) %></td>
        <td><%= Html.Encode(String.Format("{0:F}", item.StandardCost)) %></td>
        <td><%= Html.Encode(String.Format("{0:F}", item.ListPrice)) %></td>
        <td><%= Html.Encode(item.Size) %></td>
        <td><%= Html.Encode(item.SizeUnitMeasureCode) %></td>
        <td><%= Html.Encode(item.WeightUnitMeasureCode) %></td>
        <td><%= Html.Encode(String.Format("{0:F}", item.Weight)) %></td>
        <td><%= Html.Encode(item.DaysToManufacture) %></td>
        <td><%= Html.Encode(item.ProductLine) %></td>
        <td><%= Html.Encode(item.Class) %></td>
        <td><%= Html.Encode(item.Style) %></td>
        <td><%= Html.Encode(item.ProductSubcategoryID) %></td>
        <td><%= Html.Encode(item.ProductModelID) %></td>
        <td><%= Html.Encode(String.Format("{0:g}", item.SellStartDate)) %></td>
        <td><%= Html.Encode(String.Format("{0:g}", item.SellEndDate)) %></td>
        <td><%= Html.Encode(String.Format("{0:g}",
        item.DiscontinuedDate)) %></td>
        <td><%= Html.Encode(item.rowguid) %></td>
        <td><%= Html.Encode(String.Format("{0:g}", item.ModifiedDate)) %></td>
    </tr>

<% Next%>

</table>

</asp:Content>
```

Code snippet Views\Products\Index.aspx

This view presents the list of Products in a simple table. The bulk of the work is done by a for each loop, which iterates over the list of products and renders an HTML table row for each one.

C#

```
<% foreach (var item in Model) { %>

    <tr>
       <!-- ... -->
       <td><%= Html.Encode(item.ProductID) %></td>
       <td><%= Html.Encode(item.Name) %></td>
       <!-- ... -->
    </tr>

<% } %>
```

VB

```
<% For Each item In Model%>

    <tr>
        <!-- ... -->
        <td><%= Html.Encode(item.ProductID) %></td>
        <td><%= Html.Encode(item.Name) %></td>
        <!-- ... -->

    </tr>

<% Next%>
```

> *Visual Studio is able to infer the type of model because you created a strongly typed view. In the page directive you can see that this view doesn't inherit from* System.Web.Mvc.Page. *Instead, it inherits from the generic version, which states that the model will be an* IEnumerable *collection of* Product *objects. This in turn exposes a* Model *property with that type. Note that you can still pass the wrong type of item to the view from the controller. In the case of a strongly typed view this will result in a run time exception.*

Each of the properties of the products is HTML encoded before it is rendered using the Encode method on the Html helper property. This prevents common issues with malicious code injected into the application masquerading as valid user data. ASP.NET MVC is able to take advantage of the new <%: ... %> markup, which uses a colon in the place of the equals sign in ASP.NET 4 to more easily perform this encoding. Here is the same snippet again taking advantage of this technique:

C#

```
<% foreach (var item in Model) { %>

    <tr>
        <!-- ... -->
        <td><%: item.ProductID %></td>
        <td><%: item.Name %></td>
        <!-- ... -->
    </tr>

<% } %>
```

VB

```
<% For Each item In Model%>

    <tr>
        <!-- ... -->
        <td><%: item.ProductID %></td>
        <td><%: item.Name %></td>
```

```
            <!-- ... -->

        </tr>

    <% Next%>
```

In addition to the `Encode` method there is one other `Html` helper method being used by this view. This is the `ActionLink` helper. This method will emit a standard HTML anchor tag designed to trigger the specified action. Two forms are in use here. The simplest of these is the one designed to create a new Product record:

C#
```
<p>
  <%= Html.ActionLink("Create New", "Create") %>
</p>
```

VB
```
<p>
  <%=Html.ActionLink("Create New", "Create")%>
</p>
```

The first parameter is the text that will be rendered inside the anchor tag. This is the text that will be presented to the user. The second parameter is the name of the action to trigger. Because no controller has been specified the current controller is assumed.

The more complex use of `ActionLink` is used to render the edit and delete links for each product.

C#
```
<td>
  <%= Html.ActionLink("Edit", "Edit", new { id=item.ProductID }) %> |
  <%= Html.ActionLink("Details", "Details", new { id=item.ProductID })%>
</td>
```

VB
```
<td>
  <%=Html.ActionLink("Edit", "Edit", New With {.id = item.ProductID})%> |
  <%=Html.ActionLink("Details", "Details", New With {.id = item.ProductID})%>
</td>
```

The first two parameters are the same as before and represent the link text and the action name, respectively. The third parameter is an anonymous object that contains data to be passed to the action method when it is called.

When you run the application and enter /products/ in your address bar you will be presented with the page displayed in Figure 21-6. Trying to click any of the links will cause a run time exception because the target action does not yet exist.

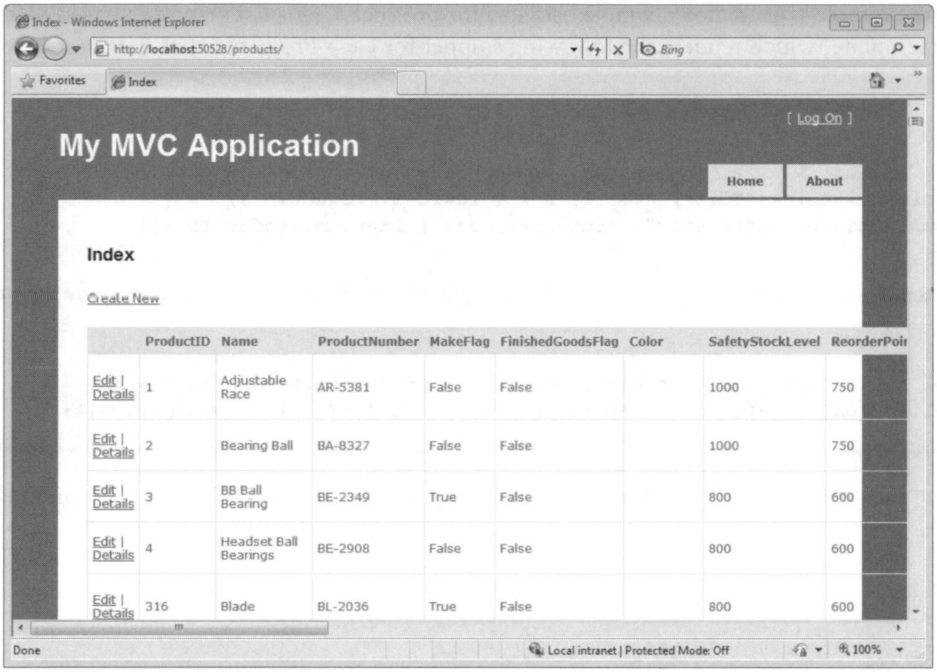

FIGURE 21-6

> *Once you have a view and a controller you can use the shortcut Ctrl+M, Ctrl+G to toggle between the two.*

ADVANCED MVC

This section provides an overview for some of the more advanced features of ASP.NET MVC.

Routing

As you were navigating around the MVC site in your web browser you might have noticed that the URLs are quite different from a normal ASP.NET web site. They do not contain file extensions and they do not match up with the underlying folder structure. These URLs are mapped to action methods and controllers with a set of classes that belong to the routing engine, which is located in the `System.Web.Routing` assembly.

> *The routing engine was originally developed as a part of the ASP.NET MVC project but was released as a standalone library before MVC shipped. Although it is not described in this book it is possible to use the routing engine with ASP. NET Web Forms projects.*

In the previous example you created a simple list view for products. This list view was based on the standard List template, which renders the following snippet for each Product in the database being displayed:

C#

```
<td>
  <%= Html.ActionLink("Edit", "Edit", new { id=item.ProductID }) %> |
  <%= Html.ActionLink("Details", "Details", new { id=item.ProductID })%>
</td>
```

VB

```
<td>
  <%=Html.ActionLink("Edit", "Edit", New With {.id = item.ProductID})%> |
  <%=Html.ActionLink("Details", "Details", New With {.id = item.ProductID})%>
</td>
```

If you examine the generated HTML markup of the final page you should see that this becomes the following:

HTML

```
<td>
  <a href="/Products/Edit/2">Edit</a> |
  <a href="/Products/Details/2">Details</a>
</td>
```

These URLs are made up of three parts:

➤ "Products" is the name of the controller. There is a corresponding ProductsController in the project.

➤ "Edit" and "Details" are the names of action methods on the controller. The ProductsController will have methods called Edit and Details.

➤ "2" is a parameter that is called "id."

Each of these components is defined in a *route*, which is set up in the Global.asax.cs file (or the Global.asax.vb file for VB) in a method called RegisterRoutes. When the application first starts it calls this method and passes in the System.Web.Routing.RouteTable.Routes static collection. This collection contains all of the routes for the entire application.

Available for download on Wrox.com

C#

```
public static void RegisterRoutes(RouteCollection routes)
{
    routes.IgnoreRoute("{resource}.axd/{*pathInfo}");

    routes.MapRoute(
        "Default",
        "{controller}/{action}/{id}",
        new { controller = "Home", action = "Index", id = "" }
    );

}
```

Code snippet Global.asax.cs

VB

```vb
Shared Sub RegisterRoutes(ByVal routes As RouteCollection)
    routes.IgnoreRoute("{resource}.axd/{*pathInfo}")

    routes.MapRoute( _
        "Default", _
        "{controller}/{action}/{id}", _
        New With {.controller = "Home", .action = "Index", .id = ""} _
    )

End Sub
```

Code snippet Global.asax.vb

The first method call tells the routing engine that it should ignore all requests for .axd files. When an incoming URL matches this route the engine will completely ignore it and allow other parts of the application to handle it. This method can be very handy if you want to integrate Web Forms and MVC into a single application. All you need to do is ask the routing engine to ignore .aspx and .asmx files.

The second method call defines a new Route and adds it to the collection. This overload of MapRoute method takes three parameters. The first parameter is a name, which can be used as a handle to this route later on. The second parameter is a URL template. This parameter can have normal text along with special tokens inside of braces. These tokens will be used as placeholders that are filled in when the route matches a URL. Some tokens are reserved and will be used by the MVC routing engine to select a controller and execute the correct action. The final parameter is a dictionary of default values. You can see that this "Default" route matches any URL in the form /controller/action/id where the default controller is "Home," the default action is "Index," and the "id" parameter defaults to an empty string.

When a new HTTP request comes in, each route in the RouteCollection tries to match the URL against its URL template in the order that they are added. The first route that is able to do so fills in any default values that haven't been supplied. Once these values have all been collected then a Controller is created and an action method is called.

Routes are also used to generate URLs inside of views. When a helper needs a URL it will consult each route (in order again) to see if it is able to build a URL for the specified controller, action, and parameter values. The first route to match will generate the correct URL. If a route encounters a parameter value that it doesn't know about, it becomes a query string parameter in the generated URL.

The following snippet declares a new route for an online store that allows for two parameters: a category and a subcategory. Assuming that this MVC application has been deployed to the root of a web server, requests for the URL http://servername/Shop/Accessories/Helmets will go to the "List" action on the "Products" controller with the parameters Category set to "Accessories" and Subcategory set to "Helmets."

C#

```csharp
public static void RegisterRoutes(RouteCollection routes)
{
    routes.IgnoreRoute("{resource}.axd/{*pathInfo}");

    routes.MapRoute(
```

```
      "ProductsDisplay",
      "Shop/{category}/{subcategory}",
      new {
        controller = "Products",
        action = "List",
        category = "",
        subcategory = ""
      }
    );

    routes.MapRoute(
      "Default",
      "{controller}/{action}/{id}",
      new { controller = "Home", action = "Index", id = "" }
    );
}
```

Code snippet Global.asax.cs

VB

```
Shared Sub RegisterRoutes(ByVal routes As RouteCollection)
    routes.IgnoreRoute("{resource}.axd/{*pathInfo}")

    routes.MapRoute( _
      "ProductsDisplay", _
      "Shop/{category}/{subcategory}", _
      New With { _
      .controller = "Products", .action = "List", _
      .category = "", .subcategory = "" _
      })

    routes.MapRoute( _
      "Default", _
      "{controller}/{action}/{id}", _
      New With {.controller = "Home", .action = "Index", .id = ""} _
    )

End Sub
```

Code snippet Global.asax.vb

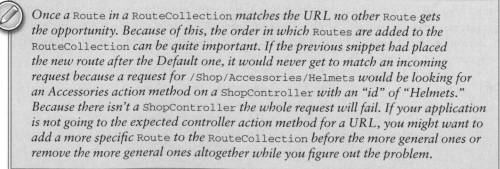

Once a Route *in a* RouteCollection *matches the URL no other* Route *gets the opportunity. Because of this, the order in which* Routes *are added to the* RouteCollection *can be quite important. If the previous snippet had placed the new route after the Default one, it would never get to match an incoming request because a request for* /Shop/Accessories/Helmets *would be looking for an Accessories action method on a* ShopController *with an "id" of "Helmets." Because there isn't a* ShopController *the whole request will fail. If your application is not going to the expected controller action method for a URL, you might want to add a more specific* Route *to the* RouteCollection *before the more general ones or remove the more general ones altogether while you figure out the problem.*

Finally, you can also add constraints to the Route that will prevent it from matching a URL unless some other condition is met. This can be a good idea if your parameters are going to be converted into complex data types such as date times later on and require a very specific format. The most basic kind of restraint is a string, which is interpreted as a regular expression that a parameter must match for the route to take effect. The following route definition uses this technique to ensure that the `zipCode` parameter is exactly five digits:

C#

```csharp
routes.MapRoute(
  "StoreFinder",
  "Stores/Find/{zipCode}",
  new { controller = "StoreFinder", action = "list" },
  new { zipCode = @"^\d{5}$" }
);
```

VB

```vb
routes.MapRoute( _
 "StoreFinder", _
 "Stores/Find/{zipCode}", _
 New With {.controller = "StoreFinder", .action = "list"}, _
 New With {.zipCode = "^\d{5}$"} _
)
```

The other type of constraint is a class that implements `IRouteConstraint`. This interface defines a single method `Match` that returns a Boolean value indicating whether the incoming request satisfies the constraint. There is one implementation of `IRouteConstraint` out of the box called `HttpMethodConstraint`. This constraint can be used to ensure that the correct HTTP method, such as GET, POST, HEAD, or DELETE is used. The following route only accepts HTTP POST requests:

C#

```csharp
routes.MapRoute(
  "PostOnlyRoute",
  "Post/{action}",
  new { controller = "Post" },
  new { post = new HttpMethodConstraint("POST") }
);
```

VB

```vb
routes.MapRoute(
  "PostOnlyRoute", _
  "Post/{action}", _
  New With {.controller = "Post"}, _
  New With {.post = New HttpMethodConstraint("POST")} _
)
```

The URL routing classes are very powerful and flexible, and allow you to easily create "pretty" URLs. This can aid users navigating around your site and even improve your site's ranking with search engines.

Action Method Parameters

All of the action methods in previous examples do not accept any input from outside of the application to perform their tasks; they rely entirely on the state of the model. In real-world applications this is an unlikely scenario. The ASP.NET MVC framework makes it very easy to parameterize action methods from a variety of sources.

As mentioned in the previous section, the "Default" route exposes an "id" parameter, which defaults to an empty string. To access the value of the "id" parameter from within the action method you can just add it to the signature of the method itself as the following snippet shows:

C#

```csharp
public ActionResult Details(int id)
{
    using (var db = new ProductsDataContext())
    {
        var product = db.Products.SingleOrDefault(x => x.ProductID == id);

        if (product == null)
            return View("NotFound");

        return View(product);
    }
}
```

Code snippet Controllers\ProductsController.cs

VB

```vb
Public Function Details(ByVal id As Integer) As ActionResult
    Using db As New ProductsDataContext
        Dim product = db.Products.FirstOrDefault(Function(p As Product)
        p.ProductID = id)

        Return View(product)
    End Using
End Function
```

Code snippet Controllers\ProductsController.vb

When the MVC framework executes the Details action method it will search through the parameters that have been extracted from the URL by the matching route. These parameters are matched up with the parameters on the action method by name and then passed in when the method is called. As the details method shows, the framework is even able to convert the type of the parameter on the fly. Action methods can also retrieve parameters from the query string portion of the URL and from HTTP POST data using the same technique.

If the conversion cannot be made for any reason, an exception is thrown.

Additionally, an action method can accept a parameter of the `FormValues` type that will aggregate all of the HTTP POST data into a single parameter. If the data in the `FormValues` collection represents the properties of an object, you can simply add a parameter of that type and a new instance will be created when the action method is called. The Create action, shown in the following snippet, uses this to construct a new instance of the `Product` class and then save it:

C#

```csharp
public ActionResult Create()
{
    return View();
}

[HttpPost]
public ActionResult Create([Bind(Exclude="ProductId")]Product product)
{
    if (!ModelState.IsValid)
        return View();

    using (var db = new ProductsDataContext())
    {
        db.Products.InsertOnSubmit(product);
        db.SubmitChanges();
    }
    return RedirectToAction("List");
}
```

Code snippet Controllers\ProductsController.cs

VB

```vb
<HttpPost()>
Function Create(<Bind(Exclude:="id")> ByVal product As Product)

    If (Not ModelState.IsValid) Then
        Return View()
    End If

    Using db As New ProductsDataContext
        db.Products.InsertOnSubmit(product)
        db.SubmitChanges()
    End Using
    Return RedirectToAction("List")
End Function
```

Code snippet Controllers\ProductsController.vb

> *There are two Create action methods here. The first one simply renders the "Create" view. The second one is marked up with an `HttpPostAttribute`, which means that it will only be selected if the HTTP request uses the POST verb. This is a common practice in designing ASP.NET MVC web sites. In addition to `HttpPostAttribute` there are also corresponding attributes for the GET, PUT, and DELETE verbs.*

Model Binders

The process of creating the new Product instance is the responsibility of a *model binder*. The model binder matches properties in the HTTP POST data with properties on the type that it is attempting to create. This works in this example because the template that was used to generate the "Create" view renders the HTML INPUT fields with the correct name as this snippet of the rendered HTML shows:

HTML

```
<p>
  <label for="ProductID">ProductID:</label>
  <input id="ProductID" name="ProductID" type="text" value="" />
</p>
<p>
  <label for="Name">Name:</label>
  <input id="Name" name="Name" type="text" value="" />
</p>
```

A number of ways exist to control the behavior of a model binder including the BindAttribute, which is used in the Create method shown previously. This attribute is used to include or exclude certain properties and to specify a prefix for the HTTP POST values. This can be very useful if multiple objects in the POST collection need to be bound.

Model binders can also be used from within the action method to update existing instances of your model classes using the UpdateModel and TryUpdateModel methods. The chief difference is that TryUpdateModel will return a Boolean value indicating whether or not it was able to build a successful model and UpdateModel will just throw an exception if it can't. The Edit action method shows this technique:

Available for download on Wrox.com

C#

```
[HttpPost]
public ActionResult Edit(int id, FormCollection formValues)
{
  using (var db = new ProductsDataContext())
  {
    var product = db.Products.SingleOrDefault(x => x.ProductID == id);

    if (TryUpdateModel(product))
    {
      db.SubmitChanges();
      return RedirectToAction("Index");
    }
    return View(product);
  }
}
```

Code snippet Controllers\ProductsController.cs

Available for download on Wrox.com

VB

```
<HttpPost()>
Function Edit(ByVal id As Integer, ByVal formValues As FormCollection)
  Using db As New ProductsDataContext
```

```vb
      Dim product = db.Products.FirstOrDefault(Function(p As Product)
      p.ProductID = id)

      If TryUpdateModel(product) Then
        db.SubmitChanges()
        Return RedirectToAction("Index")
      End If
      Return View(product)
    End Using
  End Function
```

Code snippet Controllers\ProductsController.vb

Areas

An *area* is a self-contained part of an MVC application that manages its own models, controllers, and views. You can even define routes specific to an area. To create a new area, select Add ➪ Area from the project context menu in the Solution Explorer. The Add Area dialog, shown in Figure 21-7, prompts you to provide a name for your area.

FIGURE 21-7

After you click Add, many new files are added to your project to support the area. Figure 21-8 shows a project with two areas added to it named Shop and Blog, respectively.

In addition to having its own controllers and views, each area has a class called *AreaName*AreaRegistration that inherits from the abstract base class AreaRegistration. This class contains an abstract property for the name of your area and an abstract method for integrating your area with the rest of the application. The default implementation registers the standard routes.

FIGURE 21-8

C#

```csharp
public class BlogAreaRegistration : AreaRegistration
{
    public override string AreaName
    {
      get
      {
        return "Blog";
      }
    }

    public override void RegisterArea(AreaRegistrationContext context)
    {
      context.MapRoute(
        "Blog_default",
        "Blog/{controller}/{action}/{id}",
```

Available for
download on
Wrox.com

```
            new { action = "Index", id = "" }
        );
    }
}
```

VB

```vb
Public Class BlogAreaRegistration
    Inherits AreaRegistration

    Public Overrides ReadOnly Property AreaName() As String
        Get
            Return "Blog"
        End Get
    End Property

    Public Overrides Sub RegisterArea(ByVal context As AreaRegistrationContext)
        context.MapRoute( _
          "Blog_default", _
          "Blog/{controller}/{action}/{id}", _
          New With {.action = "Index", .id = ""} _
        )
    End Sub
End Class
```

> The `RegisterArea` *method of the* `BlogAreaRegistration` *class defines a route in which every URL is prefixed with* `/Blog/` *by convention. This can be useful while debugging routes but is not necessary as long as area routes do not clash with any other routes.*

In order to link to a controller which is inside another area, you need to use an overload of `Html.ActionLink` that accepts a `routeValues` parameter. The object you provide for this parameter must include an `area` property set to the name of the area which contains the controller you are linking to.

C#

```csharp
<%= Html.ActionLink("Blog", "Index", new { area = "Blog" }) %>
```

VB

```vb
<%= Html.ActionLink("Blog", "Index", New With {.area = "Blog"})%>
```

One issue that is frequently encountered when adding area support to a project is that the controller factory becomes confused when multiple controllers have the same name. To avoid this issue you can limit the namespaces that a route will use to search for a controller to satisfy any request. The following code snippet limits the namespaces for the global routes to `MvcApplication.Controllers`, which will not match any of the area controllers.

Available for download on Wrox.com

C#

```
routes.MapRoute(
  "Default",
  "{controller}/{action}/{id}",
  new { controller = "Home", action = "Index", id = "" },
  null,
  new[] { "MvcApplication.Controllers" }
);
```

Code snippet Global.asax.cs

Available for download on Wrox.com

VB

```
routes.MapRoute( _
  "Default", _
  "{controller}/{action}/{id}", _
  New With {.controller = "Home", .action = "Index", .id = ""}, _
  Nothing, _
  New String() {"MvcApplication.Controllers"} _
)
```

Code snippet Global.asax.vb

> *The* `AreaRegistrationContext` *automatically includes the area namespace when you use it to specify routes so you should only need to supply namespaces to the global routes.*

Validation

In addition to just creating or updating it, a model binder is able to decide whether the model instance that it operating on is valid. The results of this decision are found in the `ModelState` property. Model binders can pick up some simple validation errors by default, usually with regard to incorrect types. Figure 21-9 shows the result of attempting to save a Product when the form is empty. Most of these validation errors are based on the fact that these properties are non-nullable value types and require a value.

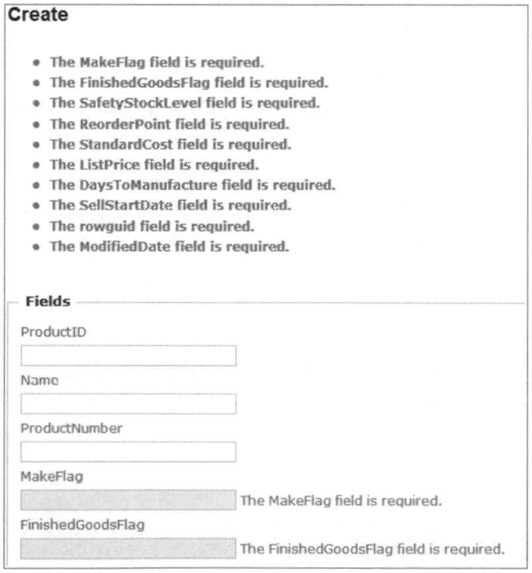
Create
The MakeFlag field is required.
The FinishedGoodsFlag field is required.
The SafetyStockLevel field is required.
The ReorderPoint field is required.
The StandardCost field is required.
The ListPrice field is required.
The DaysToManufacture field is required.
The SellStartDate field is required.
The rowguid field is required.
The ModifiedDate field is required.
Fields
ProductID
Name
ProductNumber
MakeFlag
The MakeFlag field is required.
FinishedGoodsFlag
The FinishedGoodsFlag field is required.

FIGURE 21-9

The user interface for this error report is provided by the `Html.ValidationSummary` call, which is made on the view. This helper method examines the `ModelState` and if it finds any errors it renders them as a list along with a header message.

You can add additional validation hints to the properties of the model class by marking them up with using the attributes in the `System.ComponentModel.DataAnnotations` assembly. Because the `Product` class is created by LINQ to SQL you should not update it directly. The LINQ to SQL generated classes are defined as partial so you can extend them but there is no easy way to attach metadata to the generated properties this way. Instead, you need to create a *metadata proxy* class with the properties you want to mark up, provide them with the correct data annotation attributes, and then mark up the partial class with a `MetadataTypeAttribute` identifying the proxy class. The following code snippet shows this technique being used to provide some validation metadata to the `Product` class:

C#

```csharp
[MetadataType(typeof(ProductValidationMetadata))]
public partial class Product
{
}

public class ProductValidationMetadata
{
    [Required, StringLength(256)]
    public string Name { get; set; }

    [Range(0, 100)]
    public int DaysToManufacture { get; set; }
}
```

Code snippet Models\Product.cs

VB

```vbnet
Imports System.ComponentModel.DataAnnotations

<MetadataType(GetType(ProductMetaData))>
Partial Public Class Product

End Class

Public Class ProductMetaData
    <Required(), StringLength(256)>
    Property Name As String

    <Range(0, 100)>
    Property DaysToManufacture As Integer
End Class
```

Code snippet Models\Product.vb

Now, attempting to create a new Product with no name and a negative "Days to Manufacture" produces the errors shown in Figure 21-10.

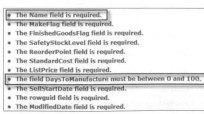

FIGURE 21-10

> *You might notice that along with the error report at the top of the page, for each field which has a validation error, the textbox is colored red and has an asterisk after it. The first effect is caused by the* Html.TextBox *helper, which accepts the value of the property that it is attached to. If it encounters an error in the model state for its attached property, it adds an* input-validation-error *CSS class to the rendered* INPUT *control. The default stylesheet defines the red background. The second effect is caused by the* Html.ValidationMessage *helper. This helper is also associated with a property and renders the contents of its second parameter if it detects that its attached property has an error associated with it.*

Partial Views

At times you have large areas of user interface markup that you would like to reuse. In the ASP.NET MVC framework a re-usable section of view is called a partial view. Partial views act very similar to views except that they have an .ascx extension and inherit from System.Web.Mvc.ViewUserControl. To create a partial view, check the Create a Partial View checkbox on the same Add View dialog that you use to create other views.

To render a partial view you can use the Html.RenderPartial method. The most common overload of this method accepts a view name and a model object. Just as with a normal view, a partial view can be either controller-specific or shared. Once the partial view has been rendered, its HTML markup is inserted into the main view. This code snippet renders a "Form" partial for the current model:

C#

```
<% Html.RenderPartial("Form", Model); %>
```

VB

```
<% Html.RenderPartial("Form", Model) %>
```

> *You can call a partial view directly from an action using the normal View method. If you do this, only the HTML rendered by the partial view will be included in the HTTP response. This can be very useful if you are returning data to jQuery.*

Custom View Templates

When you use the Add View dialog to add items to your project, Visual Studio 2010 is actually executing a T4 template, which determines the code that will be generated. The View Content drop-down determines which template will be run. If you want to edit them you can find them in the C:\Program Files\Microsoft Visual Studio 10.0\Common7\IDE\ItemTemplates\language\Web\MVC\v2\CodeTemplates\AddView folder where language is either "CSharp" or "VisualBasic."

Editing these files directly will make the change across all MVC projects on the local machine, but you cannot use this technique to create project-specific templates. It is also very hard to version control these files effectively with the rest of your application. You can get around both of these issues by creating a `CodeTemplates\AddView` folder under the root of your project and copying the T4 templates into it as shown in Figure 21-11 When the Add View dialog is populating the View Content drop-down list it will use these templates instead of the global ones.

Additionally, you can create your own templates by adding T4 template files into this folder. Figure 21-11 shows the template file `MyViewTemplate.tt` and Figure 21-12 shows "MyViewTemplate" showing up in the drop-down list.

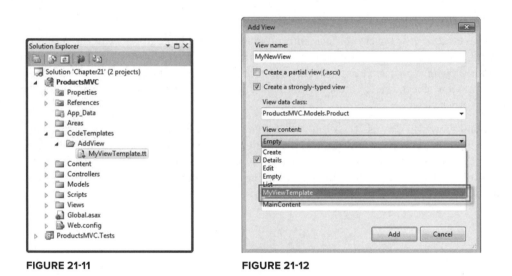

FIGURE 21-11   **FIGURE 21-12**

Custom templates can be host specific and the `Host` is of type `MvcTextTemplateHost`, which contains all of the properties defined by the Add View dialog. See Chapter 14, "Code Generation with T4," for more information about creating T4 templates.

Dynamic Data Templates

Dynamic Data is a feature of ASP.NET Web Forms that allows you to render UI based on metadata associated with the model. Although ASP.NET MVC does not integrate directly with Dynamic Data, a number of new features in ASP.NET MVC 2.0 are similar in spirit. Templates in ASP.NET MVC 2.0 are able to render parts of your model in different ways, whether they are small and simple such as a single string property or large and complex like the whole product class. The templates are exposed by Html helper methods. There are templates for display and templates for editing purposes.

Display Templates

The Details view that is created by the Add View dialog contains code to render each property. Here is the markup for just two of these properties:

C#

```
<p>
  ProductID:
  <%= Html.Encode(Model.ProductID) %>
</p>
<p>
  Name:
  <%= Html.Encode(Model.Name) %>
</p>
```

VB

```
<p>
  ProductID:
  <%= Html.Encode(Model.ProductID) %>
</p>
<p>
  Name:
  <%= Html.Encode(Model.Name) %>
</p>
```

With the new templates feature you can change this to the following:

C#

```
<p>
  <%= Html.LabelFor(x => x.ProductID) %>
  <%= Html.DisplayFor(x => x.ProductID) %>
</p>
<p>
  <%= Html.LabelFor(x => x.Name) %>
  <%= Html.DisplayFor(x => x.Name) %>
</p>
```

VB

```
<p>
  <%: Html.LabelFor(Function(x As ProductsMVC.Product) x.ProductID)%>
  <%: Html.DisplayFor(Function(x As ProductsMVC.Product) x.ProductID) %>
</p>
<p>
  <%: Html.LabelFor(Function(x As ProductsMVC.Product) x.Name)%>
  <%: Html.DisplayFor(Function(x As ProductsMVC.Product) x.Name) %>
</p>
```

This has a number of immediate advantages. First, the label is no longer hard coded into the view. Because the label is now strongly typed it will be updated if you refactor your model class. In addition to this you can apply a System.ComponentModel.DisplayName attribute to your model (or to a model metadata proxy) to change the text that is displayed to the user. This helps to ensure consistency across the entire application. The following code snippet shows the Product metadata proxy with a couple of `DisplayNameAttributes` and Figure 21-13 shows the rendered result:

C#

```
public class ProductValidationMetadata
{
    [DisplayName("ID")]
    public int ProductID { get; set; }

    [Required, StringLength(256)]
    [DisplayName("Product Name")]
    public string Name { get; set; }

    [Range(0, 100)]
    public int DaysToManufacture { get; set; }
}
```

VB

```
Public Class ProductMetaData
    <DisplayName("ID")>
    Property ProductID As Integer

    <Required(), StringLength(256)> _
    <DisplayName("Product Name")>
    Property Name As String

    <Range(0, 100)>
    Property DaysToManufacture As Integer
End Class
```

The `DisplayFor` helper is also providing a lot of hidden flexibility. It is selecting a template based on the type of the property that it is displays. You can override each of these type-specific views by creating a partial view named after the type in the `Shared\DisplayTemplates` folder. Figure 21-14 shows a String template and Figure 21-15 shows the output result.

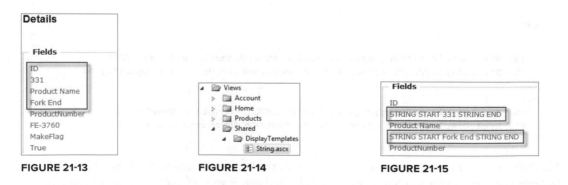

FIGURE 21-13   **FIGURE 21-14**   **FIGURE 21-15**

C#

```
<%@ Control Language="C#" Inherits="System.Web.Mvc.ViewUserControl" %>

STRING START
<%= Html.Encode(ViewData.TemplateInfo.FormattedModelValue) %>
STRING END
```

VB

```
<%@ Control Language="VB" Inherits="System.Web.Mvc.ViewUserControl" %>

STRING START
<%= Html.Encode(ViewData.TemplateInfo.FormattedModelValue) %>
STRING END
```

> *You can also create controller-specific templates by putting them inside a* `DisplayTemplates` *subfolder of the controller-specific Views folder.*

Although the display template is selected based on the type of the property by default you can override this by either supplying the name of the template to the `DisplayFor` helper or applying a `System.ComponentModel.DataAnnotations.UIHintAttribute` to the property. This attribute takes a string that identifies the type of template to use. When the framework needs to render the display for the property it tries to find the display template described by the UI Hint. If one is not found it looks for a type-specific template. If a template still hasn't been found, the default behavior is executed.

If you are simply applying `LabelFor` and `DisplayFor` for every property on your model, you can use the `Html.DisplayForModel` helper method. This method renders a label and a display template for each property on the model class. You can prevent a property from being displayed by this helper by annotating it with a `System.ComponentModel.DataAnnotations.ScaffoldColumnAttribute` passing it the value `false`.

> *If you want to change the way the* `DisplayForModel` *is rendered, you can create a type-specific template for it. If you want to change the way it renders generally, create an* `Object` *display template.*

A number of built-in display templates are available that you can use out of the box. Be aware that if you want to customize the behavior of one of these you will need to re-create it from scratch.

➤ **String:** No real surprises, just renders the string contents itself. This template does HTML encode the property value, though.

➤ **Html:** The same as string but without the HTML encoding. This is the rawest form of display that you can have. Be very careful using this template because it is a vector for malicious code injection such as Cross Site Scripting Attacks (XSS).

➤ **EmailAddress:** Renders an e-mail address as a mailto: link.

➤ **Url:** Renders a URL as an HTML anchor.

➤ **HiddenInput:** Does not render the property at all unless the `ViewData.ModelMetaData` `.HideSurroundingHtml` property is `false`.

➤ **Decimal:** Renders the property to two decimal places.

➤ **Boolean:** Renders a read-only checkbox for non-nullable values and a read-only drop-down list with True, False, and Not Set options for nullable properties.

➤ **Object:** Renders complex objects and null values.

Edit Templates

It probably comes as no surprise that there are corresponding `EditorFor` and `EditorForModel` Html helpers that handle the way properties and objects are rendered for edit purposes. Editor templates can be overridden by supplying partial views in the EditTemplates folder. Edit templates are able to use the same UI hint system that display templates use. Just as with display templates, you can use a number of built-in editor templates out of the box:

➤ **String:** Renders a standard textbox, initially populated with the value if provided and named after the property. This ensures that it will be used correctly by the model binder to rebuild the object on the other side.

➤ **Password:** The same as string but renders an HTML PASSWORD input instead of a textbox.

➤ **MultilineText:** Creates a multi-line textbox. There is no way to specify the number of rows and columns for this textbox here. It is assumed that you will use CSS to do that.

➤ **HiddenInput:** Similar to the display template, renders an HTML HIDDEN input.

➤ **Decimal:** Similar to the display template but renders a textbox to edit the value.

➤ **Boolean:** If the property type is non-nullable this renders a checkbox control. If this template is applied to a nullable property it renders a drop-down list containing the same three items as the display template.

➤ **Object:** Renders complex editors.

> *Brad Wilson has a good, multi-part, in-depth tutorial on ASP.NET MVC 2.0 Templates on his blog starting at* `http://bradwilson.typepad.com/` `blog/2009/10/aspnet-mvc-2-templates-part-1-introduction.html`.

jQuery

jQuery is an open-source JavaScript framework that is included by default with the ASP.NET MVC framework. The basic element of jQuery is the function `$()`. This function can be passed a JavaScript DOM element or a string describing elements via a CSS selector. The `$()` function returns a jQuery object that exposes a number of functions that affect the elements contained. Most of these functions also return the same jQuery object so these function calls can be chained together. As an example, the following snippet selects all of the H2 tags and adds the word "section" to the end of each one:

JavaScript

```
$("h2").append(" section");
```

To make use of jQuery you need to create a reference to the jQuery library found in the /Scripts folder by adding the following to the head section of your page:

HTML

```
<script type="text/javascript" src="/Scripts/jquery-1.3.2.js"></script>
```

It is possible to use jQuery to make an HTTP request by using the `$.get` and `$.post` methods. These methods accept a URL and can optionally have a callback function to provide the results to. The following view renders the time inside two div tags called `server` and `client`, respectively. There is also a button called `update`, which when clicked makes a GET request to the `/time` URL. When it receives the results it updates the value displayed in the client div but not the server one. In addition to this it uses the `slideUp` and `slideDown` functions to animate the client time in the UI.

C#

```
<%@ Page Language="C#" Inherits="System.Web.Mvc.ViewPage<System.String>" %>

<!DOCTYPE html PUBLIC "-//W3C//DTD XHTML 1.0 Transitional//EN"
"http://www.w3.org/TR/xhtml1/DTD/xhtml1-transitional.dtd">
<html xmlns="http://www.w3.org/1999/xhtml">
<head runat="server">
  <title>Index</title>
  <script type="text/javascript" src="/Scripts/jquery-1.3.2.js"></script>
  <script type="text/javascript">
    $(document).ready(function () {
      $('#updater').click(UpdateNow);
    });

    function UpdateNow() {
      $.get('/time', function (data) {
        $('#clientTime').slideUp('fast', function () {
          $('#clientTime').empty().append(data).slideDown();
        });
      });
    }
  </script>
</head>
<body>
    <div>
        <h2>
            Server</h2>
        <div id="serverTime">
            <%:Model %></div>
        <h2>
            Client</h2>
```

```
            <div id="clientTime">
                <%:Model %></div>
            <input type="button" value="Update" id="updater"  />
        </div>
    </body>
    </html>
```

Here is the action method that controls the previous view. It uses the IsAjaxRequest extension method to determine if the request has come from jQuery. If it has, it returns just the time as a string, otherwise it returns the full view.

C#

```
public ActionResult Index()
{
    var now = DateTime.Now.ToLongTimeString();
    if (Request.IsAjaxRequest())
      return Content(now);
    return View(now as object);
}
```

VB

```
Function Index() As ActionResult
    Dim timeNow = Now.ToString()
    If Request.IsAjaxRequest() Then
      Return Content(timeNow)
    End If
    Return View(CType(timeNow, Object))
End Function
```

jQuery is a rich client-side programming tool with an extremely active community and a large number of plug-ins. For more information about jQuery including a comprehensive set of tutorials and demos see http://jquery.com.

SUMMARY

The ASP.NET MVC framework makes it easy to build highly testable, loosely coupled web applications that embrace the nature of HTTP. The 2.0 release has a lot of productivity gains including Templates and Visual Studio integration. For more information about ASP.NET MVC, see http://asp.net/mvc.

Silverlight

WHAT'S IN THIS CHAPTER?

➤ Creating your First Silverlight application

➤ Using the Navigation Framework

➤ Theming your Silverlight application

➤ Running a Silverlight application outside of the browser

Although it's a rather new technology, Silverlight has been getting a lot of traction from within Microsoft and the developer community due to its huge potential as a development platform. New major versions are released very regularly (there were only nine months between the version 2 and version 3 releases), demonstrating that it is progressing fast. At the time of writing Silverlight had reached version 4, which is already showing a lot of maturity for a reasonably young technology.

Previously, it was quite a chore to configure Visual Studio 2008 for Silverlight development, requiring Service Pack 1 along with the Silverlight Tools to be installed just to get started. Visual Studio 2010 comes already configured for Silverlight development "out of the box," making it very easy to get started. Also, Visual Studio 2008 had no designer for Silverlight user interfaces (initially there was a preview view but this was later abandoned), requiring developers to write the XAML and run their application to view the results, or use Expression Blend if they had access to it (which did have a designer). This has been vastly improved in Visual Studio 2010, with a very capable designer now available making it much easier for developers to create user interfaces in Silverlight.

Because Silverlight is effectively a subset of Windows Presentation Foundation (WPF) you will find that many of the Visual Studio features for WPF detailed in Chapter 18 also apply to Silverlight, and thus aren't repeated here. Of course, Silverlight has no Windows Forms interoperability (due to it running in a sandboxed environment and not using the full .NET Framework), but the other Visual Studio features detailed for WPF development can also be used when developing Silverlight applications. This chapter takes you through the features of Visual Studio that are specific to Silverlight and don't apply to WPF.

WHAT IS SILVERLIGHT?

When starting Silverlight development you will notice its similarity to WPF. Both technologies revolve around their use of XAML for defining the presentation layer, and are very similar to develop with. However, they do differ greatly in how they are each intended to be used. Silverlight could essentially be considered a trimmed-down version of WPF, designed to be deployed via the Web and run in a web browser — what is generally called a Rich Internet Application (RIA). WPF, on the other hand, is for developing rich client (desktop) applications. It could be pointed out that WPF applications can be compiled to an XBAP (XAML Browser Application) and deployed and run in the same manner as Silverlight applications, but these require the .NET Framework to be installed on the client machine and can only be run on Windows — neither of which is true for Silverlight applications.

One of the great benefits of Silverlight is that it doesn't require the .NET Framework to be installed on the client machine (which can be quite a sizable download if it isn't installed). Instead, the Silverlight run time is just a small download (about 5 MB), and installs itself as a browser plug-in. If the user navigates to a web page that has Silverlight content but the client machine doesn't have the Silverlight run time installed, the user is prompted to download and install it. The install happens automatically once the user agrees to it, and the Silverlight application opens when the install completes. With such a small download size for the run time, the Silverlight plug-in can be installed and running the Silverlight application in under two minutes. This makes it very easy to deploy your application. Though not as prevalent as Adobe Flash, Silverlight is rapidly expanding its install base and eventually it's expected that its install base will come close to that of Flash.

One of the advantages Silverlight applications (and RIA applications in general) have over ASP.NET applications is that they allow you to write rich applications that run solely on the client, and communicate with the server only when necessary (generally to send or request data). Essentially, you can write web applications in much the same way as you write desktop applications. This includes the ability to write C# or VB.NET code that runs on the client — enabling you to reuse your existing codebase and not have to learn new languages (such as JavaScript).

Another great benefit of Silverlight is that Silverlight applications will run in all the major web browsers, and most excitingly will also run on Mac as well as Windows, enabling you to build cross-browser and cross-platform applications very easily. Support for Linux is being provided by Moonlight (developed by the Mono team at Novell), although its development is running somewhat behind the versions delivered by Microsoft. This means that Silverlight can be the ideal way to write Web-deployed cross-platform applications. Silverlight applications render exactly the same across different web browsers, removing the pain of regular web development where each browser can render your application differently.

The downsides of Silverlight are that it only includes a subset of the .NET Framework in order to minimize the size of the run time download, and that the applications are run in a sandboxed environment — preventing access to the client machine (a good thing for security, but reduces the uses of the technology). There are tradeoffs to be made when choosing between WPF and Silverlight, and if you choose Silverlight you should be prepared to make these sacrifices to obtain the benefits.

Ultimately, you could say that Silverlight applications are a cross between rich client and web applications, bringing the best of both worlds together.

GETTING STARTED WITH SILVERLIGHT

Visual Studio 2010 already comes configured with the main components you need for Silverlight development. Silverlight is supported out of the box with Visual Studio 2010, but if a new version of Silverlight has been released that you want to target you will need to download the SDK for that version. The best place to check if a new SDK has been released and download any required (or related) components is `http://www.silverlight.net/getstarted`.

Create a new project and select the Silverlight category (see Figure 22-1). You will find a number of project templates for Silverlight to start your project.

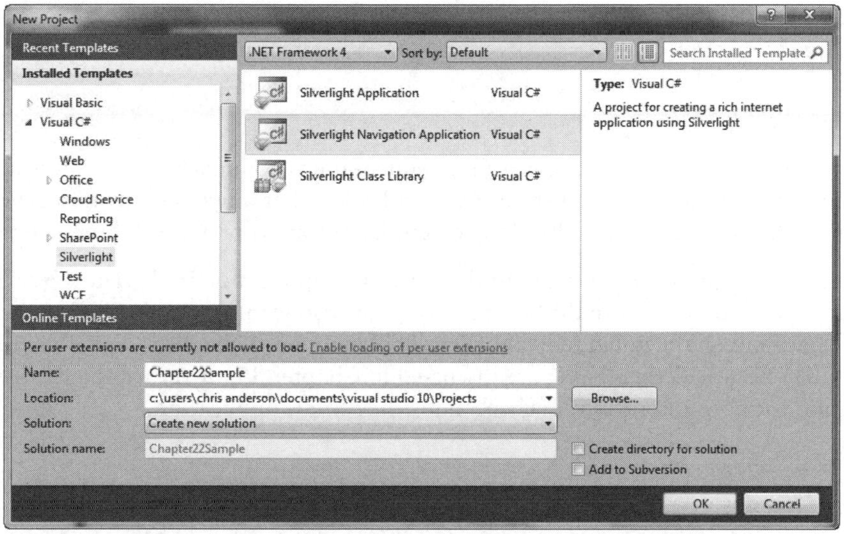

FIGURE 22-1

The Silverlight application project template is essentially a blank slate, providing a basic project to start with (best if you are creating a simple gadget). The Silverlight Navigation Application project template, however, provides you with a much better structure if you are planning to build an application with more than one screen/view, providing a user interface framework for your application and some sample views. The Silverlight Class Library project template generates exactly the same output as a standard Class Library project template, but targets the Silverlight run time instead of the full .NET Framework.

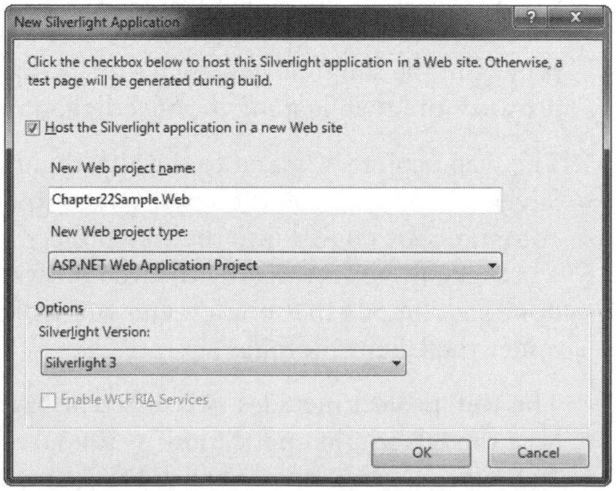

Use the Silverlight Navigation Application template for your sample project because it gives you a good base to work from. When you create the project you are presented with the template wizard screen shown in Figure 22-2 to configure the project.

FIGURE 22-2

Most of the options in this window are dedicated to configuring the web project that will be generated in the same solution as the Silverlight project. Designed primarily to be accessed via a web browser, Silverlight applications need to be hosted by a web page. Therefore, you also need a separate web project with a page that can act as the host for the Silverlight application in the browser.

So that the wizard generates a web project to host the Silverlight application, select the Host the Silverlight application in a new Web site option. If you are adding a Silverlight project to a solution with an existing web project that will host the application, you can uncheck this option and manually configure the project link in the project properties (for the Silverlight application). A default name for the web project will already be set in the New Web Project Name textbox, but you can change this if you want. The final option for configuring the web project is to select its type. The options you have are:

➤ ASP.NET Web Application Project

➤ ASP.NET Web Site Project

➤ ASP.NET MVC Web Project

Which of these web project types you choose to use is up to you, and has no impact on the Silverlight project at all. The sample application uses the Web Application Project, but how you intend to develop the web site that will host the application will ultimately determine the appropriate web project type.

In the Options group are some options that pertain to the Silverlight application itself. The Silverlight Version drop-down list allows you to choose the Silverlight version you want to target. The versions available in this list will depend on the individual Silverlight SDKs you have installed, defaulting to the latest version available. Because RIA Services are discussed in Chapter 35, disregard the Enable WCF RIA Services option for now and leave it unchecked for the sample application.

> *You can change the properties in the Options group at a later point in time via the project properties pages for the Silverlight project (see Figure 22-4).*

Let's take a tour through the structure of the solution that has been generated (shown in Figure 22-3). As was previously noted you have two projects: the Silverlight project and a separate web project to host the compiled Silverlight application. The web project is the startup project in the solution because it's really this that is opening in the browser and then loading the Silverlight application.

The web project is linked to the Silverlight project such that once the Silverlight application is compiled its output (that is, the .xap file) is automatically copied into the web project (into the ClientBin folder), where it can be accessed by the web browser. If you haven't already done so, compile the solution and you will see the .xap file appear under the ClientBin folder.

The web project includes two different pages that can be used to host the Silverlight application: a standard HTML page and an ASPX page. Both will do exactly the same thing, so it's up to you which one you use and you can delete the other.

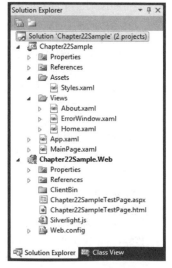

FIGURE 22-3

Looking at the Silverlight project now, you will see an `App.xaml` file and a `MainPage.xaml` file — very similar to the initial structure of a WPF project. The `MainPage.xaml` file will fill the browser window, show a header at the top with buttons to navigate around the application, and host different "views" inside the Frame control that it contains. So you could think of `MainPage.xaml` as being the shell for the content in your application.

The project template includes two default content views: a Home view and an About view. Modifying and adding new views is covered in the next section. This folder also contains `ErrorWindow.xaml`, which inherits from ChildWindow (essentially a modal dialog control in Silverlight) and pops up when an unhandled exception occurs (the unhandled exception event is handled in the code-behind for `App.xaml` and displays this control).

The Assets folder contains `Styles.xaml`, which comprises the theme styles used by the application. This is discussed in the "Theming" section in this chapter.

Now take a look at what options are available in the project properties pages of the Silverlight project. The property page unique to Silverlight applications is the Silverlight page that is shown in Figure 22-4.

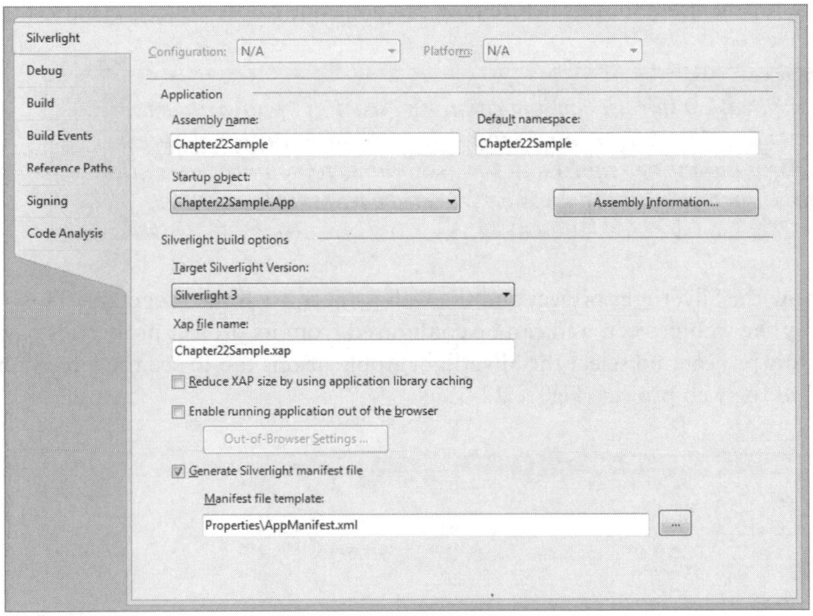

FIGURE 22-4

A number of options are of particular interest here. The Xap file name option allows you to set the name of the `.xap` file that your Silverlight project and all its references (library and control assemblies, and so on) will be compiled into. A `.xap` file is simply a zip file with a different extension, and opening it in a zip file manager enables you to view its contents. If your project is simple (that is, was created using the Silverlight Application project template and doesn't reference any control libraries), it will probably only contain your project's assembly and a manifest file. However, if you reference other assemblies in your project (such as if you use the DataGrid control that exists in the System.Windows. Controls.Data.dll assembly) you will find that your `.xap` file blows out in size very quickly (because these are also included in the `.xap` file). This would mean that each time you make a minor change to your project and deploy it that the users will be re-downloading the assemblies (such as the assembly containing the DataGrid) that haven't changed simply because they are included again in the .xap file. Fortunately, there is a way to improve this scenario, and that's to use application library caching. This is very easy to turn on, simply requiring the Reduce XAP size by using application library caching option to be checked. The next time the project is compiled the referenced assemblies will be separated out into different files and downloaded separately from the application's .xap file.

One caveat is that for assemblies to be cached they must have an extension map XML file, which is included in the .xap file and points to the zip file containing the assembly. Most controls from Microsoft will already have one of these, so you should not have to worry about this issue. Now when you compile your project again, take a look at the ClientBin folder under the web project. You will find one or more .zip files — one for each external assembly referenced by your Silverlight project, which isn't included in the core Silverlight run time. Your .xap file will also be much smaller because it will no longer contain these assemblies. The first time the user runs your application all the required pieces will be downloaded. Then when you update your project and compile it only the .xap file will need to be downloaded again. The benefits of this include less bandwidth being used for both the server and the client (updates will be much smaller to download), and updates will be much quicker, meaning less time for the users to wait before they can continue to use your application.

> *Unfortunately, application library caching cannot be used in applications that are configured to run in Out Of Browser mode (detailed later in this chapter), because Out Of Browser mode requires all the assemblies to be in the* .xap *file. If you attempt to set both options, a message box appears stating as such.*

Now let's return to see how the Silverlight project and the web project are linked together. This project link is managed by the web project, and can be configured from its project properties page. Open the properties for this project and select the Silverlight Applications tab to see the Silverlight projects currently linked to the web project (Figure 22-5).

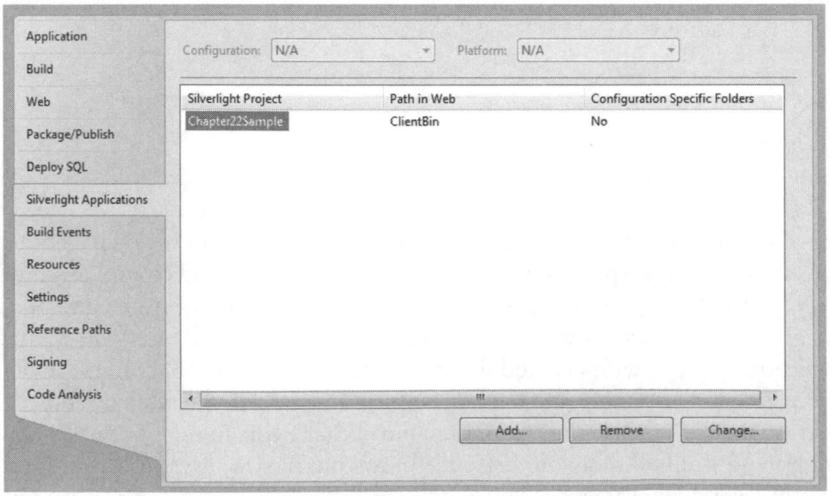

FIGURE 22-5

You will most likely only need to use this property page if the web project needs to host multiple Silverlight applications, or you have added a Silverlight project to a solution already containing a web project and you need to link the two. Project links can only be added or removed (not modified), so you will generally find you will use this property page only when a Silverlight project has been added or removed from the solution.

This property page displays the existing links in the list that this web project has to Silverlight projects in the solution. You have three options here: you can add another link to a Silverlight project, you can remove a project link, or you can change a project link (although this change option is not what you might initially expect, as discussed shortly).

Click the Add button to link another Silverlight project to the web project. Figure 22-6 shows the window used to configure the new link.

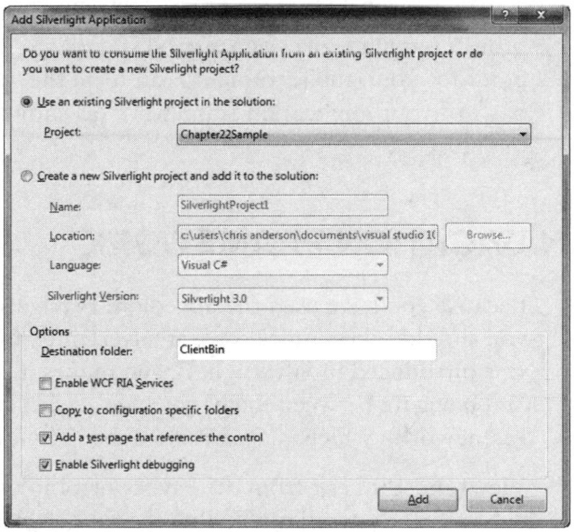

You have two choices when adding a link to a Silverlight project. The first is to link to a Silverlight project already in the solution, where you can simply select a project from the drop-down list to link to. You also have the choice to create a new Silverlight project and have it automatically link to the current web project. Unfortunately, you don't have the ability to select the project template to use, so it will only generate a new project based upon the Silverlight Application project template, somewhat limiting its use.

The Destination Folder option enables you to specify the folder underneath the web project

FIGURE 22-6

that this Silverlight project will be copied to when it has been compiled. The test pages that are generated (if selected to be created) to host the Silverlight application will point to this location.

If the Copy to configuration specific folders option is set, the Silverlight application will not be copied directly under the specified destination folder, but an additional folder will be created underneath it with the name of the current configuration (Debug, Release, and so on)? and the Silverlight application will be copied under it instead. Note that when this setting is turned on, the test pages will still point to the destination folder, not the subfolder with the name of the current configuration which will now be where the Silverlight application is located. If you want to use this option you will need to manually update the test pages to point to the path as per the current configuration, and update this each time you switch between configurations. By default, this option is not set, and it is probably best not to use it unless necessary.

Selecting the Add a test page that references the control option adds both an HTML page and an ASPX page to the web project, already configured to host the output of the Silverlight project being linked (you can delete the one you don't want to use).

The Enable Silverlight debugging option turns on the ability to debug your Silverlight application (that is, stop on breakpoints, step through code, and so on). The downside to enabling this option is that it disables JavaScript debugging for the web project, because enabling debugging for both at the same time is not possible.

Returning to the list of linked Silverlight projects (Figure 22-5), the Remove button removes a link as you'd expect, but the Change button probably won't do what you'd initially assume it would. This button is used simply to toggle between using and not using configuration-specific folders (described earlier).

Now that you have learned the structure of the project you can try running it. You can see that the Silverlight Navigation Application project template gives you a good starting point for your application and can form the basis of your application framework (as shown in Figure 22-7).

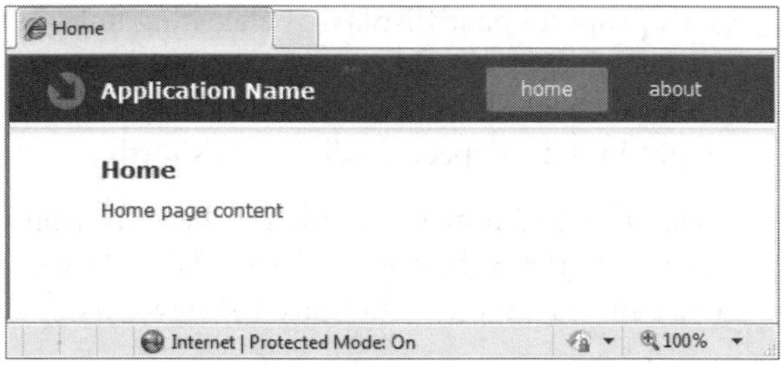

FIGURE 22-7

NAVIGATION FRAMEWORK

Because you have used the Silverlight Navigation Application project template for your project you should take a quick look at Silverlight's Navigation Framework. The Navigation Framework was introduced in Silverlight 3, and makes it easy to create an application with multiple views and navigate between them. MainPage.xaml contains a Frame control (a part of the Navigation Framework), which is used to host the individual views when they are required to be shown.

Views must inherit from the Page control in order to be hosted in the frame. If you take a look at Home.xaml you will notice that the root element is navigation:Page instead of UserControl. To create a new view, right-click the Views folder and select Add ➪ New Item. Select the Silverlight Page item template, give it a name (such as Test.xaml), and click OK. Add content to the view as required.

Each view needs a URI to point to it, and this URI will be used when you want to navigate to that view. You may want to set up a mapping from a chosen URI to the path (within the project) of its corresponding view file. These mappings are defined on the UriMapper property of the Frame control (in MainPage.xaml). These mappings allow wildcards, and a wildcard mapping has already been created that allows you to simply use the name of the XAML file (without the .xaml on the end). It will look for a XAML file with that name with a .xaml extension in the Views folder. This means you don't need to set up a mapping if you want to navigate to your Test.xaml file using /Test as the URI.

Now you need to add a button that allows you to navigate to the new view. In MainPage.xaml you will find some HyperlinkButton controls (named Link1 and Link2). Copy one of these and paste it as a new line below it (you may want to create another divider element by copying the existing one too). Change the NavigateUri to one that maps to your view (in this case it will be /Test), give the control a new name, and set the text to display on the button (in the Content property).

Now run the project. The new button will appear in the header area of the application, and clicking it navigates to the new view.

Note how the bookmark on the URL (the part after the # in the URL in the address bar of the browser) changes as you navigate between pages. You can also use the browser's Back and Next buttons to navigate backward and forward through the history of which views were previously navigated to. It also enables deep linking, such that views have a unique URL that can automatically be opened to. The Navigation Framework provides all of this functionality.

THEMING

Like WPF, Silverlight has extensive styling and theming capabilities, although their styling models are implemented slightly differently from one another. Silverlight introduced the Visual State Manager (VSM), a feature that WPF did not originally have (until WPF 4), which enables a control contract to be explicitly defined for the boundary between the control's behavior (that is, the code) and its look (that is, the XAML). This permits a strict separation to be maintained between the two. This contract defines a model for control templates called the Parts and States model, which consists of parts, states, transitions, and state groups. Further discussion of this is beyond the scope of this chapter, however the VSM in Silverlight manages this model. This is considered a much better way of managing styles than WPF's original method of using triggers, and thus the VSM has been incorporated into WPF 4. However, until Silverlight 4, Silverlight did not support implicit styling (unlike WPF, which did), where it could be specified that all controls of a given type should use a particular style (making applying a theme to your project somewhat difficult). To make theming easier, Microsoft created the ImplicitStyleManager control, which shipped in the Silverlight Toolkit control library. Silverlight 4 finally introduced implicit styling, making the ImplicitStyleManager control somewhat redundant, but you'll still use it here to demonstrate theming that works across all versions of Silverlight.

You can download the free Silverlight Toolkit from CodePlex here: `http://silverlight.codeplex.com`. It also contains numerous useful controls that aren't included in the Silverlight SDK (such as charts, tab control, TreeView, and so on).

So despite their differences, WPF and Silverlight both have controls in their respective toolkit projects that enable similar styling and theming behavior between the two.

Now take a look at applying a different theme to your project in order to completely change the way the controls look. Silverlight has the same themes available as demonstrated in Chapter 18 (in fact, the themes were originally developed for Silverlight and ported to WPF), and can be found in the Silverlight Toolkit. You will call these *control themes* to separate them from the *application themes* that are discussed shortly.

You have a couple of ways to use these control themes. One is to take one of the XAML theming files from the Silverlight Toolkit, copy it into your project's root folder, and include it in your project (setting its Build Action to Content at the same time). For this example you will use the `System.Windows.Controls.Theming.ExpressionDark.xaml` theme file. Now add a reference to the `System.Windows.Controls.Theming.Toolkit.dll` from the Silverlight Toolkit (which enables you to use the ImplicitStyleManager control). Unfortunately, you can't specify the theme at the application level because the ImplicitStyleManager control has some limitations imposed by Silverlight, therefore in the root element of all of the views to be themed you will need to add the following namespace prefix and property value definitions:

```
xmlns:theming="clr-namespace:System.Windows.Controls.Theming; assembly=
System.Windows.Controls.Theming.Toolkit"

theming:ImplicitStyleManager.ResourceDictionaryUri=
"System.Windows.Controls.Theming.ExpressionDark.xaml"
theming:ImplicitStyleManager.ApplyMode="OneTime"
```

Now when you compile and run your project you will find all the controls in the views that have had their themes set are now using the themes from the specified theme file.

> You may find that the project doesn't compile due to missing references that the theme file is using. Because the theme file has styles for many different controls, it is referencing the assemblies that contain those controls. You can either add a reference to the required assemblies, or if you don't want to use them, you can remove the styles for those controls (and their related namespace prefix definitions) from the theme file.

If you create your project using the Silverlight Navigation Application template or the Silverlight Business Application template you can also take advantage of some alternative *application themes* that have been created to give your application a whole new look. You can find the application theme styles in the `Styles.xaml` file under the Assets folder in your Silverlight project. The `App.xaml` file merges the styles from this file into its own if your project is based on the Silverlight Navigation Application project template. `MainPage.xaml` uses the styles that have been defined in `Styles.xaml` to specify its layout and look. Therefore, all you need to do is replace this file with one with the same styles defined but with different values in order to completely change the way the application looks. A number of alternative application theme files for projects based upon the Silverlight Navigation Application project template have been created by Microsoft and the community, and can be downloaded from `http://gallery.expression.microsoft.com` (look in the Themes category). For example, simply replacing the `Styles.xaml` file for the project shown in Figure 22-7 with the theme file from the gallery called "Frosted Cinnamon Toast" completely changes the way it looks, as shown in Figure 22-8.

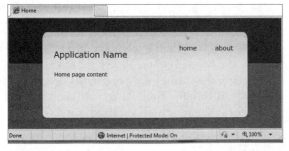

FIGURE 22-8

ENABLING RUNNING OUT OF BROWSER

Though Silverlight was initially designed as a browser-based plug-in, Silverlight 3 introduced the ability to run a Silverlight application outside the browser as if it were a standard application, and it was no longer necessary to run your Silverlight application within a browser. In fact, you don't even need to be online to run a Silverlight application once it has been installed to run in Out-Of-Browser mode. Out-Of-Browser applications are delivered initially via the browser, and can then be installed on the machine (if enabled by the developer). This install process can be initiated from the right-click menu or from code — the only criteria being that the install process must be user initiated (so random applications can't install themselves on users' machines without their approval).

By default, your Silverlight application will not be configured for Out-Of-Browser mode, and you must explicitly enable this in your application for the feature to be available. The easiest way to enable this is in the project properties for the Silverlight application, as was shown in Figure 22-4. When you put a check in the Enable Running the Application Out of the Browser option the Out-of-Browser Settings button becomes enabled, and clicking this button pops up the window shown in Figure 22-9.

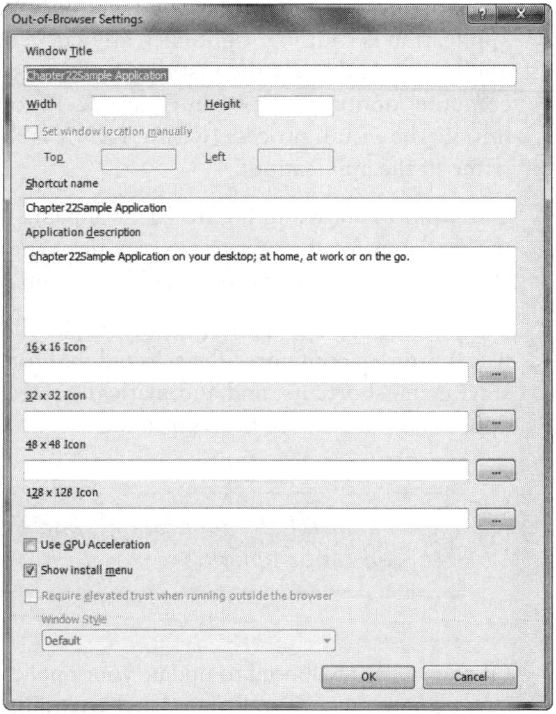

This window enables you to configure various options for when the application is running in Out-Of-Browser mode. Most of the options are fairly self-explanatory. You can set the window title and its starting dimensions (the window is resizable). You can also configure the start menu/desktop shortcuts, set the text for the shortcut (the shortcut name), set the text that will appear when the mouse hovers over the icon (the application description), and set the various-sized icons to use for the shortcut. These icons must be PNG

FIGURE 22-9

files that have already been added as files in your Silverlight project. Select the appropriate image for each icon size. If you leave any of these icons blank, it simply uses the default Out-Of-Browser icon for that icon size instead. The two checkboxes at the bottom enable you to set whether Out-Of-Browser mode should use GPU acceleration (for Silverlight applications running inside the browser this setting is set on the Silverlight plug-in itself), and the Show install menu checkbox specifies whether the user should have the option to install the application via the right-click menu (otherwise, the install process must be initiated from code).

> *Note that your Silverlight application is still sandboxed when running outside the browser and will have no more access to the user's computer than it did while running inside the browser. So although it may appear to be running as if it were a standard application, it's still restricted by the same security model as when it's running inside the browser. However, Silverlight 4 introduced the ability for Out-Of-Browser applications to obtain elevated trust privileges, including COM automation and local file access.*

Once you've configured the Out-Of-Browser settings you can now run the project and try it out. When your application is running, right-click anywhere on your application and select the Install XXXX onto your computer option as shown in Figure 22-10 to initiate the install process (where XXXX is the name of the application).

FIGURE 22-10

FIGURE 22-11

The window shown in Figure 22-11 appears with options for the user to select which types of shortcuts to the application should be set up.

This installs the application locally (under the user's profile), configures the selected desktop/ start menu shortcuts, and automatically starts the application in Out-Of-Browser mode.

> *To uninstall the application, simply right-click it and select the Remove this Application option.*

Of course, you will need to update your application at some point in time and have the existing instances that were installed updated accordingly. Luckily, this is very easy to do, but does require some code. This code could be used anywhere in your application, but you'll put it in the code-behind for the App.xaml file, and start the update available check as soon as the application has started as follows:

VB

```
Private Sub Application_Startup(ByVal o As Object, ByVal e As StartupEventArgs) _
                                                      Handles Me.Startup
    Me.RootVisual = New MainPage()

    If Application.Current.IsRunningOutOfBrowser Then
```

```
                Application.Current.CheckAndDownloadUpdateAsync()
        End If
End Sub

Private Sub App_CheckAndDownloadUpdateCompleted(ByVal sender As Object, _
                        ByVal e As _
                        System.Windows.CheckAndDownloadUpdateCompletedEventArgs) _
                        Handles Me.CheckAndDownloadUpdateCompleted
        If e.UpdateAvailable Then
            MessageBox.Show("A new version of this application is available and " &
                            "has been downloaded.  Please close the application and " &
                            "restart it to use the new version.",
                            "Application Update Found", MessageBoxButton.OK)
        End If
End Sub
```

C#
```
private void Application_Startup(object sender, StartupEventArgs e)
{
    this.RootVisual = new Page();

    if (Application.Current.IsRunningOutOfBrowser)
    {
        Application.Current.CheckAndDownloadUpdateCompleted +=
                Current_CheckAndDownloadUpdateCompleted;
        Application.Current.CheckAndDownloadUpdateAsync();
    }
}

private void Current_CheckAndDownloadUpdateCompleted(object sender,
                        CheckAndDownloadUpdateCompletedEventArgs e)
{
    if (e.UpdateAvailable)
    {
        MessageBox.Show("A new version of this application is available and " +
            "has been downloaded.  Please close the application and restart " +
            "it to use the new version.", "Application Update Found",
            MessageBoxButton.OK);
    }
}
```

As you can see, if the application is running in Out-Of-Browser mode you check to see if there are any updates. This asynchronously goes back to the URL that the application was installed from and checks if there is a new version (during which the application continues to load and run). If so it automatically downloads it. Whether or not an update was found, it raises the CheckAndDownloadUpdateCompleted event once the check (and potential download of a new version) is complete. Then you just need to see if an update had been found, and notify the user if so. The update is automatically installed the next time the application is run, so in order to start using the new version the user will need to close the application and reopen it again.

To test the update process, start by including the update check code in your application. Run the application and install it using the method described earlier. Close both it and the instance that was running in the browser and return to Visual Studio. Make a change to the application (one that allows you spot the difference if it is updated correctly) and recompile it. Now run the previously installed version (from the Start menu or desktop icon). The application starts, and shortly afterwards the message box appears stating that the new version has been downloaded and to restart the application. When you reopen the application again you should see that you are indeed now running the new version.

SUMMARY

In this chapter you have seen how you can work with Visual Studio 2010 to build applications with Silverlight, and run them both within and outside the browser. To learn about one of the many means of communicating between the client and the server and transferring data see Chapter 35, "WCF RIA Services."

Dynamic Data

➤ Creating a data-driven web application without writing any code using Dynamic Data's scaffolding functionality

➤ Customizing the data model and presentation layer of a Dynamic Data application

➤ Adding Dynamic Data features to an existing web application

Most developers spend an inordinately large amount of their time writing code that deals with data. In fact, this is so fundamental to what many of us do on a daily basis that an acronym has appeared to describe this type of code — *CRUD*. CRUD stands for *Create*, *Read*, *Update*, *Delete*, which are the four basic functions that can be performed on data.

For example, consider a simple application to maintain a Tasks or To Do list. At the very least the application must provide the following functionality:

➤ **Create:** Create a new task and save it in the database.

➤ **Read:** Retrieve a list of tasks from the database and display them to the user. Retrieve and display all the properties of an individual task.

➤ **Update:** Modify the properties of an existing task and save the changes to the database.

➤ **Delete:** Delete a task from the database that is no longer required.

ASP.NET Dynamic Data is a framework that takes away the need to write much of this low-level CRUD code. Dynamic Data can discover the data model and automatically generate a fully functioning, data-driven web site at run time. This allows developers to focus instead on writing rock-solid business logic, enhancing the user experience, or performing some other high-value programming task.

LESS IS MORE: SCAFFOLDING AND CONVENTION OVER CONFIGURATION

Scaffolding is the name for the mechanism that ASP.NET Dynamic Data uses to dynamically generate web pages based on the underlying database. The generated pages include all of the functionality you would expect in any decent data-driven application including paging and sorting. In addition to the benefits of freeing developers from writing low-level data access code, scaffolding provides built-in data validation based on the database schema and full support for foreign keys and relationships between tables.

Scaffolding was popularized by the Ruby on Rails web development framework. Along with scaffolding, ASP.NET Dynamic Data includes several other principles and practices that are clearly inspired by Ruby on Rails. One such principle is *Convention over Configuration*, which means that certain things are implicitly assumed through a standard convention. For example, at run time, Dynamic Data will detect the file `List.aspx` under the folder called Products and use it to render a custom web page for the Product database table. Because the folder name is the same (pluralized) name as the database table, there is no need to explicitly tell Dynamic Data that this file exists, or that it is associated with the Product table.

Less code means fewer places for mistakes.

This chapter demonstrates how to use Dynamic Data scaffolding to create a data-driven web application with little or no code. You also learn how flexible Dynamic Data is by customizing the data model and web pages.

Although Dynamic Data is somewhat synonymous with scaffolding and building a data-driven web application from scratch, at the end of this chapter you will see that you can get a number of benefits by adding Dynamic Data functionality to your existing web application.

CREATING A DYNAMIC DATA WEB APPLICATION

Before you can create and run a Dynamic Data web application you will need a database. The examples in this chapter use the SQL Server 2008 AdventureWorksLT database, which you can download from the CodePlex web site at `http://msftdbprodsamples.codeplex.com/`.

Once you've downloaded your database, open Visual Studio and select File ⇨ New ⇨ Project. In the Web project category of both Visual Basic and C# you will see two project templates for Dynamic Data that reflect the two major data access options supported by Microsoft. The first, LINQ to SQL, is provided by the aptly named Dynamic Data Linq to SQL Web Application template. The second template, Dynamic Data Entities Web Application, supports the ADO.NET Entity Framework.

> *If you prefer working with Web Site projects instead of Web Application projects you can still use Dynamic Data. Under the New Web Site dialog you will find two equivalent templates for creating a new LINQ to SQL or Entities Dynamic Data Web Site project.*

LINQ TO SQL VERSUS THE ADO.NET ENTITY FRAMEWORK

LINQ to SQL and the ADO.NET Entity Framework are the two main data access options that are currently being promoted by Microsoft. Both have their pros and cons, and both work perfectly well for many of the more common scenarios.

LINQ to SQL works only with Microsoft SQL Server database, and only supports a direct mapping of a single database table to a single .NET class. Because LINQ to SQL is so tightly coupled to SQL Server, it is known to generate very efficient T-SQL code.

On the other hand, the ADO.NET Entity Framework allows for a data model that is different from the underlying database schema. You can map multiple database tables to a single .NET class, or a single database table to multiple .NET classes. The Entity Framework also supports a number of different databases including Oracle, MySQL, and DB2.

You can find out more about LINQ to SQL in Chapter 28 and the ADO.NET Entity Framework in Chapter 29.

Select the Dynamic Data Linq to SQL Web Application project and click OK. When the new project is created it will generate a large number of files and folders, as shown in Figure 23-1. Most of these files are templates that can be modified to customize the user interface. These are located under the DynamicData root folder and are discussed later in this chapter.

The project template will also create a standard web form, `Default.aspx`, as the start page for the web application. As with the standard ASP.NET Web Application project, the application encourages best practices by making use of the master page feature and an external CSS file, and includes the JQuery JavaScript library. See Chapter 20 for further information on any of these features.

Adding a Data Model

Once you have created your new project you will need to specify the database and create a new data model. Right-click the App_Data folder and select Add Existing Item, then browse to the `AdventureWorksLT2008_Data.mdf` file you downloaded earlier and click Add.

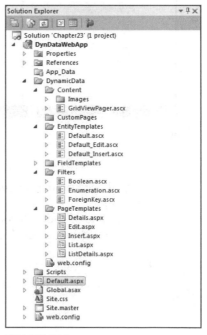

FIGURE 23-1

The next step is to create the data model. Right-click the project in the Solution Explorer and select Add ➪ New Item. Select the LINQ to SQL Classes item from the Data category and name it `AdventureWorksDM.dbml`. If you had chosen to create an Entities Dynamic Data project earlier you would select the ADO.NET Entity Data Model instead.

After you click Add, the new item will open in the Object Relational Designer. Double-click the AdventureWorksLT database file you added earlier to open it in the Server Explorer and then expand the Tables node. Select all tables, except the first two, and drag them onto the Designer. This populates the LINQ to SQL data model as shown in Figure 23-2.

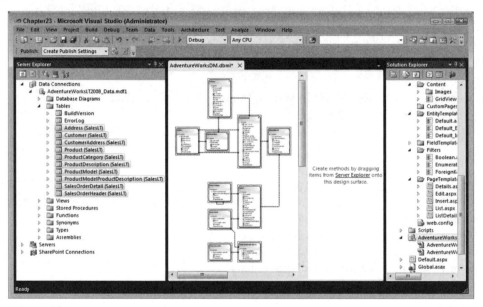

FIGURE 23-2

Finally, you'll need to register your data model with Dynamic Data and enable scaffolding. Open the `Global.asax.cs` (or `Global.asax.vb` if you are using Visual Basic) and locate the following line of code. Uncomment this line and change the `YourDataContextType` to `AdventureWorksDMDataContext`. Lastly, change the `ScaffoldAllTables` property to `true`.

C#

```
DefaultModel.RegisterContext(typeof(AdventureWorksDMDataContext),
                    new ContextConfiguration()
                    { ScaffoldAllTables = true });
```

Code snippet Global.asax.cs

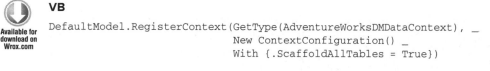

VB

```
DefaultModel.RegisterContext(GetType(AdventureWorksDMDataContext), _
                             New ContextConfiguration() _
                             With {.ScaffoldAllTables = True})
```

Code snippet Global.asax.vb

That is all you need to do to get a data-driven web application with full CRUD support up and running.

Exploring a Dynamic Data Application

When you run the application, it opens with the home page, `Default.aspx`, which displays a list of hyperlinks for all the tables you added to the data model (see Figure 23-3). Note that the names listed on this page are pluralized versions of the table name.

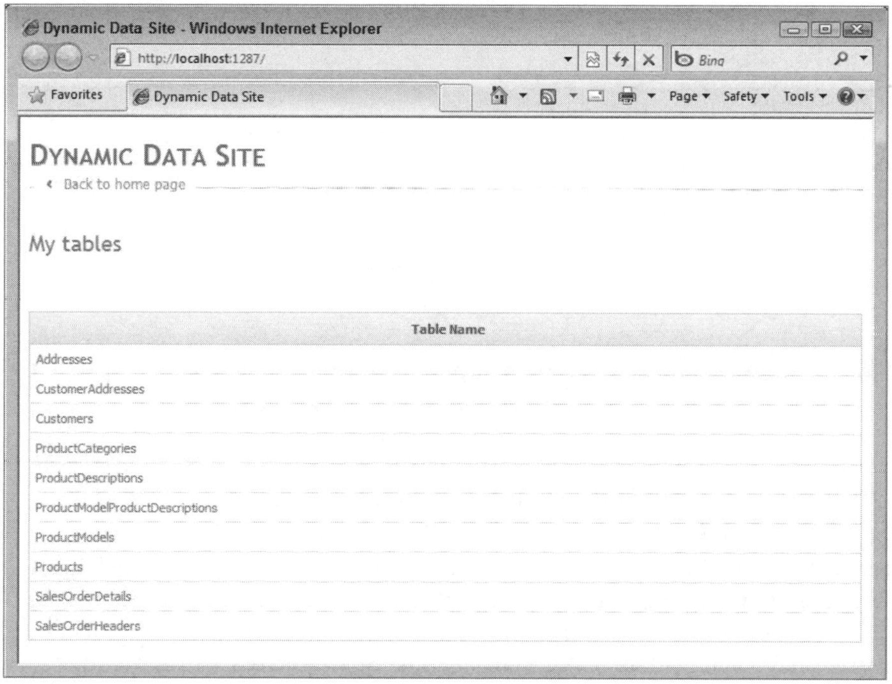

![Dynamic Data Site screenshot showing the home page with a list of table names: Addresses, CustomerAddresses, Customers, ProductCategories, ProductDescriptions, ProductModelProductDescriptions, ProductModels, Products, SalesOrderDetails, SalesOrderHeaders]

FIGURE 23-3

When you click one of these links, you are taken to the `List.aspx` page, shown in Figure 23-4, for the selected table. This page, along with the `Details.aspx` page for an individual record, represents the "Read" function of your CRUD application and includes support for paging and filtering of the records by foreign key. This page also displays links to view details, edit, or delete a record. Any foreign keys are displayed as links to a details page for that foreign key record.

> *You may notice that some database fields are missing from the web page, such as ProductID and ThumbNailPhoto. By default, Dynamic Data will not scaffold Identity columns, binary columns, or computed columns. This can be overridden, as you will find out later in this chapter.*

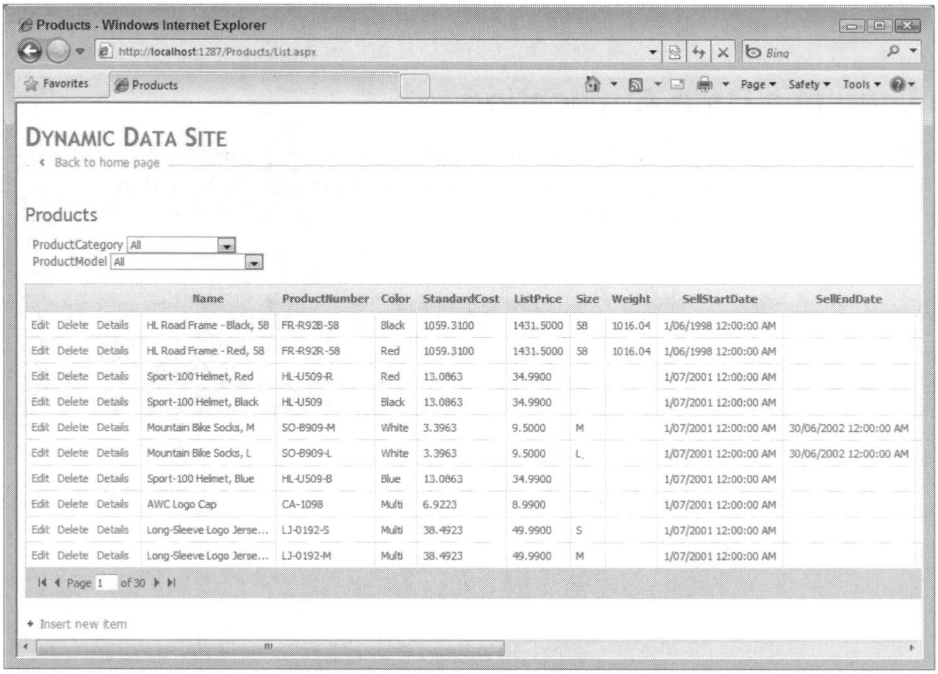

FIGURE 23-4

The "Update" CRUD function is accessed by clicking the Edit link against a record. This displays the `Edit.aspx` page, as shown in Figure 23-5. You will notice that the textboxes are different widths — this is determined based on the length of the database field. This page also includes a number of ASP.NET validation controls, based on database field information. For example, the ProductNumber field has a `RequiredFieldValidator` because the underlying database field is not nullable. Likewise, the Weight field uses a `CompareValidator` to ensure that the value entered is a decimal.

Foreign keys are also handled by drop-down selectors. For example, in Figure 23-5 the ProductCategory and ProductModel fields are foreign keys. Tables that use the selected table as a foreign key are displayed as hyperlinks. This can be seen in the SalesOrderDetails field in Figure 23-5.

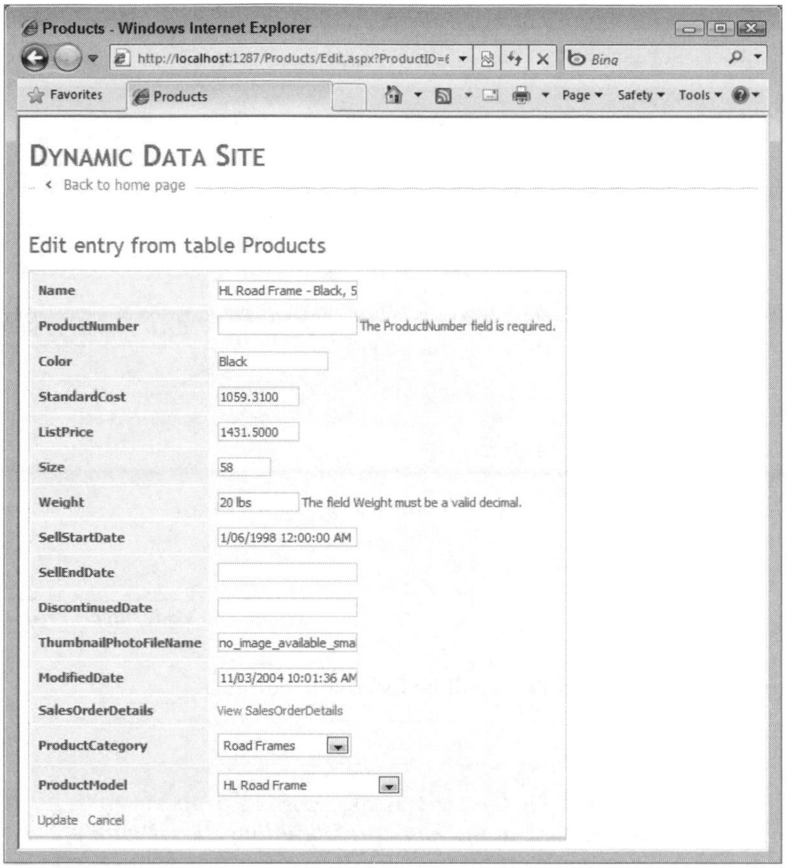

FIGURE 23-5

CUSTOMIZING THE DATA MODEL

While scaffolding an entire database makes for an impressive demo, it is unlikely that you would actually want to expose every table and field in your database to end users. Fortunately, Dynamic Data has been designed to handle this scenario, and many others, by customizing the data model.

Scaffolding Individual Tables

Before you begin customizing the data model you should disable automatic scaffolding of all tables. Open the `Global.asax.cs` file and change the `ScaffoldAllTables` property to `false`.

The next step is to selectively enable scaffolding for individual tables. Begin by adding a new class file to the project called `Product.cs`. This class must be a partial class, because Product is already defined in the LINQ to SQL data model. To enable scaffolding for the Product table, decorate the class with the `ScaffoldTable` attribute. Once completed, the class should look similar to the following code:

C#

```
using System.ComponentModel.DataAnnotations;

namespace DynDataWebApp
{
    [ScaffoldTable(true)]
    public partial class Product
    {
    }
}
```

Code snippet Product.cs

VB

```
Imports System.ComponentModel.DataAnnotations

<ScaffoldTable(True)> _
Partial Public Class Product
End Class
```

Code snippet Product.vb

If you run the application now only the Product table will be listed and editable.

> *You can achieve the same result by leaving the* ScaffoldAllTables *property to* true *and selectively hiding tables by decorating their corresponding classes with the* ScaffoldTable *attribute set to* false.

Customizing Individual Data Fields

In many cases you will want certain fields in a table to be either read only or hidden. This is particularly useful if the table contains sensitive data such as credit card information.

For example, when you edit a record in the Products table, it displays a link to the SalesOrderDetails table. This link is disabled because the SalesOrderDetails table has not been enabled for scaffolding. Therefore displaying this field provides the user with no useful information. Also the ModifiedDate field, while useful for end users to know, is not something that you would typically want them to edit directly. Therefore it would be better to display this field as read only and allow the database to modify it with an Update trigger.

These requirements are supported by Dynamic Data by adding a *metadata class* to your data model class. In the Product.cs file add a new class to the bottom of the file called ProductMetadata. This class can be associated by applying the MetadataType attribute to the Product class.

In the `ProductMetadata` class, create public fields with the same name as each data field that you want to customize. Because Dynamic Data will read the type of this field from the data model class rather than the metadata class, you can use `object` as the type for these fields.

Add the `ScaffoldColumn` attribute to the `SalesOrderDetails` field and set it to `false` to hide the field. To make the `ModifiedDate` field read only, decorate it with an `Editable` attribute that is set to `false`.

The following code shows these changes:

C#

```csharp
namespace DynDataWebApp
{
    [ScaffoldTable(true)]
    [MetadataType(typeof(ProductMetadata))]
    public partial class Product
    {
    }
    public class ProductMetadata
    {
        [ScaffoldColumn(false)]
        public object SalesOrderDetails;

        [Editable(false)]
        public object ModifiedDate;
    }
}
```

Code snippet Product.cs

VB

```vb
<ScaffoldTable(True)> _
<MetadataType(GetType(ProductMetadata))> _
Partial Public Class Product
End Class
Public Class ProductMetadata
    <ScaffoldColumn(False)> _
    Public SalesOrderDetails As Object

    <Editable(False)> _
    Public ModifiedDate As Object
End Class
```

Code snippet Product.vb

Figure 23-6 shows the results of these changes in action. On the left is the original edit screen for the Product table. On the right is the new edit screen after the data model has been customized.

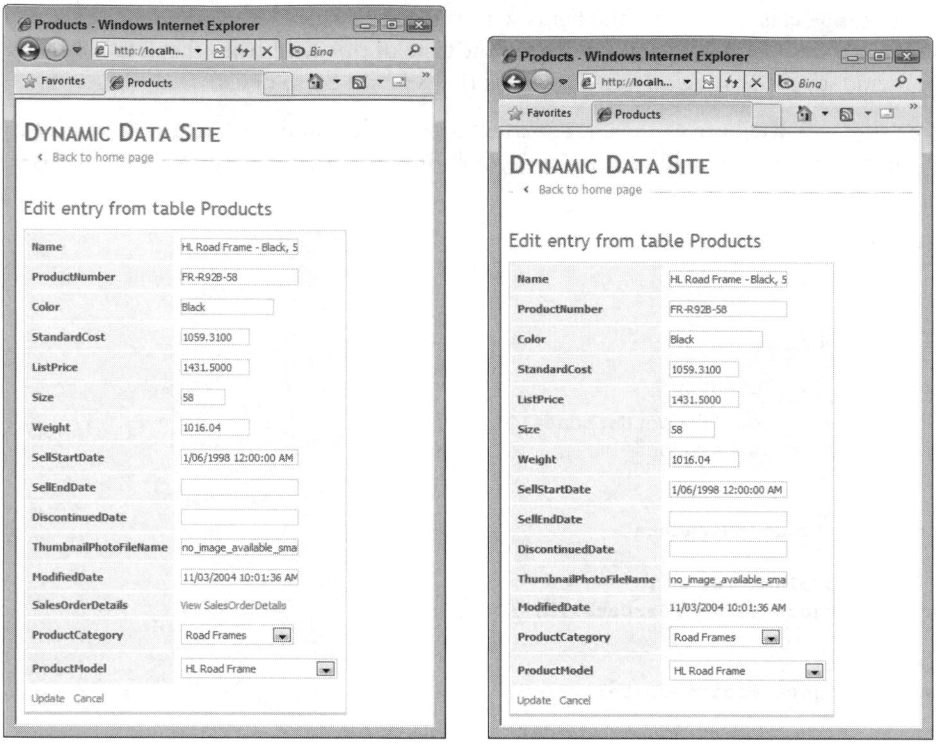

FIGURE 23-6

Adding Custom Validation Rules

As mentioned earlier in this chapter, Dynamic Data includes some built-in support for validation rules that are inferred from the underlying database schema. For example, if a field in a database table is marked as not nullable, a `RequiredFieldValidator` will be added to the Update page.

However, in some cases there are business rules about the format of data that isn't supported by the built-in validation rules. For example, in the Product table, the values saved in the ProductNumber field all follow a specific format that begins with two uppercase letters followed by a hyphen. This format can be enforced by decorating the ProductNumber field with a `RegularExpression` attribute, as shown in the following code:

Available for download on Wrox.com

C#

```
[ScaffoldTable(true)]
[MetadataType(typeof(ProductMetadata))]
public partial class Product
{
}

public class ProductMetadata
```

```
    {
        [RegularExpression("^[A-Z]{2}-[A-Z0-9]{4}(-[A-Z0-9]{1,2})?$",
         ErrorMessage="Product Number must be a valid format")]
        public object ProductNumber;
    }
```

Code snippet Product.cs

VB

```
<ScaffoldTable(True)> _
<MetadataType(GetType(ProductMetadata))> _
Partial Public Class Product
End Class

Public Class ProductMetadata
    <RegularExpression("^[A-Z]{2}-[A-Z0-9]{4}(-[A-Z0-9]{1,2})?$", _
     ErrorMessage:="Product Number must be a valid format")> _
    Public ProductNumber As Object
End Class
```

Code snippet Product.vb

There is also a Range attribute, which is useful for specifying the minimum and maximum allowed values for a numeric field. Finally, you can apply the Required or StringLength attributes if you want to enforce these constraints on a field in the data model without specifying them in the underlying database.

Although useful, the attribute-based validations don't support all scenarios. For example, a user could attempt to enter a date for the Product SellEndDate that is earlier than the SellStartDate value. Due to a database constraint on this field, this would result in a runtime exception rather than a validation error, which is presented to the user.

For each field that is in the data model, LINQ to SQL defines two methods that are called during an edit — the OnFieldNameChanging method, which is called just before the field is changed, and the OnFieldNameChanged method, which is called just after. To handle complex validation rules, you can complete the appropriate partial method declaration in the data model.

The following code shows a validation rule that ensures a value entered for the Product SellEndDate field is not earlier than the SellStartDate:

C#

```
[ScaffoldTable(true)]
[MetadataType(typeof(ProductMetadata))]
public partial class Product
{
    partial void OnSellEndDateChanging(DateTime? value)
    {
        if (value.HasValue && value.Value < this._SellStartDate)
```

```
        {
            throw new ValidationException(
                    "Sell End Date must be later than Sell Start Date");
        }
    }
}
```

Code snippet Product.cs

VB

```
<ScaffoldTable(True)> _
<MetadataType(GetType(ProductMetadata))> _
Partial Public Class Product
    Private Sub OnSellEndDateChanging(ByVal value As Nullable(Of DateTime))
        If value.HasValue AndAlso value.Value < Me._SellStartDate Then
            Throw New ValidationException( _
                    "Sell End Date must be later than Sell Start Date")
        End If
    End Sub
End Class
```

Code snippet Product.vb

Figure 23-7 shows how this custom validation rule is enforced by Dynamic Data.

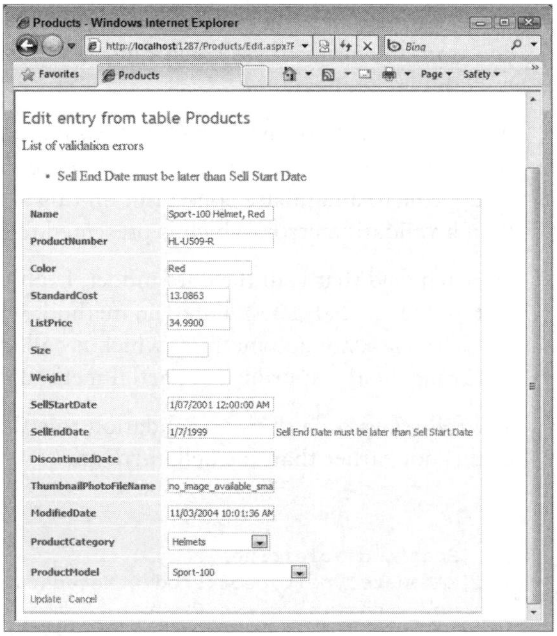

Customizing the Display Format

The default way that some of the data types are formatted is less than ideal. For example, the Product StandardCost and ListPrice fields, which use the SQL money data type, are displayed as numbers to four decimal places. Also, the Product SellStartDate and SellEndDate fields, which have a SQL datetime data type, are formatted showing both the date and time, even though the time portion is not really useful information.

The display format of these fields can be customized in two ways: globally for a specific data type by customizing the field template; or on an individual field basis by customizing the data model. Field template customization is discussed later in this chapter.

FIGURE 23-7

First, to specify how the fields will be formatted in the user interface, decorate the corresponding property in the data model with the DisplayFormat attribute. This attribute has a DataFormatString property that accepts a .NET format string. The attribute also includes a number of additional parameters to control rendering including the `HtmlEncode` parameter, which indicates whether the field should be HTML encoded, and the `NullDisplayText` attribute, which sets the text to be displayed when the field's value is null. The following code shows how the `DisplayFormat` attribute can be applied:

C#

```csharp
[DisplayFormat(DataFormatString="{0:C}")]
public object ListPrice;

[DisplayFormat(DataFormatString="{0:MMM d, yyyy}",
               NullDisplayText="Not Specified")]
public object SellEndDate;
```

Code snippet Product.cs

VB

```vb
<Display(Name:="List Price")> _
<DisplayFormat(DataFormatString:="{0:C}")> _
Public ListPrice As Object

<Display(Name:="Sell End Date")> _
<DisplayFormat(DataFormatString:="{0:MMM d, yyyy}",
               NullDisplayText:="Not Specified")> _
Public SellEndDate As Object
```

Code snippet Product.vb

> *By default, the display format will only be applied to the Read view. To apply this formatting to the Edit view set the* `ApplyFormatInEditMode` *property to* true *on the* `DisplayFormat` *attribute.*

Second, it's unlikely that you'll want to use the database field names in the user interface. It would be much better to provide descriptive names for all of your fields. You can use the `Display` attribute to control how the field labels are rendered. This attribute accepts a number of parameters, including `Name`, to specify the actual label and `Order` to control the order in which fields should be listed. In the following code, the ProductNumber field has been given a display name of "Product Code" and an order value of 1 to ensure it is always displayed as the first field:

C#

```csharp
[Display(Name="Product Code", Order=1)]
public object ProductNumber;
```

Code snippet Product.cs

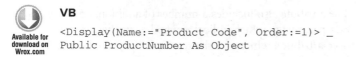

VB

```vb
<Display(Name:="Product Code", Order:=1)> _
Public ProductNumber As Object
```

Code snippet Product.vb

Figure 23-8 shows how these display formatting changes are rendered by Dynamic Data.

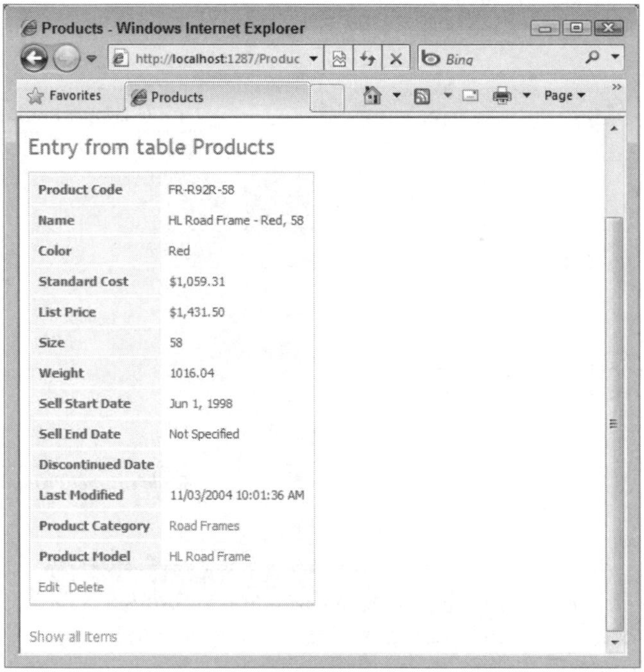

Products - Windows Internet Explorer

http://localhost:1287/Produc ▾   🔍 Bing

⭐ Favorites   📄 Products

Entry from table Products

Product Code	FR-R92R-58
Name	HL Road Frame - Red, 58
Color	Red
Standard Cost	$1,059.31
List Price	$1,431.50
Size	58
Weight	1016.04
Sell Start Date	Jun 1, 1998
Sell End Date	Not Specified
Discontinued Date	
Last Modified	11/03/2004 10:01:36 AM
Product Category	Road Frames
Product Model	HL Road Frame
Edit Delete	

Show all items

FIGURE 23-8

CUSTOMIZING THE PRESENTATION

Chances are the way that Dynamic Data renders a web site by default will not be exactly what you require. The previous section demonstrated how many aspects of the data model could be customized to control how the database tables and fields are rendered. However, limitations exist as to what can be achieved simply by customizing the data model. Fortunately, Dynamic Data uses a rich template system that is fully customizable and allows you complete control over the UI.

The Dynamic Data template files are stored under a number of subfolders in the DynamicData folder, which is in the root of the web application. Following the Convention over Configuration principle, these template files do not need to be manually registered with Dynamic Data. Instead, each different type of template should be stored in a specific folder and the framework will use the location, as well as the template filename, to determine when to load it at run time.

Page Templates

Page templates are used to provide the default rendering of a database table. The master page templates are stored in the `DynamicData\PageTemplates` folder. Dynamic Data ships with the following five page templates for viewing and editing data:

➤ **Details.aspx:** Renders a read-only view of an existing entry from a table.

➤ **Edit.aspx:** Displays an editable view of an existing entry from a table.

➤ **Insert.aspx:** Displays a view that allows users to add a new entry to a table.

➤ **List.aspx:** Renders an entire table using a grid view with support for paging and sorting.

➤ **ListDetails.aspx:** Used when Dynamic Data is configured with the combined-page mode, where the Detail, Edit, Insert, and List tasks are performed by the same page. This mode can be enabled by following the comment instructions in the `Global.asax` file.

You can edit any of these default page templates if there are changes that you would like to affect all tables by default. You can also override the default page templates by creating a set of custom templates for a table. Custom pages templates are stored under the `DynamicData\CustomPages` folder.

In the AdventureWorksLT database, the SalesOrderHeader table is a good candidate for a custom page template. Before creating the template, you will need to enable scaffolding for this table. Create a new data model partial class for the SalesOrderHeader table and enable scaffolding as shown in the following listing:

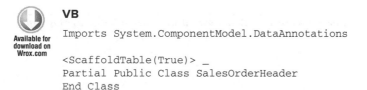

C#

```csharp
using System.ComponentModel.DataAnnotations;

namespace DynDataWebApp
{
    [ScaffoldTable(true)]
    public partial class SalesOrderHeader
    {
    }
}
```

Code snippet SalesOrderHeader.cs

VB

```vb
Imports System.ComponentModel.DataAnnotations

<ScaffoldTable(True)> _
Partial Public Class SalesOrderHeader
End Class
```

Code snippet SalesOrderHeader.vb

Next, create a subfolder called SalesOrderHeaders under the `DynamicData\CustomPages` folder. This folder will contain the custom templates for the SalesOrderHeader table. Copy the existing `List.aspx` template from the `DynamicData\PageTemplates` folder to the `DynamicData\CustomPages\SalesOrderHeaders` folder.

> *The folder name for custom page templates should generally be named with the plural form of the table name. The exception to this is if the data model is using the ADO.NET Entity Framework version 3.5, or if the default option Pluralize or Singularize Generated Object Names has been changed. In this case the folder name should have the same name as the table.*

Because the template was copied, and therefore a duplicate class was created, your application will no longer compile. The easiest way to fix this is to change the namespace to any unique value in both the markup and code-behind files of the new template, as shown in the following code:

C#

```
<%@ Page Language="C#" MasterPageFile="~/Site.master" CodeBehind="List.aspx.cs"
    Inherits="DynDataWebApp._SalesOrderHeaders.List" %>
```

Code snippet DynamicData\CustomPages\SalesOrderHeaders\List.aspx

```
namespace DynDataWebApp._SalesOrderHeaders
{
    public partial class List : System.Web.UI.Page
    {
        // Code snipped
    }
}
```

Code snippet DynamicData\CustomPages\SalesOrderHeaders\List.aspx.cs

VB

```
<%@ Page Language="VB" MasterPageFile="~/Site.master" CodeBehind="List.aspx.vb"
    Inherits="DynDataWebApp._SalesOrderHeader.List" %>
```

Code snippet DynamicData\CustomPages\SalesOrderHeaders\List.aspx

```
Namespace _SalesOrderHeader
    Class List
        Inherits Page
        ' Code Snipped
    End Class
End Namespace
```

Code snippet DynamicData\CustomPages\SalesOrderHeaders\List.aspx.vb

You can now customize the template in whatever manner you wish. For example, you may want to reduce the number of columns that appear in the List view, while still ensuring that all data fields appear in the Insert and Edit views. This degree of customization is only possible by creating a table-specific page template.

Make this change by locating the GridView control in List.aspx. Disable the automatic rendering of all data fields by adding the property AutoGenerateColumns="False". Then, manually specify the fields that you want to display by adding a set of DynamicField controls as shown in the following code:

Available for
download on
Wrox.com

```
<asp:GridView ID="GridView1" runat="server" DataSourceID="GridDataSource"
            EnablePersistedSelection="True" AllowPaging="True"
            AllowSorting="True" CssClass="DDGridView"
            AutoGenerateColumns="False" RowStyle-CssClass="td"
            HeaderStyle-CssClass="th" CellPadding="6">
  <Columns>
    <asp:TemplateField>
      <ItemTemplate>
        <asp:DynamicHyperLink runat="server" Text="Details" />
      </ItemTemplate>
    </asp:TemplateField>
    <asp:DynamicField DataField="AccountNumber" HeaderText="Account No" />
    <asp:DynamicField DataField="PurchaseOrderNumber" HeaderText="PO Number" />
    <asp:DynamicField DataField="OrderDate" DataFormatString="{0:d-MMM-yyyy}"
                HeaderText="Order Date" />
    <asp:DynamicField DataField="ShipDate" DataFormatString="{0:d-MMM-yyyy}"
                HeaderText="Ship Date" />
    <asp:DynamicField DataField="SubTotal" DataFormatString="{0:c}"
                HeaderText="Sub Total" />
    <asp:DynamicField DataField="TaxAmt" DataFormatString="{0:c}"
                HeaderText="Tax Amount" />
    <asp:DynamicField DataField="Freight" DataFormatString="{0:c}"
                HeaderText="Freight" />
  </Columns>

  <HeaderStyle CssClass="th" />

  <PagerStyle CssClass="DDFooter"/>
  <PagerTemplate>
    <asp:GridViewPager runat="server" />
  </PagerTemplate>
  <EmptyDataTemplate>
    There are currently no items in this table.
  </EmptyDataTemplate>
  <RowStyle CssClass="td" />
</asp:GridView>
```

Code snippet DynamicData\CustomPages\SalesOrderHeaders\List.aspx

Figure 23-9 shows the customized List view of the SalesOrderHeader table with this reduced set of columns.

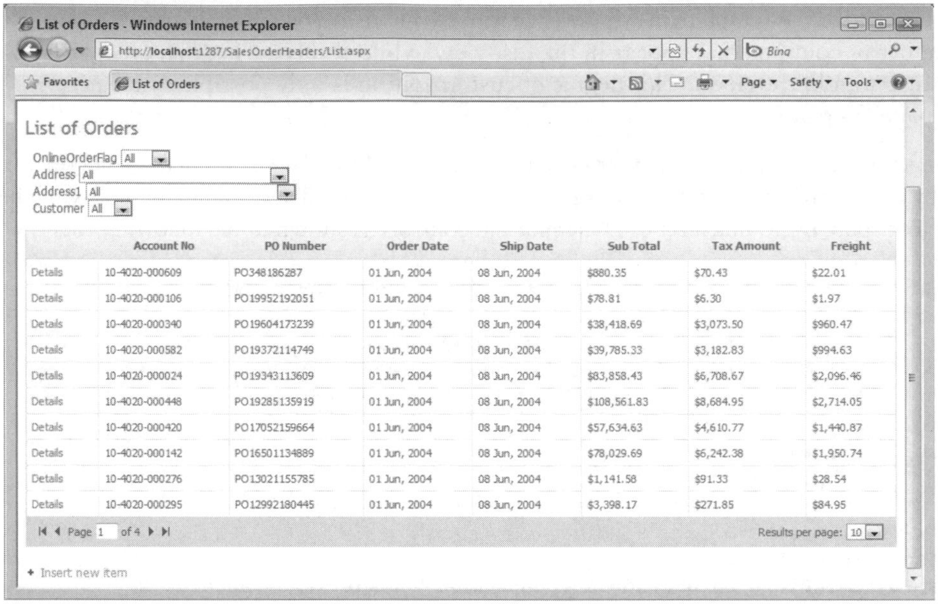

FIGURE 23-9

Field Templates

Field templates are used to render the user interface for individual data fields. There are both view and edit field templates. The field templates are named according to the name of the data type, with the suffix _Edit for the edit view. For example, the view template for a Text field is called Text.ascx, and renders the field using an ASP.NET Literal control. The corresponding edit template is called Text_Edit.ascx, and it renders the field using an ASP.NET TextBox control. The edit template also contains several validation controls, which are enabled as required and handle any validation exceptions thrown by the data model.

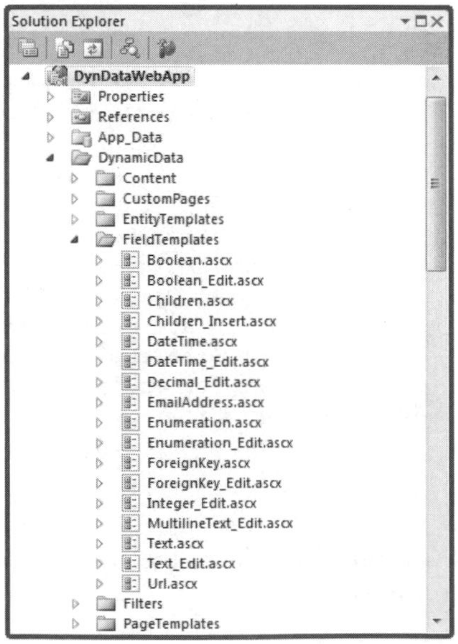

Dynamic Data ships with a large number of field templates, as shown in Figure 23-10. As with page templates, you can customize the default field templates or create new ones. All field templates, including any new templates that you create, are stored in the DynamicData\FieldTemplates folder.

Several date fields in the SalesOrderHeader table of the AdventureWorksLT database are rendered with both the date and time, even though the time portion is not relevant.

The DateTime field template in Dynamic Data displays a simple TextBox control for its Edit view. If the data field only requires the date to be entered, and not the time, it would be nice to display a Calendar control instead of a TextBox.

FIGURE 23-10

Begin by creating a copy of the `DateTime.ascx` template and renaming it to `DateCalendar.ascx`. Then open both the markup file and the code-behind file for `DateCalendar.ascx` and rename the class from `DateTimeField` to `DateCalendarField` as shown in the following code:

C#

```
<%@ Control Language="C#" CodeBehind="DateCalendar.ascx.cs"
            Inherits="DynDataWebApp.DateCalendarField" %>
```

Code snippet DynamicData\FieldTemplates\DateCalendar.ascx

```
namespace DynDataWebApp
{
    public partial class DateCalendarField : FieldTemplateUserControl
    {
        // Code snipped
    }
}
```

Code snippet DynamicData\FieldTemplates\DateCalendar.ascx.cs

VB

```
<%@ Control Language="VB" CodeBehind="DateCalendar.ascx.vb"
            Inherits="DynDataWebApp.DateCalendarField" %>
```

Code snippet DynamicData\FieldTemplates\DateCalendar.ascx

```
Class DateCalendarField
    Inherits FieldTemplateUserControl
    ' Code Snipped
End Class
```

Code snippet DynamicData\FieldTemplates\DateCalendar.ascx.vb

Next, create a copy of the `DateTime_Edit.ascx` template and rename it to `DateCalendar_Edit.ascx`. As before, open both the markup file and the code-behind file for `DateCalendar_Edit.ascx` and rename the class from `DateTime_EditField` to `DateCalendar_EditField`. The following code shows how it should look once renamed:

C#

```
<%@ Control Language="C#" CodeBehind="DateCalendar_Edit.ascx.cs"
            Inherits="DynDataWebApp.DateCalendar_EditField" %>
```

Code snippet DynamicData\FieldTemplates\DateCalendar_Edit.ascx

```
namespace DynDataWebApp
{
    public partial class DateCalendar_EditField : FieldTemplateUserControl
```

```
        {
            // Code snipped
        }
    }
```

Code snippet DynamicData\FieldTemplates\DateCalendar_Edit.ascx.cs

VB

```
<%@ Control Language="VB" CodeBehind="DateCalendar_Edit.ascx.vb"
            Inherits="DynDataWebApp.DateCalendar_EditField" %>
```

Code snippet DynamicData\FieldTemplates\DateCalendar.ascx

```
Class DateCalendar_EditField
    Inherits FieldTemplateUserControl
    ' Code Snipped
End Class
```

Code snippet DynamicData\FieldTemplates\DateCalendar.ascx.vb

At this point you could replace the TextBox control in the `DateCalendar_Edit.ascx` file with a standard Calendar web server control. However, this would require a number of changes in the code-behind file to get it working with this new type of control. A far easier solution is to use the Calendar control from the AJAX Control Toolkit. This is a Control Extender, which means it attaches to an existing TextBox on a web page and provides new client-side functionality. You can find more information about Control Extenders and the AJAX Control Toolkit in Chapter 20.

You can download the AJAX Control Toolkit from `http://ajaxcontroltoolkit.codeplex.com/`. Follow the instructions in Chapter 20 to add the controls in the AJAX Control Toolkit to the Visual Studio Toolbox. Once this has been done, add a CalendarExtender control onto the `DateCalendar_Edit.ascx` template. Then set the `TargetControlID` property and `Format` property as shown in the following code:

```
<cc1:CalendarExtender ID="CalendarExtender1" TargetControlID="TextBox1"
        Format="d-MMM-yyyy" runat="server">
</cc1:CalendarExtender>
```

Code snippet DynamicData\FieldTemplates\DateCalendar_Edit.ascx

The final step is to associate some fields in the data model with the new field templates. In this example, the OrderDate, ShipDate, and DueDate fields from the SalesOrderHeader table should be associated. Modify the SalesOrderHeader partial class and create a metadata class, as described earlier in the chapter. The `UIHint` attribute is used to associate the specified fields with the custom field template, as shown in the following code:

C#

```csharp
namespace DynDataWebApp
{
    [ScaffoldTable(true)]
    [MetadataType(typeof(SalesOrderHeaderMetadata))]
    public partial class SalesOrderHeader
    {
    }
    public class SalesOrderHeaderMetadata
    {
        [DisplayFormat(DataFormatString = "{0:dd-MMM-yyyy}",
                        ApplyFormatInEditMode = true)]
        [UIHint("DateCalendar")]
        public object OrderDate;

        [DisplayFormat(DataFormatString = "{0:dd-MMM-yyyy}",
                        ApplyFormatInEditMode = true)]
        [UIHint("DateCalendar")]
        public object DueDate;

        [DisplayFormat(DataFormatString = "{0:dd-MMM-yyyy}",
                        ApplyFormatInEditMode = true)]
        [UIHint("DateCalendar")]
        public object ShipDate;
    }
}
```

Code snippet SalesOrderHeader.cs

VB

```vbnet
<ScaffoldTable(True)> _
<MetadataType(GetType(SalesOrderHeaderMetadata))> _
Partial Public Class SalesOrderHeader
End Class
Public Class SalesOrderHeaderMetadata
    <DisplayFormat(DataFormatString:="{0:dd-MMM-yyyy}",
                ApplyFormatInEditMode:=True)> _
    <UIHint("DateCalendar")> _
    Public OrderDate As Object

    <DisplayFormat(DataFormatString:="{0:dd-MMM-yyyy}",
                ApplyFormatInEditMode:=True)> _
    <UIHint("DateCalendar")> _
    Public DueDate As Object

    <DisplayFormat(DataFormatString:="{0:dd-MMM-yyyy}",
                ApplyFormatInEditMode:=True)> _
    <UIHint("DateCalendar")> _
    Public ShipDate As Object
End Class
```

Code snippet SalesOrderHeader.vb

Figure 23-11 shows the custom field template in the Edit view of an entry in the SalesOrderHeader table.

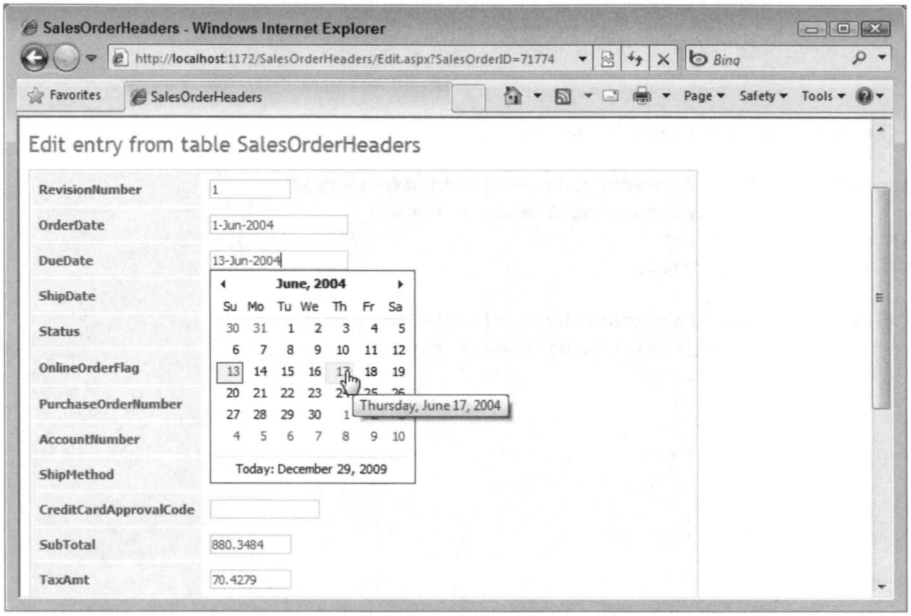

FIGURE 23-11

Entity Templates

Entity templates are used to render the user interface for an individual entry from a table. The default entity templates are stored in the `DynamicData\EntityTemplates` folder, and include templates to create, edit, and display a record. These templates work with the default page templates, and render the UI using a two-column HTML table; label in the left column, data field in the right.

Customizing the existing entity templates affects all tables. You can also create a new custom entity template for a specific table. This allows you to provide a completely different layout when editing an entry from a database table compared to when the entry is simply viewed.

To create a new entity template, right-click the `DynamicData\EntityTemplate` folder and select Add ➪ New Item. Choose a new Web User Control and name it `SalesOrderHeaders.ascx`.

The default templates use an EntityTemplate control, which is more or less equivalent to a Repeater web server control. This control dynamically generates all of the fields for this table from the data model. In this case, instead of using an EntityTemplate control, you can manually specify the fields to be displayed. The following code lists a custom markup for the entity template that displays a subset of the data:

Available for download on Wrox.com

```
<tr>
   <td class="DDLightHeader">
      <asp:Label ID="Label1" runat="server" Text="Customer" />
   </td>
```

```
            <td>
                Acct No:
                <asp:DynamicControl ID="DynamicControl1" runat="server"
                    DataField="AccountNumber" />
                <br/>
                PO No:
                <asp:DynamicControl ID="DynamicControl2" runat="server"
                    DataField="PurchaseOrderNumber" />
            </td>
        </tr>
        <tr>
            <td class="DDLightHeader">
                <asp:Label ID="Label2" runat="server" Text="Dates" />
            </td>
            <td>
                Ordered:
                <asp:DynamicControl ID="DynamicControl3" runat="server"
                    DataField="OrderDate" />
                <br/>
                Due:
                <asp:DynamicControl ID="DynamicControl4" runat="server"
                    DataField="DueDate" />
                <br/>
                Shipped:
                <asp:DynamicControl ID="DynamicControl5" runat="server"
                    DataField="ShipDate" />
            </td>
        </tr>
        <tr>
            <td class="DDLightHeader">
                <asp:Label ID="Label3" runat="server" Text="Amount" />
            </td>
            <td>
                Sub Total:
                <asp:DynamicControl ID="DynamicControl6" runat="server"
                    DataField="SubTotal" DataFormatString="{0:c}" />
                <br/>
                Tax:
                <asp:DynamicControl ID="DynamicControl7" runat="server"
                    DataField="TaxAmt" DataFormatString="{0:c}" />
                <br/>
                Freight:
                <asp:DynamicControl ID="DynamicControl8" runat="server"
                    DataField="Freight" DataFormatString="{0:c}" />
            </td>
        </tr>
```

Code snippet DynamicData\EntityTemplates\SalesOrderHeader.ascx

Finally, change the web user control to inherit from System.Web.DynamicData.EntityTemplate
UserControl instead of System.Web.UI.UserControl:

Available for download on Wrox.com

C#

```
public partial class SalesOrderHeaders :
        System.Web.DynamicData.EntityTemplateUserControl
```

Code snippet DynamicData\EntityTemplates\SalesOrderHeader.ascx.cs

Available for download on Wrox.com

VB

```
Public Class SalesOrderHeaders
    Inherits System.Web.DynamicData.EntityTemplateUserControl
```

Code snippet DynamicData\EntityTemplates\SalesOrderHeader.ascx.vb

You can now build and run the project to test the new entity template. Figure 23-12 shows the default entity template (left) and the new customized template (right) for the SalesOrderHeader table. The Edit and Insert views are unchanged, because the read-only Details template was the only template that was customized.

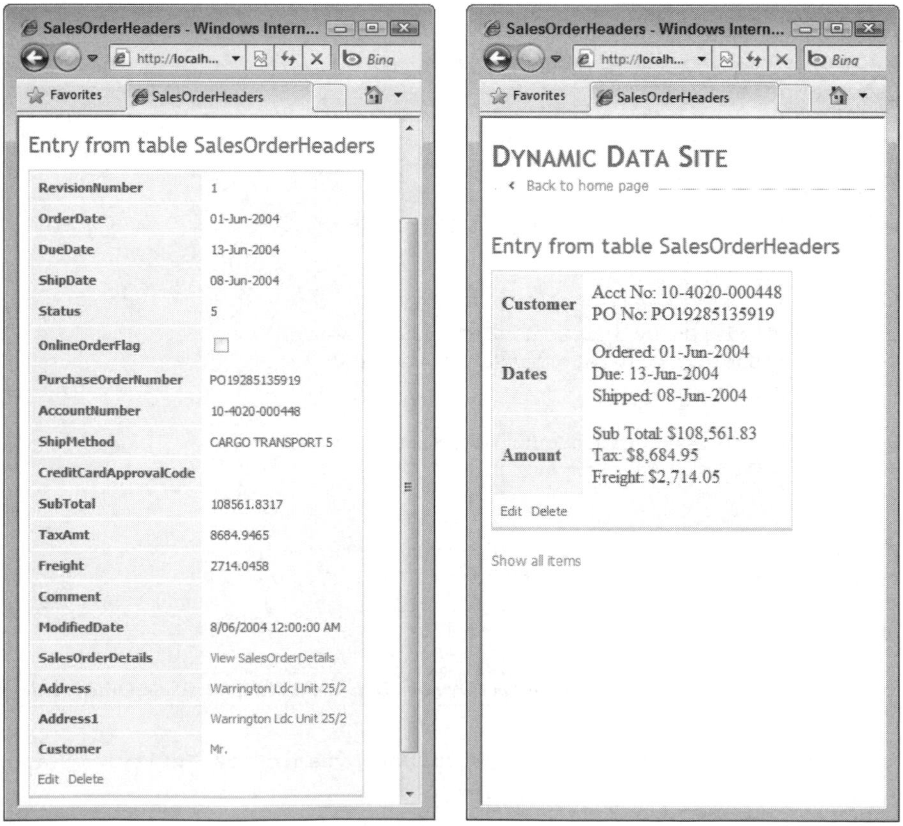

FIGURE 23-12

Filter Templates

Filter templates are used to display a control that filters the rows that are displayed for a table. Dynamic Data ships with three filter templates, stored in the `DynamicData\Filters` folder. These filters have self-explanatory names — the `Boolean` filter is used for Boolean data types, the `Enumeration` filter is used when the data type is mapped to an enum, and the `ForeignKey` filter is used for foreign key relationships.

Figure 23-13 shows the four filter templates that are rendered by default for the SalesOrderHeader table. The first filter, OnlineOrderFlag, is a Boolean filter and only contains three options — All, True, and False. The remaining three filters are generated from foreign keys, and each has a large number of entries.

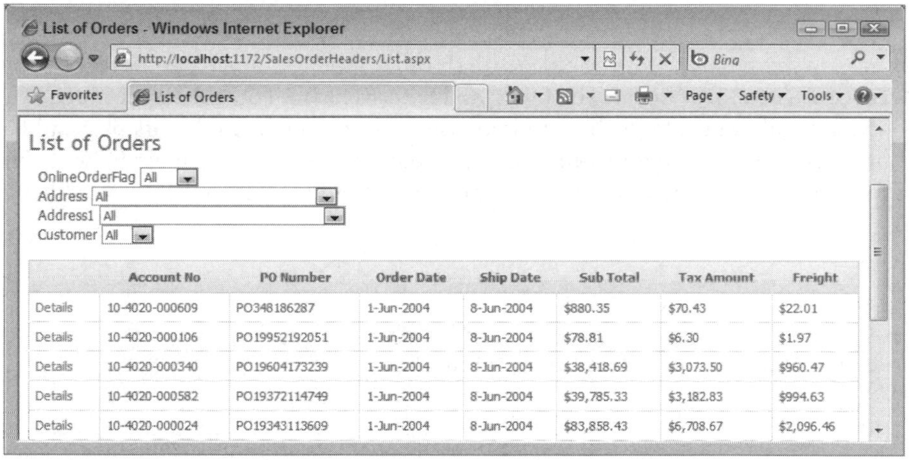

FIGURE 23-13

> *You may have noticed that the values displayed in the Customer drop-down list are simply the customer's title (Mr, Mrs, and so on), which are next to useless. To select the field that is displayed for foreign keys, Dynamic Data finds the first field on the table with a string type. This can be overridden to any other field on the table by decorating the data model class with a `DisplayColumn` attribute. However, in the case of the Customer table what you really want is to display a string containing a number of fields (FirstName, LastName). To do this, simply override the `ToString` method of the Customer data model class.*

Unfortunately, drop-down lists are only useful if they contain fewer than a couple of hundred entries. Anything more than this and the rendering of the web page will slow down and the list will be difficult to navigate. As the number of customers in the database grows to thousands, or more, the use of a drop-down list for the Address, Address1, and Customer foreign keys will render this page unusable.

If you wanted to keep these filters, you could do something advanced such as customize the default ForeignKey filter with a search control that performed a server callback and displayed a list of valid entries that matched the search, all within an AJAX request of course! However, such an exercise is well beyond the scope of this book, so instead you can learn how to control which fields are rendered as filters.

> *The remainder of this section assumes you have created a custom page template for the SalesOrderDetail table, as described earlier in this chapter.*

Open the custom `List.aspx` template for the SalesOrderHeader table from `DynamicData\CustomPages\SalesOrderHeaders`. Locate the QueryableFilterRepeater control on this page. This control is used to dynamically generate the list of filters. Delete this control, and in its place add a DynamicFilter control as shown in the following code. The `DataField` property must be set to the correct data field for the filter, and the `FilterUIHint` property should be set to the correct filter template.

Available for download on Wrox.com

```
Online Order:
<asp:DynamicFilter ID="OnlineOrderFilter" runat="server"
        DataField="OnlineOrderFlag" FilterUIHint="Boolean"
        OnFilterChanged="DynamicFilter_FilterChanged">
</asp:DynamicFilter>
```

Code snippet DynamicData\CustomPages\SalesOrderHeader\List.aspx

Next, locate the QueryExtender control toward the bottom of the page. This control is used to "wire up" the DynamicFilter control to the data source, so that the correct query will be used when the filter changes. Modify the `ControlID` property to match the name of the DynamicFilter control you just added, as shown in the following code:

Available for download on Wrox.com

```
<asp:QueryExtender TargetControlID="GridDataSource" ID="GridQueryExtender"
                    runat="server">
    <asp:DynamicFilterExpression ControlID="OnlineOrderFilter" />
</asp:QueryExtender>
```

Code snippet DynamicData\CustomPages\SalesOrderHeader\List.aspx

Finally, you will need to remove some code that was only required by the QueryableFilterRepeater control. Open the code-behind file (`List.aspx.cs` or `List.aspx.vb`) and remove the `Label_PreRender` method. When you save the changes and run the project, you will see only a single filter displayed for the SalesOrderHeader table, as shown in Figure 23-14.

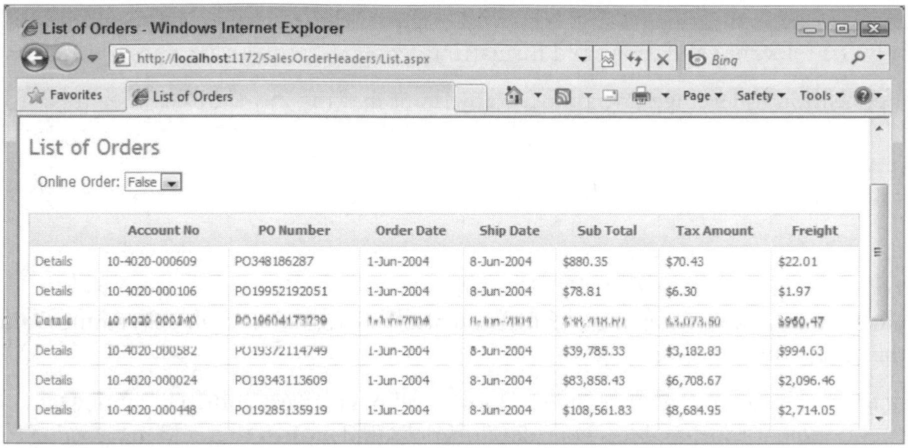

FIGURE 23-14

ENABLING DYNAMIC DATA FOR EXISTING PROJECTS

Dynamic Data is undoubtedly a very powerful way to create a new data-driven web application from scratch. However, with the version of Dynamic Data that ships with Visual Studio 2010, you can use some of the features of Dynamic Data in an existing Web Application or Web Site project.

The `EnableDynamicData` extension method has been introduced to enable this functionality. This method can be called on any class that implements the `System.Web.UI.INamingContainer` interface. This includes the Repeater, DataGrid, DataList, CheckBoxList, ChangePassword, LoginView, Menu, SiteMapNodeItem, and RadioButtonList controls.

Adding this functionality to an existing web control does not require the application to be using LINQ to SQL or the Entity Framework. In fact, the application could be using any data access option including plain old ADO.NET. This is because the Dynamic Data functionality that is enabled in this way does not include any of the scaffolding functionality. Instead, it enables both field templates and the validation and display attributes that were described earlier in this chapter.

For example, to enable Dynamic Data on a GridView control, call the `EnableDynamicData` extension method as shown in the following code:

C#

```
GridView1.EnableDynamicData(typeof(Product));
```

VB

```
GridView1.EnableDynamicData(GetType(Product))
```

You can now create a `Product` class with public properties that match the data displayed in GridView1. Each of these properties can be decorated with attributes from the `System.ComponentModel.DataAnnotations` namespace, such as `Required`, `StringLength`,

`RegularExpression`, or `DisplayFormat`. ASP.NET will interpret these attributes at run time and automatically apply the relevant validations and formatting.

This allows any application to leverage Dynamic Data without making any significant changes to the application.

SUMMARY

In this chapter you learned how to use ASP.NET Dynamic Data to create a data-driven web application with little or no code. More importantly, you also learned how flexible Dynamic Data is by customizing the data model and web pages.

By freeing developers from needing to write reams of low-level data access code, Dynamic Data allows for faster development time, and lets your developers build features that add more value to end users.

SharePoint

➤ Setting up a development environment for SharePoint

➤ Developing custom SharePoint components such as Web Parts, lists, and workflows

➤ Debugging and testing SharePoint projects

➤ Packaging and deploying SharePoint components

Over the past couple of years the level of interest — and number of deployments — in Microsoft SharePoint has reached the point where SharePoint is now one of Microsoft's fastest growing product lines.

SharePoint is really a collection of related products and technologies that broadly service the areas of document and content management, web-based collaboration, and search. SharePoint is also a very flexible application hosting platform, which allows you to develop and deploy everything from individual Web Parts to full-blown web applications.

Although it can be used to host web sites for anonymous external visitors, SharePoint is much more ideally suited for web sites that involve registered users, particularly those that service the needs of employees within an organization. SharePoint provides much of the low-level integration code that is often required in these environments including built-in authentication and authorization, integration with Microsoft Office, access to external data, provisioning of sites, and collaborative workflow.

This chapter runs through the SharePoint development tools in Visual Studio 2010, and demonstrates how to build, debug, and deploy SharePoint solutions.

> *In addition to using Visual Studio 2010, you can create SharePoint solutions using the free SharePoint Designer 2010. SharePoint Designer provides a very different implementation approach by presenting the elements of a SharePoint solution in a high-level logical way that hides many of the underlying implementation details. It also includes some excellent WYSIWYG tools to browse and edit components in existing SharePoint sites. As such, SharePoint Designer is often considered the tool of choice for non-developers (IT Professionals and end-users). However, it is still useful to developers as certain development and configuration tasks, such as building page layouts and master pages, are much easier to perform using SharePoint Designer. Typically, you'll find more experienced SharePoint developers using both tools to provision their solutions.*

PREPARING THE DEVELOPMENT ENVIRONMENT

One of the common complaints about previous versions of SharePoint has been the requirement to use Windows Server for the local development environment. This is because SharePoint 2007 and earlier could only run on a server operating system and you needed to have SharePoint running locally to perform any debugging and integration testing.

Fortunately, this has been addressed in SharePoint 2010. In addition to Windows Server 2008, you can install SharePoint on either Windows 7 or Windows Vista (Service Pack 1 or later). Unfortunately, you will need some reasonably powerful hardware for your local development machine. SharePoint 2010 requires a 64-bit operating system and a recommended 4GB of RAM for SharePoint Foundation and 6GB to 8GB of RAM for SharePoint Server.

SHAREPOINT SERVER VERSUS SHAREPOINT FOUNDATION

SharePoint 2010 comes in two editions: SharePoint Server and SharePoint Foundation. SharePoint Foundation was called Windows SharePoint Services (WSS) in previous versions and is the free version that is targeted at smaller organizations or deployments. It includes support for Web Parts and web-based applications, document management, and web collaboration functionality such as blogs, wikis, calendars, and discussions.

SharePoint Server, on the other hand, is aimed at large enterprises and advanced deployment scenarios. It has a cost for the server product itself as well as requiring a client access license (CAL) for each user. SharePoint Server includes all the features of SharePoint Foundation as well as providing multiple SharePoint sites, enhanced navigation, indexed search, access to backend data, personalization, and Single Sign On.

It is recommended that unless you are building a solution that requires the advanced features of SharePoint Server, you should take advantage of the lower system requirements and install SharePoint Foundation on your development machine. Since SharePoint Server is built on top of SharePoint Foundation, anything that can run under SharePoint Foundation will also run under SharePoint Server.

Installing the Prerequisites

SharePoint 2010 was in Beta at the time of writing, and as such, some of the instructions may have changed in the final release. If any important changes are required, you will be able to find corrections and updated instructions at www .wrox.com. Just search for this book by the ISBN number 978-0-470-54865-3, and look for Chapter 24 under errata.

The installation of SharePoint is quite straightforward if you are targeting Windows Server. The setup ships with a Prerequisite Installer tool (`PrerequisiteInstaller.exe`), which checks and installs the required prerequisites. However, at the time of writing with SharePoint 2010 Beta 2, this tool does not run on Windows 7 or Windows Vista. If you are installing SharePoint 2010 onto one of these client operating systems you must install and configure a large number of prerequisites manually.

Regardless of which operating system you are using, you must first install the WCF Hotfix for Microsoft Windows. You can download it from the following links:

➤ For Windows Vista or Windows Server 2008:
   `http://go.microsoft.com/fwlink/?linkID=160770`

➤ For Windows 7 or Windows Server 2008 R2:
   `http://go.microsoft.com/fwlink/?LinkID=166231`

The following instructions assume that your copy of SharePoint is in the form of a self-extracting executable called `SharePoint.exe` for SharePoint Foundation or `OfficeServer.exe` for SharePoint Server. If instead you are installing from a CD/DVD of SharePoint you can skip the following step, because the contents and folder structure on the disc will be the same as the extracted files.

Begin by creating a folder for the installation files, for example `c:\SharePoint`, and copy the setup executable to this folder. Next, extract the installation files by running the following from a command prompt (for SharePoint Foundation):

```
c:\SharePoint\SharePoint.exe /extract:c:\SharePoint
```

For SharePoint Server, replace `SharePoint.exe` with `OfficeServer.exe`.

If you are installing SharePoint on Windows Server you can now run the Prerequisite Installer tool (`PrerequisiteInstaller.exe`) and then proceed to the next section ("Installing SharePoint 2010"). Otherwise, if you are targeting Windows Vista or Windows 7, you must manually install the prerequisites as described in the remainder of this section.

The following prerequisites are required for Windows Vista only:

➤ **.NET Framework 3.5 SP1:** If you have installed Visual Studio 2010 this will already be installed. Available via `professionalvisualstudio.com/link/1024A`.

➤ **Windows PowerShell 2.0:** Available via `professionalvisualstudio.com/link/1024B`.

➤ **Windows Installer 4.5 Redistributable:** Available via `professionalvisualstudio.com/link/1024C`.

The following prerequisites are required for Windows 7 and Windows Vista:

➤ **Microsoft FilterPack 2.0:** This is shipped with the SharePoint installation files. Run the installer package at `c:\SharePoint\PrerequisiteInstallerFiles\FilterPack\FilterPack.msi`.

➤ **Microsoft Sync Framework:** If you have installed Visual Studio 2010 this will already be installed. Available via `professionalvisualstudio.com/link/1024D`.

➤ **SQL Server 2008 Native Client:** If you have installed Visual Studio 2010 this will already be installed. Available via `professionalvisualstudio.com/link/1024E`.

➤ **Windows Identity Foundation Runtime:** Formerly known as codename "Geneva" Framework. Available via `professionalvisualstudio.com/link/1024F`.

➤ **ADO.NET Data Services:** Select the run time only. Available via `professionalvisualstudio.com/link/1024G`.

➤ **Chart Controls:** This is not required for SharePoint Foundation. Available via `professionalvisualstudio.com/link/1024H`.

➤ **Microsoft ADOMD.NET:** This is not required for SharePoint Foundation. Available via `professionalvisualstudio.com/link/1024I`.

The final step is to enable all of the required Windows Features. Figure 24-1 lists the features that must be enabled using the Programs and Features Control Panel item. You can also download a batch script that will automatically enable these features from `professionalvisualstudio.com/link/1024J`.

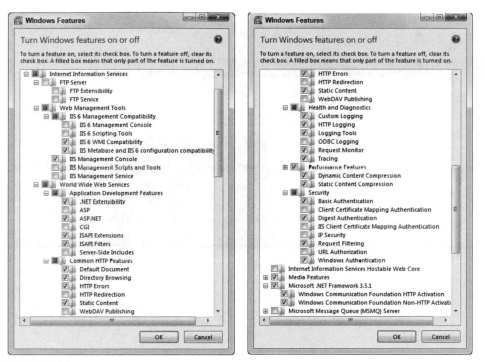

FIGURE 24-1

Installing SharePoint 2010

Now that the prerequisites have been installed you can install either SharePoint Foundation or SharePoint Server. If you are installing on Windows Server you can simply launch the installer, `setup.exe`. However, if you are installing to Windows 7 or Windows Vista you will see the error shown in Figure 24-2 if you try to run the installer.

FIGURE 24-2

To remove this limitation, you will need to edit the configuration file, `config.xml`, which is located in the `c:\SharePoint\files\Setup` folder. Add the following line to the `<configuration>` tag:

```
<Setting Id="AllowWindowsClientInstall" Value="True"/>
```

Once you have saved the configuration file, run `setup.exe`. Follow the instructions on the installer and select the Standalone installation (Install single server standalone using default settings). After the installer has completed, you will be prompted to run the SharePoint Products Configuration Wizard. Once the wizard has completed, the default SharePoint site will open in a new browser window, as shown in Figure 24-3.

FIGURE 24-3

EXPLORING SHAREPOINT 2010

The first time you peak under the covers at SharePoint it can be somewhat overwhelming. One reason for this is because so much of the terminology used by SharePoint is unfamiliar to web developers, even those who know ASP.NET inside out. Before you begin developing a SharePoint solution it's helpful to understand the meaning of SharePoint components such as content types, Features, event receivers, lists, workflows, and Web Parts.

The Server Explorer in Visual Studio 2010 has been enhanced to provide the ability to explore a SharePoint site and browse through its components. To connect to a SharePoint site, or develop and debug a SharePoint solution, you must run Visual Studio with administrator rights. Right-click the Visual Studio 2010 shortcut and select Run as Administrator.

> *To always launch Visual Studio 2010 with administrator rights, right-click the shortcut and select Properties, and then select the Compatibility tab and check the Run This Program as an Administrator checkbox.*

Open the Server Explorer by selecting View ⇨ Server Explorer. You can only connect to SharePoint if you have installed SharePoint locally. By default, a connection to the local SharePoint installation is automatically listed under the SharePoint Connections node. You can add a connection to a remote server by right-clicking the SharePoint Connections node and selecting Add Connection.

When you select a SharePoint component in the Server Explorer, the properties of that component will be listed in the Properties window. The Server Explorer provides read-only access to SharePoint. Figure 24-4 shows the Server Explorer and the properties for a SharePoint site.

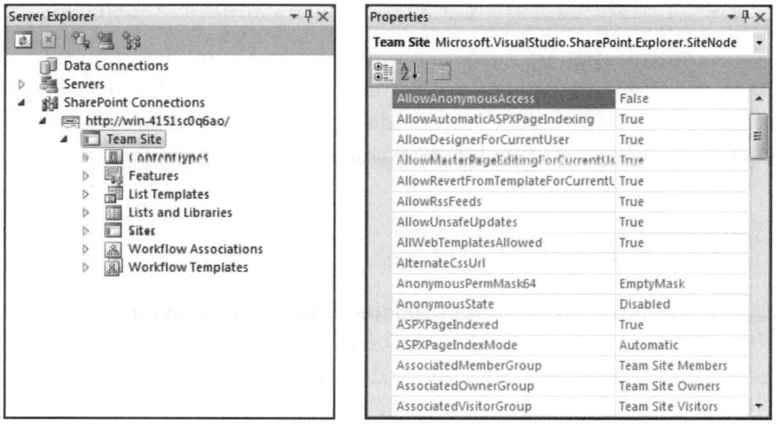

FIGURE 24-4

Now that you've seen how to connect to and browse a SharePoint site, it's worth spending some time understanding some of the main concepts used in SharePoint.

Content types provide a way to define distinct types of SharePoint content, such as a document or an announcement. A content type has a set of fields associated with it that define the metadata of the content. For example, the Document content type shown in Figure 24-5 has fields such as the title and the date the document was last modified. A content type has properties that define settings such as the template to use for displaying, editing, or creating a new instance of that content type.

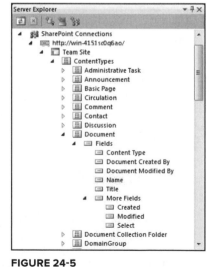

FIGURE 24-5

Features are a collection of resources that describe a logical set of functionality. For example, SharePoint ships with Features such as discussion lists, document libraries, and survey lists. Features contain templates, pages, list definitions, event receivers, and workflows. A Feature can also include resources such as images, JavaScript files, or CSS files.

Features also contain *event receivers*, which are event handlers that are invoked when a Feature is activated, deactivated, installed, uninstalled, or upgraded. Event receivers can also be created for other SharePoint items such as lists or SharePoint sites.

Lists are fundamental to SharePoint and are used almost everywhere. Features such as surveys, issues, and *document libraries* are all built upon lists. A *list definition* specifies the fields, forms, views

(.aspx pages), and content types associated with the list. A concrete implementation of a list definition is called a *list instance*.

Workflows under SharePoint 2010 are used to automate business processes. SharePoint workflows are actually built upon the same workflow engine (Windows Workflow Foundation) that ships with .NET v3.5. Workflows can be associated with a particular SharePoint site, list, or content type.

Finally, *Web Parts* are web server controls that are hosted on a Web Part page in SharePoint. Users can personalize a Web Part page and choose to display one or more Web Parts on that page. Web Parts can display anything as simple as a static label that provides some content for a web page, through to a complete data entry form for submitting line of business data.

CREATING A SHAREPOINT PROJECT

Now that you have some background on the main concepts behind SharePoint development, you can create your first SharePoint solution. In Visual Studio 2010 select File ➪ New ➪ Project. Filter the project types by selecting Visual C# or Visual Basic followed by SharePoint, and then 2010. The available SharePoint project types will be displayed, as shown in Figure 24-6.

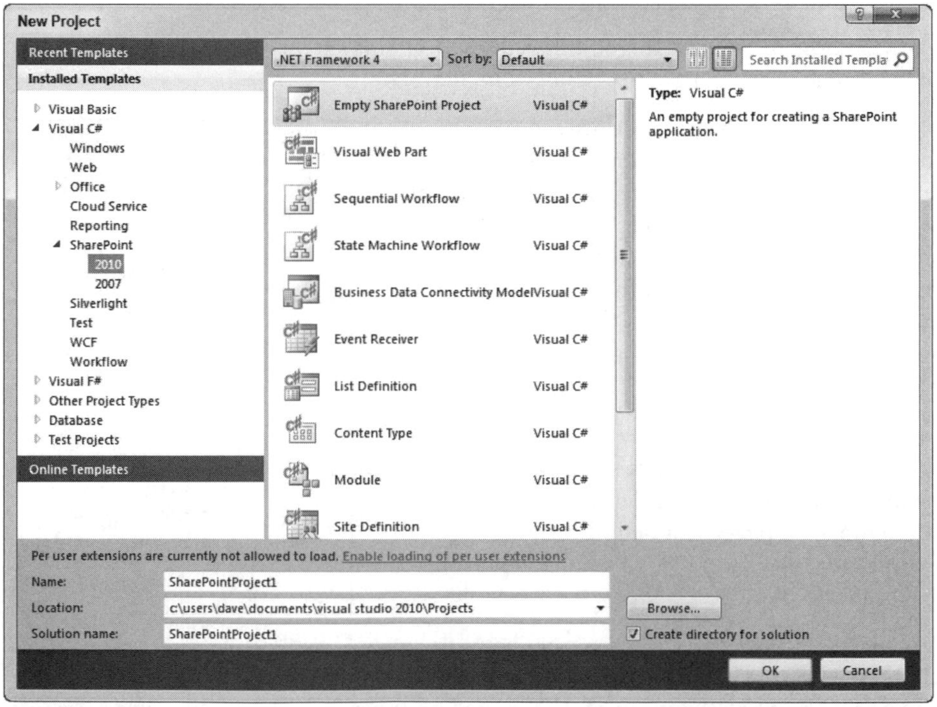

FIGURE 24-6

A number of SharePoint project templates ship with Visual Studio 2010. Most of the SharePoint components that can be created with these project templates can also be created as individual items in an existing SharePoint solution. For this reason, select a new Empty SharePoint Project.

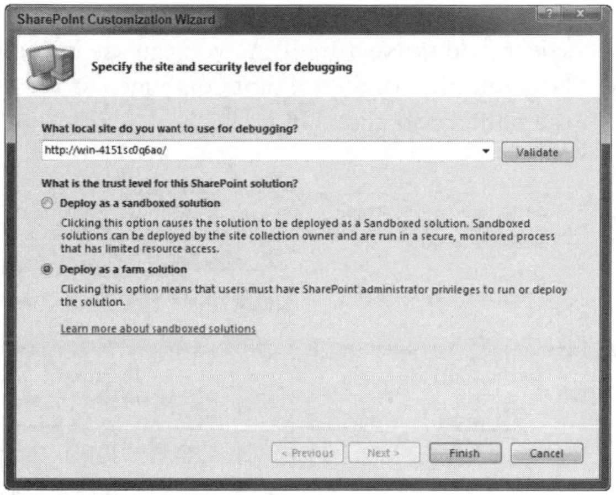

When you click OK, Visual Studio launches the SharePoint Customization Wizard, shown in Figure 24-7. You will be prompted to specify the site and a security level for debugging. Because it is not possible to debug SharePoint sites running on remote computers you will only be able to select a local SharePoint site. You must also select the trust level that the SharePoint solution will be deployed with during debugging. Select Deploy as a Farm Solution and click Finish.

FIGURE 24-7

> *Sandboxed solutions run in a partially trusted environment with access to a limited subset of functionality. The sandbox environment monitors a range of performance-related measures including CPU execution time, memory consumption, and database query time. In addition, sandbox solutions cannot be activated unless they pass a validation process. This provides SharePoint administrators with the confidence that a rogue component won't impact the rest of the SharePoint environment.*

When the SharePoint project is created you will notice two unique nodes listed in the Solution Explorer. These nodes are found in every SharePoint project and cannot be deleted, moved, or renamed.

The *Features* node can contain one or more SharePoint features. As mentioned in the previous section, a Feature is a collection of resources that describe a logical set of functionality. Any time you add a new item, such as a visual Web Part or a content type, it is added to a Feature under the Features node. Depending on the *scope* of the item, it will either be added to an existing Feature or a new Feature will be created. Features are discussed in the "Working with Features" section later in this chapter.

The *Package* node contains a single file that serves as the deployment mechanism for a SharePoint project. A package has a .wsp extension and is logically equivalent to an installer file. The package contains a set of Features, site definitions, and additional assemblies that are deployed to a SharePoint site. Packages are discussed in the "Packaging and Deployment" section later in this chapter.

To add a SharePoint component to this solution, right-click the project in the Solution Explorer and select Add ⇨ New Item. As you can see in Figure 24-8, Visual Studio ships with templates for a large number of SharePoint components. Select a new Application Page item, enter `MyPage.aspx` as the name, and click OK.

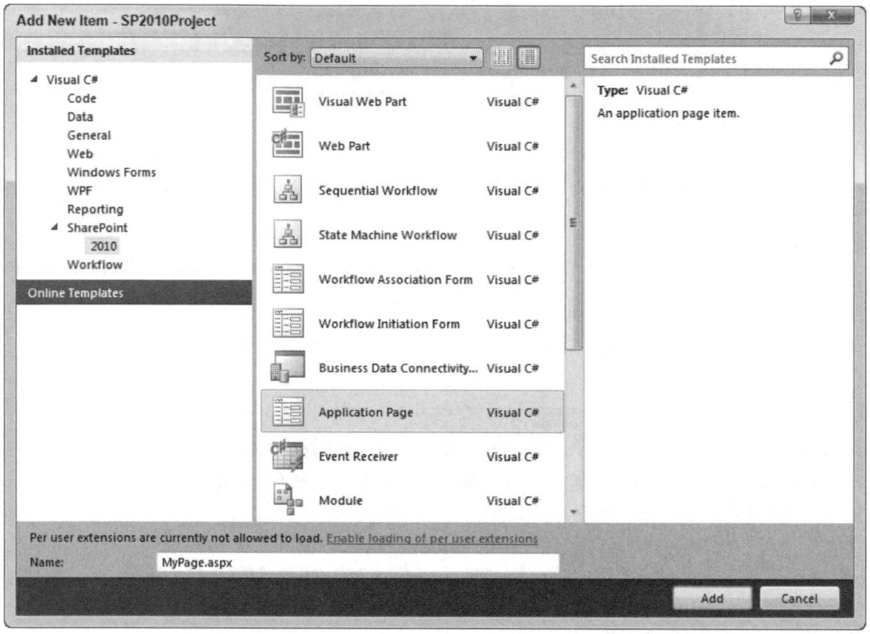

FIGURE 24-8

An *application page* is one of the two types of ASP.NET web pages that are found in SharePoint sites. Most of the pages that end users interact with in SharePoint are actually *content pages*. Visual Studio does not include a template for content pages. Instead, content pages are created and edited by tools such as the SharePoint Designer or using the SharePoint Foundation object model. Content pages can be added to a SharePoint page library, and they can also host dynamic Web Parts.

> The SharePoint Foundation 2010 object model consists of over 70 namespaces and provides an API that allows you to perform most administrative and user-tasks programmatically. The bulk of the classes are contained in the `Microsoft.SharePoint.dll` and `Microsoft.SharePoint.Client.dll` assemblies. These classes can only be used to work with a local SharePoint Foundation or SharePoint Server environment.

Although application pages cannot do many of the things that content pages can, they do have much better support for custom application code. For this reason, application pages are often used for non-user administration functions.

When the application page is added to the project it is not added to the root of the project. Instead, it is placed into a subfolder with the same name as your project, under a new folder called Layouts. The Layouts folder cannot be changed, but you can rename the subfolder at any time.

The Layouts folder is an example of a *SharePoint Mapped Folder*. A SharePoint Mapped Folder is essentially a shortcut to a standard SharePoint folder, and saves you from having to specify the full path to the folder in your SharePoint solution. You can add additional Mapped Folders to your project by right-clicking the project and selecting Add ➪ SharePoint Mapped Folder. The dialog box with all of the available SharePoint folders will be displayed, as shown in Figure 24-9.

Application pages are rendered using a SharePoint master page at run time and as such contain several ASP.NET Content controls as placeholders for different regions on the master page. You can add static content, standard HTML controls, and ASP.NET web controls onto an application page in addition to editing the code behind the page.

As with any other project type, press F5 to build and run the project in Debug mode. Visual Studio will automatically package and deploy the application page to the local SharePoint installation and then open the browser at

FIGURE 24-9

the SharePoint site home page. You must manually navigate to the application page at `http://`*ServerName*`/_layouts/`*ProjectName*`/MyPage.aspx` to view it (see Figure 24-10). You can debug the application page in the same way you would debug any other ASP.NET web form.

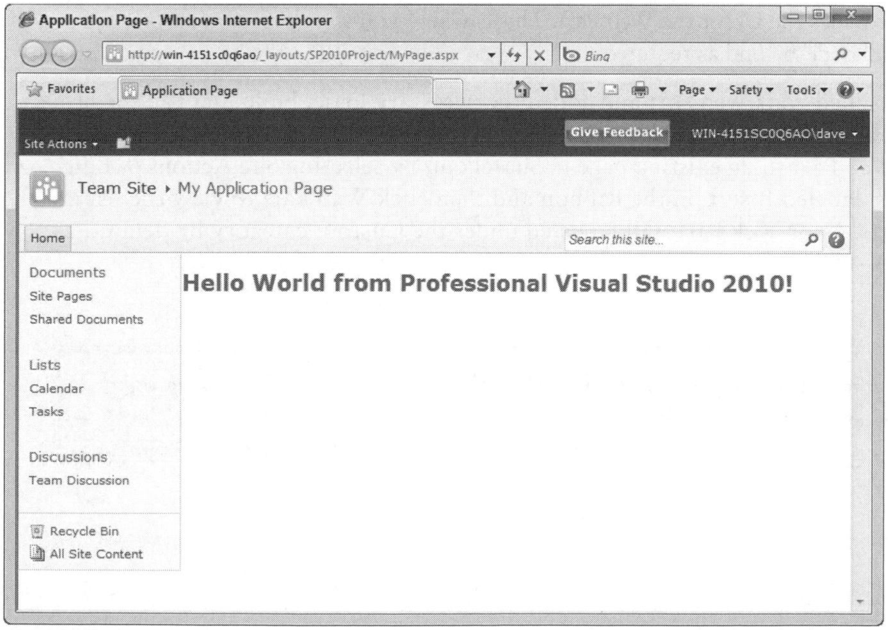

FIGURE 24-10

BUILDING CUSTOM SHAREPOINT COMPONENTS

This section walks you through the development activities associated with some of the more common SharePoint components.

Developing Web Parts

Two types of Web Parts can be created in Visual Studio 2010: ASP.NET Web Parts (also known as Visual Web Parts) and SharePoint-based Web Parts.

ASP.NET Web Parts, which are new to SharePoint 2010, inherit from `System.Web.UI.WebControls` `.WebParts.WebPart` and can be used outside of SharePoint in any ASP.NET web application that implements the ASP.NET Web Parts functionality. However, ASP.NET Web Parts cannot be used in a sandboxed solution. Visual Studio 2010 includes a designer for ASP.NET Web Parts.

SharePoint-based Web Parts are a legacy control and inherit from the `Microsoft.SharePoint` `.WebPartPages.WebPart` class. SharePoint-based Web Parts can only be used in SharePoint sites. There is no designer support for SharePoint-based Web Parts in Visual Studio 2010. Instead, you must build up the design in code by overriding the `CreateChildControls()` or `Render()` methods.

ASP.NET Web Parts are recommended for new Web Part development. To create a new ASP.NET Web Part right-click the project in the Solution Explorer and select Add ⇨ New Item. Select the Visual Web Part template, enter `MyWebPart` as the name, and click Add.

Several files are added to the project when a new Web Part is created. `MyWebPart.cs` (or `MyWebPart.vb` if you are using VB) is the entry point for the Web Part and the class that is instantiated when the Web Part is loaded at run time. `Elements.xml` and `MyWebPart.webpart` are XML-based manifest files that provide metadata to SharePoint about the Web Part. Finally, `MyWebPartUserControl.ascx` is the .NET user control that provides the UI for the Web Part. This is where you should customize the layout and add web control and code-behind as required.

Once you have designed your Web Part and added the necessary logic, build and run the project. Visual Studio will automatically package and deploy the Web Part to the local SharePoint site. You can add the Web Part to an existing page in SharePoint by selecting Site Actions ⇨ Edit Page. Click the tab labeled Insert on the Ribbon and then click Web Part to view the list of available Web Parts. Your Web Part will be listed under the Custom category by default, as shown in Figure 24-11.

> *You can change the category that your Web Part appears under by editing the* `Elements.xml` *file.*

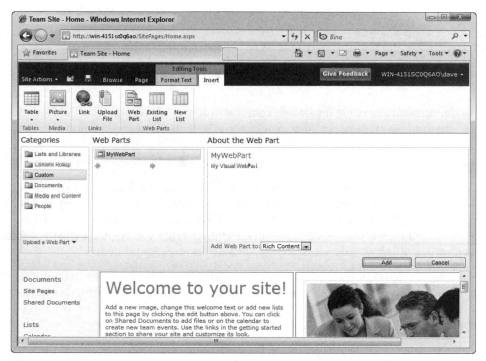

FIGURE 24-11

Creating Content Types and Lists

Content types and lists are two of the fundamental building blocks of SharePoint and are used to implement many of the features that are provided out-of-the-box.

Create a new custom content type by right-clicking the project in the Solution Explorer and selecting Add ➪ New Item. Select the Content Type template, enter `MyContentType` as the name, and click Add. In the SharePoint Customization Wizard choose Task as the base content type to inherit from and click Finish. Visual Studio will create the custom content type, which is simply an XML-based definition of the content type in the `Elements.xml` file.

Next, create a custom field that can be used by the new content type. From the Add New Item dialog, select a new Empty Element, enter `Owner` as the name, and click Add. Add the following line of XML to the `Elements.xml` file that was created, within the `<Elements>` node:

```
<Field ID="{3BA8B2E2-4BEA-4305-ACD2-9511C5E45738}"
       Type="User"
       Name="Owner"
       DisplayName="Task Owner">
</Field>
```

> *Each custom field that you create must have a unique ID. You can generate a new GUID within Visual Studio by selecting Tools ➪ Create GUID.*

Now go back to the `Elements.xml` file for `MyContentType`. Add the following line of XML under the `<FieldRefs>` node so that the Owner custom field is available to the new content type:

```
<FieldRef ID="{3BA8B2E2-4BEA-4305-ACD2-9511C5E45738}" Name="Owner"/>
```

Next, create a new SharePoint list definition for this content type. From the Add New Item dialog, select a new List Definition From Content Type, specify `MyCustomTasksList` as the name, and click Add. Visual Studio will display the SharePoint Customization Wizard, as shown in Figure 24-12. Enter a display name, and then ensure that the custom content type that you created earlier is selected in the drop-down. Also confirm that the checkbox to add a list instance is checked.

Finally, you'll need to customize the list instance so that a useful title is displayed. By default, the title of list instance is **ProjectName - ListInstanceName**. Open the `Elements.xml` file under the list instance, ListInstance1, and edit the `Title` attribute in the XML. Save the file and press F5 to build and run the project.

When the SharePoint site opens, you will see a new list in the left-hand column of the Home page. Click the list and then click the Items tab in the Ribbon. Click the New Item button to display the New Item dialog shown in Figure 24-13. Note the new custom field is shown at the bottom of the dialog.

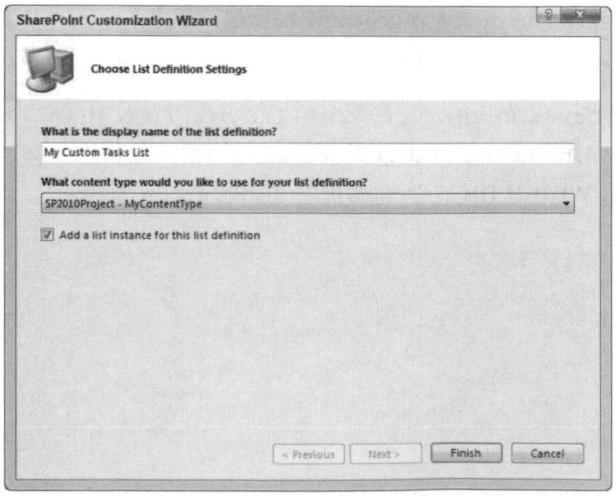

FIGURE 24-12

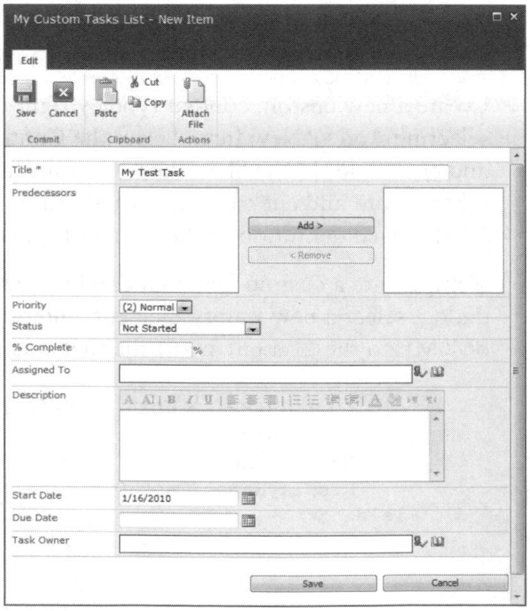

FIGURE 24-13

You can customize many aspects of the list, including which fields should be displayed in the default view, by modifying the list definition `Schema.xml` file.

Adding Event Receivers

Event receivers can be added to many different SharePoint types, including lists, items in a list, workflows, Features, and SharePoint site administrative tasks. This walkthrough adds a new event receiver to the custom list that was created in the previous section.

Begin by selecting a new Event Receiver from the Add New Item dialog. When you click Add, the SharePoint Customization Wizard is displayed, as shown in Figure 24-14. Select List Item Events Task as the type of event receiver and the custom task list as the event source. Tick the checkbox next to the An item was added event and click Finish.

Visual Studio will create the new event receiver as a class that inherits from the `Microsoft .SharePoint.SPItemEventReceiver` base class. The `ItemAdded` method will be overridden. Modify this by adding the following code that sets the Due Date of a new task to 5 days from the Start Date:

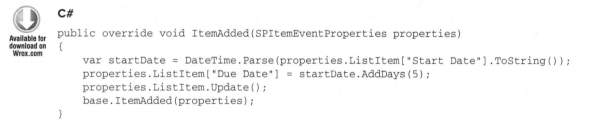

FIGURE 24-14

Available for download on Wrox.com

C#

```csharp
public override void ItemAdded(SPItemEventProperties properties)
{
    var startDate = DateTime.Parse(properties.ListItem["Start Date"].ToString());
    properties.ListItem["Due Date"] = startDate.AddDays(5);
    properties.ListItem.Update();
    base.ItemAdded(properties);
}
```

Code snippet MyEventReceiver.cs

Available for download on Wrox.com

VB

```vb
Public Overrides Sub ItemAdded(ByVal properties As SPItemEventProperties)
    Dim startDate = DateTime.Parse(properties.ListItem("Start Date").ToString())
    properties.ListItem("Due Date") = startDate.AddDays(5)
    properties.ListItem.Update()
    MyBase.ItemAdded(properties)
End Sub
```

Code snippet MyEventReceiver.vb

You may be prompted with a deployment conflict, shown in Figure 24-15, when you try to build and run the project. Check the option so that you are not prompted more than once and click Resolve Automatically.

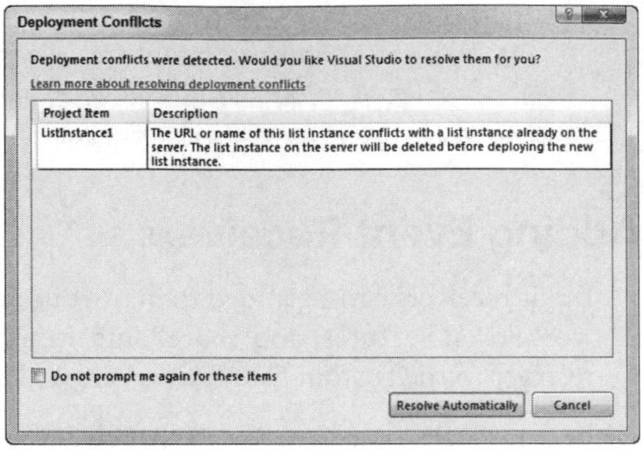

Now when you add a new task to the custom tasks list the Due Date will be automatically set when the item is saved.

Creating SharePoint Workflows

Visual Studio 2010 includes support for two types of SharePoint workflows: a sequential workflow and a state machine workflow.

FIGURE 24-15

A sequential workflow represents the workflow as a set of steps that are executed in order. For example, a document is submitted that generates an e-mail to an approver. The approver opens the document in SharePoint and either approves or rejects it. If approved, the document is published. If rejected, an e-mail is sent back to the submitter with the details of why it was rejected.

A state machine workflow represents the workflow as a set of states, transitions, and actions. You define the start state for the workflow and it will transition to a new state based on an event. For example, you may have states such as Document Created and Document Published, and events that control the transition to these states such as Document Submitted and Document Approved.

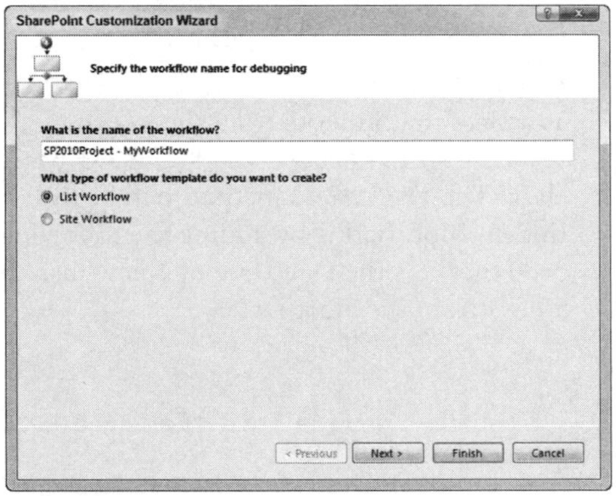

To create a new SharePoint workflow right-click the project in the Solution Explorer and select Add ⇨ New Item. Select the Sequential Workflow template, enter `MyWorkflow` as the name, and click Add.

FIGURE 24-16

Visual Studio will launch the SharePoint Customization Wizard. On the first screen enter a meaningful name for the workflow and ensure the type of workflow template to create is set to List Workflow, as shown in Figure 24-16.

On the next screen, specify the automatic workflow association that should be created when a debug session is started. The default options, shown in Figure 24-17, will associate the workflow with the Shared Documents document library. Leave the defaults and click Next.

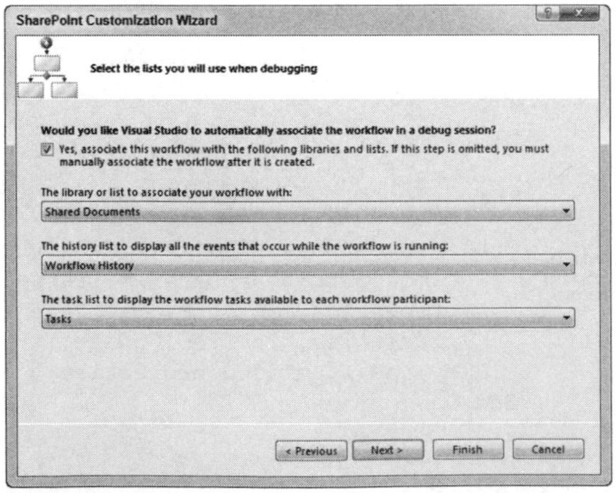

FIGURE 24-17

The final step in the SharePoint Customization Wizard is to specify how the workflow is started. Leave the defaults (manually started as well as when an item is created) and click Finish. Visual Studio will create the workflow and open it in the Workflow Designer, as shown in Figure 24-18.

Because workflows in SharePoint are built on the Windows Workflow engine, we won't spend time in this chapter exploring how you can customize the workflow. Instead, refer to Chapter 32 for a detailed look at Windows Workflow. One thing to note though: SharePoint 2010 workflows only run on version 3.5 of Windows Workflow.

You can test your workflow by running it against the local SharePoint installation. When you run the solution, Visual Studio will automatically package and deploy the workflow with the associations

FIGURE 24-18

that were specified earlier. When you add a new document to the Shared Documents library the workflow will be invoked. You can debug the workflow by setting breakpoints in the code-behind and stepping through the execution in the same way you would any other Visual Studio project.

WORKING WITH FEATURES

Features are primarily targeted at SharePoint Administrators and provide them with a way to manage related items. Every time you create an item in a SharePoint project it is added to a Feature.

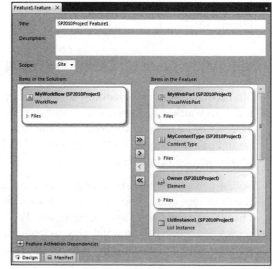

Features are stored under the Features node in your SharePoint project. Visual Studio includes a Feature Designer (shown in Figure 24-19), which is displayed when you double-click a Feature.

The Feature Designer allows you to set a title and description for the Feature that will be displayed in SharePoint. You can also set the scope of the Feature to an entire server farm, all web sites in a site collection, a specific web site, or all web sites in a web application.

You can choose to include or exclude certain items in a Feature with the Feature Designer. For example, in Figure 24-19, all SharePoint items in

FIGURE 24-19

the project except for `MyWorkflow` have been included in the Feature. If you have more than one Feature in a project, you can also set dependencies that ensure one Feature cannot be activated unless another Feature has been.

In SharePoint, Administrators can activate or deactivate Features using the Manage Site Features or Site Collection Features administration screens under Site Actions ⇨ Site Settings (see Figure 24-20).

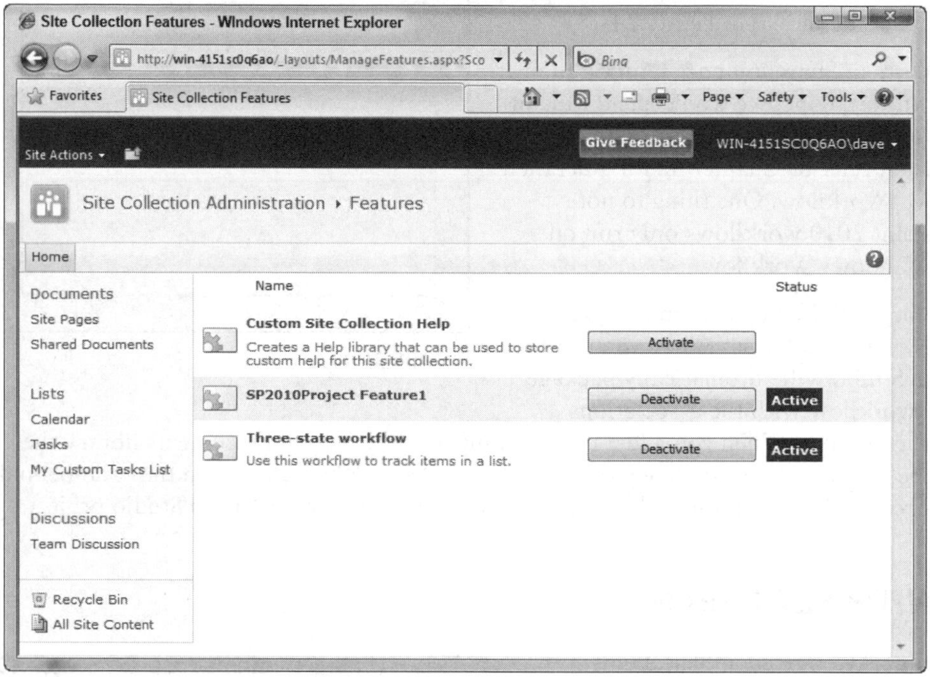

FIGURE 24-20

PACKAGING AND DEPLOYMENT

SharePoint provides a custom packaging format called Windows SharePoint Package (WSP). WSP files can contain Features, site definitions, templates and application pages, and additional required assemblies. WSP files are created in the `bin/debug` or `bin/release` folder when you build a SharePoint solution with Visual Studio. The WSP file can then be installed on a remote SharePoint server by an administrator.

When you create a SharePoint project, a package definition file is also created in the project under the Packages node. The package definition file describes what should go into the WSP file. Visual Studio includes a Package Designer and Packaging Explorer tool window to assist with building packages. If you double-click the package file it opens the file with these design tools. Figure 24-21 shows a package file that includes an application page and a single Feature.

When you press F5 in a SharePoint project, Visual Studio is saving you a whole lot of time by automatically deploying all of the items in your project to the local SharePoint installation. The deployment steps are specified under a SharePoint-specific project property page, shown in Figure 24-22. To display this property page, right-click the project in the Solution Explorer and select Properties.

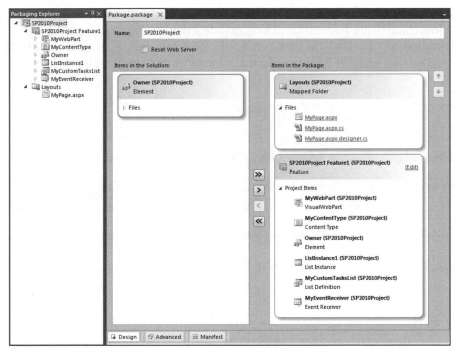

FIGURE 24-21

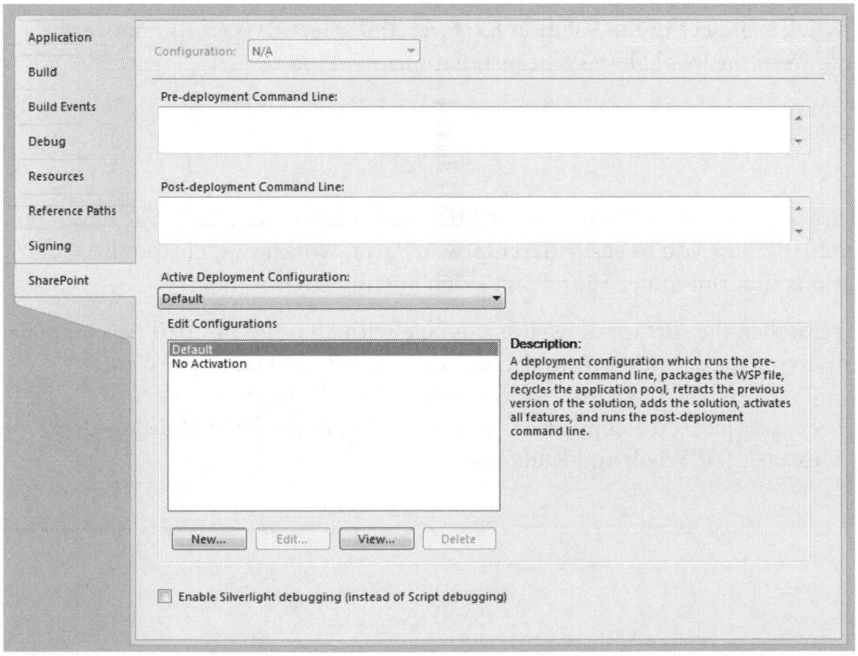

FIGURE 24-22

You can specify a command-line program or script to run before and after Visual Studio deploys the solution to the local SharePoint installation. The actual deployment steps are specified as a deployment configuration. Double-click the configuration in the Edit Configurations list to display the list of deployment steps. Figure 24-23 shows the default deployment configuration.

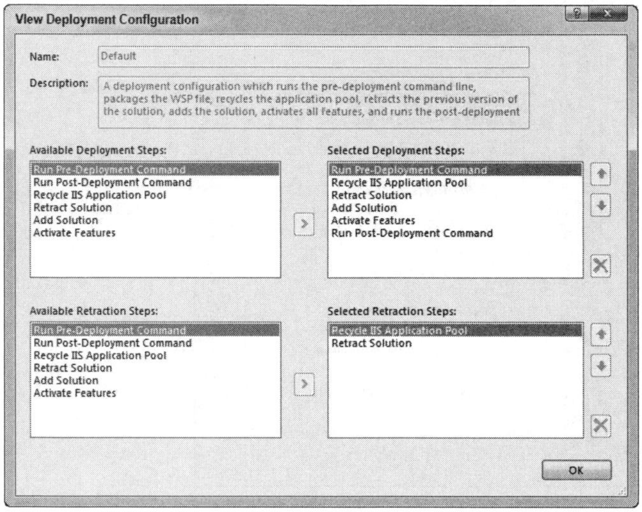

FIGURE 24-23

Finally, you can right-click a project in the Solution Explorer and select Retract to remove the SharePoint components from the local SharePoint installation.

SUMMARY

In this chapter you learned how to build solutions for Microsoft SharePoint 2010. The development tools in Visual Studio 2010 allow you to easily develop Web Parts, workflows, custom lists, and complete web applications that run under SharePoint's rich hosting environment.

This chapter has just scratched the surface of what is possible with SharePoint 2010 development. If you are interested in diving deeper into this topic, visit the SharePoint Developer Center at http://msdn.microsoft.com/sharepoint, the SharePoint Dev Wiki at http://www.sharepointdevwiki.com, or pick up a copy of *Professional SharePoint 2010 Development* by Tom Rizzo, Reza Alirezaei, Jeff Fried, and Paul Swider.

Windows Azure

WHAT'S IN THIS CHAPTER?

➤ Understanding Windows Azure

➤ Building, testing, and deploying applications using Windows Azure

➤ Storing data in Windows Azure tables, blobs, and queues

➤ Using SQL Azure from your application

➤ Understanding the AppFabric

Over the past couple of years, the adoption of cloud computing has really taken off with Google, Amazon, and a host of other providers entering the market. Microsoft's approach mirrors their own approach to desktop, mobile, and server computing, in so far as they are offering a development platform on top of which both ISVs and Microsoft itself can build great software. Without going into a formal definition of Cloud Computing, it is important to recognize that you might choose to run your application in the cloud for a number of reasons. These include the need for high availability, the ability to scale to meet the demand for your application, and of course, cost reduction.

This chapter is broken into three sections that cover the Windows Azure Platform, SQL Azure, and the AppFabric. The Windows Azure Platform hosts your web application, allowing you to dynamically vary the number of concurrent instances running. It also provides storage services in the form of tables, blobs, and queues. SQL Azure provides a true database service hosted in the cloud. Finally, you can use the AppFabric to authenticate users, control access to your application and services, and simplify the process of exposing services from within your organization.

THE WINDOWS AZURE PLATFORM

As with most Microsoft technologies, getting started with the Windows Azure platform is as easy as creating a new application, building it, and then running it. You will notice that there is a new node in the New Project dialog entitled Cloud Service, which has a single project template, also called Cloud Service, as shown in Figure 25-1.

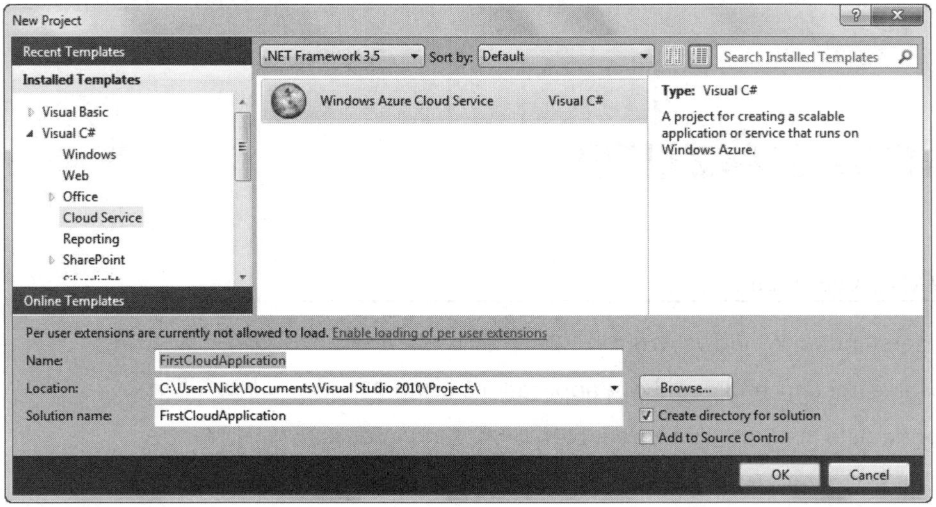

FIGURE 25-1

After selecting the Cloud Service project template you are prompted to add one or more Roles to your application. An Azure project can be broken into different Roles based on the type of work they are going to do and whether they accept user input. Simply put, Web Roles can accept user input via an inbound connection (for example, http on port 80), whereas Worker Roles cannot. A typical scenario would consist of a Web Role that is used to accept data. This may be a web site or a web service of some description. The Web Role would hand off the data, for example, via a queue, to a Worker Role, which would then carry out any processing that is to be done. This separation means that the two tiers can be scaled out independently, improving the elasticity of the application.

In Figure 25-2, both an ASP.NET Web Role and a Worker Role have been added to the cloud services solution by selecting the role and clicking the right arrow button. Clicking the edit symbol on the selected role allows you to rename the role before clicking OK to complete the creation of your application.

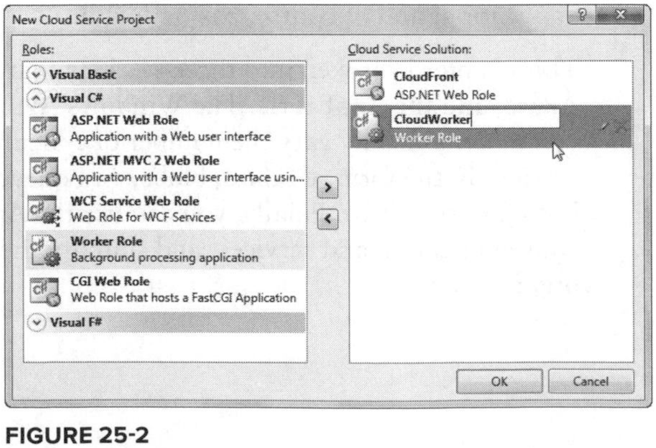

FIGURE 25-2

As you can see in Figure 25-3, the application created consists of a project for each role selected (CloudFront and CloudWorker, respectively) and an additional project, FirstCloudApplication, that defines the list of roles and other information about your Azure application.

The CloudFront project is essentially just an ASP.NET web application project. In fact, if you right-click this project and select Set as Startup Project you can run this project as with any normal ASP.NET project. On the other hand, the CloudWorker project is simply a class library with a single class, WorkerRole, which contains the entry point for the worker.

To run your Azure application, make sure the FirstCloudApplication project is set as the Startup Project and then press F5 to start debugging. If this is your first time running an Azure application you will notice a dialog appears that initializes the Development Storage. This process takes a minute or two to complete; once done you will notice that two icons have been added to the Windows taskbar.

FIGURE 25-3

The first allows you to control the Development Storage services, a set of three local services that mirror the table, blob, and queue storage available in the Azure platform. The second allows you to monitor the Development Fabric, a local replica of the Azure hosting environment in which you can run, debug, and test your application.

After the Development Storage has been initialized you should notice that the `Default.aspx` page of the CloudFront project launches within the browser. Although you will only see a single browser instance, in fact, multiple instances of the web role are all running in what's called the Development Fabric.

The Development Fabric

In the FirstCloudApplication project are two files that define attributes about your Azure application. The first, `ServiceDefinition.csdef`, defines the structure and attributes of the roles that make up your application. For example, if one of your roles needs to write to the file system you can stipulate a `LocalStorage` property, giving the role restricted access to a small amount of disk space in which to read and write temporary files. This file also defines any settings that the roles will require at run time. Defining settings is a great way to make your roles more adaptable at run time without having to rebuild and publish them.

The second file is the `ServiceConfiguration.cscfg` file, which defines the run time configuration of the roles. This includes the number of instances of each role that should be running, as well as any settings that you have defined in the `ServiceDefinition` file. If you modify values in this configuration file, for example, changing the count attribute of the `Instances` element to 4 for both roles, and re-run your application, it will run with the new configuration values in the local Development Fabric.

If you right-click the Development Fabric icon in the Windows taskbar and select Show Development Fabric UI, you will see a hierarchical representation of the running applications within the Development Fabric, as shown in Figure 25-4. As you drill down into the deployments you can see the FirstCloudApplication and then the two roles, CloudFront and CloudWorker.

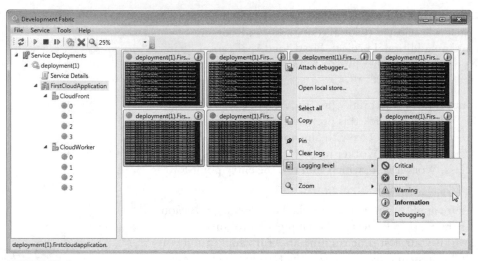

FIGURE 25-4

Within each of the roles you can see the number of running (green dot) instances, which in Figure 25-4 is 4. In the right pane you can see the log output for each of the running instances. Clicking the title bar on any of the instances toggles that instance to display in the full pane. The icon in the top-right corner of each instance indicates the logging level. You can adjust this by right-clicking the title and selecting the desired value from the Logging Level menu item.

Table, Blob, and Queue Storage

So far you have a web role with no content and a worker role that doesn't do anything. You can add content to the web role by simply adding controls to the `Default.aspx` page in the same way that you would for a normal web application. Start by adding a textbox called JobDetailsText and a button called SubmitJob. Double-click the button to bring up the code-behind file.

You can pass data between web and worker roles by writing to table (structured data), blob (single binary objects), or queue (messages) storage. You work with this storage within the Azure platform via its REST interface. However, as .NET developers this is not a pleasant or efficient coding experience. Luckily, the Azure team has put together a wrapper for this functionality that makes it easy for your application to use Windows Azure storage. If you look at the references for both the Web and Worker Role projects, you will see a reference for `Microsoft.WindowsAzure.Storage.dll`, which contains the wrapper classes and methods that you can use from your application.

In the code-behind file for the `Default.aspx` page, enter the following code, which obtains a queue reference and then adds a simple message. Note that you may need to add using statements to your code file where necessary.

C#

```csharp
protected void SubmitJob_Click(object sender, EventArgs e){
    // read account configuration settings
    var storageAccount = CloudStorageAccount.
                     FromConfigurationSetting("DataConnectionString");
```

Available for
download on
Wrox.com

```
        // create queue to communicate with worker role
        var queueStorage = storageAccount.CreateCloudQueueClient();
        var queue = queueStorage.GetQueueReference("sample");
        queue.CreateIfNotExist();
        queue.AddMessage(new CloudQueueMessage(this.JobDetailsText.Text));
    }
```

Code snippet Default.aspx.cs

VB

```
Protected Sub SubmitJob_Click(ByVal sender As Object,
                            ByVal e As EventArgs) Handles SubmitJob.Click
    ' read account configuration settings
    Dim storageAccount = CloudStorageAccount.
                    FromConfigurationSetting("DataConnectionString")

    ' create queue to communicate with worker role
    Dim queueStorage = storageAccount.CreateCloudQueueClient()
    Dim queue = queueStorage.GetQueueReference("sample")
    queue.CreateIfNotExist()
    queue.AddMessage(New CloudQueueMessage(Me.JobDetailsText.Text))
End Sub
```

Code snippet Default.aspx.vb

This code takes the value supplied in the JobDetailsText textbox and adds it to the queue, wrapped in as a message.

You also need to update the worker role to pop messages off the queue and carry out the appropriate actions. The following code retrieves the next message on the queue, and simply writes the response out to the log, before deleting the message off the queue. If you don't delete the message from the queue it is pushed back onto the queue after a configurable timeout, so as to ensure all messages are handled at least once even if a worker role dies mid-processing.

C#

```
private CloudQueue queue;
public override bool OnStart(){
    DiagnosticMonitor.Start("DiagnosticsConnectionString");

    Microsoft.WindowsAzure.CloudStorageAccount.
            SetConfigurationSettingPublisher((configName, configSetter) =>{
        configSetter(Microsoft.WindowsAzure.ServiceRuntime.RoleEnvironment.
            GetConfigurationSettingValue(configName));
            });

    Trace.TraceInformation("Worker entry point called");

    // read account configuration settings
    var storageAccount = CloudStorageAccount.
                    FromConfigurationSetting("DataConnectionString");
```

```csharp
        // create queue to communicate with web role
        var queueStorage = storageAccount.CreateCloudQueueClient();
        var queue = queueStorage.GetQueueReference("sample");
        queue.CreateIfNotExist();
        return base.OnStart();
    }

public override void Run(){
    Trace.TraceInformation("CloudWorker entry point called");
    while (true){
        try{
            // Pop the next message off the queue
            CloudQueueMessage msg = queue.GetMessage();
            if (msg != null){
                // Parse the message contents as a job detail
                string jd = msg.AsString;
                Trace.TraceInformation("Processed {0}", jd);
                // Delete the message from the queue
                queue.DeleteMessage(msg);
            }
            else{
                Thread.Sleep(10000);
            }
            Trace.TraceInformation("Working");
        }
        catch (Exception ex){
            Trace.TraceError(ex.Message);
        }
    }
}
```

Code snippet WorkerRole.cs

VB

Available for
download on
Wrox.com

```vb
Private queue As CloudQueue
Public Overrides Function OnStart() As Boolean
    DiagnosticMonitor.Start("DiagnosticsConnectionString")

    CloudStorageAccount.SetConfigurationSettingPublisher(
            Function(configName, configSetter)
                configSetter(RoleEnvironment.
                    GetConfigurationSettingValue(configName)))
    Trace.TraceInformation("Worker entry point called")

    ' read account configuration settings
    Dim storageAccount = CloudStorageAccount.
                    FromConfigurationSetting("DataConnectionString")
    ' create queue to communicate with web role
    Dim queueStorage = storageAccount.CreateCloudQueueClient()
    queue = queueStorage.GetQueueReference("sample")
    queue.CreateIfNotExist()
    Return MyBase.OnStart()
End Function
```

```vb
Public Overrides Sub Run()
    Trace.TraceInformation("CloudWorker entry point called.")
    Do While (True)
        Try
            ' Pop the next message off the queue
            Dim msg As CloudQueueMessage = queue.GetMessage()
            If (msg IsNot Nothing) Then
                ' Parse the message contents as a job detail
                Dim jd As String = msg.AsString
                Trace.TraceInformation("Processed {0}", jd)
                ' Delete the message from the queue
                queue.DeleteMessage(msg)
            Else
                Thread.Sleep(10000)
            End If
            Trace.TraceInformation("Working")
        Catch ex As StorageClientException
            Trace.TraceError(ex.Message)
        End Try
    Loop
End Function
```

Code snippet WorkerRole.vb

You will notice that this code overrides two methods, OnStart and Run. The former is used to load configuration values and set up local variables for working with Windows Azure storage, whereas the Run method contains an infinite while loop that continues to process messages off the queue.

Before you can run your modified roles you need to specify the location of the queue storage that you are going to be using. Though this will eventually be an Azure storage account, during development you need to specify the details of the local Development Storage. You do this in the ServiceConfiguration file:

```xml
<?xml version="1.0"?>
<ServiceConfiguration serviceName="FirstCloudApplication"
xmlsn="http://schemas.microsoft.com/ServiceHosting/2008/10/ServiceConfiguration">
<Role name="CloudFront">
<Instances count="2" />
<ConfigurationSettings>
<Setting name="DataConnectionString" value="UseDevelopmentStorage=true" />
<Setting name="DiagnosticsConnectionString" value="UseDevelopmentStorage=true" />
<!-- <Setting name="DeploymentConnectionString" value="DefaultEndpointsProtocol=
https;AccountName=[YOUR_ACCOUNT_NAME];AccountKey=[YOUR_ACCOUNT_KEY]" /> -->
</ConfigurationSettings>
</Role>
<Role name="CloudWorker">
<Instances count="2" />
<ConfigurationSettings>
<Setting name="DataConnectionString" value="UseDevelopmentStorage=true" />
<Setting name="DiagnosticsConnectionString" value="UseDevelopmentStorage=true" />
</ConfigurationSettings>
</Role>
</ServiceConfiguration>
```

You will notice that for both the CloudWorker and CloudFront roles, settings for `DataConnectionString` and `DiagnosticsConnectionString` have been defined. In this case, the value has been set to use the development storage account. When you go to deploy to Windows Azure, you will need to replace this with a connection string that includes the account name and key, in the format illustrated by the `DeploymentConnectionString`. Before these values will be accessible to your roles you also need to update the `ServiceDefinition` file to indicate which settings are defined for each role:

```
<?xml version="1.0" encoding="utf-8"?>
<ServiceDefinition name="FirstCloudApplication"
xmlsn="http://schemas.microsoft.com/ServiceHosting/2008/10/ServiceDefinition">
<WebRole name="CloudFront" enableNativeCodeExecution="false">
<InputEndpoints>
<!-- Must use port 80 for http and port 443 for https when running in the cloud -->
<InputEndpoint name="HttpIn" protocol="http" port="80" />
</InputEndpoints>
<ConfigurationSettings>
<Setting name="DataConnectionString" />
<Setting name="DiagnosticsConnectionString" />
</ConfigurationSettings>
</WebRole>
<WorkerRole name="CloudWorker" enableNativeCodeExecution="false">
<ConfigurationSettings>
<Setting name="DataConnectionString" />
<Setting name="DiagnosticsConnectionString" />
</ConfigurationSettings>
</WorkerRole>
</ServiceDefinition>
```

With these changes, try running your Azure application and noting that when you hit the Submit button you will see a "Processed" message appear in one of the running instances of the worker role in the Development Fabric UI.

Application Deployment

Once you have built your Azure application using the Development Fabric and Development Storage, you will want to deploy it to the Windows Azure Platform. Before doing so you will need to provision your Windows Azure account with both a hosting and a storage service. Start by going to http://www.azure.com and signing in using your Live Id to your Windows Azure account. After logging in, click on the "Go to the Windows Azure Developer portal" link. This opens the Windows Azure portal, which looks similar to Figure 25-5.

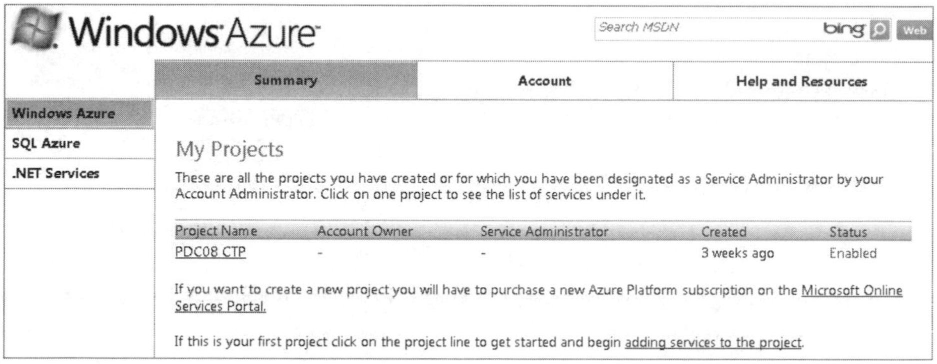

FIGURE 25-5

Click the project name, followed by the New Service button, and then select the type of service you want to add. The FirstCloudApplication requires both hosting and storage so you will need to add one of each. Once you have added a Storage Account service you should see a configuration screen similar to Figure 25-6.

FIGURE 25-6

You will need to copy the account information and storage endpoints across into your `ServiceConfiguration` file. Once you have done this you can again run your Azure application. This time it will still run within your local Development Fabric but it will use the Azure storage instead of the Development Storage. This is a good test to ensure your application will deploy correctly to the cloud.

Once you have set up your hosting service account you will see a screen similar to Figure 25-7.

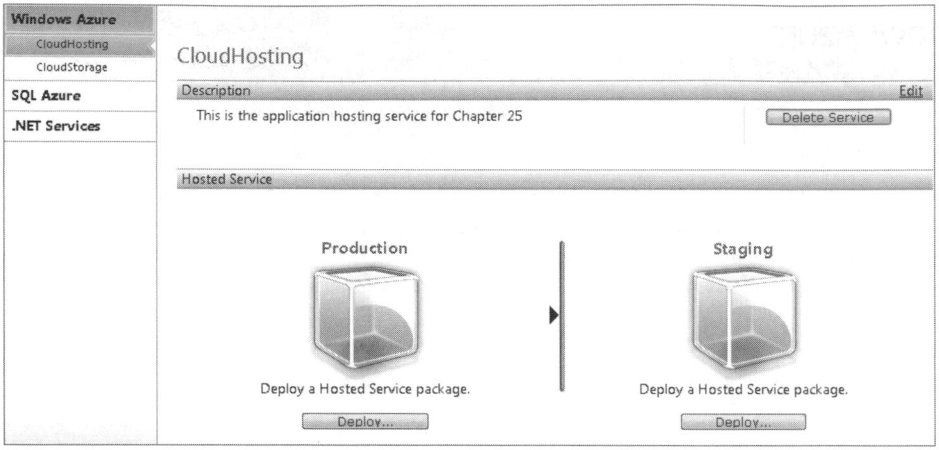

FIGURE 25-7

In Figure 25-7 you can see that you in fact have two environments into which you can deploy: Production and Staging. As with all good deployment strategies, Azure supports deploying into Staging and then once you are comfortable, migrating that into Production.

Return to Visual Studio 2010, right-click the FirstCloudApplication project, and select Publish. This builds your application and generates a deployment package and a configuration file. These are displayed in a Windows Explorer dialog once completed. Return to Windows Azure and click the Deploy button under the Staging node (in Figure 25-7). You are prompted to select the deployment package and configuration file. Once you complete the upload you are returned to the hosting service page where you will see that the Staging environment has been updated, as in Figure 25-8.

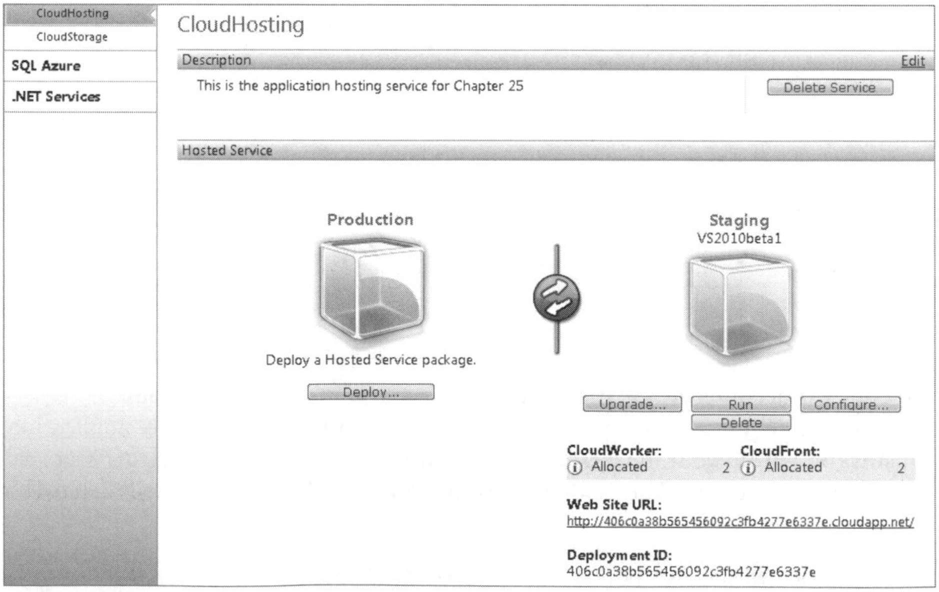

FIGURE 25-8

Unlike other ASP.NET web applications that start running as soon as they are completely deployed, Azure applications need to be started. You do this by clicking the Run button. The screen will refresh with all roles stating that they are initializing. Eventually, they will update to Started, at which point all roles are ready to receive input or do work.

The last stage in this process is to promote what's running in the Staging environment into Production. The word "promote" is important because this transition is all handled by an intelligent router. Because the cut over from one to the other will at some point (depending on how quickly the router effects the change) be close to instantaneous, there should never be any time at which someone hitting the site receives a 404 or missing page. To promote Staging into Production, select the round rotating button situated in between the product and staging areas of the Azure portal.

Tuning Your Application

Over time, demand for your application may vary, or you may need to adjust application settings specified in the `ServiceConfiguration` file. You can do this dynamically by clicking the Configure button (see the Staging deployment in Figure 25-8). Figure 25-9 shows the configuration screen where you can modify the configuration XML, or upload an alternative configuration file. You should only modify your staging deployment using this method because you don't want to affect the running of your Production deployment. The recommend approach is to start with identical Production and Staging deployments, modify the Staging configuration, allow it to initialize and start, then switch that deployment into Production. You can then modify the second deployment so that they are in sync.

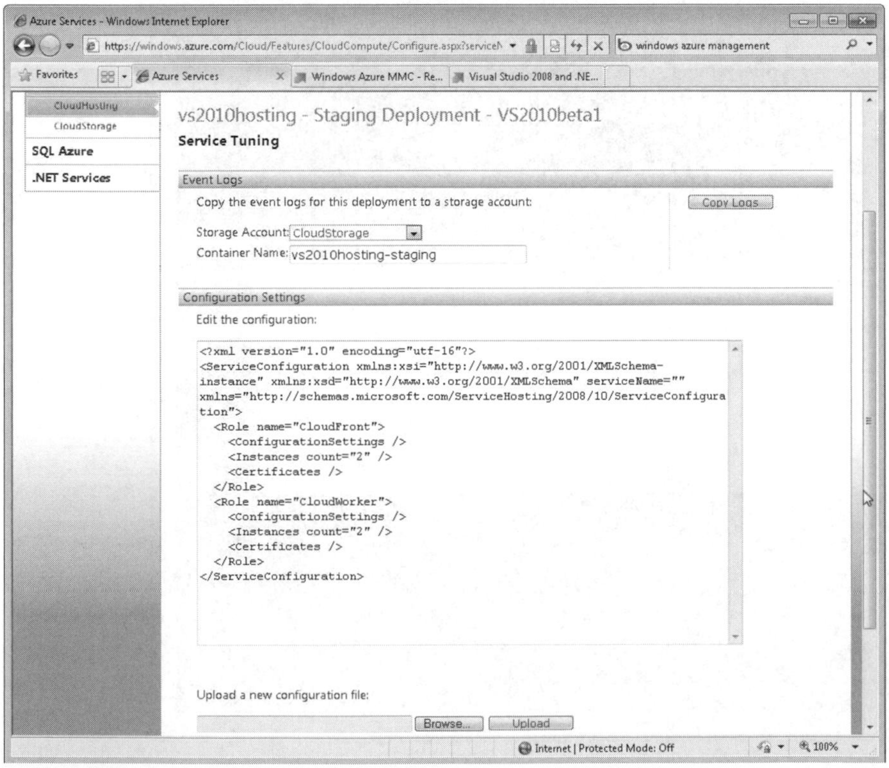

FIGURE 25-9

This screen also allows you to export logs generated by the roles within your application to a storage account. After copying the logs you will then need to retrieve the logs from the relevant storage account. You can do this using the CloudDrive sample in the Azure SDK, which can be used to map a storage account as a local drive that you can query in Powershell.

SQL AZURE

In addition to Azure table, blob, and queue storage, the Windows Azure Platform offers true relational data hosting in the form of SQL Azure. You can think of each SQL Azure database as being a hosted instance of a SQL Server 2008 database that is running in high-availability mode. This means that at any point in time there are three synchronized instances of your database. If one of these instances fails, a new instance is immediately brought online and the data is synchronized to ensure the availability of your data.

To create a SQL Azure database, sign into the Windows Azure portal and navigate to the SQL Azure tab. Once there you can manage your SQL Azure accounts, where you can create and delete databases. After creating a database you can retrieve the connection string that you need in order to connect to the database by selecting the database and clicking the Connection String button, as shown in Figure 25-10.

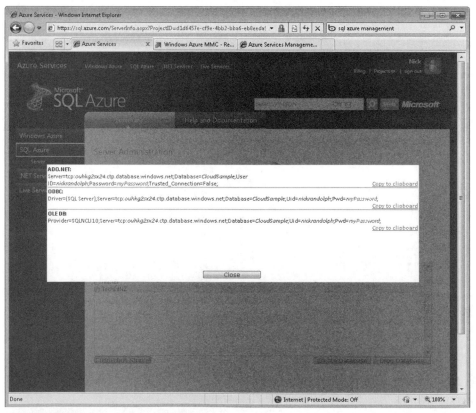

FIGURE 25-10

At the time of writing you have a number of ways to interact with a SQL Azure database. Although SQL Azure is based on SQL Server 2008, a number of limitations exist that prevent most graphical tools, such as SQL Server Management Studio (Object Browser) and Visual Studio 2010, from working properly. You can, however, connect a SQL Server Management Studio Query Window to a SQL Azure database and execute T-SQL statements against your database. Some third-party tools and Visual Studio 2010 add-ins, such as the SQL Azure Migration Wizard, the SQL Azure Manager, and the SQL Azure Explorer, are available that can assist with working with SQL Azure.

From your application you can connect to SQL Azure using the connection string retrieved from the Windows Azure portal page. You can use most frameworks that are based on top of ADO.NET such as LINQ to SQL, Entity Framework, or simply plain ADO.NET to create, update, read, or delete data in your SQL Azure database.

APPFABRIC

The third component of the Windows Azure Platform is the AppFabric. This in turn is made up of the Service Bus and the Access Control Service. In an environment where organizations are increasingly looking to host some or all of their applications in the cloud, significant challenges are posed around connectivity and security. The AppFabric provides a solution to allow enterprises to connect applications and unify application security.

Service Bus

Though most organizations have connectivity to the Internet, connectivity between offices or with individuals on the road is often the cause of frustration. Increasingly, companies operate behind one or more firewall devices that not only restrict the flow of traffic but also do network address translation. This means that computers sitting behind these devices cannot be easily addressable from outside the company network. In addition, as the number of public IPv4 addresses dwindles, more connections are dynamically allocated an IP address. This makes hosting an application within the company network that is publicly accessible almost impossible.

The Service Bus allows a service to be registered at a specific publicly addressable URL via the service registry. Requests made to this URL are directed to the service via an existing outbound connection made by the service itself. Working with the Service Bus can be as simple as changing your existing WCF bindings across to the new relay bindings. As part of running your service it registers with the service registry and initiates the outbound connection required for all further communications.

Access Control Service

Where an organization wants to integrate multiple cloud-based applications and/or an on-premise application there needs to be some way of controlling who (authentication) has access to particular resources (authorization). This is the function of the Access Control Service (ACS). Though still in its infancy, the ACS is capable of verifying a user's identity through the validation of input claims, performing claims translation, and the supply of output claims for specific applications. For example, you could sign into an application providing your e-mail address and a password. These input claims would be used to authenticate you, as well as determine that you belong in the fancy-hat group in application xyz that you are trying to access. The output claims may consist of your e-mail address and the fancy-hat group. Note that because there is a previously established trust relationship between application xyz and ACS (validated through signing of the output claims), application xyz can trust the output claims.

SUMMARY

In this chapter you learned about the Windows Azure Platform and how it represents Microsoft's entry into the cloud computing space. Using Visual Studio 2010, you can adapt an existing, or create a new, application or service for hosting in the cloud. The local Development Storage and Fabric provide a great local testing solution, which means when you publish your application to Windows Azure you can be confident that it will work without major issues.

Even if you don't want to migrate your entire application into the cloud, you can use SQL Azure and the AppFabric offerings to host your data, address connectivity challenges, or unify your application security.

PART VI
Data

▶ **CHAPTER 26:** Visual Database Tools

▶ **CHAPTER 27:** Datasets and Data Binding

▶ **CHAPTER 28:** Language Integrated Queries (LINQ)

▶ **CHAPTER 29:** The ADO.NET Entity Framework

▶ **CHAPTER 30:** Reporting

Visual Database Tools

➤ Understanding the data-oriented tool windows within Visual Studio 2010

➤ Creating and designing databases

➤ Navigating your data sources

➤ Entering and previewing data using Visual Studio 2010

Database connectivity is essential in almost every application you create, regardless of whether it's a Windows-based program or a web site or service. When Visual Studio .NET was first introduced, it provided developers with a great set of options to navigate to the database files on their file systems and local servers, with a Server Explorer, data controls, and data-bound components. The underlying .NET Framework included ADO.NET, a retooled database engine that is more suited to the way applications are built today.

Visual Studio 2010 took those features and smoothed out the kinks, adding tools and functionality to the IDE to give you more direct access to the data in your application. This chapter looks at how you can create, manage, and consume data using the various tool windows provided in Visual Studio 2010. These can be collectively referred to as the Visual Database Tools.

DATABASE WINDOWS IN VISUAL STUDIO 2010

A number of windows specifically deal with databases and their components. From the Data Sources window that shows project-related data files and the Data Connections node in the Server Explorer, to the Database Diagram Editor and the visual designer for database schemas, you'll find most of what you need directly within the IDE. In fact, it's unlikely that you'll need to venture outside of Visual Studio to work with your data.

Figure 26-1 shows the Visual Studio 2010 IDE with a current database-editing session. Notice how the windows, toolbars, and menus all update to match the particular context of editing a database table. In the main area is the list of columns belonging to the table, a Table Designer menu has been added, and there is a Column Properties editing region below. The normal Properties tool window contains the properties for the current table. The next few pages take a look at each of these windows and describe their purposes so you can use them effectively.

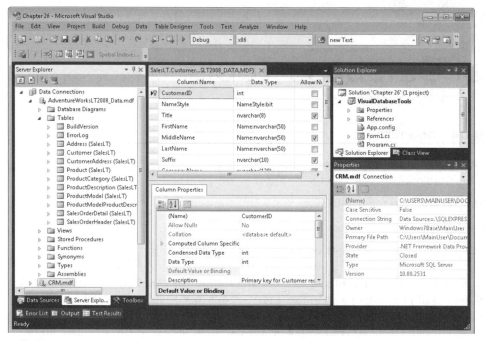

FIGURE 26-1

Server Explorer

In Chapter 12, you saw how the Server Explorer can be used to navigate the components that make up your system (or indeed the components of any server to which you can connect). One component of this tool window that was omitted from that discussion is the Data Connections node. Through this node, Visual Studio 2010 provides a significant subset of the functionality that is available through other products, such as SQL Server Management Studio, for creating and modifying databases.

Figure 26-1 shows the Server Explorer window with an active database connection (`AdventureWorksLT2009_Data.mdf`) and another database that Visual Studio is not currently connected to (`CRM.mdf`). The database icon displays whether or not you are actively connected to the database, and contains a number of child nodes dealing with the typical components of a modern database, such as Tables, Views, and Stored Procedures. Expanding these nodes lists the specific database components along with their details. For example, the Tables node contains a node for the Customer table, which in turn has nodes for each of the columns, such as CustomerID, FirstName, and LastName. Clicking these nodes enables you to quickly view the properties within the Properties tool window. This is the default database view; you can switch to either Object Type or Schema view by selecting Change View, followed by the view to change to, from the right-click context menu off the database node. Each of these views simply groups the information about the database in a different hierarchy.

To add a new database connection to the Server Explorer window, click the Connect to Database button at the top of the Server Explorer (third icon in from the left), or right-click the Data Connections root node and select the Add Connection command from the context menu.

If this is the first time you have added a connection, Visual Studio asks you what type of data source you are connecting to. Visual Studio 2010 comes packaged with a number of Data Source connectors, including Access, SQL Server, and Oracle, as well as a generic ODBC driver. It also includes a data source connector for Microsoft SQL Server Database File and Microsoft SQL Server Compact databases.

The Database File option was introduced in SQL Server 2005 and borrows from the easy deployment model of its lesser cousins, Microsoft Access and MSDE. With SQL Server Database File, you can create a flat file for an individual database. This means you don't need to attach it to a SQL Server instance, and it's highly portable — you simply deliver the .mdf file containing the database along with your application. Alternatively, using a SQL Server Compact (SSC) database can significantly reduce the system requirements for your application. Instead of requiring an instance of SQL Server to be installed, the SSC runtime can be deployed alongside your application.

Once you've chosen the data source type to use, the Add Connection dialog appears. Figure 26-2 shows this dialog for a SQL Server Database File connection, with the settings that are appropriate to that data source type. You are taken directly to this dialog if you already have data connections defined in Visual Studio.

The Change button takes you to the Data Sources page, enabling you to add different types of database connections to your Visual Studio session. Note how easy it is to create a SQL Server Database File. Just type or browse to the location where you want the file and specify the database name for a new database. If you want to connect to an existing database, use the Browse button to locate it on the file system.

Generally, the only other task you need to perform is to specify whether your SQL Server configuration is using Windows or SQL Server Authentication. The default

FIGURE 26-2

installation of Visual Studio 2010 includes an installation of SQL Server 2005 Express, which uses Windows Authentication as its base authentication model.

> *The Test Connection button displays an error message if you try to connect to a new database. This is because it doesn't exist until you click OK, so there's nothing to connect to!*

When you click OK, Visual Studio attempts to connect to the database. If successful, it adds it to the Data Connections node, including the children nodes for the main data types in the database, as discussed earlier. Alternatively, if the database doesn't exist, Visual Studio prompts you asking if it should go ahead and create it. You can also create a new database by selecting the Create New SQL Server Database item from the right-click menu off the Data Connections node in the Server Explorer.

Table Editing

The easiest way to edit a table in the database is to double-click its entry in the Server Explorer. An editing window is then displayed in the main workspace, consisting of two components. The top section is where you specify each field name, data type, and key information such as length for text fields, and whether the field is nullable.

Right-clicking a field gives you access to a set of commands that you can perform against that field, as shown in Figure 26-3. This context menu contains the same items as the Table Designer menu that is displayed while you're editing a table, but it is usually easier to use the context menu because you can clearly see which field you're modifying.

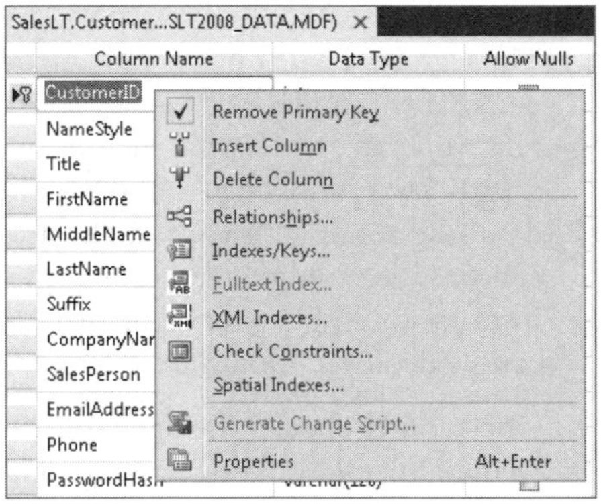

FIGURE 26-3

The lower half of the table editing workspace contains the Column Properties window for the currently selected column. Unlike the grid area that simply lists the Column Name, Data Type, and whether the column allows nulls, the column properties area allows you to specify all of the available properties for the particular Data Source type.

Figure 26-4 shows a sample Column Properties window for a field, CustomerID, that has been defined with an identity clause that is automatically incremented by 1 for each new record added to the table.

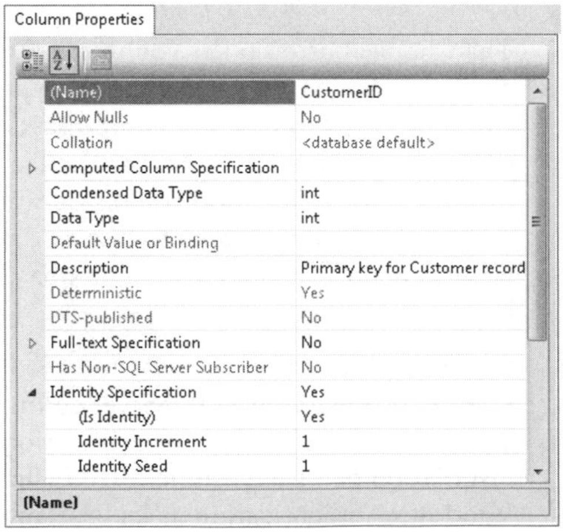

Relationship Editing

Most databases that are likely to be used by your .NET solutions are relational in nature, which means

FIGURE 26-4

you connect tables together by defining relationships. To create a relationship, open one of the tables that will be part of the relationship and click the Relationships button on the toolbar, or use the Table Designer ➪ Relationships menu command. The Foreign Key Relationships dialog is displayed (see Figure 26-5), containing any existing relationships that are bound to the table you selected.

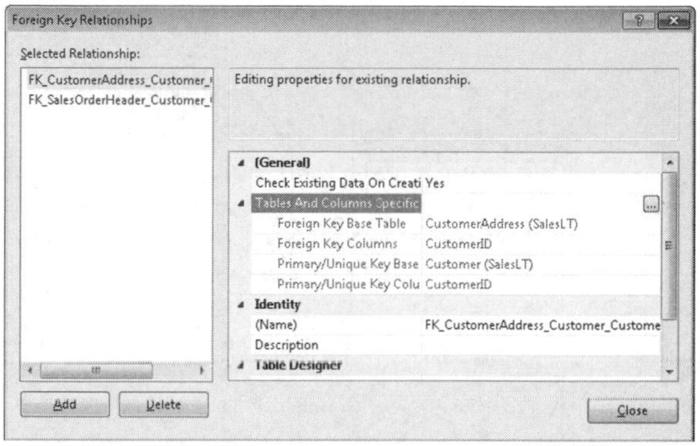

Click the Add button to create a new relationship, or select one of the existing relationships to edit. Locate the Tables and Columns Specification entry in the property grid and click its associated ellipsis to set the tables and columns that should connect to each other. In the Tables and Columns dialog, shown in Figure 26-6, first choose which table contains the primary key to which the table you selected will connect. Note that for new relationships the Foreign key table field is populated with the current table name and cannot be changed.

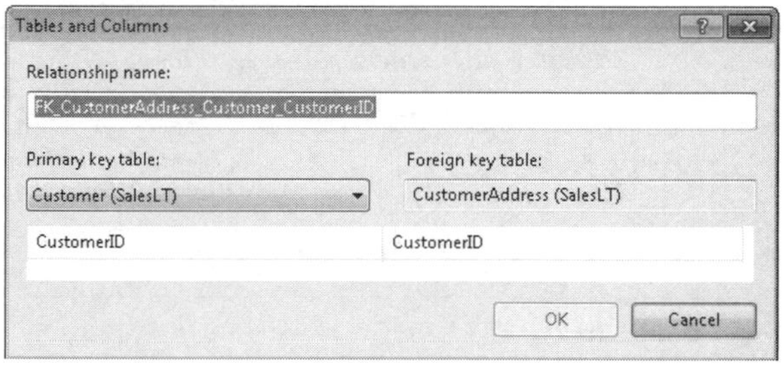

FIGURE 26-5

FIGURE 26-6

Once you have the Primary key table, you then connect the fields in each table that should bind to each other. You can add multiple fields to the relationship by clicking the blank row that is added as you add the previous field. When you are satisfied with the relationship settings, click OK to save it and return to the Foreign Key Relationships dialog.

Views

Views are predefined queries that can appear like tables to your application and can be made up of multiple tables. Use the Data ➪ Add New ➪ View menu command or right-click the Views node in Server Explorer and choose Add New View from the context menu.

The first task is to choose which tables, other views, functions, and synonyms will be included in the current view. When you've chosen which components will be added, the View editor window is displayed (see Figure 26-7). This editor should be familiar to anyone who has worked with a visual database designer such as Access. The tables and other components are visible in the top area, where you can select the fields you want included. The top area also shows connections between any functions and tables. The View in Figure 26-7 connects three tables by linking all rows in the Customer table with the CustomerAddress and Address tables. Figure 26-7 also shows that by right-clicking the connector between tables you can change the type of join used. If you need to add additional tables, right-click the design surface and select Add Table.

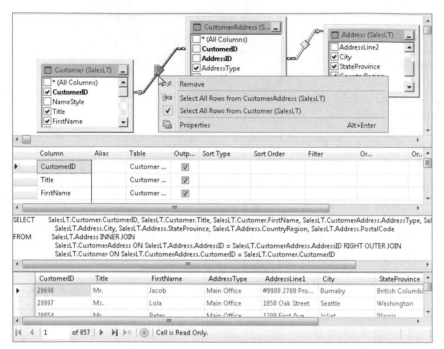

FIGURE 26-7

The middle area shows a tabular representation of your current selection, and adds columns for sorting and filtering properties, and the area directly beneath the tabular representation shows the SQL that is used to achieve the view you've specified. Changes can be made in any of these three panes with the other panes being dynamically updated with the changes.

The bottom part of the view designer can be used to execute the view SQL and preview the results. To execute this view, select Execute SQL from the right-click context menu on any of the panes, or click the button with the same name from the View Designer toolbar.

Stored Procedures and Functions

To create and modify stored procedures and functions, Visual Studio 2010 uses a text editor such as the one shown in Figure 26-8. Since there is no IntelliSense to help you create your procedure and function definitions, Visual Studio doesn't allow you to save your code if it detects an error.

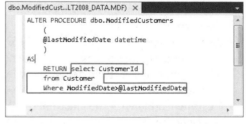

FIGURE 26-8

To help you write and debug your stored procedures and functions, there are shortcuts to Insert SQL, Run Selection, and Execute from the right-click context menu for the text editor. Inserting SQL displays the Query Builder shown earlier in Figure 26-7 as a modal dialog. Run Selection attempts to execute any selected SQL statements, displaying the results in the Output window. Finally, the Execute shortcut runs the entire stored procedure or function. If they accept input parameters, a dialog similar to

Figure 26-9 is displayed, in which you can specify appropriate test values. Again, the results are displayed in the Output window.

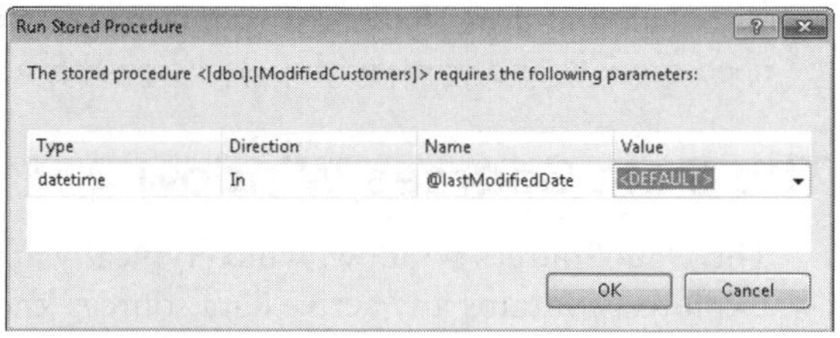

Database Diagrams

You can also create a visual representation of your database tables via database diagrams. To create a diagram, use the Data ⇨ Add New ⇨

FIGURE 26-9

Diagram menu command or right-click the Database Diagrams node in the Server Explorer and choose Add New Diagram from the context menu.

When you create your first diagram in a database, Visual Studio may prompt you to allow it to automatically add necessary system tables and data to the database. If you disallow this action, you won't be able to create diagrams at all; so it's just a notification, rather than an optional action to take.

The initial process of creating a diagram enables you to choose which tables you want in the diagram, but you can add tables later through the Database Diagram menu that is added to the IDE. You can use this menu to affect the appearance of your diagram within the editor too, with zoom and page break preview functionality as well as being able to toggle relationship names on and off.

Because database diagrams can be quite large, the IDE has an easy way of navigating around the diagram. In the lower-right corner of the Database Diagram editor in the workspace is an icon displaying a four-way arrow. Click this icon and a thumbnail view of the diagram appears, as shown in Figure 26-10.

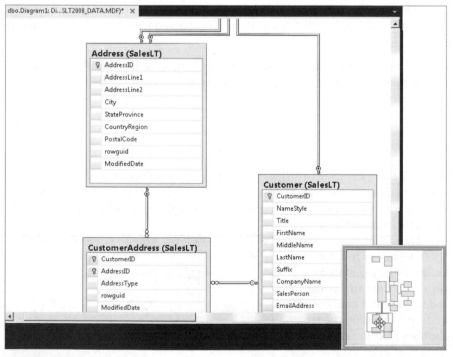

FIGURE 26-10

Just click and drag the mouse pointer around the thumbnail until you position the components you need to view and work with in the viewable area of the IDE.

The Data Sources Window

The Data Sources window, which typically appears in the same tool window area as the Solution Explorer, contains any active data sources known to the project, such as datasets (as opposed to the Data Connections in the Server Explorer, which are known to Visual Studio overall). To display the Data Sources tool window, use the Data ⇨ Show Data Sources menu command.

The Data Sources window has two main views, depending on the active document in the workspace area of the IDE. When you are editing code, the Data Sources window displays tables and fields with icons representing their types. This aids you as you write code because you can quickly reference the type without having to look at the table definition. This view is shown on the right image of Figure 26-11.

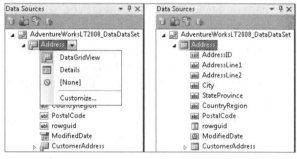

FIGURE 26-11

When you're editing a form in Design view, however, the Data Sources view changes to display the tables and fields with icons representing their current default control types (initially set in the Data UI Customization page of Options). The left image of Figure 26-11 shows that the text fields use TextBox controls, whereas the ModifiedDate field uses a DateTimePicker control. The icons for the tables indicate that all tables will be inserted as DataGridView components by default as shown in the drop-down list.

In the next chapter you learn how to add and modify data sources, as well as use the Data Sources window to bind your data to controls on a form. Data classes or fields can simply be dragged from the Data Sources window onto a form in order to wire up the user interface.

EDITING DATA

Visual Studio 2010 also has the capability to view and edit the data contained in your database tables. To edit the information, use the Data ⇨ Show Table Data menu command after you highlight the table you want to view in the Server Explorer. You will be presented with a tabular representation of the data in the table as shown in Figure 26-12, enabling you to edit it to contain whatever default or test data you need to include. By using the buttons at the bottom of the table, you can navigate around the returned records and even create new rows. As you edit information, the table editor displays indicators next to fields that have changed.

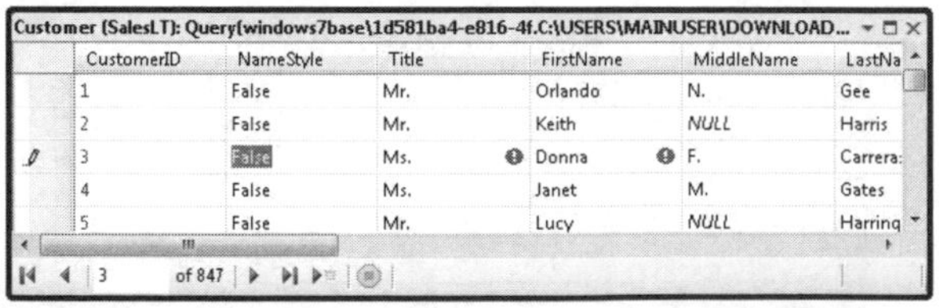

CustomerID	NameStyle	Title		FirstName		MiddleName	LastNa
1	False	Mr.		Orlando		N.	Gee
2	False	Mr.		Keith		NULL	Harris
3	False	Ms.		Donna		F.	Carrera
4	False	Ms.		Janet		M.	Gates
5	False	Mr.		Lucy		NULL	Harring

Customer (SalesLT): Query[windows7base\1d581ba4-e816-4f.C:\USERS\MAINUSER\DOWNLOAD...

◄◄ ◄ 3 of 847 ► ►► ►►

FIGURE 26-12

You can also show the diagram, criteria, and SQL panes associated with the table data you're editing by right-clicking anywhere in the table and choosing the appropriate command from the Pane submenu. This can be useful for customizing the SQL statement that is being used to retrieve the data — for example, to filter the table for specific values, or just to retrieve the first 50 rows.

PREVIEWING DATA

You can also preview data for different data sources to ensure that the associated query will return the information you expect. In the database schema designer, right-click the query you want to test and choose Preview Data from the context menu. Alternatively, select Preview Data from the right-click context menu off any data source in the Data Sources tool window.

The Preview Data dialog is displayed with the object list defaulted to the query you want to test. Click the Preview button to view the sample data, shown in Figure 26-13. A small status bar provides information about the total number of data rows that were returned from the query, as well as how many columns of data were included.

If you want to change to a different query, you can do so with the Select an object to preview drop-down list. This list contains other queries in the same data source, other data sources, and elsewhere in your solution. If the query you're previewing requires parameters, you can set their values in the Parameters list in the top-right pane of the dialog. Clicking the Preview button submits the query to the appropriate data source and displays the subsequent results in the Results area of the Preview Data dialog box.

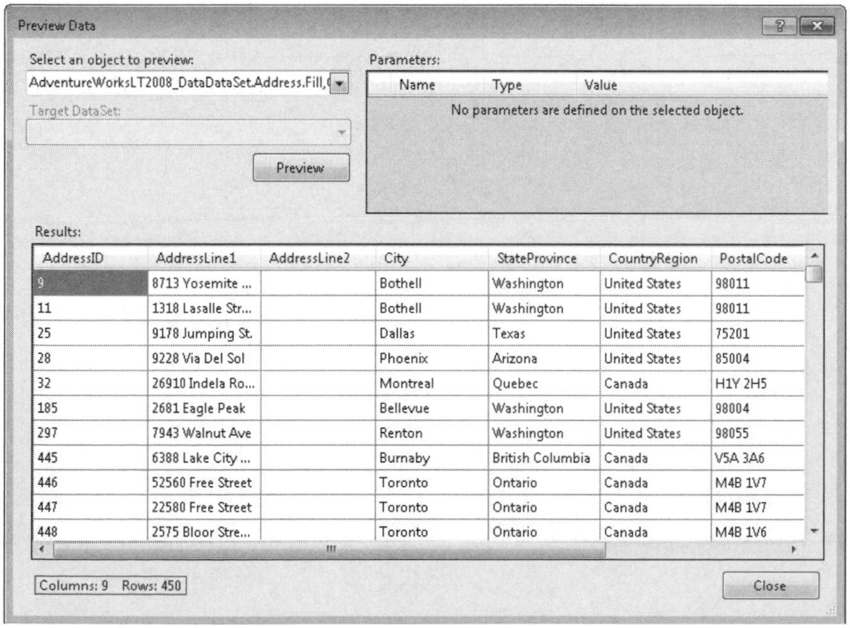

FIGURE 26-13

SUMMARY

With the variety of tools and windows available to you in Visual Studio 2010, you can easily create and maintain databases without having to leave the IDE. You can manipulate data as well as define database schemas visually using the Properties tool window in conjunction with the Schema Designer view.

Once you have your data where you want it, Visual Studio keeps helping you by providing a set of drag-and-drop components that can be bound to a data source. These can be as simple as a checkbox or textbox, or as feature-rich as a DataGridView component with complete table views. In the next chapter you learn how being able to drag whole tables or individual fields from the Data Sources window onto a form and have Visual Studio automatically create the appropriate controls for you is a major advantage for rapid application development.

DataSets and DataBinding

WHAT'S IN THIS CHAPTER?

➤   Creating DataSets

➤   Connecting visual controls to a DataSet with DataBinding

➤   How BindingSource and BindingNavigator controls work together

➤   Chaining BindingSources and using the DataGridView

➤   Using Service and Object data sources

A large proportion of applications use some form of data storage. This might be in the form of serialized objects or XML data, but for long-term storage that supports concurrent access by a large number of users, most applications use a database. The .NET Framework includes strong support for working with databases and other data sources. This chapter examines how to use DataSets to build applications that work with data from a database.

In the second part of this chapter you see how to use DataBinding to connect visual controls to the data they are to display. You see how they interact and how you can use the designers to control how data is displayed.

The examples in this chapter are based on the sample AdventureWorksLT database that is available as a download from http://professionalvisualstudio.com/link/1029A.

DATASETS OVERVIEW

The .NET Framework DataSet is a complex object that is approximately equivalent to an in-memory representation of a database. It contains DataTables that correlate to database tables. These in turn contain a series of DataColumns that define the composition of each DataRow. The DataRow correlates to a row in a database table. It is also possible to establish relationships between DataTables within the DataSet in the same way that a database has relationships between tables.

One of the ongoing challenges for the object-oriented programming paradigm is that it does not align smoothly with the relational database model. The DataSet object goes a long way toward bridging this gap, because it can be used to represent and work with relational data in an object-oriented fashion. However, the biggest issue with a raw DataSet is that it is weakly typed. Although the type of each column can be queried prior to accessing data elements, this adds overhead and can make code very unreadable. Strongly typed DataSets combine the advantages of a DataSet with strong typing (in other words, creating strongly typed properties for all database fields) to ensure that data is accessed correctly at design time. This is done with the custom tool MSDataSetGenerator, which converts an XML schema into a strongly typed DataSet, essentially replacing a lot of run time type checking with code generated at design time. In the following code snippet, you can see the difference between using a raw DataSet, in the first half of the snippet, and a strongly typed DataSet, in the second half:

Available for download on Wrox.com

VB

```
'Raw DataSet
Dim nontypedAwds As DataSet = RetrieveData()
Dim nontypedcustomers As DataTable = nontypedAwds.Tables("Customer")
Dim nontypedfirstcustomer As DataRow = nontypedcustomers.Rows(0)
MessageBox.Show(nontypedfirstcustomer.Item("FirstName"))

'Strongly typed DataSet
Dim awds As AdventureWorksLTDataSet = RetrieveData()
Dim customers As AdventureWorksLTDataSet.CustomerDataTable = awds.Customer
Dim firstcustomer As AdventureWorksLTDataSet.CustomerRow = customers.Rows(0)
MessageBox.Show(firstcustomer.FirstName)
```

Code snippet CustomersForm.vb

Available for download on Wrox.com

C#

```
// Raw DataSet
DataSet nontypedAwds = RetrieveData();
DataTable nontypedcustomers = nontypedAwds.Tables["Customer"];
DataRow nontypedfirstcustomer = nontypedcustomers.Rows[0];
MessageBox.Show(nontypedfirstcustomer["FirstName"].ToString());

// Strongly typed DataSet
AdventureWorksLTDataSet awds = RetrieveData();
AdventureWorksLTDataSet.CustomerDataTable customers = awds.Customer;
AdventureWorksLTDataSet.CustomerRow firstcustomer =
                customers.Rows[0] as AdventureWorksLTDataSet.CustomerRow;
MessageBox.Show(firstcustomer.FirstName);
```

Code snippet CustomersForm.cs

Using the raw DataSet, both the table lookup and the column name lookup are done using string literals. As you are likely aware, string literals can be a source of much frustration and should be used only within generated code, and preferably not at all.

Adding a Data Source

You can manually create a strongly typed DataSet by creating an XSD using the XML schema editor. To create the DataSet, you set the custom tool value for the XSD file to be the MSDataSetGenerator. This will create the designer code file that is needed for strongly typed access to the DataSet.

Manually creating an XSD is difficult and not recommended unless you really need to; luckily in most cases, the source of your data will be a database, in which case Visual Studio 2010 provides a wizard that you can use to generate the necessary schema based on the structure of your database. Through the rest of this chapter, you see how you can create data sources and how they can be bound to the user interface. To get started, create a new project called CustomerObjects, using the Windows Forms Application project template.

 Although this functionality is not available for ASP.NET projects, a workaround is to perform all data access via a class library.

To create a strongly typed DataSet from an existing database, select Add New Data Source from the Data menu, and follow these steps:

1. The first step in the Data Source Configuration Wizard is to select the type of data source to work with — a Database, Service, Object, or SharePoint data source. In this case, you want to work with data from a database, so select the Database icon and click Next.

2. With the introduction of the ADO.NET Entity Framework there are now two different data models that you can choose to represent the mapping between database data and .NET entities, being a Dataset or an Entity Data Model. The Entity Framework is covered in Chapter 29. Double-click the DataSet icon to continue.

3. The next screen prompts you to select the database connection to use. To create a new connection, click the New Connection button, which opens the Add Connection dialog. The attributes displayed in this dialog are dependent on the type of database you are connecting to. By default, the SQL Server provider is selected, which requires the Server name, authentication mechanism (Windows or SQL Server), and Database name in order to proceed. There is a Test Connection that you can use to ensure you have specified valid properties.

4. After you specify a connection, it is saved as an application setting in the application configuration file.

   When the application is later deployed, the connection string can be modified to point to the production database. This process can often take longer than expected to ensure that various security permissions line up. Because the connection string is stored in the configuration file as a string without any schema, it is quite easy to make a mistake when making changes to it. In Chapter 37 you learn more about connection strings and how you can customize them for different data sources.

> *A little-known utility within Windows can be used to create connection strings, even if Visual Studio is not installed. Known as the Data Link Properties dialog, you can use it to edit Universal Data Link files, files that end in .udl. When you need to create or test a connection string, you can simply create a new text document, rename it to something.udl, and then double-click it. This opens the Data Link Properties dialog, which enables you to create and test connection strings for a variety of providers. Once you have selected the appropriate connection, this information will be written to the UDL file as a connection string, which can be retrieved by opening the same file in Notepad. This can be particularly useful if you need to test security permissions and resolve other data connectivity issues.*

5. After specifying the connection, the next stage is to specify the data to be extracted. At this stage you are presented with a list of tables, views, stored procedures, and functions from which you can select what to include in the DataSet. Figure 27-1 shows the final stage of the Data Source Configuration Wizard with a selection of columns from the Customer table in the AdventureWorksLT database. Checking the Enable Local Database Caching checkbox gives you offline, or disconnected, support for working with your data. This makes use of Synchronization Services for ADO.NET to synchronize data between your application and the database, and is covered in more detail in Chapter 34.

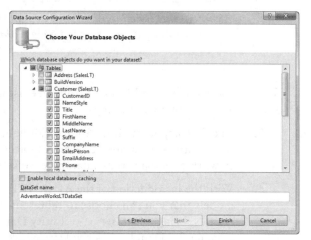

FIGURE 27-1

> *You will probably want to constrain the DataSet so it doesn't return all the records for a particular table. You can do this after creating the DataSet, so for the time being simply select the information you want to return. The editor's design makes it easier to select more information here and then delete it from the designer, rather than create it afterwards.*

6. Click Finish to add the new DataSet to the Data Sources window, shown in Figure 27-2, where you can view all the information to be retrieved for the DataSet. Each column is identified with an icon that varies depending on the data type of the column. In the left image (displayed when using a design surface) the icons represent the default visual control that will be used to represent the column; in the right image (displayed when in a code window) the icons indicate the data type.

FIGURE 27-2

The DataSet Designer

The Data Source Configuration Wizard uses the database schema to guess the appropriate .NET type to use for the DataTable columns. In cases where the wizard gets information wrong, it can be useful to edit the DataSet without the wizard. To do this, right-click the DataSet in the Data Sources window and select Edit DataSet with Designer from the context menu. Alternatively, you can open the Data Sources window by double-clicking the XSD file in the Solution Explorer window. This opens the DataSet editor in the main window, as shown in the example in Figure 27-3.

FIGURE 27-3

Here you start to see some of the power of using strongly typed DataSets. Not only has a strongly typed table (Customer) been added to the DataSet, you also have a CustomerTableAdapter. This TableAdapter is used for selecting from and updating the database for the DataTable to which it is attached. If you have multiple tables included in the DataSet, you will have a TableAdapter for each. Although a single TableAdapter can easily handle returning information from multiple tables in the database, it becomes difficult to update, insert, and delete records.

As you can see in Figure 27-3, the CustomerTableAdapter has been created with `Fill` and `GetData` methods, which are called to extract data from the database. The following code shows how you can use the `Fill` method to populate an existing strongly typed DataTable, perhaps within a DataSet. Alternatively, the `GetData` method creates a new instance of a strongly typed DataTable:

VB

```
Dim ta As New AdventureWorksLTDataSetTableAdapters.CustomerTableAdapter

'Option 1 - Create a new CustomerDataTable and use the Fill method
Dim customers1 As New AdventureWorksLTDataSet.CustomerDataTable
ta.Fill(customers1)

'Option 2 - Use the GetData method which will create a CustomerDataTable for you
Dim customers2 As AdventureWorksLTDataSet.CustomerDataTable = ta.GetData
```

In Figure 27-3, the `Fill` and `GetData` methods appear as a pair because they make use of the same query. The Properties window can be used to configure this query. A query can return data in one of three ways: using a text command (as the example illustrates), a stored procedure, or TableDirect (where the contents of the table name specified in the `CommandText` are retrieved). This is specified in the CommandType field. Although the `CommandText` can be edited directly in the Properties window, it is difficult to see the whole query and easy to make mistakes. Clicking the ellipsis button (at the top right of Figure 27-3) opens the Query Builder window, shown in Figure 27-4.

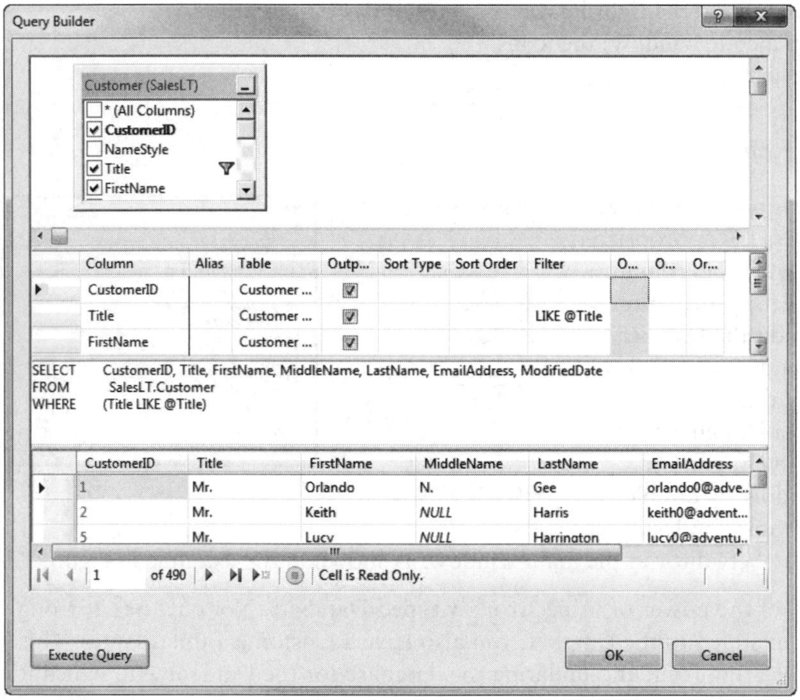

FIGURE 27-4

The Query Builder dialog is divided into four panes. In the top pane is a diagram of the tables involved in the query, and the selected columns. The second pane shows a list of columns related to the query. These columns are either output columns, such as FirstName and LastName, or a condition, such as the Title field, or both. The third pane is, of course, the SQL command that is to be executed. The final pane includes sample data that can be retrieved by clicking the Execute Query button. If there are parameters to the SQL statement (in this case, `@Title`), a dialog is displayed, prompting for values to use when executing the statement.

To change the query, you can make changes in any of the first three panes. As you move between panes, changes in one field are reflected in the others. You can hide any of the panes by unchecking that pane from the Panes item of the right-click context menu. Conditions can be added using the Filter column. These can include parameters (such as `@Title`), which must start with the `@` symbol.

Returning to the DataSet designer, and the Properties window associated with the `Fill` method, click the ellipsis to examine the list of parameters. This shows the Parameters Collection Editor, as shown in Figure 27-5. Occasionally, the Query Builder doesn't get the data type correct for a parameter, and you may need to modify it using this dialog.

Also from the Properties window for the query, you can specify whether the `Fill` and/or `GetData` methods are created, using the `GenerateMethods` property, which has values `Fill`, `Get`, or `Both`. You can also specify the names and accessibility of the generated methods.

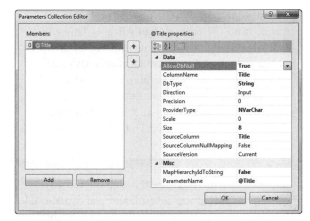

FIGURE 27-5

BINDING DATA

The most common type of application is one that retrieves data from a database, displays the data, allows changes to be made, and then persists those changes back to the database. The middle steps that connect the in-memory data with the visual elements are referred to as DataBinding. DataBinding often becomes the bane a of developer's existence because it has been difficult to get right. Most developers at some stage or another have resorted to writing their own wrappers to ensure that data is correctly bound to the controls on the screen. Visual Studio 2010 dramatically reduces the pain of getting two-way DataBinding to work. The examples used in the following sections again work with the AdventureWorksLT sample database. For simplicity, you'll work with a single Windows application, but the concepts discussed here can be extended over multiple tiers.

In this example, you build an application to assist you in managing the customers for AdventureWorks. To begin, you need to ensure that the `AdventureWorksLTDataSet` contains the Customer and Address tables. (You can reuse the `AdventureWorksDataSet` from earlier by clicking the Configure DataSet with Wizard icon in the Data Source window and editing which tables are included in the DataSet.) With the form designer (any empty form in your project will do) and Data Sources window open, set the mode for the Customer table to Details using the drop-down list. Before creating the editing controls, tweak the list of columns for the Customer table. You're not that interested in the CustomerID, NameStyle, PasswordHash, PasswordSalt, or rowguid fields, so set them to None (again using the drop-down list for those nodes in the Data Sources window). ModifiedDate should be automatically set when changes are made, so this field should appear as a label, preventing the ModifiedDate from being edited.

Now you're ready to drag the Customer node onto the form design surface. This will automatically add controls for each of the columns you have specified. It will also add a `BindingSource`, a `BindingNavigator`, an `AdventureWorksDataSet`, a `CustomerTableAdapter`, a `TableAdapter Manager`, and a `ToolStrip` to the form as shown in Figure 27-6.

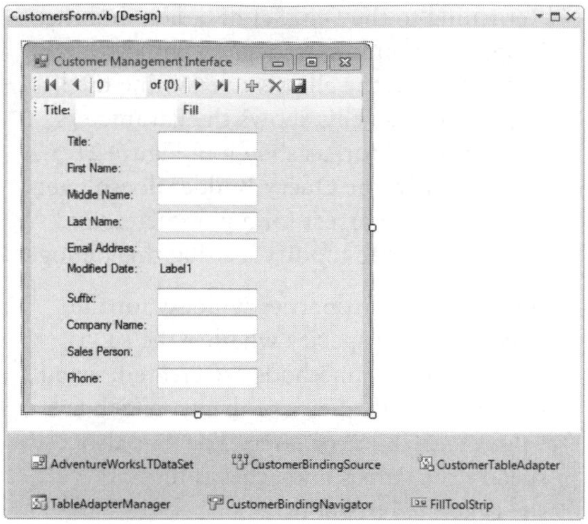

FIGURE 27-6

At this point you can build and run this application and navigate through the records using the navigation control, and you can also take the components apart to understand how they interact. Start with the `AdventureWorksDataSet` and the `CustomerTableAdapter`, because they carry out the background grunt work of retrieving information and persisting changes to the database. The `AdventureWorksDataSet` that is added to this form is actually an instance of the `AdventureWorksDataSet` class that was created by the Data Source Configuration Wizard. This instance will be used to store information for all the tables on this form. To populate the DataSet, call the `Fill` method. If you open the code file for the form, you will see that the `Fill` command has been called from the `Click` event handler of the Fill button that resides on the toolstrip.

Available for download on Wrox.com

VB

```
Private Sub FillToolStripButton_Click(ByVal sender As Object,
                                      ByVal e As EventArgs) _
                                          Handles FillToolStripButton.Click
    Try
        Me.CustomerTableAdapter.Fill(Me.AdventureWorksLTDataSet.Customer,
                                     TitleToolStripTextBox.Text)
    Catch ex As System.Exception
        System.Windows.Forms.MessageBox.Show(ex.Message)
    End Try
End Sub
```

Code snippet CustomersForm.vb

Available for download on Wrox.com

C#

```
private void fillToolStripButton_Click(object sender, EventArgs e){
    try{
        this.customerTableAdapter.Fill(
            this.adventureWorksLTDataSet.Customer, titleToolStripTextBox.Text);
    }
    catch (System.Exception ex){
        System.Windows.Forms.MessageBox.Show(ex.Message);
    }
}
```

Code snippet CustomersForm.cs

As you extend this form, you'll add a `TableAdapter` for each table within the `AdventureWorksDataSet` that you want to work with.

BindingSource

The next item of interest is the `CustomerBindingSource` that was automatically added to the non-visual part of the form designer. This control is used to wire up each of the controls on the design surface with the relevant data item. In fact, this control is just a wrapper for the `CurrencyManager`. However, using a `BindingSource` considerably reduces the number of event handlers and custom code that you have to write. Unlike the `AdventureWorksDataSet` and the `CustomerTableAdapter` — which are instances of the strongly typed classes with the same names — the `CustomerBindingSource` is just an instance of the regular `BindingSource` class that ships with the .NET Framework.

Take a look at the properties of the `CustomerBindingSource` so you can see what it does. Figure 27-7 shows the Properties window for the `CustomerBindingSource`. The two items of particular interest are the `DataSource` and `DataMember` properties. The drop-down list for the `DataSource` property is expanded to illustrate the list of available data sources. The instance of the `AdventureWorksDataSet` that was added to the form is listed under CustomerForm List Instances. Selecting the `AdventureWorksDataSet` type under the Project Data Sources node creates another instance on the form instead of reusing the existing `DataSet`. In the DataMember field, you need to specify the table to use for DataBinding. Later, you'll see how the DataMember field can be used to specify a foreign key relationship so you can show linked data.

So far you have specified that the `CustomerBindingSource` will bind data in the Customer table of the `AdventureWorksDataSet`. What remains is to bind the individual controls on the form to the `BindingSource` and the appropriate column in the Customer table. To do this you need to specify a DataBinding for each control. Figure 27-8 shows the Properties grid for the FirstNameTextBox, with the DataBindings node expanded to show the binding for the `Text` property.

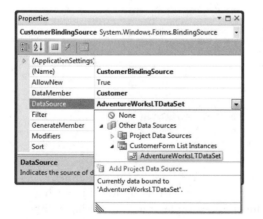

FIGURE 27-7

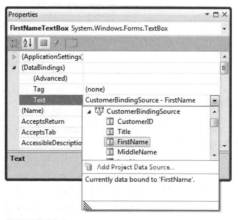

FIGURE 27-8

From the drop-down list you can see that the `Text` property is being bound to the FirstName field of the `CustomerBindingSource`. Because the `CustomerBindingSource` is bound to the Customer table, this is actually the FirstName column in that table. If you look at the designer file for the form, you can see that this binding is set up using a new `Binding`, as shown in the following snippet:

```
Me.FirstNameTextBox.DataBindings.Add(
                 New System.Windows.Forms.Binding("Text",
                                           Me.CustomerBindingSource,
                                           "FirstName", True))
```

A `Binding` is used to ensure that two-way binding is set up between the Text field of the FirstNameTextBox and the FirstName field of the `CustomerBindingSource`. The controls for the other controls all have similar bindings between their `Text` properties and the appropriate fields on the `CustomerBindingSource`.

When you run the current application you will notice that the Modified Date value is displayed as in the default string representation of a date, for example, "13/10/2004." Given the nature of the application, it might be more useful to have it in a format similar to "Friday, 13 October 2004." To do this you need to specify additional properties as part of the DataBinding. Select the ModifiedDateLabel1 and in the Properties tool window, expand the DataBindings node and select the Advanced item. This opens up the Formatting and Advanced Binding dialog as shown in Figure 27-9.

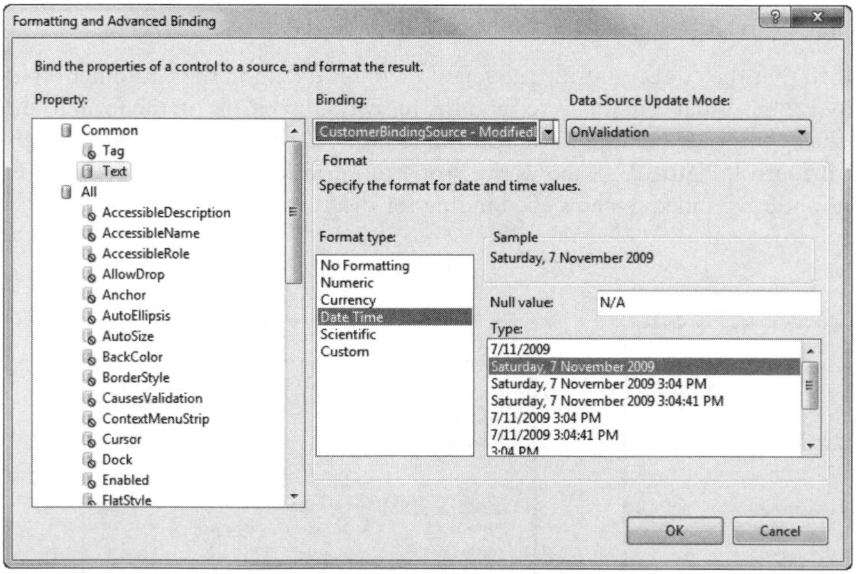

FIGURE 27-9

In the lower portion of Figure 27-9 you can see that we have selected one of the predefined formatting types, Date Time. This then presents another list of formatting options in which "Saturday, 7 November 2009" has been selected — this is an example of how the value will be formatted. In this dialog we have also provided a Null value, "N/A," which will be displayed if there is no Modified Date value for a particular row. In the following code you can see that three additional parameters have been added to create the DataBinding for the Modified Date value:

VB

```vb
Me.ModifiedDateLabel1.DataBindings.Add(
        New System.Windows.Forms.Binding("Text",
                Me.CustomerBindingSource,
                "ModifiedDate", True,
                System.Windows.Forms.DataSourceUpdateMode.OnValidation,
                "N/A", "D"))
```

The `OnValidation` value simply indicates that the data source will be updated when the visual control has been validated. This is actually the default and is only specified here so that the next two parameters can be specified. The `"N/A"` is the value you specified for when there was no Modified Date value, and the `"D"` is actually a shortcut formatting string for the date formatting you selected.

BindingNavigator

Although the `CustomerBindingNavigator` component, which is an instance of the `BindingNavigator` class, appears in the non-visual area of the design surface, it does have a visual representation in the form of the navigation toolstrip that is initially docked to the top of the form. As with regular toolstrips, this control can be docked to any edge of the form. In fact, in many ways the `BindingNavigator` behaves the same way as a toolstrip in that buttons and other controls can be added to the Items list. When the `BindingNavigator` is initially added to the form, a series of buttons are added for standard data functionality, such as moving to the first or last item, moving to the next or previous item, and adding, removing, and saving items.

What is neat about the `BindingNavigator` is that it not only creates these standard controls, but also wires them up for you. Figure 27-10 shows the Properties window for the `BindingNavigator`, with the Data and Items sections expanded. In the Data section you can see that the associated `BindingSource` is the `CustomerBindingSource`, which will be used to perform all the actions implied by the various button clicks. The Items section plays an important role, because each property defines an action, such as AddNewItem. The value of the property defines the ToolStripItem to which it will be assigned — in this case, the BindingNavigatorAddNewItem button.

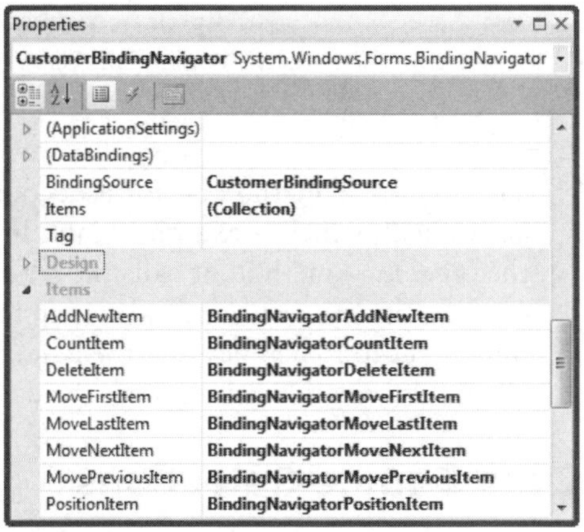

FIGURE 27-10

Behind the scenes, when this application is run and this button is assigned to the `AddNewItem` property, the `OnAddNew` method is wired up to the `Click` event of the button. This is shown in the following snippet, extracted using Reflector from the `BindingNavigator` class. The `AddNewItem` property calls the `WireUpButton` method, passing in a delegate to the `OnAddNew` method:

VB

```vb
Public Property AddNewItem As ToolStripItem
    Get
        If ((Not Me.addNewItem Is Nothing) AndAlso Me.addNewItem.IsDisposed) Then
```

```
                    Me.addNewItem = Nothing
              End If
              Return Me.addNewItem
          End Get
          Set(ByVal value As ToolStripItem)
              Me.WireUpButton(Me.addNewItem, value, _
                                           New EventHandler(AddressOf Me.OnAddNew))
          End Set
      End Property

      Private Sub OnAddNew(ByVal sender As Object, ByVal e As EventArgs)
          If (Me.Validate AndAlso (Not Me.bindingSource Is Nothing)) Then
                Me.bindingSource.AddNew
                Me.RefreshItemsInternal
          End If
      End Sub

      Private Sub WireUpButton(ByRef oldButton As ToolStripItem, _
                         ByVal newButton As ToolStripItem, _
                         ByVal clickHandler As EventHandler)
          If (Not oldButton Is newButton) Then
                If (Not oldButton Is Nothing) Then
                    RemoveHandler oldButton.Click, clickHandler
                End If
                If (Not newButton Is Nothing) Then
                    AddHandler newButton.Click, clickHandler
                End If
                oldButton = newButton
                Me.RefreshItemsInternal
          End If
      End Sub
```

The OnAddNew method performs a couple of important actions. First, it forces validation of the active field, which is examined later in this chapter. Second, and the most important aspect of the OnAddNew method, it calls the AddNew method on the BindingSource. The other properties on the BindingNavigator also map to corresponding methods on the BindingSource, and it is important to remember that the BindingSource, rather than the BindingNavigator, does the work when it comes to working with the data source.

Data Source Selections

Now that you have seen how the BindingSource works, it's time to improve the user interface. At the moment, the Sales Person is being displayed as a textbox, but this should actually be limited to just the sales staff at AdventureWorks. As such, instead of a textbox, it would be much better to have the list of staff displayed as a drop-down box from which the user can select.

Start by removing the SalesPersonTextBox from the form. Next, add a ComboBox control from the toolbox. With the new ComboBox selected, note that a smart tag is attached to the control. Expanding this tag and checking the Use Data Bound Items checkbox opens the Data Binding Mode options, as shown in Figure 27-11.

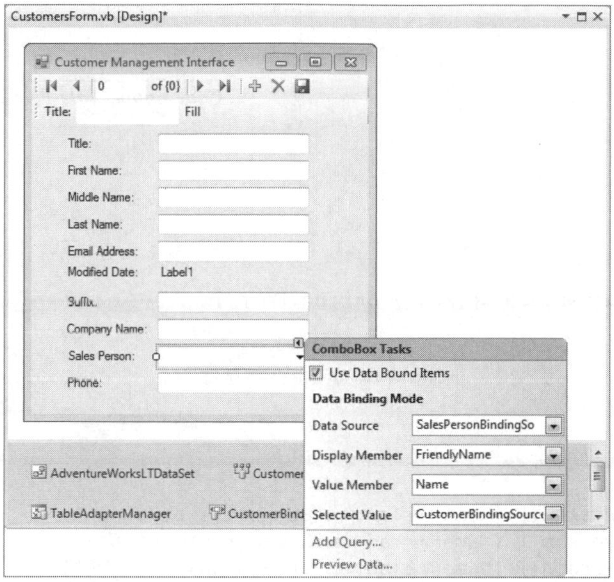

FIGURE 27-11

You need to define four things to get the DataBinding to work properly. The first is the data source for the list of staff the user should be able to select from. Unfortunately, the list of staff is not contained in a database table (this may be the case if the list of staff comes from a separate system such as Active Directory). For the purpose of this example the list staff is defined by a fixed array of `SalesPerson` objects.

Available for download on Wrox.com

VB

```
Public Class SalesPerson
    Public ReadOnly Property FriendlyName
        Get
            Return Name.Replace("adventure-works\", String.Empty)
        End Get
    End Property

    Public Property Name As String

    Public Shared Function Staff() As SalesPerson()
        Return {
            New SalesPerson() With {.Name = "adventure-works\pamela0"},
            New SalesPerson() With {.Name = "adventure-works\david8"},
            New SalesPerson() With {.Name = "adventure-works\jillian0"},
            New SalesPerson() With {.Name = "adventure-works\garrett1"},
            New SalesPerson() With {.Name = "adventure-works\jae0"},
            New SalesPerson() With {.Name = "adventure-works\linda3"},
            New SalesPerson() With {.Name = "adventure-works\josé1"},
            New SalesPerson() With {.Name = "adventure-works\michael9"},
            New SalesPerson() With {.Name = "adventure-works\shu0"}
        }
```

```
        End Function
End Class
```

Code snippet SalesPerson.vb

C#

```
public class SalesPerson{
    public string FriendlyName{
        get{
            return Name.Replace(@"adventure-works\", String.Empty);
        }
    }

    public string Name { get; set; }

    public static SalesPerson[] Staff(){
        return new SalesPerson[]{
                        new SalesPerson() {Name= @"adventure-works\pamela0"},
                        new SalesPerson() {Name= @"adventure-works\david8"},
                        new SalesPerson() {Name= @"adventure-works\jillian0"},
                        new SalesPerson() {Name= @"adventure-works\garrett1"},
                        new SalesPerson() {Name= @"adventure-works\jae0"},
                        new SalesPerson() {Name= @"adventure-works\linda3"},
                        new SalesPerson() {Name= @"adventure-works\josé1"},
                        new SalesPerson() {Name= @"adventure-works\michael9"},
                        new SalesPerson() {Name= @"adventure-works\shu0"}
                    };
    }
}
```

Code snippet SalesPerson.cs

Expanding the Data Source drop-down allows you to select from any of the existing project data sources. Although the list of staff, returned by the `Staff` method on the `SalesPerson` class, is contained in the project, it can't yet be used as a data source. First, you need to add a new Object data source to your project. You can do this directly from the Data Source drop-down by selecting the Add Project DataSource link. This displays the Data Source Configuration Wizard as you saw earlier in this chapter. However, this time you will select Object as the type of data source. You will then have to select which object(s) you want to include in the data source, as shown in Figure 27-12.

FIGURE 27-12

When you select SalesPerson and click Finish the data source will be created and automatically assigned to the Data Source property of the Sales Person drop-down. The Display Member and Value Member properties correspond to which properties on the SalesPerson object you want to be displayed and used to determine the selected item. In this case, the SalesPerson defines a read-only property, FriendlyName (which simply removes the adventure-works prefix), which should be displayed in the drop-down. However, the Value property needs to be set to the Name property so that it matches the value specified in the SalesPerson field in the Customer table. Lastly, the Selected Value property needs to be set to the SalesPerson property on the CustomerBindingSource. This is the property that is get/set to determine the Sales Person specified for the displayed Customer.

Although you have wired up the Sales Person drop-down list, if you run what you currently have, there would be no items in this list, because you haven't populated the SalesPersonBindingSource. The BindingSource object has a DataSource property, which you need to set in order to populate the BindingSource. You can do this in the Load event of the form:

Available for download on Wrox.com

VB

```vb
Private Sub CustomerForm_Load(ByVal sender As Object,
                             ByVal e As EventArgs) Handles MyBase.Load
    Me.SalesPersonBindingSource.DataSource = SalesPerson.Staff
End SubPrivate
```

Code snippet CustomersForm.vb

Available for download on Wrox.com

C#

```csharp
private void CustomerForm_Load(object sender, EventArgs e){
    this.salesPersonBindingSource.DataSource = SalesPerson.Staff();
}
```

Code snippet CustomersForm.cs

Now when you run the application, instead of having a textbox with a numeric value, you have a convenient drop-down list from which to select the SalesPerson.

Saving Changes

Now that you have a usable interface, you need to add support for making changes and adding new records. If you double-click the Save icon on the CustomerBindingNavigator toolstrip, the code window opens with a code stub that would normally save changes to the Customer table. As you can see in the following snippet, there are essentially three steps: the form is validated, each of the BindingSources has been instructed to end the current edit, and then the UpdateAll method is called on the TableAdapterManager:

VB

```vb
Private Sub CustomerBindingNavigatorSaveItem_Click(ByVal sender As Object,
                                    ByVal e As System.EventArgs) _
                          Handles CustomerBindingNavigatorSaveItem.Click
    Me.Validate()
```

```
        Me.CustomerBindingSource.EndEdit()
        Me.TableAdapterManager.UpdateAll(Me.AdventureWorksLTDataSet)
End Sub
```

C#

```
private void customerBindingNavigatorSaveItem_Click(object sender, EventArgs e){
    this.Validate();
    this.customerBindingSource.EndEdit();
    this.tableAdapterManager.UpdateAll(this.adventureWorksLTDataSet);
}
```

This code will run without modification but it won't update the ModifiedDate field to indicate the Customer information has changed. You need to correct the Update method used by the CustomerTableAdapter to automatically update the ModifiedDate field. Using the DataSet designer, select the CustomerTableAdapter, open the Properties window, expand the UpdateCommand node, and click the ellipsis button next to the CommandText field. This opens the Query Builder dialog that you used earlier in this chapter. Uncheck the boxes in the Set column for the rowguid row (because this should never be updated). In the New Value column, change @ModifiedDate to getdate() to automatically set the modified date to the date on which the query was executed. This should give you a query similar to the one shown in Figure 27-13.

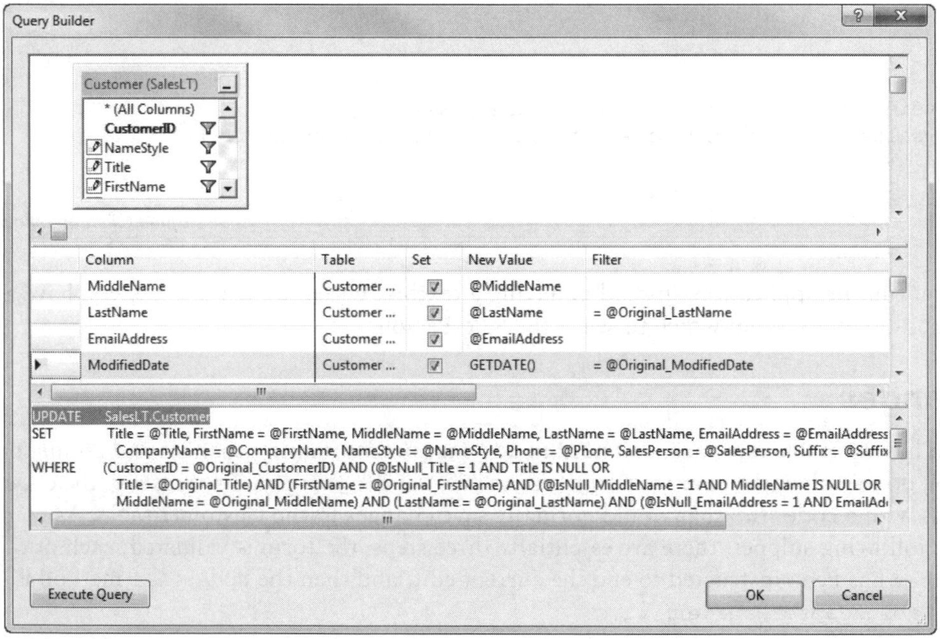

FIGURE 27-13

With this change, when you save a record the ModifiedDate will automatically be set to the current date.

Inserting New Items

You now have a sample application that enables you to browse and make changes to an existing set of individual customers. The one missing piece is the capability to create a new customer. By default, the Add button on the `BindingNavigator` is automatically wired up to the `AddNew` method on the `BindingSource`, as shown earlier in this chapter. In this case, you actually need to set some default values on the record that is created in the Customer table. To do this, you need to write your own logic behind the Add button.

The first step is to remove the automatic wiring by setting the `AddNewItem` property of the `CustomerBindingNavigator` to (None), otherwise, you will end up with two records being created every time you click the Add button. Next, double-click the Add button to create an event handler for it. You can then modify the default event handler as follows to set initial values for the new customer, as well as create records in the other two tables:

VB

```vb
Private Sub BindingNavigatorAddNewItem_Click(ByVal sender As System.Object, _
                                ByVal e As System.EventArgs) _
                                Handles BindingNavigatorAddNewItem.Click
    Dim drv As DataRowView

    'Create record in the Customer table
    drv = TryCast(Me.CustomerBindingSource.AddNew, DataRowView)
    Dim customer = TryCast(drv.Row, AdventureWorksLTDataSet.CustomerRow)
    customer.rowguid = Guid.NewGuid
    customer.PasswordHash = String.Empty
    customer.PasswordSalt = String.Empty
    customer.ModifiedDate = Now
    customer.FirstName = "<first name>"
    customer.LastName = "<last name>"
    customer.NameStyle = False
    Me.CustomerBindingSource.EndEdit()
End Sub
```

C#

```csharp
private void bindingNavigatorAddNewItem_Click(object sender, EventArgs e){
    DataRowView drv;

    //Create record in the Customer table
    drv = this.customerBindingSource.AddNew() as DataRowView;
    var customer = drv.Row as AdventureWorksLTDataSet.CustomerRow;
    customer.rowguid = Guid.NewGuid();
    customer.PasswordHash = String.Empty;
    customer.PasswordSalt = String.Empty;
    customer.ModifiedDate = DateTime.Now;
    customer.FirstName = "<first name>";
    customer.LastName = "<last name>";
    customer.NameStyle = false;
    this.customerBindingSource.EndEdit();
}
```

From this example, it seems that you are unnecessarily setting some of the properties — for example, `PasswordSalt` and `PasswordHash` being equal to an empty string. This is necessary to ensure that the new row meets the constraints established by the database. Because these fields cannot be set by the user, you need to ensure that they are initially set to a value that can be accepted by the database. Clearly, for a secure application, the `PasswordSalt` and `PasswordHash` would be set to appropriate values.

Running the application with this method instead of the automatically wired event handler enables you to create a new Customer record using the Add button. If you enter values for each of the fields, you can save the changes.

Validation

In the previous section, you added functionality to create a new customer record. If you don't enter appropriate data upon creating a new record — for example, if you don't enter a first name — this record will be rejected when you click the Save button. The schema for the `AdventureWorksDataSet` contains a number of constraints, such as `FirstName` can't be null, which are checked when you perform certain actions, such as saving or moving between records. If these checks fail, an exception is raised. You have two options. One, you can trap these exceptions, which is poor programming practice, because exceptions should not be used for execution control. Alternatively, you can preempt this by validating the data prior to the schema being checked. Earlier in the chapter, when you learned how the `BindingNavigator` automatically wires the `AddNew` method on the `BindingSource`, you saw that the `OnAddNew` method contains a call to a `Validate` method. This method propagates up and calls the `Validate` method on the active control, which returns a Boolean value that determines whether the action will proceed. This pattern is used by all the automatically wired events and should be used in the event handlers you write for the navigation buttons.

The `Validate` method on the active control triggers two events — `Validating` and `Validated` — that occur before and after the validation process, respectively. Because you want to control the validation process, add an event handler for the `Validating` event. For example, you could add an event handler for the `Validating` event of the FirstNameTextBox control:

VB

```vb
Private Sub FirstNameTextBox_Validating(ByVal sender As System.Object, _
                        ByVal e As System.ComponentModel.CancelEventArgs) _
                                    Handles FirstNameTextBox.Validating
        Dim firstNameTxt As TextBox = TryCast(sender, TextBox)
        If firstNameTxt Is Nothing Then Return
        e.Cancel = (firstNameTxt.Text = String.Empty)
End Sub
```

C#

```csharp
private void firstNameTextBox_Validating(object sender, CancelEventArgs e){
    var firstNameTxt = sender as TextBox;
    if (firstNameTxt == null) return;
    e.Cancel = (firstNameTxt.Text == String.Empty);
}
```

Though this prevents users from leaving the textbox until a value has been added, it doesn't give them any idea why the application prevents them from proceeding. Luckily, the .NET Framework includes an ErrorProvider control that can be dragged onto the form from the Toolbox. This control behaves in a manner similar to the tooltip control. For each control on the form, you can specify an Error string, which, when set, causes an icon to appear alongside the relevant control, with a suitable tooltip displaying the Error string. This is illustrated in Figure 27-14, where the Error string is set for the FirstNameTextBox.

FIGURE 27-14

Clearly, you want only to set the Error string property for the FirstNameTextBox when there is no text. Following from the earlier example in which you added the event handler for the Validating event, you can modify this code to include setting the Error string:

VB

```vb
Private Sub FirstNameTextBox_Validating(ByVal sender As System.Object, _
                        ByVal e As System.ComponentModel.CancelEventArgs) _
                                    Handles FirstNameTextBox.Validating
    Dim firstNameTxt As TextBox = TryCast(sender, TextBox)
    If firstNameTxt Is Nothing Then Return
    e.Cancel = (firstNameTxt.Text = String.Empty)

    If String.IsNullOrWhiteSpace(firstNameTxt.Text) Then
        Me.ErrorProvider1.SetError(firstNameTxt, "First Name must be specified")
    Else
        Me.ErrorProvider1.SetError(firstNameTxt, Nothing)
    End If
End Sub
```

C#

```csharp
private void firstNameTextBox_Validating(object sender, CancelEventArgs e){
    var firstNameTxt = sender as TextBox;
    if (firstNameTxt == null) return;
    e.Cancel = (firstNameTxt.Text == String.Empty);

    if (String.IsNullOrEmpty(firstNameTxt.Text)){
        this.errorProvider1.SetError(firstNameTxt, "First Name must be specified");
    }
    else{
        this.errorProvider1.SetError(firstNameTxt, null);
    }
}
```

You can imagine that having to write event handlers that validate and set the error information for each of the controls can be quite a lengthy process. Rather than having individual validation event handlers for each control, you may want to rationalize them into a single event handler that delegates the validation to a controller class. This helps ensure your business logic isn't intermingled within your user interface code.

Customized DataSets

At the moment, you have a form that displays some basic information about a customer. However, it is missing some of her address information, namely her Main Office and/or Shipping addresses. If you look at the structure of the AdventureWorksLT database you will notice that there is a many-to-many relationship between the Customer and Address tables, through the CustomerAddress linking table. The CustomerAddress has a column AddressType that indicates the type of address. While this structure supports the concept that multiple Customers may have the same address, the user interface you have built so far is only interested in the address information for a particular customer. If you simply add all three of these tables to your DataSet you will not easily be able to use data binding to wire up the user interface. As such it is worth customizing the generated DataSet to merge the CustomerAddress and Address tables into a single entity.

Open up the DataSet designer by double-clicking the `AdventureWorksLTDataSet.xsd` in the Solution Explorer. Select the AddressTableAdapter, which you should already have from earlier in the chapter, expand out the SelectCommand property in the Properties tool window, and then click the ellipses next to the CommandText property. This will again open up the Query Builder. Currently, you should only have the Address table in the diagram pane. Right-click in that pane, select Add Table, and then select the CustomerAddress table. Check all fields in the CustomerAddress table except AddressID and then go to the Criteria pane and change the Alias for the rowguid and ModifiedDate columns coming from the CustomerAddress table. The result should look similar to Figure 27-15.

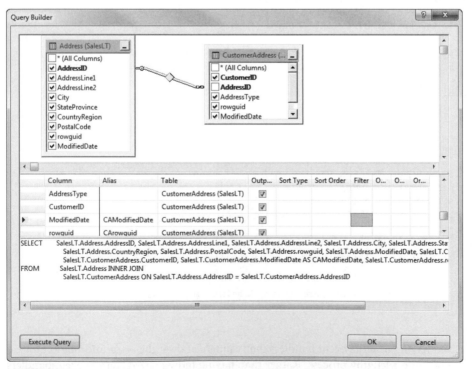

FIGURE 27-15

When you click the OK button you will be prompted to regenerate the `Update` and `Insert` statements. The code generator can't handle multiple table updates so will fail regardless of which option you select. This means that you need to manually define the update, insert, and delete statements. You can do this by defining stored procedures within the AdventureWorksLT database and then to update the CommandType and CommandText for the relevant commands in the AddressTableAdapter as shown in Figure 27-16.

Now that your DataSet contains both Customer and Address DataTables, the only thing missing is the relationship connecting them. As you have customized the Address DataTable the designer hasn't been able to automatically create the relationship. To create a relation, right-click anywhere on the DataSet design surface and select Add ➪ Relation. This opens the Relation dialog as shown in Figure 27-17.

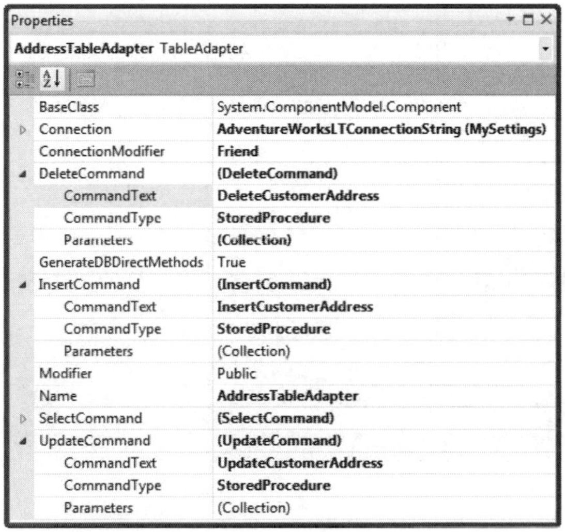

Properties	
AddressTableAdapter TableAdapter	
BaseClass	System.ComponentModel.Component
▷ Connection	**AdventureWorksLTConnectionString (MySettings)**
ConnectionModifier	**Friend**
◢ DeleteCommand	**(DeleteCommand)**
CommandText	**DeleteCustomerAddress**
CommandType	**StoredProcedure**
Parameters	**(Collection)**
GenerateDBDirectMethods	True
◢ InsertCommand	**(InsertCommand)**
CommandText	**InsertCustomerAddress**
CommandType	**StoredProcedure**
Parameters	(Collection)
Modifier	Public
Name	**AddressTableAdapter**
▷ SelectCommand	**(SelectCommand)**
◢ UpdateCommand	**(UpdateCommand)**
CommandText	**UpdateCustomerAddress**
CommandType	**StoredProcedure**
Parameters	(Collection)

FIGURE 27-16

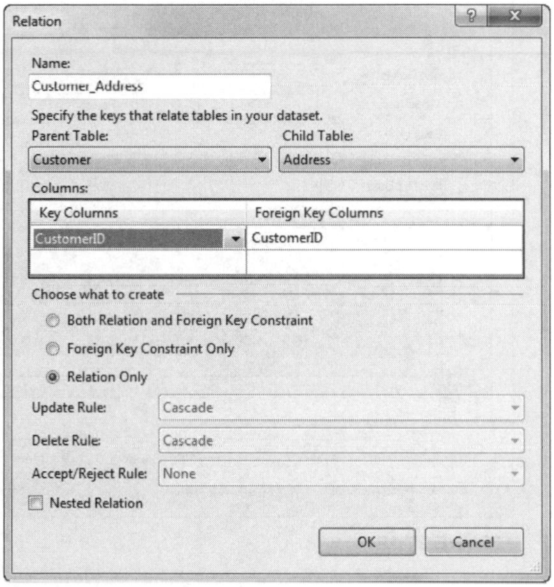

Relation

Name:
Customer_Address

Specify the keys that relate tables in your dataset.

Parent Table: Child Table:
Customer   Address

Columns:

Key Columns	Foreign Key Columns
CustomerID	CustomerID

Choose what to create

○ Both Relation and Foreign Key Constraint
○ Foreign Key Constraint Only
● Relation Only

Update Rule: Cascade
Delete Rule: Cascade
Accept/Reject Rule: None
☐ Nested Relation

OK   Cancel

FIGURE 27-17

In accordance with the way the Address DataTable has been created by combining the CustomerAddress and Address tables, make the Customer DataTable the parent and the Address the child. When you accept this dialog you will see a relationship line connecting the two DataTables on the DataSet design surface.

BindingSource Chains and the DataGridView

After completing the setup of the DataSet with the Customer and Address DataTables you are ready to data bind the Address table to your user interface. So far you've been working with simple input controls such as textboxes, drop-down lists, and labels, and you've seen how the BindingNavigator enables you to scroll through a list of items. Sometimes it is more convenient to display a list of items in a grid. This is where the DataGridView is useful, because it enables you to combine the power of the BindingSource with a grid layout.

In this example, you extend the Customer Management interface by adding address information using a DataGridView. Returning to the Data Sources window, select the Address node from under the Customer node. From the drop-down list, select DataGridView and drag the node into an empty area on the form. This adds the appropriate BindingSource and TableAdapter to the form, as well as a DataGridView showing each of the columns in the Address table, as shown in Figure 27-18.

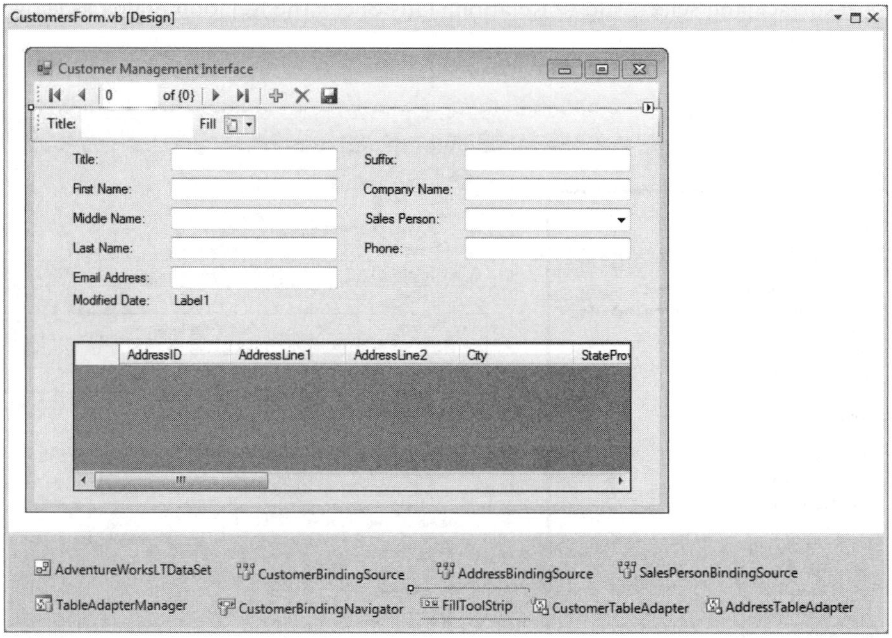

FIGURE 27-18

If you recall from earlier, the CustomerBindingSource has the AdventureWorksLTDataSet as its DataSource, with the Customer table set as the DataMember. This means that controls that are data bound using the CustomerBindingSource are binding to a field in the Customer table. If you look at the AddressBindingSource you will see that its DataSource is actually the CustomerBindingSource, with its DataMember set to Customer_Address, which is the relationship you created between the two DataTables. As you would expect, any control being data bound using the AddressBindingSource is binding to a field in the Address table. However, the difference is that unlike the CustomerBindingSource, which returns all Customers, the AddressBindingSource is only populated with the Addresses that are associated with the currently selected Customer.

Unlike working with the Details layout, when you drag the DataGridView onto the form it ignores any settings you might have specified for the individual columns. Instead, every column is added to the grid as a simple text field. To modify the list of columns that are displayed, you can either use the smart tag for the newly added DataGridView or select Edit Columns from the right-click context menu. This will open the Edit Columns dialog (shown in Figure 27-19), in which columns can be added, removed, and reordered.

After specifying the appropriate columns, the finished application can be run, and the list of orders will be visible for each customer in the database.

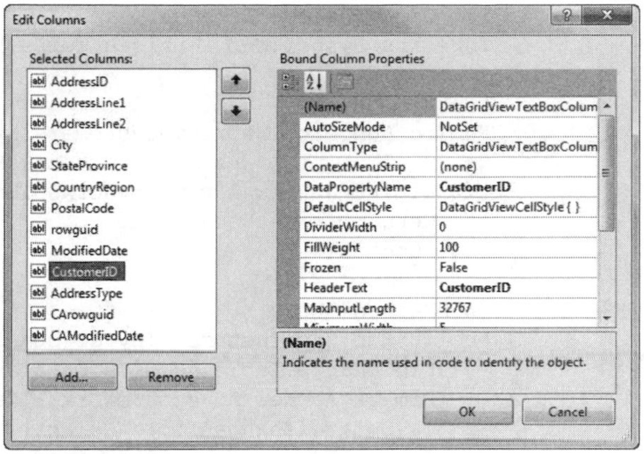

FIGURE 27-19

WORKING WITH DATA SOURCES

In this chapter you have been working with a strongly typed DataSet that contains a number of rows from the Customer table, based on a `Title` parameter. So far the example has only had one tier, which is the Windows Forms application itself. In this section you see how you can use Visual Studio 2010 to build a multi-tier application.

Start by creating two new projects, CustomerBrowser (Windows Forms Application) and CustomerService (ASP.NET Web Service Application). Change the Application Type of the initial project to Class Library by double-clicking the Properties node in Solution Explorer and then changing the Application type field on the Application tab.

> *Because this section involves working with ASP.NET applications, it is recommended that you run Visual Studio 2010 in Administrator mode if you are running Windows Vista. This will allow the debugger to be attached to the appropriate process.*

In the Web Service project, you will add a reference to the class library project. You also need to modify the `Service` class file so it has two methods, in place of the default `HelloWorld` web method:

Available for download on Wrox.com

VB

```vb
Imports System.Web.Services
Imports System.Web.Services.Protocols
Imports System.ComponentModel
Imports CustomerObject

<System.Web.Services.WebService(Namespace:="http://tempuri.org/")> _
<System.Web.Services.WebServiceBinding(ConformsTo:=WsiProfiles.BasicProfile1_1)> _
<ToolboxItem(False)> _
```

```vb
Public Class CustomerService
    Inherits System.Web.Services.WebService

    <WebMethod()> _
    Public Function RetrieveCustomers(ByVal Title As String) _
                    As AdventureWorksLTDataSet.CustomerDataTable
        Dim ta As New AdventureWorksLTDataSetTableAdapters.CustomerTableAdapter
        Return ta.GetData(Title)
    End Function

    <WebMethod()> _
    Public Sub SaveCustomers(ByVal changes As Data.DataSet)
        Dim changesTable As Data.DataTable = changes.Tables(0)
        Dim ta As New AdventureWorksLTDataSetTableAdapters.CustomerTableAdapter
        ta.Update(changesTable.Select)
    End Sub
End
```

Code snippet CustomerService.asmx.vb

C#

```csharp
namespace CustomerService{
    [WebService(Namespace = "http://tempuri.org/")]
    [WebServiceBinding(ConformsTo = WsiProfiles.BasicProfile1_1)]
    [System.ComponentModel.ToolboxItem(false)]
    public class CustomerService : System.Web.Services.WebService{
        [WebMethod]
        public AdventureWorksLTDataSet.CustomerDataTable RetrieveCustomers
                                                         (string title){
            var ta = new CustomerObject.AdventureWorksLTDataSetTableAdapters.
                                        CustomerTableAdapter();
            return ta.GetData(title);
        }

        [WebMethod()]
        public void SaveCustomers(DataSet changes){
            var changesTable = changes.Tables[0] as DataTable;
            var ta = new CustomerObject.AdventureWorksLTDataSetTableAdapters.
                                        CustomerTableAdapter();
            ta.Update(changesTable.Select());
        }
    }
}
```

Code snippet CustomerService.asmx.cs

The first web method, as the name suggests, retrieves the list of customers based on the Title that is passed in. In this method, you create a new instance of the strongly typed TableAdapter and return the DataTable retrieved by the GetData method. The second web method is used to save changes to a DataTable, again using the strongly typed TableAdapter. As you will notice, the DataSet that is passed in as a parameter to this method is not strongly typed. Unfortunately, the generated strongly typed DataSet doesn't provide a strongly typed GetChanges method, which will be used later to generate a DataSet containing only data that has changed. This new DataSet is passed into the SaveCustomers method so that only changed data needs to be sent to the web service.

The Web Service Data Source

These changes to the web service complete the server side of the process, but your application still doesn't have access to this data. To access the data from your application, you need to add a data source to the application. Again, use the Add New Data Source Wizard, but this time select Service from the Data Source Type screen. To add a Web Service Data Source you then need to click Advanced, followed by Add Web Reference. Clicking the "Web services in this solution" link displays a list of web services available in your solution. The web service that you have just been working on should appear in this list. When you click the hyperlink for that web service, the Add Reference button is enabled, as shown in Figure 27-20.

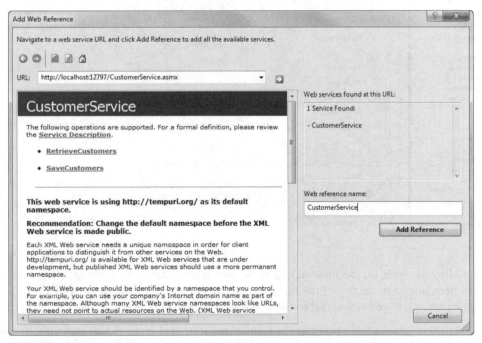

FIGURE 27-20

> *If an error is displayed when clicking the hyperlink you may need to build and run the ASP.NET Web Service Application project. This starts the service running so that the schema information can be correctly extracted by the Add Web Reference dialog.*

Clicking the Add Reference button adds an AdventureWorksDataSet to the Data Sources window under the CustomerService node. Expanding this node, you will see that the data source is very similar to the data source you had in the class library.

Browsing Data

To actually view the data being returned via the web service, you need to add some controls to your form. Open the form so the designer appears in the main window. In the Data Sources window, click the Customer node and select Details from the drop-down. This indicates that when you drag the Customer node onto the form, Visual Studio 2010 will create controls to display the details of the Customer table (for example, the row contents), instead of the default DataGridView. Next, select the attributes you want to display by clicking them and selecting the control type to use. When you drag the Customer node onto the form, you should end up with the layout similar to Figure 27-21.

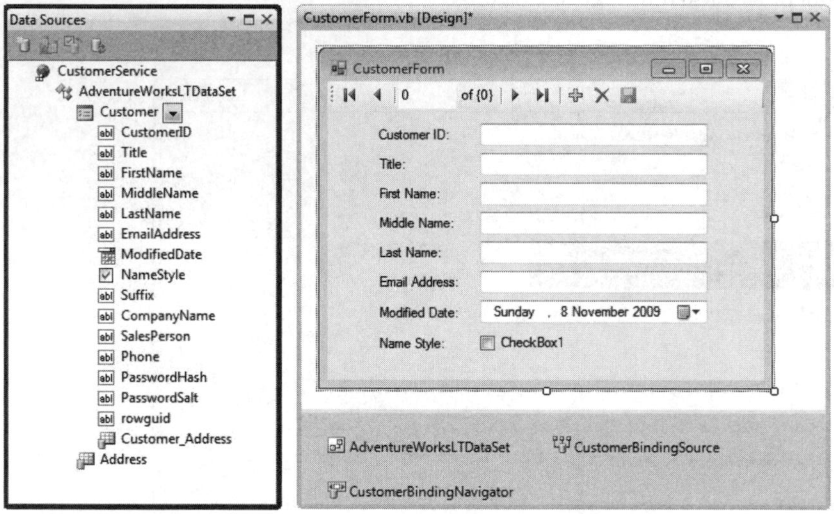

FIGURE 27-21

In addition to adding controls for the information to be displayed and edited, a Navigator control has also been added to the top of the form, and an `AdventureWorksDataSet` and a `CustomerBindingSource` have been added to the non-visual area of the form.

The final stage is to wire up the `Load` event of the form to retrieve data from the web service, and to add the Save button on the navigator to save changes. Right-click the save icon and select Enabled to enable the Save button on the navigator control, and then double-click the save icon to generate the stub event handler. Add the following code to load data and save changes via the web service you created earlier:

VB

Available for
download on
Wrox.com

```vb
Public Class CustomerForm
    Private Sub CustomerForm_Load(ByVal sender As System.Object,
                    ByVal e As System.EventArgs) Handles Me.Load
```

```vb
                    Me.CustomerBindingSource.DataSource = _
                        My.WebServices.CustomerService.RetrieveCustomers("%mr%")
        End Sub

        Private Sub CustomerBindingNavigatorSaveItem_Click _
                            (ByVal sender As System.Object,
                             ByVal e As System.EventArgs)
                            Handles CustomerBindingNavigatorSaveItem.Click
            Me.CustomerBindingSource.EndEdit()
            Dim ds = CType(Me.CustomerBindingSource.DataSource, _
                    CustomerService.AdventureWorksLTDataSet.CustomerDataTable)
            Dim changesTable As DataTable = ds.GetChanges()
            Dim changes As New DataSet
            changes.Tables.Add(changesTable)
            My.WebServices.CustomerService.SaveCustomers(changes)
        End Sub
End Class
```

Code snippet CustomersForm.vb

C#

```csharp
private void CustomersForm_Load(object sender, EventArgs e){
    var service = new CustomerService.CustomerService();
    this.CustomerBindingSource.DataSource = service.RetrieveCustomers("%mr%"); ;
}

private void CustomerBindingNavigatorSaveItem_Click(object sender, EventArgs e){
    this.CustomerBindingSource.EndEdit();
    var ds = this.CustomerBindingSource.DataSource
                    as CustomerService.AdventureWorksLTDataSet.CustomerDataTable;
    var changesTable = ds.GetChanges();
    var changes = new DataSet();
    changes.Tables.Add(changesTable);
    var service = new CustomerService.CustomerService();
    service.SaveCustomers(changes);
}
```

Code snippet CustomersForm.cs

To retrieve the list of customers from the web service, all you need to do is call the appropriate web method — in this case, RetrieveCustomers. Pass in a parameter of %mr%, which indicates that only customers with a Title containing the letters "mr" should be returned. The Save method is slightly more complex, because you have to end the current edit (to make sure all changes are saved), retrieve the DataTable, and then extract the changes as a new DataTable. Although it would be simpler to pass a DataTable to the SaveCustomers web service, only DataSets can be specified as parameters or return values to a web service. As such, you can create a new DataSet and add the changed DataTable to the list of tables. The new DataSet is then passed into the SaveCustomers method. As mentioned previously, the GetChanges method returns a raw DataTable, which is unfortunate because it limits the strongly typed data scenario.

This completes the chapter's coverage of the strongly typed DataSet scenario, and provides you with a two-tiered solution for accessing and editing data from a database via a web service interface.

SUMMARY

This chapter provided an introduction to working with strongly typed DataSets. Support within Visual Studio 2010 for creating and working with strongly typed DataSets simplifies the rapid building of applications. This is clearly the first step in the process of bridging the gap between the object-oriented programming world and the relational world in which the data is stored.

Hopefully this chapter has given you an appreciation for how the `BindingSource`, `BindingNavigator`, and other data controls work together to give you the ability to rapidly build data applications. Because the new controls support working with either DataSets or your own custom objects, they can significantly reduce the amount of time it takes you to write an application.

28

Language Integrated
Queries (LINQ)

WHAT'S IN THIS CHAPTER?

➤ Querying objects with LINQ

➤ Writing and querying XML with XLINQ

➤ Querying and updating data with LINQ to SQL

Language Integrated Queries (LINQ) was designed to provide a common programming model for querying data. In this chapter you see how you can take some very verbose, imperative code and reduce it to a few declarative lines. This enables you to make your code more descriptive rather than prescriptive; that is, describing what you want to occur, rather than detailing how it should be done.

Although LINQ provides an easy way to filter, sort, and project from an in-memory object graph, it is more common for the data source to be either a database or a file type, such as XML. In this chapter you are introduced to LINQ to XML, which makes working with XML data dramatically simpler than with traditional methods such as using the document object model, XSLT, or XPath. You also learn how to use LINQ to SQL to work with traditional databases, such as SQL Server, allowing you to write LINQ statements that will query the database, pull back the appropriate data, and populate .NET objects that you can work with. In Chapter 29 you are introduced to the ADO.NET Entity Framework for which there is also a LINQ provider. This means that you can combine the power of declarative queries with the fidelity of the Entity Framework to manage your data object life cycle.

LINQ PROVIDERS

One of the key tenets of LINQ is the ability to abstract away the query syntax from the underlying data store. LINQ sits behind the various .NET languages such as C# and VB and combines various language features, such as extension methods, type inferences, anonymous types, and Lambda expressions, to provide a uniform syntax for querying data.

A number of LINQ-enabled data sources come with Visual Studio 2010 and the .NET Framework 4.0: Objects, DataSets, SQL, Entities, and XML; each with its own LINQ provider that's capable of querying the corresponding data source. LINQ is not limited to just these data sources, and providers are available for querying all sorts of other data sources. For example, there is a LINQ provider for querying SharePoint. In fact, the documentation that ships with Visual Studio 2010 includes a walkthrough on creating your own LINQ provider.

In this chapter you see some of the standard LINQ operations as they apply to standard .NET objects. You'll then see how these same queries can be applied to both XML and SQL data sources. As you will see, the syntax for querying the data remains constant, with only the underlying data source changing.

OLD-SCHOOL QUERIES

Instead of walking through exactly what LINQ is, this section starts with an example that demonstrates some of the savings that these queries offer. The scenario is one in which a researcher is investigating whether or not there is a correlation between the length of a customer's name and the customer's average order size by analyzing a collection of customer objects. The relationship between a customer and the orders is a simple one-to-many relationship as shown in Figure 28-1.

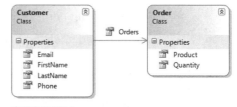

FIGURE 28-1

In the particular query you are examining, the researchers are looking for the average Milk order for customers with a first name greater than or equal to five characters, ordered by the first name:

C#

```
private void OldStyleQuery(){
    Customer[] customers = BuildCustomers();
    List<SearchResult> results = new List<SearchResult>();
    SearchForProduct matcher = new SearchForProduct() { Product = "Milk" };
    foreach (Customer c in customers){
        if (c.FirstName.Length >= 5){
            Order[] orders = Array.FindAll(c.Orders, matcher.ProductMatch);
            if (orders.Length > 0){
                SearchResult cr = new SearchResult();
                cr.Customer = c.FirstName + " " + c.LastName;
                foreach (Order o in orders){
                    cr.Quantity += o.Quantity;
```

```
                          cr.Count++;
                      }
                      results.Add(cr);
                  }
              }
          }
          results.Sort(CompareSearchResults);
          ObjectDumper.Write(results, Writer);
      }
```

Code snippet MainForm.cs

VB

```
Private Sub OldStyleQuery()
    Dim customers As Customer() = BuildCustomers()

    Dim results As New List(Of SearchResult)
    Dim matcher As New SearchForProduct() With {.Product = "Milk"}

    For Each c As Customer In customers
        If c.FirstName.Length >= 5 Then
            Dim orders As Order() = Array.FindAll(c.Orders, _
                                        AddressOf matcher.ProductMatch)
            If orders.Length > 0 Then
                Dim cr As New SearchResult
                cr.Customer = c.FirstName & " " & c.LastName
                For Each o As Order In orders
                    cr.Quantity += o.Quantity
                    cr.Count += 1
                Next
                results.Add(cr)
            End If
        End If
    Next
    results.Sort(AddressOf CompareSearchResults)

    ObjectDumper.Write(results, Writer)
End Sub
```

Code snippet MainForm.vb

Before we jump in and show how LINQ can improve this snippet, let's examine how this snippet works. The opening line calls out to a method that simply generates `Customer` objects. This will be used throughout the snippets in this chapter. The main loop in this method iterates through the array of customers searching for those customers with a first name longer than five characters. Upon finding such a customer, you use the `Array.FindAll` method to retrieve all orders where the predicate is true. Prior to the introduction of anonymous methods you couldn't supply the predicate function inline with the method. As a result, the usual way to do this was to create a simple class that could hold the query variable (in this case, the product, Milk) that you were searching for, and that had a method that accepted the type of object you were searching through, in this case an `Order`. With the introduction of Lambda expressions, you can now rewrite this line:

C#

```
var orders = Array.FindAll(c.Orders, order=>order.Product =="Milk");
```

VB

```
Dim orders = Array.FindAll(c.Orders,
                           Function(o As Order) o.Product = "Milk")
```

Here you have also taken advantage of type inferencing to determine the type of the variable orders, which is of course still an array of orders.

Returning to the snippet, once you have located the orders you still need to iterate through them and sum up the quantity ordered and store this, along with the name of the customer and the number of orders. This is your search result, and as you can see you are using a `SearchResult` object to store this information. For convenience, the `SearchResult` object also has a read-only `Average` property, which simply divides the total quantity ordered by the number of orders. Because you want to sort the customer list, you use the `Sort` method on the `List` class, passing in the address of a comparison method. Again, using Lambda expressions, this can be rewritten as an inline statement:

C#

```
results.Sort((r1, r2) => string.Compare(r1.Customer, r2.Customer));
```

VB

```
results.Sort( Function(r1 as SearchResult, r2 as SearchResult) _
                           String.Compare(r1.Customer, r2.Customer))
```

The last part of this snippet is to print out the search results. This is using one of the samples that ships with Visual Studio 2010 called `ObjectDumper`. This is a simple class that iterates through a collection of objects printing out the values of the public properties. In this case the output would look like Figure 28-2.

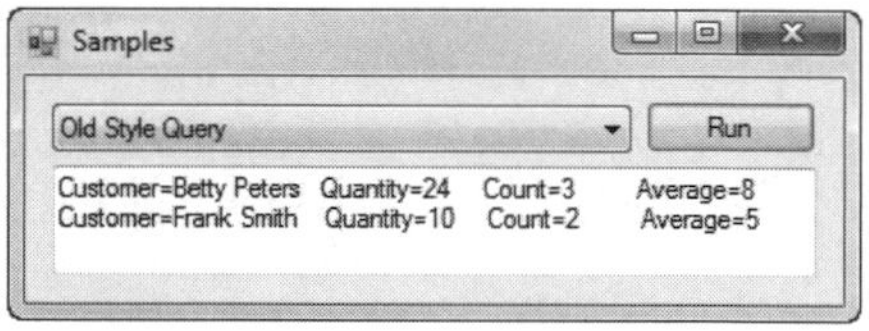

FIGURE 28-2

As you can see from this relatively simple query, the code to do this in the past was quite prescriptive and required additional classes in order to carry out the query logic and return the results. With the power of LINQ you can build a single expression that clearly describes what the search results should be.

QUERY PIECES

This section introduces you to a number of the query operations that make up the basis of LINQ. If you have written SQL statements, these will feel familiar, although the ordering and syntax might take a little time to get used to. You can use a number of query operations, and numerous reference web sites provide more information on how to use them. For the moment, you will focus on those operations necessary to improve the search query introduced at the beginning of this chapter.

From

Unlike SQL, where the first statement is `Select`, in LINQ the first statement is typically `From`. One of the key considerations in the creation of LINQ was providing IntelliSense support within Visual Studio 2010. If you've ever wondered why there is no IntelliSense support in SQL Management Studio for SQL Server 2005 for writing queries, this is because to determine what to select, you need to know where the data is coming from. By reversing the order of the statements, LINQ is able to generate IntelliSense as soon as you start typing.

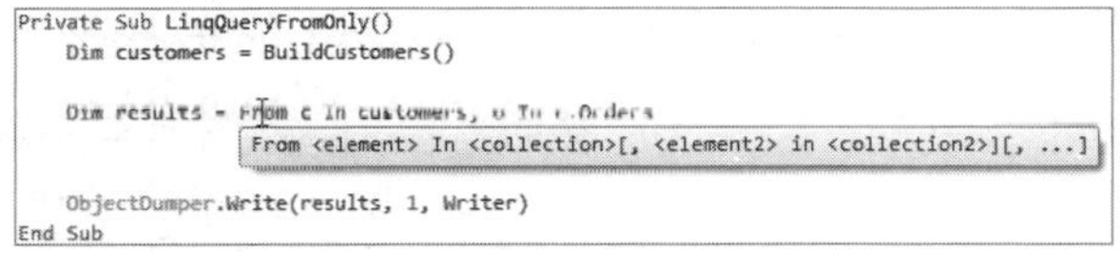

As you can see from the tooltip in Figure 28-3, the `From` statement is made up of two parts, `<element>` and `<collection>`. The latter is the source collection from which you will be extracting data, and the former is essentially an iteration variable that can be used to refer to the items being queried. This pair can then be repeated for each source collection.

FIGURE 28-3

In this case you can see you are querying the customers collection, with an iteration variable c, and the orders collection c.Orders using the iteration variable o. There is an implicit join between the two source collections because of the relationship between a customer and that customer's orders. As you can imagine, this query will result in the cross-product of items in each source collection. This will lead to the pairing of a customer with each order that this customer has.

Note that you don't have a `Select` statement, because you are simply going to return all elements, but what does each result record look like? If you were to look at the tooltip for results, you would see that it is a generic IEnumerable of an anonymous type. The anonymous type feature is heavily used in LINQ so that you don't have to create classes for every result. If you recall from the initial code, you had to have a `SearchResult` class in order to capture each of the results. Anonymous types mean that you no longer have to create a class to store the results. During compilation, types containing the relevant properties are dynamically created, thereby giving you a strongly typed result set along with IntelliSense support. Though the tooltip for results may report only that it is an IEnumerable of an anonymous type, when you start to use the results collection you will see that the type has two properties, c and o, of type Customer and Order, respectively. Figure 28-4 displays the output of this code, showing the customer-order pairs.

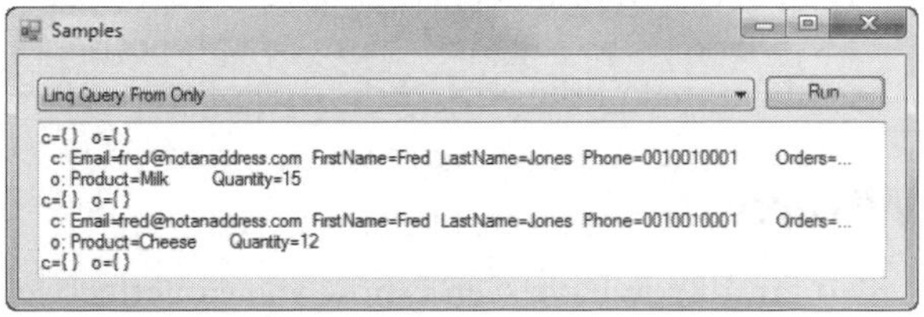

FIGURE 28-4

C# actually requires a `Select` clause to be present in all LINQ, even if you are returning all objects in the `From` clause.

Select

In the previous code snippet the result set was a collection of customer-order pairs, when in fact what you want to return is the customer name and the order information. You can do this by using a `Select` statement in a way similar to the way you would when writing a SQL statement:

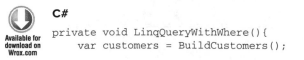

C#

```csharp
private void LinqQueryWithSelect(){
    var customers = BuildCustomers();
    var results = from c in customers
                  from o in c.Orders
                  select new{c.FirstName,
                             c.LastName,o.Product,o.Quantity};
    ObjectDumper.Write(results, Writer);
}
```

Code snippet MainForm.cs

VB

```vb
Private Sub LinqQueryWithSelect()
    Dim customers = BuildCustomers()

    Dim results = From c In customers, o In c.Orders
                  Select c.FirstName, c.LastName, o.Product, o.Quantity

    ObjectDumper.Write(results, Writer)
End Sub
```

Code snippet MainForm.vb

Now when you execute this code the result set is a collection of objects that have `FirstName`, `LastName`, `Product`, and `Quantity` properties. This is illustrated in the output shown in Figure 28-5.

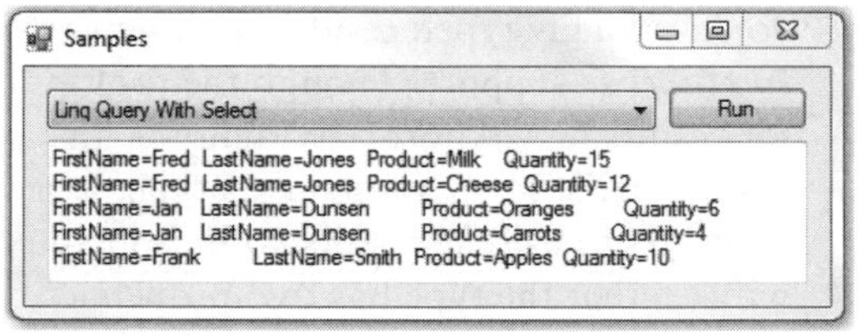

FIGURE 28-5

Where

So far all you have seen is how you can effectively flatten the customer-order hierarchy into a result set containing the appropriate properties. What you haven't done is filter these results so that they only return customers with a first name greater than or equal to five characters, and who are ordering `Milk`. The following snippet introduces a `Where` statement, which restricts the source collections on both these axes:

C#

```csharp
private void LinqQueryWithWhere(){
    var customers = BuildCustomers();

    var results = from c in customers
```

```
                                 from o in c.Orders
                                 where c.FirstName.Length >= 5 &&
                                       o.Product == "Milk"
                                 select new { c.FirstName, c.LastName, o.Product, o.Quantity };

                ObjectDumper.Write(results, Writer);
            }
```

Code snippet MainForm.cs

VB

```
Private Sub LinqQueryWithWhere()
    Dim customers = BuildCustomers()

    Dim results = From c In customers, o In c.Orders
                  Where c.FirstName.Length >= 5 And
                        o.Product = "Milk"
                  Select c.FirstName, c.LastName, o.Product, o.Quantity

    ObjectDumper.Write(results, Writer)
End Sub
```

Code snippet MainForm.vb

The output of this query is similar to the previous one in that it is a result set of an anonymous type with the four properties FirstName, LastName, Product, and Quantity.

Group By

You are getting close to your initial query, except that your current query returns a list of all the Milk orders for all the customers. For a customer who might have placed two orders for Milk, this will result in two records in the result set. What you actually want to do is to group these orders by customer and take an average of the quantities ordered. Not surprisingly, this is done with a Group By statement, as shown in the following snippet:

C#

```
private void LinqQueryWithGroupingAndWhere(){
    var customers = BuildCustomers();

    var results = from c in customers
                  from o in c.Orders
                  where c.FirstName.Length >= 5 &&
                        o.Product == "Milk"
                  group o by c into avg
                  select new { avg.Key.FirstName, avg.Key.LastName,
                               avg = avg.Average(o => o.Quantity) };
    ObjectDumper.Write(results, Writer);
}
```

Code snippet MainForm.cs

VB

```vb
Private Sub LinqQueryWithGroupingAndWhere()
    Dim customers = BuildCustomers()

    Dim results = From c In customers, o In c.Orders _
                  Where c.FirstName.Length >= 5 And _
                        o.Product = "Milk" _
                  Group By c Into avg = Average(o.Quantity) _
                  Select c.FirstName, c.LastName, avg

    ObjectDumper.Write(results)
End Sub
```

Code snippet MainForm.vb

What is a little confusing about the Group By statement is the syntax that it uses. Essentially, what it is saying is "group by dimension X" and place the results "Into" an alias that can be used elsewhere. In this case the alias is avg, which will contain the average you are interested in. Because you are grouping by the iteration variable c, you can still use this in the Select statement, along with the Group By alias. Note that the C# example is slightly different in that although the grouping is still done on c, you then have to access it via the Key property of the alias. Now when you run this you get the output shown in Figure 28-6, which is much closer to your initial query.

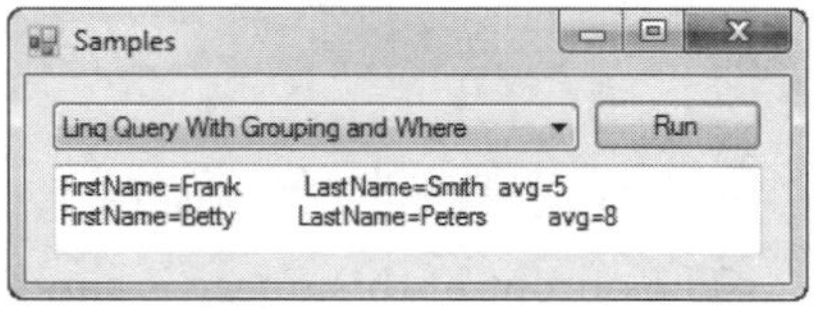

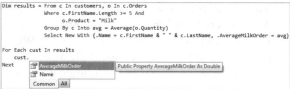

FIGURE 28-6

Custom Projections

You still need to tidy up the output so that you are returning a well-formatted customer name and an appropriately named average property, instead of the query results, FirstName, LastName, and avg. You can do this by customizing the properties that are contained in the anonymous type that is created as part of the Select statement projection. Figure 28-7 shows how you can create anonymous types with named properties.

FIGURE 28-7

This figure also illustrates that the type of the AverageMilkOrder property is indeed a Double, which is what you would expect based on the use of the Average function. It is this strongly typed behavior that can really assist you in the creation and use of rich LINQ statements.

Order By

The last thing you have to do with the LINQ statement is to order the results. You can do this by ordering the customers based on their FirstName property, as shown in the following snippet:

C#

```csharp
private void LinqQueryWithGroupingAndWhere(){
    var customers = BuildCustomers();

    var results = from c in customers
                  from o in c.Orders
                  orderby c.FirstName
                  where c.FirstName.Length >= 5 &&
                        o.Product == "Milk"
                  group o by c into avg
                  select new { Name = avg.Key.FirstName + " " + avg.Key.LastName,
                               AverageMilkOrder = avg.Average(o => o.Quantity) };
    ObjectDumper.Write(results, Writer);
}
```

Code snippet MainForm.cs

VB

```vb
Private Sub FinalLinqQuery()
    Dim customers = BuildCustomers()

    Dim results = From c In customers, o In c.Orders
                  Order By c.FirstName
                  Where c.FirstName.Length >= 5 And
                        o.Product = "Milk
                  Group By c Into avg = Average(o.Quantity)
                  Select New With {.Name = c.FirstName & " " & c.LastName,
                                   .AverageMilkOrder = avg}

    ObjectDumper.Write(results)
End Sub
```

Code snippet MainForm.vb

One thing to be aware of is how you can easily reverse the order of the query results. Here you can do this either by supplying the keyword Descending (Ascending is the default) at the end of the Order By statement, or by applying the Reverse transformation on the entire result set:

```
Order By c.FirstName Descending
```

or

```
ObjectDumper.Write(results.Reverse)
```

As you can see from the final query you have built up, it is much more descriptive than the initial query. You can easily see that you are selecting the customer name and an average of the order quantities. It is clear that you are filtering based on the length of the customer name and on orders for Milk, and that the results are sorted by the customer's first name. You also haven't needed to create any additional classes to help perform this query.

DEBUGGING AND EXECUTION

One of the things you should be aware of with LINQ is that the queries are not executed until they are used. In fact, each time you use a LINQ query you will find that the query is re-executed. This can potentially lead to some issues in debugging and some unexpected performance issues if you are executing the query multiple times. In the code you have seen so far, you have declared the LINQ statement and then passed the results object to the `ObjectDumper`, which in turn iterates through the query results. If you were to repeat this call to the `ObjectDumper`, it would again iterate through the results.

Unfortunately, this delayed execution can mean that LINQ statements are hard to debug. If you select the statement and insert a breakpoint, all that will happen is that the application will stop where you have declared the LINQ statement. If you step to the next line, the results object will simply state that it is an "In-Memory Query." In C# the debugging story is slightly better because you can actually set breakpoints within the LINQ statement. As you can see from Figure 28-8, the breakpoint on the conditional statement has been hit. From the call stack you can see that the current execution point is no longer actually in the `FinalQuery` method; it is in fact within the `ObjectDumper.Write` method.

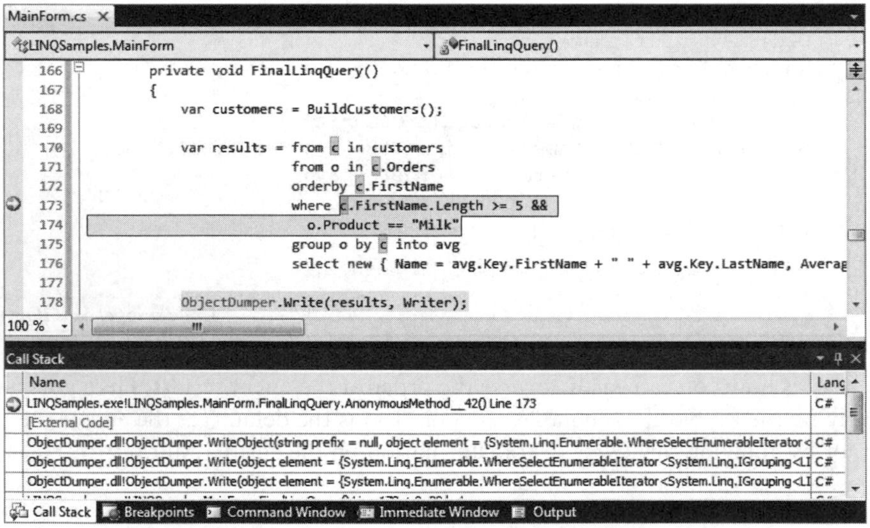

FIGURE 28-8

If you need to force the execution of a LINQ you can call `ToArray` or `ToList` on the results object. This will force the query to execute, returning an Array or List of the appropriate type. You can then use this array in other queries, reducing the need for the LINQ to be executed multiple times.

> *When setting a breakpoint within a LINQ in C# you need to place the cursor at the point you want the breakpoint to be set and press F9 (or use the right-click context menu to set a breakpoint), rather than clicking in the margin. Clicking in the margin sets a breakpoint on the whole LINQ, which is not what you want.*

LINQ TO XML

If you have ever worked with XML in .NET, you will recall that the object model isn't as easy to work with as you would imagine. For example, to create even a single XML element you need to have an XmlDocument:

```
Dim x as New XmlDocument
x.AppendChild(x.CreateElement("Customer"))
```

As you will see when you start to use LINQ to query and build XML, this object model doesn't allow for the inline creation of elements. To this end, a new XML object model was created that resides in the System.Xml.Linq assembly presented in Figure 28-9.

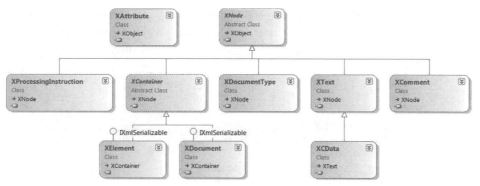

FIGURE 28-9

As you can see from Figure 28-9, there are classes that correspond to the relevant parts of an XML document: XComment, XAttribute, and XElements. The biggest improvement is that most of the classes can be instantiated by means of a constructor that accepts Name and Content parameters. In the following C# code, you can see that an element called Customers has been created that contains a single Customer element. This element, in turn, accepts an attribute, Name, and a series of Order elements.

C#

```
XElement x = new XElement("Customers",
                new XElement("Customer",
                    new XAttribute("Name","Bob Jones"),
```

```
                                        new XElement("Order",
                                                new XAttribute("Product", "Milk"),
                                                new XAttribute("Quantity", 2)),
                                        new XElement("Order",
                                                new XAttribute("Product", "Bread"),
                                                new XAttribute("Quantity", 10)),
                                        new XElement("Order",
                                                new XAttribute("Product", "Apples"),
                                                new XAttribute("Quantity", 5))
                                        )
                        );
```

Though this code snippet is quite verbose and it's hard to distinguish the actual XML data from the surrounding .NET code, it is significantly better than with the old XML object model, which required elements to be individually created and then added to the parent node.

> *While it is possible to write the same code in VB using the* XElement *and* XAttribute *constructors, the support for XML literals (as discussed in the next section) makes this somewhat redundant.*

VB XML Literals

One of the biggest innovations in the VB language is the support for XML literals. As with strings and integers, an XML literal is treated as a first-class citizen when you are writing code. The following snippet illustrates the same XML generated by the previous C# snippet as it would appear using an XML literal in VB:

VB

```
Dim cust = <Customers>
                <Customer Name="Bob Jones">
                    <Order Product="Milk" Quantity="2"/>
                    <Order Product="Bread" Quantity="10"/>
                    <Order Product="Apples" Quantity="5"/>
                </Customer>
            </Customers>
```

Not only do you have the ability to assign an XML literal in code, you also get designer support for creating and working with your XML. For example, when you enter the > on a new element, it will automatically create the closing XML tag for you. Figure 28-10 illustrates how the Customers XML literal can be condensed in the same way as other code blocks in Visual Studio 2010.

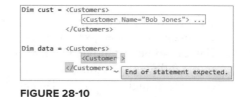

FIGURE 28-10

You can also see in Figure 28-10 that there is an error in the XML literal being assigned to the data variable. In this case there is no closing tag for the Customer element. Designer support is invaluable for validating your XML literals, preventing run time errors when the XML is parsed into XElement objects.

Paste XML as XElement

Unfortunately, C# doesn't have native support for XML literals, which makes generating XML a painful process, even with the new object model. Luckily, there is a time-saving add-in that will paste an XML snippet from the clipboard into the code window as a series of `XElement` objects. This can make a big difference if you have to create XML from scratch. The add-in, PasteXmlAsLinq in the LinqSamples folder, is available in the C# samples that ship with Visual Studio 2010. Simply open the sample in Visual Studio 2010, build the solution, navigate to the output folder, and copy the output files (namely `PasteXmlAsLinq.Addin` and `PasteXmlAsLinq.dll`) to the add-ins folder for Visual Studio 2010. When you restart Visual Studio 2010 you will see a new item, Paste XML as XElement, in the Edit menu when you are working in the code editor window, as you can see in Figure 28-11.

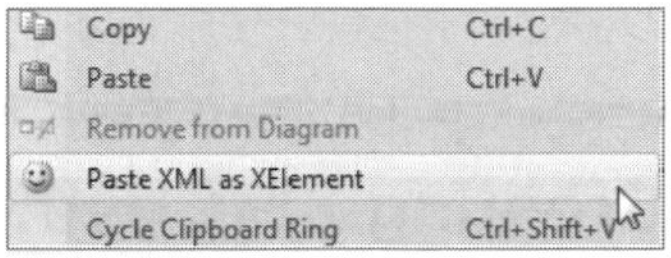

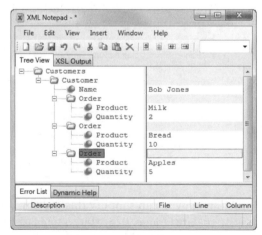

FIGURE 28-11

> *Visual Studio 2010 looks in a variety of places, defined in the Options dialog (Tools menu), for add-ins. Typically, it looks in an add-ins folder located beneath the Visual Studio root documents directory. For example:* `C:\users\username\Documents\Visual Studio 2010\Addins`. *If the* `Addins` *folder doesn't exist, you may need to create it.*

To work with this add-in, all you need to do is to create the XML snippet in your favorite XML editor. In Figure 28-12 we have used XML Notepad, which is a freely available download from `www.microsoft.com`, but you can also use the built-in XML editor within Visual Studio 2010.

Once you have created the XML snippet, copy it to the clipboard (for example, by pressing Ctrl1C). Then place your cursor at the point at which you want to insert the snippet within Visual Studio 2010 and select Paste XML as XElement from the Edit menu. (Of course, if you use this option frequently you may want to assign a shortcut key to it so that you don't have to navigate to the menu.) The code generated by the add-in will look similar to the following:

FIGURE 28-12

C#

```csharp
XElement xml = new XElement("Customers",
                new XElement("Customer",
                    new XAttribute("Name", "Bob Jones"),
                    new XElement("Order",
                        new XAttribute("Product", "Milk"),
                        new XAttribute("Quantity", "2")
```

```
    ),
    new XElement("Order",
        new XAttribute("Product", "Bread"),
        new XAttribute("Quantity", "10")
    ),
    new XElement("Order",
        new XAttribute("Product", "Apples"),
        new XAttribute("Quantity", "5")
))));
```

Code snippet MainForm.cs

Creating XML with LINQ

Although creating XML using the new object model is significantly quicker than previously possible, the real power of the new object model comes when you combine it with LINQ in the form of LINQ to XML (XLINQ). By combining the rich querying capabilities with the ability to create complex XML in a single statement, you can now generate entire XML documents in a single statement. Let's continue with the same example of customers and orders. In this case you have an array of customers, each of whom has any number of orders. What you want to do is create XML that lists the customers and their associated orders. You'll start by creating the customer list, and then introduce the orders.

To begin with, create an XML literal that defines the structure you want to create:

C#

```
XElement customerXml = new XElement("Customers",
                        new XElement("Customer",
                            new XAttribute("Name", "Bob Jones")));
```

VB

```
Dim customerXml = <Customers>
                      <Customer Name="Bob Jones">
                      </Customer>
                  </Customers>
```

Although you can simplify this code by condensing the `Customer` element into `<Customer Name="Bob Jones" />`, you're going to be adding the orders as child elements, so you will use a separate closing XML element.

Expression Holes

If you have multiple customers, the `Customer` element is going to repeat for each one, with Bob Jones being replaced by different customer names. Before you deal with replacing the name, you first need to get the `Customer` element to repeat. You do this by creating an expression hole, using a syntax familiar to anyone who has worked with ASP:

C#

```
XElement customerXml = new XElement("Customers",
                          from c in customers
                          select new XElement("Customer",
                                     new XAttribute("Name",
                                                    "Bob Jones")));
```

VB

```
Dim customerXml = <Customers>
                          <%= From c In customers _
                              Select <Customer Name="Bob Jones">
                                     </Customer> %>
                      </Customers>
```

Here you can see that in the VB code, `<%= %>` has been used to define the expression hole, into which a LINQ statement has been added. This is not required in the C# syntax because the LINQ statement just becomes an argument to the XElement constructor. The Select statement creates a projection to an XML element for each customer in the Customers array, based on the static value "Bob Jones". To change this to return each of the customer names you again have to use an expression hole. Figure 28-13 shows how Visual Studio 2010 provides rich IntelliSense support in these expression holes.

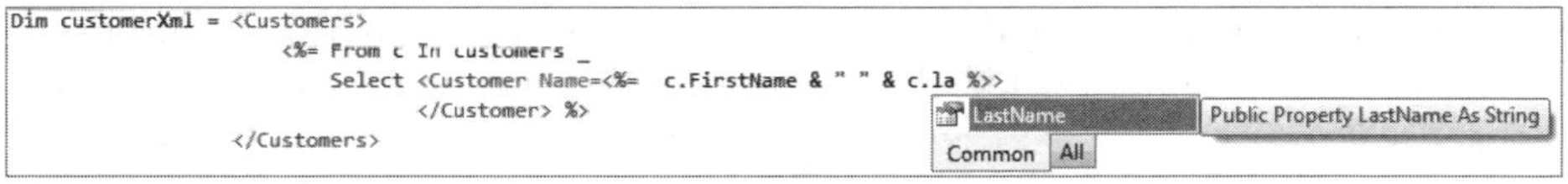

FIGURE 28-13

The following snippet uses the loop variable Name so that you can order the customers based on their full names. This loop variable is then used to set the Name attribute of the customer node.

C#

```
XElement customerXml = new XElement("Customers",
                          from c in customers
                          let name = c.FirstName + " " + c.LastName
                          orderby name
                          select new XElement("Customer",
                                  new XAttribute("Name", name),
                                      from o in c.Orders
                                      select new XElement("Order",
                                              new XAttribute("Product", o.Product),
                                              new XAttribute("Quantity",
                                                             o.Quantity)))));
```

Code snippet MainForm.cs

Available for download on Wrox.com

VB

```vb
Dim customerXml = <Customers>
                       <%= From c In customers _
                           Let Name = c.FirstName & " " & c.LastName _
                           Order By Name _
                           Select <Customer Name=<%= Name %>>
                                       <%= From o In c.Orders _
                                           Select
                                           <Order
                                                Product=<%= o.Product %>
                                                Quantity=<%= o.Quantity %>
                                                  /> %>
                                  </Customer> %>
                   </Customers>
```

Code snippet MainForm.vb

The other thing to notice in this snippet is that you have included the creation of the Order elements for each customer. Although it would appear that the second, nested LINQ statement is independent of the first, there is an implicit joining through the customer loop variable c. Hence, the second LINQ statement is iterating through the orders for a particular customer, creating an Order element with attributes Product and Quantity.

As you can see, the C# equivalent is slightly less easy to read but is by no means more complex. There is no need for expression holes, because C# doesn't support XML literals; instead, the LINQ statement just appears nested within the XML construction. For a complex XML document this would quickly become difficult to work with, which is one reason VB now includes XML literals as a first-class language feature.

QUERYING XML

In addition to enabling you to easily create XML, LINQ can also be used to query XML. The following Customers XML is used in this section to discuss the XLINQ querying capabilities:

```xml
<Customers>
    <Customer Name="Bob Jones">
        <Order Product="Milk" Quantity="2"/>
        <Order Product="Bread" Quantity="10"/>
        <Order Product="Apples" Quantity="5"/>
    </Customer>
</Customers>
```

The following two code snippets show the same query using VB and C#, respectively. In both cases the customerXml variable (an XElement) is queried for all Customer elements, from which the Name attribute is extracted. The Name attribute is then split over the space between names, and the result is used to create a new Customer object.

C#

```csharp
var results = from cust in customerXml.Elements("Customer")
                let  nameBits = cust.Attribute("Name").Value.Split(' ')
                select new Customer() {FirstName = nameBits[0],
                                       LastName=nameBits[1] };
```

Code snippet MainForm.cs

VB

```vb
Dim results = From cust In customerXml.<Customer>
                Let nameBits = cust.@Name.Split(" "c)
                Select New Customer() With {.FirstName = nameBits(0),
                                            .LastName = nameBits(1)}
```

Code snippet MainForm.vb

As you can see, the VB XML language support extends to enabling you to query elements using .<elementName> and attributes using .@attributeName. Figure 28-14 shows the IntelliSense for the customerXml variable, which shows three XML query options.

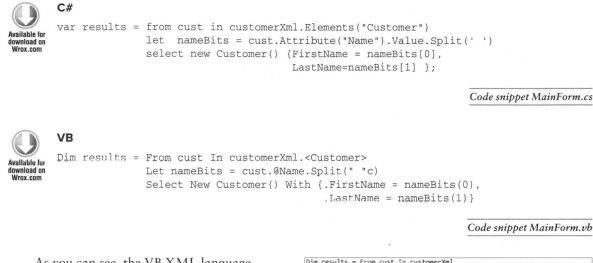

FIGURE 28-14

You have seen the second and third of these options in action in the previous query to extract attribute and element information, respectively. The third option enables you to retrieve all sub-elements that match the supplied element. For example, the following code retrieves all orders in the XML document, irrespective of which customer element they belong to:

```vb
Dim allOrders = From cust In customerXml.<Order>
                Select New Order With {.Product = cust.@Product,
                                       .Quantity = CInt(cust.@Quantity)}
```

SCHEMA SUPPORT

Although VB enables you to query XML using elements and attributes, it doesn't actually provide any validation that you have entered the correct element and attribute names. To reduce the chance of entering the wrong names, you can import an XML schema, which will extend the default IntelliSense support to include the element and attribute names. You import an XML schema as you would any other .NET namespace. First you need to add a reference to the XML schema to your project, and then you need to add an Imports statement to the top of your code file.

> *Unlike other import statements, an XML schema import can't be added in the Project Properties Designer, which means you need to add it to the top of any code file in which you want IntelliSense support.*

If you are working with an existing XML file but don't have a schema handy, manually creating an XML schema just so you can have better IntelliSense support seems like overkill. Luckily, the VB team has included the XML to Schema Inference Wizard in Visual Studio 2010. Once installed, this wizard enables you to create a new XML schema based on an XML snippet or XML source file, or from a URL that contains the XML source. In this example, you're going to start with an XML snippet that looks like the following:

Available for download on Wrox.com

```
<c:Customers xmlns:c="http://www.professionalvisualstudio.com/chapter28/customers">
    <c:Customer Name="Bob Jones">
        <c:Order Product="Milk" Quantity="2" />
        <c:Order Product="Cereal" Quantity="10" />
    </c:Customer>
    <c:Customer Name="Alastair Kelly">
        <c:Order Product="Milk" Quantity="9" />
        <c:Order Product="Bread" Quantity="7" />
    </c:Customer>
</c:Customers>
```

Code snippet customers.xml

Note that unlike the previous XML snippets, this one includes a namespace — this is necessary, because the XML schema import is based on importing a namespace (rather than importing a specific XSD file). To generate an XML schema based on this snippet, start by right-clicking your project in the Solution Explorer and selecting Add New Item. With the XML to Schema Inference Wizard installed, there should be an additional XML To Schema item template, as shown in Figure 28-15.

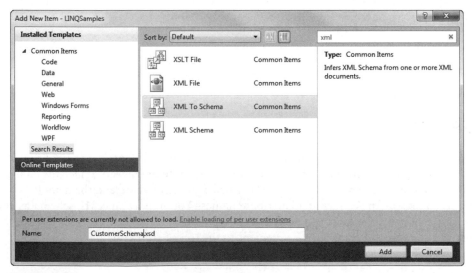

FIGURE 28-15

Selecting this item and clicking OK prompts you to select the location of the XML from which the schema should be generated. Select the Type or Paste XML button and paste the customers XML snippet from earlier into the text area provided. Once you click OK, this generates the `CustomersSchema.xsd` file containing a schema based on the XML resources you have specified.

The next step is to import this schema into your code file by adding an `Imports` statement to the XML namespace, as shown in Figure 28-16.

FIGURE 28-16

Figure 28-16 also contains an alias, c, for the XML namespace, which will be used throughout the code for referencing elements and attributes from this namespace. In your XLINQs you will now see that when you press < or @, the IntelliSense list will contain the relevant elements and attributes from the imported XML schema. In Figure 28-17, you can see these new additions when you begin to query the `customerXml` variable. If you were in a nested XLINQ statement (for example, querying orders for a particular customer), you would see only a subset of the schema elements (that is, just the `c:Order` element).

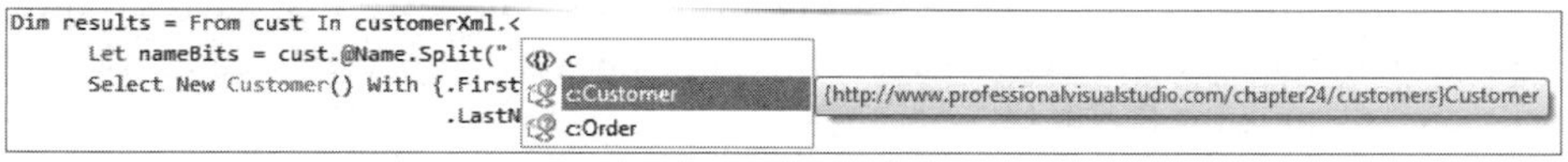

```
Dim results = From cust In customerXml.<
    Let nameBits = cust.@Name.Split("        c
    Select New Customer() With {.First    c:Customer    {http://www.professionalvisualstudio.com/chapter24/customers}Customer
                             .LastN    c:Order
```

FIGURE 28-17

> *It is important to note that importing an XML schema doesn't validate the elements or attributes you use. All it does is improve the level of IntelliSense available to you when you are building your XLINQ.*

LINQ TO SQL

You may be thinking that we are about to introduce you to yet another technology for doing data access. In fact, what you will see is that everything covered in this chapter extends the existing ADO.NET data access model. LINQ to SQL is much more than just the ability to write LINQ statements to query information from a database. It provides an object to a relational mapping layer, capable of tracking changes to existing objects and allowing you to add or remove objects as if they were rows in a database.

Let's get started and look at some of the features of LINQ to SQL and the associated designers on the way. For this section you're going to use the AdventureWorksLT sample database (downloadable from `http://professionalvisualstudio.com/link/1029A`). You're going to end up performing a similar query to what you've seen earlier in the chapter, which was researching customers with a first name greater than or equal to five characters and the average order size for a particular product. Earlier, the product was Milk, but because you are dealing with a bike company you will use the "HL Touring Seat/Saddle" product instead.

Creating the Object Model

For the purpose of this chapter you will be using a normal Visual Basic Windows Forms application from the New Project dialog. You will also need to create a Data Connection to the AdventureWorksLT database (covered in Chapter 27). The next step is to add new LINQ to SQL Classes item, named `AdventureLite.dbml`, from the Add New Item dialog. This will create three files which will be added to your project. These are `AdventureLite.dbml`, which is the mapping file; `AdventureLite.dbml .layout`, which like the class designer is used to lay out the mapping information to make it easier to work with; and finally, `AdventureLite.designer.vb`, which contains the classes into which data is loaded as part of LINQ to SQL.

> *These items may appear as a single item,* `AdventureLite.dbml`, *if you don't have the Show All Files option enabled. Select the project and click the appropriate button at the top of the Solution Explorer tool window.*

Unfortunately, unlike some of the other visual designers in Visual Studio 2010 that have a helpful wizard to get you started, the LINQ to SQL designer initially appears as a blank design surface, as you can see in the center of Figure 28-18.

FIGURE 28-18

On the right side of Figure 28-18, you can see the properties associated with the main design area, which actually represents a DataContext. If you were to compare LINQ with ADO.NET, a LINQ statement equates approximately to a command, whereas a DataContext roughly equates to the connection. It is only roughly because the DataContext actually wraps a database connection in order to provide object life cycle services. For example, when you execute a LINQ to SQL statement it is the DataContext that ends up executing the request to the database, creating the objects based on the return data and then tracking those objects as they are changed or deleted.

If you have worked with the class designer you will be at home with the LINQ to SQL designer. As the instructions in the center of Figure 28-18 indicate, you can start to build your data mappings by dragging items from the Server Explorer (or manually creating them by dragging the item from the Toolbox). In your case you want to expand the Tables node, select the Customer, SalesOrderHeader, SalesOrderDetail, and Product tables, and drag them onto the design surface. You will notice from Figure 28-19 that a number of the classes and properties have been renamed to make the object model easier to read when you are writing LINQ statements. This is a good example of the benefits of separating the object model (for example, Order or OrderItem) from the underlying data (in this case, the SalesOrderHeader and SalesOrderDetail tables). Because you don't need all the properties that are automatically created, it is recommended that you select them in the designer and delete them. The end result should look like Figure 28-19.

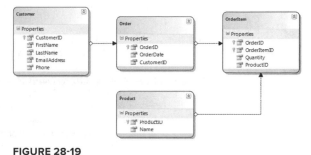

FIGURE 28-19

It is also worth noting that you can modify the details of the association between objects. Figure 28-20 shows the Properties tool window for the association between `Product` and `OrderItem`. Here we have set the generation of the `Child Property` to `False` because we won't need to track back from a `Product` to all the `OrderItems`. We have also renamed the `Parent Property` to `Product` to make the association more intuitive (although note that the name in the drop-down at the top of the Properties window uses the original SQL Server table names).

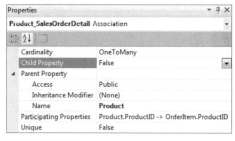

FIGURE 28-20

As you can see, you can control whether properties are created that can be used to navigate between instances of the classes. Though this might seem quite trivial, if you think about what happens if you attempt to navigate from an `Order` to its associated `OrderItems`, you can quickly see that there will be issues if the full object hierarchy hasn't been loaded into memory. For example, in this case if the `OrderItems` aren't already loaded into memory, LINQ to SQL intercepts the navigation, goes to the database, and retrieves the appropriate data in order to populate the `OrderItems`.

The other property of interest in Figure 28-20 is the `Participating Properties`. Editing this property launches an Association Editor window where you can customize the relationship between two LINQ to SQL classes. You can also reach this dialog by right-clicking the association on the design surface and selecting Edit Association. If you drag items from Server Explorer onto the design surface, you are unlikely to need the Association Editor. However, it is particularly useful if you are manually creating a LINQ to SQL mapping, because you can control how the object associations align to the underlying data relationships.

Querying with LINQ to SQL

In the previous chapters you have seen enough LINQ statements to understand how to put together a statement that filters, sorts, aggregates, and projects the relevant data. With this in mind, examine the following LINQ to SQL snippet:

C#

```csharp
public void SampleLinqToSql(){
    using (var aw = new AdventureLiteDataContext()){

        var custs = from c in aw.Customers
                    from o in c.Orders
                    from oi in o.OrderItems
                    where c.FirstName.Length>=5 &&
                        oi.Product.Name == "HL Touring Seat/Saddle"
                    group oi by c into avg
                    let name = avg.Key.FirstName + " " + avg.Key.LastName
                    orderby name
                    select new { Name = name,
                            AverageOrder = avg.Average(oi => oi.Quantity) };
        foreach (var c in custs){
            MessageBox.Show(c.Name + " = " + c.AverageOrder);
        }
    }
}
```

Code snippet MainForm.cs

VB

```vb
Using aw As New AdventureLiteDataContext
    Dim custs = From c In aw.Customers, o In c.Orders, oi In o.OrderItems
                Where c.FirstName.Length >= 5 And
                    oi.Product.Name = "HL Touring Seat/Saddle"
                Group By c Into avg = Average(oi.Quantity)
                Let Name = c.FirstName & " " & c.LastName
                Order By Name
                Select New With {Name, .AverageOrder = avg}

    For Each c In custs
        MessageBox.Show(c.Name & " = " & c.AverageOrder)
    Next
End Using
```

Code snippet MainForm.vb

The biggest difference here is that instead of the `Customer` and `Order` objects existing in memory before the creation and execution of the LINQ statement, now all the data objects are loaded at the point of execution of the LINQ statement. The `AdventureLiteDataContext` is the conduit for opening the connection to the database, forming and executing the relevant SQL statement against the database, and loading the return data into appropriate objects.

You will also note that the LINQ statement has to navigate through the Customers, Orders, OrderItems, and Product tables in order to execute the LINQ statement. Clearly, if this were to be done as a series of SQL statements, it would be horrendously slow. Luckily, the translation of the LINQ statement to SQL commands is done as a single unit.

> *There are some exceptions to this; for example, if you call* ToList *in the middle of your LINQ statement this may result in the separation into multiple SQL statements. Though LINQ to SQL does abstract you away from having to explicitly write SQL commands, you still need to be aware of the way your query will be translated and how it might affect your application performance.*

To view the actual SQL that is generated, you can use the QueryVisualizer sample that ships with Visual Studio 2010 (located in the `LinqSamples` folder of the `CSharpSamples.zip` file found at `C:\Program Files\Microsoft Visual Studio 10.0\Samples\1033`). Open and build this sample and drop the generated file, `LinqToSqlQueryVisualizer.dll`, into your visualizers folder (typically `c:\Users\<username>\Documents\Visual Studio 2010\Visualizers`). When you restart Visual Studio 2010 you will be able to make use of this visualizer to view the actual SQL that is generated by LINQ to SQL for your LINQ statement. Figure 28-21 illustrates the default data tip for the same LINQ to SQL statement in C# (VB is the same, except you don't see the generated SQL in the first line of the data tip).

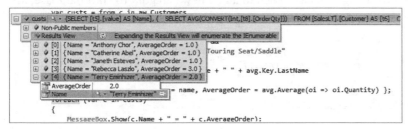

FIGURE 28-21

After adding the visualizer you will see the magnifying glass icon in the first line of the data tip. Clicking this opens up the LINQ to SQL Debug Visualizer so that you can see the way your LINQ to SQL statement is translated to SQL. Figure 28-22 illustrates this visualizer showing the way that the query is parsed by the compiler in the top half of the screen, and the SQL statement that is generated in the lower half of the screen. Clicking the Execute button displays the QueryResult window (inset into Figure 28-22) with the output of the SQL statement. Note that you can modify the SQL statement, allowing you to tweak it until you get the correct results set. This can quickly help you correct any errors in your LINQ statement.

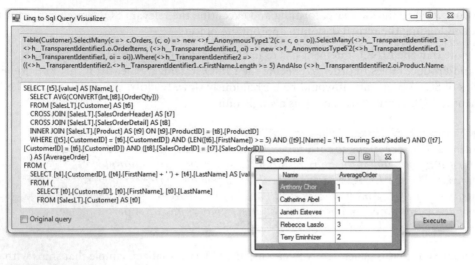

FIGURE 28-22

Inserts, Updates, and Deletes

You can see from the earlier code snippet that the DataContext acts as the conduit through which LINQ to SQL queries are processed. To get a better appreciation of what the DataContext does behind the scenes, let's look at inserting a new product category into the AdventureWorksLT database. Before you can do this you will need to add the ProductCategory table to your LINQ to SQL design surface. In this case you don't need to modify any of the properties, so just drag the ProductCategory table onto the design surface. Then to add a new category to your database, all you need is the following code:

Available for
download on
Wrox.com

C#

```csharp
using(var aw = new AdventureLiteDataContext()){
    var cat = new ProductCategory();
    cat.Name = "Extreme Bike";
    aw.ProductCategories.InsertOnSubmit(cat);
    aw.SubmitChanges();
}
```

Code snippet MainForm.cs

Available for
download on
Wrox.com

VB

```vb
Using aw As New AdventureLiteDataContext
    Dim cat As New ProductCategory
    cat.Name = "Extreme Bike"
    aw.ProductCategories.InsertOnSubmit(cat)
    aw.SubmitChanges()
End Using
```

Code snippet MainForm.vb

This code inserts the new category into the collection of product categories held in memory by the DataContext. When you then call SubmitChanges on the DataContext it is aware that you have added a new product category so it will insert the appropriate records. A similar process is used when making changes to existing items. In the following example you retrieve the product category you just inserted using the Contains syntax. Because there is likely to be only one match, you can use the FirstOrDefault extension method to give you just a single product category to work with:

Available for
download on
Wrox.com

C#

```csharp
using (var aw = new AdventureLiteDataContext()){
    var cat = (from pc in aw.ProductCategories
                  where pc.Name.Contains("Extreme")
                  select pc).FirstOrDefault();
    cat.Name = "Extreme Offroad Bike";
    aw.SubmitChanges();
}
```

Code snippet MainForm.cs

Available for
download on
Wrox.com

VB

```vb
Using aw As New AdventureLiteDataContext
    Dim cat = (From pc In aw.ProductCategories
                  Where pc.Name.Contains("Extreme")).FirstOrDefault
    cat.Name = "Extreme Offroad Bike"
    aw.SubmitChanges()
End Using
```

Code snippet MainForm.cs

Once the change to the category name has been made, you just need to call SubmitChanges on the DataContext in order for it to issue the update on the database. Without going into too much detail the DataContext essentially tracks changes to each property on a LINQ to SQL object so that it knows which objects need updating when SubmitChanges is called. If you want to delete an object, you simply need to obtain an instance of the LINQ to SQL object, in the same way as for doing an update, and then call DeleteOnSubmit on the appropriate collection. For example, to delete a product category you would call aw.ProductCategories.DeleteOnSubmit(categoryToDelete), followed by aw.SubmitChanges.

Stored Procedures

One of the questions frequently asked about LINQ to SQL is whether you can use your own stored procedures in place of the run time-generated SQL. The good news is that for inserts, updates, and deletes you can easily specify the stored procedure that should be used. You can also use existing stored procedures for creating instances of LINQ to SQL objects. Let's start by adding a simple stored procedure to the AdventureWorksLT database. To do this, right-click the Stored Procedures node under the database connection in the Server Explorer tool window and select Add

New Stored Procedure. This opens a code window with a new stored procedure template. In the following code you have selected to return the five fields that are relevant to your `Customer` object:

```
CREATE PROCEDURE dbo.GetCustomers
AS
BEGIN
    SET NOCOUNT ON
    SELECT c.CustomerID, c.FirstName, c.LastName, c.EmailAddress, c.Phone
    FROM SalesLT.Customer AS c
END;
```

Once you have saved this stored procedure it will appear under the Stored Procedures node. If you now open up the AdventureLite LINQ to SQL designer, you can drag this stored procedure across into the right-hand pane of the design surface. In Figure 28-23 you can see that the return type of the `GetCustomers` method is set to Auto-generated Type. This means that you will only be able to query information in the returned object. Ideally, you would want to be able to make changes to these objects and be able to use the DataContext to persist those changes back to the database.

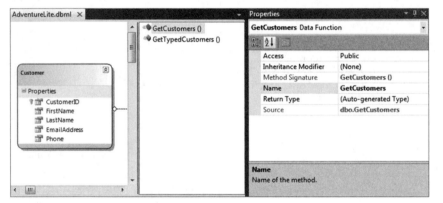

FIGURE 28-23

The second method, `GetTypedCustomers`, actually has the Return Type set as the `Customer` class. To create this method you can either drag the `GetCustomers` stored procedure to the right pane, and then set the Return Type to `Customer`, or you can drag the stored procedure onto the `Customer` class in the left pane of the design surface. The latter will still create the method in the right pane, but it will automatically specify the return type as the `Customer` type.

> *Note that you don't need to align properties with the stored procedure columns, because this mapping is automatically handled by the DataContext. This is a double-edged sword: clearly it works when the column names map to the source columns of the LINQ to SQL class but it may cause a run time exception if there are missing columns or columns that don't match.*

Once you have defined these stored procedures as methods on the design surface, calling them is as easy as calling the appropriate method on the DataContext:

Available for download on Wrox.com

C#

```
using (var aw = new AdventureLiteDataContext()){
    var customers = aw.GetCustomers();
    foreach (var c in customers){
        MessageBox.Show(c.FirstName);
    }
}
```

Code snippet MainForm.cs

Available for download on Wrox.com

VB

```
Using aw As New AdventureLiteDataContext
    Dim customers = aw.GetCustomers

    For Each c In customers
        MsgBox(c.FirstName)
    Next
End Using
```

Code snippet MainForm.vb

Here you have seen how you can use a stored procedure to create instances of the LINQ to SQL classes. If you instead want to update, insert, or delete objects using stored procedures, you follow a similar process except you need to define the appropriate behavior on the LINQ to SQL class. To begin with, create an insert stored procedure for a new product category:

```
CREATE PROCEDURE dbo.InsertProductCategory
   (
   @categoryName nvarchar(50),
   @categoryId int OUTPUT
   )
AS
BEGIN
    INSERT INTO SalesLT.ProductCategory (Name) VALUES (@categoryName)
    SELECT @categoryId=@@identity
END;
```

Following the same process as before, you need to drag this newly created stored procedure from the Server Explorer across into the right pane of the LINQ to SQL design surface. Then in the Properties tool window for the `ProductCategory` class, modify the `Insert` property. This will open the dialog shown in Figure 28-24. Here you can select whether you want to use the run time-generated code or customize the method that is used. In Figure 28-24 the `InsertProductCategory` method has been

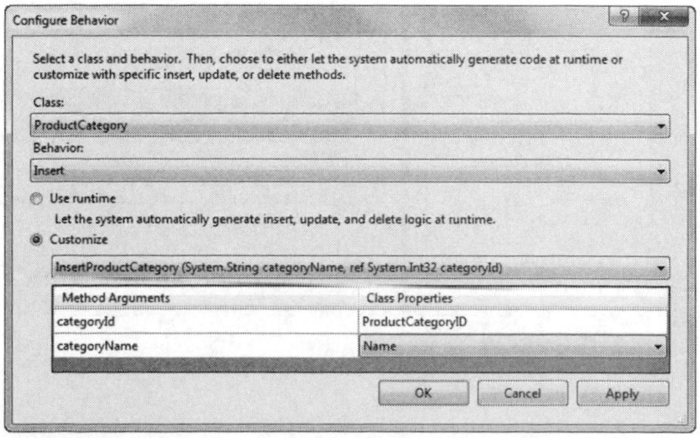

FIGURE 28-24

selected. Initially, the Class Properties will be unspecified, because Visual Studio 2010 wasn't able to guess at which properties mapped to the method arguments. It's easy enough to align these to the id and name properties. Now when the DataContext goes to insert a ProductCategory it will use the stored procedure instead of the run time-generated SQL statement.

Binding LINQ to SQL Objects

The important thing to remember when using DataBinding with LINQ to SQL objects is that they are in fact normal .NET objects. This means that you can create a new object data source via the Data Sources tool window. In the case of the examples you have seen so far, you would go through the Add New Data Source Wizard, selecting just the Customer object. Because the Order and OrderItem objects are accessible via the navigation properties Orders and then OrderItems, you don't need to explicitly add them to the Data Source window.

Once you have created the object data source (see the left side of Figure 28-25), you can then proceed to drag the nodes onto your form to create the appropriate data components. Starting with the Customer node, use the drop-down to specify that you want a DataGridView, then drag it onto your form. Next, you need to specify that you want the Orders (a child node under Customer) to appear as details and then drag this to the form as well. You will notice that you don't get a binding navigator for this binding source, so from the Toolbox add a BindingNavigator to your form and set its BindingSource property to be the OrdersBindingSource that was created when you dragged over the Orders node. Lastly, you want to display all the OrderItems in a DataGridView, so use the drop-down to set this and then drag the node onto the form. After doing all this you should end up with something similar to Figure 28-25. Note that we have also included a button that you will use to load the data and we have laid the Order information out in a panel to improve the layout.

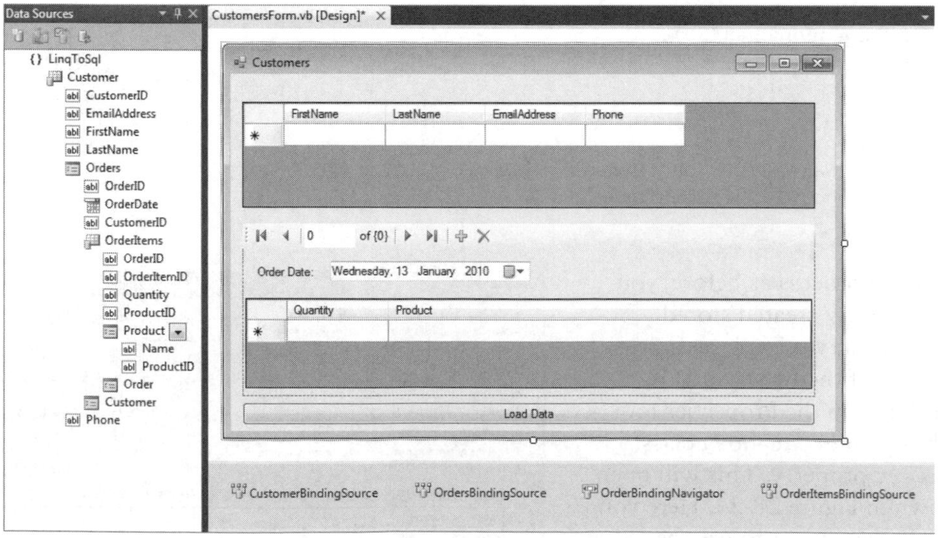

FIGURE 28-25

One of the things you will have noticed is that the columns on your OrderItems data grid don't match those in Figure 28-25. By default, you will get Quantity, Order, and Product columns. Clearly, the last two columns are not going to display anything of interest, but you don't really have an easy way to display the Name of the product in the order with the current LINQ to SQL objects. Luckily, there is an easy way to effectively hide the navigation from OrderItem to Product so that the name of the product will appear as a property of OrderItem.

You do this by adding your own property to the `OrderItem` class. Each LINQ to SQL class is generated as a partial class, which means that extending the class is as easy as right-clicking the class in the LINQ to SQL designer and selecting View Code. This generates a custom code file, in this case `AdventureLite.vb` (or `AdventureLite.cs`), and includes the partial class definition. You can then proceed to add your own code. In the following snippet we have added the `Product` property that will simplify access to the name of the product being ordered:

C#

```csharp
partial class OrderItem{
    public string ProductName{
        get{
            return this.Product.Name;
        }
    }
}
```

Code snippet AdventureLite.cs

VB

```vb
Partial Class OrderItem
    Public ReadOnly Property ProductName() As String
        Get
            Return Me.Product.Name
        End Get
    End Property
End Class
```

Code snippet AdventureLite.vb

For some reason this property, perhaps because it is added to a second code file, will not be detected by the Data Sources tool window. However, you can still bind the Product column to this property by manually setting the `DataPropertyName` field in the Edit Columns dialog for the data grid.

The last thing to do is to actually load the data when the user clicks the button. To do this you can use the following code:

C#

```csharp
private void btnLoadData_Click(object sender, EventArgs e){
    using (var aw = new AdventureLiteDataContext()){
```

```
        var cust = aw.Customers;
        this.customerBindingSource.DataSource = cust;
    }
}
```

VB

```
Private Sub btnLoad_Click(ByVal sender As System.Object, _
                    ByVal e As System.EventArgs) Handles btnLoad.Click
    Using aw As New AdventureLiteDataContext
        Dim custs = From c In aw.Customers
        Me.CustomerBindingSource.DataSource = custs
    End Using
End Sub
```

You will notice that your application will now run, and when the user clicks the button the customer information will be populated in the top data grid. However, no matter which customer you select, no information will appear in the Order information area. The reason for this is that LINQ to SQL uses lazy loading to retrieve information as it is required. Using the data visualizer you were introduced to earlier, if you inspect the query in this code you will see that it contains only the customer information:

```
SELECT [t0].[CustomerID], [t0].[FirstName], [t0].[LastName], [t0].[EmailAddress],
[t0].[Phone]
FROM [SalesLT].[Customer] AS [t0]
```

You have two ways to resolve this issue. The first is to force LINQ to SQL to bring back all the Order, OrderItem, and Product data as part of the initial query. To do this, modify the button click code to the following:

C#

```
private void btnLoadData_Click(object sender, EventArgs e){
    using (var aw = new AdventureLiteDataContext()){
        var loadOptions =new System.Data.Linq.DataLoadOptions();
        loadOptions.LoadWith<Customer>(c=>c.Orders);
        loadOptions.LoadWith<Order>(o=>o.OrderItems);
        loadOptions.LoadWith<OrderItem>(o=>o.Product);
        aw.LoadOptions = loadOptions;

        var cust = aw.Customers;
        this.customerBindingSource.DataSource = cust;
    }
}
```

VB

```
Private Sub btnLoad_Click(ByVal sender As System.Object,
                    ByVal e As System.EventArgs) Handles btnLoad.Click
    Using aw As New AdventureLiteDataContext
        Dim loadOptions As New System.Data.Linq.DataLoadOptions
```

```
loadOptions.LoadWith(Of Customer)(Function(c As Customer) c.Orders)
loadOptions.LoadWith(Of Order)(Function(o As Order) o.OrderItems)
loadOptions.LoadWith(Of OrderItem)(Function(oi As OrderItem) _
                    oi.Product)
aw.LoadOptions = loadOptions

Dim custs = From c In aw.Customers
Me.CustomerBindingSource.DataSource = aw.Customers
    End Using
End Sub
```

Essentially what this code tells the DataContext is that when it retrieves `Customer` objects it should forcibly navigate to the `Orders` property. Similarly, the `Order` objects navigate to the `OrderItems` property, and so on. One thing to be aware of is that this solution could perform really badly if there are a large number of customers. In fact as the number of customers and orders increases, this will perform progressively worse, so this is not a great solution; but it does illustrate how you can use the `LoadOptions` property of the DataContext.

The other alternative is to not dispose of the DataContext. You need to remember what is happening behind the scenes with DataBinding. When you select a customer in the data grid, this will cause the OrderBindingSource to refresh. It tries to navigate to the `Orders` property on the customer. If you have disposed of the DataContext, there is no way that the `Orders` property can be populated. So the better solution to this problem is to change the code to the following:

C#

```
private AdventureLiteDataContext aw = new AdventureLiteDataContext();
private void btnLoadData_Click(object sender, EventArgs e){
    var cust = aw.Customers;
    this.customerBindingSource.DataSource = cust;
}
```

Code snippet CustomersForm.cs

VB

```
Private aw As New AdventureLiteDataContext()
Private Sub btnLoad_Click(ByVal sender As System.Object, _
                    ByVal e As System.EventArgs) Handles btnLoad.Click
    Dim custs = From c In aw.Customers
    Me.CustomerBindingSource.DataSource = custs
End Sub
```

Code snippet CustomersForm.vb

Because the DataContext will still exist, when the binding source navigates to the various properties, LINQ to SQL will kick in, populating these properties with data. This is much more scalable than attempting to populate the whole customer hierarchy when the user clicks the button.

LINQPAD

While the intent behind LINQ was to make code more readable, in a lot of cases it has made writing and debugging queries much harder. The fact that LINQ expressions are only executed when the results are iterated can lead to confusion and unexpected results. One of the most useful tools to have by your side when writing LINQ expressions is Joseph Albahari's LINQPad (`www.linqpad.net`). Figure 28-26 illustrates how you can use the editor in the top-right pane to write expressions.

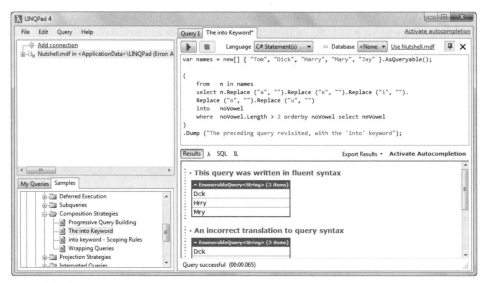

FIGURE 28-26

In the lower-right pane you can see the output from executing the expression. You can tweak your LINQ expression to get the correct output without having to build and run your entire application.

SUMMARY

In this chapter you were introduced to Language Integrated Queries (LINQ), a significant step toward a common programming model for data access. You can see that LINQ statements help to make your code more readable, because you don't have to code all the details of how the data should be iterated, the conditional statements for selecting objects, or the code for building the results set.

You were also introduced to the new XML object model, the XML language integration within VB, how LINQ can be used to query XML documents, and how Visual Studio 2010 IntelliSense enables a rich experience for working with XML in VB.

Finally, you were introduced to LINQ to SQL and how you can use it as a basic object-relational mapping framework. Although you are somewhat limited in being able only to map an object to a single table, it can still dramatically simplify working with a database.

In the next chapter you see how powerful LINQ is as a technology when you combine it with the ADO.NET Entity Framework to manage the life cycle of your objects. With much more sophisticated mapping capabilities, this technology will dramatically change the way you will work with data in the future.

The ADO.NET Entity Framework

WHAT'S IN THIS CHAPTER?

➤ Understanding the Entity Framework

➤ Creating an Entity Framework model

➤ Querying Entity Framework models

One of the core requirements in business applications (and many other types of applications) is the ability to store and retrieve data in a database. However, that's easier said than done, because the relational schema of a database does not blend well with the object hierarchies that we prefer to work with in code. To create and populate these object hierarchies required a lot of code to be written to transfer data from a data reader into a developer-friendly object model, which was then usually difficult to maintain. In fact, it was such a source of constant frustration that many developers turned to writing code generators or various other tools that automatically created the code to access a database based on its structure. However, code generators usually created a 1:1 mapping between the database structure and the object model, which was hardly ideal either, leading to a problem called "object relational impedance mismatch," where how data was stored in the database did not necessarily have a direct relationship with how developers wanted to model the data as objects. This led to the concept of Object Relational Mapping, where an ideal object model could be designed for working with data in code, which could then be mapped to the schema of a database. Once the mapping is complete, the Object Relational Mapper (ORM) framework should take over the burden of translating between the object model and the database, leaving developers to focus on actually solving the business problem (rather than focusing on the technological issues of working with data).

To many developers, ORMs are the Holy Grail for working with data in a database as objects, and there's no shortage of debate over the strengths and pitfalls of the various ORM tools available, and how an ideal ORM should be designed. We won't buy into these arguments in this chapter, but simply look at how to use the ADO.NET Entity Framework — Microsoft's ORM tool and framework.

Looking through history, the .NET Framework added a number of means to access data in a database since its inception, all under the banner of ADO.NET. First, we had low-level access through SqlConnection (and connections for other types of databases) using means like data readers. Then we had a higher-level means of accessing data using Typed DataSets. LINQ to SQL appeared in the .NET Framework 3.5, providing the first built-in way to work with data as objects.

However, for a long time Microsoft did not include an ORM tool in the .NET Framework (despite a number of earlier attempts to do so with the failed ObjectSpaces). There were already a number of ORMs available for use with the .NET Framework, with nHibernate and LLBLGen Pro being among the most popular. Microsoft did eventually manage to release its own, which it called the ADO.NET Entity Framework, and shipped it with the .NET Framework 3.5 SP1.

The Entity Framework's eventual release (despite being long awaited) was not smooth sailing either — with controversy generated before it was even released by a vote of no confidence petition signed by many developers, including a number of Microsoft MVPs. Indeed, it was the technology that provided the catalyst leading to the rise of the ALT.NET movement. However, since then there have been many improvements in the .NET Framework 4's Entity Framework implementation in order to reduce these perceived shortcomings.

This chapter takes you through the process of creating an Entity Framework model of a database, and how to query and update the database via it. The Entity Framework is a huge topic, with entire books devoted to its use. Therefore, it would be impossible to go through all its features, so this chapter focuses on discussing some of its core features and how to get started and create a basic entity model.

The Entity Framework model you create in this chapter will go on to be used in a number of subsequent chapters in this book where database access is required in the samples.

WHAT IS THE ENTITY FRAMEWORK?

Essentially, the Entity Framework is an Object Relational Mapper. Object Relational Mapping enables you to create a conceptual object model, map it to the database, and the ORM framework will take care of translating your queries over the object model to queries in the database, returning the data as the objects that you've defined in your model.

Comparison with LINQ to SQL

A common question from developers is regarding the Entity Framework's relationship with LINQ to SQL, and which technology they should use when creating data-centric applications. Let's take a look at the advantages each have over the other.

LINQ to SQL advantages over the Entity Framework:

➤ Easy to get started and query

Entity Framework advantages over LINQ to SQL:

➤ Enables you to build a conceptual model of the database rather than purely working with a 1:1 domain model of the database as objects (such as having one object mapped to multiple database tables, inheritance support, and defining complex properties).

➤ Able to generate a database from your entity model.

➤ Support for databases other than just SQL Server.

➤ Support for many-to-many relationships.

➤ Lazy loading and eager loading support.

➤ Synchronization to get database updates will not lose your customizations to your model.

➤ Will continue to evolve, whereas LINQ to SQL development will from now on be minimal.

Entity Framework Concepts

Here are some of the important concepts involved in the Entity Framework and some of the terms that are used throughout this chapter:

➤ **Entity Model:** The entity model you create using the Entity Framework consists of three parts:

➤ **Conceptual model:** Represents the object model, including the entities, their properties, and the associations between them.

➤ **Store model:** Represents the database structure, including the tables/views/stored procedures, columns, foreign keys, and so on.

➤ **Mapping:** Provides the glue between the store model and the conceptual model (that is, between the database and the object model), by mapping one to the other.

Each of these parts is maintained by the Entity Framework as XML using a domain-specific language (DSL).

➤ **Entity:** Entities are essentially just objects (with properties) to which a database model is mapped.

➤ **Entity Set:** An entity set is a collection of a given entity. You can think of it as an entity being a row in a database, and an entity set being the table.

➤ **Association:** Associations define relationships between entities in your entity model, and are conceptually the same as relationships in a database. Associations are used to traverse the data in your entity model between entities.

➤ **Mapping:** Mapping is the core concept of ORM. It's essentially the translation layer from a relational schema in a database to objects in code.

GETTING STARTED

To demonstrate some of the various features in the Entity Framework, the example in this section uses the AdventureWorksLT sample database developed by Microsoft as one of the sample databases for SQL Server. AdventureWorksLT is a simpler version of the full AdventureWorks database, making it somewhat easier to demonstrate the concepts of the Entity Framework without the additional complexity that using the full database would create.

The AdventureWorksLT database is available for download from the CodePlex web site as a database script here:
http://professionalvisualstudio.com/link/1029A

Adventure Works Cycles is a fictional bicycle sales chain, and the AdventureWorksLT database is used to store and access its product sales data.

Follow the instructions from the CodePlex web site detailing how to install the database from the downloaded script in a SQL Server instance (SQL Server Express Edition is sufficient) that is on or can be accessed by your development machine.

Now move on to creating a project that contains an Entity Framework model of this database. Start by opening the New Project dialog and creating a new project. The sample project you create in this chapter uses the WPF project template. You'll be displaying data in a WPF DataGrid control defined in the `MainWindow.xaml` file named `dgEntityFrameworkData`.

Now that you have a project that will host and query an Entity Framework model, it's time to create that model.

CREATING AN ENTITY MODEL

You have two ways of going about creating an entity model. The usual means to do so is to create the model based on the structure of an existing database; however, with the Entity Framework it is also possible to start with a blank model and have the Entity Framework generate a database structure from it.

The sample project uses the first method to create an entity model based on the AdventureWorksLT database's structure.

The Entity Data Model Wizard

Open the Add New Item dialog for your project, navigate to the Data category, and select ADO.NET Entity Data Model as the item template (as shown in Figure 29-1). Call it `AdventureWorksLTModel .edmx`.

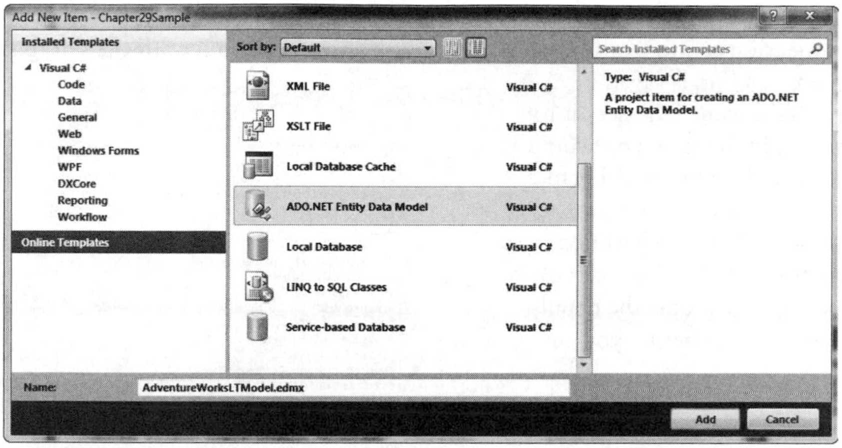

FIGURE 29-1

This will start the Entity Data Model Wizard that will help you get started building an Entity Framework model.

This will show the dialog shown in Figure 29-2 that enables you to select whether you want to automatically create a model from a database (Generate from Database), or start with an empty model (Empty Model).

The Empty Model option is useful when you want to take the approach of creating your model from scratch, and either mapping it manually to a given database, or letting the Entity Framework create a database based on your model.

However, as previously stated you will be creating an entity model from the AdventureWorksLT database, so for the purpose of this example use the Generate from Database option, and get the wizard to help you create the entity model from the database.

Moving onto the next step, you now need to create a connection to the database (as shown in Figure 29-3). You can find the most recent database connection you've created in the drop-down list, but if it's not there (such as if this is the first time you've created a connection to this database) you will need to create a new connection. To do so, click the New Connection button and go through the standard procedure of selecting the SQL Server instance, authentication credentials, and finally, selecting the database.

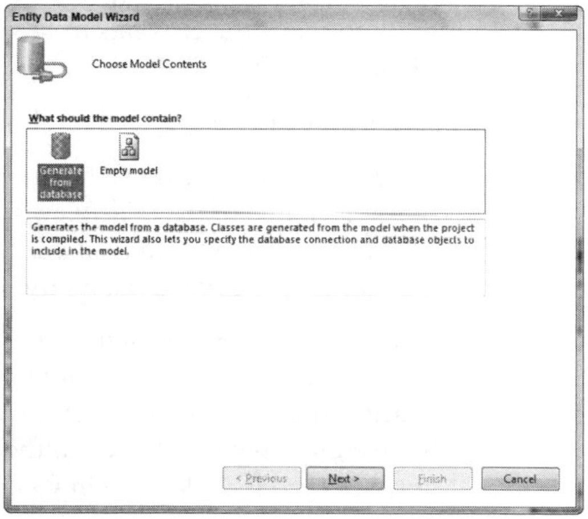

FIGURE 29-2

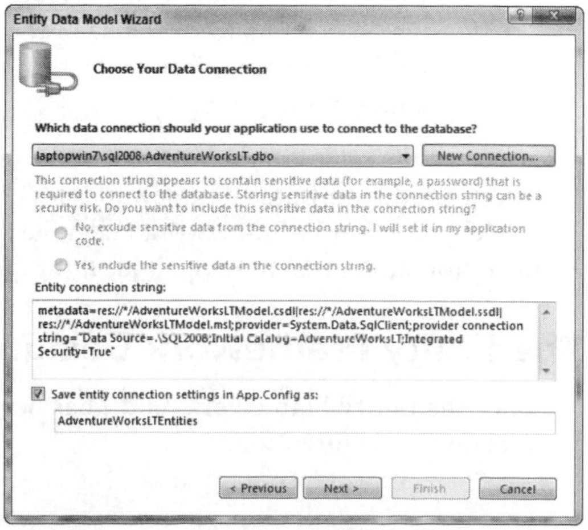

FIGURE 29-3

If you are using a username and password as your authentication details, you can choose not to include those in the connection string (containing the details required to connect to the database) when it is saved, because this string is saved in plain text that would enable anyone who sees it to have access to the database. In this case you would have to provide these credentials to the model before querying it in order for it to create a connection to the database. If you don't select the checkbox to save the connection settings in the `App.config` file you will also need to pass the model the details on how to connect to the database before you can query it.

In the next step, the wizard uses the connection created in the previous step to connect to the database and retrieve its structure (that is, its tables, views, and stored procedures), which is displayed in a tree for you to select the elements to be included in your model (see Figure 29-4).

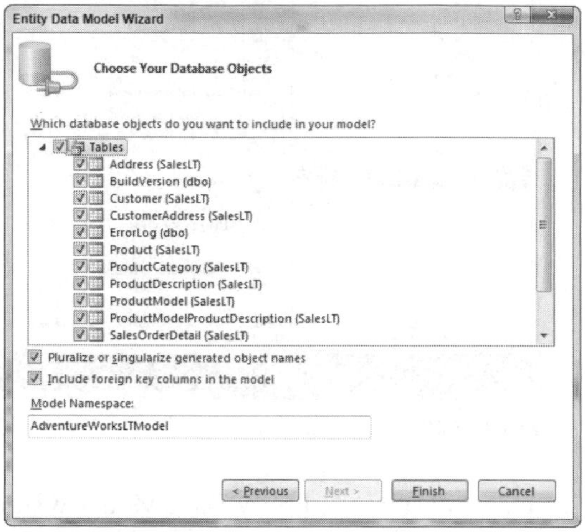

FIGURE 29-4

Other options that can be specified on this screen include:

> **Pluralize or Singularize Generated Object Names:** This option (when selected) intelligently takes the name of the table/view/stored procedure and pluralizes or singularizes the name based on how that name is used in the model (collections will use the plural form, entities will use the singular form, and so on).

> **Include Foreign Key Columns in the Model:** The previous version of the Entity Framework did not create properties for foreign key columns in the entities — opting to create a relationship instead. However, in numerous scenarios this was not ideal, making it messy to do some simple tasks due to the absence of these properties. In this new version you can now select to include them in your entities by selecting this option.

> **Model Namespace:** This enables you to specify the namespace in which all the classes related to the model will be created. By default, the model will exist in its own namespace (which defaults to the name of the model entered in the Add New Item dialog) rather than the default namespace of the project to avoid conflict with existing classes with the same names in the project.

Select all the tables in the database to be included in the model. Clicking the Finish button in this screen creates an Entity Framework model that maps to the database. From here you can view the model in the Entity Framework and adjust it as per your requirements and tidy it up as per your tastes (or standards) to make it ideal for querying in your code.

The Entity Framework Designer

Once the Entity Framework model has been generated, it opens in the Entity Framework designer, as shown in Figure 29-5.

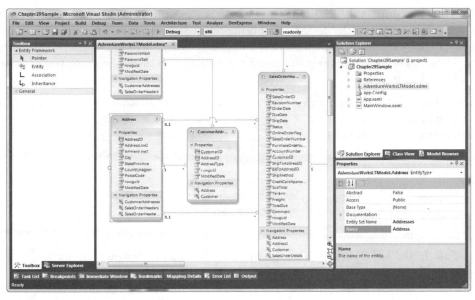

FIGURE 29-5

You'll note that the designer has automatically laid out the entities that were created by the wizard, showing the associations it has created between them.

You can move entities around on the designer surface, and the designer will automatically move the association lines and try and keep them neatly laid out. Entities will automatically snap to a grid, which you can view by right-clicking the designer surface and selecting Grid ⇨ Show Grid from the context menu. You can disable the snapping by right-clicking the designer surface and unchecking Grid ⇨ Snap to Grid from the context menu to have finer control over the diagram layout, but you will find that entities line up better (and hence make the diagram neater) by leaving the snapping on.

As you move entities around (or add additional entities to) the diagram, you may find it gets a little messy, with association lines going in all directions to avoid getting "tangled." To get the designer to automatically lay out the entities neatly again according to its own algorithms, you can right-click the designer surface and select Diagram ⇨ Layout Diagram from the context menu.

Entity Framework models can quickly become large and difficult to navigate in the Entity Framework designer. Luckily, the designer has a few tools to make navigating it a little easier. The designer enables you to zoom in and out using the zoom buttons in its bottom-right corner (below the vertical scrollbar — see Figure 29-6). The button sandwiched between these zoom in/out buttons zooms to 100% when clicked.

FIGURE 29-6

To zoom to a predefined percentage, right-click the designer surface and select one of the options in the Zoom menu. In this menu you will also find a Zoom to Fit option (to fit the entire entity model within the visible portion of the designer), and a Custom option that pops up a dialog enabling you to type a specific zoom level.

In addition, selecting an entity in the Properties tool window (from the drop-down object selector) automatically selects that entity in the designer and brings it into view; right-clicking the entity in the Model Browser tool window (described shortly) and selecting the Show in Designer menu item does the same. These make it easy to navigate to a particular entity in the designer, so you can make any modifications as required.

You can minimize the space taken by entities by clicking the icon in the top-right corner of the entity. Alternatively, you can roll up the Properties/Navigation Properties groupings by clicking the +/– icons to their left. Figure 29-7 shows an entity in its normal expanded state, with the Properties/Navigation Properties groupings rolled up and completely rolled up.

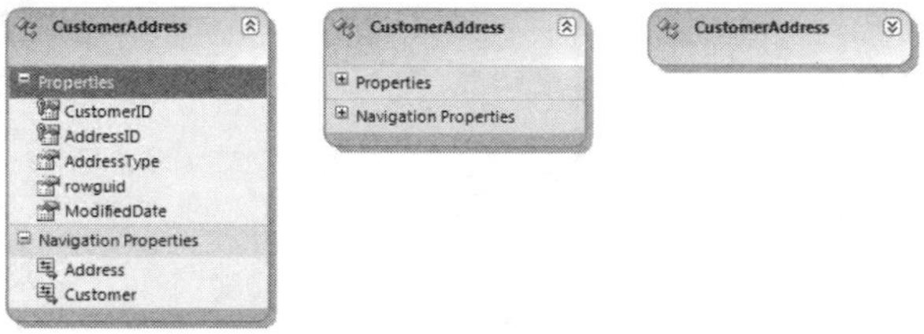

FIGURE 29-7

You can expand all the collapsed entities in one go by right-clicking the designer surface and selecting Diagram ⇨ Expand All from the context menu. Alternatively, you can collapse all the entities in the diagram by right-clicking the designer surface and selecting Diagram ⇨ Collapse All from the context menu.

A visual representation of an entity model (as provided by the Entity Framework designer) can serve a useful purpose in the design documentation for your application. The designer provides a means to save the model layout to an image file to help in this respect. Right-click anywhere on the designer surface and select Diagram ⇨ Export as Image from the context menu. This pops up the Save As dialog for you to select where to save the image. Note that it defaults to saving as a bitmap (.bmp) — if you open the Save As Type drop-down list you will find that it can also save to JPEG, GIF, PNG, and TIFF. PNG is probably the best choice for quality and file size.

It can often be useful (especially when saving a diagram for documentation) to display the property types against each property for an entity in the designer. You can turn this on by right-clicking the designer surface and selecting Scalar Property Format ⇨ Display Name and Type from the context menu. You can return to displaying just the property name by selecting the Scalar Property Format ⇨ Display Name item from the right-click context menu.

As with most designers in Visual Studio, the Toolbox and Properties tool windows are integral parts of working with the designer. The Toolbox (as shown in Figure 29-8) contains three controls: Entity, Association, and Inheritance. How to use these controls with the designer is covered shortly. The Properties tool window displays the properties of the selected item(s) in the designer (an entity, association, or inheritance), enabling you to modify their values as required.

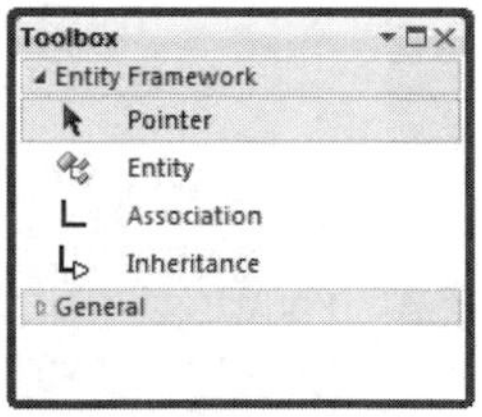

FIGURE 29-8

In addition to the Toolbox and Properties tool windows, the Entity Framework designer also incorporates two other tool windows specific to it — the Model Browser tool window and the Mapping Details tool window — for working with the data.

The Model Browser tool window (as shown in Figure 29-9) enables you to browse the hierarchy of both the conceptual entity model of the database and its storage model. Clicking an element in the Store model hierarchy shows its properties in the Properties tool window; however, these can't be modified (because this is an entity modeling tool, not a database modeling tool). The only changes you can make to the Store model is to delete tables, views, and stored procedures (which won't modify the underlying database). Clicking elements in the Conceptual model hierarchy also shows their properties in the Properties tool window (which can be modified), and its mappings are displayed in the Mapping Details tool window. Right-clicking an entity in the hierarchy and selecting the Show in Designer menu item from the context menu brings the selected entity/association into view in the designer.

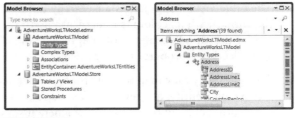

FIGURE 29-9

The second picture in Figure 29-9 demonstrates the searching functionality available in the Model Browser tool window. As previously discussed, because your entity model can get quite large, it can be difficult to find exactly what you are after. Therefore, a good search function is very important. Type your search term in the search textbox at the top of the window and press Enter. In this example the search term was Address, which highlighted all the names in the hierarchy (including entities, associations, properties, and so on) that contained the search term. You'll note that the vertical scrollbar has the places in the hierarchy (which has been expanded) highlighted where the search terms have been found, making it easy to see where the results were found throughout the hierarchy. The number of results is shown just below the search textbox, next to which are an up arrow and a down arrow to enable you to navigate through the results. When you are finished searching you can click the cross icon next to these to return the window to normal.

The Mapping Details tool window (as shown in Figure 29-10) enables you to modify the mapping between the conceptual model and the storage model for an entity. Selecting an entity in the designer, the Model Browser tool window, or the Properties tool window shows the mappings in this tool window between the properties of the entity to columns in the database. You have two ways of mapping the properties of an entity to the database: either via tables and views, or via functions (that is, stored procedures). On the left side of the tool window are two icons, enabling you to swap the view between mapping to tables and views, to mapping to functions. However, we'll focus here just on the features of mapping entity properties to tables and views.

FIGURE 29-10

The table/view mapping has a hierarchy (under the Column column) showing the table(s) mapped to the entity, with its columns underneath it. To these columns you can map properties on your entity (under the Value/Property column) by clicking in the cell, opening the drop-down list that appears, and selecting a property from the list.

A single entity may map to more than one database table/view (bringing two or more tables/views into a single entity, as previously discussed). To add another table/view to the hierarchy to map to your entity, click in the bottom row where it says <Add a Table or View> and select a table/view from the drop-down list. When you add a table to the Mapping Details tool window for mapping to an entity, it automatically matches columns with the same name to properties on the entities and creates a mapping between them. Delete a table from the hierarchy by selecting its row and pressing the Delete key.

Conditions are a powerful feature of the Entity Framework that enable you to selectively choose which table you want to map an entity to at run time based on one or more conditions that you specify. For example, say you have a single entity in your model called Product that maps to a table called Products in the database. However, you have additional extended properties on your entity that map to one of two tables based on the value of the `ProductType` property on the entity — if the product is of a particular type it will map the columns to one table, if it's another type it will map the columns to the other table. You can do this by adding a condition to the table mapping. In the Mapping Details window click in the row directly below a table to selectively map where it says <Add a Condition>. Open the drop-down list that appears, which will contain all the properties on the entity. Select the property to base your condition on (in the given example it would be the `ProductType` property), select an operator, and enter a value to compare the property to. Note that there are only two operators: equals (=) and Is. You can add additional conditions as necessary to determine whether the table should be used as the source of the data for the given properties.

> *Note that a number of advanced features are available in the Entity Framework, but not available in the Entity Framework designer (such as working with the store schema, annotations, referencing other models, and so on). However, these actions can be performed by modifying the schema files (which are XML files) directly.*

Creating/Modifying Entities

The Entity Data Model Wizard gave you a good starting point by building an entity model for you. In some cases this may be good enough and you can start writing the code to query it, but you can now take the opportunity to go through the created model and modify its design as per your requirements.

Because the Entity Framework is providing you with a conceptual model to design and work with, you are no longer limited to having a 1:1 relationship between the database schema and an object model in code, so the changes you make in the entity model won't affect the database in any way. So you may wish to delete properties from entities, change their names, and so on, and it will have no effect on the database. In addition, because any changes you make are in the conceptual model, updating the model from the database will not affect the conceptual model (only the storage model), so your changes won't be lost.

Changing Property Names

Often you will find yourself working with databases that have tables and columns containing prefixes or suffixes, over/under use of capitalization, or even names that no longer match their actual function. This is where the use of an ORM like the Entity Framework can demonstrate its power, because you can change all of these in the conceptual layer of the entity model to make the model nice to work with in code (with more meaningful and standardized names for the entities and associations), without needing to modify the underlying database schema. Luckily, the tables and columns in the AdventureWorksLT database have reasonably friendly names, but if you wanted to do so it would simply be a case of double-clicking the property in the designer (or selecting it and pressing F2), which changes the name display to a textbox enabling you to make the change. Alternatively, you can select the property in the designer, the Model Browser tool window, or the Properties tool window, and update the Name property in the Properties tool window.

Adding Properties to an Entity

Let's now look at the process of adding properties to an entity. Three types of properties exist:

➤ **Scalar properties:** Properties with a primitive type, such as string, integer, Boolean, and so on.

➤ **Complex properties:** A grouping of scalar properties in a manner similar to a structure in code. Grouping properties together in this manner can make your entity model a lot more readable and manageable.

➤ **Navigation properties:** Used to navigate across associations. For example, the SalesOrderHeader entity contains a navigation property called SalesOrderDetails that enables you to navigate to a collection of the SalesOrderDetail entities related to the current SalesOrderHeader entity. Creating an association between two entities automatically creates the required navigation properties.

The easiest way to try this for yourself is to delete a property from an existing entity and add it back again manually. Delete a property from an entity (select it in the designer and press the Delete key). Now to add it back again, right-click the entity and select Add ➾ Scalar Property from the context menu. Alternatively, a much easier and less frustrating way when you are creating a lot of properties is to simply select a property or the Properties header and press the Insert key on your keyboard. A new property will be added to the entity, with the name displayed in a textbox for you to change as required.

The next step is to set the type of the property, for which you'll have to move over to the Properties tool window to set. The default type is string, but you can change this to the required type by setting its Type property.

Properties that you want to designate as entity keys (that is, properties that are used to uniquely identify the entity) need their Entity Key property set to True. The property in the designer will have a picture of a little key added to its icon, making it easy to identify which properties are used to uniquely identify the entity.

You can set numerous other properties on a property, including assigning a default value, a maximum length (for strings), and whether it's nullable. You can also assign the scope of the getter and setter for the property (public, private, and so on), useful for, say, a property that will be mapped to a column with a calculated value in the database where you don't want the consuming application to attempt to set the value (by making the setter private).

The final task is to map the property to the store model. You do this as described earlier in the chapter using the Mapping Details tool window.

Creating Complex Types

Create a complex type on the Customer entity grouping the various customer name-related properties together in a complex type and thus making the Customer entity neater. Though you can create a complex type from scratch, the easiest way to create a complex type is to refactor an entity by selecting the scalar properties on the entity to be included in the complex type and having the designer create the complex type from those properties. Follow these instructions to move the name-related properties on the Customer entity to a complex type:

➤ Select the name-related properties on the Customer entity (FirstName, LastName, MiddleName, NameStyle, Suffix, Title) by selecting the first property, and while holding down the Ctrl key selecting the other properties (so they are all selected at the same time).

➤ Right-click one of the selected properties and select the Refactor into New Complex Type menu item.

➤ In the Model Browser will be the new complex type that it created, with its name displayed in a textbox for you to name to something more meaningful. For this example, simply call it CustomerName.

➤ The Entity Framework designer will have created a complex type, added the selected properties to it, removed the selected properties from the entity, and added the complex type that it just created as a new property on the entity in their place. However, this property will just have ComplexProperty as its name, so you will want to rename it to something more meaningful. Select the property in the designer, press F2, and enter Name in the textbox.

You will now find that by grouping the properties together in this way, the entity will be easier to work with in both the designer and in code.

Creating an Entity

So far you've been modifying existing entities as they were created by the Entity Data Model Wizard. However, let's now take a look at the process of creating an entity from scratch and then mapping it to a table/view/stored procedure in your storage model. Most of these aspects have already been covered, but we'll walk through the required steps to get an entity configured from scratch.

You have two ways of manually creating entities. The first is to right-click the designer surface and select Add ⇨ Entity from the context menu. That pops up the dialog shown in Figure 29-11, which

FIGURE 29-11

helps you set up the initial configuration of the entity. When you enter a name for the entity in the Entity Name field you'll notice that the Entity Set field automatically updates to the plural form of the entity name (although you can change this entity set name to something else if required). The Base Type drop-down list enables you to select an existing entity in your entity model that this entity will inherit from (discussed shortly). There is also a section enabling you to specify the name and type of a property to automatically create on the entity and set as an entity key.

The other way of creating an entity is to drag and drop the Entity component from the Toolbox onto the designer surface. However, you'll note that it doesn't bring up the dialog from the previous method, instead opting to immediately create an entity with a default name, entity set name, and entity key property. You will then have to use the designer to modify its configuration to suit your needs.

The steps needed to finish configuring the entity are as follows:

➤ If required, create an inheritance relationship by specifying that the entity should inherit from a base entity.

➤ Create the required properties on the entity, setting at least one as an entity key.

➤ Map these properties to the storage schema (using the Mapping Details tool window).

➤ Create any associations with other entities in the model.

➤ Validate your model to ensure that the entity is mapped correctly.

> *All entities must have an entity key that can be used to uniquely identify the entity. Entity keys are conceptually the same as a primary key in a database.*

As discussed earlier, you aren't limited to mapping to a single database table/view per entity. This is one of the benefits of building a conceptual model of the database — you may have related data spread across a number of database tables, but through having a conceptual entity model layer in the Entity Framework you are able to bring those different sources together into a single entity to make working with the data a lot easier in code.

> *Make sure you don't focus too much on the structure of the database when you are creating your entity model — the advantage of designing a conceptual model is that it enables you to design the model based on how you plan to use it in code. Therefore, focus on designing your entity model, and then you can look at how it will map to the database.*

Creating/Modifying Entity Associations

You have two ways of creating an association between
two entities. The first is to right-click the header of
one of the entities and select Add ⇨ Association from
the context menu. This displays the dialog shown in
Figure 29-12.

This dialog includes:

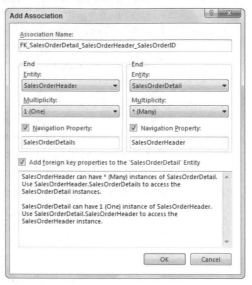

FIGURE 29-12

➤ **Association Name:** Give the association a
name — this will become the name of the
foreign key constraint in the database if you
update the database from the model.

➤ **Endpoints:** These specify the entities at each
end of the association, the type of relationship
(one-to-one, one-to-many, and so on), and the
name of the navigation properties that it will
create on both entities to navigate from one
entity to the other over the association.

➤ **Add foreign key properties to the entity:**
This enables you to create a property on the
"foreign" entity that will act as a foreign key and map to the entity key property over the
association. If you've already added the property that will form the foreign key on the
associated entity, you should uncheck this checkbox.

The other way to create an association is to click the Association component in the Toolbox, click
one entity to form an end on the association, and then click another entity to form the other end of
the association (if it is a one-to-many relationship, select the "one" entity first). Using this method
gives the association a default name, creates the navigation properties on both entities, and assumes
a one-to-many relationship. It will not create a foreign key property on the "foreign" entity. You can
then modify this association as required using the Properties tool window.

*Note that you cannot use the association component in a drag-and-drop fashion
from the Toolbox.*

Despite having created the association, you aren't done yet (unless you used the first method and
also selected the option to create a foreign key property for the association). Now you need to map
the property that acts as the foreign key on one entity to the entity key property on the other. The
entity whose primary key is one endpoint in the association is known, but you have to tell the Entity
Framework explicitly which property to use as the foreign key property. You can do this by selecting
the association in the designer and using the Mapping Details tool window to map the properties.

Once this is done, you may want to define a referential constraint for the association, which you can
assign by clicking the association in the designer and finding the Referential Constraint property in
the Properties tool window.

Entity Inheritance

In the same way that classes can inherit from other classes (a fundamental object-oriented concept), so can entities inherit from other entities. You have a number of ways of specifying that one entity should inherit from another, but the most straightforward method is to select an entity in the designer, find its Base Type property in the Properties tool window, and select the entity from the drop-down list that this entity should inherit from.

Validating an Entity Model

At times your entity model may be invalid (such as when a property on an entity has not been mapped to the storage model, or its type cannot be converted from/to the mapped column's data type in the database); however, despite having an invalid entity model your project will still compile.

You can run a check to see if your model is valid by right-clicking the designer surface and selecting the Validate menu item from the context menu. This checks for any errors in your model and displays them in the Error List tool window.

You can also set the Validate On Build property for the conceptual model to True (click an empty space on the designer surface, and then you can find the property in the Properties tool window), which will automatically validate the model each time you compile the project. However, again, an invalid model will not stop the project from successfully compiling.

Updating an Entity Model with Database Changes

The structure of databases tends to be updated frequently throughout the development of projects, so you need a way to update your model based on the changes in the database. To do so, right-click the designer surface and select the Update Model from Database menu item. This opens the Update Wizard (as shown in Figure 29-13) that will obtain the schema from the database, compare it to the current storage model, and extract the differences. These differences are displayed in the tabs in the wizard — the Add tab contains database objects that aren't in your storage model, the Refresh tab contains database objects that are different in the database from their corresponding storage model objects, and the Delete tab contains database objects that are in the storage model but no longer in the database.

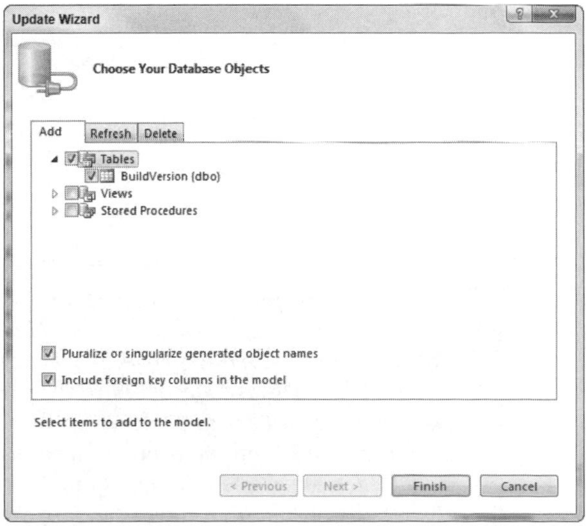

Select the items from these three tabs that you want to add, refresh, or delete, and click the Finish button to have your entity model updated accordingly.

FIGURE 29-13

QUERYING THE ENTITY MODEL

Now that you've created your entity model you will no doubt want to put it to the test by querying it, working with and modifying the data returned, and saving changes back to the database. The Entity Framework provides a number of ways to query your entity model, including LINQ to Entities, Entity SQL, and query builder methods. However, this chapter focuses specifically on querying the model with LINQ to Entities.

LINQ to Entities Overview

LINQ was covered in the previous chapter, specifically focusing on the use of LINQ to Objects, LINQ to SQL, and LINQ to XML; however, the Entity Framework has extended LINQ with its own implementation called LINQ to Entities. LINQ to Entities enables you to write strongly typed LINQ queries against your entity model, and have it return the data as objects (entities). LINQ to Entities handles the mapping of your LINQ query against the conceptual entity model to a SQL query against the underlying database schema. This is an extraordinarily powerful feature of the Entity Framework, abstracting away the need to write SQL to work with data in a database.

Getting an Object Context

To connect to your entity model you need to create an instance of the object context in your entity model. So that the object context is disposed of once you're finished you'll use a `using` block to maintain the lifetime of the variable:

VB

```vb
Using context As New AdventureWorksLTEntities()
    'Queries go here
End Using
```

C#

```csharp
using (AdventureWorksLTEntities context = new AdventureWorksLTEntities())
{
    // Queries go here
}
```

> *Note that any queries placed within the scope of the* using *block for the object context aren't necessarily executed while the object context is in scope. As detailed in the "Debugging and Execution" section of Chapter 28, the execution of LINQ queries is deferred until the results are iterated (i.e., the query is not run against the database until the code needs to use its results). This means that if the variable containing the context has gone out of scope before you are actually using the results, the query will fail. Therefore, ensure that you have requested the results of the query before letting the context variable go out of scope.*

If you need to specify the connection to the database (such as if you need to pass in user credentials or use a custom connection string rather than what's in the App.config file) you can do so by passing the connection string to the constructor of the object context (in this case AdventureWorksLTEntities).

CRUD Operations

It would be hard to argue against the most important database queries being the CRUD (Create/Read/Update/Delete) operations. Read operations return data from the database, whereas the Create/Update/Delete operations make changes to the database. Create some LINQ to Entities queries to demonstrate retrieving some data from the database (as entities), modify these entities, and then save the changes back to the database.

> *While you are getting up to speed on writing LINQ to Entities queries, you may find LINQPad to be a useful tool, providing a "scratchpad" where you can write queries against an entity model and have them executed immediately so you can test your query. You can get LINQPad from* http://www.linqpad.net.

Data Retrieval

Just like SQL, LINQ to Entity queries consist of selects, where clauses, order by clauses, and group by clauses. Take a look at some examples of these. The results of the queries can be assigned to the ItemsSource property of the DataGrid control created earlier in the MainWindow.xaml file, enabling you to visualize the results:

VB

```
dgEntityFrameworkData.ItemsSource = qry
```

C#

```
dgEntityFrameworkData.ItemsSource = qry;
```

There are actually a number of ways to query the entity model within LINQ to Entities, but we'll just focus on one method here. We'll also assume that the query is between the using block demonstrated previously, with the variable containing the instance of the object context simply called context.

To return the entire collection of customers in the database you can write a select query like so:

VB

```
Dim qry = From c In context.Customers
          Select c
```

C#

```
var qry = from c in context.Customers
          select c;
```

You can filter the results with a where clause, which can even include functions/properties such as StartsWith, Length, and so on. This example returns all the customers whose last name starts with A:

VB

```
Dim qry = From c In context.Customers
          Where c.Name.LastName.StartsWith("A")
          Select c
```

C#

```
var qry = from c in context.Customers
          where c.Name.LastName.StartsWith("A")
          select c;
```

You can order the results with an order by clause — in this example you are ordering the results by the customer's last name:

VB

```
Dim qry = From c In context.Customers
          Order By c.Name.LastName Ascending
          Select c
```

C#

```
var qry = from c in context.Customers
          orderby c.Name.LastName ascending
          select c;
```

You can group and aggregate the results with a group by clause — in this example you are grouping the results by the salesperson, returning the number of sales per salesperson. Note that instead of returning a Customer entity you are requesting that LINQ to Entities returns an implicitly typed variable containing the salesperson and his sales count:

VB

```
Dim qry = From c In context.Customers
          Group c By salesperson = c.SalesPerson Into grouping = Group
          Select New With
          {
                .SalesPerson = salesperson,
                .SalesCount = grouping.Count()
          }
```

C#

```
var qry = from c in context.Customers
          group c by c.SalesPerson into grouping
          select new
          {
              SalesPerson = grouping.Key,
              SalesCount = grouping.Count()
          };
```

> *It can be very useful to monitor the SQL queries generated and executed by the Entity Framework to ensure that the interaction between the entity model and the database is what you'd expect. For example, you may find that because an association is being lazy loaded, when traversing the entity hierarchy across this association in a loop that you are actually making repeated and excessive trips to the database. Therefore, if you have SQL Server Standard or higher you can use the SQL Profiler to monitor the queries being made to the database and adjust your LINQ queries if necessary. If you are using SQL Server Express you can download a free open source SQL Server profiler called SQL Express Profiler from* http://code.google.com/p/sqlexpressprofiler/downloads/list.

Saving Data

The Entity Framework employs change tracking — where you make changes to data in the model, it will track the data that has changed, and when you request that the changes are saved back to the database it will commit the changes to the database as a batch. This commit is via the SaveChanges() method on the object context:

VB

```
context.SaveChanges()
```

C#

```
context.SaveChanges();
```

A number of ways to update data exists (for different scenarios), but for purposes of simplicity this example takes the simple straightforward approaches.

Update Operations

Assume you want to modify the name of a customer (with an ID of 1), which you've retrieved like so:

VB

```
Dim qry = From c In context.Customers
          Where c.CustomerID = 1
          Select c

Dim customer As Customer = qry.FirstOrDefault()
```

C#

```
var qry = from c in context.Customers
          where c.CustomerID == 1
          select c;

Customer customer = qry.FirstOrDefault();
```

All you need to do is modify the name properties on the customer entity you've retrieved, the Entity Framework will automatically track that this customer has changed, and then call the `SaveChanges()` method on the object context:

VB

```
customer.Name.FirstName = "Chris"
customer.Name.LastName = "Anderson"

context.SaveChanges()
```

C#

```
customer.Name.FirstName = "Chris";
customer.Name.LastName = "Anderson";

context.SaveChanges();
```

Create Operations

To add a new entity to an entity set, simply create an instance of the entity, assign values to its properties, and then save the changes:

VB

```
Customer customer = new Customer()
customer.Name.FirstName = "Chris"
customer.Name.LastName = "Anderson"
customer.Name.Title = "Mr."
customer.PasswordHash = "*****"
customer.PasswordSalt = "*****"
customer.ModifiedDate = DateTime.Now
context.Customers.AddObject(customer)

context.SaveChanges()
```

C#

```
Customer customer = new Customer();
customer.Name.FirstName = "Chris";
customer.Name.LastName = "Anderson";
customer.Name.Title = "Mr.";
customer.PasswordHash = "*****";
customer.PasswordSalt = "*****";
customer.ModifiedDate = DateTime.Now;
context.Customers.AddObject(customer);

context.SaveChanges();
```

After the changes are saved back to the database your entity will now have the primary key that was automatically generated for the row by the database assigned to its `CustomerID` property.

Delete Operations

To delete an entity, simply use the `DeleteObject()` method on its containing entity set:

VB

```
context.Customers.DeleteObject(customer)
```

C#

```
context.Customers.DeleteObject(customer);
```

Navigating Entity Associations

Of course, working with data rarely involves the use of a single table/entity, which is where the navigation properties used by associations are very useful indeed. A customer can have one or more addresses, which is modeled in your entity model by the Customer entity having an association with the CustomerAddress entity (a one-to-many relationship), which then has an association with the Address entity (a many-to-one relationship). The navigation properties for these associations make it very easy to obtain the addresses for a customer.

Start by using the query from earlier to return a customer entity:

VB

```
Dim qry = From c In context.Customers
          Where c.CustomerID = 1
          Select c

Dim customer As Customer = qry.FirstOrDefault()
```

C#

```
var qry = from c in context.Customers
          where c.CustomerID == 1
          select c;

Customer customer = qry.FirstOrDefault();
```

You can enumerate and work with the addresses for the entity via the navigation properties like so:

VB

```
For Each customerAddress As CustomerAddress In customer.CustomerAddresses
    Dim address As Address = customerAddress.Address
    'Do something with the address entity
Next customerAddress
```

C#

```
foreach (CustomerAddress customerAddress in customer.CustomerAddresses)
{
    Address address = customerAddress.Address;
    // Do something with the address entity
}
```

Note how you navigate through the CustomerAddress entity to get to the Address entity for the customer. Because of these associations there's no need for joins in the Entity Framework.

However, there is an issue here with what you're doing. What is happening here is as you navigate through the CustomerAddress entity to the Address entity is that it's doing another database query to get the collection of CustomerAddress entities for the customer, and then in the for loop doing yet another database query for each CustomerAddress entity to get the corresponding Address entity! This is known as lazy loading — where the entity model only requests data from the database when it actually needs it. This can have some advantages in certain situations, however, in this scenario it results in a lot of calls to the database, increasing the load on the database server, reducing the performance of your application, and reducing your application's scalability. If you then did this for a number of customer entities in a loop, that would add even more strain to the system. So it's definitely not an ideal scenario as is.

Instead, you can request from the entity model when querying for the customer entity that it eagerly loads its associated CustomerAddress entities and their Address entities. This will request all the data in one database query, thus removing all the aforementioned issues, because when navigating through these associations the entity model will now have the entities in memory and not have to go back to the database to retrieve them. The way to request that the model does this is to use the `Include` method, specifying the path (as a string) of the navigation properties (dot notation) to the associated entities whose data you also want to retrieve from the database at the same time as the actual entities being queried:

VB

```vb
Dim qry = From c In context.Customers
                        .Include("CustomerAddresses")
                        .Include("CustomerAddresses.Address")
        Where c.CustomerID = 1
        Select c

Dim customer As Customer = qry.FirstOrDefault()
```

C#

```csharp
var qry = from c in context.Customers
                        .Include("CustomerAddresses")
                        .Include("CustomerAddresses.Address")
        where c.CustomerID == 1
        select c;

Customer customer = qry.FirstOrDefault();
```

ADVANCED FUNCTIONALITY

There's too much functionality available in the Entity Framework to discuss in detail in this chapter, but here's an overview of some of the more notable advanced features available that you can investigate further if you wish.

Updating a Database from an Entity Model

As mentioned earlier, it's possible with the Entity Framework to create an entity model from scratch, and then have the Entity Framework create a database according to your model. Alternatively, you can start with an existing database, but then get the Entity Framework to update the structure of your database based on the new entities/properties/associations that you've added to your entity model. To update the structure of the database based on additions to your model, you can use the Generate Database Wizard by right-clicking the designer surface and selecting the Generate Database from Model menu item.

Adding Business Logic to Entities

Though you are fundamentally building a data model with the Entity Framework rather than business objects, it is possible to add business logic to your entities. The entities generated by the Entity Framework are partial classes, enabling to you extend them and add your own code. This code may respond to various events on the entity, or it may add methods to your entity that the client application can use to perform specific tasks or actions.

For example, you might want to have the Product entity in your AdventureWorksLT entity model automatically assign the value of the `SellEndDate` property when the `SellStartDate` property is set (only if the `SellEndDate` property does not have a value). Alternatively, you may have some validation logic or business logic that you want to execute when the entity is being saved.

Each property on the entity has two partial methods that you can extend: a `Changing` method (before the property is changed) and a `Changed` method (after the property is changed). You can extend these partial methods in your partial class to respond accordingly to the value of a property being changed.

Plain Old CLR Objects (POCO)

One of the big complaints with the first version of the Entity Framework was that your entities had to inherit from `EntityObject` (or implement a set of given interfaces), meaning that they had a dependency on the Entity Framework — which made them unfriendly for use in projects where test-driven development (TDD) and domain-driven design (DDD) practices were employed. In addition, many developers wanted their classes to be persistence ignorant — that is, contain no logic or awareness of how they were persisted.

By default, the entities generated from the Entity Model Data Wizard in the Entity Framework v4 still inherit from `EntityObject`, but you now have the ability to use your own classes that do not need to inherit from `EntityObject` or implement any Entity Framework interfaces, and whose design is completely under your control. These types of classes are often termed Plain Old CLR Objects, or POCO for short.

SUMMARY

In this chapter you learned that the Entity Framework is an Object Relational Mapper (ORM) that enables you to create a conceptual model of your database in order to interact with databases in a more productive and maintainable manner. You then went on to learn how to create an entity model, and how to write queries against it in code.

30

Reporting

WHAT'S IN THIS CHAPTER?

➤ Designing Reports

➤ Generating Reports

➤ Deploying Reports

One of the key components of almost every business application is reporting. Businesses put data into the system in order to get useful information out of it, and this information is generally in the form of reports. Numerous reporting tools and engines are available, and it can often be hard to choose which one is best for your application or system (they tend to work in different ways and have different pros/cons).

Visual Studio 2010 contains a built-in report designer that saves to files using the RDL file specification — and reports built using this designer can be generated using the local report engine, or rendered on a remote report server running SQL Server Reporting Services.

The professional versions of Visual Studio 2010 (and higher) also come with another well-known reporting tool called Crystal Reports. However, this chapter specifically looks at Visual Studio's report designer, and how to use it to design and generate reports (using the local report engine).

GETTING STARTED WITH REPORTING

When you start designing reports, you will either want to add a report to an existing project or start a completely new project (such as for a reporting application). If it is the latter, the easiest way to get started is to create a new project using the Reports Application project template. This creates a Windows Forms project already set up with the necessary assembly references, a form with the Report Viewer control on it, and an empty report. Let's look at the former scenario and how to manually get started (which really isn't much extra work).

Reports can be viewed in either a Windows Forms application or an ASP.NET application using the Report Viewer control. There are two Report Viewer controls — one for use in web projects and one for use in Windows Forms projects, and both are almost identical in appearance and how you use them to render reports.

> *To render reports in a WPF application, you can use the Windows Forms interoperability feature detailed in Chapter 18 and use the Windows Forms control (because there is no Report Viewer control in WPF). Displaying reports in Silverlight applications is a bit harder because Silverlight has no Report Viewer control either (nor support for printing). In this case it is probably best to render reports to PDF, stream them through to the client using a HTTP handler, and display them in a different browser window.*

Now you need to add some assembly references to your project that are required for using the Report Viewer control and the report engine. If you are working with an ASP.NET project you will need to add a reference to `Microsoft.Reporting.WebForms.dll`, or if you are working with a Windows Forms project you will need to add a reference to `Microsoft.Reporting.WinForms.dll`. Alternatively, the Report Viewer control should be in your Toolbox for both project types, and dropping it onto your report will automatically add the required assembly reference to your project.

Now add a report definition file to your project. Add a new item to your project, and select the Reporting subsection as shown in Figure 30-1.

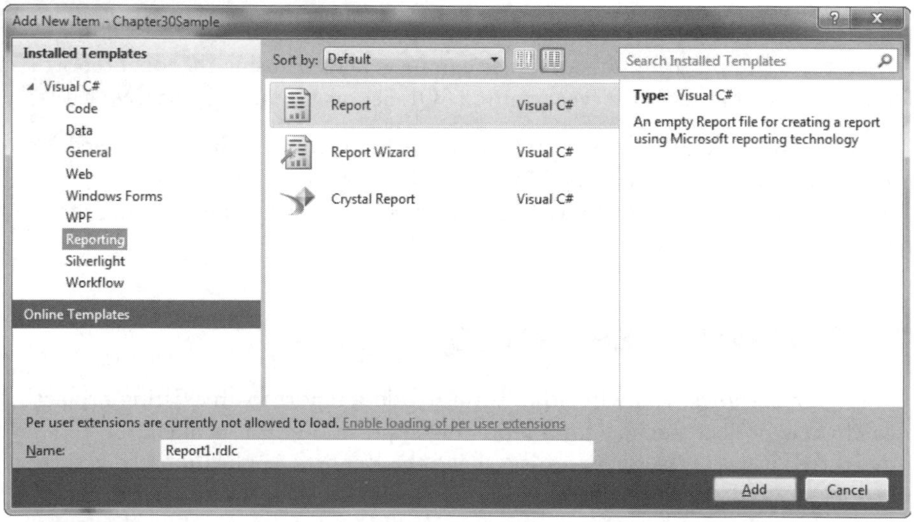

FIGURE 30-1

Two items here are of interest: the Report item and the Report Wizard item. Selecting the Report item creates an empty report definition file — essentially a blank slate that you can start working with. Selecting the Report Wizard item creates a report definition file and automatically starts the Report Wizard (detailed later in this chapter), which will design a report layout for you based upon your choices. You will generally want to start your report by using the Report Wizard, and then modify its output to suit your requirements.

Before you get into designing the report, it is important to clarify the different parts of a reporting system, the terms you use when you reference each, and how they hang together (because this can be somewhat confusing initially). There are six main parts:

➤ Report Designer

➤ Report Definition File

➤ Data Sources

➤ Reporting Engine

➤ Report

➤ Report Viewer

You use the *report designer* to design the *report definition file* (at design time), creating its structure and specifying the various rules of how the report will be laid out. At run time, you pass the *report definition file* and one or more *data sources* to the *reporting engine*. The *reporting engine* uses the two to generate the *report*, which it then renders in the *Report Viewer* (or a specified alternative output format such as PDF).

> *Where this can become confusing is that the Report Viewer is the local report engine. So you are passing the report definition file and the data sources to the Report Viewer and it then both renders and displays it. From a conceptual perspective, however, it's probably best to think of these as separate components and it will make more sense.*

DESIGNING REPORTS

Take a look now at how to go about designing a report. You will look at the manual process of designing a report, and then later take a look at how the Report Wizard automates the design process. For now, you will be working with an empty report that was created by adding a new item to the project and using the Report item template. When you create this item it will immediately be opened in the report designer as shown in Figure 30-2.

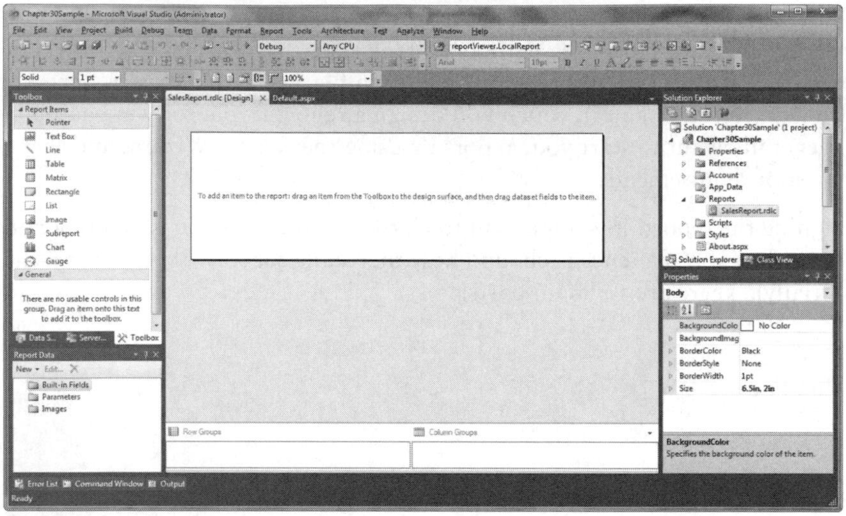

FIGURE 30-2

In the document area you have the design surface upon which you lay out the report. On the bottom left is the Report Data tool window, which will contain the data fields that you can drag onto your report. If you accidentally close this window you can open it again by using the View ➪ Report Data menu. Above it, the Toolbox window contains the controls that can be added to the report surface. When you are working with the design surface of a report you will note that a Report menu is also added to the menu bar.

> *Due to the nature of the local report engine, which can't query data sources itself (as discussed shortly), there unfortunately is no way to preview the report in the designer. This means that in order to view the output of your report you must have already set up a form with a Report Viewer control, and have written the code that populates the data structures and initiates the rendering process. This can make the report design process a little painful, and it is possibly worthwhile creating a temporary project that makes it easy to test your report. You can find the code required to do so later in this chapter.*

Defining Data Sources

Before you can design a report you need to start with a data source, because it is the data source that will dictate a large portion of the report's design. At design time the data sources won't contain any data, but the report needs the data sources for their structure.

An important concept to understand when starting with the *local* report engine is that you must pass it the data when generating the report — it doesn't query the data sources itself. The upside of this is that the data can come from a wide variety of sources; all you need to be able to do is to query the data, and you can then manipulate it and pass it to the report engine in a structure that it understands. The main structures you can use to populate your report that the report engine will understand include DataSets, objects, and Entity Framework entities.

The server *report engine (SQL Server Reporting Services) can query SQL Server databases itself (and some other various data sources via OLEDB and ODBC), and the query to obtain the data used by the report is stored in the report definition file. You can spot report definition files that are for use by SQL Server Reporting Services fairly easily because they will have an* `.rdl` *extension, whereas the files for use by the local report engine have an* `.rdlc` *extension (the c stands for client-side processing). It's reasonably easy to convert reports from using the local report engine to using SQL Server Reporting Services, because the underlying file formats are based upon the same Report Definition Language (RDL). The reason you might use SQL Server Reporting Services over the local report engine is to reduce the load on your server (such as the web server), and offload that to a separate server. Generating reports can be quite resource- and CPU-intensive, so you can make your system a lot more scalable by delegating this task to another server. SQL Server Reporting Services requires a full SQL Server license, but if you're using SQL Server Express Edition you can use a limited version of it if you install the free SQL Server Express Edition with Advanced Services.*

You can use an Entity Framework model for the data source for your report; however, a limitation of the local report engine is that you can't join data from separate data sources (in this case entities) in the report, which is often required in reporting (unless you have imported views from your database into your Entity Framework model that align with the requirements for your report). Therefore, you will need to either create a Typed DataSet or create a class to populate with the joined data, which you can then pass to the report engine.

As an example, you will simply be using the AdventureWorksLT Entity Framework model that you created in Chapter 29 as the source of the data for this report. The first step is to add an entity from this model as a data source for the report. To do so, click the New menu in the Report Data tool window, and select the Dataset menu item. This displays the Dataset Properties window shown in Figure 30-3.

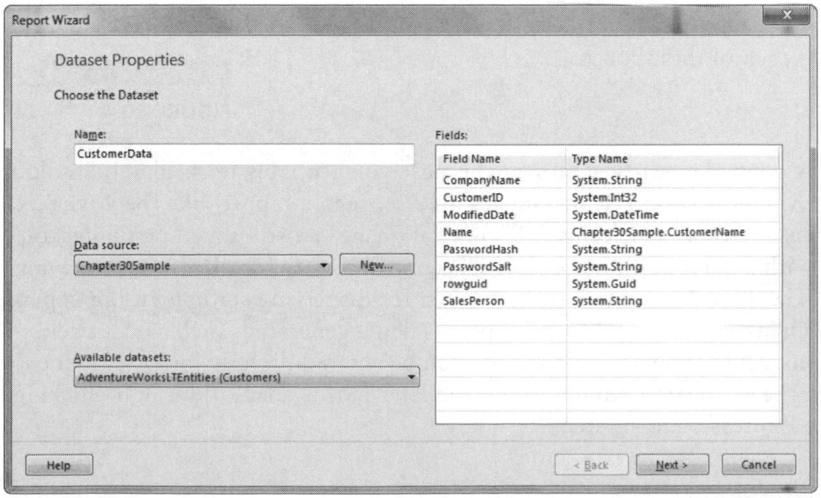

FIGURE 30-3

You should give the data source a meaningful name, because you will be referencing the data source name in code when you are passing the local report engine the data to populate it with. Enter this name in the Name textbox. Now you need to select the location of the data source from the Data Source drop-down list. The data source will usually be in your project, so you can select it from the list.

Click the New button to add a source of data to your project (such as to create a new entity model if it doesn't already exist). This opens the Data Source Configuration Wizard detailed in Chapter 27. You will assume the Entity Framework model of the AdventureWorksLT database that you created in Chapter 29 already exists in your project, so you can skip this step and simply select the type of entity objects that you will be passing to the report (for this example you want the Product entities) from the Available Datasets drop-down box. Finding which item to select when dealing with Entity Framework entities can be rather confusing initially, but the parent entity is the first part of the item name, and the name of the actual entity you want to use in the report is in the brackets following it. So to select the Product entity in the AdventureWorksLTEntities model you select the AdventureWorksLTEntities (Product) item. When you select the item the list of the fields it contains are displayed in the Fields list. This data source will now be displayed in the Report Data tool window, and will list the fields under it that you can use in your report.

If this data source changes (such as if a new field has been added to it), right-click it and select the Refresh item from the context menu to update it to its new structure.

Reporting Controls

If you take a look at the Toolbox tool window you will see that it contains the various types of controls that you can use in your report, as shown in Figure 30-4.

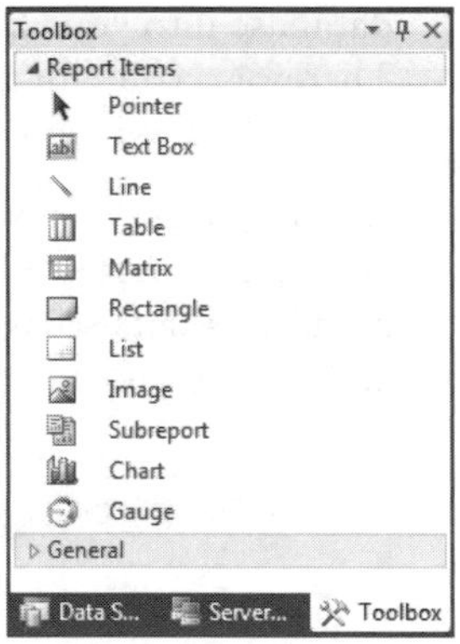

To use a control, simply drag and drop it on your report at the required position, and then you can set its properties using the Properties tool window. Alternatively you can select the control in the Toolbox and draw the control on the report design surface. Another method is to right-click anywhere on your report, select the Insert submenu, and select the control you want to insert.

Now take a closer look at each of these controls.

Text Box

The name of the Text Box control is a little confusing because you probably immediately think of a control that the user can enter text into (which makes little sense in a report) like the Text Box control in Windows Forms and other platforms. This mental image is also backed up by its icon (which shows a textbox with a caret in it), but in fact this control is only for displaying text, not for accepting text entry. The Text Box control isn't used just for displaying static text, but can also contain expressions (which are evaluated when the report is being generated, such as data field values, aggregate functions, and formulas). Expressions can be entered directly into the textbox, or they can be created using the expression builder (discussed later in this chapter) by right-clicking the textbox and selecting the Expression menu item.

FIGURE 30-4

When you drag a data field onto the report, a textbox is created at that location containing a placeholder. The placeholder has an expression behind it, which will get and display the value for that field. A placeholder is essentially a way of hiding expressions in textboxes in order to reduce the report design's complexity. You could think of it like a parameterless function, which has a name (referred to as a label), and contains code (known as an expression). In the report designer the textbox will display the label instead of the (potentially long and complex) expression.

> *If you drag a data field onto your report and it displays <<Expr>> this means it has had to create a complex expression to refer to that field (such as getting the field's value in the first row in the dataset), which is hidden behind the <<Expr>> placeholder it has created. Unless this is the behavior you are after (such showing a value in a report header or footer), it probably should be placed in a table, matrix, or a list in order to display the value of that field for each row in the dataset. If this is the behavior you are after, first click the <<Expr>> placeholder, then right-click, select the Placeholder Properties menu item, and give it a meaningful name by entering one in the Label textbox.*

You can also drag a data field into an existing textbox. This will create a placeholder with an expression behind it to display the value of that field in the dropped location in the textbox. You may do this if, for example, you wanted to display the value of that field inline with some static text, or even combine the values of multiple fields in the one textbox.

> *You can quickly create an expression to display a data field value by typing the name of the field surrounded by square brackets (for example, [EmailAddress]). This text will automatically be turned into a placeholder, with an expression behind it to display the corresponding field's value.*

To create a placeholder manually, put the textbox in edit mode (where it is displaying a cursor for you to type), then right-click and select the Create Placeholder menu item. Creating placeholders and expressions is discussed in detail later in this chapter.

The format of the text in the Text Box (as a whole) can be set in a number of ways. The formatting properties for the textbox can be found in the Properties tool window, and there is also a Font tab in the Text Box Properties window for the Text Box (right-click the textbox, and select the Text Box Properties menu item). Another way is to use the formatting options found on the Report Formatting toolbar. This is the easiest way, but has another side benefit. If you select the textbox in the designer and choose formatting options from this toolbar, it will apply those formatting options to all its text. However, the text within a textbox doesn't need to be all the same format, and selecting text *within* the textbox and choosing formatting options using this toolbar will apply that formatting to just the selected text. Of course you can use standard formatting shortcut keys too, such as Ctrl+B for bold text, and so on.

When you are displaying the value of a number or date data field you quite often need to format it for display in the report. If your textbox contains just an expression, select the textbox, right-click, select the Text Box Properties menu item, and select the Number tab (shown in Figure 30-5). Alternatively, if the textbox contains text or other field values, you can format just the value of the placeholder by selecting the placeholder in the textbox, right-clicking, selecting the Placeholder Properties menu item, and selecting the Number tab. Then select how you want the field to be formatted from the options available. If a standard format isn't available, you can select Custom from the Category list and enter a format string, or you can even write an expression to format the value by clicking the *fx* button.

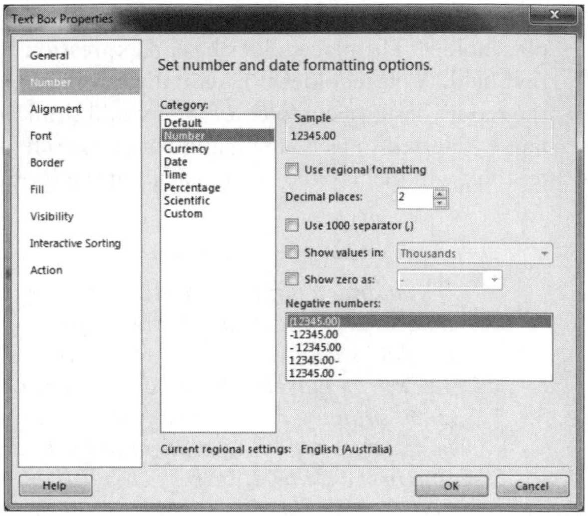

FIGURE 30-5

Line/Rectangle

The Line and Rectangle controls are shapes that you can use to draw on your report. The Line control is often used as a separator between various parts of a report. The Rectangle control is generally used to encapsulate an area in a report. The Rectangle control is a container control, meaning other controls can be placed on it, and when it is moved they will be moved along with it.

Table

The Table control is used to display the data in a tabular form, with fixed columns and a varying number of rows (depending on the data being used to populate the report). In addition to the data, tables can also display column headers, row group headers, and totals rows.

By default, each of the cells in a table is a Text Box control (and thus each cell has the same features described for the Text Box control). However, a cell can contain any control from the Toolbox (such as an Image control, Chart, Gauge, and so on) by simply dragging the control from the Toolbox into the cell.

FIGURE 30-6

When you first drop a Table control onto your report you will see that it contains a header row and a data row, as shown in Figure 30-6.

To display data in the table, drag a field from the appropriate data source in the Report Data tool window and drop it on a column in the table. You'll see that it has created a placeholder with an expression behind it to display the value of that field in the data row, and that it has also automatically filled in the header row for that column to give it a title. This header name is the name of the field, but assuming the field name follows Pascal case naming rules you will find spaces have been intelligently inserted into the name before capital letters (so the ProductNumber field will automatically have Product Number inserted as its header). If this header name isn't suitable, you can change it by typing a new one in its place.

Product Number	Name	
[ProductNumber]	[Name]	

FIGURE 30-7

Another means of setting which field should be displayed in a column is to mouse over a cell in the data row and click the icon that appears in its top right-hand corner. This is shown in Figure 30-7. This displays a menu from which you can select the field to display in that column.

> *If you have multiple datasets in your report and you haven't specified the dataset that is the source of data for the table, clicking this icon first requires you to drill down selecting the dataset first (before the field). The dataset selected will then be set as the source of the data for the table, and the next time you click the icon it will only display the fields from that dataset accordingly.*

The table will have three columns when you drop it onto a report, but you can add additional columns by simply dragging another field from the Report Data tool window over the table such that the insertion point drawn on the table is at its right edge (shown in Figure 30-8).

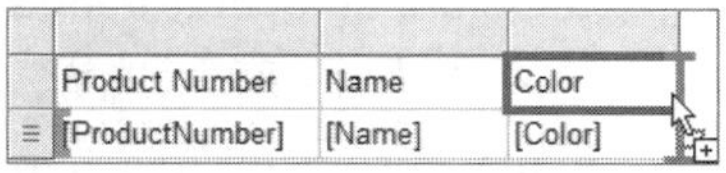

Product Number	Name	Color
[ProductNumber]	[Name]	[Color]

FIGURE 30-8

You can insert a column in the table by the same means, but positioning the insertion point at the location where the column should be inserted. Alternatively, you can add or insert a new column by right-clicking on a gray column handle, selecting the Insert Column submenu, and selecting the location (Left or Right) relative to the column that is selected.

To delete an unwanted column, right-click the gray column handle and select Delete Columns from the menu.

> *Note that tables can only contain data from a single dataset; therefore, you can't join data from multiple data sources in the one table (such as including data from an Orders data source and a Customers data source to show each order and the name of the customer that placed the order in the table). Therefore you will need to do this join in the data that you have passed to populate the report with.*

You can find which dataset is the source of the data for a table by selecting it and finding the DataSetName property in the Properties tool window. You can change which data source it uses by selecting an alternative one from the drop-down list.

Often you will find that you need to display aggregate values at the bottom of the table, such as in a totals row. There are two ways to implement this. If you have a numeric field that you want to sum all the values in that column, right-click the cell (not the placeholder, but the entire cell) and select the Add Total menu item at the bottom of the menu (this menu item will only be enabled for numeric fields). A new row will be added below the data row to display the totals, and a SUM aggregate expression for that field will be inserted, as shown in Figure 30-9.

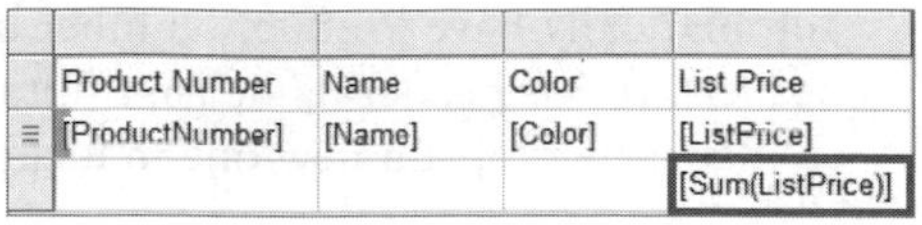
Product Number
Name
Color
List Price
[ProductNumber]
[Name]
[Color]
[ListPrice]
[Sum(ListPrice)]

FIGURE 30-9

Because the Add Total menu item is only enabled for numeric fields, you may need to create the totals row manually (such as if you want a count of items for example). Right-click the data row's handle, and select Insert Row ➪ Outside Group - Below. Then you can write the aggregate expression in the newly inserted row as required.

If you want to change the type of aggregate function used by the total, you will need to modify the expression. Instead of manually making the change, a quicker way to do this is to select the placeholder (and not the cell), right-click, select the Summarize By submenu, and select the alternative aggregate function from the submenu.

A table can filter and sort data from the data source before displaying it. Both of these can be configured in the Tablix Properties window (right-click the gray handle area for the table and select the Tablix Properties menu item). The Filter tab enables you to specify filters (each consisting of an expression, an operator, and a value). The Sorting tab enables you to specify one or more fields to sort the data by and the sort order for each.

You may also want to group rows in a table, showing a group header between each grouping. For example, you may want to group orders by customer, and show the customer's name in the group header row (which therefore doesn't need to be displayed as a column). You can have multiple levels of grouping, enabling complex nested hierarchies to be created. Again, there are multiple ways to set the grouping for a table. One is to select the table and drag a field from the Report Data tool window onto the Row Groups pane at the bottom of the report designer *above* the (Details) entry already there. Another way (that gives you additional options for the grouping) is to right-click the data row's gray handle and select Add Group ➪ Parent Group from the menu. This displays the Tablix Group window shown in Figure 30-10.

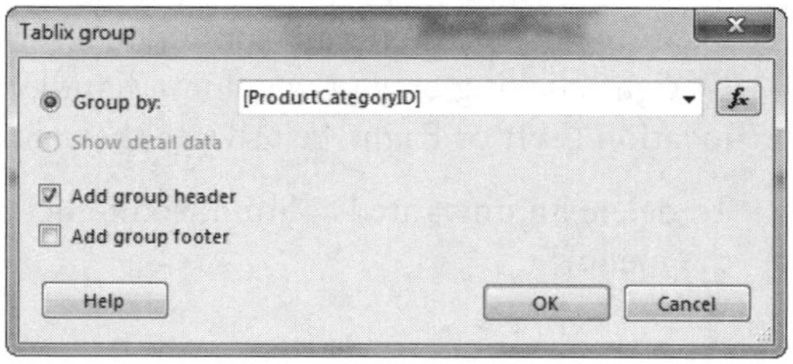
Tablix group
Group by:
[ProductCategoryID]
Show detail data
Add group header
Add group footer
Help
OK
Cancel

FIGURE 30-10

Here you can select the field or an expression to group by, and there is also the option to add a group header and/or footer row. For example, these additional options may be useful if you want to display the value of the group field in a header above the data for a group, and totals in the footer below it.

By default (even if you select to create a group header row or if there is a column displaying the group field's value) a new column will be inserted to the left of the data configured to show the value of the group field. You can safely delete this column without affecting the grouping if this is not the behavior you are after.

> *When you add a group that has a group header row, here are some things that may improve your report layout. First delete the column it added, and then set the first cell in the group header row to display the value of the field it is grouping by. Then select all the cells in the group header row, right-click, and select the Merge Cells menu item to turn them into a single cell (enabling the grouping field's value to stretch across the columns). You may also want to add a border or background color to the group header row so it stands out.*

By default there is no formatting applied to the table apart from a solid light gray border around the cells (or technically the control in each cell). Often you will want to have a border around the table, between columns, or even between individual cells. Or perhaps you want a line between the table header and the data, and/or the table footer and the data. In all of these cases the easiest way to set the borders is to select the cells to apply a border to and use the Report Borders toolbar (as shown in Figure 30-11) to set them.

FIGURE 30-11

Often you will also want to set a background color for the header row (and a foreground color to match). The easiest way to do this is to select the cells and use the Background Color/Foreground Color buttons from the Report Formatting toolbar to select the color to use (shown in Figure 30-12).

FIGURE 30-12

Matrix

The Matrix control is used for cross-tab reports (similar to Pivot Tables in Excel). Essentially, a Matrix control groups data in two dimensions (both rows and columns), and you use it when you have two variables and an aggregate field for each combination of the two. So, for example, if you wanted to see the total sales per product category in each country, this would be the perfect control to use (see Figure 30-13). The variables would be the product category and the country, and the aggregate is the total revenue (of the products in that category to that country). Matrices are one of the most important and powerful controls in reporting, because they really help enable useful information to be extracted from raw data.

	United Kingdom	United States
Bike Racks	$1584.00	$720.00
Bottles and Cages	$86.35	$71.86
Bottom Brackets	$777.52	$542.65
Brakes	$383.40	$447.30
Caps	$91.70	$185.67
Chains	$48.58	$48.58
Cleaners	$137.40	$114.48

FIGURE 30-13

What stands out about using the Matrix control (over the Table control) is that you don't know what columns there will be at design time. Both the number of rows and columns for the matrix (and their headers) will be dictated by the data.

The matrix is closely related to the Table control, and in fact both (along with the List control discussed shortly) are the same core control under the covers (called a Tablix). However, they are templated as separate controls in order to distinguish their different uses. If you were to delete the column group (and its related rows and columns), you effectively turn the Matrix control into a table.

When you drop a Matrix control on your report you will see that it contains both a column header and a row header that intersect on a data cell (as shown in Figure 30-14), and that both the Row Groups and Column Groups panes at the bottom of the designer have grouping entries (whereas the Table control only had a row grouping entry).

FIGURE 30-14

For this example, you will be using the example of displaying the total sales per product category in each country described earlier. Your data source (a collection of custom objects specifically created and populated as the source of data for this report) contains four fields: ProductCategory, Country, Revenue, and OrderQuantity. What you need to do is drag the ProductCategory field from the Report Data tool window onto the row header (marked Rows), and the Country field onto the column header (marked Columns). Then drag the Revenue field (or the OrderQuantity field — either one) onto the data cell (marked Data), and you're done! Assuming the field you are aggregating is numeric, it will have automatically applied a SUM aggregate to the Revenue field.

The designer will have automatically inserted a header label into the top left-hand cell, but generally you will want to delete it.

The matrix in the report designer will now look like Figure 30-15, and after adding some formatting you will get an output similar to that shown previously in Figure 30-13 when you generate the report.

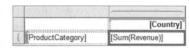

FIGURE 30-15

Like with the Table control, you can display totals, but the Matrix control enables you to have column totals as well as row totals. When you right-click the data cell you will find that the Add Total menu item is actually a submenu (unlike the Table control), from which you can select a Row total or a Column total.

The Matrix control doesn't limit you to having just one aggregate per "intersection." For example, you may want to show both the total revenue and quantity for each country/product category. Simply drag another field to aggregate (such as the OrderQuantity

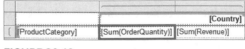

FIGURE 30-16

field) next to the Revenue field in the matrix, and it too will appear for each country (as shown in Figure 30-16).

You can also extend the matrix to show additional "dimensions" by having multiple row or column groups. Again, simply drag the additional fields to group by into the appropriate position in the row/column grouping header area.

List

Lists are a more freeform means of displaying data than the Table and Matrix controls, and thus provide a lot of flexibility in the display of the data. If you were to drop a field directly onto a report you would find that it only displays the field's value in the dataset's first row, but the List control enables you to define a template (as shown in Figure 30-17), and enumerates through the data source, populating and displaying that template for each row (or group).

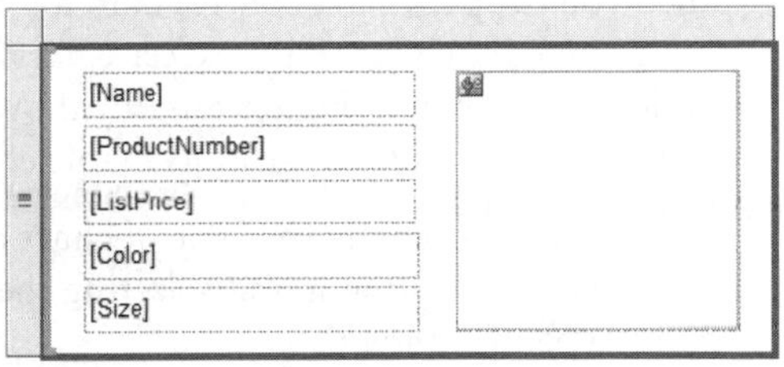

FIGURE 30-17

Being yet another form of the same base control used by the Table and Matrix controls, you will find that the List control shares many of the same features that they have.

Image

The Image control is used to display an image in your report. The source of this image can be from within your project (as an embedded image resource in your project), an external image (specified by a file system path or URL), or from a database field (a blob). When you drop this control on a report, a window is displayed enabling you to set these options (and others such as its size, border, and so on) as shown in Figure 30-18.

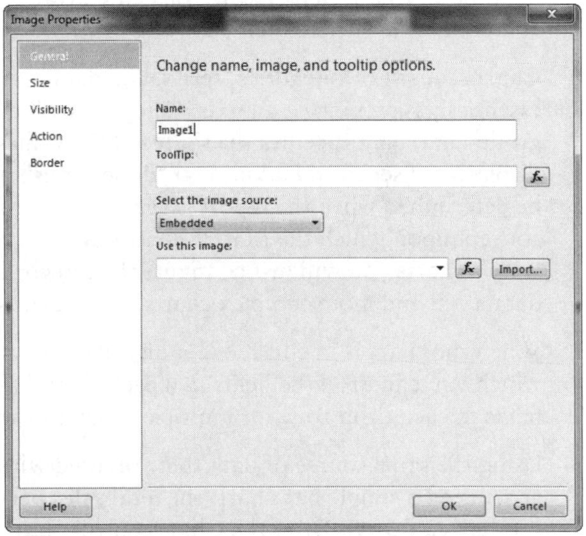

The options that appear will depend on the source you have selected for the image from the Select the Image Source drop-down box.

If you want to show external images (for example, from a file path) there are two things you must note. You must add a protocol prefix to the location you specify (for example, file://, http://, and so on), and

FIGURE 30-18

you must also set the `EnableExternalImages` property on the `LocalReport` object to true because this is not enabled by default.

```
reportViewer.LocalReport.EnableExternalImages = true;
```

Subreport

The Subreport control is used as a placeholder where the contents of another report can be inserted into this report (enabling complex reports to be created). This is discussed in detail later in this chapter.

Chart

Charts provide a much more visual representation of data, enabling patterns and anomalies in the data to be easily identified.

When you drop a Chart control onto a report it will immediately open the Select Chart Type window (as shown in Figure 30-19), allowing you to select from a wide range of available chart types.

You can always change the type of chart at a later point by right-clicking it and selecting the Change Chart Type menu item.

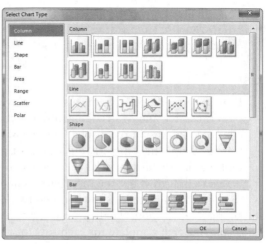

FIGURE 30-19

Double-clicking a chart will (like other controls) put it into edit mode (as shown in Figure 30-20), and you will find it consists of a number of sub-controls. Depending on the type of chart you choose it will have different controls arranged on its surface. All chart types, however, have a title and legend in addition to the chart itself. You can rearrange these components (or delete them) as you see fit.

Charts consist of categories, series, and data — each essentially representing an axis. Categories are used to group data, data specifies the source of the values to display, and series add additional "dimensions" that will be determined when the report is generated (the same concept upon which the Matrix control works). For simple charts you will just configure the categories and data axes, and more complex charts will use the series axis also.

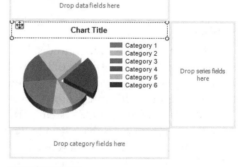

FIGURE 30-20

When the chart is in edit mode it displays drop zones (one for each axis) alongside the chart, upon which you can drop the fields that each should use. For more advanced charts you can drop multiple fields in each drop zone for multiple groupings/value displays.

Using the same source of data that you used when generating the matrix report, you will start by generating a simple bar chart (the total sales per product category). Drop the Chart control onto the report, set it to be a 3-D Clustered Bar chart, and double-click it to put it into edit mode. Drop the ProductCategory field onto the Category zone, and the Revenue field onto the Data zone. Change the chart and axes titles as you see fit, and another thing you will want to do (in order to show a label for every product category) is to right-click the vertical axis, select Axis Labels from the menu, and change the Interval from Auto to 1. Now when you generate the report you will get an output similar to Figure 30-21.

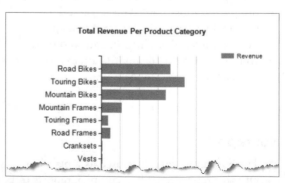

FIGURE 30-21

Note that currently the legend is of no real value, because in a bar chart it is designed to show the series group values (which you aren't using in this chart).

Now generate a chart that works much like the Matrix control, by setting the series grouping to add an additional dimension to your previous chart (so that it now displays the total quantity of sales for each product category per country). Drag the Country field onto the Series zone and run the report again. Now you will have the total sales for each product category split out per country, as shown in Figure 30-22.

Note how the legend now shows which bar color represents each country, because you are now making use of the series axis.

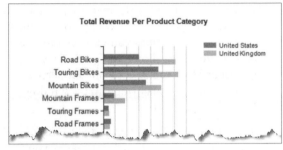

FIGURE 30-22

Gauge

The Gauge control is yet another means of visually representing the data. Gauges are generally designed to display a single value (although some gauges can each display a fixed number of separate values). This can be quite useful in displaying Key Performance Indicators (KPIs), for example.

When you drop a Gauge control onto a report it immediately opens the Select Gauge Type window, as shown in Figure 30-23, allowing you to select from a number of different linear and radial gauge types.

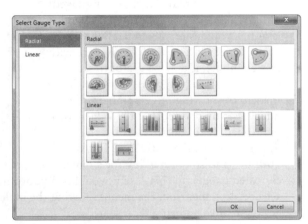

FIGURE 30-23

> Note that, unlike the Chart control, you cannot change the type of gauge once it has been created.

For this example you will use the Radial with Mini Gauge gauge. When you put the gauge into edit mode (by double-clicking it) it displays a drop zone above it (as shown in Figure 30-24), which will have one or more field placeholders (depending on how many values the gauge can display). Your selected gauge can display two values (one in the main gauge and one in the mini gauge), so it will have two field placeholders. When you drop a field from the Report Data window onto a field placeholder, you will note that it

FIGURE 30-24

automatically applies an aggregate because it is only displaying a single value in its related gauge. Numeric fields will automatically have a SUM aggregate applied, and other fields will have a COUNT aggregate applied.

Gauges have a fixed scale, and you must specify the minimum and maximum values that it will display. The nature of the Gauge control means that it won't automatically determine these values. To change these values you will need to select the scale itself (as shown in Figure 30-24), then right-click and select Scale Properties from the menu. This brings up the window shown in Figure 30-25.

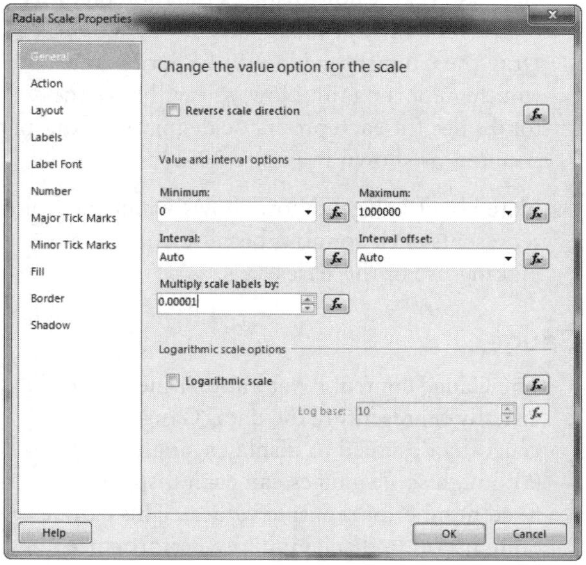

Your example will have expected values of up to 1 million, so you will set that as your maximum value. You will leave the interval options to be automatically determined (this will alter which scale labels are displayed), although you can change these if the output is not as you desire. When dealing with very small or very large values (as you are with this example), it may be useful to set the value of the Multiply Scale Labels By option. Instead of showing large numbers on the intervals, you can set that the value labels be multiplied by 0.00001, meaning that it will display 1 instead of 100000, 2 instead of 200000, and so on (making for a much less cluttered gauge). In this case it would be important to add a label to the gauge (right-click it and select Add Label from the menu) showing the multiplier that should be used with the label values to get the real value being represented.

FIGURE 30-25

You can also add one or more ranges to your gauge. For example, you might want to indicate that a range of values is acceptable by shading an area under the scale green, and shade another area red indicating the value should be of concern. Right-click your gauge and select Add Range from the menu. This automatically inserts a range into your gauge — to configure it right-click and select Range Properties from the menu. From this window you can enter at what values the range should start and end, and you will most likely (depending on your needs) want to change the start and end width of the range (generally so they are the same value). From the Fill tab you can change the color of the range to match its meaning (generally green = good, red = bad).

The final output of your gauge is shown in Figure 30-26.

FIGURE 30-26

Expressions, Placeholders, and Aggregates

Expressions provide the flexibility and power in your report, and are used everywhere from getting a value from a dataset, aggregating data, transforming data, and performing calculations, through to decision-making processes using conditional statements (IIF, and so on). Anything dynamically inserted into the report when it is being generated is handled by an expression. You might think of expressions as a formula that returns a value. Almost everything in a report can be controlled by an expression, including most control properties. So far you've already seen the expressions generated when you drag a field onto the report, and how the expression is "hidden" behind a placeholder, which can be used to hide its complexity. All expressions start with an equals (=) sign and return a single value.

Expressions can be categorized into simple expressions and complex expressions. Simple expressions refer only to a single field, which may have an aggregate function applied. Simple expressions will display a simplified version of the underlying expression as the label of the placeholder when displayed in the report designer. An example of a simple expression is:

```
=Fields!Revenue.Value
```

This will display in the report designer simply as [Revenue].

Complex expressions, however, either reference multiple fields or include operators, and appear in the report designer with <<Expr>> as their default placeholder label (although this can be changed in the placeholder properties to something more meaningful). Complex expressions essentially use VB for their syntax, although they still must consist of only a single line of code that returns a value. They can, however, make calls to more complicated multiline functions if necessary, as will be discussed in the next section. An example of a complex expression is:

```
=Fields!ProductCategory.Value + " sold to " + Fields!Country.Value
```

Now take a look at the process of creating an expression. As previously noted, when you drop a field onto a report it creates an expression that returns the value of that field from the dataset. To see this in action, drop a table on a report and then drop a field from the Report Data window into one of its cells. As discussed earlier in the chapter, what is being displayed in the cell is a placeholder label. When you right-click the placeholder you can select Expression from the menu to view and edit its underlying expression. This displays the Expression Builder window as shown in Figure 30-27.

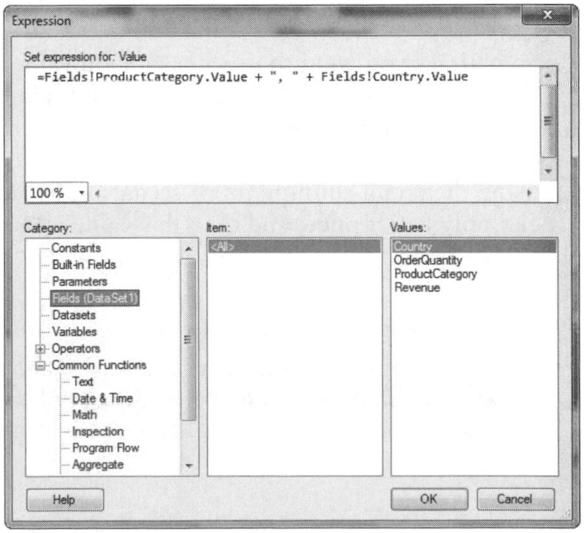

FIGURE 30-27

As its name might suggest, the Expression Builder helps you build expressions. At the top is the code area where you can type in the expression, and below it is the category tree, category items list, and a values list (which is only shown when values are available). The code area supports IntelliSense, tooltips (displaying function parameters), and syntax checking (squiggly red underlines to show errors), although unfortunately it doesn't support syntax highlighting. The lower "builder areas" help you build an expression, which is especially helpful when you don't know the syntax or what functionality is available. The Category tree allows you to drill down to select a category (such as a dataset, an operator type, a function type, and so on). The Item list displays what is available in that category, and the Values list (if values are available) displays the values for that item. For functions and operators it will display some helpful information on the selected item (what it does and examples of how it is used) in place of the Values list.

You will note when you are creating a report that many properties have an *fx* button next to them (in the dialog windows), or an Expression entry (in their drop-down list in the Properties tool window). This means that those properties can have expressions assigned to determine the value that should be applied to them, and clicking this button or selecting this item from the drop-down list will open the Expression Builder window in which you can create an expression to control the value of that property. This is extremely useful in conditional formatting scenarios, such as toggling the visibility or color of a control based upon the data being displayed.

In conditional formatting scenarios you will find the IIF function (Inline If) very useful to choose between two values based upon the result of a given expression (with the result being applied as the value of the property). Other "program flow" functions that you will find useful are the Choose and Switch functions.

Sometimes you want to use a calculated value in multiple places in a report, and rather than have the report recalculate the value multiple times, you'd like to calculate it once and reuse the value (speeding up the generation of the report in the process). This is where variables can be useful. Being named variables you may think that you can change their values (such as using them in a running totals scenario), but unfortunately that isn't the case. Their value can only be set once, and then this value is used from that point on without it needing to be recalculated.

Running totals are actually implemented in a report using the RunningValue function (built into the reporting engine) in an expression.

There are two types of variables: report variables and group variables, with their name matching their scope. The value of report values are set in the Report ⇨ Report Properties window, in the Variables tab shown in Figure 30-28.

The variables defined here will be available anywhere in the report. A new entry will be created when you click the Add button, where you can give the variable a name and a value. If it's a constant value you can specify its value there, or you can click the *fx* button to create an expression that calculates the value. This calculation will only be performed once, and the value will be reused on subsequent references of the variable.

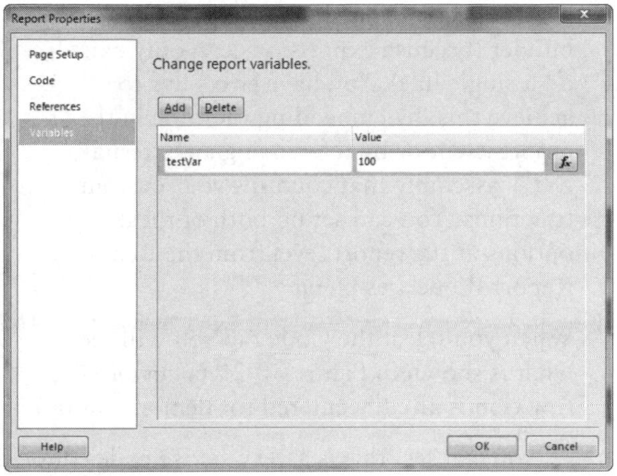

FIGURE 30-28

> The variables that are available to an expression can be found in the Expression Builder under the Variables category.

So if you've created a variable called `testVar`, you can use it in an expression like so:

```
=Variables!testVar.Value
```

Another use for report variables is to define constant values for use in your report, enabling you to centrally define values that are used in multiple places in your report without "hard coding" them in those places.

The other type of variable is the group variable. This works in much the same way as the report variables, except the scope of the calculated value is just the current grouping in a Table/Matrix/List control (and any child groupings). Its value is calculated each time the grouping changes, so if you have a calculation to make for each grouping (whose value is reused throughout that grouping), this is how you would implement it. To create a group variable, open the Group Properties window, go to the Variables tab, and then create and use the variable in the same way as demonstrated for the report variable. You can test the behavior of how the calculated value is reused and subsequently recalculated when the group changes by creating the following expression and seeing when its output changes:

```
=Round(Rnd() * 100)
```

Custom Code

Sometimes the built-in functions of the reporting engine are not enough to suit your purposes. When you need a complex multiline function to perform a calculation or make a decision, this must be written outside the expression builder (because expressions can only exist on a single line). You have two ways to achieve this: by embedding the code in the report itself, or by referencing an external .NET assembly that contains your custom functions. You can set up both of these options at the report level from the Report ➪ Report Properties menu.

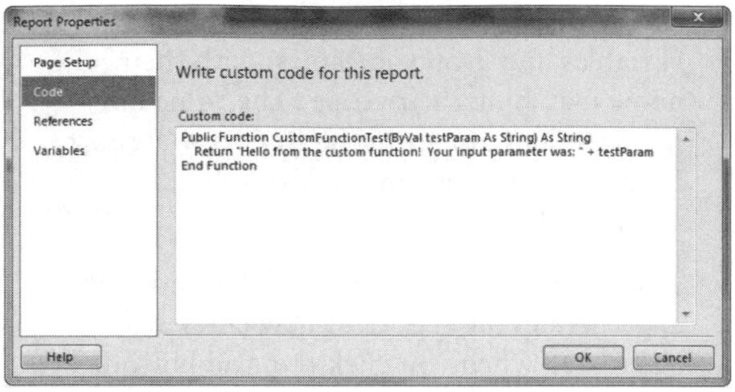

When you select the Code tab you will see what is shown in Figure 30-29 (a custom function is already entered for demonstration).

FIGURE 30-29

As you can see, this is a very sparse code editor. There is no syntax highlighting, error checking, or IntelliSense, so it isn't very friendly to use. If there is an error in your code it will be caught when the project is compiled and the compilation will fail (pointing out the cause of the error in the Error List tool window). After you've written your functions in here (using VB as the language) you can add a textbox to your report, open the expression builder, and call them like so:

```
=Code.CustomFunctionTest("Test Input")
```

> Note that the IntelliSense in the expression builder doesn't show the available function names when you type Code. in the editor, nor does it show what parameters the function takes. In addition, the only assemblies automatically referenced for use are the System.Convert, System.Math, and Microsoft.VisualBasic — if you need to use assemblies other than these you will need to add references to them in the References tab, which is discussed shortly.

Calling the function shown in Figure 30-29 with this expression displays the following in the textbox:

```
Hello from the custom function!  Your input parameter was: Test Input
```

If you want to reuse the custom functions among multiple reports you are better off writing the code in a .NET assembly, and referencing it from each report that requires its functions. You can create a Class Library project, write the code (in either VB or C#), and then reference it in your report. Unfortunately, you will face a few difficulties in ensuring that the report can find the assembly and configuring its code access security settings so that the report has the permissions to execute its functions — so it's not a completely straightforward process. However, you are about to walk through the process required to get it working here.

Create a new project using the Class Library template called CustomReportingFunctions. Create a class called MyFunctions, and add the following function to it:

VB

```
Public Shared Function CustomFunctionTest(ByVal testParam As String) As String
    Return "Your input parameter was: " + testParam
End Function
```

C#

```
public static string CustomFunctionTest(string testParam)
{
    return "Your input parameter was: " + testParam;
}
```

You will also need to add the following attribute to the assembly to enable it to be called by the reporting engine. This is added to AssemblyInfo.vb for VB developers (under the My Project folder, requiring the Show All Files option to be on in order to be seen), and to AssemblyInfo.cs for C# developers (under the Properties folder).

VB

```
<Assembly: System.Security.AllowPartiallyTrustedCallers>
```

C#

```
[assembly: System.Security.AllowPartiallyTrustedCallers]
```

In order for the report to find the assembly, it must be installed in the Global Assembly Cache (GAC). This means you need to give the assembly a strong name, by going to the Properties of the custom functions assembly, opening the Signing tab, checking in the Sign the Assembly checkbox, and choosing/creating a strong name key file. Now you can compile the project, and then install the assembly in GAC by opening the Visual Studio Command Prompt, entering

```
gacutil -i <assembly_path>
```

and replacing <assembly_path> with the actual path to the compiled assembly.

> *Each time you update this assembly, remember to install it into the GAC again.*

Now you can reference the assembly in the report. Open up the Report Properties window and go to the References tab (as shown in Figure 30-30). Click the Add button, then click the ellipsis button on the blank entry that appears. Find the assembly (you may need to browse by file to find it) and click OK.

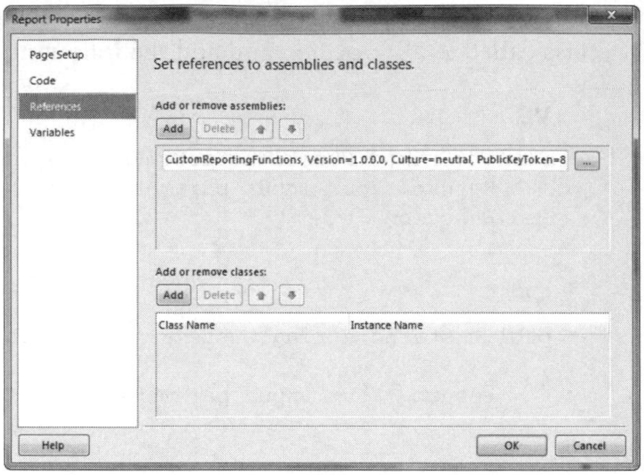

Note the Add or Remove Classes area below the Add or Remove Assemblies area. This is used to automatically create instances of classes in the referenced assemblies. You made your function shared (or static as it is referred to in C#) so you don't need an instance of the `MyFunctions` class. However, if the function was not shared/static and you needed a class instance you need to configure these instances here (because a class cannot be instantiated in an expression). To do this, specify the class name (including its

FIGURE 30-30

namespace) and give it an instance name (that is, the name of the variable that you will use in your expressions to refer to the instance of the class). The reporting engine will handle instantiating the class, and will assign the reference to a variable with the given name so you can use it in your expressions.

Now you are ready to reference your function in an expression, although slightly differently from how you used the function when it was embedded in the report. You need to refer to the function by its full namespace, class, and function name. For example:

```
=CustomReportingFunctions.MyFunctions.CustomFunctionTest("Test Input")
```

You are almost done, but not quite. The final piece of the puzzle is to specify that the assembly should be run with full trust in the domain of the report engine. This is done when initiating the report rendering process (which is covered later in this chapter) and requires the strong name of the assembly.

VB

```
Dim customAssemblyName As String = "CustomReportingFunctions, Version=1.0.0.0, " & _
                            "Culture=neutral, PublicKeyToken=b9c8e588f9750854"

Dim customAssembly As Assembly = Assembly.Load(customAssemblyName)
Dim assemblyStrongName As StrongName = CreateStrongName(customAssembly)
reportEngine.AddFullTrustModuleInSandboxAppDomain(assemblyStrongName)
```

C#

```
string customAssemblyName = "CustomReportingFunctions, Version=1.0.0.0, " +
                        "Culture=neutral, PublicKeyToken=b9c8e588f9750854";

Assembly customAssembly = Assembly.Load(customAssemblyName);
StrongName assemblyStrongName = CreateStrongName(customAssembly);
reportEngine.AddFullTrustModuleInSandboxAppDomain(assemblyStrongName);
```

There are two things you will note from this code. The first is that you are loading the custom assembly from the GAC using its name (in order to obtain its strong name so you can notify the reporting engine that it's trusted), including its version, culture, and public key token. This string can be obtained by copying it from where you added the assembly reference to the report in its Report Properties dialog box.

The second is the use of the GetStrongName function to return the StrongName object, the code for which is below:

VB

```vb
Private Shared Function CreateStrongName(ByVal assembly As Assembly) As StrongName
    Dim assemblyName As AssemblyName = assembly.GetName()

    If assemblyName Is Nothing Then
        Throw New InvalidOperationException("Could not get assembly name")
    End If

    ' Get the public key blob
    Dim publicKey As Byte() = assemblyName.GetPublicKey()

    If publicKey Is Nothing OrElse publicKey.Length = 0 Then
        Throw New InvalidOperationException("Assembly is not strongly named")
    End If

    Dim keyBlob As New StrongNamePublicKeyBlob(publicKey)

    ' Finally create the StrongName
    Return New StrongName(keyBlob, assemblyName.Name, assemblyName.Version)
End Function
```

Code snippet CreateStrongName.vb

C#

```csharp
private static StrongName CreateStrongName(Assembly assembly)
{
    AssemblyName assemblyName = assembly.GetName();

    if (assemblyName == null)
        throw new InvalidOperationException("Could not get assembly name");

    // Get the public key blob
    byte[] publicKey = assemblyName.GetPublicKey();

    if (publicKey == null || publicKey.Length == 0)
        throw new InvalidOperationException("Assembly is not strongly named");

    StrongNamePublicKeyBlob keyBlob = new StrongNamePublicKeyBlob(publicKey);

    // Finally create the StrongName
    return new StrongName(keyBlob, assemblyName.Name, assemblyName.Version);
}
```

Code snippet CreateStrongName.cs

Now when you run the report you will have the same output as when you embedded the code in the report, but in a more reusable and maintainable form.

Report Layout

Generally reports are produced in order to be printed, therefore you must consider how the printed report will look in your report design. The first thing to ensure is that the dimensions of your report match the paper size that it will be printed on. Open the Report Properties window via the Report ⇨ Report Properties menu. The selected tab will be the Page Setup tab, from which you can select the paper size, the margins, and the orientation of the page (portrait or landscape).

Many reports tend to extend beyond one page, and it can be useful to show something at the top and bottom of each page to show which company and report it belongs to, and where that page belongs within the report (in case the pages are dropped, for example). So far you have been dealing just with the body of the report, but you can add a page header and footer to the report to use for these purposes. Page headers tend to be used for displaying the company logo, name, and information about the company (like a letterhead). Page footers tend to be used to display page numbers, the report title, and perhaps some totals for the information displayed on that page.

Add a page header to your report via the Report ⇨ Add Page Header menu command. This adds a page header area in the report designer above the report body (see Figure 30-31), which you can resize to your needs, and upon which you can place various controls such as textboxes and images. You can even place other controls such as a Table or Gauge, although it's rare to do so. If you drag a field from the Report Data tool window directly onto the page header you will note that it creates a complex expression (as it does on the report body), so add a table first if you want to display some totals, for example.

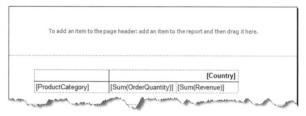

FIGURE 30-31

Adding a page footer is much the same process. Select the Report ⇨ Add Page Footer menu to add a page footer area in the report designer below the body of the report (see Figure 30-32).

FIGURE 30-32

You can use the built-in report fields to display information such as the page number, number of pages, report name, the time the report was generated, and so on, which can be used anywhere in your report. You can find them in the Report Data tool window, under the Built-in Fields category.

> *The value for the Report Name field is retrieved from the filename of the report with the extension removed.*

Generally you will want to show the page numbers in the form as Page 1 of 6. However, the page number and page count fields are separate, so it's best to drop a textbox in the footer and drop both fields in that:

```
Page [&PageNumber] of [&TotalPages]
```

The values in the square brackets will automatically turn into placeholders with the correct expressions behind them (the & specifies that these are global variable references) that get the values from the built-in fields. You can alternatively drag these fields from the Report Data tool window into the textbox and add the static text in between.

> *Be careful that you don't remove the page header or footer once you've created it (by selecting Remove Page Header or Remove Page Footer from the Report menu) because this will delete the content of the header/footer and adding it back again won't restore its content. There is no warning displayed when you do this, so if you do so by accident use the Undo function to restore it to its previous state.*

One question you may now have is how to create report headers and footers (that only appear on the first/last page of the report, rather than each page). An example of a report header would be to display the title of the report and other report information at the top of the report (on the first page only), and an example of a report footer would be to display some totals at the end of the report (on the last page only).

The report designer doesn't support report headers/footers as special areas of the report in the same way it does for page headers/footers because you can simply include them in the body of the report. By putting the report header content at the top of the body of your report it will only display once, then it will display the content (which may expand to cover multiple pages), and finally at the bottom of your report you can put the report footer content. The only issue to deal with is that you won't want the page header on the first page of your report (because you will only want the report header), and you won't want the page footer on the last page (because you will only want the report footer). To do this, right-click your report header and select Header Properties from the menu. From the General tab (which will be the one selected), uncheck the Print on First Page checkbox. The process is much the same for the page footer: right-click your report footer, select Footer Properties from the menu, and then uncheck the Print on Last Page checkbox.

The final thing you must consider with your report layout is where the page breaks will occur. For example, you may want a table to appear all on the same page where possible rather than half on one page and half on another. Or perhaps you have its data grouped, and you want each group to start on a new page. You can do this by setting page break options on the controls that support them (Table, Matrix, List, Rectangle, Gauge, and Chart). Each of these controls has the PageBreak property (select the control in the report designer and find the property in the Properties tool window). This gives you the option to start a new page before it displays the control, after it displays the control, or both before and after it displays the control. You can set KeepTogether to true so that if the output of the control stretches across two pages it will attempt to display it all on the one page by starting it on the next page instead. When you are grouping data in a table, matrix, or list, you can also set the page break options for the group. When you view the properties of a group (right-click the group in the Row Groups pane at the bottom of the designer and select Group Properties from the menu) you will note a Page Breaks tab. Here you can select whether there should be a page break between each group, and you can also select whether there should be an additional page break before and/or after each group.

Subreports

Subreports is a feature that enables you to insert the contents of one report into another. You can insert the contents (excluding headers and footers) of any report into another by adding a Subreport control to your main report and setting its ReportPath property to the path of the other report to display in that area. By merging a number of reports into a single output report you are able to create quite complex report structures. Other uses of subreports include creating master-detail reports, drill-down reports, and splitting reports into predefined "components" that can be used by multiple reports — enabling each component to be defined once and used multiple times. This also has the advantage that changes can be made in a single place and automatically picked up by the other reports (such as a standard report header with company information, used by all the reports).

First look at a scenario where the contents of the subreport are not linked to the "master" report. Create a new report, and simply put a textbox on it with some text. Now add a Subreport control to your main report, and set the ReportName property to the filename of the other report (but without the extension).

> *Unfortunately the report to be used as the subreport must be located in the same folder as the main report.*

When you run the project and view the report you will see that the contents of the subreport are merged into the main report.

Getting a little more complicated now, hook up a data source to the subreport and show some data in it (in a standalone fashion from the main report). The issue now is, because the data sources aren't shared between the main report and the subreport, how do you pass the data to that report? You do this by handling the SubreportProcessing event on the LocalReport object in the code that configures the Report Viewer control (discussed in full later in this chapter). You will need to add an event handler for this event like so:

VB
```
AddHandler reportViewer.LocalReport.SubreportProcessing, AddressOf ProcessSubreport
```

C#
```
reportViewer.LocalReport.SubreportProcessing += ProcessSubreport;
```

and add a function for this event handler that adds the data to the
`SubreportProcessingEventArgs` object passed in as a parameter (including the name of the
dataset), like so:

VB

```
Private Sub ProcessSubreport(ByVal sender As System.Object,
                            ByVal e As SubreportProcessingEventArgs)
    e.DataSources.Add(New ReportDataSource("DataSetName", data))
End Sub
```

C#

```
private void ProcessSubreport(object sender, SubreportProcessingEventArgs e)
{
    e.DataSources.Add(new ReportDataSource("DataSetName", data));
}
```

When you run the project now the subreport will be populated with data.

Now take a look at the slightly more complex scenario where what is displayed in the subreport is
dependent on data in the main report. Say, for example, the main report is displaying the details
of each customer, but you also want to show the orders each customer made in the last month
underneath their details using a subreport. So that the subreport knows which customer to retrieve
the order details for, you need to make use of Report Parameters.

> Note that there are a lot of overheads in implementing this scenario in this way.
> There will be multiple calls to the database — one for each customer to return
> their order details, which will put strain on the database server. A better, more
> efficient way for this scenario would be to return a joined customer details
> + orders dataset from the database, and use the Table control to group by
> customer and display their order details. However, this scenario is just used as
> an example of how to pass information from the main report to subreports.

Create a report (which will be the main report) to display the details of each customer (in a list),
and another report (the subreport) that displays the orders that a customer has made. Under the
customer details fields (but still in the list), add a Subreport control that points to the subreport
you created, and hook up the code-behind as previously described. What you will note is that
when handling the `SubreportProcessing` event to return the order details data to the subreport,
you need to know which customer to return the data for (the subreport will be rendered for each
customer, therefore this event handler will be called to return the order details for each
customer). This is where you need to create a Report Parameter for the subreport that the main report will use
to pass the current customer's ID to it.

To add a new parameter to the subreport, go to the Report Data tool window, right-click the
Parameters folder, and select Add Parameter from the menu. Create the parameter with CustomerID
as its name, and set its data type to Integer.

Back on the main report, select the Subreport control in the designer, right-click and select Subreport Properties from the menu, and go to the Parameters tab. Click the Add button, specify CustomerID as the parameter name, and enter [CustomerID] as its value. Now each time it renders the subreport, it will pass it the current value of the customer ID field.

The final thing to do is retrieve the value of that parameter in your `ProcessSubreport` event handler, and filter the results returned accordingly, like so:

VB

```
Private Sub ProcessSubreport(ByVal sender As System.Object,
                             ByVal e As SubreportProcessingEventArgs)
    Dim customerID As Integer =
        Convert.ToInt32(e.Parameters("CustomerID").Values(0))
    Dim fromDate As DateTime = DateTime.Today.AddMonths(-1)

    Dim qry = From co In context.SalesOrderHeaders
            Where co.CustomerID = customerID AndAlso co.OrderDate > fromDate
            Select co

    e.DataSources.Add(New ReportDataSource("OrderData", qry))
End Sub
```

C#

```
public void ProcessSubreport(object sender, SubreportProcessingEventArgs e)
{
    int customerID = Convert.ToInt32(e.Parameters["CustomerID"].Values[0]);
    DateTime fromDate = DateTime.Today.AddMonths(-1);

    var qry = from co in context.SalesOrderHeaders
            where co.CustomerID == customerID && co.OrderDate > fromDate
            select co;

    e.DataSources.Add(new ReportDataSource("OrderData", qry));
}
```

The Report Wizard

The easiest place to start when designing a report is to make use of the Report Wizard. The Report Wizard leads you through all the main steps to generate a report, and based upon your input will generate the report for you that you can then customize to your needs.

The Report Wizard takes you through the following steps:

➤ **Choosing/creating a data source:** Enables you to select an existing data source or create a new one as the source of data for the report. This step is exactly the same as was detailed earlier in the "Defining Data Sources" section of this chapter.

➤ **Arranging fields:** Drag fields into the Values list to create a simple table, add fields in the Row Groups list to group the rows of the table by those fields, and add fields to the Column Groups list to group the columns by those fields (which will turn it into a matrix).

➤ **Choose the layout:** Gives you the option to add subtotals and grand totals rows/columns.

➤ **Choose a style:** Allows you to choose different colors and styles used in the output. If you want to create your own color scheme you can do so by modifying the `StyleTemplates` `.xml` file in the `C:\Program Files\Microsoft Visual Studio 10.0\Common7\IDE\` `PrivateAssemblies\1033` folder on your machine (this path may differ on your machine based upon where Visual Studio has been installed).

To start the Report Wizard you will need to create a new report file (you cannot use the Report Wizard on an existing file or after it has already been run). Add a new item to your project, and from the Reporting subsection add a new Report Wizard item.

The Report Wizard takes you through its series of steps to generate a basic report. Once you have completed the steps, it generates the report and opens it in the report designer for you to modify as required.

> *This is a great place to start when learning how to design reports, and when you become more familiar and comfortable with the process and designing more complicated reports you will find yourself using it less and less.*

RENDERING REPORTS

Now that you have designed your report, it's time to actually generate it by populating it with data. This is where the Report Viewer control is used, because it contains the local engine for generating the report from the report definition files and the data sources.

The Report Viewer Controls

There are two versions of the Report Viewer control: one for use in web applications and one for use in Windows applications. However, the way you use them to generate and display reports is virtually identical.

The Windows version of the control is shown in Figure 30-33.

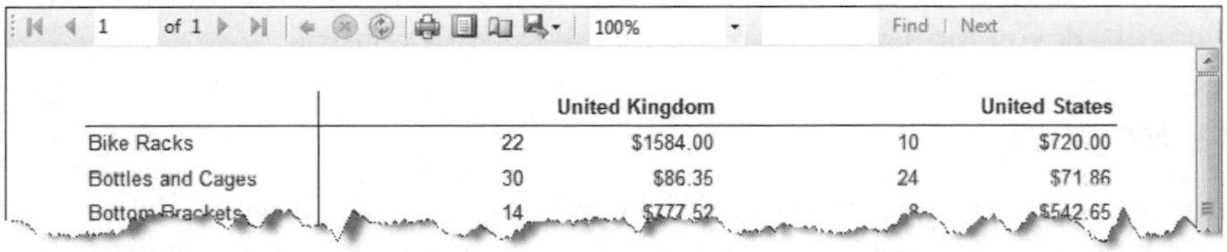

		United Kingdom		United States
Bike Racks	22	$1584.00	10	$720.00
Bottles and Cages	30	$86.35	24	$71.86
Bottom Brackets	14	$777.52	8	$542.65

FIGURE 30-33

The Report Viewer contains a toolbar with various functions (such as Refresh, Export, Print, and so on), and a view of the report (page by page). Individual functions on this toolbar can be turned off via properties on the Report Viewer control, and each raises an event when clicked (although the corresponding behavior is performed by the Report Viewer control automatically unless cancelled in the event handler).

To use the Report Viewer control in your Windows Forms project, simply drop it on your form from the Toolbox.

The web version also looks quite similar (shown in Figure 30-34), but displays the report output in a browser.

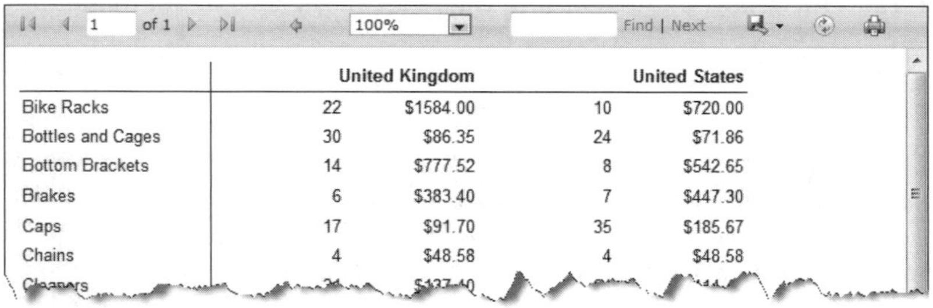

FIGURE 30-34

To use the web version of the Report Viewer control, you can drop it on a page from the Toolbox (in the Reporting tab). This adds a namespace prefix (rsweb) for the `Microsoft.ReportViewer` `.WebForms` assembly/namespace, and the following tag to use the Report Viewer control:

```
<rsweb:ReportViewer ID="reportViewer" runat="server" />
```

The web version of the Report Viewer control also requires a Script Manager to be on the page. If you don't have one on the page already, drag this from the Toolbox (under the AJAX Extensions tab) and onto the page.

When you display a report in the web version of the Report Viewer control you will find that it displays a Print button on the toolbar only in Internet Explorer (IE), and not in other browsers such as Firefox. This is because, in order to print the report from the browser, the Report Viewer needs an ActiveX control to do the printing and ActiveX controls only work in IE. Because printing can't be done from other browsers the Print button won't be displayed. When you click the Print button in IE the first time it will ask you for permission to install the ActiveX control.

Generating the Report

The process of generating a report is essentially to tell the report engine which report definition file to use, and pass it the data (objects, entities, data tables, and so on) to populate the report with.

By default the report definition file is embedded into the assembly, although it often is best to have it as a separate file so it can be easily updated when necessary without having to recompile the assembly. However, embedding it into the assembly means that there are fewer files to distribute, and it may in some circumstances be preferable that the report definition file cannot (easily) be tampered with. Set the Build Action on the report definition file to Embedded Resource in order for it to be embedded in the assembly (which is the default value), or otherwise set it to be Content.

The following code is what is required to generate a report from a file-based report definition file and populate it with some data (the data variable contains a collection of entities from the Entity Framework model, which is used to populate the CustomerData data source in the report):

VB

```
Dim reportEngine As LocalReport = reportViewer.LocalReport
reportEngine.ReportPath = "CustomerReport.rdlc"
reportEngine.DataSources.Add(New ReportDataSource("CustomerData", data))
reportViewer.RefreshReport() 'Only for Windows Report Viewer
```

C#

```
LocalReport reportEngine = reportViewer.LocalReport;
reportEngine.ReportPath = "CustomerReport.rdlc";
reportEngine.DataSources.Add(new ReportDataSource("CustomerData", data));
reportViewer.RefreshReport(); // Only for Windows Report Viewer
```

Here you get the existing `LocalReport` object from the Report Viewer control, assign values to its properties, and then use the `RefreshReport` function on the Report Viewer control to start the report engine generating the report.

If you have chosen to embed the report in your assembly, then instead of setting the `ReportPath` property on the `LocalReport` object you will need to set the `ReportEmbeddedResource` property instead. This must be the qualified resource path (which is case sensitive), including the namespace and the extension of the report like so:

VB

```
reportEngine.ReportEmbeddedResource = "Chapter30Sample.CustomerReport.rdlc"
```

C#

```
reportEngine.ReportEmbeddedResource = "Chapter30Sample.CustomerReport.rdlc";
```

If you have one or more subreports in your report you will also have to handle the `SubreportProcessing` event of the `LocalReport` object as was demonstrated when discussing the Subreport control. If you are using custom assemblies, you will need to include the code to specify that the custom assembly is trusted. In addition, you may need to set the properties on the `LocalReport` object to enable the report to use external images, hyperlinks, and so on. However, the code provided here is the core code required to generate a report and display it in the Report Viewer control.

Rendering Reports to Different Formats

It's not necessary to display a report in the Report Viewer control. In some instances you may want to generate the report and e-mail it as a PDF without any user interaction, or return a PDF'd report as a result of a web service call. The Report Viewer control enables you to export the report to various formats (Excel, PDF, Word, and so on) as an option on its toolbar, and this can also be done via code. This is possible by creating a `LocalReport` object, setting the required properties, and then using the `Render` function on the `LocalReport` object to render it to a specified format (which is output to a stream or byte array).

The `Render` function has a number of overloads, but the simplest one to use is to just pass it the output format (in this case PDF) and it will return a byte array containing the report. For example:

VB

```
Dim reportOutput As Byte() = reportEngine.Render("PDF")
```

C#

```
byte[] reportOutput = reportEngine.Render("PDF");
```

The report engine can generate the report in a number of formats. Valid values include:

➤ **PDF:** Output to an Adobe Acrobat file

➤ **Word:-** Output to a Microsoft Word document

➤ **Excel:** Output to an Microsoft Excel spreadsheet

➤ **Image:** Output to a TIFF image file

To output to a stream (such an HTTP Response stream or a file stream) you can turn the bytes into a stream:

VB

```
Dim stream As MemoryStream = New MemoryStream(reportOutput)
stream.Seek(0, SeekOrigin.Begin)
```

C#

```
MemoryStream stream = new MemoryStream(reportOutput);
stream.Seek(0, SeekOrigin.Begin);
```

Alternatively, for larger reports (where this may be too memory-intensive) you can write directly to a stream from the `Render` function using one of its overloads, passing in a callback function that creates and returns the stream to write to as the value for the `createStream` parameter:

VB

```
Private Function CreateReportFileStream(ByVal fileName As String,
                                        ByVal extension As String,
                                        ByVal encoding As Encoding,
                                        ByVal mimeType As String,
                                        ByVal willSeek As Boolean) As Stream
    Return New FileStream(fileName & "." & extension, FileMode.Create)
End Function
```

C#

```
private Stream CreateReportFileStream(string fileName, string extension,
                            Encoding encoding, string mimeType, bool willSeek)
{
    return new FileStream(fileName + "." + extension, FileMode.Create);
}
```

Then you can call the render function like so:

VB

```
Dim warnings As Warning() = Nothing
reportEngine.Render("PDF", Nothing, AddressOf CreateReportFileStream, warnings)
```

C#

```
Warning[] warnings;
reportEngine.Render("PDF", null, CreateReportFileStream, out warnings);
```

DEPLOYING REPORTS

Now that you've designed your report you can deploy it to users as a part of your application. However, the Report Viewer control is not a part of the .NET Framework, and thus it needs to be installed separately. A search for "Report Viewer redistributable" on the Web should help you find the installer for the Report Viewer assemblies.

An alternative is to simply distribute the Report Viewer assemblies that you have referenced with your application. Note, however, that this won't include the .cab installer for the ActiveX control that, when using the web report viewer control in web applications, will enable reports to be printed (in IE only). If this is a feature you require in your application then it's best to use the Report Viewer redistributable installer instead.

SUMMARY

In this chapter you've seen how to use Visual Studio's report designer to design a report, populate it with data, and display the output to the user. Unfortunately, reporting is an incredibly complex topic, and it is impossible to cover it completely and go through every option available in one chapter. Hopefully this has been a good introduction to the topic, however, and will guide you in the right direction for designing your own reports.

PART VII
Application Services

▶ **CHAPTER 31:** Windows Communication Foundation (WCF)

▶ **CHAPTER 32:** Windows Workflow Foundation (WF)

▶ **CHAPTER 33:** Client Application Services

▶ **CHAPTER 34:** Synchronization Services

▶ **CHAPTER 35:** WCF RIA Services

31

Windows Communication Foundation (WCF)

WHAT'S IN THIS CHAPTER?

➤   Understanding WCF services

➤   Creating a WCF service

➤   Configuring WCF service endpoints

➤   Hosting a WCF service

➤   Consuming a WCF service

Most systems require a means to communicate between their various components — most commonly between the server and the client. Many different technologies enable this sort of communication, but Windows Communication Foundation (WCF) brings a unified architecture to implementing them. This chapter takes you through the architecture of WCF services and how to create, host, and consume WCF services in your system.

WHAT IS WCF?

Within the .NET Framework there are a variety of ways that you can communicate among applications, including (but not limited to) remoting, web services, and a myriad of networking protocols. This has often frustrated application developers who not only had to pick the appropriate technology to use, but also had to write plumbing code that would allow their applications to use different technologies depending on where or how they would be deployed. For example, when users are connected directly to the intranet it is probably better for them to use a remoting or direct TCP/IP connection for their speed benefits. However, these aren't the ideal solution for communication when the application is outside the corporate firewall, in which case a secured web service would be preferable.

WCF is designed to solve this sort of problem by providing a means to build messaging applications that are technology-agnostic, which can then be configured (in text-based configuration files) to what technologies each service will support and how they will be used. Therefore, you only need to write the one service and it can support all the various communication technologies supported by WCF. WCF is essentially a unified communication layer for .NET applications.

GETTING STARTED

A WCF service can be added to an existing project (such as a web application), or it can be created as a standalone project. For the purposes of this example you will be creating a standalone service so you can easily see how a single service can be configured and hosted in many communication scenarios.

When you open the New Project dialog and click the WCF category (under either the VB or C# languages), you will notice a number of different WCF project types as shown in Figure 31-1.

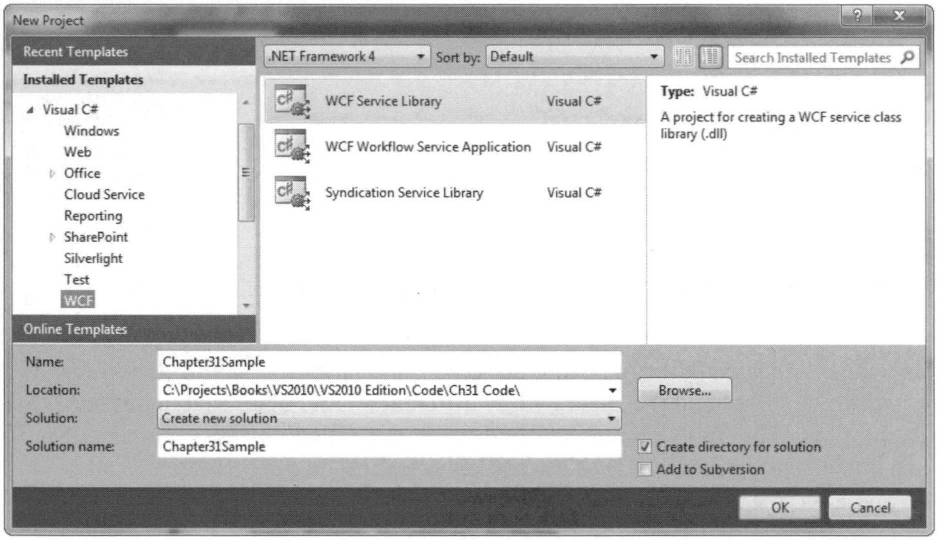

FIGURE 31-1

The WCF Workflow Service Application project template provides an easy way to expose a Windows Workflow (WF) publicly, and this is discussed in Chapter 32. The Syndication Service Library project template is used to expose data as an RSS feed. However, the project template you will be using in the example for in this chapter is the WCF Service Library project template.

> *If you look in the Web category in the New Project dialog, you will see that there is also a WCF Service Application project template, which wasn't under the WCF category. This project template creates a WCF service that is already configured to be hosted within an ASP.NET web application.*

By default, a new WCF Service Library will include `IService1.vb` and `Service1.vb` (or `.cs` if you are using C#), which define the contract and the implementation of a basic service, respectively. When you open these files you will see that they already expose some operations and data as an example of how to expose your own operations and data yourself. This can be all cleared out until you simply have an interface with nothing defined (but with the `ServiceContract` attribute left in place), and a class that simply implements that interface. Or you can delete both files and start anew.

When you want to add additional services to your project you will find a WCF Service item template in the Add New Item dialog that will add both an interface and a class to your project to use for the contract and implementation of the service.

DEFINING CONTRACTS

This example project will expose some data from the Entity Framework model that you created in Chapter 29 for the AdventureWorksLT database, and expose some operations that can be performed on that data. The way that you do so is by creating *contracts* that will define the operations and the structure of the data that will be publicly exposed. Three core types of contracts exist: *service contracts*, *data contracts*, and *message contracts*.

➤ A service contract is a group of operations, essentially detailing the capabilities of the service.

➤ A data contract details the structure of the data being passed between the service and the client.

➤ A message contract details the structure of the messages passed between the service and the client. This is useful when the service must conform to a given message format. This is an advanced topic, and not required for basic services, so we won't cover this type of contract in this chapter.

These contracts are defined by decorating the classes/interfaces in the service with special attributes.

In this chapter you walk through an example of creating a WCF service exposing customer data from the AdventureWorksLT database to client applications. To do this you will expose operations for working with the customer data, which will expose the actual customer data itself in the database.

For the purpose of this example you'll start fresh — so delete `IService1` (`.vb` or `.cs`) and `Service1` (`.vb` or `.cs`). Add a new item to the project using the WCF Service item template, called CustomerService. This will add two new files to your project — `CustomerService` (`.vb` or `.cs`) and `ICustomerService` (`.vb` or `.cs`).

> *There are two primary angles that you can take when designing services. You can take either an implementation-first approach (where you write the code first and then apply attributes to it to create the contract), or you can take a contract-first approach (where you design the schema/WSDL first and generate the code from it). An in-depth discussion of these approaches is beyond the scope of this chapter; however, WCF can support both approaches. The example in this chapter follows the contract-first approach.*

Creating the Service Contract

Focus on defining the service contract first. The operations you want to expose externally are:

➤   AddCustomer

➤   GetCustomer

➤   UpdateCustomer

➤   DeleteCustomer

➤   GetCustomerList

You may recognize the first four operations as standard CRUD (Create, Read, Update, and Delete) operations when you are working with data. The final operation will return a list of all the customers in the database.

Now that you know what operations are required you can define your service contract.

> *You may have noted from the sample implementation in the WCF project template that all of the service attributes were defined in the interface. However, creating an interface to decorate with the contract attributes is not essential — in fact, you don't need to create an interface at all, and you can decorate the class itself with the attributes instead. However, standard practice (and best practice) dictates that the contract should be defined as (and in) an interface, so you will be following this best practice in the example.*

You will define your operations in the ICustomerService interface. However, these operations will expose data using a data class that you haven't defined as yet — in the meantime, create a stub data class and you can flesh it out shortly. Add a new class to the project called `CustomerData` and leave it as it is to act as your stub. Each of the operations needs to be decorated with the `OperationContract` attribute:

VB

```vb
<ServiceContract([Namespace]:="http://www.professionalvisualstudio.com")>
Public Interface ICustomerService
    <OperationContract()>
    Function AddCustomer(ByVal customer As CustomerData) As Integer

    <OperationContract()>
    Function GetCustomer(ByVal customerID As Integer) As CustomerData

    <OperationContract()>
    Sub UpdateCustomer(ByVal customer As CustomerData)

    <OperationContract()>
    Sub DeleteCustomer(ByVal customerID As Integer)

    <OperationContract()>
```

```
        Function GetCustomerList() As List(Of CustomerData)
    End Interface
```

C#

```csharp
[ServiceContract(Namespace="http://www.professionalvisualstudio.com")]
public interface ICustomerService
{
    [OperationContract]
    int AddCustomer(CustomerData customer);

    [OperationContract]
    CustomerData GetCustomer(int customerID);

    [OperationContract]
    void UpdateCustomer(CustomerData customer);

    [OperationContract]
    void DeleteCustomer(int customerID);

    [OperationContract]
    List<CustomerData> GetCustomerList();
}
```

Both the `ServiceContract` and `OperationContract` attributes have a number of properties that you can apply values to, enabling you to alter their default behavior. For example, both have a name property (enabling you to specify the name of the service/operation as seen externally). Of particular note is the `ServiceContract`'s `Namespace` property, which you should always explicitly specify (as has been done in the preceding code). If a namespace has not been explicitly set, the schema and WSDL generated for the service will use `http://tempuri.org` as its namespace. However, to reduce the chance of collisions with other services it's best to use something unique such as your company's URL.

Now that you've defined your contract you need to actually implement these operations. Open the `CustomerService` class, which implements the ICustomerService interface. VB will implement the methods automatically (you may need to press Enter after the `Implements ICustomerService` for these to actually be implemented), and in C# you can use the smart tag (Ctrl+.) to have the methods automatically implemented. The service contract is now complete and ready for the operations to be implemented (that is, write the code that performs each operation). However, before you do so you still need to define the properties of the data class, and at the same time you should also define the data contract.

Creating the Data Contract

You are returning objects containing data from some of the operations you expose in your service, and accepting objects as parameters. Therefore, you should specify the structure of these data objects being transferred by decorating their classes with data contract attributes.

> *From the .NET Framework 3.5 SP1 onward it is no longer essential that you explicitly define a contract for your data classes if the classes are public and each has a default constructor (this is referred to as having an inferred data contract instead of a formal data contract). However, it is useful (and recommended) to create a formal contract anyway — especially if you need to conform to a specific message format in your communication, have non-.NET clients access your service, or want to explicitly define what properties in the data class are included in the message. Because explicitly specifying the data contract is generally recommended, this is the approach you will be taking in the example.*

This example requires only one data class — the `CustomerData` class that you already created (although no properties have been defined on it as yet), which you will now decorate with the data contract attributes. Whereas the service contract attributes were found in the `System.ServiceModel` namespace, data contract attributes are found in the `System.Runtime.Serialization` namespace, so C# developers will need to start by adding a using statement for this namespace in their classes:

```
using System.Runtime.Serialization;
```

Each data class first needs to be decorated with the `DataContract` attribute, and then you can decorate each property to be serialized with the `DataMember` attribute:

VB

```vb
<DataContract([Namespace]:="http://www.professionalvisualstudio.com")>
Public Class CustomerData
    <DataMember()> Public Property CustomerID As Integer
    <DataMember()> Public Property Title As String
    <DataMember()> Public Property FirstName As String
    <DataMember()> Public Property MiddleName As String
    <DataMember()> Public Property LastName As String
    <DataMember()> Public Property Suffix As String
    <DataMember()> Public Property CompanyName As String
    <DataMember()> Public Property EmailAddress As String
    <DataMember()> Public Property Phone As String
End Class
```

C#

```csharp
[DataContract(Namespace="http://www.professionalvisualstudio.com")]
public class CustomerData
{
    [DataMember] public int CustomerID { get; set; }
    [DataMember] public string Title { get; set; }
    [DataMember] public string FirstName { get; set; }
    [DataMember] public string MiddleName { get; set; }
    [DataMember] public string LastName { get; set; }
    [DataMember] public string Suffix { get; set; }
    [DataMember] public string CompanyName { get; set; }
    [DataMember] public string EmailAddress { get; set; }
    [DataMember] public string Phone { get; set; }
}
```

If you don't want a property to be serialized, simply don't apply the `DataMember` attribute to it. Like the service contract attributes you can also set the value of each of the various properties each attribute has. For example, the `DataContract` attribute enables you to set properties such as the namespace for the class's data contract (the `Namespace` property), and an alternative name for the class's data contract (the `Name` property). The `DataMember` attribute also has a number of properties that you can set, such as the member's name (the `Name` property), and whether the member must have a value specified (`IsRequired`).

> *When defining your data contract you might ask why you are decorating the data classes directly and aren't defining the contract on an interface as you did with the service contract (which was considered good practice). This is because only concrete types can be serialized — interfaces cannot (and thus cannot be specified as parameter or return types in WCF calls). When an object with only an interface specifying its type is to be deserialized, the serializer would not know which type of concrete object it should create the object as. There is a way around this but it's beyond the scope of this chapter. Note that if you try to create an interface and decorate it with the `DataContract` attribute, this will generate a compile error.*

You must be aware of some caveats when designing your data contracts. If your data class inherits from another class that isn't decorated with the `DataContract` attribute, you will receive an error when you attempt to run the service. Therefore, you must either also decorate the inherited class with the data contract attributes, or remove the data contract attributes from the data class (although this is not recommended) so the data contract is inferred instead.

If you choose to have inferred data contracts and not decorate the data classes with the data contract attributes, all public properties will be serialized. You can, however, exclude properties from being serialized if you need to by decorating them with the `IgnoreDataMember` attribute. A caveat of inferred data contracts is that the data classes must have a default constructor (that is, one with no parameters), or have no constructors at all (in which case a default constructor will be created for it by the compiler). If you do not have a default constructor in a data class with an inferred contract, you will receive an error when you attempt to run the service. Note that when an object of that type is passed in as an operation's parameter, the default constructor will be called when the object is created, and any code in that constructor will be executed.

> *Although it's not strictly required, it's best that you keep your data contract classes separate from your other application classes, and that you use them only for passing data in and out of services (as data transfer objects, aka DTOs). This way you minimize the dependencies between your application and the services that it exposes or calls.*

CONFIGURING WCF SERVICE ENDPOINTS

A WCF service has three main components: the Address, the Binding, and the Contract (easily remembered by the mnemonic ABC):

➤ The address specifies the location where the service can be found (the where) in the form of a URL.

➤ The binding specifies the protocol and encoding used for the communication (the how).

➤ The contract details the capabilities and features of the service (the what).

The configurations of each of these components combine to form an *endpoint*. Each combination of these components forms a separate endpoint, although it may be easier to consider it as each service having multiple endpoints (that is, address/binding combinations). What makes WCF so powerful is that it abstracts these components away from the implementation of the service, enabling them to be configured according to which technologies the service will support.

With this power, however, comes complexity, and the configuration of endpoints can become rather complex. In particular, many different types of bindings are supported, each having a huge number of options. However, WCF 4.0 simplifies this configuration over previous versions by providing default endpoints, standard endpoints, default protocol mappings, default binding configurations, and default behavior configurations — all of which ease the amount of configuration required. Because endpoint configuration can become very complex, this chapter focuses on just the most common requirements.

Endpoints for the service are defined in the `App.config` file. Though you can open the `App.config` file and edit it directly, Visual Studio comes with a configuration editor tool to simplify the configuration process. Right-click the `App.config` file in the Solution Explorer, and select Edit WCF Configuration from the context menu. This opens the Microsoft Service Configuration Editor, as shown in Figure 31-2.

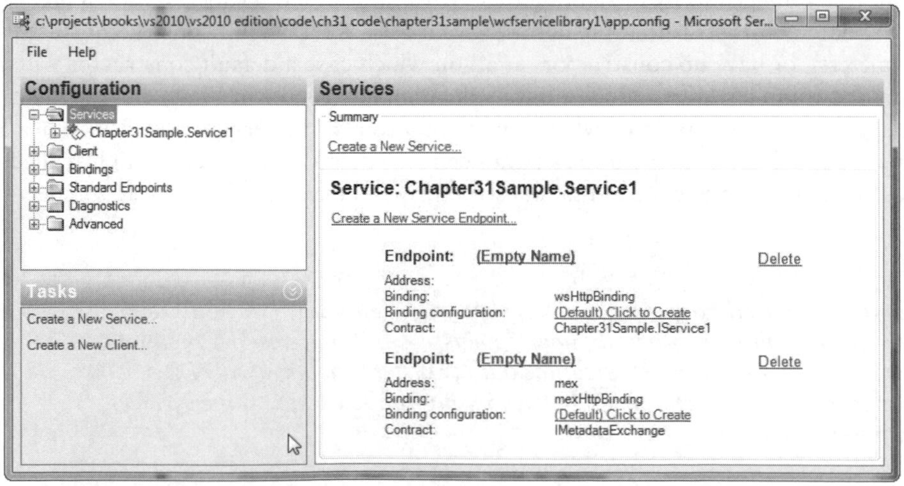

FIGURE 31-2

The node you are most interested in is the Services node. Selecting this node displays a summary in the Services pane of all the services that have been configured and their corresponding endpoints. You will find that a service is already listed here, although it is the configuration for the default service that was created by the project template (Service1), which no longer exists. Therefore, you can delete this service from the configuration and start anew (click the service and press Delete).

> *If you try running the service (detailed in the next section) without properly configuring an endpoint for it (or have an incorrect name for the service in the configuration), you will receive an error stating that the WCF Service Host cannot find any service metadata. If you receive this error, ensure that the service name (including its namespace) in the configuration matches its name in the actual service implementation.*

The first step is to define your service in the configuration. From the Tasks pane, click the Create a New Service hyperlink. This starts the New Service Element Wizard. In the service type field you

can directly type the qualified name of your service (that is, include its namespace), or click the Browse button to discover the services available (it's best to use the Browse function because this automatically fills in the next step for you). If you use this option you must have compiled your project first, and then you can navigate down into the bin\Debug folder to find the assembly, and drill through it to display the services within that assembly (as shown in Figure 31-3). Now you have specified the service implementation, but next you need to specify the contract, binding, and address for the endpoint.

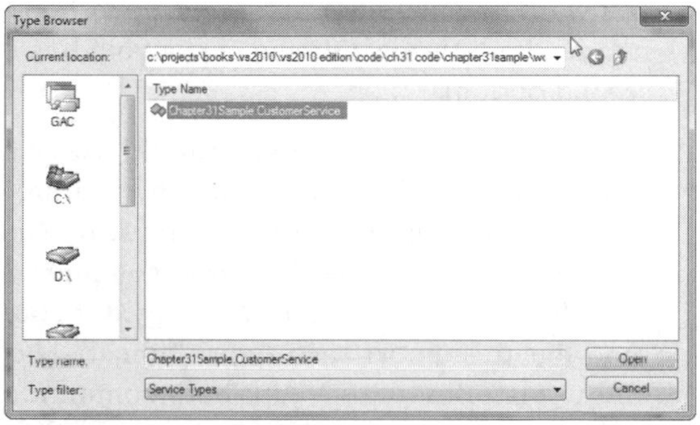

FIGURE 31-3

If you used the Browse button in the previous step (recommended), this next step (specifying the service contract) will have already been filled in for you (as shown in Figure 31-4). Otherwise, fill this in now.

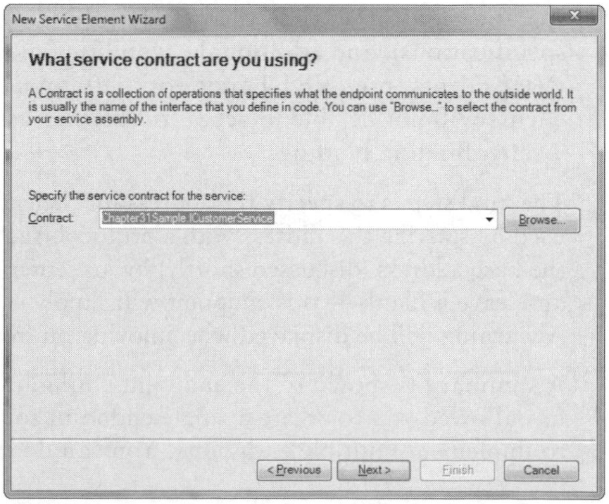

The next step states that it allows you to either create a new binding configuration, or use an existing binding configuration (as shown in Figure 31-5). However, the first option is probably a bit misleading, because it doesn't create a new binding configuration but instead helps you (via a wizard) choose which of the default binding configurations you want to use for the endpoint. Each

FIGURE 31-4

binding has a default/standard binding configuration, but additional configurations can be created for a binding (under the Bindings node in the Configuration tree) that enable you to configure exactly how a binding behaves. The custom bindings configuration can become rather complex, with a myriad of options available. However, in many cases you will find that you will just need a default binding (unless you actually have a specific need to change its behavior). In this chapter, assume that the default bindings are satisfactory for your needs.

So the actual options you have on this screen (in spite of the text displayed) are to either

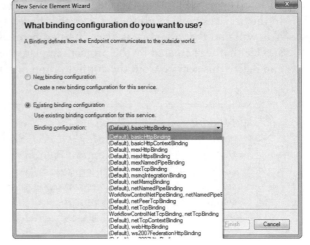

FIGURE 31-5

run another part of the wizard that will help you decide which of the default binding configurations you want (the first option), or to simply choose from a list of the existing binding configurations (that is, both the default and custom binding configurations) if you know which one you want (the second option).

Choosing which binding you should use really depends on your usage scenario for the service. The wizard will help you choose a binding, with a description under each option detailing the purpose for the option. You must remember, however, that not all clients may support the binding you choose — therefore, you must also consider what clients will be using your service and choose the binding accordingly. Of course, you can add additional endpoints with different bindings to support each type of client. The most common bindings are basicHttpBinding and wsHttpBinding — with both communicating over HTTP. The basicHttpBinding binding is used to communicate in the same manner as the ASMX web services (which conform to the WS-I Basic Profile 1.1). The wsHttpBinding binding implements a number of additional specifications other than the basicHttpBinding binding (including reliability and security specifications), and additional capabilities such as supporting transactions. However, older .NET clients (pre-.NET Framework 3.0), non-.NET clients, mobile clients, and Silverlight clients will not be able to access the service using this binding. For this example, choose the wsHttpBinding binding.

The final step is to specify the address for the endpoint. You can specify the entire address to be used by starting the address with a protocol (such as http://), or specify a relative address to the base address (discussed shortly) by just entering a name. In this case, delete the default entry and leave it blank — this endpoint will simply use the base address that you are about to set up. A warning will be displayed when moving on from this step, but it can be safely ignored.

A summary is shown of the endpoint configuration, and you can finish the wizard. This wizard has allowed you to create a single endpoint for the service, but chances are you will need to implement multiple endpoints. You can do this easily by using the New Service Endpoint

Element Wizard to create additional endpoints. Underneath the service node that was created will be an Endpoints node. Select this, and then click the Create a New Service Endpoint hyperlink in the Tasks pane. This opens the wizard that will help you to create a new endpoint.

As was mentioned earlier you now need to configure a base address for the endpoint. Because you chose to use the wsHttpBinding binding you will use a standard http URL that you will make the service accessible by. Under the newly created service node is a Host node. Select this, and from the Host pane that appears click the New button to add a new base address to the list (which is currently empty). A dialog appears asking for the base address, and contains a default entry. The address you enter here will largely depend on the binding that was selected earlier. Because you chose one of the HTTP bindings, use `http://localhost:8733/Chapter31Sample` as the base address (port 8733 was chosen at random) for this example.

Your service is now configured with the endpoints that it will support. There is another topic related to service configuration that is worth touching upon — that of behaviors. In essence, WCF behaviors modify the execution of a service or an endpoint. You will find that a service behavior containing two element extensions has already been configured for the service by the project template. If you expand the Advanced node and select the Service Behaviors node under it, you will find a behavior has been defined containing the `serviceMetadata` and `serviceDebug` element extensions. The `serviceMetadata` behavior element extension enables metadata for the service to be published. Your service must publish metadata in order for it to be discoverable and able to be added as a service reference for a client project (that is, create a proxy). You could set this up as a separate endpoint with the mexHttpBinding binding, but this behavior will merge this binding with the service without requiring it to be explicitly configured on the service itself. This makes it easy to ensure all your services are discoverable. Clicking the serviceMetadata node in the tree will show all its properties — ensure that the `HttpGetEnabled` and the `HttpsGetEnabled` properties are set to True. The other behavior element is the `serviceDebug` behavior extension. When debugging your service it can be useful for a help page to be displayed in the browser when you navigate to it (essentially publishing its WSDL at the HTTP get URL). You can do this by setting both the `HttpHelpPageEnabled` and `HttpsHelpPageEnabled` properties to True. Another useful property to set to true while debugging is the `IncludeExceptionDetailsInFaults` property, enabling you to view a stack trace of what exception occurred in the service from the client. Although this behavior is very useful in debugging, it's recommended that you remove it before deploying your service (for security purposes).

HOSTING WCF SERVICES

With these changes made you can now build and run the WCF Service Library. Unlike a standard class library, a WCF Service Library can be "run" because Visual Studio 2010 ships with the WCF Service Host utility. This is an application that can be used to host WCF services for the purpose of debugging them. Figure 31-6 shows this utility appearing in the taskbar.

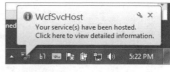

FIGURE 31-6

As the balloon in Figure 31-6 indicates, clicking the balloon or the taskbar icon brings up a dialog showing more information about the service that is running. If the service doesn't start correctly, this dialog can help you work out what is going wrong.

> *If you aren't running under elevated privileges, you may end up with an error from the WCF Service Host relating to the registration of the URL you specified in the configuration file. The issue is a result of security policies on the computer that are preventing the WCF Service Host from registering the URL you have specified. If you receive this error you can resolve it by executing the following command using an elevated permissions command prompt (that is, while running as administrator), replacing the parameters according to the address of the service and your Windows username.*
>
> ```
> netsh http add urlacl url=http://+:8733/Chapter31Sample
> user=<username>
> ```
>
> *This command will allow the specified user to register URLs that match the URL prefix. Now when you try to run your WCF Service Library again it should start successfully.*

In addition to hosting your WCF service, Visual Studio 2010 also launches the WCF Test Client utility as you can see in Figure 31-7. This utility automatically detects the running services, and provides a simple tree representation of the services and their corresponding operations.

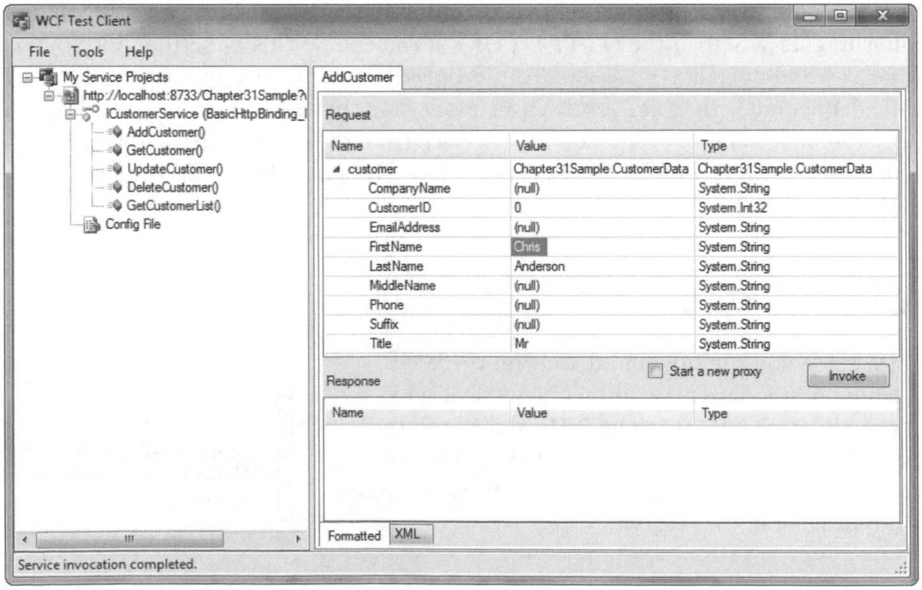

FIGURE 31-7

When you double-click a service operation you will see the tab on the right-hand side of the dialog change to display the request and response values. Unlike the very basic test page for ASP.NET Web Services, the WCF Test Client can help you simulate calls to WCF services that contain complex types. In Figure 31-7, you can see that in the Request section each parameter is displayed, and the `customer` object parameter of the `AddCustomer` operation has been broken down with data entry fields for each of its properties (those that were marked with the `DataMember` attribute). After setting values for each of these properties you can then invoke the operation by clicking the Invoke button. Figure 31-8 also shows that any return value will be displayed in a similar layout in the Response section of the tab.

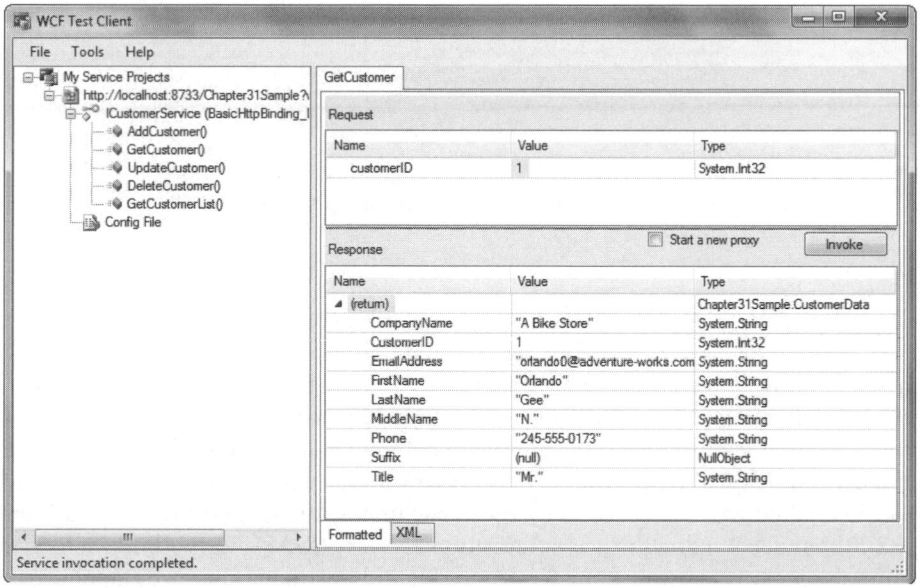

FIGURE 31-8

If you are trying to isolate an issue it can be useful to see exactly what information is traveling down the wire for each service request. You can do this using third-party tools such as Fiddler, but for a simple XML representation of what was sent and received you can simply click the XML tab. Figure 31-9 shows the body XML for both the request and the response. You will notice that there is additional XML due to the request and response each being wrapped in a SOAP envelope.

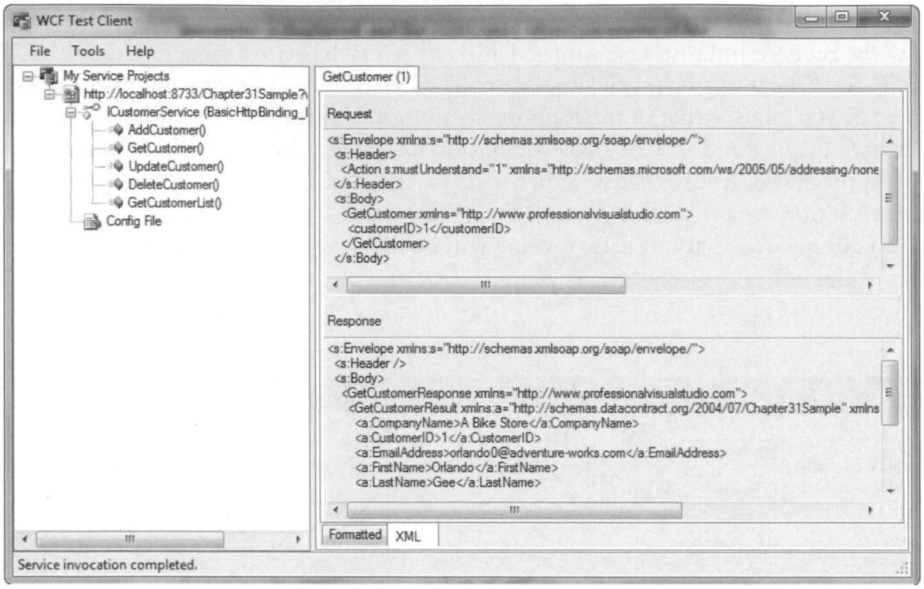

FIGURE 31-9

This is fine while you are debugging the service, but in production you will need to properly host your service. You have a lot of ways to host your service, and how you choose to do so really depends on your scenario. If it's a situation where the service is acting as a server (which clients communicate with) and communicates via HTTP, then Internet Information Services (IIS) is probably your best choice. If your service is being used to communicate between two applications, your application itself can be used to host the service. Other options you may wish to consider are hosting the service in a Windows Service, or (if the host machine is running Windows Vista/7 or Windows Server 2008) under Windows Process Activation Services (WAS). We will take a look at the two most common scenarios: hosting your service in IIS, and hosting it in a .NET application (which will be a console application).

The first example shows how to host your WCF service in IIS. The first step is to set up the folder and files required. Create a new folder (under your IIS wwwroot folder, or anywhere you choose) with a name of your own choosing, and create another folder under this called bin. Copy the compiled service assembly (that is, the `.dll` file) into this folder. Also take the `App.config` file and copy it into the folder one level higher (that is, the first folder you created), and rename it to `web.config`.

Now you need to create a simple text file (in the Visual Studio IDE, Notepad, or a text editor of your choice) and call it `CustomerService.svc` (it can be any name, but it does require the `.svc` extension). Put this line as the contents of the file:

```
<%@ServiceHost Service="Chapter31SampleCS.CustomerService"%>
```

Essentially, this specifies that IIS should host the service called Chapter31SampleCS. CustomerService (which it expects to find in one of the assemblies in the bin folder).

In summary, you should have a `CustomerService.svc` file and a `web.config` file in a folder, and the service assembly (`dll`) in the bin folder below it. Ensure (in the folder permissions) that the IIS process has read access to this folder.

Now you need to configure the service in IIS. Open IIS, and under the default web site add a new application. Give it a name (such as CustomerService), and specify the folder created earlier as its physical path. Also make sure you select to use the ASP.NET v4.0 application pool (so it will use V4 of the .NET Framework), and that should be it!

You can then navigate to the service's URL in a browser to see if it works, and use the WCF Test Client to actually test the operations.

> *If you create the project using the WCF Service Application project template, the correct structure and required files will already be created for you and ready to host under IIS.*

The other example goes through hosting the WCF service in a .NET application (known as a self-hosted service). You can either put the service code (created previously) directly in this project, or reference the service project you created earlier. For this example, just create a simple console application to act as the host, and reference the existing service project. Create a new console application project in Visual Studio called CustomerServiceHost, and add a reference to the service project. You will also need to add a reference to the System.ServiceModel assembly. Copy the `App.config` file from the service project into this project (so you can use the service configuration previously set up).

Use the following code to host the service:

VB

```vb
Imports System.ServiceModel
Imports Chapter31SampleVB

Module CustomerServiceHost
    Sub Main()
        Using svcHost As New ServiceHost(GetType(CustomerService))
            Try
                'Open the service, and close it again when the user presses a key
                svcHost.Open()

                Console.WriteLine("The service is running...")
                Console.ReadLine()

                'Close the ServiceHost.
                svcHost.Close()

            Catch ex As Exception
                Console.WriteLine(ex.Message)
                Console.ReadLine()
            End Try
```

```
        End Using
    End Sub
End Module
```

C#

```csharp
using System;
using System.ServiceModel;
using Chapter31SampleCS;

namespace CustomerServiceHost
{
    class Program
    {
        static void Main(string[] args)
        {
            using (ServiceHost serviceHost =
                            new ServiceHost(typeof(CustomerService)))
            {
                try
                {
                    // Open the service, and close it again when the user
                    // presses a key
                    serviceHost.Open();

                    Console.WriteLine("The service is running...");
                    Console.ReadLine();

                    serviceHost.Close();
                }
                catch (Exception ex)
                {
                    Console.WriteLine(ex.Message);
                    Console.ReadLine();
                }
            }
        }
    }
}
```

In summary, the configuration for the service is being read from the `.config` file (although it could also be specified programmatically), so you just need to create a service host object (passing in the type of the service to be hosted), and open the host. When you are done you just need to close the host and clean up!

Now you can run the project and access the service using the URL specified in the `.config` file. As you can see, very little code is required to host a WCF service.

CONSUMING A WCF SERVICE

Now that you have successfully created your WCF service it's time to access it within an application. To do so add a Windows Forms project to your solution called CustomerServiceClient.

The next thing is to add a reference to the WCF service to the Windows Forms application. Right-click the project node in the Solution Explorer tool window and select Add Service Reference. This opens the dialog shown in Figure 31-10, in which you can specify the WCF service you want to add a reference to. As you can see, there is a very convenient Discover button that you can use to quickly locate services contained within the current solution.

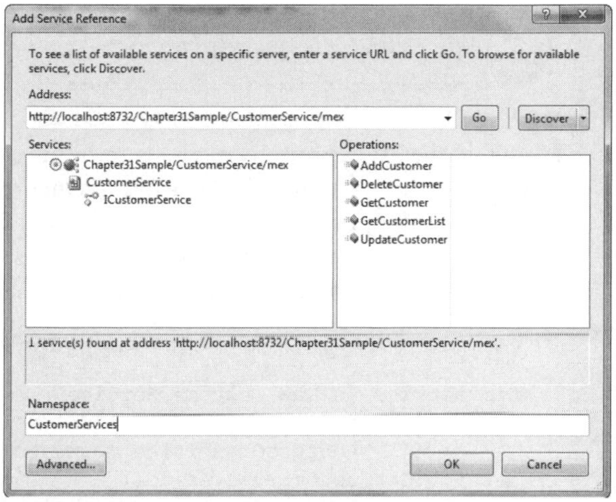

Select the ICustomerService node in the Services tree, change the namespace to CustomerServices, and click the OK button to complete the process. The next step is to create a form that will display/edit data from the service. Put the code to communicate with the service in the code behind for this form. Start by adding a using/Imports statement to the top of the code for the namespace of the service:

FIGURE 31-10

VB

```
Imports CustomerServiceClient.CustomerServices
```

C#

```
using CustomerServiceClient.CustomerServices;
```

Let's say you have a BindingSource control on your form called customerDataBindingSource, whose DataSource property you want to set to the list of customers to be retrieved from the service. All you need to do is create an instance of the service proxy and call the operation, and the data will be returned.

VB

```
Dim service As New CustomerService
customerDataBindingSource.DataSource = service.GetCustomerList()
```

C#

```
CustomerService service = new CustomerService();
customerDataBindingSource.DataSource = service.GetCustomerList();
```

You can now run this application and it will communicate with the WCF service. This example demonstrated communicating with the WCF service synchronously (that is, the UI thread was paused until a response had been received from the server), but this has the disadvantage of making your application unresponsive to the user until the response from the service had been received. Though calling the service synchronously is easy code to write, it doesn't provide for a very nice user experience. Fortunately, you can also call WCF services asynchronously. This allows the client to make a request to a service, and continue on running without waiting for the response. When a response has been received, an event will be raised that can be handled by the application from which it can act upon that response.

Silverlight clients only support asynchronous service calls.

To enable the asynchronous methods to be created on the service proxy you must specifically request them by selecting the Generate Asynchronous Operations checkbox in the Configure Service Reference dialog (detailed later in this section). To call the WCF service asynchronously you create an instance of the service, handle the Completed event for the associated operation, and then call the operation method that is suffixed with Async:

VB

```
Dim service As New CustomerService
AddHandler service.GetCustomerListCompleted, _
          AddressOf service_GetCustomerListCompleted
service.GetCustomerListAsync()
```

C#

```
CustomerService service = new CustomerService();
service.GetCustomerListCompleted += service_GetCustomerListCompleted;
service.GetCustomerListAsync();
```

The operation call will return immediately, and the event handler specified will be called when the operation is complete. The data that has been returned from the service will be passed into the event handler via e.Results:

VB

```
Private Sub service_GetCustomerListCompleted(ByVal sender As Object, _
                                    ByVal e As
GetCustomerListCompletedEventArgs)
    customerDataBindingSource.DataSource = e.Result
End Sub
```

C#

```
private void service_GetCustomerListCompleted(object sender,

GetCustomerListCompletedEventArgs e)
{
    customerDataBindingSource.DataSource = e.Result;
}
```

When you add a reference to the WCF service to your rich client application you will notice that an App.config file was added to the project (if it didn't already exist). In either case, if you take a look at this file you'll see that it now contains a system.serviceModel element that contains bindings and client elements. Within the bindings element you can see that there is a wsHttpBinding element (this is the default WCF binding), which defines how to communicate with the WCF service. Here you can see that the subelements override some of the default values. The Client element contains an endpoint element. This element defines the Address (which in this case is a URL), a Binding (which references the customized wsHttpBinding defined in the bindings element), and a Contract (which is the CustomerServices.ICustomerService interface of the WCF service that is to be called). Because this information is all defined in the configuration file, if any of these elements changes (for example, the URL of the endpoint) you can just modify the configuration file instead of having to recompile the entire application.

When you make changes to the service you will need to update the service proxy that was created by Visual Studio when you added the service reference to your project (otherwise it will remain out of date and not show new operations added to it, and so on). You can do this by simply right-clicking the service reference (under the Service References node in your project) and selecting the Update Service Reference item from the context menu.

If you right-click a service reference (under the Service References node in your project) you will also find a Configure Service Reference option. This will bring up the dialog shown in Figure 31-11 (which can also be accessed from the Add Service Reference dialog by clicking the Advanced button).

This dialog allows you to configure how the service proxy is generated, with a variety of options available. Of particular interest is the Reuse types in referenced assemblies option. This option (when enabled) means that if the service reference generator finds that a type (that is, class/object) consumed/returned by the service is defined in an assembly referenced by the client, the proxy code generated will return/accept objects of that type instead of creating a proxy class

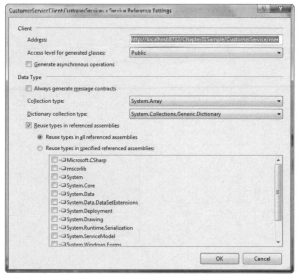

FIGURE 31-11

for it. The big benefit of this is where you manage both ends of the system (both server and client) and want to pass objects between them that have associated business logic (such as validation logic, business rules, and so on). The usual process is to (on the client side) copy the property values from a proxy object into a business object (when requesting data), and then copy property values from a business object into a proxy object (to pass data back to the server). However, this option means that you can have both the server and the client reference an assembly that contains the types to be passed between them (with corresponding business logic code for both ends), and simply pass the objects backward and forward between the server and the client without requiring a proxy class as an intermediary (on the client side). This saves you from having to write a lot of property mapping code, which becomes a maintenance burden and has a high potential to contain incorrect mappings.

SUMMARY

In this chapter you learned how to create a WCF service, host it, consume it, and configure it for different purposes/uses. However, WCF isn't the end of the story for communication layers — in fact, a number of technologies are built on top of WCF to enhance its capabilities. These include WCF Data Services and WCF RIA Services, with the latter detailed in Chapter 35.

Windows Workflow Foundation (WF)

WHAT'S IN THIS CHAPTER?

- ➤ Understanding Windows Workflow Foundation
- ➤ Creating a basic workflow
- ➤ Hosting and executing a workflow
- ➤ Hosting the workflow designer in your application

Windows Workflow Foundation (WF) is a powerful platform for designing and running workflows — a central tenet in many business applications. WF was introduced with the .NET Framework 3.0, and has been completely redesigned and rewritten for its .NET Framework 4.0 version to overcome some of the problems it had in its previous incarnations. Unfortunately, this has rendered it incompatible with workflows created in those previous versions, but leaving it a much more robust technology as a result. This chapter takes you through using the WF designer, and the process of creating and running workflows using WF.

WHAT IS WINDOWS WORKFLOW FOUNDATION?

Before discussing Windows Workflow, you should first examine exactly what workflow is. A workflow is essentially a model of the steps that form a business process. For example, this may incorporate document approvals, job status tracking, and so on.

A well-designed workflow requires a clear separation between the steps in the business process (the *work* to be done), and the business rules/logic that binds them (the *flow*).

Windows Workflow is a complete workflow solution, including both the design and the run time components required to design/create and run workflows. These workflows can then be hosted in an application, or exposed publicly as a service.

> *One of the powerful features of WF is that you can host both the WF run time and the WF designer in your application, enabling end users to reconfigure workflows themselves through the WF designer hosted in your application.*

Using WF requires you to break your business process into discrete tasks (known as activities), which can then be declaratively connected and controlled in a configurable workflow using the WF designer.

You can use WF in your own products, but you will also find it embedded in various Microsoft products, including Sharepoint and Windows Server AppFabric.

WHY USE WINDOWS WORKFLOW?

A common question raised by those who investigate WF is regarding why should they use it, rather than embed business logic directly in the code. It's a very valid question, and whether or not you should use it really comes down to the business problem that you are attempting to solve and the business process you need to model. This chapter covers some of the scenarios in which it might be appropriate to use WF, but you will first look at some of the benefits you would gain with using it.

One of the primary scenarios where you would achieve the most benefits from using WF is where you have a business process that frequently changes (or the rules within the business process frequently change). Alternatively, you may have an application that is deployed to different customers, each of whom has different business processes. The business logic/rules that form workflows in WF are defined declaratively rather than being embedded in code, which has the advantage of enabling the workflow to be reconfigured without requiring the application to be recompiled. This, combined with the ability to host the WF designer in your own application, enables you to design highly configurable applications.

Another scenario where using WF provides a lot of advantages is where you are modeling long-running processes. Some workflows can run from seconds, to minutes, hours, days, and even years. WF provides a framework for managing these long-running processes, enabling a workflow to be persisted while waiting for an event (rather than remaining memory resident), and able to be continued after a machine restart.

An advantage of being able to design and visualize your workflows in the WF designer is that the workflow diagram can be used as a form of documentation of the business process/logic. This diagram can be exported from the WF designer as an image, and used in documentation or presentations. This helps provide a high degree of transparency for the business process you are modeling.

Ultimately, it's not appropriate to use WF in all applications that incorporate a business process that requires modeling. If any of the benefits listed previously are core requirements in your application, you should seriously consider designing your workflows and activities using WF. However, if none of the listed benefits are necessary (nor likely to be in the future), it's really a decision you need to make based on whether you think it will improve the development practices of your team, and whether you believe that the imposition of such a framework will still provide more benefits through its use to outweigh the potential problems that it may create (which are not unheard of).

WORKFLOW CONCEPTS

Before you get into the practical aspects of designing and executing workflows, you first run through some of the important concepts around workflows, and the terminology that is involved.

Activities

An activity is a discrete unit of work; that is, it performs a task. An activity doesn't have to just perform a single task — in fact an activity can contain other activities (known as a composite activity), which can each contain activities themselves, and so on. A workflow is an activity itself, and so are control flow activities (discussed shortly). You can think of an activity as the fundamental building block of workflows.

Activities can have input and output arguments, which enable the flow of data in and out of the activity, and can return a value. An activity can also have variables, which (like in code) store a value that any activities the activity contains can also get/set. The activity in which a variable is defined designates its scope.

> *You can think of activities as being much like a method in regular code.*

WF includes a base library of predefined activities that cover a wide variety of tasks, which you can use in your workflow. These include activities that:

➤ Control execution flow (If, DoWhile, ForEach, Switch, and so on)

➤ Provide messaging functionality (for communicating with services)

➤ Persist the current workflow instance to a database

➤ Provide transaction support

➤ Enable collection management (add/remove items in a collection, clear a collection, and determine whether an item exists in the collection)

➤ Provide error handling (try, catch, throw, rethrow)

➤ Provide some primitive functionality (delays, variable assigning, write to console, and so on)

Of course, despite this wide range of predefined activities available to you, you will no doubt want to create custom activities to suit your own requirements, especially when you have complex logic to implement. These are written in code, will appear in the Toolbox in the WF designer, and you can drag and drop them into your workflow.

When creating your own custom activities, you have a number of custom activity types to choose from: `Activity`, `CodeActivity`, `NativeActivity`, and `DynamicActivity` (the custom activity inherits from one of these base classes).

Activities based on the `Activity` class are composed of other activities, and are designed visually in the WF designer. As previously stated, workflows are activities themselves, so your workflow is actually based on the `Activity` class. Activities composed in this manner can be used in other activities too.

An activity that is based on `CodeActivity`, as its name suggests, is an activity whose action(s)/logic is defined in code. This code is actually a class that inherits from `CodeActivity` and overrides the `Execute` method in which the code to be executed should be placed.

Activities don't necessarily have to be executed synchronously, blocking the continuing execution of the workflow while performing a long-running task, or waiting for an operation to complete, a response or input to be received, or an event to be raised. You can create asynchronous activities by inheriting from the `AsyncCodeActivity` class. This is much like the `CodeActivity` class, except rather than having a single `Execute` method to be overridden, it has a `BeginExecute` and an `EndExecute` method instead. When an asynchronous activity is executed, it will do so on a separate thread from the scheduler and return immediately. It can then continue to execute without blocking the execution of the main workflow. The scheduler that invoked it will be notified when it has completed executing.

> *Note that a workflow cannot be persisted or be unloaded while an asynchronous activity is executing.*

An activity that is based on the `NativeActivity` class is much like one that inherits from `CodeActivity`, but whereas `CodeActivity` is limited to interacting with arguments and variables, `NativeActivity` has full access to all the functionality exposed by the workflow run time (which passes it a `NativeActivityContext` object that provides it with this access). This includes the ability to schedule and cancel child activity execution, aborting activity execution, access to activity bookmarks, and scheduling and tracking functions.

Control Flow Activities

Control flow activities are used to control the flow of activities — essentially providing the binding between them that organizes them into a workflow and forming the logic/rules of the process being modeled. Control flow activities are just standard activities themselves, but designed to control the execution/flow of the activities it contains (by scheduling the execution of those activities).

There are two primary types of control flow activities (essentially workflow types): Sequence and Flowchart. A Sequence executes the activities that it contains (as its name suggests) in sequence. It's not possible to go backward and return to a previous step in a sequence; execution can only move forward through the sequence. A Flowchart, however, enables the execution to return to a previous step, making it more suited to decision making (that is, business) processes than sequences.

If you've worked with previous versions of WF, you will note that there is no longer a state machine control flow activity. There is, however, expected to be an out-of-band release of a state machine control flow activity at some stage in the near future.

You are not limited to using a single control flow activity in a workflow — because they are activities, you can mix and match them as required in the same workflow.

Expressions

Expressions are VB code (only) that return a value, and are used in the designer to control the values of variables and arguments. You can think of them much like formulas in, say, Excel. Expressions are generally bound to an activity's input arguments, used to set the value of variables, or used to define conditions on activities (such as the If activity).

Workflow Run Time/Scheduler

The workflow run time (also known as the scheduler) is the engine that takes a workflow definition file and executes it in the context of a host application. The host application starts a given workflow in the workflow run time using the `WorkflowInvoker`, the `WorkflowApplication`, or the `WorkflowServiceHost` classes.

The `WorkflowInvoker` class is used in a "hands off" approach to executing the workflow, leaving the workflow run time to handle the entire execution of the workflow. The `WorkflowApplication` class is used when requiring a "hands on" approach to executing the workflow (such as resuming a persisted instance), enabling the execution to be controlled by the host. The `WorkflowServiceHost` class is used when hosting the workflow as a service to be used by client applications.

Bookmarks

A bookmark marks a place in the workflow, from which its execution can be resumed at a later point in time. Bookmarks enable a workflow instance to be "paused" while it's waiting for input to be received, specifying a point from which it will be resumed when that input has been received. A bookmark is given a name and specifies a callback function, pinpointing the activity that is currently executing and specifying the method in the activity that should be called when the workflow is resumed.

Creating a bookmark stops the workflow from executing, and releases the workflow thread (although the workflow isn't complete, but simply paused), enabling the workflow to be persisted and unloaded. The host is then tasked with capturing the input that the workflow is waiting on, and resuming that workflow's instance execution again from the bookmark position (passing in any data to the callback method received from the awaited input).

Bookmarks are particularly useful in long-running processes where the workflow is waiting for an input to be received, that potentially may not be received for quite some time. In the meantime, it releases the resources that it's using (freeing them up for use by other workflows), and its state can be persisted to disk (if required).

Persistence

Persistence enables the current state of a workflow instance and its metadata (including the values of in-scope variables, arguments, bookmark data, and so on) to be serialized and saved to a data store (known as an *instance store*) by a *persistence provider*, to be retrieved and resumed at a later point in time. To persist a workflow instance, the workflow execution must be idle (such as if it's waiting for input), and a bookmark must be defined to mark the current execution point in the workflow.

Persistence is particularly important when you have long-running workflows, where you want to be able to unload workflows that are idle and waiting for input, or if the machine/server may restart in the times that the workflow is idle, or if the execution may even continue on a different server (such as in a server farm).

> *Note that the workflow itself is not persisted to the instance, only its state. You need to be aware of the consequences of modifying the workflow while instances are still alive and persisted, and cater accordingly.*

WF comes with a default persistence provider called `SqlWorkflowInstanceStore` that handles persisting a workflow instance to a SQL Server database. You can also create your own custom persistence provider by inheriting from the `InstanceStore` class.

You have two ways to persist a workflow instance. One is to use the predefined Persist activity from the Toolbox in your workflow, which will persist the workflow instance when executed by the run time. The other option is for the host to register an event handler for the `PersistableIdle` event, which is raised by the run time when the workflow instance is idle (but not yet complete). The host can then choose whether or not to persist the workflow instance, returning a value from the `PersistIdleAction` enumeration that will tell the run time what it should do.

Tracking

WF enables you to implement tracking in your workflows, where various aspects of the execution of a workflow can be logged for analysis. Tracking provides transparency over your workflow, enabling you to see what it has done in the past and its current execution state by the workflow run time emitting *tracking records*.

You can specify the granularity at which the tracking records will be emitted by configuring a *tracking profile*, which can be defined either in the `App.config` file or through code. This will enable you to specify which tracking records you want the workflow run time to emit. The types of tracking records that can be emitted include workflow life cycle records (such as when a workflow starts or finishes), activity life cycle records (such as when an activity is scheduled or completes, or when an error occurs), bookmark resumption records, and custom tracking records (which you can emit from your custom activities). These tracking records can include associated data, such as the current values of variables and arguments.

Where tracking records are written is determined by specifying a *tracking participant*. By default, the WF run time emits tracking records to the Windows Event Log. You can create your own tracking participants if you, for example, want to write tracking records to a different source, such as a database.

You can also trace the execution of a workflow for troubleshooting and diagnostic purposes, which makes use of the standard .NET trace listeners. Tracing can be configured in the `App.config` file.

GETTING STARTED

Start by opening the New Project dialog and navigating to the Workflow category under your favorite language (as shown in Figure 32-1).

FIGURE 32-1

As you can see, you have four project types to choose from as follows:

➤ **Activity Designer Library:** Enables you to create and maintain a reusable library of activity designers to customize how their corresponding activities look and behave in the WF designer.

➤ **Activity Library:** Creates a project that enables you to create and maintain a reusable library of activities (consisting of other activities) that you can then use in your workflows. Think of it much like a class library but for workflows.

➤ **Workflow Console Application:** Creates an empty workflow hosted in a console application.

➤ **WCF Workflow Service Application:** Creates a workflow hosted and publicly exposed as a WCF service.

> You aren't limited to hosting workflows in a console application or WCF service — you can also host them in other platforms such as Windows Forms, WPF, or ASP.NET applications. Add a workflow to an existing project using the Add New Item dialog and selecting Activity from the Workflow category (there is no Workflow item, because a workflow is essentially an activity itself, containing other activities).

For the sample project, you will use the simplest option to get up and running, by using the Workflow Console Application project template. As you can see from Figure 32-2, the project it generates is very simple, containing `Program.cs/Module1.vb` and `Workflow1.xaml`. The `Program` class (for C# developers), or `Module1` module (for VB developers), as found in any console application, contains the entry point for the application (that is, the static/shared `Main` method), which is automatically configured to instantiate and execute the workflow. The `Workflow1.xaml` file is the file where you will define your workflow.

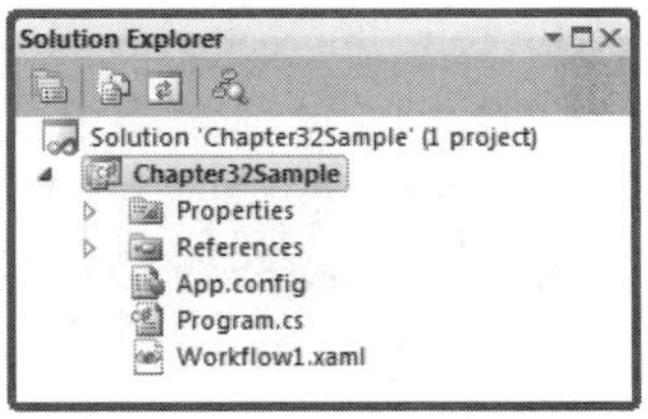

FIGURE 32-2

> Note that the workflow file is a XAML file — a file format you may recognize because it is used to define user interfaces in WPF and Silverlight. However, in this case it is used to declaratively define a workflow. You can view and edit the underlying XAML for a workflow by right-clicking the file and selecting View Code from the context menu.

Before you do anything else, compile and run the application as is to see the result. You should find that a console window briefly appears before the application automatically ends (because it is not currently configured to actually do anything).

The name `Workflow1.xaml` isn't very meaningful, so you will no doubt want to change that to something more appropriate. Unfortunately Visual Studio doesn't help you much in this respect (unlike with forms and classes), because changing the filename will not automatically change the class created behind the scenes for the workflow, nor will it change any references to the class when you change its name in the designer. For example, to rename the workflow and its corresponding class to `SimpleProcessWorkflow`, you will need to:

➤ Change the name of the file (in the Solution Explorer).

➤ Change the name of the corresponding class (by clicking the design surface, and assigning the name to the `Name` property in the Properties tool window).

➤ Change all existing references to the workflow class. In this case where you haven't done anything with your project as yet, the only reference will be in the `Program` class (for C# developers) or `Module1` module (for VB developers), which will need to be updated accordingly. Note that the class name will not appear in IntelliSense and will indicate an error when you enter it, if you have not compiled the project after changing the class name (because it's only then that the compiler will regenerate the class).

THE WORKFLOW FOUNDATION DESIGNER

The WF designer enables you to drop control flow activities and standard activities (from the Toolbox) on a workflow design surface, and connect them to form the workflow. It's much like building a form where you drop controls from the Toolbox onto the design surface, but in this case you are building a workflow. When you first create the project, the empty workflow is displayed in the designer, as shown in Figure 32-3.

FIGURE 32-3

At the bottom of the designer, you will note the three hyperlink buttons: Variables, Arguments, and Imports. Clicking one of these buttons pops up a pane at the bottom of the designer that will enable to you modify their respective configurations.

Variables can be defined for use by activities within a given scope (which is defined by a parent activity to which the variables are attached). Add a variable by simply popping up the Variables pane (as shown in Figure 32-4), clicking in the area that says Create Variable, and entering a name for it. You can set the type for the variable by clicking in the Variable Type column and selecting the type from the drop-down list. If the type that you need doesn't appear in the list, you can click the Browse for Types item, which will pop up a dialog enabling you to type in the qualified name of the type, or navigate through the referenced assemblies tree to find it. Clicking in the Scope column displays a drop-down list that will allow you to modify the scope of the variable (by selecting the activity it belongs to). This activity and its child activities will therefore have access to the variable. Clicking in the Default column enables you to enter an expression (in VB code) that will set the default value of the variable.

Note that the default value column accepts expressions rather than values. If you want to assign a value to the variable rather than an expression you will need to enter the literal value, not simply the value itself. The literal values for numeric values are identical, but if the variable is a string, you will need to enclose it in double quotes. This also applies when setting the default value of arguments.

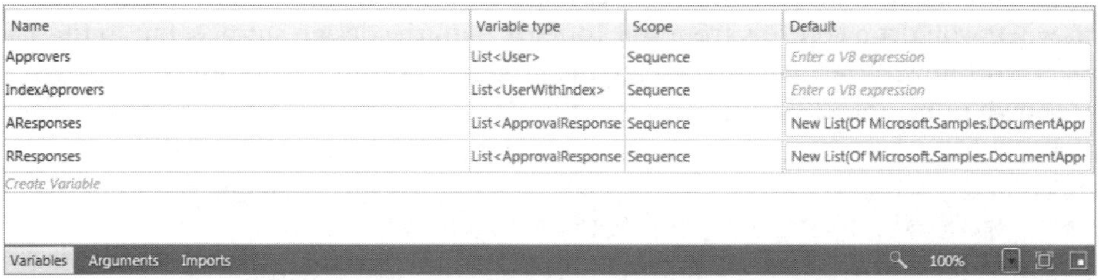

Name	Variable type	Scope	Default
Approvers	List<User>	Sequence	*Enter a VB expression*
IndexApprovers	List<UserWithIndex>	Sequence	*Enter a VB expression*
AResponses	List<ApprovalResponse>	Sequence	New List(Of Microsoft.Samples.DocumentAppr
RResponses	List<ApprovalResponse>	Sequence	New List(Of Microsoft.Samples.DocumentAppr
Create Variable			

Variables   Arguments   Imports   🔍 100%

FIGURE 32-4

The Arguments pane (as shown in Figure 32-5) enables you to define the input and output arguments for an activity (which enable the flow of data in and out of the activity). There are four types of arguments (that is, argument directions): Input arguments, Output arguments, In/Out arguments, and Property arguments.

➤ **Input** arguments can conceptually be considered the same as passing parameters into methods by value in regular code.

➤ **Output** arguments can conceptually be considered the same as output parameters in methods in regular code, whose values are set in the method and returned to the caller.

➤ **In/Out** arguments can conceptually be considered the same as passing parameters into methods by reference in regular code.

➤ **Property** arguments can conceptually be considered the same as assigning property values on an object in regular code.

Add an argument by simply popping up the Arguments pane, clicking in the area that says Create Argument, and entering a name for it. Specify the type of argument by clicking in the Direction column and selecting a type from the drop-down list. You can set the type for the argument by clicking in the Argument Type column and selecting the type from the drop-down list. As with variables, you can also assign an expression to the default value of the argument (for In and Property arguments only).

Note that activities can also have a return value.

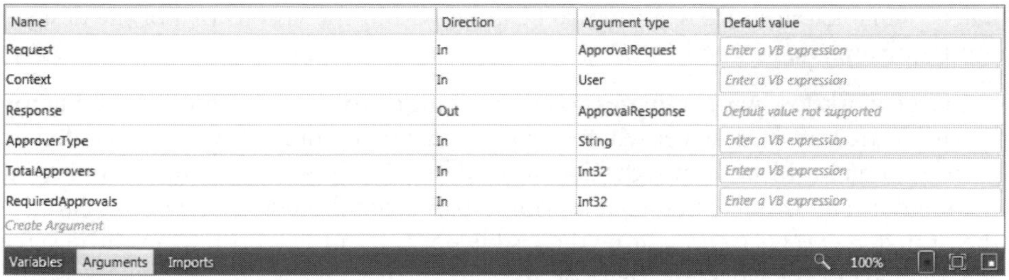

FIGURE 32-5

The Imports pane (as shown in Figure 32-6) enables you to import namespaces (the same as defining using statements in C#) for use in expressions. At the top of the panel is a combo box where you can type a namespace to import and add to the list, or select a namespace from the drop-down list.

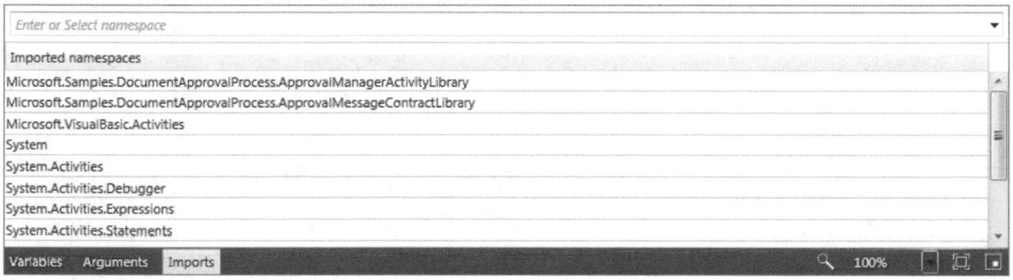

FIGURE 32-6

Workflows can become quite large and potentially unwieldy as they increase in complexity, but luckily the WF designer contains a few tools to help you manage and navigate through the model. You will find that some activities have an icon in their top-right corner, enabling you to roll them up to just display their title (that is, collapse them), or to expand them if they are collapsed. Because you can nest activities within activities (and so on), potentially creating rather deep and complex hierarchies, it can be useful to hide some of this complexity by collapsing activities when you are not actively editing them. Collapsing activities can reduce the amount of space they take in the workflow diagram, and can also be used to hide the complexity of the hierarchy of sub-activities contained within them. You can then expand the activities again by clicking this same icon (whose arrows will have changed direction according to the state of the activity).

In the top-right corner of the designer, you will find an Expand All hyperlink button and a Collapse All hyperlink button (both of which change to read Restore when clicked). It can often be useful to "roll up" the entire workflow (using the Collapse All hyperlink button) to its top-level activities, from which you can then drill down through specific activities by expanding them as required to follow a specific logical path. In addition, you can also use the Expand All hyperlink button to expand all the activities that form the workflow, enabling you to get a picture of the full extent of the workflow.

You can zoom in and out of the view of the workflow using the drop-down list in the bottom-right side of the designer (that lists zoom percentages), and clicking the magnifying glass icon to its left resets the view back to 100%. The icon to the right of the drop-down list will automatically select a zoom level that will enable the entire workflow to be fitted within the visible area of the designer window (without requiring you to scroll).

When you have a large workflow with activities you don't want to collapse, with it far too big to fit entirely in the visible area of the designer window, you can make use of the Overview window by clicking the rightmost icon in the bottom-right side of the designer. This will pop up a window in the designer (as shown in Figure 32-7) that enables you to pan around the workflow by clicking and dragging the orange rectangle (representing the visible portion of the workflow in the designer) around to display the part of the workflow that you want to currently view.

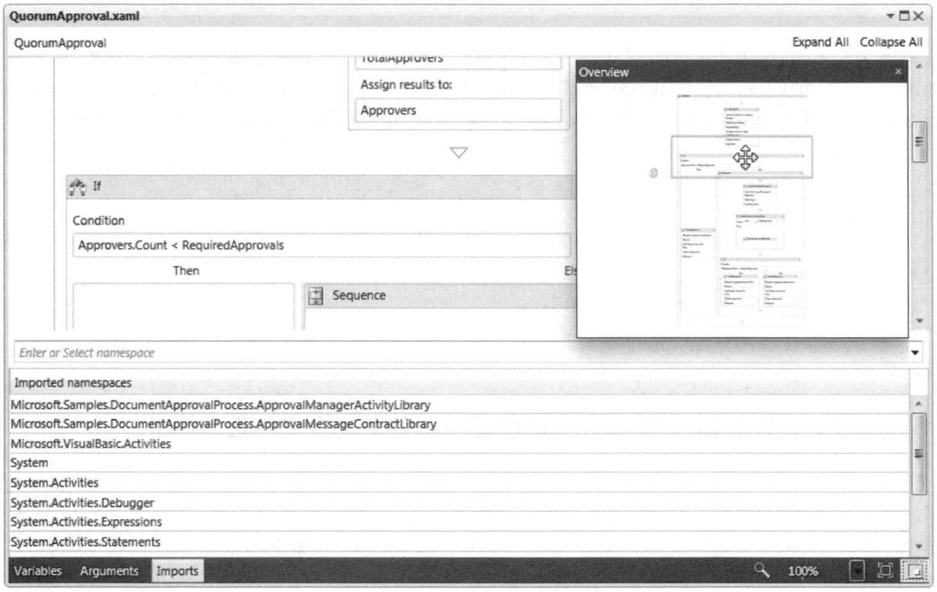

FIGURE 32-7

As previously discussed, one of the advantages of using WF is that the diagram of the workflow can be used as a form of documentation for your business process/logic/rules. It can often be useful to place this diagram in documentation or presentations, and the way to do this is quite easy. Right-click anywhere on the design surface. Two items appear in the context menu that you can use for this purpose: Save as Image and Copy as Image. Selecting the Copy as Image menu item copies a picture of the entire diagram to the clipboard, whereas the Save as Image menu item shows a dialog box enabling you to save the diagram to your choice of a JPEG, PNG, GIF, or XPS document. You can then paste the diagram into your document or presentation (if you copied it to the clipboard), or import it if you had saved it to disk.

CREATING A WORKFLOW

This section walks through the process of creating a very simple workflow that demonstrates a number of the features of WF. For this example, you will simply be writing output to the console window and receiving input from the user, but doing so in a workflow rather than regular code.

Designing a Workflow

The first thing you want to do is to drop a control flow activity onto the designer that will schedule the execution of the activities that it contains. For this example, you will use a Sequence activity for this purpose. You will find the Sequence activity under the Control Flow category in the Toolbox. Drag and drop it into your SimpleProcessWorkflow workflow, as demonstrated in Figure 32-8.

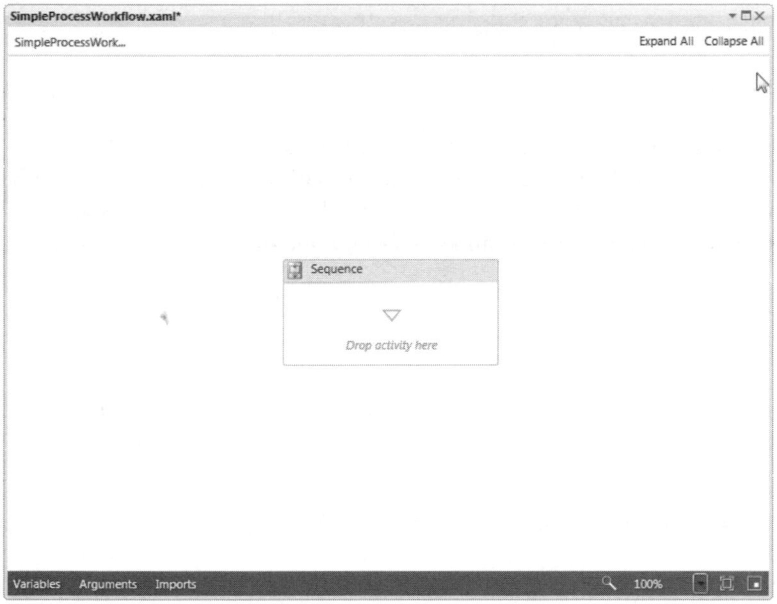

FIGURE 32-8

At this point, it would be useful to give it a meaningful name — click in its header and change it to SimpleProcessSequence. You can also simply select the activity and set its `DisplayName` property in the Properties tool window.

For this initial example, you'll get the workflow to execute a do/while loop that will write a message to the console five times. To do this, you then need to drop a DoWhile activity into the Sequence activity from the Control Flow category in the Toolbox. Once you've done that, you will find that both the new activity and the Sequence activity are now displaying as invalid (a red icon with an exclamation mark appears in the right side of the headers of both activities). This is because an expression needs to be assigned to the condition of the DoWhile activity before it can be considered valid.

> *If you attempt to compile the application that has an invalid activity, it will still compile but when you try to run it you will receive a run time error. You can, however, see a list of all the validation errors in a workflow as errors in the Error List tool window.*

Because you want to place more than one activity in the DoWhile activity, add a Sequence activity as its child. Call this sequence WriteHelloWorldSequence.

Now find the WriteLine activity in the Toolbox (under the Primitives category), and drag and drop that into the WriteHelloWorldSequence activity. To make it write Hello World to the output each time it's executed, set its Text argument to `"Hello World"` (with the argument accepting an expression and being a string value that you are assigning, you need to assign it as a literal value by enclosing it in quotes).

So that the output can be seen more easily, drop a Delay activity (from the Primitives category in the Toolbox) into the WriteHelloWorldSequence activity, following the WriteLine activity. The `Delay` activity's `Duration` argument accepts a `TimeSpan` type — you'll use an expression to specify its value as 200 milliseconds because it's more readable than the literal value:

```
TimeSpan.FromMilliseconds(200)
```

To control the number of times this loop will execute, add a variable called `Counter` to the SimpleProcessSequence activity (which will be available to all the activities in the sequence). Select the SimpleProcessSequence activity and pop up the Variables pane. Click where it says Create Variable, enter `Counter` as its name, a type of `Int32`, and a default value of `0`.

Back in the DoWhile activity, you can now specify the following expression as its condition:

```
Counter < 5
```

The final step is to actually increment the `Counter` variable. Add an Assign activity (from the Primitives category in the Toolbox) to the sequence (following the Delay activity), setting its `To` argument to `Counter`, and its `Value` argument to `Counter + 1`.

Your simple workflow is now complete, and should look like Figure 32-9.

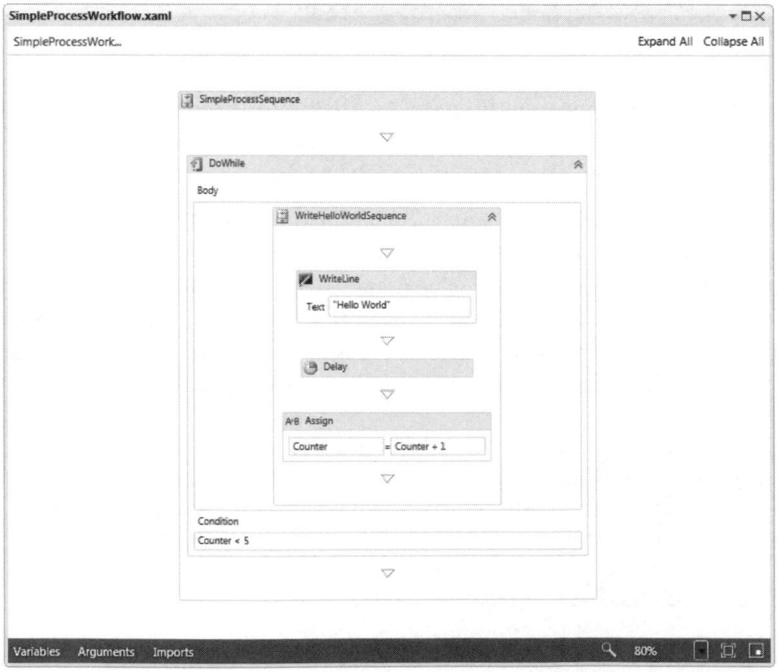

FIGURE 32-9

Now you can run your application, which will execute the workflow with the results shown in Figure 32-10.

Writing Code Activities

Now create a custom activity whose work is defined in code to get input from the user. Add a new item to your project, select the Code Activity item template from the Workflow category in the Add New Item dialog (as shown in Figure 32-11), and call it UserInput.

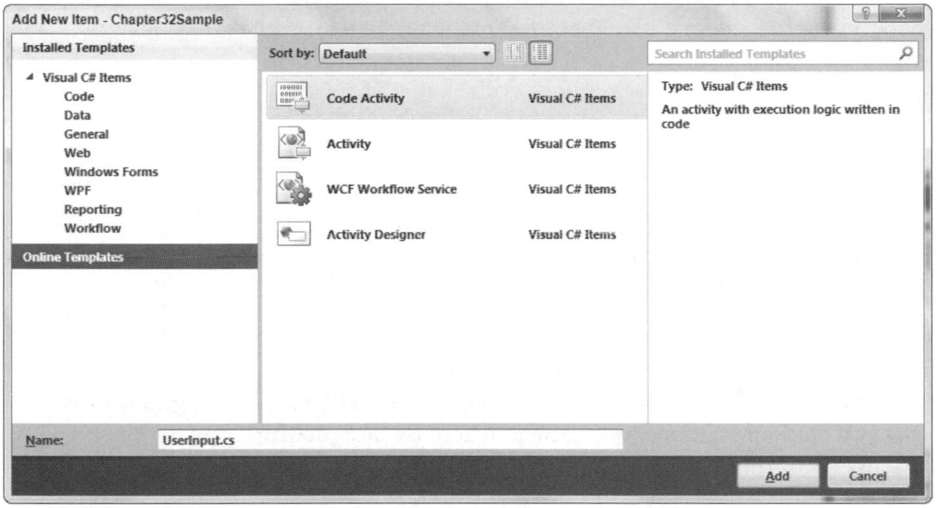

FIGURE 32-10

FIGURE 32-11

This creates a class that inherits from System.Activities.CodeActivity, and overrides the Execute method into which you can write the code that this activity will execute. It also includes a sample input argument called Text (defined as a property on the class), which you can delete because this activity won't require any inputs (also delete the line of code in the Execute method that retrieves its value).

This activity will obtain input from the user that other activities in the workflow can use. You can return the value either as an output argument or as a return value. Either way is acceptable, so for this example return the value.

To return a value, instead of inheriting from the CodeActivity class you will need to inherit from its generic version instead (into which you pass the type that the activity will return). Change the class to inherit from the generic CodeActivity class, passing in the type of the return value. Change the Execute method to return a type instead of void (C# developers), or to a function that returns

a type (VB developers). Then it's simply a case of returning the value returned from the `Console`
`.ReadLine()` function in the `Execute` method:

VB

```
Public NotInheritable Class UserInput
    Inherits CodeActivity(Of String)

    Protected Overrides Function Execute(ByVal context As CodeActivityContext) _
                                                                As String
        Return Console.ReadLine()
    End Function
End Class
```

C#

```
public sealed class UserInput : CodeActivity<string>
{
    protected override string Execute(CodeActivityContext context)
    {
        return Console.ReadLine();
    }
}
```

If you switch back now to the workflow in the designer, you will find that
the activity is nowhere to be found in the Toolbox. However, once you
compile your project, it will appear in the Toolbox, under the category with
the same name as your project, as shown in Figure 32-12.

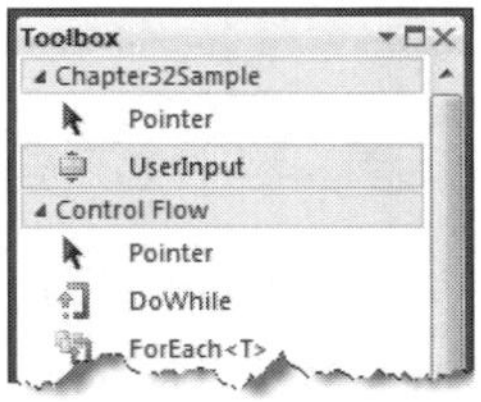

Drop the activity from the Toolbox into your workflow, in the main
SimpleProcessSequence sequence activity after the DoWhile activity. You
will note that there is no nice designer user interface for the activity (just a
simple block), but you could design one by creating an activity designer for
it. However a discussion of this is beyond the scope of this chapter.

FIGURE 32-12

When you select it, the Properties tool window will have a property called `Result`, in which an
expression to work with the return value of the `Execute` method in the activity can be specified.
What you want to do is assign the return value to a variable, which activities following it in the
sequence can use. Create a new variable in the Variables pane called `UserInputValue` with a type of
`String`. In the Properties tool window, you can now simply set `UserInputValue` as the expression
for the `Result` property, which will assign the return value from the activity to the `UserInputValue`
variable. You can prove this works by adding a WriteLine activity following the UserInput activity
that then writes the value of this variable back out to the console.

Executing a Workflow

If you inspect the `Main` method (the entry point of the application) in the `Program.cs` file (for C#
developers) or `Module1.vb` (for VB developers) you will find the code used to execute the workflow:

VB

```
WorkflowInvoker.Invoke(New SimpleProcessWorkflow())
```

C#

```csharp
WorkflowInvoker.Invoke(new SimpleProcessWorkflow());
```

This is making use of the `WorkflowInvoker` class to invoke the workflow, which, as described earlier in this chapter, has no control over the actual execution of the workflow other than simply initiating its execution.

If you want more control over the execution of a workflow, however (such as if you need to resume execution from a bookmark, or persist/unload a workflow), you will need to turn to the `WorkflowApplication` class to invoke your workflow instead. Basic use of the `WorkflowApplication` class to invoke a workflow and handle its `Complete` event is as follows:

VB

```vb
Dim syncEvent As New AutoResetEvent(False)

Dim app As New WorkflowApplication(New SimpleProcessWorkflow())

app.Completed = Function(args)
                    Console.WriteLine("Workflow instance has completed!")
                    Thread.Sleep(1000)
                    syncEvent.Set()
                    Return Nothing
                End Function

app.Run()
syncEvent.WaitOne()
```

C#

```csharp
AutoResetEvent syncEvent = new AutoResetEvent(false);

WorkflowApplication app = new WorkflowApplication(new SimpleProcessWorkflow());

app.Completed = (e) =>
{
    Console.WriteLine("Workflow instance has completed!");
    Thread.Sleep(1000);
    syncEvent.Set();
};

app.Run();
syncEvent.WaitOne();
```

> *Note that you will need to add an Imports/using statement to the* `System` `.Threading` *namespace at the top of the file for the code snippets above to work.*

This code assigns a delegate that will be run when the workflow has completed executing. Because the `Run` method returns immediately, you will wait for the workflow to complete executing before continuing (and exiting the application) using the `WaitOne` method on a `AutoResetEvent`, which is notified in the `Completed` handler that it can enable the thread execution to continue.

> *Although we are referring to "events" here, you'll note from the code snippets that they aren't events at all. Instead, they are properties to which you can assign delegates. However, for the purposes of simplifying their description we'll continue to refer to them as events.*

Executing a workflow via the `WorkflowApplication` class actually invokes it on a background thread, with the `Run` method returning immediately. The host can attach event handlers to various events raised by the `WorkflowApplication` class (such as when a workflow instance has completed, is idle, thrown an unhandled exception, and so on), and also gains the ability to abort/cancel/terminate a workflow instance, load one from a instance store, persist it, unload it, and resume from a bookmark.

You can pass input arguments into a workflow, and obtain output argument values from it. Input arguments are exposed as properties from your workflow class, so assign values to these before invoking the workflow. Output arguments are returned in a dictionary (which is the return value of the `WorkflowInvoker.Invoke` method), each having a string key with the name of the argument, and a corresponding object value that you can cast to the appropriate type.

As previously noted, workflows/activities are XAML files. By default, the XAML file is compiled into the application (as a resource), but what if you want to take advantage of the fact that you can reconfigure a workflow without recompiling the application? In that case, you would have to have the XAML file as a content file in your project instead, and dynamically load it into your application from file. This is where the `ActivityXamlServices` class is useful. Load the XAML file as an activity using the `ActivityXamlServices` class, and then invoke (that is, execute) the activity that it returns with the `WorkflowInvoker` or `WorkflowApplication` class:

VB

```
Dim activity As Activity = ActivityXamlServices.Load("SimpleProcessWorkflow.xaml")
WorkflowInvoker.Invoke(activity)
```

C#

```
Activity activity = ActivityXamlServices.Load("SimpleProcessWorkflow.xaml");
WorkflowInvoker.Invoke(activity);
```

> *Loading and executing a workflow from a file becomes a little more complicated when it uses custom activities (such as the UserInput activity), because the run time will need a reference to the assemblies containing those custom activities so it can use them. However, going into this further is beyond the scope of this chapter.*

Debugging Workflows

In addition to having a rich designer support for building workflows, WF also includes debugging capabilities. To define a breakpoint in a workflow, simply select the activity and press F9, or select

Breakpoint ⇨ Insert Breakpoint from the right-click context menu. Figure 32-13 demonstrates what an activity looks like when it has a breakpoint set on it (on the left), and how the activity is highlighted when stepping through the workflow and it is the current execution item (on the right).

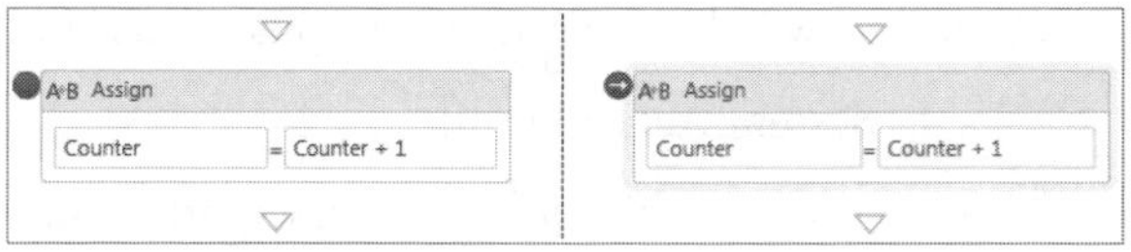

FIGURE 32-13

As in a normal debugging session, in a workflow you step through code using shortcut keys. Pressing F10 steps through the workflow, and pressing F11 steps into the current activity. You can view the values of variables currently in scope in the Locals tool window.

Of course, your custom code activities can be debugged as normal by setting breakpoints in the code editor and stepping through the code.

Testing Workflows

Having a well-defined testing framework is extremely important in business applications, with it especially vital that the underlying business logic for the application is well covered with tests. Therefore, it is essential with your workflow being at the core of your business logic that it should be testable too. Luckily, this is indeed possible, and you can use your favorite unit testing framework — going so far as to use Test Driven Development (TDD) practices if you want. As discussed in the "Executing a Workflow" section, by using the `WorkflowInvoker.Invoke` method to execute your workflow, you can pass input argument values into the workflow and obtain the resulting output argument values (in a dictionary). Therefore, testing your workflow is as easy as supplying input argument values and asserting that the corresponding output argument values are as expected.

HOSTING THE WORKFLOW DESIGNER

One of the benefits in having a declarative configurable workflow is that it can be reconfigured at will to support changing business requirements without the application needing to be recompiled. This means (in theory) that an end user given the right tools (that is, the WF designer) should be able to modify the workflow without requiring a developer to be involved (creating custom activities is a different story, however). Of course it's probably asking too much to have a casual end user use the WF designer and modify a workflow without training — it really is a tool designed to be used by developers. That said, with a little training, IT-savvy users (such as business analysts and so on) could successfully take on this task.

If this is the case, it is quite easy to host the WF designer in your own application and expose it to the end user for modification. The WF designer is a WPF component that you can host in your own WPF applications, making it available to the users to modify a workflow as required. You can also host the WF designer in Windows Forms using the WPF interoperability described in Chapter 18. This chapter, however, will focus on hosting it natively in a WPF application.

> *The coverage of this topic assumes you have some experience working with WPF and XAML. See Chapter 18 for more information on these topics.*

Create a new WPF project, called WFDesignerHost. Add the following assembly references to the project:

➤ System.Activities.dll

➤ System.Activities.Core.Presentation.dll

➤ System.Activities.Presentation.dll

You will also need to add a reference to any assemblies that contain custom activities that you want to be used in the workflows through your application.

The designer has three main (separate) components: the Toolbox, the Properties window, and the designer surface. Let's create a user interface that instantiates and displays the three of these.

Open up the `MainWindow.xaml` file and set the name of the Grid control to WFLayoutGrid. Also add three columns to this Grid (you will no doubt want to define some appropriate widths for these columns at a later point in time). Host the Toolbox in the first column, the designer surface in the second, and the Properties window in the third. The Toolbox can be created either declaratively in XAML or in code, but the designer surface and Properties window can only be created in code. For the purpose of this example, you'll create all three of these controls in code.

Open up the code behind the `MainWindow.xaml` file. Import the following namespaces:

VB

```vb
Imports System.Activities
Imports System.Activities.Core.Presentation
Imports System.Activities.Presentation
Imports System.Activities.Presentation.Toolbox
Imports System.Activities.Statements
Imports System.Linq
Imports System.Reflection
Imports System.Windows
Imports System.Windows.Controls
```

C#

```csharp
using System;
using System.Activities;
using System.Activities.Core.Presentation;
using System.Activities.Presentation;
using System.Activities.Presentation.Toolbox;
using System.Activities.Statements;
using System.Linq;
using System.Reflection;
using System.Windows;
using System.Windows.Controls;
```

First, you need to register the designer metadata:

VB

```vb
Private Sub RegisterMetadata()
    Dim metaData As New DesignerMetadata()
    metaData.Register()
End Sub
```

C#

```csharp
private void RegisterMetadata()
{
    DesignerMetadata metaData = new DesignerMetadata();
    metaData.Register();
}
```

Now add the Toolbox to the page. You will find that the Toolbox is not automatically populated with activities — instead you need to populate it yourself with the activities you want to make available to the user. The following code handles this by creating an instance of the Toolbox and adding all the activities in the same assembly as the Sequence activity to it.

VB

```vb
Private Sub AddToolboxControl(ByVal parent As Grid, ByVal row As Integer,
                              ByVal column As Integer)
    Dim toolbox As New ToolboxControl()

    Dim category As New ToolboxCategory("Activities")
    toolbox.Categories.Add(category)

    Dim query = From type In Assembly.GetAssembly(GetType(Sequence)).GetTypes()
                Where type.IsPublic AndAlso
                Not type.IsNested AndAlso
                Not type.IsAbstract AndAlso
                Not type.ContainsGenericParameters AndAlso
                (GetType(Activity).IsAssignableFrom(type) OrElse
                    GetType(IActivityTemplateFactory).IsAssignableFrom(type))
                Order By type.Name
                Select New ToolboxItemWrapper(type)

    query.ToList().ForEach(Function(item)
                              category.Add(item)
                              Return Nothing
                           End Function)

    Grid.SetRow(toolbox, row)
    Grid.SetColumn(toolbox, column)
    parent.Children.Add(toolbox)
End Sub
```

C#

```csharp
private void AddToolboxControl(Grid parent, int row, int column)
{
    ToolboxControl toolbox = new ToolboxControl();

    ToolboxCategory category = new ToolboxCategory("Activities");
    toolbox.Categories.Add(category);

    var query = from type in Assembly.GetAssembly(typeof(Sequence)).GetTypes()
                where type.IsPublic &&
```

```
                            !type.IsNested &&
                            !type.IsAbstract &&
                            !type.ContainsGenericParameters &&
                            (typeof(Activity).IsAssignableFrom(type) ||
                            typeof(IActivityTemplateFactory).IsAssignableFrom(type))
                            orderby type.Name
                            select new ToolboxItemWrapper(type);

                query.ToList().ForEach(item => category.Add(item));

                Grid.SetRow(toolbox, row);
                Grid.SetColumn(toolbox, column);
                parent.Children.Add(toolbox);
        }
```

Now you add the designer and the Properties window (both are controls returned from instantiating the `WorkflowDesigner` class):

VB

```vb
Private Sub AddDesigner(ByVal parent As Grid,
                        ByVal designerRow As Integer,
                        ByVal designerColumn As Integer,
                        ByVal propertiesRow As Integer,
                        ByVal propertiesColumn As Integer)
    Dim designer As New WorkflowDesigner()
    designer.Load(New Sequence())

    Grid.SetRow(designer.View, designerRow)
    Grid.SetColumn(designer.View, designerColumn)
    parent.Children.Add(designer.View)

    Grid.SetRow(designer.PropertyInspectorView, propertiesRow)
    Grid.SetColumn(designer.PropertyInspectorView, propertiesColumn)
    parent.Children.Add(designer.PropertyInspectorView)
End Sub
```

C#

```csharp
private void AddDesigner(Grid parent, int designerRow, int designerColumn,
                                int propertiesRow, int propertiesColumn)
{
    WorkflowDesigner designer = new WorkflowDesigner();
    designer.Load(new Sequence());

    Grid.SetRow(designer.View, designerRow);
    Grid.SetColumn(designer.View, designerColumn);
    parent.Children.Add(designer.View);

    Grid.SetRow(designer.PropertyInspectorView, propertiesRow);
    Grid.SetColumn(designer.PropertyInspectorView, propertiesColumn);
    parent.Children.Add(designer.PropertyInspectorView);
}
```

Now call these three functions from the window's New method/constructor, like so:

VB
```vb
Public Sub New()
    InitializeComponent()

    RegisterMetadata()
    AddToolboxControl(WFLayoutGrid, 0, 0)
    AddDesigner(WFLayoutGrid, 0, 1, 0, 2)
End Sub
```

C#
```csharp
public MainWindow()
{
    InitializeComponent();

    RegisterMetadata();
    AddToolboxControl(WFLayoutGrid, 0, 0);
    AddDesigner(WFLayoutGrid, 0, 1, 0, 2);
}
```

Now you can run the project and test it. Your final user interface should look something like Figure 32-14 (which can, of course, be improved upon by spending some time styling the page).

FIGURE 32-14

SUMMARY

In this chapter, you learned that Windows Workflow is a means of defining a business process, which is especially useful to use when you have a business process that changes frequently or is a long running process. You also learned how to create and run a basic workflow, and how to host the workflow designer in your own application. Windows Workflow is quickly becoming the standard for implementing workflows on the Microsoft platform, enabling you to reuse the skills you have gained here to also build workflows in the various products that support it.

33

Client Application Services

WHAT'S IN THIS CHAPTER?

➤ Accessing client application services

➤ Managing application roles

➤ Persisting user settings

➤ Specifying a custom login dialog

A generation of applications built around services and the separation of user experience from backend data stores has seen requirements for occasionally connected applications emerge. Occasionally connected applications are those that continue to operate regardless of network availability. In Chapter 34 you will learn how data can be synchronized to a local store to allow the user to continue to work when the application is offline. However, this scenario leads to discussions (often heated) about security. Because security (that is, user authentication and role authorization) is often managed centrally, it is difficult to extend so that it incorporates occasionally connected applications.

In this chapter you become familiar with the client application services that extend ASP.NET Application Services for use in client applications. ASP.NET Application Services is a provider-based model for performing user authentication, role authorization, and profile management that has in the past been limited to web services and web sites. In Visual Studio 2010, you can configure your rich client application, either Windows Forms or WPF, to make use of these services throughout your application to validate users, limit functionality based on what roles users have been assigned, and save personal settings to a central location.

CLIENT SERVICES

Over the course of this chapter you are introduced to the different application services via a simple WPF application. In this case it is an application called ClientServices, which you can create by selecting the (C# or VB) WPF Application template from the File ➪ New ➪ Project menu item.

To begin using the client application services, you need to enable the checkbox on the Services tab of the project properties designer, as shown in Figure 33-1. The default authentication mode is to use Windows authentication. This is ideal if you are building your application to work within the confines of a single organization and you can assume that everyone has domain credentials. Selecting this option ensures that those domain credentials are used to access the roles and settings services. Alternatively, you can elect to use Forms authentication, in which case you have full control over the mechanism that is used to authenticate users. We return to this topic later in the chapter.

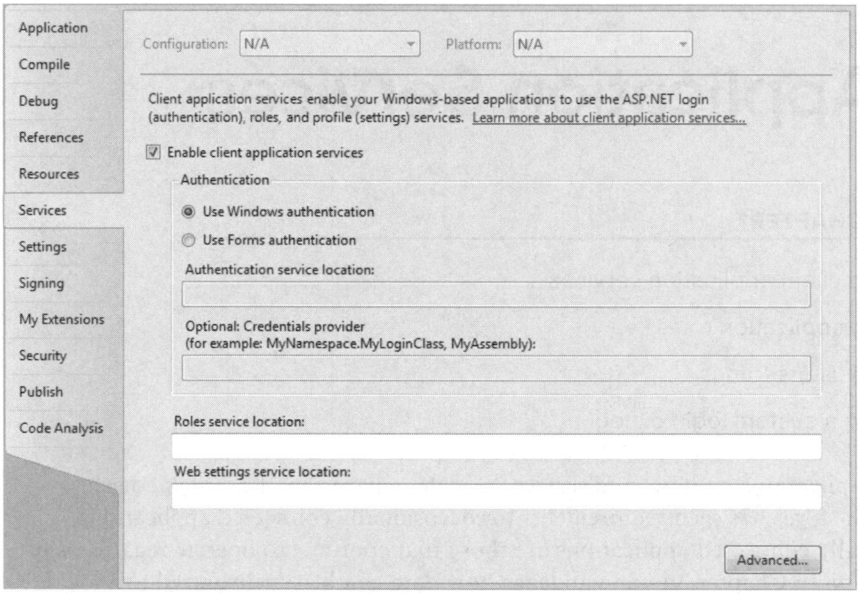

FIGURE 33-1

> *You can also add the client application services to existing applications via the Visual Studio 2010 project properties designer in the same way as for a new application.*

You will notice that when you enabled the client application services, an `app.config` file was added to your application if one did not already exist. Of particular interest is the `<system.web>` section, which should look similar to the following snippet:

Available for download on Wrox.com

```
<system.web>
    <membership defaultProvider="ClientAuthenticationMembershipProvider">
        <providers>
            <add name="ClientAuthenticationMembershipProvider" type=
            "System.Web.ClientServices.Providers.ClientWindowsAuthentication
```

```
MembershipProvider, System.Web.Extensions, Version=4.0.0.0, Culture=neutral,
PublicKeyToken=31bf3856ad364e35" serviceUri="" connectionStringName="Default
Connection" credentialsProvider=""/>
        </providers>
    </membership>
    <roleManager defaultProvider="ClientRoleProvider" enabled="true">
        <providers>
            <add name="ClientRoleProvider"
type="System.Web.ClientServices.Providers.ClientRoleProvider, System.Web.Ext
ensions, Version=4.0.0.0, Culture=neutral, PublicKeyToken=31bf3856ad364e35"
serviceUri="" cacheTimeout="86400" connectionStringName="DefaultConnection"/>
        </providers>
    </roleManager>
 </system.web>
```

Code snippet app.config

Here you can see that providers have been defined for membership and role management.
You can extend the client application services framework by building your own providers
that can talk directly to a database or to some other remote credential store such as Active
Directory. Essentially, all the project properties designer does is modify the app.config file
to use the providers that ship with the .NET Framework and define associated properties. To
implement your own providers, you need to create concrete classes that implement the abstract
methods defined in the System.Web.Security.RoleProvider, System.Web.Security
.MembershipProvider, or System.Configuration.SettingsProvider classes (depending on
which provider you are implementing).

After you define the default role and membership providers, you use the client application services
to validate the application user. To do this, you need to invoke the ValidateUser method on the
System.Web.Security.Membership class, as shown in the following snippet:

C#

```
using System.Web.Security;
public partial class MainWindow : Window{
    public MainWindow(){
        InitializeComponent();
    }
    private void Window_Loaded(object sender, RoutedEventArgs e){
        if (Membership.ValidateUser(null, null)){
            MessageBox.Show("User is valid");
        }
        else{
            MessageBox.Show("Unable to verify user, application exiting");
            this.Close();
            return;
        }
    }
}
```

Code snippet MainWindow.cs

VB

```vb
Imports System.Web.Security
Class MainWindow
    Private Sub Window_Loaded(ByVal sender As System.Object,
                        yVal e As System.Windows.RoutedEventArgs) Handles Me.Loaded
        If Membership.ValidateUser(Nothing, Nothing) Then
            MessageBox.Show("User is valid")
        Else
            MessageBox.Show("Unable to verify user, application exiting")
            Me.Close()
            Return
        End If
    End Sub
End Class
```

Code snippet MainWindow.vb

Interestingly, there is no overload of the `ValidateUser` method that accepts no arguments; instead, when using Windows authentication, you should use `Nothing` (VB) or `null` (C#) for the username and password arguments. In this case, `ValidateUser` does little more than prime the `CurrentPrincipal` of the application to use the client application services to determine which roles the user belongs to, and by default will return true. You see later that using this method is the equivalent of logging the user in to the application.

> *The preceding code snippet, and others throughout this chapter, may require you to import the* `System.Web.Security` *namespace into this class file. You may also need to manually add a reference to* `System.Web.dll` *in order to resolve type references.*

The client application services include what is often referred to as an application framework for handling security. VB has for a long time had its own application framework for Windows Forms Applications that is enabled and disabled via the Application tab on the project properties designer. This framework already includes limited support for handling user authentication, but it conflicts with the client application services. Figure 33-2 shows how you can elect to use an application-defined authentication mode so that you can use both the Windows application framework and the client application services in your application.

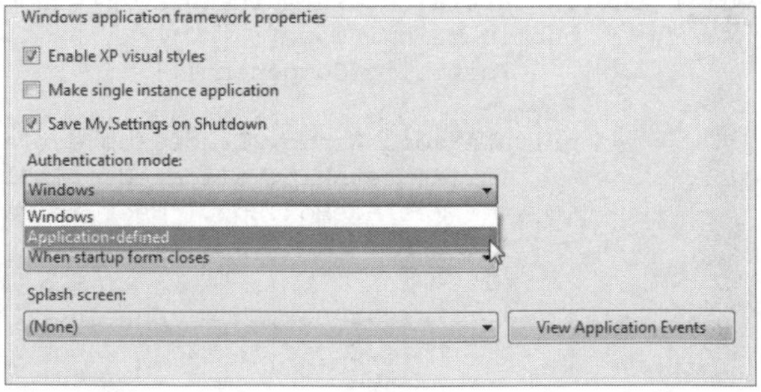

Windows application framework properties

☑ Enable XP visual styles
☐ Make single instance application
☑ Save My.Settings on Shutdown

Authentication mode:

Windows
Windows
Application-defined
When startup form closes

Splash screen:

(None) ▾ [View Application Events]

FIGURE 33-2

Note that this setting is available only if you are developing a Windows Forms Application in VB.

ROLE AUTHORIZATION

So far, you have seen how to enable the client application services, but they haven't really started to add value because the user was already authenticated by the operating system when you were using Windows authentication for the client application. What isn't handled by the operating system is specifying which roles a user belongs to and thus what parts or functions within an application the user can access. Although this could be handled by the client application itself, it would be difficult to account for all permutations of users and the system would be impractical to manage, because every time a user was added or changed roles a new version of the application would have to be deployed. Instead, it is preferable to have the correlations between users and roles managed on the server, allowing the application to work with a much smaller set of roles through which to control access to functionality.

The true power of the client application services becomes apparent when you combine the client-side application framework with the ASP.NET Application Services. To see this, you should add a new project to your solution using the (VB or C#) ASP.NET Empty Web Application template (under the Web node in the New Project dialog), calling it ApplicationServices.

Right-click the newly created project in Solution Explorer and select Properties to bring up the project properties designer. Because you will be referencing this web application from other parts of the solution, it is preferable to use a predefined port and virtual directory with the Visual Studio Development Server. On the Web tab, set the specific port to 12345 and the virtual path to /ApplicationServices.

ASP.NET Application Services is a provider-based model for authenticating users, managing roles, and storing profile (a.k.a. settings) information. Each of these components can be engaged independently, and you can either elect to use the built-in providers or create your own. To enable the role management service for access via client application services, add the following snippet before the `<system.web>` element in the `web.config` file in the ApplicationServices project:

Available for download on Wrox.com

```
<system.web.extensions>
    <scripting>
        <webServices>
            <roleService enabled="true"/>
        </webServices>
    </scripting>
</system.web.extensions>
```

Code snippet web.config

Because you want to perform some custom logic to determine which roles a user belongs to, you will need to create a custom role provider, called `CustomRoles`, to take the place of the default role provider. This is done by adding a new class to your project and implementing the `RoleProvider` abstract class. For this role provider, you are interested only in returning a value for the `GetRolesForUser` method; all other methods can be left as method stubs.

Available for download on Wrox.com

C#

```
public class CustomRoles: RoleProvider{
    public override string[] GetRolesForUser(string username){
        if (username.ToLower().Contains("nick")){
            return new string[] { "All Nicks" };
```

```
        }
        else{
            return new string[] { };
        }
    }
}
```

Code snippet CustomRoles.cs

VB

```
Public Class CustomRoles
    Inherits RoleProvider

    Public Overrides Function GetRolesForUser(ByVal username As String) As String()
        If username.ToLower.Contains("nick") Then
            Return New String() {"All Nicks"}
        Else
            Return New String() {}
        End If
    End Function
End Function
```

Code snippet CustomRoles.vb

You now have a custom role provider and have enabled role management. The only thing missing is the glue that lets the role management service know to use your role provider. You provide this by adding the following `roleManager` node to the `<system.web>` element in the `web.config` file:

```
<roleManager enabled="true" defaultProvider="CustomRoles">
    <providers>
        <add name=" CustomRoles" type="AuthenticationServices.CustomRoles"/>
    </providers>
</roleManager>
```

Code snippet web.config

The last thing to do is to make use of this role information in your application. You do this by first configuring your application with the URI to use for loading role information. On the Services tab of the ClientServices project properties (shown in Figure 33-1), enter `http://localhost:12345/ApplicationServices`. Next, you need to add a call to `IsUserInRole` to the `Window_Loaded` method:

C#

```
private void Window_Loaded(object sender, RoutedEventArgs e){
    if (Membership.ValidateUser(null, null))
    { // Commented out for brevity.
    }
    if (Roles.IsUserInRole("All Nicks")){
        MessageBox.Show("User is a Nick, so should have Admin rights.");
    }
}
```

Code snippet MainWindow.cs

VB

```vb
Private Sub Window_Loaded(ByVal sender As System.Object,
                        ByVal e As System.Windows.RoutedEventArgs) Handles Me.Loaded
    If Membership.ValidateUser(Nothing, Nothing) Then
        '. Commented out for brevity .
    End If
    If Roles.IsUserInRole("All Nicks") Then
        MessageBox.Show("User is a Nick, so should have Admin rights.")
    End If
End Sub
```

Code snippet MainWindow.vb

To see your custom role provider in action, set a breakpoint in the `GetRolesForUser` method. For this breakpoint to be hit, you have to have both the client application and the web application running in debug mode. To do this, right-click the Solution node in the Solution Explorer window and select Properties. From the Startup Project node, select Multiple Startup Projects and set the action of both projects to start. Now when you run the solution, you will see that the `GetRolesForUser` method is called with the Windows credentials of the current user, as part of the validation of the user.

USER AUTHENTICATION

In some organizations it would be possible to use Windows authentication for all user validation. Unfortunately, in many cases this is not possible, and application developers have to come up with their own solutions for determining which users should be able to access a system. This process is loosely referred to as *forms-based authentication*, because it typically requires the provision of a username and password combination via a login form of some description. Both ASP.NET Application Services and the client application services support forms-based authentication as an alternative to Windows authentication.

To begin with, you will need to enable the membership management service for access by the client application services. Adding the `<authenticationService>` element to the `<system .web.extensions>` element in the `web.config` file does this. Note that we have disabled the SSL requirement, which is clearly against all security best practices and not recommended for production systems.

```xml
<system.web.extensions>
      <scripting>
            <webServices>
                  <authenticationService enabled="true" requireSSL="false"/>
                  <roleService enabled="true"/>
```

Code snippet web.config

The next step is to create a custom membership provider that will determine whether a specific username and password combination is valid for the application. To do this, add a new class, `CustomAuthentication`, to the ApplicationServices application and set it to inherit from the

`MembershipProvider` class. As with the role provider you created earlier, you are just going to provide a minimal implementation that validates credentials by ensuring the password is the reverse of the supplied username, and that the username is in a predefined list.

C#

Available for download on Wrox.com

```csharp
public class CustomAuthentication : MembershipProvider{
    private string[] mValidUsers = { "Nick" };

    public override bool ValidateUser(string username, string password)
    {
        var reversed = new string(password.Reverse().ToArray());
        return (from user in mValidUsers
                where string.Compare(user, username, true) == 0 &&
                      user == reversed
                select user).Count() > 0;
    }
    // The rest of the implementation has been omitted for brevity
}
```

Code snippet CustomAuthentication.cs

VB

Available for download on Wrox.com

```vb
Public Class CustomAuthentication
    Inherits MembershipProvider
    Private mValidUsers As String() = {"Nick"}

    Public Overrides Function ValidateUser(ByVal username As String,
                                    ByVal password As String) As Boolean
        Dim reversed As String = New String(password.Reverse.ToArray)
        Return (From user In mValidUsers
                Where String.Compare(user, username, True) = 0 And
                      user = reversed).Count > 0
    End

    'The rest of the implementation has been omitted for brevity
End Class
```

Code snippet CustomAuthentication.vb

As with the role provider you created, you will also need to inform the membership management system that it should use the membership provider you have created. You do this by adding the following snippet to the `<system.web>` element in the `web.config` file:

Available for download on Wrox.com

```xml
<membership defaultProvider="CustomAuthentication">
    <providers>
        <add name="CustomAuthentication"
  type="ApplicationServices.CustomAuthentication"/>
    </providers>
</membership>
<authentication mode="Forms"/>
```

Code snippet web.config

Back on the client application, only minimal changes are required to take advantage of the changes to the authentication system. On the Services tab of the project properties designer, select Use Forms Authentication. This enables both the Authentication Service Location textbox and the Optional: Credentials Provider textbox. For the time being, just specify the authentication service location as `http://localhost:12345/ApplicationServices`.

Previously, using Windows authentication, you performed the call to `ValidateUser` to initiate the client application services by supplying `Nothing` as each of the two arguments. You did this because the user credentials could be automatically determined from the current user context in which the application was running. Unfortunately, this is not possible for Forms authentication, so you need to supply a username and password:

C#

```
private void Window_Loaded(object sender, RoutedEventArgs e){
    if (Membership.ValidateUser("Nick", "kciN")){
        MessageBox.Show("User is valid");
```

Code snippet MainWindow.cs

VB

```
Private Sub Window_Loaded(ByVal sender As System.Object,
                    ByVal e As System.Windows.RoutedEventArgs) _
                    Handles Me.Loaded
    If Membership.ValidateUser("Nick", "kciN") Then
        MessageBox.Show("User is valid")
```

Code snippet MainWindow.vb

If you specify a breakpoint in the `ValidateUser` method in the ApplicationServices project, you will see that when you run this solution the server is contacted in order to validate the user. You see later that this information can then be cached locally to facilitate offline user validation.

SETTINGS

In the .NET Framework v2.0, the concept of settings with a User scope was introduced to allow per-user information to be stored between application sessions. For example, window positioning or theme information might have been stored as a user setting. Unfortunately, there was no way to centrally manage this information. Meanwhile, ASP.NET Application Services had the notion of profile information, which was essentially per-user information, tracked on a server, that could be used by web applications. Naturally, with the introduction of the client application services, it made sense to combine these ideas to allow settings to be saved via the Web. These settings have a scope of User (Web).

As with the membership and role services, you need to enable the profile service for access by the client application services. You do this by adding the `<profileService>` element to the `<system .web.extensions>` element in the `web.config` file:

```
<system.web.extensions>
    <scripting>
        <webServices>
            <profileService enabled="true"
                            readAccessProperties="Nickname"
                            writeAccessProperties="Nickname" />
            <authenticationService enabled="true" requireSSL="false"/>
```

Code snippet web.config

Following the previous examples, you will build a custom profile provider that uses an in-memory dictionary to store user nicknames. Note that this isn't a good way to track profile information, because it would be lost every time the web server recycled and would not scale out to multiple web servers. Nevertheless, you need to add a new class, CustomProfile, to the ApplicationServices project and set it to inherit from ProfileProvider.

C#

```csharp
using System.Web.Profile;
using System.Configuration;
public class CustomProfile : ProfileProvider{
    private Dictionary<string, string> nicknames =
                                new Dictionary<string, string>();

    public override System.Configuration.SettingsPropertyValueCollection
        GetPropertyValues(System.Configuration.SettingsContext context,
            System.Configuration.SettingsPropertyCollection collection){
        var vals = new SettingsPropertyValueCollection();
        foreach (SettingsProperty setting in collection){
            var value = new SettingsPropertyValue(setting);
            if (nicknames.ContainsKey(setting.Name)) {
                value.PropertyValue = nicknames[setting.Name];
            }
            vals.Add(value);
        }
        return vals;
    }

    public override void SetPropertyValues(SettingsContext context,
                        SettingsPropertyValueCollection collection){
        foreach (SettingsPropertyValue setting in collection){
            nicknames[setting.Name] = setting.PropertyValue.ToString();
        }
    }

    // The rest of the implementation has been omitted for brevity
}
```

Code snippet CustomProfile.cs

VB

```vb
Imports System.Configuration

Public Class CustomProfile
    Inherits ProfileProvider
    Private nicknames As New Dictionary(Of String, String)

    Public Overrides Function GetPropertyValues(ByVal context As SettingsContext, _
                    ByVal collection As SettingsPropertyCollection) _
                                            As SettingsPropertyValueCollection
        Dim vals As New SettingsPropertyValueCollection
        For Each setting As SettingsProperty In collection
            Dim value As New SettingsPropertyValue(setting)
            If nicknames.ContainsKey(setting.Name) Then
                value.PropertyValue = nicknames.Item(setting.Name)
            End If
            vals.Add(value)
        Next
        Return vals
    End Function

    Public Overrides Sub SetPropertyValues(ByVal context As SettingsContext, _
                        ByVal collection As SettingsPropertyValueCollection)
        For Each setting As SettingsPropertyValue In collection
            nicknames.Item(setting.Name) = setting.PropertyValue.ToString
        Next
    End Sub

    'The rest of the implementation has been omitted for brevity
End Class
```

Code snippet CustomProfile.vb

The difference with the profile service is that when you specify the provider to use in the `<system .web>` element in the `web.config` file, you also need to declare what properties can be saved via the profile service (see the following snippet). For these properties to be accessible via the client application services, they must have a corresponding entry in the `readAccessProperties` and `writeAccessProperties` attributes of the `<profileService>` element, shown earlier.

```xml
<profile enabled="true" defaultProvider="CustomProfile">
    <providers>
        <add name="CustomProfile" type="ApplicationServices.CustomProfile"/>
    </providers>
    <properties>
        <add name="Nickname" type="string"
            readOnly="false" defaultValue="{nickname}"
            serializeAs="String" allowAnonymous="false" />
    </properties>
</profile>
```

Code snippet web.config

As an aside, the easiest way to build a full profile service is to use the utility `aspnet_regsql.exe` (typically found at `c:\Windows\Microsoft.NET\Framework\v4.0.21006\aspnet_regsql.exe`) to populate an existing SQL Server database with the appropriate table structure. You can then use the built-in `SqlProfileProvider` (`SqlMembershipProvider` and `SqlRoleProvider` for membership and role providers, respectively) to store and retrieve profile information. To use this provider, change the profile element you added earlier to the following:

```
<profile enabled="true" defaultProvider="CustomProfile">
    <providers>
        <add name="SqlProvider"
            type="System.Web.Profile.SqlProfileProvider"
            connectionStringName="SqlServices"
            applicationName="SampleApplication"
            description="SqlProfileProvider for SampleApplication" />
```

Note that the `connectionStringName` attribute needs to correspond to the name of a SQL Server connection string located in the `connectionStrings` section of the `web.config` file.

To use the custom profile provider you have created, in the client application, you need to specify the web settings service location on the Services tab of the project properties designer. This location should be the same as for both the role and authentication services: `http://localhost:12345/ApplicationServices`.

This is where the Visual Studio 2010 support for application settings is particularly useful. If you now go to the Settings tab of the project properties designer and click the Load Web Settings button, you are initially prompted for credential information, because you need to be a validated user to access the profile service. Figure 33-3 shows this dialog with the appropriate credentials supplied.

After a valid set of credentials is entered, the profile service is interrogated and a new row is added to the settings design surface, as shown in Figure 33-4. Here you can see that the scope of this setting is indeed User (Web) and that the default value, specified in the `web.config` file, has been retrieved.

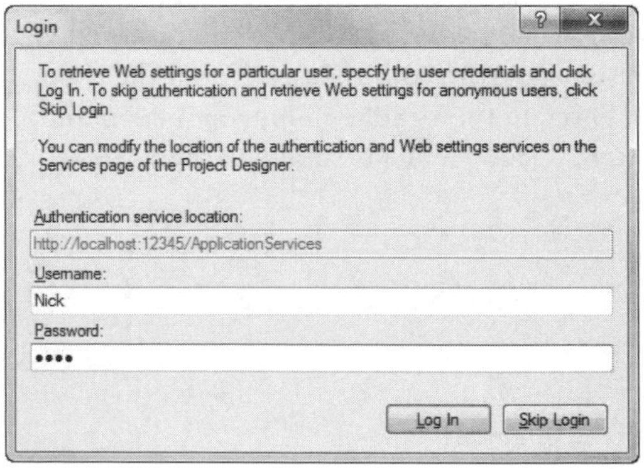

FIGURE 33-3

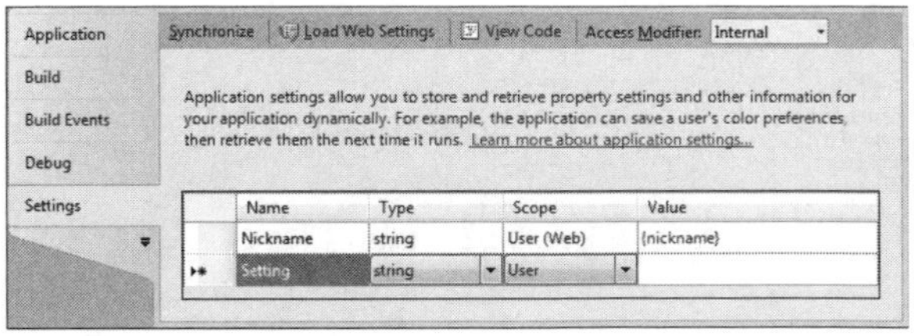

FIGURE 33-4

If you take a look at the `app.config` file for the client application, you will notice that a new `sectionGroup` has been added to the `configSections` element. This simply declares the class that will be used to process the custom section that has been added to support the new user settings.

```
<configSections>
    <sectionGroup name="userSettings"
                type="System.Configuration.UserSettingsGroup, System,
                    Version=4.0.0.0, Culture=neutral,
                    PublicKeyToken=b77a5c561934e089" >
        <section name="ClientServices.Properties.Settings"
                type="System.Configuration.ClientSettingsSection, System,
                    Version=4.0.0.0, Culture=neutral,
                    PublicKeyToken=b77a5c561934e089" allowExeDefinition=
                    "MachineToLocalUser" requirePermission="false" />
    </sectionGroup>
</configSections>
```

Toward the end of the app.config file, you will see the custom section that has been created. As you would expect, the name of the setting is Nickname and the value corresponds to the default value specified in the web.config file in the ApplicationServices project.

```
<userSettings>
    <ClientAppServicesVB.MySettings>
        <setting name="Nickname" serializeAs="String">
            <value>{nickname}</value>
        </setting>
    </ClientAppServicesVB.MySettings>
</userSettings>
```

To make use of this in code you can use the same syntax as for any other setting. Here you simply retrieve the current value, request a new value, and then save this new value:

Available for download on Wrox.com

C#

```
private void Window_Loaded(object sender, RoutedEventArgs e){
    // Commented out for brevity
    MessageBox.Show(My.Settings.Nickname)
    Properties.Settings.Default.Nickname = "Not the default Name";
    My.Settings.Save()
```

Code snippet MainWindow.cs

Available for download on Wrox.com

VB

```
Private Sub Window_Loaded(ByVal sender As System.Object,
                    ByVal e As System.Windows.RoutedEventArgs) _
                                Handles Me.Loaded
    ' Commented out for brevity
    MessageBox.Show(My.Settings.Nickname)
    My.Settings.Nickname = InputBox("Please specify a nickname:", "Nickname")
    My.Settings.Save()
```

Code snippet MainWindow.vb

If you run this application again, the nickname you supplied the first time will be returned.

LOGIN FORM

Earlier, when you were introduced to Forms authentication, you used a hard-coded username and password to validate the user. Although it would be possible for the application to prompt the user for credentials before calling ValidateUser with the supplied values, there is a better way that uses the client application services framework. Instead of calling ValidateUser with a username/password combination, you go back to supplying Nothing as the argument values and define a credential provider; then the client application services will call the provider to determine the set of credentials to use.

C#

```csharp
private void Window_Loaded(object sender, RoutedEventArgs e){
    if (Membership.ValidateUser(null, null)){
        MessageBox.Show("User is valid");
```

Code snippet MainWindow.cs

VB

```vb
Private Sub Window_Loaded(ByVal sender As System.Object,
                    ByVal e As System.Windows.RoutedEventArgs) _
                                            Handles Me.Loaded
    If Membership.ValidateUser(Nothing, Nothing) Then
        MessageBox.Show("User is valid")
```

Code snippet MainWindow.vb

This probably sounds more complex than it is because it is relatively easy to create a credentials provider. Start by adding a login form to the client application. Do this by selecting the Login Form template from the Add New Item dialog and calling it LoginForm. Unfortunately, this template is only available for VB developers as a Windows Forms form. If you want to create a WPF version or are working in C# you will need to add a new Window to the ClientServices project and add a TextBox (name it UsernameTextBox), a PasswordBox (name it PasswordTextBox), and two Buttons (name them OK and Cancel). While you have the designer open, click the OK button and change the DialogResult property to OK.

To use this login form as a credential provider, modify it to implement the IClientFormsAuthenticationCredentialsProvider interface. An alternative strategy would be to have a separate class that implements this interface and then displays the login form when the GetCredentials method is called. The following code snippet contains the code-behind file for the LoginForm class, showing the implementation of the IClientFormsAuthenticationCredentialsProvider interface:

C#

```csharp
using System.Web.ClientServices.Providers;
public partial class LoginForm : Window,
                        IClientFormsAuthenticationCredentialsProvider {
    public LoginForm(){
```

```
        InitializeComponent();
    }

    private void OK_Click(object sender, RoutedEventArgs e){
        this.DialogResult = true;
        this.Close();
    }

    private void Cancel_Click(object sender, RoutedEventArgs e){
        this.DialogResult = false;
        this.Close();
    }

    public ClientFormsAuthenticationCredentials GetCredentials(){
        if (this.ShowDialog() ?? false) {
            return new ClientFormsAuthenticationCredentials(
                            UsernameTextBox.Text,
                            PasswordTextBox.
                            Password,
                            false);
        }
        else{
            return null;
        }
    }
}
```

Code Snippet LoginForm.xaml.cs

VB

Available for download on Wrox.com

```
Imports System.Web.ClientServices.Providers

Public Class LoginForm
    Implements IClientFormsAuthenticationCredentialsProvider

    Public Function GetCredentials() As ClientFormsAuthenticationCredentials _
            Implements IClientFormsAuthenticationCredentialsProvider.GetCredentials
        If Me.ShowDialog() = Forms.DialogResult.OK Then
            Return New ClientFormsAuthenticationCredentials(UsernameTextBox.Text,
                                                    PasswordTextBox.Text,
                                                    False)
        Else
            Return Nothing
        End If
    End Function
End Class
```

Code snippet LoginForm.vb

> *You will notice that the C# and VB code snippets are quite different. This is because the C# uses a new WPF window, while the VB snippet uses the Windows Form Login Form template.*

As you can see from this snippet, the GetCredentials method returns ClientFormsAuthenticationCredentials if credentials are supplied, or Nothing (VB)/null (C#) if Cancel is clicked. Clearly this is only one way to collect credentials information, and there is no requirement that you prompt the user for this information. (The use of dongles or employee identification cards are common alternatives.)

With the credentials provider created, it is just a matter of informing the client application services that they should use it. You do this via the Optional: Credentials Provider field on the Services tab of the project properties designer, as shown in Figure 33-5.

Now when you run the application, you are prompted to enter a username and password to access the application. This information is then passed to the membership provider on the server to validate the user.

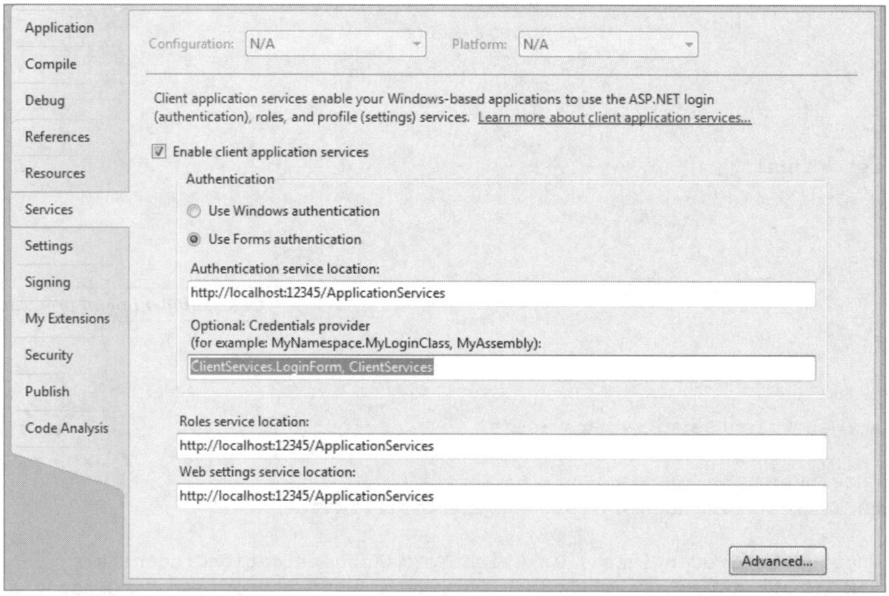

FIGURE 33-5

OFFLINE SUPPORT

In the previous steps, if you had a breakpoint in the role provider code on the server, you may have noticed that it hit the breakpoint only the first time you ran the application. The reason for this is that it is caching the role information offline. If you click the Advanced button on the Services tab of the project properties designer, you will see a number of properties that can be adjusted to control this offline behavior, as shown in Figure 33-6.

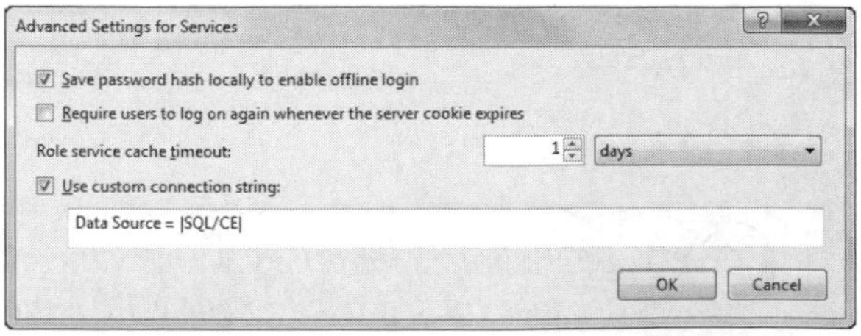

FIGURE 33-6

It's the role service cache timeout that determines how frequently the server is queried for role information. Because this timeout determines the maximum period it will take for role changes to be propagated to a connected client, it is important that you set this property according to how frequently you expect role information to change. Clearly, if the application is running offline, the changes will be retrieved the next time the application goes online (assuming the cache timeout has been exceeded while the application is offline).

Clicking the Save Password Hash checkbox means that the application doesn't have to be online for the user to log in. The stored password hash is used only when the application is running in offline mode, in contrast to the role information, for which the cache is queried unless the timeout has been exceeded.

Whether the application is online or offline is a property maintained by the client application services, because it is completely independent of actual network or server availability. Depending on your application, it might be appropriate to link the two as shown in the following example, where offline status is set during application startup or when the network status changes. From the project properties designer, click the View Application Events button on the Application tab (VB), or open App.xaml and add an event handler for the Startup event. This displays a code file in which the following code can be inserted:

C#

```
using System.Net.NetworkInformation;
public partial class App : Application{
    private void Application_Startup(object sender, StartupEventArgs e){
        NetworkChange.NetworkAvailabilityChanged +=
        new NetworkAvailabilityChangedEventHandler
                                (NetworkChange_NetworkAvailabilityChanged);
        this.UpdateConnectivity();
    }

    private void NetworkChange_NetworkAvailabilityChanged(object sender,
                                    NetworkAvailabilityEventArgs e){
        this.UpdateConnectivity();
    }

    private void UpdateConnectivity(){
        System.Web.ClientServices.ConnectivityStatus.IsOffline =
    !System.Net.NetworkInformation.NetworkInterface.GetIsNetworkAvailable();
    }
}
```

Code snippet Application.xaml.cs

VB

```
Class Application
    Private Sub MyApplication_Startup(ByVal sender As Object,
            ByVal e As System.Windows.StartupEventArgs) Handles Me.Startup
        AddHandler System.Net.NetworkInformation.NetworkChange.
        NetworkAvailabilityChanged, _
                    AddressOf MyApplication_NetworkAvailabilityChanged
        UpdateConnectivity()
    End Sub
```

```
    Private Sub MyApplication_NetworkAvailabilityChanged(
        ByVal sender As Object,
        ByVal e As System.Net.NetworkInformation.NetworkAvailabilityEventArgs)
        UpdateConnectivity()
    End Sub

    Private Sub UpdateConnectivity()
        System.Web.ClientServices.ConnectivityStatus.IsOffline = Not _
        My.Computer.Network.IsAvailable()
    End Sub
End Class
```

Code snippet Application.xaml.vb

You should note that this is a very rudimentary way of detecting whether an application is online, and that most applications require more complex logic to determine if they are, in fact, connected. The other thing to consider is that when the application comes back online, you may wish to confirm that the user information is still up to date using the RevalidateUser method on the ClientFormsIdentity object (only relevant to Forms authentication):

C#

```
(System.Threading.Thread.CurrentPrincipal.Identity as
            System.Web.ClientServices.ClientFormsIdentity).RevalidateUser()
```

VB

```
CType(System.Threading.Thread.CurrentPrincipal.Identity,
            System.Web.ClientServices.ClientFormsIdentity).RevalidateUser()
```

The last property in the Advanced dialog determines where the cached credential and role information is stored. This checkbox has been enabled because we chose to use Windows authentication earlier in the example. If you are using Forms authentication you can clear this checkbox. The client application services will use .clientdata files to store per-user data under the Application.UserAppDataPath, which is usually something like C:\Users\Nick\AppData\ Roaming\ClientServices\1.0.0.0 (this will differ on Windows XP). Using a custom connection string enables you to use a SQL Server Compact Edition (SSCE) database file to store the credentials information. This is required for offline support of Windows authentication.

> *Unfortunately, the designer is limited in that it doesn't enable you to specify any existing connections you may have. If you modify the* app.config *file, you can tweak the application to use the same connection.*
>
> *This might be a blessing in disguise, because the |SQL/CE| datasource property (which is the default) actually lets the client application services manage the creation and setup of the SSCE database file (otherwise you have to ensure that the appropriate tables exist).*
>
> *You will notice that the files that are created are* .spf *instead of the usual* .sdf *file extension — they are still SSCE database files that you can explore with Visual Studio 2010.*

SUMMARY

In this chapter, you have seen how the ASP.NET Application Services can be extended for use with client applications. With built-in support for offline functionality, the client application services enable you to build applications that can seamlessly move between online and offline modes. Combined with the Microsoft ADO.NET Synchronization Services, they provide the necessary infrastructure to build quite sophisticated occasionally connected applications.

34

Synchronization Services

WHAT'S IN THIS CHAPTER?

➤ What an occasionally connected application is and why you would build an application that way

➤ Wiring up Synchronization Services to build an occasionally connected application

➤ Separating Synchronization Services across multiple tiers

➤ Performing both single and bi-directional synchronization

Application design has gone through many extremes, ranging from standalone applications that don't share data, to public web applications in which everyone connects to the same data store. More recently, we have seen a flurry of peer-to-peer applications in which information is shared between nodes but no central data store exists. In the enterprise space, key buzzwords such as Software as a Service (SaaS) and Software and Services (S+S) highlight the transition from centralized data stores, through an era of outsourced data and application services, toward a hybrid model where data and services are combined within a rich application.

One of the reasons organizations have leaned toward web applications in the past has been the need to rationalize their data into a single central repository. Although rich client applications can work well across a low-latency network using the same data repository, they quickly become unusable if every action requires data to be communicated between the client and server over a slow public network. To reduce this latency, an alternative strategy is to synchronize a portion of the data repository to the client machine and to make local data requests. This will not only improve performance, because all the data requests happen locally, but it will also reduce the load on the server. In this chapter, you discover how building applications that are only occasionally connected can help you deliver rich and responsive applications using the Microsoft Synchronization Services for ADO.NET.

OCCASIONALLY CONNECTED APPLICATIONS

An occasionally connected application is one that can continue to operate regardless of connectivity status. You have a number of different ways to access data when the application is offline. Passive systems simply cache data that is accessed from the server, so that when the connection is lost at least a subset of the information is available. Unfortunately, this strategy means that a very limited set of data is available and is really only suitable for scenarios where there is an unstable or unreliable connection, rather than completely disconnected applications. In the latter case, an active system that synchronizes data to the local system is required. The Microsoft Synchronization Services for ADO.NET (Sync Services) is a synchronization framework that dramatically simplifies the problem of synchronizing data from any server to the local system.

SERVER DIRECT

To get familiar with the Sync Services, you will use a simple database that consists of a single table that tracks customers. You can create this using the Server Explorer within Visual Studio 2010. Right-click the Data Connections node and select Create New SQL Server Database from the shortcut menu. Figure 34-1 shows the Create New SQL Server Database dialog in which you can specify a server and a name for the new database.

When you click OK, a database with the name CRM is added to the SQL Server Express instance and a data connection is added to the Data Connections node in the Server Explorer. From the Tables node, under the newly created data connection, select Add New Table from the right-click shortcut menu and create columns for CustomerId (primary key), Name, Email, and Phone so that the table matches what is shown in Figure 34-2.

FIGURE 34-1

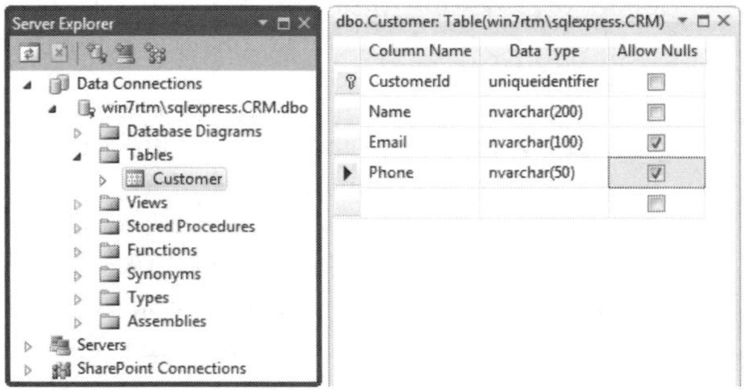

FIGURE 34-2

Now that you have a simple database to work with, it's time to create a new Windows Forms Application. In this case the application is titled QuickCRM, and in the Solution Explorer tool window of Figure 34-3 you can see that we have renamed Form1 to MainForm and added two additional forms, ServerForm and LocalForm.

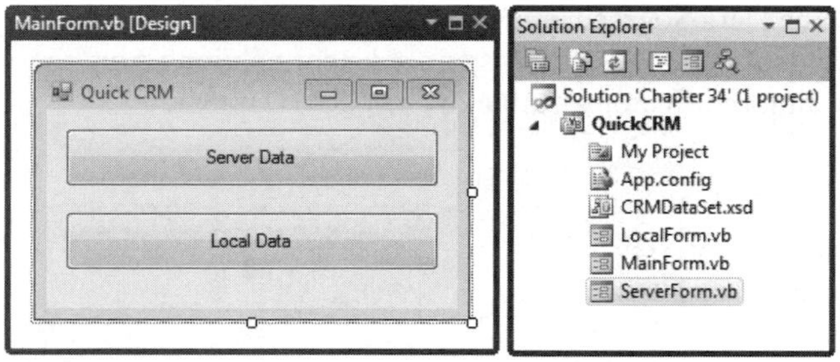

FIGURE 34-3

MainForm has two buttons, as shown in the editor area of Figure 34-3, and has the following code to launch the appropriate forms:

VB

Available for download on Wrox.com

```vb
Public Class MainForm
    Private Sub ServerButton_Click(ByVal sender As System.Object,
                                    ByVal e As System.EventArgs) _
                        Handles ServerButton.Click
        My.Forms.ServerForm.Show()
    End Sub

    Private Sub LocalButton_Click(ByVal sender As System.Object,
                                    ByVal e As System.EventArgs) _
                        Handles LocalButton.Click
        My.Forms.LocalForm.Show()
    End Sub
End Class
```

Code snippet MainForm.vb

C#

Available for download on Wrox.com

```csharp
public partial class MainForm : Form {
    public MainForm(){
        InitializeComponent();
    }

    private void ServerButton_Click(object sender, EventArgs e){
        (new ServerForm()).ShowDialog();
    }
    private void LocalButton_Click(object sender, EventArgs e){
        (new LocalForm()).ShowDialog();
    }
}
```

Code snippet MainForm.cs

Before looking at how you can use Sync Services to work with local data, take a look at how you might have built an always-connected, or server-bound, version. From the Data menu, select

Add New Data Source and step through the Data Source Configuration Wizard, selecting the DataSet option, followed by the CRM database created earlier, saving the connection string to the application configuration file, and adding the Customer table to the CRMDataSet.

Open the ServerForm designer by double-clicking it in the Solution Explorer tool window. If the Data Sources tool window is not already visible, select Show Data Sources from the Data menu. Using the drop-down on the Customer node, select Details and then select None from the CustomerId node. Dragging the Customer node across onto the design surface of the ServerForm adds the appropriate controls so that you can locate, edit, and save records to the Customer table of the CRM database, as shown in Figure 34-4.

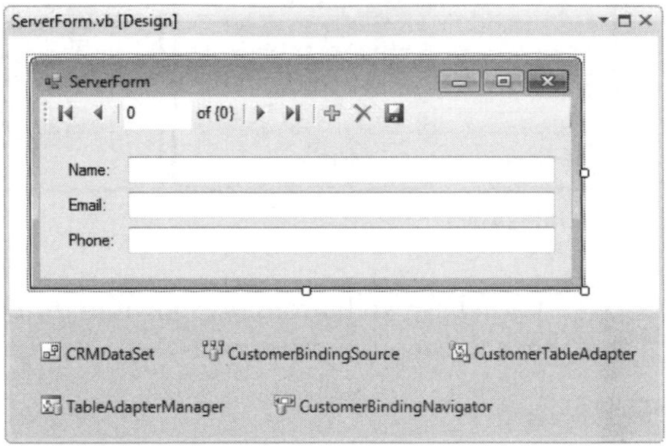

FIGURE 34-4

You will recall from the table definition that the CustomerId can't be null, so you need to ensure that any new records are created with a new ID. To do this you tap into the `CurrentChanged` event on the `CustomerBindingSource` object. You can access this either directly in the code-behind of the ServerForm or by selecting `CustomerBindingSource` and finding the `CurrentChanged` event in the Properties tool window.

Available for download on Wrox.com

VB

```
Private Sub CustomerBindingSource_CurrentChanged _
                     (ByVal sender As System.Object, ByVal e As System.EventArgs) _
                                     Handles CustomerBindingSource.CurrentChanged
    If Me.CustomerBindingSource.Current Is Nothing Then
        Return
    End If

    Dim c As CRMDataSet.CustomerRow = CType(CType(Me.CustomerBindingSource.Current,
                                       DataRowView).Row,CRMDataSet.CustomerRow)
    If c.RowState = DataRowState.Detached Then
        c.CustomerId = Guid.NewGuid
    End If
End Sub
```

Code snippet ServerForm.vb

Available for download on Wrox.com

C#

```
private void customerBindingSource_CurrentChanged(object sender, EventArgs e){
    if (this.customerBindingSource.Current == null){
        return;
    }

    var c = (this.customerBindingSource.Current as DataRowView)
                .Row as CRMDataSet.CustomerRow;
```

```
    if (c.RowState == DataRowState.Detached){
        c.CustomerId = Guid.NewGuid();
    }
}
```

Code snippet ServerForm.cs

This completes the part of the application that connects directly to the database to access the data. You can run the application and verify that you can access data while the database is online. If the database goes offline or the connection is lost, an exception is raised by the application when you attempt to retrieve from the database or save new changes.

GETTING STARTED WITH SYNCHRONIZATION SERVICES

To get started with Sync Services you need to add a Local Database Cache item to your project. In the past you would have done this via the Add New Item dialog. However, in Visual Studio 2010 you can do this using the same process as you would for adding a data source that connects to a SQL Server database. Run the Data Source Configuration Wizard by selecting Add New Data Source from either the Data Sources tool window or the Data menu. Step through the wizard specifying the connection string and selecting the Customer table. On what would normally be the final screen, where you specify the name of the dataset to be created, check the Enable Local Database Caching box, as shown in Figure 34-5.

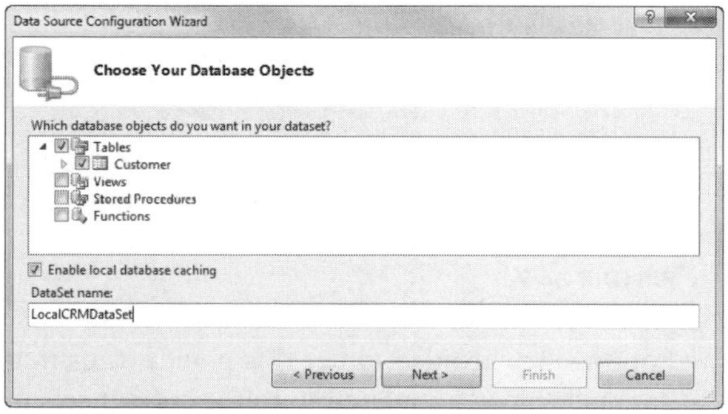

FIGURE 34-5

Now when you select Next you are presented with a new step in the wizard that allows you to configure the way that data is synchronized between the server and your local database cache. In Figure 34-6 you can see that for each table you can toggle the synchronization mode between Incremental and Snapshot. The former is better for tables that contain a large quantity of data that changes frequently; the latter is for tables that contain small reference sets that change infrequently and don't require change tracking.

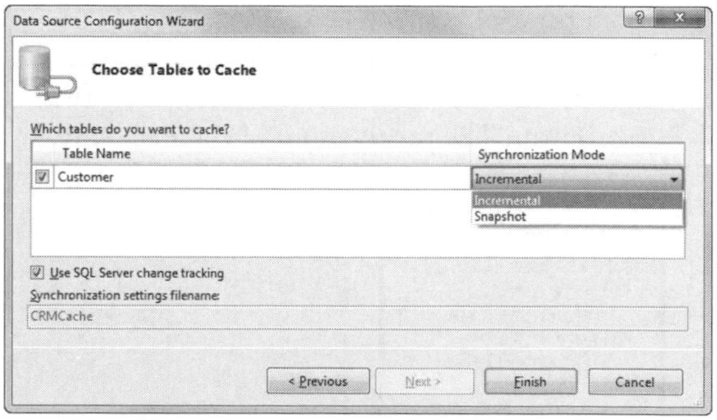

FIGURE 34-6

The other option presented in Figure 34-6 is whether to enable SQL Server change tracking. Sync Services relies on being able to track changes to the data in order to synchronize those changes between the server and the client. Out of the box it supports two mechanisms for doing this. You can either enable change tracking, in which case changes on the server are automatically tracked by the SQL Server database, or you can configure Sync Services to track changes within your database tables. The former is only available with SQL Server 2008, and the latter requires additional fields, triggers, and tables in order to provide equivalent change tracking capabilities. If you are going to be deploying the database to SQL Server 2008, it is recommended that you enable change tracking.

When you click Finish you are prompted to confirm that you want to apply the server changes immediately (Figure 34-7). If you're working on a database shared by others, you may want to review the generated scripts before allowing them to execute. For this example leave both checkboxes checked, which will create the database scripts (including undo scripts) and add them to your project, as well as execute them on the server database, to either enable change tracking or to create the additional change tracking columns, triggers, and tables.

Clicking OK both persists this configuration in the form of synchronization classes and invokes a synchronization between the server and the local data file, as shown in Figure 34-8.

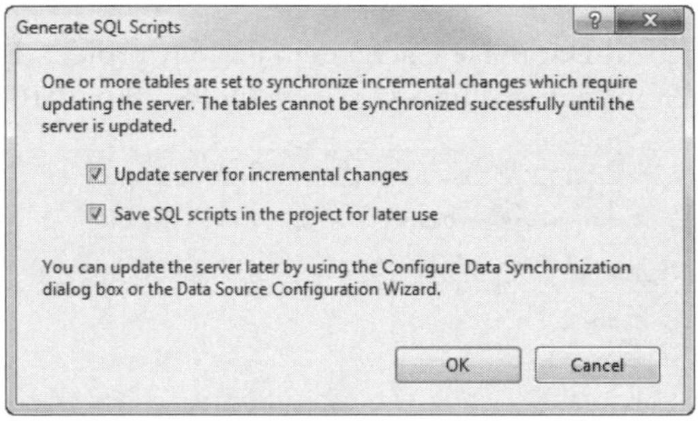

FIGURE 34-7

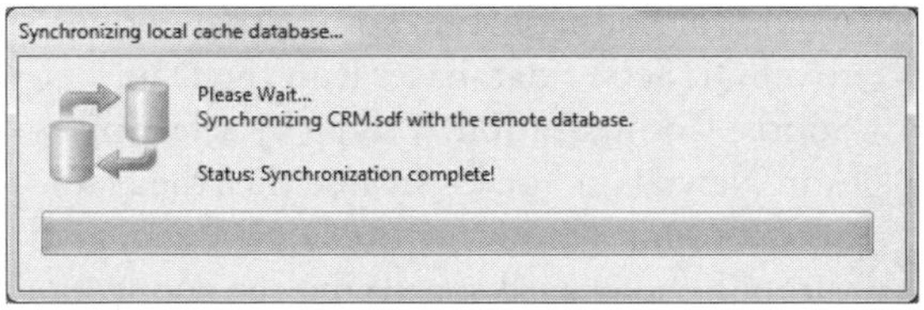

FIGURE 34-8

Forcing synchronization at this point means that the newly created SQL Server Compact (SSC) database file is populated with the correct schema and any data available on the server. The LocalCRMDataSet is also added to your project.

If you now look at the Data Sources tool window, you will see that there is a LocalCRMDataSet node that contains a Customer node. As you did previously, set the Customer node to Details and the CustomerId node to None. Then drag the Customer node across onto the designer surface of the LocalForm. The result should be a form similar to the one shown in Figure 34-9.

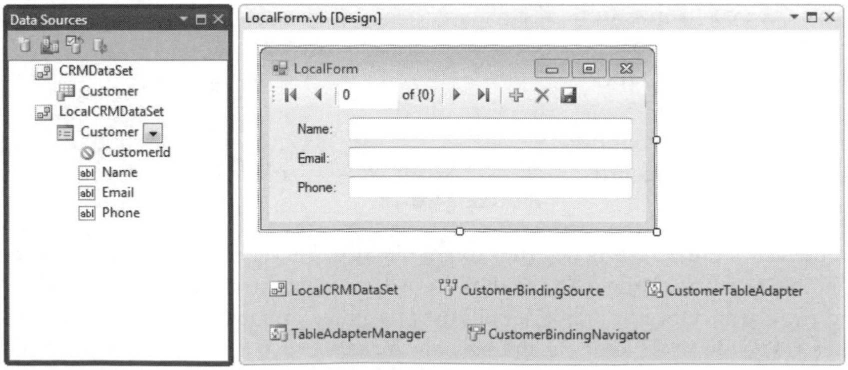

FIGURE 34-9

Adding these components brings the same components to the design surface and the same code to the form as when you were connecting directly to the server. The difference here is that a CustomerTableAdapter connects to the local database instead of the server. As before, you need to add the code to specify the CustomerId for new records in the `CurrentChanged` event of the `CustomerBindingSource`.

The last thing you need to add to this part of the project is a mechanism to invoke the synchronization process. Simply add a button, `SynchronizeButton`, to the bottom of the LocalForm and double-click it to generate the click-event handler. Then add the following code to trigger a synchronization.

VB

```vb
Private Sub SynchronizeButton_Click(ByVal sender As System.Object,
                                    ByVal e As System.EventArgs)
                                          Handles SynchronizeButton.Click
    Dim syncAgent As New CRMCacheSyncAgent()
    Dim syncStats As Microsoft.Synchronization.Data.SyncStatistics =
                                          syncAgent.Synchronize()

    Me.CustomerTableAdapter.Fill(Me.LocalCRMDataSet.Customer)
End Sub
```

Code snippet LocalForm.vb

C#

```csharp
private void SynchronizeButton_Click(object sender, EventArgs e){
    var syncAgent = new CRMCacheSyncAgent();
    var syncStats = syncAgent.Synchronize();

    this.customerTableAdapter.Fill(this.localCRMDataSet.Customer);
}
```

Code snippet LocalForm.cs

Pay particular attention to the next-to-last line of this snippet, in which you use the CustomerTableAdapter to fill the Customer table. This is important: without this line the user interface will not reflect changes in the SSC database that have been made by the synchronization process.

SYNCHRONIZATION SERVICES OVER N-TIERS

So far, the entire synchronization process is conducted within the client application with a direct connection to the server. One of the objectives of an occasionally connected application is to be able to synchronize data over any connection, regardless of whether it is a corporate intranet or the public Internet. Unfortunately, with the current application you need to expose your SQL Server so that the application can connect to it. This is clearly a security vulnerability, which you can solve by taking a more distributed approach. Sync Services has been designed with this in mind, allowing the server components to be isolated into a service that can be called during synchronization.

Sync Services supports separating the synchronization process so that the client application communicates via a WCF service, instead of directly to the server database. To do this, you need to create a WCF service that implements the four methods that makes up Sync Service, as shown in the following `IServiceCRMCacheSyncContract` interface.

VB

```vb
<ServiceContractAttribute()> _
Public Interface IServiceCRMCacheSyncContract
    <OperationContract()> _
    Function ApplyChanges(ByVal groupMetadata As SyncGroupMetadata, _
                          ByVal dataSet As DataSet, _
                          ByVal syncSession As SyncSession) As SyncContext
    <OperationContract()> _
    Function GetChanges(ByVal groupMetadata As SyncGroupMetadata, _
                        ByVal syncSession As SyncSession) As SyncContext
    <OperationContract()> _
    Function GetSchema(ByVal tableNames As Collection(Of String), _
                       ByVal syncSession As SyncSession) As SyncSchema
    <OperationContract()> _
    Function GetServerInfo(ByVal syncSession As SyncSession) As SyncServerInfo
End Interface
```

The WCF Service essentially acts as a remote proxy for the server provider used by Sync Service. To use the WCF Service, you first need to add it to the client project using Add Service Reference (right-click your project and select this option from the context menu). Then you need to set the Remote Provider on the Sync Agent to be a new instance of the `ServerSyncProviderProxy`. The constructor for the `ServerSyncProviderProxy` class takes a single parameter which should be the proxy class that was generated for the WCF Service using Add Service Reference. Now, when you call `Synchronize`, Sync Services will use the Remote Provider to call the methods on the WCF Service. The WCF Service will in turn communicate with the server database carrying out the synchronization logic.

BACKGROUND SYNCHRONIZATION

You may have noticed that when you click the synchronize button, the user interface appears to hang until the synchronization completes. Clearly this wouldn't be acceptable in a real-world application, so you need to synchronize the data in the background, thereby allowing the user to continue working. By adding a BackgroundWorker component (in the Components group in the Toolbox) to the LocalForm, you can do this with only minimal changes to your application. The following code illustrates how you can wire up the events of the BackgroundWorker, which has been named `bgWorker`, to use the Sync Service implementation. This makes use of an additional button, `SynchronizeInBackgroundButton`, that was added to the `LocalForm`:

VB

```vb
Private Sub SynchronizeInBackgroundButton_Click(ByVal sender As System.Object, _
                                    ByVal e As System.EventArgs) _
                    Handles SynchronizeInBackgroundButton.Click
    Me.SynchronizeButton.Enabled = False
    Me.SynchronizeInBackgroundButton.Enabled = False
```

```vb
        Me.bgWorker.RunWorkerAsync(New CRMCacheSyncAgent())
End Sub


Private Sub bgWorker_DoWork(ByVal sender As System.Object,
                        ByVal e As System.ComponentModel.DoWorkEventArgs) _
                                            Handles bgWorker.DoWork
    Dim syncAgent As Microsoft.Synchronization.SyncAgent =
                        TryCast(e.Argument, Microsoft.Synchronization.SyncAgent)
    If syncAgent Is Nothing Then Return
    syncAgent.Synchronize()
End Sub

Private Sub bgWorker_RunWorkerCompleted(ByVal sender As System.Object,
                ByVal e As System.ComponentModel.RunWorkerCompletedEventArgs) _
                                        Handles bgWorker.RunWorkerCompleted
    Me.CustomerTableAdapter.Fill(Me.LocalCRMDataSet.Customer)

    Me.SynchronizeInBackgroundButton.Enabled = True
    Me.SynchronizeButton.Enabled = True
End Sub
```

Code snippet LocalForm.vb

C#

```csharp
private void SynchronizeInBackgroundButton_Click(object sender, EventArgs e){
    this.SynchronizeButton.Enabled =false;
    this.SynchronizeInBackgroundButton.Enabled = false;
    this.bgWorker.RunWorkerAsync(new CRMCacheSyncAgent());
}

private void bgWorker_DoWork(object sender, DoWorkEventArgs e){
    var syncAgent = e.Argument as Microsoft.Synchronization.SyncAgent;
    if (syncAgent == null) return;
    syncAgent.Synchronize();
}

private void bgWorker_RunWorkerCompleted(object sender,
                                    RunWorkerCompletedEventArgs e){
    this.customerTableAdapter.Fill(this.localCRMDataSet.Customer);

    this.SynchronizeInBackgroundButton.Enabled = true;
    this.SynchronizeButton.Enabled = true;
}
```

Code snippet LocalForm.cs

In this snippet you are not reporting any progress, but Sync Services does support quite a rich event model that you can hook into in order to report on progress. If you want to report progress via the BackgroundWorker component, you need to enable its WorkerReportsProgress property. The following code illustrates how you can hook into the ApplyChanges event on the client component of Sync Services in order to report progress (in this case to a label called "SyncProgressLabel" added to the form). Other events correspond to different points in the synchronization process.

VB

```vb
Private Sub bgWorker_DoWork(ByVal sender As System.Object, _
                        ByVal e As System.ComponentModel.DoWorkEventArgs) _
        Handles bgWorker.DoWork
    Dim syncAgent As Microsoft.Synchronization.SyncAgent = _
                        TryCast(e.Argument, Microsoft.Synchronization.SyncAgent)
    If syncAgent Is Nothing Then Return
    Dim clientProvider As _
            Microsoft.Synchronization.Data.SqlServerCe.SqlCeClientSyncProvider = _
            CType(syncAgent.LocalProvider, _
                Microsoft.Synchronization.Data.SqlServerCe.SqlCeClientSyncProvider)
    AddHandler clientProvider.SyncProgress, AddressOf SyncProgress
    syncAgent.Synchronize()
End Sub
Private Sub SyncProgress(ByVal sender As Object, _
                ByVal e As Microsoft.Synchronization.Data. SyncProgressEventArgs)
    Dim progress = 0
    If (e.GroupProgress.TotalChanges > 0) Then
        progress = (e.GroupProgress.TotalChanges -
                        e.GroupProgress.TotalChangesPending) _
                    * 100 / e.GroupProgress.TotalChanges
    End If
    Me.bgWorker.ReportProgress(progress, e.SyncStage.ToString())
End Sub

Private Sub bgWorker_ProgressChanged(ByVal sender As Object, _
                    ByVal e As System.ComponentModel.ProgressChangedEventArgs) _
                                            Handles bgWorker.ProgressChanged
    Me.SyncProgressLabel.Text = e.UserState.ToString
End Sub
```

Code snippet LocalForm.vb

C#

```csharp
private void bgWorker_DoWork(object sender, DoWorkEventArgs e){
    var syncAgent = e.Argument as Microsoft.Synchronization.SyncAgent;
    if (syncAgent == null) return;
    var clientProvider = syncAgent.LocalProvider as
            Microsoft.Synchronization.Data.SqlServerCe.SqlCeClientSyncProvider;
    clientProvider.SyncProgress += SyncProgress;

    syncAgent.Synchronize();
}

private void SyncProgress(object sender,
                        Microsoft.Synchronization.Data.SyncProgressEventArgs e){
    var progress = 0;
    if(e.GroupProgress.TotalChanges>0){
        progress = (e.GroupProgress.TotalChanges -
                    e.GroupProgress.TotalChangesPending)
```

```
                    *100 /e.GroupProgress.TotalChanges;
    }
    this.bgWorker.ReportProgress(progress, e.SyncStage.ToString());
}

private void bgWorker_ProgressChanged(object sender, ProgressChangedEventArgs e){
    this.SyncProgressLabel.Text = e.UserState.ToString();
}
```

Code snippet LocalForm.cs

CLIENT CHANGES

Working through the example so far, you may have been wondering why none of the changes you have made on the client are being synchronized to the server. If you go back to Figure 34-6, you will recall that you selected Incremental from the top drop-down, which might lead you to believe that changes from both the client and server will be synchronized. This is not the case and it is the wording above this control that gives it away. For whatever reason, this control only enables you to select options pertaining to "Data to download." To get changes to propagate in both directions, you have to override the default behavior for each table that is going to be synchronized. Again, right-click the CRMCache object in the Solution Explorer and select View Code. In the following code, we have set the SyncDirection property of the CustomerSyncTable to be bidirectional. You may also want to do this for the ServerCRMCache item so that both synchronization mechanisms will allow changes to propagate between client and server.

Available for
download on
Wrox.com

VB

```
Partial Public Class CRMCacheSyncAgent
    Partial Class CustomerS yncTable
        Private Sub OnInitialized()
            Me.SyncDirection = _
                        Microsoft.Synchronization.Data.SyncDirection.Bidirectional
        End Sub
    End Class
End Class
```

CRMCache.vb

Available for
download on
Wrox.com

C#

```
partial class CRMCacheSyncAgent{
    partial class CustomerSyncTable{
        private void OnInitialized(){
            this.SyncDirection =
                        Microsoft.Synchronization.Data.SyncDirection.Bidirectional;
        }
    }
}
```

CRMCache.cs

If you were synchronizing other tables, you would need to set `SyncDirection` on each of the corresponding SyncTables. An alternative implementation would be to place this code in the `OnInitialized` method of the SyncAgent itself, setting the SyncDirection on each sync table (for example the `CustomerSyncTable`). Whichever way you choose, you still need to apply the `Bidirectional` value to all tables you want to synchronize in both directions.

SUMMARY

In this chapter you have seen how to use the Microsoft Synchronization Services for ADO.NET to build an occasionally connected application. While you have other considerations when building such an application, such as how to detect network connectivity, you have seen how to perform synchronization as a background task and how to separate the client and server components into different application tiers. With this knowledge, you can begin to work with this new technology to build richer applications that will continue to work regardless of where they are being used.

WCF RIA Services

WHAT'S IN THIS CHAPTER?

➤ Understanding WCF RIA Services

➤ Creating a domain service

➤ Exposing data

➤ Consuming WCF RIA Services in Silverlight

In Chapter 31 you saw how WCF provided a standardized means of communication in a technology-agnostic manner. WCF RIA Services (commonly referred to as just RIA Services) is a layer on top of WCF that provides a prescriptive pattern and framework for designing data-driven applications that consume data from a server. WCF RIA Services currently target Silverlight applications, but with a view to support additional presentation technologies. This chapter looks at how to use RIA Services to create an end-to-end Silverlight application.

GETTING STARTED

RIA Services is currently most closely associated with and focused toward Silverlight for the client platform, so you will start by creating a Silverlight project. You will find a Business Application template (as shown in Figure 35-1 under the Silverlight category), which will create all the solution structure required to start with RIA Services (a Silverlight project, an ASP.NET web application, and the RIA Services link between the two).

FIGURE 35-1

This creates a Silverlight project and an ASP.NET project — with the structure of the ASP.NET project shown in Figure 35-2.

The ASP.NET project already supports and implements some basic functionality using the RIA Services pattern. You'll note from Figure 35-2 that there is a Services folder and a Models folder in the project. The Services folder already contains two domain services (AuthenticationService and UserRegistrationService) for providing authentication and user registration operations to the client. The Models folder contains two data classes (User and RegistrationData) that are passed between the server and the client. You will also find a Shared folder under the Models folder, which has a file called User.shared.vb or User.shared.cs that contains code to be shared between the server and the client projects.

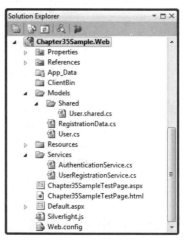

FIGURE 35-2

As demonstrated in Chapter 22, the Silverlight and the ASP.NET projects are linked together such that the Silverlight application is copied to somewhere in the ASP.NET project when the project/solution is compiled (configured in the project properties for the ASP.NET project). However, by introducing RIA Services into the picture you will now have another link between the projects. This link is configured in the project properties of the Silverlight project to select the ASP.NET project that will be acting as the server that it will be communicating with, and from which project the RIA Services build task will generate the code based on, as shown in Figure 35-3.

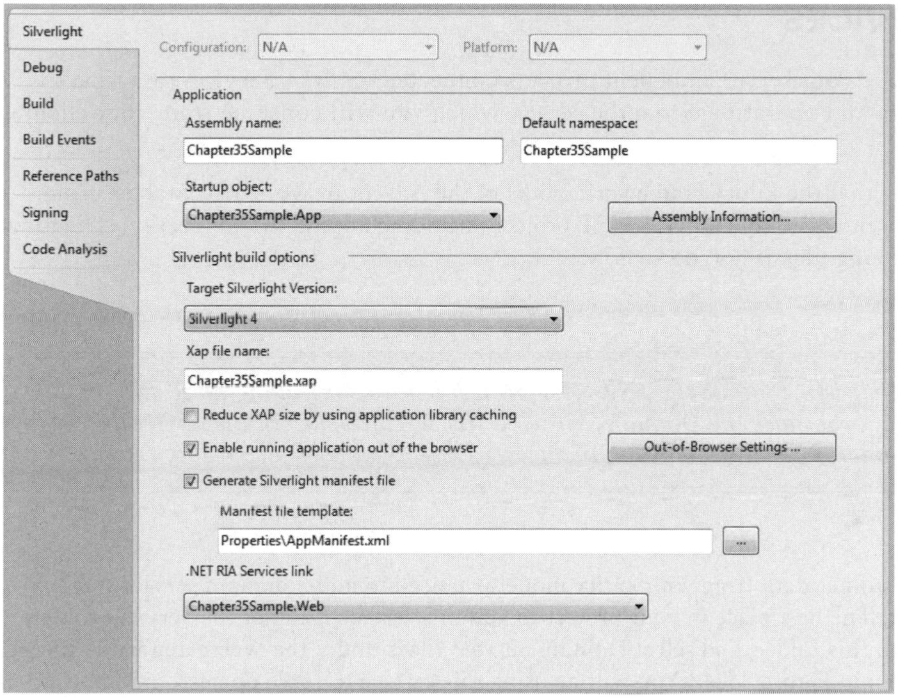

FIGURE 35-3

This link will already be set up by using the Business Application project template; however, if you have an existing Silverlight project or web application that you want to use RIA Services with you can manually link the projects together by linking the Silverlight project to an ASP.NET project with this option.

Now you are ready to start writing some code. The example you work through in this chapter demonstrates some of the key concepts of the RIA Services pattern. Your aim will be to expose customer data and operations from the server and make the data and operations accessible from the client.

You will be using your Entity Framework model of the AdventureWorksLT database that you created back in Chapter 29. It's not necessary to pass entities from your model back and forth between the server and the client, and in many cases it's considered bad practice. The entities are essentially a model of your data layer, which conceptually is not something that the presentation layer should be exposed to. Whether or not you pass entities or POCO (Plain Old CLR Objects) objects of your own design (referred to as *presentation model types* in RIA Services) back and forth is a decision you will have to make, dependant on many factors. Using entities will make development much faster, but will also be less flexible than using presentation model types. RIA Services works just as well using presentation model types as it does with entities, despite more work being involved in initially creating the Domain Services. Therefore, the best practice would be to use presentation model types as the data transfer mechanism; however, we will focus on using entities in this chapter because they provide the easiest means to get started.

DOMAIN SERVICES

Now that you have your server and client projects connected via RIA Services, it's time to expose some data and operations from the server, which you will consume from your client at a later point.

Start by assuming that the Entity Framework model of the AdventureWorksLT database from Chapter 29 has been added to your ASP.NET project (including adding the connection string that it uses to the web.config file). If not, do so now.

> Ensure that you compile the ASP.NET project before continuing on to the next step, otherwise the Domain Service Class Wizard will not display your entity model in the available DataContexts/ObjectContexts drop-down list.

To expose the customer data from your entity model you need to add a domain service to your ASP.NET project. The best place in your project to add this service is under the Services folder. Add a new item to this folder, and select Domain Service Class under the Web category as the item template (as shown in Figure 35-4). You will be using this service to serve up customer data, so call it CustomersService (.cs or .vb).

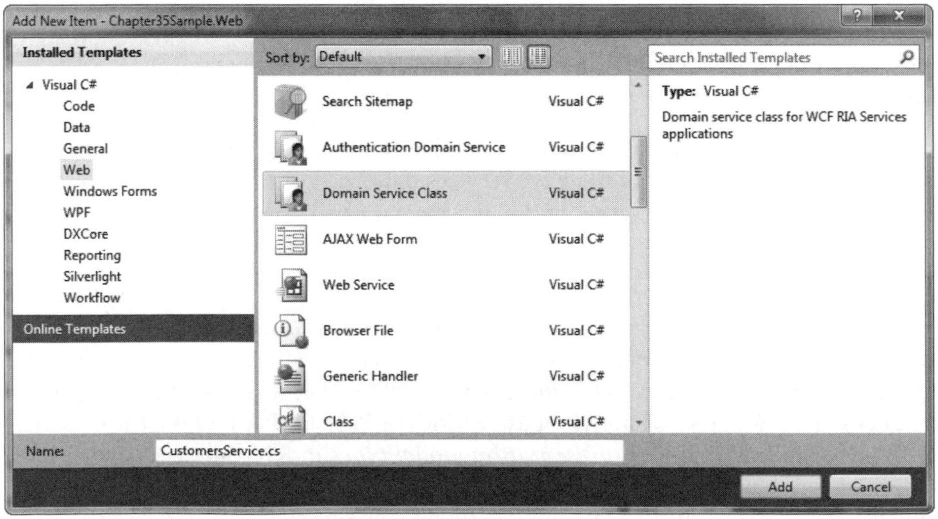

FIGURE 35-4

Clicking OK initiates the Domain Service Class Wizard, shown in Figure 35-5.

If it hasn't automatically selected your Entity Framework model for the AdventureWorksLT database in the Available DataContexts/ ObjectContexts drop-down list, select it now. All the entities from your entity model will be displayed in the list. Here you can select one or more entities that you want to expose from your domain service. When you select an entity the wizard creates a domain operation to return a collection of that entity from the domain service. If you select the Enable Editing option for an entity, the wizard also creates Insert, Update, and Delete domain operations for that entity on the domain service.

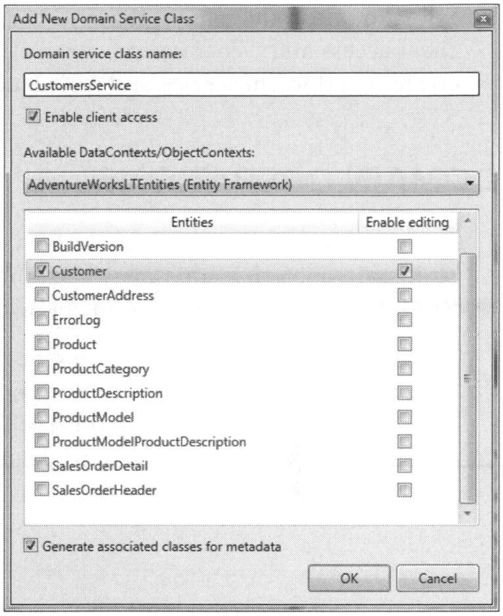

FIGURE 35-5

> If you're using POCO/presentation model types instead of Entity Framework or LINQ-to-SQL types, you can select the <empty domain service class> option from the Available DataContexts/ObjectContexts drop-down list and implement the domain operations yourself.

You should ensure that the Enable client access checkbox is checked. This will ensure that the EnableClientAccess attribute is applied to the service when it is created, which means that code will be generated on the client by the RIA Services code generator to enable it to access the domain service.

You will note that there is also a Generate associated classes for metadata checkbox on the wizard. Metadata classes enable you to add special attributes to properties on the data class being transferred (such as how the entity should be created on the client, and data validation rules) without the need to modify the source object (which is important when, for example, you regenerate your object's code with a code generator or an ORM). Instead, you can apply attributes to the properties in a metadata class that correlate with the properties on the actual class, and these attributes will control how the associated entity is created on the client, and apply other attributes (such as validation rules) to the entity it creates on the client. You will find a more thorough explanation of metadata classes in Chapter 23 (Dynamic Data).

It's not essential to generate metadata classes for your entities, although it does provide a degree of control over the data passed between the server and the client, so it is recommended that you create them.

Select the Customer entity, select the Enable Editing checkbox for it, and ensure both the Enable client access and Generate associated classes for metadata checkboxes are selected. Clicking OK creates the domain service and metadata classes for you.

DOMAIN OPERATIONS

Domain operations are operations on a domain service that can be called from the client. The types of domain operations that exist in a domain service can each be considered to be a CRUD (Create, Read, Update, Delete) operation, an invoke operation, or a custom operation.

The names and/or the method signature of these operations are convention-based so RIA Services can implicitly determine what type of operation it is and generate the correct corresponding operation in the client project. If for some reason you don't want to use the given conventions you can decorate the operation (that is, the method) with an attribute to specify what type of operation is being represented.

> *Some people prefer to decorate their operations even when they follow the naming/signature convention in order to explicitly define what type of operation is being represented.*

Let's now take a look at what domain operations have been generated for you in your domain service by the wizard, and what other types of operations you can create.

Query Operations

When you open the `CustomersService` (`.cs` or `.vb`) file you will see that the basic CRUD operations have been implemented for your Customer entity. The default `Read` (aka `Get` or `Query`) operation returns a collection of entities with the following method signature:

VB
```
Public Function GetCustomers() As IQueryable(Of Customer)
```

C#
```
public IQueryable<Customer> GetCustomers()
```

Note how the `GetCustomers` operation returns an IQueryable collection of the Customer entity. This is one of the most powerful features of RIA Services, in that this feature enables you to write a LINQ query on the client that can be used to filter and shape the entities that it wants returned. This LINQ query is actually serialized and sent to the server before being executed. Where you will see the power of this feature is when you try to implement filtering/paging/grouping/sorting on the client. Instead of requiring a raft of complex operations on the server to implement these behaviors, you only need the one simple operation that returns an IQueryable collection, and then a LINQ query can be provided by the client to filter/shape the results on the server before returning them. Alternatively, you can modify the Get operation and add your own parameters to it, which the operation can use to filter and shape the results to return to the client.

Insert/Update/Delete Operations

The insert (also known as create), update, and delete operations are automatically called when you submit a change set to the server (based on the actions taken upon the results of a query operation on the client), and cannot be called explicitly from the client. These actions are covered later in the chapter, but for now take a look at the operations that have been implemented for you automatically by the Domain Service Class Wizard and how they are implemented. The operations that were created for you have the following method signatures:

VB

```
Public Sub InsertCustomer(ByVal customer As Customer)
Public Sub UpdateCustomer(ByVal currentCustomer As Customer)
Public Sub DeleteCustomer(ByVal customer As Customer)
```

C#

```
public void InsertCustomer(Customer customer)
public void UpdateCustomer(Customer currentCustomer)
public void DeleteCustomer(Customer customer)
```

Each of these accepts an entity of the given type, and performs the appropriate server-side action on that entity. They each have a convention for its naming, they must not return a value, and their method signature must accept an entity as the only parameter. The naming convention and alternative attribute is as follows:

➤   The method name of insert operations must start with Insert, Create, or Add. Otherwise, apply the Insert attribute to the method.

➤   The method name of update operations must start with Update, Change, or Modify. Otherwise, apply the Update attribute to the method.

➤   The method name of delete operations must start with Delete or Remove. Otherwise, apply the Delete attribute to the method.

Other Operation Types

Other types of operations supported by RIA Services (but not fully detailed here) are as follows:

➤   An invoke operation is essentially the same as a service operation in a standard WCF Service (that is, a method exposed by the service). Invoke operations are created as methods on the domain context on the client, and are called immediately (that is, they aren't queued until changes are submitted to the server).

➤   A custom operation is one that is called at any time on the client, but whose execution is deferred on the server until a changeset is submitted. Custom operations act upon entities, and are actually created as methods on their associated entities on the client in addition to being created as methods on the domain context that is generated for the domain service.

CONSUMING A DOMAIN SERVICE IN SILVERLIGHT

Before you look at actually consuming a domain service in the Silverlight project, take a look at what RIA Services has generated for you. As mentioned earlier in the chapter, RIA Services automatically generates code in the Silverlight project to communicate with the server. This code is generated in a folder called Generated_Code, which is not added to the project, but can be seen if you select the Silverlight project in the Solution Explorer and click the Show All Files button. Code is generated by RIA Services in files under this folder (as shown in Figure 35-6), with the primary code generated file being `<web project name>.g.vb` (or `.cs`). For example, for the sample project, the primary code gen file is `Chapter35Sample.Web.g.vb` (or `.cs`).

FIGURE 35-6

You can open this file to inspect its contents and see what the code generator has created for you. Of particular interest, you will note that the entities (or presentation model classes) exposed by domain services in the web project will have a corresponding class generated in this file (decorated with attributes from the metadata classes or the classes themselves). You will also find that for each domain service on the client there will be a corresponding *domain context* class created, which handles communicating with the domain service from the client. The operations exposed by a domain service will be created on the corresponding domain context, and you call the operations on the domain context instead of attempting to reference the domain service itself.

> Note that corresponding operations for the Insert/Update/Delete operations on the domain service are not created on the domain context, because these operations are managed by the changeset. Changes made to a collection of entities retrieved from the server via a query operation are handled by the RIA Services framework in a changeset, and when `SubmitChanges` is called on the domain context, the framework will handle calling the Insert/Update/Delete operations on the domain service as required.

If you follow standard RIA Services naming conventions, a domain service called CustomersService in the web project will result in a corresponding domain context in the Silverlight project called CustomersContext.

Now, attempt to populate a data grid with a list of customers retrieved from the server. You have two primary means of doing so: either using a declarative XAML-based approach or a code-based approach. The XAML-based approach is the easiest way to get started, so this section will use that approach.

The easiest way to get started with the XAML-based approach is to simply use the Data Sources window (as detailed in Chapter 18), and drag and drop an entity exposed by a domain context from this window and onto your page. You will find that a data source has already been created in your project for each data context created by the RIA Services code generator (as shown in Figure 35-7), so you don't need to worry about creating the data sources yourself.

FIGURE 35-7

For this example you will be consuming the CustomersService that exposes the Customer entities from the Entity Framework model on the server, so drag and drop the Customer entity (from the CustomersContext data source, that is, the selected item in Figure 35-7) onto the page. This will create a data grid with a column for each property on the entity. Now if you look at the XAML you can see how it ties together:

```
<riaControls:DomainDataSource AutoLoad="True" QueryName="GetCustomersQuery"
        Name="CustomerDomainDataSource" Height="0" Width="0">
    <riaControls:DomainDataSource.DomainContext>
        <my:CustomersContext />
    </riaControls:DomainDataSource.DomainContext>
</riaControls:DomainDataSource>

<data:DataGrid AutoGenerateColumns="False" Height="250"
        ItemsSource="{Binding ElementName=CustomerDomainDataSource, Path=Data}"
        Name="CustomerDataGrid" RowDetailsVisibilityMode="VisibleWhenSelected">
    <data:DataGrid.Columns>
        <!--This code has been removed for purposes of brevity-->
    </data:DataGrid.Columns>
</data:DataGrid>
```

The DomainDataSource control being used is a part of the RIA Services framework, and provides the bridge to declaratively access the domain context in XAML. The DomainDataSource control is specifying that it should use the CustomersContext (which corresponds to the CustomersService on the server) as its domain context, and that the query operation that should be called on this domain context is GetCustomersQuery. The `AutoLoad` property on the DomainDataSource control is set to True, meaning this query will be called as soon as the page is loaded. Finally, the `ItemsSource` property is set on the data grid, where it uses element name binding to bind to the DomainDataSource control and use that as its source of data.

Now you can run your project, and you will find that the data grid is automatically populated with the results of the query from the server (as shown in Figure 35-8).

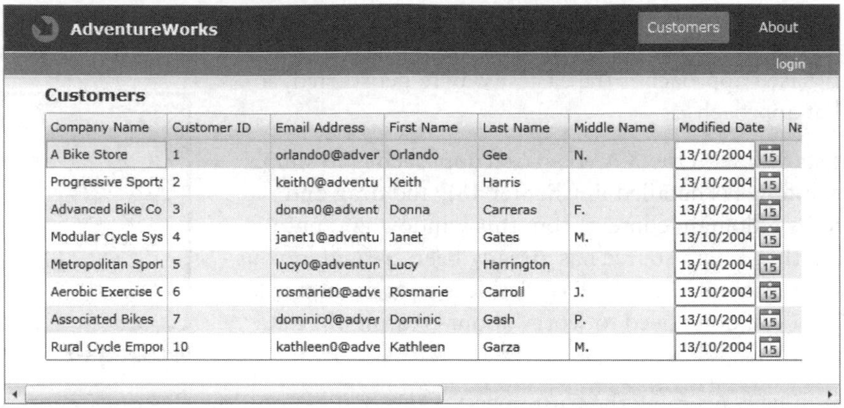

FIGURE 35-8

As discussed previously, the advantage of returning an IQueryable from a domain service operation is that RIA Services enables you to specify filtering, sorting, grouping, and paging options — all of which will be performed on the server. This is also very easy to do in XAML by specifying descriptors on the DomainDataSource — let's take a look at performing each of these in turn.

Add a textbox to the page that will automatically filter the customers by the company name, and call it searchTextBox. Now you can add a filter descriptor to the DomainDataSource that specifies the name of the property to filter (PropertyPath) and the operator specifying how the matching will be done (Operator). You can then add a ControlParameter to the filter descriptor, which links to the textbox (by providing the name of the textbox), uses the text in the textbox as the search criteria (by providing the name of the property on the textbox to get the value from), and runs the filter each time the text is changed (by providing the name of the event on the textbox that will invoke the filtering when raised).

```
<riaControls:DomainDataSource AutoLoad="True" QueryName="GetCustomersQuery"
                              Name="CustomerDomainDataSource" Height="0" Width="0">
    <riaControls:DomainDataSource.DomainContext>
        <my:CustomersContext />
    </riaControls:DomainDataSource.DomainContext>

    <riaControls:DomainDataSource.FilterDescriptors>
        <riaControls:FilterDescriptor PropertyPath="CompanyName"
                    Operator="Contains"
                    Value="{Binding ElementName=searchTextBox, Path=Text}" />
    </riaControls:DomainDataSource.FilterDescriptors>
</riaControls:DomainDataSource>
```

Sorting is automatically handled by the data grid (click the column headers to sort by that column), and if the results are paged it will automatically go back to the server to get the new page of results according to the current page and sort criteria. You can, however, specify the initial sorting using sort descriptors on the DomainDataSource, by providing the name of the property to sort on, and the sort direction:

```xml
<riaControls:DomainDataSource AutoLoad="True" QueryName="GetCustomersQuery"
                              Name="CustomerDomainDataSource" Height="0" Width="0">
    <riaControls:DomainDataSource.DomainContext>
        <my:CustomersContext />
    </riaControls:DomainDataSource.DomainContext>

    <riaControls:DomainDataSource.SortDescriptors>
        <riaControls:SortDescriptor PropertyPath="CompanyName" Direction="Ascending" />
    </riaControls:DomainDataSource.SortDescriptors>
</riaControls:DomainDataSource>
```

Grouping again is handled in a similar manner by providing group descriptors, and simply providing the name of the property to group on:

```xml
<riaControls:DomainDataSource AutoLoad="True" QueryName="GetCustomersQuery"
                              Name="CustomerDomainDataSource" Height="0" Width="0">
    <riaControls:DomainDataSource.DomainContext>
        <my:CustomersContext />
    </riaControls:DomainDataSource.DomainContext>

    <riaControls:DomainDataSource.GroupDescriptors>
        <riaControls:GroupDescriptor PropertyPath="SalesPerson" />
    </riaControls:DomainDataSource.GroupDescriptors>
</riaControls:DomainDataSource>
```

Paging the data in the grid (to display, for example, 20 customers at a time) is easy with the DataPager control. Add the control to your page, bind its Source property to the DomainDataSource control, and provide its PageSize property with the number of items to be displayed in the data grid:

```xml
<data:DataPager PageSize="20"
                Source="{Binding Data, ElementName=CustomerDomainDataSource}"/>
```

Note that the page size specifies how many items should be displayed in the grid, not how many items should be retrieved from the server. If you just set the PageSize property the entire collection will still be retrieved from the server and paged on the client instead. To retrieve just a single page of items at a time and go back to the server to retrieve more items when navigating between pages, you will need to set the LoadSize property on the DomainDataSource control. Generally, you will want to set both properties to the same value. Now, it will retrieve and display a single page of items, and it will request and display a new page of items from the server each time you navigate to a new page with the DataPager control.

In the background, any changes you make to the data in the data grid (such as adding rows, deleting rows, and updating values) will be tracked in a changeset by the RIA Services framework. Submitting these changes back to the server is a case of calling the SubmitChanges() method on the domain context. Add a button to the page called SubmitButton. In its Click event handler (in the code-behind), add the following line of code:

VB

```vb
CustomerDomainDataSource.SubmitChanges()
```

C#

```
CustomerDomainDataSource.SubmitChanges();
```

Clicking the button will now submit any changes you've made back to the server.

> 🖉 *You can also reject any changes made using the* RejectChanges() *method on the DomainDataSource control.*

The final page that implements loading, filtering, sorting, grouping, paging, and saving the data is shown in Figure 35-9.

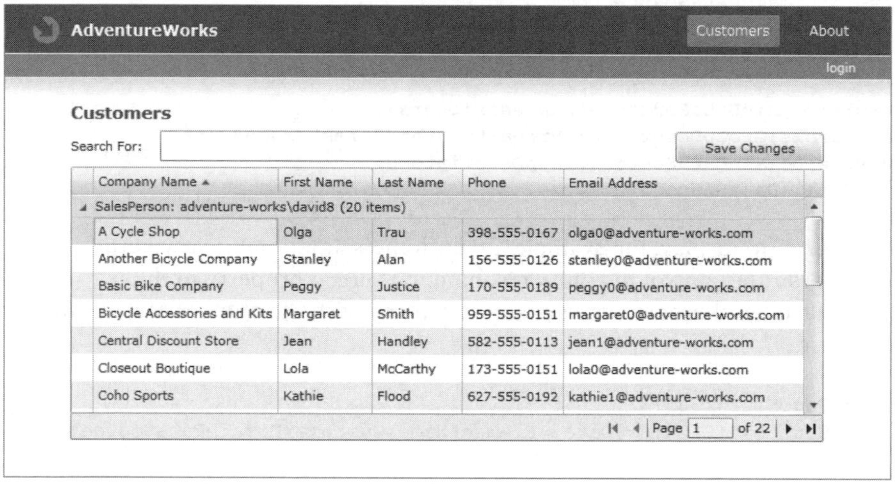

FIGURE 35-9

As you can see, RIA Services is an extremely powerful framework for managing data, greatly simplifying functionality that was once complex to implement, and making it very quick and easy to create very functional business applications.

> 🖉 *The DomainDataSource control makes it very easy to consume data from RIA Services in a Silverlight application; however, at times you may wish to interact with the domain service in code instead. This is possible by creating an instance of the corresponding domain context and using the methods on it. However, note that communication with the domain service is performed asynchronously, requiring your code to be structured accordingly.*

SUMMARY

In this chapter you learned how WCF RIA Services can vastly simplify architecting and developing an end-to-end data-driven Silverlight application, through its combination of prescriptive design patterns, code generation, and feature-rich framework. RIA Services provides many more features than described here, including decorating classes and their properties with attributes (such as validation rules which RIA Services enforces), using metadata classes (i.e., classes associated with the entities being passed between the server and the client that attributes can be applied to and projected onto the associated entities such that the original entities don't need to be modified), sharing code between the server and the client, built-in authentication and security functionality, and much more. However, this chapter should help you get started using RIA Services to provide a means for communicating between your Silverlight application and the server.

PART VIII
Configuration and Resources

▶ **CHAPTER 36:** Configuration Files

▶ **CHAPTER 37:** Connection Strings

▶ **CHAPTER 38:** Resource Files

36

Configuration Files

WHAT'S IN THIS CHAPTER?

➤ Understanding the .NET configuration system

➤ Using configuration files within your application

➤ Storing custom types in configuration files

One of the challenges of building applications is adjusting the way the application functions on the fly without having to rebuild it. There's a long history of applications using configuration files to control the way an application runs. .NET applications use a series of XML configuration files that can be adjusted to determine application behavior. This chapter explores the structure of these configuration files and demonstrates how you can store custom information using a configuration section handler.

.CONFIG FILES

The .NET Framework configuration system consists of several configuration files (discussed in the following sections) that can be used to adjust one or more applications on a computer system. Part of this system is an inheritance model that ensures that configurations can be applied at the appropriate level. This model is such that sections defined in a configuration file at a lower level will override the same sections specified in a file higher up the chain. If no configuration file defines a value or section, the default values are taken from the schema files to which the configuration files must adhere.

Machine.Config

At the root of the inheritance model is the `machine.config` file (located in the *systemroot*Microsoft .NET\Framework*versionNumber*\CONFIG\ folder, or *systemroot*\Microsoft .NET\

Framework64*versionNumber*\CONFIG\ for 64-bit machines), which defines configuration settings for the entire system. All configuration files inherit from this file and can override these settings.

Web.Config

Web applications are configured via the `web.config` file. This file can be located in a number of locations, depending on the scope to which the settings need to be applied. To apply a configuration to all web applications on a machine, place the `web.config` file in the same directory as the `machine.config` file. In most cases the settings need to be applied at a much finer granularity. As such, the `web.config` file can also be placed in any virtual directory or subdirectory to control web applications at that level. If it is placed in the root folder for a web site, the configuration will be applied to all ASP.NET applications in that web site.

A word of caution: When you are working with virtual directories that do not align with the directory structure on the computer, it's possible to have an application that has different configurations depending on how it is referenced. For example, consider `C:\inetpub\wwwroot\MainApplication\Contacts\Contact.aspx`, which has been set up with both `MainApplication` and `Contacts` as virtual directories. You can reference the contact page as either:

```
http://localhost/MainApplication/Contacts/Contact.aspx
```

or:

```
http://localhost/Contacts/Contact.aspx
```

In the first case, the configuration settings that are applied are inherited from the MainApplication folder and may be overridden by a configuration file in the Contacts folder. However, in the second case, settings are applied only from the configuration file within the Contacts folder.

> *Making changes to a* `web.config` *file causes the ASP.NET application to be restarted. This is quite an effective way to force a web application to flush its cache and behave as if it were being accessed for the first time, without having to restart the entire server.*

App.Config

Windows applications can be configured via an application configuration file, which also inherits from `machine.config`. Because the output assembly name is known only when an application is compiled, this file starts off as `app.config` and is renamed to *`application`*`.exe.config` as part of the build process. For example, an application with `AccountingApplication.exe` as the main executable would have a configuration file entitled `AccountingApplication.exe.config`. This configuration file is automatically loaded based on its name when the application is loaded. If an `app.config` files is added to a dll, it will be renamed to `assembly.dll.config` during the build process.

Security.Config

In conjunction with the application configuration files are a number of security configuration files. These also follow an inheritance path but across a different dimension. Instead of being application-focused, the security configuration files are broken down into enterprise (Enterprisesec.config), machine (Security.config), and user (Security.config). The enterprise- and machine-level files are both stored in the same location as the machine.config file, whereas the user-level file is stored under the user-specific application data folder.

ApplicationHost.Config

IIS7 changes the way configuration information is stored to use a set of configuration files that work in parallel with those for ASP.NET and the .NET Framework. Because IIS and the .NET Framework are versioned independently, configuration information specific to the individual technologies are held in the machine.config/web.config and the applicationHost.config files, respectively. However, because there is an interrelationship between IIS and ASP.NET, the applicationHost.config file does fit into the configuration file inheritance hierarchy. Because the applicationHost.config file is specific to an instance of IIS, it fits into the inheritance hierarchy after both the machine.config and web.config files located at the machine level (that is, located in the *systemroot*\Microsoft .NET\Framework*versionNumber*\CONFIG\ folder).

The applicationHost.config file can be found in the *systemroot*\System32\InetSrv\Config folder, and the corresponding schema files can be found in the Schema subdirectory. There are also administration.config and redirection.config files in this folder that are responsible for IIS feature delegation and configuration file redirection, respectively.

CONFIGURATION SCHEMA

A configuration file, whether it is a machine.config, a web.config, or an application configuration file, needs to adhere to the same configuration schema that determines which elements should be included. The schema is located at C:\Program Files\Microsoft Visual Studio 10.0\Xml\Schemas\DotNetConfig.xsd (C:\Program Files (x86)\Microsoft Visual Studio 10.0\Xml\Schemas\DotNetConfig.xsd on 64-bit machines) and is broken down into a number of sections.

Section: configurationSections

Configuration files can be customized to contain any structured XML data. In order to do this, you must define a custom section in the configurationSections block within the configuration file. This defines both the name of the configuration section and the class that is to be called in order to process the section.

The configurationSections section in the machine.config file defines the handlers for each of the standard configuration sections discussed here. You can define your own configuration sections in your application configuration file so long as you specify which class will be used to validate and process that section. For example, the following code snippet defines the section handler for the ConfigurationApplication.My.MySettings configuration section, along with the corresponding section. The schema of this section must correspond to what the System.Configuration .ClientSettingsSection class expects, rather than the normal configuration file schema.

```
<configuration>
<configSections>
<section name="ConfigurationApplication.My.MySettings"
                type="System.Configuration.ClientSettingsSection,
System, Version=2.0.0.0, Culture=neutral, PublicKeyToken=b77a5c561934e089"
                requirePermission="false" />
</configSections>
.
<ConfigurationApplication.My.MySettings>
<setting name="PrimaryServer" serializeAs="String">
<value>www.builttoroam.com</value>
</setting>
</ConfigurationApplication.My.MySettings>
</configuration>
```

It is also possible to include configSections in a sectionGroup element that can be used to help lay out configuration information. The preceding example can be extended as follows:

```
<configuration>
<configSections>
<sectionGroup name="applicationSettings"
                    type="System.Configuration.ApplicationSettingsGroup,
System, Version=2.0.0.0, Culture=neutral, PublicKeyToken= b77a5c561934e089" >
<section name="ConfigurationApplication.My.MySettings"
                type="System.Configuration.ClientSettingsSection,
System, Version=2.0.0.0, Culture=neutral, PublicKeyToken=b77a5c561934e089"
                requirePermission="false" />
<section name="ReferencedAssembly.My.MySettings"
                type="System.Configuration.ClientSettingsSection,
System, Version=2.0.0.0, Culture=neutral, PublicKeyToken=b77a5c561934e089"
                requirePermission="false" />
</sectionGroup>
</configSections>
.
<applicationSettings>
<ConfigurationApplication.My.MySettings>
<setting name="PrimaryServer" serializeAs="String">
<value>www.builttoroam.com</value>
</setting>
</ConfigurationApplication.My.MySettings>
<ReferencedAssembly.My.MySettings>
<setting name="SecondaryServer" serializeAs="String">
<value>www.peaksite.com</value>
</setting>
</ReferencedAssembly.My.MySettings>
</applicationSettings>
</configuration>
```

Where used, the configSections element must appear as the first child of the configuration element.

Section: startup

The `startup` configuration section determines the version of the framework that is either required (`requiredRuntime`) or supported (`supportedRuntime`) by the framework. By default, a .NET application will attempt to execute using the same version of the framework on which it was built. Any application being built with support for multiple versions of the framework should indicate this with the `supportedRuntime` element, defining the most preferred framework version first:

```
<configuration>
<startup>
<supportedRuntime version="v4.0.20409"/>
<supportedRuntime version="v2.0.50727"/>
<supportedRuntime version="v1.1.4322"/>
</startup>
</configuration>
```

This configuration section would be used by an application that has been tested for versions 4.0, 2.0, and 1.1 of the .NET Framework. Anomalies were detected in the testing for version 1.0 of the .NET Framework, so it has been omitted from the `supportedRuntime` list. The version number must correspond exactly to the installation directory for that framework version (for example, version 4.0 of the .NET Framework typically installs to `C:\WINDOWS\Microsoft.NET\Framework\v4.0.20409\`).

Section: runtime

Garbage collection is a feature of the .NET Framework that distinguishes it from non-managed environments. The process of collecting and disposing of unreferenced objects is usually done in parallel with the main application on a separate thread. This means that the user should not see any performance issues as a result of this process being run. However, there may be circumstances when this process should be run inline with the main application. The `runtime` section of the configuration file can be used to provide limited control over how the .NET runtime engine operates. Among other things, you can specify whether the garbage collection should be done concurrently with the main application.

This section can also be used to specify a location in which to search for assemblies that may be required by an application. This attribute can be useful if an application references assemblies that are in a non-standard location. The following code illustrates the use of the `codeBase` attribute to locate the `ImportantAssembly.dll`, as well as to dictate that garbage collection be done inline with the main application thread:

```
<configuration>
<runtime>
<assemblyBinding xmlns="urn:schemas-microsoft-com:asm.v1">
<dependentAssembly>
<assemblyIdentity name="ImportantAssembly"
                  publicKeyToken="32ab4ba45e0a69a1"
                  culture="neutral" />
<codeBase version="2.0.0.0" href="./ImportantAssembly.dll"/>
</dependentAssembly>
</assemblyBinding>
```

```
<gcConcurrent enabled="false"/>
</runtime>
</configuration>
```

Section: system.runtime.remoting

The `remoting` section of the configuration file can be used to specify information about remote objects and channels required by the application. For example, the default HTTP channel can be directed to listen to port 8080 by means of the following configuration snippet:

```
<configuration>
<system.runtime.remoting>
<application>
<channels>
<channel port="8080" ref="http"/>
</channels>
</application>
</system.runtime.remoting>
</configuration>
```

Section: system.net

Because of the current demand for more secure operating environments, organizations often use proxies to monitor and protect traffic on their networks. This can often result in applications not functioning correctly unless they have been configured to use the appropriate proxies. The networking section of the configuration files can be used to adjust the proxy that an application uses when making HTTP requests.

The .NET Framework ships with an `SmtpClient` class that can be used to send mail from within an application. Obviously, doing this requires information such as the server and the credentials to use when sending mail. Although such information can be hard-coded within an application, a more flexible approach would be to specify it in a configuration file that can be adjusted when the application is deployed. The following configuration snippet illustrates the use of the default proxy (although it bypasses the proxy for local addresses and the DeveloperNews web site) and specifies the default SMTP settings to be used by the SMTP client:

```
<configuration>
<system.net>
<defaultProxy>
<proxy usesystemdefaults="true"
                proxyaddress="http://192.168.200.222:3030"
                bypassonlocal="true" />
<bypasslist>
<add address="[a-z]+\.developernews\.com" />
</bypasslist>
</defaultProxy>
<mailSettings>
<smtp deliveryMethod="network">
<network host="smtp.developernews.com"
   port="25" defaultCredentials="true" />
</smtp>
```

```
    </mailSettings>
    </system.net>
    </configuration>
```

Section: cryptographySettings

Although the .NET Framework contains base implementations for a number of cryptographic algorithms, such as the hashing function, sometimes it is necessary to override these algorithms. When this is required, the cryptographySettings section of the configuration file can be included to remap existing algorithm names, or map new names, to another implementation class.

Section: system.diagnostics

Debugging is always the hardest part of writing an application. It is made even more difficult when the application is in production and the error cannot be replicated in the debugging environment. One technique that is particularly important for debugging this type of error is to use trace statements:

```
    Trace.WriteLine("The application made it this far before crashing.")
```

Both trace and debug statements work very similarly to events and event handlers. For the preceding WriteLine statement to have any effect, an object must be listening for this WriteLine. This is typically done by a TraceListener class. The framework supports a number of default trace listeners that can be wired up to the application via the diagnostics section of the configuration file, as shown in the following section in which an EventLog trace listener has been attached to the application:

```
    <configuration>
    <system.diagnostics>
    <trace autoflush="true" indentsize="0">
    <listeners>
    <add name="MyEventListener"
    type="System.Diagnostics.EventLogTraceListener, system,
    version=1.0.3300.0, Culture=neutral, PublicKeyToken=b77a5c561934e089"
    initializeData="DeveloperApplicationEventLog"/>
    </listeners>
    </trace>
    </system.diagnostics>
    </configuration>
```

The initializeData attribute specifies a text string to be passed into the constructor for the trace listener. In the case of the event-log listener, this text corresponds to the name of the event log into which trace statements will be inserted.

Other elements can also be added to the diagnostics section of the configuration file — for example, to determine the level of trace logging to perform, which will determine how verbose the trace messages are; or to control whether or not the debug assertion dialog is displayed for an application.

Section: system.web

The system.web section of the configuration file is used to control how web applications behave. This is the section that can have quite a deep hierarchy, because configuration settings can be specified on a machine, web server, web site, web application, or even subfolder basis. Because this section controls the security requirements for a web application, it is often used to restrict access to certain areas of the web application.

webServices

Although web service applications use several configuration settings, such as `authentication` and `impersonation` sections, the `system.web` section of the configuration file contains some settings that are particular to the way that web services operate. For example, the following code snippet enables the use of `SOAP` and `Documentation` protocols, but removes the `POST` and `GET` protocols for the application:

```
<configuration>
<system.web>
<webServices>
<protocols>
<add name="HttpSoap"/>
<remove name="HttpPost"/>
<remove name="HttpGet"/>
<add name="Documentation"/>
</protocols>
</webServices>
</system.web>
</configuration>
```

By default, only `SOAP` and `Documentation` are enabled for web services. Quite often, for debugging purposes, it is convenient to allow the `POST` protocol so that the web service can be tested via a web browser. You should do this on an application basis by including the appropriate section in the configuration file within the application folder.

Section: compiler

The `compiler` section of the configuration file is used to list the compilers installed on a computer. The following snippet shows how the VB.NET compiler is referenced in the `machine.config` file. Within an application, this information can be accessed via the `CodeDomProvider` framework class.

```
<configuration>
<system.codedom>
<compilers>
<compiler language="vb;vbs;visualbasic;vbscript" extension=".vb"
type="Microsoft.VisualBasic.VBCodeProvider, System, Version=2.0.0.0,
Culture=neutral, PublicKeyToken=b77a5c561934e089" />
</compilers>
</system.codedom>
</configuration>
```

Configuration Attributes

All configuration elements can specify a `configSource`, which is simply a redirection to a separate file. This can be useful if a configuration file becomes unwieldy in length. The following code snippet illustrates how a section of a configuration file can be extracted and subsequently referenced by means of this attribute:

```
<!-Original Configuration File->
<configuration>
.
<WindowsApplication1.My.MySettings>
<setting name="Button1_Text" serializeAs="String">
<value>Press Me!</value>
</setting>
</WindowsApplication1.My.MySettings>
</configuration>

<!-Reduced Configuration File using configSource->
<configuration>
.
<WindowsApplication1.My.MySettings configSource="MySettings.Config" />
</configuration>

<!-Code from MySettings.Config->
<WindowsApplication1.My.MySettings>
<setting name="Button1_Text" serializeAs="String">
<value>Press Me!</value>
</setting>
</WindowsApplication1.My.MySettings>
```

Note a couple of limitations to using a `configSource`:

➤ There is no merging of configuration sections between the referenced file and the original configuration file. If you include the section in both files, a configuration error will be generated when you attempt to run the application.

➤ This attribute cannot be applied to configuration section groups. This can be a significant limitation, because the purpose of a section group is to group items that relate similar configuration sections. A logical separation could see all items in a particular section group in a separate configuration file.

➤ If the attribute is used within a `web.config` file, changing the referenced configuration file will not restart the ASP.NET application. In order for the configuration information to be reread, you need to either manually restart the ASP.NET application or modify the `web.config` file itself.

Each element within the configuration file inherits a number of attributes that can be set to control whether or not that element can be overridden. To prevent an element, or even an entire section, from being overridden, you can lock it. Five different locking attributes (outlined in Table 36-1) can be used to specify any number of configuration attributes and elements that are to be locked.

Being able to lock configuration items is particularly relevant when you're dealing with web applications, which might contain a deep hierarchy of configuration inheritance. Windows applications inherit only from the `machine.config` file, so it is unlikely that you will need to lock items.

TABLE 36-1: Locking Attributes

CONFIGURATION ELEMENT	DESCRIPTION
LockItem	Locks the element to which this attribute is applied, including all other attributes provided on that element and all child elements
LockAttributes	Locks the comma-delimited list of attributes provided
LockAllAttributesExcept	Locks all attributes except those provided in the comma-delimited list
LockElements	Locks the comma-delimited list of child elements provided
LockAllElementsExcept	Locks all child elements except those provided in the comma-delimited list

APPLICATION SETTINGS

Applications frequently have settings that do not fit into the default configuration schema. The four mechanisms for storing this information are discussed in the following sections.

Using appSettings

The first technique is to use the predefined `appSettings` section of the configuration file. This section can be used to store simple name-value pairs of application settings, which might be useful for storing the name of the server, as in the following example:

```
<configuration>
<appSettings>
<add key="Server" value="http://www.builttoroam.com"/>
</appSettings>
</configuration>
```

This value can easily be accessed within code by means of the `AppSettings` property of the `ConfigurationManager` class (which requires a reference to the `System.Configuration` assembly):

VB

```
Dim server As String = ConfigurationManager.AppSettings("Server")
```

C#

```
var server = ConfigurationManager.AppSettings["Server"];
```

One of the weaknesses of this approach is that the name of the setting is specified as a string, rather than as a strongly typed property. It also assumes that the value will be a string, which is often not the case.

> *In the case of web applications, you should use the* WebConfigurationManager *class instead of the* ConfigurationManager *class because it provides access to additional configuration information specific to ASP.NET applications.*

Project Settings

Using the Settings tab of the project properties designer, you can define application settings of a variety of types. Figure 36-1 illustrates how the PrimaryServer setting would appear in this designer.

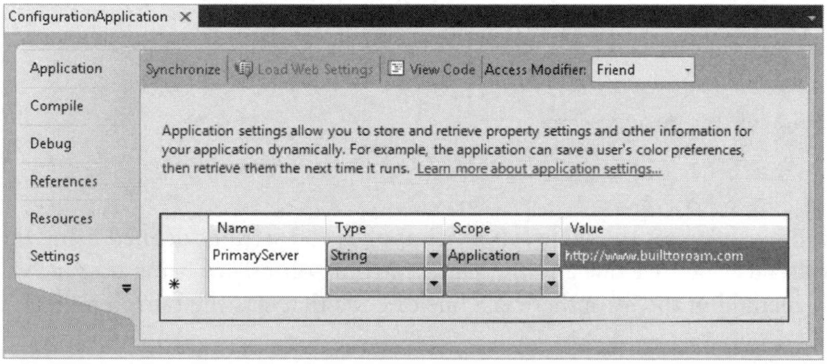

FIGURE 36-1

Adding application settings via this designer does not use the appSettings section as you might expect. Instead, it defines a new section in the configuration, as discussed earlier in the section on the configSection element and shown in the following snippet:

```
<configuration>
...
<ConfigurationApplication.My.MySettings>
<setting name="PrimaryServer" serializeAs="String">
<value>www.builttoroam.com</value>
</setting>
</ConfigurationApplication.My.MySettings>
</configuration>
```

To access this setting in code, you can make use of the generated strongly typed access properties.

VB

```
Dim primaryServer as String = My.Settings.PrimaryServer
```

C#

```
string primaryServer = Properties.Settings.Default.PrimaryServer;
```

Dynamic Properties

The third mechanism for storing application-specific information is the use of dynamic properties. These are typically used to dynamically set designer properties. For example, you could set the text on a Button1 using the following configuration block:

```
<configuration>
...
<applicationSettings>
<ConfigurationApplication.My.MySettings>
<setting name="Button1_Text" serializeAs="String">
<value>Press Me Now!</value>
</setting>
</ConfigurationApplication.My.MySettings>
</applicationSettings>
</configuration>
```

You will note that the preceding code uses the same syntax as application settings defined using the project properties designer. In fact, they are one and the same, the only difference being that in the `InitializeComponent` method of the form there is a line of code that sets the button text:

VB

```
Me.Button1.Size =
          Global.ConfigurationApplication.My.MySettings.Default.Button1_Size
```

C#

```
this.button1.Size =
          global::ConfigurationApplication.Properties.Settings.
          Default.Button1_Size;
```

When this application is deployed, the text displayed on Button1 is dynamically loaded from the configuration file. In the following steps, for example, you set the size of a control, Button1, to be dynamically loaded from the configuration file:

1. Select Button1 on the designer surface and press F4 to display the Properties window. Locate the `ApplicationSettings` item within the Data category or in the alphabetic list, as shown in Figure 36-2.

2. Click the ellipsis button (. . .) next to the `PropertyBinding` row. This opens a dialog that lists the available properties for Button1, along with any application settings that have been assigned, as shown in Figure 36-3.

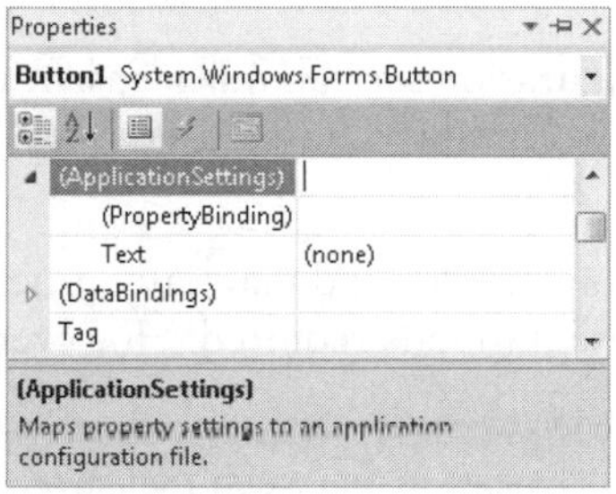

Properties

Button1 System.Windows.Forms.Button

▲ (ApplicationSettings)
    (PropertyBinding)
    Text   (none)
▷ (DataBindings)
  Tag

(ApplicationSettings)
Maps property settings to an application
configuration file.

FIGURE 36-2

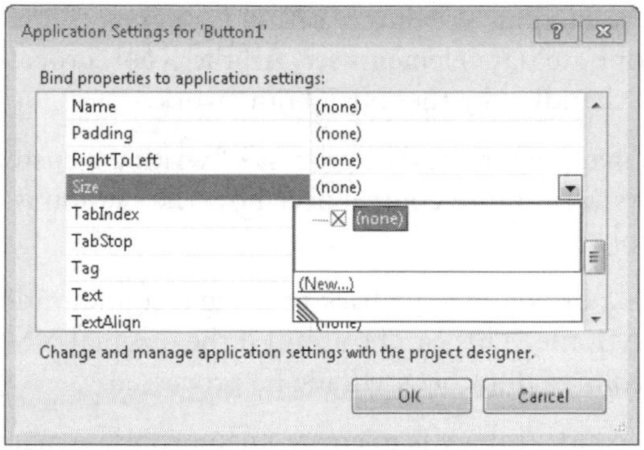

Application Settings for 'Button1'

Bind properties to application settings:

Name	(none)
Padding	(none)
RightToLeft	(none)
Size	(none)
TabIndex	—✕ (none)
TabStop	
Tag	
Text	(New...)
TextAlign	(none)

Change and manage application settings with the project designer.

OK   Cancel

FIGURE 36-3

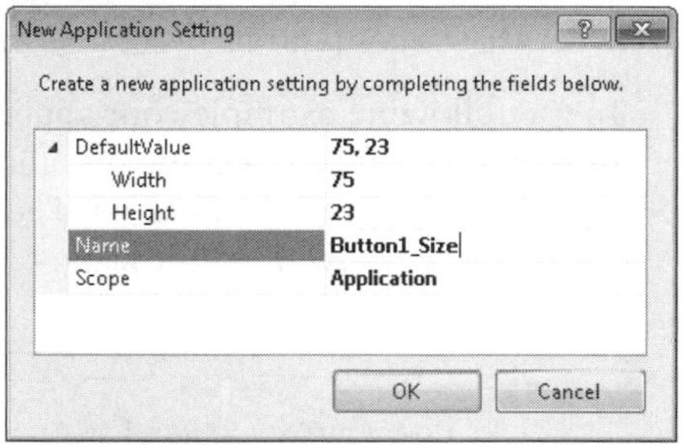

3. Select the drop-down next to the Size property and select New. This opens a dialog in which you can specify a default value, a name for the application setting, and the scope of the setting.

4. Specify a name for the application setting — for example, Button1_Size, and set the scope to Application. You can modify the default value or simply accept the value that has been extracted from the current properties of Button1, as shown in Figure 36-4.

New Application Setting

Create a new application setting by completing the fields below.

▲ DefaultValue   75, 23
    Width   75
    Height   23
Name   **Button1_Size**
Scope   **Application**

OK   Cancel

FIGURE 36-4

5. Click OK on both dialogs. If you open the app.config file that will be available from the Solution Explorer window, you will see a section that defines the Button1_Size setting.

Custom Configuration Sections

Developers often want to include more structured information in the configuration file than can be stored in the appSettings section. To solve this problem and eliminate any need for additional configuration files, you can create a custom configuration section. The new configuration section must be defined at the top of the configuration file via the configSection element, complete with a reference to a class that should be used to process that portion of the configuration file.

In the past this process was fairly complex, because the class needed to implement the IConfigurationSectionHandler interface. This exposed a simple method, Create, which was called the first time that section was referenced in code. There was little support from the framework to process the section, and a class implementing this interface often resorted to parsing the XML block to determine settings.

Visual Studio 2010 provides much better support for creating custom configuration sections via the ConfigurationSection and ConfigurationElement classes. These provide the bases for creating classes that map to the structure of the data being stored in the configuration files. Instead of mapping a class that processes the configuration section, you can now create a much simpler class that maps to the section. When the section is referenced in code, an instance of this class is returned with the appropriate data elements set. All the XML processing that would have been necessary in the past is now handled by the .NET Framework.

Although this mapping makes the process of writing a custom configuration section much easier, you may sometimes want more control over how the section is read. Two options can be used to give you this control:

➤ The first option is to go back to using a configuration section handler and manually process the XML file. This can be useful if the original XML representation is required. However, it still requires that the XML file be processed.

➤ The second strategy is to create an appropriate mapping class as an in-between measure. Instead of referencing this class directly, another class can be generated that exposes the configuration information in the right way.

If you need to use either of these options, it might be worth taking a step back and determining whether the configuration section structure is actually in a format suited to the data being stored.

In the following example your application requires a list of registered entities with which to work. One type of entity is a company, and you need to be provided with both the company name and the date on which it was registered. The XML snippet that you would like to have in the configuration file might look like the following:

```
<RegisteredEntities>
<Companies>
<add CompanyName="Random Inc" RegisteredDate="31/1/2005" />
<add CompanyName="Developer Experience Inc" RegisteredDate="1/8/2004" />
</Companies>
</RegisteredEntities>
```

Once generated, the corresponding classes that would map to the preceding snippet might look like the following (again, this requires a reference to the System.Configuration assembly):

VB

```
Public Class RegisteredEntities
    Inherits ConfigurationSection

<ConfigurationProperty("Companies")> _
    Public ReadOnly Property Companies() As Companies
        Get
            Return CType(MyBase.Item("Companies"),Companies)
        End Get
    End Property
End Class

<ConfigurationCollectionAttribute(GetType(Company))> _
Public Class Companies
    Inherits ConfigurationElementCollection

    Protected Overrides Function CreateNewElement() As ConfigurationElement
        Return New Company
```

```
        End Function

        Protected Overrides Function GetElementKey _
                            (ByVal element As ConfigurationElement) As Object
            Return CType(element, Company).CompanyName
        End Function

        Public Sub Add(ByVal element As Company)
            Me.BaseAdd(element)
        End Sub

    End Class

    Public Class Company
        Inherits ConfigurationElement

    <ConfigurationProperty("CompanyName",DefaultValue:="Random Inc",
    IsKey:=true, IsRequired:=true)> _
        Public Property CompanyName() As String
            Get
                Return CType(MyBase.Item("CompanyName"),String)
            End Get
            Set
                MyBase.Item("CompanyName") = value
            End Set
        End Property

    <ConfigurationProperty("RegisteredDate",DefaultValue:="31/1/2005",
    IsKey:=false, IsRequired:=false)> _
        Public Property RegisteredDate() As String
            Get
                Return CType(MyBase.Item("RegisteredDate"),String)
            End Get
            Set
                MyBase.Item("RegisteredDate") = value
            End Set
        End Property
    End Class
```

Code snippet RegisteredEntities.vb

C#

```
class RegisteredEntities : ConfigurationSection{
    [ConfigurationProperty("Companies")]
    public Companies Companies{
        get{
            return base["Companies"] as Companies;
        }
    }
}

[ConfigurationCollection(typeof(Company))]
class Companies : ConfigurationElementCollection{
```

```csharp
        protected override ConfigurationElement CreateNewElement(){
            return new Company();
        }

        protected override object GetElementKey
                (ConfigurationElement element){
            return (element as Company).CompanyName;
        }

        public void Add(Company element){
            BaseAdd(element);
        }
    }

    class Company : ConfigurationElement{
        [ConfigurationProperty("CompanyName", DefaultValue = "Random Inc",
                            IsKey = true, IsRequired = true)]
        public string CompanyName{
            get{
                return base["CompanyName"] as string;
            }
            set{
                base["CompanyName"] = value;
            }
        }

        [ConfigurationProperty("RegisteredDate", DefaultValue = "31/1/2005",
                            IsKey = false, IsRequired = true)]
        public string RegisteredDate{
            get{
                return base["RegisteredDate"] as string;
            }
            set{
                base["RegisteredDate"] = value;
            }
        }
    }
}
```

Code snippet RegisteredEntities.cs

The code contains three classes that are required in order to correctly map the functionality of this section. The registered entities section corresponds to the RegisteredEntities class, which contains a single property that returns a company collection. A collection is required here because you want to be able to support the addition of multiple companies. This functionality could be extended to clear and/or remove companies, which might be useful if you had a web application for which you needed to control which companies were available to different portions of the application. Lastly, there is the Company class that maps to the individual company information being added.

To access this section from within the code, you can simply call the appropriate section using the ConfigurationManager framework class:

VB

```
Dim registered as RegisteredEntities= _
    ctype(configurationmanager.GetSection("RegisteredEntities"),RegisteredEntities)
```

C#

```
var registered =
    ConfigurationManager.GetSection("RegisteredEntities") as RegisteredEntities;
```

> *In order for the .NET configuration system to correctly load your configuration file with the RegisteredEntities section you will also need to register this section in the configSections. You can do this by adding* `<section name="Registered Entities" type="ConfigurationApplication.RegisteredEntities, ConfigurationApplication, Version=1.0.0.0, Culture=neutral, PublicKeyToken=null"/>` *to the configSections immediately before the* `</configSections>` *tag.*

Automation Using SCDL

You just saw how custom configuration sections can be written and mapped to classes. Although this is a huge improvement over writing section handlers, it is still a fairly laborious process that is prone to error. Furthermore, debugging the configuration sections is nearly impossible because it's difficult to track what's going wrong.

As part of another project to support ASP.NET developers, a development manager for the ASP.NET team at Microsoft recognized that the process of creating these mapping classes was mundane and could easily be automated. To this end, he created a small application entitled SCDL (`http://blogs.msdn.com/dmitryr/archive/2005/12/07/501365.aspx`) that could take a snippet of configuration data, such as the `RegisteredEntities` section discussed previously, and output both the mapping classes and a schema file that represented the section supplied. Once generated, this code can be included in the application. Furthermore, if the snippet of configuration data is to be included as a non-compiled file within the solution, it is possible to automate the generation of the mapping classes via a pre-build `batch` command. If changes need to be made to the structure of the section, they can be made in the snippet. That way, the next time the solution is built the mapping classes will be updated automatically.

IntelliSense

Even after you get the custom configuration sections correctly mapped, there is still no support provided by Visual Studio 2010 for adding the custom section to the configuration file. Unlike the rest of the configuration file, which has support for IntelliSense and will report validation issues, your custom section will not be able to be validated.

To get IntelliSense and validation for your custom configuration section, you need to indicate the structure of the configuration section to Visual Studio 2010. You can do this by placing an appropriate schema (as generated by the SCDL tool) in the XML Schemas folder, which is usually located at `C:\Program Files\Microsoft Visual Studio 10.0\Xml\Schemas\`. Unfortunately, this is where it gets a little bit more complex, because it is not enough to place the file in that folder; you also need to tell it that the schema should be included in the catalog used for parsing configuration files. To register your schema, follow these steps:

1. Generate your schema file from your configuration snippet:

```
Scdl.exe snippet.scdl snippet.vb snippet.xsd
```

2. Copy the schema file (in this case, `snippet.xsd`) to the schema folder.

3. Create a new text file called `Config.xsd` and include the following lines. Note that if your schema is called something different, you should update these lines appropriately. You may also add additional lines to include more than one schema. Do not remove the `DotNetConfig` `.xsd` line because that will remove validation for the standard configuration sections.

```
<?xml version="1.0" encoding="utf-8" ?>
<xs:schema xmlns:xs="http://www.w3.org/2001/XMLSchema">
<xs:include schemaLocation="DotNetConfig.xsd"/>
<xs:include schemaLocation="snippet.xsd"/>
</xs:schema>
```

4. Open `Catalog.xml` in a text editor and replace `DotNetConfig.xsd` with `Config.xsd`. This effectively remaps the validation, and IntelliSense, for configuration files to use `Config.xsd` instead of `DotNetConfig.xsd`. However, because this file sources both `DotNetConfig.xsd` and your schema information, you will get validation for both your configuration section and the standard configuration sections.

USER SETTINGS

Because configuration files are commonly used to store settings that control how an application runs, it is often necessary to be able to dynamically change these to suit the way an individual uses the application. Rather than having to build an entirely different framework for accessing and saving these settings, you can simply change the scope of your settings. Figure 36-5 illustrates that on the Settings tab of the Project Properties page you can indicate whether you want a setting to have Application or User scope.

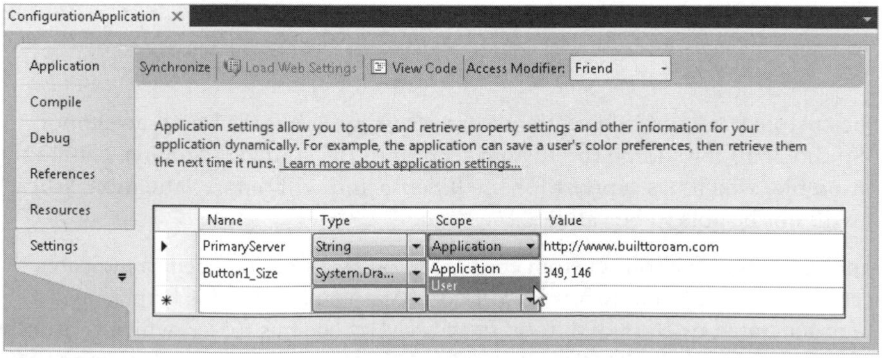

FIGURE 36-5

In essence, by changing the scope of a setting you are making the choice as to whether you want the setting to be read-only — in other words, it applies to the application regardless of which user is using the application — or read-write. When you access a project setting from code you will notice that if you try to assign a value to an Application setting you will get a compile error, whereas with a User setting you can assign a new value. Assigning a new value to the User setting only changes the value for that setting for the duration of that application session. If you want to persist the new value between sessions you should call the Save method on the designer-generated Settings object, as shown in the following code snippet:

VB

```
Properties.Settings.Default.BackgroundColor = Color.Blue;
Properties.Settings.Default.Save();
```

Table 36-2 lists the other methods that are defined on the Settings object that may be useful when manipulating User settings.

TABLE 36-2: Settings Objects Methods

METHOD NAME	FUNCTIONALITY
Save	Persists the current value of the setting.
Reload	Restores the persisted value of the setting.
Reset	Returns the persisted, and in-memory, value of a setting to the default value (this is the value you define during development in the Settings tab of the Project Properties page). You do not need to call Save after calling Reset.
Upgrade	When versioning your application you can call Upgrade to upgrade user settings to new values associated with your application. Note that you may want to be discriminate on when you call this method because you may inadvertently clear user settings.
(event) SettingChanging	Event raised when a setting is about to change.
(event) PropertyChanged	Event raised when a setting has changed.
(event) SettingsLoaded	Event raised when settings are loaded from persisted values.
(event) SettingsSaving	Event raised prior to current values being persisted.

When building an application that makes use of User-scoped settings it is important to test the application as if you were using it for the first time. The first time you run your application there will be no user-specific settings, which means your application will either use the values in the application configuration file or the default values that are coded in the designer-generated file. If you have been testing your application, the Synchronize button on the Settings tab of the Project Properties page (shown in the top-left corner of Figure 36-5) will remove any user-specific settings that may have been persisted during earlier executions of your application.

REFERENCED PROJECTS WITH SETTINGS

As applications grow, it is necessary to break up the logic into assemblies that are referenced by the main application. In the past, if these referenced assemblies wanted to use an application setting, there were a number of gotchas that made it problematic. With Visual Studio 2010, it is now possible to share application settings among assemblies using the project properties designer. Figure 36-6 shows the Settings tab of the project properties designer for a reference assembly. In this case the Access Modifier drop-down has been set to Public to allow access to these settings from the main application.

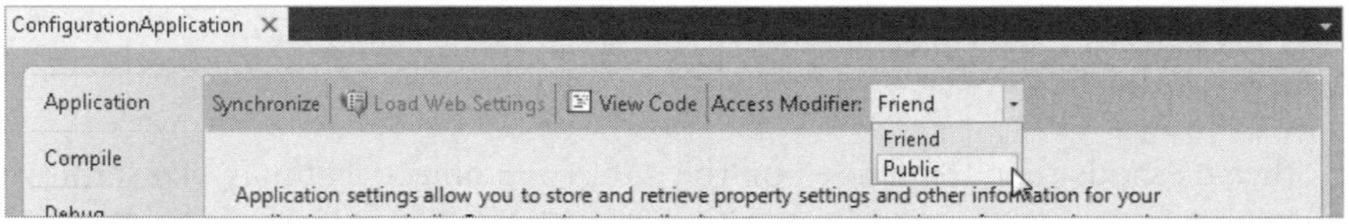

FIGURE 36-6

To access this property from the main application, you can again use the generated strongly typed access properties:

VB

```
ReferencedAssembly.My.MySettings.Default.SecondaryServer
```

C#

```
ReferencedAssembly.Properties.Settings.Default.SecondaryServer
```

A word of caution about using the project properties designer and referenced application settings: If you examine the code-behind file for the settings designer, you will note that for each of the settings you have defined there is a strongly typed access property, as previously discussed. What is important is the `DefaultSettingValueAttribute` that is applied. This is significant because it determines the value that will be returned by this property if the configuration file does not have any value specified. In the following snippet, the default value of `www.peaksite.com` will be returned if there is no `SecondaryServer` element defined in the configuration file:

VB

```
Namespace My
    Partial Friend NotInheritable Class MySettings
        Inherits Global.System.Configuration.ApplicationSettingsBase
    .
<Global.System.Configuration.ApplicationScopedSettingAttribute(), _
Global.System.Diagnostics.DebuggerNonUserCodeAttribute(), _
Global.System.Configuration.DefaultSettingValueAttribute("www.peaksite.com")> _
        Public ReadOnly Property SecondaryServer() As String
            Get
                Return CType(Me("SecondaryServer "),String)
            End Get
        End Property
    End Class
End Namespace
```

Now, you might ask why this is important when you're dealing with referenced application settings. It is because although the project properties designer enables you to specify that you want to allow access to settings from another assembly, it doesn't enable you to indicate that an application does, in fact, reference settings from another assembly. The upshot is that when it compiles the application it takes only the `app.config` file in the application project folder, rather than combining the elements from the `app.config` files in the referenced assembly folder.

Unfortunately, because of the default value attribute you are unlikely to notice this until the application is deployed and you realize that some of the settings are missing from the `app.config` file. Because of this, you should make sure you manually combine these files. In this case the result would be this:

```
<configuration>
.
<applicationSettings>
<ConfigurationApplication.My.MySettings>
<setting name="PrimaryServer" serializeAs="String">
<value>www.softteq.com</value>
</setting>
</ConfigurationApplication.My.MySettings>
<ReferencedAssembly.My.MySettings>
<setting name="SecondaryServer" serializeAs="String">
<value>www.peaksite.com</value>
</setting>
</ReferencedAssembly.My.MySettings>
</applicationSettings>
</configuration>
```

SUMMARY

In this chapter you have learned how configuration files can be used not only to control how your application runs, but also to store settings that may need to be adjusted at runtime. You should now be able to store simple name-value information, as well as more structured information, within the configuration file.

37

Connection Strings

WHAT'S IN THIS CHAPTER?

> ➤ Creating connection strings for use in your application

> ➤ Working with the Visual Studio 2010 Connection dialogs to specify how to connect to a data source

> ➤ Accessing connection strings from within code

A large proportion of applications need to persist data, and the obvious candidate for enterprise software is a relational database. The .NET Framework provides support for working with SQL Server, SQL Server Compact Edition, Oracle, ODBC, and OLE DB databases. Many other databases are also supported through third-party providers. To connect to any of these databases, you need to specify a connection string that determines the location, the database, authentication information, and other connection parameters. This chapter explains how to create and store connection strings. In addition, you learn about encrypting and working with connection strings in code.

CONNECTION STRING WIZARD

Connection strings are similar to XML in that, although they can be read, it is neither an enjoyable experience nor recommended to work with them directly. Because connection strings are strings, it is easy to introduce errors, misspell words, or even omit a parameter. Unlike XML, which can easily be validated against a schema, connection strings are harder to validate. The connection string wizard built into Visual Studio 2010 enables you to specify database connections without having to manually edit the connection string itself.

You can invoke the connection string wizard in a number of ways, as you will experience when you start working with any of the data controls in either the Windows Form or Web Form designers. For the purposes of illustrating the wizard, follow these steps to add a new data source to an existing Windows Forms application. You'll connect to the sample AdventureWorksLT database, which you will need to download from the Codeplex web site (www.codeplex.com and search for AdventureWorksLT).

1. From the Data menu within Visual Studio 2010, select Add New Data Source, which opens the Data Source Configuration Wizard.

2. Selecting Database, followed by either DataSet or Entity Data Model, prompts you to specify a database connection to use. If a connection already exists, you can select it from the drop-down and the associated connection string will appear in the lower portion of the window, as shown in Figure 37-1.

    The connection string connects to the AdventureWorksLT database using the SQL Server Express capability of attaching a database file. Later in this chapter you look at the properties of a SQL Server connection string in more detail.

3. To create a new connection, click the New Connection button to open the Add Connection dialog, in which you can specify the properties of the connection string. Figure 37-2 shows the dialog as it would appear for a SQL Server Database File connection. This dialog is specific to the database source being configured.

    Notice in Figure 37-2 that only the basic connection properties (such as the database filename and authentication information) are presented.

4. Click the Advanced button to open the Advanced Properties window, shown in Figure 37-3, where you can configure all properties for a SQL Server connection. At the bottom of this window is the connection string being constructed. The default values are omitted from the

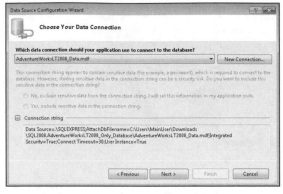

FIGURE 37-1

FIGURE 37-2

FIGURE 37-3

connection string. Once a value is set, it appears in the connection string and in bold in the Properties window. The list of available properties is again based on the data source being used.

5. Click OK to return to the Add Connection window, where you can change the type of data source by clicking the Change button. This opens the Change Data Source dialog, shown in Figure 37-4.

The list on the left contains all the data sources currently registered in the `machine.config` file. For a given data source, such as Microsoft SQL Server, there may be multiple data providers — in this case, the SQL Server and OLE DB providers.

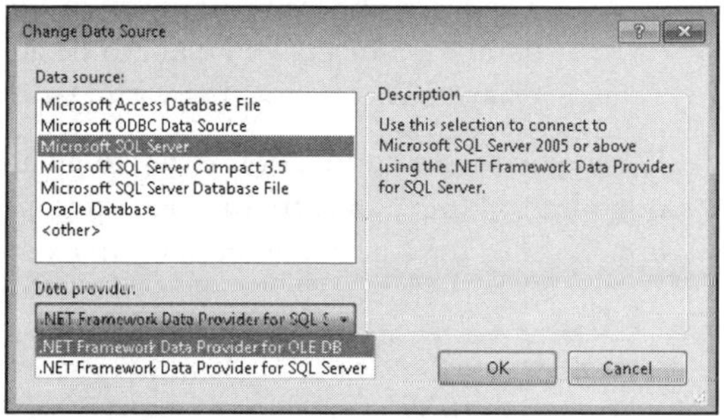

FIGURE 37-4

Selecting an alternative data source-data provider combination results in a different Add Connection dialog, displaying parameters that are relevant to that database connection. In most cases it is necessary to open the Advanced Properties window to configure the connection itself.

---

6. After specifying the data source and connection settings using the Add Connection dialog, return to the Data Source Configuration Wizard. If you are creating a new connection, you are given the option to save the connection string in the application configuration file, as shown in Figure 37-5. Unless you can guarantee that the location of the database, the authentication mode, or any other connection property will not change at a later stage, it is a good idea to store the connection string in the configuration file. Saving the connection string to the configuration file has the added benefit that the same configuration string can be reused throughout the application.

If you don't save the connection string to the configuration file, it is explicitly assigned to the connection object you are creating, which makes reuse difficult. Alternatively, saving the

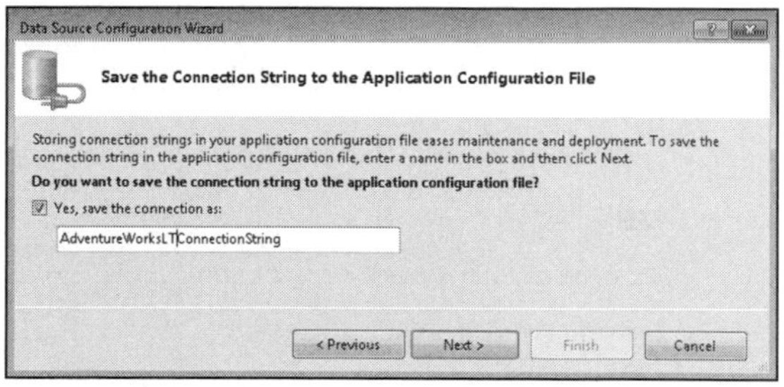

FIGURE 37-5

connection string in the configuration file means that other connection objects can access the same string. If the database connection changes at a later stage, you can easily update it in a single location.

7. The Data Source Configuration Wizard continues to step you through selecting which database objects you want to be added to your data source. This is covered in more detail in Chapter 27 on working with DataSets.

When you save a connection string to an application configuration file, it is added to the `connectionStrings` configuration section, as illustrated in the following snippet from an `app.config` file (the same section can exist in a `web.config` file for a web application):

```
<?xml version="1.0" encoding="utf-8" ?>
<configuration>
<appSettings />
<connectionStrings>
<add
      name="Connection_Strings.Properties.Settings.
      AdventureWorksLTConnectionString"
      connectionString="Data Source=.\SQLEXPRESS;AttachDbFilename=C:\Users\
MainUser\Downloads\SQL2008.AdventureWorksLT2008_Only_Database\AdventureWorks
LT2008_Data.mdf;Integrated Security=True;Connect Timeout=30;User Instance=Tr
ue" providerName="System.Data.SqlClient" />
</connectionStrings>
</configuration>
```

The `connectionStrings` section of a configuration file uses the standard element collection pattern, which allows multiple connection strings to be specified and then referenced in code. For example, the preceding connection string can be accessed in code as follows (this assumes your project has a reference to the System.Configuration assembly):

C#
```
private void OpenConnectionClick(object sender, EventArgs e){
    var sqlCon = new System.Data.SqlClient.SqlConnection();
    sqlCon.ConnectionString = ConfigurationManager.
    ConnectionStrings["AdventureWorksLTConnectionString"].ConnectionString;
    sqlCon.Open();
}
```

VB
```
Private Sub OpenConnectionClick(ByVal sender As System.Object,
                        ByVal e As System.EventArgs) _
                                        Handles BtnOpenConnection.Click
    Dim sqlCon As New SqlClient.SqlConnection
    sqlCon.ConnectionString = ConfigurationManager.ConnectionStrings _
                ("AdventureWorksLTConnectionString").ConnectionString
    sqlCon.Open()
End Sub
```

A nice artifact of working with the connection string wizard is that it also adds strongly typed support for accessing the connection string from within your code. This means that you can access the connection string using the following strongly typed methods, rather than call them using a string constant:

C#

```
Properties.Settings.Default.AdventureWorksLTConnectionString;
```

VB

```
My.Settings.AdventureWorksLTConnectionString
```

The other advantage of saving the connection string in the configuration file is that when you are editing the project settings, the connection strings are listed alongside other settings for the project as shown in Figure 37-6. Not only can you modify the connection string directly, but you also have a shortcut to the connection string wizard, via the ellipsis button to the right of the connection string value, which enables you to adjust the connection properties without fear of corrupting the connection string. Note that the ellipsis button is not visible until you click into the cell containing the connection string value.

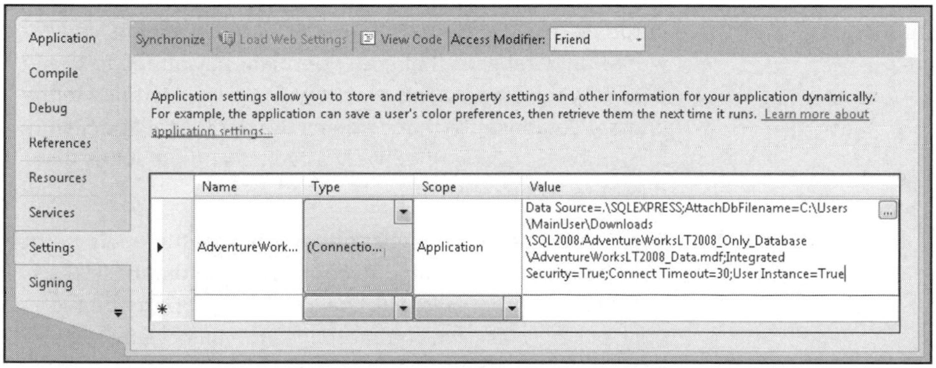

FIGURE 37-6

You will notice in Figure 37-6 that the name of the connection string excludes the rather lengthy prefix, `Connection_Strings.Properties.Settings`, which is in the application configuration file. This prefix is used to determine which connection strings should be included in both the project properties designer and for providing strongly typed support.

> *Given the inherent danger of getting data source properties wrong when manually editing the connection strings in the configuration file versus the benefits of using either the Add Data Source Wizard or the project properties designer, it is highly recommended that you avoid the manual approach wherever possible.*

SQL SERVER FORMAT

Probably the most familiar data provider is the SQL Server database provider, so Table 37-1 details some of the common connection properties you may need to specify to connect to your database server.

TABLE 37-1: Some Common Connection Properties

CONNECTION PROPERTY	DESCRIPTION
Asynchronous Processing	Determines whether the connection will support asynchronous database calls. Most applications try to deliver a responsive user interface, so it is important for it not to freeze when retrieving data. In the past this could only be achieved by doing the data processing in a separate thread from the user interface. The data access methods, such as ExecuteNonQuery, now support calls using the Begin and End asynchronous pattern. For example, BeginExecuteNonQuery will return immediately so the user interface does not block while the data access is performed.
AttachDBFilename	Introduced in SQL Server 2005, this property means you can work with databases that aren't permanently attached to a SQL Server instance. This property is a path reference to the primary database file that contains the database. Specifying AttachDBFilename effectively attaches and detaches the database when required.
Connect Timeout	Determines the maximum length of time that the Open method will block when attempting to connect to the database. This should not be confused with the Timeout property on the SQLCommand class, which determines the timeout for a given command to execute.
Data Source	The host name or IP address of the instance of SQL Server that the connection will be accessing. In cases where multiple instances exist on a given machine, or where SQL Server has been assigned an instance name other than the default instance, this needs to be specified as part of the Data Source field. For example, 192.168.205.223\InstanceName.
Initial Catalog	Specifies the name of the database to connect to.
Integrated Security	If IntegratedSecurity is used, the Windows credentials of the current user will be used to connect to the database server. To provide user ID and password, this property must be set to false. Also be aware that when working with ASP.NET using Windows authentication without impersonation, if IntegratedSecurity is enabled, the authenticated web user's credentials will be used to access the database server.

CONNECTION PROPERTY	DESCRIPTION
MultipleActiveResultSets	Allows multiple result sets to be returned across a given connection. For example, a single database command might contain two SELECT statements. If the MultipleActiveResultSets property is enabled, the results of both SELECT statements will be returned and can be used to populate a DataSet. This property is compatible only with SQL Server 2005 and above.
Password	Used for the SQL Server user account used to access the database server.
User ID	Specifies the SQL Server account used to access the database server. Mixed-mode authentication for the SQL Server must be enabled, and the IntegratedSecurity property must be set to false.

Each connection string property must be specified as it appears in the preceding table, but they can be in any order in the connection string. A semicolon is used to separate each property. An example connection string might be as follows:

```
Data Source=.;Initial Catalog=AdventureWorksLT;Integrated Security=True;
MultipleActiveResultSets=True
```

IN-CODE CONSTRUCTION

Although the connection string wizard in Visual Studio 2010 provides a convenient tool for writing connection strings, it is often necessary to build one dynamically — a feat easily done with the SqlConnectionStringBuilder class. In fact, string builder classes also exist for Oracle, ODBC, and OLE DB, and they all derive from the generic DBConnectionStringBuilder class, which exposes the ConnectionString property.

This example demonstrates creating a connection builder object, based on an existing connection string, and changing the authentication mode to use the user ID and password provided by the user before assigning the new connection string to the connection object. In addition, the example demonstrates the use of the MultipleActiveResultSets property to retrieve multiple tables from the database using a single command object:

C#
```
private void LoadDataClick(object sender, EventArgs e){
    //Update the connection string based on user settings
    var sqlbuilder = new System.Data.SqlClient.SqlConnectionStringBuilder
(Properties.Settings.Default.AdventureWorksLTConnectionString);
    if (!string.IsNullOrEmpty(this.TxtUserId.Text)){
```

```
        sqlbuilder.IntegratedSecurity = false;
        sqlbuilder.UserID = this.TxtUserId.Text;
        sqlbuilder.Password = this.TxtPassword.Text;
    }
    sqlbuilder.MultipleActiveResultSets = true;

    //Create the connection based on the updated connection string
    var sqlCon = new System.Data.SqlClient.SqlConnection();
    sqlCon.ConnectionString = sqlbuilder.ConnectionString;

    //Set the command and create the dataset to load the data into
    var sqlcmd = new System.Data.SqlClient.SqlCommand(
                            "SELECT * FROM Person.Contact;" +
                            "SELECT * FROM Person.ContactType", sqlCon);

    var ds = new DataSet();
    var rds = new System.Data.SqlClient.SqlDataAdapter(sqlcmd);

    //Open connection, retrieve data, and close connection
    sqlCon.Open();
    rds.Fill(ds);
    sqlCon.Close();
}
```

VB

```
Private Sub LoadDataClick (ByVal sender As System.Object, _
                        ByVal e As System.EventArgs) Handles Button1.Click
    'Update the connection string based on user settings
    Dim sqlbuilder As New SqlClient.SqlConnectionStringBuilder _
                        (My.Settings.AdventureWorksLTConnectionString)
    If Not Me.TxtUserId.Text = "" Then
        sqlbuilder.IntegratedSecurity = False
        sqlbuilder.UserID = Me.TxtUserId.Text
        sqlbuilder.Password = Me.TxtPassword.Text
    End If
    sqlbuilder.MultipleActiveResultSets = True

    'Create the connection based on the updated connection string
    Dim sqlCon As New SqlClient.SqlConnection
    sqlCon.ConnectionString = sqlbuilder.ConnectionString

    'Set the command and create the dataset to load the data into
    Dim sqlcmd As New SqlClient.SqlCommand("SELECT * FROM Person.Contact;" & _
                                    "SELECT * FROM Person.ContactType", _
                                    sqlCon)

    Dim ds As New DataSet
    Dim rds As New SqlClient.SqlDataAdapter(sqlcmd)

    'Open connection, retrieve data, and close connection
    sqlCon.Open()
    rds.Fill(ds)
    sqlCon.Close()
End Sub
```

The important thing to note about this code sample is that the `MultipleActiveResultSets` property is enabled, which means that multiple SELECT statements can be specified in the `SqlCommand` object. The `SqlCommand` object is then used by the `SqlDataAdapter` object to fill the DataSet. The `DataSet` object will contain two data tables, each populated by one of the SELECT statements.

ENCRYPTING CONNECTION STRINGS

Although best practices state that you should use Windows authentication and integrated security wherever possible, this is not always the case; sometimes you have to resort to specifying a user ID and password in a connection string. It is recommended that this information not be hard-coded into your application, because it can easily be extracted from the assembly. As such, this information needs to be either specified by the users each time they use the system, or added to the connection string in the configuration file. The upshot of this is that you need a mechanism for encrypting configuration sections. This walk-through shows you how to encrypt a section of a configuration file for a web application, StagingWebsite, which has a `web.config` file as follows:

```
<?xml version="1.0"?>
<configuration>
<connectionStrings>
<add name="AdventureWorksLTConnectionString" connectionString="Data Source=
.\SQLEXPRESS;AttachDbFilename=C:\Users\MainUser\Downloads\SQL2008.Adventure
WorksLT2008_Only_Database\AdventureWorksLT2008_Data.mdf;Integrated Security
=True;Connect Timeout=30;User Instance=True"
                providerName="System.Data.SqlClient" />
</connectionStrings>
<!-
.
->
</configuration>
```

Using the command prompt, execute the following commands in sequence, replacing `UserName` with the name of the account that the web application will run as (for example, the AspNet account):

1. `cd\WINDOWS\Microsoft.NET\Framework\v2.0.50739`

2. `aspnet_regiis -pa "NetFrameworkConfigurationKey" "UserName"`

3. `aspnet_regiis -pe "connectionStrings" -app "/StagingWebsite"`

Executing these commands modifies the `web.config` file as follows (if you get an error saying that the RSA key container was not found, you may need to execute `aspnet_regiis -pc "NetFrameworkConfigurationKey" -exp` to create the key container):

```
<?xml version="1.0"?>
<configuration>
<connectionStrings configProtectionProvider="RsaProtectedConfigurationProvider">
<EncryptedData Type="http://www.w3.org/2001/04/xmlenc#Element"
   xmlns="http://www.w3.org/2001/04/xmlenc#">
<EncryptionMethod Algorithm="http://www.w3.org/2001/04/xmlenc#tripledes-cbc" />
<KeyInfo xmlns="http://www.w3.org/2000/09/xmldsig#">
<EncryptedKey xmlns="http://www.w3.org/2001/04/xmlenc#">
<EncryptionMethod Algorithm="http://www.w3.org/2001/04/xmlenc#rsa-1_5" />
```

```
<KeyInfo xmlns="http://www.w3.org/2000/09/xmldsig#">
<KeyName>Rsa Key</KeyName>
</KeyInfo>
<CipherData>
<CipherValue>Y4Be/ND8fXTK13r0CASBK0oaOSvbyijYCVUudf1AuQl
pU2HRsTyEpR2sVpxrOukiBhvcGyWlv4EM0AB9p3Ms8FgIA3Ou6mGORhxfO9eIUGD+M5tJSe6wn/
9op8mFV4W7YQZ4WIqLaAAu7MKVI6KKK/ANIKpV8l2NdMBT3uPOPi8=</CipherValue>
</CipherData>
</EncryptedKey>
</KeyInfo>
<CipherData>
<CipherValue>BeKnN/kQIMw9rFbck6IwX9NZA6WyOCSQlziWzCLA8Ff/JdA0W/dWIidnjae1
vgpS8ghouYn7BQocjvc0uGsGgXlPfvsLq18//1ArZDgiHVLAXjW6b+eKbE5vaf5ss6psJdCRRB0ab5xao
NAPHH/Db9UKMycWVqP0badN+qCQzYyU2cQFvK1S7Rum8VwgZ85Qt+FGExYpG06YqVR9tfWwqZmYwtW8iz
r7fijvspm/oRK4Yd+DGBRKuXxD6EN4kFgJUil7ktzOJAwW1y4bVpmwzwJT9N6yig54lobhOahZDP05gtk
Lor/HwD9IKmRvO1jv</
    CipherValue>
</CipherData>
</EncryptedData>
</connectionStrings>
<!—
.
—>
</configuration>
```

As you can see from this example, the connection string is no longer readable in the configuration file. The commands you executed did two things. Ignoring the first command (because it simply changes the directory so you can access the asp_regiis executable), the second command permits access to the key container NetFrameworkConfigurationKey for the user Nick. This key container is the default container for the RSAProtectedConfigurationProvider, which is specified in the machine.config file. For your application to be able to decrypt data from the configuration file, the user that the application is running as must be able to access the key container. To determine the identity of this user, execute the following command:

```
System.Security.Principal.WindowsIdentity.GetCurrent( ).Name
```

The third command encrypts the connectionStrings section of the configuration file for the web application StagingWebsite. Other sections of the configuration file can also be encrypted using the same command. If at some later stage you need to decrypt the configuration section, execute the same command, but with –pd instead of –pe. For example:

```
aspnet_regiis -pd "connectionStrings" -app "/StagingWebsite"
```

SUMMARY

This chapter showed you how to use Visual Studio 2010 to take charge of your application and configure it to connect to a database using a connection string. With the built-in support of the data classes in the .NET Framework, connection strings can be dynamically created and modified so you never have to handcraft a connection string again.

38

Resource Files

WHAT'S IN THIS CHAPTER?

➤ Understanding what an application resource is

➤ Defining and using resources within your application

➤ Defining culture-specific resources

➤ Extending the default resource types

Developers often overlook the humble XML resource file, because it is often hidden by Visual Studio 2010 so as not to clutter the solution. Because its most common use is as a backing file for forms or web pages, you can write large applications without interacting directly with resource files. However, resource files are an important tool that you need to be able to use in order to write applications that can be easily maintained and translated into other languages.

The first part of this chapter explains why resource files are important and describes the features that enable developers to work with them. The remainder of the chapter explains how you can use resource files to localize an application for different languages and cultures.

WHAT ARE RESOURCES?

A resource is any data required by an application, whether it is a string, an icon, an image, or even an audio clip. Resources are non-executable and support the running of the application through the provision of data such as location, size, and other physical properties of controls. Though most resources are strings, images, audio clips, or icons, there is no reason why a resource could not be a more complex object that supports serialization.

Three types of resource files can be compiled into an application: text, resx (XML resource file), and resources (binary resource file) file formats. Whole files can also be embedded as application resources where needed. Most developers who use Visual Studio 2010 will use resx files and embedded file resources.

Text File Resources

Text files are the most basic sort of resource because they are limited to providing string values. In applications for which a large number of string literals need to be managed, using a simple text file can be the easiest way to do it because that way they are not cluttered among the other resources of the application.

The format of strings defined in a text resource file is a name-value pair, where the name is used to reference the resource in code, as shown in the following example:

```
Error_Unable_To_Connect = Unable to connect to specified server
```

Because each name-value pair is delimited by a new line, this character cannot be added to the string. However, C-style escape characters can be used to insert new lines (\n) or tabs (\t) into the text.

You can add comments to the resource file by prefixing a line with a semicolon, as shown here:

```
;Error message to be displayed when a connection could not be made to the server
Error_Unable_To_Connect = Unable to connect to specified server
```

Text resource files should be saved with the file extension of .txt or .restext. The latter is useful when you want to distinguish text resource files from regular text files.

Although text resource files are easy to edit and update, it is harder to integrate them into your application. As text files, they cannot be directly compiled into an application; they must instead be converted into either resx or resources files. Do this using the Resource Generator utility, resgen.exe, located in the \bin folder of the Windows SDK (located at C:\Program Files\Microsoft SDKs\ Windows\v7.0A\bin):

```
resgen StringResources.txt StringResources.resources
```

Include the output file — in this case, StringResources.resources — in your application to give yourself access to those resources.

A prebuild event can be used to convert text resource files into a resources file that can be compiled into the main application build. This will ensure that the resources files contained in the application are always up to date. To do this, include the text resource file in the application and set the build action property to None. Navigate to the Project Properties window for the project that contains the text resource file and on the Compile tab select Build Events (VB) or the Build Events tab (C#). In the prebuild events, enter the Resgen command required to compile your text resource file:

```
"C:\Program Files\Microsoft SDKs\Windows\v7.0A\bin\resgen.exe"
    "$(ProjectDir)StringResources.txt" "$(ProjectDir)StringResources.resources"
```

Building the application generates the resources file that needs to be included within your application with the build action property set to Embedded Resource. Figure 38-1 illustrates how both the text file and the resources file are included within an application with appropriate build action properties.

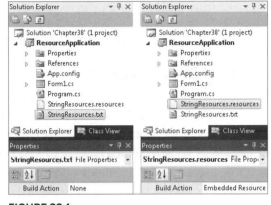

Resx Resource Files

A much more user-friendly format for resources is the XML resource file, commonly referred to as a resx file. This is a simple XML data file that contains name-value pairs of XML nodes. The advantage of this format is that the value is not restricted to just a string; it can be of any type that is serializable or that can be represented as a string.

FIGURE 38-1

The following XML snippet shows a resource named HelloWorld, with an associated value and comment. As you can see from the code, no information is available about the type of data contained within the resource, because it is a string resource:

```
<data name="HelloWorld">
<value>Say Hello</value>
<comment>This is how we say hello</comment>
</data>
```

The next snippet illustrates how a more complex data type can be stored in a resource file as a string representation. It also shows how an assembly alias can be used to reference an external assembly that contains type information. When this resource is accessed, the type information will be used to convert the string value to an object of this type:

```
<assembly alias="System.Drawing" name="System.Drawing, Version=4.0.0.0,
Culture=neutral, PublicKeyToken=b03f5f7f11d50a3a" />
<data name="Button1.Location" type="System.Drawing.Point, System.Drawing">
<value>71, 43</value>
</data>
```

Although resx files can be included in an application without your having to use the Resource File Generator (Resgen), they are still converted prior to being compiled into the application. During the build process, resources files are generated for each resx file in the application. These are subsequently linked into the application.

Binary Resources

The third resource format is the binary resource file, indicated by the .resources file extension. Behind the scenes, Visual Studio 2010 converts all resx files into .resources files as an intermediate step during compilation (you can see these files in the \obj\debug folder for your project), and as you saw earlier in this chapter, you must manually convert text resources into `.resources` files using Resgen. You can also integrate other binary resources into your project by simply including the `.resources` file and setting the build action to `Embedded Resource`.

Adding Resources

Visual Studio 2010 supports a rich user interface for adding and modifying resource files. It is still possible to view the contents of a resource file within the IDE. However, unless the resource is a string, or has a string representation, it is not possible to modify the value within the resource file. The resource editor provides support for strings, images, icons, audio files, and more.

Double-clicking the My Project (VB) or Properties (C#) node for a project in the Solution Explorer opens the project properties editor, from which you can select the Resources tab to open the default, or project, resource file. For C# projects you will then need to click the presented link to create the resource file (VB projects already have a default resource file). When the default resource file opens, you will see that in the top left-hand corner of the resource editor is a drop-down list that navigates among resources of different types, as shown in Figure 38-2. Double-clicking any resx file within the Solution Explorer also brings up this resource editor.

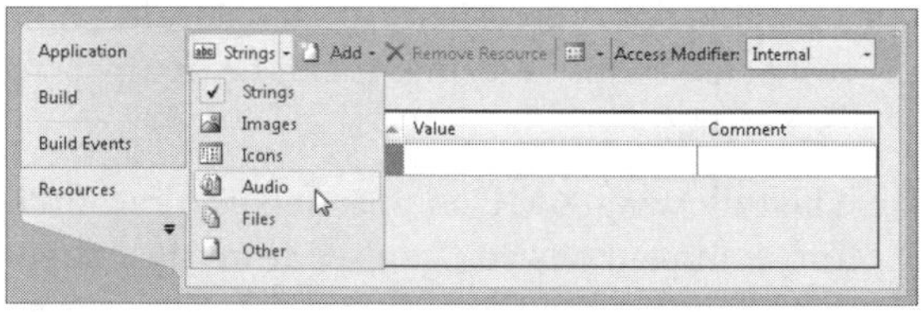

FIGURE 38-2

The editor displays the resource in an appropriate format, according to its type. For example, strings are presented in an editable textbox, whereas images are presented as thumbnails that can be opened and edited. Adding new resources is as simple as selecting the Add Resource drop-down, choosing the appropriate resource type, and adding the necessary information. Once you have added a resource, it appears in the resource editor, as shown in Figure 38-3.

Figure 38-3 shows an additional column that gives you the option to specify a comment alongside your resource. Unfortunately, the resource editor is the only place in Visual Studio 2010 where this comment is displayed.

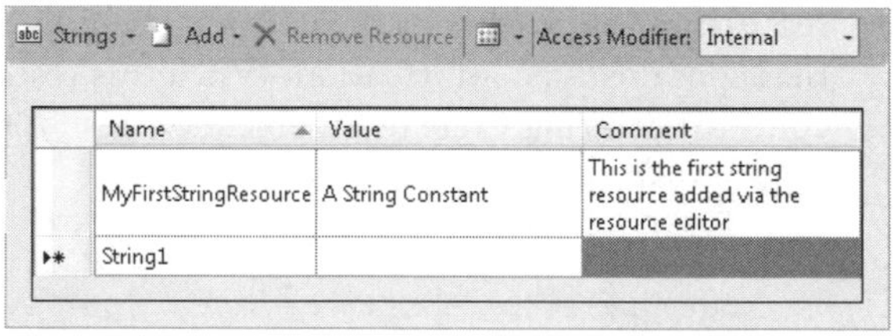

FIGURE 38-3

Embedding Files as Resources

It is often necessary to embed an entire file in an application. You can do this by including the file in the application and modifying the build action. Depending on the file type, when the item is included in the application, the build action (click the file and open the Properties window) is normally set to either `Compile` or `None`. If this is changed to `Embedded Resource`, the entire file is added to the application as an embedded resource.

Alternatively, you can use the resource editor shown in Figure 38-2 to add a file resource. When images, icons, and other files are added to an existing resource file by means of the resource editor, they are added as a `resxfileref` item. The file will appear in the resources directory, but the build action will be None. When the application is built, these files are compiled into the resources file prior to being linked into the application. In the past, the data from these files was pulled out and added to the resx file as a binary block. This meant that, once added, the data couldn't be easily modified. With the file reference item, the data remains in an associated file and can easily be updated.

Naming Resources

Resources are named for the resource file to which they belong and the root namespace. For example, if you have a resource file called Sample.resources in a project called MyProject, the full resource name will be MyProject.Sample.

This is particularly important to remember when you make a file an embedded resource by changing the build action. You can access any file by prefixing the filename with the project name. Unlike with resource files, the name of the file retains the extension. For example, if you have a file called ASimpleDataDocument.doc in a project called MyProject, it will need to be referenced as MyProject.ASimpleDataDocument.doc.

> *Any directory structure will be ignored for the purpose of naming embedded resources.*

Accessing Resources

The method that you use to access resources depends on how they are embedded in the application. You have already seen that you have two ways to embed resources: the first is to add a file to the project and set the build action to Embedded Resource; the second is via the resource editor. To access resources added by a change to the build action, you need to use the GetManifestResourceNames and GetManifestResourceStream methods. The following code retrieves the names of all the resources in the assembly by querying the manifest. It then creates a stream for accessing the relevant resource file. As discussed in the previous section, the name of the embedded resource file returned by the GetManifestResourceNames method and accepted by the GetManifestResourceStream method is in the form *Root namespace .Filename .File_extension* (for example, MyProject. ASimpleDataDocument.doc).

VB
```
Dim names = Reflection.Assembly.GetExecutingAssembly.GetManifestResourceNames
Dim resources = From n In names
                Select Assembly.GetExecutingAssembly.GetManifestResourceStream(n)
For Each r In resources
    Using strm As New IO.StreamReader(r)
        MsgBox(strm.ReadToEnd)
    End Using
Next
```

C#

```
var names = Assembly.GetExecutingAssembly().GetManifestResourceNames();
var resources = from n in names
                select Assembly.GetExecutingAssembly().GetManifestResourceStream(n);
foreach (var r in resources){
    using (var strm = new StreamReader(r)){
        MessageBox.Show(strm.ReadToEnd());
    }
}
```

Resources added via the resource editor can be accessed in code by means of a resource manager, which you can easily create from the name of the resource file to which they belong and a reference to the assembly from which the resource should be extracted:

VB

```
Dim res As New ResourceManager("WorkingWithResources.Resources",
                               Assembly.GetExecutingAssembly)
```

C#

```
var res = new ResourceManager("WorkingWithResources.Properties.Resources",
                              Assembly.GetExecutingAssembly());
```

Once created, resources can be extracted by means of either the `GetObject` or `GetString` function:

```
res.GetObject("StringResource")
```

For more complex resources, such as files, you may also want to use the `GetStream` function. All three functions take the name of the resource as the only parameter.

Designer Files

The Resource Generator utility, Resgen, has a number of improvements that enable you to build strongly typed wrapper classes for your resource files. When you add a resx file to your application, Visual Studio 2010 automatically creates a designer file that wraps the process of creating a resource manager and accessing the resources by name. The accessor properties are all strongly typed and are generated by the designer to reduce the chance of invalid type conversions and references. For example, if you have a string resource, `StringResource`, contained in a resource file, `MyResources`, you can use the following code to access the string:

VB

```
My.Resources.MyResources.MyStringResource
```

C#

```
MyResources.StringResource
```

You will notice that the designer-generated code is different for VB and C#. This is because C# uses the generic ResXFileCodeGenerator custom tool whereas VB uses the VbMyResourcesResXFileCodeGenerator custom tool to integrate the resource file into the `My` namespace.

Unfortunately, Visual Studio 2010 does not automatically generate the designer file for text resource files, because text resource files cannot be explicitly added to the application. The process of generating a resource file from the text file can be extended to include the generation of the designer file.

A new argument has been added to Resgen that facilitates the generation of this designer file:

```
resgen sample.txt sample.resources /str:vb
```

Both of the output files need to be added to the application so that the resources are accessible. To ensure that the resources can be correctly accessed, you must ensure that the naming used within the designer file matches the naming of the compiled resources. You can provide additional parameters to control the namespace, class name, and output filename:

```
resgen sample.txt defaultnamespace.sample.resources
    /str:vb,defaultnamespace,sample,sample.vb
```

In this case, the fully qualified output class would be `defaultnamespace.sample`, and the use of this file would allow access to resources without an exception being raised. Once the correct command has been determined, you can update your prebuild event to include the generation of the designer file. This way, every time the file is modified and saved and the application is compiled, the designer file will be re-created.

RESOURCING YOUR APPLICATION

Writing an application often requires data such as images, icons, or sounds (collectively known as *resources*) to enhance the appearance of the application. Furthermore, best coding practices suggest that the use of constant strings throughout your application be avoided. In either case, you can put together a custom solution that stores these resources in files that need to be shipped with the application.

An alternative is to include them in a resource file that can be compiled into your application. This way you not only have the resources in a format that you can work with, but they are also automatically available within your application.

In Visual Studio 2010, forms are initially represented by two files: the generated designer file (for example, `Form1.Designer.vb`) and the code-beside file (for example, `Form1.vb`). When a control, such as a button, is first added to the form, a resource file (for example, `Form1.resx`) is automatically created for the form. By default, this resource file contains very little data, because most properties are hard-coded into the designer file. This file becomes very important when localization is turned on for the form. When this is done, via the properties grid shown in Figure 38-4, the designer properties for the controls on the form are persisted to the resource file.

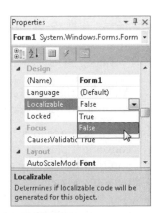

FIGURE 38-4

The following code snippet shows the designer-generated method `InitializeComponent`, which creates and sets properties on Button1. This is how the code would appear with the `Localizable` property on the form set to `False`:

```
Private Sub InitializeComponent()
    Me.Button1 = New Button
    '
    'Button1
    '
    Me.Button1.Location = New Point(71, 43)
    Me.Button1.Size = New Size(185, 166)
    Me.Button1.Text = "Button1"
    Me.Button1.TabIndex = 0
    Me.Button1.Name = "Button1"
    Me.Button1.UseVisualStyleBackColor = True
    '
    'Form1
    '
    Me.Controls.Add(Me.Button1)
End Sub
```

Once the `Localizable` property of the form has been set to `True`, the form uses the new `ComponentResourceManager` class to load and apply properties found in the associated resource file. (This framework class is covered in more detail later in this chapter.)

```
Private Sub InitializeComponent()
    Dim resources As New ComponentResourceManager(GetType(Form1))
    Me.Button1 = New Button
    '
    'Button1
    '
    resources.ApplyResources(Me.Button1, "Button1")
    Me.Button1.Name = "Button1"
    Me.Button1.UseVisualStyleBackColor = True
    '
    'Form1
    '
    Me.Controls.Add(Me.Button1)
End Sub
```

Although the resource files generated by the forms designer can be manually edited, this is not encouraged because changes may be overwritten the next time the file is regenerated by the designer.

When resource files are used properly, they can provide a number of benefits because they are a convenient place to store strings, icons, images, and other data that might be referenced by an application. The use of resource files, both for tracking form properties and for application data, is a must for any application that needs to be translated for a foreign culture (we use the term "culture" here because more than language can differ among countries and ethnic groups). Resource files enable developers to provide alternative data for different cultures. When the application is run, the .NET Framework uses the current culture information to determine which data to load, based upon the resource fallback process (the fallback process is discussed in the section "Loading Culture

Resource Files" later in this chapter). Common examples of information that might need to be varied among cultures are prompts, titles, error messages, and button images.

Control Images

A number of Windows Forms controls have images as properties. For example, the PictureBox control has Image, ErrorImage, and InitialImage properties. If you click the ellipsis in the value column of the Properties window for any of these properties, you see the dialog shown in Figure 38-5, which enables you to select an image for the specified property.

Before selecting an image, you have to decide whether you want to store it in the resource file associated with the current form (that is, a Local resource) or in a project-level resource file. The former option stores the image in a Base64-encoded block within the actual resource file,

FIGURE 38-5

whereas the latter adds the image to the project and adds an appropriate reference to the selected resource file. Clearly the latter is normally preferable, because it means that you can change the image without having to import it again.

SATELLITE RESOURCES

One of the big advantages of placing data in a resource file is the resulting capability to translate the data for foreign cultures. Instead of all the languages being included in a single resource file, each culture's data is stored in a resource file that has a suffix defined by that culture.

Cultures

Cultures are defined by a combination of two lowercase letters, which represent the language, and two uppercase letters, which represent the country or region of the culture. These two pairs of letters are separated by a hyphen. For example, U.S. English and Australian English are represented as en-US and en-AU, respectively. The corresponding resource files for these cultures would be MyResource .en-US.resx and MyResource.en-AU.resx. You can find a full list of culture identifiers at http:// msdn2.microsoft.com/en-us/library/system.globalization.cultureinfo.aspx. If you are curious, you can look over all the available cultures, which are returned by CultureInfo.GetCultures (CultureTypes.AllCultures). About 220 cultures exist, and they can be classified as follows:

➤ **Invariant culture:** No language or country identifier (for example, Form1.resx). Data is not dependent upon culture — for example, this might be the company logo, which will not vary and is not dependent upon culture information.

➤ **Neutral culture:** Language identifier (for example, Form1.en.resx). Data is dependent upon language alone — for example, a simple warning message that merely needs to be translated.

➤ **Specific culture:** Language and country identifier (for example, `Form1.en-US.resx`). Data is dependent upon both language and country/region — for example, form layout, color, and prompts should all be translated and adjusted for specific regions.

Creating Culture Resources

If you are creating additional resource files for a form, it is important to ensure that the `Localizable` property is set to `True`. You have three ways to create culture-specific resource files:

➤ If you know the identifier of the culture for which you want to generate a resource file, you can simply save the resx file to filename.*culture_identifier*.resx. For example, if you were converting the resource file `Form1.resx` to Australian English, you would save it as `Form1.en-AU.resx`. You will notice that when you do this, Visual Studio removes the original resx file from the solution and adds the new culture-specific resx file. To get both files to show up nested under the Form1 node, you actually need to exclude the new resx file, refresh the solution view (by closing and reopening the solution), and then put both files back into the project.

➤ Visual Studio supports a much better way to create culture-specific resource files for forms. From the Properties window for the form you can select `Language`. The name of this property is slightly misleading because it adjusts not only the language, but also the country/region of the form in designer mode. This property is initially set to `(Default)` and should always be returned to this setting after you have finished generating or modifying resource files for specific cultures. To generate the resource file for Australian English, select `English (Australia)` from the Language drop-down and make the appropriate changes to the form. Once you are comfortable with the new layout, save it and reset the `Language` property to `(Default)`.

➤ The last way to generate culture-dependent resource files is to use `WinRes.exe`. Although it's not added to the Start menu, it is available under the Windows SDK folder (located at `C:\Program Files\Microsoft SDKs\Windows\v7.0A\bin`) and is a graphical utility for generating resource files for forms. This utility can load an existing resource file, allow properties of all controls on the form to be modified, and then save the changes to a particular culture resource file. Before opening a form's resource file using this utility, make sure that the `Localizable` property is set to `True`; otherwise the file will not load properly.

Loading Culture Resource Files

At this point you might be wondering how resource files interact, and whether culture-specific resource files have to be created and compiled at the same time as the main application. The answer to both of these questions lies in the resource fallback process, which is the mechanism by which the `ResourceManager` class loads resources.

The fallback process has three levels, based upon the current user interface culture (UI culture) of the executing thread. This can be accessed in code via the `CultureInfo.CurrentUICulture` property. Be aware that this is different from `CultureInfo.CurrentCulture`, which is the current culture used in string comparisons, date formats, and so on. Unlike the current culture, which is based upon the regional settings of the computer (which you can adjust using Control Panel ⇨ Regional Settings), the default UI culture is dependent upon the Windows user interface language pack that is currently selected. Unless you have a Windows Multilingual User Interface Pack installed, you will not be able to modify the default UI culture for your applications.

Although you can't change the default user interface culture, you can adjust this property in code. A word of caution here, however: without the interface pack installed, some cultures may not display correctly.

```
Thread.CurrentThread.CurrentUICulture = New CultureInfo("en-US")
```

Using the current user interface culture, the fallback process tries to locate resources based on a culture match. For example, if the UI culture is en-US, the process would start off by looking for specific culture resources that match both language (English) and country (U.S.). When no resource can be located, the process falls back to neutral culture resources that match just the language (English). If the fallback process still can't locate a resource, the process falls back to *invariant culture*, indicating there is no match for language or country.

Satellite Culture Resources

So far we have mentioned only how a resource can be converted into a new culture and added to an application. Although this method gives you control over which cultures are deployed with your application, it would be better if you didn't have to rebuild your entire application whenever a culture resource needed to be modified, or when you decided to add support for a new culture.

When Visual Studio 2010 compiles culture resources, it splits the resource files into a hub-and-spoke arrangement, using satellite assemblies to contain culture resources. At the hub is the main assembly that would contain the invariant resources. Satellite assemblies are then created for each culture for which a resource has been created. The naming of the satellite assembly is of the form "MyApp.resources.dll" and it is located in a subdirectory named according to the culture under the main output path. Although there is an implicit relationship between specific cultures and neutral cultures (for example, between en-US and en), satellite assemblies for both types should reside in a subdirectory under the main output path.

Another alternative is for the main assembly and/or satellite assemblies to be installed into the Global Assembly Cache (GAC). In this case, each assembly must be strongly named so that it is unique within the cache.

Clearly, the resource fallback process needs to accommodate assemblies both in the GAC and in subdirectories. Hence, for each culture level (specific, neutral, and invariant) the GAC is checked first, followed by the culture subdirectory. Finally, if no resource is found, an exception is raised.

Note that culture resource files do not have to contain all the resources defined in the default resource file. The resource fallback process will load the resource from the default resource file if it is not located in a more specific resource file, so it makes sense to save in the specified culture only those resources that are different.

ACCESSING SPECIFICS

Numerous shortcuts have been built into the .NET Framework to support the most common tasks related to accessing resources. These shortcuts include single-line image loading, cross-assembly referencing, and the use of the `ComponentResourceManager` class.

Bitmap and Icon Loading

Images and icons are two of the most common data types held in resource files. Therefore, both the `Bitmap` and `Icon` classes in the framework support a constructor that can create an instance directly from a resource without the need for a resource manager. For example, if you have an image, `MyImage.bmp`, that you included in your project by setting the build action to `Embedded Resource`, you can access the image directly using the following code:

```
Dim img As New Bitmap(GetType(ThisClass), "MyImage.bmp")
```

Here the class, `ThisClass`, can be any class in the root namespace of the project that contains the embedded resource.

Cross-Assembly Referencing

In Visual Studio 2010, you can control the accessibility level for resource files. With the Access Modifier option in the resource editor, as shown in Figure 38-6, you can choose between keeping a resource internal to the assembly it is defined in (Friend [VB] or Internal [C#]) or making it publicly accessible (Public).

If you set the Access Modifier to Public, you can then access this resource from another assembly by prefixing the resource name with the assembly name. For example, in the following code the `MyPerson` resource is located in the `CustomResourceType` assembly:

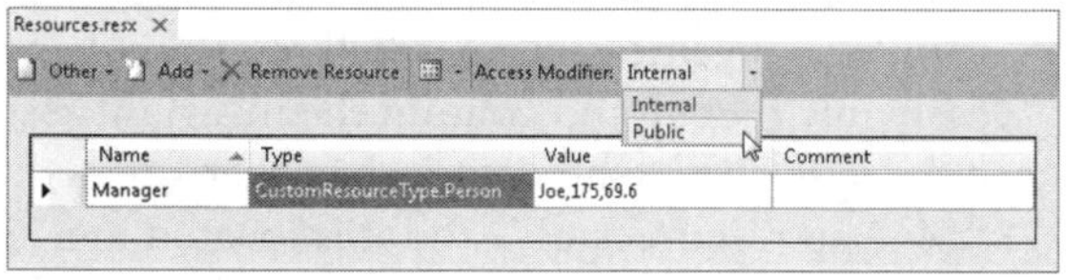

FIGURE 38-6

```
Dim p As Person = CustomResourceType.My.Resources.MyPerson
```

ComponentResourceManager

In the first example in this chapter, after localization was turned on, a `ComponentResourceManager` object was used to retrieve resources associated with the form. The `ComponentResourceManager` extends the base `ResourceManager` by providing additional functionality for retrieving and applying component properties. Here are the original four lines required to set the properties defined for Button1:

```
Me.Button1.Location = New Point(71, 43)
Me.Button1.Size = New Size(185, 166)
Me.Button1.Text = "Button1"
Me.Button1.TabIndex = 0
```

Using the `ComponentResourceManager`, they can be condensed into just one line:

```
resources.ApplyResources(Me.Button1, "Button1")
```

In previous versions of Visual Studio, the code generated when localization was turned on was much more verbose. For each property, a separate call was made to the `ResourceManager` to retrieve it by name, as shown in this code snippet:

```
Me.Button1.Location = CType(resources.GetObject("Button1.Location"), Point)
Me.Button1.Size = CType(resources.GetObject("Button1.Size"), Size)
Me.Button1.TabIndex = CType(resources.GetObject("Button1.TabIndex"), Integer)
Me.Button1.Text = resources.GetString("Button1.Text")
```

It is still possible to write this code because the `GetObject` method is still available on the `ComponentResourceManager`. The issue with writing this code is that each property that is going to be localized needs to be known at compile time. Because of this, every property on every control was added to the resource file. This added excess properties (even when they were no different from the default values) to the resource file. It also added huge overhead during the loading up of a form, because each property was set via a resource property.

The `ApplyResources` method in the `ComponentResourceManager` class works in reverse. When you specify a control name, which must be unique on a form, all resources that start with that prefix are extracted. The full resource name is then used to determine the property to set on the control. For example, a resource with the name `Button1.Location` would be extracted for the control called Button1, and the value used to set the `Location` property on that control.

This process eliminates the need to have all properties specified in a resource file. It also creates the need for culture resource files to specify additional properties that might not have been defined in the default resource file.

You might be wondering whether any additional penalties exist in using the `ComponentResourceManager`. To set a property on a control using the name of the property, the `ComponentResourceManager` uses *reflection* to find the appropriate property. Once it has been retrieved, it can be invoked. Each search that is done in order to set the property is relatively expensive. However, given the reduced number of properties to be set, the tradeoff is definitely worthwhile, because the application can easily be localized without recompilation of the main application.

CODING RESOURCE FILES

In addition to the rich visual tools that Visual Studio 2010 now provides for editing resource files, it is possible to use code to create resource files. The .NET Framework provides support for reading and writing resource files using two interfaces: IResourceReader and IResourceWriter. Once the resource files have been created, they need to be added to the application or manually linked so that they can be referenced within the application.

> ➤ **IResource Reader:** The reader interface ensures that resource readers have the following methods:

>> ➤ **GetEnumerator:** The `GetEnumerator` method retrieves an `IDictionaryEnumerator` object that permits the developer to iterate over each of the resources in the resource file.

>> ➤ **Close:** The `Close` method is used to close the resource reader and release any associated resources.

> ➤ **IResource Writer:** The writer interface ensures that resource writers have the following methods:

>> ➤ **AddResource:** Three overloads to the `AddResource` method support adding resources to the resource file. Both of the framework implementations of this interface have either an additional overload of this method or an alternative method for adding resources. The overloads that are part of this interface support adding resources in a name-value pair. Each method has the resource name as the first parameter and a value, such as a string, byte array, or object, as the second parameter. The final implementation that takes an object as a parameter may need to be serializable or converted to a string via a type converter.

>> ➤ **Close:** The `Close` method writes resources out to the stream before closing it.

>> ➤ **Generate:** Unlike the `Close` method, the `Generate` method simply writes the resources out to the stream without closing it. Once this method is called, any other method will cause an exception to be raised.

ResourceReader and ResourceWriter

ResourceReader and ResourceWriter are an implementation of the IResource interfaces to support reading and writing directly to resources files. Although reading and writing to this format is the most direct approach, because it reduces the need to use Resgen to generate the resources file, it does limit the quality of information that can be retrieved in reading from the file. Each resource is treated as a series of bytes where the type is unknown.

ResxResourceReader and ResxResourceWriter

ResxResourceReader and ResxResourceWriter are more versatile implementations of the IResource interfaces. In addition to supporting the IResource interface, ResxResourceWriter supports an additional overload of the `AddResource` method, whereby a ResxDataNode can be added. A ResxDataNode is very similar to a dictionary entry, because it has a key (in this case, the `Name` property) and a value (which you must set when the node is created). However, the difference is that this node can support additional properties such as a comment and, as an alternative to a value, a file reference (for example, one that indicates where an image needs to be added to a resource file).

As mentioned previously, it is possible to add a file reference to a resx file so that the file is still editable, yet has the benefit of being compiled into the resource file by `resgen.exe`. The supporting class in the framework is `ResxFileRef`. This can be instantiated and added as a resource via the ResxResourceWriter. This inserts an XML node similar to the following snippet:

```
<data name="Figure_11_2" type="ResXFileRef, System.Windows.Forms">
<value>.\Resources\CompanyLogo.tif;System.Drawing.Bitmap, System.Drawing,
Version=4.0.0.0, Culture=neutral, PublicKeyToken=b03f5f7f11d50a3a</value>
</data>
```

❌ *Resource files are the best means of storing static application data. Although they are linked in to the application as part of the compilation process, their contents can easily be extracted and made human-readable. Because of this, however, resource files are not suitable for storing secure data such as passwords and credit card information.*

CUSTOM RESOURCES

Although Visual Studio provides good support for international application development using resource files, at times it is not possible to get the level of control required using the default behavior. This section delves a little deeper into how you can serialize custom objects to the resource file and how you can generate designer files, which give you strongly typed accessor methods for resource files you have created.

Visual Studio 2010 enables you to store strings, images, icons, audio files, and other files within a resource file. You can do all this using the rich user interface provided. To store a more complex data type within a resource file you need to serialize it into a string representation that can be included within the resource file.

The first step in adding any data type to a resource file is to make that data type serializable. You can do this easily by marking the class with the `Serializable` attribute. Once it is marked as serializable, you can add the object to a resource file using an implementation of the IResourceWriter interface — for example, ResXResourceWriter:

VB
```
<Serializable()> _
Public Class Person
    Public Property Name As String
    Public Property Height As Integer
    Public Property Weight As Double
End Class
Dim p As New Person
p.Name = "Bob"
p.Height = 167
p.Weight = 69.5
Dim rWriter As New ResXResourceWriter("foo.resx")
rWriter.AddResource("DefaultPerson", p)
rWriter.Close()
```

C#

```
[Serializable()]
public class Person{
    public string Name { get; set; }
    public int Height { get; set; }
    public double Weight { get; set; }
}
var p = new Person(){
                Name = "Bob",
                Height = 167,
                Weight = 69.5};
var rWriter = new ResXResourceWriter("foo.resx");
rWriter.AddResource("DefaultPerson", p);
rWriter.Close();
```

However, serializing an object this way has a couple of drawbacks:

➤ You need to use code to write out this resource file before the build process so that the resource file can be included in the application. Clearly this is an administrative nightmare, because it is an additional stage in the build process.

➤ Furthermore, the serialized representation of the class is a binary blob and is not human-readable. The assumption here is that what is written in the generating code is correct. Unfortunately, this is seldom the case, and it would be easier if the content could be human-readable within Visual Studio 2010.

A workaround for both of these issues is to define a TypeConverter for the class and use that to represent the class as a string. This way, the resource can be edited within the Visual Studio resource editor. TypeConverters provide a mechanism through which the framework can determine whether it is possible to represent a class (in this case a Person class) as a different type (in this case as a string). The first step is to create a TypeConverter using the ExpandableObjectConverter, as follows:

VB

```
Imports System.ComponentModel
Imports System.ComponentModel.Design.Serialization
Imports System.Globalization

Public Class PersonConverter
    Inherits ExpandableObjectConverter

    Public Overrides Function CanConvertFrom(ByVal context As _
                                              ITypeDescriptorContext, _
                                              ByVal t As Type) As Boolean
        If t Is GetType(String) Then Return True
        Return MyBase.CanConvertFrom(context, t)
    End Function
    Public Overrides Function ConvertFrom( _
                                ByVal context As ITypeDescriptorContext, _
                                ByVal info As CultureInfo, _
                                ByVal value As Object) As Object
        If (TypeOf (value) Is String) Then
```

```vbnet
        Try
            If value Is Nothing Then Return New Person()
            Dim vals = CStr(value).Split(",""c)
            If vals.Length <> 3 Then Return New Person()
            Return New Person With {.Name = vals(0), _
                                    .Height = Integer.Parse(vals(1)), _
                                    .Weight = Double.Parse(vals(2))}
        Catch
            Throw New ArgumentException("Can not convert '" & _
                                        value.ToString & _
                                        "' to type Person")
        End Try
    End If
    Return MyBase.ConvertFrom(context, info, value)
End Function
Public Overrides Function ConvertTo(ByVal context As ITypeDescriptorContext, _
                                    ByVal culture As CultureInfo, _
                                    ByVal value As Object, _
                                    ByVal destType As Type) As Object
    If (destType Is GetType(String) And TypeOf (value) Is Person) Then
        Dim c = TryCast(value, Person)
        Return c.Name & "," & c.Height.ToString & "," & c.Weight.ToString
    End If
    Return MyBase.ConvertTo(context, culture, value, destType)
End Function
End Class
```

C#

```csharp
public class PersonConverter : ExpandableObjectConverter{
    public override bool CanConvertFrom(ITypeDescriptorContext context,
                                        Type t){
        if (typeof(string) == t) return true;
        return base.CanConvertFrom(context, t);
    }

    public override object ConvertFrom(ITypeDescriptorContext context,
                                       CultureInfo culture, object value){
        if (value is string){
            try{
                if (value == null) return new Person();
                var vals = (value as string).Split(',');
                if (vals.Length != 3) return new Person();
                return new Person{
                        Name = vals[0],
                        Height = int.Parse(vals[1]),
                        Weight = double.Parse(vals[2])
                    };
            }
            catch (Exception){
                throw new ArgumentException("Can not convert '" +
                                        value.ToString() + "' to type Person");
            }
        }
}
```

```
        return null;
    }

    public override object ConvertTo(ITypeDescriptorContext context,
                          CultureInfo culture, object value, Type destType){
        if (typeof(string) == destType && value is Person){
            var c = value as Person;
            return c.Name + "," + c.Height.ToString() + "," + c.Weight.ToString();
        }
        return base.ConvertTo(context, culture, value, destType);
    }
}
```

The class being represented also needs to be attributed with the `TypeConverter` attribute:

VB
```
<System.ComponentModel.TypeConverter(GetType(PersonConverter))> _
<Serializable()> _
Public Class Person
    Public Property Name As String
    Public Property Height As Integer
    Public Property Weight As Double
End Class
```

C#
```
[System.ComponentModel.TypeConverter(typeof(PersonConverter))]
[Serializable()]
public class Person{
    public string Name { get; set; }
    public int Height { get; set; }
    public double Weight { get; set; }
}
```

Now you can add this item to a resource file using the string representation of the class. For example, an entry in the resx file might look like this:

```
<assembly alias="CustomResourceType" name="CustomResourceType, Version=1.0.0.0,
Culture=neutral, PublicKeyToken=null" />
<data name="Manager" type="CustomResourceType.Person, CustomResourceType">
<value>Joe,175,69.5</value>
</data>
```

> *Creating custom resource types is a difficult process, because Visual Studio 2010 doesn't refresh your `TypeConverter` after it has been loaded the first time. You can either strongly name the assembly in which the `TypeConverter` is located and increment the version number each time you change it, or you will have to restart Visual Studio in order for the changes to take effect.*

SUMMARY

This chapter demonstrated how important XML resource files are in building an application that can both access static data and be readily localized into foreign languages and cultures. The rich user interface provided by Visual Studio 2010 enables you to easily add resources such as images, icons, strings, audio files, and other files to an application.

The built-in support for localizing forms and generating satellite assemblies empowers developers to write applications that can target a global market. You have also seen that the user interface provided within Visual Studio 2010 is extensible, meaning that you can modify it to interact with your own custom resource types.

PART IX
Debugging

▶ **CHAPTER 39:** Using the Debugging Windows

▶ **CHAPTER 40:** Debugging with Breakpoints

▶ **CHAPTER 41:** DataTips, Debug Proxies, and Visualizers

▶ **CHAPTER 42:** Debugging Web Applications

▶ **CHAPTER 43:** Advanced Debugging Techniques

39
Using the Debugging Windows

WHAT'S IN THIS CHAPTER?

➤ Learning basic debugging concepts in Visual Studio, including breakpoints and DataTips

➤ Understanding the debugging windows in Visual Studio

➤ Using and unwinding exceptions during a debug session

Debugging an application is one of the more challenging tasks developers have to tackle, but correct use of the Visual Studio 2010 debugging windows will help you analyze the state of the application and determine the cause of any bugs. This chapter examines the numerous windows available in Visual Studio 2010 to support you in building and debugging applications.

THE CODE WINDOW

The most important window for debugging purposes is the code window. With the capability to set breakpoints and step through code, this window is the starting point for almost all debugging activities. Figure 39-1 shows a simple snippet of code with both a breakpoint and the current execution point visible.

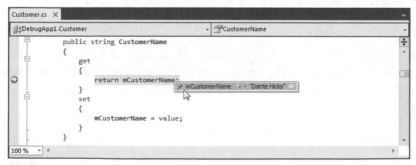

FIGURE 39-1

Breakpoints

The first stage in debugging an application is usually to identify the area that is causing the error by setting a breakpoint and gradually stepping through the code. Setting breakpoints and working with the current execution point are covered in more detail in the next chapter. Although you can't see the color in Figure 39-1, breakpoints are marked in the code window with a red dot in the margin of the page and red highlighting of the code itself.

When a breakpoint is encountered, the current execution point is marked with a yellow arrow in the margin and the actual code is also highlighted in yellow. As discussed in the next chapter, this marker can be dragged forward and backward to control the order of execution. However, this should be done sparingly because it modifies the behavior of the application.

DataTips

After hitting a breakpoint, the application is paused, or is in *Break mode*. In this mode, you can retrieve information about current variables simply by hovering your mouse over the variable name. Figure 39-1 shows that the value of the `mCustomerName` variable is currently "Dante Hicks." This debugging tooltip is commonly referred to as a *DataTip*, and can be used to view not only the values of simple types, such as strings and integers, but also to drill down and inspect more complex object types, such as those made up of multiple nested classes.

> *DataTips are used to both query and edit the value of a variable.*

In Chapter 41 you learn how the layout of this DataTip can be customized using type proxies and type visualizers.

THE BREAKPOINTS WINDOW

When debugging a complex issue, it is possible to set numerous breakpoints to isolate the problem. Unfortunately, this has two side effects. One, the execution of the application is hampered, because you have to continually press F5 to resume execution. Two, and more significantly, the execution of the application is slowed considerably by the presence of *conditional breakpoints*, which enable you to specify an expression that is executed to determine if the application should be paused. The more complex the breakpoint conditions are, the slower the application will run. Because these breakpoints can be scattered through multiple source files, it becomes difficult to locate and remove breakpoints that are no longer required.

The Breakpoints window, shown in Figure 39-2, is accessible via Debug ➪ Windows ➪ Breakpoints and provides a useful summary of all the breakpoints currently set within the application. Using this window, breakpoints can easily be navigated to, disabled, and removed.

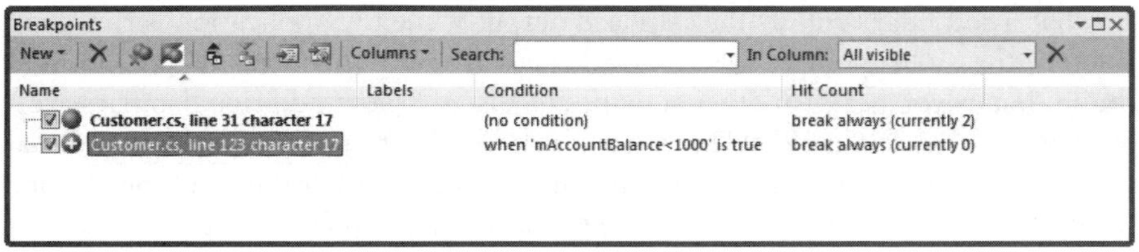

FIGURE 39-2

Figure 39-2 shows two currently active breakpoints in the `Customer.cs` file. The first is a regular breakpoint with no conditions. The second has a condition whereby the application will break only if the `mAccountBalance` variable has a value less than 1000. This condition is also in bold, because the application is currently in Break mode at that breakpoint.

The Breakpoints window, like most other debugging windows, is made up of two regions: the toolbar and the breakpoint list. Several new functions have been added to the toolbar in Visual Studio 2010, including search, and import and export of breakpoints. These functions are explained further in Chapter 40.

Each item in the breakpoint list is represented by a checkbox that indicates whether the breakpoint is enabled, an icon and breakpoint descriptor, and any number of columns that show properties of the breakpoint. The columns can be adjusted using the Columns drop-down from the toolbar. You can set additional breakpoint properties by right-clicking the appropriate breakpoint.

THE OUTPUT WINDOW

One of the first debugging windows you will encounter when you run your application for the first time is the Output window. By default, the Output window appears every time you build your application, and shows the build progress. Figure 39-3 shows the successful build of a sample solution. The final line of the Output window indicates a summary of the build, which in this case indicates three successfully built projects. In the output there is also a summary of the warnings and errors encountered during the build. In this case there were no errors, but there were three warnings. Although the Output window can be useful if for some reason the build fails unexpectedly, most of the time the errors and warnings are reported in the Error List.

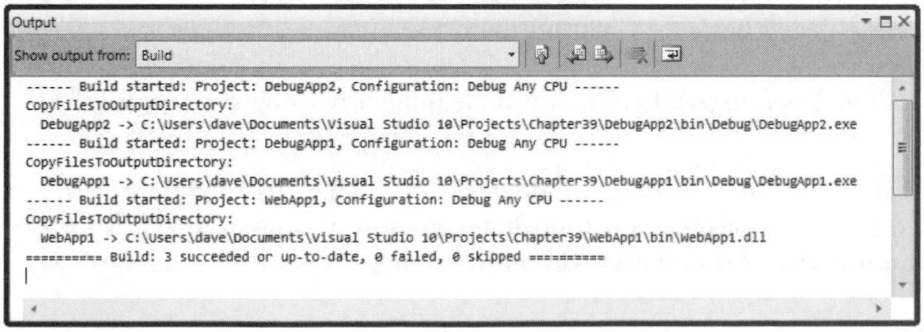

FIGURE 39-3

The Output window has a secondary role as the standard output while the application is running. The drop-down on the left of the toolbar can be used to toggle between output sources. Figure 39-3 shows the output of the build, but as you perform other activities in Visual Studio additional entries are created in the drop-down list. For example, when you run your application in Debug mode, Visual Studio creates an entry called Debug, which displays any messages that either the run time or your code has emitted using `Debug.Write` or `Debug.WriteLine`. Likewise, a Refactor entry is created to show the results of any recent refactoring operation that was performed.

> *The output from external tools such as `.bat` and `.com` files is normally displayed in the Command window. The output from these tools can also be displayed in the Output window by setting the Use Output Window option in the Tools ⇨ External Tools dialog box.*

The other icons on the toolbar, in order from left to right, enable you to navigate to the source of a build message, go to the previous message, go to the next message, clear the window contents, and toggle word wrapping for the Output window.

THE IMMEDIATE WINDOW

Quite often when you are writing code or debugging your application, you will want to evaluate a simple expression either to test a bit of functionality or to remind yourself of how something works. This is where the Immediate window (Debug ⇨ Windows ⇨ Immediate) comes in handy. This window enables you to run expressions as you type them. Figure 39-4 shows a number of statements — from basic assignment and print operations through to more advanced object creation and manipulation.

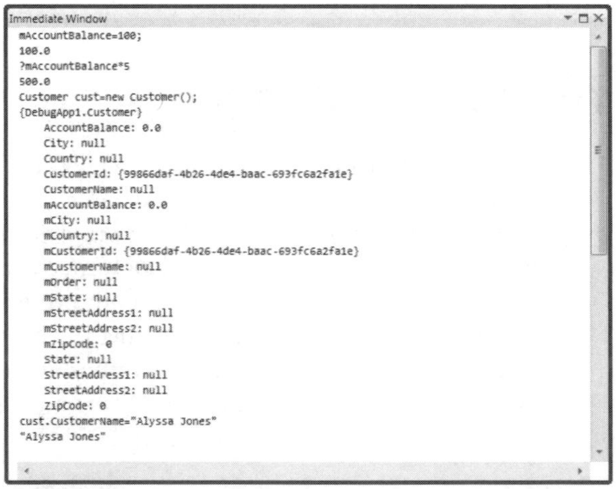

Figure 39-4 shows a new `Customer` object being created in a C# project within the Immediate window. Within a Visual Basic project you can't do explicit variable

```
Immediate Window
  mAccountBalance=100;
100.0
  ?mAccountBalance*5
500.0
  Customer cust=new Customer();
{DebugApp1.Customer}
    AccountBalance: 0.0
    City: null
    Country: null
    CustomerId: {99866daf-4b26-4de4-baac-693fc6a2fa1e}
    CustomerName: null
    mAccountBalance: 0.0
    mCity: null
    mCountry: null
    mCustomerId: {99866daf-4b26-4de4-baac-693fc6a2fa1e}
    mCustomerName: null
    mOrder: null
    mState: null
    mStreetAddress1: null
    mStreetAddress2: null
    mZipCode: 0
    State: null
    StreetAddress1: null
    StreetAddress2: null
    ZipCode: 0
  cust.CustomerName="Alyssa Jones"
"Alyssa Jones"
```

FIGURE 39-4

declaration (for example, Dim x as Integer). Instead it is done implicitly using the assignment operator.

One of the more useful features of the Immediate window is that it can be used while you are writing code. When you create new objects in the Immediate window at design time, it invokes the constructor and creates an instance of that object without running the rest of your application.

If you invoke a method or property that contains an active breakpoint, Visual Studio changes to Debug mode and breaks at the breakpoint. This is especially useful if you are working on a particular method that you want to test without running the entire application.

The Immediate window supports a limited form of IntelliSense, and you can use the arrow keys to track back through the history of previous commands executed.

> *IntelliSense is only supported in the Immediate window when running in Debug mode, not during design-time debugging.*

The Immediate window also enables you to execute Visual Studio commands. To submit a command, you must enter a greater than symbol (>) at the start of the line. There is an extremely large set of commands available; in fact, almost any action that can be performed within Visual Studio is accessible as a command. Fortunately, IntelliSense makes navigating this list of available commands a little more manageable.

There is also a set of almost 100 predefined aliases for commands. One of the more well-known aliases is "?", which is a shortcut for the `Debug.Print` command that prints out the value of a variable. You can see the full list of predefined aliases by entering >alias, as shown in Figure 39-5.

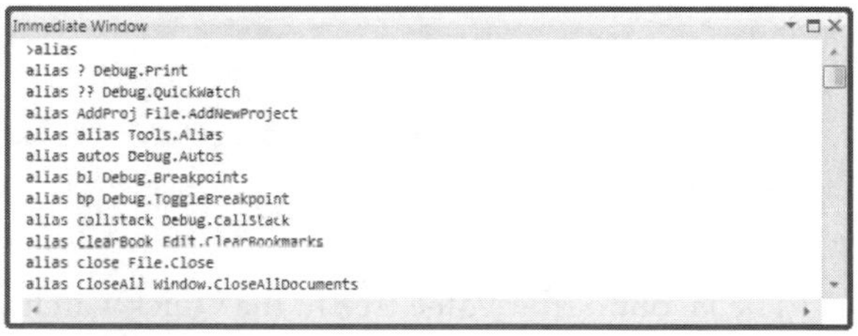

FIGURE 39-5

THE WATCH WINDOWS

Earlier in this chapter you saw how DataTips can be used in the code window to examine the content of a variable by hovering the mouse over a variable name. When the structure of the object is more complex it becomes difficult to navigate the values using just the DataTip. Visual Studio 2010 has a series of Watch windows that can be used to display variables, providing an easy-to-use interface for drilling down into the structure.

QuickWatch

The QuickWatch window (Debug ⇨ QuickWatch) is a modal dialog that can be launched by right-clicking the code window. Whatever you have selected in the code window is inserted into the Expression field of the dialog, as shown in Figure 39-6 where a `Customer` object is visible. Previous expressions you have evaluated appear in the drop-down associated with the Expression field.

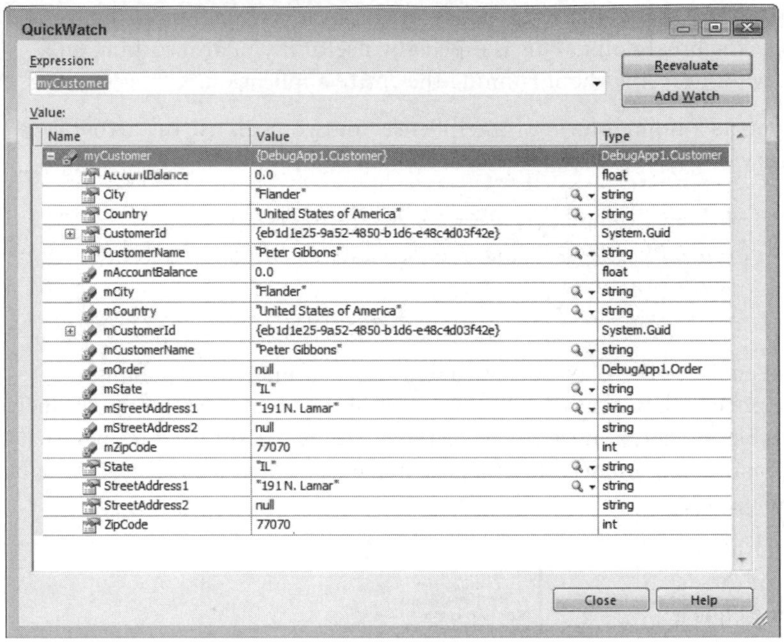

FIGURE 39-6

The layout of the Value tree in the QuickWatch window is similar to the DataTip. Each row shows the variable name, the current value, and the type of object. The value of the variable can be adjusted by typing in the Value column.

Use the Add Watch button to add the current expression to one of the Watch windows. These are variables to be continuously watched.

Watch Windows 1–4

Unlike the QuickWatch window, which is modal and shows a variable value at a particular execution point, the Watch windows can be used to monitor a variable value as you step through your code. Although there are four Watch windows, a single window is sufficient in most cases. Having four separate windows means that you can have different sets of variables in the different windows, which might be useful if you are working through a more complex issue that involves multiple classes.

Figure 39-7 shows an `Order` and `Customer` class in a Watch window (Debug ➪ Windows ➪ Watch 1 to Watch 4). Similar to both the QuickWatch window and the DataTips discussed previously, the user interface can be used to drill down into more complex data types.

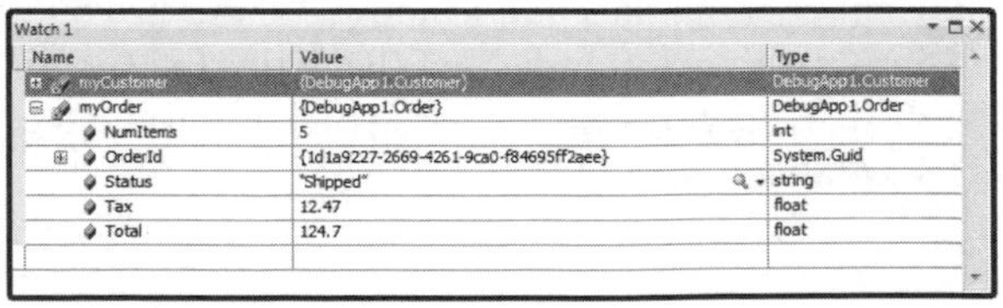

FIGURE 39-7

Additional variables to be watched can be added either by typing into the Name column on an empty line or by right-clicking the variable in the code window and selecting Add Watch from the context menu.

Autos and Locals

The Autos and Locals windows are two special Watch windows in which the variables are automatically added by the debugger. The Autos window (Debug ⇨ Windows ⇨ Autos) contains variables that are used in the current, preceding, and future lines of code. Similarly, the Locals window (Debug ⇨ Windows ⇨ Locals) shows all variables used in the current method. Other than being automatically generated, these windows behave the same as the Watch windows.

THE CODE EXECUTION WINDOWS

In addition to inspecting the contents of variables during a debugging session, it is essential that you carefully evaluate the logic of your code to ensure that everything is executed in the order that you expect. Visual Studio 2010 has a group of debugger windows that show exactly what was loaded and being executed at the time you paused the program execution. This allows you to better understand the runtime behavior of your source code and quickly track down logic errors.

Call Stack

As applications grow in complexity, it is quite common for the execution path to become difficult to follow. The use of deep inheritance trees and interfaces can often obscure the execution path. This is where the call stack is useful. Each path of execution must have a finite number of entries on the stack (unless a cyclic pattern emerges, in which case a stack overflow is inevitable). The stack can be viewed using the Call Stack window (Debug ⇨ Windows ⇨ Call Stack), shown in Figure 39-8.

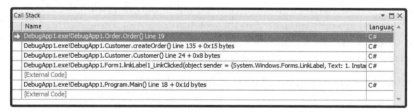

FIGURE 39-8

Using the Call Stack window, it is easy to navigate up the execution path to determine from where the current executing method is being called. You can do this by clicking any of the rows in the call stack, known as a *stack frame*. Other options available from the call stack, using the right-click context menu, enable viewing the disassembler for a particular stack frame, setting breakpoints, and varying what information is displayed.

Threads

Most applications make use of multiple threads at some point. In particular for Windows applications, in order for the user interface to always appear responsive, it is important to run time-consuming tasks on a thread separate from the main application. Of course, concurrent execution of threads makes debugging more difficult, especially when the threads are accessing the same classes and methods.

Figure 39-9 shows the Threads window (Debug ➪ Windows ➪ Threads), which lists all the active threads for a particular application. Notice that in addition to the threads created in the code, additional background threads have been created by the debugger. For simplicity, the threads used by this application, including the main user interface thread, have been given names so they can easily be distinguished.

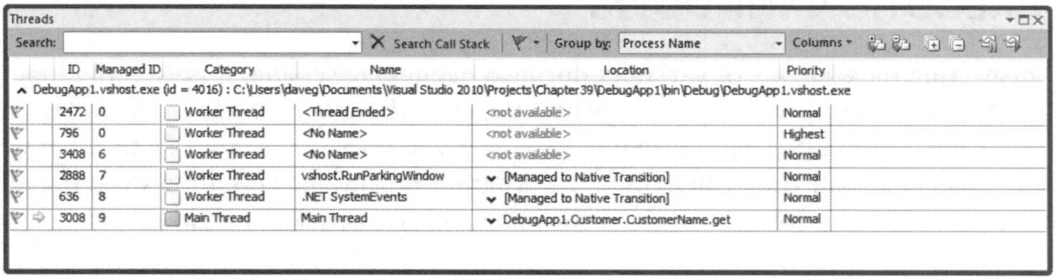

FIGURE 39-9

The Threads window shows a yellow arrow next to the thread that is currently being viewed in the code window. To navigate to another thread, simply double-click that thread to bring the current location of that thread into view in the code window and update the call stack to reflect the new thread.

In Break mode, all threads of an application are paused. However, when you are stepping through your code with the debugger, the next statement to be executed may or may not be on the same thread you are interested in. If you are only interested in the execution path of a single thread, and the execution of other threads can be suspended, right-click the thread in the Threads window and select Freeze from the context menu. To resume the suspended thread, select Thaw from the same menu.

Debugging multi-threaded applications is explained further in Chapter 43.

Modules

The Modules window (Debug ➪ Windows ➪ Modules), shown in Figure 39-10, displays a list of assemblies that are referenced by the running application. Those assemblies that make up the application will also have debugging symbols loaded, which means that they can be debugged without dropping into the disassembler. This window is particularly useful if you want to find out what version of an assembly is currently loaded and where it has been loaded from.

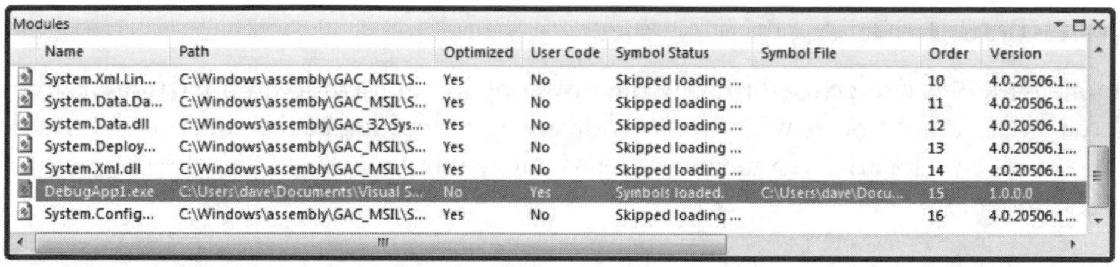

FIGURE 39-10

In Figure 39-10 the symbols have been loaded for the DebugApp1.exe application. All the other assemblies have been skipped, because they contain no user code and are optimized. If an appropriate symbol file is available, it is possible to load it for an assembly via the Load Symbols option from the right-click context menu.

Processes

Building multi-tier applications can be quite complex, and it is often necessary to have all the tiers running. To do this, Visual Studio 2010 can start multiple projects at the same stage, enabling true end-to-end debugging. Alternatively, you can attach to other processes to debug running applications. Each time Visual Studio attaches to a process, that process is added to the list in the Processes window (Debug ⇨ Windows ⇨ Processes). Figure 39-11 shows a solution containing two Windows applications and a web application.

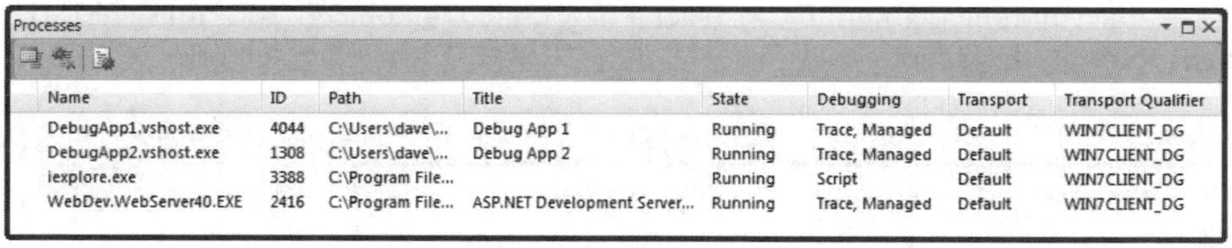

FIGURE 39-11

The toolbar at the top of the Processes window enables you to detach or terminate a process that is currently attached, or attach to another process.

THE MEMORY WINDOWS

The next three windows are typically used for low-level debugging when all other alternatives have been exhausted. Stepping into memory locations, using a disassembler, or looking at registry values requires a lot of background knowledge and patience to analyze and make use of the information that is presented. Only in very rare cases while developing managed code would you be required to perform debugging at such a low level.

Memory Windows 1–4

The four Memory windows can be used to view the raw contents of memory at a particular address. Where the Watch, Autos, and Locals windows provide a way of looking at the content of variables, which are stored at specific locations in memory, the Memory window shows you the big picture of what is stored in memory.

Each of the four Memory windows (Debug ➪ Windows ➪ Memory 1 to Memory 4) can examine different memory addresses to simplify debugging your application. Figure 39-12 shows an example of the information that can be seen using this window. The scrollbar on the right of

FIGURE 39-12

the window can be used to navigate forward or backward through the memory addresses to view information contained in neighboring addresses.

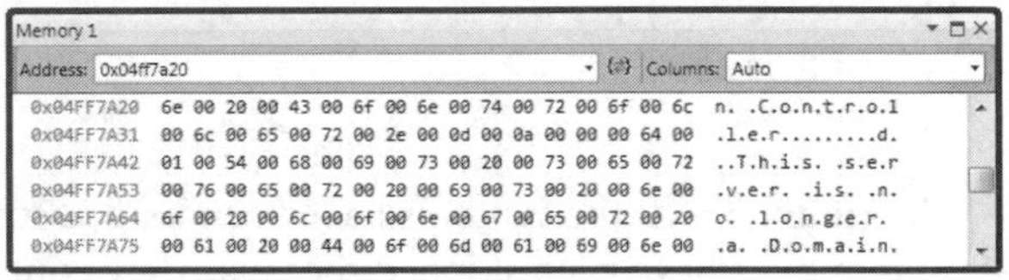

Disassembly

Interesting debates arise periodically over the relative performance of two different code blocks. Occasionally this discussion devolves to talking about which MSIL instructions are used, and why one code block is faster because it generates one fewer instruction. Clearly, if you are calling that code block millions of times, disassembly might give your application a significant benefit. However, more often than not, a bit of high-level refactoring saves much more time and involves much less arguing. Figure 39-13 shows the Disassembly window (Debug ➪ Windows ➪ Disassembly) for a LinkLabel click — the run time is about to construct a new `Customer` object. You can see MSIL instructions that make up this action.

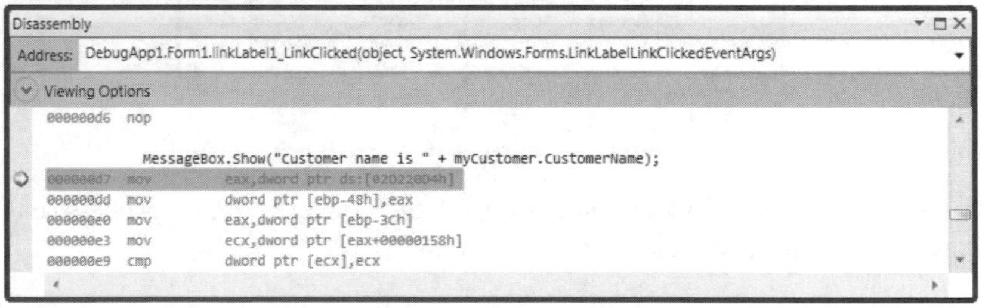

FIGURE 39-13

You can see from Figure 39-13 that a breakpoint has been set on the call to the constructor and that the execution point is at this breakpoint. While still in this window you can step through the lines of MSIL and review what instructions are being executed.

Registers

Using the Disassembly window to step through MSIL instructions can become very difficult to follow as different information is loaded, moved, and compared using a series of registers. The

Registers window (Debug ⇨ Windows ⇨ Registers), shown in Figure 39-14, enables the contents of the various registers to be monitored. Changes in a register value are highlighted in red, making it easy to see what happens as each line is stepped through in the Disassembly window.

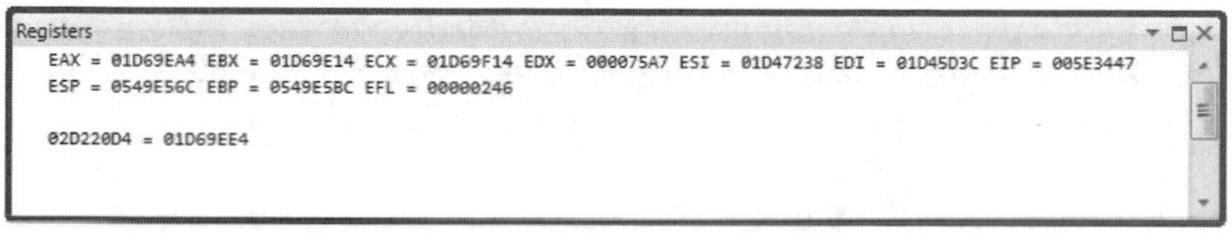

FIGURE 39-14

INTELLITRACE (ULTIMATE EDITION ONLY)

One of the more interesting new features in the Ultimate edition of Visual Studio is IntelliTrace. One of the limitations of traditional debuggers is that they only show a snapshot of the state of the application at a single point in time. The IntelliTrace feature of Visual Studio collects information during the debugging session, thereby allowing you to go back to an earlier point and view the application state at that time.

> *You can think of IntelliTrace as your very own black box flight recorder for debugging.*

IntelliTrace has two data collection levels. By default it collects information about diagnostic events only, such as entering Break mode, stepping through code in the debugger, or when an exception is thrown. You can also configure IntelliTrace to collect very detailed information, such as the details of every function call, including the parameters passed to that function and the values that were returned.

The IntelliTrace Events window (Debug ⇨ Windows ⇨ IntelliTrace Events) shown in Figure 39-15, enables you to navigate to past diagnostic events. When you click a past event, the execution point in the code window changes from a yellow arrow to a red arrow with a stopwatch icon. The call stack is also updated to reflect the historical state of the application.

If you have enabled the detailed data collection level, you will be able to use the Autos and Locals windows to inspect the contents of variables that have been collected.

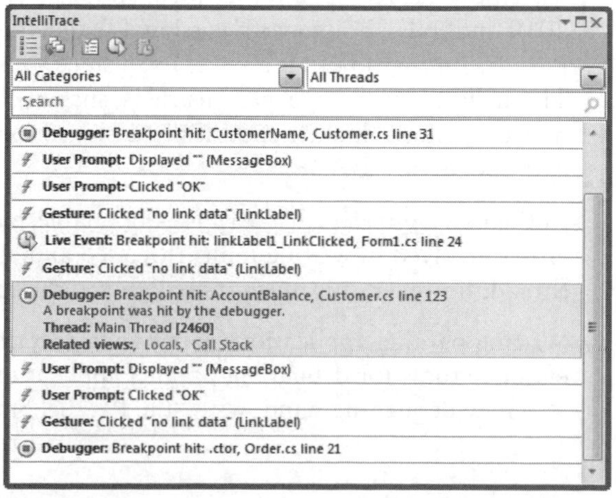

FIGURE 39-15

You can change the data collection level or disable it completely from the IntelliTrace tab in the options menu (Tools ➪ Options). You can also configure IntelliTrace to exclude certain assemblies from the data collection.

> You can expect a reasonable performance impact if you enable the detailed data collection level. You must also ensure that you have enough free disk space to collect this data. The Edit and Continue functionality is also disabled for the detailed level.

IntelliTrace can also debug logs created by the new Visual Studio software test tools, Test and Lab Manager. Chapter 55 provides more information on IntelliTrace.

THE PARALLEL DEBUGGING WINDOWS

Nowadays it is almost impossible to purchase a new computer that has a single processor. The trend to *many-core* CPUs, which has been necessary due to physical limitations that have been reached in CPU architecture, will certainly continue into the future as the primary way for hardware vendors to release faster computers.

Unfortunately, software that has not been written to explicitly run on multiple CPUs will not run faster on a many-core machine. This will be a problem for many users who have been conditioned over the past couple of decades to expect their applications to run faster when they upgrade to newer hardware.

The solution is to ensure that our applications can execute different code paths concurrently on multiple CPUs. The traditional approach is to develop software using multiple threads or processes. Unfortunately, writing and debugging multi-threaded applications is very difficult and error prone, even for an experienced developer.

Microsoft has recognized this issue, and has introduced a number of new features with Visual Studio 2010 and .NET Framework version 4.0 aimed to simplify the act of writing such software. The *Task Parallel Library* (TPL) is a set of extensions to the .NET Framework to provide this functionality. The TPL includes new language constructs, such as the `Parallel.For` and `Parallel.ForEach` loops, and new collections that are specifically designed for concurrent access including `ConcurrentDictionary` and `ConcurrentQueue`.

In the new `System.Threading.Tasks` namespace are several new classes that greatly simplify the effort involved in writing multi-threaded and asynchronous code. The `Task` class is very similar to a thread; however, it is much more lightweight and therefore performs much better at run time.

Writing parallel applications is only one part of the overall development life cycle — you also need effective tools for debugging parallel applications. To that end Visual Studio 2010 has introduced two new debugging windows — the Parallel Stacks window and the Parallel Tasks window.

Parallel Stacks

You will recall from earlier in the chapter, the Call Stacks window can be used to view the execution path of the current line of code when debugging. One of the limitations of this window is that you can see only a single call stack at a time. To see the call stack of other threads, you must use the Threads window or Debug Location toolbar to switch the debugger to a different thread.

The Parallel Stacks window (Debug ➪ Windows ➪ Parallel Stacks), shown in Figure 39-16, is one of the more useful windows for debugging multi-threaded and parallelized applications. It provides not just a way to view multiple call stacks at once, but also provides a graphical visualization of the code execution including showing how multiple threads are tied together and the execution paths that they share.

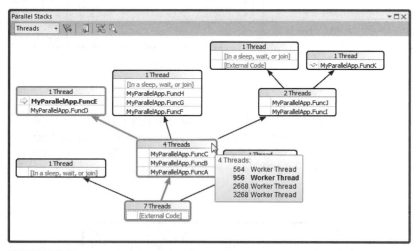

FIGURE 39-16

The Parallel Stacks window in Figure 39-16 shows an application that is currently executing seven threads. The call graph is read from bottom to top. The Main thread appears in one box, and four others threads are grouped together in another box. The reason these four threads are grouped is because they share the same call stack (that is, each thread called FuncA, which then called FuncB, which in turn called FuncC). After these threads executed FuncC, their code paths diverged. One thread executed FuncD, which then called FuncE. A different thread executed FuncF, FuncG, and then FuncH. The other two threads executed FuncI, which called FuncJ, and so on. You can see how visualizing all of the call stacks at once provides a much better understanding on the state of the application as a whole and what has led to this state, rather than just the history of an individual thread.

A number of other icons are used on this screen. The execution point of the current thread is shown with a yellow arrow. In Figure 39-16, this is against FuncE in a box on the left-hand side of the diagram. Each box that the current thread has progressed through as part of its execution path is highlighted in blue. The wavy lines (also known as the cloth thread icon) shown against the call to FuncK in the top-right box indicates that this is the current execution point of a non-current thread.

As shown in Figure 39-16, you can hover over the thread count label at the top of each box to see the Thread ID's of the applicable threads. You can also right-click any entry in a call stack to access various functions such as navigating to the applicable line of source code in the code editor or switching the visualization to a different thread.

If you are working with an application that uses numerous threads or tasks, or has a very deep call stack, you may find that the Parallel Stacks call graph visualization does not fit in the one window. In this case you can click the icon in the bottom-right corner of the window to display a thumbnail view, which enables you to easily pan around the visualization. You can see this in Figure 39-17.

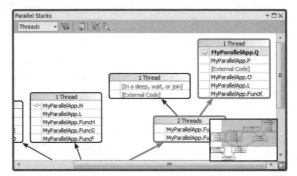

FIGURE 39-17

Parallel Tasks

At the beginning of this section of the chapter we explained the new Task Parallel Library in .NET version 4.0, which includes the Task class found in System.Threading.Tasks and the new Parallel.For loops. The Parallel Tasks window (Debug ➪ Windows ➪ Parallel Tasks), shown in Figure 39-18, assists you in debugging applications that use these new features by displaying a list with the state of all the current tasks.

	ID	Status	Location	Task	Thread Assignment	AppDomain
➡	1	▶ Running	MyParallelApp.FuncE	FuncA(1)	3720 (Worker Thread)	1 (MultiThreadedApp.vshost.exe)
⛿	2	▶ Running	MyParallelApp.FuncH	FuncA(2)	3132 (Worker Thread)	1 (MultiThreadedApp.vshost.exe)
⛿	3	⏳ Waiting	MyParallelApp.FuncJ	FuncA(3)	1268 (Worker Thread)	1 (MultiThreadedApp.vshost.exe)
⛿	4	⏳ Waiting	MyParallelApp.FuncK	FuncA(4)	3164 (Worker Thread)	1 (MultiThreadedApp.vshost.exe)

FIGURE 39-18

The application that has been paused in Figure 39-18 has created four tasks, two of which are running and two of which are in a waiting state. You can click the flag icon to flag one or more tasks for easier tracking.

> Parallel.For, Parallel.ForEach, *and the Parallel LINQ library (PLINQ)*
> *use the* System.Threading.Tasks.Task *class as part of their underlying*
> *implementation.*

EXCEPTIONS

Visual Studio 2010 has a sophisticated exception handler that provides you with a lot of useful information. Figure 39-19 shows the Exception Assistant dialog that appears when an exception is raised. In addition to providing more information, it also displays a series of actions. The Actions list varies depending on the type of exception being thrown. In this case, the two options are to view details of the exception or copy it to the clipboard.

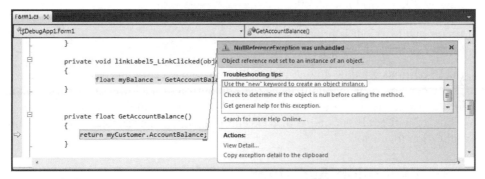

FIGURE 39-19

If you select the View Detail action item from the exception, you are presented with a modal dialog that provides a breakdown of the exception that was raised. Figure 39-20 shows the attributes of the exception, including the Stack Trace, which can be viewed in full by clicking the down arrow to the right of the screen.

Of course, at times exceptions are used to control the execution path in an application. For example, some user input may not adhere to a particular formatting constraint, and instead of using a Regular Expression to determine whether it matches, a parse

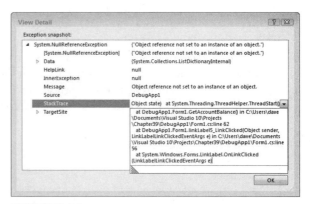

FIGURE 39-20

operation has been attempted on the string. When this fails, it raises an exception, which can easily be trapped without stopping the entire application.

By default, all exceptions are trapped by the debugger, because they are assumed to be exceptions to the norm that shouldn't have happened. In special cases, such as invalid user input, it may be important to ignore specific types of exceptions. This can be done via the Exceptions window, accessible from the Debug menu.

Figure 39-21 shows the Exceptions window (Debug ➪ Exceptions), which lists all the exception types that exist in the .NET Framework. Each exception has two debugging options. The debugger can be set to break when an exception is thrown, regardless of whether it is handled. If the Just My Code option has been enabled, checking the User-unhandled box causes the debugger to break for any exception that is not handled within a user code region. More information on Just My Code is provided in Chapter 41, which examines debugging attributes.

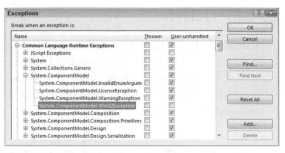

FIGURE 39-21

Unfortunately, the Exceptions window doesn't pick up any custom exception types that you may have created, but you can add them manually using the Add button in the lower-right corner of the window. You need to ensure that you provide the full class name, including the namespace; otherwise, the debugger will not break on handled exceptions. Clearly, unhandled exceptions will still cause the application to crash.

Customizing the Exception Assistant

As with a lot of the configurable parts within Visual Studio 2010, the information displayed by the Exception Assistant is stored in an XML file (C:\Program Files\Microsoft Visual Studio 10.0\Common7\IDE\ExceptionAssistantContent\1033\DefaultContent.xml). This file can be modified either to alter the assistant information for existing exception types or to add your own custom exception types. If you have your own exception types, it is better practice to create your own XML document. Simply placing it in the same directory as the DefaultContent.xml is sufficient to register it with Visual Studio for the next time your application is debugged. An example XML file is provided in the following code listing:

```xml
<?xml version="1.0" encoding="utf-8" ?>
<AssistantContent Version="1.0" xmlns="urn:schemas-microsoft-com:xml-msdata:
  exception-assistant-content">
  <ContentInfo>
    <ContentName>Additional Content</ContentName>
    <ContentID>urn:exception-content-microsoft-com:visual-studio-7-default-
    content</ContentID>
    <ContentFileVersion>1.0</ContentFileVersion>
    <ContentAuthor>David Gardner</ContentAuthor>
    <ContentComment>My Exception Assistant Content for Visual Studio
    </ContentComment>
  </ContentInfo>
  <Exception>
    <Type>DebugApp1.myException</Type>
    <Tip HelpID="http://www.professionalvisualstudio.com/MyExceptionHelp.htm">
      <Description>Silly error, you should know better...</Description>
    </Tip>
  </Exception>
</AssistantContent>
```

This example registers help information for the exception type `myException`. The `HelpID` attribute is used to provide a hyperlink for more information about the exception. When this exception is raised, the debugger displays the window shown in Figure 39-22.

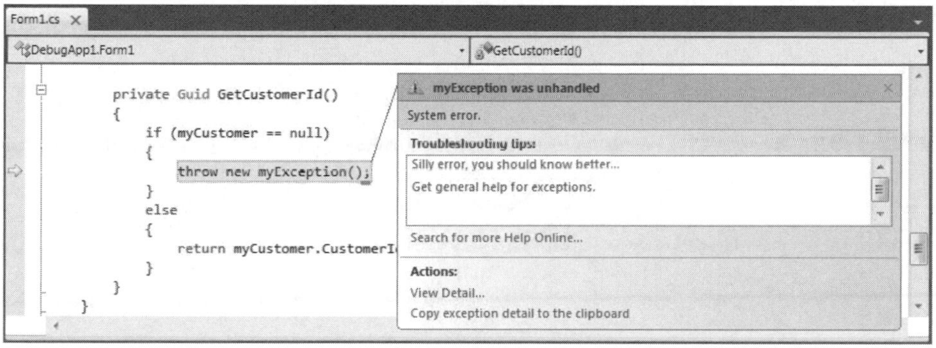

FIGURE 39-22

Unwinding an Exception

In Figure 39-23, there is an additional item in the Actions list of an exception helper window, which is to enable editing. This is effectively the capability to unwind the execution of the application to just before the exception was raised. In other words, you can effectively debug your application without having to restart your debugging session.

FIGURE 39-23

The Enable Editing option appears only if you have configured Visual Studio to break when an exception is thrown, as discussed earlier in this chapter. As with many of the debugging features, both the Exception Assistant and the capability to unwind exceptions can also be disabled via the Debugging tab of the Options window.

> *An alternative way to unwind the exception is to select the Unwind to This Frame item from the right-click context menu off the Call Stack window after an exception has been raised. This can be useful to check what the state of the application was just before the exception was thrown. You can only unwind an exception if it is handled (that is, contained within a try . . . catch block). You should also ensure that the debugger is set to break when the exception is thrown. You can do this via the Debug ⇨ Exceptions window.*

SUMMARY

This chapter has described each of the debugging windows in detail so you can optimize your debugging experience. Although the number of windows can seem somewhat overwhelming at first, they each perform an isolated task or provide access to a specific piece of information about the running application. As such, you will easily learn to navigate between them, returning to those that provide the most relevant information for you.

The following chapter provides more detail about how you can customize the debugging information. This includes changing the information displayed in the DataTip and visualizing more complex variable information.

40

Debugging with Breakpoints

WHAT'S IN THIS CHAPTER?

➤ Using breakpoints, conditional breakpoints, and tracepoints to pause code execution

➤ Controlling the program execution during debug by stepping through code

➤ Modifying your code while it is running using the Edit and Continue feature

Long gone are the days where debugging an application involved adding superfluous output statements to track down where an application was failing. Visual Studio 2010 provides a rich interactive debugging experience that includes breakpoints, tracepoints, and the Edit and Continue feature. This chapter covers how you can use these features to debug your application.

BREAKPOINTS

A *breakpoint* is used to pause, or break, an application at a particular point of execution. An application that has been paused is said to be in Break mode, causing a number of the Visual Studio 2010 windows to become active. For example, the Watch window can be used to view variable values. Figure 40-1 shows a breakpoint that has been added to the constructor of the Customer class. The application breaks on this line if the Customer class constructor is called.

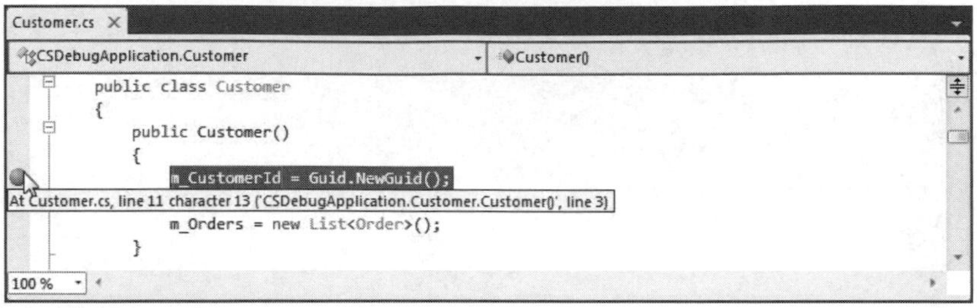

FIGURE 40-1

Setting a Breakpoint

Breakpoints can be set either through the Debug menu, using the Breakpoint item from the right-click context menu, or by using the keyboard shortcut, F9. The Visual Studio 2010 code editor also provides a shortcut for setting a breakpoint using a single mouse click in the margin.

An application can only be paused on a line of executing code. This means that a breakpoint set on either a comment or a variable declaration will be repositioned to the next line of executable code when the application is run.

Simple Breakpoints

A breakpoint can be set on a line of code by placing the cursor on that line and enabling a breakpoint using any of the following methods:

➤ Selecting Toggle Breakpoint from the Debug menu.

➤ Selecting Insert Breakpoint from the Breakpoint item on the right-click context menu.

➤ Pressing F9.

➤ Clicking once in the margin of the code window with the mouse. Figure 40-1 shows the location of the mouse cursor immediately after a breakpoint has been set using the mouse.

Selecting Location from the Breakpoint item on the right-click context menu for the line of code with the breakpoint set displays the File Breakpoint dialog, shown in Figure 40-2. Here you can see that the breakpoint is set at line 11 of the Customer.cs file. There is also a character number, which provides for the case in which multiple statements appear on a single line.

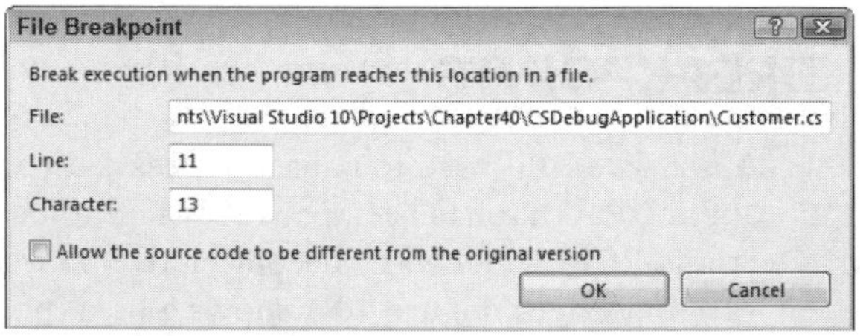

FIGURE 40-2

Function Breakpoints

Another type of breakpoint that can be set is a function breakpoint. The usual way to set a breakpoint on a function is to select the function signature and either press F9 or use the mouse to create a breakpoint. In the case of multiple overloads, this would require you to locate all the overloads and add the appropriate breakpoints. Setting a function breakpoint enables you to set a breakpoint on one or more functions by specifying the function name.

To set a function breakpoint, select Break at Function from the New Breakpoint item on the Debug menu. This loads the New Breakpoint dialog shown in Figure 40-3, in which you can specify the name of the function on which to break. There is a toggle to enable IntelliSense checking for the function name. The recommendation is to leave this checked, because it becomes almost impossible to set a valid breakpoint without this support.

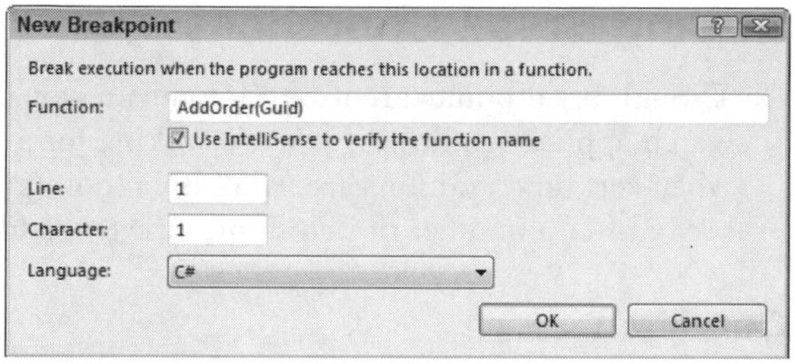

FIGURE 40-3

Unfortunately, the IntelliSense option doesn't give you true IntelliSense as you type, unlike other debugging windows. However, if you select the name of the function in the code window before creating the breakpoint, the name of the function is automatically inserted into the dialog.

When setting a function breakpoint, you can specify either the exact overload you want to set the breakpoint on or just the function name. In Figure 40-3, the overload with a single Guid parameter has been selected. Notice that unlike a full method signature, which requires a parameter name, to select a particular function overload, you should provide only the parameter type. If you omit the parameter information, and there are multiple overloads, you are prompted to select the overloads on which to place the breakpoint, as illustrated in Figure 40-4.

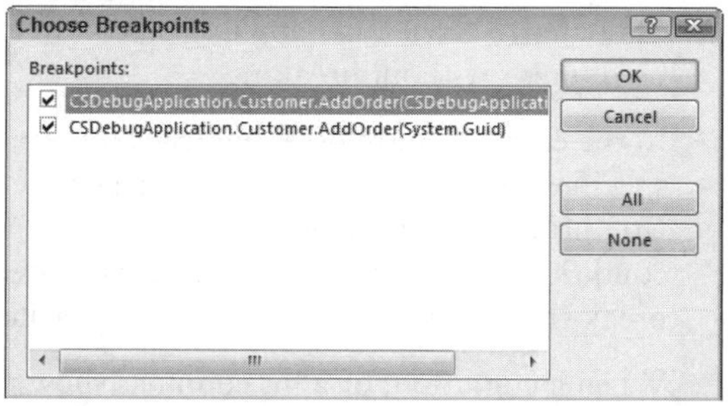

FIGURE 40-4

Address Breakpoint

Another way to set a breakpoint is via the Call Stack window. When the application is in Break mode, the call stack shows the current list of function calls. After selecting any line in the call stack, a breakpoint can be set in the same way as a file breakpoint, as described earlier (toggle Breakpoint from the Debug menu, use the F9 keyboard shortcut, or use Insert Breakpoint from the context menu). Figure 40-5 shows a short call stack with a new breakpoint set on a control event on Form1.

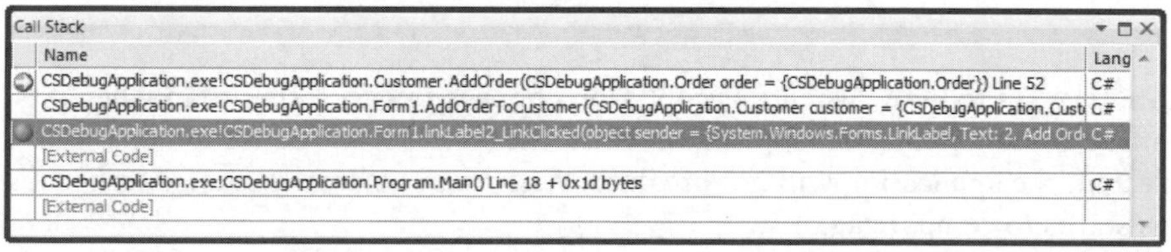

Call Stack	▾ □ ×
Name	Lang ▲
CSDebugApplication.exe!CSDebugApplication.Customer.AddOrder(CSDebugApplication.Order order = {CSDebugApplication.Order}) Line 52	C#
CSDebugApplication.exe!CSDebugApplication.Form1.AddOrderToCustomer(CSDebugApplication.Customer customer = {CSDebugApplication.Cust	C#
CSDebugApplication.exe!CSDebugApplication.Form1.linkLabel2_LinkClicked(object sender = {System.Windows.Forms.LinkLabel, Text: 2, Add Ord	C#
[External Code]	
CSDebugApplication.exe!CSDebugApplication.Program.Main() Line 18 + 0x1d bytes	C#
[External Code]	

FIGURE 40-5

The call stack is generated using function addresses. As such, the breakpoint that is set is an address breakpoint. This type of breakpoint is only useful within a single debugging session, because function addresses are likely to change when an application is modified and rebuilt.

Adding Break Conditions

Though breakpoints are useful for pausing an application at a given point to review variables and watch application flow, if you are looking for a particular scenario it may be necessary to break only when certain conditions are valid. Breakpoints can be tailored to search for particular conditions, to break after a number of iterations, or even be filtered based on process or machine name.

Condition

A breakpoint condition can be specified by selecting Condition from the Breakpoint item on the right-click context menu for the breakpoint. This brings up the Breakpoint Condition dialog shown in Figure 40-6, which accepts a Boolean expression that determines whether the breakpoint will be hit. If the expression evaluates to `false`, the application continues past the breakpoint without breaking.

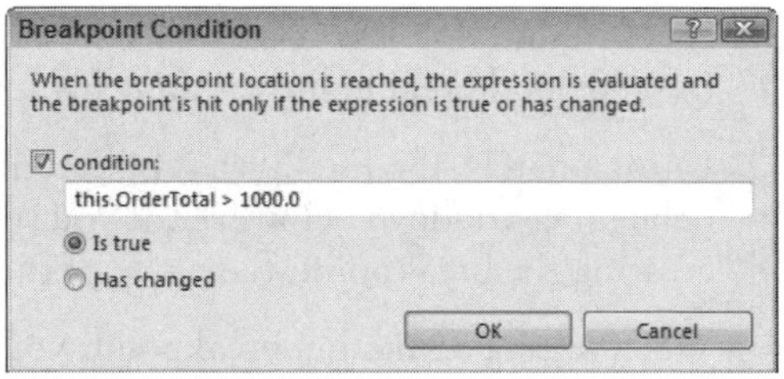

Breakpoint Condition

When the breakpoint location is reached, the expression is evaluated and the breakpoint is hit only if the expression is true or has changed.

☑ Condition:

    this.OrderTotal > 1000.0

◉ Is true
◯ Has changed

        OK   Cancel

FIGURE 40-6

In the case of Figure 40-6, which is for a breakpoint set within the `Order` class, the condition specifies that the order total must be greater than 1000. As with most debugging windows, the Condition field provides rich IntelliSense support to aid writing valid conditions. If an invalid condition is specified, the debugger throws an appropriate error message and the application will break the first time the breakpoint is reached.

When a condition, or a hit count, as shown in the next section, is placed on a breakpoint, the breakpoint changes appearance. The solid red dot is replaced with a red dot with a white cross. When you move your mouse across this dot, the tooltip provides useful information about the breakpoint condition, as illustrated in Figure 40-7.

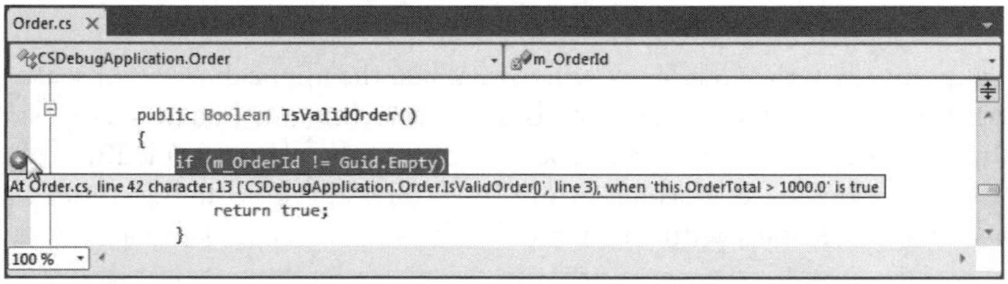

```
Order.cs ×
⚙ CSDebugApplication.Order                    ⚬ m_OrderId
⊟          public Boolean IsValidOrder()
           {
●              if (m_OrderId != Guid.Empty)
At Order.cs, line 42 character 13 ('CSDebugApplication.Order.IsValidOrder()', line 3), when 'this.OrderTotal > 1000.0' is true
               return true;
           }
100 %   ◂
```

FIGURE 40-7

Sometimes it is more relevant to know when this condition changes status, rather than when it is true. The Has Changed option breaks the application when the status of the condition changes. If this option is selected, the application will not break the first time the breakpoint is hit, because there is no previous status to compare against.

> *Using multiple breakpoints with complex conditions can significantly slow down the execution of your application, so it is recommended that you remove breakpoints that are no longer relevant in order to speed up the running of your application.*

Hit Count

Though it's perhaps not as useful as breakpoint conditions, it is also possible to break after a particular number of iterations through a breakpoint. To do this, select Hit Count from the Breakpoint item on the right-click context menu. Figure 40-8 shows the Breakpoint Hit Count dialog, which can be used to specify when the breakpoint should be hit.

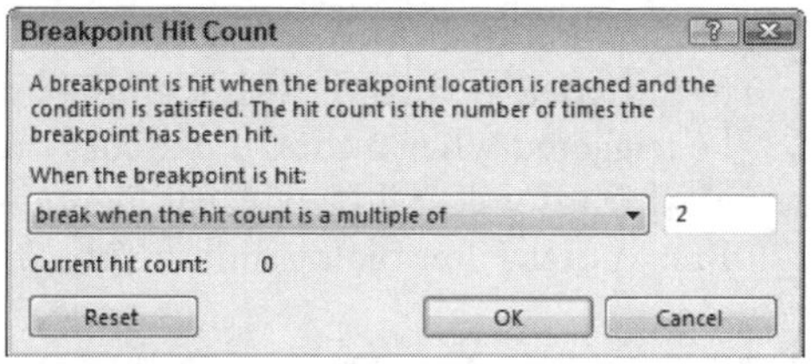

FIGURE 40-8

Every time the application is run, the hit count is reset to zero, and it can be manually reset using the Reset button. The hit count is also unique to each breakpoint. The hit count condition is one of four options:

➤ **Always:** Disregard the hit count.

➤ **Is equal to:** Break if the hit count is equal to the value specified.

➤ **Multiple of:** Break if the hit count is a multiple of the value specified (as shown in Figure 40-8).

➤ **Is greater than or equal to:** Break if the hit count is greater than or equal to the value specified.

Figure 40-9 shows the Breakpoints window, which provides additional information about the status of each of the breakpoints. In this case, the breakpoint is set to break every second time. The current hit count is 2.

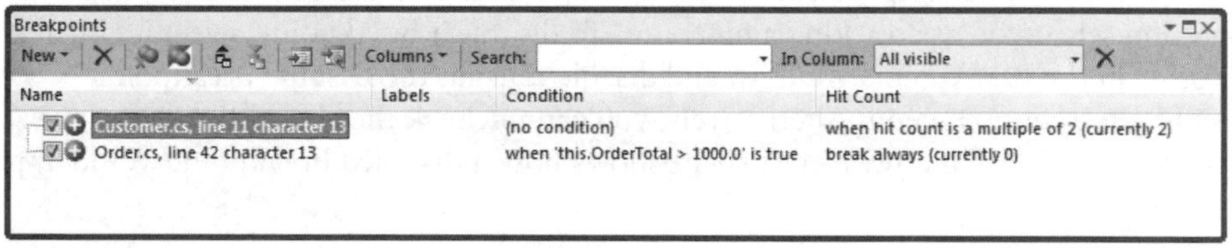

FIGURE 40-9

Filter

A single solution may contain multiple applications that need to be run at the same time. This is a common scenario when building a multi-tier application. When the application is run, the debugger can attach to all these processes, enabling them to be debugged. By default, when a breakpoint is reached all the processes will break. This behavior can be controlled from the Debugging (General) node in the Options window, accessible from the Options item on the Tools menu. Unchecking the Break All Processes When One Process Breaks checkbox enables processes to be debugged individually.

If a breakpoint is set in a class library that is used by more than one process, each process will break when it reaches that breakpoint. Because you might be interested in debugging only one of these processes, you can place a filter on the breakpoint that limits it to the process you are interested in. If you are debugging applications on multiple machines, it is also possible to specify a machine name filter.

In fact, filtering can be useful for a multi-threaded application for which you want to limit the breakpoints to a particular thread. Although the breakpoint will only be triggered when a thread matches the filter criteria, all threads will still be paused. Figure 40-10 shows the Breakpoint Filter dialog and the possible filter conditions.

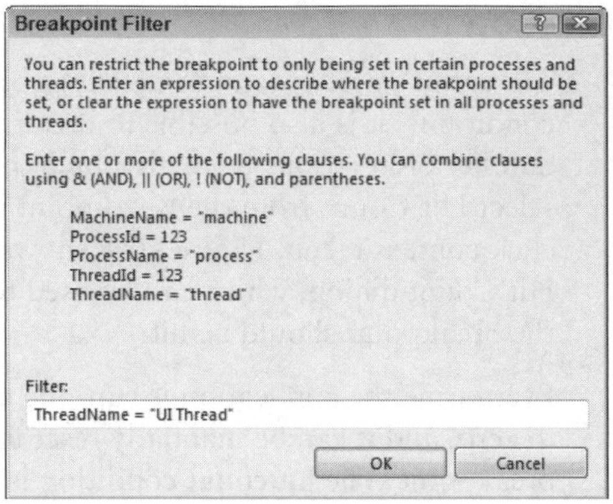

Working with Breakpoints

It's often necessary to adjust a breakpoint, because it might be in the wrong location or no longer relevant. In most cases it is easiest to remove the breakpoint, but in some cases — for example, when you have a complex breakpoint condition — it might be necessary to adjust the existing breakpoint.

Breakpoint Filter

You can restrict the breakpoint to only being set in certain processes and threads. Enter an expression to describe where the breakpoint should be set, or clear the expression to have the breakpoint set in all processes and threads.

Enter one or more of the following clauses. You can combine clauses using & (AND), || (OR), ! (NOT), and parentheses.

    MachineName = "machine"
    ProcessId = 123
    ProcessName = "process"
    ThreadId = 123
    ThreadName = "thread"

Filter:

    ThreadName = "UI Thread"

[OK] [Cancel]

FIGURE 40-10

Deleting Breakpoints

To remove a breakpoint that is no longer required, select it, either in the code editor or in the Breakpoints window, and remove it using the Toggle Breakpoint item from the Debug menu. Alternatively, the Delete Breakpoint item from the right-click context menu or the Delete Breakpoint icon from the Breakpoints window toolbar will remove the breakpoint.

Disabling Breakpoints

Instead of deleting a breakpoint, simply disabling the breakpoint can be useful when you have a breakpoint condition set or you are tracking a hit count. To disable a breakpoint, select it either in the code editor or in the Breakpoints window, and disable it using the Disable Breakpoint item from the right-click context menu. Alternatively, you can uncheck the checkbox against the breakpoint in the Breakpoints window. Figure 40-11 shows how a disabled breakpoint would appear in the code window.

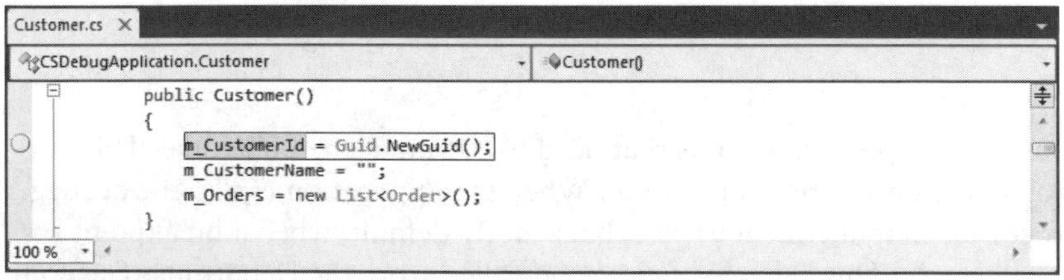

```
Customer.cs  X

CSDebugApplication.Customer                          Customer()

        public Customer()
        {
            m_CustomerId = Guid.NewGuid();
            m_CustomerName = "";
            m_Orders = new List<Order>();
        }
100 %
```

FIGURE 40-11

Changing Breakpoint Locations

The location of a breakpoint can be modified by selecting Location from the Breakpoint item on the right-click context menu. Depending on what type of breakpoint has been set, the dialog shows the location of the breakpoint as either a line and character position in a file or function, or as an address within an assembly. If the location is either a file or function position, the breakpoint can be adjusted so it is in the correct location. Address breakpoints are harder to relocate, because you need to ensure that the new address is a valid location for a breakpoint.

Labeling Breakpoints

One new feature introduced in Visual Studio 2010 is the ability to assign a label to a breakpoint. This is particularly useful if you want to group a set of related breakpoints together. Once labeled, you can search for and perform a bulk action on all breakpoints with a specific label.

To assign a label to a breakpoint, right-click the breakpoint and choose Edit Labels. This displays the Edit Breakpoint Labels dialog, shown in Figure 40-12, where you can attach one or more labels to the breakpoint.

FIGURE 40-12

After you have labeled your breakpoints you can perform bulk actions on them by opening the Breakpoints window (Debug ➪ Windows ➪ Breakpoints). This window, shown in Figure 40-13, allows you to filter the list by typing a label in the Search box and pressing Enter. You can then select one of the actions from the toolbar, such as Enable or Disable All Breakpoints Matching the Current Search Criteria.

> By default, the search will be performed across all columns that are shown in the Breakpoint window. You can limit the search to specific columns by changing the In Column drop-down from All Visible to a specific column.

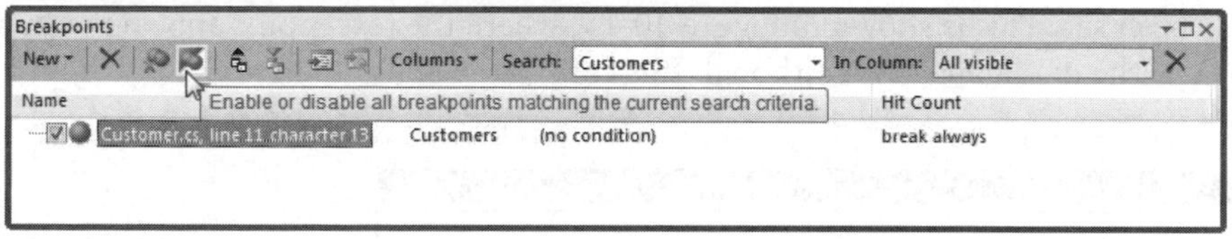

FIGURE 40-13

Import and Export of Breakpoints

Another new debugging feature in Visual Studio 2010 is the import and export of breakpoints. This feature allows you to back up and restore breakpoints, and share them among developers. This functionality was previously impossible, because the location of breakpoints is stored in the binary solution user options file (.suo), along with a whole raft of other user-specific information.

Export of breakpoints is performed from the Breakpoints window (Debug ➪ Windows ➪ Breakpoints). If you only want to export a subset of your breakpoints, first filter the list by entering a search criteria. Once the list of breakpoints that you want to export is shown, click the button labeled Export All Breakpoints Matching the Current Search Criteria from the toolbar.

Import of breakpoints can also be performed from the Breakpoints window by clicking the appropriate button on the toolbar.

TRACEPOINTS

A *tracepoint* differs from a breakpoint in that it triggers an additional action when it is hit. In fact, for purposes such as applying filters, conditions, and hit counts, a tracepoint can be thought of as a breakpoint.

Tracepoints can be compared to using either `Debug` or `Trace` statements in your code, but tracepoints can be dynamically set as the application is being debugged and will not affect your code.

Creating a Tracepoint

Tracepoints can be created from either an existing breakpoint or the Breakpoint right-click context menu. To create a tracepoint from an existing breakpoint, select When Hit from the Breakpoint right-click context menu. The resulting dialog, shown in Figure 40-14, gives you the option of printing a message to the console window or running a macro. Alternatively, to create a tracepoint at a new location, select Insert Tracepoint from the Breakpoint item on the right-click context menu. This again loads the dialog shown in Figure 40-14 so you can customize the tracepoint action.

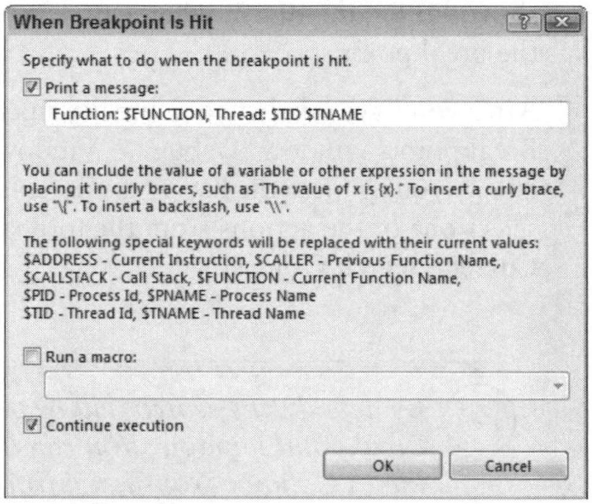

FIGURE 40-14

Once you set a tracepoint, the code window changes the appearance of that line of code to indicate that a tracepoint has been set. This is shown in Figure 40-15, where the tracepoint appears with a diamond in the margin (the diamond is red, although this can't be seen in the figure).

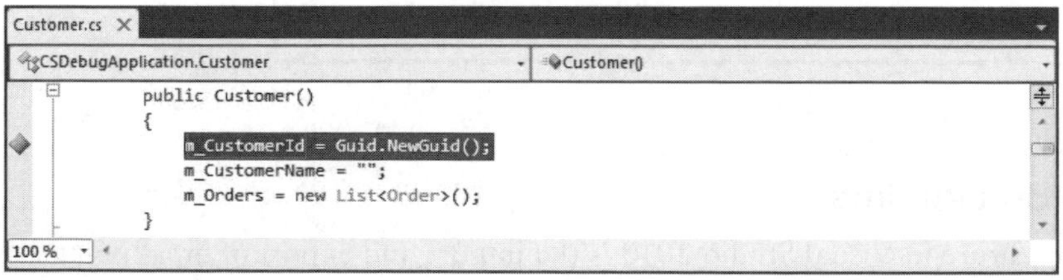

FIGURE 40-15

Tracepoint Actions

Two types of actions can be performed when a tracepoint is hit: either print a message to the console window or run a macro. In the dialog shown in Figure 40-14, you can indicate which action should be run when the tracepoint is hit. If both actions are unchecked, the tracepoint will fall back to being a breakpoint.

By default, once a tracepoint action has been indicated, the Continue Execution checkbox will be checked so the application will not break at this point. Unchecking this option causes the application to break at the tracepoint as if it were a breakpoint. The action defined will be performed prior to the application breaking. The appearance of this tracepoint will be the same as that of a breakpoint, because the visual cue indicates that the debugger will not stop at the tracepoint, rather than indicating that there are actions associated with the tracepoint.

Output Messages

As the dialog in Figure 40-14 suggests, a number of keywords can be used in conjunction with your trace message. However, a couple of keywords are not listed by the dialog: $FILEPOS, which gives the location of the current file, and $TICKS, which can be used as a relative time indicator.

Macros

Tracepoints can execute any Visual Studio macro, which includes macros you may have created. Because macros can be used to modify source code, be careful which macros you execute within a tracepoint. Modifying code while debugging an application may result in the source code being out of sync with the running application. Visual Studio macros are discussed in Chapter 52.

EXECUTION CONTROL

After reaching a breakpoint, it is often useful to be able to step through code and review both variable values and program execution. Visual Studio 2010 not only enables you to step through your code, it also permits you to adjust the execution point to backtrack or even repeat operations. The line of code that is about to be executed is highlighted and an arrow is displayed to the left, as shown in Figure 40-16.

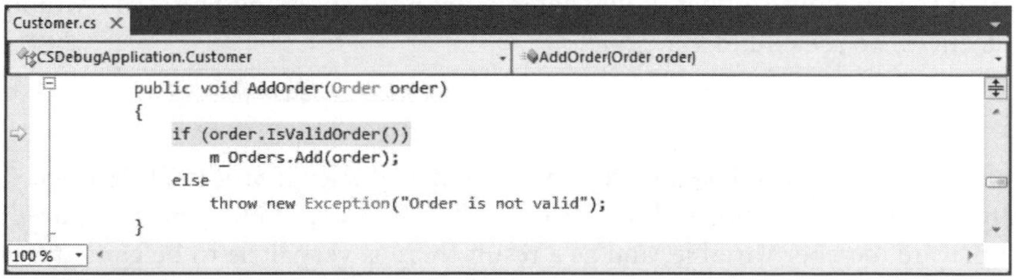

FIGURE 40-16

Stepping Through Code

The first step in manipulating the execution point is simply to step through code in the expected order of execution. Three size increments can be used to step the debugger forward. It is important to remember that when stepping through code it is actually being run, so variable values may change as you progress through the application.

Stepping Over (F10)

Stepping Over is fully executing the line that currently has focus and progressing to the next line in the current code block. If the end of the code block has been reached, Stepping Over returns to the calling code block.

Stepping Into (F11)

Stepping Into behaves the same as Stepping Over when the line is a simple operator, such as a numeric operation or a cast. When the line is more complex, Stepping Into steps through all user code. For example, in the following code snippet, pressing F10 through the TestMethod only steps through the lines of code within TestMethod. Pressing F11 steps through TestMethod until the MethodA call is made, and then the debugger steps through MethodA before returning to TestMethod:

C#

```
public void TestMethod()
{
    int x = 5 + 5;
    MethodA();
}

private void MethodA()
{
    Console.WriteLine("Method A being executed");
}
```

Stepping Out (Shift+F11)

If you step into a long method by accident, it is quite often convenient to be able to step back out of that method without having to either step over every line in that method or setting a breakpoint at the end of the method. Stepping Out moves the cursor out of the current method to where it was being called. Considering the previous snippet, if you entered MethodA, pressing Shift+F11 would immediately return the cursor to the end of TestMethod.

Step Filtering

One very welcome feature that was introduced with Service Pack 1 of Visual Studio 2008 is the ability to automatically step over properties and operators. In many cases, public properties are simply wrappers for a private member variable, and as a result there is very little to be gained from stepping into them while debugging. This debugger option is especially useful if you are calling a method that passes a number of properties as parameters, such as the method call listed here:

C#

```
printShippingLabel(cust.name, shipTo.street, shipTo.city, shipTo.state,
    shipTo.zipCode);
```

With the Step Over Properties and Operators option enabled, the debugger steps directly into the first line of the printShippingLabel method if you hit F11. If you need to, you can manually step into a specific property by right-clicking the code editor window and selecting Step Into Specific. This displays a submenu with each of the available properties listed, as shown in Figure 40-17.

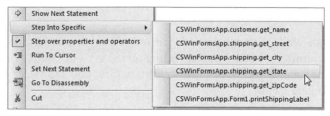

⇨	Show Next Statement	
	Step Into Specific ▶	CSWinFormsApp.customer.get_name
✓	Step over properties and operators	CSWinFormsApp.shipping.get_street
◆≣	Run To Cursor	CSWinFormsApp.shipping.get_city
⇨	Set Next Statement	CSWinFormsApp.shipping.get_state
⬚	Go To Disassembly	CSWinFormsApp.shipping.get_zipCode
✂	Cut	CSWinFormsApp.Form1.printShippingLabel

FIGURE 40-17

The Step Over Properties and Operators option is enabled by default. You can enable or disable it during debugging by right-clicking anywhere in the code editor window and selecting it from the context menu, or from the Options dialog window (Tools ➪ Options, then select Debugging from the treeview on the left-hand side).

Moving the Execution Point

As you become familiar with stepping in and out of functions, you will find that you are occasionally overzealous and accidentally step over the method call you are interested in. In this case, what you really want to do is go back and review the last action. Though you can't actually unwind the code and change the application back to its previous state, you can move the execution point so the method is reevaluated.

To move the current execution point, select and drag the yellow arrow next to the current line of execution (refer to Figure 40-16) forward or backward in the current method. Use this functionality with care, because it can result in unintended behavior and variable values.

EDIT AND CONTINUE

One of the most useful features of Visual Studio 2010 debugging is Edit and Continue. Both C# and Visual Basic have support for Edit and Continue, enabling you to make changes to your application on the fly. Whenever your application is paused, you can make changes to your code and then resume execution. The new or modified code is dynamically added to your application, with the changes taking immediate effect.

Rude Edits

At this point, you are likely wondering whether any limitations exist on the changes that you can make. The answer is yes, and there are quite a few types of *rude edits*, which refer to any code change that requires the application to be stopped and rebuilt. A full list of rude edits is available from the Visual Studio 2010 help resource under the Edit and Continue topic, but they include the following:

➤ Making changes to the current, or active, statement

➤ Changes to the list of global symbols — such as new types or methods — or changing the signatures of methods, events, or properties

➤ Changes to attributes

Stop Applying Changes

When changes are made to the source code while the application is paused, Visual Studio has to integrate, or apply, the changes into the running application. Depending on the type or complexity of the changes made, this could take some time. If you want to cancel this action, you can select Stop Applying Code Changes from the Debug menu.

SUMMARY

Most developers who use Visual Studio 2010 will use breakpoints to track down issues with their application. In this chapter, you learned how to optimize the use of breakpoints to reduce the amount of time spent locating the issue.

The following chapter examines data tips and explains how to create debugging proxy types and visualizers. This allows you to customize the debugging experience and reduce the time spent wading through unnecessary lines of code.

41

DataTips, Debug Proxies, and Visualizers

WHAT'S IN THIS CHAPTER?

➤ Inspecting the contents of your variables usingDataTips

➤ Applying attributes to your classes and member variables to customize the debugger behavior

➤ Creating type proxies and visualizers to represent complex variables and data types in a useful way within the debugger

Other than writing code, debugging is likely the most time-consuming activity when writing an application. If you consider all the time you spend stepping through code, looking at the Watch window to see the value of a variable, or even just running the application looking for any exceptions being raised, you will realize that this is one of the most time-consuming parts of writing software.

Previous chapters have focused on how you can use the various debugging windows to retrieve information about the current status of your application, and how you can set breakpoints and tracepoints to generate debugging information. This chapter goes beyond what is provided out of the box, and looks at how you can customize the debugging experience to reduce the time spent wading through unnecessary lines of code.

Using debugging proxy types and visualizers, you can represent complex variables and data types in a useful way within the debugger. This allows you to filter out unnecessary information and zero in on the most relevant properties of an object, thereby making it easier to determine when your application is not functioning correctly and be able to trace the source of the issue.

DATATIPS

You have many ways to inspect the value of variables within Visual Studio while debugging. For many types, the easiest way to inspect a variable is simply hover the mouse over it, which displays the value of

FIGURE 41-1

the variable in a *DataTip*. Figure 41-1 shows a DataTip for a string property.

In addition to viewing the value of the variable, you can right-click the DataTip and perform a number of actions. These include copying the value that is being displayed, adding the variable to the Watch window, or even editing the current value of the variable in the case of simple types such as strings or integers.

One new feature of Visual Studio 2010 is the introduction of pinned and floating DataTips. You can think of these as the electronic equivalents of Post-It notes for Visual Studio. To create a pinned DataTip, click the pin icon in the right-hand side of the DataTip. The DataTip will now stay pinned to that line of code in the source file of the code editor and will become visible anytime a debugging session is underway.

Figure 41-2 shows a Visual Studio workspace with two pinned DataTips for the variables `c.CustomerName` and `o1.Total`. A menu will appear when you hover over a pinned DataTip. Clicking the icon with double arrows will display a text input field below the DataTip where you can enter some text. You can also click the pin icon in the menu to covert the pinned DataTip to a floating DataTip. The DataTip for the `c` variable in Figure 41-2 is a floating DataTip.

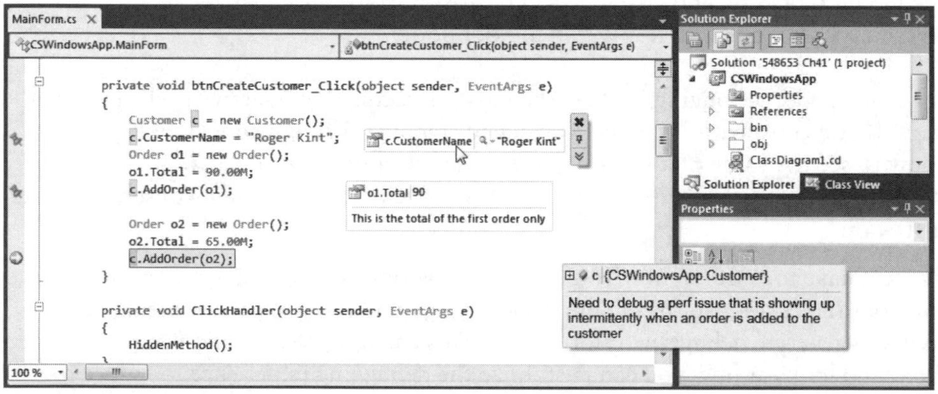

FIGURE 41-2

You can drag a pinned DataTip to any line of code in the source file to which it has been pinned, but not anywhere outside of the code editor window. Pinned DataTips will also disappear if you switch to a different source code file. Floating DataTips, on the other hand, are always visible during a debugging session and can be dragged to any location on your monitor.

A blue pin icon will appear in the margin of the code editor for each pinned DataTip. This icon will still be visible once the debug session has finished; you can hover the mouse over it and the DataTip will appear with the value during the last debug session.

You can close an individual pinned or floating DataTip by clicking the x icon, or close all of them by selecting Debug ⇨ Clear All DataTips from the menu. You will also see a menu option to clear all DataTips pinned to the current source file in the code editor if it contains any.

Finally, DataTips can be imported and exported to an external XML file, which can be useful for backup purposes, or sharing them among developers. This is done by selecting Import DataTips or Export DataTips from the Debug menu.

DEBUGGER ATTRIBUTES

This section outlines a number of debugging attributes that can be applied to code to affect the way the debugger steps through it. Some of the debugging attributes can also be used to customize the appearance of your types when you hover over them in Break mode.

> *The debugging attribute classes are contained within the* System.Diagnostics *namespace. Rather than specify the full namespace for each attribute, the source code examples in this chapter assume that it has been added as an import.*

DebuggerBrowsable

The first attribute you can apply to fields and properties is the DebuggerBrowsable attribute. In .NET Framework 2.0, this attribute was only interpreted by the C# debugger and had no effect when applied to Visual Basic code. This limitation has been removed in newer versions of the .NET Framework. The DebuggerBrowsable attribute takes a single parameter that determines how the member is displayed in the variable tree. In the following code snippet, the field Orders is set to Collapsed:

C#

```
public class Customer
{
    [DebuggerBrowsable(DebuggerBrowsableState.Collapsed)]
    public List<Order> Orders;
}
```

VB

```
Public Class Customer
    <DebuggerBrowsable(DebuggerBrowsableState.Collapsed)> _
    Public Orders As List(Of Order)
End Class
```

Figure 41-3 (left) shows the same snippet of code with DebuggerBrowsable initially set to Collapsed (or not specified). Figure 41-3 (center) shows the same snippet with DebuggerBrowsable set to the RootHidden value, where the actual Orders item does not appear, just the contents of the collection. Finally, in Figure 41-3 (right) the Never value is used for DebuggerBrowsable, in which case the Orders member does not appear at all.

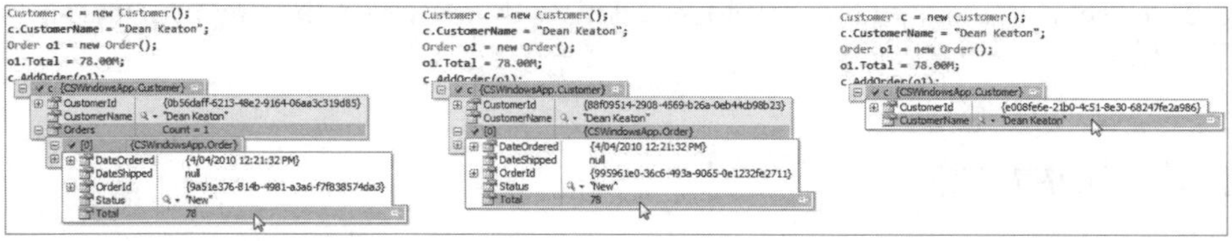

FIGURE 41-3

DebuggerDisplay

When you hover your mouse over a variable while you are in Break mode, the first thing you will see in the tooltip is the type of object you are hovering over. In Figure 41-3, a mouse was initially hovering over the Customer class, followed by the Order class. This information is not particularly useful, because most of the time you have a fairly good idea about the type of object you are dealing with. It would be better for this single line to contain more useful information about the object. This is the case for well-known types, such as strings and integers, where the actual value is displayed.

The DebuggerDisplay attribute can be used to change the single-line representation of the object from the default full class name. This attribute takes a single parameter, which is a string. The format of this string can accept member injections using the String.Format breakout syntax. For example, the attributes applied to the Customer and Order classes might be as follows:

C#

```
[DebuggerDisplay("Customer {CustomerName} has {Orders.Count} orders")]
public class Customer

[DebuggerDisplay("Order made on {DateOrdered} which is worth ${Total}")]
public class Order
```

VB

```
<DebuggerDisplay("Customer {CustomerName} has {Orders.Count} orders")> _
Public Class Customer

<DebuggerDisplay("Order made on {DateOrdered} which is worth ${Total}")> _
Public Class Order
```

This would give you the debugger output shown in Figure 41-4, which indicates that customer Michael McManus has one order, which, as you can see from the description, was made on April 4 and is worth $120.

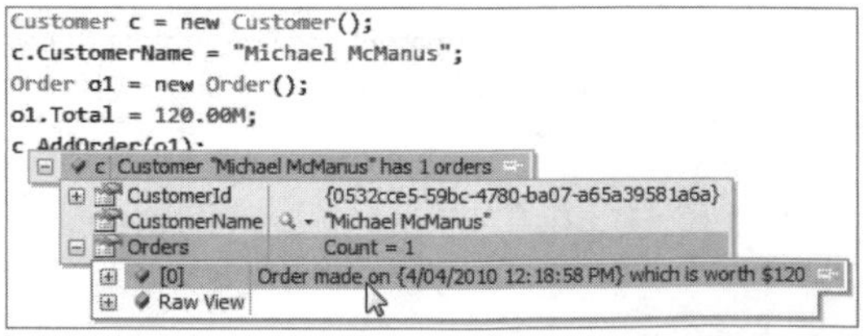

FIGURE 41-4

Looking back at the syntax for the `DebuggerDisplay` attribute, you can see that the output string consists of both static text and field and property information from the object. For example, the `CustomerName` property for the `Customer` object is referenced using the `{CustomerName}` syntax within the static text.

DebuggerHidden

The `DebuggerHidden` attribute can be added to code that you don't want to step through when debugging. Code marked with this attribute is stepped over and does not support breakpoints. If this code makes a call to another method, the debugger steps into that method. Taking the following code snippet, a breakpoint can be set in both `ClickHandler` and `NotSoHiddenMethod`:

C#

```csharp
private void ClickHandler(object sender, EventArgs e)
{
    HiddenMethod();
}

[DebuggerHidden()]
public void HiddenMethod()
{
    Console.WriteLine("Can't set a breakpoint here");
    NotSoHiddenMethod();
}

public void NotSoHiddenMethod()
{
    Console.WriteLine("Can set a breakpoint here!");
}
```

VB

```vb
Private Sub ClickHandler(ByVal sender As Object, ByVal e As EventArgs)
    HiddenMethod()
End Sub

<DebuggerHidden()> _
Public Sub HiddenMethod()
    Console.WriteLine("Can't set a breakpoint here")
    NotSoHiddenMethod()
End Sub

Public Sub NotSoHiddenMethod()
    Console.WriteLine("Can set a breakpoint here!")
End Sub
```

If you step through this code, the debugger goes from the call to `HiddenMethod` in the `ClickHandler` method straight to `NotSoHiddenMethod`. The call stack at this point is shown in Figure 41-5, and you can see that `HiddenMethod` does not appear in the stack.

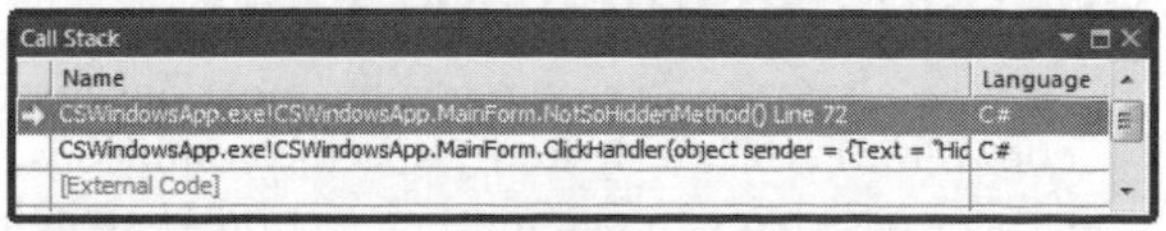

FIGURE 41-5

As with all of the `System.Diagnostic` attributes, the CLR will ignore this, so you will still see the method call in the stack trace of any exceptions thrown at run time.

DebuggerStepThrough

Like the `DebuggerHidden` attribute, when the `DebuggerStepThrough` attribute is applied to a piece of code, that code is stepped over when debugging, regardless of whether this code calls other methods.

Similar to the `DebuggerHidden` attribute, breakpoints cannot be set within a block of code marked with the `DebuggerStepThrough` attribute. However, if a breakpoint is set within a section of code that is called by that code, the attributed code will be marked as *external code* in the call stack. This is illustrated in Figure 41-6, which shows the code that was listed in the previous section. However, in this case `DebuggerStepThrough` has been set on `HiddenMethod` instead of `DebuggerHidden`.

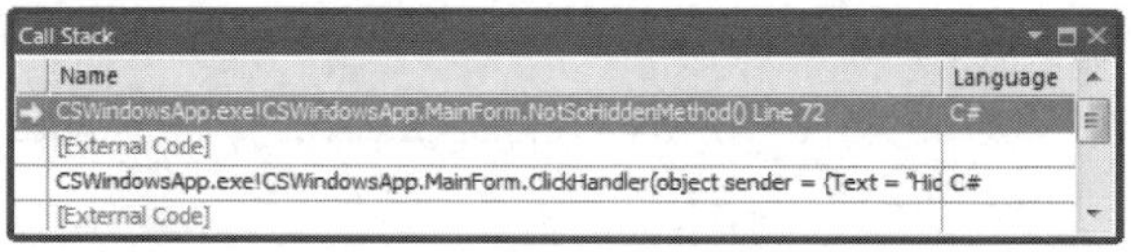

FIGURE 41-6

Visual Studio 2010 supports the Just My Code option, configurable from the Debugging node in the Options dialog (select Tools ➪ Options). Unchecking this option makes all code contained within your application appear in the call stack, as shown in Figure 41-7. This includes designer and other generated code that you might not want to debug. Once this option is unchecked, breakpoints can also be set in blocks of code marked with this attribute.

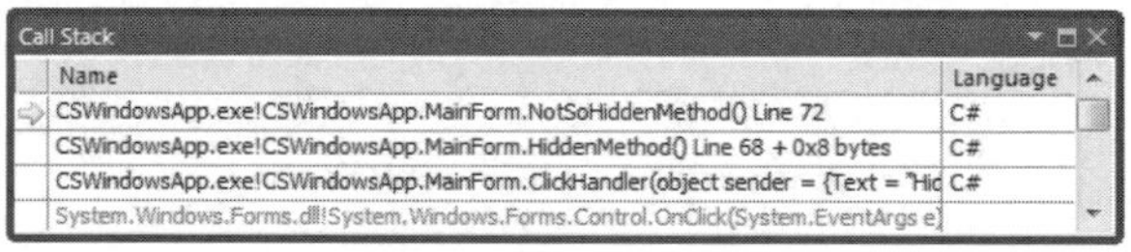

FIGURE 41-7

> *You can also right-click the call stack and select "Show External Code" to reveal any hidden or designer code.*

DebuggerNonUserCode

The `DebuggerNonUserCode` attribute combines the `DebuggerHidden` and `DebuggerStepThrough` attributes. In the default Visual Studio configuration, code marked with this attribute appears as external code in the call stack. As was the case with the `DebuggerStepThrough` attribute, you cannot set breakpoints in blocks of code marked with this attribute. Stepping through code steps into any code called by that block of code in the same way it does for the `DebuggerHidden` attribute.

DebuggerStepperBoundary

`DebuggerStepperBoundary` is the most obscure of all of the `Debugger` attributes, because it comes into effect only under specific conditions. It is used to avoid a misleading debugging experience that can occur when a context switch is made on a thread within the boundaries of the

DebuggerNonUserCode attribute. It is entirely possible in this scenario that the next user-supplied code module stepped into may not actually relate to the code that was in the process of being debugged. To avoid this invalid debugging behavior, the DebuggerStepperBoundary attribute, when encountered under this scenario, will escape from stepping through code and instead resume normal execution of the code.

TYPE PROXIES

So far, you have seen how you can modify the tooltip to show information that is more relevant to debugging your application. However, the attributes discussed so far have been limited in how they control what information is presented in the expanded tree. The DebuggerBrowsable attribute enables you to hide particular members, but there is no way to add more fields. This is where the DebuggerTypeProxy attribute can be used to provide you with complete control over the layout of the tooltip.

The other scenario where a type proxy is useful is where a property of a class changes values within the class. For example, the following snippet from the Customer class tracks the number of times the OrderCount property has been accessed. Whenever the tooltip is accessed, the CountAccessed property is incremented by one:

C#

```csharp
public class Customer
{
    private int m_CountAccessed;
    public int OrderCount
    {
        get
        {
            m_CountAccessed++;
            return this.Orders.Count;
        }
    }

    public int CountAccessed
    {
        get
        {
            return this.m_CountAccessed;
        }
    }
}
```

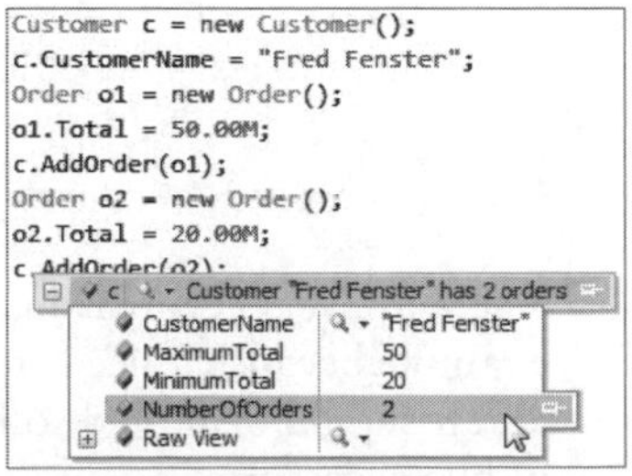

Figure 41-8 illustrates the tooltip you want to be shown for the Customer class. Instead of showing the full list of orders to navigate through, it provides a summary about the number of orders, the maximum and minimum order quantities, and a list of the items on order.

The first line in the tooltip is the same as what you created using the DebuggerDisplay attribute. To generate the rest of the tooltip,

```
Customer c = new Customer();
c.CustomerName = "Fred Fenster";
Order o1 = new Order();
o1.Total = 50.00M;
c.AddOrder(o1);
Order o2 = new Order();
o2.Total = 20.00M;
c.AddOrder(o2);
```

✔ c	⚙ ▾ Customer "Fred Fenster" has 2 orders	
⚙ CustomerName	⚲ ▾ "Fred Fenster"	
⚙ MaximumTotal	50	
⚙ MinimumTotal	20	
✔ NumberOfOrders	2	
⚙ Raw View	⚲ ▾	

FIGURE 41-8

you need to create an additional class that will act as a substitute when it comes to presenting this information. You then need to attribute the Customer class with the DebuggerTypeProxy attribute so the debugger knows to use that class instead of the Customer class when displaying the tooltip. The following code snippet shows the CustomerProxy class that has been nested within the Customer class:

C#

```csharp
[DebuggerDisplay("Customer {CustomerName} has {Orders.Count} orders")]
[DebuggerTypeProxy(typeof(Customer.CustomerProxy))]
public class Customer
{
    private int m_CountAccessed;
    public int OrderCount
    {
        get
        {
            m_CountAccessed++;
            return this.Orders.Count;
        }
    }

    public int CountAccessed
    {
        get
        {
            return this.m_CountAccessed;
        }
    }

    public class CustomerProxy
    {
        public string CustomerName;
        public int NumberOfOrders;
        public decimal MaximumTotal = decimal.MinValue;
        public decimal MinimumTotal = decimal.MaxValue;

        public CustomerProxy(Customer c)
        {
            this.CustomerName = c.m_CustomerName;
            this.NumberOfOrders = c.m_Orders.Count;
            foreach (Order o in c.m_Orders)
            {
                this.MaximumTotal = Math.Max(o.Total, this.MaximumTotal);
                this.MinimumTotal = Math.Min(o.Total, this.MinimumTotal);
            }
        }
    }
}
```

There are very few reasons why you should create public nested classes, but a type proxy is a good example because it needs to be public so it can be specified in the DebuggerTypeProxy attribute, and it should be nested so it can access private members from the Customer class without using the public accessors.

Raw View

On occasion, you might want to ignore the proxy type. For example, this might be true if you are consuming a third-party component that has a proxy type defined for it that disguises the underlying data structure. If something is going wrong with the way the component is behaving, you might need to review the internal contents of the component to trace the source of the issue.

In Figure 41-8, you may have noticed at the bottom of the tooltip was a node titled Raw View. Expanding this node displays the debugger tooltip as it is normally shown, without any proxy types or debugger display values.

In addition, you can turn off all type proxies in Visual Studio through the Tools ⇨ Options menu. Under the Debugging node, check the box that says Show Raw Structure of Objects in Variables Windows. Doing this prevents all type proxies and debugger displays from being shown.

VISUALIZERS

This part of the chapter looks at a feature in Visual Studio 2010 that can be used to help debug more complex data structures. Two of the most common data types programmers work with are Strings and DataTables. Strings are often much larger than the area that can be displayed within a tooltip, and the structure of the DataTable object is not suitable for displaying in a tooltip, even using a type proxy. In both of these cases, a visualizer has been created that enables the data to be viewed in a sensible format.

Once a visualizer has been created for a particular type, a magnifying glass icon appears in the first line of the debugger tooltip. Clicking this icon displays the visualizer. Figure 41-9 shows the Text Visualizer dialog that appears.

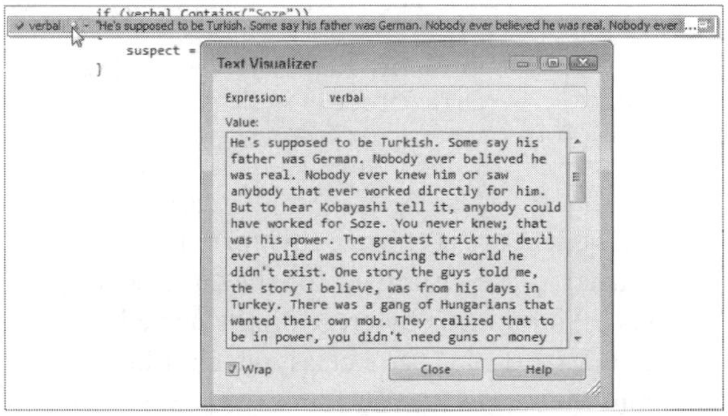

FIGURE 41-9

Before you can start writing a visualizer, you need to add a reference to the `Microsoft.VisualStudio.DebuggerVisualizers` namespace. To do this, right-click the project in the Solution Explorer and select Add Reference from the context menu. You should also add this namespace as an import to any classes for which you plan to create debugger visualizers.

> 🖉 *The version of* `Microsoft.VisualStudio.DebuggerVisualizers` *that ships with Visual Studio 2010 is valid only for projects that target version 4.0 of the Microsoft .NET Framework.*

A visualizer is typically made up of two parts: the class that acts as a host for the visualizer and is referenced by the `DebuggerVisualizer` attribute applied to the class being visualized, and the form that is then used to display, or visualize, the class. Figure 41-10 shows a simple form, `CustomerForm`, which can be used to represent the customer information. This is just an ordinary Windows Form with a couple of TextBox controls, a DataGridView control, and a Button. The only unique aspect to this form is that it has been marked as `Serializable`, and its constructor has been changed to accept a `Customer` object, from which the customer information is extracted and displayed, as shown in the following code:

C#

```csharp
[Serializable()]
public partial class CustomerForm : Form
{
    public CustomerForm(Customer c)
    {
        InitializeComponent();

        this.txtCustomerId.Text = c.CustomerId.ToString();
        this.txtCustomerName.Text = c.CustomerName;
        this.dgOrders.DataSource = c.Orders;
    }

    private void btnOk_Click(object sender, EventArgs e)
    {
        this.DialogResult = DialogResult.OK;
        this.Close();
    }
}
```

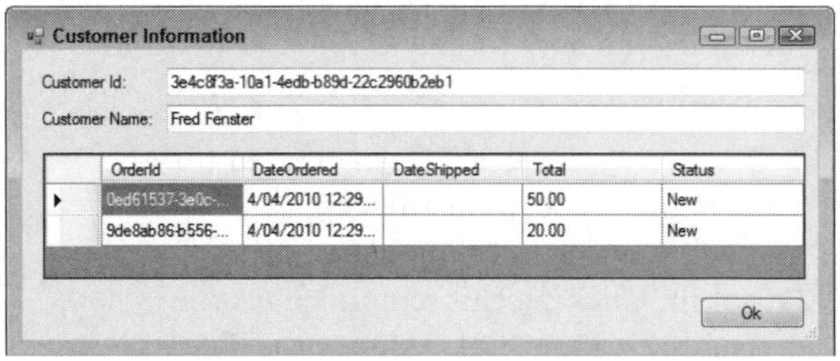

The next stage is to wire this form up to be used as the visualizer for the `Customer` class. You do this by creating the nested `CustomerVisualizer` class, which inherits from the `DialogDebuggerVisualizer` abstract class, as shown in the following code:

FIGURE 41-10

C#

```csharp
[Serializable()]
[DebuggerDisplay("Customer {CustomerName} has {Orders.Count} orders")]
[DebuggerTypeProxy(typeof(Customer.CustomerProxy))]
[DebuggerVisualizer(typeof(Customer.CustomerVisualizer))]
public class Customer
{
    //...
    public class CustomerVisualizer : DialogDebuggerVisualizer
    {
        protected override void Show(
                        IDialogVisualizerService windowService,
                        IVisualizerObjectProvider objectProvider)
```

```
        {
            Customer c = (Customer)objectProvider.GetObject();
            CustomerForm cf = new CustomerForm(c);
            windowService.ShowDialog(cf);
        }
    }
}
```

Unlike the type proxy, which interacts with the actual Customer object being debugged, visualizers need to be able to serialize the class being debugged so the class can be moved from the process being debugged to the process that is doing the debugging, and will subsequently be shown in the visualizer. As such, both the Customer and Order classes need to be marked with the Serializable attribute.

The Show method of the CustomerVisualizer class does three things. To display the Customer object being debugged, first you need to get a reference to this object. You do this via the GetObject method on the ObjectProvider object. Because the communication between the two processes is done via a stream, this method does the heavy lifting associated with deserializing the object so you can work with it.

Next you need to pass the Customer object to a new instance of the CustomerForm. Finally, use the ShowDialog method on the WindowService object to display the form. It is important that you display the form using this object because it will ensure that the form is displayed on the appropriate UI thread.

Lastly, note that the CustomerVisualizer class is referenced in the DebuggerVisualizer attribute, ensuring that the debugger uses this class to load the visualizer for Customer objects.

As a side note, if you write components and want to ship visualizers separately from the components themselves, visualizers can be installed by placing the appropriate assembly into either the C:\ Program Files\Microsoft Visual Studio 10.0\Common7\Packages\Debugger\Visualizers directory (Program Files (x86) on 64-bit Windows), or the Documents\Visual Studio 2010\ Visualizers directory.

ADVANCED TECHNIQUES

Thus far, this chapter has covered how to display and visualize objects you are debugging. In earlier chapters, you learned how to modify field and property values on the object being debugged via the data tip. The missing link is being able to edit more complex data objects. The final section in this chapter looks at how to extend your visualizer so you can save changes to the Customer object.

Saving Changes to Your Object

When you created the CustomerVisualizer, you had to retrieve the Customer object from the communication stream using the GetObject method. This essentially gave you a clone of the Customer object being debugged to use with the visualizer. To save any changes you make in the CustomerVisualizer, you need to send the new Customer object back to the process being debugged. You can do this using the ReplaceObject method on the ObjectProvider, which gives you a CustomerVisualizer.

Before you can call the `ReplaceObject` method you will need to make some changes to pass the modified `Customer` object back to the visualizer. This has been done by saving the `Customer` object to an internal variable when it is initially passed into the class, and exposing this variable via a read-only property. This is shown in the following code:

C#

```csharp
[Serializable()]
public partial class CustomerForm : Form
{
    public CustomerForm(Customer c)
    {
        InitializeComponent();

        this.txtCustomerId.Text = c.CustomerId.ToString();
        this.txtCustomerName.Text = c.CustomerName;
        this.dgOrders.DataSource = c.Orders;

        m_ModifiedCustomer = c;
    }

    private Customer m_ModifiedCustomer;
    public Customer ModifiedCustomer
    {
        get
        {
            m_ModifiedCustomer.CustomerId = new Guid(txtCustomerId.Text);
            m_ModifiedCustomer.CustomerName = txtCustomerName.Text;
            m_ModifiedCustomer.Orders = (List<Order>)dgOrders.DataSource;
            return m_ModifiedCustomer;
        }
    }

    private void btnOk_Click(object sender, EventArgs e)
    {
        this.DialogResult = DialogResult.OK;
        this.Close();
    }
}
```

You can now easily access the modified `Customer` object and save the changes back by calling the `ReplaceObject` method as shown here:

C#

```csharp
[Serializable()]
[DebuggerDisplay("Customer {CustomerName} has {Orders.Count} orders")]
[DebuggerTypeProxy(GetType(Customer.CustomerProxy))]
[DebuggerVisualizer(GetType(Customer.CustomerVisualizer))]
public class Customer
{
    ...

    public class CustomerVisualizer : DialogDebuggerVisualizer
```

```
    {
        protected override void Show(
                            IDialogVisualizerService windowService,
                            IVisualizerObjectProvider objectProvider)
        {
            Customer c = (Customer)objectProvider.GetObject();
            CustomerForm cf = new CustomerForm(c);
            if (windowService.ShowDialog(cf) ==
                                System.Windows.Forms.DialogResult.OK)
                objectProvider.ReplaceObject(cf.ModifiedCustomer);
        }
    }
}
```

> An alternate method would be to use data binding for all of the Customer fields
> on the form with a BindingSource object. This BindingSource object could be
> exposed with a public modifier, thereby making it accessible from the visualizer
> class. All that is needed then is to set the Customer object as the DataSource
> of this BindingSource object by the visualizer class, and it will automatically
> synchronize changes back to the original Customer object.

SUMMARY

Debugging applications is one of the most time-consuming and frustrating activities in the development cycle. In this chapter, you learned how you can take charge of Visual Studio 2010 by customizing the debugging experience.

Using debugging proxy types and visualizers, you can control how information is presented to you while you are debugging your application. This means that you can easily determine when your application is not functioning correctly and be able to trace the source of the issue.

42

Debugging Web Applications

WHAT'S IN THIS CHAPTER?

➤ Using Visual Studio to debug both server-side ASP.NET code and client-side JavaScript running in a web browser

➤ Enabling and viewing ASP.NET trace logs for an individual web page or the entire application

➤ Configuring Health Monitoring so that you are notified as soon as a problem occurs in an ASP.NET application

With Visual Studio 2010, debugging solutions for the Web is just as straightforward as doing the same for Windows-based applications. You can use most of the same debugging windows already discussed in previous chapters, as well as deal with errors through the Exception Assistant. However, there are some differences and additional features specific to web applications that you can use to target your debugging practices more closely to the web paradigm.

In addition to the standard debugging techniques, ASP.NET also provides you with a comprehensive tracing capability, and even the capability to perform health monitoring on your system to ensure it is running in the manner you expect, and exposing problematic scenarios when it doesn't.

> *If you are using Windows Vista or Windows 7 with UAC, and you use IIS rather than the built-in web development server for debugging, then you must launch Visual Studio with administrator rights. Right-click the Visual Studio 2010 shortcut and select Run as Administrator. To always launch as administrator, right-click the shortcut and select Properties, and then select the Compatibility tab and check the Run This Program as an Administrator checkbox.*

DEBUGGING SERVER-SIDE ASP.NET CODE

Before you can perform any level of debugging in a web application, you first need to ensure that ASP.NET debugging is enabled in your web-application or web site project. For web application projects, enable debugging options by right-clicking the project entry in the Solution Explorer and selecting Properties. Select the Web tab option page and ensure that the ASP.NET debugger option is checked, as illustrated in Figure 42-1.

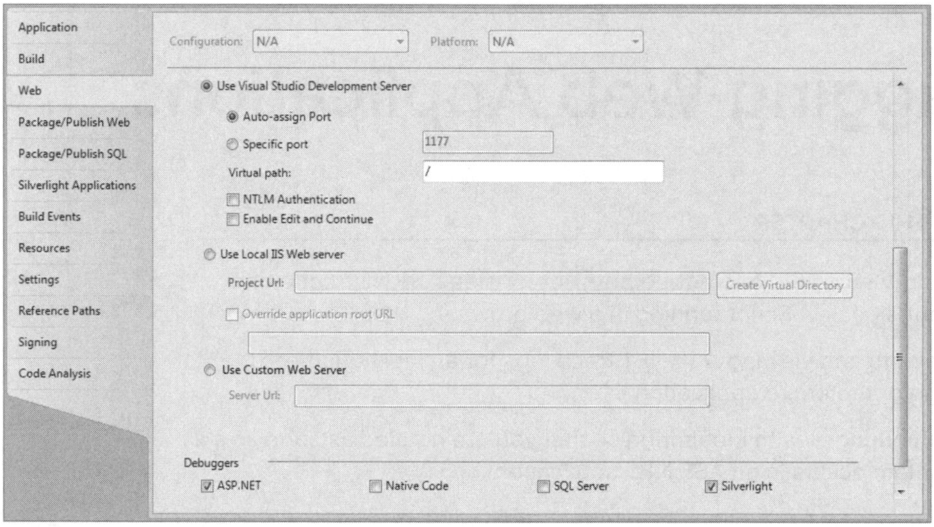

FIGURE 42-1

If you want to be able to include unmanaged code, stored procedures, or Silverlight in your debugging of the web applications, you can activate the Native Code, SQL Server, and Silverlight debuggers here. Native code and SQL Server debugging are explained in the next chapter and Silverlight debugging is discussed later in this chapter.

> *Enabling debugging in other web application projects, such as ASP.NET Web Service or ASP.NET MVC applications, is exactly the same as for standard ASP.NET web applications. In fact, from a debugging perspective, there are really no differences between any of these project types.*

Because web site projects do not have a project file, you must use a slightly different procedure to enable debugging. Enable debugging in web site projects by right-clicking the project entry in the Solution Explorer and selecting Property Pages from the context menu. When the Property Pages dialog is displayed, navigate to the Start Options page, and ensure that the ASP.NET debugger option is checked, as shown in Figure 42-2.

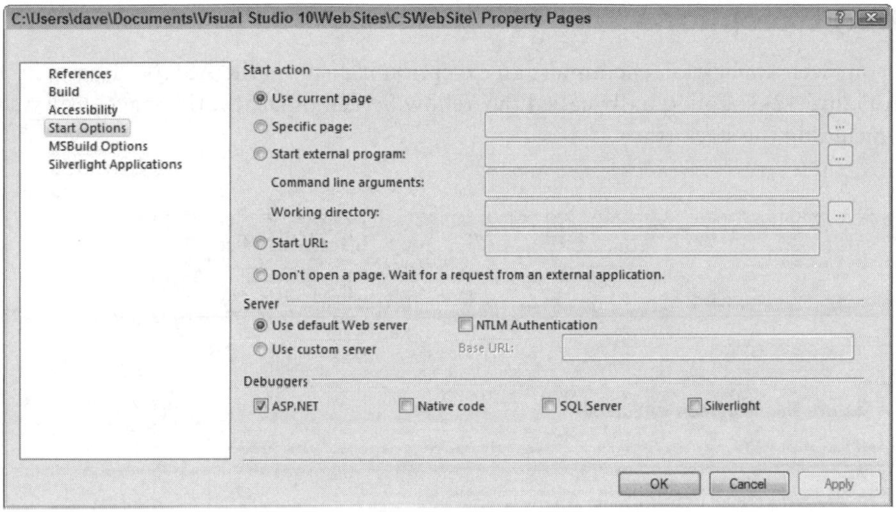

FIGURE 42-2

As with web application projects, you can also customize how a web site project is to be started, including not opening any specific page, but running the server so it listens for a request from another application.

In addition to enabling the ASP.NET debugger in the property pages, you must enable the compiler debug option in the web.config file. Locate the compilation node within system.web and set the debug attribute to true. The following code shows a minimal web.config file with the debug option enabled, ready for hooking the debugger to the application:

```xml
<?xml version="1.0"?>
<configuration>
    <system.web>
        <compilation debug="true" targetFramework="4.0" />
    </system.web>
    <system.webServer>
        <modules runAllManagedModulesForAllRequests="true" />
    </system.webServer>
</configuration>
```

Note that even when you activate the ASP.NET debugger in the Start Options, without setting the debug attribute to true you will be unable to debug the application. However, Visual Studio will detect this discrepancy and present you with a dialog informing you that in order to debug you will need to change the web.config file. It also provides an option for Visual Studio to automatically change this attribute for you.

> *You should never deploy an ASP.NET application into production with the* debug="true" *option set within the* web.config *file. Doing so will cause your application to run slower, use more memory, and prevent some items from being cached.*

Web Application Exceptions

By default, when your web application encounters an exception it displays the ASP.NET server error page, as shown in Figure 42-3. Colloquially called the Yellow Screen of Death, this page displays the exception details including the stack trace.

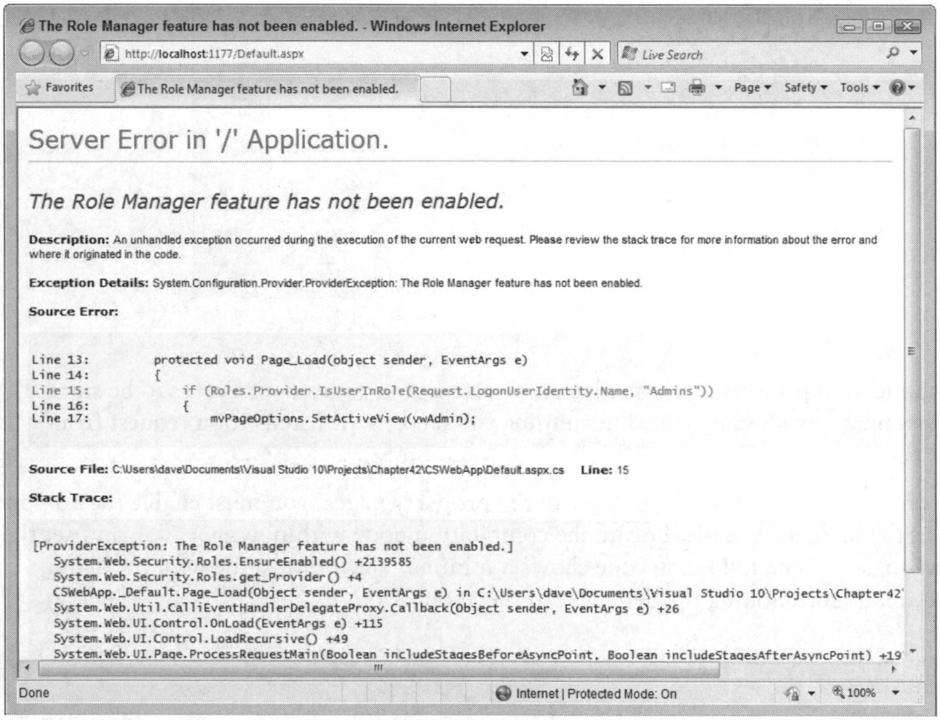

FIGURE 42-3

The server error page is generated under both debug and normal execution. Although it is useful to have this information during development, it is not something that you should be displaying to your end users. Fortunately, there is an easy way to configure redirections for exceptions, including standard HTTP errors, by editing the `customErrors` section in the `web.config` file.

Modifying the previous `web.config` file to include these redirection options for 403 (access denied) and 404 (page not found) can result in a configuration similar to the following:

```xml
<?xml version="1.0"?>
<configuration>
    <system.web>
        <compilation debug="true" targetFramework="4.0" />
        <customErrors mode="RemoteOnly" defaultRedirect="GenericErrorPage.htm">
            <error statusCode="403" redirect="AccessDenied.html" />
            <error statusCode="404" redirect="PageNotFound.html" />
        </customErrors>
```

```
        </system.web>
        <system.webServer>
            <modules runAllManagedModulesForAllRequests="true" />
        </system.webServer>
    </configuration>
```

The mode attribute of the customErrors section defines three options for displaying a custom error page instead of the default server error page. These are:

➤ **On:** The custom error page will always be displayed.

➤ **Off:** The server error page will always be displayed.

➤ **RemoteOnly:** The server error page will be displayed if the browser request is coming from the local computer; otherwise, the custom error page will be displayed.

The server error page is useful in production scenarios where you cannot run the application in Debug mode. However, when debugging, it is much more useful to break execution as soon as an exception occurs. You can do this by enabling the Break When an Exception Is Thrown option for the Common Language Runtime. Figure 42-4 shows how this option is set in the Exceptions dialog under the Debug ➪ Exceptions menu item.

FIGURE 42-4

Once you have enabled this option, when an exception occurs, Visual Studio drops back into the IDE and positions the workspace so the statement at issue is visible. Just like Windows-based applications, Visual Studio can aid you when errors occur by displaying the Exception Assistant. As shown in Figure 42-5, web errors are fully detailed and include information about which part of the statement is in error.

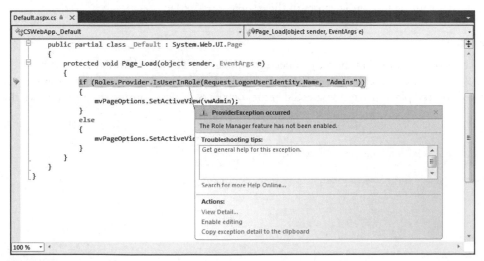

FIGURE 42-5

You can gather additional information on the error by clicking the View Detail link, which provides you with a comprehensive exception object visualizer that you can navigate to determine the content of the error at hand.

Edit and Continue

Edit and Continue, which enables you to modify code when the application is paused in a debug session, is disabled by default in ASP.NET web applications. This useful feature can be enabled by right-clicking the project entry in the Solution Explorer and selecting Properties. Under the Web tab option page, check the Enable Edit and Continue option. This is only supported for the built-in Visual Studio development web server.

Web site projects do not support Edit and Continue, however, because they naturally support a very iterative style of development; it is not such a useful feature for those projects. Edit and Continue is explained in more detail in Chapter 40.

Error Handling

Although debugging your applications is indeed easy with the tools Visual Studio 2010 provides, it is always best to try to avoid error situations proactively. You can do this in web applications with structured Try-Catch exception handling, but you will also want to make your solutions more solid by including code to handle any errors that fall outside any Catch conditions.

> *Notice we are using the term* error handling *and not* exception handling *here. This is because it is broader than trapping program exceptions and also covers HTML errors, such as Page Not Found and Authentication Required.*

You can catch errors on two levels — on an individual page you can intercept unexpected errors and produce a custom-built error, or you can catch errors on an application-wide level through the implementation of a routine to handle errors in the `global.asax` file.

Page-Level Errors

To handle an error on an individual page, you need to implement an event handler routine that intercepts the `MyBase.Error` event. When this event is raised, you can then perform whatever actions you need to take place when unexpected errors occur. A typical routine might look like this:

C#

```csharp
void Page_Error(object sender, EventArgs e)
{
    Response.Write("An unexpected error has occurred.");
    Server.ClearError();
}
```

VB

```
Private Sub Page_Error(ByVal sender As Object, ByVal e As System.EventArgs) _
    Handles MyBase.Error
    Response.Write("An unexpected error has occurred.")
    Server.ClearError()
End Sub
```

As discussed previously, you can also set custom redirections for standard HTTP error codes in the web.config file, so you should use this method only for errors that are not already handled and are specific to the individual page.

Application-Level Errors

At the web application level, you can also trap a series of errors through the global.asax file. By default, Visual Studio 2010 web projects do not include this file, so you'll first need to add it to the project through the Add New Item dialog. Select the Global Application Class item, leave the name as global.asax, and click Add to add the file to your project.

When this class is added to the project, the template includes stubs for the commonly encountered application events, including the error event. To handle any errors that are not catered to elsewhere in the project, add your processing code to this Application_Error routine, like so:

C#

```
protected void Session_End(object sender, EventArgs e)
{
    Server.Transfer("UnexpectedError.aspx");
}
```

VB

```
Sub Application_Error(ByVal sender As Object, ByVal e As EventArgs)
    Server.Transfer("UnexpectedError.aspx")
End Sub
```

This sample routine simply transfers the user to an errors page that determines what to do by interrogating the Server.GetLastError property.

DEBUGGING CLIENT-SIDE JAVASCRIPT

One of the most useful features of Visual Studio 2010 for front-end web developers is the excellent support for debugging client-side JavaScript code. Combined with the IntelliSense support for JavaScript, this significantly eases the difficulty of developing JavaScript code.

> *JavaScript debugging works only if you are using Internet Explorer as your web browser during the debug session.*

Setting Breakpoints in JavaScript Code

Setting breakpoints for JavaScript code is no different from setting any other breakpoint. Within the editor window, any breakpoints in JavaScript code are displayed with a white circle in the center, as shown in Figure 42-6.

 JavaScript debugging will be disabled if the Silverlight debugger is enabled.

FIGURE 42-6

JavaScript breakpoints have the same functionality as standard breakpoints. This includes setting conditions, hit counts, or even running a macro as part of a tracepoint.

When the debugger hits a breakpoint, it pauses execution and displays the HTML code that has been rendered on the client, as shown in Figure 42-7. This provides a true debug experience, because it includes all client-side elements such as the ViewState and server controls rendered in HTML.

Visual Studio 2010 also has comprehensive watch visualizers for client-side elements. Figure 42-7 demonstrates this with a tooltip that shows the properties and methods of the document object.

FIGURE 42-7

It is also possible to set both client-side JavaScript breakpoints and Visual Basic or C# server-side breakpoints at the same time on the same page. This enables you to step through both server-side and client-side code in a single debug session.

Debugging Dynamically Generated JavaScript

Several scenarios exist where ASP.NET sends down to the client JavaScript that has been dynamically generated on the server. For example, the ASP.NET AJAX controls such as the Update

Panel will generate client-side JavaScript files that are actually stored as resources in the ScriptManager control.

When you are running a web application in Debug mode, the Visual Studio Solution Explorer shows a list of all the script references that the page you are debugging has loaded, as shown in Figure 42-8. Double-clicking any of the links under the Script Documents node displays the JavaScript code and enables you to set breakpoints within those scripts.

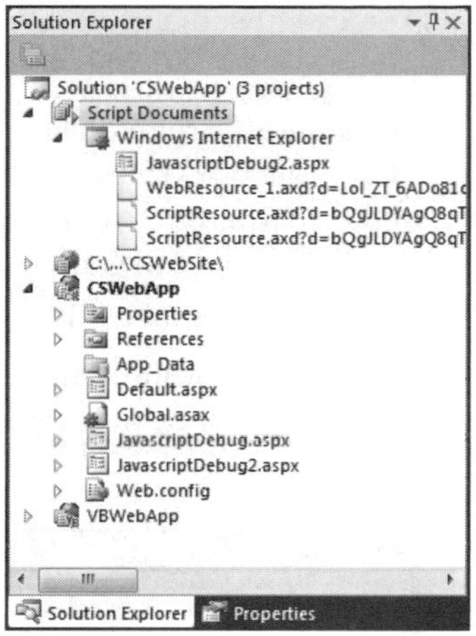

Debugging ASP.NET AJAX JavaScript

ASP.NET AJAX provides both Debug and Release versions of its client JavaScript libraries. The Release version is optimized for performance and minimizes the size of the JavaScript that must be downloaded to the client. The Debug version is more verbose and provides additional debugging features at runtime, such as type and argument checking.

FIGURE 42-8

If debugging is enabled in the `web.config` file, ASP.NET AJAX uses a debug version of the client libraries. You can also enable the debug version on a per-page basis by setting `ScriptMode="Debug"` on the ScriptManager control.

ASP.NET AJAX also includes the `Sys.Debug` class, which can be used to add debug statements to your client JavaScript. This class can be used to display the properties of objects at run time, generate trace messages, or use assertions.

DEBUGGING SILVERLIGHT

Visual Studio 2010 includes a native debugger that makes it easy to debug Silverlight applications. When you create a new Silverlight application, Visual Studio prompts you either to generate an HTML test page to host the Silverlight application, or to utilize an existing or new web project, as shown in Figure 42-9.

In Figure 42-9, we've chosen to create a test page that hosts the Silverlight application in the web application project that is part of the existing solution, and to enable Silverlight debugging in this web application. If you select either of the other two options, you will not need to perform any additional steps to enable Silverlight debugging.

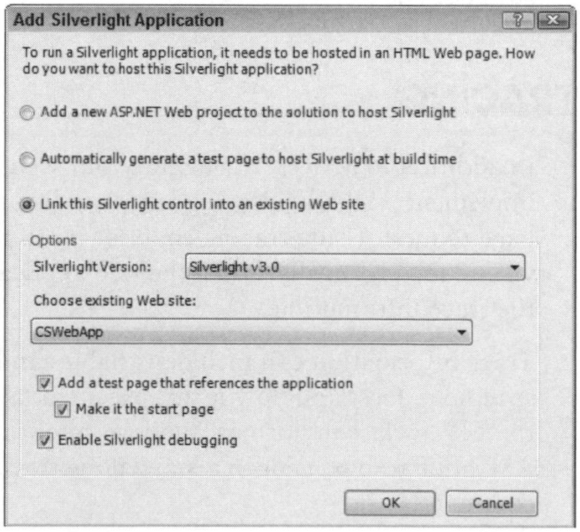

FIGURE 42-9

You can always enable or display support for Silverlight debugging in an existing web application project under the Web option page of the project properties.

Once the Silverlight debugger is enabled, you are able to set breakpoints in the code-behind class files of the XAML pages. When the breakpoint is encountered during debugging, the session pauses and displays the current line of code, as shown in Figure 42-10. You will be able to step through the code, view the call stack, and interrogate the properties of objects, just as you would with any Web or Windows Forms application.

The only major limitations with Silverlight debugging are that Edit and Continue are not supported and JavaScript debugging is disabled.

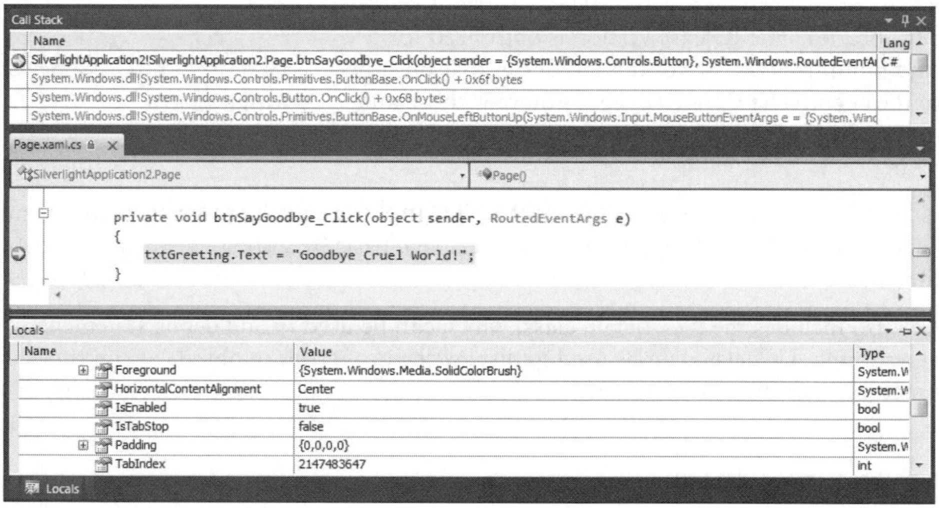

FIGURE 42-10

TRACING

In addition to actively debugging your web applications when things go wrong, you can also implement ASP.NET tracing functionality to look at the information produced in an individual page request. Using tracing enables you to add debug statements to your code that are only viewable when viewing locally; when the web application is deployed to the remote server, users do not see the trace information.

Trace information can include variables and simple objects to help you determine the state of the specific request and how it was executed. Note that ASP.NET tracing is different from using the Trace class in normal Windows applications in that its output is produced on the actual ASP.NET web page or in a standalone trace viewer, rather than the output windows that Trace commands use.

Page-Level Tracing

To implement page-level tracing, you simply need to include a `trace` attribute in the `@Page` directive at the top of the page you want to trace. A simple ASPX page with tracing activated might look like the following:

```
<%@ Page Language="C#" AutoEventWireup="true" Trace="true"
TraceMode="SortByCategory" CodeBehind="ShowTrace.aspx.cs"
Inherits="CSWebApp.ShowTrace" %>

<!DOCTYPE html PUBLIC "-//W3C//DTD XHTML 1.0 Transitional//EN"
"http://www.w3.org/TR/xhtml1/DTD/xhtml1-transitional.dtd">

<html xmlns="http://www.w3.org/1999/xhtml" >
<head runat="server">
    <title>Trace Example Page</title>
</head>
<body>
    <form runat="server">
    <div>Hello!</div>
    </form>
</body>
</html>
```

In addition, you can specify how the tracing messages associated with the page request should appear by using the `TraceMode` attribute. Set this to `SortByTime` to output the tracing messages in the order that they were produced, or `SortByCategory` to categorize them into different message types. Figure 42-11 shows the trace output for the sample page defined in the previous code when sorted by category.

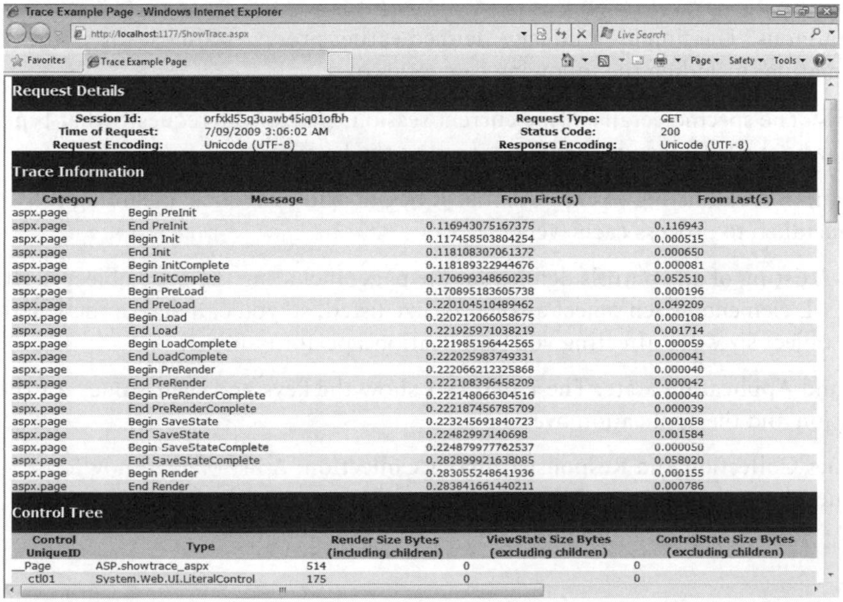

FIGURE 42-11

Application-Level Tracing

Application-level tracing can be enabled through the `web.config` file. Within the `system.web` node, you need to include a trace node that contains the attribute enabled with a value of `true`. When using application-level tracing, you can control how the tracing is produced through the `pageOutput` attribute. When set to `true`, you receive the tracing information at the bottom of every page (similar to how it appears in Figure 42-11), whereas a value of `false` ensures that the tracing information never appears on the page, and is instead only accessible through the Trace Viewer (covered later in this chapter). You can also restrict the amount of information to trace with the `requestLimit` attribute. Including a trace node for the `web.config` file you saw earlier in this chapter results in a configuration like the following:

```
<?xml version="1.0"?>
<configuration>
    <system.web>
        <compilation debug="true" targetFramework="4.0" />
        <customErrors mode="RemoteOnly" defaultRedirect="GenericErrorPage.htm">
            <error statusCode="403" redirect="AccessDenied.html" />
            <error statusCode="404" redirect="PageNotFound.html" />
        </customErrors>
        <trace enabled="true" pageOutput="false" traceMode="SortByCategory"/>
    </system.web>
    <system.webServer>
        <modules runAllManagedModulesForAllRequests="true" />
    </system.webServer>
</configuration>
    </system.web>
</configuration>
```

Trace Output

Tracing output is voluminous. The simple Hello page defined earlier produces almost three full printed pages of information, including the following categories of data:

➤ **Request Details:** The specific details of the current session, time of the request, what type of request it was, and the HTTP code that is returned to the browser.

➤ **Trace Information:** A full listing of each event as it begins and then ends, including the amount of time taken to process each event.

➤ **Control Tree:** A listing of all controls defined on the page, including the page object itself, as well as HTML elements. Each object also has a size listed, so you can determine whether any abnormal object sizes are affecting your application's performance.

➤ **Session State and Application State:** These two lists show the keys and their values for the individual session and the application overall.

➤ **Request Cookies Collection and Response Cookies Collection:** A list of any known ASP.NET request and response cookies on the system that your application may be able to access.

➤ **Headers Collection:** A list of the HTTP headers included in the page.

➤ **Response Headers Collection:** The HTTP headers associated with the response, indicating what type of object is being returned.

➤ **Form Collection:** A list of any forms defined in the page.

➤ **Querystring Collection:** A list of any query strings used in the page request.

➤ **Server Variables:** A list of all server variables known to the ASP.NET server and application you're currently executing.

As you can see, when tracing is implemented for a web page or application, you gain access to an enormous amount of information that you can then use to determine how your application is performing. You can see whether problems exist in the various collections in the way of missing or extraneous data, as well as analyze the Trace Information list to determine whether there are any abnormally long processing times for any specific events.

The Trace Viewer

The Trace Viewer is a custom handler included in your web application when you have application tracing activated. When tracing is being reported at the application level, you can navigate to this page and view all page tracing output as it occurs. To view the Trace Viewer, browse to the `trace.axd` page in the root directory of your web site.

The Trace Viewer provides a summary table of all requests made in the application, along with the time the request was made and the HTTP status code returned in the response. It also provides a link to detailed information for each request (which is the same information that you can see on a page trace discussed earlier), as shown in Figure 42-12.

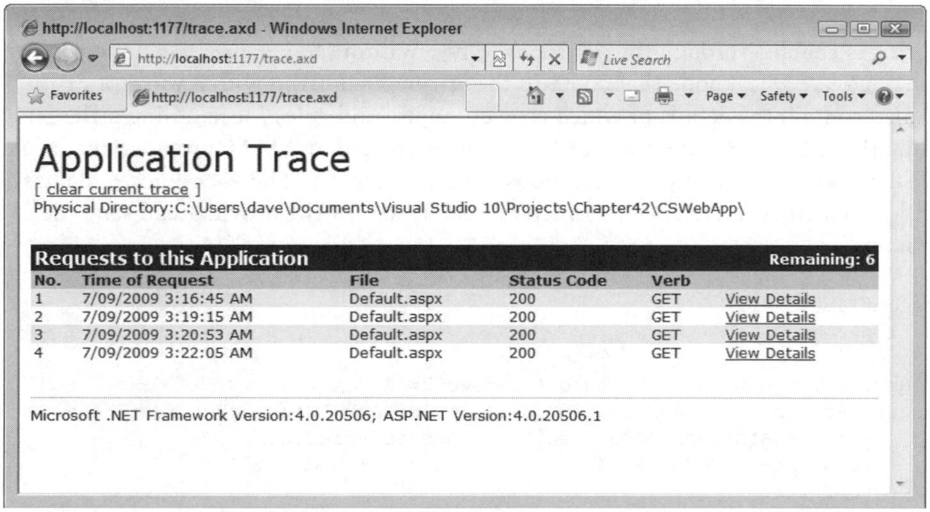

FIGURE 42-12

Custom Trace Output

You can supplement the default trace information with your own custom-built trace messages, using the `Trace.Warn` and `Trace.Write` methods. Both have the same set of syntactical overloads, and the only real difference is that messages outputted using the `Warn` method are displayed in red text.

The simplest form for these commands is to include a message string like so:

```
Trace.Warn("Encountered a potential issue")
```

However, you can categorize your warnings and messages by using the second and third forms of the methods, including a category and optionally an error object as well:

```
Trace.Warn("MyApp Error Category", "Encountered a potential issue", myAppException)
```

HEALTH MONITORING

ASP.NET includes a built-in framework for generating and capturing events for the purposes of monitoring a web application. This feature, called Health Monitoring, allows you to become more proactive in managing your production web applications, enabling you to be notified as soon as a problem occurs.

> *The Health Monitoring provides much more than just alerting you that an exception has occurred. You can also instrument your code and generate alerts for custom events; for example, if a user fails to log on or attempts to access a restricted area.*

Health Monitoring is enabled through the `web.config` file. Within the `system.web` node you need to include a `healthMonitoring` node that contains the attribute `enabled` with a value of `true`. This node will also contain the details of which provider to use and rules for handling different events. Extending the `web.config` file from earlier, we have created an SMTP provider and a rule that e-mails the details of any unhandled exceptions to the webmaster. The `web.config` file has also been modified to include a reference to an SMTP server, so that the provider can send the e-mail notifications.

```xml
<?xml version="1.0"?>
<configuration>
    <system.web>
        <compilation debug="true" targetFramework="4.0" />
        <customErrors mode="RemoteOnly" defaultRedirect="GenericErrorPage.htm">
            <error statusCode="403" redirect="AccessDenied.html" />
            <error statusCode="404" redirect="PageNotFound.html" />
        </customErrors>
        <trace enabled="true" pageOutput="false" traceMode="SortByCategory"/>
        <healthMonitoring enabled="true">
            <providers>
                <add name="SMTPProvider"
                    type="System.Web.Management.SimpleMailWebEventProvider"
```

```
                            from="server@yourdomain.com"
                            to="webmaster@yourdomain.com"
                            subjectPrefix="Exception on WebApp:"
                            bufferMode="Critical Notification"/>
                </providers>
                <rules>
                    <clear />
                    <add name="All Errors Default"
                         eventName="All Errors"
                         provider="SMTPProvider" />
                </rules>
            </healthMonitoring>
        </system.web>
        <system.net>
            <mailSettings>
                <smtp><network host="mail.yourdomain.com"/></smtp>
            </mailSettings>
        </system.net>
        <system.webServer>
            <modules runAllManagedModulesForAllRequests="true" />
        </system.webServer>
    </configuration>
```

Once this is in place, anytime an exception is generated and not handled, an e-mail is sent to the specified address. This e-mail message contains a large amount of useful troubleshooting information, including the exception details and stack trace. Figure 42-13 shows an example message.

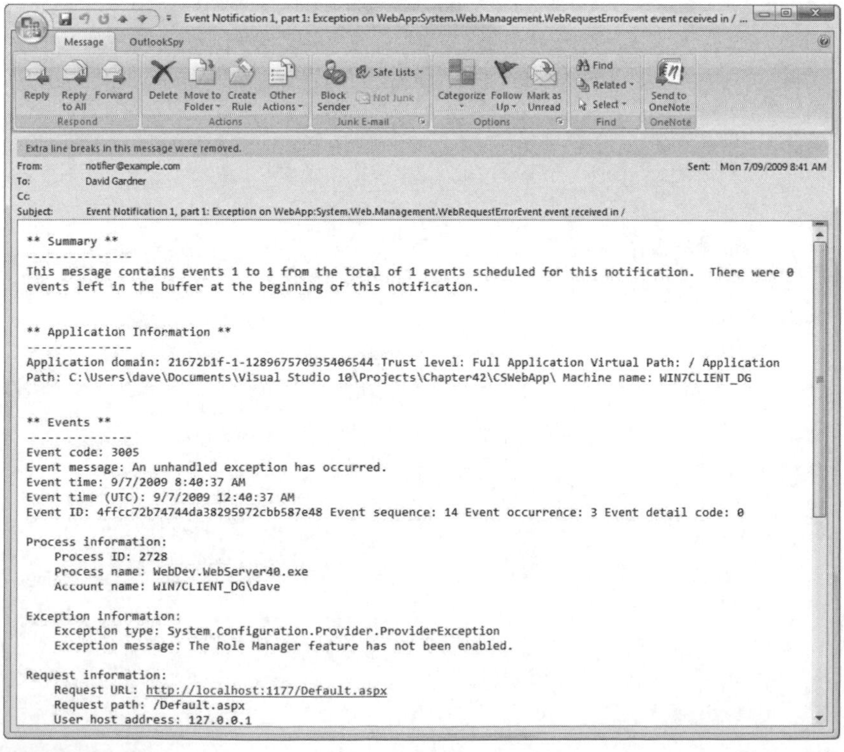

FIGURE 42-13

In addition to the SMTP provider, there is also an Event Log, WMI, and SQL Server provider. Quite complex rules can be enabled to direct the notifications to one of more of these providers. If none of these meet your needs, you can even write your own custom provider.

SUMMARY

With the combination of Visual Studio 2010 and ASP.NET server-side capabilities, you have a wide array of tools to help you look after your web solutions. These features enhance the already impressive feature set available with normal Windows application debugging, with web-specific features such as JavaScript and Silverlight debugging, page- and application-level error handling, and the capability to trace code, which you can use to monitor the way pages are being executed in your web applications without interrupting your end users.

In addition, the ASP.NET Health Monitoring framework enables you to proactively manage your production web applications by notifying you as soon as a problem occurs.

Advanced Debugging Techniques

As you've seen throughout the last several chapters, Visual Studio 2010 comes with a great variety of ways to debug and run through your applications, including catching errors and displaying them to you for action before the code executes too far; a number of techniques for effectively debugging web applications; and other features, such as breakpoints and visualizing errors.

However, there is still more functionality to be found in Visual Studio that you can use to customize your experience with debugging projects, databases, unmanaged code, and even the .NET Framework itself. In this chapter you'll find advanced techniques for debugging your projects regardless of language or technology.

START ACTIONS

Visual Studio provides several ways to launch applications at the start of a debugging session. For most projects the default start option will be sufficient, which in the case of a Windows executable will launch the program directly. In the case of a web application, Visual Studio opens the default web browser and loads the current page, or navigates to the root path of the web application if there is no active page.

In some scenarios you may want a different action to occur during a debugging session. For example, you may need to always open a specific web page when the web application is started. In these scenarios you can change the start options on the Debug or Web project property page. Figure 43-1 shows the start actions for a Windows Forms project.

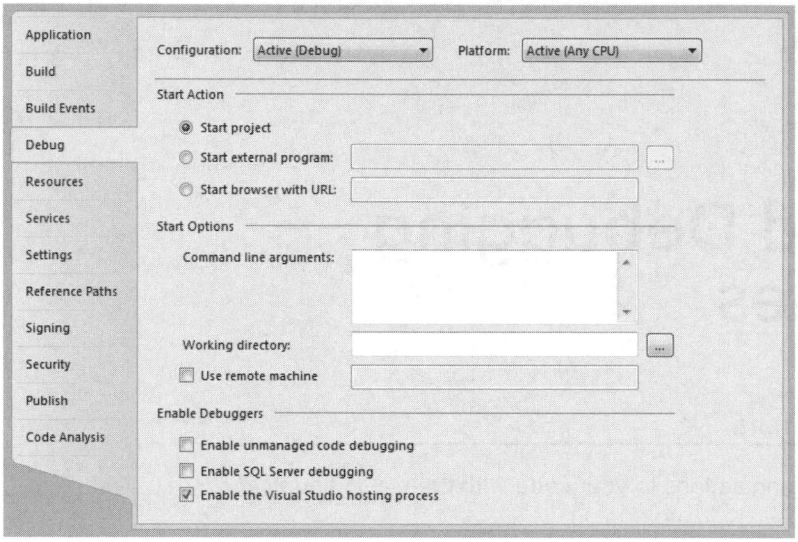

FIGURE 43-1

In addition to starting the project directly, you can also choose to start an external program that presumably will subsequently call your project into the execution process. Alternatively, you can choose to launch the default web browser on your system with a specific URL, again with the assumption that the URL will ultimately invoke your project.

Often, applications are built with the capability to exhibit different behavior depending on command-line arguments. If your project is of this variety and you need to test the different configurations, you can use the Command Line Arguments textbox to specify which set of arguments is to be included in the execution of the project. You should enter the command-line arguments in exactly the same way you expect the end user to do so when that user is invoking your application once it has been deployed.

You can override the default directory from which the application should be executed by setting the Working Directory option. This equates to the same setting when you edit a Windows shortcut. In addition, you can also specify a different machine to control the debugging process of the application by activating the Use Remote Machine option. Note that you will need to explicitly specify the remote computer path, because it does not have an associated browse option.

The final section of the Debug page pertains to the different kinds of debugging that will be performed during the execution of your application. By default, the only debugging process active is the debugging of managed code inside the Visual Studio environment, but you can optionally include native unmanaged code or SQL Server stored procedures. These debuggers are discussed later in the chapter.

> *The configuration and platform settings are available only when you have the Show Advanced Build Configurations setting activated. You can find this in the Projects and Solutions ⇨ General options page and it is on by default for all environment configurations except for Visual Basic programmers.*

The start actions for ASP.NET web applications are found on the Web property page for the project, as shown in Figure 43-2. The default is to launch the web site with whichever page is currently open in the code editor or web designer. This can be changed to always use a specific page or URL. The other option is to start an external program or wait for a request from an external application. This is particularly useful when debugging a web service that is invoked by another application.

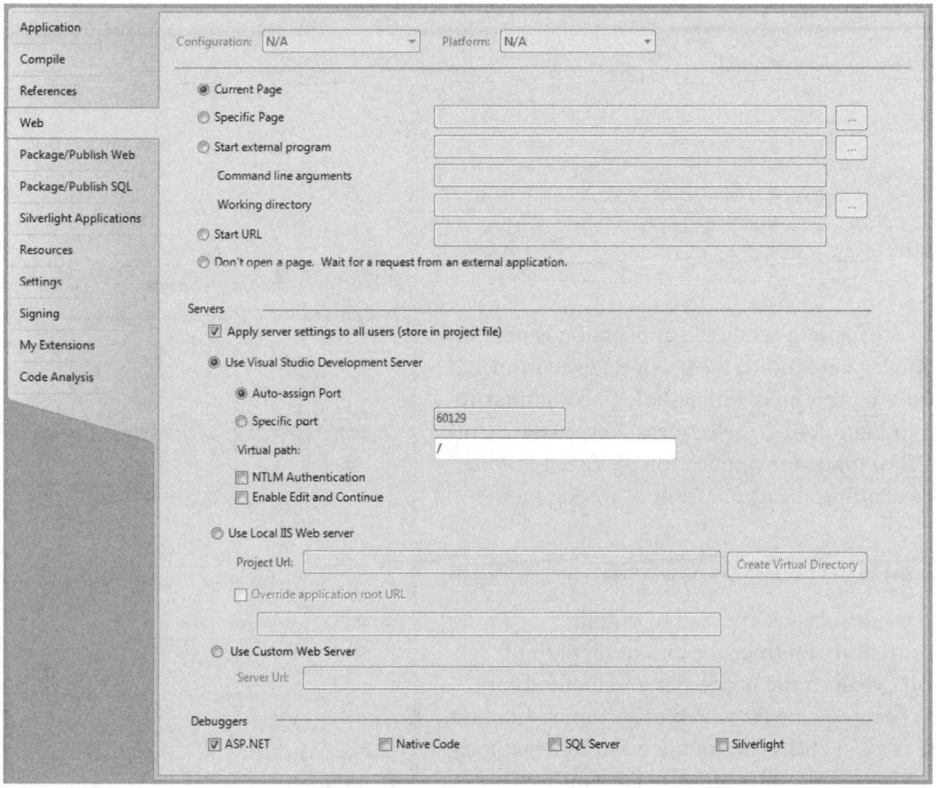

FIGURE 43-2

ASP.NET web application projects can also choose from one of three web server options. The built-in Visual Studio Development Server is the most convenient, because it does not require installation or configuration. Unlike IIS, the Visual Studio Development Server supports Edit and Continue. The Custom Web Server option enables you to specify a remote web server to debug against.

DEBUGGING WITH CODE

Three classes ship with the .NET Framework under the `System.Diagnostics` namespace that can be used to build debugging support directly into your code — the `Debug`, `Debugger`, and `Trace` classes. When used properly, these classes provide a very powerful way for you to interact with the debugger.

The functionality provided by all three of these classes is exposed through static/shared methods and properties, which makes it easy to add them to your code.

The Debugger Class

The `Debugger` class provides programmatic access to certain debugger functions within Visual Studio. For example, the following code snippet checks whether the application is running under a debugger and, if not, launches one and attaches to the process:

C#

```
if (!Debugger.IsAttached)
{
    Debugger.Launch();
}
```

VB

```
If Not Debugger.IsAttached() Then
    Debugger.Launch()
End If
```

When this code is executed while the application is running normally outside Visual Studio, the program execution pauses, and you are presented with a dialog box similar to the one shown in Figure 43-3. Selecting a New Instance of Visual Studio 2010 loads the application in Visual Studio and continues executing the application in Debug mode.

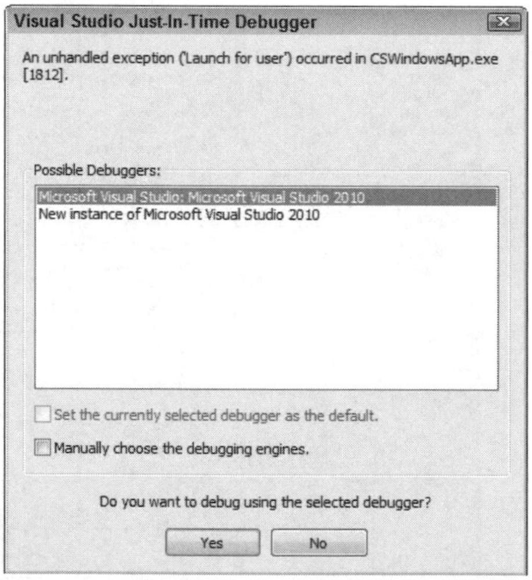

FIGURE 43-3

The Debug and Trace Classes

The `Debug` and `Trace` classes are used to output debugging information and trace the execution path of your application. Most of the properties and methods are common across the two classes, which may seem redundant. However, there is a key difference in the way these methods are implemented and the results presented to you.

The `Debug` class should be used if you only need to output information while running in Debug mode. The `Trace` class can be used if you want output in both the Debug and Release versions. While you are debugging an application during development, both your tracing and debugging output go to the Output window in Visual Studio. However, in Release mode, any `Debug` statements will be suppressed by the compiler and not invoked during execution. This ensures that you can include a large amount of debug code in your application without increasing the size or decreasing the performance of your release code.

> *The ability to use* Trace *and* Debug *statements in different build configurations is specified through compiler directives. Within Visual Studio, you can enable or disable these directives from the project properties pages. These settings are found on the Build property page for C# projects, and under the Advanced Compiler Options button on the Compile property page for Visual Basic projects.*

The methods that are available to output debug messages in the Debug and Trace classes are listed in Table 43-1.

TABLE 43-1: Methods for Outputting Debug Messages

METHOD	OUTPUTS
Write	The text or string representation and an optional category.
WriteIf	The text and an optional category, if the condition specified as an argument evaluates to true.
WriteLine	The text followed by a carriage return and an optional category.
WriteLineIf	The text followed by a carriage return and an optional category, if the condition specified as an argument evaluates to true.

You can also offset the output by increasing or decreasing the indenting through the Indent and Unindent methods.

You can use the Assert method on the Debug and Trace classes to create an assertion, which tests a condition that was specified as an argument. If the condition evaluates to true, no action occurs. If the condition evaluates to false, the assertion fails. If you are running in Debug mode, your program pauses execution, and a dialog box is displayed, as shown in Figure 43-4.

Selecting Abort terminates the application execution. Retry breaks at the statement and Ignore continues execution.

While running in Debug mode, all output from the Debug and Trace classes is displayed in the Output window. However, with a Release build all trace output is collected by a listener. A listener is simply

FIGURE 43-4

an object that receives trace output and writes it to an output device. An output device could be a text file, Windows event log, or some other custom logging repository.

Finally, Trace Switches are available, which allow you to enable, disable, and filter tracing output. Trace Switches can be declaratively enabled within the app.config file for an application.

DEBUGGING RUNNING APPLICATIONS

Sometimes you'll need to debug an application that is running outside Visual Studio. Many reasons exist for why you would want to do this, such as if a defect appears only when an application is executed in production. Fortunately, Visual Studio provides a simple method for attaching and debugging a Windows executable or web application that is actively running.

Attaching to a Windows Process

Attaching to a running Windows process is a fairly straightforward task in Visual Studio. Ideally, you will have the original source code open in Visual Studio, in which case you will be able to debug the process as if you had launched it in Debug mode from Visual Studio.

> *If you are debugging an executable without access to the source code, the available debugging features are limited. If the executable was built without debug information or symbols, available features are further limited and it is unlikely that you will gain much useful information by debugging it in this way. Therefore, it is recommended that when you perform a release build you should in fact perform two builds: one with and one without debug symbols. The symbols should be archived in a safe location so that they can be accessed if you ever need to attach to a running process or debug a memory dump.*

From the Debug menu, use the Attach to Process command. This displays the Attach to Process dialog window (see Figure 43-5), from which you can browse all active processes. Locate the application that you want to debug from the Available Processes list and click the Attach button.

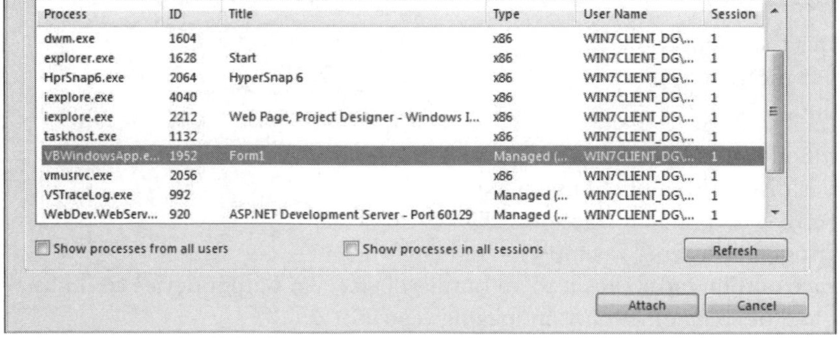

FIGURE 43-5

Because attaching to an application requires these manual steps, it is not well suited if you are trying to debug a problem that occurs during startup. Also, if you are debugging an application that does not require any user input and finishes quickly, you may not have time to attach to it. In both these scenarios it would be better to either launch the application in Debug mode from within Visual Studio, or create a custom build with a `Debug.Break()` statement in the startup code of the application.

Once you've finished debugging an attached process, you should always cleanly detach from the process by selecting Debug ➪ Detach All. You can also choose to end the application by selecting Debug ➪ Terminate All.

Attaching to a Web Application

Attaching to an ASP.NET web application is almost as easy as attaching to a Windows application. However, before you attach to a web application, you must ensure that it has debugging enabled by editing the `web.config` file for the application. Locate the Compilation node within `system.web` and set the `debug` attribute to `true`. The following listing shows a minimal `web.config` file with the Debug option set, ready for attaching the debugger to the application:

```
<configuration>
    <appSettings/>
    <connectionStrings/>
    <system.web>
        <compilation debug="true" />
    </system.web>
</configuration>
```

ASP.NET automatically detects any changes to `web.config` settings and applies them immediately. Therefore, you don't need to restart the computer or the IIS service for this change to take effect. As discussed in Chapter 42, this change can have an adverse affect on performance, so you should never leave it enabled in production.

Once you have enabled debugging you can attach to the web application. The process you'll need to attach to is the ASP.NET worker process, which will either be the native process within IIS (called `w3wp.exe` for IIS 6.0 or higher, or `aspnet_wp.exe` on older versions of IIS) or the built-in Visual Studio 2010 development server `WebDev.WebServer.exe`.

> *Because the IIS process normally runs under the* `ASPNET` *or* `NETWORK SERVICE` *account, you will need to be running Visual Studio with Administrator rights to attach the debugger to it.*

To begin debugging, select Attach to Process from the Debug menu in Visual Studio 2010. Select the Show Processes in All Sessions checkbox if you are attaching to ASP.NET under IIS. Locate the ASP.NET worker process from the Available Processes list and click the Attach button. As shown in Figure 43-6, you may be prompted to restart Visual Studio with elevated rights.

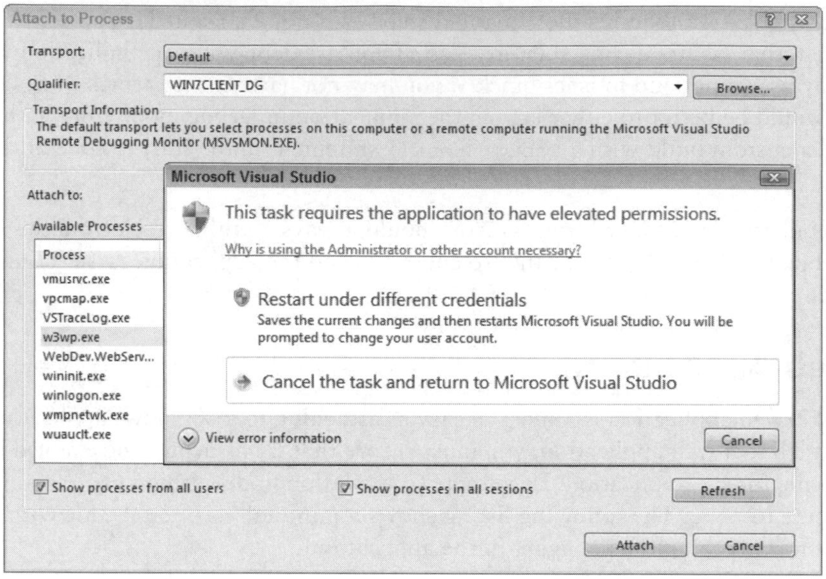

FIGURE 43-6

Remote Debugging

Remote debugging enables you to attach to an application that is executing on another machine. This can be useful for those cases where a bug is manifesting itself only on a non-programmer's computer, or if you need to debug a Windows Service or ASP.NET web application that is running on a production server.

Debugging a remote application is no different from debugging a local application. Once you have attached to the remote application you can set breakpoints, watch variables, and step through code. However, before you can attach to a remote process you must ensure that the Remote Debugging Monitor is running on the machine to be debugged.

The Remote Debugging Monitor, `msvsmon.exe`, is a small executable that is shipped with Visual Studio 2010. By default you will find the 32-bit version installed in the directory `C:\Program Files\Microsoft Visual Studio 10.0\Common7\IDE\Remote Debugger\x86`.

> *The x64 version of* `msvsmon.exe` *is not installed by default with Visual Studio 2010 unless you are running a 64-bit version of Windows. The IA-64 version of* `msvsmon.exe` *is available only with Visual Studio Team System.*

You can simply copy this folder over to the remote machine and run it locally, or create a share and run it from a UNC path. You can also choose to install the Remote Debugging Monitor on the remote machine by running the setup MSI file that is on the Visual Studio installation DVD media under the `Remote Debugger` directory.

When you launch `msvsmon.exe` on a remote computer for the first time, it attempts to configure the Windows Firewall to open the network ports necessary to enable remote debugging. In some environments, such as on a Windows Server 2003, it prompts you to make the necessary changes as shown in Figure 43-7. On the Developer's machine, Visual Studio makes the necessary changes to the Windows Firewall to enable it to connect to a remote machine.

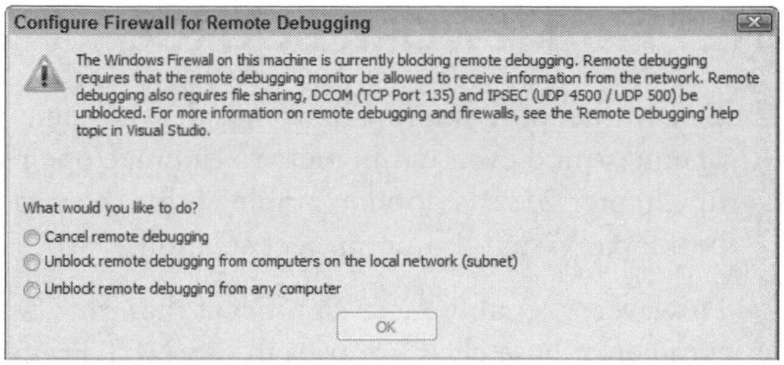

FIGURE 43-7

Once you have started the Remote Debugging Monitor it simply listens on the network for incoming debugging requests. By default, remote requests must be authenticated, and only users who are Administrators have the necessary permissions to attach and debug applications. These security settings can be changed from the Tools ➪ Options menu, as shown in Figure 43-8.

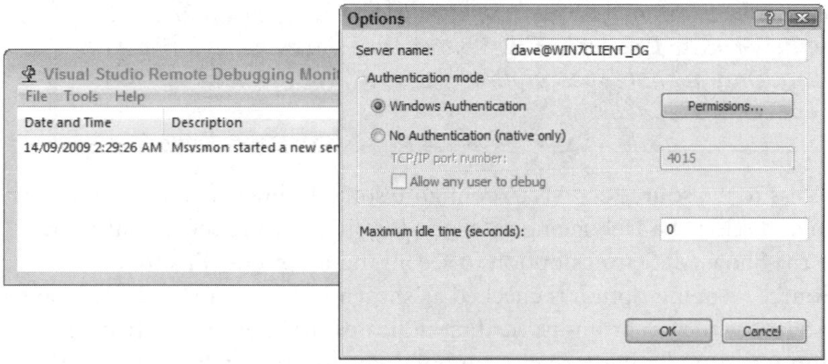

FIGURE 43-8

> If you enable the No Authentication mode, your machine will be vulnerable to any user on the network. A remote user could launch applications on your computer, access data, or perform untold mischievous or destructive actions by using a debugger. You have been warned!

Once you have the Remote Debugging Monitor running on the remote machine, you can attach to an application on that machine through the Debug ➪ Attach to Process menu. Enter the computer name or IP address of the remote machine in the field marked Qualifier. Visual Studio will connect to the Remote Debugging Monitor, authenticate you, and finally display the list of processes running on the remote machine. Simply select a process to attach to and you will be able to debug as if you had attached to a local process.

.NET FRAMEWORK SOURCE

One of the more interesting trends that has emerged from Microsoft in recent years is an increased openness and even willingness to embrace open source. The ASP.NET MVC Framework, covered in Chapter 21, is a good example of this, because the source code for this has been released as a buildable Visual Studio project solution.

However, arguably more significant than this has been the release of the source code for a large number of base class libraries in the .NET Framework. Available under the read-only Microsoft Reference License, it enables you to step into and debug the .NET Framework code as part of a debugging session. Though you could always infer the programmer's intent by using Reflector, there is no comparison to browsing the actual source code, *including the inline documentation*. The really good news is that this documentation is quite comprehensive.

> *The source code is not available for every assembly that ships as part of the .NET Framework, nor is it available for every version that has been released. For the assemblies that are available, there has often been a delay between when the framework was publicly released and when the source code became available. You can find the list of currently available assemblies at* `http://referencesource.microsoft.com/netframework.aspx`.

The first step to enabling access to the source code is to configure some Debugger settings. Open the Tools ⇨ Options menu item and select the Debugging category. If you are using the Visual Basic Profile, you'll need to select the Show All Settings option to see all these options. Ensure that the Enable .NET Framework Source Stepping option is checked as shown in Figure 43-9. When you check this option you may be presented with two prompts; the first indicates that the Enable Just My Code option has been disabled, and the second advises that a symbol cache location default has been set.

Secondly, navigate to the Symbols category in the Options dialog (see Figure 43-10) and check the symbol cache location that was automatically added. You can modify the cache location if required, but ensure that you have full read/write access to the target directory. If you are configuring these options while running in Debug mode, you also have the option to download the symbols immediately by clicking the Load all symbols button. Otherwise, if you are not running a debug session, the symbols applicable to the current project are downloaded as soon as you click OK.

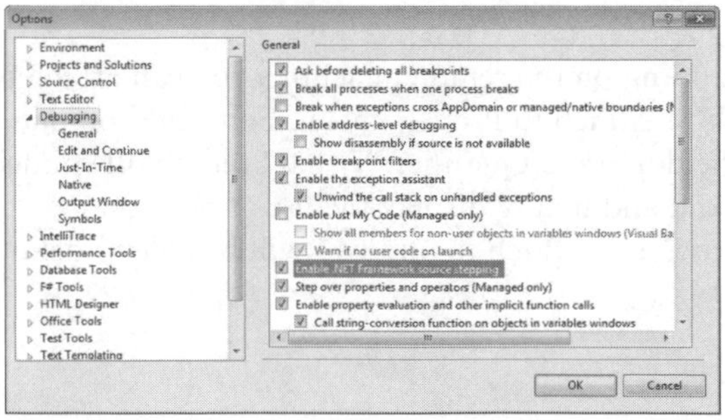

FIGURE 43-9

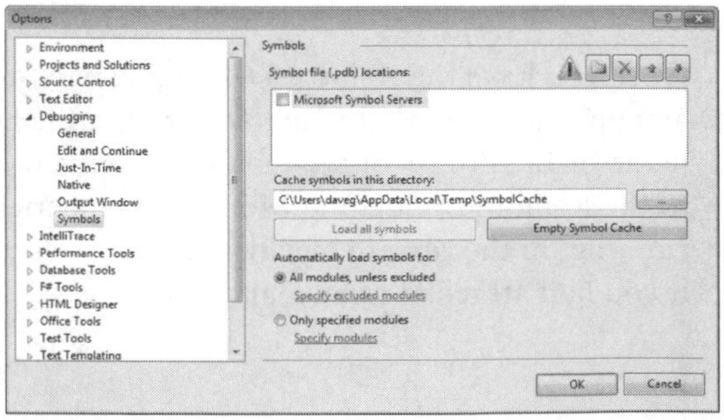

FIGURE 43-10

You will now be able to step into and browse the .NET Framework base class libraries during a debugging session. Set a breakpoint in your application code and run in Debug mode. When the breakpoint is hit, open the Call Stack window (Debug ➪ Windows ➪ Call Stack) to display the execution path. If the symbols have been loaded, the code that is available for debugging will not be grayed out, and you will be able to double-click the entry in the Call Stack, or step into the source code during your debug session, as shown in Figure 43-11. If this is the first time you are viewing the code, you are prompted to accept the Microsoft Reference Library license.

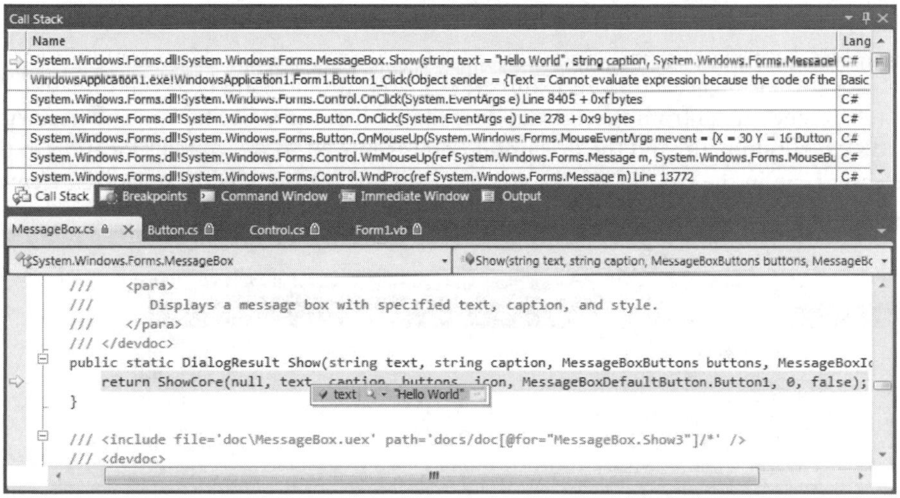

FIGURE 43-11

MULTI-THREADED AND PARALLELIZED APPLICATION DEBUGGING

Multi-threaded applications have traditionally been notoriously difficult to debug properly. Seemingly fundamental tasks, such as keeping track of which thread you are currently inspecting and what other threads are currently executing, are some of the reasons why this task is so hard. Fortunately, Visual Studio 2010 has improved the support available for debugging multi-threaded applications.

Chapter 39 discussed the Threads debug window, which lists all the active threads for a particular application. Functionality accessed through this window includes the ability to set a friendly name for a thread. You can also set flags on individual threads, which means that you don't have to spend as much time trying to keep track of thread IDs.

To further improve debugging, you can now identify each thread within the source code editor window. This is enabled from the Threads window by right-clicking any entry and selecting Show Threads in Source. The result of this is shown in Figure 43-12, where a cloth thread icon (consisting of a red and blue wavy line) is displayed in the gutter. The thread icon indicates that a thread, or several threads, is stopped at this location. When you hover over the thread icon, a tooltip is displayed that identifies which threads are stopped here. The thread names listed are the friendly names that have been entered in the Threads window.

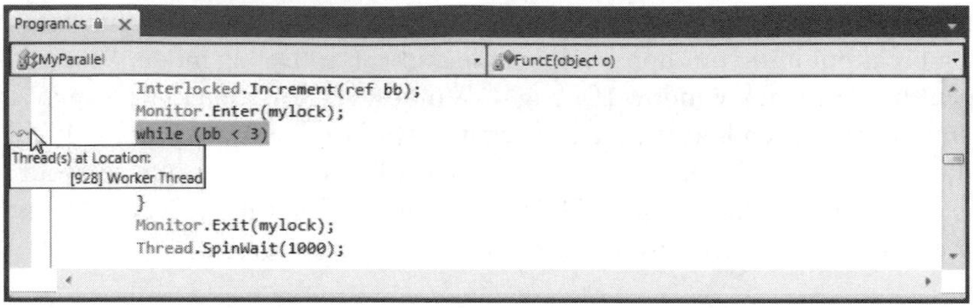

FIGURE 43-12

Within the Debug Location toolbar, shown in Figure 43-13, you can navigate between threads. When you select a different thread from the Thread drop-down list, the Call Stack is updated with the selected thread's execution path, and the execution point is moved to the current location in the source code. The call graph in the Parallel Stacks window will also be updated to reflect the newly selected current thread.

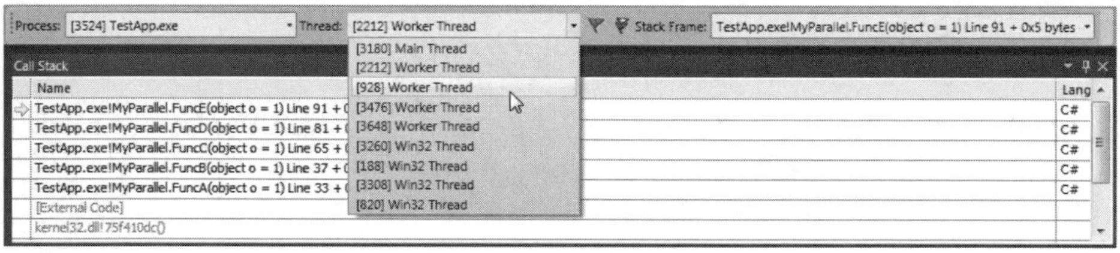

FIGURE 43-13

You can also flag both threads and tasks from the Threads and Parallel Tasks windows. Flagging enables you to keep track of a thread or task within a debugging session, and filter out some of the tasks or threads you are not interested in. In Figure 43-14, we have flagged the first two tasks in the Parallel Tasks window. By selecting the Show Only Flagged option on the toolbar of the Parallel Stacks window, we have filtered the call graph to hide the tasks that we are not interested in.

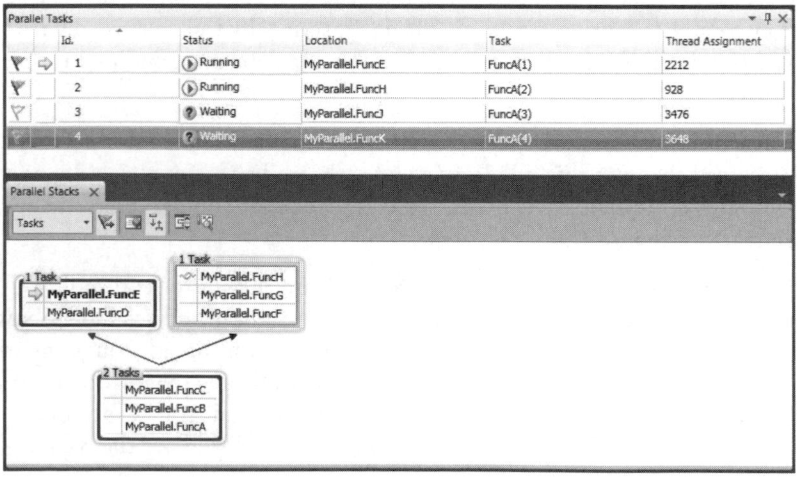

FIGURE 43-14

Though debugging multi-threaded and parallelized applications is still not a trivial task, these features do make it much easier to drill down on specific threads and tasks, and filter out the unimportant information from the Visual Studio debugger windows.

DEBUGGING SQL SERVER STORED PROCEDURES

Another very useful feature of the debugging model found in Visual Studio 2010 is the capability to debug stored procedures in SQL Server databases. You'll need to first check the Enable SQL Server Debugging setting in the Debug property page of your project, as shown in Figure 43-15. Once activated, whenever your code encounters a stored procedure, you can debug the procedure code inline with your own code.

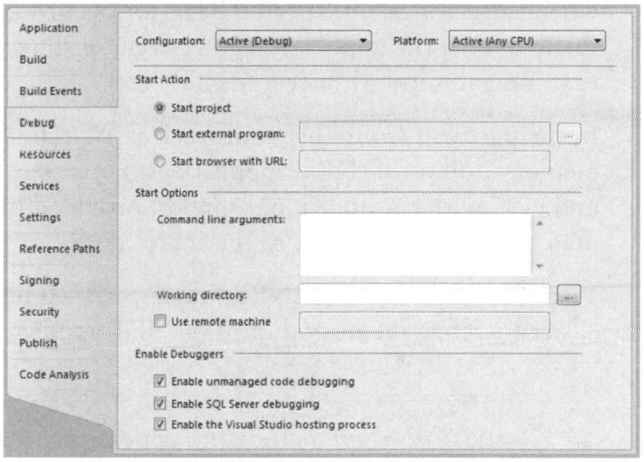

You can even include breakpoints within a stored procedure so you can trace through the SQL Server code without halting the application code execution.

FIGURE 43-15

Your Windows account must be a member of the sysadmin group on SQL Server in order to debug stored procedures.

MIXED-MODE DEBUGGING

A mixed-mode application is any application that combines managed code (Visual Basic, C#, Managed C++, and so on) with native code (typically C++). Debugging a mixed-mode application is not all that different from debugging a pure managed-code application; however, you must first configure the application to support native code debugging. Figure 43-15, in the previous section, shows the unmanaged code debugger enabled, along with the SQL Server debugger.

Mixed-mode debugging has a couple of limitations that you should be aware of. First, it is only available on Windows 2000 or higher operating systems. Also, when debugging a mixed-mode application, you may find that some operations, such as stepping through code, run very slowly. This can be improved by unchecking the option to Enable Property Evaluation and Other Implicit Function Calls in the Debugger option page.

> *Because native call stacks and managed call stacks are different, the debugger cannot always provide a single complete call stack for mixed code. Though rare, it is possible that there will be some discrepancies in the call stack. You can find more information on this in the MSDN library.*

POST-MORTEM DEBUGGING

Even with the most well tested of applications, it is inevitable that there will be latent bugs within your code that will show up after the software has been released. Fortunately, it is possible to debug many of the errors on user computers after they have occurred.

Post-mortem debugging involves inspecting a dump of the application's memory that was taken when the error or unexpected behavior occurred. This could be when an unhandled exception is thrown, or if the application enters a hung state, or simply if the application is exhibiting behavior that indicates it may have a memory leak.

In the past you would use tools such as WinDbg with the Son of Strike (SOS) extension to debug memory dumps of .NET applications. However, WinDbg was designed for native code debugging, and even with the additional support provided by SOS it was still difficult to perform tasks such as matching the MSIL back to the source code.

Visual Studio 2010 and .NET Framework 4.0 have introduced new functionality that makes it much easier to debug memory dumps of .NET applications.

> *Post-mortem debugging, as described here, only works for .NET version 4.0 applications and web sites. It is also much better if your application is compiled in a debug configuration. If not, you will not have access to a lot of very useful information.*

Generating Dump Files

You have several ways to generate dump files, including the Windows Task Manager, WinDbg, and Visual Studio itself. On Windows Vista or later operating systems, the simplest method is to right-click the process in the Windows Task Manager and select Create Dump File.

One of the more functional tools for generating dumps is the `adplus.vbs` script, which is a command-line interface to WinDbg. The adplus script and WinDbg are installed with the Debugging Tools for Windows, which is available from `http://www.microsoft.com/whdc/DevTools/Debugging/`. You must install the version that matches the processor architecture on the target machine (x86, x64, Itanium).

To generate the dump file, open a command prompt, change directory to the install location of the Debugging Tools, and enter the following command:

```
adplus -hang -pn processname.exe
```

This command attaches to the application called *processname.exe* in non-invasive mode, generates the dump, and then detaches. The application will continue to run after this.

If you are debugging a hung application, an application that is using an excessive amount of memory, or an application that is exhibiting unexpected behavior, you should take one or more memory dumps at the appropriate times. It may involve a degree of trial and error to ensure that you generate a dump that contains useful information.

If you are debugging a specific exception that is being thrown in an application, you will need to use the -c switch to pass in a file that configures adplus to generate a dump file when that exception is thrown.

You can also use Visual Studio 2010 to generate a dump file during a debug session. To do so, pause execution and select Debug ➪ Save Dump As.

Debugging Dump Files

To get the most out of post-mortem debugging you will need to configure Visual Studio to load your symbol files. Symbol files have a PDB extension and are generated as part of a debug build. You will find them in the debug output build directory; there is one for each assembly that was built.

Under Visual Studio select Tools ➪ Options and then select the Symbols category under Debugging. You can specify either a URL or a local directory as the location of your symbol files. The public Microsoft Symbol Servers will already be included; add your own local symbol directories, as shown in Figure 43-16.

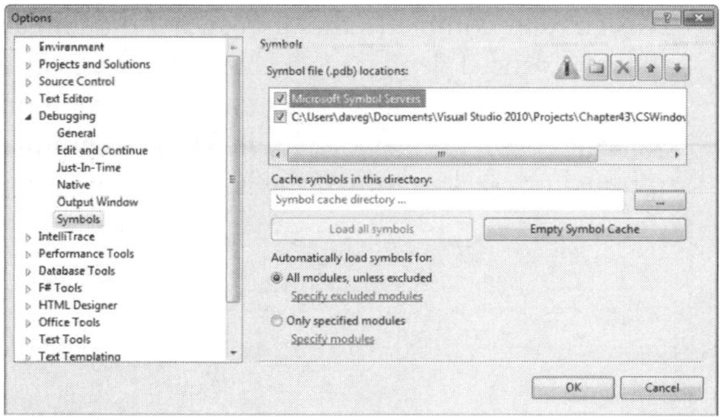

FIGURE 43-16

Now that you have generated your dump file and set up the symbols, you use Visual Studio to begin post-mortem debugging. Select File ➪ Open ➪ File and locate the dump file. Once opened, Visual Studio displays the dump summary page as shown in Figure 43-17.

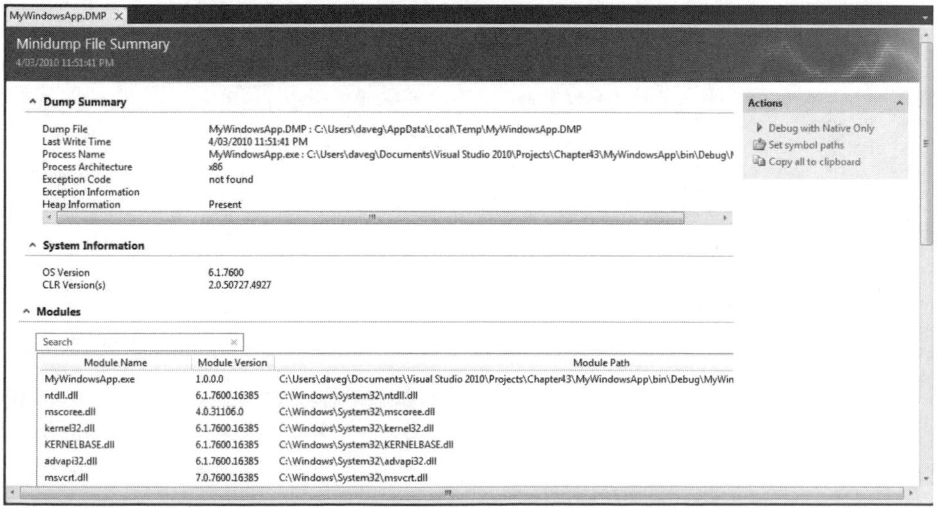

FIGURE 43-17

Click the Debug with Mixed link to load the dump and all symbols and begin debugging. This link is only displayed if the dump is from a managed application that targets the .NET Framework 4.0; otherwise you can only use the Debug with Native Only option.

Debugging a dump file is much the same as any other debugging session — you can display the call stack, inspect the contents of variables, and view the threads. The one main limitation is that because you are looking at a snapshot, and not a live application, you cannot step through the source code.

SUMMARY

This chapter completes the discussion on debugging your projects and applications, offering details about advanced debugging techniques. Visual Studio 2010 is capable of meeting a wide spectrum of debugging scenarios, such as multi-threaded applications, stored procedures, unmanaged code, and even the .NET Framework itself. These techniques provide you with a set of very effective debugging options for tracking down the issues in your projects regardless of language or technology.

PART X
Build and Deployment

▶ **CHAPTER 44:** Upgrading with Visual Studio 2010

▶ **CHAPTER 45:** Build Customization

▶ **CHAPTER 46:** Assembly Versioning and Signing

▶ **CHAPTER 47:** Obfuscation, Application Monitoring, and Management

▶ **CHAPTER 48:** Packaging and Deployment

▶ **CHAPTER 49:** Web Application Deployment

44

Upgrading with Visual Studio 2010

WHAT'S IN THIS CHAPTER?

➤ Taking advantage of the new IDE when working on older projects

➤ Updating projects to use the latest runtime and libraries

Each time a new version of Visual Studio is released, there is always a delay before developers start to use it. This is primarily due to the need to upgrade existing applications to a new version of the .NET Framework at the same time. For example, the migration from Visual Studio 2003 to Visual Studio 2005 required upgrading applications to version 2.0 of the .NET Framework. Since the introduction of multi-targeting in Visual Studio 2008, you have been able to upgrade to the latest IDE independently of moving to the .NET Framework version. This is particularly important if you still need to target older versions of Windows for which there is no support for the newer .NET Framework versions.

In this chapter, you see how easy it is to migrate existing .NET applications into Visual Studio 2010. This is done it two parts: upgrading to Visual Studio 2010 and then upgrading the .NET Framework version the application makes use of to 4.0.

UPGRADING FROM VISUAL STUDIO 2008

To begin with, let's start with a solution that contains a good mix of application types. Figure 44-1 shows a Visual Studio 2008 solution that contains Class Library, Unit Test, WCF Web Site, Web Application, Windows Application, Workflow Application, and WPF Application projects. The WCF Web Site, Web Application, Unit Test, and Workflow Application projects all reference the Class Library project and the Windows Application and WPF Application projects reference the WCF Service Application project.

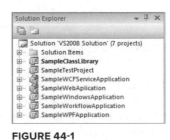

FIGURE 44-1

> *The tools required to develop Windows Mobile device applications are not included in the initial release of Visual Studio 2010. This means that you cannot upgrade existing device applications from Visual Studio 2008 to Visual Studio 2010.*

Upgrading this solution is as simple as opening it in Visual Studio 2010. This automatically invokes the Visual Studio Conversion Wizard, as shown in Figure 44-2. The wizard is relatively straightforward, with the only option being whether or not a backup is made of the solution before upgrading. If your solution is in source control, you can ignore this because you will be able to revert to the checked-in version if something goes wrong with the upgrade process. If your solution is not in source control, it is highly recommended that you allow Visual Studio to make this backup for you so you will have a working version if something goes wrong.

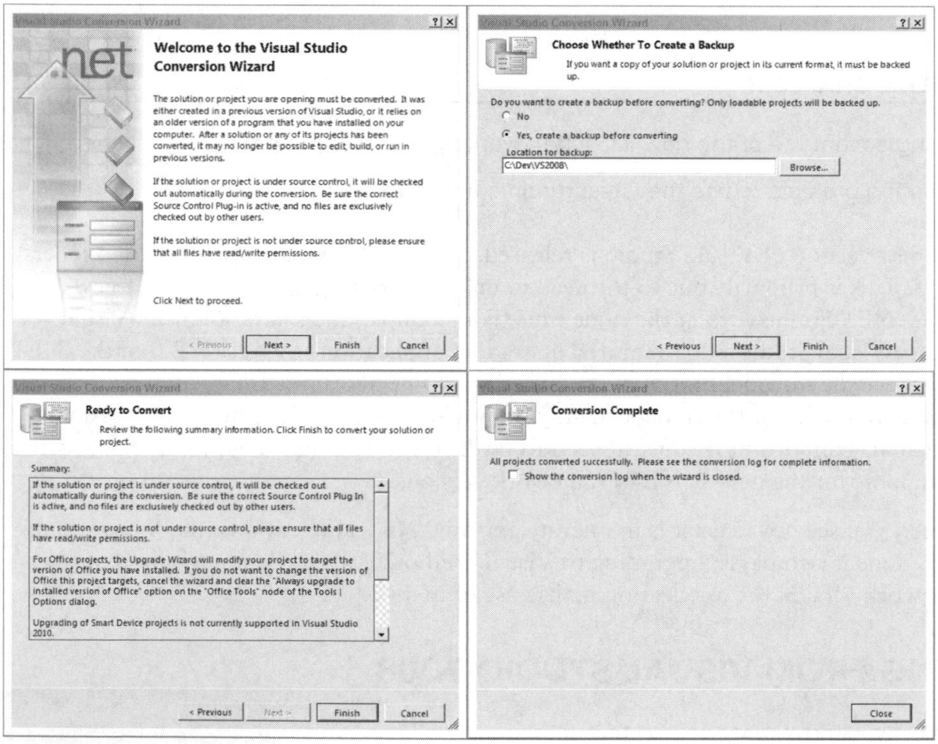

FIGURE 44-2

The Summary screen indicates that your solution will be checked out of source control so that changes can be made. It also indicates that in some cases there may be some framework and reference changes made as part of the upgrade. What you can't see in the screenshot is the list of projects that will be upgraded as part of the process.

> *If you have a Web Site project in your solution, you will be prompted to upgrade it to version 4.0 of the framework during this upgrade process. If you opt not to make the change now, you can still change the target framework version later.*

Even if the Conversion Wizard reports no errors, it is still recommended that you look through the conversion log after the wizard closes. This log (UpgradeLog.XML, found in the solution folder) looks similar to Figure 44-3 and typically lists the solution and project files as the only things that have been upgraded. If you are upgrading a pre–Visual Studio 2005 solution, you may find some conversion issues, because some known breakages between the framework versions exist. Despite being able to target multiple versions of the .NET Framework, Visual Studio 2010 is limited to version 2.0 and above. So, if you have a solution that uses a version prior to this, the Conversion Wizard will attempt to upgrade it.

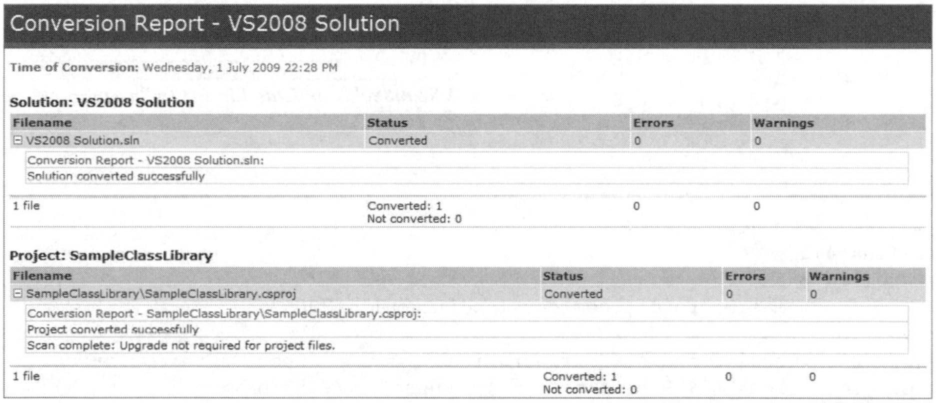

Conversion Report - VS2008 Solution

Time of Conversion: Wednesday, 1 July 2009 22:28 PM

Solution: VS2008 Solution

Filename	Status	Errors	Warnings
⊟ VS2008 Solution.sln	Converted	0	0
Conversion Report - VS2008 Solution.sln:			
Solution converted successfully			
1 file	Converted: 1 Not converted: 0	0	0

Project: SampleClassLibrary

Filename	Status	Errors	Warnings
⊟ SampleClassLibrary\SampleClassLibrary.csproj	Converted	0	0
Conversion Report - SampleClassLibrary\SampleClassLibrary.csproj:			
Project converted successfully			
Scan complete: Upgrade not required for project files.			
1 file	Converted: 1 Not converted: 0	0	0

FIGURE 44-3

With the multi-targeting capabilities of Visual Studio 2010, upgrading a solution does not mean updating the version of the framework that you are developing for. So, the question is what has been changed and what effect this might have. The answer is that there are minimal changes to both the solution and project files. In the solution file the changes may be as subtle as the header. For example, the following:

```
Microsoft Visual Studio Solution File, Format Version 10.00
# Visual Studio 2008
```

becomes:

```
Microsoft Visual Studio Solution File, Format Version 11.00
# Visual Studio 2010
```

The changes to the project file include some additional elements and attributes. For example, the following:

```
<Project
  ToolsVersion="3.5"
  DefaultTargets="Build"
  xmlns="http://schemas.microsoft.com/developer/msbuild/2003">
  <PropertyGroup>
    <Configuration Condition=" '$(Configuration)' == '' ">Debug</Configuration>
    <Platform Condition=" '$(Platform)' == '' ">AnyCPU</Platform>
    <ProductVersion>9.0.30729</ProductVersion>
    <SchemaVersion>2.0</SchemaVersion>
    <ProjectGuid>{8735A946-4A21-4921-A4F9-E9645ABCF9ED}</ProjectGuid>
    <OutputType>Library</OutputType>
    <AppDesignerFolder>Properties</AppDesignerFolder>
    <RootNamespace>ClassLibrary1</RootNamespace>
    <AssemblyName>ClassLibrary1</AssemblyName>
    <TargetFrameworkVersion>v3.5</TargetFrameworkVersion>
    <FileAlignment>512</FileAlignment>
  </PropertyGroup>
  ...
```

VS2008Solution\ClassLibrary1\ClassLibrary1.csproj

becomes:

```
<Project
  ToolsVersion="4.0"
  DefaultTargets="Build"
  xmlns="http://schemas.microsoft.com/developer/msbuild/2003">
  <PropertyGroup>
    <Configuration Condition=" '$(Configuration)' == '' ">Debug</Configuration>
    <Platform Condition=" '$(Platform)' == '' ">AnyCPU</Platform>
    <ProductVersion>9.0.30729</ProductVersion>
    <SchemaVersion>2.0</SchemaVersion>
    <ProjectGuid>{8735A946-4A21-4921-A4F9-E9645ABCF9ED}</ProjectGuid>
    <OutputType>Library</OutputType>
    <AppDesignerFolder>Properties</AppDesignerFolder>
    <RootNamespace>ClassLibrary1</RootNamespace>
    <AssemblyName>ClassLibrary1</AssemblyName>
    <TargetFrameworkVersion>v3.5</TargetFrameworkVersion>
    <FileAlignment>512</FileAlignment>
    <FileUpgradeFlags>
    </FileUpgradeFlags>
    <OldToolsVersion>3.5</OldToolsVersion>
    <UpgradeBackupLocation />
  </PropertyGroup>
  ...
```

Upgraded\ClassLibrary1\ClassLibrary1.csproj

> *If you have developers working with a mix of Visual Studio 2008 and Visual Studio 2010, you can have them all work off a common set of project files by having two solution files, one for each version of Visual Studio. Even after upgrading the project to Visual Studio 2010, they can still be opened in both versions of the IDE. Unfortunately, the same is not true of MSBuild — once you upgrade your projects, you must also upgrade your build process in order to use MSBuild version 4.0.*

UPGRADING TO .NET FRAMEWORK 4.0

Once you have migrated your application across to Visual Studio 2010 and tidied up your build environment, you should consider the upgrade path to .NET Framework 4.0. Unlike the upgrade to version 2.0 of the .NET Framework, where there were a number of breaking changes, the upgrade to version 4.0 should be relatively painless. Although you may still need to make some changes, for the most part your existing application should be easily upgradeable.

In most cases, upgrading your application is just a matter of changing the Target Framework project property. Figure 44-4 shows the project properties dialog for a C# Class Library project. On the Application tab there is a drop-down that lists the different target frameworks that are available for you to select.

> *For VB projects, this drop-down list is in the Advanced Compile Options dialog box, which you can access from the Compile tab in the project properties designer.*

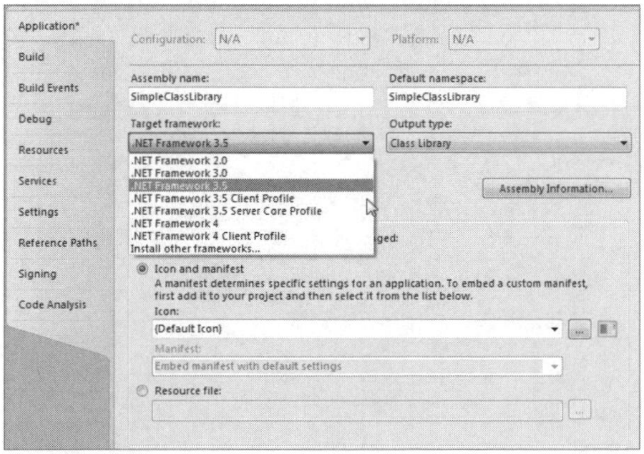

FIGURE 44-4

As soon as you select a new framework version, the dialog in Figure 44-5 appears. If you select Yes, all pending changes to the project will be saved and the project will be closed, updated, and reopened with the new target framework version. It is recommended that you immediately attempt a rebuild to ensure that the application still compiles.

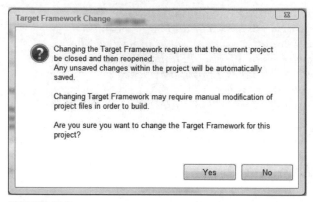

FIGURE 44-5

SUMMARY

In this chapter, you have seen how you can upgrade existing .NET applications to Visual Studio 2010 and version 4.0 of the framework. Using the latest toolset and framework version clearly has some advantages in performance, functionality, and usability. However, don't overlook the limitations that using the latest .NET Framework might impose. If your target market still uses old operating systems, such as Windows 2000, you may want to stay on version 2.0 of the framework, because this is supported on these platforms. Visual Studio 2010 allows you to have the best of both worlds, only upgrading as and when you want to.

45

Build Customization

WHAT'S IN THIS CHAPTER?

➤ Customizing the build environment

➤ Performing actions at the beginning and the end of the build

➤ Creating custom MSBuild scripts

Although you can build most of your projects using the default compilation options set up by Visual Studio 2010, occasionally you'll need to modify some aspect of the build process to achieve what you want. This chapter looks at the various build options available to you in both Visual Basic and C#, outlining what the different settings do so you can customize them to suit your own requirements.

In addition, you learn how Visual Studio 2010 uses the MSBuild engine to perform its compilations and how you can get under the hood of the configuration files that control the compilation of your projects.

GENERAL BUILD OPTIONS

Before you even get started on a project, you can modify some settings in the Options pages for Visual Studio 2010. These options apply to every project and solution that you open in the IDE, and as such can be used to customize your general experience when it comes to compiling your projects.

The first port of call for professional Visual Basic developers should be the General page of the Projects and Solutions group. By default, the Visual Basic development settings of the IDE hide some of the build options from view, so the only way to show them is to activate the Show Advanced Build Configurations option.

When this is active, the IDE displays the Build Configuration options in the My Project pages, and the Build ⇨ Configuration Manager menu command also becomes accessible. Other language environments don't need to do this, because these options are activated on startup (although you could certainly turn them off if you didn't want them cluttering your menus and pages).

Two other options on this page relate to building your projects. One allows Visual Studio to automatically show the Output window when you start a build and the other allows Visual Studio to automatically show the Error window if compilation errors occur during the build process. By default, all language configurations have both of these options turned on.

The Build and Run options page (shown in Figure 45-1) in the Projects and Solutions group has many more options available to you to customize the way your builds take place.

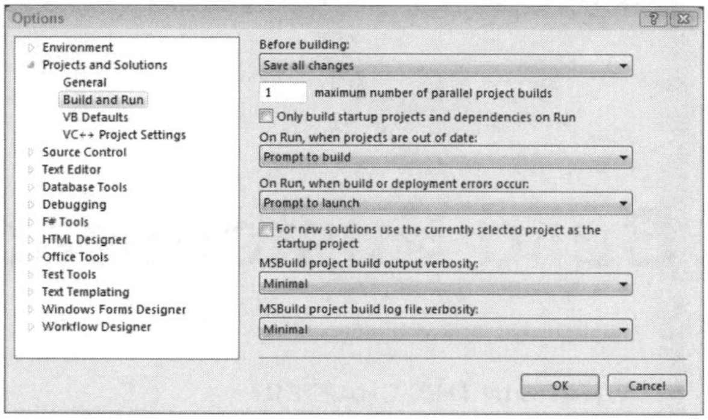

FIGURE 45-1

It's unclear from this page, but some of these options affect only C11 projects, so it's worth running through each option, what it does, and what languages it affects:

➤ **Before Building:** This tells Visual Studio how to handle changes that have been made to any part of your project before the build process. You have four options:

➤ **Save All Changes** automatically saves any changes without prompting you. This is perhaps the best option, because you don't have to remember to save your work. This is the default setting.

➤ **Save Changes to Open Documents Only** also automatically saves changes, but only to open documents. This excludes some changes to solution and project files.

➤ **Prompt to Save All Changes** gives you the chance to save any changes before the build commences. When the build process is started, it displays a dialog prompting you to save the changes or not. If you decline to save the changes, the build still continues but uses the last saved version of the file. This option can be good to use when you want to know when you've made changes (perhaps inadvertently) to the source code.

➤ **Don't Save Any Changes,** as it suggests, doesn't save changes to any files, open in the editor or otherwise.

➤ **Maximum Number of Parallel Project Builds:** This controls how many simultaneous build processes can be active at any one time (assuming the solution being compiled has multiple projects).

➤ **Only Build Startup Projects and Dependencies on Run:** This option only builds the part of the solution directly connected to the startup projects. This means that any projects that are not dependencies for the startup projects are excluded from the default build process. This option is active by default, so if you have a solution that has multiple projects called by the startup projects through late-bound calls or other similar means, they will not be built automatically. You can either deactivate this option or manually build those projects separately.

➤ **On Run, When Projects Are Out of Date:** This option is used for C++ projects only and gives you three options for out-of-date projects (projects that have changed since the last build). The default is Prompt to Build, which forces the build process to occur whenever you run the application. The Never Build option always uses the previous build of out-of-date projects, and the Prompt to Build gives you an option to build for each out-of-date project. Note that this only applies to the Run command, and if you force a build through the Build menu, projects are rebuilt according to the other settings in the build configuration and on this Options page.

➤ **On Run, When Build or Deployment Errors Occur:** This controls the action to take when errors occur during the build process. Despite official documentation to the contrary, this option does indeed affect the behavior of builds in Visual Basic and C#. Your options here are the default Prompt to Launch, which displays a dialog prompting you for which action to take; Do Not Launch, which does not start the solution and returns to design time; and Launch Old Version, which ignores compilation errors and runs the last successful build of the project.

The option to launch an old version enables you to ignore errors in subordinate projects and still run your application; but because it doesn't warn you that errors occurred, you run the risk of getting confused about what version of the project is active.

Note that when you use the Prompt to Launch option, if you subsequently check the Do Not Show This Dialog Again option in the prompt dialog, this setting is updated to either Do Not Launch or Launch Old Version, depending on whether or not you to choose to continue.

> *It is recommended that you set this property to Do Not Launch because this can improve the efficiency with which you write and debug code — one fewer window to dismiss!*

➤ **For New Solutions Use the Currently Selected Project as the Startup Project:** This option is useful when you're building a solution with multiple projects. When the solution is being built, the Visual Studio build process assumes that the currently selected project is the startup project and determines all dependencies and the starting point for execution from there.

➤ **MSBuild Project Build Output Verbosity:** Visual Studio 2010 uses the MSBuild engine for its compilation. MSBuild produces its own set of compilation outputs, reporting on the state of each project as it's built. You have the option to control how much of this output is reported to you:

   ➤ By default, the MSBuild verbosity is set to Minimal, which produces only a very small amount of information about each project, but you can turn it off completely by setting this option to Quiet, or expand on the information you get by choosing one of the more detailed verbosity settings.

➤ MSBuild output is sent to the Output window, which is accessible via View ➪ Other Windows ➪ Output (under some environmental setups this will be View ➪ Output). If you can't see your build output, make sure you have set the Show Output From option to Build (see Figure 45-2).

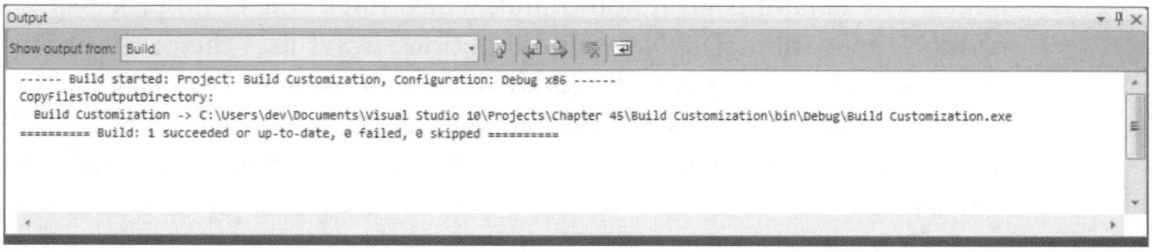

```
Output                                                                              ▾ ⅇ ×
Show output from:  Build                           ▾  🔄 🔄 🔄  🔄 🔄
    ------ Build started: Project: Build Customization, Configuration: Debug x86 ------
    CopyFilesToOutputDirectory:
      Build Customization -> C:\Users\dev\Documents\Visual Studio 10\Projects\Chapter 45\Build Customization\bin\Debug\Build Customization.exe
    ========== Build: 1 succeeded or up-to-date, 0 failed, 0 skipped ==========
```

FIGURE 45-2

➤ **MSBuild Project Log File Verbosity:** When Visual Studio builds a C++ project, it generates a text-based log file of MSBuild activities as well as the normal information that goes to the Output window. The amount of information that goes into this text file can be controlled independently using this option. One way to take advantage of this is to have more detailed information go into the log file and leave the Output window set to Minimal, which streamlines the normal development experience but gives you access to more detailed information when things go wrong. If you do not want Visual Studio to produce this separate log file, you can turn it off using the Projects and Solutions ➪ VC++ Project Settings ➪ Build Logging setting.

It's also worth taking a look at the other Options pages in the Projects and Solutions category, because they control the default Visual Basic compilation options (Option Explicit, Option Strict, Option Compare, and Option Infer), and other C++-specific options relating to build. Of note for C++ developers is the capability to specify PATH variables for the different component types of their projects, such as executables and include files, for different platform builds; and whether to log the build output (see the preceding list).

MANUAL DEPENDENCIES

Visual Studio 2010 is able to detect inter-project dependencies between projects that reference each other. This is then used to determine the order in which projects are built. Unfortunately, in some circumstances Visual Studio can't determine these dependencies, such as when you have custom steps in the build process. Luckily, you can manually define project dependencies to indicate how projects are related to each other. You can access the dialog shown in Figure 45-3 by selecting either the Project ➪ Project Dependencies or Project ➪ Build Order menu commands.

Note that these menu commands are available only when you have a solution with multiple projects in the IDE.

You first select the project that is dependent on others from the drop-down, and then check the projects it depends on in the bottom list. Any dependencies that are automatically detected by Visual Studio 2010 will already be marked in this list. The Build Order tab can be used to confirm the order in which the projects will be built.

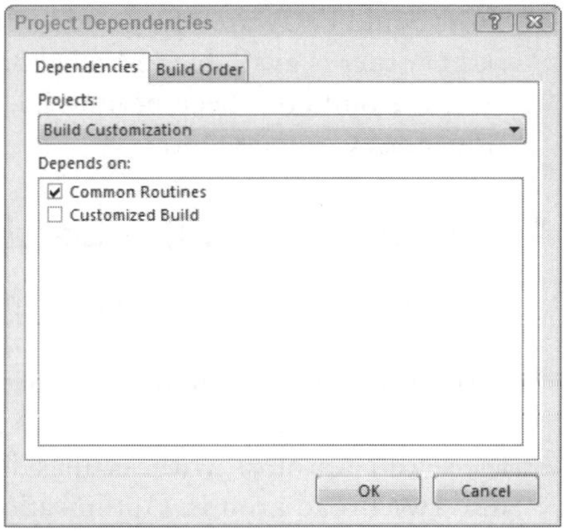

THE VISUAL BASIC COMPILE PAGE

Visual Basic projects have an additional set of options that control how the build process will occur. To access the compile options for a specific project, open My Project by double-clicking its entry in the Solution Explorer. When the project Options page is shown, navigate to the Compile page from the list on the left side (see Figure 45-4).

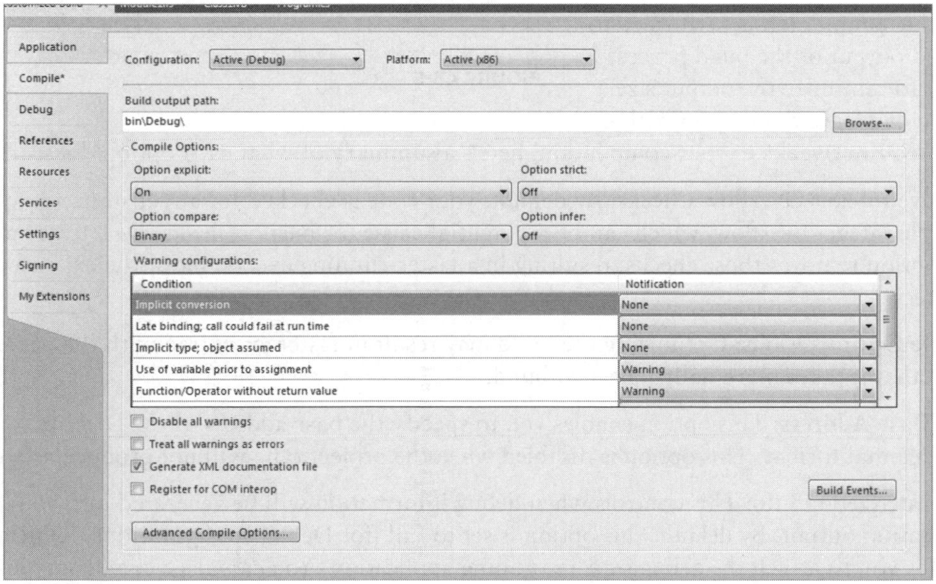

FIGURE 45-3

FIGURE 45-4

The Build Output Path option controls where the executable version (application or DLL) of your project is stored. For Visual Basic, the default setting is the `bin\Debug\` or `bin\Release\` directory (depending on the current configuration), but you can change this by browsing to the desired location.

> *It is recommended that you enable the Treat All Warnings as Errors option because this will, in most cases, encourage you to write better, less error-prone code.*

You should be aware of two additional sets of hidden options. The Build Events button in the lower-right corner is available to Visual Basic developers who want to run actions or scripts before or after the build has been performed. They are discussed in a moment. The other button is labeled Advanced Compile Options.

Advanced Compiler Settings

Clicking the Advanced Compile Options button displays the Advanced Compiler Settings dialog (see Figure 45-5) in which you can fine-tune the build process for the selected project, with settings divided into two broad groups: Optimizations and Compilation Constants.

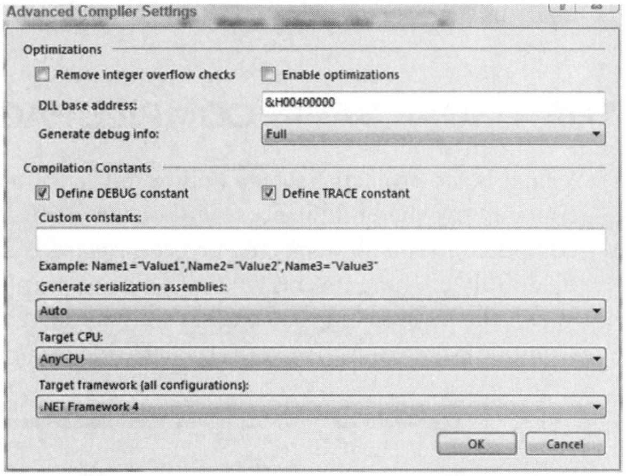

FIGURE 45-5

Optimizations

The settings in the Optimizations group control how the compilation is performed to make the build output or the build process itself faster or to minimize the output size. Normally, you can leave these options alone, but if you do require tweaks to your compilation, here's a summary of what each option does:

➤ **Remove Integer Overflow Checks:** By default, your code is checked for any instance of a possible integer overflow, which can be a potential cause for memory leaks. Deactivating this option removes those checks, resulting in a faster-running executable at the expense of safety.

➤ **Enable Optimizations:** Optimizing the build may result in faster execution with the penalty being that it takes marginally longer to build.

➤ **DLL Base Address:** This option enables you to specify the base address of the DLL in hexadecimal format. This option is disabled when the project type will not produce a DLL.

➤ **Generate Debug Info:** This controls when debug information will be generated into your application output. By default, this option is set to full (for Debug configurations), which enables you to attach the debugger to a running application. You can also turn debugging information off completely or set the option to pdb-only (the default for Release configurations) to only generate the PDB debugging information. The latter means that you can still debug the application when it is started from within Visual Studio 2010 but you will only be able to see the disassembler if you try to attach to a running application.

Compilation Constants

Compilation constants can be used to control what information is included in the build output and even what code is compiled. The Compilation Constants options control the following:

> ➤ **Define DEBUG Constant and Define TRACE Constant:** Enable debug and trace information to be included in the compiled application based on the DEBUG and TRACE flags, respectively.

> ➤ **Custom Constants:** If your application build process requires custom constants, you can specify them here in the form ConstantName="Value". If you have multiple constants, they should be delimited by commas.

The last three options don't really fall under compilation constants, but they do allow you to further customize the way the project builds.

> ➤ **Generate Serialization Assemblies:** By default this option is set to Auto, which enables the build process to determine whether serialization assemblies are needed, but you can change it to On or Off if you want to hard-code the behavior.

> *Serialization assemblies are created using the* Sgen.exe *command-line tool. This tool generates an assembly that contains an* XmlSerializer *for serializing (and deserializing) a specific type. Normally these assemblies are generated at run time the first time an* XmlSerializer *is used. Pre-generating them at compile time can improve the performance of the first use. Serialization assemblies are named* TypeName.XmlSerializers.dll. *See the documentation of* Sgen.exe *for more info.*

> ➤ **Target CPU:** Depending on what CPU types are known to your system, this option enables you to optimize the build output to a specific platform. The default option of AnyCPU provides output that can be run on any CPU that supports the .NET Framework.

> ➤ **Target Framework:** This is the only option in this dialog that applies to all configurations and is used to determine what version of the base class libraries the project is compiled against.

Build Events

You can perform additional actions before or after the build process by adding them to an events list. Click the Build Events button on the My Project Compile page to display the Build Events dialog. Figure 45-6 shows a post-build event that executes the project output after every successful build.

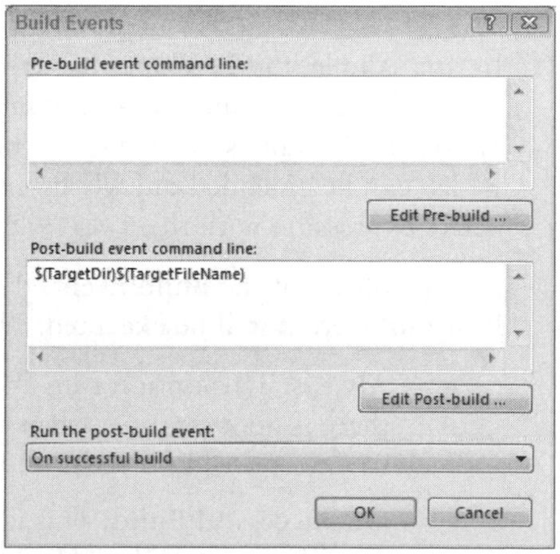

Each action you want to perform should be on a separate line, and can be added directly into either the Pre-build Event Command Line text area or the Post-build Event Command Line text area, or you can use the Edit Pre-build and Edit Post-build buttons to access the known predefined aliases that you can use in the actions.

FIGURE 45-6

> 🖊 *If your pre- or post-build event actions are batch files, you must prefix them with a call statement. For example, if you want to call* `archive_previous_build.bat` *before every build, you need to enter* `call archive_previous_build.bat` *into the Pre-build Event Command Line text box. In addition to this, any paths that contain spaces should be encased in double-quotes. This applies even if the path with spaces comes from one of the built-in macros.*

Shown in Figure 45-7, the Event Command Line dialog includes a list of macros you can use in the creation of your actions. The current value is displayed for each macro so you know what text will be included if you use it.

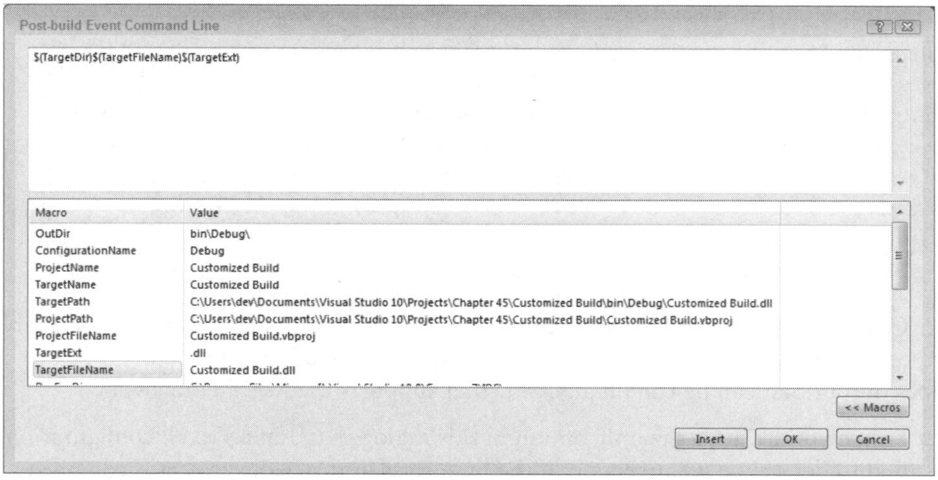

FIGURE 45-7

In this sample, the developer has created a command line of `$(TargetDir)$(TargetFileName)$(TargetExt)`, assuming that it would execute the built application when finished. However, analyzing the values of each of the macros, it's easy to see that the extension will be included twice, which can be amended quickly by either simply removing the `$(TargetExt)` macro or replacing the entire expression with the `$(TargetPath)` macro.

At the bottom of the Build Events dialog there is an option to specify the conditions under which the Post Build Event will be executed. The valid options are:

➤ **Always:** This option runs the Post Build Event script even if the build fails. Remember that there is no guarantee when this event fires that Visual Studio has produced any files at all, so your post-build script should be able to handle this scenario.

➤ **On Successful Build:** This is the default option. It causes the Post Build Event script to be run whenever the build is considered to be successful. Note that this means that it will run even if your project is up to date (and therefore is not rebuilt).

➤ **When the Build Updates the Project Output:** This option is very similar to On Successful Build, except that it only fires the Post Build Event script when the project output files have changed. This is a great option for keeping a local cache of archived builds of your projects because it means you will only copy a file into the archive if it has changed since the last build.

There are no filter options for determining if the Pre-Build Event will be executed.

C# BUILD PAGES

C# provides its own set of build options. In general, the options are the same as those available to a Visual Basic project, but in a different location because C# programmers are more likely to tweak the output than Visual Basic developers, who are typically more interested in rapid development than in fine-tuning performance.

Instead of a single Compile page in the project property pages, C# has a Build page and a Build Events page. The Build Events page acts in exactly the same way as the Build Events dialog in Visual Basic, so refer to the previous discussion for information on that page.

As you can see in Figure 45-8, many of the options on the Build page have direct correlations to settings found in the Compile page or in the Advanced Compiler Settings area of Visual Basic. Some settings, such as Define DEBUG Constant and Define TRACE Constant, are identical to their Visual Basic counterparts.

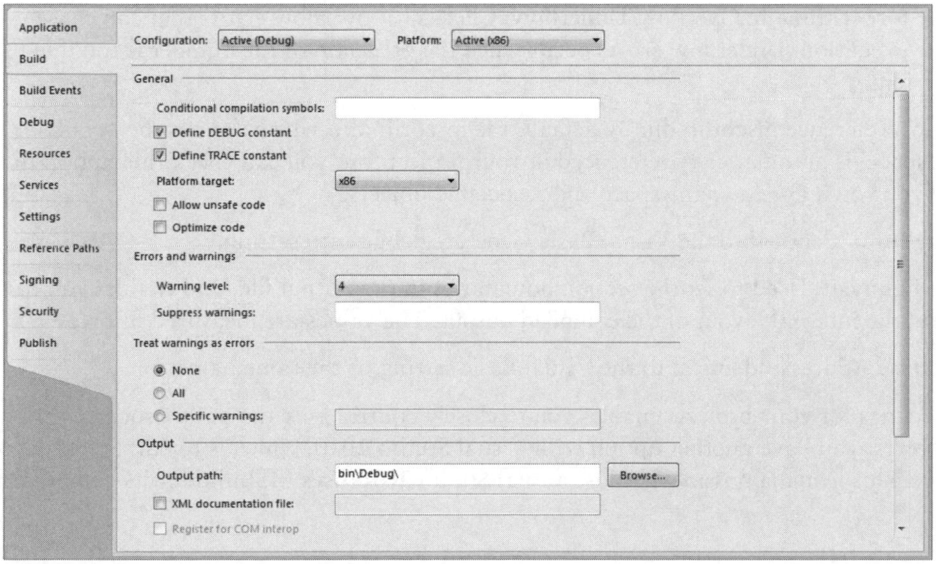

FIGURE 45-8

However, some are renamed to fit in with a C-based vocabulary; for example, "Optimize code" is equivalent to "Enable optimizations." As with the Visual Basic compile settings, you can determine how warnings are treated, and you can specify a warning level.

Clicking the Advanced button on the Build page invokes the Advanced Build Settings dialog, shown in Figure 45-9, which includes settings that are not accessible to Visual Basic developers. These settings give you tight control over how the build will be performed, including information on the internal errors that occur during the compilation process and what debug information is to be generated.

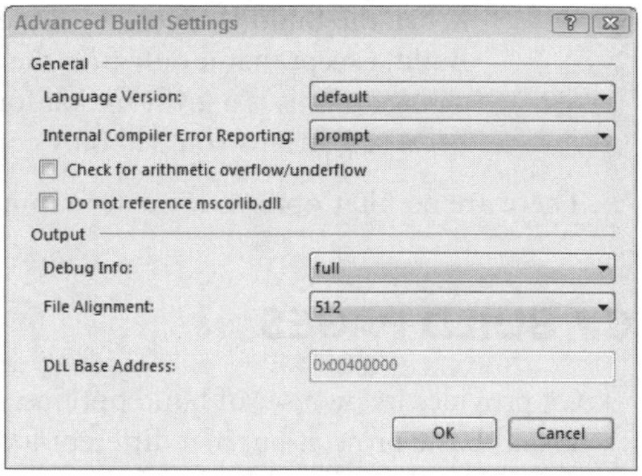

These settings are mostly self-explanatory, so the following list is a quick summary of what effect each one has on the build:

FIGURE 45-9

➤ **Language Version:** Specifies which version of the C# language to use. The default is to use the current version. In Visual Studio 2010, the other options are ISO-1 and ISO-2, which restricts the language features to those defined in the corresponding ISO standard.

➤ **Internal Compiler Error Reporting:** If errors occur during the compilation (not compilation errors, but errors with the compilation process itself), you can have information sent to Microsoft so it can add it to its revision of the compiler code. The default setting is Prompt, which asks you whether you want to send the information to Microsoft.

Other values include None, which won't send the information; Send, to automatically send the error information; and Queue, which adds the details to a queue to be sent later.

➤ **Check for Arithmetic Overflow/Underflow:** Checks for overflow errors that can cause unsafe execution. Underflow errors occur when the precision of the number is too fine for the system.

➤ **Do Not Reference mscorlib.dll:** By default, the mscorlib.dll, which defines the `System` namespace, is automatically referenced in your project, but you can check this option to build your own `System` namespace and associated objects.

➤ **Debug Info:** Identical to the Visual Basic Generate debug info setting.

➤ **File Alignment:** Used to set the section boundaries in the output file, and enables you to control the internal layout of the compiled output. The values are measured in bytes.

➤ **DLL Base Address:** Identical to the Visual Basic setting of the same name.

Using these settings for your projects enables you to closely control how the build process will perform. However, you have another option with Visual Studio 2010, which is to edit the build scripts directly. This is made possible because Visual Studio 2010 uses MSBuild for its compilations.

MSBUILD

Visual Studio 2010 uses MSBuild, which is the compilation engine Microsoft originally released with Visual Studio 2005. It uses XML-based configuration files to identify the layout of a build project, including all of the settings discussed earlier in this chapter, as well as what files should be included in the actual compilation.

In fact, since Visual Studio 2005, Visual Studio uses MSBuild configuration files as its project definition files, in place of the old project file formats used by previous versions of Visual Studio. This enables the MSBuild engine to be used automatically when compiling your applications within the IDE because the same settings file is used for both your project definition in the IDE and the build process.

How Visual Studio Uses MSBuild

As already mentioned, the contents of Visual Studio 2010 project files are based on the MSBuild XML Schema and can be edited directly in Visual Studio so you can customize how the project is loaded and compiled.

However, to edit the project file you need to effectively remove the project's active status from the Solution Explorer. Right-click the project you want to edit in the Solution Explorer, and choose the Unload Project command from the bottom of the context menu that is displayed.

The project will be collapsed in the Solution Explorer and marked as unavailable. In addition, any open files that belong to the project will be closed while it is unloaded from the solution. Right-click the project entry again and an additional menu command will be available to edit the project file (see Figure 45-10).

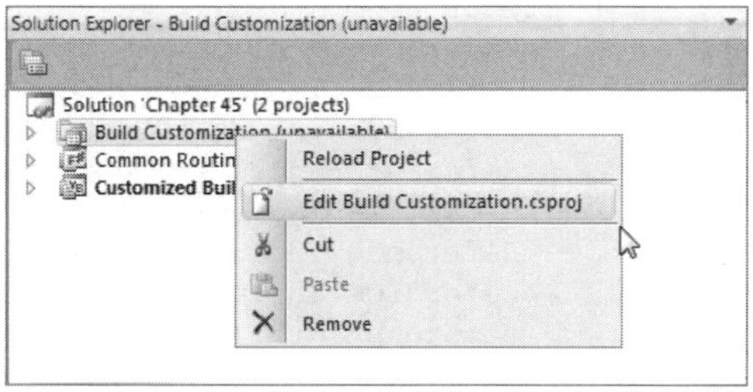

FIGURE 45-10

The XML-based project file will be correspondingly opened in the XML editor of Visual Studio 2010, enabling you to collapse and expand nodes. The following listing is a sample MSBuild project file for an empty C# project:

```xml
<?xml version="1.0" encoding="utf-8"?>
<Project
  ToolsVersion="4.0"
  DefaultTargets="Build"
  xmlns="http://schemas.microsoft.com/developer/msbuild/2003">
  <PropertyGroup>
    <Configuration Condition=" '$(Configuration)' == '' ">Debug</Configuration>
    <Platform Condition=" '$(Platform)' == '' ">x86</Platform>
    <ProductVersion>8.0.30703</ProductVersion>
    <SchemaVersion>2.0</SchemaVersion>
    <ProjectGuid>{04ABE6E2-5500-467B-BB01-0BBF0258E94A}</ProjectGuid>
    <OutputType>Exe</OutputType>
    <AppDesignerFolder>Properties</AppDesignerFolder>
    <RootNamespace>ConsoleApplication</RootNamespace>
    <AssemblyName>ConsoleApplication</AssemblyName>
    <TargetFrameworkVersion>v4.0</TargetFrameworkVersion>
    <TargetFrameworkProfile>Client</TargetFrameworkProfile>
    <FileAlignment>512</FileAlignment>
  </PropertyGroup>
  <PropertyGroup Condition=" '$(Configuration)|$(Platform)' == 'Debug|x86' ">
    <PlatformTarget>x86</PlatformTarget>
    <DebugSymbols>true</DebugSymbols>
```

```xml
      <DebugType>full</DebugType>
      <Optimize>false</Optimize>
      <OutputPath>bin\Debug\</OutputPath>
      <DefineConstants>DEBUG;TRACE</DefineConstants>
      <ErrorReport>prompt</ErrorReport>
      <WarningLevel>4</WarningLevel>
   </PropertyGroup>
   <PropertyGroup Condition=" '$(Configuration)|$(Platform)' == 'Release|x86' ">
      <PlatformTarget>x86</PlatformTarget>
      <DebugType>pdbonly</DebugType>
      <Optimize>true</Optimize>
      <OutputPath>bin\Release\</OutputPath>
      <DefineConstants>TRACE</DefineConstants>
      <ErrorReport>prompt</ErrorReport>
      <WarningLevel>4</WarningLevel>
   </PropertyGroup>
   <ItemGroup>
      <Reference Include="System" />
      <Reference Include="System.Core" />
      <Reference Include="System.Xml.Linq" />
      <Reference Include="System.Data.DataSetExtensions" />
      <Reference Include="Microsoft.CSharp" />
      <Reference Include="System.Data" />
      <Reference Include="System.Xml" />
   </ItemGroup>
   <ItemGroup>
      <Compile Include="Program.cs" />
      <Compile Include="Properties\AssemblyInfo.cs" />
   </ItemGroup>
   <Import Project="$(MSBuildToolsPath)\Microsoft.CSharp.targets" />
   <!-- To modify your build process, add your task inside one of the targets
        below and uncomment it. Other similar extension points exist, see
        Microsoft.Common.targets.
   <Target Name="BeforeBuild">
   </Target>
   <Target Name="AfterBuild">
   </Target>
   -->
</Project>
```

ConsoleApplication\ConsoleApplication.csproj

The XML contains the information about the build. In fact, most of these nodes directly relate to settings you saw earlier in the Compile and Build pages, but also include any Framework namespaces that are required. The first `PropertyGroup` element contains project properties that apply to all build configurations. This is followed by two conditional elements that define properties for each of the two build configurations, Debug and Release. The remaining elements are for project references and project-wide namespace imports.

When the project includes additional files, such as forms and user controls, each one is defined in the project file with its own set of nodes. For example, the following listing shows the additional XML that is included in a standard Windows Application project, identifying the Form, its designer code file, and the additional application files required for a Windows-based application:

```
<ItemGroup>
  <Compile Include="Form1.cs">
    <SubType>Form</SubType>
  </Compile>
  <Compile Include="Form1.Designer.cs">
    <DependentUpon>Form1.cs</DependentUpon>
  </Compile>
  <Compile Include="Program.cs" />
  <Compile Include="Properties\AssemblyInfo.cs" />
  <EmbeddedResource Include="Properties\Resources.resx">
    <Generator>ResXFileCodeGenerator</Generator>
    <LastGenOutput>Resources.Designer.cs</LastGenOutput>
    <SubType>Designer</SubType>
  </EmbeddedResource>
  <Compile Include="Properties\Resources.Designer.cs">
    <AutoGen>True</AutoGen>
    <DependentUpon>Resources.resx</DependentUpon>
  </Compile>
  <None Include="Properties\Settings.settings">
    <Generator>SettingsSingleFileGenerator</Generator>
    <LastGenOutput>Settings.Designer.cs</LastGenOutput>
  </None>
  <Compile Include="Properties\Settings.Designer.cs">
    <AutoGen>True</AutoGen>
    <DependentUpon>Settings.settings</DependentUpon>
    <DesignTimeSharedInput>True</DesignTimeSharedInput>
  </Compile>
</ItemGroup>
```

WindowsFormsApplication\WindowsFormsApplication.csproj

You can also include additional tasks in the build process in the included Target nodes for
`BeforeBuild` and `AfterBuild` events. However, these actions will not appear in the Visual Studio
2010 Build Events dialog discussed earlier. The alternative is to use a `PropertyGroup` node that
includes `PreBuildEvent` and `PostBuildEvent` entries. For instance, if you wanted to execute the
application after it was successfully built, you could include the following XML block immediately
before the closing `</Project>` tag:

```
<PropertyGroup>
  <PostBuildEvent>"$(TargetDir)$(TargetFileName)"</PostBuildEvent>
</PropertyGroup>
```

Once you've finished editing the project file's XML, you need to re-enable it in the solution by
right-clicking the project's entry in the Solution Explorer and selecting the Reload Project command.
If you still have the project file open, Visual Studio asks if you want to close it to proceed.

The MSBuild Schema

An extended discussion on the MSBuild engine is beyond the scope of this book. However, it's
useful to understand the different components that make up the MSBuild project file so you can
look at and update your own projects.

Four major elements form the basis of the project file: *items*, *properties*, *targets*, and *tasks*. Brought together, you can use these four node types to create a configuration file that describes a project in full, as shown in the previous sample C# project file.

Items

Items are those elements that define inputs to the build system and project. They are defined as children of an ItemGroup node, and the most common item is the Compile node used to inform MSBuild that the specified file is to be included in the compilation. The following snippet from a project file shows an Item element defined for the Form1.cs file of a WindowsApplication project:

```
<ItemGroup>
  <Compile Include="Form1.cs">
    <SubType>Form</SubType>
  </Compile>
</ItemGroup>
```

Properties

PropertyGroup nodes are used to contain any properties defined to the project. Properties are typically key/value pairings. They can only contain a single value and are used to store the project settings you can access in the Build and Compile pages in the IDE.

PropertyGroup nodes can be optionally included by specifying a Condition attribute, as shown in the following sample listing:

```
<PropertyGroup Condition=" '$(Configuration)|$(Platform)' == 'Release|x86' ">
  <DebugType>pdbonly</DebugType>
  <Optimize>true</Optimize>
  <OutputPath>bin\Release\</OutputPath>
  <DefineConstants>TRACE</DefineConstants>
  <ErrorReport>prompt</ErrorReport>
  <WarningLevel>4</WarningLevel>
</PropertyGroup>
```

This XML defines a PropertyGroup that will only be included in the build if the project is being built as a Release for the x86 platform. Each of the six property nodes within the PropertyGroup uses the name of the property as the name of the node.

Targets

Target elements enable you to arrange tasks (discussed in the next section) into a sequence. Each Target element should have a Name attribute to identify it, and it can be called directly, thus enabling you to provide multiple entry points into the build process. The following snippet defines a Target with a name of BeforeBuild:

```
<Target Name="BeforeBuild">
</Target>
```

Tasks

Tasks define actions that MSBuild will execute under certain conditions. You can define your own tasks or take advantage of the many built-in tasks, such as Copy. Shown in the following snippet, Copy can copy one or more files from one location to another:

```
<Target Name="CopyFiles">
    <Copy
        SourceFiles="@(MySourceFiles)"
        DestinationFolder="\\PDSERVER01\SourceBackup\"
    />
</Target>
```

Assembly Versioning via MSBuild Tasks

One aspect of most automated build systems is planning application versioning. In this section, you see how you can customize the build process for your project so that it can accept an external version number. This version number will be used to update the AssemblyInfo file, which will subsequently affect the assembly version. Start by looking at the AssemblyInfo.cs file, which typically contains assembly version information such as the following.

[Assembly: AssemblyVersion("1.0.0.0")]

CustomizedBuild\Properties\AssemblyInfo.cs

What the build customization needs to do is replace the default version number with a number supplied as part of the build process. To do this we have elected to use a third-party MSBuild library entitled MSBuildTasks, which is a project on Tigris (http://msbuildtasks.tigris.org/). This includes a FileUpdate task that can be used to match on a regular expression. Before we can use this task, we need to import the MSBuildTasks Targets file. This file is installed into the default MSBuild extensions path by the MSBuildTasks MSI.

```
<Project ToolsVersion="4.0" DefaultTargets="Build"
xmlsn="http://schemas.microsoft.com/developer/msbuild/2003">
    <!-- Required Import to use MSBuild Community Tasks -->
    <Import Project="$(MSBuildExtensionsPath)\MSBuildCommunityTasks\
    MSBuild.Community.Tasks.Targets"/>
    <PropertyGroup>
        . . .
```

CustomizedBuild\CustomizedBuild.csproj

Because we want to update the AssemblyInfo file before the build, we could add a call to the FileUpdate task in the BeforeBuild target. This would make it harder to maintain and debug later on. A much better approach is to create a new target for the FileUpdate task and then make the BeforeBuild target depend upon it, as follows:

```
<Import Project="$(MSBuildToolsPath)\Microsoft.CSharp.targets" />
<Target Name="BeforeBuild" DependsOnTargets="UpdateAssemblyInfo">
</Target>
<Target Name="UpdateAssemblyInfo">
    <Message Text="Build Version: $(BuildVersion)" />
    <FileUpdate Files="Properties\AssemblyInfo.cs"
                Regex="\d+\.\d+\.\d+\.\d+"
                ReplacementText="$(BuildVersion)" />
</Target>
```

Available for download on Wrox.com

CustomizedBuild\CustomizedBuild.csproj

You will notice here that we are using a property called $(BuildVersion), which doesn't yet exist. If we run MSBuild against this project now, it will replace the version numbers in our AssemblyInfo file with a blank string. This unfortunately will not compile. We could simply define this property with some default value like this:

```
<PropertyGroup>
    <BuildVersion>0.0.0.0</BuildVersion>
    <Configuration Condition=" '$(Configuration)' == '' ">Debug</Configuration>
```

This will work but it means that when building our project in Visual Studio 2010 it will always have the same version. Luckily the MSBuildTasks library has another task called Version, which will generate a version number for us. Here is the code:

```
<Target Name="BeforeBuild" DependsOnTargets="GetVersion;UpdateAssemblyInfo">
</Target>
...
<Target Name="GetVersion" Condition=" $(BuildVersion) == ''">
    <Version BuildType="Automatic" RevisionType="Automatic" Major="1" Minor="3" >
        <Output TaskParameter="Major" PropertyName="Major" />
        <Output TaskParameter="Minor" PropertyName="Minor" />
        <Output TaskParameter="Build" PropertyName="Build" />
        <Output TaskParameter="Revision" PropertyName="Revision" />
    </Version>
    <CreateProperty Value="$(Major).$(Minor).$(Build).$(Revision)">
        <Output TaskParameter="Value" PropertyName="BuildVersion" />
    </CreateProperty>
</Target>
```

Available for download on Wrox.com

CustomizedBuild\CustomizedBuild.csproj

The new GetVersion target will only be executed if $(BuildVersion) is not specified. It calls into the Version task from MSBuildTasks, which sets the major version number to 1 and the minor version number to 3 (you could, of course, configure these instead of hard-coding them). The Build and Revision numbers are automatically generated according to a simple algorithm. These components of the version are then put together in a CreateProperty task, which comes with MSBuild, to create the full $(BuildVersion) that we need. Finally, this task has been added to the list of targets that BeforeBuild depends on.

Now when we build the project in Visual Studio 2010, we will get an automatically generated version number as per usual. In your automated build process you can specify the version number as an argument to the MSBuild call. For example:

```
MSBuild CustomizedBuild.csproj /p:BuildVersion=2.4.3154.9001
```

SUMMARY

The default build behavior can be customized with an enormous range of options in Visual Studio 2010 thanks to the power and flexibility of the MSBuild engine. Within the project file you can include additional actions to perform both before and after the build has taken place, as well as include additional files in the compilation.

46

Assembly Versioning and Signing

WHAT'S IN THIS CHAPTER?

➤   Versioning Assemblies

➤   Signing an Assembly to give it a Strong Name

➤   Managing Strongly Named Assemblies in the Global
     Assembly Cache

When you create a .NET assembly, you can optionally sign it to provide it with a strong name. An assembly without a strong name is identified by its filename, which often is not enough to uniquely identify it. This means that other projects that depend on your assembly cannot be guaranteed to consume the correct version. A strongly named assembly can be uniquely identified by dependent projects and even system administrators, who can apply a security policy to your assembly.

In this chapter, you learn how to use Visual Studio 2010 to set the assembly version number, and how you can use a digital signature to sign your assembly so that it can't be tampered with. This will also result in a strongly named assembly, which can be added to the Global Assembly Cache.

ASSEMBLY NAMING

Every .NET assembly, whether it is an executable or a class library, contains a manifest that has information about the assembly's identity. Primarily this includes the name and version number of the assembly, but also includes culture and public key if it is a strongly named assembly. This information can be easily viewed by opening an assembly in Red Gate's .NET Reflector, as shown in Figure 46-1.

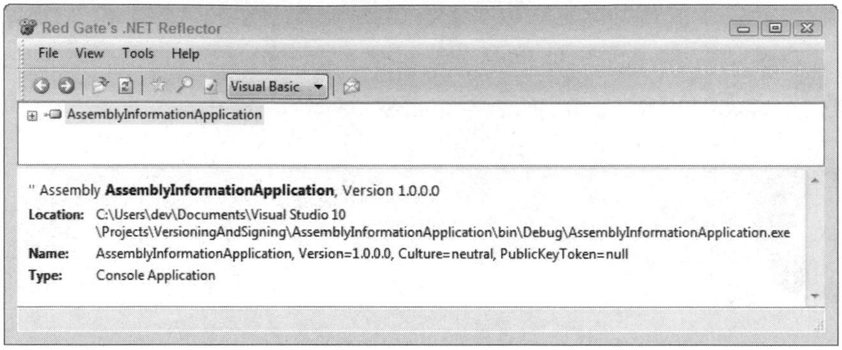

FIGURE 46-1

In Figure 46-1, the assembly `AssemblyInformationApplication.exe` does not have a public key. Other assemblies, such as `System.Data`, have a full name such as:

```
System.Data, Version=2.0.0.0, Culture=neutral, PublicKeytoken=b77a5c561934e089
```

You specify the name of your assembly in Visual Studio 2010 via the project properties editor, as shown in Figure 46-2. You can see in this figure the Assembly Name field on the main Application tab and the Assembly Version in the inset, which is accessible via the Assembly Information button.

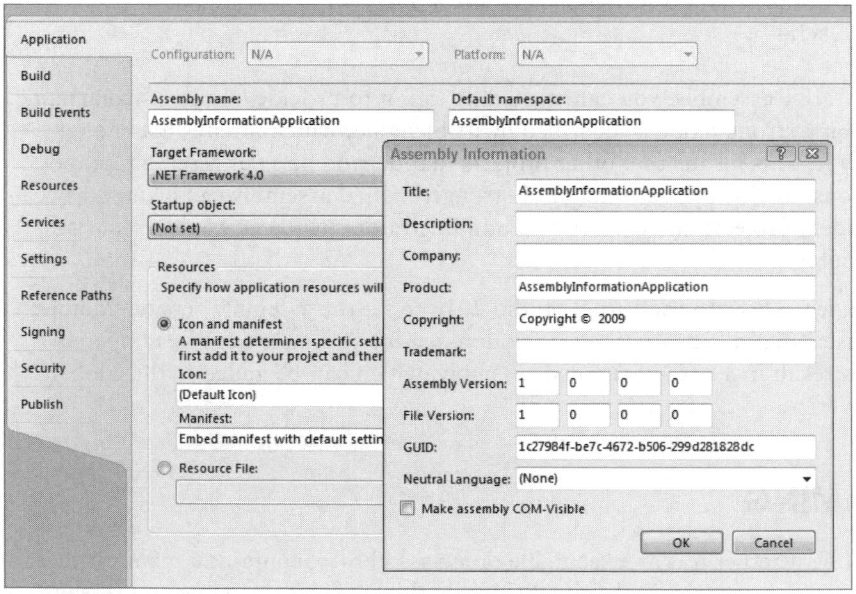

FIGURE 46-2

The assembly properties that are presented in the inset dialog in Figure 46-2 all appear in the `AssemblyInfo` file that is added to your project by default.

> *If you are using a C# project, you can find the* `AssemblyInfo.cs` *file by expanding the Properties item found underneath the project in Solution Explorer. If you are using VB, you can find the* `AssemblyInfo.vb` *file under My Project but only once Show All Files has been checked for the project.*

The following snippet illustrates the `AssemblyVersion` and `AssemblyFileVersion` assembly attributes that are used to define the version and file version of the assembly:

VB

```
' Version information for an assembly consists of the following four values:
'
'       Major Version
'       Minor Version
'       Build Number
'       Revision
'
' You can specify all the values or you can default the Build and Revision Numbers
' by using the '*' as shown below:
' <Assembly: AssemblyVersion("1.0.*")>
<Assembly: AssemblyVersion("1.0.0.0")>
<Assembly: AssemblyFileVersion("1.0.0.0")>
```

C#

```
// Explanatory comments removed
[assembly: AssemblyVersion("1.0.0.0")]
[assembly: AssemblyFileVersion("1.0.0.0")]
```

In case you were wondering what the difference is between the version and file version of an assembly, it comes down to usage. The assembly version information is used by the .NET Framework when resolving assembly and type information. On the other hand, the file version is what is displayed in Windows Explorer when you look at the file properties.

> *There is much debate over whether the assembly version and file version number should be in sync, but essentially it is up to you. Some developers prefer keeping them in sync because it means that they can determine the assembly version via Windows Explorer. Alternatively, other organizations use the file version to represent changes to an assembly (for example, a hotfix or service pack), whereas the assembly version is used for new versions of the application.*

As the comments in the VB snippet explain, assembly version numbers have four components — Major, Minor, Build, and Revision. Again, how you increment these is completely up to you. In fact, you could even elect for Visual Studio 2010 to increment them for you by specifying an * for the build and/or revision numbers. One fairly common strategy is to use the Major and Minor numbers to represent the actual version of the product being worked on. Incrementing just the Minor number would perhaps represent minor fixes and minimal new functionality (similar to a service pack), whereas the Major number would represent new core functionality.

This leaves the Build and Revision numbers that can be used to perhaps tie into the build process. For example, the Build number might represent the week number into development for a particular release, whereas the Revision number might represent the most recent revision number in the source repository. This last value then becomes very important because it can be used, in isolation, to access the exact source code from the repository that was used to build a particular version.

VERSION CONSISTENCY

The default project configuration doesn't lend itself easily to having a consistent version number across all projects within a solution. However, using the ability to include linked files in a project, you can coerce Visual Studio 2010 into giving you version consistency. This is particularly important if you have an automated build system that automatically increments the version number. Instead of having to update any number of `AssemblyInfo` files, it can simply modify a single file and have all projects be updated.

You need to start by creating an additional `AssemblyInfo` file, say `GlobalAssemblyInfo.vb`, in the solution folder. To do this, right-click the Solution node and select Add New Item. The new

item will be added to a Solution Items folder in your solution. Into this file you need to move the `AssemblyVersion` and `AssemblyFileVersion` attributes from the `AssemblyInfo` file in your projects (you will also need to import the `System.Reflection` namespace unless you fully qualify the attribute names).

Once you have done this, you then need to add this file into each of your projects. You do this via the Add Existing Item right-click menu item for the projects in the Solution Explorer tool window. When you have located the `GlobalAssemblyInfo.vb` or `GlobalAssemblyInfo.cs` file, make sure you select the Add As Link item from the Add drop-down, as shown in Figure 46-3.

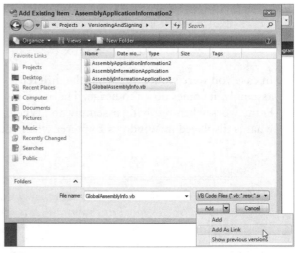

FIGURE 46-3

This one `GlobalAssemblyInfo` file can be used in any number of projects, the one limitation being that it is specific to VB or C#. If you have a solution that uses a mix of VB and C# projects, you will need to have a central

`GlobalAssemblyInfo` file for each language — this is still better than having to maintain the version information in a separate file for each project. Note that you can include other assembly attributes in these central files, such as the `AssemblyCopyright`, `AssemblyCompany`, and `AssemblyTrademark`, if appropriate.

STRONGLY NAMED ASSEMBLIES

A strong name consists of the parts that uniquely identify an assembly's identity. This includes the plain-text name and a version number. Added to these elements are a public key and a digital signature. These are generated with a corresponding private key. Because of this private/public key system coupled with a digital signature, strong names can be relied on to be completely unique. Further, by signing your assembly you are preventing someone from maliciously tampering with your code. .NET assemblies are relatively easy to reverse engineer, modify, and compile as a modified assembly. The hash that is created as part of the signing process changes as the assembly is modified — in effect providing a security mechanism against unauthorized modifications.

Using a strong name can also ensure that the version of your assembly is the one that has been shipped. No modification can be made to it without affecting its signature and thus breaking its compatibility with the generated strong name.

As mentioned previously, using strong names also gives administrators the ability to explicitly set security policy against your solutions by referring to their unique names. This can give a corporation confidence that once deployed, the software will run as expected because it cannot be tampered with without affecting the signing of the strong name.

> *Once you start using strong-named assemblies in your solution, you will have to use strong-named files right down the chain of references, because allowing an unsigned assembly as part of the chain would break the very security that strong-naming your assembly was intended to implement.*

THE GLOBAL ASSEMBLY CACHE

Every computer that has the .NET Framework installed has a system-wide cache, called the Global Assembly Cache (GAC), which can be used to store assemblies that are to be shared by multiple applications. Assemblies that are added to the GAC are accessible from any .NET application on the same system. This itself can be a huge saving for organizations where you have common functionality that you want to share between applications.

In this cache (usually stored in a folder within the `Windows` directory) you'll find the common language run time components as well as other globally registered binary files that you, and anyone else, can consume. If an assembly is only going to be used by a single application, it should be deployed in that application's folder.

> *It is important to note here that adding assemblies to the GAC is not recommended unless you really need to share assemblies between applications, and they are too large to redistribute alongside each application.*

If you do decide to share the assembly between applications, you will need to know how to store it in the GAC. Your assembly must also be strong-named. You don't have a choice in the matter, because the cache interrogates all files to ensure that their integrity is valid; hence, it needs the strong-name versioning to compare against. Instructions on how to strongly name your assemblies appear at the end of this chapter.

Once you have a strongly named assembly you can add it to the GAC by using the `gacutil.exe` command-line tool like this:

```
gacutil.exe /i AssemblyInformationApplication.dll
```

If an assembly with the same strong name already exists, you can force a reinstall with the `/f` option. To uninstall the assembly you use this command:

```
gacutil.exe /u AssemblyInformationApplication
```

> `Gacutil.exe` *is a part of the Microsoft .NET Framework Software Developer Kit (SDK) and not a part of the standard redistributable. This means that you can only rely on it being present in development environments. For deployment to the GAC on client machines, you should use an MSI file. See Chapter 48 for more details.*

SIGNING AN ASSEMBLY

Previously, signing an assembly in Visual Studio required the generation of a strong-name key (`.snk`) file via an external utility and then editing the assembly attributes of your application's configuration file. Thankfully, Visual Studio has built-in support for signing all managed code projects using the Signing tab in the project properties editor, as you can see from Figure 46-4.

The Signing tab enables you to sign the assembly in the lower half of the page. You first should select the Sign the Assembly checkbox to indicate that you will be generating a strong name. You will then need to select the strong-name key file to use when signing the assembly.

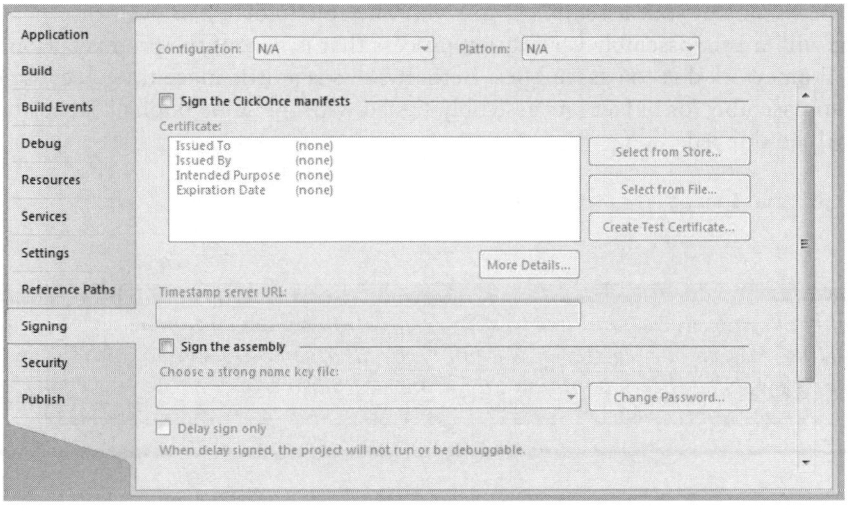

FIGURE 46-4

Existing key files in either the older `.snk` paired key file format or the new `.pfx` format can be used. From the drop-down list, select the Browse option to locate the file in your file system and click OK in the dialog to save the key file to the Signing page settings.

Alternatively, you can create a new strong-named key by selecting the New option from the drop-down list. When you choose New, you will be able to create a new `.pfx` formatted strong-named file. Figure 46-5 shows the Create Strong Name Key dialog. You can simply choose a filename to use for the key or you can additionally protect the key file with a password. If you do decide to add a password, you will be prompted to enter the password if you build your application on any other computer the first time. Thereafter, Visual Studio will remember the password.

FIGURE 46-5

Either way, once you've created and selected the key file, it will be added to your project in the Solution Explorer, enabling you to easily include it for deployment projects.

One of the main reasons you might want to sign your assemblies is to ensure that they cannot be modified. For this reason, most organizations place a high level of security around the strong-name key file that is used to sign their assemblies. As such, it is likely that you won't have access to the private key to successfully sign the assembly. When you're in this situation, you still need to dictate that the application be digitally signed. However, instead of providing the full strong-name key file, which contains the public and private key information, you provide only a file containing the public key information and select the Delay Sign Only checkbox. Later, perhaps as part of your build process, you would need to sign the assemblies using the full key:

```
sn -R AssemblyInformationApplication MyOrganisationsStrongkey.snk
```

If you select to delay the signing of your assemblies, you won't be able to debug or even run the application, because it will fail the assembly verification process that is part of the pre-execution checks that the .NET Framework does on assemblies. Actually, this is a little inaccurate because it is possible to register your assembly (or in fact any assembly signed with the same public key) so that the verification step will be skipped:

```
sn -Vr AssemblyInformationApplication.exe
```

 You should only ever register assemblies to skip verification on development machines. Further, you can unregister an assembly (or all assemblies signed with the same public key) using the sn *command with the* -Vu *parameter.*

SUMMARY

Strongly naming your assembly and thus safeguarding it from improper use is now straightforward to implement, and can be done completely from within the Visual Studio 2010 IDE. The Signing page gives you the ability to both create and set the key file without having to edit the application's assembly attributes directly.

47

Obfuscation, Application Monitoring, and Management

WHAT'S IN THIS CHAPTER?

➤ Exploring the features of Dotfuscator Software Services - Community Edition, a free post-build hardening and application monitoring tool that ships with Visual Studio

➤ Understanding how obfuscation can be used to prevent your assemblies from being easily decompiled

➤ Using tamper defense to protect your application assemblies from unauthorized modification

➤ Configuring application expiry to encode a specific date after which your application can't be executed

➤ Setting up usage tracking to determine what applications and features are being used

If you've peeked under the covers at the details of how .NET assemblies are executed, you will have picked up on the fact that instead of compiling to machine language (and regardless of the programming language used), all .NET source code is compiled into the Microsoft Intermediary Language (MSIL, or just IL, for short). The IL is then *just-in-time* compiled when it is required for execution. This two-stage approach has a number of significant advantages, such as allowing you to dynamically query an assembly for type and method information, using reflection. However, this is a double-edged sword, because this same flexibility means that once-hidden algorithms and business logic can easily be reverse-engineered and modified, legally or otherwise. This chapter introduces tools and techniques that will help to protect your source code from prying eyes and monitor the execution of your applications.

THE MSIL DISASSEMBLER

Before looking at how you can protect your code from other people and monitor its behavior "in the wild," this section describes a couple of tools that can help you build better applications. The first tool is the Microsoft .NET Framework IL Disassembler, or IL Dasm. This is included as part of the Microsoft Windows SDK, which is installed by default with Visual Studio 2010. You can find it under Start ➪ All Programs ➪ Microsoft Visual Studio 2010 ➪ Microsoft Windows SDK Tools ➪ IL Disassembler. In Figure 47-1, a small class library has been opened using this tool, and you can immediately see the namespace and class information contained within this assembly.

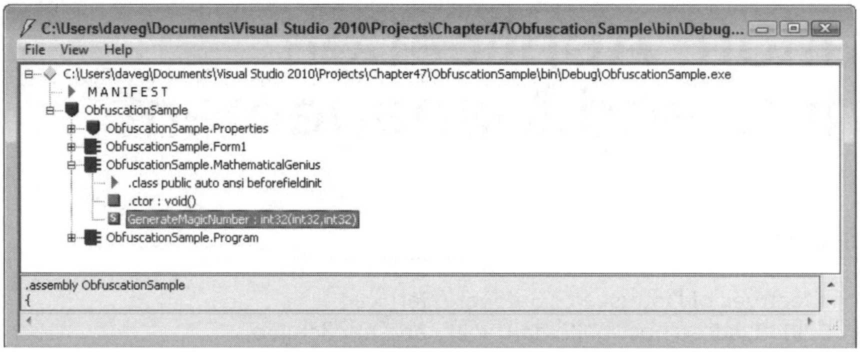

FIGURE 47-1

To compare the IL that is generated, the original source code for the `MathematicalGenius` class is as follows:

C#

```
namespace ObfuscationSample
{
    public class MathematicalGenius
    {
        public static Int32 GenerateMagicNumber(Int32 age, Int32 height)
        {
            return (age * height) + DateTime.Now.DayOfYear;
        }
    }
}
```

VB

```
Namespace ObfuscationSample
    Public Class MathematicalGenius
        Public Shared Function GenerateMagicNumber(ByVal age As Integer, _
                                        ByVal height As Integer) As Integer
            Return (age * height) + Today.DayOfWeek
```

```
        End Function
      End Class
    End Namespace
```

Double-clicking the `GenerateMagicNumber` method in IL Dasm opens up an additional window that shows the IL for that method. Figure 47-2 shows the IL for the `GenerateMagicNumber` method, which represents your super-secret, patent-pending algorithm. In actual fact, anyone who is prepared to spend a couple of hours learning how to interpret MSIL could quickly work out that the method simply multiplies the two `int32` parameters, `age` and `height`, and then adds the current day of the year to the result.

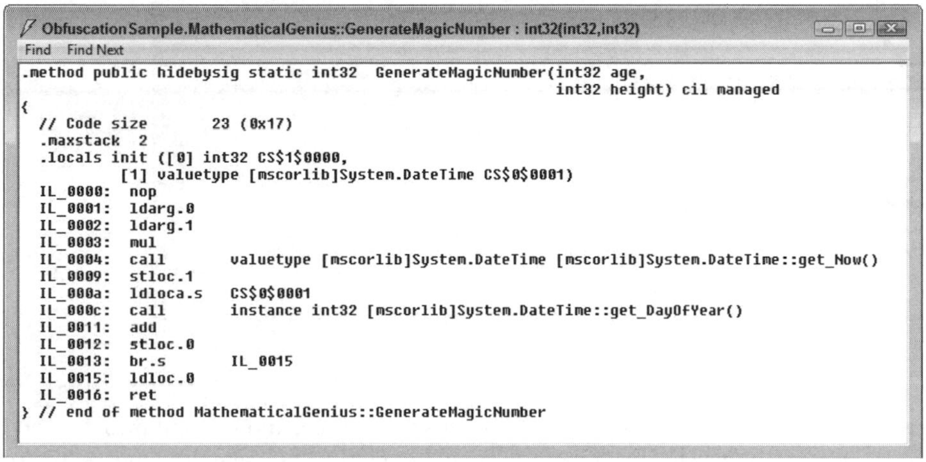

```
ObfuscationSample.MathematicalGenius::GenerateMagicNumber : int32(int32,int32)          [_][□][×]
Find  Find Next
.method public hidebysig static int32  GenerateMagicNumber(int32 age,
                                                            int32 height) cil managed
{
  // Code size       23 (0x17)
  .maxstack  2
  .locals init ([0] int32 CS$1$0000,
           [1] valuetype [mscorlib]System.DateTime CS$0$0001)
  IL_0000:  nop
  IL_0001:  ldarg.0
  IL_0002:  ldarg.1
  IL_0003:  mul
  IL_0004:  call       valuetype [mscorlib]System.DateTime [mscorlib]System.DateTime::get_Now()
  IL_0009:  stloc.1
  IL_000a:  ldloca.s   CS$0$0001
  IL_000c:  call       instance int32 [mscorlib]System.DateTime::get_DayOfYear()
  IL_0011:  add
  IL_0012:  stloc.0
  IL_0013:  br.s       IL_0015
  IL_0015:  ldloc.0
  IL_0016:  ret
} // end of method MathematicalGenius::GenerateMagicNumber
```

FIGURE 47-2

For those who haven't spent any time understanding how to read MSIL, a decompiler can convert this IL back into one or more .NET languages.

DECOMPILERS

One of the most widely used decompilers is .NET Reflector from Red Gate Software (available for download at `www.red-gate.com/products/reflector/`). Reflector can be used to decompile any .NET assembly into C#, Visual Basic, Managed C11, and even Delphi. In Figure 47-3, the same assembly you just accessed is opened using IL Dasm, in Reflector.

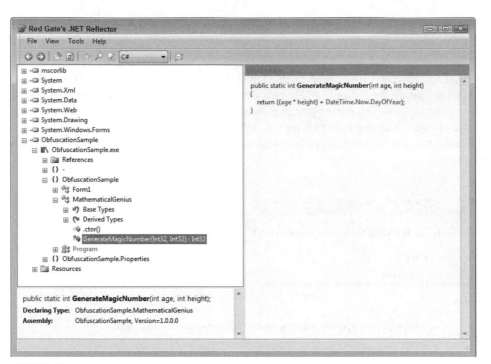

FIGURE 47-3

In the pane on the left of Figure 47-3, you can see the namespaces, type, and method information in a layout similar to IL Dasm. Double-clicking a method should open the Disassembler pane on the right, which displays the contents of that method in the language specified in the toolbar. In this case, you can see the C# code that generates the magic number, which is almost identical to the original code.

> *You may have noticed in Figure 47-3 that some of the .NET Framework base class library assemblies are listed, including System, System.Data, and System.Web. Because obfuscation has not been applied to these assemblies, they can be decompiled just as easily using Reflector. However, Microsoft has made large portions of the actual .NET Framework source code publicly available, which means you can browse the original source code of these assemblies including the inline comments. This is shown in Chapter 43.*

If the generation of the magic number were a real secret on which your organization made money, the ability to decompile this application would pose a significant risk. This is made worse when you add the Reflector.FileDisassembler add-in, written by Denis Bauer (available at www.denisbauer.com/NETTools/FileDisassembler.aspx). With this add-in, an entire assembly can be decompiled into source files, complete with a project file.

OBFUSCATING YOUR CODE

So far, this chapter has highlighted the need for better protection for the logic that is embedded in your applications. Obfuscation is the art of renaming symbols and modifying code paths in an assembly so that the logic is unintelligible and can't be easily understood if decompiled. Numerous products can obfuscate your code, each using its own tricks to make the output less likely to be understood. Visual Studio 2010 ships with the Community Edition of Dotfuscator Software Services from PreEmptive Solutions, which this chapter uses as an example of how you can apply obfuscation to your code.

> *Obfuscation does not prevent your code from being decompiled; it simply makes it more difficult for a programmer to understand the source code if it is decompiled. Using obfuscation also has some consequences that need to be considered if you need to use reflection or strong-name your application.*

Dotfuscator Software Services

Although Dotfuscator can be launched from the Tools menu within Visual Studio 2010, it is a separate product with its own licensing. The Community Edition (CE) contains only a subset of the functionality of the commercial edition of the product, the Dotfuscator Suite. If you are serious about trying to hide the functionality embedded in your application, you should consider upgrading. You can find more information on the commercial version of Dotfuscator at www.preemptive. com/products/dotfuscator/compare-editions.

Dotfuscator CE uses its own project format to keep track of which assemblies you are obfuscating and any options that you specify. After starting Dotfuscator from the Tools menu, it opens with a new unsaved project. Select the Input Assemblies node in the navigation tree, and then click the button with an ellipsis (...) under the Assembly Name listing to add the .NET assemblies that you want to obfuscate. Figure 47-4 shows a new Dotfuscator project into which has been added the assembly for the application from earlier in this chapter.

> *Unlike other build activities that are typically executed based on source files, obfuscation is a post-build activity that works with an already compiled set of assemblies. Dotfuscator takes an existing set of assemblies, applies the obfuscation algorithms to the IL, and generates a set of new assemblies.*

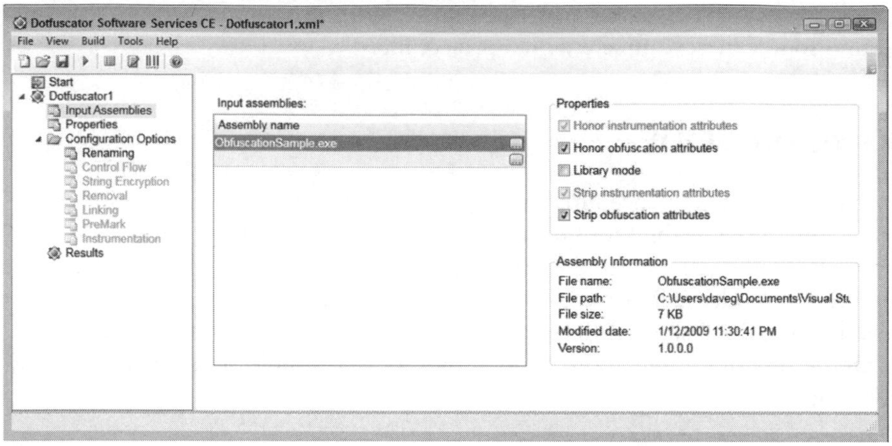

FIGURE 47-4

Without needing to adjust any other settings, you can select Build Project from the Build menu, or click the "play" button (fourth from the left) on the toolbar, to obfuscate this application. If you have saved the Dotfuscator project, the obfuscated assemblies will be added to a Dotfuscated folder under the folder where the project was saved. If the project has not been saved, the output is written to `c:\Dotfuscated`.

If you open the generated assembly using Reflector, as shown in Figure 47-5, you will notice that the `GenerateMagicNumber` method has been renamed, along with the input parameters. In addition, the namespace hierarchy has been removed and classes have been renamed. Although this is a rather simple example, you can see how numerous methods with similar, non-intuitive names could cause confusion and make the source code very difficult to understand when decompiled.

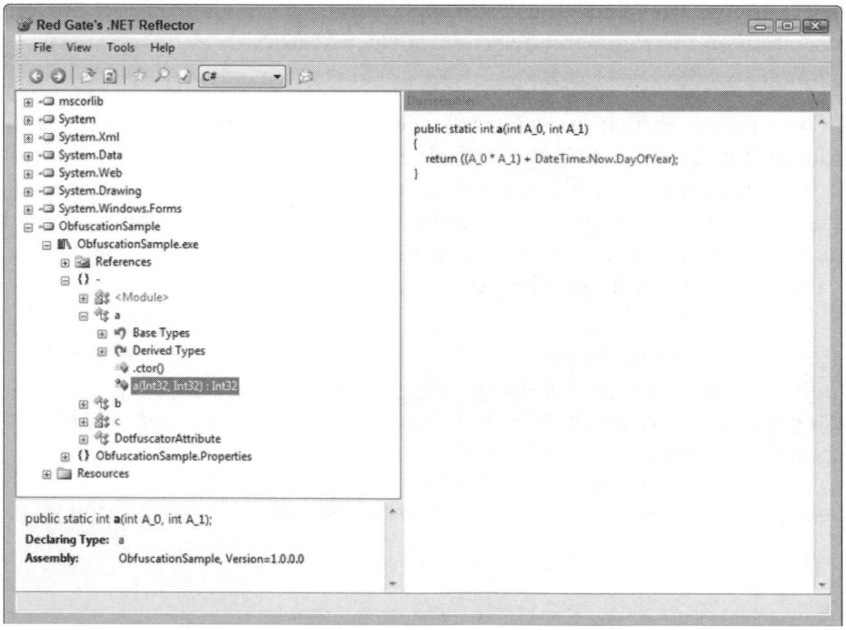

FIGURE 47-5

> *The free version of Dotfuscator only obfuscates assemblies by renaming classes, variables, and functions. The commercial version employs several additional methods to obfuscate assemblies, such as modifying the control flow of the assembly and performing string encryption. In many cases, control flow will actually trigger an unrecoverable exception inside decompilers, effectively preventing automated decompilation.*

The previous example obfuscated the public method of a class, which is fine if the method will only be called from assemblies obfuscated along with the one containing the class definition. However, if this was a class library or API that will be referenced by other, unobfuscated applications, you would see a list of classes that have no apparent structure, relationship, or even naming convention. This would make working with this assembly very difficult. Luckily, Dotfuscator enables you to control what is renamed during obfuscation. Before going ahead, you will need to refactor the code slightly to pull the functionality out of the public method. If you didn't do this and you excluded this method from being renamed, your secret algorithm would not be obfuscated. By separating the logic into another method, you can obfuscate that while keeping the public interface unchanged. The refactored code would look like the following:

C#

```csharp
namespace ObfuscationSample
{
    public class MathematicalGenius
    {
        public static Int32 GenerateMagicNumber(Int32 age, Int32 height)
        {
            return SecretGenerateMagicNumber(age, height);
        }

        private static Int32 SecretGenerateMagicNumber(Int32 age, Int32 height)
        {
            return (age * height) + DateTime.Now.DayOfYear;
        }
    }
}
```

Code Snippet MathematicalGenius.cs

VB

```vb
Namespace ObfuscationSample
    Public Class MathematicalGenius
        Public Shared Function GenerateMagicNumber(ByVal age As Integer, _
                                    ByVal height As Integer) As Integer
            Return SecretGenerateMagicNumber(age, height)
        End Function

        Private Shared Function SecretGenerateMagicNumber(ByVal age As Integer, _
```

```
                                                        ByVal height As Integer) As Integer
                Return (age * height) + Today.DayOfWeek
            End Function
        End Class
    End Namespace
```

Code Snippet MathematicalGenius.vb

After rebuilding the application, you will need to reopen the Dotfuscator project by selecting it from the Recent Projects list. You have several different ways of selectively applying obfuscation to an assembly. First, you can enable Library mode on specific assemblies by selecting the appropriate checkbox on the Input Assemblies screen (see Figure 47-4). This has the effect of keeping the namespace, class name, and all public properties and methods intact, while renaming all private methods and variables. Second, you can manually select which elements should not be renamed from within Dotfuscator. To do this, open the Renaming item from the navigation tree, shown in Figure 47-6.

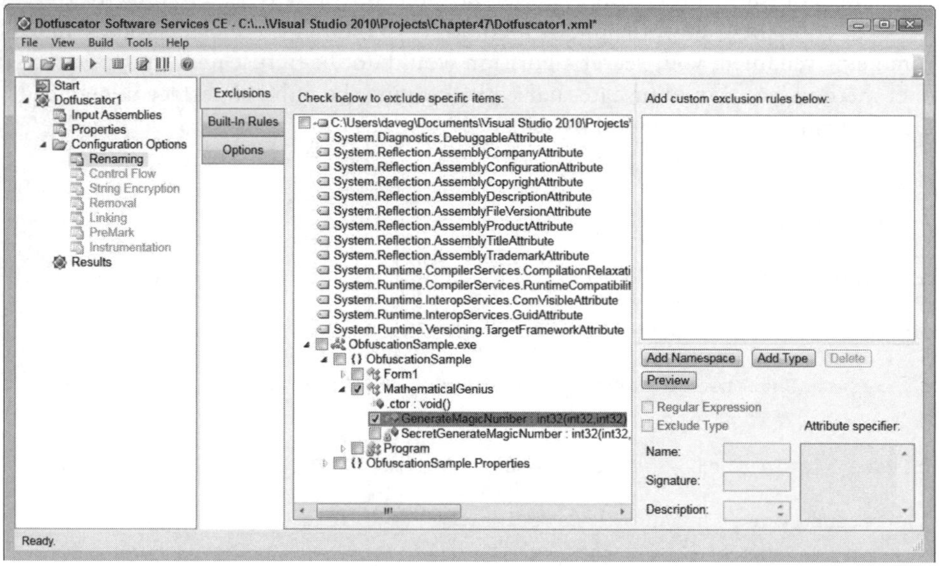

FIGURE 47-6

The Renaming dialog opens on the Exclusions tab where you can see the familiar tree view of your assembly, with the attributes, namespaces, types, and methods listed. As the name of the tab suggests, this tree enables you to exclude certain elements from being renamed. In Figure 47-6, the GenerateMagicNumber method, as well as the class that it is contained in, is excluded (otherwise, you would have ended up with something like b.GenerateMagicNumber, where b is the renamed class). In addition to explicitly choosing which elements will be excluded, you can also define custom rules that can include regular expressions.

After you build the Dotfuscator project, click the Results item in the navigation tree. This screen shows the actions that Dotfuscator performed during obfuscation. The new name of each class, property, and method is displayed as a sub-node under each renamed element in the tree. You will see that the MathematicalGenius class and the GenerateMagicNumber method have not been renamed, as shown in Figure 47-7.

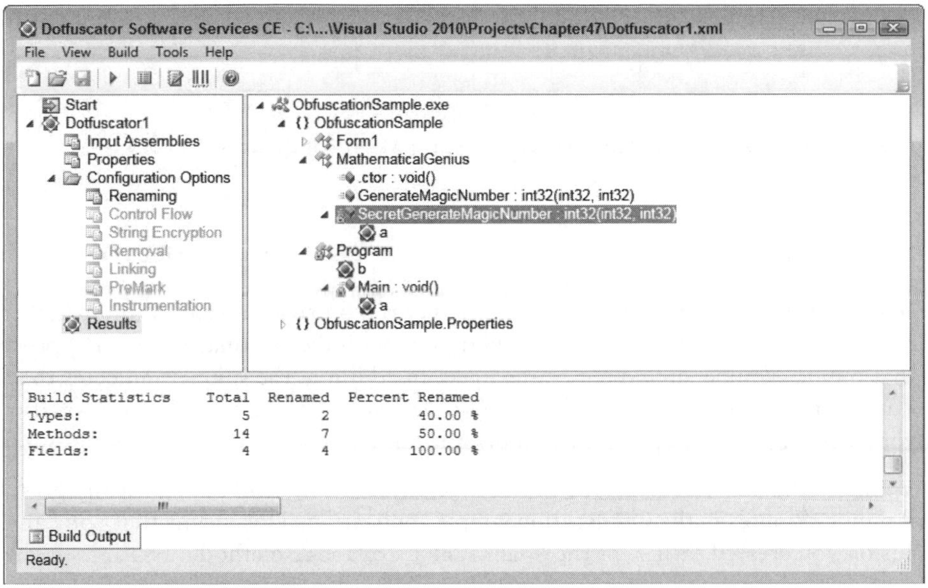

FIGURE 47-7

The `SecretGenerateMagicNumber` method has been renamed to a, as indicated by the sub-node with the Dotfuscator icon.

Obfuscation Attributes

In the previous example you saw how to choose which types and methods to obfuscate within Dotfuscator. Of course, if you were to start using a different obfuscating product you would have to configure it to exclude the public members. It would be more convenient to be able to annotate your code with attributes indicating whether a symbol should be obfuscated. You can do this by using the `Obfuscation` and `ObfuscationAssemblyAttribute` attributes from the `System.Reflection` namespace.

The default behavior in Dotfuscator is to override exclusions specified in the project with the settings specified by any obfuscation attributes. In Figure 47-4 is a series of checkboxes for each assembly added to the project, of which one is Honor Obfuscation Attributes. You can change the default behavior so that any exclusions set within the project take precedence by unchecking the Honor Obfuscation Attributes option on a per-assembly basis.

ObfuscationAssemblyAttribute

The `ObfuscationAssemblyAttribute` attribute can be applied to an assembly to control whether it should be treated as a class library or as a private assembly. The distinction is that with a class library it is expected that other assemblies will be referencing the public types and methods it exposes. As such, the obfuscation tool needs to ensure that these symbols are not renamed.

Alternatively, as a private assembly, every symbol can be potentially renamed. The following is the syntax for `ObfuscationAssemblyAttribute`:

C#

```
[assembly: ObfuscateAssemblyAttribute(false, StripAfterObfuscation=true)]
```

VB

```
<Assembly: ObfuscateAssemblyAttribute(False, StripAfterObfuscation:=True)>
```

The two arguments that this attribute takes indicate whether it is a private assembly and whether to strip the attribute off after obfuscation. The preceding snippet indicates that this is not a private assembly, and that public symbols should not be renamed. In addition, the snippet indicates that the obfuscation attribute should be stripped off after obfuscation — after all, the less information available to anyone wishing to decompile the assembly, the better.

Adding this attribute to the `AssemblyInfo.cs` or `AssemblyInfo.vb` file will automatically preserve the names of all public symbols in the ObfuscationSample application. This means that you can remove the exclusion you created earlier for the `GenerateMagicNumber` method.

ObfuscationAttribute

The downside of the `ObfuscationAssemblyAttribute` attribute is that it exposes all the public types and methods regardless of whether they existed for internal use only. On the other hand, the `ObfuscationAttribute` attribute can be applied to individual types and methods, so it provides a much finer level of control over what is obfuscated. To illustrate the use of this attribute, refactor the example to include an additional public method, `EvaluatePerson`, and place the logic into another class, `HiddenGenius`:

Available for download on Wrox.com

C#

```
namespace ObfuscationSample
{
    [System.Reflection.ObfuscationAttribute(ApplyToMembers=true, Exclude=true)]
    public class MathematicalGenius
    {
        public static Int32 GenerateMagicNumber(Int32 age, Int32 height)
        {
            return HiddenGenius.GenerateMagicNumber(age, height);
        }

        public static Boolean EvaluatePerson(Int32 age, Int32 height)
        {
            return HiddenGenius.EvaluatePerson(age, height);
        }
    }

    [System.Reflection.ObfuscationAttribute(ApplyToMembers=false, Exclude=true)]
    public class HiddenGenius
    {
        public static Int32 GenerateMagicNumber(Int32 age, Int32 height)
        {
```

```csharp
            return (age * height) + DateTime.Now.DayOfYear;
        }

        [System.Reflection.ObfuscationAttribute(Exclude=true)]
        public static Boolean EvaluatePerson(Int32 age, Int32 height)
        {
            return GenerateMagicNumber(age, height) > 6000;
        }
    }
}
```

Code Snippet MathematicalGenius.cs

VB

Available for
download on
Wrox.com

```vb
Namespace ObfuscationSample
    <System.Reflection.ObfuscationAttribute(ApplyToMembers:=True,Exclude:=True)> _
    Public Class MathematicalGenius
        Public Shared Function GenerateMagicNumber(ByVal age As Integer, _
                                    ByVal height As Integer) As Integer
            Return HiddenGenius.GenerateMagicNumber(age, height)
        End Function

        Public Shared Function EvaluatePerson(ByVal age As Integer, _
                                    ByVal height As Integer) As Boolean
            Return HiddenGenius.EvaluatePerson(age, height)
        End Function
    End Class

    <System.Reflection.ObfuscationAttribute(ApplyToMembers:=False,Exclude:=True)> _
    Public Class HiddenGenius
        Public Shared Function GenerateMagicNumber(ByVal age As Integer, _
                                    ByVal height As Integer) As Integer
            Return (age * height) + Today.DayOfWeek
        End Function

        <System.Reflection.ObfuscationAttribute(Exclude:=True)> _
        Public Shared Function EvaluatePerson(ByVal age As Integer, _
                                    ByVal height As Integer) As Boolean
            Return GenerateMagicNumber(age, height) > 6000
        End Function
    End Class
End Namespace
```

Code Snippet MathematicalGenius.vb

In this example, the MathematicalGenius class is the class that you want to expose outside of this library. As such, you want to exclude this class and all its methods from being obfuscated. You do this by applying the ObfuscationAttribute attribute with both the Exclude and ApplyToMembers parameters set to True.

The second class, HiddenGenius, has mixed obfuscation. As a result of some squabbling among the developers who wrote this class, the EvaluatePerson method needs to be exposed, but all other methods in this class should be obfuscated. Again, the `ObfuscationAttribute` attribute is applied to the class so that the class does not get obfuscated. However, this time you want the default behavior to be such that symbols contained in the class are obfuscated, so the `ApplyToMembers` parameter is set to `False`. In addition, the `Obfuscation` attribute is applied to the `EvaluatePerson` method so that it will still be accessible.

Words of Caution

In a couple of places it is worth considering what will happen when obfuscation — or more precisely, renaming — occurs, and how it will affect the workings of the application.

Reflection

The .NET Framework provides a rich reflection model through which types can be queried and instantiated dynamically. Unfortunately, some of the reflection methods use string lookups for type and member names. Clearly, the use of renaming obfuscation will prevent these lookups from working, and the only solution is not to mangle any symbols that may be invoked using reflection. Note that control flow obfuscation does not have this particular undesirable side-effect. Dotfuscator's *smart obfuscation* feature attempts to automatically determine a limited set of symbols to exclude based on how the application uses reflection. For example, say that you are using the field names of an enum type. Smart obfuscation will detect the reflection call used to retrieve the enum's field name, and then automatically exclude the enum fields from renaming.

Strongly Named Assemblies

One of the purposes behind giving an assembly a strong name is that it prevents the assembly from being tampered with. Unfortunately, obfuscating relies on being able to take an existing assembly and modify the names and code flow, before generating a new assembly. This would mean that the assembly no longer has a valid strong name. To allow obfuscation to occur you need to delay signing of your assembly by checking the Delay Sign Only checkbox on the Signing tab of the Project Properties window, as shown in Figure 47-8.

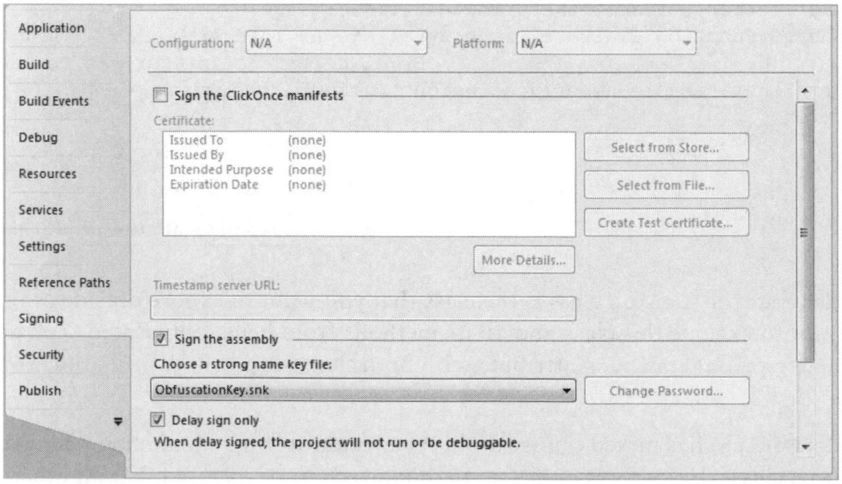

FIGURE 47-8

After building the assembly, you can then obfuscate it in the normal way. The only difference is that after obfuscating you need to sign the obfuscated assembly, which you can do manually using the Strong Name utility, as shown in this example:

```
sn -R ObfuscationSample.exe ObfuscationKey.snk
```

> *The Strong Name utility is not included in the default path, so you will either need to run this from a Visual Studio Command Prompt (Start ⇨ All Programs ⇨ Microsoft Visual Studio 2010 ⇨ Visual Studio Tools), or enter the full path to* `sn.exe`.

Debugging with Delayed Signing

As displayed on the Project Properties window, checking the Delay Sign Only box prevents the application from being able to be run or debugged. This is because the assembly will fail the strong-name verification process. To enable debugging for an application with delayed signing, you can register the appropriate assemblies for verification skipping. This is also done using the Strong Name utility. For example, the following code will skip verification for the `ObfuscationSample.exe` application:

```
sn -Vr ObfuscationSample.exe
```

Similarly, the following will reactivate verification for this application:

```
sn -Vu ObfuscationSample.exe
```

This is a pain for you to have to do every time you build an application, so you can add the following lines to the post-build events for the application:

```
"$(DevEnvDir)..\..\..\Microsoft SDKs\Windows\v7.0A\bin\sn.exe" -Vr "$(TargetPath)"
"$(DevEnvDir)..\..\..\Microsoft SDKs\Windows\v7.0A\bin\sn.exe" -Vr
"$(TargetDir)$(TargetName).vshost$(TargetExt)"
```

> *Depending on your environment, you may need to modify the post-build event to ensure that the correct path to* `sn.exe` *is specified.*

The first line skips verification for the compiled application. However, Visual Studio uses an additional vshost file to bootstrap the application when it executes. This also needs to be registered to skip verification when launching a debugging session.

APPLICATION MONITORING AND MANAGEMENT

The version of Dotfuscator that ships with Visual Studio 2010 has a whole lot of new functionality for adding run time monitoring and management functionality to your applications. As with obfuscation, these new capabilities are injected into your application as a post-build step, which means you typically don't need to modify your source code in any way to take advantage of them.

The new application monitoring and management capabilities include:

➤ **Tamper Defense:** Exits your application, and optionally notifies, if it has been modified in an unauthorized manner.

➤ **Application Expiry:** Configure an expiration date for your application, after which it will no longer run.

➤ **Application Usage Tracking:** Instrument your code to track usage, including specific features within your application.

To enable the new monitoring and management functionality you must enable instrumentation for your Dotfuscator project. Select the Instrumentation item from the navigation tree and select the Options tab. Select the Enable Instrumentation option as shown in Figure 47-9.

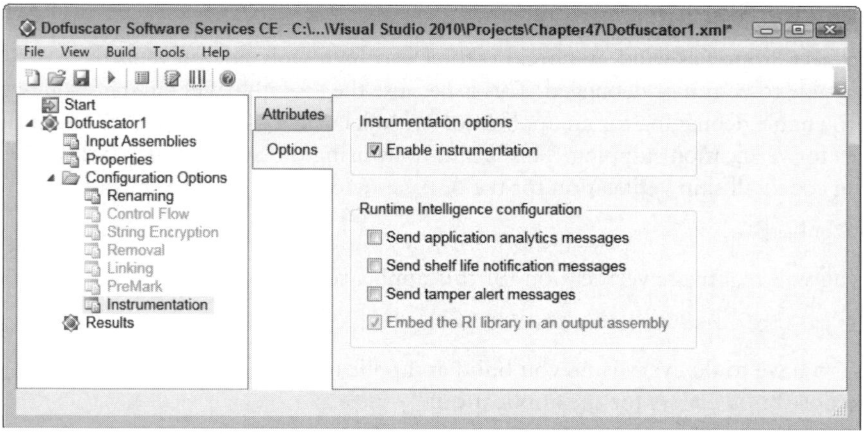

FIGURE 47-9

Once instrumentation has been enabled, you can specify the new functionality to be injected into your application by adding Dotfuscator attributes — either as a custom attribute within your source code, or through the Dotfuscator UI.

Tamper Defense

Tamper defense provides a way for you to detect when your applications have been modified in an unauthorized manner. Whereas obfuscation is a *preventative control* designed to reduce the risks that stem from unauthorized reverse engineering, tamper defense is a *detective control* designed to reduce the risks that stem from unauthorized modification of your managed assemblies. The pairing of preventative and detective controls is a widely accepted risk management pattern, for example, fire prevention and detection.

Tamper defense is applied on a per-method basis, and tamper detection is performed at run time when a protected method is invoked.

To add tamper defense to your application, select the Instrumentation item from the navigation menu and then select the Attributes tab. You will see a tree that contains the assemblies you have added to the Dotfuscator project with a hierarchy of the classes and methods that each assembly contains. Navigate to the `HiddenGenius.GenerateMagicNumber` function, right-click it, and select Add Attribute. This displays the list of available Dotfuscator attributes as shown in Figure 47-10.

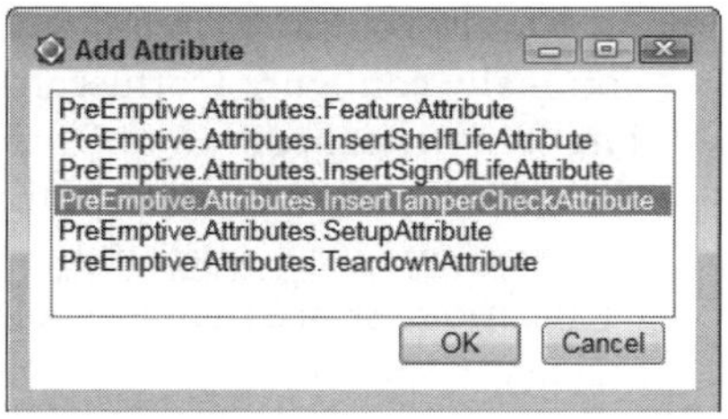

Select the `InsertTamperCheckAttribute` attribute and click OK. The attribute is added to the selected method and the attribute properties are listed as shown in Figure 47-11. Finally, select the `ApplicationNotificationSinkElement` property and change the value to `DefaultAction`.

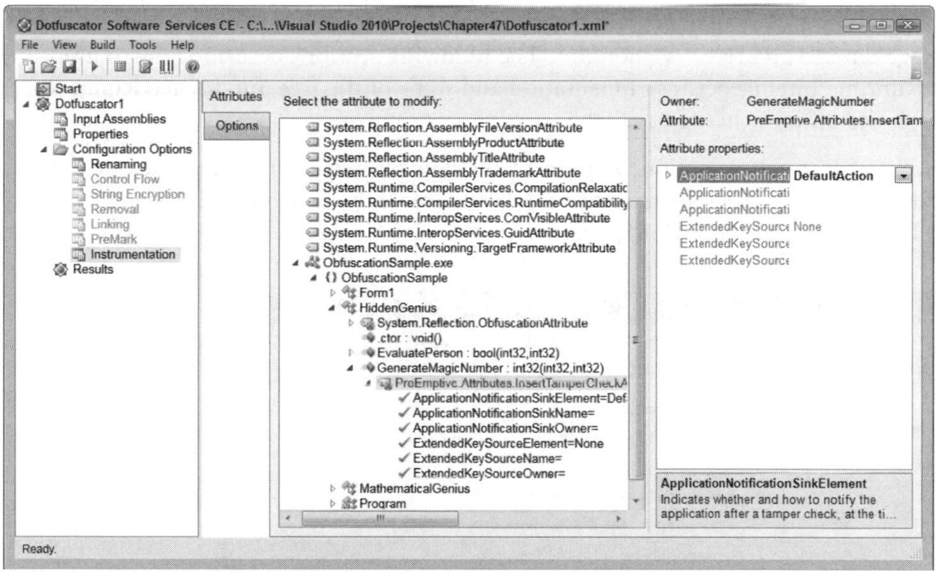

FIGURE 47-10

FIGURE 47-11

You can now build the Dotfuscator project to inject the tamper defense functionality into your application.

To help you test the tamper defense functionality, Dotfuscator ships with a simple utility that simulates tampering of an assembly. Called TamperTester, you can find this utility in the same directory in which Dotfuscator is installed (by default `C:\Program Files\Microsoft Visual Studio 10.0\PreEmptive Solutions\Dotfuscator Community Edition`). This should be run from the command line with the name of the assembly and the output folder as arguments:

```
tampertester ObfuscationSample.exe c:\tamperedapps
```

> Make sure you run the TamperTester utility against the assemblies that were generated by Dotfuscator and not the original assemblies built by Visual Studio.

By default, your application will immediately exit if the method has been tampered with. You can optionally configure Dotfuscator to generate a notification message to an endpoint of your choosing. The commercial edition of Dotfuscator includes two primary extensions to the CE version; it allows you to add a custom handler to be executed when tampering is detected supporting a custom real-time tamper defense in lieu of the default exit behavior; and PreEmptive Solutions offers a notification service that accepts tamper alerts and automatically notifies your organization as an incident response.

Runtime Intelligence Instrumentation and Analytics

The term *Runtime Intelligence* (RI) refers to technologies and managed services for the collection, integration, analysis, and presentation of application usage patterns and practices. In Visual Studio 2010, Dotfuscator CE can inject RI instrumentation into your assemblies to stream session and feature usage data to an arbitrary endpoint. The following sections describe how to use Dotfuscator's Runtime Intelligence instrumentation and some of the free and for-fee Runtime Intelligence analytics options that are available.

To use Dotfuscator CE instrumentation, you must first enable it within your Dotfuscator project. Click the Instrumentation item in the navigation tree and select the Options tab. Ensure that all the options under Runtime Intelligence Configuration are enabled, as shown in Figure 47-12.

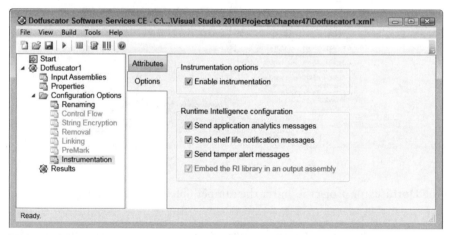

FIGURE 47-12

Next you must add some attributes to your assemblies to ensure that they can be uniquely identified and any instrumentation data can be accessed. Under the Attributes tab of the Instrumentation node is the class hierarchy of any assemblies you have added to Dotfuscator. Right-click each of the top-level nodes (the node that contains the full path to your assembly), select Add Attribute, and add a new `BusinessAttribute` attribute.

Select `CompanyKey` from the attribute properties listing. This attribute provides a unique identifier for your company and should be the same across all of your assemblies. You can click the button labeled with the ellipsis to generate a new `CompanyKey`. Also enter a value for the `CompanyName` property that will be displayed in the portal and any reports.

Repeat this to add a new `ApplicationAttribute` attribute to your assemblies. The `GUID` property of this attribute should contain a unique identifier that is the same across all assemblies within this application. As with the `CompanyKey` property, you can generate a new value for the `GUID` property by clicking the button labeled with the ellipsis. You should also enter values for the `Name` and `Version` properties, but the `ApplicationType` property can be left blank.

Once you have added these attributes, your project should look similar to Figure 47-13.

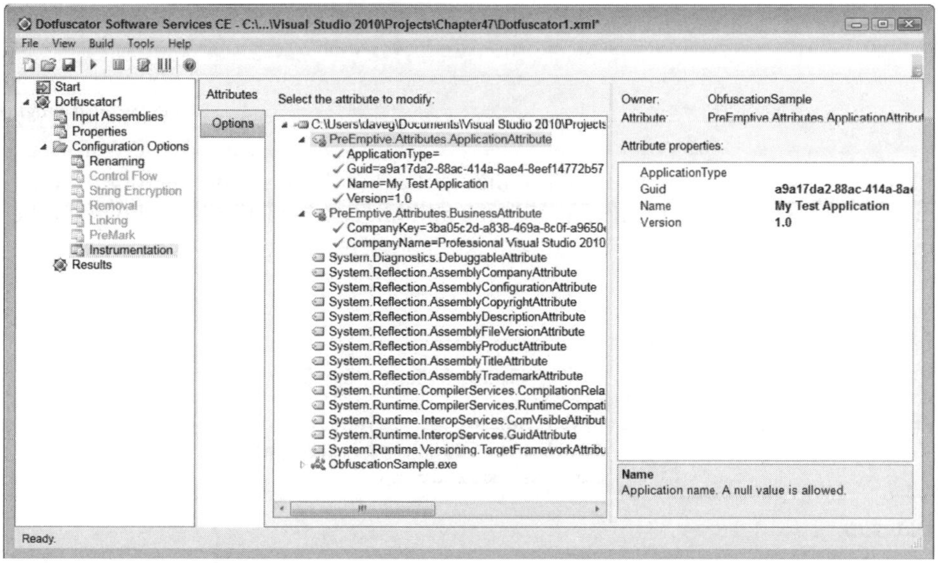

FIGURE 47-13

The final step is to add `SetupAttribute` and `TeardownAttribute` attributes to your application. These attributes can be added to any method and are usually defined once each per application, though that is not strictly necessary if your application has multiple entry and exit points. `SetupAttribute` should be placed on a method that is called soon after application startup. Likewise, the `TeardownAttribute` attribute must be added to a method that is called just before the application exits. It is sometimes a good idea to create methods specifically for these attributes.

For a C# Windows Forms application, you can place the attributes on the `Main` method; alternatively, you can modify the `Program.cs` class by adding the `AppStart` and `AppEnd` methods as shown in the following listing:

C#

Available for
download on
Wrox.com

```csharp
static class Program
{
    static void Main()
    {
        Application.EnableVisualStyles();
        Application.SetCompatibleTextRenderingDefault(false);
        AppStart();
```

```
        Application.Run(new Form1());
        AppEnd();
    }

    static void AppStart()
    {
    }

     static void AppEnd()
    {
    }
}
```

Code Snippet Program.cs

For a VB Windows Forms application, you can use the Application Events functionality provided the Windows application framework to specify `Startup` and `Shutdown` methods as shown in the following listing:

VB

```
Imports Microsoft.VisualBasic.ApplicationServices
Namespace My
    Partial Friend Class MyApplication
        Private Sub MyApp_Startup(ByVal sender As Object, _
                        ByVal e As StartupEventArgs) _
                        Handles Me.Startup

        End Sub

        Private Sub MyApp_Shutdown(ByVal sender As Object, _
                        ByVal e As System.EventArgs) _
                        Handles Me.Shutdown

        End Sub
    End Class
End Namespace
```

Code Snippet ApplicationEvents.vb

Once you have a `startup` and `shutdown` method defined in your application, you can add the `SetupAttribute` and `TeardownAttribute` attributes. Locate your startup method in the tree, then right-click it and select Add Attribute. Select `SetupAttribute` and click OK. In the attribute properties you will need to specify a value for the `CustomEndpoint` property, which instructs Dotfuscator where to send any instrumentation messages. Click the ellipsis button and select PreEmptive's Free Runtime Intelligence Services from the list.

> *You shouldn't collect information about application usage without asking permission from your users, otherwise your application could be flagged as spyware. The* SetupAttribute *provides three properties to help configure this —* OptInSourceElement, OptInSourceName, *and* OptInSourceOwner.

The Runtime Intelligence Service is a managed service provided by PreEmptive Solutions that aggregates and manages Runtime Intelligence data generated by your application, and a web portal that includes runtime analytics. PreEmptive Solutions offers a free and a commercial version of its Runtime Intelligence Service.

> *The free version of PreEmptive's Runtime Intelligence Service is suitable only for preliminary testing purposes because it lacks sufficient security and does not include any guarantees of uptime or data retention. You should transition to the commercial version or find/build an alternative for production deployment.*

Finally, add the `TeardownAttribute` attribute to the appropriate method and then build the Dotfuscator project. Run the application a couple of times to generate some instrumentation messages. You can also use the TamperTester utility described in the previous section to create a "tampered" version of the application that generates Tamper notifications.

Once you have run the application a number of times, open your browser and visit `http:/free. runtimeintelligence.com`. You can log on to the portal using the unique identifier you generated earlier for the `CompanyKey` property.

The Welcome screen, which is displayed after you log on, shows the number of notification messages that are queued waiting to be loaded into the database. You may need to wait until any pending messages are loaded before you can view any data.

On the Application Overview menu you can view summary graphs that show data such as the application usage over time, and the operating systems and .NET Framework versions used by your users. The Application Scorecard report, shown in Figure 47-14, displays a list of all the applications registered under this Company Key, along with key metrics about their usage.

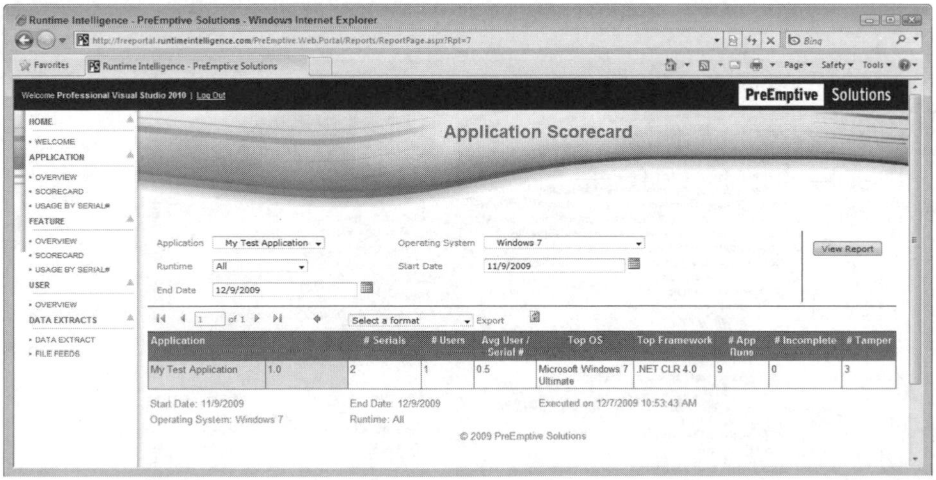

FIGURE 47-14

Later in this chapter you see how the usage tracking can be extended to cover usage of specific features within your application.

Application Expiry

The application expiry feature, also known as *Shelf Life*, allows you to specify an expiration date for your application, after which it will no longer run. This can be useful in a number of scenarios, such as when releasing beta or trial versions of software.

Application expiry requires a Shelf Life Activation Key (SLAK). This key is issued by PreEmptive, and can be requested by visiting `http://www.preemptive.com/products/shelflife`.

Two attributes are available to help implement application expiry. The `InsertShelfLifeAttribute` attribute enforces the expiration dates, ensuring that the application will not run after the specified date. It can also send a notification to an arbitrary endpoint when an expired application is executed. The `InsertSignOfLifeAttribute` attribute sends a notification to the Runtime Intelligence service every time your application is executed. This allows you to find out how often an application was executed.

Before adding the application expiry attributes, you should set up your assembly with the `BusinessAttribute`, `ApplicationAttribute`, `SetupAttribute`, and `TeardownAttribute` attributes, as described in the previous section on Runtime Intelligence.

It's a good idea to add the application expiry attributes to a method that is called shortly after the application is started. You may also want to add it to a method that is called regularly, just in case your users leave your application running after the expiry date. In Figure 47-15, the `InsertShelfLifeAttribute` and `InsertSignOfLifeAttribute` attributes have been added to the `Form1.InitializeComponent` method. This ensures that the application expiry date will be checked every time Form1 is invoked.

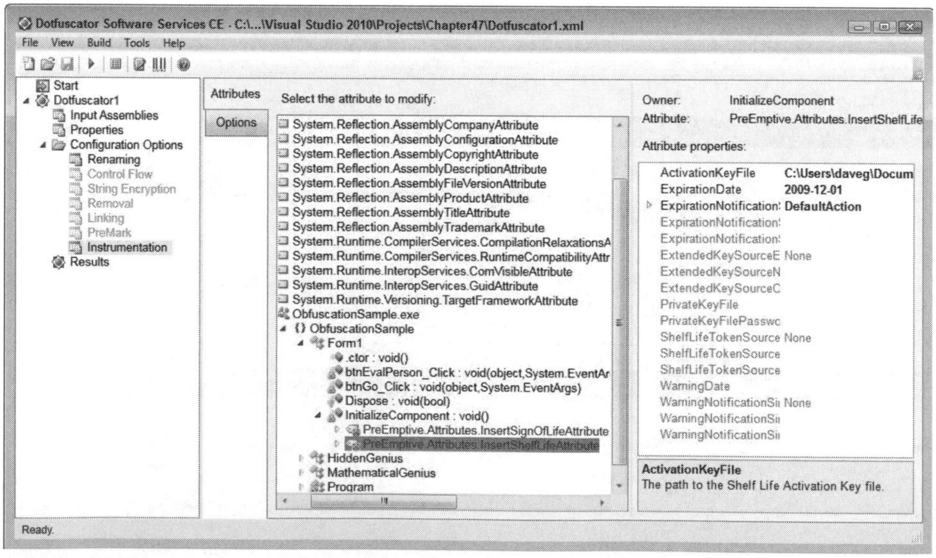

FIGURE 47-15

Both attributes require a Shelf Life Activation Key. Once you have obtained this key from PreEmptive, save it to your local disk and set the path to this file in the `ActivationKeyFile` property. Setting the `ExpirationDate` property to a date in the past is a good way to test this feature.

When an application expires, the behavior is determined by two settings. First, if you have Send Shelf Life Notification Messages checked on the Instrumentation Options tab, it will send a notification message to the endpoint you have specified. Second, if you have set the `ExpirationNotificationSinkElement` property to `DefaultAction`, the application will immediately exit.

The commercial edition of Dotfuscator allows you to specify a warning date and add custom handlers that are executed when the warning date or expiration date are reached. You could use this to deactivate specific features or display a friendly message to the users advising them that the application has expired.

The commercial version of Dotfuscator also allows your application to obtain the shelf life information from an external location, such as a web service or configuration file. This allows you to support other expiration scenarios such as expiring 30 days from installation or renewing annual subscriptions.

Application Usage Tracking

Earlier in this chapter you saw how to add the `SetupAttribute` and `TeardownAttribute` attributes to your application. By adding these attributes your application can send notification messages, and thereby allow you to track usage data and system environment statistics for your applications. These attributes are also used to determine application stability, because a missing Teardown notification indicates that the application may have crashed or a user may have gotten frustrated and simply forced an exit.

In addition to tracking application startup and shutdown, Dotfuscator allows you to further instrument your code to track usage of specific features within your application. With Dotfuscator CE, you can add up to ten `FeatureAttribute` attributes to your methods, each one specifying the same or a different feature. This allows you to aggregate your application's methods into a logical, high-level "feature" grouping that is independent of the actual class hierarchy of your code.

In Figure 47-16, you can see that a `FeatureAttribute` attribute has been added to the `EvaluatePerson` and the `GenerateMagicNumber` methods of the `MathematicalGenius` class. These features have been given a descriptive name, which is displayed when viewing the usage reports. These attributes also have the `FeatureEventType` property set to `Tick`, which simply tracks that the feature has been used.

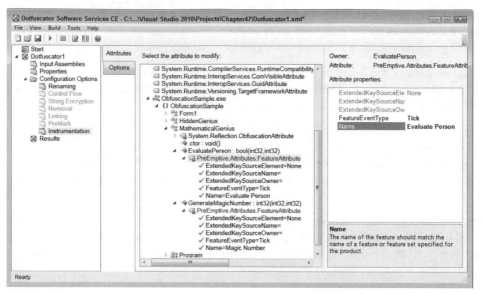

FIGURE 47-16

In addition to Tick feature tracking, you can also track the amount of time a feature was used. In this case you will need to add two `FeatureAttribute` attributes — one with the `FeatureEventType` property set to `Start` and the other set to `Stop`. This generates two instrumentation messages and allows the Runtime Intelligence analytics service to calculate feature usage duration.

The commercial edition of Dotfuscator includes:

➤ Unlimited feature tracking

➤ Injection of the Microsoft WMI SDK for hardware and software stack detection

➤ Extensible data capture to include custom data values

➤ An SSL runtime data transmission option

Runtime Intelligence data can be used to improve the development process, provide greater visibility into application usage for IT operations, and serve as an additional data source for business activity and performance monitoring. Microsoft's own Customer Experience Improvement Program (CEIP) relies on this kind of usage data (for a description of its program, visit `http://www.microsoft.com/products/ceip/`).

As managed code moves beyond the desktop and the in-house server to the web client (Silverlight), the cloud (Azure), and your mobile devices, Runtime Intelligence will likely become an increasingly important part of your application life cycle management toolkit.

SUMMARY

This chapter introduced two tools, IL Dasm and Reflector, which demonstrated how easy it is to reverse-engineer .NET assemblies and learn their inner workings. You also learned how to use Dotfuscator Software Services to:

➤ Protect your intellectual property using obfuscation

➤ Harden your applications against modification using tamper defense

➤ Monitor and measure application usage with Runtime Intelligence instrumentation

➤ Enforce your application's end-of-life with shelf life

48

Packaging and Deployment

WHAT'S IN THIS CHAPTER?

➤ Creating installers for your projects

➤ Customizing the installation process

➤ Verifying the presence of application prerequisites

➤ Installing Windows Services

➤ Deploying projects over the web with ClickOnce

➤ Updating ClickOnce projects

One area of software development that is often overlooked is how to deploy the application. Building an installer is a simple process and can transform your application from an amateur utility to a professional tool. This chapter looks at how you can build a Windows Installer for any type of .NET application.

Visual Studio 2010 also includes support for a ClickOnce deployment, which can be used to build applications that can be dynamically updated. This is particularly important for rich client applications that periodically need updating, because it solves the problem of how to roll out those updates.

WINDOWS INSTALLERS

Windows Installer has been a standard part of Windows since Windows 2000. It is the component that manages the installation, maintenance, and removal of software packages. Visual Studio 2010 comes with a rich user interface for building installation packages for a variety of different applications that target the Windows Installer infrastructure. This chapter demonstrates building installers for desktop applications and windows services. The next chapter contains information about packaging and deploying web applications.

Building an Installer

To build an installer with Visual Studio 2010, you need to add an additional project to the application that you want to deploy. Figure 48-1 shows the available setup and deployment project types. The Setup Project should be used for Windows Forms or service applications, and the Web Setup Project should be used for ASP.NET web sites or web services. If you want to build an installer that will be integrated into a larger installer, you may want to build a merge module. Alternatively, a CAB Project can be used to create a package that can be deployed via a web browser. The Setup Wizard steps you through the process of creating the correct project for the type of application you're deploying.

FIGURE 48-1

Web Setup Projects are covered in the next chapter.

In this case, you are going to use the Setup Wizard to create an installer for a simple C# Windows Forms Application, CallCentre. After acknowledging the Setup Wizard splash screen, the first decision is specifying whether you want to create an installer or a redistributable package. For an installer, you need to choose between a Windows application or a web application installer. The basic difference is that the Windows application installer places the application in the appropriate folder within Program Files, whereas the web application installer creates a virtual directory under the root folder for the specified web site. In the case of a redistributable package, the choice is between a merge module, which can be integrated into a larger installer, or a CAB file.

> *A merge module is a special type of installer that contains the instructions for installing a shared component. Once a merge module has been created, it can be included within a number of installers providing re-use and simplified maintenance. Merge modules must be included within an installer file. They cannot be installed by themselves.*
>
> *A CAB project produces a collection of* .cab *files, which contain a set of compressed files. The* .cab *files can be downloaded individually or opened from a number of disks. Typically, the contents of the* .cab *files are copied to the local file system when the installer runs.*

Regardless of the type of deployment project you are creating, the next step in the Setup Wizard is the most important because it determines the set of files to be deployed. Figure 48-2 shows the third screen in the Setup Wizard, which prompts you to select which files or project outputs will be included in the deployment project. In this case, the primary output for your CallCentre Application has been selected, because you want to include the main executable and any assemblies on which this executable depends. The Content Files item has also been selected, which will include any files with the build action set to Content. In the remaining step in the Setup Wizard, you can choose to add files

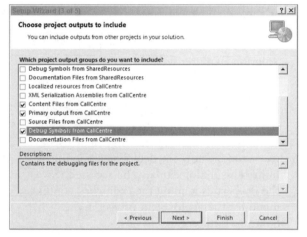

FIGURE 48-2

that were not part of any existing project. For example, this might include release notes, licensing information, getting started samples, or documentation and README files.

> *Occasionally you may choose to deploy debug symbols with your application, because this can aid you in diagnosing a failing application in production. However, it is not generally deemed a good practice to do this, because you should incorporate sufficient logging or other diagnostic instrumentation for this purpose.*

Once the deployment project has been created, it is added to the Solution Explorer, as shown in Figure 48-3. Although you didn't explicitly add any files or output from the SharedResources class library to the deployment project, it has been added as a detected dependency. If the dependencies are guaranteed to exist on the target computer, they can be manually excluded from the deployment project by selecting the Exclude item from the right-click context menu. For example, if this were an add-in for another application that already has a copy of the SharedResources assembly, you could exclude that from the dependency list. The resulting installer would be smaller, and thus easier to deploy.

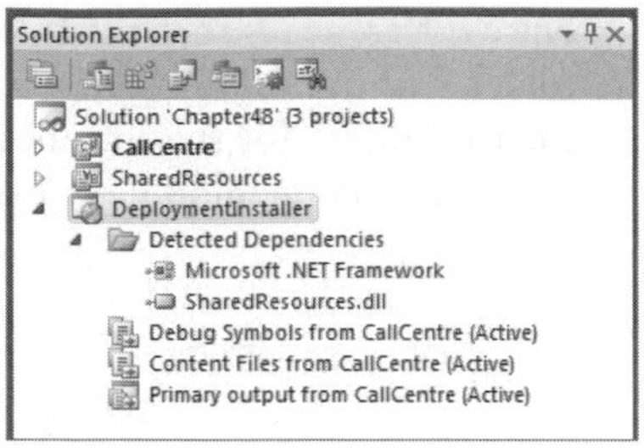

FIGURE 48-3

> If the dependencies between your projects vary, it may be necessary to force a recalculation of these dependencies. You can do this by selecting Refresh Dependencies from the right-click shortcut menu on the Detected Dependencies node.

When a deployment project (DeploymentInstaller) is selected, a number of new icons appear across the top of the Solution Explorer window, as shown in Figure 48-3. Unlike other project types, where the project properties appear in the main editor area, clicking the first icon (Properties) opens the Property Pages dialog, as shown in Figure 48-4. This can be used to customize how the deployment module is built. This dialog can also be accessed via the Properties item on the right-click context menu for the deployment project in the Solution Explorer.

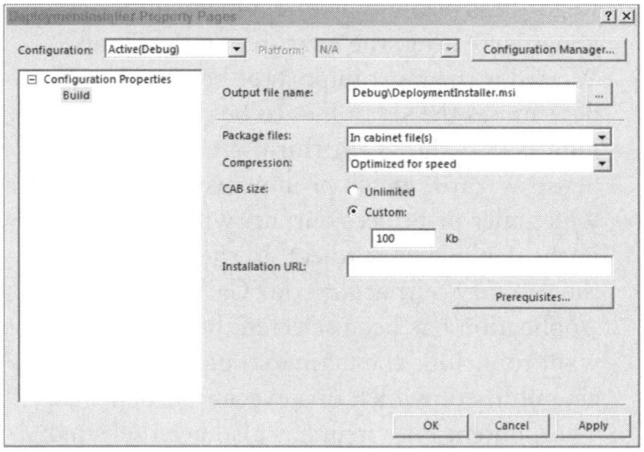

FIGURE 48-4

By default, the Package Files property is set to "In setup file," so all executables and associated dependencies are placed into the `.msi` file that is created. The deployment project also creates a `Setup.exe` file that checks for minimum requirements, such as the presence of the .NET Framework, prior to calling the `.msi` file to install the application. Although the compression can be adjusted to optimize for file size, including everything into a single distributable might be an issue for large projects. An alternative, as shown in Figure 48-4, is to package the application into a series of CAB files. In this scenario, the size of the CAB file is limited to 100Kb, which will aid deployment over a slow network. Another scenario where this would be useful is if you were planning to deploy your application via CD or DVD, and your application exceeded the capacity of a single disc.

The final property on this page is the Installation URL. If you are planning to deploy your application via a web site, you can elect to package everything into a single file, in which case you do not need to specify the Installation URL, because you can simply add a reference to the `Setup.exe` file to the appropriate web site and a user can install the application simply by clicking the link. Alternatively, you can package your application into smaller units that can be incrementally downloaded. To do this, you must specify the Installation URL from which they will be installed.

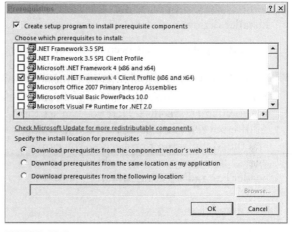

As just discussed, the default deployment project creates a `Setup.exe` file. The Prerequisites button opens a dialog like the one shown in Figure 48-5, where you can configure the behavior of this file. You can indicate that a setup file should not be created, in which case the application can be installed by double-clicking the `.msi` file. This, of course, removes the initial check to ensure that the .NET Framework has been installed.

FIGURE 48-5

In addition to the .NET Framework, you can also specify that other components, such as SQL Server Compact 3.5, need to be installed. These checks will be carried out, and the user prompted to install any missing components before the main installer file is invoked. Depending on how you want to deploy your application, having all the prerequisites in the same location as your application may be useful and will eliminate time spent looking for the appropriate download.

Returning to the Solution Explorer and your DeploymentInstaller project (and just to confuse matters), there is an additional Properties window for deployment projects that can be opened by selecting the appropriate project and pressing F4. This opens the standard Properties window, shown in Figure 48-6, which can be used to tailor the deployment details for the application it is installing.

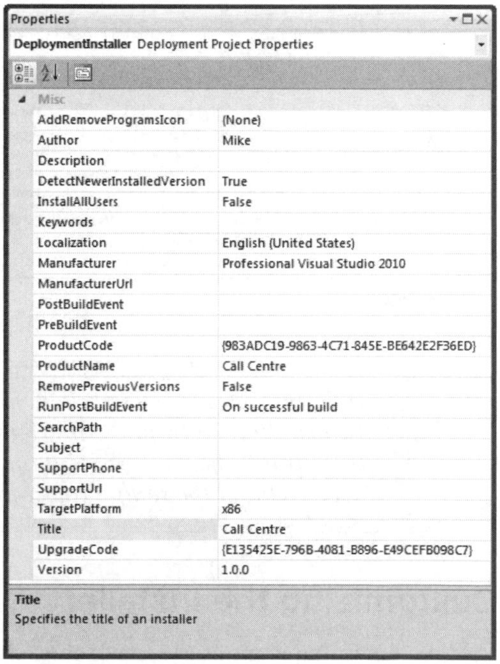

The properties for the deployment project shown on this screen configure the appearance, icons, and behavior of the installation wizard. It is highly

FIGURE 48-6

recommended that you adjust these properties so your application is easily identifiable in the Add/Remove Programs dialog, and so that the installation looks professional rather than half-finished. As you can see from Figure 48-7, some of these properties are used to tailor the installer dialog.

Once the application has been installed, some of these properties also appear in the Programs and Features dialog (Add/Remove Programs under Windows 7) accessible via the Control Panel, as shown in Figure 48-8. Here you can see the AddRemoveProgramsIcon, the ProductName, and the Manufacturer properties. You can display more properties by right-clicking the header bar and selecting More.

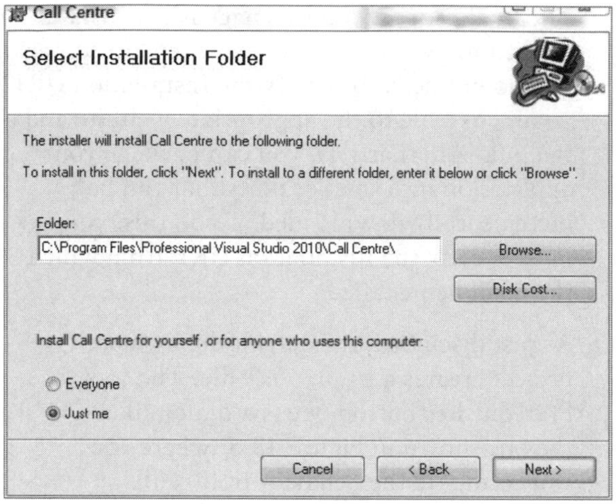

FIGURE 48-7

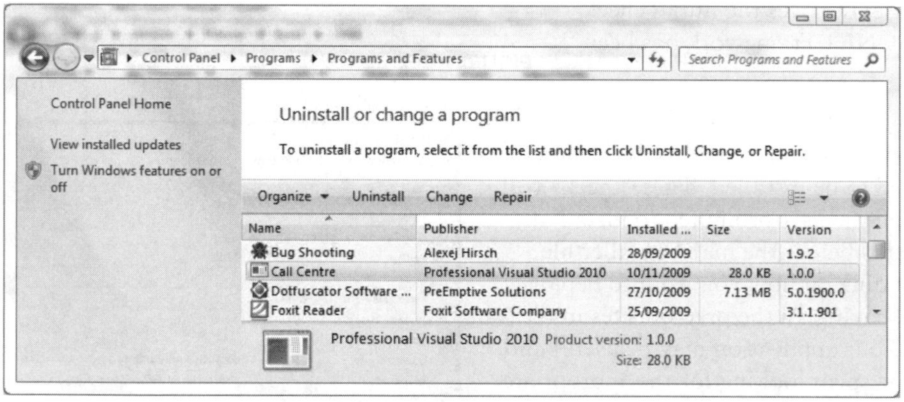

FIGURE 48-8

> In order to test your installer, you can select the Install (and subsequently Uninstall) item from the shortcut menu that is displayed when you right-click the setup Project in the Solution Explorer. If this option is disabled, you may need to build the setup Project first.

Customizing the Installer

The remaining icons at the top of the Solution Explorer are used to customize what is included in the deployment package. In addition to the shortcut icons, these views of the deployment project can be accessed via the View item on the right-click context menu. Start with the File System view, which indicates where files will be installed on the target machine. By default, the primary output for a Windows application is added to the Application Folder, as shown in Figure 48-9. Selecting this node and looking at the Properties window shows that this folder has a default location of `[ProgramFilesFolder][Manufacturer]\[ProductName]`. This location is made up of three predefined installation variables: `ProgramFilesFolder`, `Manufacturer`, and `ProductName`, which will be evaluated and combined during installation. As you can see in Figure 48-7, the installation wizard allows users to change this location when they install the application.

Earlier, you saw that the CallCentre Application had a dependency on the SharedResources assembly. In Figure 48-9 this assembly has been removed from the Application Folder and placed instead in the Global Assembly Cache Folder. When this application is installed, the main executable will be installed in the relevant directory under Program Files, but the SharedResources assembly will be installed in the Global Assembly Cache so it is available to any .NET application. To achieve this, you first need to create the new folder in the File System view by selecting the Global Assembly Cache Folder from the Add Special Folder item on the right-click context menu. You can install files to a number of other special folders as part of the installer. The next step is to move the SharedResources assembly to the Global Assembly Cache by selecting the assembly in the right pane of the File System view and changing the Folder property from Application Folder to Global Assembly Cache Folder. Alternatively, you can drag the item from the Application Folder to the Global Assembly Cache Folder.

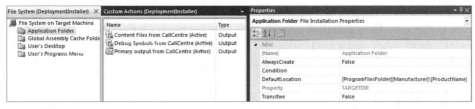

FIGURE 48-9

In addition to installing files on the target machine, you can also add keys to the registry. Some developers argue for and other developers argue against the use of the registry. Although it can provide a convenient store for per-user configuration information, the application settings with user scope are an alternative that makes them easier to manage. The Registry view, as shown in Figure 48-10, can be used to add registry keys and values. To add a new key, right-click the appropriate node in the Registry tree and select Add Key from the context menu. To add a new value, select the appropriate key in the Registry tree and select the type of value from the New item on the right-click context menu off the right pane shown in Figure 48-10. The Name and Value can then be set using the Properties window.

Figure 48-11 shows the File Types view of the deployment project. This view is used to add file extensions that should be installed. For example, in this case you are installing the extension `.call`. You can specify an icon for this type of file, as well as specify the executable that should be called for this file type. In most cases this will be the primary output for your application. To add a new file type, right-click the root node of the File Types tree and select Add File Types from the context menu. This creates a node for the new file type and for the default action (in bold) for that file type. For the `.call` extension, the default action is Open, and it can be executed by double-clicking a file of the appropriate file type. The Open action also appears, again in bold, in the right-click context menu for a file with the `.call` extension. You can add other actions for this file type by selecting Add Action from the right-click context menu for the file type. An alternative action can be made the default by selecting Set as Default from that action's context menu. You can change the order in which the actions appear in the context menu by moving the action up or down in the tree.

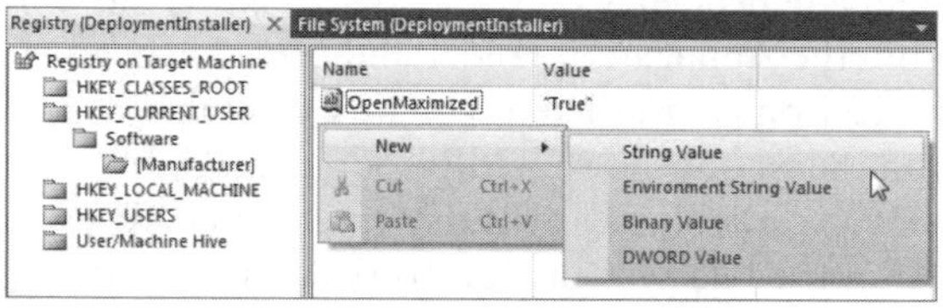

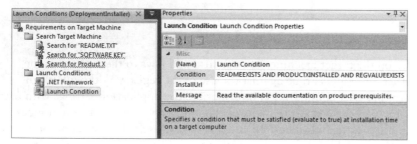

FIGURE 48-10 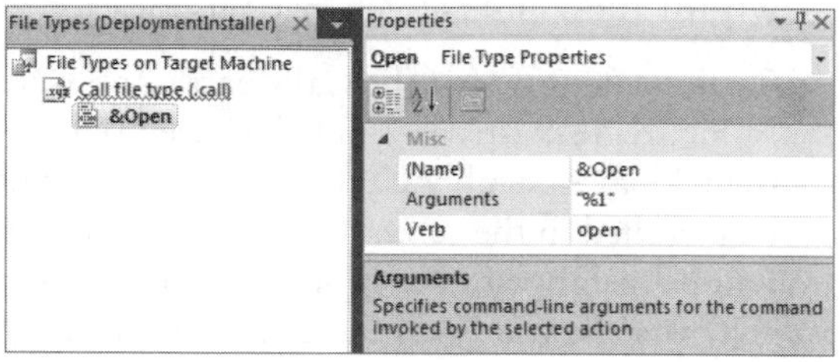   FIGURE 48-11

.NET applications can be autonomous so that their list of dependencies may only contain the .NET Framework. However, web applications require IIS, and more complex applications may require SQL Server to be installed. You can check for these dependencies by using a launch condition via the view shown in Figure 48-12. By default, the .NET Framework is added to this launch condition. Previously you saw that `Setup.exe` also did a check for the .NET Framework and would install it if it was not found. Launch conditions are embedded in the `.msi` file and, unlike conditions in the `Setup.exe` file, are validated even if the `.msi` file is installed directly. The only limitation is that the launch conditions only provide a warning message and a URL reference for more information. In the case of the .NET framework launch condition, this message and URL are already provided for you.

FIGURE 48-12

> When the `Setup.exe` file checks for the .NET Framework it is limited to searching for or installing a specific version. The .NET Framework launch condition can be configured to detect a specific version as well, but if your application is able to target multiple versions, you can instead set the Version property of the launch condition to Any. This allows your application to be deployed as long as there is any version of the .NET Framework installed.

The tree in the left pane of Figure 48-12 is actually split into two sections. The top half of the tree is used to specify searches to be performed on the target machine. Searches can be carried out for files, for installed components or applications, and for registry values. Properties for a file search include the search folder, version and modification dates, and file size. To search for an installed component, you need to know the Component ID, which is embedded in the `.msi` file used to install the product. This information can be retrieved using a product such as Orca, which is included in the Windows SDK Components for Windows Installer Developers that you can download from the Microsoft web site (`www.microsoft.com/downloads/`). A registry search requires properties indicating the key, name, and value to search for. In each of these cases, the search needs to be assigned a `Property` identifier. If the search is successful, the installer property with that identifier is `True`.

The `Property` identifiers assigned to searches on the target machine can be used by a launch condition in the lower half of the tree. As you can see in Figure 48-12, there are conditions that check for the .NET Framework, as well as a custom launch condition. The `Condition` property is set to a logical AND operation across the three search results. If any of the searches fail, the associated property identifier is replaced with `False`, making the whole logical expression false. This will prevent the application from installing, and a warning message will be displayed.

Note that some other views have a `Condition` property for some of the tree nodes. For example, in the File System view, each file or output has a `Condition` property that can be specified. If this condition fails, the file is not installed on the target machine. In each of these cases the syntax of the `Condition` property must be valid for the `MsiEvaluateCondition` function that is called as part of the installation process. This function accepts standard comparison operators, such as equals (=), not equals (<>), less than (<), and greater than (>), as well as Boolean operators NOT, AND, OR, and XOR. There are also some predefined Windows installer properties that can be included in the condition property. The following is a subset of the full list, which you can find in the documentation for the Windows Installer SDK:

➤ `ComputerName`: Target computer name

➤ `VersionNT`: Version of Windows on the target computer

➤ `VersionNT64`: The same value as `VersionNT` but this property is only set for 64-bit operating systems

➤ `ServicePackLevel`: The service pack that has been installed

➤ `LogonUser`: The username of the current user

➤ `AdminUser`: Whether the current user has administrative privileges

➤ `COMPANYNAME`: The company name, as specified in the installation wizard

➤ `USERNAME`: The username, as specified in the installation wizard

One of the main reasons for creating an installer is to make the process of deploying an application much smoother. To do this, you need to create a simple user interface into which an end user can specify values. This might be the installation directory or other parameters that are required to configure the application. Clearly, the fewer steps in the installer the easier the application will be to install. However, it can be better to prompt for information during the installation than for the user to later sit wondering why the application is not working. The User Interface view, shown in Figure 48-13, enables you to customize the screens that the user sees as part of the installation process.

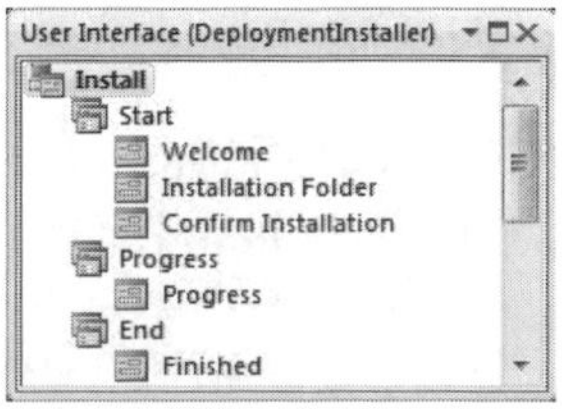

FIGURE 48-13

Two user interfaces are defined in this view: the standard installation and an Administrative install (not visible). Both processes follow the same structure: Start, where you typically collect information from the user before installing the product; Progress, used for providing a visual cue as to the installation's progress; and End, at which point the user is presented with a summary of the installation. The Administrative install is typically used when a network setup is required, and can be invoked by calling `msiexec` with the `/a` flag.

You can customize either of the installation processes by adding and/or removing dialogs from the user interface tree. To add a new dialog, right-click any of the three stages in the installation process and select Add Dialog from the context menu. This displays a list of the predefined dialogs from which you can choose. Each of the dialogs has a different layout; some are used for accepting user input and others are used to display information to the user. Input controls are allocated a property identifier so that the value entered during the installation process can be used later in the process. For example, a checkbox might be used to indicate whether the tools for a product should be installed. A condition could be placed on an output in the File System view so the tools are installed only if the checkbox is enabled.

Adding Custom Actions

It is often necessary to perform some actions either before or after the application is installed. To do this, you can create a custom action to be executed as part of the install or uninstall process. Adding a custom action entails creating the code to be executed and linking the appropriate installer event so that the code is executed. Custom actions use an event model similar to what Windows components use to link the code that you write to the appropriate installer event. To add a custom action to an installer event, you need to create a class that inherits from the `Installer` base class. This base class exposes a number of events for which you can write event handlers. Because writing custom installer actions is quite a common task, the Add New Item dialog includes an Installer Class template item under the General node. The new class (added to the SharedResources project) opens using the component designer, as shown in Figure 48-14.

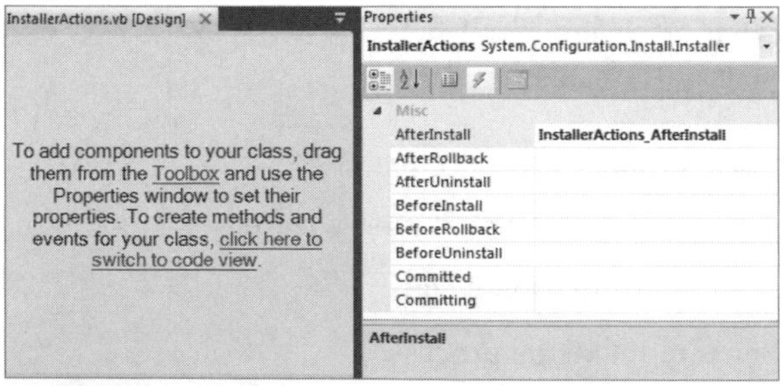

FIGURE 48-14

From the Events tab of the Properties window, select the installer event for which you want to add an event handler. If no event handler exists, a new event handler will be created and opened in the code window. The following code is automatically generated when an event handler is created. A simple message box is inserted to notify the user that the `AfterInstall` event handler has completed:

C#

```csharp
using System.ComponentModel;
using System.Configuration.Install;
using System.Windows.Forms;

public partial class InstallerActions
{
  public InstallerActions()
  {
    InitializeComponent()
  }

  private void InstallerActions_AfterInstall(object sender, InstallEventArgs e)
  {
    MessageBox.Show("Installation process completed!");
  }
}
```

Code snippet SharedResources\InstallerActions.cs

VB

```vb
Imports System.ComponentModel
Imports System.Configuration.Install
Imports System.Windows.Forms

Public Class InstallerActions

    Public Sub New()
        MyBase.New()

        InitializeComponent()
    End Sub

    Private Sub InstallerActions_AfterInstall(ByVal sender As Object, _
                                    ByVal e As InstallEventArgs) _
                                            Handles Me.AfterInstall
        MessageBox.Show("Installation process completed!")
    End Sub
End Class
```

Code snippet SharedResources\InstallerActions.vb

As with forms and other components, the rest of this class is stored in a designer class file where the partial InstallerActions class inherits from the Installer class and is attributed with the RunInstaller attribute. This combination ensures that this class is given the opportunity to handle events raised by the installer.

The InstallerActions class you have just created was added to the SharedResources assembly. For the events to be wired up to the InstallerActions class, the installer needs to know that there is a class that contains custom actions. To make this association, add the SharedResources assembly to the Custom Actions view for the deployment project by right-clicking any of the nodes shown in Figure 48-15 and selecting Add Custom Action from the context menu. In this case, you want to wire up the SharedResources. In Figure 48-15, this association has been made only for the Install action. If you want to wire up the `Custom Action` class for all of the actions, you need to add the custom action to the root Custom Actions node.

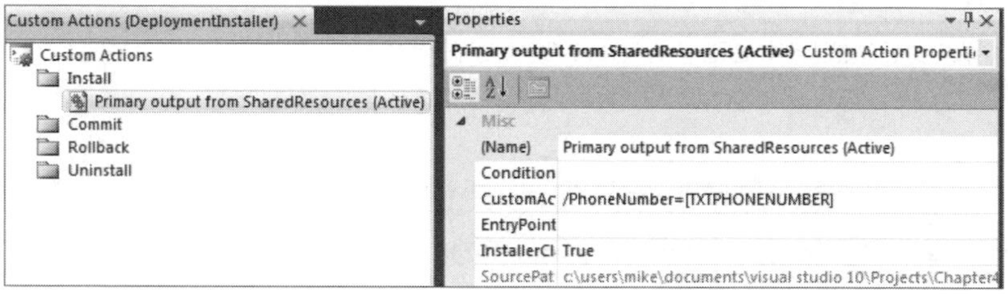

FIGURE 48-15

To complete this discussion, understand that it is important to be able to pass information collected from the user during the Start phase of the installation process to the custom action. Unfortunately, because the custom action is invoked after the installer has finished, you have to use a special channel to pass installer properties to the custom action event handler. In the Custom Actions view (refer to Figure 48-15), select Properties Window from the right-click context menu for the Primary output node. The `CustomActionData` property is used to define name/value pairs that will be sent through to the custom installer. For example, you might have `/PhoneNumber= "+1 425 001 0001"`, in which case you can access this value in the event handler as follows:

Available for download on Wrox.com

C#

```
private void CustomActions_AfterInstall(object sender, InstallEventArgs e)
{
  MessageBox.Show("Number: " + this.Context.Parameters["PhoneNumber"].ToString());
}
```

Code snippet SharedResources\CustomActions.cs

Available for download on Wrox.com

VB

```
Private Sub CustomActions_AfterInstall(ByVal sender As Object, _
                                        ByVal e As InstallEventArgs) _
                                                     Handles Me.AfterInstall
    MessageBox.Show("Number: " & Me.Context.Parameters("PhoneNumber").ToString)
End Sub
```

Code snippet SharedResources\CustomActions.vb

Of course, hard-coded values are not a good idea and it would be better if this were a user-specified value. To use a property defined in the installer user interface, replace the specified string with the property identifier in square brackets. For example, `/PhoneNumber=[TXTPHONENUMBER]` would include the text in the `TXTPHONENUMBER` textbox.

The Service Installer

You can create an installer for a Windows Service the same way you would create an installer
for a Windows application. However, a Windows Service installer not only needs to install the
files into the appropriate location, but it also needs to register the service so it appears in the services
list. You can do this using the `ServiceInstaller` and `ServiceProcessInstaller` components
from the `System.ServiceProcess` namespace (you'll probably need to add these to the Toolbox,
because they are not visible by default). An instance of each of these components needs to be
dragged onto the designer surface of a custom installer, as shown in Figure 48-16.

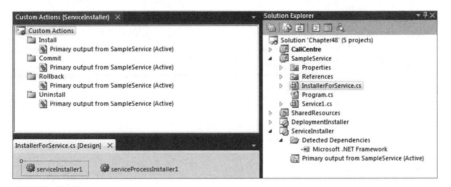

FIGURE 48-16

The `ServiceInstaller` class is used to specify the display name (the name of the service as it
will appear in the Windows services list), the service name (the name of the service class that will
be executed when the service is run), and the startup type (whether it is manually started or
automatically started when Windows starts up). For each service you want to install, you need to
create a separate instance of the `ServiceInstaller` class, specifying a different display and service
name. Only a single instance of the `ServiceProcessInstaller` class is required, which is used
to specify the account information that the service(s) will run as. In the following example, the
`InstallerForService` constructor specifies that the class `Service1` should be installed as a service,
and that it should automatically start using the `NetworkService` account:

C#

```
[RunInstaller(true)]
public partial class InstallerForService : System.Configuration.Install.Installer
{
    const string SERVICE_DISPLAY_NAME = "My Generic Service";
    const string START_AFTER_INSTALL = "STARTAFTERINSTALL";
    const string NET_PROCESS_NAME = "Net";
    const string NET_START = "Start \"{0}\"";
    const int NET_WAIT_TIMEOUT = 5000;
    const string NET_WAIT_ERROR = "WARNING: Process took longer than " +
        "expected to start, it may need to be restarted manually";


    public InstallerForService()
```

```csharp
  {
    InitializeComponent();

    serviceInstaller1.DisplayName = SERVICE_DISPLAY_NAME;
    serviceInstaller1.ServiceName = typeof(Service1).ToString();
    serviceInstaller1.StartType = ServiceStartMode.Automatic;
    serviceProcessInstaller1.Account = ServiceAccount.NetworkService;
  }

  private void InstallerForService_AfterInstall(object sender, InstallEventArgs e)
  {
    var startString = Context.Parameters[START_AFTER_INSTALL];
    if (startString == "") return;
    var shouldStart = Boolean.Parse(startString);
    if (!shouldStart) return;

    var proc = Process.Start(CreateNetStartProcessInfo());

    if (!proc.WaitForExit(NET_WAIT_TIMEOUT))
      MessageBox.Show(NET_WAIT_ERROR);
  }

  private ProcessStartInfo CreateNetStartProcessInfo()
  {
    return new ProcessStartInfo(NET_PROCESS_NAME,
      String.Format(NET_START, SERVICE_DISPLAY_NAME))
      {
        WindowStyle = ProcessWindowStyle.Hidden
      };

  }
}
```

Code snippet Windows Service\InstallerForService.cs

VB

```vb
Public Class InstallerForService

    Const SERVICE_DISPLAY_NAME = "My Generic Service"
    Const START_AFTER_INSTALL = "STARTAFTERINSTALL"
    Const NET_PROCESS_NAME = "Net"
    Const NET_START = "Start ""{0}"""
    Const NET_WAIT_TIMEOUT = 5000
    Const NET_WAIT_ERROR = "WARNING: Process took longer than " &
      "expected to start, it may need to be restarted manually"


    Public Sub New()
        MyBase.New()

        'This call is required by the Component Designer.
```

```
        InitializeComponent()

        'Add initialization code after the call to InitializeComponent
        ServiceInstaller1.DisplayName = SERVICE_DISPLAY_NAME
        ServiceInstaller1.ServiceName = GetType(Service1).ToString
        ServiceInstaller1.StartType = ServiceStartMode.Automatic
        ServiceProcessInstaller1.Account = ServiceAccount.NetworkService


    End Sub

    Private Sub InstallerForService_AfterInstall(ByVal sender As System.Object, _
                ByVal e As System.Configuration.Install.InstallEventArgs) _
                Handles MyBase.AfterInstall
        Dim startString = Context.Parameters(START_AFTER_INSTALL)
        If startString = "" Then Return

        Dim shouldStart = Boolean.Parse(startString)
        If Not shouldStart Then Return

        Dim proc = Process.Start(CreateNetStartProcessInfo())

        If Not proc.WaitForExit(NET_WAIT_TIMEOUT) Then
            MessageBox.Show(NET_WAIT_ERROR)
        End If

    End Sub


    Private Function CreateNetStartProcessInfo() As ProcessStartInfo
        Dim startInfo = New ProcessStartInfo(NET_PROCESS_NAME, _
            String.Format(NET_START, SERVICE_DISPLAY_NAME))
        startInfo.WindowStyle = ProcessWindowStyle.Hidden
        Return startInfo
    End Function
End Class
```

Code snippet Windows Service\InstallerForService.vb

Also included in this listing is an event handler for the AfterInstall event that is used to start the service on completion of the installation process. By default, even when the startup is set to automatic, the service will not be started by the installer. However, when uninstalling the service, the installer does attempt to stop the service.

The user interface for this deployment project includes a Checkboxes (A) dialog using the User Interface view for the project. Refer to Figure 48-13 for a view of the default user interface. Right-click the Start node and select Add Dialog from the context menu. Highlight the dialog titled Checkboxes (A) from the Add Dialog window and click OK. This inserts the new dialog at the end of the installation process. The order of the dialogs can be adjusted using the Move Up/Down items from the right-click context menu on the nodes in the User Interface window.

Selecting Properties Window from the right-click context menu on the new dialog brings up the Properties window. Set the property identifier for Checkbox1 to STARTAFTERINSTALL and then set the Visible property for the remaining checkboxes to false. As discussed earlier in the chapter, you also needed to add /STARTAFTERINSTALL=[STARTAFTERINSTALL] to the CustomActionData property for the assembly in the Custom Actions view of the deployment project. With this user input you can decide whether to start the service when the installer completes.

CLICKONCE

Using a Windows installer is a sensible approach for any application development. However, deploying an installer to thousands of machines, and then potentially having to update them, is a daunting task. Although management products help reduce the burden associated with application deployment, web applications often replace rich Windows applications because they can be dynamically updated, affecting all users of the system. *ClickOnce,* introduced in version 2.0 of the .NET Framework, enables you to build self-updating Windows applications. This section shows you how to use Visual Studio 2010 to build applications that can be deployed and updated using ClickOnce.

One Click to Deploy

To demonstrate the functionality of ClickOnce deployment, this section uses the same application used to build the Windows Installer, CallCentre, which simply displays an empty form. To deploy this application using ClickOnce, select the Publish option from the right-click context menu of the project. This opens the Publish Wizard, which guides you through the initial configuration of ClickOnce for your project.

The first step in the Publish Wizard allows you to select a location to deploy to. You can choose to deploy to a local web site, an FTP location, a file share, or even a local folder on your machine. Clicking Browse opens the Open Web Site dialog, which assists you in specifying the publishing location.

The next step asks you to specify where the users are expecting to install the application from. The default option is for users to install from a CD or DVD-ROM disc. More commonly, you will want to install from a file share on a corporate intranet or a web site on the Internet. Note that the location you publish to and the location the users install from can be different. This can very useful while testing new releases.

The contents of the final step will change depending on the installation option selected. If your application will be installed from a CD or DVD-ROM, this step asks if the application should automatically check for updates. If this option is enabled you must provide a location for the application to check. In the case that your users will be installing from a file share or web site, it is assumed that the application will update from the location that it was originally installed from. Instead, the final question relates to whether or not the application will be available offline. If the offline option is selected, an application shortcut is added to the Start menu and the application can be removed in the Add/Remove programs dialog in the operating system. The user will be able to run the application even if the original installation location is no longer available. If the application is only available online, no shortcut is created and the users have to visit the install location every time they want to run the application.

The last screen in the wizard allows you to verify the configuration before publishing the application. After the application has been published, you can run the Setup.exe bootstrap file that is produced to install the application. If you are installing from a web site, you will get a default.htm file generated as well. This file, shown in Figure 48-17, uses some JavaScript to detect a few dependencies and provides an Install button that launches the `Setup.exe`.

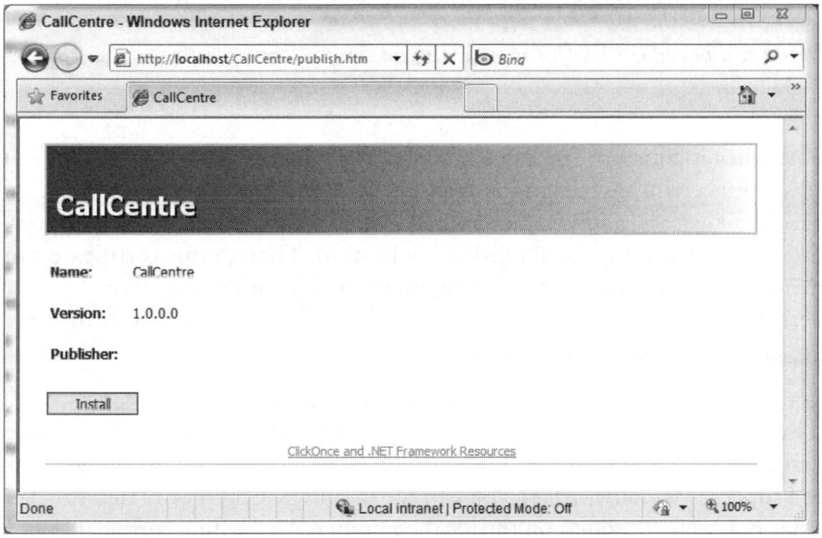

FIGURE 48-17

Clicking the Install button at this location displays a dialog prompting you to run or save `Setup.exe`. Selecting Run (or running `Setup.exe` from a different kind of install) shows the Launching Application dialog, shown in Figure 48-18, while components of your application are being retrieved from the installation location.

After information about the application has been downloaded, a security warning is launched, as shown in Figure 48-19. In this case, the security warning is raised because, although the deployment manifest has been signed, it has been signed with a certificate that is not known on the machine on which it is being installed.

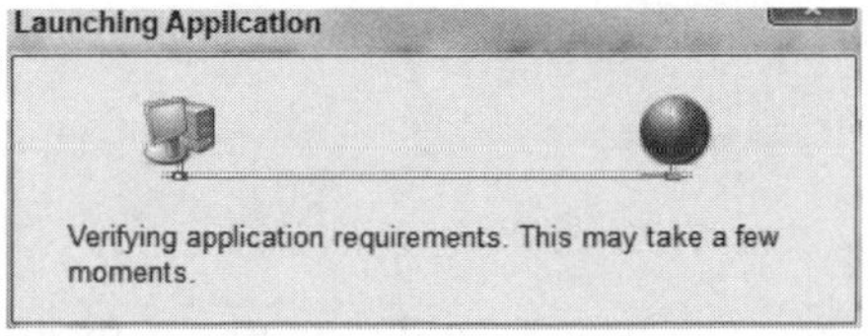

FIGURE 48-18

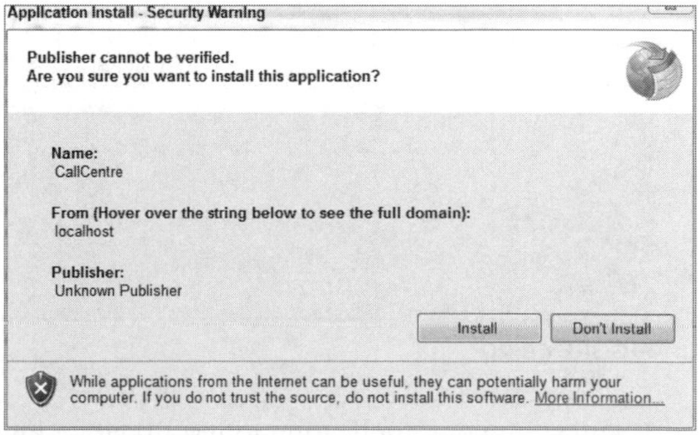

FIGURE 48-19

> *The deployment manifest of a ClickOnce application is an XML file that describes the application to be deployed along with a reference to the current version. Although it is not required, each deployment manifest can be signed by the publisher to provide the manifest with a strong name. This prevents the manifest from being tampered with after it is deployed.*

Three options are available when it comes to signing the deployment manifest. By default, Visual Studio 2010 creates a test certificate to sign the manifest, which has the format `application name_TemporaryKey.pfx` and is automatically added to the solution (this happens when the application is first published using the Publish Now button). Though this certificate can be used during development, it is not recommended for deployment. The other alternatives are to purchase a third-party certificate, from a company such as VeriSign, or to use the certificate server within Windows Server to create an internal certificate.

The advantage of getting a certificate from a well-known certificate authority is that it can automatically be verified by any machine. Using either the test certificate or an internal certificate requires installation of that certificate in the appropriate certificate store. Figure 48-20 shows the Signing tab of the Project Properties window, where you can see that the ClickOnce manifest is being signed with a certificate that has been generated on the local computer. An existing certificate can be used by selecting it from the store or from a file. Alternatively, another test certificate can be created.

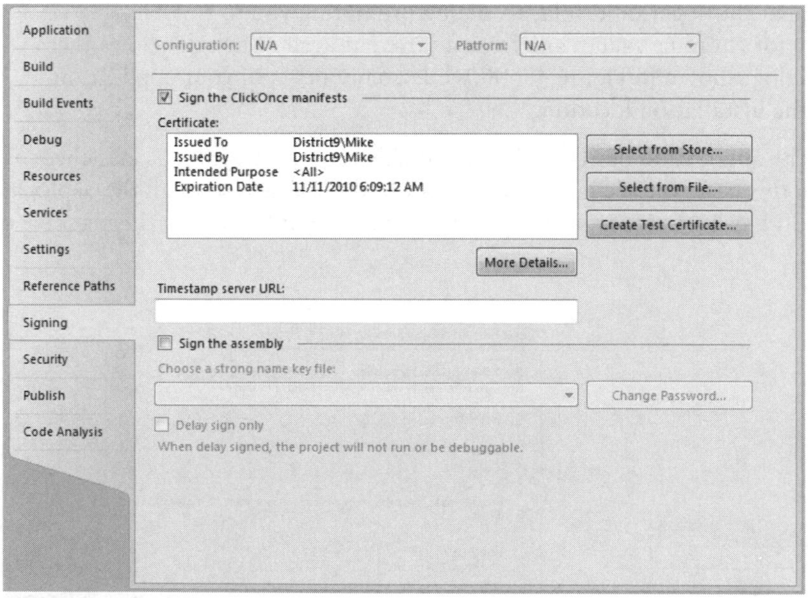

FIGURE 48-20

If you want your application to install with a known publisher, you need to add the test certificate into the root certificate store on the machine on which you're installing the product. Because this also happens to be the deployment machine, you can do this by clicking More Details. This opens a dialog that outlines the certificate details, including the fact that it can't be authenticated. (If you are using the certificate created by default by Visual Studio 2010, you will need to use the Select from File button to re-select the generated certificate, and then use the More Details button. There seems to be an issue here, in that the details window does not show the Install Certificate button without this additional step.) Clicking Install Certificate enables you to specify that the certificate should be installed into the Trusted Root Certification Authorities store. This is not the default certificate store, so you need to browse for it. Because this is a test certificate, you can ignore the warning that is given, but remember that you should not use this certificate in production. Now when you publish your application and try to install it, you will see that the dialog has changed, looking similar to the one shown in Figure 48-21.

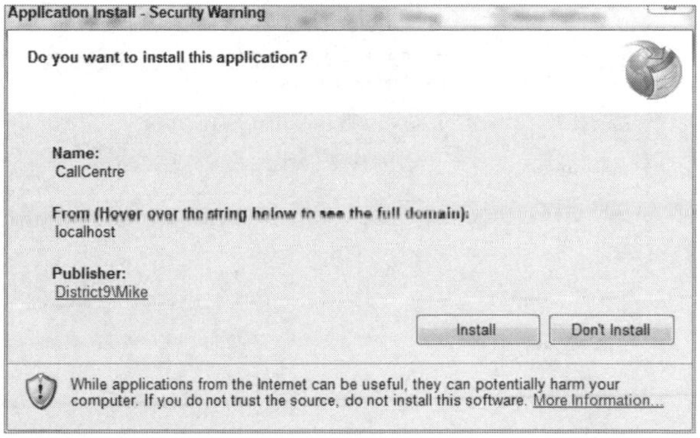

FIGURE 48-21

Although you have a known publisher, you are still being warned that additional security permissions need to be granted to this application in order for it to execute. Clicking the rather minimalist More Information hyperlink opens a more informative dialog, shown in Figure 48-22. As with the security coding within Windows Server 2008 and Windows 7, there are three icons: green for positive security, red for potential security weaknesses, and yellow for informative or best practice guidance.

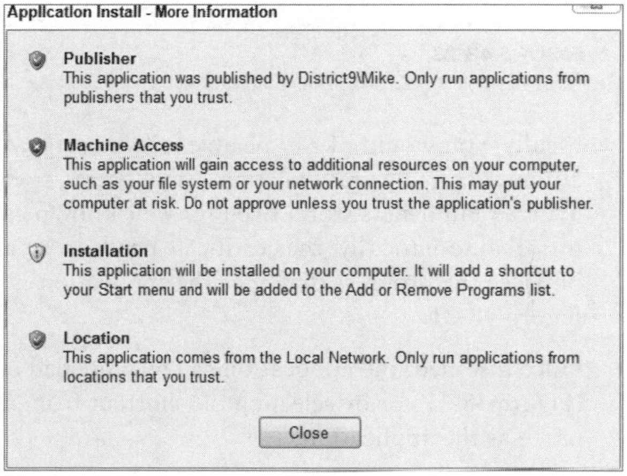

ClickOnce deployment manifests are rated on four security dimensions. You've just seen how you can specify a well-known publisher,

FIGURE 48-22

critical for safe installation of an application. By default, ClickOnce publishes applications as full trust applications, giving them maximum control over the local computer. This is unusual, because in most other cases Microsoft has adopted a security-first approach. To run with full trust, the application requires additional security permissions, which might be exploited. The Sample Application will be available online and offline; and though this isn't a major security risk, it does modify the local file system. Lastly, the location from which the application is being installed is almost as important as the publisher in determining how dangerous the application might be. In this case, the application was published within the local network so it is unlikely to be a security threat.

Because this application doesn't really do anything, you can decrease the trust level that the application requires. As shown in Figure 48-23, this application is made a partial trust application based on the Local Intranet zone. This changes the Machine Access icon to green, leaving only the Installation icon yellow. Unfortunately, the only way you can get this to be green would be to not install the application, which means that it would not be available offline.

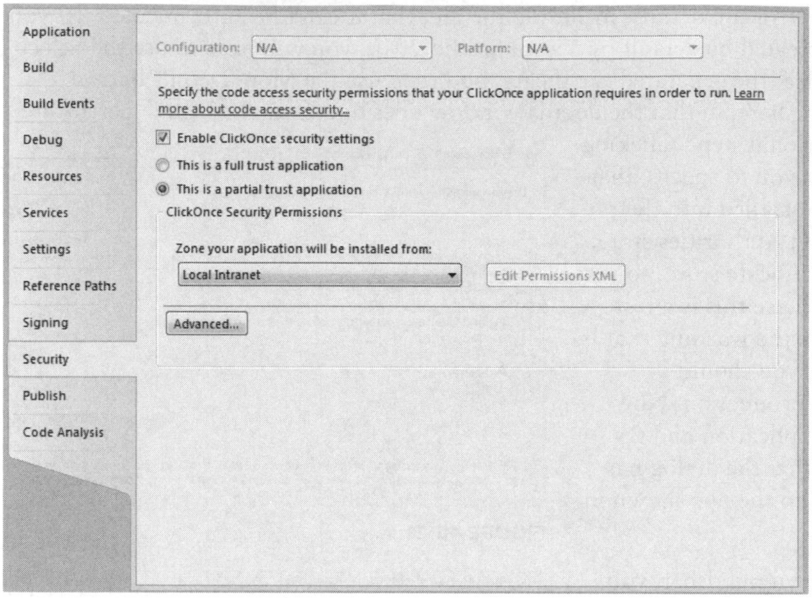

FIGURE 48-23

Ideally, you would like to be able to bypass the Application Install dialog and have the application automatically be granted appropriate permissions. You can do this by adding the certificate to the Trusted Publishers store. Even for well-known certificate authorities, in order for the application to install automatically, the certificate needs to be added to this store. With this completed, you will only see the progress dialog as the application is downloaded, rather than the security prompt in Figure 48-21.

Once installed, the application can be launched either by returning to the installation URL (Figure 48-17) or by selecting the shortcut from the newly created Start Menu folder with the same name as the application.

One Click to Update

At some point in the future you might make a change to your application — for example, you might add a button to the simple form you created previously. ClickOnce supports a powerful update process that enables you to publish the new version of your application in the same way you did previously, and existing versions can be upgraded the next time they are online. As long as you are content with the current set of options, the update process is just the Publish process. When using the Publish Wizard to update an existing application, all of the values previously used to publish the application are preconfigured for you.

You can check the settings in the Publish tab of the Project Properties designer (Figure 48-24). The designer shows the publish location, the installation location, and the install mode of the application. There is also a setting for the Publish Version. This value is not shown in the Publish Wizard, but by default this version starts at 1.0.0.0 and increments the right-most number every time the application is published.

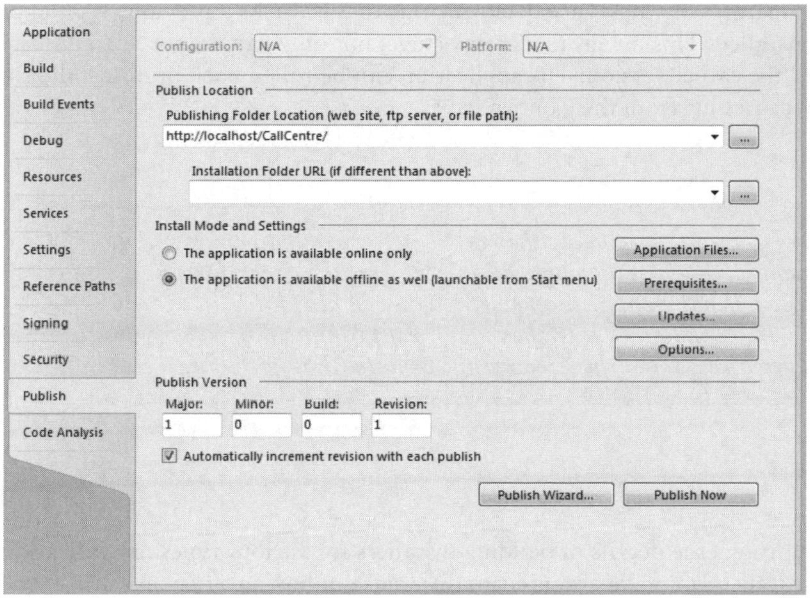

FIGURE 48-24

Along the right are a number of buttons that bring up more advanced options, most of which are not exposed by the wizard. The Application Updates dialog (Figure 48-25) allows you to configure how the application updates itself. In Figure 48-25, the application will update once a month after it has started. You can also specify a minimum required version, which will prevent older clients from executing until they are updated.

With this change, now when you publish a new version of your application, any existing users will be prompted to update their application to the most recent version, as shown in Figure 48-26.

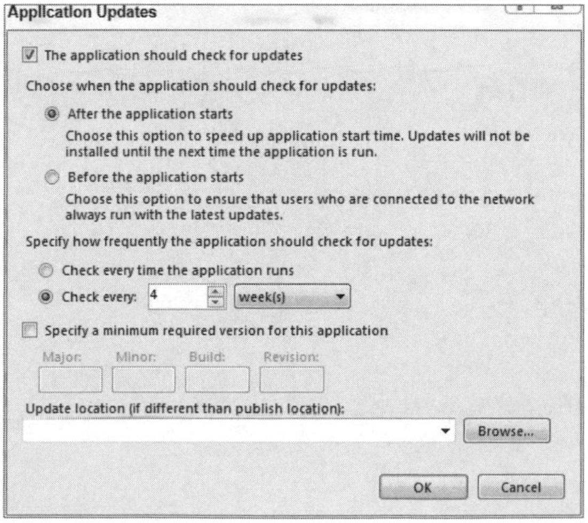

FIGURE 48-25

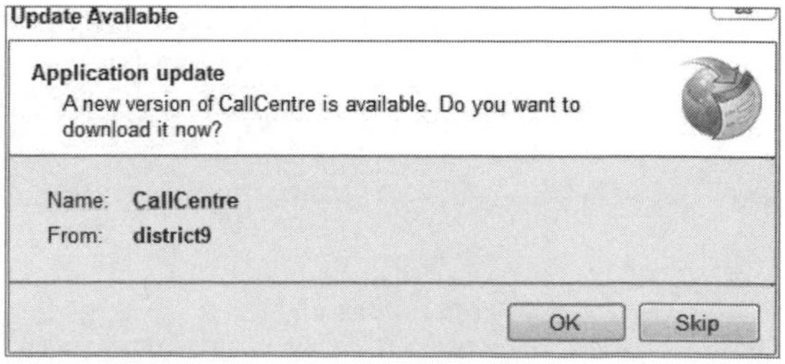

FIGURE 48-26

One of the most powerful features of ClickOnce deployment is that it tracks a previous version of the application that was installed. This means that at any stage, not only can it do a clean uninstall, but it can also roll back to the earlier version. The application can be rolled back or uninstalled from the Programs and Features list from the Control Panel.

> *Note that for users to receive an update they do need to be able to contact the original deployment URL when the application performs the check for a new version (in this case when the application starts). You can also force all users to upgrade to a particular version (that is, they won't get prompted) by specifying the minimum required version in the Application Updates dialog (Figure 49-25).*

SUMMARY

This chapter walked you through the details of building installers for various types of applications. Building a good-quality installer can make a significant difference in how professional your application appears. ClickOnce also offers an important alternative for those who want to deploy their application to a large audience, and with the changes introduced with version 3.5 of the .NET Framework, it can now be used for a much wider range of applications.

49

Web Application Deployment

WHAT'S IN THIS CHAPTER?

➤ Publishing Web Site and Web Application projects

➤ Publishing database scripts with Web Applications

➤ Copying Web Site changes to a remote server

➤ Creating Web Application packages for deployment with the Web Deployment Tool

➤ Managing configuration files for multiple deployment environments

➤ Keeping machines up to date with the Web Platform Installer

➤ Extending the Web Platform Installer to include your own applications

In the previous chapter you saw how to deploy your Windows application using either an installer or ClickOnce. But how do you go about deploying web applications? This chapter walks you through deploying Web Site and Web Application projects. It also covers packaging web applications for remote deployment with the new Web Deployment Tool and integrating with the Web Platform Installer.

One of the most important aspects of building your application is to think about how you will package it so that it can be deployed. Though a large proportion of web applications are only for internal release, where a simple copy script might be sufficient, if you do want to make your web application available for others to purchase and use, you really need to focus on making the deployment process as simple as possible.

After the release of Visual Studio 2005, Microsoft released Web Deployment Projects as a more advanced way of managing the deployment of Web Site and Web Application projects. When Visual Studio 2008 was released, these projects were updated but not included in the final release. At the time of writing, Microsoft has not announced any plans to include Web Deployment Projects in Visual Studio 2010.

WEB SITE DEPLOYMENT

Web projects created with Visual Studio 2010 fall into two broad categories: Web Application projects and Web Site projects. This section demonstrates tools that are specifically for deploying and maintaining Web Site projects.

Publish Web Site

The simplest way to deploy a web site from Visual Studio 2010 is to publish it via the Publish Web Site item on the Build menu. Selecting this option presents you with the dialog shown in Figure 49-1. It has only a few basic options that allow you to publish debugging information, allow in-place updating of your web site, and enforce different naming policies and security requirements.

Usually you will simply use the Target Location box to specify the location that you want to publish to. This location can be a local instance of IIS, an FTP site, elsewhere on the file system, or a remote instance of IIS. Clicking the ellipsis button next to the Target Location textbox in Figure 49-1 brings up a dialog to specify the details of where you want to publish to, as shown in Figure 49-2.

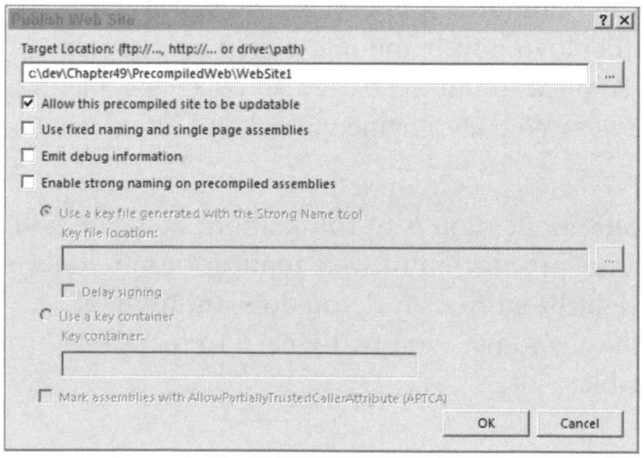

FIGURE 49-1

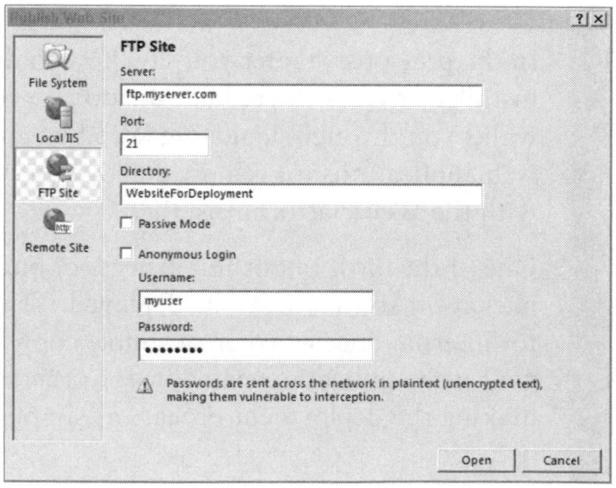

FIGURE 49-2

> *Here we are publishing to a private FTP account, and if this is the first time we are publishing this site we may have to define this folder as an IIS application in order for the web site to function.*

Copy Web Site

Once a web site has been published, it is important that you have some way of updating it. One option is to go through the process of publishing your web site again. However, this will publish the entire web site, even if only a single file needs to be updated. An alternative is to use the Copy Web Site tool, shown in Figure 49-3, to synchronize files between your development project and the web site. You can access this tool from the right-click context menu in the Solution Explorer, or via the web site menu.

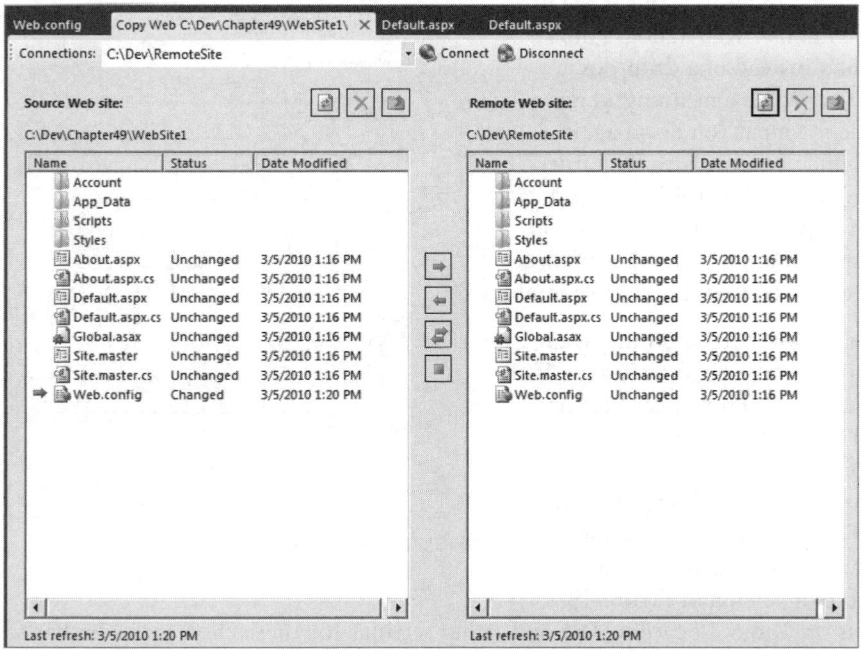

FIGURE 49-3

To view the existing files on the remote web site, you need to either select a recent connection from the drop-down list or click the Connect button. This will open a dialog similar to Figure 49-2, where you can specify how to connect to the remote web site. Once you have connected you can see which files are out of sync. You can then use the right and left arrows to move files between your local project and the remote web site.

WEB APPLICATION DEPLOYMENT

Web application projects are quite different from Web Site projects and come with a different set of tools for deployment. Visual Studio 2010 introduces the capability to deploy with the new Web Deployment Tool, which is used to easily import and export IIS applications along with their dependencies — such as IIS meta-data and databases — from the command line, IIS 7.0 management console, Powershell cmdlets, or directly from Visual Studio itself. It also provides the ability to manage several versions of configuration data for different environments in a clean manner without duplication.

Publishing a Web Application

The quickest way to deploy a Web Application project is to simply publish it directly from Visual Studio. Select the Publish item from the right-click context menu in Solution Explorer to display the Publish Web dialog shown in 49-4. If this is the first time you have run the Publish Web dialog, Publish Profile will be a textbox instead of a drop-down enabling you to give the profile a meaningful name. Each time you do a deployment you do so against a particular profile, which encapsulates the target environment settings. A Web Application project can maintain a collection of profiles, which allows you deploy the one web application to a number of target environments and keep the settings for each separate.

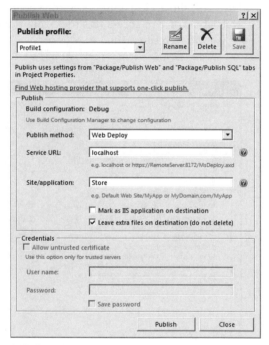

Four options for Publish Method determine what you see in the lower part of the dialog window: Web Deploy FTP, File System, and Front-Page Server Extensions (FPSE). The File System and Front-Page Server Extensions options both allow you to enter the target location for the web application to be published. The FTP option offers the same but also allows you to enter FTP credentials. Each of these provides a cut down version of Figure 49-2

FIGURE 49-4

if you click the ellipsis on Target Location. The only other settings for these choices is whether to simply replace any files in the target location or clear all of the files from the target location before deployment.

The final publishing method option is Web Deploy MSDeploy.exe, also known as the Web Deployment Tool, is designed to help administrators and developers more easily package and deploy web application projects. It does this by packaging all of the necessary files for your application along with all of the required meta-data to install and configure it into a single zip file. This zip file can then be installed via the IIS7.0 interface, the command line, Powershell cmdlets, or directly from Visual Studio itself.

To deploy directly to a server that is running MSDeploy, you will need:

➤ A service reference where MSDeploy will be listening

➤ A site and application name used to identify the remote application

➤ A username and password for the remote instance of MSDeploy

All of this information will be provided by your server administrator or hosting provider.

Once you have published your web application successfully at least once, the Web One Click Publish toolbar will become available. This toolbar, shown in Figure 49-5, allows you to select a publishing profile and click the Publish button to instantly publish your web application. If you don't see the toolbar, you can enable it by selecting View ➪ Toolbars ➪ Web One Click Publish from the main menu.

FIGURE 49-5

> *If you start the Publish process from the main menu or from the project right-click context menu, you will get the option to examine the profile properties before the application is deployed. When you use the Web One Click Publish toolbar, however, the deployment starts immediately.*

Packaging a Web Application

Even if you do not have direct access to the target environment, you can still create packages that can be managed by the Web Deployment Tool. This is as simple as selecting Create Package from the right-click context menu of the Web Application project in the Solution Explorer window.

By default, this generates a zip file along with some support material in the obj\Debug\Package\ folder. The support material includes a sample .cmd file along with a parameters file, which can be used to install the package from the command line on the target server.

> *These packages are precisely what get deployed to a remote server during an MSDeploy Publish.*

Configuring Web Application Packages

One important aspect of deploying and packaging web applications is configuring what gets deployed. You can reach the Package/Publish settings tab pictured in Figure 49-6 from the normal project properties pages, or by selecting the Package/Publish Settings item in the right-click context menu of the project in the Solution Explorer window.

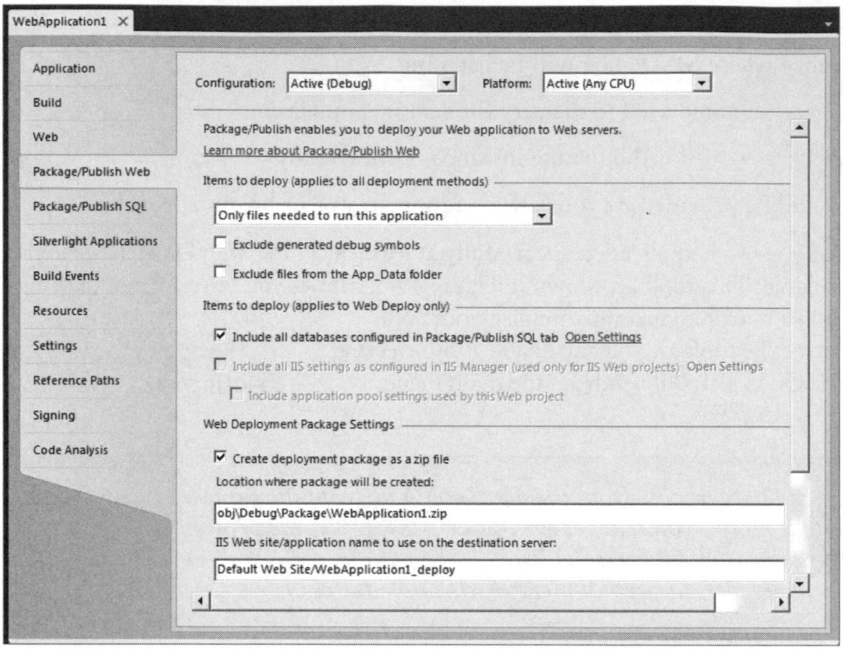

FIGURE 49-6

The first option to configure is which files to actually deploy. The three options are as follows:

➤ **Only files needed to run the application** will include only the files that are actually necessary to running the application. This can exclude files with a build action of None. This is the most exclusive option and is the default.

➤ **All files in this project** will include any file that appears as a part of the project in the Solution Explorer window.

➤ **All files in this project folder** will include any file that is found in the project folder even if it is not a part of the project. This is the least restrictive option.

You also have options to exclude generated debug files and files in the App_Data folder. To deploy databases you should use the Package/Publish SQL options, which are discussed in the next section.

A Web Deployment Package is also able to copy IIS meta-data, but only if your project is being developed in IIS. To configure this, go to the Web properties page and change the Servers option to Use Local IIS Web Server.

Finally, you can opt to provide a location for the deployment package to be created and a web site/application name to apply to the package when it is deployed to an IIS server.

Packaging SQL Server Data

One common problem when deploying web applications is that they frequently rely on a database server to store data and so the deployment process has to find a way to manage the deployment of a database schema, and potentially data as well. Web Deployment Packages allow you to specify database scripts to set up or update your databases, and the Web Deployment Tool manages the process of running these scripts against a database server during the deployment process.

To add a database to your deployment package, use the Package/Publish SQL property page for the web project shown in Figure 49-7. Use the Add and Remove buttons on the right-hand side to maintain a list of connections that are to be deployed. If you already have a set of connection strings in the `web.config` file, you can import them directly into this list using the Import from Web.Config button provided. You can also use the checkboxes to decide whether or not to include each connection string in the deployment.

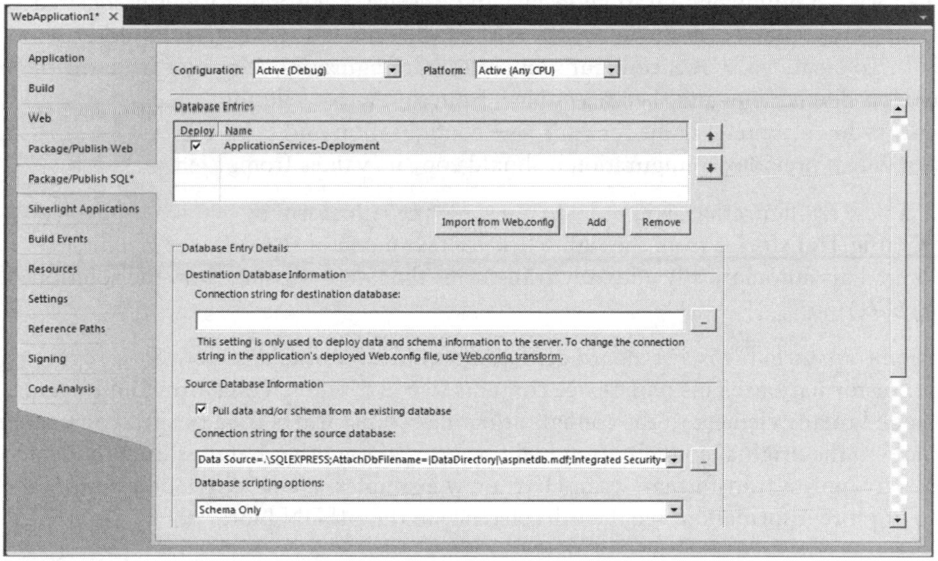

FIGURE 49-7

When you have a connection string highlighted in the top section, the bottom section displays deployment details relating to that connection string. The first option allows you to provide a different connection string for the deployment package.

The next option allows you pull a schema and/or data from an existing database while creating the deployment package. To do this, you need to simply provide a connection string and select whether schema, data, or both should be deployed. In addition to these automatically generated database scripts, you can add your own database scripts to the deployment. This can be useful if you are using a tool that produces change scripts for your database.

> When you use Visual Studio to extract schema information or data from an existing SQL Server, it generates scripts suitable for deploying a brand new database. To update an existing database, you need to create your own scripts and add them to the package.

web.config Transformations

One other problem that many projects face is how to maintain different versions of application configuration between different environments. This problem is commonly handled by keeping several copies of the `web.config` file around — one for each environment — and then remembering to rename the correct version for the target environment every time the application is deployed. Even if you make this a part of your build process, this can be problematic because any change to the web.config file potentially needs to be replicated to each of the other environment-specific configuration files. Visual Studio 2010 introduces a new capability called Web.config Transformation, which allows you to have a single configuration file and then specify only the differences for each environment.

When a web application project is first created it includes a web.config file along with two config transforms, one for each build configuration: Debug and Release. Each transform is associated with a single configuration and appears under the web.config file in the Solution Explorer (see Figure 49-8). To create your own configuration, select Configuration Manager from the Configuration drop-down menu and then select New from the Active solution configuration drop-down. Enter a name for your new configuration and optionally select which previous configuration it should copy its values from.

FIGURE 49-8

Once you have a new configuration, you can add a new config transform by selecting Add Config Transforms from the right-click context menu of the web.config file in Solution Explorer. This automatically adds any transforms that were missing from the solution's Configuration collection.

The configuration transform file is a standard configuration file, but it adds a new XML namespace for specifying transformations. This namespace contains two attributes, Transform and Locator, which can be added to any element in the configuration file. Transform is used to specify a change that is to be made to the original configuration file. Locator, on the other hand, is used to identify particular nodes to apply a transformation to. Here a few examples, along with a description of what they do. For more information, see the full reference in the MSDN Library.

```
<appSettings>
  <add xdt:Transform="Remove"xdt:Locator="Condition(@name='UseMockDatabase')"/>
</appSettings>
```

This locates an add node under appSettings with the name attribute set to UseMockDatabase and removes it from the output configuration file.

```
<connectionStrings>
  <add name="AdventureWorks" xdt:Transform="Replace" xdt:Locator="Match(name)"
  connectionString="Data Source=UAT_DB; Initial Catalog=AdventureWorks; ~CA
  Integrated Security=true"/>
</connectionStrings>
```

This updates the contents the AdventureWorks connection string to point to a UAT database server.

```
<system.web>
  <compilation xdt:Transform="RemoveAttributes(debug)" />
</system.web>
```

This removes the debug attribute from the compilation node under system.web.

```
<authorization>
  <deny users="*" xdt:Transform="Insert"/>
</authorization>
```

This inserts a new node at the bottom of the authorization element that denies access to all users.

WEB PROJECT INSTALLERS

In addition to using the Web Deployment Tool, you can create a standard Windows Installer package to manage a web application or web site deployment. To do this, you will need to create a Web Setup Project from the Other Project Types Setup and Deployment node in the New Project dialog. This is essentially a normal setup project that has been configured with the relevant output folder (see the File System view) and user interface (see the User Interface view) for deploying web applications. Once you have created the setup project, you will need to add the appropriate project outputs. The left image of Figure 49-9 shows the Add Project Output Group dialog for adding a web site to the setup project. Because a web site contains only content files, this is the only option available.

Alternatively, when you are using a Web Application Project, you will want to select the primary output as well as the content files, as shown in the right image of Figure 49-9.

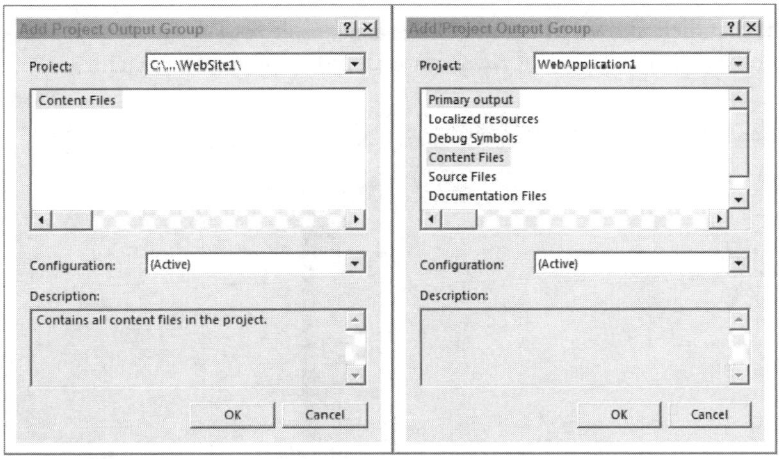

FIGURE 49-9

One of the unique features of the Web Setup Project is the screen that is added to the user interface to enable the user to define the web site, virtual directory, and application pool that will be used by the web application being installed. Figure 49-10 illustrates this dialog as part of the installation process.

In older versions of Visual Studio, the web site installation wizard would only prompt the user to specify the name of the virtual directory into which the application was to be installed, and this directory would then be created in the default web site. If multiple web sites were hosted on the same server (often the case with products such as SharePoint installed), this

FIGURE 49-10

could result in the application being installed on the wrong web site. Being able to specify the web site during installation reduces any post-installation administration that would have been required in the past.

THE WEB PLATFORM INSTALLER

Web applications tend to rely on a large number of technologies and tools to function correctly both during development and in production. Even once your environment is correctly set up for a single application, relationships and dependencies between applications need to be understood and managed. Finally, there are always new tools, libraries, and applications being made available on the Internet, which you can build on when creating your own projects. As your environment becomes more complex it can be quite a challenge to keep everything working correctly and up to date.

The Microsoft Web Platform Installer, shown in Figure 49-11, is a simple tool designed to manage the software that you have installed on your web servers and development machine.

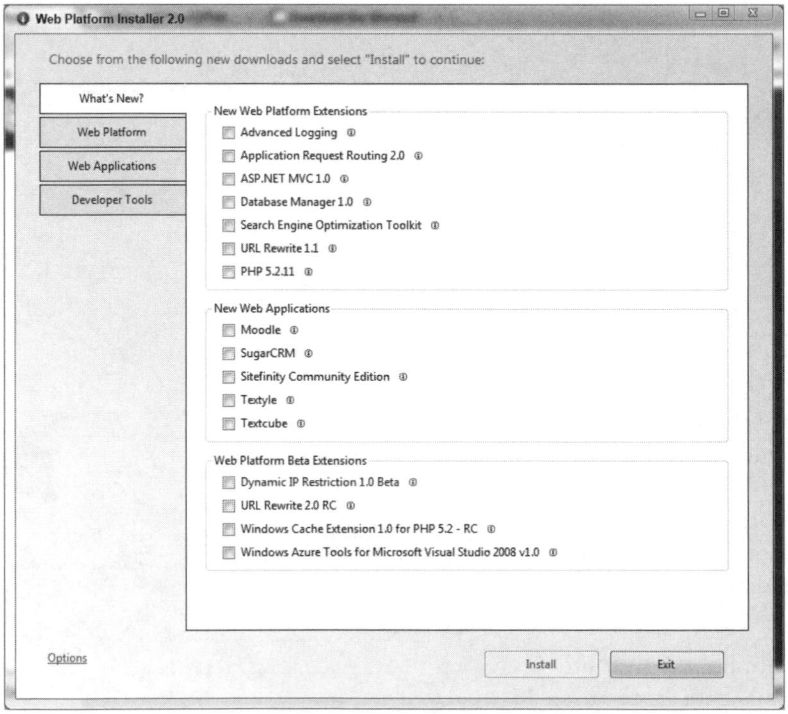

FIGURE 49-11

Once you have downloaded the Web Platform Installer from `http://www.microsoft.com/web`, you can run it as many times as you like. It is able to detect which components you already have on your machine and you can check and uncheck components to add and remove them, respectively. It is even able to take care of dependencies between components and install everything you need.

The Web Platform Installer is able to manage components beyond just the Web Platform itself. Also available is a collection of applications from the Microsoft Web Application Gallery found at `http://www.microsoft.com/web/gallery`. These applications are filed under various categories under the Web Applications tab. Just like the components in the Web Platform, these applications can have their own prerequisites and the Web Platform Installer takes care of ensuring they are installed.

If you are already packaging your web application for deployment with MSDeploy, it is ready to be distributed using the Web Platform Installer. You can get your application added to the Web Application Gallery by filling in a simple form on the Microsoft Web portal. Once your application is approved, it will show up ready to be installed on any machine with the Web Platform Installer on it.

Extending the Web Platform Installer

As mentioned in the previous section, it is quite easy to have your application included in the Web Application Gallery to make it available to a large audience. There are some scenarios in which you would like to take advantage of the Web Platform Installer but do not want to make your application publicly available. This might be because your application is being used privately within your company or it might be because your application is not yet ready for release and you want to test the deployment procedure.

The Web Platform Installer relies on atom feeds to ensure that the list of components and products that it installs are always kept up to date. Each entry in these feeds corresponds to an application or component in the user interface of the Web Platform Installer. The Web Platform and Web Application tabs each come from different feeds at `http://www.microsoft.com/web/webpi/2.0/WebProductList.xml` and `http://www.microsoft.com/web/webpi/2.0/WebApplicationList.xml`, respectively. In addition to these two feeds, each installation of the Web Platform Installer can specify additional feeds that reference more components.

Here is a sample feed for a simple timesheets web application:

```
<?xml version="1.0" encoding="utf-8"?>
<feed xmlns="http://www.w3.org/2005/Atom">
  <version>1.0.0</version>
  <title>AdventureWorks Product WebPI Feed</title>
  <link href="http://www.professionalvisualstudio.com/SampleProductFeed.xml" />
  <updated>2009-11-01T16:30:00Z</updated>
  <author>
    <name>Adventure Works</name>
    <uri>http://www.professionalvisualstudio.com</uri>
  </author>
  <id>http://www.professionalvisualstudio.com/SampleProductFeed.xml</id>

  <entry>
```

```xml
<productId>TimeSheets</productId>
<title>Adventure Works Timesheets</title>

<summary>The Adventure Works corporate Timesheeting system</summary>
<longSummary>The Adventure Works corporate Timesheeting system</longSummary>
<productFamily>Human Resources</productFamily>

<version>1.0.0</version>
<images>
  <icon>c:\AdventureWorksIcon.png</icon>
</images>
<author>
  <name>Adventure Works IT</name>
  <uri>http://www.professionalvisualstudio.com</uri>
</author>
<published>2009-11-01T12:30:00Z</published>

<discoveryHint>
  <or>
    <discoveryHint>
      <registry>
        <keyPath>HKEY_LOCAL_MACHINE\SOFTWARE\AdventureWorks\Timesheets</keyPath>
        <valueName>Version</valueName>
        <valueValue>1.0.0</valueValue>
      </registry>
    </discoveryHint>
    <discoveryHint>
      <file>
        <filePath>%ProgramFiles%\AdventureWorks\Timesheets.exe</filePath>
      </file>
    </discoveryHint>
  </or>
</discoveryHint>

<dependency>
  <productId>IISManagementConsole</productId>
</dependency>

<installers>
  <installer>
    <id>1</id>
    <languageId>en</languageId>
    <architectures>
      <x86 />
    </architectures>
    <osList>
      <os>
        <!-- the product is supported on Vista/Windows Server SP1 + -->
        <minimumVersion>
          <osMajorVersion>6</osMajorVersion>
          <osMinorVersion>0</osMinorVersion>
          <spMajorVersion>0</spMajorVersion>
        </minimumVersion>
        <osTypes>
```

```
                        <Server />
                        <HomePremium />
                        <Ultimate />
                        <Enterprise />
                        <Business />
                      </osTypes>
                    </os>
                  </osList>
                  <eulaURL>http://www.professionalvisualstudio.com/eula.html</eulaURL>

                  <installerFile>
                    <!-- size in KBs -->
                    <fileSize>1024</fileSize>
                    <installerURL>http://www.professionalvisualstudio.com/Timesheets_x86.msi
                    </installerURL>
                    <sha1>111222FFF000BBB444555EEEAAA777888999DDDD</sha1>
                  </installerFile>

                  <installCommands>
                    <msiInstall>
                      <msi>%InstallerFile%</msi>
                    </msiInstall>
                  </installCommands>
                </installer>
              </installers>
          </entry>

          <tabs>
            <tab>
            <groupTab>
            <id>AdventureWorksHRTab</id>
            <name>Adventure Works Human Resources</name>
            <description>Adventure Works HR Apps</description>
            <groupingId>HRProductFamilyGrouping</groupingId>
            </groupTab>
            </tab>
          </tabs>

          <groupings>
            <grouping>
              <id>HRProductFamilyGrouping</id>
              <attribute>productFamily</attribute>
              <include>
                <item>Human Resources</item>
              </include>
            </grouping>
          </groupings>
      </feed>
```

The first part specifies some standard information about the feed itself, including the date it was last updated and author information. This is all useful if the feed is consumed using a normal feed reader. Following this is a single `entry` node containing information about the application itself. The Web Platform Installer is able to use the value of `productId` to refer to the application in other places, including being listed as a dependency for other components.

The discoveryHint node is used to determine if this application is already installed. The sample application can be detected by looking for a specific registry key value or by looking for a specific application by name. If either one of these items is found, the Web Platform Installer considers this application to be already installed. In addition to these two kinds of hints, you can use an msiProductCode hint to detect applications that are installed via MSI.

The sample timesheets application has a dependency on the IIS Management Console. Each component that your application relies upon can be specified by its productId. If it is not already installed on the target machine, the Web Platform Installer will install it for you. In addition to dependencies, you can specify incompatibilities for your application, which will prevent both applications from being installed at once.

The last component of the application entry is the installers element. There should be one installer element for each installer that you want to make available and they should all have different identifiers. Each installer can be targeted at a specific range of languages, operating systems, and CPU architectures. If the target environment doesn't fall into this range, the installer will not be shown. Each installer should specify an installer file, which will be downloaded to a local cache before the specified installCommands are executed against it.

> *An installer file requires a size and a SHA1 hash so that the Web Platform Installer can verify that the file has been downloaded correctly. Microsoft provides a tool called File Checksum Integrity Verifier (fciv.exe), which can be used to generate the hash. You can download this tool from* http://download.microsoft.com.

The final two elements relate to what is displayed in the Web Platform Installer user interface. Each tab element adds to the list of tabs on the left. In the example, we are adding a tab based on a grouping of products, which is defined below in the groupings element based on the productFamily attribute.

To add this feed to a Web Platform Installer instance, click the Options link in the lower left-hand corner to bring up the Options page. Enter the URL to the atom feed into the textbox and click the Add Feed button. When you click OK the Web Platform Installer refreshes all of the feeds and reloads all of the applications including the new Adventure Works timesheets application shown in Figure 49-12.

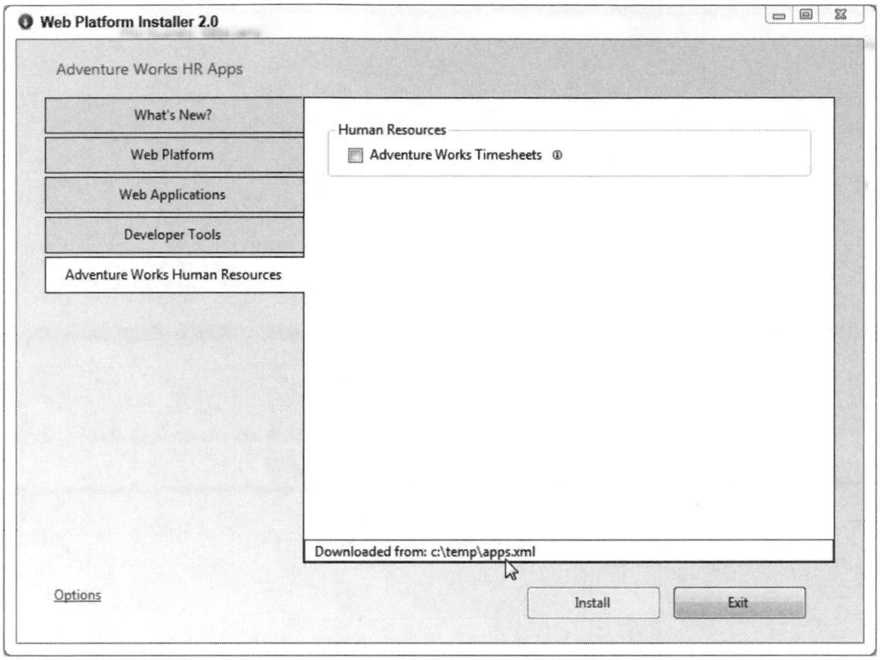

FIGURE 49-12

SUMMARY

This chapter showed you how to use a number of the features of Visual Studio 2010 to package your web applications and get them ready for deployment. The new Web Deployment Tool makes deployment to a number of environments and machines quick and painless, and the One Click Publish toolbar makes it easy to manage the different publishing profiles. Finally, the Web Platform Installer provides you with an easy way to reach a large number of potential customers or to manage your own suite of enterprise applications.

PART XI
Customizing and Extending Visual Studio

▶ **CHAPTER 50:** The Automation Model

▶ **CHAPTER 51:** Add-Ins

▶ **CHAPTER 52:** Macros

▶ **CHAPTER 53:** Managed Extensibility Framework (MEF)

50

The Automation Model

WHAT'S IN THIS CHAPTER?

➤ Understanding the Visual Studio extensibility options

➤ Working with the Visual Studio automation model

Often you will find yourself performing repetitive tasks when working in Visual Studio, and wish you could bundle all those tasks into a single automated task, streamlining your workflow, decreasing your frustration at doing the same thing repeatedly, and consequently increasing your productivity. Alternatively, perhaps you want to add functionality to Visual Studio to share with other developers in your company (or even around the world). Fortunately, Visual Studio has been designed to be very extensible — in fact, many features that you may have thought were built into Visual Studio are actually extensions themselves! This extensibility is exposed to make it very easy to add the functionality to Visual Studio that suits your requirements. Extensibility points include automating tasks, adding new tool windows, adding features to the code editor, adding your own menu items (including items to the code editor's context menu), creating debug visualizers, creating your own wizards, extending existing dialogs, and even adding your own editors/designers and programming languages! This chapter looks at the options available for extending Visual Studio, and takes a look at the automation model used by both macros and add-ins.

VISUAL STUDIO EXTENSIBILITY OPTIONS

Unfortunately, the extensibility story in Visual Studio is a bit murky, because a number of different means exist to extend Visual Studio and it can be hard to determine which method you should use for what you want to achieve. Here are the various extensibility options available for Visual Studio, and the context in which it is most appropriate to use each:

➤ **Macros** are the easiest way to automate Visual Studio, and can be thought of as a scripting language for the IDE. Macros are best suited to quickly automating a task (such as manipulating the text in the code editor, or automating a repeated set of tasks in the IDE). Macros are rather limited in their capabilities, and suited only to simple automation tasks. Macros must be written in VB — no other language is supported. Macros can be shared between developers, but require sharing macro project files (including their source code). Chapter 52 covers how to develop macros for Visual Studio 2010.

➤ **Add-ins** are more powerful than macros (despite both working against the Visual Studio automation model), enabling you to also create tool windows and wizards, and integrate other features seamlessly within the IDE itself. Add-ins are compiled projects (in your favorite .NET language or Visual C++), enabling you to ship a binary to other developers rather than the code itself. Chapter 51 covers how to develop add-ins for Visual Studio 2010.

➤ **VSPackages** are a part of the Visual Studio SDK (a separate download and install), and provide even more power than add-ins. VSPackages enable you to access the core internal interfaces in Visual Studio, and thus are ideally suited to integrating your own editors, designers, and programming languages into Visual Studio. Coverage of VSPackages, however, is beyond the scope of this book. More information of VSPackages can be found in the book *Professional Visual Studio Extensibility* by Keyvan Nayyeri.

➤ **Managed Extensibility Framework (MEF) component parts** enable you to extend the new WPF-based code editor in Visual Studio 2010 in order to change its appearance and behavior. If you want to add features to the code editor, this is the best option for your need. Chapter 53 covers how to develop code editor extensions for Visual Studio 2010.

The next few chapters take you through some of the various ways in which you can extend Visual Studio, including using add-ins, macros, and the Managed Extensibility Framework (MEF). However, we continue in this chapter by looking at the core Visual Studio 2010 automation model that both macros and add-ins rely upon to interact with Visual Studio.

THE VISUAL STUDIO AUTOMATION MODEL

The Visual Studio automation model, also known as Development Tools Extensibility (abbreviated as DTE, which you will see used in the automation model), is an object model exposed by Visual Studio that you can program against to interact with the IDE. This object model allows you to perform many actions in Visual Studio to achieve a required behavior, handle events raised by Visual Studio (such as when a command has been activated), and various other functions such as displaying a custom dockable tool window within the Visual Studio IDE.

This object model is the means by which both add-ins and macros interact with the Visual Studio IDE, so this section takes a deeper look at its structure and the functionality that it exposes.

An Overview of the Automation Model

The Visual Studio automation model (DTE) is a COM-based object model that has been added to with each new version of Visual Studio, over time making it somewhat confusing and messy.

DTE consists of various COM interfaces and their associated implementations covering the facets of functionality in Visual Studio. Because the concrete classes mostly implement a corresponding interface, you can expect to see lots of pair classes: an interface and its implementation. For example, the root object is the DTE class, which implements the _DTE interface.

By their very nature, interfaces don't support extensibility and should never be changed, because any change in their structure breaks the structure of any class that implements the original interface. As Visual Studio matured and new versions were released (each requiring new functionality to be added to the existing classes in the object model), this created a problem. Microsoft couldn't update the existing interfaces or it would cause problems with existing add-ins, so instead it decided to create new versions of the interfaces with each new Visual Studio version by deriving from the previous version and adding the new requirements to it. These new interfaces were suffixed with a revision number so they didn't have the same name as their predecessor, thus creating the messy and unfriendly model we have today where multiple interfaces/classes represent the same part of the object model.

For example, you can check out the Debugger, Debugger2, Debugger3, Debugger4, and Debugger5 interfaces. The Debugger interface was a part of Visual Studio 2003 and was the original interface. Debugger2 is an updated version of Debugger for Visual Studio 2005, Debugger3 came with Visual Studio 2008, Debugger4 came with Visual Studio 2008 SP1, and Debugger5 came with Visual Studio 2010. The root DTE interface also has a revision called DTE2, and you will normally use this rather than its predecessor.

What this means in practical terms is that navigating the object model hierarchy isn't straightforward. The model will expose the methods on the classes in the early manifestation of the model, but you will need to cast the object to a more recent interface to access the functions it exposes. For example, the first iteration of the Solution object didn't provide the ability to create a solution folder — this didn't come until later where the AddSolutionFolder method was exposed on the object by the Solution2 interface. So the following macro code will *not* work:

```
Public Sub AddSolutionFolder()
    DTE.Solution.AddSolutionFolder("TestFolder") 'Will not work
End Sub
```

but this macro code will:

```
Public Sub AddSolutionFolder()
    Dim solution As Solution2 = DirectCast(DTE.Solution, Solution2)
    solution.AddSolutionFolder("TestFolder")
End Sub
```

As you can see, this makes using the automation model difficult with it commonly necessary to cast objects to interfaces, also creating somewhat messy code.

Because the underlying automation model is COM-based and we are using managed code to interact with it, we need to use interop assemblies to provide the bridge between our managed code and the COM object model. Unfortunately, like the object model itself, these are somewhat messy too. An additional interop assembly has been added with each version of Visual Studio, so your project will need to reference each interop assembly, from the base interop assembly up to the one released with the lowest version of Visual Studio that your add-in or macro will support. For example, add-ins or macros that support only Visual Studio 2010 will need to have references to your project to `EnvDTE.dll` (from Visual Studio 2003), `EnvDTE80.dll` (from Visual Studio 2005), `EnvDTE90.dll` (from Visual Studio 2008), `EnvDTE90a.dll` (from Visual Studio 2008 SP1), and `EnvDTE100.dll` (from Visual Studio 2010).

> *It's worth noting that the Visual Studio SDK is now somewhat taking the place of the Visual Studio automation model going forward, with fewer new features in Visual Studio being added to the automation model and more focus and emphasis being placed on using VSPackages instead (in the Visual Studio SDK). However, despite its flaws, the Visual Studio automation model is still very functional and able to perform most common tasks when integrating with Visual Studio.*

Let's now take a look at some of the various functional areas of Visual Studio that the automation model exposes to us, including solutions and projects, documents and windows, commands, debuggers, and events. All of these exist under the root `DTE` object (which should be cast to `DTE2` to expose the more recent revision of this object).

> *Code examples are macro code, with macros discussed in detail in Chapter 52. Most examples output information using the `Debug.Print` command, which you can view in the Output window in the Macros IDE.*

Solutions and Projects

The `DTE.Solutions` object enables you to automate the currently open solution, such as enumerate the projects that it contains, create a new project in the solution (or remove a project), add a solution folder, get/update solution configuration and properties, get/update its build configuration, or even open a new solution in the Visual Studio IDE and work with that. The following code demonstrates enumerating the projects in a solution, printing the project names and the number of project items in each project to the Output window:

```
Public Sub EnumerateProjects()
    For Each project As Project In DTE.Solution.Projects
        Debug.Print(project.Name & " contains " & _
                    project.ProjectItems.Count.ToString() & " project items")
    Next project
End Sub
```

> *Note that you can also enumerate the projects in the active solution using the `DTE.ActiveSolutionProjects` collection.*

You can also automate the projects in the solution. This includes enumerating the project items in a project, and the files it contains. You can also get/update the project's configuration and properties, and add or remove items from the project:

```
Public Sub EnumerateProjectsItems()
    Dim project As Project = DTE.Solution.Projects.Item(1) 'Get first project

    For Each projectItem As ProjectItem In project.ProjectItems
        Debug.Print(projectItem.Name)
    Next projectItem
End Sub
```

Windows and Documents

Windows in Visual Studio are either tool windows (such as the Solution Explorer, Tasks window, and so on) or document windows (files open in the code editor or a designer). Working with all types of windows is relatively simple.

You can enumerate through all the open windows and get details of each window as follows:

```
Public Sub EnumerateOpenWindows()
    'This includes both tool windows and document windows
    For Each window As Window2 In DTE.Windows
        Debug.Print(window.Caption & " | State = " & window.WindowState.ToString())
    Next window
End Sub
```

Next, take a look at how to work with tool windows. Use the following code to get a reference to a window (whether or not it's open) and interact with the window itself (activating it, showing it, hiding it, collapsing it, pinning it, and so on):

```
Public Sub ShowandDockTaskListWindow()
    Dim window As Window2 = DTE.Windows.Item(Constants.vsWindowKindTaskList)
    window.Visible = True 'Show it
    window.IsFloating = False 'Dock it
    window.AutoHides = False 'Pin it
    window.Activate()
End Sub
```

You can get a reference to a specific tool window (such as the Task List), and interact with its functionality (such as adding tasks to the Task List):

```
Public Sub AddTaskToTaskList()
    Dim tasksWindow As TaskList = DTE.ToolWindows.TaskList
    tasksWindow.TaskItems.Add("", "", "Created by a macro")
End Sub
```

As you can see, working with the tool windows is fairly straightforward. Now look at how to work with document windows. You can get a reference to the active window in the IDE like so:

```
Dim window As Window2 = DTE.ActiveWindow
```

You can even obtain a reference to the Visual Studio IDE window itself to manipulate:

```
Dim window As Window2 = DTE.MainWindow
```

It's possible to automate the document windows in Visual Studio, including opening or closing a document window, activating it, and getting the project item object opened in the document window. The following example enumerates through the open document windows, printing the filename and its path to the output window:

```
Public Sub EnumerateOpenDocuments()
    For Each document As Document In DTE.Documents
        Debug.Print(document.Name & ", Path=" & document.Path)
    Next document
End Sub
```

To get a reference to the active document window, use:

```
Dim document As Document = DTE.ActiveDocument
```

You can use the `DTE.WindowConfigurations` collection to manipulate the configuration of windows in the IDE.

Commands

Every executable action in Visual Studio is represented by a command. For example, all menu items execute a command when selected. Every command has a unique name, numeric ID (within its grouping), and GUID designating its grouping. Visual Studio has thousands of commands, as you can see by enumerating the `DTE.Commands` collection like so:

```
Public Sub EnumerateCommands()
    For Each command As Command In DTE.Commands
        Debug.Print(command.Name & ", ID=" & command.ID & ", GUID=" & command.Guid)
    Next command
End Sub
```

To perform an action in Visual Studio through your add-in or macro, you will need to get a reference to the appropriate command and execute it. For example, say you want to comment out the selected code in the code editor. This command is called `Edit.CommentSelection`, and you can execute it using the following code:

```
Public Sub ExecuteCommentSelectionCommand()
    DTE.ExecuteCommand("Edit.CommentSelection")
End Sub
```

Finding the command name for a specific action can be difficult considering the number of commands that exist. The easiest way to find the name of a command so you can use it is to record a macro (see Chapter 52) of you performing the action, and inspect the code the macro recorder generates.

You can also listen for commands being executed, which are raised by Visual Studio as events that you can handle. An event will be raised before the command is executed, and another event will be raised after the command has completed. For example, you may want to do something particular when text is pasted into the code editor (that is, respond to the `Edit.Paste` command). Handling events is covered later in this chapter.

Debugger

You can control the various functions of the Visual Studio debugger using the `DTE.Debugger` automation object. This allows you to work with breakpoints, control code execution, and examine various aspects of the application being debugged (including processes and threads).

The following code demonstrates enumerating through all the breakpoints in the current solution:

```
Public Sub EnumerateBreakpoints()
    For Each breakpoint As Breakpoint2 In DTE.Debugger.Breakpoints
        Debug.Print(breakpoint.Name & " | File: " & breakpoint.File & _
                    " | Function: " & breakpoint.FunctionName & _
                    " | Line: " & breakpoint.FileLine)
    Next breakpoint
End Sub
```

You can also control the execution of code when debugging an application, such as starting debugging, terminating debugging, stepping over a line of code, running to the current cursor position, and so on. The following code demonstrates starting the current solution in the debugger:

```
Public Sub RunApplicationInDebugger()
    DTE.Debugger.Go()
End Sub
```

Events

The automation model enables you to listen for various actions in Visual Studio and respond to them by raising events that you can handle. The events are categorized into a number of objects according to their functional area under the `DTE.Events` object, including `DocumentEvents`, `WindowEvents`, `BuildEvents`, `SolutionEvents`, `ProjectsEvents`, `DebuggerEvents`, and many others. Chapter 51 demonstrates handling events in add-ins. In macros, the `EnvironmentEvents` module that is automatically added to each macro project defines event variables that you can create event handler methods for (using the `Handles` keyword). The following code captures the `DocumentOpened` event on the `DTE.Events.DocumentEvents` object (an instance of which has previously been created and stored in the `DocumentEvents` variable in the default `EnvironmentEvents` module). Place it in the `EnvironmentEvents` module, save the module, and close the Macros IDE:

```
Private Sub DocumentEvents_DocumentOpened(ByVal Document As EnvDTE.Document) _
                                Handles DocumentEvents.DocumentOpened
    MsgBox("Document opened: " & Document.Name & " at " & DateTime.Now)
End Sub
```

This event handler will be raised whenever you open a new document in the Visual Studio IDE.

SUMMARY

In this chapter you were introduced to the various means of extending the functionality of Visual Studio 2010, and you then took a look at the structure and capabilities of the Visual Studio automation model, which both add-ins and macros use to extend Visual Studio. The following two chapters look at these two means of extending Visual Studio using this object model.

51

Add-Ins

WHAT'S IN THIS CHAPTER?

- ➤ Understanding the structure of add-ins
- ➤ Creating add-ins
- ➤ Testing and debugging add-ins
- ➤ Deploying add-ins

As detailed in Chapter 50, Visual Studio add-ins are components that run within Visual Studio and extend its functionality via the Visual Studio automation model.

This chapter takes you through the process of creating a Visual Studio add-in that integrates with the Visual Studio IDE to display a tool window (that enables you to store some notes), perform actions in Visual Studio (copy selected text from the code editor), and handle Visual Studio events (capture the cut and copy command events from the code editor).

DEVELOPING AN ADD-IN

When you create a Visual Studio add-in project, the Add-in Wizard appears and helps you to create the appropriate structure and base functionality in your add-in based on your input to its questions. From there you are on your own to implement the functionality from this base framework. You start from the base that it gives you and gradually add functionality to make it a useful tool.

The Add-in Wizard

Start by creating a new project, using the Visual Studio Add-in project template in the Extensibility project category (under the Other Project Type category), as shown in Figure 51-1.

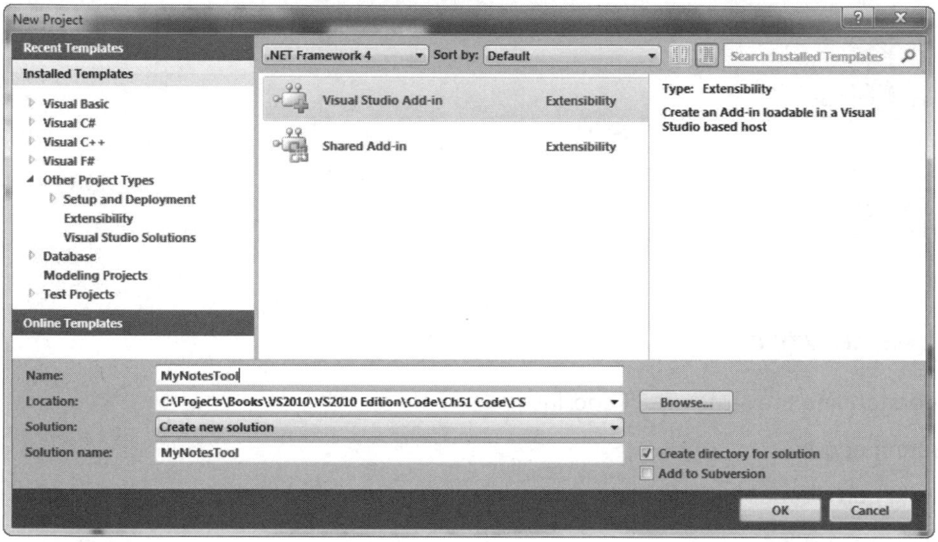

FIGURE 51-1

> You'll note that the Extensibility category also contains a Shared Add-in project template. This template is similar to the Visual Studio Add-in, but is used for creating add-ins for the various applications in Microsoft Office instead of Visual Studio (although this has largely been taken over by VSTO).

Clicking OK starts the Add-in Wizard. The wizard consists of seven steps (including a welcome step and summary step). This section goes through each of these steps in the wizard and the options that each step provides.

There is a welcome page at the start, which gives a short description of the wizard (as shown in Figure 51-2).

In the next step of the Add-in Wizard (as shown in Figure 51-3) you need to choose a development language for your add-in (because the Visual Studio Add-in project template was not under a particular language category in the New Project dialog). You have four options — Visual C#, Visual Basic, Visual C++/CLR, and Visual C++/ATL. Visual Studio generates the project in the language that you choose here.

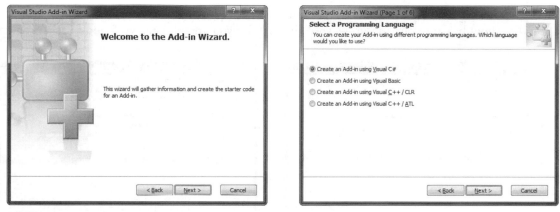

FIGURE 51-2

FIGURE 51-3

Now you need to choose an application host for your add-in (as shown in Figure 51-4). Two application hosts are available for your add-ins: the Visual Studio IDE and the Visual Studio Macros IDE (which is discussed in the next chapter). You can check or uncheck each host to select or deselect it. Your add-in will be available to the application host(s) that you select here.

Now you can enter a name and description for your add-in (as shown in Figure 51-5). This information is what end users see in the Add-in Manager dialog in Visual Studio for your add-in.

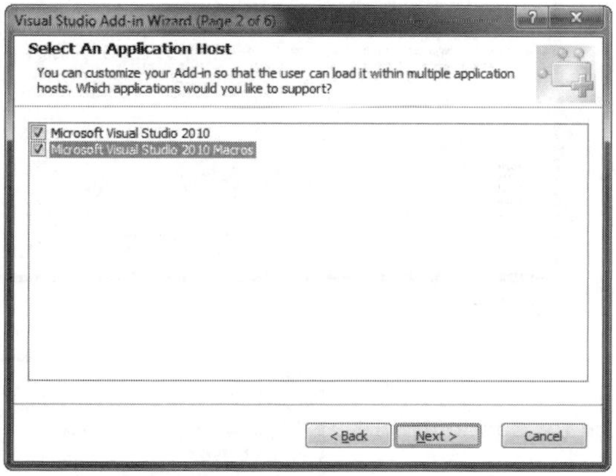

FIGURE 51-4

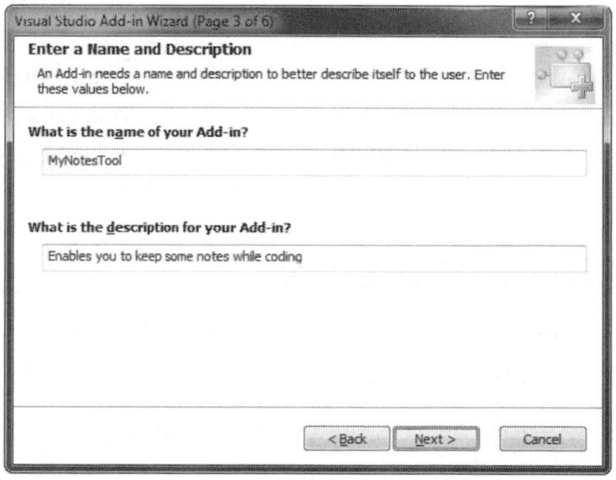

FIGURE 51-5

The next step contains the options for how your add-in will load and interact with Visual Studio. You can check three options to include in your add-in (as shown in Figure 51-6). The first option specifies that your add-in will have a menu item in the Tools menu that can be used to activate it. The second option indicates that you would like to load your add-in when the Visual Studio IDE or Visual Studio Macros IDE starts, and the third option is used to specify that your add-in doesn't show any modal user interfaces, and thus can be used with command-line builds.

The next step (as shown in Figure 51-7) enables you to display some information in the Visual Studio About box for your add-in — especially useful if you are releasing your add-in as a product.

FIGURE 51-6

FIGURE 51-7

In the final step you will see a summary of what you have chosen in your wizard (as shown in Figure 51-8). At this stage, you can go back and change your options or click the Finish button to go ahead and generate the solution and initial code for your add-in.

After you click the Finish button, Visual Studio generates a solution with the required files for creating the add-in, configured according to the options you've selected for the add-in.

Project Structure

Once the project has been created, you will find the project structure, shown in Figure 51-9.

As you can see, the project consists of a `Connect.cs` (or `Connect.vb`) file, and two files with the `.AddIn` extension.

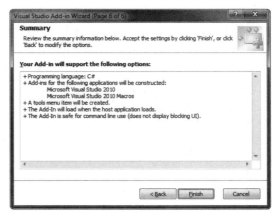

FIGURE 51-8

FIGURE 51-9

The `Connect.cs/Connect.vb` file contains the core class that controls the add-in. The `.AddIn` files are used to enable Visual Studio to discover the add-in so it can load it. One is located in your project folder, but you'll note that the other is a linked file (`MyNotesTool - For Testing.AddIn`), located in the `My Documents\Visual Studio 2010\Addins` folder of your Windows user profile. As its name suggests, this file is used so that Visual Studio can discover your add-in during its testing and debugging. The reason the file is in this folder is that it is one of the paths that Visual Studio looks in to discover add-in files. If you open both files, you will find that they are identical with one exception — the Assembly node of the linked file includes the full path to the compiled add-in assembly, whereas the other only includes the name of the assembly (expecting it to be in the same folder as the `.AddIn` file). We take a closer look at `.AddIn` files later in this chapter.

Testing Your Add-in

First, check to make sure everything works OK by simply running your project. This starts a new instance of Visual Studio 2010 in which you can test and debug the add-in. If you selected the options in the wizard to start automatically when the IDE is started and to create a Tool menu item, you should see a menu item at the top of the Tools menu for your add-in, with a default smiley face icon (which you can change to your own icon), as shown in Figure 51-10.

If you haven't selected the add-in to load automatically with the IDE, you can start it from the Add-in Manager (Tools ➪ Add-in Manager) and put a check mark in the checkbox next to its name, as shown in Figure 51-11.

FIGURE 51-10

FIGURE 51-11

> *If your add-in is not appearing in the Add-in Manager, Visual Studio is unable to find the* `.AddIn` *file. Go to Tools ➪ Options and select the Add-in/Macro Security category (under the Environment category, as shown in Figure 51-12). Make sure that the path where the testing* `.AddIn` *file is located is listed in the Add-in File Paths list. It's also possible that the environment variables used in this dialog are not declared in your system, so check these too.*

FIGURE 51-12

Close the debugging instance of Visual Studio to finish debugging the add-in.

The .AddIn File

As mentioned earlier in this chapter, there are two `.AddIn` files in your solution: one in the project folder, and a linked file that has been placed in the `My Documents\Visual Studio 2010\ Addins` folder on your machine.

In early versions of Visual Studio, you had to register the COM component by hand for an add-in on the machine, making deployment a little difficult (the add-in couldn't be deployed using a simple XCOPY). `.AddIn` files were designed to make the process of deploying add-ins easier. By placing the `.AddIn` file in a folder that Visual Studio is configured to look in, Visual Studio will use it to discover your add-in and load it (without worrying about the need to register the add-in). Essentially, `.AddIn` files point Visual Studio to where your add-in is (which will usually be in the same path as the `.AddIn` file).

`.AddIn` files are XML files, and in addition to pointing Visual Studio to the location of your add-in, they also contain configuration information such as what hosts the add-in should be accessible to (including different versions of Visual Studio), what will appear in the Add-in Manager to describe the add-in, and startup options for the add-in.

If you open up an `.AddIn` file, you will find XML similar to the following:

```xml
<?xml version="1.0" encoding="UTF-16" standalone="no"?>
<Extensibility xmlns="http://schemas.microsoft.com/AutomationExtensibility">
    <HostApplication>
        <Name>Microsoft Visual Studio Macros</Name>
        <Version>10.0</Version>
    </HostApplication>
    <HostApplication>
        <Name>Microsoft Visual Studio</Name>
        <Version>10.0</Version>
    </HostApplication>
    <Addin>
        <FriendlyName>My Notes</FriendlyName>
        <Description>My Notes</Description>
        <Assembly>MyNotesTool.dll</Assembly>
        <FullClassName>MyNotesTool.Connect</FullClassName>
        <LoadBehavior>5</LoadBehavior>
        <CommandPreload>1</CommandPreload>
        <CommandLineSafe>1</CommandLineSafe>
    </Addin>
</Extensibility>
```

Of particular note are the `HostApplication` nodes, listing each host application name and its specific version that the add-in should be accessible to. The preceding file is making the add-in available to both Visual Studio 2010 and the Visual Studio Macros 2010 IDE. If you want to make your add-in accessible to other versions of Visual Studio, simply add additional `HostApplication` nodes, with the corresponding version number for that version of Visual Studio (Visual Studio 2008 = 9.0, Visual Studio 2005 = 8.0). Of course you must make sure that you don't use features specific to Visual Studio 2010, and remove references to the higher EnvDTE dlls than the lowest version you are supporting.

If you are upgrading an add-in from a previous version of Visual Studio, you will need to add another HostApplication *node to the existing* .AddIn *file, with a value of 10.0 in the* Version *node so that it will run under Visual Studio 2010.*

The Connect Class

This section looks at the structure of the core class that manages the add-in. The Connect.cs class (or Connect.vb) manages the life cycle of the add-in, and you can find a number of methods that handle the event notifications from the IDTExtensibility2 and IDTCommandTarget interfaces that are implemented by the class.

The IDTExtensibility2 interface exposes handlers for the events raised by Visual Studio that notifies the add-in at each point in its life cycle. The following methods form the IDTExtensibility2 interface:

➤ **OnConnection:** Called when the add-in is being loaded by Visual Studio.

➤ **OnStartupComplete:** Called when Visual Studio has finished loading.

➤ **OnAddInsUpdate:** Called when the collection of add-ins in Visual Studio has changed.

➤ **OnBeginShutdown:** Called when Visual Studio is shutting down.

➤ **OnDisconnection:** Called when the add-in is being unloaded by Visual Studio.

The IDTCommandTarget interface exposes handlers for the events of named commands used by the add-in. The following methods form the IDTCommandTarget interface:

➤ **Exec:** Called when a command used by the add-in is called from Visual Studio (such as when the menu item created under the Tools menu is selected). Visual Studio will pass this method the name of the command so you can respond accordingly.

➤ **QueryStatus:** Called when the status of a command (such as whether or not it is available) is requested by Visual Studio.

Creating a Tool Window

Now that you have looked at the structure and life cycle of an add-in, it's time to add some functionality to interact with the Visual Studio IDE and implement some useful behavior. The sample you work through in this chapter creates a dockable tool window in Visual Studio that will enable you to place some notes while working in Visual Studio. Unfortunately, the Add-in Wizard doesn't provide options to help in creating your own tool window (which is one of the more common requirements when writing add-ins), so you will have to do this yourself. This section takes you through the steps to do so.

Despite Visual Studio 2010 having a complete user interface overhaul to use WPF, unfortunately you still have to use Windows Forms for your tool windows when creating add-ins. To use WPF for your tool windows, you will have to use VSPackages in the Visual Studio 2010 SDK when extending Visual Studio instead.

Add a new Windows Forms User Control item to your project, and call it `NotesUserControl` (`.cs` or `.vb`). Add a RichTextBox control to the user control, name it `rtbNotes`, set the `BorderStyle` property to None, and dock it to fill the area of the control.

Now return to the `Connect.cs` (or `.vb`) file, and add the following method to it to simplify the process of creating the tool window:

VB

```
Private toolWindow As Window2 = Nothing

Private Function CreateToolWindow(ByVal guid As String,
                                  ByVal windowTitle As String,
                                  ByVal classPath As String) As Object
    Dim windowObject As Object = Nothing

    Dim windows As Windows2 = DirectCast(_applicationObject.Windows, Windows2)
    Dim assemblyLocation As String = Assembly.GetCallingAssembly().Location

    toolWindow = DirectCast(windows.CreateToolWindow2(_addInInstance,
                                                      assemblyLocation, classPath,
                                                      windowTitle, guid,
                                                      windowObject), Window2)

    Return windowObject
End Function
```

C#

```
Private Window2 toolWindow = null;

private object CreateToolWindow(string guid, string windowTitle, string classPath)
{
    object windowObject = null;

    Windows2 windows = (Windows2)_applicationObject.Windows;
    string assemblyLocation = Assembly.GetCallingAssembly().Location;

    toolWindow = (Window2)windows.CreateToolWindow2(_addInInstance,
        assemblyLocation, classPath, windowTitle, guid, ref windowObject);

    return windowObject;
}
```

> *A reference needs to be maintained to the user control at the class level because windows of add-ins are not destroyed/cleaned up during the life cycle of the add-in — instead they are merely hidden.*

You will create the tool window when the menu item in the Tools menu is selected. You are notified of this in the `Exec` method, and you'll notice that the wizard already created the code to respond to this (although it currently does nothing). Use the following code to create the tool window and have it displayed in Visual Studio (the code to be added to the method has been bolded):

VB

```
Private notesUserControl As NotesUserControl

Public Sub Exec(ByVal commandName As String,
                ByVal executeOption As vsCommandExecOption,
                ByRef varIn As Object, ByRef varOut As Object,
                ByRef handled As Boolean) Implements IDTCommandTarget.Exec
    handled = False
    If executeOption = vsCommandExecOption.vsCommandExecOptionDoDefault Then
        If commandName = "MyNotesTool.Connect.MyNotesTool" Then
            ' An ID that uniquely identifies this tool window
            Dim windowID As String = "{fb9e4681-681d-4216-9a28-0f09f3528360}"

            ' Create the tool window if it hasn't already been created
            If toolWindow Is Nothing Then
                notesUserControl = DirectCast(CreateToolWindow(windowID,
                    "My Notes" , "MyNotesTool.NotesUserControl" ), NotesUserControl )
            End If

            ' Make the tool window visible if it's currently hidden
            toolWindow.Visible = True

            handled = True
            Return
        End If
    End If
End Sub
```

C#

```
private NotesUserControl notesUserControl;

public void Exec(string commandName, vsCommandExecOption executeOption,
                ref object varIn, ref object varOut, ref bool handled)
{
    handled = false;
    if (executeOption == vsCommandExecOption.vsCommandExecOptionDoDefault)
    {
        if (commandName == "MyNotesTool.Connect.MyNotesTool")
        {
            // An ID that uniquely identifies this tool window
            string windowID = "{fb9e4681-681d-4216-9a28-0f09f3528360}" ;

            // Create the tool window if it hasn't already been created
            if (toolWindow == null)
            {
                notesUserControl = ( NotesUserControl)
                    CreateToolWindow(windowID, "My Notes" ,
                                "MyNotesTool.NotesUserControl" );

            }
```

```
            // Make the tool window visible if it's currently hidden
            toolWindow.Visible = true;

            handled = true;
            return;
        }
    }
}
```

As you can see from the code, it's now a relatively easy process to create the window. You pass an ID that uniquely identifies this tool window, a window title, and the qualified name of the user control class to the `CreateToolWindow` method you created earlier, and it handles calling the extensibility model to create the tool window in Visual Studio.

Now, run your project and select the menu item for the add-in under the Tools menu. The user control will display as a tool window (as shown in Figure 51-13), which you can then move around and dock to the IDE as if it were any other tool window.

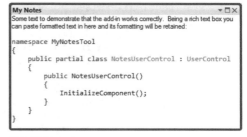

FIGURE 51-13

 Visual Studio will remember the location of the window (using its unique ID to store and retrieve these details), so the next time you load Visual Studio the window will appear where you last placed it (although this only works when the add-in is not being debugged). However, for it to be displayed when Visual Studio is started, you will have to create the tool window when the add-in is started (rather than when its menu item is selected).

Accessing the Visual Studio Automation Model

You can now add your own additional functionality to the tool window (in the user control) such as loading and saving the text to a text file (if you want) as if you were programming a standard application. However, this example doesn't currently demonstrate integrating with the functionality of Visual Studio and the events it raises, so add a feature to demonstrate this by creating a button to take selected code from the code editor and insert it into the notes at the current caret position.

To get to the Visual Studio object model from the user control, you'll have to make the class-level variable `_applicationObject` in the `Connect` class static and expose it publicly by wrapping it in a property as shown in the following code:

VB

```
Private Shared _applicationObject As DTE2

Public ReadOnly Property ApplicationObject() As DTE2
    Get
```

```
            Return _applicationObject
        End Get
End Property
```

C#

```csharp
private static DTE2 _applicationObject;

public static DTE2 ApplicationObject
{
    get { return Connect._applicationObject; }
}
```

Add a ToolStrip control to the user control with a button that will copy the selected text in the code editor and insert it into the textbox when clicked. In the event handler for this button, add the following code:

VB

```vb
Private Sub btnCopy_Click(ByVal sender As System.Object,
                          ByVal e As System.EventArgs) Handles btnCopy.Click
    If Not Connect.ApplicationObject.ActiveDocument Is Nothing Then
        Dim selection As TextSelection = DirectCast(
            Connect.ApplicationObject.ActiveDocument.Selection, TextSelection)

        rtbNotes.SelectedText = selection.Text
    End If
End Sub
```

C#

```csharp
private void btnCopy_Click(object sender, EventArgs e)
{
    if (Connect.ApplicationObject.ActiveDocument != null)
    {
        TextSelection selection =
            Connect.ApplicationObject.ActiveDocument.Selection as TextSelection;

        rtbNotes.SelectedText = selection.Text;
    }
}
```

This will take the selected text from the active code editor document and insert it at the current caret position in the rich textbox in the user control. Note that the code will be unformatted (that is, no syntax coloring) when it's put into the rich textbox. Alternatively, you can use the following code to copy the text out of the code editor and paste it into the rich textbox, which would retain the syntax coloring but lose the existing contents of the clipboard:

VB

```vb
Private Sub btnCopy_Click(ByVal sender As System.Object,
                          ByVal e As System.EventArgs) Handles btnCopy.Click
    If Not Connect.ApplicationObject.ActiveDocument Is Nothing Then
```

```
        Connect.ApplicationObject.ActiveDocument.Selection.Copy()
        rtbNotes.Paste()
    End If
End Sub
```

C#

```
private void btnCopy_Click(object sender, EventArgs e)
{
    if (Connect.ApplicationObject.ActiveDocument != null)
    {
        Connect.ApplicationObject.ActiveDocument.Selection.Copy();
        rtbNotes.Paste();
    }
}
```

Handling Visual Studio Events

As a final example, handle an event raised by Visual Studio. You'll handle the Cut and the Copy command events (before the command is actually executed), get the selected text from the code editor, and automatically insert it into the rich textbox.

First, you need to get a reference to the commands whose events you want to capture (the Cut and Copy commands), and then the command events objects themselves. C# developers will also add an event handler for the BeforeExecute event for each command.

VB

```
Private WithEvents cutEvent As CommandEvents = Nothing
Private WithEvents copyEvent As CommandEvents = Nothing

Private Sub EnableAutoCopy()
    ' Enable the event listening for the Cut and Copy commands
    Dim cmdCut As Command = Connect.ApplicationObject.Commands.Item("Edit.Cut", 0)
    Dim cmdCopy As Command = Connect.ApplicationObject.Commands.Item("Edit.Copy",
                                                                        0)

    cutEvent = Connect.ApplicationObject.Events.CommandEvents(cmdCut.Guid,
                                                                cmdCut.ID)
    copyEvent = Connect.ApplicationObject.Events.CommandEvents(cmdCopy.Guid,
                                                                cmdCopy.ID)
End Sub
```

C#

```
private CommandEvents cutEvent = null;
private CommandEvents copyEvent = null;

private void EnableAutoCopy()
{
    // Enable the event listening for the Cut and Copy commands
    Command cmdCut = Connect.ApplicationObject.Commands.Item("Edit.Cut", 0);
```

```
        cutEvent = Connect.ApplicationObject.Events.get_CommandEvents(cmdCut.Guid,
                                                                      cmdCut.ID);
        cutEvent.BeforeExecute += new
            _dispCommandEvents_BeforeExecuteEventHandler(OnBeforeCutCopy);

        Command cmdCopy = Connect.ApplicationObject.Commands.Item("Edit.Copy", 0);

        copyEvent = Connect.ApplicationObject.Events.get_CommandEvents(cmdCopy.Guid,
                                                                       cmdCopy.ID);
        copyEvent.BeforeExecute += new
            _dispCommandEvents_BeforeExecuteEventHandler(OnBeforeCutCopy);
    }
```

Now you can define the event handler method that will handle the BeforeExecute event for both commands, extracting the selected text from the code editor and inserting it into the rich textbox:

VB

```
    Private Sub OnBeforeCutCopy(ByVal guid As String, ByVal id As Integer,
                                ByVal customIn As Object, ByVal customOut As Object,
                                ByRef cancel As Boolean) _
                                Handles cutEvent.BeforeExecute, copyEvent.BeforeExecute
        Dim codeWindow As TextWindow = TryCast(
            Connect.ApplicationObject.ActiveWindow.Object, EnvDTE.TextWindow)

        If Not codeWindow Is Nothing Then
            rtbNotes.SelectedText = codeWindow.Selection.Text &
                Environment.NewLine & Environment.NewLine
        End If
    End Sub
```

C#

```
    private void OnBeforeCutCopy(string guid, int id, object customIn,
                                 object customOut, ref bool cancel)
    {
        TextWindow codeWindow = Connect.ApplicationObject.ActiveWindow.Object
                                                          as EnvDTE.TextWindow;

        if (codeWindow != null)
        {
            rtbNotes.SelectedText = codeWindow.Selection.Text +
                Environment.NewLine + Environment.NewLine;
        }
    }
```

Finally, you need to clean things up when the add-in is unloaded and release any event handlers you have active (the CloseToolWindow method will be called from the Connect class in the OnDisconnection method):

VB

```
    private void DisableAutoCopy()
    {
        if (cutEvent != null)
```

```
                Marshal.ReleaseComObject(cutEvent);

        if (copyEvent != null)
            Marshal.ReleaseComObject(copyEvent);

        cutEvent = null;
        copyEvent = null;
    }

    public void CloseToolWindow()
    {
        DisableAutoCopy();
    }
```

C#

```
    private void DisableAutoCopy()
    {
        if (cutEvent != null)
            Marshal.ReleaseComObject(cutEvent);

        if (copyEvent != null)
            Marshal.ReleaseComObject(copyEvent);

        cutEvent = null;
        copyEvent = null;
    }

    public void CloseToolWindow()
    {
        DisableAutoCopy();
    }
```

DEPLOYING ADD-INS

Despite being a COM component (which typically require registration in Windows), Visual Studio add-ins are very easy to deploy thanks to the `.AddIn` file, which enables Visual Studio to discover your add-in and use it.

As discussed earlier in the chapter, Visual Studio will look in each of the paths listed in the Options dialog (see Figure 51-12) for files with an `.AddIn` extension. Therefore, when deploying your add-in, you will need to place the `.AddIn` file and the add-in assembly (that is, the `.dll` file) into one of these paths (typically a user profile's `My Documents\Visual Studio 2010\Addins` folder), enabling Visual Studio to discover and load your add-in when it starts up.

You can use a simple XCOPY operation to deploy your add-in to another user's machine, but the best way would be to create a setup program to do this for you. You could use a standard Windows installer package (`.msi`), but in this instance it's probably better to use a *Visual Studio Content Installer* package. Unfortunately, it's a manual process to create a Visual Studio Content Installer package, but they're very easy to create. They essentially consist of your files packed into a zip file, but with a `.vsi` extension, and a specially formatted XML file (also included in the zip file) with a `.vscontent` extension that contains the details of the files to be installed (from the zip file) and where they are to be installed to.

Start by creating an XML file in your project with the name `MyNotesTool.vscontent`, and add the following content:

```
<VSContent xmlns="http://schemas.microsoft.com/developer/vscontent/2005">
  <Content>
    <FileName>MyNotesTool.Addin</FileName>
    <FileName>MyNotesTool.dll</FileName>
    <DisplayName>My Notes</DisplayName>
    <Description>
      Enables you to keep notes in a tool window in
      Visual Studio while you code.
    </Description>
    <FileContentType>Addin</FileContentType>
    <ContentVersion>2.0</ContentVersion>
  </Content>
</VSContent>
```

Now, in Windows Explorer (or your favorite zip tool), combine the `MyNotesTool.AddIn` file, the `MyNotesTool.dll` file, and the `MyNotesTool.vscontent` file into a zip file, and name it `MyNotesTool.vsi` (do not include the `.zip` extension). Now when someone double-clicks this `.vsi` file, the add-in will automatically be installed and ready for them to use when they next open Visual Studio.

SUMMARY

In this chapter, you were introduced to Visual Studio add-ins, and went through the process of creating one that displayed a dockable tool window, retrieved text from the code editor, and responded to some code editor events. Finally, you looked at the best way to deploy your add-in to other developers.

Macros

WHAT'S IN THIS CHAPTER?

➤ Understanding macros

➤ Creating macros

➤ Testing and debugging macros

➤ Deploying macros

Like add-ins, macros are another common extensibility option built into Visual Studio. As discussed in Chapter 50, macros have many benefits over add-ins (quick to create, and Visual Studio actions can be recorded to a macro), but also many downsides (they must be written in VB, can't be compiled, and have limited abilities). It's a tradeoff as to which means you use to automate Visual Studio based upon your requirements. If you perform the same set of actions repetitively in Visual Studio, macros are a great way to reduce these down to a single action.

This chapter takes you through the process of recording a macro and running it again, creating macros from scratch, and deploying macros to other developers once you've created them.

UNDERSTANDING MACROS

A Visual Studio macro (it's actually called VSMacro but is commonly known just as a macro among developers) is code that can be run by the Visual Studio IDE to automate a task. The code is not compiled, but is interpreted — it's essentially a scripting language for Visual Studio. A macro is implemented as a public method in a module that takes no parameters and does not return a value. Like add-ins, macros use the Development Tools Extensibility (DTE) API to automate the Visual Studio IDE. Macros can't display any user interface elements in

Visual Studio (such as a tool window) — if you need this sort of functionality, you should consider creating an add-in instead.

Macros exist in code modules, and these code modules are contained in macro projects. Macro project files have a `.vsmacros` extension, and are much like a standard Visual Studio project file (in concept); however, the various modules and associated files in the project are embedded into this project file (rather than existing in their own individual files). In addition, a code module can contain one or more macros, so you can include multiple macros in a module.

If you are a VB developer, you will have no problem coding macros, because VB is the native language used by macros. Unfortunately, C# is not supported as a macro language, and therefore C# developers will need to learn VB or create add-ins instead.

THE MACRO EXPLORER TOOL WINDOW

Before you look at the tools for creating macros, take a look at the Macro Explorer tool window that can help you manage and run the macros available to you. If the tool window is not visible, select the View ➪ Other Windows ➪ Macro Explorer menu item to display it in the IDE.

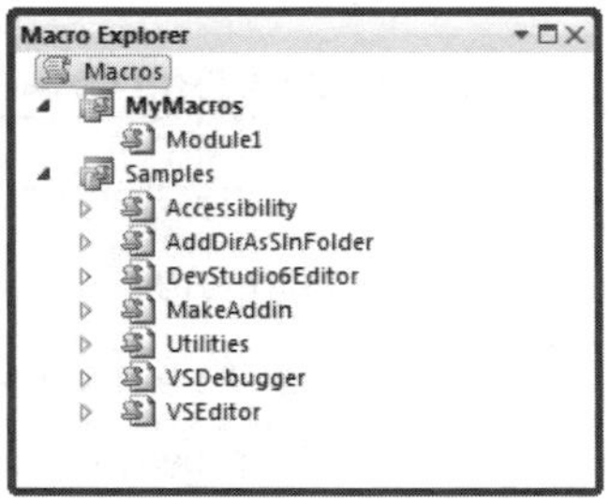

As you can see from Figure 52-1, there is a top-level Macros node under which macro projects live. Each macro within that project is listed as well.

FIGURE 52-1

This dialog is very useful in enabling you to select and run a macro (simply double-click the macro to run it), and edit a macro (right-click the macro and select Edit from the context menu). When you select to edit a macro, its code will be opened in the Macros IDE, which is discussed in the next section of this chapter.

You'll notice that two projects are already displayed in the Macro Explorer: MyMacros and Samples. MyMacros is the default project in which to create your macros (although you can create additional macro projects as required). The Samples macro project consists of example macros that you can use to help you learn how to write macros and work with the Visual Studio automation model.

THE MACROS IDE

As you can see in Figure 52-2, the Visual Studio Macros IDE is quite similar to the Visual Studio IDE, despite being a completely separate program. It being a somewhat familiar user interface should help you navigate your way around the IDE.

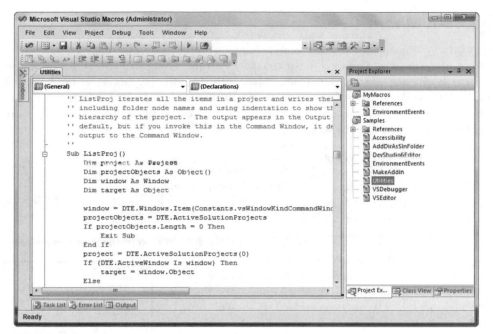

FIGURE 52-2

Of particular note is the Project Explorer tool window (akin to the Solution Explorer tool window in the Visual Studio IDE, on the right side of the screen). This window enables you to navigate the various macro projects and the modules/files they contain. You'll note that as opposed to the Macro Explorer in the main Visual Studio IDE, which displays the available macros under each macro project, this window displays the modules and files within each macro project. The Macro Explorer hides the modules from you, and just collates all the macro functions across all the modules to be displayed under the macro project. When you open a module, it's just the same as opening a code file in Visual Studio.

> *The Visual Studio Macros IDE can't run as a standalone program and can only be loaded via Visual Studio.*

CREATING A MACRO

You have two ways of creating a macro: one is to start from scratch and write the code yourself, and the other is to record a set of actions in Visual Studio using the macro recorder for later playback. This section looks at both methods, starting with recording macros because that's the easiest way to get started creating macros.

How to Record a Macro

If you simply want to automate a predefined set of actions in Visual Studio, the easiest way to create a macro to perform those actions is to use the macro recorder to record you performing those actions, and then play it back when required. The macro recorder will take all the actions you do in the Visual Studio IDE while it's recording and document them in code form. If necessary, you can then tweak the code that the macro recorder generated to work exactly the way you want. This can save you having to learn the Visual Studio automation model and manually write code against it. It's also a great way of learning how to create macros.

To record a macro, select Tools ⇨ Macros ⇨ Record Temporary Macro (or press Ctrl1Shift1R). This immediately starts the recorder, which will be recording everything you now do in the Visual Studio IDE. A toolbar (shown in Figure 52-3) is displayed, enabling you to pause, stop, cancel, or continue recording the macro.

FIGURE 52-3

After performing the actions that you want to record, click the stop button in the macro recorder toolbar (or press Ctrl1Shift1R again). Now, if you look in the Macro Explorer you will see that a module has been created in the MyMacros project (by default) called RecordingModule, and that a macro called TemporaryMacro has been created (as shown in Figure 52-4).

You should now rename the macro by right-clicking it, selecting Rename from the context menu (or simply selecting it and pressing F2), and entering a new name in the textbox for it so it isn't overwritten the next time you try to record a macro. You can now run the macro by double-clicking its name and testing it.

FIGURE 52-4

> You can change the project that the macro is recorded to by right-clicking the project in the Macro Explorer and selecting the Set as Recording Project menu item. However, the module that the macro is recorded to cannot be set, and will always go into RecordingModule.

Although the macro recorder can help a lot in creating a macro, it won't capture every action you perform in Visual Studio, and more than likely won't be able to capture everything (such as all the logic) that you want it to do. That's when you will have to turn to modifying the code it outputs to add the appropriate additional logic that you require.

How to Develop a Macro

When you create a macro, you can choose to create a new macro project (useful if you want to distribute this macro to other developers), or use an existing one. If you want to create a new macro project, you will no doubt be surprised to find no option to create one within the Macros IDE.

Instead, you will have to do it back in the Visual Studio IDE from either the Macro Explorer by right-clicking the root Macros node and selecting New Macro Project from the context menu, or using the Tools ⇨ Macros ⇨ New Macro Project menu item. This will show a dialog enabling you to give the project a name, and then the project will be created along with a default module called Module1 (which you will ideally rename to something more meaningful). Otherwise, you can simply use one of the existing macro projects (with the MyMacros project probably being the best choice). Then you can start adding public functions to the code module — with each becoming a macro.

> *Two good ways exist to get up to speed with writing macros. The first is to look at the samples (all the macros in the Samples macro project) and how they work. Try to find one that does something similar to what you need to do and work from that. Another good way to get started is to just use the macro recorder to record various actions when working with Visual Studio, and then examine the code that it generates. You can then take pieces of this code and use it in the macro you are working on.*

You can add additional modules as required by right-clicking the macro project and selecting Add ⇨ Add New Item from the context menu. You can also import existing code modules (such as a pre-existing code module from a standard VB project) into your macro project by right-clicking the macro project and selecting Add ⇨ Add Existing Item from the context menu, then selecting the module that you want to import from the dialog that is displayed. Of course, you could also reference a .NET assembly (written in any .NET language) containing functions that you want to use in your macro by right-clicking the References node under the macro project, selecting Add Reference from the context menu, and then selecting the assembly in the dialog that's displayed. However, if you find yourself doing this and you think that you might deploy this macro to other developers, it is probably better to create an add-in instead of a macro.

Let's work through an example of creating a very simple macro that inserts some text at the current cursor position in the code editor to state that the code below was modified (consisting of `// Modified by [Name] at [DateTime]`, with appropriate values replacing the square bracket placeholders).

Because you plan to deploy this macro to other machines, you'll create a separate macro project for it called CodeNotes (right-click the Macros node in the Macro Explorer tool window and select New Macro Project from the context menu). Rename the default module that was created under it from Module1 to CodeModificationNotes (right-click the module and select Rename from the context menu). Double-click the CodeModificationNotes module to open it in the Macros IDE. Add the following function to the module (this will be the macro):

```
Public Sub InsertCodeModificationNote()
    Const MY_NAME As String = "Chris Anderson"
    Dim textSelection As EnvDTE.TextSelection

    textSelection = CType(DTE.ActiveDocument.Selection(), EnvDTE.TextSelection)
    textSelection.Text = "// Modified by " & MY_NAME & " at " & DateTime.Now
End Sub
```

Now you can debug your macro by placing the cursor within the function and pressing F5 (Run). The Visual Studio IDE will quickly become active as the macro runs, returning to the Macros IDE when complete. If you return to the Visual Studio IDE and look in the Macro Explorer, you will note that the macro now appears under the module, and can be run by double-clicking its name.

RUNNING A MACRO

You have a number of ways to run a macro once you've created it that we've already discussed. As a recap you can:

➤ Double-click the name of the macro in Macro Explorer.

➤ Press F5 in the Macros IDE when the cursor is inside the macro code.

In addition, you can also assign keyboard shortcuts to macros that you use regularly to make them easier to activate and run. Go to Tools ➪ Options and find the Keyboard node under the Environment category. Search for your macro by its name (enter the name into the Show Commands Containing textbox) and select it from the list. Select the Press Shortcut Keys textbox, and press the key combination that you want to use to activate the macro (as shown in Figure 52-5). Ensure that the key combination isn't currently being used, or you don't mind overwriting it, and then click the

FIGURE 52-5

Assign button. Now when you press that key combination in the Visual Studio IDE the macro will run.

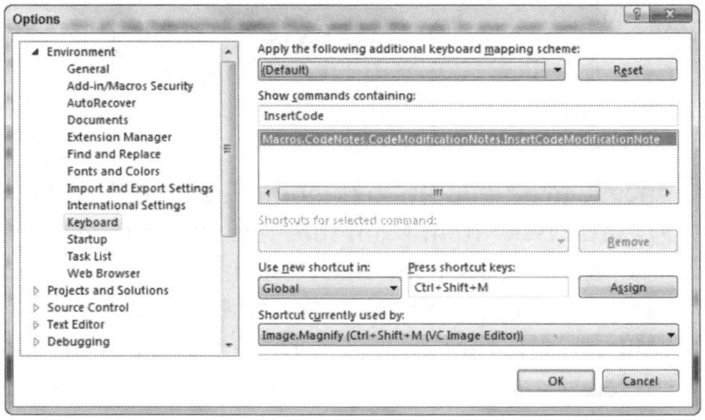

For long-running macros, a tape icon will appear in the bottom-right corner of the IDE, and in the taskbar. If you right-click this icon, you can choose to stop any macros currently running.

Debugging macros is similar to debugging any other type of .NET application. You simply start your macro project in Debug mode by pressing F5 or choosing appropriate menu items in the Macros IDE. You also have the same debugging tools as in Visual Studio, enabling you to set breakpoints, step through code, and view the value of a variable by putting your mouse over it.

DEPLOYING MACROS

Because macros can't be compiled, when you deploy a macro you are actually deploying its source code, which any user can view. Therefore, be sure you're not including any sensitive code in your macro project. You cannot deploy just a single macro — you need to deploy the entire macro project. If you have other macros in the project that you don't want distributed, you should first move the macro to a new macro project and deploy that instead.

For the macros to be available to a developer automatically in Visual Studio, the macro projects must be deployed to the `My Documents\Visual Studio 2010\Projects\VSMacros80` folder in that user's Windows profile.

As with add-ins, you can deploy your macro to another user's machine using a simple XCOPY operation, a Windows installer package (.msi), or a Visual Studio Content Installer package. Creating a Visual Studio Content Installer package is probably your best option, and is created in much the same way as the one demonstrated for add-ins. Let's take a look at deploying the macro project using a Visual Studio Content Installer package.

Create a text file called CodeNotes.vscontent in the same location as your .vsmacros file, with the following content:

```
<VSContent xmlns="http://schemas.microsoft.com/developer/vscontent/2005">
    <Content>
        <FileName>CodeNotes.vsmacros</FileName>
        <DisplayName>Code Notes</DisplayName>
        <Description>A macro project to put notes in code.</Description>
        <FileContentType>Macro Project</FileContentType>
        <ContentVersion>1.0</ContentVersion>
    </Content>
</VSContent>
```

Now, in Windows Explorer (or your favorite zip tool), combine the CodeNotes.vsmacros and CodeNotes.vscontent files into a zip file, and name it CodeNotes.vsi (do not include the .zip extension). Now when someone double-clicks this .vsi file, the macro will automatically be installed and ready to use when he or she next opens Visual Studio.

SUMMARY

This chapter discussed how macros can be used to automate repetitive tasks in Visual Studio by either recording those actions or coding them against the Visual Studio automation model. You looked at the support that Visual Studio has for macros, how to create them, run them, and finally, deploy them to other developers.

Managed Extensibility Framework (MEF)

WHAT'S IN THIS CHAPTER?

➤ Architecting extensible applications

➤ Hosting the Managed Extensibility Framework in your applications

➤ Understanding the Visual Studio 2010 Editor components

➤ Extending the Visual Studio 2010 Editor

➤ Importing Visual Studio Services

Creating loosely coupled applications that can be extended after deployment can be a difficult process. You have many design decisions to make, including identifying and loading extensions that have been deployed, and making application services available to loaded extensions. The Managed Extensibility Framework (MEF) is an open source library created by Microsoft designed to reduce the complexity of creating extensible applications. It allows you to expose reusable parts of your application to plug-ins or extensions that are discovered and loaded at run time and design your application in a very loosely coupled fashion.

Visual Studio 2010 uses the MEF library to provide extension points for the main editor control. It is expected that in future versions of Visual Studio, more areas will be exposed for this kind of extension.

This chapter is split into three sections. The first section is an introduction to how MEF works and how to use it in your own applications. The middle section describes the components of the new Visual Studio 2010 Editor control and how they interact. The final section describes the process of extending the editor with MEF and provides a complete sample which emphasizes certain types of comment in your code.

> *At the time of writing, the MEF library is still in development so some details may have changed. For the latest information about MEF, check* http://mef.codeplex.com.

GETTING STARTED WITH MEF

In this section, you create a simple application that demonstrates the manner in which most applications will utilize the capabilities offered by MEF. The MEF library is contained within the System.ComponentModel.Composition assembly, which is installed in the GAC as a part of the .NET Framework 4.0.

The key component of MEF is the CompositionContainer, which is found in the System.ComponentModel.Composition.Hosting namespace. A *composition container* is responsible for creating *composable parts* of your application, which in the default MEF implementation are just normal .NET objects. These parts might be a core aspect of your application or they might come from externally deployed extension assemblies that are loaded dynamically at run time.

Each part is able to provide one or more *exports* that other composable parts need and may require one or more externally provided *imports* that other parts provide. Imports and exports can be simple properties or fields, or they can be entire classes. When you request a part from the composition container, it will attempt to locate the part and satisfy any import dependencies it might have. Each of these imports must be provided (exported) by other parts that the container is aware of and may have import requirements of their own, which in turn must also be satisfied.

To build a bare-bones MEF application, create a new command-line project, add a reference to the System.ComponentModel.Composition assembly, and replace the contents of Program.cs (C#) or Module1.vb (VB) with the following:

Available for download on Wrox.com

C#

```csharp
using System.ComponentModel.Composition;
using System.ComponentModel.Composition.Hosting;

namespace GettingStartedCS
{
    class Program
    {
        static void Main(string[] args)
        {
            var app = new ApplicationRoot();
            app.Run();
        }
    }

    class ApplicationRoot
    {
        public void Run()
        {
```

```
            Compose();
        }

        private void Compose()
        {
            var compositionContainer = new CompositionContainer();
            compositionContainer.ComposeParts(this);
        }
    }
}
```

Code snippet GettingStarted\Program.cs

VB

```
Imports System.ComponentModel.Composition
Imports System.ComponentModel.Composition.Hosting

Module Module1

    Sub Main()
        Dim app As New ApplicationRoot
        app.Run()
    End Sub

End Module

Class ApplicationRoot
    Sub Run()
        Compose()
        Console.WriteLine("OK")
    End Sub

    Private Sub Compose()
        Dim compositionContainer As New CompositionContainer
        compositionContainer.ComposeParts(Me)
    End Sub
End Class
```

Code snippet GettingStarted\Module1.vb

> The `ComposeParts` *method is an extension method in the* `System.ComponentModel`
> `.Composition` *namespace, so if you do not have this namespace included, this code*
> *will not compile.*

All the sample does is create a `CompositionContainer` and then ask it to *compose* the `Application Root` class. The `ComposeParts` method, satisfies the import requirements of the parts that you provide it. If it cannot satisfy these requirements it will throw a `System.ComponentModel.Composition`

.CompositionException. As the ApplicationRoot class has no import requirements, the application simply writes OK to the console and ends. This is not very exciting, but it does provide a base on which you can add functionality.

Imports and Exports

The previous code sample asks the container to satisfy the import requirements of the ApplicationRoot class. Before you add an import requirement to that class, you will need an exported class to satisfy the dependency. The ApplicationRoot class prints a status message once composition is complete. You can delegate this responsibility to another class and then ask the composition container to provide an instance of that class during composition.

To make a part available to the rest of your program you can export it by applying an ExportAttribute to it. This code snippet creates a simple class and exports it:

Available for
download on
Wrox.com

C#

```csharp
[System.ComponentModel.Composition.Export]
class StatusNotificationService
{
  public void ShowStatus(string statusText)
  {
    System.Console.WriteLine(statusText);
  }
}
```

Code snippet GettingStarted\StatusNotificationService.cs

Available for
download on
Wrox.com

VB

```vbnet
<System.ComponentModel.Composition.Export()>
Public Class StatusNotificationService
    Public Sub ShowStatus(ByVal statusText As String)
        System.Console.WriteLine(statusText)
    End Sub
End Class
```

Code snippet GettingStarted\StatusNotificationService.vb

By adding an ExportAttribute onto the StatusNotificationService class, MEF is able to treat it as a composable part. Note, however, that the Export attribute is just metadata and MEF is still not aware of this part and will not use it. The simplest way to make the part available to MEF during part composition is to provide an instance of the exported class to the ComposeParts method. Change the Compose method of the ApplicationRoot class to instantiate an instance of the StatusNotification class and pass it into the ComposeParts method call as a second parameter.

Finally, to specify that the ApplicationRoot class requires an instance of this part, add a property to the ApplicationRoot class and mark it up with an ImportAttribute. Following is the full listing for the ApplicationRoot class. There is some code added after the call to Compose in the Run method that uses the newly imported part.

C#

```csharp
class ApplicationRoot
{
  public void Run()
  {
    Compose();
    NotifcationService.ShowStatus("Composition Complete");
  }

  public void Compose()
  {
    var compositionContainer = new CompositionContainer();
    var statusNotificationService = new StatusNotificationService();
    compositionContainer.ComposeParts(this, statusNotificationService);
  }

  [System.ComponentModel.Composition.Import]
  public StatusNotificationService NotifcationService { get; set; }
}
```

Code snippet GettingStarted\Program.cs

VB

```vbnet
Class ApplicationRoot
    Sub Run()
        Compose()
        NotificationService.ShowStatus("Composition Complete")
    End Sub

    Private Sub Compose()
        Dim compositionContainer As New CompositionContainer
        Dim statusNotificationService As New StatusNotificationService
        compositionContainer.ComposeParts(Me, statusNotificationService)
    End Sub

    <System.ComponentModel.Composition.Import()>
    Property NotificationService() As StatusNotificationService

End Class
```

Code snippet GettingStarted\Module1.vb

Contracts

When the composition container is attempting to resolve dependencies during a composition, it uses a string called a *contract* to match imports up to exports. By default, if no contract is supplied, MEF will use the fully qualified type name of the exported item as the contract. You can override this contract by supplying either a string or a type to the constructor of either the ImportAttribute or the ExportAttribute. The following code snippet shows three exports that all have the same contract:

C#

```csharp
class Settings
{
    [Export]
    public string Username;

    [Export(typeof(string))]
    public string Password;

    [Export("System.String")]
    public string Server;
}
```

Code snippet GettingStarted\Settings.cs

VB

```vb
Public Class Settings
    <Export()>
    Dim Username As String

    <Export(GetType(String))>
    Dim Password As String

    <Export("System.String")>
    Dim Server As String
End Class
```

Code snippet GettingStarted\Settings.vb

> It is recommended to use a type for the contract, because a fully qualified type name is more likely to be unique. If you need to use string contracts, you should come up with a way of ensuring they are all unique.

You can specify a contract that is different than the type of the export, if required. The best reason to do this is if the type implements an interface or inherits from an abstract base class. In the following sample, the SaveOperation class is not aware of the concrete message sender it will use and instead imports an abstraction: IMessageService. The CommandLineMessageService exports itself under the contract of the IMessageService interface. In this way, the SaveOperation class is able to take advantage of message sending without worrying about the details of how these messages are being sent. If you wanted to change the way the application worked later, you could implement a new IMessageService and then change which concrete type exported the contract.

C#

```csharp
public interface IMessageService
{
  void SendMessage(string message);
}

[Export(typeof(IMessageService))]
public class CommandLineMessageService : IMessageService
{
  public void SendMessage(string message)
  {
    Console.WriteLine(message);
  }
}

public class SaveOperation
{
  [Import]
  public IMessageService MessageService { get; set; }

  public void DoSave()
  {
    MessageService.SendMessage("Saving...");
    // Perform the save operation
    MessageService.SendMessage("Saved");
  }
}
```

Code snippet GettingStarted\SaveOperation.cs

VB

```vb
Public Interface IMessageService
    Sub SendMessage(ByVal message As String)
End Interface

<Export(GetType(IMessageService))>
Public Class CommandLineMessageService
    Implements IMessageService

    Public Sub SendMessage(ByVal message As String) _
      Implements IMessageService.SendMessage
        Console.WriteLine(message)
    End Sub
End Class

Public Class SaveOperation
    <Import()>
    Public Property MessageService As IMessageService

    Public Sub DoSave()
```

```
        MessageService.SendMessage("Saving...")
        ' Perform the save operation
        MessageService.SendMessage("Saved")
    End Sub
End Class
```

Code snippet GettingStarted\SaveOperation.vb

> *Exporting abstractions and strings raises a potential issue. If there are many exports with the same contract, MEF will not know which one to use to satisfy any given import. If this is the case, you can import an enumerable collection for a contract instead of a single instance using the* ImportMany *attribute. It is also possible to attach more metadata to an export, which you can use to refine the imports. See* http://mef.codeplex.com *for more information on this technique.*

Catalogs

In the sample code so far, the only way that the CompositionContainer is made aware of parts is by passing instances into the ComposeParts method. This means that your application will need to know about each part added to the container, which will not work for extensions that need to be deployed after release. It also gets a little tedious after a while.

Locating parts is the job of a *catalog*, which can be provided to the CompositionContainer constructor. If a composition container is constructed with a catalog, it will consult the catalog whenever it needs to locate an export. MEF ships with four catalogs:

➤   A TypeCatalog is created with a list of part types. The parts will be instantiated as required by the composition container to fulfill the import requirements during part composition.

➤   An AssemblyCatalog is similar to the TypeCatalog except that it scans an entire assembly looking for part types.

➤   A DirectoryCatalog scans a folder structure looking for assemblies, which can be examined for part types.

➤   An AggregateCatalog collects the parts from a number of other catalogs. This is useful because the composition container constructor is only able to accept a single catalog.

The following code sample demonstrates creating a composition container that will look for parts in the currently executing assembly and in all of the assemblies in the /Extensions folder:

C#

```csharp
var assemblyCatalog = new AssemblyCatalog(Assembly.GetExecutingAssembly());
var directoryCatalog = new DirectoryCatalog(@".\Extensions\");
```

```
var aggregateCatalog = new AggregateCatalog(assemblyCatalog, directoryCatalog);

var compositionContainer = new CompositionContainer(aggregateCatalog);
```

VB

```
Dim assemblyCatalog As New AssemblyCatalog(Assembly.GetExecutingAssembly())
Dim directoryCatalog As New DirectoryCatalog(".\Extensions\")
Dim aggregateCatalog As New AggregateCatalog(assemblyCatalog, directoryCatalog)

Dim compositionContainer As New CompositionContainer(AggregateCatalog)
```

> *You can create your own catalog by creating a new class that inherits from* `ComposablePartCatalog` *and overriding the* `Parts` *property.*

Advanced MEF

MEF supports a number of advanced scenarios that can be useful to you when you are creating host applications, or when you are creating add-ons or extensions for another host application. These include:

- ➤ Exporting properties, fields, and methods
- ➤ Importing fields, methods, and constructor arguments
- ➤ Importing collections
- ➤ Composition batches and recomposition
- ➤ Lazy imports
- ➤ Catalog filtering
- ➤ Part lifetimes
- ➤ Importing and exporting custom metadata

See the MEF Programming Guide on `http://mef.codeplex.com` for more information about these topics.

THE VISUAL STUDIO 2010 EDITOR

One of the most significant changes in Visual Studio 2010 is the new code and text editor control, which is written in managed code. This new editor uses MEF to manage its structure, which means that it imports many predefined contracts. In addition to this, it exports a number of services under predefined contracts that provide access to the presentation layer and the underlying model of the editor. The new editor is made up of four main subsystems.

The Text Model Subsystem

The *Text Model* subsystem is used to represent text and enable its modification. It is a logical model only, which doesn't have any responsibility for displaying pixels on the screen.

The chief component of this subsystem is the `ITextBuffer`, which represents a sequence of characters that should be displayed by the editor. The `ITextBuffer` can be persisted to the file system as an `ITextDocument`, but it doesn't need to be. It can be an entirely in-memory representation. To create new `ITextBuffer` instances, you can use an `ITextBufferFactoryService`. Any number of threads can make changes to an `ITextBuffer` until one of them calls the `TakeThreadOwnership` method.

Whenever an `ITextBuffer` is changed, a new version is created. Each version is represented as an immutable `ITextSnapshot`. Because these snapshots cannot change, any number of threads can refer to them safely, even if the `ITextBuffer` that they refer to is still changing.

To make a change to an `ITextBuffer`, you can use the `CreateEdit` method to create an instance of the `ITextEdit` interface. `ITextEdit` allows you to replace a span of text in the buffer with a new set of characters. The `ITextEdit` instance can be applied to the `ITextBuffer` by calling its `Apply` method. It can be abandoned by calling either the `Cancel` or `Dispose` method. Only one `ITextEdit` can be instantiated for an `ITextBuffer` at any given time, and if the buffer is owned by a particular thread, only that thread can create the edits.

> The `ITextBuffer` *interface contains* `Insert`, `Replace`, *and* `Delete` *convenience methods, which just wrap up the creation and application of an* `ITextEdit` *instance.*

All operations within a single `ITextEdit` occur relative to the initial state of the `ITextBuffer` at the time when the edit was created. Because of this you cannot insert some text and then remove it again within a single edit.

When an `ITextEdit` is applied, new instances of `ITextVersion` and `ITextSnapshot` are created and a `Changed` event is raised. The `ITextVersion` represents the changes between the current state of the `ITextBuffer` and the previous state, whereas the `ITextSnapshot` is a read-only view of the `ITextBuffer` after the edit has been applied. The changes in an `ITextVersion` are represented as a list of `ITextChange` instances which, if they are applied to a snapshot, would produce the subsequent snapshot. This collection is always `null` (`Nothing`) for the most recent version.

The Text View Subsystem

The *Text View* subsystem is responsible for managing the display of text on the screen. This includes which lines should be displayed and how text should be formatted. It is also responsible for enhancing the text with visual adornments such as the squiggly line, which notifies you of compilation errors. Finally, this subsystem manages the borders around the edges of the editor, which can be enhanced with additional information.

The main part of this subsystem is the `ITextView` interface. Instances of this interface are used to represent text visually on the screen. This is used for the main editor window but also for things like tooltip text. The `ITextView` keeps track of three different text buffers through its `TextViewModel` property. These are:

➤ The data buffer, which is the actual text

➤ The edit buffer in which text edits occur

➤ The visual buffer, which is actually displayed

Text is formatted based on *classifiers* (see "The Classification Subsystem") and decorated with adornments, which come from adornment providers attached to the text view.

The part of the text that is displayed on the screen is the *view port*. The view port relies on a logical coordinate system that has (0,0) as the top left of the text. If the editor is not zoomed or transformed in any way, each unit of distance in the view is the equivalent of a single pixel. Each line of text that is displayed on the screen is an instance of the `ITextViewLine` interface. This interface can be used to map from pixel points to characters.

Finally, the entire editor and all adornments and margins are contained within an `IWpfTextViewHost`.

> *The Text View subsystem comes in two parts. One part is technology agnostic and is found in the* `Microsoft.VisualStudio.Text.UI` *assembly. The other part is the WPF implementation and is found in the* `Microsoft.VisualStudio.Text.UI.WPF` *assembly. In most cases, the WPF-specific items contain the text "Wpf" in the name.*

The Classification Subsystem

The Classification subsystem manages the recognition and formatting of different types of text. It is also responsible for tagging text with additional metadata, which will be used by the Text View subsystem for attaching glyphs and adornments as well as text highlighting and text outlining (such as collapsed regions of code).

The Operations Subsystem

The Operations subsystem defines editor behavior and commands. It also provides the Undo capability.

EXTENDING THE EDITOR

Editor extensions are .vsix packages, which export contracts that Visual Studio components will import. When Visual Studio loads these packages, it adds their contents to a MEF catalog, which is then used to compose parts of the editor control. The Visual Studio Integration SDK comes with a number of templates to get you started creating editor controls. These appear under the Extensibility page of the New Project dialog shown in Figure 53-1.

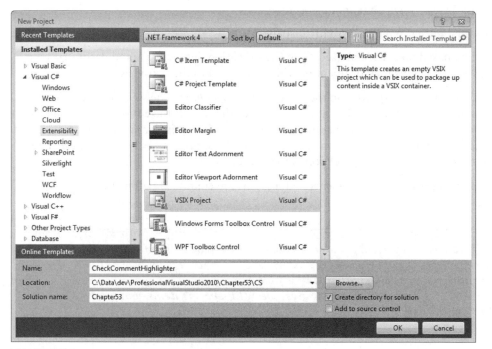

FIGURE 53-1

> The Visual Studio 2010 SDK is not installed with Visual Studio 2010. You can download a copy from http://msdn.microsoft.com/en-us/vsx/default.aspx.

If you want to start with a clean slate, you need to use the VSIX Project template. To expose editor extensions via this package, edit the source.extension.vsixmanifest file, and use the Add Content button to add the current project as an MEF Component as in Figure 53-2.

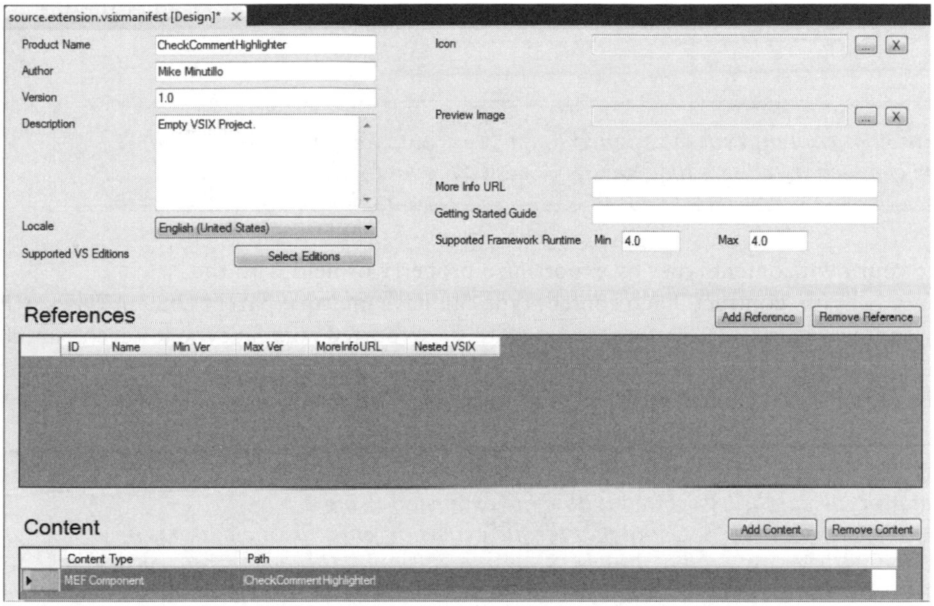

FIGURE 53-2

Once your project is set up to contain MEF content, all you need to do is to create classes that export known extension contracts and Visual Studio will pick them up. In addition to this, you can import service contracts from Visual Studio that will provide you with access to the full capabilities of the editor.

During development, editor extensions can be run and debugged in the Experimental Instance of Visual Studio. The Experimental Instance behaves like a separate installation of Visual Studio with its own settings and registry. It also manages a separate set of extensions. When you are ready to deploy your extension to the normal instance of Visual Studio, you can double-click the `.vsix` package, which is created as a part of the build process. This package is entirely self-contained, so you can use it to deploy your extension to other machines as well.

Editor Extension Points

The Visual Studio 2010 Editor looks for a number of contracts, which it uses to extend the editor behavior at run time. Usually you need to create at least two classes for each type of extension that you are exposing. One class will perform the work of the extension and the other will typically be imported by Visual Studio and asked to provide instances of your main extension class when required.

Content Types

Each `ITextBuffer` is assigned a *content type* when it is created that identifies the type of text it contains. Examples of content types include Text, Code, CSharp, or Basic. Content types are used as filters for the various editor extensions that you can create by adding a `ContentTypeAttribute` to the exported extension. An example would be an IntelliSense provider that is only valid for Xml content.

> *Even though content type is assigned to an* `ITextBuffer` *when it is created, it can be changed by calling the* `ChangeContentType` *method.*

You can create your own content types by exporting a property or field with the `ContentTypeDefinition` contract. Each content type can have multiple parent content types, which are defined by adding a `BaseDefinitionAttribute` to the exported content type for each parent type. To get a full list of content types you can import the `IContentTypeRegistryService`, which maintains a list of registered content types.

> *A content type can be associated with a file extension using a* `FileExtensionAttribute`. *Note that the file extension must be one that has been registered with Visual Studio already. Search for "ProvideLanguageExtension Attribute Class" on MSDN for more information on how to do this.*

Classification Types and Formats

A *classification type* is metadata that can be applied to any span of text. Some examples of classification types include "keyword" or "comment," both of which inherit from the classification type "code." You can create your own classification types by exporting a property or field of the `ClassificationTypeDefinition` class. This allows you to attach custom behavior to the text.

> *Classification types are not the same thing as content types. Each* `ITextBuffer` *has a single content type but may contain spans of text that have many different classifications.*

Classification types are attached to spans of text using an `IClassifier` instance. A *classifier aggregator* collects the classifications from a number of different classifiers for a text buffer and creates a unique non-overlapping set of classifications from that buffer. In effect, a classifier aggregator is a classifier itself because it also provides classifications for a span of text. To get the classifier aggregator for a particular `ITextBuffer` instance of text you can import the `IClassificationAggregatorService` and call its `GetClassifier` method, passing in the text buffer.

You can define a format for a specific classification type by deriving a new class from `ClassificationFormatDefinition` and exporting it with an `EditorFormatDefinition` contract. The base class contains a number of properties that you can use to change the way text is rendered. You associate the format definition with the classification type by using the ClassificationTypeAttribute on the exported class. This attribute accepts a string that is a comma-separated list of classification types that the format applies to. You can also use DisplayNameAttribute and UserVisibleAttribute to show this classification format in the Fonts and Settings page of the Options dialog. You can also specify a PriorityAttribute, which will help to determine when the format is applied.

Margins

A *margin* is a piece of UI around the edges of the main editor window. There are four predefined margins names: Top, Bottom, Left, and Right, which act as containers for other margins that you can define. You could define a margin that turns red when a generated file is opened to warn the user that they should not edit the file.

To create a margin, you need to make a new class that implements IWpfTextViewMargin, which contains properties for the margin size as well as for the actual UIElement that draws the margin on the screen. To register your margin with Visual Studio, you need to export a class with the IWpfTextViewMarginProvider contract. This interface contains a single method that should return an instance of your IWpfTextViewMargin. In addition to the MEF export, the margin provider can also provide the following:

➤ A NameAttribute, which is used to give the provider a human-readable name.

➤ A ContentTypeAttribute, which identifies the content type that the margin should be made available for.

➤ An OrderAttribute and a MarginContainerAttribute, which are both used to determine where the margin should be drawn. The order is specified by supplying the string name of another margin to run either Before or After. The container identifies which border the margin should be displayed against (top, bottom, left, or right).

Tags

A *tag* is a piece of metadata that is applied to a specific span of text. Examples of tags include SquiggleTag, TextMarkerTag, and OutliningRegionTag. Tags are associated with spans of text using instances of the ITagger interface. To register an ITagger, you need to create a class that implements the ITaggerProvider interface, override the CreateTagger method, and then export the new class with the ITaggerProvider contract. Your tagger provider should also be marked up with the TagTypeAttribute, which identifies the type of tag its taggers will produce.

> *Classification is a special case of tagging provided by a* ClassifactionTag.

Adornments

An *adornment* is a special effect that can be applied to a span of text or to the editor surface itself. You can define your own adornments, which are just standard WPF UIElements. Each type of adornment gets rendered in a separate layer so that different adornment types don't interfere with each other. To specify a layer on which your adornment belongs, your adornment class should export an AdornmentLayerDefinition along with a NameAttribute and an OrderAttribute. The Order can be defined as Before or After one of four built-in adornment layers: Selection, Outlining, Caret, and Text. When the adornment wants to display itself, it can request an instance of the IAdornmentLayer from the IWpfTextView by name. This interface exposes methods to add UIElements to the layer and clear all adornments out of the layer.

To create your adornment, you need to export a class with the IWpfTextViewCreationListener contract. This class should simply instantiate a new adornment whenever a text view is created. It is up to the adornment to wire itself up to events that it needs to use to redraw its contents. This class can be marked up with a standard ContentTypeAttribute to filter the content types on which it will appear. It can also include a TextViewRoleAttribute that defines for which kind of text view it should appear. The PredefinedTextViewRoles contains a list of valid values.

Mouse Processors

Mouse processors are able to capture events from the mouse. Each mouse processor should derive from MouseProcessorBase and override the event handlers that they want to handle. To expose your mouse processor to Visual Studio, you must export a class under the IMouseProcessorProvider contract. You also need to apply a ContentTypeAttribute to identify the types of content for which the mouse processor is available.

Drop Handlers

Drop handlers customize the behavior of the Visual Studio editor when content is dropped into it. Each drop handler should implement IDropHandler and you will need an IDropHandlerProvider to provide your drop handler to Visual Studio. This provider class should export the IDropHandlerProvider contract along with the following metadata:

➤ A NameAttribute to identify your drop handler.

➤ A DropFormatAttribute, which specifies the format of text for which this handler is valid. Twenty-three built-in formats are supported, which are all handled in a specific order. Check the MSDN documentation for the full list.

➤ An OrderAttribute, which identifies where in the order of drop handlers this handler should execute. You do this by providing Before and After components of the Order. Each component is just a text name for the handler. The default drop handler provided by Visual Studio is called DefaultFileDropHandler.

Editor Options

Editor options allow your extensions to expose settings. These settings can be imported into other components of the system and used to alter their behavior. This type of export is used to expose the value of your option to other components, but Visual Studio does nothing to expose these options to the user. If you want the user to be able to manage these options, you need to create your own UI.

To create a new editor option, you must derive from one of the three abstract base classes EditorOptionDefinition<T>, ViewOptionDefinition<T>, or WpfViewOptionDefintion<T> and specify the type of the option value being created (that is, Boolean or String). These base classes provide abstract properties for you to implement containing information about the option, including its current value and its default value. To make the editor option available to Visual Studio, you should export it with the `EditorOptionDefinition` contract.

IntelliSense

IntelliSense is a term that is used to describe a set of features that provide contextual information and statement completion services. No matter what type of IntelliSense extension you are providing, the components and the process are always the same:

➤ A *broker* controls the overall process.

➤ A *session* represents the sequence of events, which typically start with a user gesture triggering the presenter and end with the committal or cancellation of the selection.

➤ A *controller* determines when a session should begin and end. It also decides the manner in which the session ends.

➤ A *source* provides content for the IntelliSense session and determines the best match for display.

➤ A *presenter* is responsible for displaying the content of a session.

It is recommended that you provide at least a source and a controller when defining IntelliSense extensions. You should only provide a presenter if you want to customize the display of your feature.

To provide an IntelliSense source, you need to create a class that implements one (or more) of these interfaces: `ICompletionSource`, `IQuickInfoSource`, `ISignatureHelpSource`, or `ISmartTagSource`. Each of these interfaces defines methods that provide you with the context for the session and allow you to return the information that will be displayed.

For each of the interfaces implemented you need another class that implements the corresponding provider interface: `ICompletionSourceProvider`, `IQuickInfoSourceProvider`, `ISignatureHelpSourceProvider`, or `ISmartTagSourceProvider`. This provider class must be exported using its provider interface as a contract. In addition to the export, you can specify a `NameAttribute`, an `OrderAttribute`, and a `ContentTypeAttribute`.

To provide an IntelliSense controller, you need a class that implements `IIntellisenseController`. This interface provides methods for the controller to attach and detach `ITextBuffer`s. When the controller senses an event that should begin an IntelliSense session, it requests one from the correct type of broker: `ICompletionBroker`, `IQuickInfoBroker`, `ISignatureHelpBroker`, or `ISmartTagBroker`. The easiest way to get access to a broker is to import one into the controller provider (defined next) and pass it into the constructor of the IntelliSense controller.

Finally, you need an `IIntellisenseControllerProvider` that is exported along with a `NameAttribute`, an `OrderAttribute`, and a `ContentTypeAttribute`.

Editor Services

Visual Studio exposes a large number of editor services under well-known contracts that you can import into your extension classes. Here are a few common ones (see the MSDN documentation for a complete list):

➤ `IContentTypeRegistryService` manages the collection of content types that are available to be assigned to `ITextBuffers`. This service allows you add and remove content types, as well as query the currently registered content types.

➤ `ITextDocumentFactoryService` provides the ability to create new documents and load existing documents from the file system. It also has events for when `ITextDocuments` are created and disposed.

➤ `IClassifierAggregatorService` contains only a single method, `GetClassifier`, that returns a classifier for a given `ITextBuffer`. It will create and cache classifiers if they don't already exist.

➤ `ITextSearchService` is responsible for locating specific text within a defined region of text. It has methods to find all instances or just find the next instance.

➤ `IWpfKeyboardTrackingService` allows you to switch the keyboard tracking over to WPF in the editor. Normally Visual Studio performs its own keyboard tracking, so if you are using WPF controls that listen for keyboard events they will never be detected. This service allows you toggle the ability for WPF to have the first shot at handling keyboard events. Keyboard events that are left unhandled by WPF will be passed to Visual Studio and handled as normal.

The Check Comment Highlighter Extension

This section shows the complete source code for a sample extension with explanations along the way. In our office, whenever we come across something that doesn't seem to be quite right we attach a comment asking for an explanation using the special token `check:` followed by a few sentences going into what aspect we think is wrong. Normally, if we encounter a piece of code with a check comment and we can answer the query, we will try and find a way to refactor the code so that the answer is obvious or supply a comment explaining why the code is the way it is (on the rare occasion that the check comment exposes an error, we fix it). Using this technique, our code becomes more maintainable over time as it gets easier to read and understand. We have tools that allow us to extract a list of these comments from the code base, but it would be really handy if we could highlight them within the code editor itself. The Check Comment Margin Highlighter does just that by adding a glyph in the margin on the left (where breakpoints normally appear) for any line that contains a comment that contains the token `check:`.

The code comes in two parts: a tagger and a glyph factory. Here is the complete code listing for the tagger:

C#

```
using System;
using System.Collections.Generic;
```

```csharp
using System.ComponentModel.Composition;

using Microsoft.VisualStudio.Text;
using Microsoft.VisualStudio.Text.Classification;
using Microsoft.VisualStudio.Text.Editor;
using Microsoft.VisualStudio.Text.Tagging;
using Microsoft.VisualStudio.Utilities;

namespace CheckCommentHighlighter
{
    class CheckCommentTag : IGlyphTag { }

    class CheckCommentTagger : ITagger<CheckCommentTag>
    {
        private readonly IClassifier _classifier;

        public CheckCommentTagger(IClassifier classifier)
        {
            _classifier = classifier;
        }

        public IEnumerable<ITagSpan<CheckCommentTag>> GetTags(
            NormalizedSnapshotSpanCollection spans)
        {
            foreach (var span in spans)
            {
                foreach (var classification in
                        _classifier.GetClassificationSpans(span))
                {
                    var isComment = classification.ClassificationType
                                                  .Classification
                                                  .ToLower()
                                                  .Contains("comment");

                    if (isComment)
                    {
                        var index = classification.Span.GetText()
                                                  .ToLower().IndexOf("check:");
                        if (index != -1)
                        {
                            var tag = new CheckCommentTag();
                            var snapshotSpan = new SnapshotSpan(
                                        classification.Span.Start + index, 6);
                            yield return new TagSpan<CheckCommentTag>(
                                                    snapshotSpan,
                                                    tag);
                        }
                    }
                }
            }
        }

        public event EventHandler<SnapshotSpanEventArgs> TagsChanged;
```

```
    }


    [Export(typeof(ITaggerProvider))]
    [TagType(typeof(CheckCommentTag))]
    [ContentType("code")]
    class CheckCommentTaggerProvider : ITaggerProvider
    {
        [Import]
        private IClassifierAggregatorService AggregatorService;

        public ITagger<T> CreateTagger<T>(ITextBuffer buffer) where T : ITag
        {
            if( buffer == null )
                throw new ArgumentNullException("buffer");

            var classifier = AggregatorService.GetClassifier(buffer);

            return new CheckCommentTagger(classifier) as ITagger<T>;
        }
    }

}
```

Code snippet CheckCommentHighlighter\CheckCommentTagger.cs

VB

```
Imports System.ComponentModel.Composition
Imports Microsoft.VisualStudio.Text
Imports Microsoft.VisualStudio.Text.Tagging
Imports Microsoft.VisualStudio.Text.Editor
Imports Microsoft.VisualStudio.Text.Classification
Imports Microsoft.VisualStudio.Utilities

Friend Class CheckCommentTag
  Inherits IGlyphTag

End Class


Friend Class CheckCommentTagger
  Implements ITagger(Of CheckCommentTag)

  Private m_classifier As IClassifier

  Friend Sub New(ByVal classifier As IClassifier)
    m_classifier = classifier
  End Sub

  Private Function GetTags(ByVal spans As NormalizedSnapshotSpanCollection)
    As IEnumerable(Of ITagSpan(Of CheckCommentTag))
```

```vb
      Implements ITagger(Of CheckCommentTag).GetTags

      Dim Tags As New List(Of ITagSpan(Of CheckCommentTag))
      For Each span As SnapshotSpan In spans
        For Each classification As ClassificationSpan In
          m_classifier.GetClassificationSpans(span)

          If classification.ClassificationType.Classification.ToLower()
            .Contains("comment") Then

            Dim index As Integer = classification.Span.GetText().ToLower()
              .IndexOf("check.")

            If index <> -1 Then
              Dim snapshotSpan As New SnapshotSpan(classification.Span.Start
                  + index, 6)

            Dim tag As New CheckCommentTag
                Tags.Add(New TagSpan(Of CheckCommentTag)(snapshotSpan, tag))
            End If
          End If
        Next classification
      Next span
      Return Tags
    End Function

    Public Event TagsChanged As EventHandler(Of SnapshotSpanEventArgs)
      Implements ITagger(Of CheckCommentTag).TagsChanged

End Class

<Export(GetType(ITaggerProvider)), ContentType("code"),
  TagType(GetType(CheckCommentTag))>
Friend Class CheckCommentTaggerProvider
  Implements ITaggerProvider

  <Import()>
  Friend AggregatorService As IClassifierAggregatorService

  Public Function CreateTagger(Of T As ITag)(ByVal buffer As ITextBuffer)
    As ITagger(Of T) Implements ITaggerProvider.CreateTagger

    If buffer Is Nothing Then
      Throw New ArgumentNullException("buffer")
    End If

    Dim Classifier = AggregatorService.GetClassifier(buffer)
    Dim tagger As New CheckCommentTagger(Classifier)

    Return TryCast(tagger, ITagger(Of T))

  End Function
End Class
```

Code snippet CheckCommentHighlighter\CheckCommentTagger.vb

Three classes are defined here. The first is the `CheckCommentTag` class. It inherits from `IGlyphTag` but has no implementation on its own. It is purely a marker that identifies when a particular span of text should have this glyph applied. We could have supplied some properties on the tag class to pass information to the glyph factory later that could be used to affect the type of `UIElement` displayed.

The second class is the `CheckCommentTagger` class. This class is responsible for identifying spans of text that should have the `CheckCommentTag` applied. It does this by implementing the `ITagger<CheckCommentTag>` interface. This interface consists of a method called `GetTags` and a `TagsChanged` event. `GetTags` takes a collection of spans and returns a collection of `ITagSpans`. In this implementation, it finds all of the comments with the help of a classifier and searches for the string `check:`. If it finds this string, it creates a new `TagSpan<CheckCommentTag>` item, which it applies to just the span of text that covers the `check:` string.

The final class is `CheckCommentTaggerProvider`, which contains the MEF export metadata that Visual Studio is looking for in the extension. This class is exported using the `ITaggerProvider` contract, which means that Visual Studio will add it to an internal list of tagger providers to be called upon whenever taggers are required. Two other pieces of metadata are also attached to this class. The `TagTypeAttribute` specifies the type of tags that will be produced by any taggers that this provider creates. The `ContentTypeAttribute` supplies a filter on the kinds of content on which this tagger provider should be used. In this case, the attribute specifies that this tagger provider should only be called upon when the editor contains code, which is a common base content type provided by the editor.

The tagger provider class also has an import requirement for an `IClassifierAggregatorService`. This service is used in the construction of taggers, which occurs in the `CreateTagger<T>` method. This method is passed an `ITextbuffer` for which it is to provide a tagger. It uses the `AggregatorService` to retrieve a classifier and then uses the classifier to construct the `CheckCommentTagger` defined in the previous code snippet.

This code is enough to allow Visual Studio to mark up check comments as requiring a glyph, but if you deploy the extension as it is right now you won't see anything because there are no components offering to draw a `CheckCommentTag`. For that you need a *glyph factory*, which is the other half of the extension. Here is the code:

C#

```csharp
using System.ComponentModel.Composition;
using System.Windows;
using System.Windows.Media;
using System.Windows.Shapes;

using Microsoft.VisualStudio.Text.Editor;
using Microsoft.VisualStudio.Text.Formatting;
using Microsoft.VisualStudio.Text.Tagging;
using Microsoft.VisualStudio.Utilities;

namespace CheckCommentHighlighter
{
    class CheckCommentGlyphFactory : IGlyphFactory
    {
        public UIElement GenerateGlyph(IWpfTextViewLine line, IGlyphTag tag)
        {
```

```csharp
            var validTag = tag as CheckCommentTag != null;
            if (!validTag)
                return null;

            return new Polygon
            {
                Fill = Brushes.LightBlue,
                Stroke = Brushes.DarkBlue,
                StrokeThickness = 2,
                Points = new PointCollection
                {
                    new Point(0, 0),
                    new Point(16, 8),
                    new Point(0, 16)
                }
            };

        }
    }

    [Export(typeof(IGlyphFactoryProvider))]
    [TagType(typeof(CheckCommentTag))]
    [Name("CheckCommentGlyph")]
    [ContentType("code")]
    [Order(After="VSTextMarker")]
    class CheckCommentGlyphFactoryProvider : IGlyphFactoryProvider
    {
        public IGlyphFactory GetGlyphFactory(IWpfTextView view,
                                             IWpfTextViewMargin margin)
        {
            return new CheckCommentGlyphFactory();
        }
    }
}
```

Code snippet CheckCommentHighlighter\CheckCommentGlyphFactory.cs

VB

```vbnet
Imports System.ComponentModel.Composition
Imports System.Windows
Imports System.Windows.Media
Imports System.Windows.Shapes

Imports Microsoft.VisualStudio.Text.Editor
Imports Microsoft.VisualStudio.Text.Formatting
Imports Microsoft.VisualStudio.Text.Tagging
Imports Microsoft.VisualStudio.Utilities

Friend Class CheckCommentGlyphFactory
    Implements IGlyphFactory
```

```vb
      Public Function GenerateGlyph(ByVal line As IWpfTextViewLine,
   ByVal tag As IGlyphTag) As UIElement Implements IGlyphFactory.GenerateGlyph
            If tag Is Nothing OrElse Not (TypeOf tag Is CheckCommentTag) Then
                Return Nothing
            End If

            Dim triangle As New System.Windows.Shapes.Polygon()

            With triangle
                .Fill = Brushes.LightBlue
                .Stroke = Brushes.DarkBlue
                .StrokeThickness = 2
                .Points = New PointCollection()
                With .Points
                    .Add(New Point(0, 0))
                    .Add(New Point(16, 8))
                    .Add(New Point(0, 16))
                End With
            End With

            Return triangle
      End Function

   End Class

   <Export(GetType(IGlyphFactoryProvider)), Name("CheckCommentGlyph"),
   Order(After:="VsTextMarker"), ContentType("code"),
   TagType(GetType(CheckCommentTag))>
   Friend NotInheritable Class TodoGlyphFactoryProvider
      Implements IGlyphFactoryProvider


      Public Function GetGlyphFactory(
   ByVal view As Microsoft.VisualStudio.Text.Editor.IWpfTextView,
   ByVal margin As Microsoft.VisualStudio.Text.Editor.IWpfTextViewMargin)
   As Microsoft.VisualStudio.Text.Editor.IGlyphFactory
   Implements Microsoft.VisualStudio.Text.Editor.IGlyphFactoryProvider.GetGlyphFactory
            Return New CheckCommentGlyphFactory()

      End Function
   End Class
```

Code snippet CheckCommentHighlighter\CheckCommentGlyphFactory.vb

Just as with the code to expose the check comment tagger to Visual Studio, two classes are at work here: one class that actually creates glyphs and another class that provides instances of this glyph factory to Visual Studio on demand. The CheckCommentGlyphFactory is very simple. It just checks to ensure that the tag is of the correct type and then creates the visual element that is to be displayed. This can be any WPF UIElement. In this implementation, it is a light blue triangle pointing to the right with a dark blue border.

The second class is the actual gateway into Visual Studio. It is exported using the IGlyphFactoryProvider contract, associated with a specific tag and content type. It also specifies a name that makes it easier to identify. Finally, it specifies that it should be drawn after items in the "VSTextMarker" layer, which means it will appear to be on top of items in this layer. The actual implementation of this class is a simple factory method for instances of the `CheckCommentGlyphFactory` class.

If you run this extension it will start up in the Experimental Instance of Visual Studio. Load a code file and add a comment that starts with `Check:` and a blue triangle appears in the margin to the left as in Figure 53-3.

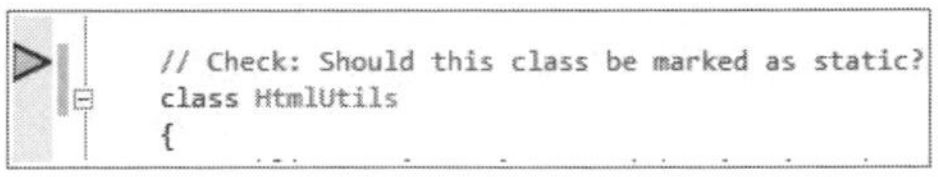

```
// Check: Should this class be marked as static?
class HtmlUtils
{
```

FIGURE 53-3

SUMMARY

The Managed Extensibility Framework simplifies the process of creating extensible applications by allowing you to think of your application as a collection of composable parts, each of which exposes exports and requires imports. Extensions can be added to your application by creating appropriate catalogs of parts and providing them to your composition container. MEF is able to cover a much wider range of capabilities than those covered in this chapter. Be sure to check out the MEF Programming Guide on `http://mef.codeplex.com` for more information.

Visual Studio 2010 is able to create a highly extensible run time by taking advantage of MEF. It watches extensions for known exported contracts, which it will use when composing the new WPF Editor control, allowing you to easily extend its behavior. In addition to this, Visual Studio exports a number of services on well-known contracts that you can import for use in your extensions. For more information about the new Visual Studio Editor and how to extend it using MEF, consult the Visual Studio 2010 Editor topic on MSDN, which contains many examples of extensions.

PART XII
Visual Studio Ultimate

▶ **CHAPTER 54:** Visual Studio Ultimate for Architects

▶ **CHAPTER 55:** Visual Studio Ultimate for Developers

▶ **CHAPTER 56:** Visual Studio Ultimate for Testers

▶ **CHAPTER 57:** Team Foundation Server

54

Visual Studio Ultimate for Architects

WHAT'S IN THIS CHAPTER?

➤ Creating models of your solution

➤ Enforcing application architecture

➤ Exploring existing architectures

The VSTS Architecture edition offered four diagrams for designing distributed systems, which were almost never used by teams in production. These four diagrams have all been dropped in Visual Studio 2010 and all of the functionality targeted for architecture tasks is brand new. This functionality can be split into two broad categories.

The first new feature is Modeling Projects, which allow you to create UML diagrams to build up an application model. There is also a new diagram that can be used to determine and enforce certain relationships between code elements in your projects.

The other new features all revolve around navigating and understanding existing code bases. This includes the ability to generate sequence diagrams from C# and VB methods, as well as Dependency Graphs of various components in your solution. Finally, Visual Studio 2010 includes the new Architecture Explorer, which is used to quickly navigate your solution.

MODELING PROJECTS

A model in software terms is an abstract representation of some process or object. You create models to better understand and communicate to others the way different parts of the application are intended to work. In Visual Studio 2010, you keep all of your models together in a Modeling Project. Modeling Projects are found on their own page in the Add New Project dialog. You can also create a new Modeling Project by adding a diagram to your solution with the Architecture ➪ New Diagram menu option. This brings up the Add New Diagram dialog shown in Figure 54-1. At the bottom of this dialog is a drop-down list allowing you to select an existing Modeling Project or offering to create a new one for you.

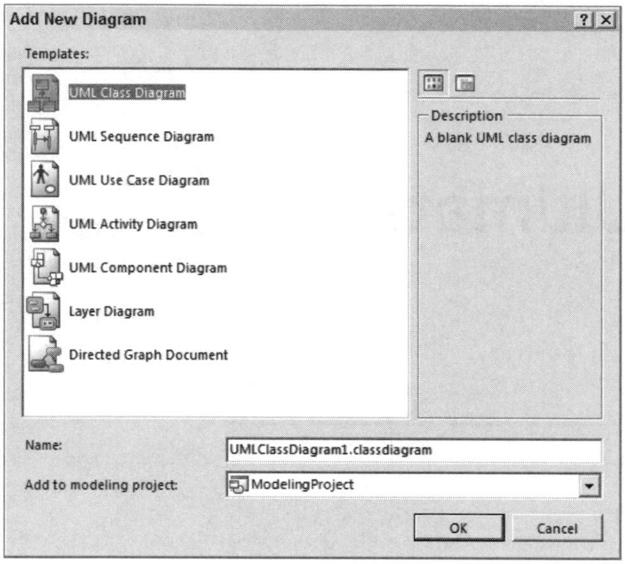

FIGURE 54-1

Many of the diagrams in a Modeling Project can easily be attached to Work Items in Team Foundation Server, which makes them a great tool for communicating with the rest of the team.

> *The ability to create Modeling Projects and their associated diagrams is limited to the Ultimate edition of Visual Studio 2010. The Premium edition includes the ability to view Modeling Projects and diagrams already created by someone else.*

UML Diagrams

The Unified Modeling Language (UML) is an industry standard for creating diagrammatic models. Visual Studio 2010 has the ability to create the most common UML diagrams, including Activity Diagrams, Component Diagrams, Class Diagrams, Sequence Diagrams, and Use Case Diagrams.

> *The Visual Studio 2010 UML diagrams adhere to the UML 2.0 standard.*

Use Case Diagrams

A Use Case Diagram (Figure 54-2) defines the users of a system (Actors) and the tasks they need to achieve with the system (Use Cases). As Figure 54-2 shows, each use case can be made up of subordinate use cases. Use Case Diagrams are typically very high level.

Modeling Use Cases helps you to focus on the objectives of the end users and ensure that their needs are being met by the application that you are providing. Additionally, it helps to identify the boundaries of your application with respect to the user's needs, which is very good for understanding the scope of what you need to build. Use Cases are typically associated with User Story and Test Case work items within TFS.

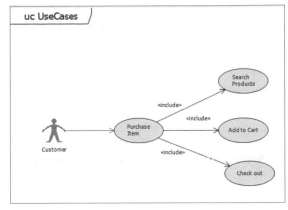

FIGURE 54-2

Activity Diagrams

An Activity Diagram (Figure 54-3) describes the actions and decisions that go into performing a single task. Activity Diagrams and Use Case Diagrams are often used to show different views of the same information. Use Cases are often better at showing the hierarchical nature of tasks that a user performs, whereas Activity Diagrams show how each of the sub-tasks are used.

Activity begins with the small black circle and follows the arrows until they reach the circle with the ring around it. Each rounded box is an activity and each diamond shape represents a decision about which activity to move to next. The small fork icon in the bottom-right corner of the Search Products activities identifies it as calling another activity.

Activity diagrams can also run activity streams in parallel as shown in Figure 54-4. This figure also shows sending and receiving events asynchronously.

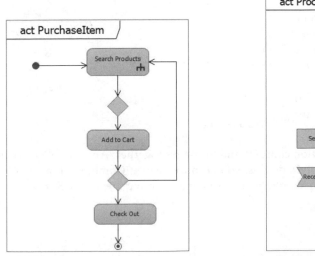

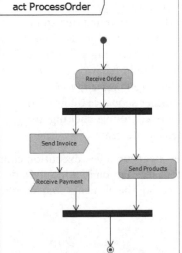

FIGURE 54-3

FIGURE 54-4

> *It is common to represent algorithms as activity diagrams.*

Sequence Diagrams

A Sequence Diagram (Figure 54-5) shows the messages passed between different components in a system or between systems during some larger activity. You use a Sequence Diagram when you want to show the flow of activities from one actor to another within a system.

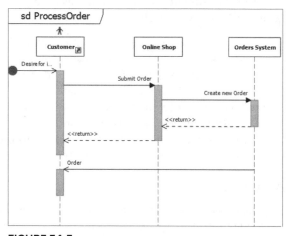

FIGURE 54-5

Running along the top of the diagram are boxes representing the different actors involved. Running down from each actor is a dashed lifeline on which hangs thicker execution contexts that show where in the process each actor is performing some operation. As you read a sequence diagram, moving down a lifeline equates to moving forward in time. Running between the lifelines are messages being passed back and forth between the different actors. Messages can be synchronous (closed arrow) or asynchronous (open arrow). Messages can be found, which means that you don't know where they come from, or lost, which means that you don't know where they go. These commonly appear at the boundaries of the activity being modeled.

An Interaction Use (Figure 54-6) is a piece of a Sequence Diagram that is separated out and can be re-used. To create an Interaction Use, select it from the Toolbox and then drag a rectangle over the lifelines that should be involved. Once an Interaction Use has been created, you can use it to generate another sequence diagram or link it to an existing one. Double-clicking an Interaction Use opens its diagram.

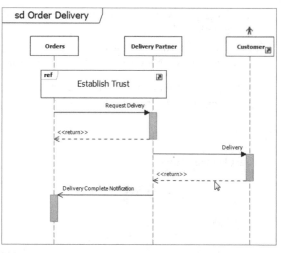

FIGURE 54-6

Sometimes you need to group a few execution contexts and messages together. An example is when you want to repeat an interaction in a loop. To do this, you need to create a Combined Fragment (Figure 54-7) by selecting the elements that should be involved and selecting one of the Surround With options.

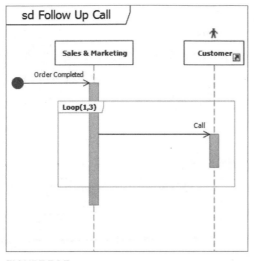

FIGURE 54-7

Although they both use the same notation, UML Sequence diagrams should not be confused with .NET Sequence diagrams. UML Sequence diagrams can only be created within Modeling Projects and can include elements from other parts of the model. .NET Sequence diagrams are generated from existing .NET code and are not a part of the model.

Component Diagrams

A component is a single unit of functionality that can be replaced within its environment. Each component hides its internal structure but publishes provided interfaces that other components can use to access its features. Additionally, each component can publish a set of required interfaces that it needs to perform its tasks. A Component Diagram (Figure 54-8) shows the components in a system along with their published and required interfaces. It also shows how published interfaces will be matched up with required interfaces.

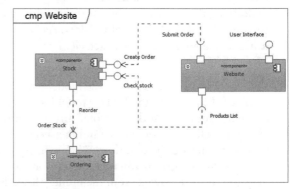

FIGURE 54-8

Modeling components helps you to think about the parts of your application as discrete units. This in turn reduces the coupling in your design, making your application easier to maintain and evolve going forward. You will typically model interactions between systems components (or between the parts inside a component) with a Sequence Diagram. You can use a Class Diagram to model the interfaces of a component along with the data that travels between the interfaces (parameters).

You can also use a Class Diagram to describe the classes that make up components' parts. Finally, you use an Activity Diagram to model the internal processing of a component.

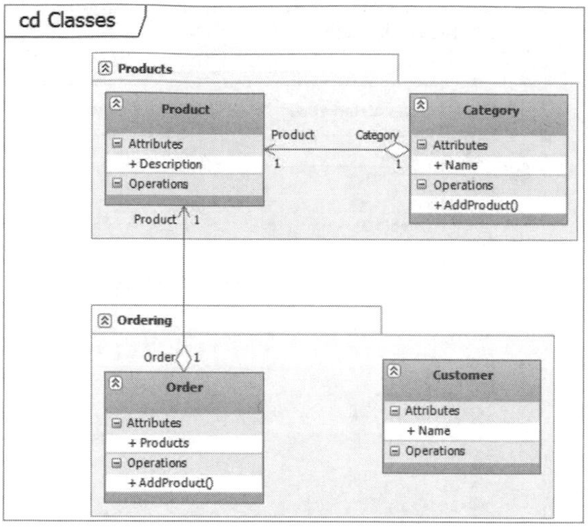

Class Diagrams

A Class Diagram (Figure 54-9) allows you to model the types in your system and the relationships between them. These are probably the most widely used of the UML diagram types in the industry. You can define classes, interfaces, and enumerations. Each of these items can be related to each other by inheritance, composition, aggregation, or just association. Each item can have attributes and operations defined on them. Finally, these items can be grouped into packages.

FIGURE 54-9

Although based on the same notation, UML Class Diagrams should not be confused with .NET Class Diagrams. A UML Class Diagram is used to define and organize elements of the model. A .NET Class Diagram performs a similar role for .NET code. Changing a .NET Class Diagram will alter the underlying .NET code.

UML Model Explorer

Each of the UML diagrams actually present different views of the same underlying model. To see the entire model, you can use the UML Model Explorer (Figure 54-10) tool window. As you add content to your model using the various diagrams, each element will also appear in the UML Model Explorer.

You can add items directly to the model using the context menu on many of the nodes in the UML Model Explorer. You can also drag elements from the Model Explorer directly onto the surface of many diagrams. Doing this creates a link between the original element and its appearance on the diagram. When you try to delete any element from a UML diagram, you have the option to simply remove it from the diagram or to remove it from the model altogether.

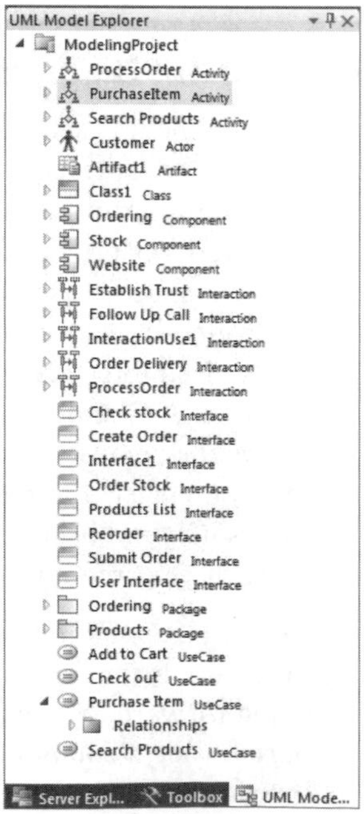

Using Layer Diagrams to Verify Application Architecture

A Layer Diagram (Figure 54-11) is a tool that helps you specify the high-level structure of a software solution. It is made up of different areas or layers of your application and defines the relationships between them.

FIGURE 54-10

Each layer is a logical group of classes that commonly share a technical responsibility, such as being used for data access or presentation.

Once you have created a new Layer Diagram, you can drag each layer onto the design surface and configure it with a name. You can draw directed or bidirectional dependency links between layers. A layer depends on another layer if any of its components have a direct reference to any of the components in the layer it depends on. If there is not an explicit dependency, it is assumed that no components match this description.

Presentation
Infrastructure
Caching
Business Logic
Logging
Security
1
Data Access

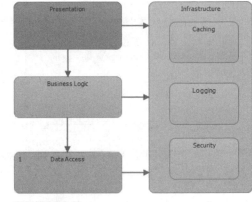

FIGURE 54-11

As is shown in Figure 54-11, layers can be nested inside one another.

Once you have created a layer diagram you use it to discover communications between layers in your compiled application and to verify that these links match the design. Before you do this, you need to associate projects with each layer by dragging them from the Solution Explorer and onto the layer itself. As you do this, entries are added to the Layer Explorer tool window (Figure 54-12) and a number inside each layer is updated to reflect the number of artifacts associated with it.

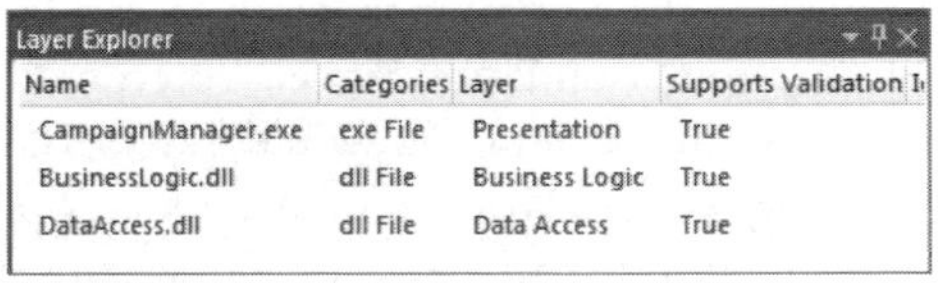

Layer Explorer
Name
Categories
Layer
Supports Validation
CampaignManager.exe
exe File
Presentation
True
BusinessLogic.dll
dll File
Business Logic
True
DataAccess.dll
dll File
Data Access
True

FIGURE 54-12

You can create new layers by dragging projects from the Solution Explorer directly onto the Layer Diagram surface.

Once the layer diagram has assemblies associated with it, you can fill in any missing dependencies by selecting Generate Dependencies from the design surface context menu. This will analyze the associated assemblies, building the project if necessary, and fill in any dependencies that are missing. Note that the tool won't ever delete unused dependencies.

When your layer diagram contains all of the layers and only the dependencies that you would expect, you can verify that your application matches the design specified by the layer diagram. To do this, you can select Validate Architecture from the design surface context menu. The tool will analyze your solution structure and any violations that are found will appear as build errors, as seen in Figure 54-13. Double-clicking one of these errors opens a Directed Graph showing the relationships between the various projects.

Error List					
⊗ 1 Error	⚠ 0 Warnings	ⓘ 0 Messages			
	Description	File	Line	Column	Project
⊗ 1	AV0001 : Invalid Dependency : CampaignManager(Assembly) --> DataAccess (Assembly)	Architecture.layerdiagram	0	0	ModelingProject
	Layers: Presentation, DataAccess | Dependencies: References				

FIGURE 54-13

> *Not all artifacts that can be linked to a layer diagram support validation. The Layer Explorer window has a Supports Validation column, which can help you determine if you have linked artifacts for which this is true.*

Modeling projects have a Boolean property called `ValidateArchitecture`, which is used to determine if all Layer Diagrams should be validated whenever the project is built. You can also request that Team Foundation Build validates your architecture by adding a property called `ValidateArchitectureOnBuild` to your `TfsBuild.proj` file or Process Template and setting it to true.

Linking to Team Foundation Server

Each of the elements of a diagram in a Modeling Project, as well as the diagrams themselves, can be linked to Work Items in Team Foundation Server. You can do this from the context menu of the item you would like to associate and selecting either Create Work Item or Link to Work Item. When a model element is associated with Work Items, it will show in the properties window for that element (Figure 54-14). You can also get a list of Work Items that an element is linked to by selecting View Work Items from the element's context menu.

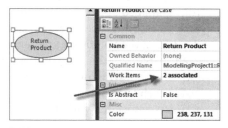

FIGURE 54-14

EXPLORING CODE

Many advanced features in Visual Studio are designed to help you understand and navigate the structure of an existing code base. Directed Graphs give you a high-level view of the relationships between various types of components within your project. The Architecture Explorer lets you deep dive into different areas while still leaving a trail of breadcrumbs to help you understand where you are. The ability to generate Sequence Diagrams lets you quickly understand how a particular method behaves, especially as it relates to other methods and classes.

The Architecture Explorer

One of the hardest aspects of navigating a new code base is understanding where you are in relation to everything else. The Architecture Explorer window (Figure 54-15) allows you to move very quickly through the code structure with single clicks, leaving a trail that always makes it easy to figure out how you got to wherever you end up. Some elements can be dragged from the Architecture Explorer directly onto the design surfaces of many of the other diagrams in this chapter.

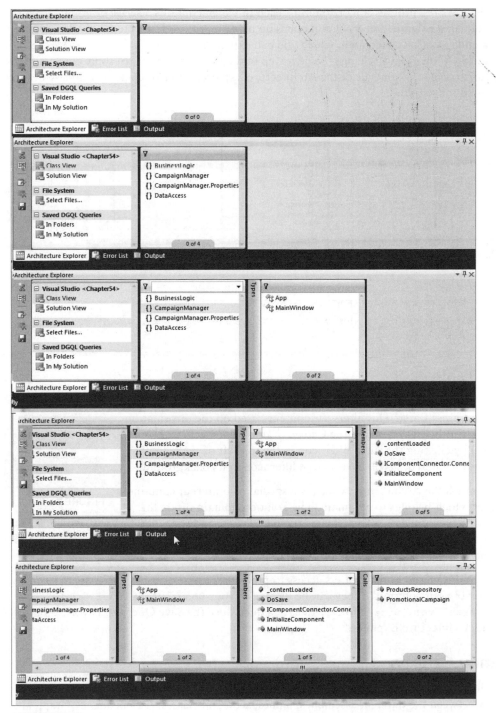

FIGURE 54-15

Figure 54-15 shows the progression of columns, each of which contains a series of nodes. Each time you click a node in a column, a new column opens up based on the node selected. Between each of the columns is a collapsed Action column, which you can expand by clicking it (Figure 54-16). Selecting a different action allows you to change the next step in the navigation path. In some cases, actions actually perform some task outside of the Architecture Explorer. Double-clicking a node will often open it in the editor window.

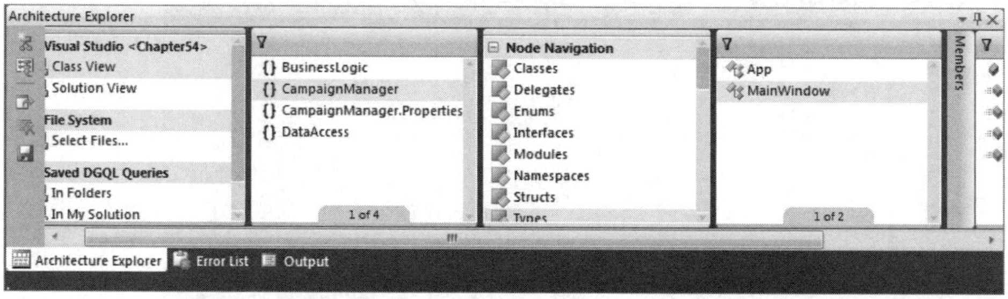

FIGURE 54-16

> You can select multiple nodes in a column to see a union of the results in the next column.

Each column in the Architecture Explorer can be independently filtered in one of two ways. The simplest way is to type into the textbox at the top of the column and press Enter. This filters the content based on the information you entered. The other way is to use the Category and Property Filter box (Figure 54-17) by clicking the small filter icon in the top-left of the column. When a column is filtered, it will have a large filter icon in its background.

FIGURE 54-17

The first column is the Architecture, which is a special column that contains views, each of which belongs to a domain. The Solution domain offers the Class View, which is based on a logical view of your classes, and the Solution View, which is based on the physical layout of your files. The File System domain allows you to load compiled assemblies from disk and analyze them in the Architecture Explorer.

The Saved DGQL Queries domain offers access to previously saved queries. These queries can be saved as a part of your solution or they can be located in your `Documents\Visual Studio 10\ArchitectureExplorer\Queries` folder. To save a query, use the Save Query to Favorites button on the left of the Architecture Explorer.

Dependency Graphs

When you inherit an existing code base, one of the more difficult tasks is trying to figure out the dependencies between the different assemblies, namespaces, and classes. A Dependency Graph allows you to visualize the dependencies between items at different levels of focus. The easiest way to create a Dependency Graph is the Architecture ➪ Generate Dependency Graph menu. This option allows you to create a Dependency Graph by assembly, by namespace, by class, or by some custom criteria that you can define. Four basic options specify the way a Dependency Graph is arranged based on the direction of arrows: top to bottom, left to right, bottom to top, and right to left. Figure 54-18 shows an example of the Left to Right view. There is also a Quick Clusters view, which attempts to arrange the items so that they are closest to the things they are connected to.

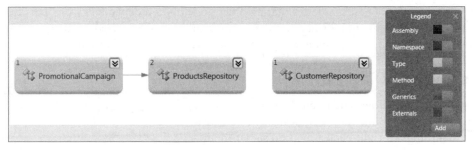

FIGURE 54-18

In addition to these views, there is a Dependency Matrix view (Figure 54-19), which shows a colored square whenever the item in the row depends on the item in the column.

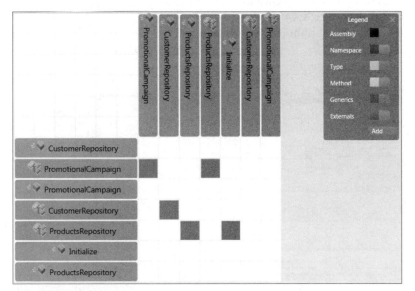

FIGURE 54-19

Visual Studio 2010 includes three analyzers for dependency graphs that can help you find potential problems with a code base. These are enabled and disabled under the Analyzers context menu and will update the legend to colorize any items that match criteria defined by the analyzer.

➤ **Circular References:** These can become difficult to detect, especially as the number of components involved grows. This analyzer will detect strongly connected items and colorize them.

➤ **Show Hubs:** A hub is a component that many other components depend on. These can be difficult to change because the impact of most changes tends to ripple out through the rest of the system.

➤ **Unreferenced Nodes:** These are nodes that no other node takes a dependency on. This can be an issue because it might indicate that the item it represents is not used by anyone else. It may also mean that the items that are dependent on it are not in the diagram.

Generate Sequence Diagram

A .NET Sequence Diagram allows you to model the implementation of a C# or VB method. The best way to create a .NET sequence diagram is to right-click a method signature in the editor window and select Generate Sequence Diagram to display the Generate Sequence Diagram dialog shown in Figure 54-20.

Once you click the OK button, Visual Studio analyzes your project and produces a .NET Sequence Diagram as in Figure 54-21. You can make changes to this sequence diagram without affecting the underlying code, so you can use this diagram to rapidly try out different ideas about how the code should work.

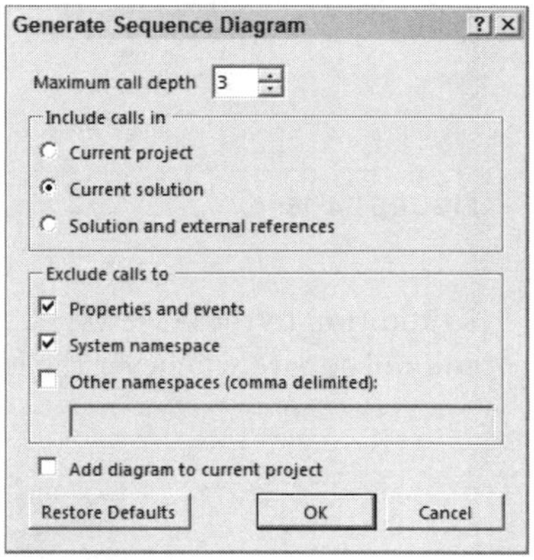

FIGURE 54-20

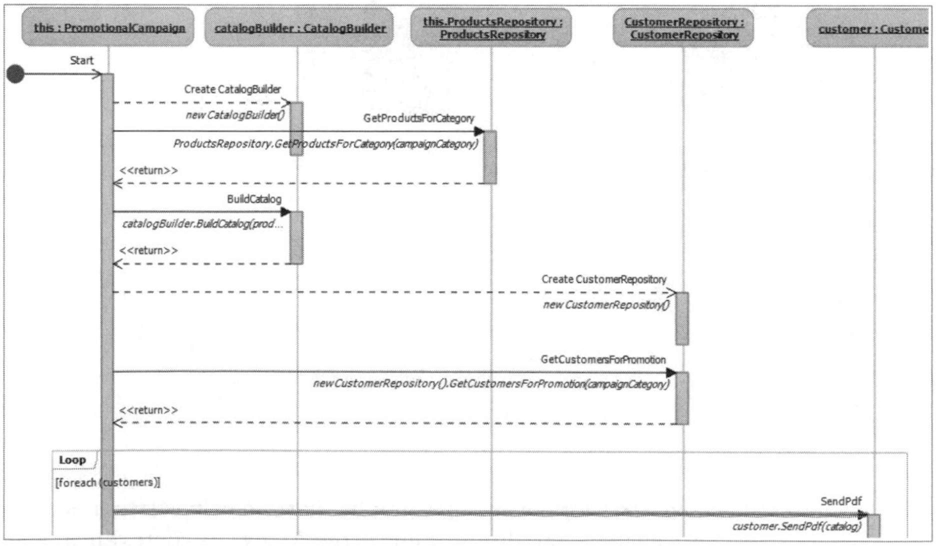

FIGURE 54-21

> *You can add a .NET Sequence Diagram to any .NET project by using the Add New Item dialog. If you add a Sequence Diagram this way, it will not be related to a specific .NET method.*

SUMMARY

Modeling Projects provide a great way for you to communicate the design of your project clearly, unambiguously, and effectively. You can use Use Case Diagrams, Activity Diagrams, and Sequence Diagrams to model user requirements from a number of different perspectives. You will use Component Diagrams, Class Diagrams, and Layer Diagrams to model the structure of your application. The ability to verify that your application meets the architecture as designed by the Layer Diagram can be a useful sanity check to ensure project quality standards remain high and architectural decisions are not abandoned once the project gets underway.

Getting up to speed with an existing code base can be very hard. Directed Graphs are an easy way to identify the relationships between various parts of your application. The new Architecture Explorer allows you to rapidly move through the connections between components in the system to find the items that you are looking for. Finally, the ability to generate a Sequence Diagram from an existing method allows you to quickly grasp the fundamentals of how a method interacts with other methods and classes within the application.

Visual Studio Ultimate for Developers

WHAT'S IN THIS CHAPTER?

➤   Analyzing code for potential problems

➤   Profiling applications to find bottlenecks

➤   Developing database projects

The Premium and Ultimate editions of Visual Studio 2010 have many advanced features for developers mainly designed to improve quality and facilitate database development. The quality tools include code metrics, static analysis, and profiling tools. It's not that you can't develop quality software with other editions or that using these tools will make sure your software performs well. Obviously, there's more to it than using a few tools, but these can be of great help and will reduce the time invested in other tasks like code review and debugging. The most interesting new debugging tool is called IntelliTrace, which allows you to capture environment information associated with failed test cases.

Chapter 26 already examined some of the tools available for working with databases in Visual Studio 2010. This chapter looks at two main areas: SQL-CLR development, and tools to help teams working with databases. The first will aid in developing and deploying .NET code that will be hosted inside SQL Server. The second will allow you to version schema changes, isolating developers and allowing them to compare changes, auto-generate data, and share their modifications easily with other developers or DBAs.

CODE METRICS

Code metrics serve as a reference to know how maintainable your code is. Visual Studio 2010 provides five metrics for your source code, which are all shown in the Code Metrics window (Figure 55-1). To open this window use the Analyze ➪ Calculate Code Metrics or the Analyze ⇨ Windows ⇨ Code Metric Results menu. Once the window is displayed, you can use the toolbar button in the top left to recalculate the metrics.

Hierarchy ▲	Maintainability Index	Cyclomatic Comple...	Depth of Inheritance	Class Coupling	Lines of Code
⊟ 🔳 Tailspin.Infrastructure (Debug)	78	387	2	112	745
⊟ { } Kona.Infrastructure	80	351	2	92	658
⊞ ⚙ Address	89	37	1	1	61
⊞ ⚙ AspNetAuthenticationService	69	9	1	4	20
⊞ ⚙ DbCommon	68	15	1	17	45
⊞ ⚙ DbCommonExtensions	50	14	1	9	42
⊞ ⚙ DbExtensions	74	2	1	5	9
⊟ ⚙ EntityBase	82	20	1	3	28
EntityBase()	98	1		0	1
EntityBase(object)	76	2		0	4
Equals(object) : bool	83	3		0	2
GetHashCode() : int	78	2		0	4
Key.get() : object	91	1		0	2
Key.set(object) : void	79	2		1	3
NewKey() : object	89	1		1	2
operator !=(EntityBase, EntityBase) : bool	85	1		0	2
operator ==(EntityBase, EntityBase) : bool	67	6		0	8
Validate() : void	100	1		0	0
IAggregateRoot	100	0	0	1	0

FIGURE 55-1

Directly from the list, you can filter any of the metrics to show methods that fall within a specified range, export to Excel, configure columns to remove metrics, or create a Team Foundation Server work item. Export to Excel is particularly useful to generate reports using pivot tables or to work with a flat view of the information using filters and sorts. For example, if you want to look for methods with more than 15 lines of code, filtering directly in the Code Metrics window will get you a lot of namespaces and types, but you will have to expand each to see whether there are any methods, whereas in Excel you can easily filter out namespaces and types and only look at methods.

As you use the metrics to make decisions about your code, bear in mind that the actual values are not as important as relative values. Having a rule that states "all methods must have less than 25 lines of code" is not as useful as one that makes relative statements such as "prefer shorter methods." You should also consider the changing values as important, so if your average Maintainability Index is going down it might be a sign you need to focus on making code easier to maintain.

> For each metric except for Maintainability Index, lower numbers are considered to be better.

Lines of Code

The name is self-explanatory; however, it's worth mentioning that the purpose of this metric should be only to get a clue of the complexity of the code, and must *not* be used to measure progress. Clearly, a method with five lines of code that calls other methods will be simpler than if you inline all 25 lines of code in that method.

```
public class OrdersGenerator
{
  public void GenerateOrder(Order order)
  {
    IsUnderCreditLimit(order);
    IsCustomerBlocked(order.Customer);
    AreProductsInStock(order);
    IsCustomerBlocked(order);
    SaveOrder(order);
  }
  // remaining methods are omitted.
}
```

If you compare a class with six methods, as shown in the preceding code, with a class having the same functionality, but with all the code inlined in one method, the latter will have 25 lines. Assuming the remaining methods have five lines each, the former will be 30 lines long, although it is simpler. You have to be careful about how to consider this metric; a longer class might be better than a short one.

> *Use the Extract Method refactoring discussed in Chapter 8 to reduce this metric. Be sure to keep an eye on extracted methods to see if they might be better off in a new class.*

Depth of Inheritance

This metric counts the base classes; some recommendations are to have a value lower than six. But this, like other metrics, has to be looked at with special care. It's hard to give a recommended value and it's relative to which classes you are inheriting from. If you inherit from LinkLabel, you will have a depth of 4, but your base classes are less likely to change than if you inherit from ProviderXComponent and have a depth of 1. It's more probable that ProviderX will change his component and break yours, while Microsoft will take more care not to break code. But you'll probably never update ProviderX's library. The point is that this metric is relative to what base classes you have.

Class Coupling

This counts the dependencies an item has on other types except for primitives and built-in types like Int32, Object, and String. The more dependencies you have, the harder it's supposed to be to maintain, because it would be more probable that changes on other types will cause a break in your code. Similarly to depth of inheritance, the importance you give is relative to the dependencies you have. A class referencing System libraries is less likely to have a break than classes referencing other types on active development. You can see a value for this metric at each level of the hierarchy (project, namespace, type, and member).

Cyclomatic Complexity

Cyclomatic Complexity is a measure of how many paths of execution there are through your code. A method with higher cyclomatic complexity is going to be harder to understand and maintain than one with a lower value. It is hard to find a recommended value for this metric because it depends on the level of your team and on the team that will maintain the product. Far more important is trending information — a steadily increasing cyclomatic complexity indicates that your code is getting harder to understand and follow. Having said that, sometimes a complex solution is warranted.

Maintainability Index

This metric is calculated using a formula that considers cyclomatic complexity, lines of code, and the Halstead volume, which is a metric that considers the total and distinct number of operators and operands. It will give you a range between 0 and 100, with the higher being easier to maintain than the lower.

Excluded Code

Code marked with the `CompilerGenerated` and `GeneratedCode` attributes won't be considered in the metrics. Datasets and Web Service Proxies are examples of code marked with the `GeneratedCode` attribute, but other generated code (like Windows Forms) isn't marked and will be considered in the metric's results.

MANAGED CODE ANALYSIS TOOL

This is a tool based on FxCop, a Microsoft internal tool released to the public a few years ago and finally integrated into the IDE. It allows you to perform static code analysis using a set of rules that define the quality decisions that you want to apply to your code. You can configure which set of rules to apply to each project from the project property page shown in Figure 55-2.

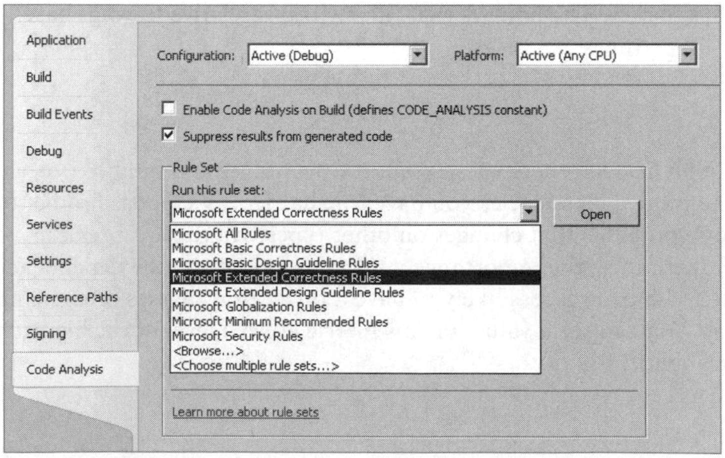

FIGURE 55-2

To use it you can right-click a project and select Run Code Analysis, or if you selected Enable Code Analysis on Build in the project's property window, you can simply compile it. The rules will be evaluated and if there is any violation (and believe me, there will be sooner or later) you will have a set of warnings in the Error List window.

> *By default each violation will appear as a warning, but you can change this behavior.*

If you right-click a warning and select Show Error Help, you will have a description of the rule, the cause, steps on how to fix violations, and suggestions on when to suppress warnings. Suppressing warnings is done with the `System.Diagnostics.CodeAnalysis.SuppressMessageAttribute`, which can be applied to the offending member or to the assembly as a whole. You can quickly and easily generate these attributes by selecting one of the Suppress Message menu options from the right-click menu in the Errors window.

More than 200 rules are conveniently organized into 11 categories, and you can add custom rules if needed. Depending on your project, you might want to exclude some categories or some particular rules. For example, if you don't need globalization and don't have plans in the future to support it, you might exclude that category. You can even create your own sets of rules (Add New Item ⇨ Code Analysis Rule Set) if the ones provided by Microsoft don't meet your needs.

When you first get started with Code Analysis tools, you should turn on all the rules and either exclude or suppress the warnings as needed. This is an excellent way of learning best practices. After a couple of iterations, new code written will be less prone to violate a rule. If you are starting a new project you might want to add a check-in policy, which prevents code with Analysis warnings from being checked in.

> *Never suppress a warning unless you have a very good reason. Finding these violations again can be quite difficult.*

C/C++ CODE ANALYSIS TOOL

This tool is similar to the Managed Code Analysis Tool, but works for unmanaged code. To activate it simply go to your C++ project's properties window, look for the Code Analysis node inside the Configuration Properties, and select Yes for Enable Code Analysis for C/C++ on Build. Every time you compile your project, the tool will intercept the process and attempt to analyze each execution path.

It will help you detect crashes that are otherwise hard to find with other techniques like debugging that are very time consuming. It's able to detect memory leaks, uninitialized variables, pointer management problems, and buffer over/under runs.

PROFILING TOOLS

Profiling tools enable you to detect and correct performance and memory issues in your projects. You can start a profiling session by selecting Launch Performance Wizard from the Analyze menu. The first step of the wizard asks you to select one of four profiling methods:

➤   CPU Sampling reports the CPU utilization at regular intervals while your application is running. This type of profiling is good for initial analysis or for identifying issues specifically related to CPU usage.

➤   Instrumentation actually inserts additional lines of code into your assembly to report on the length of time each method call takes. You can use this sort of profiling to get a detailed look at where your application spends most of its time.

➤   The .NET Memory profiler collects data about objects as they are created and as they are cleared up by the garbage collector.

➤   Concurrency profiling collects information about multi-threaded applications and provides some visualizations that you can use to explore several concurrency-related issues.

Next you need to select a project, executable, DLL, or web site to profile. With that information, the Performance Wizard creates a performance session and opens the Performance Explorer window. You could also create a blank session from the Performance Explorer or from a test in the Test Results window.

In the Performance Explorer (Figure 55-3) you can change between instrumentation and sampling. Using the combo box, you could start the wizard again or manually create a new performance session. Although you can instrument or sample a DLL, you need a point of entry for your application to run when you start the session, so be sure to include an executable, web site, or test project as a target.

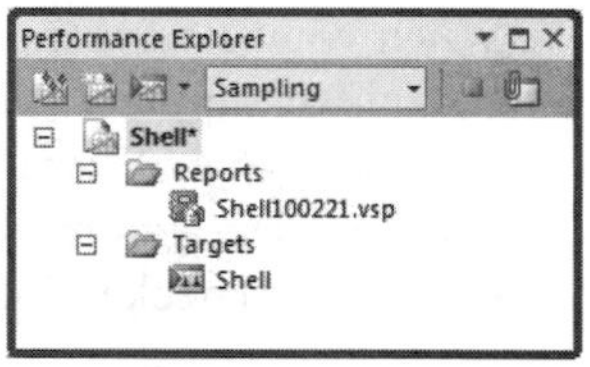

FIGURE 55-3

> If you have high code coverage, profiling unit test projects can give you a good insight into which methods take the longest to execute or use the most memory. Be wary of reacting to this information, though, because long-running methods may be called infrequently and improving an already fast method that is called many times will have a greater impact on overall application performance.

Configuring Profiler Sessions

To configure your session, simply right-click and select Properties. In the General section you can change between Sampling, Instrumentation, and Concurrency (Figure 55-4), and choose if you want to activate .NET memory profiling collection, the output for the reports, and the report names.

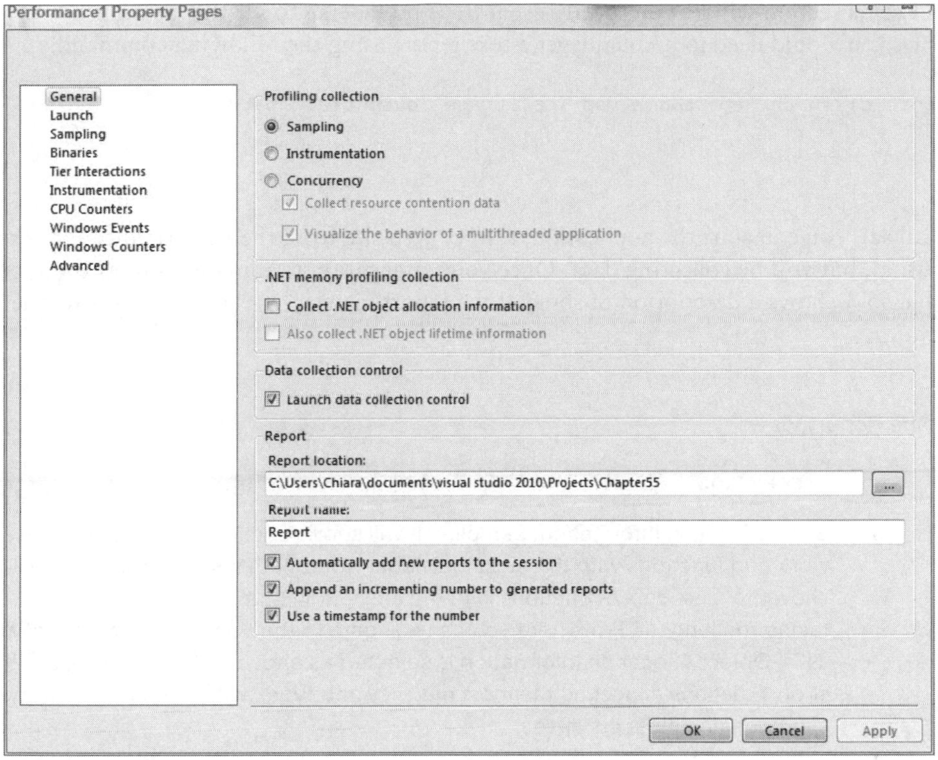

FIGURE 55-4

In the Sampling section, you can select when to take samples; by default this is set to 10,000,000 clock cycles. Depending on what you want to track, you can change the sample event to page faults, system calls, or a particular performance counter.

Enabling Tier Interaction Profiling (TIP) allows you collect information about synchronous ADO.NET calls between your application and SQL Server. This includes the number of times each query is made and how long each one took. If you are profiling an ASP.NET WebForms application, TIP is also able to provide data about page request counts and generation times.

The Instrumentation section is used to specify pre- and post-instrument events, for example signing an assembly with a strong name. These settings are set on a per-target basis. The last section in the property page, Advanced, is also used when instrumentation is selected, and there you can specify additional command arguments. To see a list of available options, search for VSInstr on MSDN. VSInstr is the tool used to instrument binaries.

The remaining sections are used to specify the collection of different counters or events. CPU Counters will let you capture additional low-level information and will be displayed as extra columns in the different report views. These are only available for instrumentation. The Windows Counters are system performance counters and you will be able to see the results in the Marks report view.

The Windows Events section will let you specify event trace providers. To see the information on Windows events, you would need to manually get a text report using the following command:

```
Vsperfreport c:\<path>ReportName.vsp /calltrace /output:c:\<path>
```

Reports

Once you are all set, you can start the application, test, or web site from the Performance Explorer. It will run as usual, but will be collecting data. Once your application terminates, a report will be generated. Table 55-1 shows a description of some of the report views and Figure 55-5 shows the Summary View.

TABLE 55-1: Some Report Views

VIEW NAME	DESCRIPTION
Summary	Shows function information. Sampling it will show functions causing the most work and functions with the most individual work. With instrumentation it will show the most called functions with the most individual work and functions taking the longest. From here you can navigate to the Functions view. If Collect .NET Object Allocation Information is selected as shown in Figure 55-4, it will show functions allocating the most memory and types with the most memory allocated and most instances.
Call Tree	Contains a hierarchy of the functions called. The Call Tree has a feature called Hot Spot that will point you to child functions taking the most time.
Modules	Shows information about the module sampled or instrumented.
Caller/Callee	Shows you which functions a particular function called and which functions called it.
Functions	Presents a list of all the functions sampled or instrumented. Double-clicking each function lets you navigate to the caller/callee window.
Allocations	Shows the number of instances and bytes allocated of a particular type.

Additional reports can be generated using the command-line tool VSPerfReport. For more information, consult the MSDN documentation.

Allocation and Object Lifetime are only available if you select Collect .NET Object Allocation Information and Also Collect .NET Object Lifetime Information, respectively, in the session's property page. Some of the report views are different depending on the configuration. To see a description of a particular column, simply hover over its title. You should go through the documentation on MSDN to get a thorough description on each report.

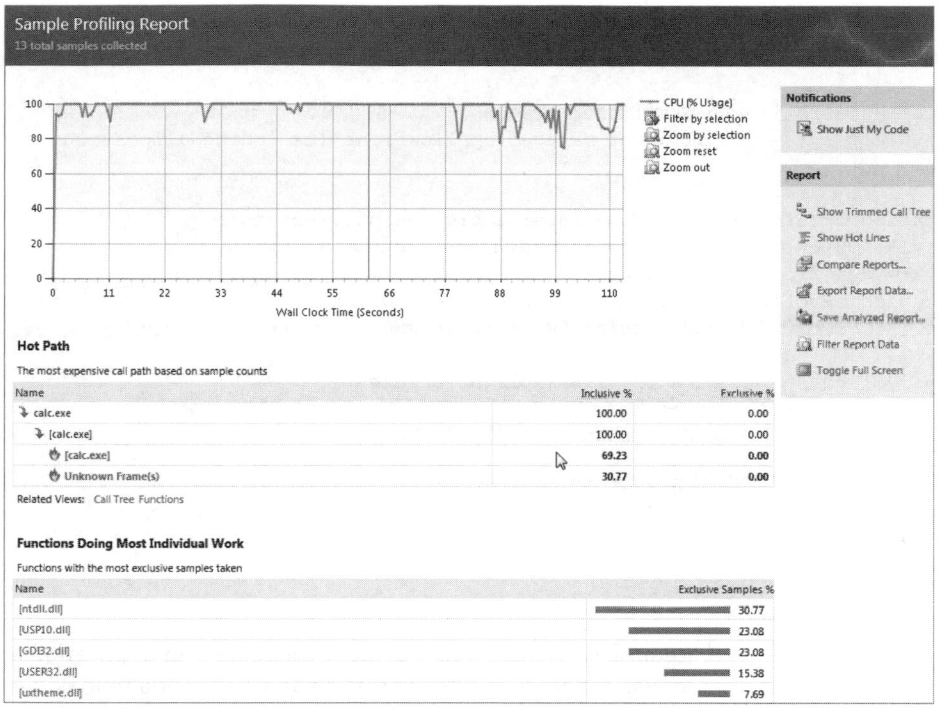

FIGURE 55-5

In all the views, you can use the filter from the toolbar to get to specific information. You can add or remove columns by right-clicking a header and sort using a particular column. Reports can be exported to either XML or CSV and successive reports can be compared against one another, allowing you to spot changes in your application's performance.

STAND-ALONE PROFILER

This is a command-line tool that is useful when you need to profile an application without installing Visual Studio on the machine — for example, in a production environment. To install this tool, you need to execute vs_profiler.exe from the Visual Studio installation media located in the Standalone Profiler folder. It will install the tools in the directory %ProgramFiles%\Microsoft Visual Studio 10.0\Team Tools\Performance Tools. If you are going to use the command-line profiler often, you could add this path to the system path.

The following commands profile an application using sampling with the default settings. The first line enables the trace. The next command switches the profiler to use CPU Sampling and to output a report. In this case the report will be saved in the ApplicationToProfile directory on a file named

`Report.vsp`. Then you launch the application, interact with it as usual, and when you are done you finally shut down the Profiler. You can then open and inspect the generated report in Visual Studio.

```
C:\ApplicationToProfile>vsperfclrenv /traceon
Enabling VSPerf Trace Profiling of managed applications (excluding allocation
profiling).
...
C:\ApplicationToProfile>vsperfcmd -start:sample -output:Report
Microsoft (R) VSPerf Command Version 10.0.30128 x86
...
C:\ApplicationToProfile>vsperfcmd -launch:Application.exe
Microsoft (R) VSPerf Command Version 10.0. 30128 x86
...
Successfully launched process ID:4144 Application.exe
C:\ApplicationToProfile>vsperfcmd -shutdown
Microsoft (R) VSPerf Command Version 10.0. 30128 x86
...
Shutting down the Profile Monitor
```

INTELLITRACE

IntelliTrace is a new tool in Visual Studio 2010 Ultimate that makes debugging your application a lot easier. It operates like a flight recorder while you are in a debug session and allows you to look back at historical values and state. In addition to this, you can save IntelliTrace sessions and load them back up at a later time. Testers who are using Microsoft Test and Lab Manager can also collect IntelliTrace information while they run through test cases, providing you with the exact state of the system when a bug is reported.

> *IntelliTrace currently supports C# and VB projects with experimental support for F#. You cannot use IntelliTrace by using the Attach To Process command or in remote debugging scenarios.*

When a debugging session is started and IntelliTrace is enabled (Tools ⇨ Options ⇨ IntelliTrace) the IntelliTrace window (Figure 55-6) is shown. This window maintains a list of diagnostic events that IntelliSense is able to detect.

As each new diagnostic event occurs, Visual Studio adds it to the end of the list. If you pause the execution or hit a breakpoint, the IntelliTrace window becomes active. If you click any of the diagnostic events, it expands to show a little more information. This expanded view contains a list of Related Views, which have been updated by IntelliTrace to reflect the state of the

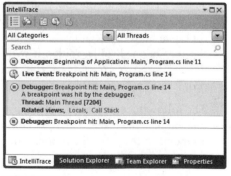

FIGURE 55-6

application at the time of the event. You can check the call-stack, add watches, check locals, and generally perform any of the tasks that you would normally be able to during a normal debugging session. When you are ready to resume execution of the application you can click the Return to Live Debugging button.

IntelliTrace is able capture two types of information during a debugging session. IntelliTrace Events are enabled by default and include Visual Studio debugger events such as application start and hitting breakpoints. Throwing and catching exceptions are also IntelliTrace events. When a tester is collecting IntelliTrace information, the beginning and end of a test along with any failures form contextual events that are covered under the label of IntelliTrace Events. Finally, the Framework itself is able to raise some diagnostic events. You can find a list of these in the IntelliTrace options.

The other type of information, that IntelliTrace can track is method calls along with parameter information. To use this information, you need to turn it on before starting the debugging session (Tools ⇨ Options ⇨ IntelliTrace). Once Call Information has been activated, you can switch the IntelliTrace window over to the Show Calls View (Figure 55-7), which shows each method call entry and exit along with a sublist of events that occurred during their execution.

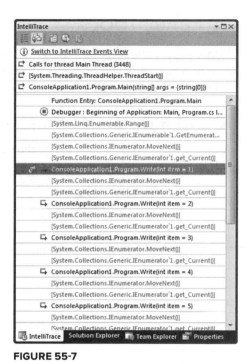

FIGURE 55-7

When you are in an IntelliTrace session with Call Information enabled, a new border is added to the editor window, which contains IntelliTrace navigational markers (Figure 55-8). You can use these to navigate the IntelliSense information from inside the editor. This border is a light grey during normal debugging, but turns a darker grey when IntelliSense is activated.

FIGURE 55-8

IntelliTrace files (.tdlog files) are stored in a default location on your hard drive and can be archived and re-opened later. When you open a .tdlog file you see the IntelliTrace Summary view. By double-clicking a thread or an exception, you can open the IntelliTrace session at the appropriate point and begin debugging again.

> *By default, IntelliTrace files are stored in the* `C:\ProgramData\Microsoft Visual Studio\10.0\TraceDebugging` *folder. You can always check where the files are stored from Tools ⇨ Options ⇨ IntelliTrace ⇨ Advanced.*

DATABASE TOOLS

Most applications require some kind of database to store data when it is not being used. Visual Studio 2010 Premium provides all of the capabilities that were previously introduced with the Database edition of VSTS and adds tools that were previously only available as Power Tools.

SQL-CLR Database Project

In the New Project dialog inside the Database node are two nodes for C# and VB SQL-CLR Database projects. These are used to create managed classes to use inside a SQL Server. When you create a new project of this type, you will be prompted for a connection and to enable CLR debugging. Use CLR debugging only on development database servers and isolated from other developers, as explained later in the "Best Practices" section.

You can add to this project some types like Aggregates, User-Defined Functions, Stored Procedures, Triggers, User-Defined Types, and Classes. You can think of this as a normal VB/C# project; you can add classes, references, and even web references. You can create unit tests for your methods as explained in Chapter 11, refactor your code, and build, in the same way you would for other library projects. However, the debugging history is a bit different, because your code is running in an SQL Server context. First you will need to allow VS to remote debug the code. This is needed only the first time you debug your project. However, the point of entry for your code will be through a script that will use any of your managed objects. As you may have noticed when you created the project, there's already a file named `Test.sql`, which is used to create and test your types.

The test scripts can grow quickly, and long script files are not easy to maintain. You can add new test scripts and right-click to set them as Default Debug Script. This is similar to the way you would set an ASP.NET page as the start page. You can set a breakpoint on the script or the classes you are testing and hit F5 (or from the menu Debug ➪ Start Debugging). This will build the project, drop the assembly from SQL Server in case it was previously deployed by Visual Studio, and then register the assembly again with SQL Server using the Create Assembly procedure. Finally, it will attach to the `SqlServr.exe` process to allow you to debug scripts and managed code. You can also create Database Unit Tests that use your SQL objects (including SQL-CLR types) as explained in the section on Database Unit Tests in Chapter 56.

Offline Database Schema

There's another type of Database Project and it's inside the Microsoft SQL Server node, as shown in Figure 55-9. As you can see, there are three options each for SQL Server 2005 and SQL Server 2008, but it's basically the same project type; the difference between them is the use of a wizard and the SQL Server version being targeted. Some options are available only from the creation of the project using the wizard, so I suggest you start using that. These projects will let you have an offline representation of your DB schema, so that you can version it along with your code. It will create a file for each schema object and deploy the changes to a database.

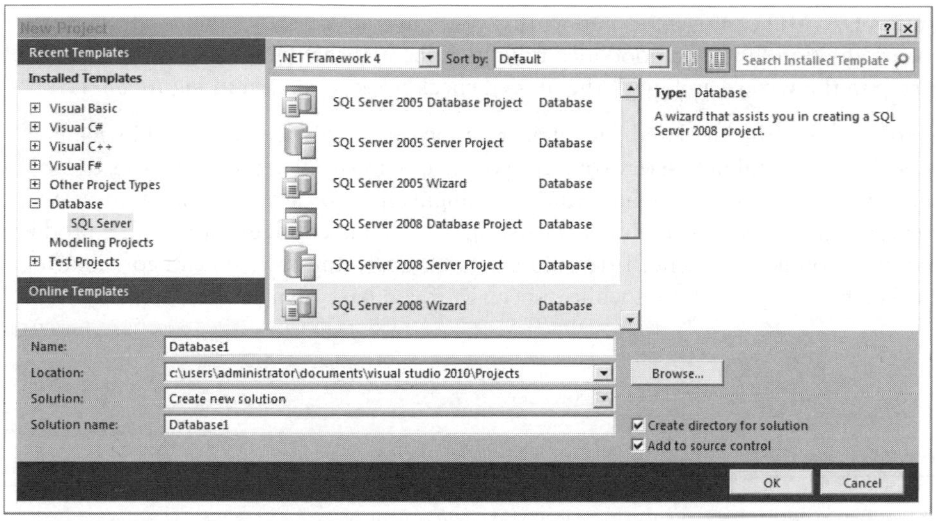

FIGURE 55-9

If you run the wizard for SQL Server 2008, the first option will let you choose whether your project will manage a single database or a SQL Server. This is the same as choosing either Database Project or Server Project in Figure 55-9. The other option on this page is to organize the files by schema or object type (tables, views, stored procedures, and so on). This is important because you can't change this option once the project is created, although you will find yourself working on the Schema View most of the time instead of doing it directly on the files — from that window you can select or deselect the filter by Schema View. However, if you select "No" to organizing by schema inside the types, you can still distinguish the schema because of the prefix added to each filename. On the other hand, if you select to organize by schema, inside of each you will have folders for each type. Figure 55-10 shows at the left the Schema View filtered by schema. You could change this option to organize all the objects by type. The Solution Explorer (at the right) shows two different projects where files are physically organized differently.

FIGURE 55-10

The database options are the next step of the wizard; if you don't know your defaults now, don't be afraid to choose something and change it once you get this information from either your DBA or your production DB. You can select to import this configuration directly from a DB. If you can connect to your production DB, it's a good idea to import them at this moment. To do this, simply go to the next step in the wizard and mark the needed checkboxes as shown in Figure 55-11.

The last step is to configure the build and deployment options. You will need more deployment configurations, so here you will only select your development database. Keep in mind this doesn't have to be the same as in the previous step — here you are configuring your development database and in the previous step, if available, you would import existing objects and configuration from a production DB. You see the three configurations needed in more detail later, so for now you can go with the default options. The final step will take a while, especially if you have many objects to import.

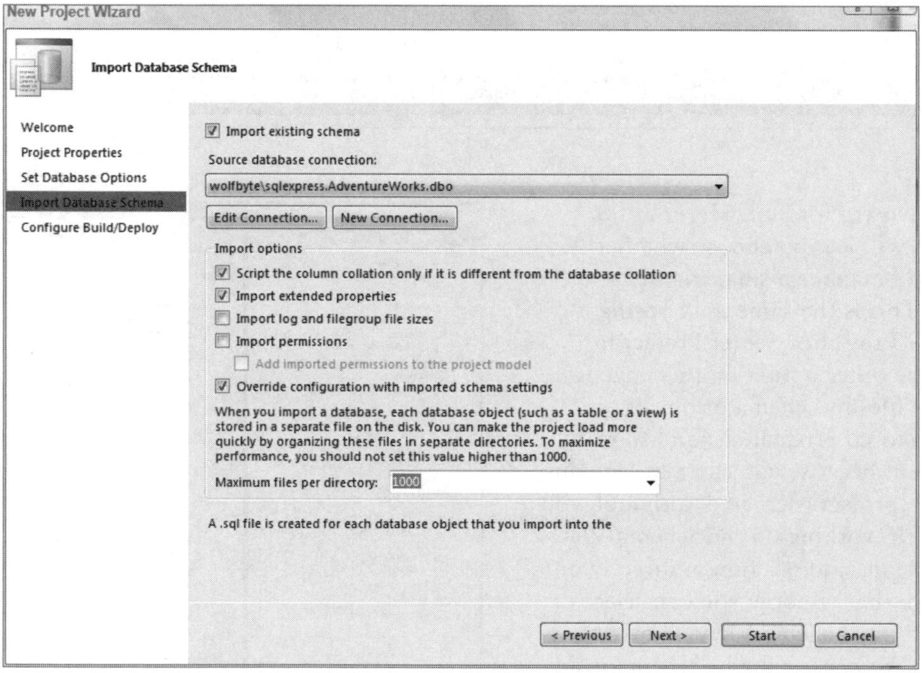

FIGURE 55-11

Once the wizard finishes, you can add, edit, or delete schema objects right from the Solution Explorer or the Schema View (View ➪ Schema View) — these will be represented as files. When you build the project, a `.sql` file containing all the DML necessary to re-create your schema will be generated and evaluated. The script can then be deployed to SQL Server. You could also choose to deploy on every build, so your DB will always get your last changes.

When working with Source Control, this type of project becomes really useful. The scenario would be that each developer works on his own server instance. One of them has made changes to the schema and his .NET code and deployed them to his instance. He then tests the .NET application and it works fine with the new database changes. Then he checks in all of his changes to the server and another developer retrieves the changes. When the second developer deploys his database instance it is also updated with the latest changes, and he will be running the new code changes along with the new schema changes applied to his SQL Server instance.

Data Generation

In addition to versioning the schema, you might want a way to generate data for testing purposes. To do this, you need to add a Data Generation Plan. If you right-click the Offline Schema project under the Add menu, you will find the option for Data Generation Plan. By default, all the tables on the schema will be selected, but you can override these settings. In the top section of Figure 55-12, only the Products table is checked. The ProductModel and ProductCategory tables are automatically added (darkened checkboxes) because of the foreign key between Products and those tables.

> *Keep in mind these generation plans are only for development and testing purposes. Don't run them on production servers.*

FIGURE 55-12

In the plan, you can select the ratio between Related Columns; for example, in Figure 55-12 we are specifying to have 10 products for each subcategory (10:1).

In the Column Details window, all columns are selected except for the ProductID, which is an identity column. You can deselect columns as long as they have either a Default value or allow nulls. In the properties window you can specify the percentage of nulls to be generated.

For each column, you can also specify the type of generator to use. By default a generator will be selected depending on the data type, or in case a column is a foreign key, the values will come from the related table's primary keys. You can use other generators. In the example in Figure 55-12, for the Name on the Products table we used a regular expression to mix first names and last names. Another option would be to use a Data Bound Generator. In that case, you would need to specify a connection string and a select query to get the values to insert. You could also create a Custom Generator and implement your own logic simply by implementing a base class and registering your assembly as a Customer Generator. For more information see "Creating Custom Generators" on MSDN.

To run the Data Generation Plan, simply select Generate Data from the Data ⇨ Data Generator menu. Remember to run this plan only on a development or testing database.

Database Refactoring

Chapter 8 introduced the topic of refactoring for normal .NET code. For databases you have only three refactoring tasks: Rename, Move Schema, and Fully-Qualify Names. You can rename tables, columns, stored procedures, constraints, and indexes, as well as other database objects. You can also rename the references to other servers or databases if a cross-database reference is used in the scripts.

To rename an object from the Schema View, right-click it and select Rename from the Refactor submenu. When renaming an object, you will see a preview of the changes as shown in Figure 55-13. In the upper pane you will see the old version, and in the lower pane you will see the new one for all the dependencies.

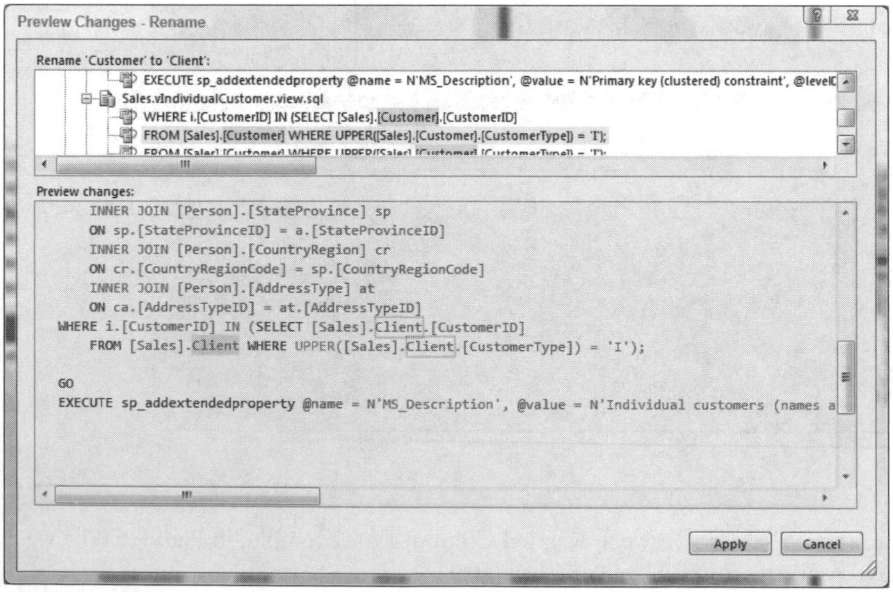

FIGURE 55-13

Renaming is easily done on an offline schema version, but for tables and columns it can be hard to deploy to the database. Because the old object will be dropped and re-created, this can result in data loss. If you have a Data Generation Plan, you can regenerate the data after the changes are deployed, but if you need to preserve your data you should either modify the deployment script or apply the refactoring manually. See "Protecting Data during a Renaming Operation" on MSDN for more information.

Schema Compare

This tool enables you to compare schemas between databases or Database Projects. To use it, select New Comparison from the Data ➪ Schema Compare menu. You will have to select a project or database as Source and a project or database as Target. When you do that, you will be presented with a window similar to the one shown in Figure 55-14. The lower pane will show both versions of the selected object with the changes highlighted. It's handy to use the filters from the toolbar; by default all objects will be shown. You should select Non Skip Objects to see only the differences.

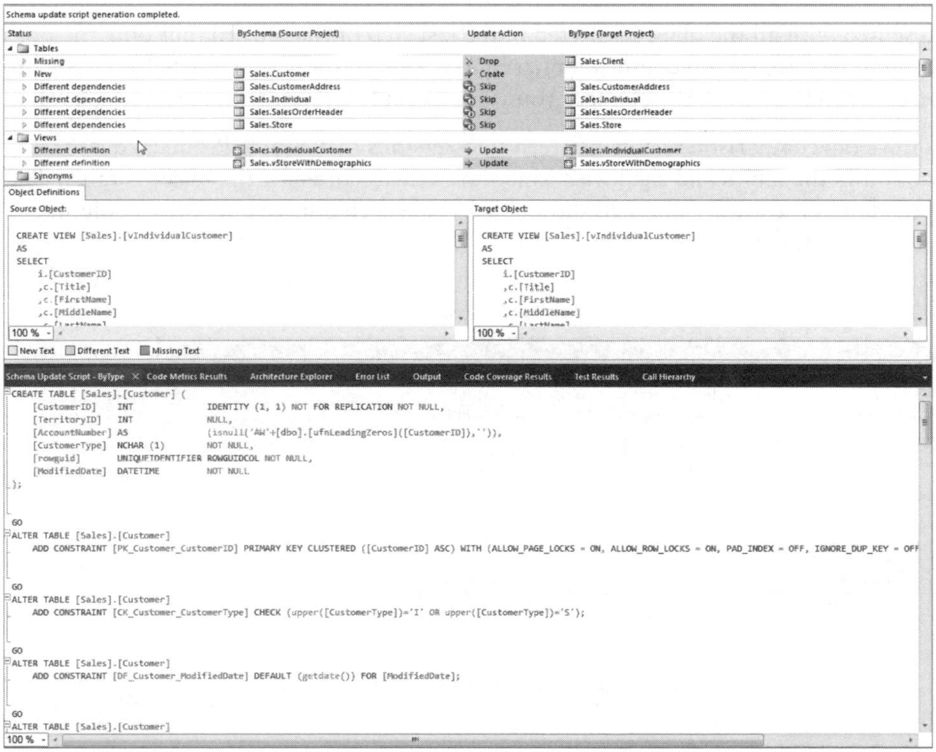

FIGURE 55-14

For each DB object, you can see the action that will be applied. Then from the toolbar you can either select Write Updates to apply all the changes or Export to Editor to get the SQL statements used for the update in case you need to do manual changes or hand it out to your DBA.

To customize the options for Schema Comparisons, go to Tools ➪ Options and to the Schema Compare node under Database Tools. By default, Block Schema Updates if Data Loss Might Occur is selected; this is recommended but can cause some updates to fail. You can uncheck this option, but be sure you're running on a test database and that you can regenerate the data. Other options such as Ignore White Space can be useful to reduce unnecessary changes.

Remember that if you are using a Database Project, the deploy option will write the changes from your Database Project to the database selected in the build option in the project's properties. This tool can be useful to see the changes or do manual tweaking.

Data Compare

This tool is useful for copying data from one database to another. Go to Data ➪ Data Compare ➪ New Data Comparison to start the wizard. You will need to select the Source and Target database and the records to compare. Depending on what you want to do, you can choose between the different Compare options, "Different Records" for updates, "Only in Source" for inserts, "Only in Target" for deletes, and Identical Records just as a reference. Finally, you can select which tables and columns to compare.

You will be presented with all the objects selected in the last step of the wizard, but only the objects with differences will be selected. I recommend filtering the view to show only the Selected Records. From there you can check/uncheck the changes you want to apply either at a table or row level.

Figure 55-15 shows the comparison results between two versions of a simple Products database. The upper pane shows the tables and the lower pane shows the records for the selected table. The Different Records tab in the lower pane will show side by side each Source and Target column, so you can see where the differences are.

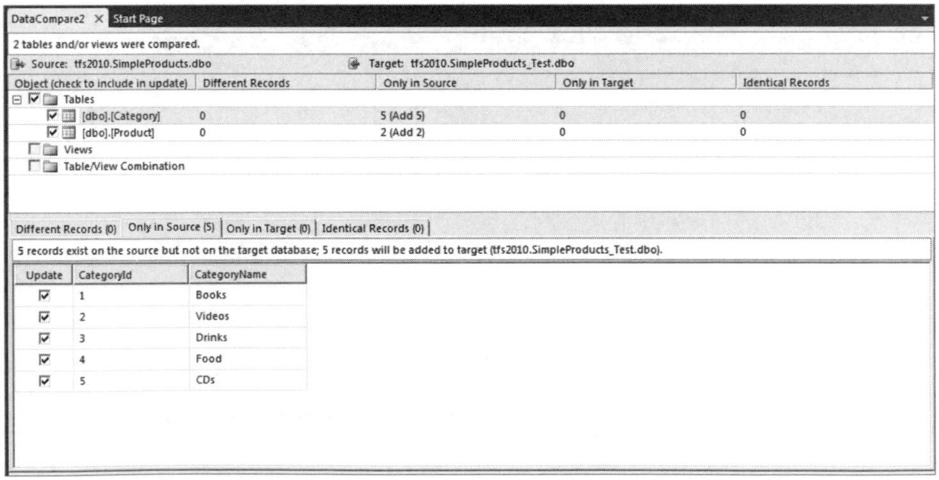

FIGURE 55-15

> *The Data Compare tool is only able to work with tables in the default schema of the database.*

From the toolbar you can select either Write Updates or Export to Editor to manually apply the changes.

Static Analysis

Visual Studio 2010 Premium and Ultimate include static analysis tools for databases as well as for code. To run the static analysis tools, select Data ➪ Static Analysis ➪ Run. Currently, 14 rules are spread across three categories to help you develop databases: Design, Naming, and Performance.

Transact-SQL Editor

This editor allows you to work with Transact-SQL (T-SQL) code directly in Visual Studio. To open it, you can double-click a `.sql` file in Solution Explorer or from the Schema View of a Database Project. Another option is to start with a blank editor — to do this go to Data ➪ Transact-SQL Editor and select New Query Connection. Now you can start to write your T-SQL, with nice coloring and most of Visual Studio's shortcuts and features like bookmarks and search and replace. From the toolbar or the T-SQL Editor menu, you can validate syntax, execute your code, include client statistics, disconnect to work offline, and reconnect once you need to run a query. When you run the queries, the results can be displayed on a grid or text format or be exported to a file. You can also change this behavior from the menu or toolbar.

Best Practices

The following is a list of best practices we compiled through our work with Database Professionals and which have worked for us on small and medium-sized projects:

➤ Each developer works with his own local SQL database instance, one for development and another for testing. This is necessary to isolate uncommitted and untested changes and avoid affecting other developers working on the database at the same time. It is strictly necessary for managed-code debugging purposes, because starting a debugging session will cause all managed threads to stop. From the project properties for Database Projects, you can specify the database to target for each Solution Configuration, but SQL-CLR projects can only target one database.

➤ Each developer works with two databases, one for development and one for unit testing because different data will be used for each.

➤ Use (local) or 127.0.0.1 for the hostname instead of, say, MikesComputer or 192.168.2.6, which would work only on one machine.

➤ If you are using database instances, be sure all your developers have an instance with the same name.

➤ All developers should have the same SQL Server version. Although SQL Server Express can be used for design-time validation and testing purposes, some features, like Text Indexing, are not supported.

➤ Clear the Block Incremental Deployment if Data Loss Might Occur checkbox in the project properties window for the Solution Configuration used for Test Databases. Because you will have a Data Generation Plan, data will be easy to re-create after changes have been made to the schema.

➤ When deploying to a production database, build the Database Project and then modify the build script to manually deploy it to the server. You can lean on the Schema Comparison tool to have a more granular view of the changes made.

SUMMARY

In this chapter, you saw a couple of advanced features that are part of Visual Studio 2010 Premium. All of these target quality improvement. Code Metrics and the Analysis Tool will analyze your code or binaries statically, collecting metrics and evaluating rules. The metrics will be useful to see how maintainable your code is. For the analysis, you have rules for different categories that will help you ensure that your code will perform well before it runs. On the other hand, the Profiling Tools will evaluate your code at run time and IntelliTrace lets you explore the execution of your application during a debugging session.

This chapter covered some of the most important features for database developers. You saw how easy it is to develop code for SQL-CLR and how the Offline Schema Projects will help you work on a team, versioning and merging your changes. Advanced features like refactoring and unit testing will change the way you develop databases, and tools like Schema Compare, Data Compare, Data Generation, and the T-SQL Editor will support the process as well.

56

Visual Studio Ultimate for Testers

WHAT'S IN THIS CHAPTER?

➤ Testing web and windows applications

➤ Identifying relationships between code and tests

➤ Planning, executing, and coordinating testing tasks

➤ Managing test environments

You can test an application in many ways. Chapter 11 introduced the concept of unit tests, which are small executable pieces of code that verify a particular aspect of behavior for a single method or class. The first part of this chapter examines the advanced tools built into Visual Studio that are available for other testing tasks, including testing web applications and databases. You also learn how to track the relationships between tests and code.

The 2010 release of Visual Studio also contains a new product called Test and Lab Manager. This tool is designed for testers to interact directly with Team Foundation Servers and manage test plans, suites, and cases. Test and Lab Manager is available with the Ultimate edition of Visual Studio and as a part of a separate pack called Test Elements.

AUTOMATED TESTS

An automated test is a piece of code that verifies the behavior of your application without any user input or control. Once the system has been asked to run an automated test, it can be left unattended until it has completed. To create a new automated test from Visual Studio

2010, use the Test ⇨ New Test menu option to display the Add New Test dialog shown in Figure 56-1.

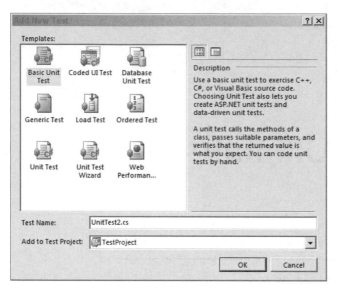

FIGURE 56-1

> Depending on which edition of Visual Studio you have, you might not have all of the tests shown in Figure 56-1. Coded UI Tests and Database Unit Tests are only available in the Premium and Ultimate editions. Web Tests and Load Tests are only available in the Ultimate edition. The rest of the automated tests are available in all three editions.

Web Performance Tests

This type of automated test simulates web requests and allows you to inspect the responses and evaluate different conditions to determine if the test passes. When you create a new Web Test, Internet Explorer opens with the Web Test Recorder enabled, as shown in Figure 56-2. Navigate to and around your site as if you were a normal user. Once done, simply click Stop. This opens the Web Test's designer shown in Figure 56-3. There you can customize your test, adding validation and extraction rules, context parameters, comments, data sources, and calls to other Web Tests, or inserting transactions. You can also specify response time goals for requests.

You will often need to run the same set of tests against different web servers; to do this you configure which server the test runs against as a context parameter. From the Web Test Designer you can right-click the main node and select Parameterize Web Servers. Visual Studio will inspect the URLs in each request and determine the context parameters it will need to create.

You can link your requests using the output from one of them as input for the next; to do this, you add extraction rules to a specific request. You can extract from fields, attributes, HTTP headers, hidden fields, and text, or even use regular expressions. The result of an extraction will set a context parameter, which can then be used, for example, as a form or query string parameter in further requests. You could add a product and then search for it using the ID in another request.

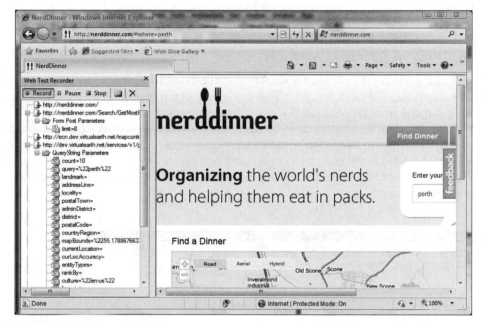

FIGURE 56-2

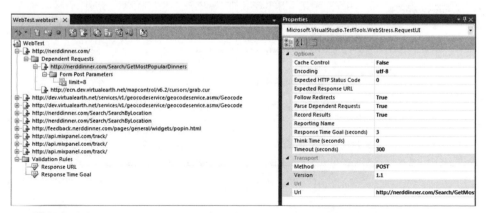

FIGURE 56-3

You can add form and query string parameters from the context menu of a request. By selecting a form or query string parameter from the properties window, you can set its value to a context parameter or bind it to a data source.

No test framework would be complete without validations. When you record a test, a Response URL Validation Rule is added asserting that the response URL is the same as the recorded response URL. This is not enough for most scenarios. From the context menu at a Web Test or request level, you can add validation rules. You can check that a form field or attribute has a certain value or that a particular tag is included, find some text, or ascertain that the request doesn't take more than a specified length of time.

Double-clicking the `.testrunconfig` file in Solution Explorer allows you to further customize how Web Tests are run. There you can choose the number of iterations, the browser and network type, and whether the test engine should simulate think times. You can have many Test Run Configurations and from the Test menu select the active one.

Web Tests, as well as any other type of test, are displayed in the Test List Editor window as you saw in Chapter 11. From there you can run your Web Test and group it inside a particular test list. You can also run it directly from the Web Test Designer. Once a test is run you can see its details by double-clicking it in the Test Results window. To open this window, select Test Results from the Test Windows menu. There you can see each request's status, total time, and bytes. When you select a request you will see the details of the selected request and received response, values of the context parameters, validations and extraction rules, and a web-browser-like view displaying the web page. An example is shown in Figure 56-4.

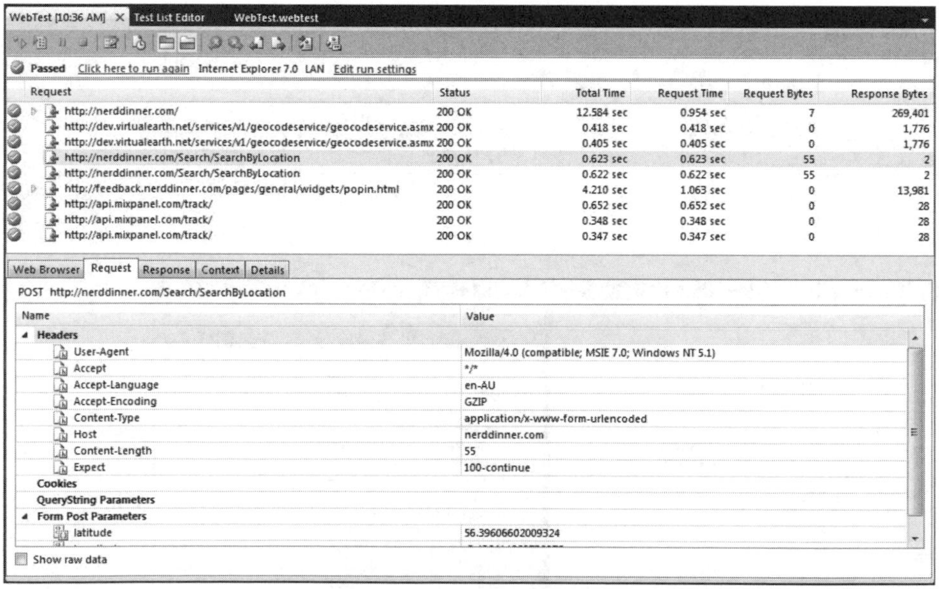

FIGURE 56-4

If you need additional flexibility, you can code the Web Tests using .NET and the Web Testing Framework. The best way to learn how to use the framework and start coding your test is by generating code for a recorded Web Test. You have this option in the Web Test context menu.

> *Although Visual Studio provides some ASP.NET-specific features, you can use Web Tests for sites built using other technologies.*

Load Tests

Whereas web and load testing are meant to test functional requirements, Load Tests will run a set of tests repeatedly so you can see how your application will perform. When you create a new Load Test, you are presented with a wizard that guides you through the necessary steps. First, you need to create a scenario; here you will define if you want to use think times. When you recorded the Web Tests, the time you took between each request was also recorded and can be used as the think time. It can be edited for each Web Test request in the properties window.

As part of the scenario, you will define the load pattern; for example, a constant load of 100 users or a load incrementing by 10 every 10 seconds until you get to 200 users. The next steps, Test, Browser, and Network Mix, define how tests will be run by virtual users, specify which browsers will be used to run the tests, and determine the kinds of network that will be simulated. In the Test Mix step you can add Generic, Ordered, and Web Tests.

In the Counter Sets step, you add the computers that you want to monitor and the performance counters you are interested in. For example, you can monitor your Database Server and IIS. In the last step, Run Settings, you can specify the test duration or test iterations, how often samples will be taken for performance counters, a test description, how many identical errors will be recorded, and the validation level. We defined a validation level for each Validation Rule in our Web Tests. Because evaluation of these rules can be expensive, in Load Tests only rules with a level equal to or below the specified validation level will be evaluated.

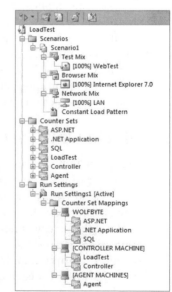

When you click Finish, you are presented with the Load Test Designer as shown in Figure 56-5. There you can add additional scenarios, counter sets, or new run settings.

When you run the tests, you will see the Load Test Monitor; by default it will show the Graphs view. In the left-side pane you have a tree view of the counters that are being collected. You can select items there to add them to the graphics. From the toolbar, you can change to Summary or Tables view, export to Excel or CSV, and add analysis notes. In the Graphs view at the bottom, you will have a legends pane as shown in Figure 56-6. There you can select/deselect the counters that you want to include in the graphs. While the test is running, the monitor is updated on each sample interval. In the Tables view, you can see the Requests, Errors, Pages, SQL Trace, Tests, Thresholds, and Transactions.

FIGURE 56-5

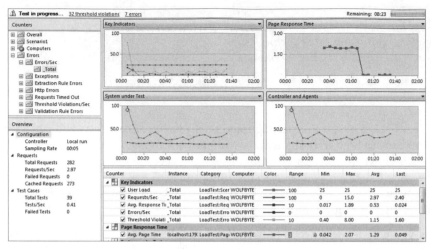

FIGURE 56-6

Thresholds are particularly important. These are values for each performance counter that will allow you to spot problems. In the graphs, you can see points where violations occurred marked with a warning or error icon.

Test Load Agent

For large-scale applications, one computer might not be enough to simulate the desired load. Visual Studio Team System 2010 Test Load Agent can distribute the work across different machines. It can simulate approximately 1,000 users per processor. This product requires a separate installation and requires one controller and at least one agent. To configure the environment, select Administer Test Controller from the Test menu. There you can select a controller and add agents. Then, from the Test Run Configuration window in the Controller and Agent node you can select to run the tests remotely and select the configured controller.

Database Unit Test

You already looked at unit testing in Chapter 11; this section expands the topic to databases. This kind of test is useful to verify the functionality and design of your schema objects and can work hand-in-hand with your Data Generation Plans and Schema Database Projects. To create a new Database Unit Test, from the Tests menu select New Test and choose the template for Database Unit Test, then create a new project if needed. For the first DB Unit Test in the project you will be prompted for a database to run the tests against. You can change this later from the Database Test Configuration option under the Test menu. It's highly recommended to have a dedicated database for test purposes for each developer. You can also select to deploy the project before running the tests. This will guarantee you are always running the tests against the latest version of the schema. Finally, you can select to use a Data Generation Plan to re-create the data for the unit tests.

To create and edit the tests, you have a designer (Figure 56-7). From there you can select the different test methods or create new ones and add new test conditions. The conditions available are Empty ResultSet, Execution Time, Inconclusive, Not Empty ResultSet, Row Count, and Scalar Value. When selected, you can configure them from the properties windows — for example, to set the value for the row count. You can also create your own test conditions. The Data Checksum and Expected Schema test conditions that were previously released as a part of the Power Tools pack are now also available by default.

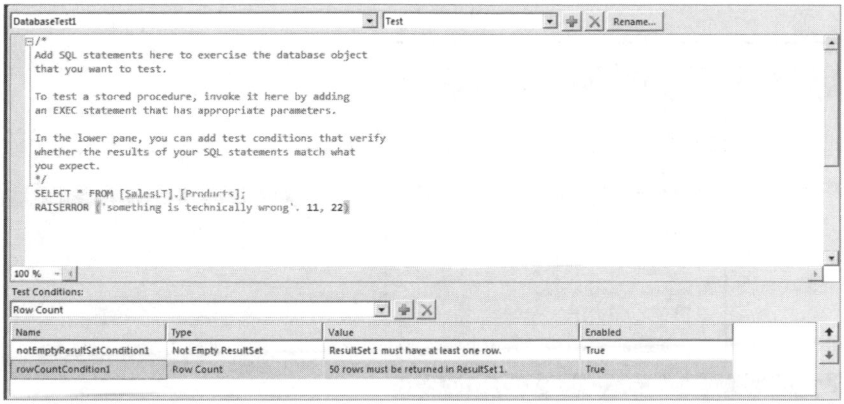

FIGURE 56-7

You have two other ways to verify your tests. One is by raising errors from your T-SQL code. The RAISERROR function will take an error message (this will be displayed on the Test Results window in case of failure), error severity, and error state. If error severity is above 10, it will cause the unit test to fail.

The other way to verify tests is from your C# or VB.NET script. If you right-click your test and select View Code, you will see it's structured as a regular unit test as explained in Chapter 11 and simply has methods that call SQL scripts. When you execute a script, you will get back in your .NET code an ExecutionResult array; each ExecutionResult object will contain a DataSet, number of rows affected, and the Execution Time. Using those properties you can make your assertions. The Execute method of the TestService also takes SqlParameters that could be passed to your script and can be returned to your C# code for further verification.

Coded UI Test

Sometimes the best way to test an application is to drive it from the outside as a user would.

When you create a new Coded UI Test, it starts the Coded UI Test Builder (Figure 56-8). Once you click the Start Recording button, the Coded UI Test Builder tracks all of the actions that you take with the mouse and keyboard.

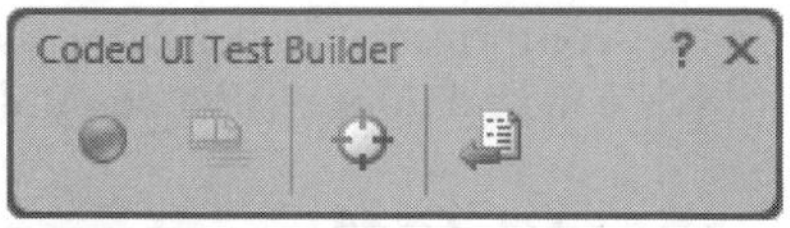

FIGURE 56-8

Open your application and use it to get into the state that you'd like to test, then click the Generate Code button. This prompts you to name your recorded method, which will be saved in the test project as a part of the UI Map. This map is a description of actions and assertions that you can use to automate and test your application.

> *Each test project contains a single UI Map, which all of the Coded UI Tests share.*

Once your application is in the desired state you can create assertions about different parts of the user interface. To do this, drag the cross-hair icon from the Coded UI Test Builder over the part of the UI that you want to make an assertion about. When you release the mouse button, the Add Assertions dialog is displayed as in Figure 56-9.

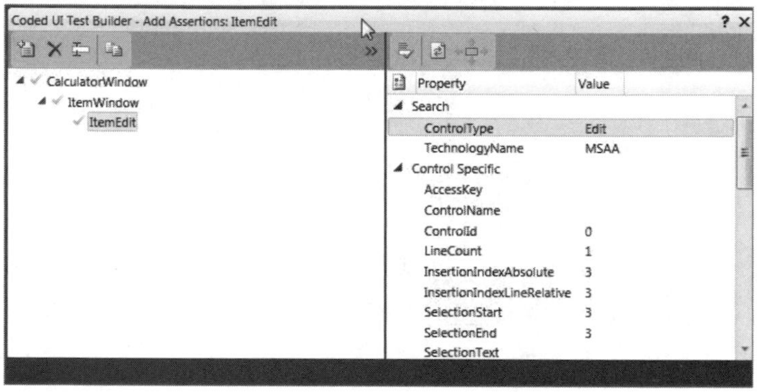

FIGURE 56-9

On the left is a collapsible panel showing the UI control map, which displays the hierarchy of all controls that have been identified so far. On the right is a list of properties that the Coded UI Test Builder has been able to identify along with their values. To make an assertion about one of these properties, you can right-click it and select Add Assertion. Each assertion has a comparator and a comparison value to be tested against.

Generic Tests

Not every kind of test is covered in Team System. This is why Microsoft included the concept of Generic Tests so that you can easily use custom tests, but still be able to use the rest of the features like Test Results, Test List, Assign Work Items, and Publish Test Results.

To configure a Generic Test, you need to specify an existing program and optionally specify its command-line arguments, additional files to deploy, and environment variables. The external application can communicate the test result back to Team System in two ways. One is with the Error Level, where a value of 0 indicates success and anything else is considered a failure. The other is to return an XML file that conforms to the SummaryResult.xsd schema located in Visual Studio's installation path. In MSDN you can find information about this schema and how to report detailed errors using XML.

Ordered Test

Ordered Tests are used when you need to group tests and run them as a whole, or if tests have dependencies on each other and need to be run in a particular order. It's a good practice to create atomic Unit Tests to be able to run them in isolation with repeatable results. I don't recommend using Ordered Tests just to deal with dependencies between Unit Tests. A good reason for creating Ordered Tests could be to create a performance session for more than one test.

In the Ordered Test Editor you will have a list of the available tests that you can add to the Ordered Test — the same test can be added more than once. You can also choose to continue after a failure. When the test is run, it executes each of the selected tests in the specified order.

RELATING CODE AND TESTS

Tests and code are heavily interconnected. Tests have no reason to exist without the code that they verify and code that is not verified by tests is potentially incorrect. Visual Studio contains two tools designed to make the link between tests and code more explicit. Code Coverage is able to determine which areas of your code are executed during a test run, which tells you if you need to add more tests to your solution. Test Impact Analysis enables you to determine which tests need to be re-run based on the areas of code that you have modified.

> *Both Code Coverage and Test Impact Analysis are available only for the Premium and Ultimate editions of Visual Studio 2010.*

Code Coverage

This is a very useful tool. It will instrument the code being tested to help you see which lines of code are really being executed. First, you need to have a Test Project on your solution. To demonstrate this, you can refer to the example described under "Your First Test Case" in Chapter 11. Assuming you have already created the `SubscriptionTest` class and `CurrentStatusTest` is passing, you will now activate Code Coverage.

To open the Test Run properties window, you can double-click the `Local.testsettings` file in Solution Explorer or go to the menu Test ➪ Edit Test Run Configurations and select your active configuration. The settings for Code Coverage (Figure 56-10) are located under the Data and Diagnostics page.

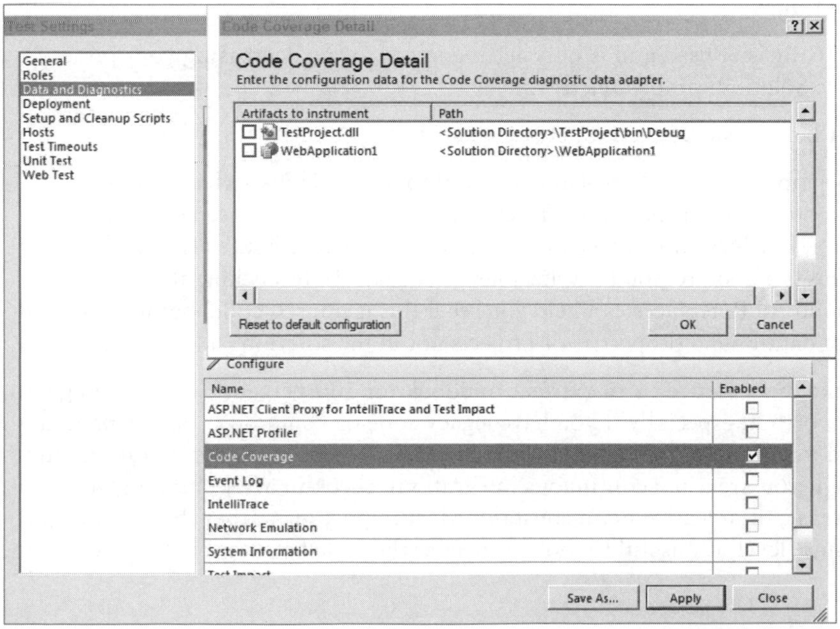

FIGURE 56-10

You need to select the assemblies to instrument. In case you are signing your assemblies, similar to the procedure when you are profiling using instrumentation, you need to resign them.

Now, simply run your test and from the Test Results window right-click it and select Code Coverage. Figure 56-11 shows the Code Coverage window, indicating the not-covered and covered blocks for each assembly, namespace, type, and member. Double-clicking a member opens the code file with the executed lines highlighted in blue (light shading in the figure) and untouched lines in red (darker shading in the figure) as shown in Figure 56-12.

Code Coverage Results				
Administrator@TFS2010 2010-02-22 01:53:52 ▾				
Hierarchy	Not Covered (Blocks)	Not Covered (% Blocks)	Covered (Blocks)	Covered (% Blocks)
⊟ 🗋 Administrator@TFS2010 2010-02-22 01:53:52	14	73.68 %	5	26.32 %
⊟ 🗋 Store.dll	14	73.68 %	5	26.32 %
⊟ { } Store	14	73.68 %	5	26.32 %
⊟ 🗋 Subscription	14	73.68 %	5	26.32 %
≡ get_CurrentStatus()	14	73.68 %	5	26.32 %

FIGURE 56-11

As you can see in Figure 56-11, the `get_CurrentStatus()` has 73.68 percent in not-covered blocks. The first option is evaluated and returned, so the remaining branches are never being touched. This is an indication that you will need additional test cases. This was covered in the "Data" section in Chapter 11, where you specify a DataSource with the additional input.

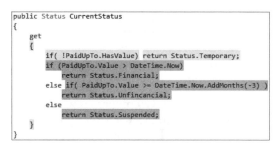

```
public Status CurrentStatus
{
    get
    {
        if( !PaidUpTo.HasValue) return Status.Temporary;
        if (PaidUpTo.Value > DateTime.Now)
            return Status.Financial;
        else if( PaidUpTo.Value >= DateTime.Now.AddMonths(-3) )
            return Status.Unfincancial;
        else
            return Status.Suspended;
    }
}
```

FIGURE 56-12

When you have code that is never touched, this can lead you to think three things:

➤ It is code that really isn't used and is only getting in your way, decreasing your project's maintainability. Solution: simply delete it.

➤ That code isn't being tested. Solution: create a new test.

➤ The code is so simple that there's probably no need to test it. Think twice about this, even for simple properties or methods. The code is likely to be referenced elsewhere in your application, in which case any errors in the code may cause issues elsewhere in your application. This is a good reason to write a new test case. Right-clicking the member and selecting Find All References can help you see if this is unused code, but it won't find references from data-bound properties or projects not in the solution.

It's not necessary to take this practice to an extreme and look for 100 percent Code Coverage. In many projects it's not worth it, especially if you have legacy code or you didn't start using unit testing. What you need to keep in mind is not to let your code coverage go down. Iteration after iteration, or better yet (if you are using continuous integration), check-in after check-in, your percentage should increase, or at least remain constant. Most important, rather than looking at the numbers at a test suite level, it's useful to look at them at the code level to see if you're missing critical test cases.

Test Impact Analysis

It is a good idea to run all of your unit tests fairly regularly as you develop new features and fix bugs to ensure you have not broken anything. Having said that, not every test needs to be re-run each time you make a change to the code. Once it has been enabled, Test Impact Analysis is able to determine which tests will be affected by changes in your code base. The Test Impact View (Figure 56-13) is split into two sections. The top section shows the list of tests that need to be re-run based on the changes you have made to the source code. When you select a test (or tests) in the top section, the bottom section shows the method or methods that have changed.

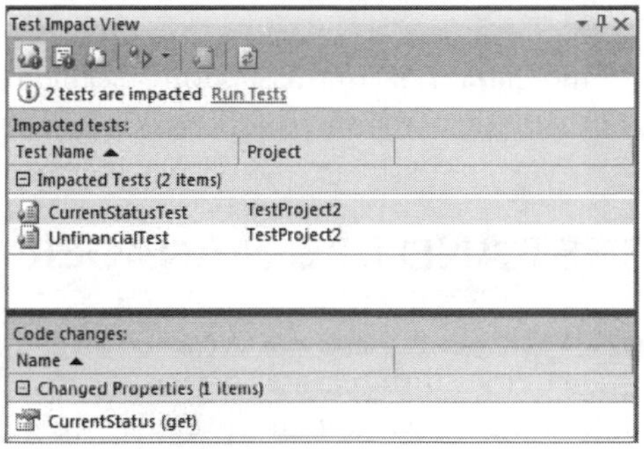

FIGURE 56-13

Test impact data is not kept up to date with every change that you make, because this would be too much of a performance drain on your development environment. This data is instead refreshed every time you build your solution and when you run tests. When test impact data is out of date, a refresh button becomes available on the Test Impact View.

> *The Test Impact View has a run button that allows you to run all of the impacted tests.*

VISUAL STUDIO TEST MANAGEMENT

The easiest way to manage your tests in Visual Studio is through the Test List Editor explained in Chapter 11. There you can add the tests to lists, select the tests or lists to run, sort, group, filter, and enable or disable them. To display the Test List Editor, select it from the Test Windows menu.

Another option is to use the Test View window, which is simpler than the Test List Editor. From there you can also run tests and filter tests, but can't group them in test lists.

When you run a set of tests you are presented with the Test Results window. In case it doesn't appear automatically, you can open it from the Test ⇨ Windows menu. There you can sort the tests and results and see error messages. You can select what tests to re-run; by default failing, inconclusive, and not-executed tests will be checked, and passed tests will be unchecked. Because the list of results can be big, you can use sorting, filtering, and grouping, or even change the view to display a left pane with the Test Lists and use the same organization defined in the Test List Editor.

From the Test Results window, you can export the Test Result to save a .trx file containing all the details and a folder with the test output. You can simply send the files to someone else who can import them from the Test Results window by selecting the .trx file. This person can see the same results the tester saw and even rerun the tests to reproduce the error on his or her machine. The latter is possible because the binaries are included with every test output.

Instead of passing Test Result files from one computer to another, it would be better to publish them to Team Foundation Server. This option is available in the Test Results window's toolbar. You will be prompted to select a team project. The team project must have a build configured, as you will see in Chapter 57 in the section "Team Foundation Build." The benefit of publishing, besides making the data available to other people, is that the data can also be used for reports.

TEST AND LAB MANAGER

Test and Lab Manager (Figure 56-14) is a new tool for you to plan, execute, and track your testing activities. It integrates directly with a Team Foundation Server and enables you to create, update, and query work items directly.

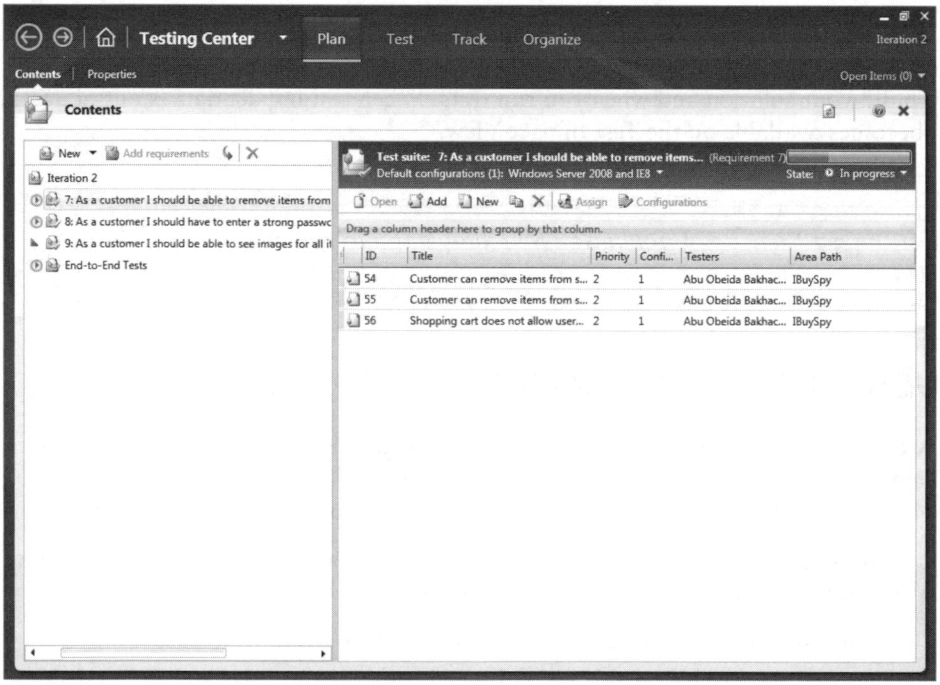

FIGURE 56-14

There are two UIs for Test and Lab Manager. When you first open the application it will look like Figure 56-14. This is the Testing Center. It has four tabs along the top that relate to the basic types of activities that the Testing Center provides for creating and running suites of tests.

Testing Center

When you first start Testing Center you are asked to create a new plan. All tests in Testing Center are organized into test plans and it is recommended that you create a test plan for each releasable version of your application. Once you have a test plan you will see the Contents View, which is shown in Figure 56-14. From here you can create new tests, add existing tests, and assign testers and configurations to your tests.

> Each plan has a state, which can be In Planning, In Progress, or Complete. This information is stored in the Team Foundation Server and can be surfaced in reports. When a plan is in progress, a percentage of how many of the planned test cases are complete is also available.

If you open an existing test case or create a new one you will see the Test Case window shown in Figure 56-15. Each test case is made up of a number of actions, which are shown toward the bottom of the window. Each action comes with a description of what the tester should do, along with a description of how to verify that the action has completed successfully.

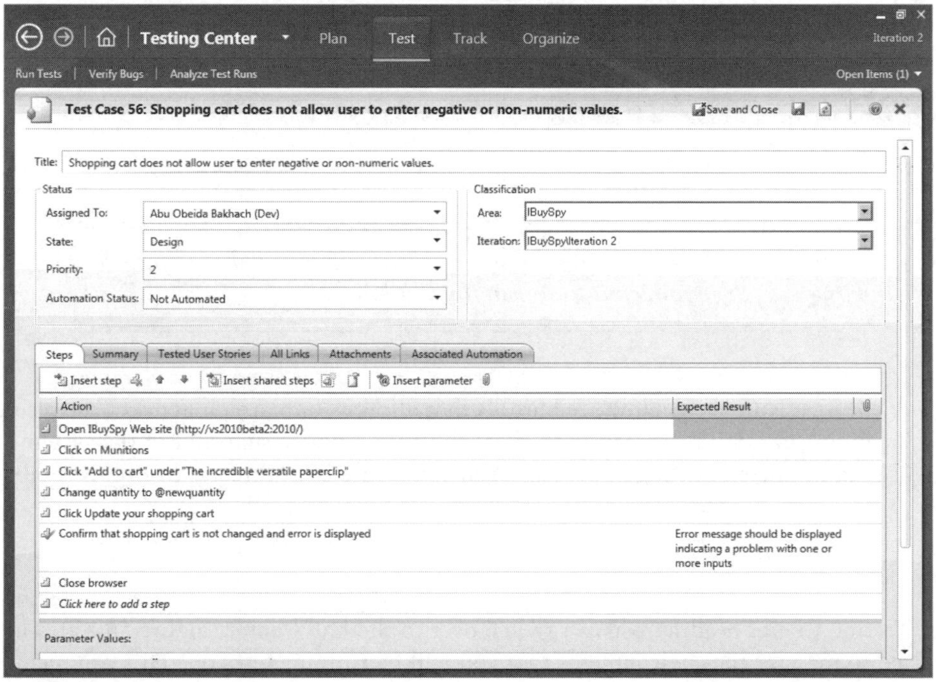

FIGURE 56-15

Actions can have parameters like the one in the fourth step of Figure 56-16. Each parameter can have multiple values defined, and there will be one iteration of the test for each value.

To run a test case, select it on the Test tab and click the Run button. This opens the Test Runner window (Figure 56-16). This window shows a list of steps and marks the progress of the tester. As you complete each step, you can mark it as passed or failed.

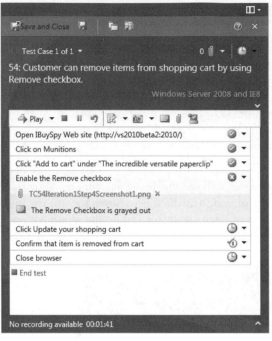

FIGURE 56-16

You can record the steps of a manual test as you go through, which allows you to automate the process when you want to re-run the test later.

On the toolbar of the Test Runner window are buttons that allow you to attach items to the results of this test run, including comments, screenshots, files, and even a whole snapshot of the system that developers can use later to help in debugging issues. You can create bugs directly from this toolbar as well.

Lab Center

If you click the Testing Center heading you can switch over to the Lab Center (Figure 56-17). The Lab Center is used to manage the environments that you will be running tests on. This can include information on physical and virtual environments.

To use the features of Lab Center, you need to install a Test Controller and associate it with a project collection in your Team Foundation Server. Once your Test Controller is available, you are able to use the Lab Center to maintain a collection of Physical Machines, Virtual Machines and Virtual Machine Templates. When a tester starts up a test he will be connected to one of these machines and if he spots an error he can take a system snapshot, which will be attached to the bug report. When a developer retrieves the bug, he can reconnect to the test machine and have it be put back into this state by the test controller.

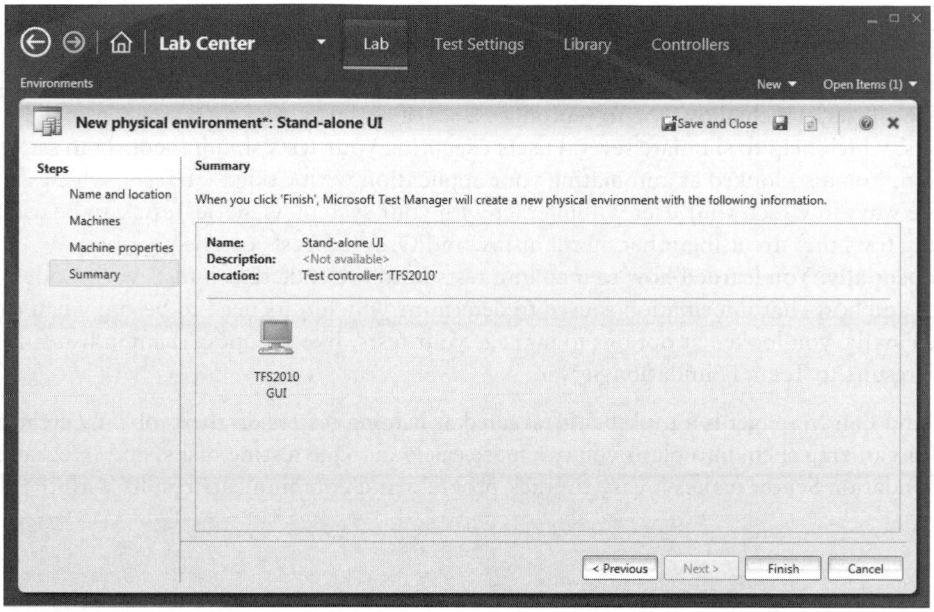

FIGURE 56-17

To configure the data that is collected on each machine in the environment, use the Data and Diagnostics page on the Test Settings tab (Figure 56-18). You can collect many different kinds of data, from mouse clicks and keyboard strokes to full video of the desktop during the test.

FIGURE 56-18

SUMMARY

In this chapter you saw the different types of automated tests included in Visual Studio 2010. You started with Web Tests, which allow you to reproduce a set of requests, and then you continued with Load Tests, which help to simulate several users executing your tests simultaneously to stress your application. You also looked at automating your application with Coded UI Tests, which helps to test the ways in which your user will interact with your system. Generic Tests can be used to wrap existing tests that are using other mechanisms, and Ordered Tests can help you run a set of tests sequentially. You learned how to map unit tests onto the code that it tests with Code Coverage tools and how that information is used to determine which tests need to be run when the code changes. Finally, you looked at options to manage your tests, like grouping them in lists and publishing the results to Team Foundation Server.

The new Test and Lab Manager is a tool that is targeted at helping testers do their jobs. By creating test cases and organizing them into plans you can more easily manage testing tasks, and integration with Team Foundation Server makes it easy to track progress and communicate results with the rest of the team.

57

Team Foundation Server

WHAT'S IN THIS CHAPTER?

➤ Managing project tasks

➤ Visualizing source code repository changes

➤ Creating build configurations

➤ Reporting progress

➤ Customizing process templates

Software projects are notoriously difficult; very few are delivered successfully on time, within budget, and up to the desired quality levels. As software projects get larger and require larger teams, the processes involved in managing them gets even more complicated, and not just for the manager, but for the developers, the testers, the architects, and the customer. Over time there have been many approaches to solving software project management problems, including quality models like CMMI, methodologies such as RUP, or Agile Practices, Scrum, and Continuous Integration. Clearly a tool to help support all the pieces necessary to ensure more successful software projects should be desired.

The most basic requirement for a software project, even for the smallest one-person project, is to have a source control repository. For bigger ones more sophisticated features are needed, such as labeling, shelving, branching, and merging. Project activities need to be created, prioritized, assigned, and tracked, and at the end of the day (or better yet even before every change is checked in to your repository) you need to ensure that everything builds and all tests are passing. To make this process smoother and improve team communication, a way to report to project managers or peer developers is also required.

Team Foundation Server (TFS) 2010 allows you to do all this. In this chapter you see how version control works, how it integrates with work item tracking, and how each change can be checked to ensure it is working before it is checked in. You also see how project managers can see reports to get a better understanding of the project status and how they can work using Excel and Project to assign work items. The team can interact using the project's portal in SharePoint and different stakeholders can get the information they need through the report server or configure it to get their reports directly by e-mail.

> TFS 2010 has a few new features that make it easier to get up and running, including reduced requirements and streamlined installation. You can even install it on a client operating system like Windows 7.

TEAM PROJECT

To begin working with TFS you need to create a *team project*. A team project contains all of the information about your project, including source code, tasks that need to be performed, instructions for building your application, documentation, quality metrics, and planning information. Each team project can also have its own SharePoint collaboration portal.

In Visual Studio 2010, team projects are grouped together under *team project collections*. All of the projects with a team project collection share basic infrastructure such as a data warehouse, a work item schema, and a pool of IDs (for work items and changeset numbers). If you have logical groups of projects within your enterprise, it is a good idea to create a team project collection for each one.

> You cannot back up and restore individual projects. This can only be done at the project collection level.

PROCESS TEMPLATES

When you create a new team project, you need to select the *process template*, which defines the way in which you intend to use the tool. Select the one that better suits your organization's process or methodology. Out of the box, Team Foundation Server comes with two templates, both based on the Microsoft Solution Framework. One flavor is for Agile Development and the other is for CMMI Process Improvement. Both options are great as starting points, but if your company has a defined process it can be incorporated into TFS or you can use a third-party process template. Figure 57-1 shows the process template selection process. The rest of this chapter uses MSF for Agile Software Development and refers to the CMMI version when necessary.

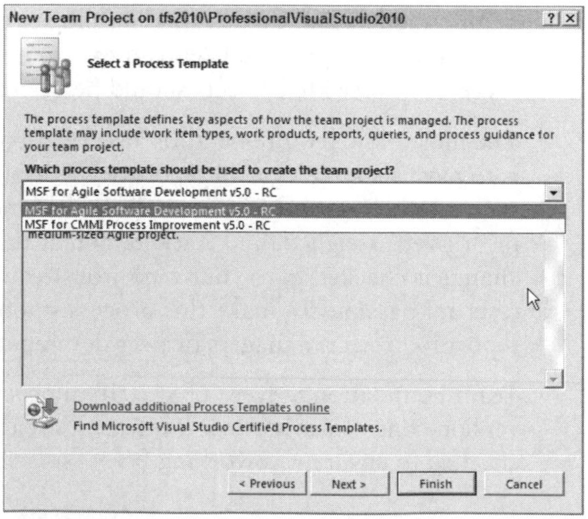

FIGURE 57-1

A process template creates the environment for the team project. This usually consists of defining work item types (as you see in the section titled "Work Item Tracking"), creating default groups and permissions, preparing a version control repository, and configuring reports and a custom SharePoint portal with document structure and process guidance. A different process could omit some of these or add custom tasks.

When the wizard finishes it opens the Guidance Page, which details the process used, defines the responsibilities of the roles involved, explains the different types of work items, and provides step-by-step guidance about specific tasks like "How to create a Vision Statement." Figure 57-2 shows the Project Guidance and the Team Explorer windows.

You navigate to the different features of TFS through the Team Explorer tool window. It has Work Item Queries, a convenient way to access the documents stored in the Team Portal, links to Reports, a list of the Team Builds, and the Source Control node.

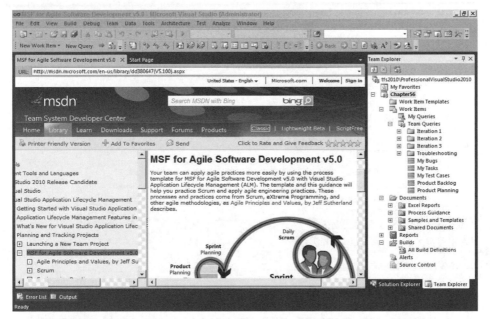

FIGURE 57-2

WORK ITEM TRACKING

Team Foundation Server allows you to manage activities using *work items*. As you see in the following sections, you can search for work items using *work item queries* and you manage them using Visual Studio, Excel, Project, or Team System Web Access. Different types of work items are defined by your process template.

> One of the most requested features leading up to TFS 2010 was hierarchical work items. TFS now provides this capability, so you can create sub-tasks and parent tasks. You can also create predecessor and successor links between work items, which enables you to manage task dependencies. These new work item links will even synchronize with Microsoft Excel and Microsoft Project providing even greater flexibility for managing work items.

Work Item Queries

The work items shown in Figure 57-3 are all tasks in the selected team project. You can look for different work items using the work item queries from Team Explorer. The template process includes 14 team queries (Figure 57-2) such as Active Bugs, Open Issues, or My Work Items.

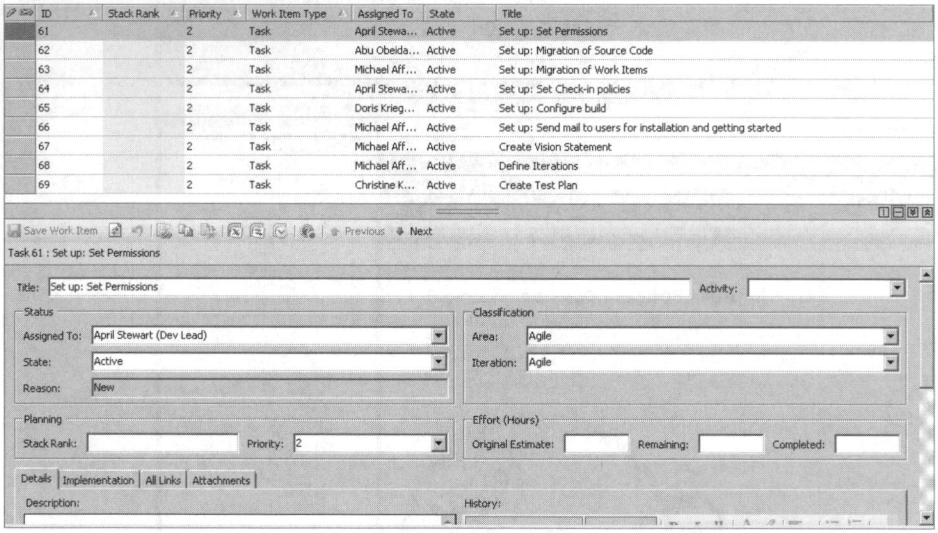

FIGURE 57-3

> There is a folder of queries called Workbook Queries, which are used to support some of the Excel workbook reports found in the Documents area.

Most of the time those queries will be enough, but you have the option to create new ones. If you're a project administrator you can add new team queries to make them available to everyone with access to this project. If you can modify the process template, you can add new team queries, so projects created with the edited templates will include them. Changes in the templates don't apply to team projects already created. If you don't have these permissions or you want to create a personal query, you can do that, too.

> *When you notice you are creating the same queries over and over from one project to another, you should add those to your process templates. Over time, there will be less need to create custom queries.*

To create a new query, right-click the My Queries node and select New Query (Figure 57-4).

Now you can visually design your query. In this case you only care about the work items of the selected project, assigned to the current user and under Iteration 1. You specify this using the @me and @Project variables. You can also specify which columns you want visible in the grid and sorting options (Figure 57-5). You can then run the new query to see a sub-list of the work items.

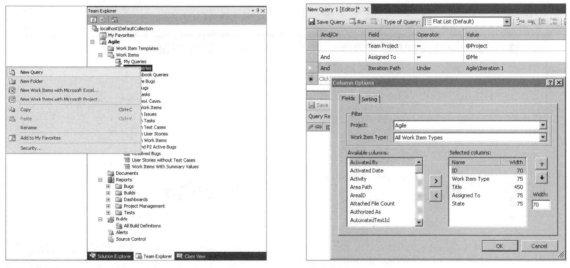

FIGURE 57-4   **FIGURE 57-5**

In Team Foundation Server 2010, queries can take advantage of the new hierarchical work item structure to show work items that are directly related, allowing you to see the impact of cutting a feature or the required tasks necessary to complete a feature. You can also show query results in a flat list, a list of work items and their direct links, or a tree of work items. Each of these is identified by a small icon that appears next to the query in the Team Explorer. You can create folder structures for your work item queries and each query or folder can be secured separately.

> *Although a folder of work item queries can be secured, there is nothing stopping unauthorized users from duplicating the queries for themselves.*

Work Item Types

In MSF for Agile Development you have six types of work items: bugs, issues, shared steps, tasks, test cases, and user stories. Each work item has different fields depending on its type. For example, a bug will have test information and a system info field, whereas a task contains effort information about estimated, remaining, and completed hours. Contrasting it with the MSF for CMMI template, you have a change-request work item, which doesn't exist in the Agile version. CMMI also has a bug work item, but in this case it is not so simple; it now requires repro steps and has other fields such as severity, priority, probability, and estimate. All these fields are customizable either at a template or team-project level.

Adding Work Items

The basic way of adding work items is via the Team ➪ Create Work Item menu option and selecting the work item type you want to add. Another convenient way to add work items is through the Test Results window (Figure 57-6).

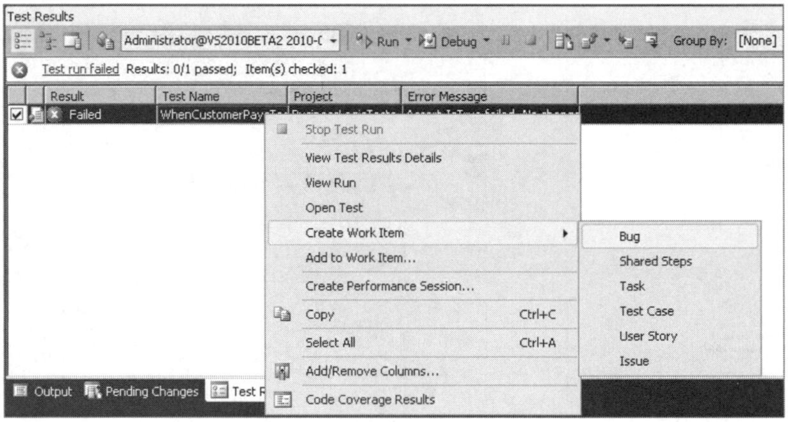

FIGURE 57-6

When you do it this way you will usually create a bug and also create a link between it and the selected test. You can navigate from the bug to the test or see the test and its related work items (Figure 57-7). If the test fails again, you

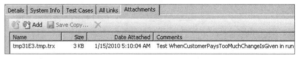

FIGURE 57-7

can see the work items associated with it and track it back to their related change sets, as you will see later in the "Version Control" section. Visual Studio 2010 is able to associate IntelliTrace information with the work item; that way the developer assigned to correct the bug can easily reproduce it.

Each work item can be related to many others with links. Team Foundation Server 2010 understands several different types of links, including Parent, Child, Predecessor, and Successor. To add a link, click the All Links tab and click the Link To button. You can also create a new work item directly linked to the current one with the New Linked Work Item button.

Work Item State

During your normal daily activity, you will be working on tasks that are described by work items that are assigned to you. Each work item is described by a simple state machine that determines the allowed new states for any given state. This state machine is a part of the work item definition and is decided by the process template. Whenever a new state is selected you can provide a reason for the state transition. For example, the Bug work item in MSF for Agile can go from Active to Resolved to Closed. It can then go back to Active again with a reason of Regression or Reactivated. The reason field allows you to differentiate between the bugs that are active because they are new and those that are active because they have re-occurred.

EXCEL AND PROJECT INTEGRATION

Looking at, adding, or editing work items can get a bit complicated and won't scale well when you have hundreds of tasks. This can be problematic especially for project managers who are not used to working inside Visual Studio. They usually prefer to work from Excel or Project. This integration is really easy using the provided add-ins.

Excel

From the Ribbon, simply click New List and choose a Team Project and Work Item Query. This will retrieve all the information from a web service and display it in Excel. Once it's there you can sort, filter, edit, and publish changes back to the server, refresh the changes made by others, add links or attachments, and choose columns to be displayed.

Another way of doing this is from Team Explorer. From a work item query's context menu, select Open in Microsoft Excel. This will create a new Excel worksheet with the information. Figure 57-8 shows both options and Figure 57-9 shows the results in Excel.

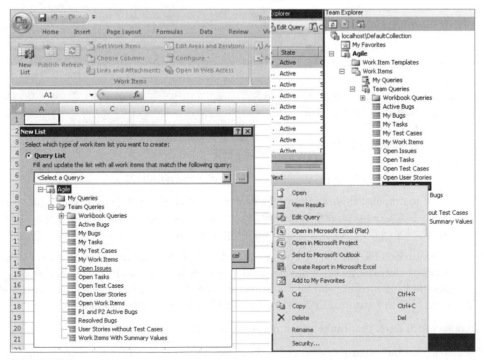

FIGURE 57-8

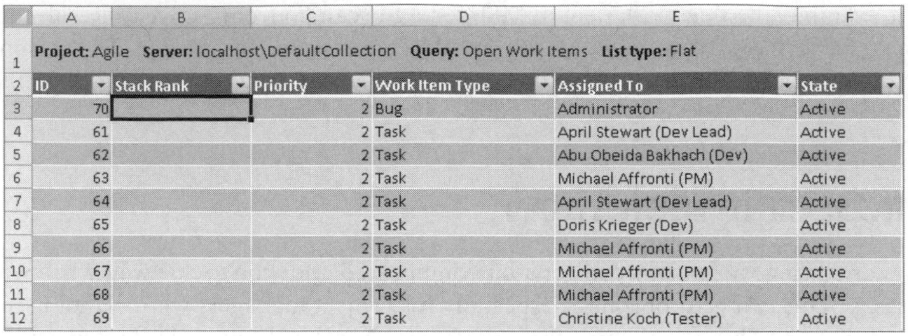

	A	B	C	D	E	F
1	**Project:** Agile **Server:** localhost\DefaultCollection **Query:** Open Work Items **List type:** Flat					
2	ID	Stack Rank	Priority	Work Item Type	Assigned To	State
3	70		2	Bug	Administrator	Active
4	61		2	Task	April Stewart (Dev Lead)	Active
5	62		2	Task	Abu Obeida Bakhach (Dev)	Active
6	63		2	Task	Michael Affronti (PM)	Active
7	64		2	Task	April Stewart (Dev Lead)	Active
8	65		2	Task	Doris Krieger (Dev)	Active
9	66		2	Task	Michael Affronti (PM)	Active
10	67		2	Task	Michael Affronti (PM)	Active
11	68		2	Task	Michael Affronti (PM)	Active
12	69		2	Task	Christine Koch (Tester)	Active

FIGURE 57-9

The MSF for Agile template creates a number of standard work item Excel workbooks, which are hosted on the SharePoint Portal. These are found in the Documents node under Excel Reports.

Project

There is also an add-in for Project. Similar to when you use Excel, you can connect to a server, choose a team project, and select a work item query, but instead of using the entire list, you have to choose each of the work items you want to import to your project, as shown in Figure 57-10.

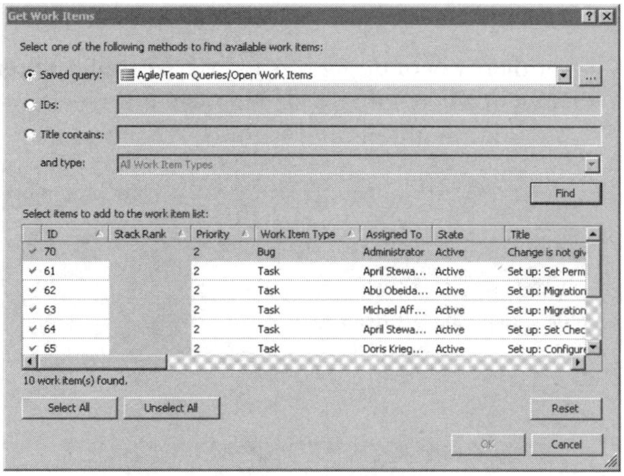

Once your work items are imported, you can edit each of their fields directly in Project. This is possible thanks to the column mappings between TFS fields and MS Project Columns. For example, Resource Names in Project will map to the Assigned To field in TFS. Fields that exist only in Team System will be mapped to Text Fields in Project; for example, Work Item Type is mapped to Text 24. This is preconfigured in the process template.

FIGURE 57-10

You can add new work items, nest them in iterations or areas, assign them to people, choose a work item type, balance workloads between resources, see project reports, and refresh the progress from the server after each developer changes the work remaining or work item state.

Unlike the previous version of TFS, the 2010 edition does understand the notions of hierarchical work items and successor and predecessor tasks. When the work items are loaded into Project, it is able to take advantage of these links to create a normal Project experience. As new associations are created and updated, Project is even able to return the updated data to TFS in a form it can understand.

Important differences still exist that make the integration a bit tricky:

➤ In Project you can have many resources for the same activity, but TFS only accepts one entry. One approach could be to add a custom field to the work item type, but then the mapping won't work because you would need to have one column in Project mapped to two fields in TFS. The workaround is to add the activity once for each resource.

➤ There's no Project server/TFS integration out of the box. A couple of third-party tools are available that do this for you. The next version of Team System will include it, as well as project management improvement across multiple projects for load balancing of resources.

> *If you are going to use Project with TFS you should look at the article "Quick Tips and Operational Differences when Tracking Tasks using Office Project and Team Foundation" on MSDN at* `http://msdn.microsoft.com/en-us/library/dd380701(VS.100).aspx`.

VERSION CONTROL

Version Control (sometimes called Source Control) is a tool that allows you to manage, share, and retain a history of changes to your source code. To interact with the TFS version control system, you use the Source Control Explorer window, shown in Figure 57-11. You can open this window from the Team Explorer window or View ➪ Other Windows ➪ Source Control Explorer.

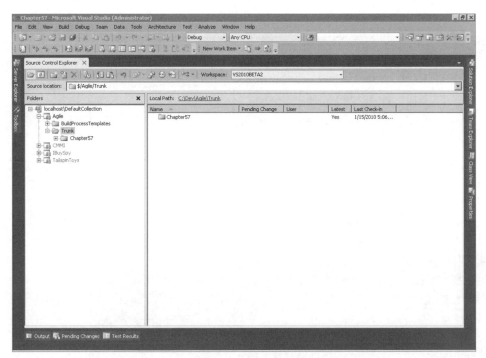

FIGURE 57-11

To work with files on your machine, you will need a *workspace* that defines a set of mappings between paths on your local file system and the remote system. You can define a different local folder for each path, but a good practice is to have only one mapping; this helps keep all the solutions and projects relative to each other even between different team projects. To define this mapping, open the workspace combo box and select Workspace.

Once your workspace is set up, you can get the latest version of the source code and start working with it, add files, check out files (mark as edit) or check in (upload/persist) changes, view change history, and compare folders.

> *In previous versions of TFS, each workspace was limited to a single user on a single machine. Visual Studio 2010 introduces the concept of a public workspace that can be shared among multiple users on the same machine.*

Working from Solution Explorer

When you create a new project you have the option to add it to Source Control. Team System will automatically bind it and add it according to the mapping previously defined. That's why you need to set the location to a folder inside your workspace (the local path you mapped to), as shown in Figure 57-12.

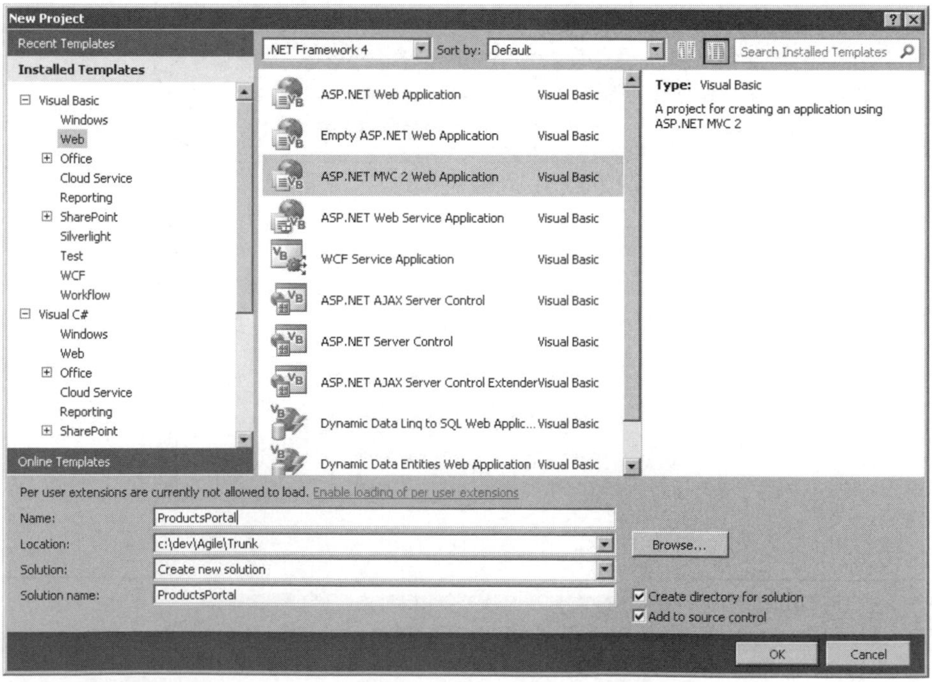

FIGURE 57-12

The Solution Explorer you are used to working with in Visual Studio will be the main place to interact with your source control system. Every time you add a new file to the solution, it will be added to source control; when you open a file and VS detects you're editing it, it will be automatically checked out for you. Once you are done working, you can simply right-click the solution and choose Check In to persist your changes in the server. See the section "Source Control" in Chapter 13 for more information on the common tasks; this chapter explains the specifics of Source Control as it relates to Team Foundation Server 2010.

> *Though it is common to work directly with TFS source control via the Solution Explorer, this can have some disadvantages because it means that Visual Studio is only able to manipulate the files that are referenced by your solution. If you have other items in source control that are not part of your solution, you need to manage these from the Source Control Explorer window.*

Check Out

Files under source control are by default read-only; in TFS terms you would say the file is *checked in*. To start editing a file you need to check it out. This is done for you automatically when you modify it from VS. When the file is a text file (that is, a C#, VB, or XML file), the IDE will do a *shared check-out*; if it's a binary file (that is, a Word document, SQL Server Compact Edition Database, or another resource) an *exclusive check-out* will be made.

Shared check-outs allow two or more developers to modify a file at the same time, whereas an exclusive check-out prevents a second developer from checking out the file. You can choose to do an exclusive check-out on a text file if you need to prevent anyone from modifying it. This is not a recommended practice, and you should only use it when you really need it. A good example of this is when you are about to update the data for a WCF reference. This sort of information is textual, but not easy to merge because many files are all updated at once. By using exclusive check-outs you can ensure that no one else is modifying the reference at the same time as you.

> *If you install the TFS2010 Power Tools you can check files in and out directly from Windows Explorer.*

Check In

To preserve your changes in the server, you will need to *check in* the edited files. You can select which files to include in this *changeset*, add comments to it, associate it with work items, and add check-in notes (Figure 57-13).

Depending on the policies defined for the team project, you might need to associate your check-in with a work item, run code analysis, have it pass tests, or at least successfully build the solution. To modify a team project's policies, open the Source Control Settings window (Team ⇨ Team Project Settings ⇨ Source Control) and go to the Check-in Policy tab. Once the policies are defined, you will get Policy Warnings (Figure 57-14); these can be overridden.

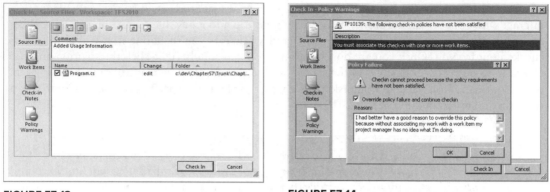

FIGURE 57-13   **FIGURE 57-14**

> *You should check in a group of files related to a logical change at the same time rather than one at a time. The set of files associated with a check-in along with any notes and work item associations become a changeset. Changesets make managing project history and merging much easier.*

Resolve Conflicts

Although shared check-outs allow multiple developers to work on the same file, this can lead to conflicts. These can easily be resolved with the help of Visual Studio. From the Pending Changes - Conflicts window (Figure 57-15) you can compare versions and look at all the changes to that file. To resolve it, you can use Auto Merge and let Visual Studio merge the changes for you, undo your local changes, discard server changes, or merge changes manually in the merge tool.

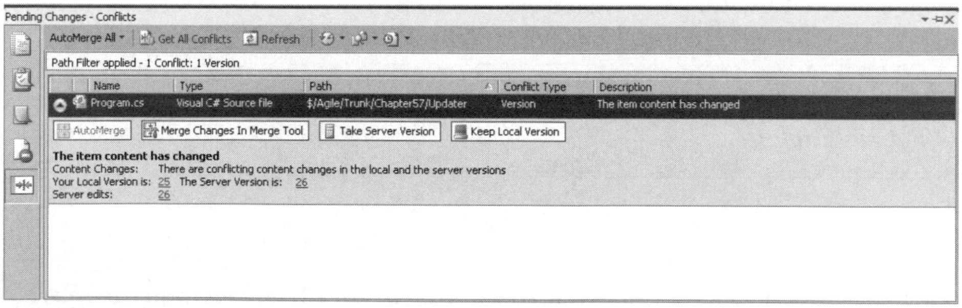

FIGURE 57-15

When the changes were made in different parts of the file (for example, two different methods), VS can automatically resolve changes, but if changes were made in the same line you have to either choose a version or manually merge both files using the Merge Changes tool.

> *Visual Studio will compare text to determine if changes overlap, but this will not guarantee the resulting file will even compile or behave as expected. This option is really useful, but has to be used with caution. Over time, you will have more confidence in choosing which files to auto-merge to save time and which are worth a quick look just to be sure.*

In the Merge Changes tool (Figure 57-16), you will have a view of "their" version (that is, the server version), your version, and a merged version. You can navigate easily between changes and conflicts. In the case of conflicts, you can manually edit the offending lines or select a version to keep. When all conflicts are resolved, you can accept the changes, keep the new file as your current version, and proceed to check-in.

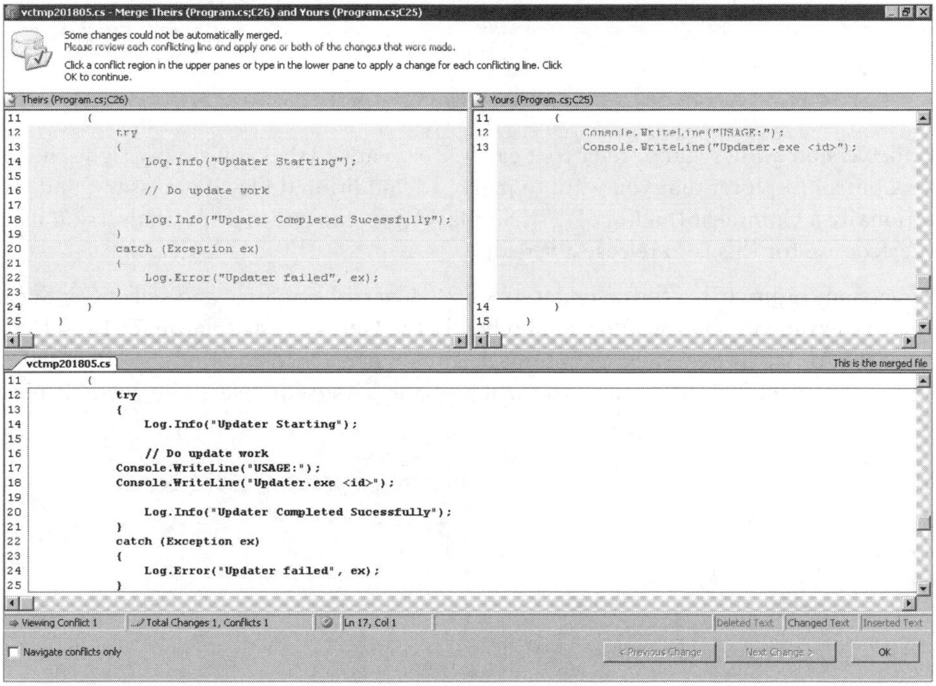

FIGURE 57-16

> *After resolving conflicts, it is recommend that you run the automated tests again to ensure there are no breaking changes. As you will see in the "Team Foundation Build" section, this test can be run automatically in the server before each check-in, but it's best to get the feedback as early as possible.*

Working Offline

Team Foundation Server uses HTTP and web services and can work perfectly through the Internet and allow for collaboration of distributed teams, but in case you don't have an available connection VS will allow you to work offline when you try to open a bound project.

All files under Source Control are read-only. When you save a file you will be warned and should simply choose Overwrite. When the connection with TFS can be reestablished, you can select to go online from Solution Explorer or by right-clicking the solution. VS will look for files in the solution without the read-only attribute; if those are not in Source Control it will add them, and if they exist it will check them out.

> *Files modified outside the solution won't be detected and you have to manually check them out. To make this easier, you can compare your local copy to the latest version by right-clicking a folder in the Source Control Explorer.*

Label

Labeling a specific version allows you to refer to it easily. To create a label you simply right-click a folder in Source Control Explorer that you want to mark, add additional files if necessary, and write a Name and optionally a Comment (Figure 57-17). Similarly, you can get to a specific version using the label. The perfect use for this is to release a version.

To get a labeled version, right-click a file or folder in Source Control Explorer and select Get Specific Version from the context menu. On the Type combo box in the Get window (Figure 57-18) select Label. You can search for labels by name, team project, and owner. Once you find the label, to be sure you are getting the exact labeled version, you will probably choose to overwrite writable files.

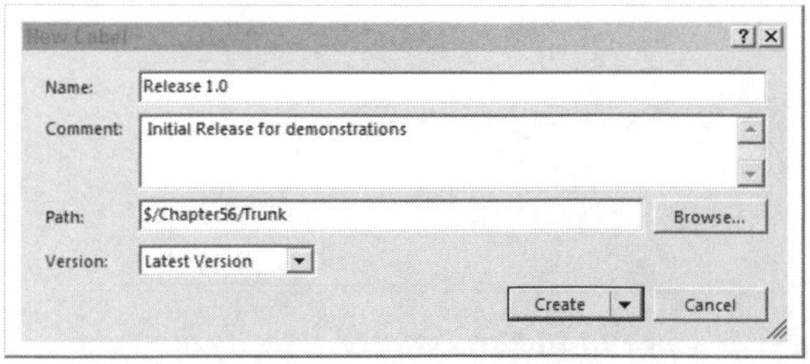

FIGURE 57-17

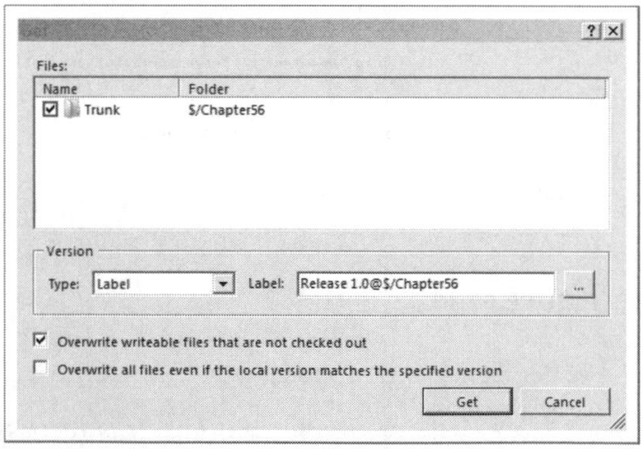

FIGURE 57-18

> *You should undo, shelve, or check-in any pending changes before getting a specific version to separate the latest changes in your workspace from the labeled version.*

If you want to get the version in a different location, you can create a branch. You see this later in the chapter.

History

Every change you make is persisted in the server and you can get to any specific version of a file; a great way to do it is through the History window. Simply right-click a file in Source Control or Solution Explorer and select View History. From there you can see how a file has evolved over time (Figure 57-19). When you right-click any version, you can compare it to your version, open it, and view details of the changeset (including the comments and related work items).

FIGURE 57-19

Toward the top of Figure 57-19 is a tab to switch between Changesets and Labels. Switching to Labels view, shown in Figure 57-20, displays a list of all of the labels that have been applied to the file. This can be very useful to quickly see all of the changes made between two versions.

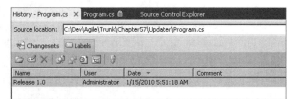

FIGURE 57-20

Annotate

The *annotate* command enables you see when and who edited each line of code (Figure 57-21). From each of the changes made, you can get to each particular changeset to see details, get that particular version, compare it to its previous version, locate the file in the History window, or annotate from that version.

Shelve

When you check in a file, that change is automatically made available to others. Sometimes you need to persist your changes without affecting everyone — a scenario that can happen when you need to work from another computer and want to upload

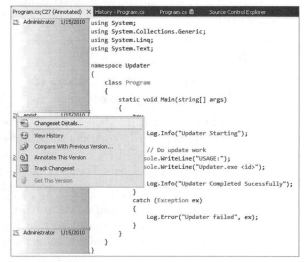

FIGURE 57-21

your changes and send them somewhere else, or when you are in the middle of something and are assigned a new task.

Shelving persists your changes in the server. You can associate a *shelveset* to work items and add comments and check-in notes, much as you would when checking in. You can optionally evaluate check-in policies before shelving and choose to undo local changes after the shelve is done. The latter is useful when you need to work on some other work item without the shelved changes interfering with what you are doing. Shelving changes is also useful if you are moving to another machine and don't want to have to make the same change in both places. To get to the changes, you can *unshelve* your shelveset and your files will be checked out again.

Each shelveset is a read-only snapshot of the files at the time when it was created. Because of this, each shelveset is not versioned and if you save a new shelveset with the same name as an existing one it will simply overwrite it. This can be extremely handy for common tasks such a Work In Progress or For Review.

> *Shelvesets are uniquely identified by a combination of their name and the name of the user who created them, so even if you use the same naming scheme for your shelvesets as another team member you won't be able to overwrite each other's work.*

Although the default behavior is for you to see the shelvesets that you have created, you can see the shelvesets that other people have created and even retrieve them, which can be useful if you need a colleague to review some code before it is checked in or to hand a task off to someone when it is not in a state that is ready to be checked in.

There is an option hidden behind the Details when unshelving a shelveset to Preserve Shelveset on Server. If you uncheck this option the shelveset is deleted from the server as you retrieve it. You can also delete shelvesets without retrieving them from the Unshelve dialog. It is a good idea to clean out shelvesets regularly that you don't need any more to make it easier for you to find the ones you actually use.

Branch

A *branch*, in source control terms, is a parallel version of your code. This is useful for different purposes. Here are a couple of examples:

> ➤ Hot fixes or bugs for stable versions while working on new ones. When you release 1.0 you label all your source code and start working on 2.0. Then a critical bug is found but version 2.0 is months away from being ready. You will branch from version 1.0 (you can get to this version using the label). Then you can fix the bug in the new branch and release version 1.1. Later you can merge the change made and integrate it with the main branch.

> ➤ Creating a branch from the latest version to do a big refactoring or a change you are not sure will work and thus don't want to affect the main branch. If it works you can merge it with the main branch and if it doesn't you can simply delete it.

You have to choose wisely what branching strategy is better for your organization, type of product, and process, or when you could substitute by simply labeling a version or shelving a change. Abuse of branching can exponentially complicate source-code management. Codeplex hosts branching guidance that provides additional scenarios (`http://www.codeplex.com/TFSBranchingGuideII`).

To create a new branch, right-click the folder you want to branch from and select Branching and Merging ➪ Branch. You will be asked which version you want to branch from and where the branch should be saved in the source control repository.

> *Branches have become first class features in TFS 2010 so the tools are able to take full advantage of them. You can mark an existing folder as a branch by supplying the required metadata, which allows branches from previous versions to take advantage of this as well.*

Once you have a few branches you can use the Branch Visualization (Figure 57-22) tool to see the hierarchy of your branches by selecting View Hierarchy from the Branching and Merging dropdown in the Source Control Explorer. You can initiate merges from this tool by dragging from one branch to a valid target branch.

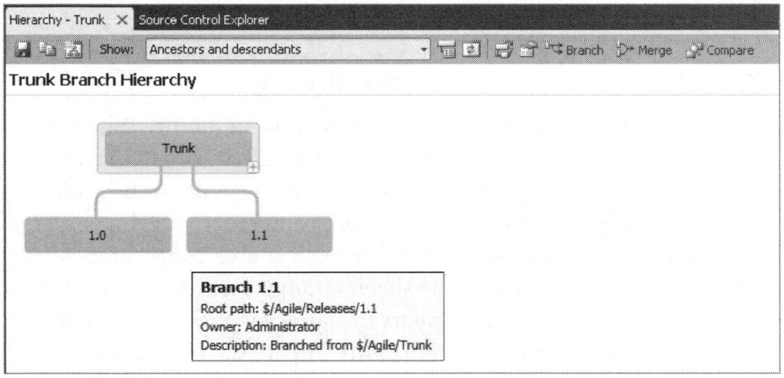

FIGURE 57-22

Another new tool in TFS 2010 is Changeset Tracking, which allows you to see where the changes in a particular changeset have come from. It has two views: Timeline Tracking (which is shown in Figure 57-23) and Hierarchy Tracking, which shows the hierarchy between the branches in a clearer fashion. Just as with the Branch Visualization view, you can initiate a merge by dragging a changeset from one branch to another.

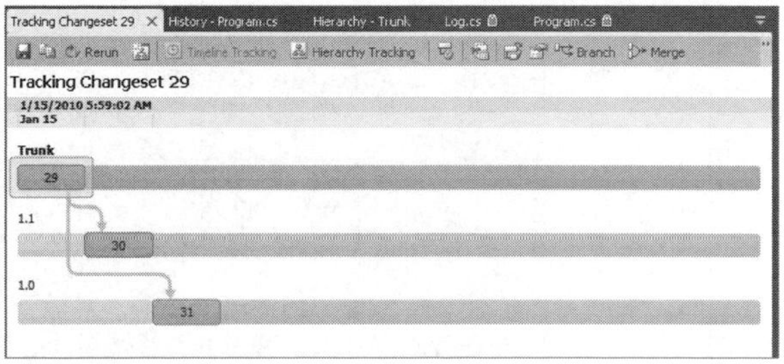

FIGURE 57-23

Merge

If you fix a bug or implement a feature in one branch, it would be advantageous to be able to apply that same changeset to other branches. This is what the *merge* operation does. To begin a merge, right-click the folder or file you want to merge and select Branching and Merging ➪ Merge. Once you have selected a source and destination for the merge, you are presented with a list of changesets that that can be applied. Select the changesets that you want and click Finish. If there are any conflicts, you will be given the opportunity to fix them.

TEAM FOUNDATION BUILD

Team Foundation Build is a tool, part of TFS, and its responsibility is to get the latest version from source control to a local workspace, build the projects as configured, run tests, do other tasks, and finally report the results and leave the output in a shared folder. Each machine that is able to build a project for you is called a *build agent*. TFS 2010 also introduces the concept of a *build controller*, which is responsible for coordinating the activities of several build agents. The information that each build agent needs to do its job is called a *build definition*.

To create a new build definition, right-click the Builds folder in Team Explorer and select New Build Definition (Figure 57-24). In the General tab you need to write the build name and optionally a description.

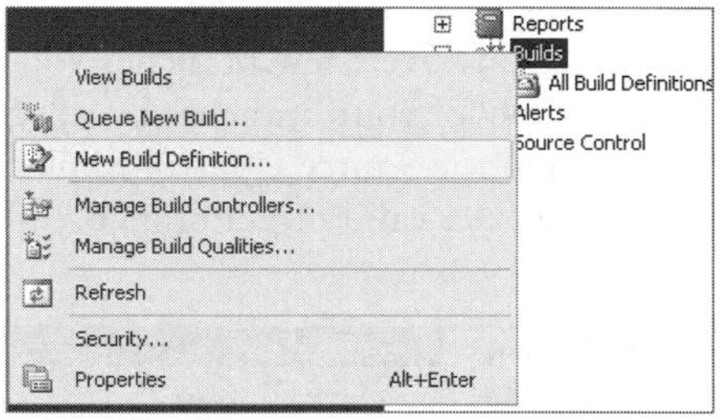

FIGURE 57-24

By default the build has to be manually queued, but in the Trigger tab you can modify this behavior. You have five options, as shown in Figure 57-25. The new option for TFS 2010 is the Gated Check-in option. When you have build definitions that are triggered this way, check-ins will not necessarily go straight into source control. Instead they will be shelved (you will be prompted about this) and built by a build agent first. If the build succeeds, the shelveset is saved into the source control repository. If it does not, you are notified and it is up to you to retrieve the shelveset, make any required changes, and check it in again. Using this type of build definition prevents the situation where the contents of the source control repository do not compile, which can significantly impact the rest of the team.

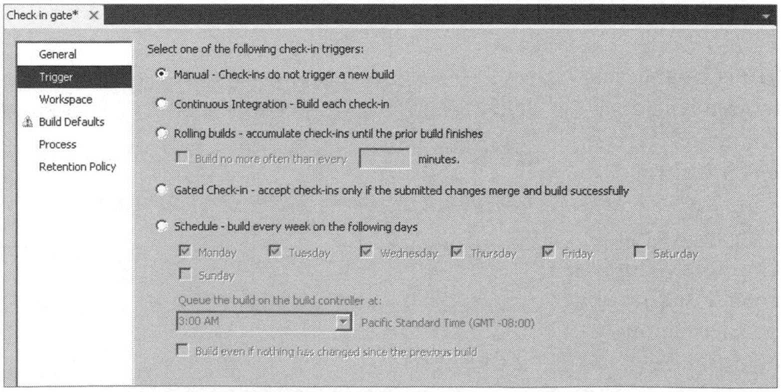

FIGURE 57-25

Depending on how big your project is, how long it takes to build and run the tests, and how often the team checks in, this option may cause some overhead. The third option, Rolling Builds, will definitely help alleviate the workload, but it's better to wait until you find you need it.

Configuring the workspace will be used in complex scenarios where you have dependencies between team projects, so the defaults in that tab might be enough. In the build defaults page, you can choose a build controller and a shared folder to drop the output into. These will be used for triggered builds, but for manual builds this can be overridden.

The Process tab, shown in Figure 57-26, allows you to configure the build process. Here you must select at least one project or solution and a configuration (like x86 | Debug or AnyCPU | Release). The rest of the values are optional but include information allowing you to specify the location of any automated test assemblies, whether or not to perform code analysis, if the build agent should publish the project symbols anywhere, how to format the build number, and more.

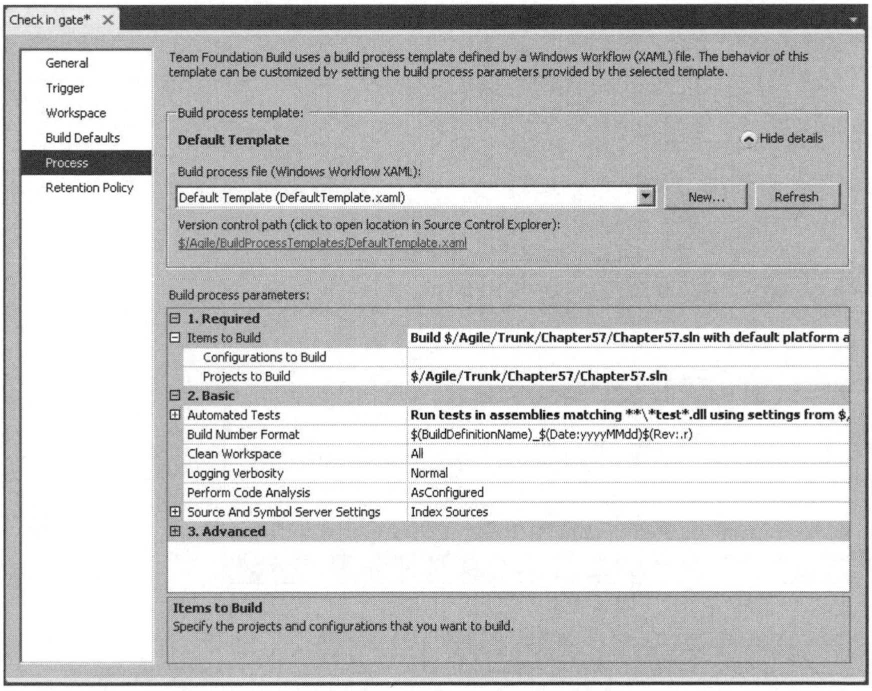

FIGURE 57-26

TFS 2010 build processes are based on a process template that is defined with Windows Workflow 4.0. You can create your own custom process template by copying the default one and making changes to it. A number of custom activities are related to Team Build and you can always create your own. If you have a build definition from a previous version of Team Build you should use the Upgrade Template, which only requires a path that contains the legacy TfsBuild.proj file.

> *By default the build process templates are located in the* $/TeamProjectName/BuildProcessTemplates *folder in the source control repository.*

The retention policy lets you choose how many of the builds left in the shared folder will be kept before some are deleted. It is recommended to use the Keep All option, at least for successful builds, until you need to reduce the number of files being kept around. There are two sets of settings. The ones under Private relate to builds that form a part of a gated check-in and are not as important to keep around.

To start a build manually, you can right-click the Builds node in the Team Explorer and select Queue New Build. Once the build is queued you can open it by double-clicking it in the Build Explorer. This opens the new Build Report, which has been greatly improved from the previous version. This report, shown in Figure 57-27, includes information on current activity, previous build statuses and durations, and provides links to a number of other areas and activities related to this build.

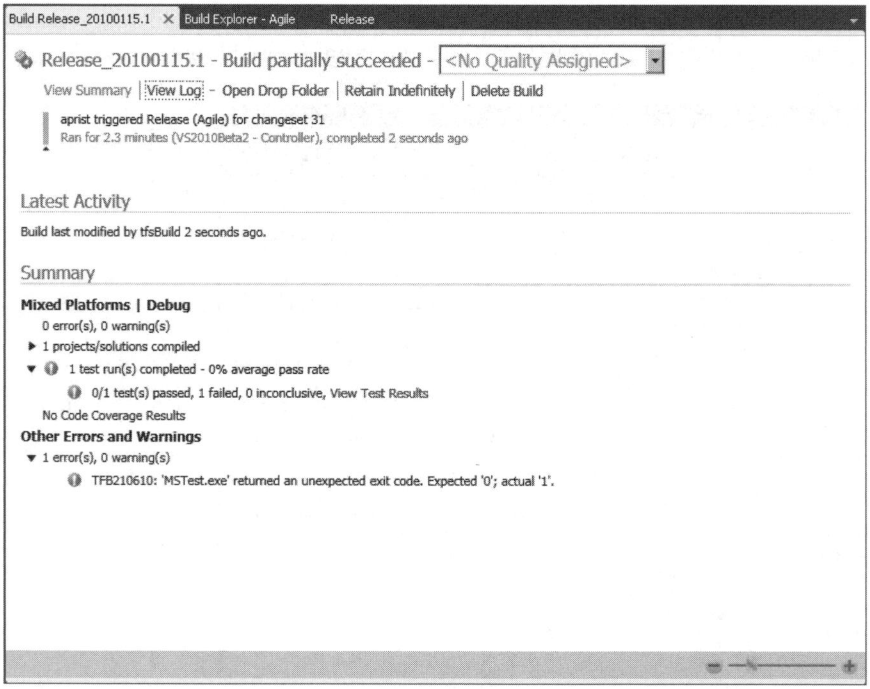

FIGURE 57-27

> *If you want to be notified of build events while you work, there is a Build Notifications system tray application that is installed with Team Explorer. Once configured, this application will adjust its icon based on whether any builds you are watching are broken, building, or if everything is built successfully.*

REPORTING AND BUSINESS INTELLIGENCE

TFS uses Report Server, which is part of Microsoft SQL Server, to provide useful information for project managers, customers, and developers. Reports can be accessed directly from Team Explorer, the reports site (`http://mytfs/reports/`), SharePoint, or Team System Web Access, or they can be configured as a subscription from the Reports site to be left in a Windows file share or sent through e-mail.

The great benefit these have is that developers can focus on their work instead of manually filling out reports. All the information is collected during their daily work, checking out and checking in code, fixing bugs, and relating what they are doing to work items. This way project managers and stakeholders can get to the information they need from the reports TFS provides.

Each process template provides its own set of reports. The CMMI version provides three additional reports and templates like Scrum for Team System from Conchango, and has reports appropriate for the Scrum methodology like Delta Report and Burndown Charts. Again, we will focus on MSF for Agile Development here.

Some of the reports included are Burndown and Burn Rate, Stories Progress, Build Success Over Time, Build Quality Indicators, Test Case Readiness, Test Plan Progress, Bug Status, Bug Trends, and Reactivations. Figure 57-28 shows how the work has been resolved over a couple of years and how much work is left. In the report you can filter by dates, work item type, iteration, and area. You can export to XML, CSV, TIFF, PDF, Web, and Excel.

You don't need two years of information to get useful reports. Depending on the nature of the data displayed, you might not see anything at the beginning. For example, the Test Failing reports will need to have at least one test in your team build process, or to have data for the Regressions report you need Passing tests that are now failing. Similarly, the Scenarios Details report will need you to register at least a Scenario Work Item. After a couple of iterations of working with TFS you will have a lot of useful metrics for free.

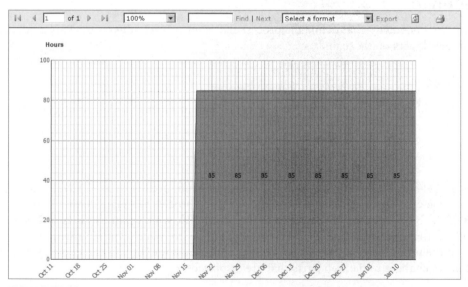

FIGURE 57-28

> *Microsoft has been very clear that you should not be accessing the data in the TFS databases directly, but should instead be using the reports and tools provided. In TFS 2010 there are new Data Warehouse Views, which have been added over the tables in each TFS database. There is some guarantee that these views will not change moving forward and they have been designed so you can create your own reports.*

TEAM PORTAL

Team Foundation uses SharePoint to create a portal for each team project. It has all the benefits of SharePoint, but is customized for each process template. The home in each team portal will include the most important reports, latest announcements, and useful links. TFS 2010 also includes the ability to create custom dashboards, which can be for specific users or for everyone on the project. To navigate to the project portal, right-click the team project in the Team Explorer and select Show Project Portal.

Documents

Depending on the process template, certain documents will be included as templates. For example, MSF for Agile Software Development includes Word documents for creating personas and scenarios. These documents are also available from the Team Explorer's document folder.

Process Guidance

Inside SharePoint are documents that define the process that your project adheres to. This guidance is available to all developers on the team.

SharePoint Lists

You can have picture libraries, discussion boards, surveys, announcements, links, events, contacts, and custom lists. This will help improve team collaboration.

Dashboards

Dashboards are SharePoint Web Part pages that have been preconfigured with useful Web Parts to give you an overview of a project's status. The MSF for Agile process template defines two dashboards out of the box including My Dashboard (Figure 57-29), which contains lists of Tasks, Bugs, and Test Cases that are assigned to you; and Project Dashboard, which contains metrics and information about the progress of the entire team. Using the SharePoint UI, you can copy an existing dashboard and make changes to the web parts that are displayed.

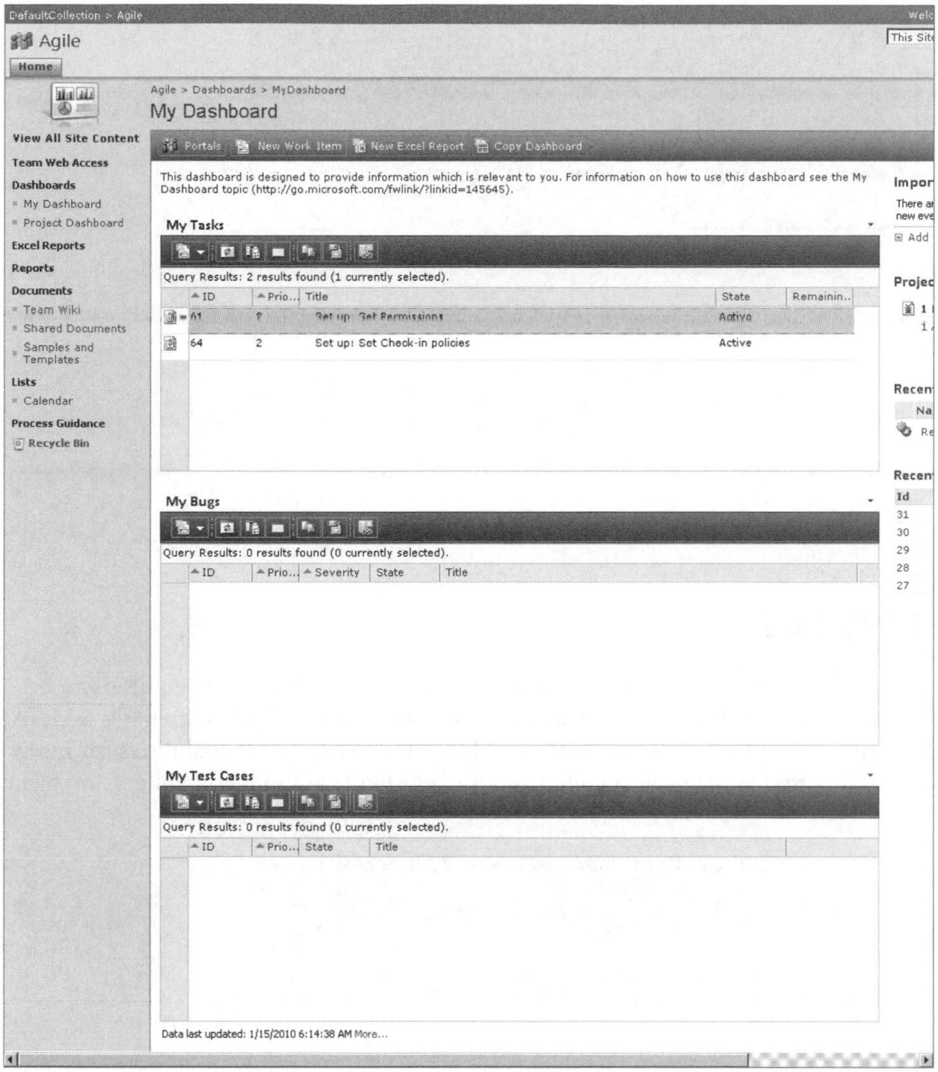

FIGURE 57-29

TEAM SYSTEM WEB ACCESS

This is a separate, free tool from Microsoft that integrates with TFS and allows you to do pretty much everything you can do from VS, but in a web interface (Figure 57-30). You can create and modify work items as well as work item queries, see the reports and documents, and initiate and monitor builds. The only area with limited functionality is Source Control. You can see history and changeset details, but you can't check out/check in documents due to the web client nature.

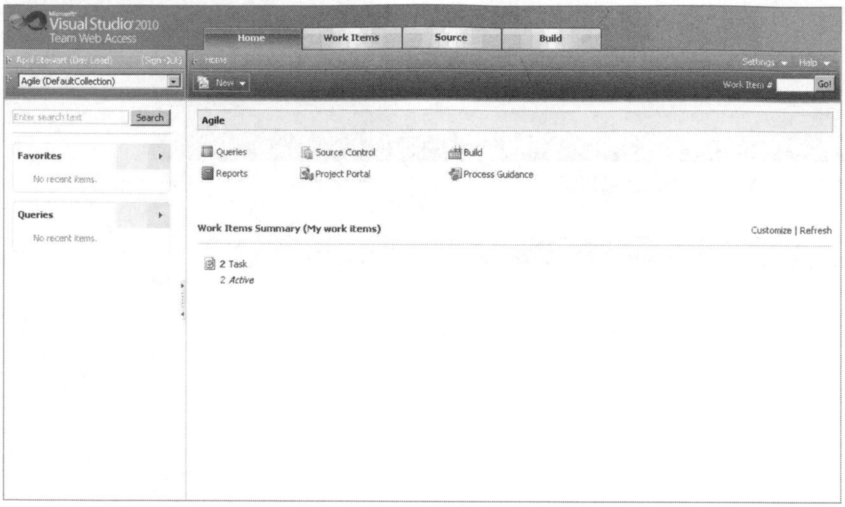

FIGURE 57-30

ADMINISTERING TFS

Keeping track of all of the settings, web sites, databases, and accounts that TFS requires can be a hassle. The Team Foundation Server Administration Console (Figure 57-31) aggregates a lot of the information about your TFS installation into one place. It also provides capabilities for many common tasks including managing project collections and configuring build controllers and agents.

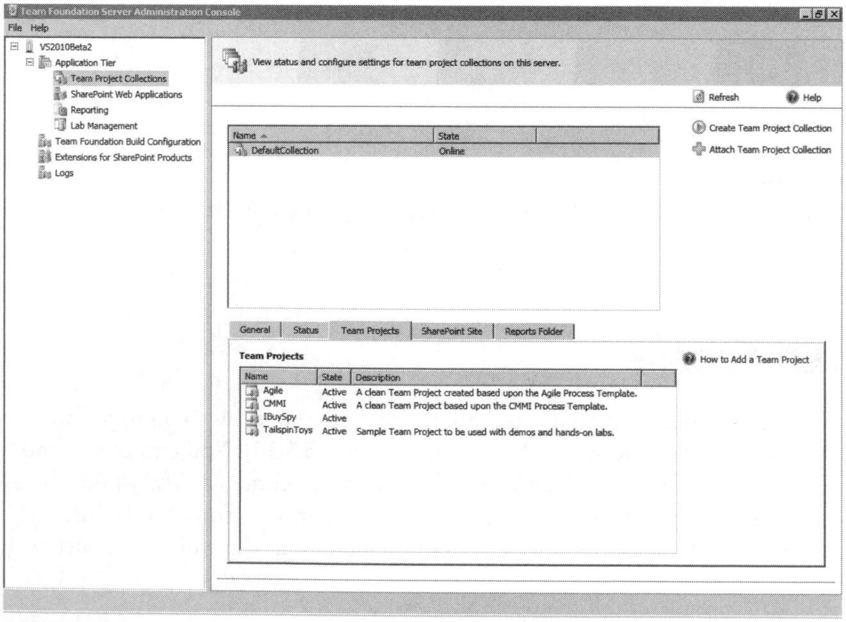

FIGURE 57-31

TFS AUTOMATION AND PROCESS CUSTOMIZATION

Throughout this chapter, you have seen how the process templates define most of the behavior of TFS; for example, they define work item types, process guidance, and reports. To close the chapter, we briefly introduce how you could customize a process template or edit work item types.

To edit either work item types or process templates, you could modify the XML that defines them, but it's easier to use the Process Editor, which is part of the Team Foundation Server Power Tools, downloadable from the Microsoft site.

Work Item Types

From the Tools ⇨ Process Editor ⇨ Work Item Types menu, you can open a work item type directly from an existing team project and start to edit it. Working this way will cause all your changes to be immediately propagated to all users. Another approach is to export the work item type to a file and then open it for editing and finally import it back to a team project. All these options are located in the same submenu.

> *It is recommended that you have a team project dedicated to testing changes before importing or editing work item types in active team projects.*

Once you are editing a work item type, either directly from a team project or from a file, you will have three tabs to work with — Fields, Layout, and Workflow (Figure 57-32).

The first tab has a list of fields with their data types and a reference name. The reference name is used to uniquely identify fields from different work item types. For example, a title for a bug and a title for a task have the same "System.Title" reference name; other fields might have the same names but refer to different things.

The second tab allows you to modify the layout. You don't have a visual designer here, but you can work in a tree designer to nest groups, columns, and controls. Each control will be mapped to a field name using the reference name. There is also a Preview Form button that allows you to see what the end product will look like.

On the third tab you can modify the workflow, and from the Toolbox you can add states and transition links. The bug shown in Figure 57-32 shows how it can transition between active and resolved. If you double-click the transition, you can define reasons, actions, and fields. The last is used to set default values to fields after a transition; for example, when the bug transitions from active to resolved, it is assigned to the person who created the bug, the Resolved By field is set to the current user, and the Resolved Date is set to the server's current date.

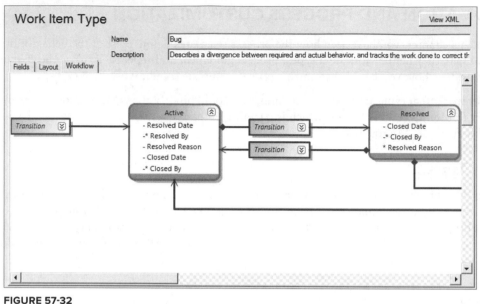

FIGURE 57-32

In the next section you see how you can include work item types on a process template.

Customizing the Process Template

To serve as an example for process template customization, you will modify MSF for Agile Development. To create a local copy you need to open the Process Template Manager from the Team ⇨ Team Project Collection Settings menu and select Process Template Manager. When the Process Template Manager dialog opens, select the desired template and click Download. Now you can open it in the Process Template Editor from the Tool ⇨ Process Editor ⇨ Process Template ⇨ Open Process Template menu and select the `processtemplate.XML` file just downloaded.

In the Process Template Editor window (Figure 57-33) you have a tree view to configure the different areas of a team project. In the Work Item Tracking node you can modify the Default Work Item List, create default work item queries, and import work item types. In Areas & Iteration you can configure default values for these lists and specify the field and column mappings for Microsoft Project Integration. You can specify permissions and settings under Source Control. In the Portal node, you can add documents that will be added to Document Libraries for SharePoint, and finally in the Reports node you can add Report Definition files.

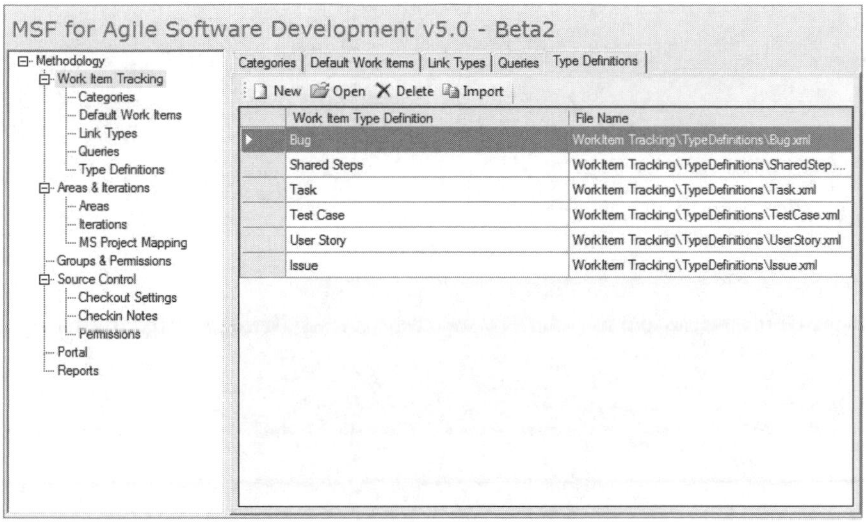

FIGURE 57-33

Although this tool can tremendously simplify the required work, you will need to edit the XML files for several tasks. For example, there's no way to specify a SharePoint template for the portal.

SUMMARY

In this chapter, you saw how Team Foundation Server can help you get the work done by integrating the different roles involved. The project managers will be filing and monitoring work items in either Excel or Project, while architects, developers, and testers will be working with the Visual Studio Projects using the version control features, easily relating changes to their assigned work items. Optionally, each change will trigger a team build that will ensure the quality standards are met. TFS will be monitoring everything and generating metrics for reports that can be viewed through the different interfaces like Visual Studio, Team Portal, and Team System Web Access. At the end of the chapter, you saw how the whole process can be customized by modifying the process templates and work item types to better suit each organization's needs.

INDEX

$( ) function, 468–470

* (asterisk), unsaved changes, 11

A

abstraction, imperative languages and, 312

Access Modifier option, 816

accessibility for users, 416–417

ACS (Access Control Service), 545–546

action methods
  Create, 457
  parameters, 456–459

ActionLink helper, 450

Actions Pane window (VSTO), 381, 386–387

ActivationKeyFile property, 957

activities (workflow), 703–704
  code, 715–719
  control flow, 704–705
      Flowchart, 704
      Sequence, 704

Activity class, 704

Activity Diagrams (UML), 1062, 1063

Add Area dialog, 459

Add button, 575–576

Add Controller dialog, 441

Add-in Manager dialog, 1011

Add-in Wizard, 1009–1012

add-ins
  Add-in Wizard, 1009–1012
  COM components, 1014
  Connect class, 1015
  deploying, 1022–1023
  disabled, 394
  extensibility and, 1002
  loading, 1011

project structure, 1012–1013
  testing, 1013–1014
  unregistering, 392–393
  Visual Studio IDE, 1011
  Visual Studio Macros IDE, 1011

Add Reference dialog, 21

.AddIn file, 1014

address breakpoint, 847

AddSolutionFolder method, 1003

Administrative install, 970

ADO.NET. *See also* Sync Services

ADO.NET Entity Framework, 621
  associations, 623
      creating, 634
      modifying, 634
      navigating, 641–642
  change tracking, 639
  Empty Model option, 625
  entities, 623
      adding properties, 631–632
      business logic, 645
      complex types, 632
      creating, 630–633, 632–633
      inheritance, 635
      modifying, 630–633
      property names, 631
  Entity Data Model Wizard, 624–625
  Entity Framework designer, 626–630
  entity models, 623
      creating, 624–635
      CRUD operations, 637–641
      database updates, 644–645
      querying, 636–642
      updating with database changes, 635
      validation, 635

ADO.NET Entity Framework (*continued*)
  entity sets, 623
  LINQ and, 587
      LINQ to Entities, 636–642
      LINQ to SQL, 622–623
  LINQ to SQL and, 487
  mapping, 623
  POCO (Plain Old CLR Objects), 645
  reports, 649
adornments in text, 1047–1048
AfterInstall event handler, 970
aggregates, reports, 661–663
Agile Software Development. *See* MSF for Agile
    Development
aliases
  commands, Immediate window, 831
  e (XML namespace), 605
alignment, text controls, 342
Allocation information, 1082
AmbientValue attribute, 31–32
anchoring controls, 349–350
animated window closing, 41
anonymous methods, 321–322
anonymous type feature (LINQ), 591
app.config file, 726, 774
AppFabric, 533, 545–546
  authentication, 533
application add-ins, 388–392
  VSTO, 388–392
Application Events, 954
Application Expiry, 950
Application Framework, 100
  security, 728
application-level add-ins (Office), 381–382
application-level errors, 877
application-level tracing, 882
application monitoring and management, 949–958
  application expiry, 956–957
  RI (Runtime Intelligence), 952–956
  Tamper defense, 950–952
  usage tracking, 957–958
application pages, SharePoint, 522
Application tab (Solution Explorer), 97–98
  Application Framework, 100
  Assembly Information, 98–99

User Account Control, 99–100
Application Usage Tracking, 950
ApplicationAttribute attribute, 953
applicationHost.config file, 775
ApplicationRoot class, 1035
  import requirements, 1036
applications. *See also* Windows Forms
    applications
  ASP.NET Dynamic Data, 489–491
  composable parts, 1034
  debugging
      multi-threaded, 897–899
      parallelized, 897–899
      running remote debugging, 894–895
      running Web applications, 893–894
      running Windows processes, 892–893
  deploying, 394–396
  occasionally connected, 746
  resourcing, 811–813
  settings, configuration files, 782–790
  themes (Silverlight), 479
ApplicationServices, 729
ApplyResources method, 817
appSettings section of configuration file,
    782–783
Architecture edition. *See* VSTS Architecture
Architecture Explorer, 1068–1070
  queries, 1070
areas (MVC), 459–461
arrays, literals, 323–324
Ascending keyword, 595
ASP (Active Server Pages), 437
ASP.NET
  applications, reports, 646
  configuration in IIS, 434
  debugging, 872–877
      Edit and Continue, 876
      error handling, 876–877
      web applications, 874–876
  RIA Services and, 758
  Web site administration, 431–434
ASP.NET AJAX
  JavaScript, debugging, 879
  Web Application projects, 427–429
      control extenders, 429–431

ASP.NET Application Services, 725
  authentication, 729
  client application services, 729
  profiles, 729
  role management, 729
ASP.NET Dynamic Data, 485
  applications, 489–491
  Convention over Configuration, 486
  data fields, customizing, 492–494
  data models
      adding, 487–489
      customizing, 491–492
      display format, 496–498
      scaffolding tables, 491–494
      validation rules, 494–496
  enabling for existing projects, 511–512
  Entities Dynamic Data project, 488
  metadata classes, 492
  presentation, 498
      entity templates, 506–508
      field templates, 502–506
      filter templates, 509–511
      page templates, 499–502
  scaffolding, 486
  web applications, creating, 486–491
ASP.NET MVC, 437, 438
  action methods, parameters, 456–459
  areas, 459–461
  Dynamic Data templates, 464
      display templates, 465–468
      edit templates, 468
  files, 439
  folders, structure, 439–440
  jQuery, 468–470
  model binders, 458–459
  models, selecting, 440–441
  partial views, 463
  request life cycle, 438–439
  routing, 451–455
  views, custom view templates, 463–464
ASP.NET Web Forms, 399, 437
ASP.NET Web Parts, 524
assemblies
  caching, XML file and, 476
  GAC, 933–934

  naming, 929–932
  signing, 934–936
  strongly named, 933
      obfuscation, 948–949
  versions, consistency, 932–933
assembly directive (T4), 276
Assembly Information, 98–99
AssemblyCleanup attribute, 207
AssemblyInfo file, 932–933
AssemblyInitialize attribute, 207
Assert class, 203
Assert method, 891
Association connector, 179
associations (Entity Framework), 634
asterisk (*), unsaved changes, 11
asynchronous methods, 698
attached properties, XAML, 358
attaching to Web applications, 893–894
attaching to Windows processes, 892–893
attributes
  AmbientValue, 31–32
  ApplicationAttribute, 953
  Browseable, 28–29
  Category, 30
  CompilerGenerated, 1078
  configuration, 780–781
  DataContract, 686
  DebuggerBrowsable, 859–860
  DebuggerDisplay, 860–861
  DebuggerHidden, 861–862
  DebuggerNonUserCode, 862
  DebuggerStepperBoundary, 862–863
  DebuggerStepThrough, 862
  DefaultValue, 30–31
  Description, 29
  DisplayName, 29
  EnableClientAccess, 761
  ExportAttribute, 1036
  FeatureAttribute, 957–958
  GeneratedCode, 1078
  InsertShelfLifeAttribute, 956
  InsertSignOfLifeAttribute, 956
  InsertTamperCheckAttribute, 951
  ObfuscationAssemblyAttribute, 945–946
  ObfuscationAttribute, 946–948

attributes (*continued*)
  OperationContract, 684
  ServiceContract, 685
  SetupAttribute, 953–956
  TeardownAttribute, 953–956
  TestClass, 200
  testing and, 200–202
      ExpectedException, 204–206
      Ignore, 201
      Owner, 201
      Priority, 201
      TestCategory, 201
      Timeout, 201
      WorkItem, 201
  TestMethod, 200
  xmlns, 356
authentication, 107
  AppFabric, 533
  ASP.NET Application Services, 729
  Forms, 726
  forms-based, 731
  NTLM, 113
  RIA Services, 758
  users, 731–733
  Web controls, 418–420
  Windows authentication, 726
authorization, roles, 729–731
automated tests, 1095–1096
automatic properties, 322–323
automation, T4 templates, 280–284
automation model. *See* DTE (Development
    Tools Extensibility)
  accessing, 1018–1020
Autos window, 833
Azure. *See* Windows Azure Platform

B

background synchronization, 752–755
BackgroundWorker, 752–755
Bauer, Denis, 940–941
BeforeExecute event, 1020
best practices for databases, 1093–1094
binary resources, 807–808
binding data, data contracts, 690

binding objects, LINQ to SQL, 614–617
BindingNavigator, 569–570
BindingSource, 567–569
  chains, 579–581
BindingSource property, 614
bitmap loading, 816
block comments, 220
block selection, code editor, 60
bookmarks, 133–135
  workflow, 705
Branch Visualization tool, 1127
branches in Version Control, 1126–1127
Break mode (debugging), 828, 845
Breakpoint Hit Count dialog, 849
breakpoints, 828, 845
  break conditions, 848
  conditional, 828
  deleting, 850
  disabling, 850
  exporting, 851–852
  filters, 849–850
  hit counts, 849
  importing, 851–852
  JavaScript, 878
  labeling, 851
  location, changing, 850–851
  setting
      address, 847
      function, 846–847
      simple, 846
  workflows, 718–719
Breakpoints window, 828–829
  breakpoint list, 829
  toolbar, 829
brokers (IntelliSense), 1049
Browseable attribute, 28–29
browsers, Silverlight, 481–484
browsing data, 584–586
Build and Run node, 49–50
Build and Run options page, 912
Build Configuration options, 912
Build Events tab (Solution Explorer), 103, 917–919
Build tab (Solution Explorer), 102–103
building first application, 9–13
builds

C# build pages, 919–920
Compile page (VB), 915–919
    Build Events, 917–919
    compilation constants, 916–917
    optimizations, 916
dependencies, manual, 914–915
general options, 911–914
MSBuild, 920–921
    Items elements, 924
    PropertyGroup nodes, 924
    Target elements, 924
    Tasks elements, 925–927
    Visual Studio's use, 921–923
parallel project builds, 912
Business Application template, 757
business logic, Entity Framework, 645

C

C#
  build pages, 919–920
  code snippets, 139–140
C/C++ Code Analysis tool, 1079
CAL (client access license), 514
Call Hierarchy window, 66–67
Call Stack window, 833, 839, 847
camel case searching, 82
catalogs (MEF), 1040–1041
Category attribute, 30
CEIP (Customer Experience Improvement
    Program), 958
certificates
  deployment and, 977–979
  Trusted Root Certification Authorities, 979
Changed event, 1042
Chart control, 658–659
charts
  categories, 658
  data, 658
  drop zones, 658
  series, 658
Check Comment Margin Highlighter, 1050–1057
CheckCommentGlyphFactory class, 1056
CheckCommentTagger class, 1054
CheckCommentTaggerProvider class, 1054

class associations, 179
class coupling, code metrics, 1077
Class Designer
  Class Details, 180
  class diagram
    creating, 176–177
    entities, 178–179
    exporting, 182
  code generation
    drag-and-drop, 182–184
    IntelliSense, 184–185
  drag and drop and, 177
  Implement Abstract Class function, 185
  layout, 181
  modeling and, 175
  Override Members function, 185
  Properties window, 181
  refactoring with, 185
  Toolbox, 178
Class Details window, 180
class diagrams
  creating, 176–177
  entities, 178–179
    connectors, 179
  exporting, 182
Class Diagrams (UML), 1062, 1066
Class Feature blocks (T4), 270–272
Class View, 8, 63–64
ClassCleanup attribute, 206–207
classes
  Activity, 704
  ApplicationRoot, 1035
  Assert, 203
  CheckCommentGlyphFactory, 1056
  CheckCommentTagger, 1054
  CheckCommentTaggerProvider, 1054
  ClassificationTypeDefinition, 1046
  CodeActivity, 704, 715
  CollectionAssert, 204
  CommandLineMessageService, 1038
  ComponentResourceManager, 812
  Connect, 1015
  CustomAuthentication, 731
  CustomerVisualizer, 866–867
  Debug, 890–891

classes (*continued*)
  Debugger, 890
  domain context, 764–765
  DynamicActivity, 704
  EventLog, 161
  Installer, 172, 971
  InstallerActions, 971
  MembershipProvider, 732
  metadata, 492
  metadata proxy, 462
  NativeActivity, 704
  RegisteredEntities, 788
  RoleProvider, 729
  SaveOperation, 1038
  SearchResult, 591
  ServerSyncProviderProxy, 752
  ServiceInstaller, 973–976
  StatusNotificationService, 1036
  StringAssert, 203–204
  SubscriptionTest, 1103
  Trace, 890–891
  WorkflowApplication, 705, 717
  WorkflowInvoker, 705
  WorkflowServiceHost, 705
Classification subsystem, 1043
classification types (Editor), 1046–1047
ClassificationTypeDefinition class, 1046
classifier aggregators, 1046
ClassInitialize attribute, 206–207
Click event handler, 37
ClickOnce, 110
  deployment, 976–980
  security, 111
  updating, 980–982
client application services, 725
  application framework, security, 728
  ASP.NET Application Services, 729
  offline support, 740–742
  users, validation, 727
client changes in Sync Services, 755–756
client services
  authentication, 107
  roles, 107
  Web settings, 107
client-side development, Web Application projects, 425–431

ClientServices, creating, 725–728
clipboard, code editor, 60
Cloud Computing, 533
Cloud Service project template (Azure), 534
CloudFront project (Azure), 535
CLR (Common Language Runtime), 394
CMMI Process Improvement, MSF and, 1112
code, linking with tests, 1103–1105
code analysis, 112–113
  C/C++ Code Analysis tool, 1079
  Managed Code Analysis tool, 1078–1079
Code Analysis Settings, 93
Code Analysis tab (Solution Explorer), 112–113
code assets, generating, 280–284
code blocks
  commenting/uncommenting, 59–60
  surrounding with snippets, 141–142
  Toolbox, 138
Code Contracts, 214–216, 258–260
Code Coverage, 1103–1104
Code Definition window, 66
code editor
  block selection, 60
  clipboard, 60
  code blocks, commenting/uncommenting, 59–60
  code formatting, 55–56
  Find All References option, 61
  floating windows, 58–59
  full-screen view, 60
  Go To Definition option, 61
  line numbers, 57
  multiline editing, 60
  Navigate Backward, 57
  Navigate Forward, 57
  outlining, 55
  reference highlighting, 57
  regions, 54–55
  split view, 58
  tab groups, 59
  tear away code windows, 58–59
  threads, 897
  window layout, 53–54
  word wrap, 57
  zooming, 57
code execution windows, Call Stack, 833
code formatting, code editor, 55–56

code generation, 263–264
  drag-and-drop, 182–184
  IntelliSense, 184–185
code metrics, 1075
  class coupling, 1077
  Cyclomatic Complexity, 1078
  depth of inheritance, 1077
  excluded code, 1078
  lines of code, 1076–1077
  maintainability index, 1078
Code Metrics window, 1075–1076
code modules, macros, 1026
code snippets
  C#, 139–140
  code blocks, 138–139
        surrounding, 141–142
  creating, 143
  IDE, 137
  Insert Snippet, 139–140
  inserting, 139
  IntelliSense, 133
  predefined, 139
  reviewing, 144–147
  shortcuts, 140
  VB, 140–141
Code Snippets Manager, 142–143
code window
  Break mode, 828
  DataTips, 828
  debugging, 827–828
CodeActivity class, 704, 715–719
Coded UI Tests, 1101–1102
CodeRush Xpress, 137
  refactoring, 149
coding resource files, 817–819
coding standards, FxCop, 254–257
coding style, StyleCop, 258
collection associations, 179
CollectionAssert class, 204
collections, initializers, 323–324
colors, editor space, 43–44
COM components
  add-ins, 1014
  registering, 1014
Command window, 61–62

IntelliSense, 62
CommandLineMessageService class, 1038
commands
  aliases, Immediate window, 831
  DTE.Commands enumeration, 1006–1007
  Find in Files, 78
  groups, 61
  Immediate window, 831
  IntelliSense, 131
  listing, 47, 61
  Lock Controls, 345
  Replace in Files, 78
  Toggle Bookmark, 133–134
commenting/uncommenting, code blocks, 59–60
comments, 1046
  block, 220
  inline commenting, 220
  single line, 220
  Task List window, 241–243
  text file resources, 806
  XML comments, 220–221
commit characters (IntelliSense), 123
Common Controls, 23
compile errors, 64
Compile page (VB), 915–916
  Build Events, 917–919
  compilation constants, 916–917
  optimizations, 916
Compile tab (Solution Explorer), 100–102
compiler debug option, enabling, 873
compiler section of configuration schema, 780
CompilerGenerated attribute, 1078
compiling
  decompilers, 939–941
  just-in-time compiling, 937
  PIAs (Primary Interop Assemblies), 315
  transformation errors, 279
completion mode (IntelliSense), 124–125
complex expressions, 661
complex properties (entities), 631
Component Diagrams (UML), 1062, 1065–1066
ComponentResourceManager class, 812, 816–817
composable parts of application, 1034
ComposeParts method, 1035

composition containers, 1034
`CompositionContainer`, 1034
`Condition` property, 969
conditional breakpoints, 828
.config files
  `app.config` file, 774
  `applicationHost.config` file, 775
  `machine.config` file, 773–774
  `security.config` file, 775
  `web.config` file, 774
configuration, help system, 85–86
configuration attributes, 780–781
configuration files, 773. *See also* .config files
  application settings, 782–790
  `appSettings` section, 782–783
  `connectionStrings` section, 798
  custom sections, 785–790
  dynamic properties, 784–785
  IntelliSense, 789–790
  project settings, 783–784
  referenced projects with settings, 792–793
  SCDL, 789
  user settings, 790–791
configuration schema
  `compiler` section, 780
  `configurationSections` block, 775–776
  `cryptographySettings` section, 779
  `runtime` block, 777–778
  `startup` block, 777
  `system.diagnostics` section, 779
  `system.net` block, 778–779
  `system.runtime.remoting` block, 778
  `system.web` section, 779–780
configuration settings, inherited, 774
`configurationSections` block of configuration
    schema, 775–776
`Connect` class, 1015
connection properties (SQL Server), 800–801
connection strings, 562
  encrypting, 803–804
  in-code construction, 801–803
Connection Strings Wizard, 795–801
`ConnectionString` property, 801
`connectionStrings` section of configuration
    files, 798

connectors to entities, 179
container controls
  composition container, 1034
  FlowLayoutPanel, 348
  Panel, 347–348
  SplitContainer, 347–348
  TableLayoutPanel, 348–349
content controls (Word), 381
content pages (SharePoint), 522
content types
  Editor, 1045–1046
  SharePoint, 519
`ContentTypeDefinition` contract, 1046
context menus, Solution Explorer, 17
contracts (MEF), 1037–1040
  `ContentTypeDefinition`, 1046
  `IGlyphFactoryProvider`, 1056
  `IMouseProcessorProvider`, 1048
  `IWpfTextviewCreationListener`, 1048
contracts (WCF), 683
  data contracts, 683, 685–687
  message contracts, 683
  service contracts, 683, 684–685
contravariance, 317, 319–321
control flow activities (WF), 704–705
  Flowchart, 704
  Sequence, 704
control images, 813
control themes (Silverlight), 479
controllers, 441
  classes, populating, 441
Controllers folder, 441
controllers (IntelliSense), 1049
controls
  Chart, 658–659
  container controls
    FlowLayoutPanel, 348
    Panel, 347–348
    SplitContainer, 347–348
    TableLayoutPanel, 348–349
  detective, 950
  DomainDataSource, 765
  drag and drop, 650
  Gauge control, 659–660
  Image control, 657

Line, 652
List, 657
Matrix control, 655–657
preventative, 950
QueryableFilterRepeater, 510
QueryExtender, 510
Rectangle, 652
Report Viewer, 645, 646
Subreport control, 657
Table control, 652–655
Text Box, 650–652
web forms
 formatting, 411–412
 positioning, 409–411
Windows Forms
 adding, 341
 aligning text controls, 342
 anchoring, 349–350
 docking, 349–350
 horizontal spacing, 343
 layering, 344
 locking design, 344–345
 positioning multiple, 342–343
 property setting, 345–346
 tab order, 344
 vertical spacing, 343
 WPF, layout controls, 358–360
Convention over Configuration, 486
covariance, 317, 318–319
Create action method, 457
CreateToolWindow method, 1016, 1018
credentials provider, 738
cross-assembly referencing, 816
CRUD (Create, Read, Update, Delete), 485
 contracts, 684
 entity models, 637–641
cryptographySettings section in
 configuration schema, 779
Crystal Reports, introduction, 645
CSS (cascading style sheets), web forms, 412–415
Ctrl key, temporary window, 40
Ctrl+Tab window, 40
culture resources, 813–814, 815
 creating, 814
 invariant cultures, 813

 loading files, 814–815
 neutral cultures, 813
 specific cultures, 814
CurrentChanged event, 748
CurrentPrincipal, 728
CurrentStatusTest, 1103
CustomActionData property, 972
CustomAuthentication class, 731
Customer Experience Improvement Program
 (CEIP), 958
CustomerBindingNavigator, 569–570
CustomerBindingSource, 567–569
CustomerTableAdapter, 563
CustomerVisualizer class, 866–867
customization, document-level, 381
CustomReportingFunctions template, 665
CVS, 246
Cyclomatic Complexity, 1078

D

dashboards (SharePoint), 1132–1133
data
 browsing, 584–586
 editing, 556–557
 previewing, 557
data binding, 565–567
 saving changes, 573–574
 validation, 576–578
 WPF, 367–370
Data Binding Mode options, 570–571
Data Compare, 1092–1093
Data Connections node (Server Explorer), 549
data contracts (WCF), 683, 685–687
Data Generation Plan, 1089–1090
Data Link Properties dialog, 562
data models, ASP.NET Dynamic Data, 487–489
 display format, 496–498
 validation rules, 494–496
data sets
 customized, 578–579
 Typed DataSets, 649
Data Source Configuration Wizard, 561, 650, 798
data sources, 581–586
 adding, 561–563

data sources (*continued*)
  reports, 647
      defining, 648–650
  selecting, 570–573
  Web Service Data Source, 583
Data Sources window, 549, 556
data types
  F#, 330
  resource files, 819
data view controls, 422–423
Database Diagram Editor, 549
database diagrams, 555–556
Database projects, 95
database tools
  Data Compare, 1092–1093
  Data Generation Plan, 1089–1090
  Offline Schema project, 1086–1089
  refactoring, 1090–1091
  Schema Compare, 1091–1092
  SQL-CLR Database projects, 1086
  static analysis, 1093
  Transact-SQL editor, 1093
Database Unit Tests, 1100–1101
databases
  best practices, 1093–1094
  SQL Azure, 544
  updating, entity models, 644–645
  windows, 549–556
DataColumns, 559–560
DataContract attribute, 686
DataGridView, 579–581
DataRows, 559–560
DataSet editor, 563–565
DataSet object, 560
DataSets
  creating, 561–563
  GeneratedCode attribute, 1078
  overview, 559–560
DataTables, 559–560
DataTips, 828
  floating, 858
  pinned, 858
  variables, 858
DDD (domain-driven design), 645
Debug class, 890–891

DEBUG constant, 102
Debug Source Files, 93
Debug tab (Solution Explorer), 103
  enable debuggers, 104–105
debugger
  DebuggerBrowsable attribute, 859–860
  DebuggerDisplay attribute, 860–861
  DebuggerHidden attribute, 861–862
  DebuggerNonUserCode attribute, 862
  DebuggerStepperBoundary attribute,
      862–863
  DebuggerStepThrough attribute, 862
  DTE.Debugger, 1007
Debugger class, 890
Debugger interface, 1003
debugging
  ASP.NET
      Edit and Continue, 876
      error handling, 876–877
      web applications, 874–876
  ASP.NET AJAX JavaScript, 879
  Assert method, 891
  Break mode, 828, 845
  breakpoints, 828, 845
      conditional, 828, 848–849
      deleting, 850
      disabling, 850
      exporting, 851–852
      importing, 851–852
      labeling, 851
      location, 850–851
      setting, 846–847
  Breakpoints window, 828–829
  client-side JavaScript, 877–878
      breakpoints, 878
  with code, Debugger class, 890
  code execution windows
      Call Stack, 833
      Modules, 834–835
      Processes, 835
      Threads, 834
  code window, 827–828
  DataTips, 828
  Debug class, 890–891
  delayed signing and, 949

dynamically-generated JavaScript, 878–879
Edit and Continue, 855–856
exceptions and, 841
    unwinding, 845
Exceptions window, 841
execution control, 853
    stepping through code, 853–855
execution point, moving, 855
first application, 9–13
Immediate window, 830–831
IntelliTrace, 837–838, 1075
LINQ, 596–597
macros, 1030
memory windows, 835
    1-4, 836
    Disassembly, 836
    Registers, 836–837
mixed-mode, 899
multi-threaded applications, 897–899
.NET Framework, 896–897
Output window, 829–830
Parallel Stacks window, 839–840
Parallel Tasks window, 840
parallel windows, 838–840
parallelized applications, 897–899
post-mortem
    dump files debugging, 901–902
    dump files generation, 900–901
Raw View, 865
rude edits, 855
running applications
    remote debugging, 894–895
    Web applications, 893–894
    Windows processes, 892–893
saving changes to object, 867–869
server-side ASP.NET code, 872–877
SharePoint, remote computers, 521
Silverlight, 477, 879–880
start actions, 887–889
Stop Applying Changes, 855
stored procedures (SQL Server), 899
Trace class, 890–891
Trace Switches, 891
tracepoints
    creating, 852

macros, 852–853
printing, 852–853
tracing, 880
    application level, 882
    page-level, 881
type proxies, 863–865
visualizers, 865–867
Watch windows
    1-4, 832–833
    Autos, 833
    Locals, 833
    QuickWatch, 831–832
web applications, 874–876
workflows, 718–719
WPF Visualizer, 376–377
declarative languages, 312
decompilers, 939–941
DefaultValue attribute, 30–31
DELETE HTTP method, 455
dependencies
  builds, manual, 914–915
  .NET applications, 968
Dependency Graphs, 1070–1072
deploying
  add-ins, 1022–1023
  applications, 394–396
  first application, 9–13
  macros, 1030–1031
  reports, 677
  Web applications, 983
    web.config transformations, 989–990
  Windows Azure applications, 540–543
deployment
  certificates, 977–979
  ClickOnce, 976–980
  outputs included, 963
depth of inheritance, 1077
Descending keyword, 595
Description attribute, 29
design-time errors, 278–279
designer files, 810–811
designing reports, 647–648
detective controls, 950
developer types, 4
developing first application, 9–13

developing macros, 1028–1030
Development Fabric (Azure), 535–536
Development Tools Extensibility. *See* DTE
    (Development Tools Extensibility)
dialogs
  Add Area, 459
  Add Controller, 441
  Add-in Manager, 1011
  Add Reference, 21
  Breakpoint Hit Count, 849
  Data Link Properties, 562
  Exception Assistant, 841
  Exceptions, 47
  Find and Replace, 74
  Find in Files, 78, 79
  Find Symbol, 81
  Foreign Key Relationships, 553
  Help Library Manager, 85
  New Project, 95–96, 353
  Preview Data, 557
  Publish Web, 986–987
  Quick Find, 73
  Remove Parameters, 154
  Rename, 154
  Reorder Parameters, 153–154
  Report Properties, 667
  Service Reference Settings, 22
  Solution Properties, 16
  Surround With, 141–142
directives, T4, 265
  `assembly`, 276
  `import`, 276–277
  `include`, 277–278
  `output`, 275–276
  `template`, 275
directories, virtual, 774
disabled add-ins, 394
disabled users, accessibility, 416–417
disabling breakpoints, 850
Disassembly window, 836
Display Items list, Text Editor, 44
`DisplayFor` helper, 466
DisplayName attribute, 29
docking, 41–43
  controls, 349–350

document-level customization, 381
document libraries, SharePoint, 519
Document Outline window, 364
  controlling outlining, 69–70
  HTML outlining, 68–69
document windows, automation, 1006
documentation. *See also* comments; XML
  comments
  GhostDoc and, 237–238
  introduction, 219
  Sandcastle and, 238–241
documents as templates, 1132
domain context class, 764–765
domain operations, 762
  delete operations, 763
  insert operations, 763
  invoke operation, 763
  query operations, 762–763
  update operations, 763
Domain Service Class Wizard, 761
domain services
  consuming, Silverlight, 764–768
  RIA Services, 760–762
DomainDataSource control, 765
Dotfuscator, 941–945
  RI (Runtime Intelligence), 952
  tamper defense, 950–952
drag and drop
  Class Designer, 177
  code generation, 182–184
  controls, 650
drop handlers, 1048
DTE (Development Tools Extensibility),
  1002–1004
  debugger, 1007
  event handling, 1007
  macros, 1025–1026
`DTE.Commands`, enumeration, 1006–1007
`DTE.Debugger`, 1007
`DTE.Events` object, 1007
`DTE.Solutions` object, 1004–1005
dump files
  debugging, 901–902
  generating, 900–901
Dynamic Data, templates, 464

display templates, 465–468
edit templates, 468
dynamic data. *See also* ASP.NET Dynamic Data
dynamic languages, 312–313
dynamic lookups, late binding and, 325–326
dynamic properties of configuration files, 784–785
`DynamicActivity` class, 704

E

Edit and Continue, 855–856
  ASP.NET debugging, 876
editing, data, 556–557
Editor
  adornments, 1047–1048
  Check Comment Margin Highlighter,
    1050–1057
  Classification subsystem, 1043
  classification types, 1046–1047
  classifiers, 1043
  content types, 1045–1046
  drop handlers, 1048
  extending, 1044
  IntelliSense, 1049
  margins, 1047
  mouse processors, 1048
  Operations subsystem, 1043
  options, 1048–1049
  services, 1050
  tags, 1047
  Text Model subsystem, 1042
  Text View subsystem, 1042–1043
editor space, 8
  colors, 43–44
  fonts, 43–44
  full-screen mode, 45
  tracking changes, 46
  visual guides, 44–45
embedding files as resources, 808–809
empty test cases, 193
Empty Web Site project template, 402
`EnableClientAccess` attribute, 761
`EnableDynamicData` method, 511–512
Encapsulate Field method of refactoring, 150–151

`Encode` method, 450
encryption, connection strings, 803–804
endpoints (WCF), 688–691
Entities Dynamic Data project, 488
entities in class diagrams, 178–179
  connectors, 179
  display style, 181
Entity Data Model Wizard, 624–625
Entity Framework designer, 626–630
entity templates, ASP.NET Dynamic Data,
    506–508
enumeration
  `DTE.Commands`, 1006–1007
  projects, 1004–1005
  windows, 1005–1006
Environment settings, source code repository, 248
environment settings, 6
  RSS feed, 7
error handling, ASP.NET debugging, 876–877
Error List, 64
Error List window, 664
`ErrorImage` property, 813
errors
  compile errors, 64
  compiling transformation, 279
  in conversion, 907
  design-time, 278–279
  executing transformation errors, 279–280
  generated code errors, 280
event handlers
  `AfterInstall`, 970
  Click, 37
  XAML editor, 361
event handling, 1020–1022
event receivers (SharePoint), 519, 527–528
`EventLog` class, 161
events
  `BeforeExecute`, 1020
  Changed, 1042
  CurrentChanged, 748
  `DTE.Events` object, 1007
  IntelliTrace, 1085
  Post Build Event, 918
  `SubreportProcessing`, 670

Excel
  document-level customization, 381
  Project integration, 1118–1119
  smart tags, 381
  work items, 1117–1118
Exception Assistant, customizing, 844–845
Exception Assistant dialog, 841
exception information, writing, 161
exceptions
  debugger, 841
  execution path, 841
  IntelliTrace, 1085
  unwinding, 845
Exceptions dialog, 47
Exceptions window, 841
excluded code, 1078
executing transformation errors, 279–280
execution control, 853
  stepping through code, 853–854
        step filtering, 854
        Stepping Into, 854
        Stepping Out, 854
        Stepping Over, 854
execution point, moving, 855
ExpectedException attribute, 204–206
Experimental Instance, 1045
expiration date, 956–957
ExportAttribute attribute, 1036
exporting
  breakpoints, 851–852
  class diagrams, 182
  composable parts and, 1034
  contracts and, 1037–1040
  settings, 51–52
Expression blocks (T4), 268
Expression Builder, 75–76, 662
  fx button, 662
expression holes, 600–601
expressions, 705
  complex, 661
  Immediate window, 830–831
  Lambda expressions, 589–590
  reports, 661–663
  simple, 661
extensibility, 1001. *See also* DTE (Development
    Tools Extensibility)

add-ins, 1002
macros, 1002, 1025–1026
MEF (Managed Extensibility Framework),
    1002, 1033
options, 1001–1002
VSPackages, 1002
extension methods, LINQ, 110
Extract Interface method of refactoring, 151–153
Extract method of refactoring, 148–150

F

F#, 327–330
  data types, 330
  Interactive window, 329
  lazy keyword, 331
  for loop, 330
  Pattern Matching, 330
Feature Designer, 529–530
FeatureAttribute attribute, 957–958
Features node (SharePoint), 521
features (SharePoint), 519, 529–530
field templates, ASP.NET Dynamic Data, 502–506
file extensions, toolbar associations, 39
files. *See also* .config files; configuration files
  .AddIn, 1014
  designer files, 810–811
  dump files
        debugging, 901–902
        generating, 900–901
  embedding as resources, 808–809
  find and replace, 78–79
  hidden, 91
  JavaScript, 129–130
  project, format, 96
  replace in, 80–81
  text file resources, 806–807
Fill method, 564
filter templates, ASP.NET Dynamic Data,
    509–511
filters
  breakpoints, 849–850
  step filtering, 854
FinalQuery method, 596
find and replace
  in files, 78–79

Find Symbol search tool, 81
options, 77
Quick Find dialog, 73
regular expressions, 76–77
replace in files, 80–81
Replace With field, 75
wildcards, 75–76
Find and Replace dialog, 74
Find in Files command, 78
Find in Files dialog, 78, 79
Find Options, 75
Find Results windows, 79–80
Find Symbol dialog, 81
Find Symbol search tool, 81
flexibility, 311
floating code editor windows, 58–59
floating tool windows, 43
Flowchart control flow activity (WF), 704
FlowLayoutPanel control, 348
folders, 90
  ASP.NET MVC, 439–440
  Controllers, 441
  Open Containing Folder option, 40
  SharePoint Mapped Folders, 523
  solution folders, 90
Font and Colors node, 43
fonts, editor space, 43–44
for loops, F#, 330
Foreign Key Relationships dialog, 553
formatting code, code editor, 55–56
forms
  login, 738–740
  Outlook, 389–392
  SnapLines, 339
  Windows Forms Designer, 338–340
Forms authentication, 726
forms-based authentication, 731
framework, versions, 19
From statement, 591
full-screen mode, editor space, 45
full-screen view, code editor, 60
function breakpoints, 846–847
functional languages, 313–314
functionality, Modeling Power Toys for Visual
  Studio 2010, 187

functions
  $( ), 468–470
  GetStrongName, 667
  Implement Abstract Class, 185
  Override Members, 185
  refactoring functions, 185
  Server Explorer window, 554–555
fx button, 662
FxCop, 245
  code analysis, 254–257
  Managed Code Analysis tool, 1078

G

GAC (Global Assembly Cache), 26, 933–934
  installers, 967
  reports, 665
gacutil.exe, 934
garbage collection, 777
Gauge control, 659–660
generated code errors, 280
GeneratedCode attribute, 1078
GenerateMagicNumber method, 939
generating reports, 674–675
Generic Tests, 1102
generic variance, 317
Generics, inheritance, 316–318
GET HTTP method, 455
Get Started tab, 34
GetCredentials method, 740
GetData method, 564
GetManifestResourceNames method,
  809–810
GetManifestResourceStream method,
  809–810
GetRolesForUser method, 729
GetStrongName function, 667
GetTags method, 1054
GhostDoc, 219, 237–238
GlobalAssemblyInfo file, 932–933
glyph factory, 1054
glyphs, WPF designer, 362
GroupBy statement, 593–594
Guidance and Resources tab, 34

H

Halstead volume, 1078
hard disabled add-ins, 394
HEAD HTTP method, 455
headers/footers in reports, 669
Health Monitoring, 884–886
Hello World, 9–13
Help Library Manager dialog, 85
help system, 83–84
  configuration, 85–86
  navigating, 84–85
  online help system, 85
  searching, 84–85
  Service Unavailable message, 83
hidden files, 91
HideSolutionNode, 92
highlighting, code editor, 57
hit counts, 849
Hopper, Grace, 312
horizontal spacing, 343
HostApplication nodes, 1014
HTML Designer, 407–409
HTML elements, positioning in web
  forms, 409–411
HTML outlining, 68–69
HTTP methods
  DELETE, 455
  GET, 455
  HEAD, 455
  POST, 455

I

IClassifier, 1046
IClassifierAggregatorService, 1050, 1054
IClientFormsAuthenticationCredentials
  Provider interface, 738
icons
  loading, 816
  projects, 16
IContentTypeRegistryService, 1050
ICustomerService interface, 684
IDE (integrated development environment)
  code snippets, 137

configuration, 7
  Start Page, 7
IDropHandler, 1048
IDropHandlerProvider, 1048
IDTCommandTarget interface, 1015
IDTExtensibility2 interface, 1015
IGlyphFactoryProvider contract, 1056
Ignore attribute, testing, 201
IIS (Internet Information Services), 401
IL Dasm, 938–939
Image control, 657
Image Library, 301
Image property, 813
images
  control images, 813
  as properties, 813
IMessageService, 1038
Immediate window, 62–63, 830–831
  commands, 831
  IntelliSense, 63, 831
IMouseProcessorProvider contract, 1048
imperative languages, 312
Implement Abstract Class function, 185
implicit line continuation, 322
ImplicitStyleManager (Silverlight), 480
Import and Export Settings Wizard, 51–52
import directive (T4), 276–277
importing
  ApplicationRoot class and, 1036
  breakpoints, 851–852
  composable parts and, 1034
  contracts and, 1037–1040
  settings, 51–52
Imports command, 603
in keyword, 319–320
include directive (T4), 277–278
inconclusive statements, 197
incremental searches, 82–83
Incremental synchronization, 749
Index method, 441
  results, 442
inheritance
  configuration settings, 774
  depth of inheritance, 1077
  entities, 635

Generics, 316–318
Inheritance connector, 179
InitialImage property, 813
InitializeComponent method, 812
inline commenting, 220
Insert Snippet, 139–140
InsertShelfLifeAttribute attribute, 956
InsertSignOfLifeAttribute attribute, 956
InsertTamperCheckAttribute attribute, 951
installation. *See also* Windows Installer
  Administrative install, 970
  licensing terms, 4
  SharePoint, 517–518
  variables, 967
  Visual Studio 2010, 3–5
    stages, 3–4
Installation URL property, 965
installation wizard, 967
Installed Templates hierarchy, 18
Installer class, 172, 971
Installer Class template, 970
InstallerActions class, 971
  SharedResources assembly, 971
installers
  building, 962–966
  custom actions, 970–972
  customization, 966–970
  GAC and, 967
  merge module, 962
  Service Installer, 973–976
  Web Application projects, 991
  Web Platform Installer, 992–997
IntelliSense
  brokers, 1049
  C#-specific options, 132
  code generation, 184–185
  code snippets, 133
  Command window, 62
  commands, 131
  commit characters, 123
  configuration files, 789–790
  controllers, 1049
  Editor, 1049
  extended, 132–133
  function breakpoints, 847

Immediate window, 63, 831
IntelliSense context, 129
JavaScript, 128–130
Options, 131–132
overview, 119–120
parameter information, 127–128
presenters, 1049
Quick Info, 128
schema definitions, 133
sessions, 1049
shortcut key, 121
sources, 1049
statement completion, 132
wavy lines, 120
word/phrase completion
    completion mode, 124–125
    in context, 121–123
    Generate From Usage, 126–127
    list members, 123–124
    stub completion, 125–126
    suggestion mode, 124–125
XAML editor, 361
XML comments, 133, 237
IntelliTrace, 837–838, 1075, 1084
  events, 1085
  exceptions, 1085
  IntelliTrace Events window, 837–838
Interaction Use (Sequence diagrams), 1064
Interactive window (F#), 329
interfaces
  Debugger, 1003
  ICustomerService, 684
  IDTCommandTarget, 1015
  IDTExtensibility2, 1015
  IWizard, 303–305
invoke operation, 763
IResourceReader, 817–819
IResourceWriter, 817–819
IsEnabled property, 357
item templates, 291–295
items, 89
ITextBuffer, 1042, 1054
ITextDocument, 1042
ITextDocumentFactoryService, 1050
ITextEdit, 1042

`ITextSearchService`, 1050
`ITextSnapshot`, 1042
`ITextVersion`, 1042
`ITextView`, 1043
IWizard interface, 303–305
`IWpfKeyboardTrackingService`, 1050
`IWpfTextviewCreationListener`
    contract, 1048
`IWpfTextViewMargin`, 1047

J

JavaScript
  ASP.NET AJAX, debugging, 879
  debugging
      breakpoints, 878
      client-side, 877–878
      dynamically-generated, 878–879
  IntelliSense, 128–130
  jQuery, 468–470
  referencing files, 129–130
  Web Application projects, 426–427
jQuery, 468–470
just-in-time compiling, 937

K

key files, 109–110
  strong-named, 935
keyboard mapping, 47
Keyboard node, 47, 61
keyboard shortcuts, 46–48
  IntelliSense, 121
  Quick Find, 74
keywords, 1046
  `in`, 319–320
  `Ascending`, 595
  `Descending`, 595
  `lazy`, 331
  `out`, 318
  `var`, 314
KPIs (Key Performance Indicators), 659

L

Lab Center, 1108–1109
labeling breakpoints, 851
labeling versions, 1124–1125
Lambda expressions, 589–590
lambdas, 321–322
languages
  declarative, 312
  dynamic, 312–313
  F#, 327–330
  functional, 313–314
  imperative, 312
  .NET Framework, 311
late binding, dynamic lookup, 325–326
Latest News tab, 34
Layer Diagrams (UML Model Explorer),
  1066–1068
layering controls, Windows Forms, 344
layers, adornments, 1048
layout, Class Designer, 181
Layout Diagram button, 181
layout of reports, 668–670
`lazy` keyword, 331
libraries, 21
licensing terms, 4
line continuation, implicit, 322
Line control, 652
line-level tracking, 46
line numbers, 45
  code editor, 57
Line Numbers checkbox, 45
lines of code (code metrics), 1076–1077
links
  Silverlight, 477
  Start Page, 34
LINQ (Language Integrated Query), 314
  anonymous type feature, 591
  debugging, 596–597
  expression holes, 600–601
  extension methods, 110
  `FinalQuery` method, 596
  `GroupBy` statement, 593–594
  `OrderBy` statement, 594–595
  properties, custom, 594
  providers, 588

`Select` statement, 592
`From` statement, 591
`Where` statement, 592–593
XML creation, 600–602
LINQ to Entities, 636–642
LINQ to SQL, 587, 605
  ADO.NET Entity Framework and, 487
  ADO.NET Entity Framework comparison, 622–623
  deletes, 610–611
  inserts, 610–611
  object binding, 614–617
  object model, 606–607
  querying, 608–610
  stored procedures, 611–614
  Stored Procedures node, 612
  updates, 610–611
LINQ to XML, 587, 597–598, 600
LINQPAD, 618
List control, 657
list members, IntelliSense, 123–124
List template, 452
listing commands, 61
lists, SharePoint, 519–521
literals
  array literals, 323–324
  XML literals, 598
load pattern, 1099
Load Test Designer, 1099
Load Test Monitor, 1099
load tests, 1099–1100
  test load agent, 1100
  thresholds, 1100
local report engine, 648
Locals window, 833
Lock Controls command, 345
locking control design, Windows Forms, 344–345
login form, 738–740
  as credential provider, 738–739
lookups, dynamic, late binding and, 325–326

M

`machine.config` file, 773–774
Macro Explorer tool window, 1026

macros
  code modules, 1026
  debugging, 1030
  deploying, 1030–1031
  developing, 1028–1030
  extensibility and, 1002
  long-running, 1030
  overview, 1025–1026
  recording, 1028
  running, 1030
  temporary, 1028
  tracepoints, 852–853
Macros IDE, 1026–1027
maintainability index, 1078
Managed Code Analysis, 1078–1079
Managed Extensibility Framework. *See* MEF (Managed Extensbility Framework)
management classes, Server Explorer, 162–164
Management Events, 164–167
manual dependencies between builds, 914–915
`MapRoute` method, overloading, 453
margins, 1047
master pages
  SharePoint, 523
  Web Application projects, 424–425
Matrix control, 655–657
MEF (Managed Extensbility Framework), 1002, 1033
  advanced scenarios, 1041
  catalogs, 1040–1041
  `CompositionContainer`, 1034
  contracts, 1037–1040
membership, providers, 727
membership management, enabling, 731
`MembershipProvider` class, 732
memory windows, 836
  1-4, 836
  Disassembly window, 836
  Registers window, 836–837
menus, 8. *See also* context menus
  Windows, 40
merge module, 962
merges (Version Control), 1128
message contracts (WCF), 683
message queues, 167–169

messages, 64
metadata
  classes, 492
  text, 1043
  WPF, 24
metadata proxy class, 462
method stubs, generating, 156
methods
  AddSolutionFolder, 1003
  ApplyResources, 817
  Assert, 891
  asynchronous, 698
  ComposeParts, 1035
  CreateToolWindow, 1016, 1018
  EnableDynamicData, 511–512
  Encode, 450
  extension, LINQ, 110
  Fill, 564
  FinalQuery, 596
  GenerateMagicNumber, 939
  GetCredentials, 740
  GetData, 564
  GetManifestResourceNames, 809–810
  GetManifestResourceStream, 809–810
  GetRolesForUser, 729
  GetTags, 1054
  IDTExtensibility 2 interface, 1015
  Index, 441
  InitializeComponent, 812
  MapRoute, 453
  parameters, entering, 180
  SaveChanges( ), 639
  Sync Services, 752
  TakeThreadOwnership, 1042
  TransformText( ), 274
  Validate, 576–577
  ValidateUser, 727
  Write( ), 274
Microsoft Code Contracts, 258–260
Microsoft .NET Framework IL Disassembler
    (IL Dasm), 938–939
Microsoft Synchronization Services for ADO.NET,
    745. See also Sync Services
Microsoft Visual SourceSafe, 246
  checking in/out, 250

history, 253
merging changes, 252–253
offline support, 253–254
Pending Changes, 250–251
pinning files, 253
repository, creating, 249
solution, 249–250
Solution Explorer, 250
Miscellaneous Files solution folder, 90
mixed-mode debugging, 899
model binders, 458–459
  validation errors, 461
Modeling Power Toys for Visual Studio 2010, 186
  functionality, 187
  visualization, 186–187
Modeling Projects (Architecture edition), 1061
  linking to Team Foundation Server, 1068
  new diagrams, 1062
Modules window, 834–835
monitoring
  applications, 949–958
  Health Monitoring, 884–886
Moonlight, 472
mouse processors, 1048
MouseProcessorBase, 1048
MSBuild, 920–921
  Items elements, 924
  PropertyGroup nodes, 924
  schema, 96
  Target elements, 924
  Tasks elements, 925
      assembly versioning, 925–927
  Visual Studio's use, 921–923
MSDataSetGenerator, 560
MSF for Agile Development, 1112
  dashboards, 1132
  Word documents, 1132
  work items, 1115–1116
      adding, 1116
      Excel, 1117–1118
      state, 1116–1117
MSF (Microsoft Solution Framework)
  Agile Development, 1112
      work items, 1115–1116
  CMMI Process Improvement, 1112

MSIL (Microsoft Intermediary Language), 937
  disassembler, 938–939
multi-threaded applications, debugging, 897–899
MVC (Model-View-Controller)
  components, 438
  SmallTalk, 438
  URLs, 451
  validation, 461–462
MVVM (Model-View-ViewModel), 352
My Extensions tab (Solution Explorer), 110
MyWizard, 301–305

N

n-tiers, Sync Services, 751–752
named parameters, 326–327
naming assemblies, 929–932
  strongly named, 933
    obfuscation, 948–949
naming resources, 809
NativeActivity class, 704
Navigate To search tool, 82
navigating
  associations (Entity Framework), 641–642
  code editor, 57
  help system, 84–85
  open items, 40–41
navigation components, Web controls, 418
Navigation Framework (Silverlight), 478
navigation properties (entities), 631
nested types, 187
.NET developers, Visual Basic Development
    Settings option, 6
.NET Framework
  applications, dependencies, 968
  assemblies, projects, 90
  debugging, 896–897
  languages, 311
  Silverlight and, 472
  upgrading to, 909–910
.NET Framework IL Disassembler (IL Dasm),
    938–939
.NET Reflector, 939–941
  assembly information, 929–930
.NET Sequence Diagrams, generating, 1072–1073

New Project dialog, 95–96, 353
New Service Element Wizard, 689
New Service Endpoint Wizard, 690–691
nodes, 16
NotesUserControl, 1016
NTLM authentication, 113
nullable optional parameters, 324–325

O

obfuscation, 941
  attributes
      ObfuscationAssemblyAttribute,
        945–946
      ObfuscationAttribute, 946–948
  delayed signing, debugging and, 949
  Dotfuscator, 941–945
  reflection model, 948
  smart obfuscation, 948
  strongly named assemblies, 948–949
ObfuscationAssemblyAttribute attribute,
    945–946
ObfuscationAttribute attribute, 946–948
object binding, LINQ to SQL, 614–617
Object Browser, 64–65
Object Lifetime information, 1082
object models, LINQ to SQL, 606–607
Object Relational Designer, 488
Object Relational Mapping, 621
ObjectDumper, 596–597
objects, serializing, 820
occasionally connected applications, 746
Office
  debugging applications, 392–394
  deploying applications, 394–396
  projects, 95
office project types, 380–382
Offline Schema project, 1086–1089
offline support, 740–742
online help, 85
Online Templates, 19
online templates, 308–309
OperationContract attribute, 684
Operations subsystem, 1043
Option Strict, 50–51

optional parameters, 326–327
  nullable, 324–325
Orca, installed components, 969
OrderBy statement, 594–595
Ordered Tests, 1102
Organize Usings, 156–157
ORM (Object Relational Mapper), 621
out keyword, 318
outlining
  code editor, 55
  controlling, 69–70
  HTML outlining, 68–69
Outlook
  add-in creation, 388–392
  form region creation, 389–392
output directive (T4), 275–276
output type, 97
Output window, 829–830
overloading methods, 453
Override Members function, 185
Owner attribute, testing, 201

P

Package Files property, 964
Package node (SharePoint), 521
Package/Publish SQL tab (Solution Explorer), 116
Package/Publish Web tab (Solution Explorer), 115
packaging (SharePoint), 530–532
packaging Web applications
  configuring packages, 987–988
  SQL Server data, 988–989
page headers, reports, 668
page-level errors, 876–877
page-level tracing, 881
page templates, ASP.NET Dynamic Data, 499–502
Panel control, 347–348
parallel debugging windows, 838–840
Parallel Stacks window, 839–840
Parallel Tasks window, 840
parallelized applications, debugging, 897–899
parameterizing web servers, 1096
parameters
  action methods, 456–459
    entering on method, 180
    IntelliSense, 127–128
    named, 326–327
    optional, 326–327
      nullable, 324–325
  subreports, 671
  templates, 298–299
partial views, MVC, 463
PasteXmlAsLinq, 599–600
Pattern Matching (F#), 330
PDB file extension, 901
Performance Explorer, 1080
  Allocation information, 1082
  Object Lifetime information, 1082
  profiler sessions, configuring, 1080–1082
  reports, 1082–1083
  Windows Events section, 1082
Performance Wizard, 1080
persistence (workflow), 706
PIAs (Primary Interop Assemblies), 315, 395
pinned windows, 8
placeholders
  reports, 661–663
  Text Box control, 651
POCO (Plain Old CLR Objects), 645
positioning, SnapLines, 339
Post Build Event, 918
POST HTTP method, 455
post-mortem debugging, dump files
  debugging, 901–902
  generating, 900–901
PowerPacks (VB), 325
prebuild events, 806
predefined code snippets, 139
Preprocessed Text Templates, 284–288
  compared to standard T4 template, 288–289
presentation, ASP.NET Dynamic Data, 498
  entity templates, 506–508
  field templates, 502–506
  filter templates, 509–511
  page templates, 499–502
presentation model types (RIA Services), 759
presenters (IntelliSense), 1049
preventative controls, 950
Preview Data dialog, 557

previewing data, 557
printing tracepoints, 852–853
`Priority` attribute, testing, 201
private members, testing, 213–214
process templates (TFS), 1112–1113
  customizing, 1136–1137
processes, debugging running applications,
    892–893
Processes window, 835
profiles, ASP.NET Application Services, 729
profiling tools, 1080
  Performance Explorer, configuring sessions,
    1080–1082
  Standalone Profiler, 1083–1084
  TIP (Tier Interaction Profiling), 1081
Project, Excel integration, 1118–1119
Project Explorer tool window, 1027
project settings of configuration files, 783–784
projects, 89. *See also* web application projects;
    Web Site project
  default locations, 48
  dependencies, 93
  enumeration, 1004–1005
  file formats, 96
  folders, 90
  icons, 16
  .NET assemblies, 90
  properties, 96–97
      Application tab, 97–100
      Build Events tab, 103
      Build tab, 102–103
      Code Analysis tab, 112–113
      Compile tab, 100–102
      Debug tab, 103–105
      My Extensions tab, 110
      Publish tab, 111–112
      Reference Paths tab, 108–109
      References tab, 105–106
      Resources tab, 106–107
      Security tab, 111
      Services tab, 107–108
      Settings tab, 108
      Signing tab, 109–110
  Solution Explorer, 90
  startup, 16

structure, add-ins, 1012–1013
templates, 295–296
    generating, 306–308
types, 94–96
Web Site, 19
promoting variable to parameter, 155
properties, 26–28
  `ActivationKeyFile`, 957
  attached, XAML, 358
  automatic, 322–323
  `BindingSource`, 614
  `Condition`, 969
  connection properties (SQL Server), 800–801
  `ConnectionString`, 801
  `CustomActionData`, 972
  entities, 631
  `ErrorImage`, 813
  `Image`, 813
  images as, 813
  `InitialImage`, 813
  Installation URL, 965
  `IsEnabled`, 357
  LINQ, custom, 594
  Package Files, 964
  projects, 96–113
      Application tab, 97–100
      Build Events tab, 103
      Build tab, 102–103
      Code Analysis tab, 112–113
      Compile tab, 100–102
      Debug tab, 103–105
      My Extensions tab, 110
      Publish tab, 111–112
      Reference Paths tab, 108–109
      References tab, 105–106
      Resources tab, 106–107
      Security tab, 111
      Services tab, 107–108
      Settings tab, 108
      Signing tab, 109–110
  solutions
      Common properties, 92–93
      Configuration properties, 93–94
  `SyncDirection`, 755–756
  unit testing, 211–212

properties (*continued*)
  `ValidateArchitecture`, 1068
  `Visibility`, 357
  web application projects
      Package/Publish SQL tab, 116
      Package/Publish Web tab, 115
      Silverlight Applications tab, 114–115
      Web tab, 113–114
  Windows Forms, 337–338
      setting for controls, 345–346
  `WorkerReportsProgress`, 752–755
  WPF, 357
Properties window, 181, 211–212, 650
  AmbientValue attribute, 31–32
  Browsable attribute, 28–29
  Category attribute, 30
  DefaultValue attribute, 30–31
  Description attribute, 29
  DisplayName attribute, 29
  WPF designer, 364–367
property element syntax, 359
property markers, 365
providers
  implementing, 727
  membership, 727
  role management, 727
proxies
  metadata proxy class, 462
  type proxies, 863–865
  Web Service Proxies, 1078
Publish Method, 986
Publish tab (Solution Explorer), 111–112
Publish Web dialog, 986–987
Publish Wizard, 976–977
publishing
  Web applications, 986–987
  Web sites, 984–985

Q

queries, 588–590. *See also* LINQ (Language
    Integrated Query)
  Architecture Explorer, 1070
  entity models, 636–642
  LINQ to SQL, 608–610
    returning data, 564
    XML, 602–603
  Query Builder, 564
  query operations, 762–763
  QueryableFilterRepeater control, 510
  QueryExtender control, 510
  QueryVisualizer, SQL, 609
  Quick Find, starting Find action, 74
  Quick Find box, 74
  Quick Find dialog, 73
  Quick Info (IntelliSense), 128
  Quick Replace, 75
  QuickCRM, 746
  QuickWatch window, 831

R

Raw View, 865
Recent Projects list, 34
Recent Templates, 19
recording macros, 1028
Rectangle control, 652
Refactor!, 137
refactoring
  Class Designer and, 185
  CodeRush Xpress, 149
  databases, 1090–1091
  Encapsulate Field method, 150–151
  Extract Interface method, 151–153
  Extract method, 148–150
  functions, 185
  Generate Method Stub, 156
  Organize Usings, 156–157
  promote variable to parameter, 155
  removing parameters, 154
  renaming parameters, 154
  reordering parameters, 153–154
  support, 147–148
reference highlighting, code editor, 57
Reference Library Controls, 23
Reference Paths tab (Solution Explorer), 108–109
referenced projects with settings in configuration
    files, 792–793
references (Solution Explorer)
  adding, 21

cross-assembly referencing, 816
service references, 22
References tab (Solution Explorer), 105–106
reflection model, obfuscation, 948
RegEx engine, 76
regions (code editor), 54–55
RegisteredEntities class, 788
Registers window, 836–837
Registry view, 967
regular expressions, 76–77
relationships, Server Explorer window, 552–553
Release mode, 93–94
remote debugging, 894–895
Remote Debugging Monitor, 894–895
Remove Parameters dialog, 154
Rename dialog box, 154
rendering reports to different formats, 675–677
Reorder Parameters dialog, 153–154
replace in files, 80–81
Replace in Files command, 78
Report Data window, 648
report definition file, 647
  SQL Server Reporting Services, 649
report designer, 647
report engine, 647
  local, 648
  server report engine, 649
Report Properties dialog, 667
Report Server, 1130–1132
Report Viewer, 647
  toolbar, 674
  Windows, 673
Report Viewer control, 645, 646
  web version, 674
  Windows Forms projects, 674
Report Wizard, 647–648, 672–673
reporting, introduction, 645
Reporting projects, 95
reports, 647
  aggregates, 661–663
  ASP.NET applications, 646
  Chart control, 658–659
  custom code, 663–668
  data sources, 647
    defining, 648–650
  deploying, 677

designing, 647–648
Entity Framework, 649
expressions, 661–663
GAC (Global Assembly Cache), 665
Gauge control, 659–660
generating, 674–675
Image control, 657
layout, 668–670
  headers/footers, 669
  page breaks, 669
  page headers, 668
Line control, 652
List control, 657
Matrix control, 655–657
Performance Explorer, 1082–1083
placeholders, 661–663
Rectangle control, 652
rendering, to different formats, 675–677
Silverlight, 646
Subreport control, 657
subreports, 670–672
Table control, 652–655
templates, 647–648
Text Box control, 650–652
Windows Forms applications, 646
WPF applications, 646
Reports Application project template, 645
repositories for source code, 246
  checking in/out, 250
  creating, 249
  environment settings for, 248
  history, 253
  merging changes, 252–253
  pending changes, 250–251
  plug-in settings, 248
  selection tips, 246–248
Resgen, 810–811
resource files
  binary formats, 805, 807–808
  coding, 817–819
  data types, 819
  designer files, 810–811
  IResourceReader, 817–819
  IResourceWriter, 817–819
  resx, 805, 807
Resource Generator utility, 810–811

ResourceReader, 818
resources
  accessing, 809–810
      specifics, 816–817
  adding, 808
  bitmap loading, 816
  ComponentResourceManager, 816–817
  cross-assembly referencing, 816
  custom, 819–822
  designer files, 810–811
  embedding files as, 808–809
  icon loading, 816
  naming, 809
  overview, 805–806
  satellite, cultures, 813–814, 815
  text files, 806–807
Resources tab (Solution Explorer), 106–107
ResourceWriter, 818
resourcing applications, 811–813
Response URL Validation Rule, 1098
resx resource files, 807
ResxResourceReader, 818–819
ResxResourceWriter, 818–819
reviewing code snippets, 144–147
RI (Runtime Intelligence), 952–956
RIA (Rich Internet Application), 472
RIA Services
  ASP.NET and, 758
  authentication, 758
  Business Application template, 757
  domain operations, 762
      delete operations, 763
      insert operations, 763
      invoke operation, 763
      query operations, 762–763
      update operations, 763
  domain services, 760–762
  introduction, 757
  presentation model types, 759
  Silverlight and, 757
      consuming domain services, 764–768
  user registration, 758
role management
  ASP.NET Application Services, 729
  providers, 727

RoleProvider abstract class, 729
roles, 107
  authorization, 729–731
routing
  MVC, 451–455
  URL components, 452
  URLs, views, 453
RSS feed
  environment settings, 7
  Latest News, 34
Ruby on Rails
  MVC (Model-View-Controller), 437
  scaffolding, 486
rude edits, 855
run time, workflow, 705
running macros, 1030
running Visual Studio 2010, 5–6
runtime block of configuration schema, 777–778
Runtime Intelligence Service, 955

S

SaaS (Software as a Service), 745
Sandcastle, 219, 238–241
satellite resources, cultures, 813–814, 815
  creating, 814
  loading files, 814–815
SaveChanges( ) method, 639
SaveOperation class, 1038
scaffolding, 486
scalar properties (entities), 631
SCC (Source Code Control), 246
SCDL, configuration data, 789
Schema Compare, 1091–1092
schema (XML), importing, 603–605
searches
  camel case, 82
  Find Options, 75
  Find Symbol search tool, 81
  help system, 84–85
  incremental, 82–83
  Navigate To search tool, 82
  Quick Find, 74–75
  Quick Replace, 75
  regular expressions, 76–77

wildcards, 75–76
SearchResult class, 591
security
  application framework, 728
  ASP.NET Web site administration, 432–433
  ClickOnce, 111
Security tab (Solution Explorer), 111
security.config file, 775
Select statement, 591, 592
Sequence control flow activity (WF), 704
Sequence Diagrams (UML), 1062, 1064–1065
sequential workflows (SharePoint), 528–529
serialization, 820
Server Explorer window, 8, 550–552
  Data Connections node, 159, 173–174, 549
  database diagrams, 555–556
  functions, 554–555
  overview, 159
  relationship editing, 552–553
  Servers node, 159–160
          Event Logs node, 160–162
          management classes, 162–164
          Management Events, 164–167
          Message Queues, 167–169
          Performance Counters, 169–172
          Services, 172–173
  SharePoint, 174
          connections, 159
  stored procedures, 554–555
  Table Designer menu, 552
  Views node, 553–554
server report engine, 649
ServerForm designer, 748
ServerSyncProviderProxy class, 752
service-based components in Windows Forms, 346
service contracts (WCF), 683, 684–685
Service Installer, 973–976
Service Reference Settings dialog, 22
service references, 22
Service Unavailable message (help), 83
ServiceContract attribute, 685
ServiceInstaller class, 973–976
services, Editor, 1050
Services tab (Solution Explorer), 107–108
sessions (IntelliSense), 1049

Settings object, 791
Settings tab (Solution Explorer), 108
Setup Wizard, 962
SetupAttribute attribute, 953–956
SharedResources assembly, 967
  InstallerActions class, 971
SharePoint
  application pages, 522
  components, custom, 524–529
  connecting to, 518
  content pages, 522
  content types, 519, 525–527
  dashboards, 1132–1133
  debugging, remote computers, 521
  development environment, 514–518
          prerequisites, 515–517
  document libraries, 519
  event receivers, 519, 527–528
  features, 519, 529–530
  Features node, 521
  installation, 517–518
  lists, 519, 525–527, 1132
          list definitions, 519–520
          list instances, 520
  Mapped Folders, 523
  master pages, 523
  overview, 513–514
  Package node, 521
  packaging, 530–532
  Prerequisite Installer tool, 515, 516
  process guidance, 1132
  projects, 95
          creating, 520–523
          Server Explorer, 174
  SharePoint Server versus SharePoint Foundation,
    514–515
  Team Foundation Build, 1132–1133
  templates, 521
  WCF Hotfix, 515
  Windows 7, 516
  Windows Vista, 516
  workflows
          sequential, 528–529
          state machine, 528–529
  WSP (Windows SharePoint Package), 530–532

SharePoint-based Web Parts, 524
SharePoint Customization Wizard, 521
SharePoint Products Configuration Wizard, 517
Shelf-Life, 956–957
  notification messages, 957
Shelf Life Activation Key (SLAK), 956–957
shortcuts
  code snippets, 140
  keyboard shortcuts, 46–48
  shortcut keys, IntelliSense, 121
ShowGrid, 339
signing assemblies, 934–936
  delayed, debugging and, 949
Signing tab (Solution Explorer), 109–110,
    934–936
Silverlight
  consuming domain services, 764–768
  debugging, 477, 879–880
  Destination folder, 477
  ImplicitStyleManager, 480
  introduction, 471
  links, 477
  Navigation Framework, 478–479
  .NET Framework and, 472
  Out-Of-Browser mode, 481–484
  overview, 472
  projects, 95
  reports, 646
  RIA Services and, 757
  rich applications, 472
  SDKs, 474
  templates, 473
      default content views, 475
  themes, 479–480
      application themes, 479
      control themes, 479
  web browsers, 472
  web project, 474
  WPF and, 471
Silverlight Applications tab (Solution Explorer),
    114–115
Silverlight Class Library project template, 473
Silverlight Navigation Application project
    template, 473
simple expressions, 661

single line comments, 220
SLAK (Shelf Life Activation Key), 956–957
.sln (solution file), contents, 91
Smart Indenting, 56
smart obfuscation, 948
smart tags
  Excel, 381
  Windows Forms, 346–347
  Word, 381
SnapLines, 339, 341–342
Snapshot synchronization, 749
SnapToGrid, 339
Snippet Editor, 144–147
soft disabling of add-ins, 394
Solution Explorer, 8
  activities, 18
  Application tab, 97–98
      Application Framework, 100
      Assembly Information, 98–99
      User Account Control, 99–100
  Build Events tab, 103
  Build tab, 102–103
  Code Analysis tab, 112–113
  Compile tab, 100–102
  context menu, 17
  Debug tab, 103
      enable debuggers, 104–105
  introduction, 15–17
  Microsoft Visual SourceSafe, 250
  My Extensions tab, 110
  Package/Publish SQL tab, 116
  Package/Publish Web tab, 115
  projects, adding, 18–20
  projects and, 90
  Publish tab, 111–112
  Reference Paths tab, 108–109
  references
      adding, 21
      service, 22
  References tab, 105–106
  Resources tab, 106–107
  Security tab, 111
  Services tab, 107–108
  Settings tab, 108
  Signing tab, 109–110

Silverlight Applications tab, 114–115
solution folders, 90
solutions and, 90
templates, 18
tool window, 16
toolbar, 16
Track Active Item option, 49
Version Control, 1120–1121
Web tab, 113–114
XML resource files, 17
solution files, format, 91–92
solution folders, 90
   Solution Explorer, 90
Solution node, visibility, 16
Solution Properties dialog, 16
solutions, 89
   Common properties, 92–93
   Configuration properties, 93–94
   as container of related projects, 90
   Solution Explorer, 90
   structure, 89–91
   temporary, 89
source code
   accessing control, 248–253
   controlling, 245–246
   repositories, 246
      checking in/out, 250
      creating, 249
      CVS, 246
      environment settings for, 248
      history, 253
      merging changes, 252–253
      Microsoft Visual SourceSafe, 246
      pending changes, 250–251
      plug-in settings, 248
      SCC (Source Code Control), 246
      selection tips, 246–248
      Subversion, 246
      TFS (Team Foundation Server), 246
Source Control. *See* Version Control
sources (IntelliSense), 1049
splash screen, 5–6
split view, code editor, 58
SplitContainer control, 347–348
SQL Azure, 533, 544–545

SQL-CLR, 1075
SQL-CLR Database projects, 1086
SQL Server
   connection properties, 800–801
   packaging data, 988–989
   stored procedures, debugging, 899
SQL Server Reporting Services, 649
SQL (Structured Query Language). *See also*
     LINQ to SQL
   QueryVisualizer, 609
S+S (Software and Services), 745
stack frame, 833
stages of installation, 3–4
Standalone Profiler, 1083–1084
start actions, debugging, 887–889
Start Page, 7, 33–34
   customizing, 34–36
   links, 34
   modifying, 35
   opening, 34
   projects
      creating, 34
      opening, 34
   Recent Projects list, 34
   tabs, 34
   user controls, 36–38
Starter Kits, 308
`startup` block of configuration schema, 777
startup projects, 16
state machine workflows (SharePoint), 528–529
Statement blocks (T4), 268–270
statements
   `From`, 591
   `GroupBy`, 593–594
   `OrderBy`, 594–595
   `Select`, 591, 592
   `Where`, 592–593
static analysis of databases, 1093
`StatusNotificationService` class, 1036
stepping through code, 853–854
   execution point, moving, 855
   step filtering, 854
   Stepping Into, 854
   Stepping Out, 854
   Stepping Over, 854

stored procedures
  LINQ to SQL, 611–614
  Server Explorer window, 554–555
  SQL Server, debugging, 899
StringAssert class, 203–204
strongly named assemblies, 933
  obfuscation, 948–949
structure of solutions, 89–91
stub completion (IntelliSense), 125–126
StyleCop, 245, 258
styles, WPF, 371
SubmitChanges, 611
Subreport control, 657
SubreportProcessing event, 670
subreports, 670–672
  parameters, 671
SubscriptionTest class, 1103
Subversion, 246
suggestion mode (IntelliSense), 124–125
Surround With dialog, 141–142
symbols, Find Symbol, 81
Syme, Don, 327
Sync Services, 746
  background synchronization, 752–755
  client changes, 755–756
  forcing synchronization, 750
  Incremental synchronization, 749
  methods, 752
  n-tiers, 751–752
  Remote Provider, 752
  Snapshot synchronization, 749
  track changes, 749
  WCF Service and, 752
SyncDirection property, 755–756
synchronization services, 745
SynchronizeButton, 751
syntax, property element syntax, 359
system.diagnostics section in configuration
    schema, 779
system.net block of configuration schema,
    778–779
system.runtime.remoting block of
    configuration schema, 778
system.web section in configuration schema,
    779–780

T

T4
  Class Feature blocks, 270–272
  directives, 265
    assembly, 276
    import, 276–277
    include, 277–278
    output, 275–276
    template, 275
  Domain Specific Languages Toolkit, 263
  Expression blocks, 268
  Statement blocks, 268–270
  templates
    automation, 280–284
    creating, 264–268
    Preprocessed Text Template comparison,
        288–289
T-SQL, code generation, 487
tab order, Windows Forms controls, 344
TabItem tags, 35
Table control, 652–655
Table Designer menu, 550
TableAdapter, 563
TableLayoutPanel control, 348–349
tags
  Editor, 1047
  TabItem, 35
TakeThreadOwnership method, 1042
Tamper Defense, 950
Task List window, comments, 241–243
Task Panes (Office), 381–382
TDD (test-driven development), 645
Team Foundation Build, 1128–1130
  build agents, 1128
  build controllers, 1128
  build definitions, 1128
  Queue New Build, 1130
  Rolling Builds, 1129
  SharePoint, 1132–1133
    dashboards, 1132–1133
    lists, 1132
    process guidance, 1132
Team Foundation Server. See TFS (Team
  Foundation Server)

team projects (TFS), 1112
Team System Edition, 191
tear away code windows, 58–59
TeardownAttribute attribute, 953–956
template directive (T4), 275
templates
  Business Application, 757
  custom view templates (MVC), 463–464
  CustomReportingFunctions, 665
  documents as, 1132
  Dynamic Data, 464
      display templates, 465–468
      edit templates, 468
  extending, 299–308
  file location, 49
  Installed Templates hierarchy, 18
  Installer Class, 970
  item templates, 291–295
  List, 452
  locations, 299
  MyWizard, 301–305
  online, 308–309
  Online Templates, 19
  parameters, 298–299
  process templates, 1112–1113
  project setup, 299–301
  project templates, 295–296
  Recent Templates, 19
  reports, 647–648
  Reports Application project template, 645
  SharePoint, 521
  Silverlight, 473
  Solution Explorer, 18
  structure, 296–298
  T4
      automation, 280–284
      creating, 264–268
  VSIX Project template, 1044
  WCF Workflow Service Application project, 682
  Web Application projects, 406
  Windows Forms applications, 336
  Workflow Console Application, 708
temporary macros, 1028
temporary solutions, 89
temporary window, 40

Test and Lab Manager, 1095, 1106
  Lab Center, 1108–1109
  Testing Center, 1106–1108
test cases
  AssemblyCleanup attribute, 207
  AssemblyInitialize attribute, 207
  ClassCleanup attribute, 206–207
  ClassInitialize attribute, 206–207
  clean up, 206–207
  empty, 193
  first, 192–199
  inconclusive statements, 197
  initialization, 206–207
  large numbers, 216–217
  TestClass attribute, 200
  TestCleanup attribute, 206
  TestContext object, 207–211
  TestInitialize attribute, 206
  TestMethod attribute, 200
  writing, 192
  writing output, 210–211
Test Controller, 1108–1109
Test Elements, Test and Lab Manager, 1095
Test Impact Analysis, 1105
Test List Editor, 216–217, 1098, 1105–1106
test load agent, 1100
Test projects, 95
Test Results window, 196, 1105
Test Run Configuration file, 198
Test Runner window, 1107–1108
test runs, 198
Test Timeouts, 199
Test View window, 211–212, 1105
Test Windows, 1105
TestCategory attribute, testing, 201
TestClass attribute, 200
TestCleanup attribute, 206
TestContext object, 207–211
testing. *See also* unit testing
  add-ins, 1013–1014
  attributes, 200–202
  workflows, 719
  writing output, 210–211
Testing Center (Test and Lab Manager),
    1106–1108

`TestInitialize` attribute, 206
TestMethod attribute, 200
tests
  attributes, 200
  automated, 1095–1096
  Coded UI Tests, 1101–1102
  Generic Tests, 1102
  link with code, 1103–1105
  load tests, 1099–1100
  Ordered Tests, 1102
  unit tests, Database Unit Tests, 1100–1101
  web performance, 1096–1099
text
  adornments, 1047–1048
  classification types, 1046–1047
  classifiers, 1043
  displaying, 1042–1043
  formatting, 1042–1043, 1043
  margins, 1047
  metadata, 1043
  modification, enabling, 1042
  recognition, 1043
  tags, 1047
  word wrapping, 45
Text Box control, 650–652
  placeholders, 651
text controls, alignment, 342
Text Editor, Display Items list, 44
text file resources, 806–807
  comments, 806
  new lines, 806
  prebuild events, 806
Text Model subsystem, 1042
Text Template Transformation, Preprocessed Text
   Templates, 284–288
Text Template Transformation Toolkit. *See* T4
Text View subsystem, 1042–1043
  classifiers, 1043
  view ports, 1043
TFS (Team Foundation Server), 34, 246,
   1111–1112
  Administration Console, 1134
  Agile Development and, 1112
  automation, 1135–1137
  Changeset Tracking, 1127

  CMMI Process Improvement and, 1112
  customization, 1135–1137
  Guidance Page, 1113
  linking to from Modeling Projects, 1068
  Merge Changes, 1122–1123
  offline work, 1124
  process templates, 1112–1113
    customizing, 1136–1137
  Report Server, 1130–1132
  Team Foundation Build, 1128–1130
  team project collections, 1112
  team projects, 1112
  Team Web Access, 1133
  Version Control, 1119–1128
  Windows Workflow 4.0, 1129
  Work Item Queries, 1113
  work item queries, 1113–1114, 1114–1115
  work items
    adding, 1116
    Excel, 1117–1118
    state, 1116–1117
    tracking, 1113–1114
    types, 1115–1116, 1135–1136
  workspaces, 1120
themes
  Silverlight, 479–480
  WPF, 371
threads, code editor window, 897
Threads window, 834
Tick feature, 958
`Timeout` attribute, testing, 201
TIP (Tier Interaction Profiling), 1081
Toggle Bookmark command, 133–134
tool windows, 8, 39
  creating, 1015–1018
  dockable, 41
  floating, 43
  location, 41
  Macro Explorer tool window, 1026
  Project Explorer, 1027
  reorganizing, 70–71
  Solution Explorer, 16
toolbars, 8
  Breakpoints window, 829
  buttons, 39

customizing, 39
file associations, 39
Solution Explorer, 16
viewing, 39
Toolbox, 8
Class Designer, 178
code block storage, 138
components
adding, 25–26
arranging, 24–25
customizing appearance, 24
docking, 41
Toolbox window, 22–24
tooltips
DataTips, 828
IntelliSense, 120
TPL (Task Parallel Library), 838
Trace class, 890–891
TRACE constant, 102
Trace Switches, 891
Trace Viewer, 883
tracepoints
creating, 852
macros, 852–853
printing, 852–853
tracing, 880
application-level, 882
output, 882–883
page-level, 881
tracking changes, 46
ADO.NET Entity Framework, 639
Sync Services, 749
tracking participant (WF), 706–707
tracking profile (WF), 706–707
tracking records (WF), 706–707
tracking usage, 957–958
Transact-SQL editor, 1093
TransformText( ) method, 274
troubleshooting
compiling transformation errors, 279
design-time errors, 278–279
executing transformation errors, 279–280
generated code errors, 280
Trusted Root Certification Authorities, 979
Type Equivalence, 395–396

type equivalence, 316
type proxies, 863–865
type referencing, 590
TypeConverter, classes as strings, 820
Typed DataSets, 649

U

UIs (user interfaces), views, 443–451
UML diagrams (Architecture edition), 1061,
1062–1066
Activity diagrams, 1063
Class diagrams, 1066
Component diagrams, 1065–1066
Sequence diagrams, 1064–1065
Use Case diagrams, 1063
UML Model Explorer, 1066
Layer Diagrams, 1066–1068
UML (Unified Modeling Language), 1062
Undo, 1043
unit testing
AssemblyCleanup attribute, 207
AssemblyInitialize attribute, 207
Assert class, 203
attributes, 200–202
ClassCleanup attribute, 206–207
ClassInitialize attribute, 206–207
clean up, 206–207
Code Contracts, 214–216
CollectionAssert class, 204
Database Unit Tests, 1100–1101
empty test cases, 193
ExpectedException attribute, 204–206
first test case, 192–199
inconclusive statements, 197
initialization, 206–207
introduction, 191
large numbers of tests, 216–217
private members, 213–214
properties, custom, 211–212
StringAssert class, 203–204
test runs, 198
TestClass attribute, 200
TestCleanup attribute, 206
TestContext object, 207–211

unit testing (*continued*)
  `TestInitialize` attribute, 206
  TestMethod attribute, 200
  writing output, 210–211
unpinned windows, 8
unsaved changes, 11
unwinding exceptions, 845
updating
  ClickOnce and, 976–982
  databases, entity models, 644–645
upgrading
  to .NET Framework 4.0, 909–910
  from Visual Studio 2008, 901–909
URIs (Uniform Resource Indicators), Silverlight
    Navigation Framework, 478
URLs (Uniform Resource Locators)
  MVC, 451
  parts of, 452
  views, 453
usage tracking, 957–958
Use Case Diagrams (UML), 1062, 1063
User Account Control settings, 99–100
user authentication, Web controls, 418–420
user controls, Start Page, 36–38
user registration, RIA Services, 758
user settings in configuration files, 790–791
users, authentication, 731–733

V

`Validate` method, 576–577
`ValidateArchitecture` property, 1068
`ValidateUser` method, 727
  overloading, 728
validation
  ASP.NET Dynamic Data, 494–496
  data binding, 576–578
  entity models, 635
  MVC, 461–462
  web forms, 416–417
`var` keyword, 314
variables
  DataTips, 858
  installation variables, 967
  promoting to parameter, 155

WF designer, 709
variance
  contravariance, 317, 319–321
  covariance, 317, 318–319
VB (Visual Basic)
  anonymous methods, 321–322
  array literals, 323–324
  code snippets, 140–141
  collections, initializers, 323–324
  Compile page, 915–916
      Build Events, 917–919
      compilation constants, 916–917
      optimizations, 916
  lambdas, 321–322
  late binding, dynamic lookup, 325–326
  line continuation, implicit, 322
  options, 50–51
  parameters
      named, 326–327
      optional, 326–327
          nullable, 324–325
  PowerPacks, 325
  properties, automatic, 322–323
  XML literals, 598
VBA (Visual Basic for Applications), 379
Version Control
  annotating, 1125
  branches, 1126–1127
  check-ins, 1121–1122
  check-outs
      exclusive, 1121
      shared, 1121
  conflict resolution, 1122–1123
  History window, 1125
  introduction, 1119–1120
  labeling versions, 1124–1125
  Merge Changes, 1122–1123
  merges, 1128
  offline work, 1124
  shelvesets, 1126
  shelving, 1125–1126
  Solution Explorer, 1120–1121
vertical spacing, 343
views
  Class View, 63–64

custom view templates (MVC), 463–464
full-screen, code editor, 60
partial views (MVC), 463
split view, code editor, 58
UIs, 443–451
virtual directories, 774
Visibility property, 357
Visual Basic Development Settings option, 6
Visual Glyphs checkbox, 45
visual guides in editor space, 44–45
Visual Studio 2008, upgrading from, 901–909
Visual Studio 2010
    installation, 3–5
    running, 5–6
    setup, launching, 3–4
Visual Studio Content Installer package,
    1022–1023
    macros, 1031
Visual Studio Conversion Wizard, 906–907
Visual Studio IDE, add-ins, 1011
Visual Studio Macros IDE, add-ins, 1011
visualization, Modeling Power Toys for Visual
    Studio 2010, 186–187
visualizers, 865–867
visually impaired users, 416–417
VSIX Project template, 1044
VSM (Visual State Manager), 479
VSMacro, 1025–1026
VSPackages, extensibility, 1002
VSTO (Visual Studio Tools for Office), 18
    Actions Pane window, 381, 386–387
    add-ins
        disabled, 394
        unregistering, 392–393
    application-level add-ins, 381–382, 388–392
    applications
        debugging, 392–394
        deploying, 394–396
    document-level customization, 381
        creating, 382–387
    documents, protecting design, 385–386
    Explorer window, 388
    initial version, 379
    Inspector window, 388
    Outlook, form region creation, 389–392
    Task Panes, 381–382

VSTS Architecture, 1061
    Dependency Graphs, 1070–1072
    Modeling Projects, 1061
    .NET Sequence Diagrams, 1072–1073
    UML diagrams, 1062–1066
    UML Model Explorer, Layer Diagrams,
        1066–1068
VSTS Premium edition, Code Analysis tab,
    112–113
VSTS Ultimate edition, Code Analysis tab,
    112–113

W

warnings, 64
Watch windows
    1-4, 832–833
    Autos window, 833
    Locals window, 833
    Modules window, 834–835
    Processes window, 835
    QuickWatch window, 831
    Threads window, 834
wavy lines, IntelliSense and, 120
WCF RIA Services. See RIA Services
WCF Service Library, 683, 691–696
WCF Test Client, 692–693
WCF (Windows Communication Foundation), 22
    contracts, 683
        data contracts, 683, 685–687
        message contracts, 683
        service contracts, 683, 684–685
    Hotfix, 515
    overview, 681–682
    project types, 682
    projects, 95
    services
        consuming, 696–699
        endpoints, 688–691
        hosting, 691–696
        Sync Services and, 752
WCF Workflow Service Application project
    template, 682
Web Application projects
    ASP.NET AJAX, 427–429
        control extenders, 429–431

Web Application projects (*continued*)
  client-side development, 425–431
  creating, 404–405
  installers, 991–991
  JavaScript, 426–427
  master pages, 424–425
  output, 991
  properties
        Package/Publish SQL tab, 116
        Package/Publish Web tab, 115
        Web tab, 113–114
  Silverlight Applications tab, 114–115
  templates, 406
Web Application *versus* Web Site projects,
    400–401
Web applications
  debugging, 874–876
  deploying, 983
        web.config transformations, 989–990
  packaging
        configuring packages, 987–988
        SQL Server data, 988–989
  publishing, 986–987
Web browsers, Silverlight, 472
Web controls, 417–424
  data components, 420–423
  data helper controls, 423
  data view controls, 422–423
  navigation components, 418
  user authentication, 418–420
  Web Parts controls, 423–424
Web forms
  controls
        formatting, 411–412
        positioning, 409–411
  CSS tools, 412–415
  HTML Designer, 407–409
  HTML elements, positioning, 409–411
  validation tools, 416–417
Web pages, scaffolding, 486
Web Parts, development, 524–525
Web Parts controls, 423–424
Web performance tests, 1096–1099
Web Platform Installer, 992–997
Web projects, 95

  Silverlight, 474
Web servers, parameterizing, 1096
Web Service Data Source, 583
Web Service Proxies, GeneratedCode
        attribute, 1078
Web settings, 107
Web Setup Project, 991
Web site administration, ASP.NET, 431–434
Web Site project, 19, 116–117
  creating, 401–404
  Empty Web Site project template, 402
Web sites
  copying, 985
  location, 984
  publishing, 984–985
Web tab (Solution Explorer), 113–114
Web Test Designer, 1096
Web Test Recorder, 1096
Web Testing Framework, 1098
Web Tests
  customizing, 1098
  Test List Editor, 1098
web.config, transformations, 989–990
web.config file, 774
WebPartZone containers, 424
WF designer, 709–712
  Arguments pane, 710
  code activities, writing, 715–719
  hosting, 719–722
  workflow
        creating, 712
        designing, 713–715
        executing, 716–718
  WriteLine activity, 714
WF (Windows Workflow Foundation).
    See also workflow
  activities, code, 715–719
  bookmarks, 705
  expressions, 705
  introduction, 701–702
  library, 703
  reasons for using, 702–703
  tracking, 706–707
  WCF and, 682
Where statement, 592–593

wildcards in searches, 75–76
Windows
  authentication, 726
  menu, 40
  projects, 95
windows
  animation, 41
  Breakpoints, 828–829
  Call Hierarchy window, 66–67
  Class Details, 180
  Close All But This option, 40
  Code Definition window, 66
  code editor, 53–54
  code execution, Call stack, 833
  Code Metrics, 1075–1076
  Command window, 61–62
  Ctrl+Tab, 40
  Data Sources, 549, 556
  databases, 549–556
  debugging, 827–828
      Call Stack, 839
      Exceptions window, 841
      parallel debugging windows, 838–840
      Parallel Stacks, 839–840
      Parallel Tasks, 840
  Document Outline window, 68–70
  enumeration, 1005–1006
  Error List, 664
  Find Results, 79–80
  Immediate window, 62–63, 830–831
  IntelliTrace Events, 837–838
  Macro Explorer tool window, 1026
  memory windows, 836
      Disassembly, 836
      Registers, 836–837
  memory windows, 1-4, 836
  navigating open items, 40–41
  Open Containing Folder option, 40
  Output, 829–830
  pinned, 8
  Project Explorer, 1027
  Properties window, 181, 211–212, 650
  Report Data, 648
  Server Explorer, 550–556
  Solution Explorer tool window, 16

tear away code windows, 58–59
temporary, 40
Test Results, 196
Test View, 211–212
tool windows, 8, 39
      creating, 1015–1018
      floating, 43
      reorganizing, 70–71
unpinned, 8
viewing, 39
Watch windows
      Autos, 833
      Locals, 833
      Modules, 834–835
      QuickWatch, 831
      Threads, 834
Watch windows, 1-4, 832–833
Watch windows, Processes, 835
Windows 7, SharePoint, 516
Windows Azure Platform, 533
  AppFabric, 545–546
  application tuning, 543–544
  applications, deploying, 540–543
  blobs, 536–540
  Cloud Service project template, 534
  CloudFront project, 535
  Development Fabric, 535–536
  Development Storage, 535
  queues, 536–540
  roles, 534
  SQL Azure, 544–545
  tables, 536–540
Windows Forms
  Appearance properties, 338
  applications, 335
      templates, 336
  controls
      adding, 341
      aligning text controls, 342
      anchoring, 349–350
      docking, 349–350
      horizontal spacing, 343
      hosting in WPF, 374–375
      layering, 344
      locking design, 344–345

Windows Forms (*continued*)
    positioning multiple, 342–343
    property setting, 345–346
    resizing, 337
    tab order, 344
    vertical spacing, 343
  hosting WPF controls, 372–374
  interoperability, 372–375
  Layout properties, 338
  projects, creating, 335–336
  reports, 646
  service-based components, 346
  smart tag tasks, 346–347
  visual design, 336–337
  Window Style properties, 338
Windows Forms Designer, 338–340
  GridSize property, 339
  SnapLines, 339
Windows Forms User Control items, 1016
Windows Installer, 961–962
Windows SDK Components for Windows
    Installer Developer, Orca, 969
Windows Vista, SharePoint, 516
wizards
  Add-in Wizard, 1009–1012
  Connection Strings Wizard, 795–801
  Data Source Configuration Wizard, 561,
    650, 798
  Domain Service Class Wizard, 761
  Entity Data Model Wizard, 624–625
  Import and Export Settings, 51–52
  installation wizard, 967
  New Service Element Wizard, 689
  New Service Endpoint Wizard, 690–691
  Performance Wizard, 1080
  Publish Wizard, 976–977
  Report Wizard, 647–648, 672–673
  SharePoint Customization Wizard, 521
  SharePoint Products Configuration Wizard, 517
  Visual Studio Conversion Wizard, 906–907
  XML to Schema Inference Wizard, 604
WMI (Windows Management Instrumentation),
    162–163
Word
  content controls, 381
  document-level customization, 381

  smart tags, 381
word/phrase completion (IntelliSense)
  completion mode, 124–125
  in context, 121–123
  Generate From Usage, 126–127
  list members, 123–124
  stub completion, 125–126
  suggestion mode, 124–125
word wrap, 45
  code editor, 57
Word Wrap checkbox, 45
WorkerReportsProgress property, 752–755
Workflow Console Application project
    template, 708
Workflow projects, 95
WorkflowApplication class, 705, 717
WorkflowInvoker class, 705
workflows, 701–702. *See also* WF (Windows
    Workflow Foundation)
  activities, 703–704
    control flow, 704–705
  bookmarks, 705
  breakpoints, 718–719
  creating, 712
  debugging, 718–719
  designing, 713–715
  executing, 716–718
  expressions, 705
  persistence, 706
  run time, 705
  testing, 719
  tracking, 706–707
workflows (SharePoint)
  sequential, 528–529
  state machine, 528–529
WorkflowServiceHost class, 705
WorkItem attribute, testing, 201
workspaces, 1120
WPF Application, 9
  reports, 646
  styling, 371–372
WPF designer, 35, 360–364
  Apply Data Binding, 366
  Apply Resource, 366
  control template, 371
  Document Outline window, 364

glyph, 362
properties, listing, 365
Properties window, 364–367
Reset Value, 366
themes, 371
WPF Visualizer, debugging with, 376–377
WPF (Windows Presentation Foundation)
controls, 357–358
  hosting in Windows Forms, 372–374
  hosting Windows Forms, 374–375
  layout, 358–360
data binding, 367–370
metadata, 24
New Project dialog, 353
overview, 351–353
properties, 357
Silverlight and, 471
Start Page, 34
Write( ) method, 274
WSP (Windows SharePoint Package), 530–532
WSS (Windows SharePoint Services), 514

X

XAML (eXtensible Application Markup Language)
editor, 360–361
  control template, 371
  event handlers, 361
  IntelliSense, 361
XAML (eXtensible Application Markup
  Language), 312
attached properties, 358
overview, 355–356
syntax, 355
WPF and, 352
XAML page, modifying Start Page, 35
Xap file, 475
XBAP file, 354
XBAP (XAML Browser Application), 472
XCOPY, deploying add-ins, 1022–1023
XElement, XML snippets as, 599–600
XML comments, 219, 220–221
adding, 221
IntelliSense, 133, 237
tags

<c>, 222
<code>, 222–223
<example>, 223–224
<exception>, 224–225
<include>, 225–226
<list>, 226–228
<para>, 228
<param>, 228–229
<paramref>, 229–230
<permission>, 230
<remarks>, 230
<returns>, 231
<see>, 232
<seealso>, 232–233
<summary>, 233
<typeparam>, 233–234
<typeparamref>, 234–235
<value>, 235
using, 235–237
XML (eXtensible Markup Language)
creating with LINQ, 600–602
expression holes, 600–601
LINQ to XML, 597–598
literals, 598
querying, 602–603
resource files
  resx, 807
  Solution Explorer, 18
schema, importing, 603–605
schema editor, DataSets, creating, 561–563
schema files, 96
snippets, pasting as XElement, 599–600
WCF Service Library, 693
XML to Schema Inference Wizard, 604
xmlns attribute, 356

Y

yellow marks in code, 46
Yellow Screen of Death, 874

Z

zooming, code editor, 57